Frommer's

Caribbean Cruises
& Ports of Call
2004

by Heidi Sarna & Matt Hannafin

Here's what the critics say about Frommer's:

"It's possible to devote a life's study to researching cruise vacations; if you want to delve in, the most useful primer is *Frommer's Caribbean Cruises & Ports of Call*."
—Condé Nast Traveler

"Amazingly easy to use. Very portable, very complete."
—Booklist

"Detailed, accurate, and easy-to-read information for all price ranges."
—Glamour Magazine

"Hotel information is close to encyclopedic."
—Des Moines Sunday Register

"Frommer's Guides have a way of giving you a real feel for a place."
—Knight Ridder Newspapers

WILEY

Wiley Publishing, Inc.

Published by:

Wiley Publishing, Inc.
111 River St.
Hoboken, NJ 07030

ISBN 0-7645-3739-3
ISSN 1090-2600

Editor: Mike Kelly, Naomi Kraus
Production Editor: Heather Wilcox
Cartographer: John Decamillis
Photo Editor: Richard Fox
Production by Wiley Indianapolis Composition Services

For information on our other products and services or to obtain technical support,
please contact our Customer Care Department within the U.S. at 800-762-2974,
outside the U.S. at 317-572-3993 or fax 317-572-4002.

Wiley also publishes its books in a variety of electronic formats. Some content that
appears in print may not be available in electronic formats.

Manufactured in the United States of America

5   4   3

Contents

3 Things to Know Before You Go 73

4 The Cruise Experience 82

Part 2: The Cruise Lines & Their Ships

5 The Ratings (and How to Read Them) 103

6 The Mainstream Lines 114

7 The Ultraluxury Lines   274

8 Soft-Adventure Lines & Sailing Ships   334

9 European Lines ... Plus   374

Part 3: The Ports

10 The Ports of Embarkation   383

11 Caribbean Ports of Call   424

List of Maps

About the Authors

Heidi Sarna has cruised on more than 75 ships of all shapes and sizes, and she loves them all (well, okay, some more than others). Heidi's a contributing editor to *Travel Holiday* magazine, and her work has appeared in numerous magazines, major guidebooks, websites, and newspapers including the *New York Times, Star Ledger,* and *Boston Herald.* When she's not off cruising somewhere, she lives in the Big Apple with her husband, Arun, and their baby boys.

Matt Hannafin is freelance writer, editor, and musician based in New York City. A former Frommer's senior editor and former senior online writer at *Expedia Travels* magazine, he currently writes a biweekly cruise newsletter for Frommers.com and a monthly column for the *Boston Herald,* edits for several UN agencies and most of the major New York publishing houses, writes for various magazines and newspapers, and is the foremost Irish-American Persian-classical percussionist on the island of Manhattan.

Acknowledgments

A select group of experienced travel journalists and experts contributed to this book.

Michael Driscoll, editor of the probing industry newsletter *Cruise Week,* provided invaluable insight into the whims and fancies of the booking process. **Dr. Christina Colon,** respected academic, revamped the section on Mexico's burgeoning Yucatan ports for this edition, and serves always as Heidi's number-one cruise companion. Seaman **Ben Lyons,** who cruises for pleasure when not serving as a ship's officer, updated the Star Clippers review and provided insight into ship security. Thanks to **Lesley Abravanel,** *Miami Herald* columnist and author of *Frommer's South Florida,* for her downtown, late-night take on what's cool in Miami, and to cruise expert, writer, and all-around great guy **Art Sbarsky** for updating the SeaDream Yacht Club review and for his review of Radisson's new *Seven Seas Voyager.* Our appreciation goes to **Ted Scull,** a well-respected ship authority and travel writer, for his two cents (and cryptic wit) regarding Royal Olympia Cruises and anything else we need a second opinion about. Thanks to **Anne Kalosh,** U.S. editor for *Seatrade Cruise Review,* for her take on the new *Carnival Conquest.* Thanks to **Fran Golden,** travel editor at the *Boston Herald* and author of *Frommer's European Cruises* and *Frommer's Alaska Cruises,* for updating the Celebrity Cruises review, and Boston cruise columnist **Jim Burke,** for updating Crystal. A big general thanks to freelance writer and editor **Claudette Covey** for saving our butts, or at least our deadline, sanity, and eyesight. Many thanks also to the helpful public-relations staff at the cruise lines, to all the folks who contributed to past editions of this book (especially **Ken Lindley,** who provided so many wonderful port reviews), and to our editors, **Naomi Kraus** and **Mike Kelly.**

Last but not least, Heidi thanks her dear husband, **Arun,** for his support, his insight, and—most important—his prodding around deadline time, when all she really wanted to do was watch TV. For the latter reason, Matt would also like to thank Arun.

An Invitation to the Reader

In researching this book, we discovered many wonderful places—hotels, restaurants, shops, and more. We're sure you'll find others. Please tell us about them, so we can share the information with your fellow travelers in upcoming editions. If you were disappointed with a recommendation, we'd love to know that, too. Please write to:

Frommer's Caribbean Cruises & Ports of Call 2004
Wiley Publishing, Inc. • 111 River St. • Hoboken, NJ 07030

An Additional Note

Please be advised that travel information is subject to change at any time—and this is especially true of prices. We therefore suggest that you write or call ahead for confirmation when making your travel plans. The authors, editors, and publisher cannot be held responsible for the experiences of readers while traveling. Your safety is important to us, however, so we encourage you to stay alert and be aware of your surroundings. Keep a close eye on cameras, purses, and wallets, all favorite targets of thieves and pickpockets.

Frommers.com

Now that you have the guidebook to a great trip, visit our website at **www.frommers.com** for travel information on nearly 3,000 destinations. With features updated regularly, we give you instant access to the most current trip-planning information available. At Frommers.com, you'll also find the best prices on airfares, accommodations, and car rentals—and you can even book travel online through our travel booking partners. At Frommers.com, you'll also find the following:

- Online updates to our most popular guidebooks
- Vacation sweepstakes and contest giveaways
- Newsletter highlighting the hottest travel trends
- Online travel message boards with featured travel discussions

The Gulf of Mexico & the Caribbean

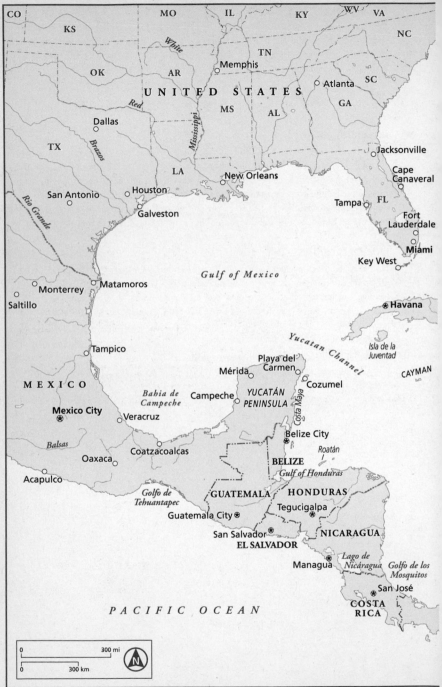

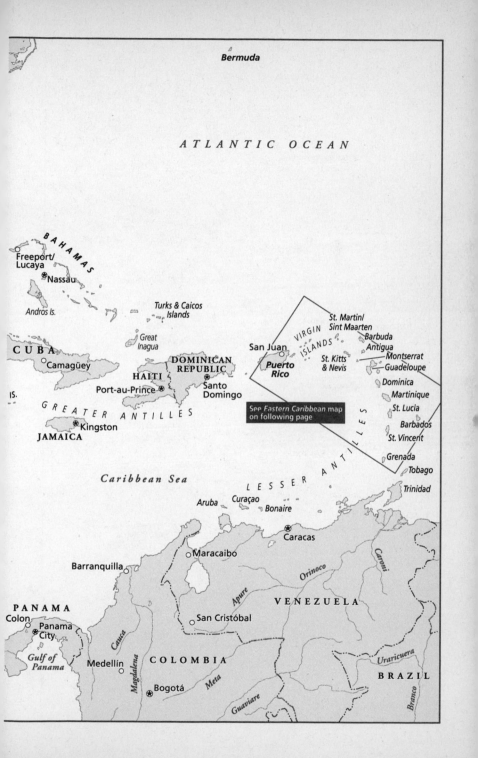

The Eastern Caribbean

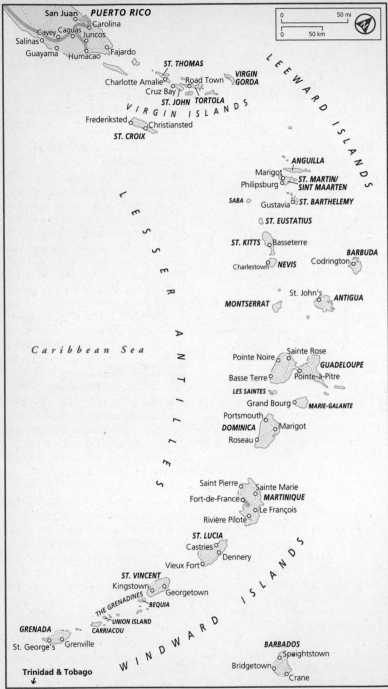

What's New in Cruising

We'll be honest. It's not the three-story show lounges or sushi bars that we remember about a cruise. It's not the rock-climbing walls or the cabin balconies or the Internet centers, either. It's simply being at sea on a ship. It's the teak decks, white steel railings, thick mooring lines, and those proud funnels. The sound of waves swooshing against a hull, a wistful horn moaning good-bye to a port. Salty sea breezes grabbing at our hair. Catching an auburn sunset melting into the horizon off the bow. These are the things about a cruise that stick with us long after we've returned home. (And yes, those great bars, restaurants, comfy cabins, spas, and cheapo rates you can snag these days certainly don't hurt.)

No other vacation, no other mode of transport creates a mood in quite the same way. No matter how high-tech ships have become, no matter how plush, there's no denying the basic pleasures of a ship at sea. Nowhere else can you be so isolated and away from it all, yet so immersed in and connected to the diverse community of cruisers and crew on board, and the swirl of activity surrounding it all. The romance and nostalgia of ocean travel, even on the newest, flashiest mega-ships, is undeniably alluring, and it's impossible not to be drawn into the spell. If you can break away from the disco and the conga lines long enough to wander out to some quiet corner of the deck, you'll see what we mean. The sea is a mesmerizing, powerful, and magical place to call home for a week.

HELPING YOU FIND YOUR IDEAL CRUISE

We've got a mission: to show you, above all else, that all cruises are not created equal. Sure, a lot of them *are* those huge Vegas-style floating resorts you see advertised on TV, but others are as far from glitz as you can get. Some are intimate tall ships with masts and sails that take old (and young) salts on nostalgic seagoing adventures. Other ships cater to the fancy caviar and champagne crowd, while still others attract L.L. Bean types who wouldn't know a tuxedo or a sequined dress from a rutabaga. These days, cruises attract a broad swath of travelers, from young families to retired folks, and you've got more ships and itineraries to choose from than you could imagine. Chances are there's a ship out there with your name on it. We help you wade through the options and illustrate the vast differences among ships and cruise experiences. To do this, we've divided the cruise lines covered in this book into three main categories—mainstream lines, ultraluxury lines, and soft-adventure lines—and developed a rating system that judges them only against other ships in the same category, so as to offer comparisons between comparable lines and ships. (A 4th category covers some of the major European lines operating in the Caribbean, just to give you a little more than the usual choice.) It's important to compare apples with apples, and not draw irrelevant comparisons between wildly different cruises—say, between ultraluxurious Silversea and adventurous Star Clippers, or riotously mainstream Carnival and genteel, upscale Cunard. You wouldn't compare a two-seater sports car with a hulking sport utility vehicle, would you? The same idea applies here.

HELPING YOU REALISTICALLY BUDGET YOUR TRIP

This book offers something else you won't find in other cruise guides: the ability to find out how much you can *realistically* expect to pay for your cruise. Just like new-car prices, cruise line brochure prices are notoriously inflated—in fact, some lines are talking about dropping them from brochures altogether. In the meantime, you should basically just plain ignore brochure rates. Everything, and we mean everything, is discounted due to stiff competition between cruise lines. Other guidebooks print those inflated brochure prices anyway, leaving it up to you to take a guess at what the real price may be. We don't.

We've partnered with **Just Cruisin' Plus,** a major full-service travel agency specializing in cruises (**www.justcruisin plus.com**), to provide you with the actual prices consumers were paying for cruises aboard all the ships reviewed in this book. Each review shows you approximately how much you can expect to pay for an inside cabin (one without windows) and an outside cabin (with windows or a balcony). In chapter 2, we've provided a chart that shows how these prices compare with the published brochure rates. How much of a difference could it be, you ask? Think about this: The brochure rate for a 7-night western Caribbean cruise aboard Royal Caribbean's beautiful *Radiance of the Seas* is $2,099 for a low-end outside cabin. In reality, however, people who booked during our sampling period (Nov 2003 cruises, priced in mid-Apr)

were able to get that same cabin for $649. If that ain't a big difference, we don't know what is.

CRUISING TODAY: NEW SHIPS FOR PEANUTS . . .

It's mind-boggling just how many ships have been built and introduced over the past few years, all as a result of a building spree the major cruise lines started more than a decade ago. Betting on cruising's ever-increasing popularity—in 1990, just under four million North Americans had taken a cruise, but by 2000, the number had jumped to nearly seven million—the lines have nearly two dozen ships in the construction pipeline through 2004, though in 2005 and beyond, the pace of building seems to be finally slowing down. For now, throw in a recent spate of mergers that allow cruise lines to cut costs and offer lower rates, the continuing post-9/11 redeployment of many ships from Europe to the Caribbean, plus some lingering travel jitters and soft-economy woes, and you have a bargain-lover's dream: more supply than demand, resulting in lower prices. It's not an exaggeration to say this is the best time since the Stone Age to book a cruise. In fact, Carnival President and CEO Bob Dickinson summed up the dramatic situation by pointing out cruise prices haven't been this low since 1974.

And you'll find as many deals on today's newest, splashiest ships as you would on the dated, low-frills ones. Take your pick: You can choose from a head-spinning variety of Caribbean-bound ships—sailing mostly 7-night cruises, but also more 2-, 3-, 4-, 5-, 8-, 10- and 11-nighters. And they're departing from more U.S. ports than ever before. Gone are the days of having to fly to Florida to hop on your Caribbean cruise; now many of you from the northeast, mid-Atlantic, and south-central states can drive to the ship. Caribbean-bound ships now depart from Galveston, Houston, New Orleans, Baltimore, Philadelphia, Charleston, Norfolk, and New York City. Of course, many vessels continue to depart from Miami, Fort Lauderdale, Port Canaveral, and Tampa. And some Caribbean-bound cruises begin or end from West Coast ports such as Los Angeles, San Diego, and San Francisco.

A handful of ships launched in late 2002, after the 2003 edition of this book was published, including Holland America's 1,848-passenger *Zuiderdam*, NCL's 2,224-passenger *Norwegian Dawn*, and Carnival's 2,974-passenger *Conquest*.

Joining the more than 100 ships already plying Caribbean routes are 9 new Caribbean-bound megaships launched in 2003 alone. Early January brought the debut of the 91,000-ton, 1,970-passenger *Coral Princess,* a new class for Princess Cruises, with sister *Island Princess* following in May. A sister to Costa Cruises' *CostaAtlantica,* the 2,112-passenger *CostaMediterranea* was launched in June, while a new class for the line debuted with the 105,000-ton *CostaFortuna* in November. Other sister ships introduced in 2003 included the *Oosterdam* in June, sister to *Zuiderdam,* the first of Holland America's new Vista class of ships. The 110,000-ton *Carnival Glory,* sister to *Carnival Conquest,* Carnival's newest and largest supersize class, launched in July; and *Serenade of the Seas,* a third Radiance-class sister, debuted for Royal Caribbean in August. A brand-new eagerly awaited ship for ultraluxe line Crystal debuted in July; called *Crystal Serenity,* she is slightly larger than sisters *Harmony* and *Symphony.* The fifth mondo Voyager-class ship for Royal Caribbean, 3,114-passenger *Mariner of the Seas* debuted in November.

And 2004 will be pretty impressive too. At last count, 10 more are slated to debut, including the most eagerly awaited new ship: Cunard's 2,620-passenger **Queen Mary 2.** This new classic liner with a modern twist will be both the longest and tallest passenger ship in the world. In April, look for the *Westerdam,* another sister to Holland America's *Zuiderdam.* The *Diamond Princess* is slated to debut in February as the first of a new class for Princess, with a sister, *Sapphire,* to debut in May. Look for a fourth Radiance-class sister in spring, *Jewel of the Seas,* and in November, a sister to the *CostaFortuna—CostaMagica.* At press time, a third Conquest-class ship for Carnival, the 2,874-passenger *Carnival Valor,* was slated to debut in fall 2004.

Sure, there are plenty of new ships to keep us busy sailing for a good long time, but compared to just a few years ago, when 12 to 15 new ships a year was par for the course, the building frenzy is finally slowing down. Only 3 new ships are currently a sure thing for 2005, as lines such as Royal Caribbean and Princess haven't, at press time, signed off on options to build several more new ships. So far, 2006 and beyond appear to be lean years (finally) for new shipbuilding.

. . . OLD ONES FEW AND FAR BETWEEN . . .

The industry's cruise ship fleet is as young as it's ever been. Over the past few years, five lines have gone under (including Premier and Commodore, which operated older ships that are now laid up and getting rustier by the minute), and a handful of ships have been quietly put out to pasture, transferred to European- and Asian-based divisions. In this age of botox and implants, it seems youth is everything, even to cruise lines, as they continue to ditch their frumpiest, oldest, and least high-tech (though in some cases most beloved) vessels en masse. To name a few: Princess's 1970-built *Pacific Princess,* one of the original Love Boats, was retired in November of 2002, and Holland America's 17-year-old *Westerdam* was transferred to Costa Cruises in April 2002 and renamed *CostaEuropa.* What's left behind in the Caribbean market is new, new, new. And that means cabin balconies, triumphalist atria, and multiple restaurants. If you want old and classic, your options are few: NCL's *Norway,* the 51-year-old *Royal Empress* (late of Regal Cruises, and now operated by Imperial Majesty following Regal's demise), plus a very few Caribbean cruises on Cunard's venerable *QE2.* Acting as a sort of candle in the darkness on this issue, NCL announced in April 2003 that it had purchased the SS *United States,* one of the most classic extant ocean liners, laid up now for almost 30 years. To the delight of classic-ship fans everywhere, the line intends to restore her to service. See the NCL review in chapter 6 for more details.

. . . AND DIFFERENT SHIPS FOR DIFFERENT TASTES

While the mondo megaships attract most of the attention these days, they're not the only fish in the sea. In the same way that there are five-star hotels, cozy B&Bs, and roadside motels on land, cruise ships come in all shapes and sizes to please all different walks of life. Adventurous sailing ships and small expedition-style vessels navigate off-the-beaten-path ports, and ultradeluxe ships serve oceans of champagne and jumbo shrimp cocktail. You can sail on ships that require you to pack nothing more than flip-flops, bathing suits, T-shirts, and a pass-me-another-cup-of-that-rum-punch attitude, or you can fill your suitcase with sequins and silk and enough dinner conversation for a week's worth of elegant soirees. It all depends on what you like, how much you want to spend, and where you want to go.

TODAY'S ONBOARD OFFERINGS: FROM E-MAIL TO ICE SKATING

With the exception of the midsize *Seven Seas Voyager,* all of this year's new ships are massive, carrying upward of 2,000 passengers (plus about half that number in crew), weighing from 80,000 to 142,000 gross registered tons, and measuring nearly 1,000 feet long. The biggest cruise ships in the world (at least for now), Royal Caribbean's five Voyager-class ships, are nearly as long as the Empire State Building is tall. *Disney Magic, Disney Wonder, QE2,* and Princess's *Star, Golden,* and *Grand Princess* are all about twice as long as the Washington Monument is tall. Get the picture? Floating hotels, floating cities, floating galaxies—whatever you want to call them, these babies are *big.*

So, what does one of these hot new $350 million to $500 million ships come loaded with? As with the race to build the most outsized SUV, lines are forever trying to outdo each other in the size and gimmick department. Not only do megaships have three or four sprawling dining rooms, a couple of intimate alternative restaurants, easily a dozen bars and entertainment lounges, several pools, cavernous gyms and spas, Internet centers, and a mall-like string of shops, but they also have things you'd never imagine finding on a ship—or even at some resorts, for that matter. The Voyager- and Radiance-class ships have—no kidding—rock-climbing walls and miniature-golf courses, and the Voyager ships also have ice-skating rinks—you know, in case the four pools and regulation-size basketball court aren't enough for you. The

Norwegian Sun, Star, and *Dawn* each have a proper sushi restaurant and a Benihana-style teppanyaki restaurant, while *Brilliance* and *Radiance of the Seas* each have a pair of self-leveling $90,000 pool tables. The *Disney Magic* and *Wonder,* along with Sea-Dream yachts, have futuristic Segway Human Transporters (upright scooter things) for passengers to give a whirl. The *Grand* and *Golden Princess* both have a sprawling virtual-reality video arcade with dozens of machines you can climb onto and do things such as fly-fishing and skiing; plus, these ships and the newer *Coral* and *Island Princess* each sport a nine-hole minia-ture-golf course. You can tap your artistic side in the pottery studios on *Coral* and *Island Princess. Millennium* offers dining in an elegant 1900s-style restaurant designed with actual wood paneling salvaged from the classic early-20th-century liner *Olympic,* sister to the famed *Titanic.* The newest ships in the Norwegian, Carnival, Royal Caribbean, and Princess fleets even have wedding chapels on board.

On ships large and small, must-have accessories are private balconies, multiple dining venues with casual dress codes, specialty coffee cafes, well-equipped spas, cigar bars, and computer rooms with e-mail and Internet access, giving passengers more onboard choices than ever. While Internet and e-mail access is standard on the vast majority of ships today, the latest trend is offering Internet hookups in passenger cabins. And Norwegian even offers wireless access on their newest ship, *Norwegian Dawn.*

So, whatever happened to deck chairs, piña coladas, and afternoon naps? Well, for you Luddites out there, you can still choose to do nothing more than laze by the pool all day with a cold beer and a bestseller. It's up to you.

We offer one caveat to all of this choice, though: The more you choose to do, the more it may cost you. More and more things to do on board mean more and more opportunities for you to spend extra money. Cappuccinos, seaweed wraps, spinning classes, pottery-making, and Häagen-Dazs ice cream all vie for your discretionary dollars, along with the bars, shops, casinos, photo galleries, bingo games, florists, and shore excursions. Ten dollars here, 50 there—it adds up, and can easily add three or four or five hundred dollars (or more) to what seemed initially like a bargain "all-inclusive" cruise.

COVERING THE WATER-FRONT: THE PORTS OF CALL TODAY

The Caribbean is a time-tested favorite, your classic picture-perfect

C Safety at Sea in the New World (Dis)Order

Traditionally, safety-at-sea issues have included icebergs, hurricanes, fire, gastrointestinal bugs (like those widely reported on a handful of ships in fall of 2002), and petty theft. But in the wake of the September 11, 2001, terrorist attacks, the threat of terrorism immediately assumed a high place on that list, though it did so with only a fraction of the media attention paid to airport security. News stories or no, the cruise lines, port authorities, and the U.S. Coast Guard have been tackling the issue and have implemented several new security measures designed to keep cruisers safe and worry-free.

Logistically, ships are more difficult to protect than planes because of their larger passenger loads and multicountry itineraries, their numerous labyrinthine public and "crew only" areas, their regular presence at public port facilities, and the access they offer weekly to the numerous contractors who come aboard on turnaround days to refresh flowers, service machinery, and perform other needed functions. For these reasons, all the major cruise lines have their own dedicated onboard security forces (with generally five to seven members), though events over the years have periodically forced an upgrade in their operations and rules.

Terrorism played a role in the last major upgrade back in 1985, when four members of the Palestine Liberation Front hijacked the Italian ship *Achille Lauro,* killing American Leon Klinghoffer. Following this event, onboard security was substantially tightened, ex–Navy SEALs began to be favored as top-level security consultants, deck officers were drilled in how to react to takeover attempts, and alternative onboard command sites were mandated, making it difficult for a small number of terrorists to take and maintain control of a ship—a task also complicated by the presence of thousands of determined crew and passengers, and the ships' size and complex layouts. Many lines hired dedicated security personnel—in some cases Gurkhas, the famed Nepalese fighters—to assist officers and/or other staffers at the gangway and be on hand as needed.

Following September 11, 2001, all cruise ships went to security level III, the highest dictated by the Coast Guard, but because stringent security measures were already in place, onboard changes have been relatively few. The cruise lines already had used metal detectors at the gangways, required that anyone boarding be on a preapproved list, and employed computerized systems that can tell instantly who is aboard at any given time, both at initial boarding and when passengers are moving on and off ship at the ports of call. New regulations dictate a no-visitors policy, and while picture IDs have always been required when first checking in on the day of embarkation, many cruise lines today are photographing passengers digitally at embarkation. When you slide your shipboard ID card through the computer at each subsequent embarkation, your photo shows up on the gangway officer's computer. (Lines without this technology require guests to show a separate picture ID.) At press time, the U.S. Bureau of Citizenship and Immigration Services (BCIS)—formerly the INS—was trying to establish a regulation that would require all passengers to show a passport when first boarding a ship on embarkation day.

While cruise lines had always screened a significantly higher percentage of bags than airlines had (possibly due to ships' longer turnaround time in port), all bags, ship's stores, mail, and cargo are now carefully screened or X-rayed. At some ports, like the Port of Miami, specially trained dogs are also used to sniff baggage for suspicious substances. In addition, access to sensitive areas such as the bridge has been tightened in some cases—the bridge observation areas on Disney's ships, for example, have been closed for the foreseeable future.

The Coast Guard has stepped up its involvement with ships homeported in the U.S. by reviewing security plans and by generally increasing their presence in major ports of embarkation. In some ports, they have also tested ships' security systems and the no-visitors policy by trying to board clandestinely. Port facilities themselves have been upgraded, with concrete barriers placed to prevent vehicles from approaching the ships and extra security guards hired to patrol the usually open pier facilities. Even lowly garbage dumpsters have been moved to new locations farther away from the ships, to prevent their being used as hiding places for explosives.

The new protection offered in port applies when underway as well; a new 100-yard security zone is mandated around all cruise ships, and the policy is enforced by Coast Guard escorts until the ships are in open ocean. (Say good-bye to those jet skis and small powerboats you'd always see cruising beside you in Miami harbor.) A "Sea Marshall" program is also being tested or considered in a few U.S. cities, with two armed security personnel boarding with the harbor pilot as ships come into port to prevent hostile persons from taking control as the ship passes near bridges or other sensitive structures. Also, ships are now required to give 96 hours' notice of arrival in U.S. ports (rather than the previous 24 hr.), giving BCIS more time to review paperwork and see who is aboard, and make sure no one is disembarking who should not be. To help prevent ships from being used as a means of escape, the INS now sends each ship's purser the current "Prevent Departure" list before every sailing, to compare against the ship's manifest.

Since Level III guidelines apply only to U.S. ports, the cruise lines have been working diligently with foreign port officials to beef up security around the ships, and to protect passengers on shore excursions that the cruise lines sell. Ultimately, if any port's security efforts do not come up to par, the cruise lines have the flexibility to simply alter their itineraries to avoid that port.

All told, the increase in security has been a remarkable balancing act of furthering passengers' safety without infringing upon the fun of their vacation. So relax: These measures and others the companies aren't talking about are there to protect you, and to make your ship a peaceful haven from the outside world—the way it was always meant to be.

island-vacation destination. It's warm and sunny year-round and the major ports of embarkation are more accessible than ever. The big trend in the cruise world these days is **homeporting** ships in cities all around the U.S., rather than having them all sail from Miami and Fort Lauderdale. Unless you live in Kansas, there's a good chance you can drive to one of the many embarkation ports now offered, from Texas to South Carolina and New York. Another plus, Caribbean cruising is hassle-free because American, Canadian, and British citizens don't need visas to go there.

Even as cruise lines continue to offer itineraries in the far corners of the world, from Tahiti to Taormina, the Caribbean remains the most popular cruise destination. In fact, it's never been more popular, with ports along Mexico's Yucatán Peninsula, and in Belize, Honduras, and Panama among the newest additions to the Caribbean circuit. With all the new ships coming on the scene, many lines are increasing their presence here, deploying more and bigger ships. And just like the new ships, new and improved facilities are being introduced at the ports of call, as island nations recognize how lucrative cruise ship arrivals can be. Shore excursions, too, are getting more interesting and more active, with biking, horseback riding, golfing, and river-tubing trips exposing cruisers to the more natural parts of the islands.

While the Caribbean remains hot, hot, hot (and increasingly packed, packed, packed), you may notice that some of the huge ships in the Carnival, Royal Caribbean, Princess, Norwegian, and Holland America fleets visit only three ports during a typical weeklong western or eastern Caribbean cruise instead of four or five ports. What's the story? Ports too crowded?

Ships too big to dock there? Cruise lines wanting to keep passengers on board to spend more money in the shops, bars, and casinos? Passengers just *wanting* to stay on board?

All of the above, if you ask us. First-time cruisers who want to see as many islands as possible may be disappointed, but there are alternatives: Small-ship lines such as Windstar, Star Clippers, Windjammer, Clipper, American Canadian Caribbean, Sea-Dream Yacht Club, and Seabourn really pack in the ports of call, visiting a different island nearly every single day, sometimes even making two stops—one in the morning and another after lunch. Even some of the big ships, such as Royal Caribbean's *Mariner* and *Radiance of the Seas,* Celebrity's *Constellation,* Princess's *Dawn Princess,* and NCL's *Norwegian Sky,* visit five ports on their 7-night southern Caribbean itineraries; Carnival's *Jubilee* actually visits six ports.

On the other hand, if you've been to the Caribbean many times (been there, done that . . .) and are just looking for relaxation and an escape from winter weather, the big new ships may be a good choice for you, with so much happening on board that you don't have to even leave the ship to have fun. The upshot is, make sure the itinerary you choose is right for you.

To give you an even more well-rounded look at Caribbean cruises, this book includes coverage of Panama Canal itineraries and Bermuda cruises. Sure, we know Bermuda's not in the Caribbean, but the British-flavored island is a unique cruise destination; unlike other ports where visits rarely exceed 1 day, the five ships that conduct regularly scheduled weeklong cruises to Bermuda spend 3 of those days tied up at Hamilton or St. George's.

BON VOYAGE!

Just the fact that you've bought this book means you've got a hankering to cruise; now it's our job to help you find the cruise that's just right for you from among the huge selection of ships and cruise experiences in the market. We've made the reviews candid and provided lots of tips and first-hand experience to help you navigate the vast sea of choices. Together, we'll get you hooked up with the vacation of your dreams.

Bon Voyage!

The Best of Cruising

To make it easier for you to select your cruise, we've compiled these "Frommer's Favorites," our picks of the best lines, ships, and ports of call for different types of cruise experiences. You'll find more complete information in part 2, "The Cruise Lines & Their Ships," and part 3, "The Ports."

1 Our Favorite Ships

Now, this is subjective, mind you, but that's the point—even two ships that are equally well designed and equally well run will appeal differently to different people. While we love lots of ships, here are our personal favorites in each of the three main categories into which we've divided the reviews in this book.

- **Mainstream Ships:** Mainstream ships are the big boys of the industry, carrying the most passengers and providing the most diverse cruise experiences to suit many different tastes, from party-hearty to elegant and refined. Among them, our picks are Celebrity's 100% classy **Millennium-class ships** with their excellent, ultra-elegant alternative restaurants; Princess's huge but cozy **Grand-class ships** and slightly smaller *Coral Princess,* introduced this year; and Royal Caribbean's impressive **Radiance-class ships,** with all of their glass and nautically inspired public rooms and cabins. See chapter 6.
- **Ultraluxury Ships:** Got some big bucks to spend on a superluxurious cruise? These are the ships for you. Offering elegant, refined, and doting service, extraordinary dining, spacious cabins, and high-toned entertainment aboard intimately sized, finely appointed vessels, they're the Dom Perignon of cruises. Our picks overall are Windstar's intimate sailing ships *Wind Spirit,* Silversea's rich *Silver Shadow* and *Whisper,* and Radisson's lovely *Seven Seas Navigator.* See chapter 7.
- **Soft-Adventure & Sailing Ships:** Maybe you want to sail on a ship that *really* sails. If so, several lines offer cruises aboard vessels that, while they do use engines to keep their schedules, are fully capable of going it under sail alone. Among them, Star Clipper's *Royal Clipper* offers an experience that's incredibly romantic (and cushy), while Windjammer Barefoot Cruises' *Mandalay* offers an experience that is ruggedly romantic and wonderfully adventurous. See chapter 8.

2 Best Luxury Cruises

Here's the very best for the Caribbean cruiser who's used to traveling deluxe and who doesn't mind paying for the privilege. These ships have the best cuisine, accommodations, and service at sea.

- **Silversea:** Best overall highbrow, small-ship cruise line. With its cuisine, roomy suites, and over-the-top service, which includes complimentary and free-flowing Moët & Chandon champagne, the 388-passenger *Shadow* and *Whisper,* and 296-passenger *Silver Wind,* are the crème de la crème of high-end cruises. See p. 318.

• **Crystal Cruises:** The 940-passenger *Crystal Harmony* and *Crystal Symphony,* and new 1,080-passenger *Serenity* are the best midsize ships out there, big enough to offer lots of dining, entertainment, and fitness options, and small enough to bathe passengers in luxury. See p. 276.

• **Radisson Seven Seas:** Not only are cabins aboard the 490-passenger,

all-suite *Seven Seas Navigator* roomy at 301 square feet, but their huge bathrooms are the best at sea (along with the identical ones offered on fleetmate *Seven Seas Voyager* and Silversea's *Silver Shadow* and *Whisper*). To top it off, food and service on both are among the very best at sea! See p. 289.

• **Celebrity Cruises:** The 1,950-passenger Millennium-class ships and the 1,880-passenger *Galaxy* and *Mercury* are the best luxury mega-ships, featuring wonderful spas, cigar bars, modern art collections, and entertainment lounges—and prices that are far lower than you'd expect. See p. 139.

3 Best Cruises for First-Timers

Short 3- and 4-night cruises are among the best ways to test the waters. Here are our favorite shorties, as well as one particularly good weeklong cruise, any of which would be a good choice for first-timers.

• **Carnival Cruise Lines:** The 3- and 4-night Bahamas cruises on the *Fascination,* sailing from Miami, or *Fantasy,* sailing from Port Canaveral, are great choices. These flashy megas offer lots to do all day long, and their standard cabins are among the largest at sea. See p. 116.

• **Royal Caribbean International:** Like Carnival's 3- and 4-night Bahamas cruises, those out of Miami on *Majesty of the Seas* and out of Port Canaveral on *Sovereign of the Seas* are total megaship fun, with tons to do for all ages, though they're a shade more low-key than Carnival ships. See p. 242.

• **Imperial Majesty:** The *Regal Empress* may be 51 years old and

not so regal anymore, but she's a classic, and her 2-night Nassau cruises are cheap and a fun way to get your feet wet. See p. 4.

• **Disney Cruise Line:** For Disney fanatics, a 3- or 4-night Bahamas cruise on *Disney Wonder* is the closest you'll get to a Disney park at sea. Half ship, half theme park, the Disney vessels are a great segue into cruising. See p. 166.

• **Crystal Cruises:** If you're a glutton for the best of everything, the 940-passenger *Crystal Harmony* and *Symphony,* and the new 1,080-passenger *Serenity,* are unlike other high-end ships in that they're big enough to keep first-timers busy, with lots of outdoor deck space, generous fitness facilities, and more than a half dozen bars and entertainment venues, as well as pampering service and scrumptious cuisine. In 2003, the ships began offering more 7-night Caribbean cruises than ever before. See p. 276.

4 The Most Romantic Cruises

Of course, all cruises are pretty romantic when you consider the props they have to work with: the undulating sea all around, moonlit nights on deck, cozy dining and cocktailing, private cabin balconies. The majority of cruise passengers are couples, and more and more romantic pairs are getting married on board or in port, renewing their vows, or celebrating anniversaries. (For how to get married on board, see chapter 1, "Choosing Your Ideal Cruise.") Here are some great ships to get you in the mood.

- **Windstar Cruises:** Pure romance. Spend the day with your loved one in a private cove with *Wind Surf* or *Wind Spirit* anchored offshore, bobbing calmly on the waves, sails furled. Windstar offers a truly unique cruise experience, giving passengers the delicious illusion of adventure and the ever-pleasant reality of first-class cuisine, service, and itineraries. See p. 326.
- **Celebrity Cruise Lines:** If your idea of romance is a date with a big, glamorous ship, then Celebrity's **Millennium-class ships,** with their quiet alternative restaurants, cozy piano bars, intimate lounges, and great spas, are a sure thing. See p. 139.
- **Holland America Line:** This line attracts lots of 50-plus couples celebrating anniversaries and/or renewing vows, and offers several goodie packages you can buy to sweeten the moment. The midsize **Statendam-class ships,** as well as

the *Volendam* and *Zaandam* twins and *Rotterdam,* will put you in the mood with their elegant Crow's Nest observation lounges/nightclubs, with floor-to-ceiling windows, dim lighting, and cozy seating. The private cabin balconies and glamorous two-story dining rooms will help, too. See p. 175.

- **Sea Cloud Cruises:** Really, when it comes right down to it, what setting is more movie-star romantic than a zillionaire's sailing yacht? That's what you get with *Sea Cloud I,* once owned by Edward F. Hutton and Marjorie Merriweather Post, with some cabins retaining their original grandeur. See p. 378.
- **Star Clippers:** With the wind in your hair and sails fluttering overhead, the top decks of the four- and five-masted *Royal Clipper, Star Clipper,* and *Star Flyer* provide a most romantic setting. Below decks, the comfy cabins, lounge, and dining room make these ships the most comfortable adventure on the sea. See p. 349.
- **Windjammer:** If footloose and fancy-free describes you and your betrothed, then the rum-swigging, T-shirts-and-shorts-wearing ambience of *Mandalay, Legacy,* and their sister ships will be your ideal. Ultracasual and ultrafree, these eclectic sailing ships are a trip, and their itineraries are offbeat. See p. 359.

5 Best Cruises for Families with Kids

More families are cruising than ever before, and lines are beefing up their family programs to keep the kids happy and content. All the lines included here offer supervised activities for three to five age groups

between ages 2 or 3 and 17, and have well-stocked playrooms, wading pools, kids' menus, and cabins that can accommodate three to five people. They also offer group and/or private babysitting. See the box "Family

Cruising," in chapter 1, and the cruise line reviews in chapters 6 through 8, which describe children's activities in detail.

- **Disney Cruise Lines:** This family magnet offers the most sophisticated and high-tech seagoing children's program in the world, bar none. Huge play areas, family-friendly cabins, baby nursery, and the ubiquitous Mickey all spell success. Plus, the 3- and 4-night Bahamas cruises aboard the *Disney Wonder* are marketed in tandem with stays at Disney World, so you can have your ocean voyage and your Space Mountain, too. See p. 166.

- **Royal Caribbean:** The huge **Voyager-class ships** are truly theme parks at sea, with such totally bizarre features as an onboard rock-climbing wall, an ice-skating rink, an in-line skate rink, miniature golf, and a Disneyesque Main Street running down the center of each vessel, with parades and other entertainment throughout the day. The **Radiance class** is also a great family choice, offering rock climbing and miniature golf. All this is in addition to bigger-than-normal kids' playrooms, teen centers, wading pools, and video game rooms, plus regulation-size basketball, paddle ball, and volleyball courts. Even the line's older ships have impressively roomy kids' facilities. See p. 242.

- **Carnival Cruise Lines:** Despite a let-the-good-times-roll allure that appeals to adults, Carnival goes out of its way to amuse people of all ages, and does a particularly fine job with kids 2 to 15 years old. A few hundred per cruise is pretty normal, with as many as 700 to 800 kids on Christmas and New Year's cruises. The kids' facilities are the most extensive on the newest ships in the **Destiny, Spirit,** and **Conquest class,** where you'll find the biggest and brightest playrooms in the fleet, with computer stations, a climbing maze, a video wall showing movies and cartoons, arts and crafts, and oodles of toys and games, plus great water slides out on the main pool deck. See p. 116.

- **Princess Cruises:** *Grand, Golden, Sun, Dawn, Coral,* and *Island Princess* each have a spacious children's playroom and a sizable piece of fenced-in outside deck for kids, with a wading pool. Teen centers have computers, video games, and a sound system, and the ones on the *Grand* and *Golden* even have teen hot tubs and private sunbathing decks. See p. 224.

- **Norwegian Cruise Line:** The kids' facilities on the line's new *Norwegian Dawn* are fantastic, with a huge, brightly colored crafts/play area, a TV room full of beanbag chairs, an enormous ball-jump/play-gym, a nap room, a teen center, and a large outdoor play/pool area that even has a Jacuzzi just for kids. Parents will appreciate the many restaurant options on board, while kids can dine in tiny chairs at a kid-size buffet of their own. See p. 196.

6 Best Cruises for Party-Hungry Singles

A cruise can be a great social vacation for solo travelers looking to mingle, if you choose the right one.

- **Windjammer Barefoot Cruises:** If you're under about 45 (or think you are) and have an informal attitude, these cruises are a great bet, extremely dress-down and casual. Things can get very, very intimate aboard these small tall ships; it's amazing what a little wind, waves, stars, and moonlight can do. The free rum punch and $2 beers don't hurt, either! There are a handful of rowdy singles-only cruises annually—erotic tart-eating contest, anyone? See p. 359.

- **Carnival Cruise Lines:** Single men and women in their 20s, 30s, and 40s seek out Carnival's "fun ships" for their wild-and-crazy decor and around-the-clock excitement. What else would you expect from ships bearing such names as *Fantasy, Inspiration,* and *Sensation?* The Pool Deck is always bustling (especially on the 3- and 4-nighters), with music playing so loudly you'll have to go back to your cabin to think, and the discos and nightspots hop until the early morning hours. The ships are big, offering many places to meet and mingle. Who knows whom you may meet in that aerobics class, on that shore excursion, or even at your dining table? See p. 116.

- **Royal Caribbean:** This line draws a good cross section of men and women from all walks of life. As with Carnival, a decent number of passengers are singles and in their 20s, 30s, and 40s, especially on the short 3-and 4-night weekend cruises. For an exciting Saturday-night-out-on-the-town barhopping kind of thing, the **Voyager-class ships** feature a truly unique multideck, boulevard-like promenade running down the center of each ship, its ground floor lined with shops, bars, restaurants, and entertainment outlets, and multistory atria at either end. See p. 242.

- **Norwegian Cruise Line:** This line is a heavy contender in the singles sweepstakes, offering both short 3- and 4-nighters and weeklong cruises. There are tons of activities all day, hoppin' pool decks, lots of dining venues, and some of the best entertainment at sea. An added plus: The ships all have casual dress codes and open-seating dining, creating more mingling opportunities. See p. 196.

- **Crystal Cruises:** This line's elegant 940-passenger *Harmony* and *Symphony* and 1,080-passenger *Serenity* are good choices for single ladies and men over 50. Since there tend to be more older single women cruising than older single men, "gentleman hosts"—men in their 50s and 60s, semiemployed by the line (at least for one trip)—sail aboard all Panama Canal cruises and act as dancing and dinner hosts for unattached ladies. See p. 276.

7 Best Cuisine

Here's where you'll find the finest restaurants afloat, rivaling what you'd find at the best restaurants in the world's major cities.

- **Celebrity Cruise Line:** It doesn't get any better than the alternative restaurants on the **Millennium-class ships,** all supervised by chef and restaurateur Michel Roux of the Waterside Inn, one of England's few three-star Michelin restaurants. Reservations are required in these intimate, elegantly designed spots. *Millennium's* Olympic restaurant boasts the actual gilded French walnut wood paneling used aboard White Star Line's *Olympic,* sister ship to *Titanic,* while sister ships *Infinity, Summit,* and *Constellation* have restaurants themed around artifacts from the SS *United States, Normandie,* and *Ile de France.* A highly trained staff dotes on diners with tableside cooking, musicians play elegant period pieces, and the entire decadent experience takes about 3 hours. It costs $25 a person, but it's well worth it. See p. 139.

- **Silversea Cruises:** Hit it on a sunset departure from port, and the windowed, candlelit Terrace Cafe alternative restaurant on this line's four ships becomes a window to the passing scenery and a home for some of the best food at sea. Reservations are required for the fixed theme menu, with the Asian night starting with sushi and sashimi, while a French feast begins with foie gras and is followed by a scallop and ratatouille salad, beef tenderloin, and a warm chocolate tart with raspberries. (Excellent wines and all spirits are included in the cruise rates.) See p. 318.

- **Crystal Cruises:** While all the food you'll get on these ships is first-class, their reservations-only Asian specialty restaurants are the best at sea. Master Chef Nobuyuki "Nobu" Matsuhisa is behind the outstanding Asian food on *Serenity*, and the restaurant on *Harmony* serves up utterly delicious, fresh Japanese food, including sushi. The accouterments help set the tone, too—chopsticks, sake served in tiny sake cups and decanters, and sushi served on thick blocky square glass platters. An Asian-theme buffet lunch, offered at least once per cruise, gives passengers an awesome spread, from jumbo shrimp to chicken and beef satays to stir-fry dishes. See p. 276.

- **Radisson Seven Seas Cruises:** The award-winning chefs aboard all the line's Caribbean ships produce artful culinary presentations that compare favorably to those of New York's or San Francisco's top restaurants, and the waiters are some of the industry's best. See p. 289.

- **Seabourn Cruise Lines:** There's nothing quite like dining on the outdoor deck of *Legend* and *Pride*'s Veranda Café, where casual dinners are offered most nights. With the ships' wakes shushing just below, it's a rare opportunity to dine with the sea breezes and starry night sky surrounding you. Theme Caribbean, Italian, Thai, and Surf & Turf menus are featured. See p. 303.

- **Norwegian Cruise Lines:** The *Norwegian Sun* and new *Norwegian Dawn* offer the greatest range of dining choices at sea—9 restaurants on *Sun* and 10 on *Dawn*. While the fare in the main dining rooms is totally average, it's quite good in some of the alternative venues, including the sushi bar and the elegant French/continental Le Bistro. See p. 196.

- **Best Vegetarian Cuisine:** Every line offers vegetarian options with every meal, but **Holland America** also has a separate menu of vegetarian dishes from which you can order any day of the week. The tofu stroganoff on *Veendam* was the best vegetarian dish we've ever had aboard a ship. See p. 175.

8 Best Spas

If a massage is your idea of nirvana, then you're in luck. Most ships, especially those built within the past few years, have excellent spa facilities. These are the best.

- **Celebrity Cruises:** No contest: Celebrity's **Millennium-class** and **Century-class** ships have the most attractive spas at sea. The huge AquaSpas manage to combine a huge repertoire of the latest wraps, packs, soaks, and massages with striking aesthetics inspired by motifs such as Japanese gardens and bathhouses, and Moorish and Turkish spas. Facilities include saunas, mud baths, massage rooms, and Turkish baths. Each also offers a dip in the thalassotherapy pool (a souped-up hot tub the size of a swimming pool). See p. 139.

- **Windstar Cruises:** The intimate, 308-passenger *Wind Surf* has extensive spa facilities and a staff of 10, with prebookable spa packages combining six or more treatments tailored to men and women. See p. 326.
- **Royal Caribbean:** The two-level spa complex aboard the line's new **Voyager-class ships** is among the largest and best accoutered out there. A peaceful waiting area has New Age tropical bird-song music piped in overhead. Ahhhh, relaxation—until you get your bill. *Radiance* and *Brilliance of the Seas* not only have huge Africa- and India-themed solariums (respectively), but also 13 treatment rooms, including a special steamroom complex featuring heated, tiled chaise longues and special

showers simulating tropical rain and fog. See p. 242.

- **Radisson Seven Seas:** The spa aboard the 490-passenger *Seven Seas Navigator* and 700-passenger *Mariner* and *Voyager* are some of the few not run by the ubiquitous Steiner spa vendor. Instead, the Judith Jackson spa provides quality, first-rate treatments and doesn't shove its skin-care products down your throat just as you are coming out of a massage-induced trance. Innovative treatments include a relaxing 20-minute hair and scalp oil massage, and a 1-hour four-hand massage—two therapists work on you simultaneously. See p. 289.
- **Norwegian Cruise Line:** The new *Norwegian Dawn* really ratchets up the line's commitment to spa culture, with facilities located off a lofty, sunlit entrance atrium done up in greenery and a Mayan design theme. Treatment options are par for today's cruise-ship course, but a big thumbs up goes to the spa's indoor pool complex, an elegant space with a large lap pool, hot tub, jet-massage pool, and sunny windowed seating areas. See p. 196.

9 Best Gyms

If you can't bear to miss a workout, even while on a cruise, you're in luck. Most ships, especially those built within the past few years, have excellent fitness facilities.

- **Carnival Cruise Lines:** The gyms on *Destiny, Triumph,* and *Victory* are cavernous, with more than 40 state-of-the-art exercise machines, including virtual-reality stationary bikes. The huge spaces are framed in floor-to-ceiling windows and the machines are spaced far apart,

so you'll never feel cramped. See p. 116.

- **Holland America:** The oceanview gyms aboard the line's *Rotterdam, Volendam,* and *Zaandam,* as well as the new *Zuiderdam,* are downright palatial, and though there are dozens of state-of-the-art machines, they're spaced so far apart that you may wonder (as we did on a recent sailing) whether more equipment is on backorder, coming to fill all the space.

Nope—they're just spacious, and among the best gyms at sea. The adjacent aerobics room is huge, too—nearly as big as the ones we use at home. See p. 175.

• **Royal Caribbean:** Though they can get a bit cramped when busy, the gyms on the line's **Voyager-class** ships are huge, with a large indoor whirlpool, scads of aerobics and weight machines, and some of the largest aerobics studios at sea. See p. 242.

10 Best Soft-Adventure & Learning Cruises

If you want to explore more remote areas of the Caribbean where the megaships can't venture (and maybe even learn something in the process) or want a vessel that recalls the sailing days of yore, here are your best bets.

• **Windstar Cruises:** *Wind Spirit* and her larger sibling *Wind Surf* are the most high-end of the motorized sailing ships, and make stops in some of the most intriguing off-the-beaten-path ports in the Caribbean, such as Tobago and Bequia, one of the jewels of the Grenadines but a place where the megaships don't go. Other stops include the remote, little-visited Mayreau and Nevis, and the lovely little French outpost of Iles des Saintes. See p. 326.

• **Clipper Cruise Line:** Despite their names, the *Nantucket Clipper* and *Yorktown Clipper* don't have sails, but they're the perfect ships for people who like the Holland America or Princess experience but want to see what a smaller, more exploration- and education-oriented vessel can give them. Some cruises will introduce you to history and culture, but others are oriented toward pure adventure, concentrating on ports of call with rugged scenic beauty and opportunities for wildlife viewing. The company's ships call at remote islands in the Grenadines, as well as Belize and Costa Rica. See p. 343.

• **Star Clippers:** Clippers' biggest and plushest tall ship to date, the 5,000-ton, 228-passenger *Royal Clipper,* is one of the largest sailing ships ever built. Adventurous yet very comfy, the vessel visits small ports such as Iles des Saintes, Antigua, St. Kitts, Dominica, St. Lucia, Bequia, Tobago Cays, and Grenada. Slightly smaller fleet-mate *Star Clipper* also offers the same ambience and great ports. See p. 349.

• **Windjammer Barefoot Cruises:** This eclectic fleet of pirate-style sailing ships feels more adventurous than any of the others, and will take you to some of the Caribbean's less frequented islands. A typical itinerary round-trip from Grenada visits Carriacou, Palm Island, Bequia, St. Vincent, and Mayreau. Two of the line's ships—the sailing ship *Mandalay* and the nonsail passenger/cargo ship *Amazing Grace*—sail 12-night itineraries that stop at a bundle of off-the-beaten-path islands. See p. 359.

11 Best Cruises for Snorkelers & Scuba Divers

Virtually any cruise you take in the Caribbean will allow you opportunities to snorkel at one or another of the island ports. Scuba-diving excursions are fairly common, too. Grand Cayman, Bonaire, Virgin Gorda, St. Croix, and Belize offer the best waters.

• **Star Clippers:** This line's owner, Mikael Krafft, is a dedicated scuba diver, and he selects his sailing ships' itineraries through the Caribbean based in part on the accessibility of superior, intriguing, and often offbeat dive sites, including small ports that many big cruise ships can't even approach. See p. 349.

- **Windstar:** These cozy megayachts visit some of the Caribbean's best sites for snorkeling and scuba diving, including the reefs and cays of Belize. See p. 326.
- **Clipper Cruises:** Like Windstar, this line's small ships visit off-the-beaten-track sites; the *Nantucket Clipper* does weeklong cruises round-trip out of Belize City, visiting ports in both Belize and Honduras. See p. 343.

- **Windjammer Barefoot Cruises:** Windjammer's ships offer year-round diving possibilities on 6- to 13-day cruises to some 50 ports, including the rarely visited Grenadines. Divers should look for itineraries that depart from Tortola, capital of the British Virgin Islands. See p. 359.
- **Princess Cruises:** Princess's "New Waves" program allows ambitious passengers to earn PADI Open Water Diver certification, completing all coursework and dives while aboard or doing some of the homework before your cruise. The program is offered aboard all 7-night Caribbean sailings. See p. 224.

12 Best Cruises for Golfers

Many lines sell golfing shore excursions with tee times and transportation between the ship and the course, and on some ships a golf pro sails aboard, offering onboard lessons (about $80 per hour) and escorting players to the great courses on Bermuda, St. Thomas, Puerto Rico, and Jamaica. Some Royal Caribbean, Princess, and Crystal ships have putting greens on board, while others have golf simulators, state-of-the-art virtual-reality machines that allow you to play the great courses of the world without ever leaving the ship (for about $20 per half-hour).

- **Royal Caribbean:** Eight of the line's ships—*Brilliance, Radiance, Voyager, Explorer, Adventure, Navigator, Legend,* and *Splendour of the Seas*—feature a real live miniature-golf course on board. The **Radiance-** and **Voyager-class ships** also have golf simulators, and the Voyagers also have a golf-themed sports bar. The ships are so huge and well stabilized that

golfers are seldom bothered by motion. See p. 242.

- **Crystal Cruises:** The *Harmony, Symphony,* and *Serenity* each have two golf driving nets and a large putting green, so golfing fanatics can hit balls virtually all day long. An instructor is often on board giving complimentary group instruction throughout the week. See p. 276.
- **Celebrity Cruises:** On every one of their Bermuda cruises, *Zenith* and *Horizon* feature a PGA-certified pro who gives lessons at the ship's driving net. In port, the pro takes golfers to the courses for hands-on instruction. The **Century-** and **Millennium-class ships** have golf simulators. See p. 139.
- **Princess Cruises:** *Grand, Golden, Sun, Dawn, Coral,* and *Island Princess* have golf simulators on board; and *Golden, Grand, Coral,* and *Island* also have a nine-hole miniature-golf course. See p. 224.

13 Best Cruises for Gamblers

Gamblers are in luck. Most cruise ships, with the exception of the small ships in the soft-adventure category (see chapter 8, "Soft-Adventure Lines & Sailing Ships"), have casinos. The megaships have sprawling Vegas-style operations with dozens of gaming tables and hundreds of slots, as well as roulette and craps. Some of the midsize ships have more modest digs, with just a couple of blackjack and poker tables and a handful of slots. A few of the islands have casinos too, and since most ships' casinos are closed while in port, high-rollers should make sure to choose an itinerary that includes Nassau, San Juan, Aruba, Curaçao, and/or Sint Maarten. The following lines have the biggest and best in the size and flashiness departments.

- **Carnival Cruise Lines:** Fleetwide, Carnival's casinos are the best at sea: bold, bright, and glowing with neon. See p. 116.
- **Royal Caribbean International:** Fleetwide, the casinos are exciting places to play. The three-level casino on *Nordic Empress* is particularly appealing, and the mondo ones on the new **Voyager-class ships** are mind-blowing. See p. 242.
- **Princess Cruises:** All of the line's megaships attract gamblers, but the huge casinos on *Grand* and *Golden Princess* are the best of the lot. See p. 224.
- **Celebrity Cruises:** Some of the Caribbean's best casinos are aboard Celebrity's **Millennium-** and **Century-class ships.** They're large and dazzling, though in a more subdued way than their neon competition. See p. 139.

14 Best Beaches

If time logged on the beach is just as important to you as days spent at sea, you'll want to consider cruises that stop in the following ports.

- **In the Western Caribbean:** Grand Cayman and Jamaica are two of the Caribbean's best. Grand Cayman's **Seven Mile Beach** is a stretch of pristine sand easily accessible via a short taxi ride from Georgetown. Jamaica's **Negril** is also accessible via taxi, and is closer to Montego Bay than to Ocho Rios. See chapter 11.
- **In the Eastern and Southern Caribbean:** Beach bums should head to **Trunk Bay** in St. John (protected by the U.S. National Park Service), **Grand Anse Beach** in Grenada, **Shoal Bay** in Anguilla (topless and sometimes bottomless too), **Orient Beach** in St. Martin, and Aruba's 7 miles of beach—all excellent stretches of white sand. All are easily accessible via taxi. See chapter 11.

15 Best Ports for Serious Shoppers

All the ports have at least a few stores or souvenir stands, and most have a sprawling market or complex of stores near the cruise ship docks. Believe us, if a ship is coming to an island, the locals will be ready to sell you stuff.

The following are the absolute best spots for dedicated shoppers. All offer duty-free shopping and stores bursting with jewelry, perfume and cosmetics, clothing, accessories, arts and crafts, liquor, and souvenirs. Ubiquitous chains such as Little Switzerland, Colombian Emeralds, and Diamonds International sell a wide variety of duty-free gold and silver jewelry and gems. In outdoor markets and craft shops, look for local specialties such as straw hats and purses, beaded necklaces, and brightly painted folk art and carved-wood boxes, as well as your more typical souvenirs: T-shirts, snow globes, and beach towels.

The bad news: While the following islands offer lots of variety, the days of getting great deals in the Caribbean have gone the way of the eight-track player. Where there's demand (a heck of a lot of passengers pour off cruise ships these days), there are high prices. The exceptions to this are on the booze front, where you can often get some great buys.

- **St. Thomas:** Close to the cruise ship docks, Charlotte Amalie is the island's shopping mecca, and you get a bigger customs allowance than you do coming from non-U.S. ports. See p. 620.

- **The Bahamas: Nassau** and **Freeport** are veritable shopping free-for-alls. Go wild. See p. 441.
- **St. Croix: Christiansted** has shopping galore, and is also covered by the U.S. Virgin Islands customs allowance. See p. 632.
- **Puerto Rico: San Juan,** Puerto Rico's capital, is historic and a great shopping spot, with lots of antique and art galleries. The same customs deal applies here as at St. Thomas and St. Croix. See p. 573.
- **Grand Cayman: Georgetown** has numerous brand-name and other shops clustered right around its port facilities. See p. 518.
- **St. Martin/Sint Maarten:** French **Marigot** and Dutch **Philipsburg** are particularly good for European luxury items. See p. 604.
- **Aruba: Oranjestad's** Caya G. F. Betico Croes compresses six continents into one main, theme-park-like shopping street. See p. 435.

16 Best Bathrooms at Sea

Last, but not least . . . . okay, so you don't want to spend all day in them (people will start to talk), but let's admit it, bathrooms are important places. Here are our picks of the best.

- **Radisson Seven Seas:** Bigger and better than those on high-end Seabourn and Crystal ships, every single bathroom on *Seven Seas Navigator* and *Seven Seas Voyager* has a separate shower stall and a full-size bathtub long enough for a normal-size human to actually recline in, as well as a long marble counter flanked by two sets of tall shelves, and a generous collection of chichi lemon-scented soaps and shampoos by spa guru Judith Jackson. See p. 289.
- **Silversea:** *Shadow* and *Whisper* boast the exact same wonderful stateroom bathrooms the *Navigator* and *Voyager* do, only with rich

green tea–scented Bulgari bath products. See p. 318.
- **Disney:** They don't come any family-friendlier than this! The majority of *Wonder* and *Magic's* 875 cabins are equipped with *two bathrooms*—a sink and toilet in one and a shower/tub combo and a sink in the other. Both, while compact, have ample shelf space. This will cut down on family squabbles for sure! See p. 166.
- **Holland America Line:** Just outside the top level of the dining room on *Volendam* and *Zaandam* are little-girl-pink, oceanview public powder rooms. You can touch up the shadow and spray the locks like a queen in these spacious places, which are set up with four mirrored vanity tables and stools. See p. 175.

- **Royal Caribbean:** Nothing better to boost a guy's self-esteem than to use the ritzy marble urinal on *Voyager of the Seas*. The caviar of cans, the men's room outside of the Island Grill and Windjammer restaurant boasts an oceanview and a breathtaking (well, almost) forest green, malachite-like undulating marble urinal bank. See p. 242.
- **Windstar:** *Wind Surf*'s 30 suites have two full bathrooms, his and hers, each with its own shower and toilet. See p. 326.
- **Norwegian:** The new *Norwegian Dawn* has inspirational oceanview men's rooms on the Pool Deck, and bathrooms in the Garden Villas suites are out of this world, with wraparound windows, jet-massage pools, and more s-p-a-c-e than most folks would know what to do with. Located on the highest deck of the ship, they have sky-high prices to match. See p. 196.

Part 1

Planning, Booking & Preparing for Your Cruise

With advice on choosing and booking your ideal cruise and tips on getting ready for the cruise experience.

1 Choosing Your Ideal Cruise
2 Booking Your Cruise & Getting the Best Price
3 Things to Know Before You Go
4 The Cruise Experience

Choosing Your Ideal Cruise

We know you have many things you should consider before you head off for your perfect cruise—oh, you know, like should you pack a bikini or a one-piece? John Grisham or Gabriel García Márquez? The new digital camera or a disposable? But way before you deal with these decisions, you really do need to consider some important issues. What kind of itinerary are you looking for and when do you want to go? What size ship will make you most comfortable? Which are family-friendly, or accessible to travelers with disabilities? Is a particular cruise active enough for you? In this chapter, we'll address all of these issues and more.

1 When to Go

THE CARIBBEAN With temperatures in the balmy 80s (upper 20s Celsius) almost year-round, dozens of ships stay in the Caribbean full-time, and a bunch more spend the winters there after summering in Alaska or Europe: The Caribbean is the only major cruise destination that never closes; it's the sea that never sleeps. Defining seasons as "low" and "high," then, is more a matter of supply-and-demand than of weather and appeal, though there is the matter of **hurricane season** to consider. Officially, the season runs from June 1 to November 30, but it rarely causes cruisers anything more than a few days of rain and a bit of rocking and rolling. We've taken many cruises in the Caribbean during this period and have only occasionally run into stormy weather. It's rare, but it's a risk you take. The chance of getting caught in a really dangerous storm is next to nil, however, as modern communications (and generally speedy vessels) allow captains to change course and pilot their ships out of danger as soon as they get word of a storm.

Since the vast majority of cruisers now book their trips at the last minute, most lines have stopped bothering to divide rates by season at all, relying on demand to determine which deals they offer. In general, **high season** is mid-December through mid-April, the period when northerners tend to flee the cold in favor of the Caribbean's near-perfect weather. The largest number of ships are assigned to the region during these months, so even though demand is highest, it's often outpaced by supply. Within this season, the **holiday weeks** of Christmas, New Year's, Presidents' Day, and Easter are generally the busiest and most expensive, especially on the family-oriented megaships. (See chapter 2, "Booking Your Cruise & Getting the Best Price," for a full explanation of pricing.) The **summer months** of June, July, and August are the next busiest times, since families traditionally vacation during these months. Temperatures may be a bit hotter, but the islands' lush and colorful flowering trees are at their height and the winds are mildest. Since many ships migrate to Alaska and Europe for this season, demand is a bit higher for vessels that remain in the Caribbean. September, October, and early November are considered **low season** and are the times when you encounter the fewest crowds on shore and on board, and often very low rates. Sometimes, there can be a lull during the first 2 weeks of January, just after the rush of the holidays, and occasionally in late April and May, so look for good prices then as well.

PANAMA CANAL   The Panama Canal cruise season is roughly the same as the Caribbean's, generally between about November and April. A few lines, like Holland America, have ships doing Panama Canal cruises in September and October too. Many ships do only two Panama Canal cruises annually, when repositioning between the summer season in Alaska and the fall/winter season in the Caribbean.

BERMUDA   The Bermuda cruise season extends from late April to early October, with the peak between late June and late August, when the average temperature is 80°F (27°C)—10° to 15° higher than the rest of the year.

2 Choosing the Itinerary That's Best for You

If you count every little rocky outcropping and sandbar, the Caribbean has hundreds of islands, but of the 40 or 50 that make it onto the map, cruise ships regularly visit only about 25 of them. Most Caribbean cruises are 7 nights long and visit anywhere from three to six different ports, with megaships tending toward the lower number, spending the rest of their time on leisurely (and more profitable) days at sea. A handful of 2-, 3-, and 4-night cruises out of Florida visit the Bahamas or Cozumel, Mexico; 4- and 5-night cruises out of Tampa, Miami, New Orleans, and Galveston, Texas, do western Caribbean itineraries; and 10- to 14-night Caribbean cruises transit the Panama Canal, typically sailing between Florida and Acapulco, visiting three to seven ports.

While they're all appealing in some way, the Caribbean islands are not all created equal. Some islands are better for shopping, others for beaches or scenic drives. Some are quite developed, others remain natural. Some have piers that can accommodate large ships, while others require that ships anchor up to a mile offshore and shuttle passengers back and forth in small motorized launches called tenders. Big ships tend to visit the more commercialized, developed islands, which can see as many as 10 ships in a day, while the small ships are able to access more natural, off-the-beaten-path islands. Typically, the big lines divide Caribbean itineraries into eastern, western, and southern, but smaller ship lines rarely adhere to such rigid labels.

MEGASHIP ITINERARIES

WESTERN CARIBBEAN   Most western Caribbean itineraries depart from Miami, Fort Lauderdale, or Tampa, Florida (a few depart from New Orleans and Galveston, Texas), and typically visit some combination of Key West, Grand Cayman, Jamaica, and Playa del Carmen, Cozumel, or one of the other ports on Mexico's Yucatán Peninsula. This is a popular itinerary for many lines, so you'll see throngs of other cruise passengers in each port—often four or more ships will be visiting at a time. Belize City and the Bay Islands of Honduras are also popping up more frequently on western Caribbean itineraries.

EASTERN CARIBBEAN   Eastern Caribbean itineraries also typically sail out of Florida (plus East Coast ports such as New York and Charleston), and may include visits to Puerto Rico, St. Thomas, St. Martin, and Nassau or Freeport in the Bahamas—all very popular and busy ports of call. Most of the major mainstream cruise lines also maintain private islands or beaches in the Bahamas, where their ships will stop for a guaranteed beach day. Slightly more offbeat itineraries may include St. Croix in the U.S. Virgin Islands or Tortola in the British Virgin Islands.

SOUTHERN CARIBBEAN   A southern itinerary is typically round-trip out of San Juan (Puerto Rico) or sometimes Aruba, and will typically overlap with ports usually included on eastern Caribbean itineraries. Southern routes may visit St. Thomas, St. Martin, Barbados, St. Lucia, Martinique, Antigua, and maybe Dominica, Guadeloupe, Aruba, and Grenada or one of the other islands in the Grenadines.

SMALL-SHIP ITINERARIES

Most small ships cruise in the eastern and southern Caribbean, where distances between islands are shorter. Instead of Florida, they may sail out of Barbados, Grenada, St. Kitts, or San Juan, and visit more remote islands.

EASTERN CARIBBEAN   These itineraries may include St. Barts, the British Virgin Islands, and the U.S. Virgin Islands (lush St. John as well as more touristy St. Thomas).

SOUTHERN CARIBBEAN   Southern Caribbean cruises may visit Guadeloupe, Dominica, Les Saintes, St. Kitts, Nevis, Martinique, St. Lucia, St. Vincent, Grenada, and Bequia, and maybe the truly unspoiled and remote Palm, Canouan, Mayreau, and Carriacou islands.

SHORTER ITINERARIES

Today, there are more 2-, 3-, 4-, and 5-night cruise itineraries than ever before, as cruise lines continually look for new ways to fill all of their big ships. Short and affordable, **2- and 3-night cruises** offer a more action-packed, nonstop party ambience than longer 7-night Caribbean itineraries. It's obvious why: They're weekend cruises, departing Thursday or Friday afternoons, so people are ready to squeeze in as much fun, relaxation, drinking, gambling, dancing, eating, or whatever as they can. Though you definitely find more 20- and 30-somethings on these shorties than on any other type of cruise, you'll still see a wide range of ages.

The ships that offer these minicruises tend to be the oldest in their fleets and are a bit beat-up compared to the newest megas. We've also noticed that service is not as good on the weekend party cruises as on longer itineraries; the crews are overworked and probably a bit fed up with the throngs of rowdies week after week. That said, most passengers on these cruises have neither the time nor the inclination to notice the difference.

At the opposite end of the spectrum, **4- and 5-night itineraries,** which typically depart on Sunday or Monday afternoons and sail through the workweek, tend to attract an older and less party-oriented type of crowd.

Aside from the fun factor, these shorter cruises are a great way for first-timers to test the waters before committing to a full week's cruise. They're also a good idea if you're short on time or moola. The majority of the minicruises sail round-trip from Miami and Port Canaveral in southern Florida and visit the Bahamas and/or Key West and Cozumel, on Mexico's Yucatán Peninsula. Others depart from Tampa, Galveston, and San Juan. Short cruises include the same fun and games, five-course meals, and entertainment featured on weeklong cruises; there's often one formal night per cruise (though less so these days), as well as the traditional captain's cocktail party.

Many cruise lines offer weeklong **land-sea packages** that pair a cruise with a land vacation either before or after your cruise. For instance, Disney, Carnival,

Two-Nighters on the Cheap

In addition to the cruise lines profiled in this book, **Imperial Majesty Cruise Line** (© 954/956-9505; www.imperialmajesty.com) offers a year-round schedule of 2-night cruises from Fort Lauderdale, with a full day in Nassau and a full range of classic onboard entertainment—music, dancing, gambling, karaoke, bingo, spa treatments, and, of course, a midnight buffet. Imperial Majesty's one ship, the 21,909-ton, 914-passenger *Regal Empress*, was operated by Regal Cruises until that line went belly-up in May 2003. A real oldie-but-goodie, the ship was built in 1953 and still retains some of her original ocean-liner style, including rich wood paneling, sunken seating clusters in the cozy Commodore Lounge (our absolute favorite spot aboard), and its clubby library, once the ship's first-class tearoom. Regal maintained the ship extremely well, and now Imperial Majesty (which bought her at government auction for $1.75 million) is reaping the rewards. High-season rates run from $179 for an inside cabin to $279 for a standard outside and $409 for a suite.

In 2003, two new players jumped into Florida's short-cruise market. **Ocean Club Cruises** (© 866/SEA-CLUB; www.oceanclubcruises.com) offers 2-night Bahamas cruises and 3-night Bahamas/Key West cruises aboard the 15,000-ton, 850-passenger *Club Mirage*, a former ferry and Mediterranean cruise ship that has variously gone by the names *Bolero, Scandinavica, Jupiter,* and *Magic I* since her launch back in 1973. (Standard year-round rates: $349 inside, $459 standard outside, $549 suite.) Those seeking something different may want to look into **Yucatan Express**'s *Scotia Prince*, a 1,000-passenger, 200-car cruise-ferry that sails between Tampa and Merida/Progreso on Mexico's Yucatán Peninsula, November through April. Passage-only tickets transport you and your car to Mexico and then bring you back at a later date, but you can also create a more traditional cruise by booking both the out and back sailings for 4 nights total, with 11 hours in port. In its inaugural season, the company also offered extended-stay cruise/hotel packages of 7, 11, and 14 days, and something similar will likely be offered for 2004. Prices for 4-night back-to-back cruises range from $174 for an economy cabin to $749 for a suite, plus port and security charges, government taxes, and transfer charges. For information, contact Yucatan Express at © 866/670-3939 or www.yucatanexpress.com.

and Royal Caribbean will combine a 3- or 4-night cruise out of Port Canaveral with a 4- or 3-night visit to one of central Florida's theme parks, such as Walt Disney World, Universal Studios, SeaWorld, or Busch Gardens.

MATCHING YOUR HABITS TO YOUR DESTINATION

Each port has its strengths. Below is a short rundown; see the introduction to chapter 11, "Caribbean Ports of Call," for a comparison chart that rates shore excursions, activities, beaches, shopping, and dining for all the Caribbean ports. The island reviews in that chapter provide detailed information.

PORTS FOR SHOPPERS

Eastern Caribbean: Nassau, St. Thomas, St. Martin, San Juan, St. Croix. **Western Caribbean:** Grand Cayman, Cozumel. **Southern Caribbean:** Aruba, Barbados. **Bermuda.**

PORTS FOR BEACH LOVERS

Eastern Caribbean: Anguilla, British Virgin Islands, St. John, St. Martin. **Western Caribbean:** Grand Cayman, Montego Bay and Ocho Rios (Jamaica). **Southern Caribbean:** Aruba, Grenada, Bequia. **Bermuda.**

PORTS FOR SCUBA DIVERS & SNORKELERS

Eastern Caribbean: St. Croix, St. John, St. Thomas. **Western Caribbean:** Grand Cayman, Belize, Cozumel. **Southern Caribbean:** Bonaire, Curaçao, Dominica.

PORTS FOR HISTORY & ARCHAEOLOGY BUFFS

Eastern Caribbean: San Juan, Dominican Republic. **Western Caribbean:** Cozumel, Playa del Carmen, and Calica (all on Mexico's Yucatán Peninsula). **Southern Caribbean:** Barbados, Curaçao. **Bermuda.**

PORTS FOR NATURE LOVERS

Eastern Caribbean: St. John, San Juan. **Southern Caribbean:** Aruba, Dominica, St. Kitts, Grenada, Trinidad.

PORTS FOR FRANCOPHILES

Eastern Caribbean: Guadeloupe, Les Saintes, St. Martin, St. Barts, Martinique.

SHORE EXCURSIONS: THE WHAT, WHY & HOW

No matter what size ship you're on or what its itinerary, you'll be able to choose from between a few and a few dozen tours in any given port, from walking tours, bus tours, and booze cruises to more active trips such as biking, hiking, snorkeling, horseback riding, golfing, kayaking, and river tubing. Prices range from about $25 to $200 per person, and are generally run by concessionaires on the islands rather than by the cruise lines themselves.

Although many tours are excellent and can be real high-points of your cruise, others are impersonal, disappointing, and not worth the money. Choose wisely, and remember, sometimes it's best to skip the organized tours and go off exploring on your own. Aruba, Curaçao, St. Thomas, St. Martin, San Juan, Grand Cayman, Grenada, Bequia, Tortola, and Bermuda, for instance, are easily explored independently—all you need is this book and a sense of adventure. In chapters 11 and 12 we list both the best shore excursions and the best sights you can see on your own, and tell you which islands are more conducive to which kind of sightseeing.

In the past, you could only sign up for tours once aboard ship, which sometimes meant waiting in long lines and, if you put it off too long, could mean being shut out of the most popular excursions. Today, however, all the mainstream lines, except Carnival, Costa, and Royal Olympia, allow confirmed guests to **prebook shore excursions** online or via phone or fax, generally up to 10 days before your cruise. If the line you choose offers this option, we advise you to take it. If you wait until you're aboard, plan to sign up for your excursions early on embarkation day.

Because of the large numbers of passengers on a megaship, be prepared for some waiting around on excursion days, as each jumbo-size tour group is herded from the ship to the waiting army of buses or minivans.

On smaller ships, tours may never sell out because there's room to accommodate all passengers. The whole process is saner, and group sizes are usually smaller. That said, big ship or small, the attraction itself, the quality of the tour guide, and the execution of the tour are what determine whether you have an enjoyable time.

...e Cruises

...ough they're no longer the craze they were in years past, several cruise lines still offer occasional cruises designed around particular themes. Crystal and Windstar, for instance, feature an annual series of food-and-wine cruises, in which well-known chefs and sommeliers are brought on board to conduct demonstrations and tastings. Cunard and Crystal do quite a few music-theme cruises every year, featuring jazz, '50s rock 'n' roll, and Broadway, with live bands and lots of dancing. Cunard and Windjammer also throw murder-mystery cruises every so often.

Florida-based **Port Promotions** (© **800/929-4548;** www.portpromotions. com) offers an alternative to booking shore excursions through the cruise lines. Their roster of advertised excursions is pretty standard (though prices are often a little lower, buses smaller, and lunch stops better), but what makes the company interesting are its **custom-designed excursions**—golf, tennis, watersports, beach parties, hiking, culinary adventures, and other options you design in consultation with the company.

3 Choosing the Ship of Your Dreams

News flash: Not all ships are the same. Even before getting to the kind of experience offered by the cruise lines, physical factors such as the size and age of the ship figure into whether it can offer you the vacation experience you want.

BIG SHIP OR SMALL?

A cruise on a big ship with, say, 2,000-plus passengers versus a small one with only 200 is like night and day—like spending a week in a 500-room high-rise hotel in Cancún versus hiding out in a cozy New England B&B. As much as anything else, a ship's size greatly determines its personality and the kind of vacation it offers. Big ships tend to be busy, exciting affairs, while the smaller ones are most often low-key retreats with unique personalities. Big ships normally spend 2 or 3 days at sea on a weeklong cruise because they travel great distances between ports and because there's so much to do on board; small ships are more destination-oriented, visiting a different port every day.

BIG SHIPS

Today's megaships, carrying upwards of 1,800 passengers, really live up to the overused "city at sea" metaphor, providing an onboard experience that any city-dweller will recognize: food and drink available at any hour, entertainment districts filled with neon and twinkling lights, grand architecture, big crowds, and a definite buzz. The onboard atmosphere is carefree and casual by day—with passengers decked out in bathing suits, shorts, sarongs, and sandals—and dressier in the evening, though often these days that translates into the resort version of business casual. The occasional formal night calls for a suit or tuxedo for men and a cocktail dress or fancy pantsuit for women; however, because all the big ships offer casual restaurants these days, you can usually opt out of formality if it's not your thing.

In general, the megas are buzzing social hives, but just as in a metropolis like New York, you'll be able to blend in with the crowd and become an anonymous passenger among the throngs if you choose to. You often won't see the same faces

ℰ Clean Bill of Health

If you want to check out how clean a ship's water supply is, how its food-preparation and storage procedures measure up, how its personnel are trained in maintaining a hygienic environment, and how well scrubbed its spas, gyms, and pools are, check out the **Centers for Disease Control and Prevention sanitation reports.** Twice a year, the government agency makes unannounced inspections of every ship that carries more than 13 passengers and stops at both U.S. and foreign ports, then posts the results on its website. You can see who's A-OK and who has earned an unsatisfactory rating at www.cdc.gov/nceh/vsp/default.htm, which typically has records on more than 150 vessels.

If you're worried about a ship's seaworthiness from a mechanical and operational perspective, then take a look at the **U.S. Coast Guard inspection results** Web page (http://psix.uscg.mil). Click on "Vessel Search," then enter the name of the ship. Under "Vessel Service," choose "Passenger (More Than 6)." You can leave the other fields blank.

twice from day to day, and, in fact, if you don't plan specific times and places to meet up with your spouse, lover, or friend, you may roam the decks for hours looking for them. (Some passengers even bring a set of walkie-talkies to stay in touch—annoying to the rest of us, maybe, but it keeps them happy.) The megas have as many as 12 or 14 passenger decks full of shops, restaurants, bars, and lounges, plus cabins of all shapes and sizes. Most have a grand multistory atrium lobby, three or four swimming pools and hot tubs, casinos with scores of slot machines and dozens of card tables, three or four restaurants, a movie theater, a pizzeria, and a patisserie. Mammoth spas and gyms boast dozens of exercise machines and treatment rooms, and vast children's areas include splash pools, playrooms, and video arcades.

But even the megas aren't all alike. Carnival, Royal Caribbean, and Costa's ships (and to a slightly lesser degree NCL's) are the most Vegas-like in atmosphere, with over-the-top decor and a distinctly theme-park ambience, while Disney—the one you'd expect to be theme-parky—is in fact much more stylish, with its family-oriented activities and entertainment carrying the theme all by themselves. Celebrity is king in terms of sleek modern decor and a near-upscale ambience, while Princess and Holland America go for a more traditional feel— the former with a sort of Pottery Barn design sense and fun but not-too-daring activities and shows; the latter with a more traditional steamship decor (except on its newest ships, which are much more modern) and a more reserved onboard feel. As you'd expect, the largest ships offer the greatest variety of activities, with an emphasis on choice. Countless activities are offered all day long, including dance lessons, wine tastings, fashion shows, art auctions, aerobics classes, bingo, bridge, cooking demonstrations, pool games, computer classes, and trivia contests. And at night you have a choice of piano bars, discos, martini and champagne bars, sports bars, theaters, and show lounges.

As a general rule, these ships are so large that they're limited as to where they can tie up—certain islands and ports simply cannot handle them. Slightly

SHIP SIZE COMPARISONS

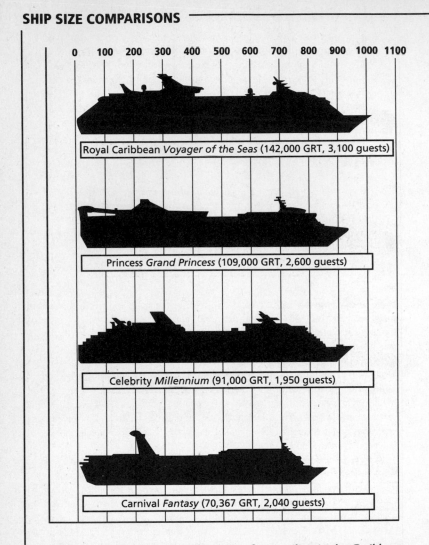

0 100 200 300 400 500 600 700 800 900 1000 1100

Royal Caribbean *Voyager of the Seas* (142,000 GRT, 3,100 guests)

Princess *Grand Princess* (109,000 GRT, 2,600 guests)

Celebrity *Millennium* (91,000 GRT, 1,950 guests)

Carnival *Fantasy* (70,367 GRT, 2,040 guests)

Ships in this chart represent the range of sizes sailing in the Caribbean in 2004. See reviews in chapters 6-9 for sizes of ships not shown here, then compare. Note that GRT= gross register tons, a measure of the interior space used to produce revenue on a vessel. One GRT=100 cubic feet of enclosed, revenue-generating space.

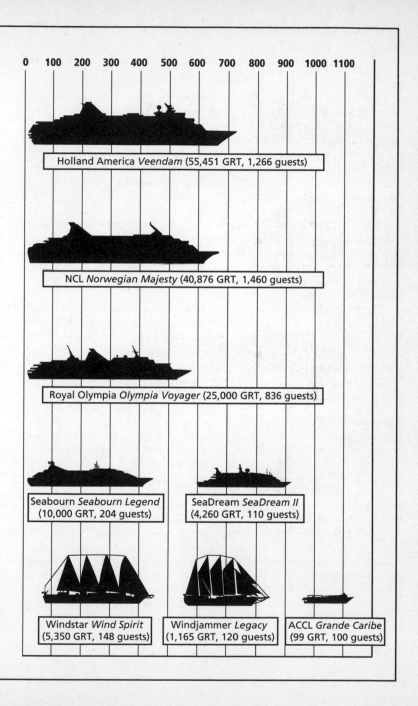

0 100 200 300 400 500 600 700 800 900 1000 1100

Holland America *Veendam* (55,451 GRT, 1,266 guests)

NCL *Norwegian Majesty* (40,876 GRT, 1,460 guests)

Royal Olympia *Olympia Voyager* (25,000 GRT, 836 guests)

Seabourn *Seabourn Legend*
(10,000 GRT, 204 guests)

SeaDream *SeaDream II*
(4,260 GRT, 110 guests)

Windstar *Wind Spirit*
(5,350 GRT, 148 guests)

Windjammer *Legacy*
(1,165 GRT, 120 guests)

ACCL *Grande Caribe*
(99 GRT, 100 guests)

smaller big ships—such as the Crystal, Royal Olympia, and Oceania vessels and the older Celebrity, Norwegian, and Holland America ships—carry "only" 700 to 1,500 passengers and so don't qualify as megaships, but they're big enough to offer a similarly exciting and active experience.

SMALL SHIPS

If the thought of sailing with thousands of other people makes you want to jump overboard, a smaller ship may be more up your alley. Small ships are ideal for those who crave a calm, intimate experience in a clublike atmosphere where conversation is king. As in a small town, you'll quickly get to know your neighbors, since you'll see the same faces at meals and on deck throughout the week.

The small ships in the Caribbean can be broken down into three groups: sailing ships, casual motorized cruisers, and small luxury ships. The Windjammer, Star Clippers, and Windstar fleets are **sailing ships** (though they rely on both sail and engine power), attracting as many passengers in their 30s as in their 70s or older, all of them looking for something a little different. Windstar is the most upscale, emphasizing fine cuisine and plusher cabin amenities such as CD players and VCRs. Windjammer is the most casual and adventurous, maintaining an anything-goes onboard atmosphere where shorts and T-shirts can be worn to dinner. Star Clippers offers an experience midway between these two, although its new *Royal Clipper* is more or less on par with Windstar's ships in terms of cabin amenities and overall decor.

Clipper and American Canadian Caribbean (ACCL) lines operate **casual motorized ships,** with a more sedate ambience, a cozy feel, and a generally over-50 clientele. Often, there will be an emphasis on learning about the history and nature of the islands being visited. The **small luxury ships** of high-end lines such as Seabourn, Silversea, Radisson, and SeaDream offer a refined, ultra-elegant ambience. Cabins are spacious, gracious waiters serve gourmet meals on fine china, and guests dress to impress.

The smallest ships have fewer activity options, but to some that's their greatest appeal. There's usually only one restaurant and one all-purpose lounge, and maybe a bar or central patch of outdoor deck where passengers can congregate to chat, read, have a drink, or listen to a presentation about their next port destination. Often a library of books and videos is either in a separate room or tucked into the corner of a lounge. A pianist or duo may entertain before dinner, and there may be a crew or passenger talent show afterward. To a greater or lesser degree, there's usually some focus on learning. On Windstar, Star Clippers, Clipper, Windjammer, and ACCL, for instance, the cruise director or captain will discuss the native wildlife or history of the next port of call—in contrast, port talks on the megaships are usually about shopping. Sometimes a naturalist, an author, or a celebrity will join the cruise to present informal lectures on a wide variety of topics. Clipper Cruise Line carries **naturalists and historians** as part of the crew, offering passengers full-time learning opportunities. Small ships generally visit a port nearly every day, and are able to easily slip in and out of more off-the-beaten-path, less spoiled ports, such as Les Saintes, Virgin Gorda, and St. Barts.

OLD SHIP OR NEW?

Depending on what you like, the age of a ship can be a plus or a minus. Aside from just being more modern in design, the newest ships come with all the bells and whistles, including Internet centers, big gyms and spas, cabin balconies, multiple restaurants and theaters, pizza and ice-cream parlors, uncluttered open expanses of deck, and big windows everywhere.

Older ships now come in two basic flavors: *really* older, meaning classic, heroic old ocean liners, and just plain old cruise ships, which have been beaten up by 20 years of Caribbean partying. Unfortunately, there are very few of the former left in the market. The 2000 edition of this book included no fewer than 12 older vessels, of which 10 have either been sold off or been lost when a line has gone out of business. This leaves only two significant graybeards—NCL's 41-year-old *Norway* (the former SS *France*) and Cunard's 34-year-old *QE2*—along with 2-night cruise specialist Imperial Majesty Cruises' 1956-vintage *OceanBreeze* (see "Two-Nighters on the Cheap," earlier in the chapter) and the dear old *Regal Empress,* which Imperial bought at auction when Regal Cruises folded in May 2003. All three offer a nostalgic glimpse back to the old days, with their long, sweeping hulls, rich wood paneling and teak decks, chunky portholes, and varnished railings. Cabin doors may still operate with a lock and key rather than a computerized key-card, and tall sills in most doorways will require some high stepping to avoid tripping (old ships are not for wheelchair users). Out on deck, there's no shortage of exposed cables, pipes, ropes, winches, and all manner of hardware. These are ships that look like ships, and for maritime buffs they're charming.

Norway, which still cuts a mean profile with her long bowed hull (though extensive renovations have made her almost unrecognizable on the inside) was slated to leave the American market in mid-2001 but was pulled back at the last minute. For her part, *QE2* manages to hold on to the past with dignity, and her long body and razor-sharp bow still turn heads. However, she's scheduled to cede her transatlantic duties to the new *QM2* this year, so could her going-away party be many years behind? The bottom line: If you want your *An Affair to Remember* ocean-liner experience, do it soon, 'cause the clock's ticking.

The other type of old ships—long-in-the-tooth cruisers—are another matter. They're just . . . old. Think about how many macarenas have been danced on their decks. That kind of hard use starts to show eventually, and ships like Royal Caribbean's *Sovereign of the Seas* and Carnival's *Holiday, Jubilee,* and *Celebration,* though all were only built between 1985 and 1988, are starting to show their age. Like *OceanBreeze* and *Club Mirage* mentioned above, these ships are now generally relegated to the short-cruise market, offering sailings of 3 and 4 nights. The plus side? You get a nice little cruise on the cheap. The negative? Only that they may feel a little dated, a little worn, especially when berthed alongside a gleaming newer ship in port.

4 Matching the Cruise to Your Needs
CRUISES FOR FAMILIES

The right cruise can be the perfect family vacation—safe, fun, and relaxing for the whole brood. Cruise lines have been going to great lengths to please parents and kids alike, as families become an ever larger and more influential segment of the cruising public.

It's the megaships that cater most to families and attract the largest numbers of them, with playrooms, video arcades, and supervised activities generally provided for children ages 3 to 17 (young children must be potty-trained), and programs broken down into several age categories. Some lines set a minimum age for children to sail aboard, but Disney offers a supervised nursery for ages 3 months and up, and it wouldn't surprise us if this became a trend. See the "Children's Program" sections in the individual cruise line reviews for details.

Disney offers the most family-friendly ships at sea today, followed by **Royal Caribbean,** whose ships (especially the Voyager- and Radiance-class ships) have huge play areas. The post-1990 **Carnival** ships do a pretty good job, too, as do the new **Norwegian** ships (especially the new *Norwegian Dawn,* with its awesome kids' center) and all **Princess** and **Celebrity** ships built after 1993, when family cruising was becoming more mainstream. Even lines traditionally geared to older folks are getting in on the kid craze. Holland America's *Maasdam, Veendam,* and *Zuiderdam,* for instance, have decent playrooms.

See the section "Best Cruises for Families with Kids" in "The Best of Cruising" for more info.

ACTIVITIES & FACILITIES   With dedicated playrooms, camplike counselors, computers, state-of-the-art video arcades, and pools at their disposal, your kids will have so much fun you may have to drag them away kicking and screaming at the end of the cruise. Chances are, even too-cool, nonchalant teens will be worn down by the endless activities and the chance to make new friends.

The youngest kids frolic in toy- and game-stocked **playrooms,** listen to stories, and go on treasure hunts; older kids keep busy with arts and crafts, **computer games,** lip-sync competitions, pool games, and volleyball; and teenagers go snorkeling, mingle at **teen parties,** or hang out at the video arcade. There's usually a TV showing movies throughout the day and, for the younger ones, there are ball bins and plastic jungle gyms to crawl around in. Many megaships have shallow kiddie pools, sometimes sequestered on an isolated patch of deck.

BABYSITTING   To ensure that parents have a good time, too, there are adults-only discos and lounges, and babysitting from about 8pm to 1 or 2am on many ships (though not all). Most mainstream lines offer **group babysitting** slumber-party style in the playroom, at a cost of about $4 to $6 per hour per child. **Private in-cabin babysitting** by a crewmember is also offered by several lines (for example, Celebrity, Royal Caribbean, and Crystal) at a steep $8 to $10 per hour for the first child, plus generally a dollar or two more for a sibling. Using a private babysitter every night could put a serious dent in your budget, but it's a nice option. While most supervised kids' programs accept only potty-trained children over age 3 (and sometimes as young as 2), a few lines such as Carnival welcome infants into the group-babysitting program, and Disney (for kids over 3 months) and Cunard (for kids over 1 year) offer actual nurseries. The counselors will even change diapers!

FAMILY-FRIENDLY CABINS   Worried about spending a whole week with the family in some cramped little box? Depending on your budget, you may not have to.

Of course, a family of four can share a cabin that has bunk-style third and fourth berths, which pull out of the walls just above the pair of regular beds, and a few lines, like Carnival and Norwegian, will even accommodate a fifth person on a rollaway bed on certain ships if space permits. But there's no other way to slice it: A standard cabin with four people in it will be cramped, and with one bathroom . . . well, you can imagine. However, when you consider how little time you'll spend in the cabin, it's doable, and many families take this option. The incentive to share one cabin is price—whether children or adults, the rates for third and fourth persons sharing a cabin with two full-fare (or even heavily discounted) passengers are usually about half of the lowest regular rates. On

Family Cruising

Here are some suggestions for better sailing and smoother seas on your family cruise.

- **Ask about children's amenities.** If you'd like a crib, for instance, check in advance with the cruise line to find out if they can provide it.
- **Pack some basic first-aid supplies, and even a thermometer.** Cruise lines have limited supplies of these items (and charge for them, too). If an accident should happen on board, virtually every ship (except the smallest ones) has its own infirmary staffed by doctors and/or nurses. Keep in mind that first aid can usually be summoned more readily aboard ship than in port.
- **Warn younger children about the danger of falling overboard,** and make sure they know not to play on the railings.
- **Make sure your kids know their cabin number** and what deck it's on. The endless corridors and doors on the megaships often look exactly alike (though some are color-coded).
- **Prepare kids for TV letdown.** Though many ships today receive satellite TV programming, you won't get the range of options you have at home.

occasion, you'll find special deals and further discounts. Norwegian Cruise Line and Royal Olympia Cruises allow children under 2 to sail free with two full-fare passengers (though you must pay port charges and government taxes for the kids, which will run about $100–$200 per person). Disney offers a reduced rate of $99 per 3- and 4-night and $119 per 7-night cruise for children under 3. *Note:* Since prices are based on double adult occupancy of cabins, single parents sailing with children usually have to pay adult prices for their kids, though deals for single parents are offered every once in a while.

If you can afford it, and if space equals sanity in your book, **consider booking a suite.** Many have a pullout couch in the living room (or, better yet, two separate bedrooms) and can accommodate up to three or four children. *Disney Magic* and *Wonder* boast the family-friendliest cabins at sea: The majority of the ships' 875 cabins are equipped with two bathrooms and a sitting area that converts to a kids' bedroom. They're like minisuites and comfortably sleep families of three or four—but, of course, you pay more for all of this. (The ships' bona fide suites accommodate families of five to seven.) Royal Caribbean and Princess's newest ships have family suites as well, but remember, they're no bargain: You pay for the larger size and beefed-up amenities.

If you have older kids, it may just be cheaper to book **connecting cabins—** two separate standard cabins with interconnecting doors, which allows you to be close to each other, but separate. You'll find connecting cabins on most ships in the Royal Caribbean, Disney, Carnival, Celebrity, Norwegian, and Holland America fleets, and on some ships in the Princess fleets. Connecting cabin information is noted in each ship review in this book.

TAKING THE KIDS ON SMALL SHIPS   If your children are at least 10 or 12, some of the casual, off-beat cruises (for example, aboard Windjammer's *Legacy* and *Polynesia* and Star Clippers' *Royal Clipper*) can be loads of fun for some kids and educational to boot. You won't find a kids' playroom stuffed with toys, TVs, video games, or many other kids on board for that matter, but these cruises are more about exploring the ports anyway, so you'll only be aboard ship in the evenings. If your child is inquisitive and somewhat extroverted, he or she may be able to talk with the crew and learn how a sailing ship operates.

CRUISES FOR HONEYMOONERS & ANNIVERSARY COUPLES

You want romance? You're in luck. All cruises are romantic, with all the elements for making your honeymoon or anniversary cuddly and cozy: moonlit nights on deck, the undulating sea all around, dining in dimly lit restaurants, exploring silky beaches and exotic ports of call, maybe even a private balcony or whirlpool tub in your cabin.

Of course, different ships are romantic to different kinds of people. The megas offer glamorous, Vegas-style romance; the small, casual ships, an intimate and Sunday-drive-in-the-country kind of romance; the ultraluxury lines, epicurean romance with gourmet cuisine, fine wine, and plush surroundings; and older ships, a nostalgic brand of romance.

Besides their inherent romantic qualities, cruises are honeymoon havens for lots of reasons—Sunday departures, for instance, which means that couples who marry on Saturday can leave on a cruise the next day. Some lines offer **honeymooner freebies** such as a special cake in the dining room one night, or, aboard Royal Caribbean, an invitation to a private cocktail party. (Couples celebrating anniversaries are often invited as well.) To get your share of freebies, be sure to tell your travel agent or the cruise line reservation agent that you'll be celebrating your honeymoon or anniversary on the cruise.

HONEYMOON & ANNIVERSARY PACKAGES   For even more romance, the lines aren't shy about selling a variety of goodies and packages geared to honeymooners and couples celebrating anniversaries and vow renewals. You'll get a pamphlet describing the available packages when you receive your cruise tickets in the mail. These packages must be ordered before the cruise, and run from around $40 per couple up into the thousands, with wedding ceremony packages naturally being the most costly.

The $169 package offered by Celebrity Cruises is typical; it includes breakfast in bed served with champagne, engraved champagne flutes, a keepsake designer floral arrangement, a red rose placed on the pillow, a pair of bathrobes, Cova pralines, and a personalized honeymoon or anniversary certificate. The $99 Costa package includes a portrait taken by the ship's photographer and a frame to go with it, his-and-hers bathrobes, an invitation to a cocktail party hosted by the captain, a bottle of sparkling wine, and fresh flowers. For $75 a couple, Carnival offers a bottle of champagne, a pair of engraved champagne flutes, two Carnival T-shirts and visors, a credit for four bar drinks, and a reusable flash camera with extra film. For the celebrating couple with a more gourmet palate, Windstar offers a bottle of Dom Perignon and caviar at $210 a pop. Other packages may include a photograph and wedding album, chocolate-covered strawberries, limousine service between the ship and airport, shore excursions, and even a pair of massages at the spa.

Some lines offer **vow-renewal packages** for couples who'd like to celebrate their marriage all over again. On Holland America ships, for example, couples can renew their vows at a special group ceremony at sea, catered with drinks and cold hors d'oeuvres; the $99 package includes a floral arrangement in the cabin, a photo and photo album, and a certificate presented by the captain. Princess offers similar (but souped-up) vow-renewal packages for $149 and $399 per couple: the former including the ceremony, an orchid bouquet and boutonniere, a bottle of Mums champagne, a framed formal portrait of the ceremony, and a commemorative certificate; the latter including all of this plus a champagne breakfast in bed, two terry-cloth robes, a visit to the spa and one half-hour massage or facial per person, canapés or petit fours in your stateroom every evening, and a personalized invitation from the captain to visit the bridge while in port.

HONEYMOONING WITH THE LUXURY LINES   High-end lines, such as Windstar, Silversea, Seabourn, Radisson, Cunard, and Crystal, don't offer special cocktail parties and the like, but their ultradeluxe amenities are especially pleasing to honeymooners. From terry bathrobes and slippers to whirlpool bathtubs, five-course dinners served in your cabin, stocked minibars, and high crew-to-passenger ratios (meaning more personalized service), extra-special touches are business as usual on these upscale lines.

CRUISES FOR 20- & 30-SOMETHINGS

So, what's young? We know a few 60-year-olds who act a lot younger than people who haven't even hit 30, so who's to say? Nevertheless, we're often asked to recommend ships geared to folks in their 20s and 30s. Here's the deal: There aren't any. That is, there aren't any that attract *only* young people. While the age of the average cruiser continues to sail downward, the majority are people in their 40s, 50s, and 60-plus. No ships attract only 20- and 30-somethings, just as you'd be hard-pressed to find a hotel that does, or even a resort. Most ships are a mixed bag of ages, and more so in the Caribbean, which tends to attract a sizable young crowd as well as lots of retirees. Alaska, Europe, and Asia itineraries, on the other hand, draw mostly an older, 50-plus crowd. All this said, here are some general guidelines about ships and the ages of the people you'll find on them.

The **youngest crowds,** in the 20s-to-40s range, are typically found on 2-, 3-, and 4-night cruises (and next on the 7-night cruises) on mainstream lines such as Carnival, Royal Caribbean, and NCL, and on soft-adventure lines like Windjammer and Star Clippers.

The **oldest folks,** upward of 60, will be the vast majority on luxury lines such as Seabourn, Cunard, and Radisson. Holland America, a mainstream line, has also traditionally attracted a mature crowd. Among the soft-adventure lines, American Canadian Caribbean has the oldest demographic, followed by Clipper.

Young-at-heart types, who may be 54 or 67 or 72 but who wear bikinis and short-shorts and drink piña coladas for lunch, will be found on the fun-loving lines such as Carnival, Royal Caribbean, NCL, Windjammer, and Star Clippers.

CRUISES FOR GAY MEN & LESBIANS

There are a number of particularly gay-friendly cruises and special chartered sailings for gay men and lesbians. For details, contact these specialists: **RSVP Vacations,** 2535 25th Ave. S., Minneapolis, MN 55406 (© **800/328-7787** or 612/ 729-1113; www.rsvpvacations.com); **Pied Piper Travel,** 330 W. 42nd St., Suite 1804, New York, NY 10036 (© **800/874-7312** or 212/239-2412; www.Pied PiperTravel.com); and **Olivia Cruises and Resorts,** 4400 Market St., Oakland,

Getting Married at Sea

If you'd like to have your marriage and honeymoon all in one, you can legally get hitched on board many ships. Princess's *Golden, Grand, Coral,* and *Island Princess;* Royal Caribbean's *Adventure, Explorer,* and *Voyager of the Seas;* Carnival's *Spirit, Pride,* and *Legend;* and NCL's *Norwegian Sun* and *Dawn* all have wedding chapels on board. Other ships hold ceremonies in lounges, which are decorated with flowers, ribbons, and other frilly wedding accouterments.

CIVIL CEREMONIES IN U.S. PORTS Passengers can have a civil ceremony performed by a local justice of the peace or church official aboard ship before departing from any U.S. port. This way, friends and family can come aboard for a few hours for a ceremony and a reception before the ship sails (though they'll have to present two forms of ID due to today's tighter security).

CEREMONIES IN THE CARIBBEAN & BERMUDA Couples can also tie the knot while in port in Bermuda and several Caribbean islands, either on the ship or ashore. (But remember that your cruise itinerary limits where and when you can tie the knot; time spent in a given port generally ranges from 3–10 hr.) The U.S. Virgin Islands—St. Croix, St. Thomas, and St. John—as well as the Bahamas and Jamaica, are some of the most popular wedding spots. Carnival may be the biggest wedding factory at sea, pulling off more than 2,200 weddings a year and offering packages aboard the ships and at beach and waterfall settings in just about every port the ships visit, from San Juan to St. Thomas, Ocho Rios and Montego Bay (Jamaica), Nassau, Grand Cayman, St. Martin, and Barbados. Royal Caribbean and Princess are also biggies in the wedding world.

Sometimes, where permitted, you can request or arrange to have a priest, rabbi, or other official of your choice. Ceremony and reception packages include not only the services of the officiant, but also floral arrangements, tuxedo/gown rental, wedding cake, photography, music, and hors d'oeuvres, and range from about $700 to $2,000 per couple (though, like weddings ashore, they can run much higher than that).

HAVING THE CAPTAIN OFFICIATE Have your heart set on the big boss performing your marriage rites at sea? If so, you've got only one choice: Princess Cruises' *Golden, Grand, Coral,* and *Island Princess* (plus sister ship *Star Princess,* which doesn't sail in the Caribbean) are currently the only ships where the captain himself performs about six or seven bona fide, 100% legal civil ceremonies a week in the ships' charming wedding chapels. Adorned with fresh flower arrangements as well as ribbons

CA 94608 (© **800/631-6277** or 510/655-0364; www.olivia.com), which caters to lesbians.

You can also contact the **International Gay and Lesbian Travel Association,** 4331 N. Federal Hwy., Suite 304, Fort Lauderdale, FL 33308 (© **800/448-8550** or 954/776-2626; www.iglta.com), which has more than 1,200 travel industry members. You may want to check out the well-known San Francisco–based strung along the aisle, the rooms are tastefully designed in warm caramel-colored wood tones and stained glass, and there is seating for a few dozen friends and family members. Assistant pursers, decked out in their handsome dress blues, are available to escort a bride down the mini-aisle. Three different ceremony packages are offered, starting at $1,400 per couple. Depending on which you choose, they include photography, video, music, and salon treatments for the bride. And if you've got friends and family on board, reception packages start at $28 per person (for 1 hr.), and include hors d'oeuvres, champagne, and wedding cake. Don't wait till the last minute if you're considering Princess for your wedding, since there's often a waiting list.

THE LEGAL DETAILS   No matter where you choose to wed, U.S. or foreign port, you must obtain a **marriage license** (or file an application) in advance of the cruise, and you must make specific arrangements for the wedding ceremony itself. Policies vary from country to country, and you need to find out what the rules are well in advance of your sailing date. To get married in the U.S. Virgin Islands, for example, you must be sure to get your license applications to the USVI Territorial Court at least 8 days before your wedding day. The license application fee is $50; contact the **USVI Territorial Court** in St. Thomas at © **340/774-6680** for an application. In Bermuda, couples are required to file a Notice of Intended Marriage with the office of the registrar general at least 6 weeks in advance. The fee is $186 and you can get a form from the **Bermuda Department of Tourism** at © **800/223-6106** or from the registrar at 441/295-5151. The Bahamas requires you to be in-country at least 24 hours before marrying there. The fee for a marriage license is $40; contact the **Bahamas Tourist Office** at © **800/422-4262** for more information.

While you could technically arrange everything yourself by calling the above numbers, you save a lot of hassle and headaches by booking wedding packages through the cruise lines. At the time of booking, the cruise line or your travel agent can fill you in on the rules and regulations of the ports visited and assist you with the paperwork—for example, by sending you a license application form—as well as providing transportation to the courthouse to be sworn in (for example, in St. Thomas). To help you with the details, Carnival and Princess have wedding departments; other lines handle wedding planning through the guest-relations office or refer you to a wedding consultant.

Out & About **travel newsletter** ($39 a year for 10 paper issues, or $20 a year for the electronic edition; to subscribe, call © **800/929-2268;** www.outandabout. com). And *Our World* **travel magazine,** 1104 N. Nova Rd., Ste. 251, Daytona Beach, FL (© **386/441-5367;** www.ourworldmagazine.com), has articles, tips, and listings on gay and lesbian travel. Subscriptions cost $25 a year for 10 paper issues or $12 a year for the electronic version.

CRUISES FOR ACTIVE PEOPLE

Sure, there are lots of activities offered on cruises—wine tastings, dancing lessons, lectures, bingo, makeup demonstrations, and lots more, including weird classics like napkin folding and vegetable carving. But on the megaships (and even on the small ships), you'll find quite a bit to do to keep your heart pumping and muscles moving too.

The newer, post-1990 megaships in the Carnival, Royal Caribbean, Princess, Celebrity, Norwegian, and Holland America fleets have **jogging tracks** and **well-equipped gyms** that rival those on shore: The biggest exceed 10,000 square feet, and all have dozens of exercise machines. Smaller ships, such as Radisson's *Seven Seas Navigator* and Seabourn's *Seabourn Legend* and *Pride,* have decent gyms, too; they're just more compact. Ships with **basketball, volleyball,** and/or **paddle-tennis courts** include Royal Caribbean's *Brilliance, Radiance, Adventure, Explorer,* and *Voyager of the Seas;* all the Princess ships reviewed in this book; all the Holland America ships except *Noordam;* NCL's *Norwegian Sky, Sun,* and *Dawn;* Crystal's *Symphony;* and the entire Carnival and Disney fleets. Princess's *Golden, Grand, Coral,* and *Island Princess* and Royal Caribbean's *Adventure, Explorer, Voyager, Splendour,* and *Legend of the Seas* even have **miniature-golf courses** on board. The enormous *Adventure, Explorer,* and *Voyager* take the cake, though, boasting an ice-skating rink, **outdoor rock-climbing wall,** and in-line skating track.

Celebrity, Norwegian, Crystal, Princess, Radisson, and Cunard have **outdoor golf cages**—areas enclosed in netting where you can whack at real golf balls. Sometimes, though, the onboard golf pro and his students monopolize these nets: For instance, on Celebrity and Cunard, you've got to pay to play.

A handful of smaller ships—those in the Windstar, Seadream, and Seabourn fleets, plus the *Radisson Diamond* and *Royal Clipper*—have retractable or floating watersports platforms to allow easy access to the sea. Weather and conditions permitting, you can swim, be taken water-skiing or on banana-boat rides, or use the kayaks, sailboats, and windsurfers provided, all free of charge and all just a few steps from your cabin. Star Clippers' *Star Clipper, Star Flyer,* and *Royal Clipper* each carry a fleet of motorized Zodiac boats on board to take passengers water-skiing or on banana-boat rides.

On shore, more and more active excursions are being offered. No need to sit on a bus for 3 hours sweating if you'd rather be working up a sweat the natural way. Along with snorkeling and diving, options such as biking, hiking, and horseback riding have become popular tours in many ports. For more details, see chapter 11, "Caribbean Ports of Call."

For fitness options on individual ships, see the reviews in chapters 6 through 8.

CRUISES FOR PEOPLE WITH DISABILITIES

Though most of the cruise industry's ships are foreign-flagged and so are not required to comply with the Americans with Disabilities Act, the newest ships have all been built with accessibility in mind, and some older ships have been refit to offer the same.

Most ships that can accommodate passengers with disabilities require wheelchair-bound passengers to be accompanied by a fully mobile companion. The vast majority of ships travel with a nurse on board at all times, and often there is a doctor too; we've listed which ships have infirmaries in the "Ships at a Glance" chart in chapter 5, but if you have special needs, check with the line to see exactly what medical services are provided. Generally, Princess and Holland America have the best medical centers.

In the ship reviews in chapters 6 through 8, we've provided information about which ships provide the best access and facilities for passengers with disabilities, but be sure to discuss your needs fully with your travel agent prior to booking.

ACCESSIBLE CABINS & PUBLIC ROOMS   On newer ships, most public rooms—dining rooms, lounges, discos, and casinos, for example—have ramps. Keep in mind that ships more than 20 years old may have raised doorways (known as sills or lips, originally created to contain water and in many cases as high as 6–8 in.) in bathrooms, at cabin entrances, and elsewhere. Most new ships have no sills or very low ones; those that do may be able to install temporary ramps to accommodate wheelchair users. This must be arranged in advance.

Most ships have a handful of cabins specifically designed for travelers with disabilities, with extra-wide doorways, large bathrooms with grab bars and roll-in showers, closets with pull-down racks, and furniture built to a lower height. The "Ships at a Glance" chart in chapter 5 lists which ships have accessible cabins, and the "Cabins" section in each of the ship reviews in chapters 6 through 8 indicates how many. The vast majority of the ships reviewed in the mainstream category (chapter 6) have accessible cabins, while most of the ships in the ultra-luxury category also do (chapter 7). None of the soft-adventure ships (chapter 8) is accessible.

ELEVATORS   Most elevators aboard today's megaships are wide enough to accommodate wheelchairs, but make sure before booking. Sailing ships and most small vessels do not have elevators. Even if a ship does have elevators, the size of today's huge megaships means your cabin could be quite a distance from the elevators and stairs, unless you specify otherwise. Cabins designed specifically for wheelchair users are intentionally located near elevators. If you don't use a wheelchair but have trouble walking, you'll want to choose a cabin close to an elevator to avoid a long hike down a corridor.

TENDERING INTO PORT   If your ship is too large to dock or if a port's docks are already taken by other vessels, your ship may anchor offshore and shuttle passengers to land via tenders (small boats). Some tenders are large and stable and others are not. But the choppiness of the water can be a factor when boarding either way, so if you use a wheelchair or have trouble walking, it may be difficult or impossible to get aboard; even calm seas can rock the boats enough to make climbing in a tricky maneuver for anyone, much less someone with a mobility problem. For liability reasons, many lines forbid wheelchairs to be carried onto tenders, meaning you may have to forgo a trip ashore and stay on board when in these ports. An exception to this is Holland America, which has a wheelchair-to-tender transport system aboard *Zuiderdam, Oosterdam, Rotterdam, Volendam,* and *Veendam.* The system works by locking a wheelchair on a lift, which transports it safely between the gangway and the tender.

It's a good idea to check with your travel agent to find out if itineraries you're interested in allow your ship to dock at a pier. Note, though, that once you're on the cruise, weather conditions and heavy port traffic may necessitate last-minute changes in the way your ship reaches a port of call. Generally, ships do pull alongside the piers in Nassau, Key West, Ocho Rios (Jamaica), Cozumel, San Juan, St. Thomas, St. Croix, Grenada, Barbados, Aruba, and Curaçao. All ships calling on Grand Cayman, Belize City, and Roatan (Honduras), on the other hand, always anchor offshore and tender passengers in.

TRAVEL-AGENT SPECIALISTS   A handful of experienced travel agencies specialize in booking cruises and tours for travelers with disabilities. **Accessible Journeys,** 35 W. Sellers Ave., Ridley Park, PA 19078 (© **800/846-4537** or 610/ 521-0339; www.disabilitytravel.com), can even provide licensed healthcare professionals to accompany those who require aid. **Flying Wheels Travel,** 143 W. Bridge St., Owatonna, MN 55060 (© **507/451-5005;** www.flyingwheelstravel. com), is another option.

2

Booking Your Cruise & Getting the Best Price

As the last few years have proven, the travel industry is greatly affected by world events. While the Caribbean cruise market hasn't suffered anywhere near as much as some sectors, they've certainly not gone unscathed. Assuming fewer people are going to book a cruise to, say, Israel or Indonesia this year, the cruise lines have pulled many ships out of the Mediterranean and Asian market, positioning them instead closer to home—many of them in the Caribbean. A spate of new shipbuilding over the past decade meant the region already faced stiff competition, so adding yet more vessels to the market caused prices to fall precipitously—according to Carnival president Bob Dickinson, recent rates have equaled those charged in 1974. The bottom line? Base cruise prices are cheap, and that fact isn't going to change anytime soon.

In this chapter, we'll show you how to get the very lowest prices, keep additional costs down, and find a reputable travel agent, online or off, to help you through the booking process. After that, we'll tip you off on how to choose your cabin and complete other arrangements once you've hunted down the (affordable) ship of your dreams.

1 Pricing & Booking: The Short Explanation

Cheap. That about sums up the price of a cruise these days. While you can be sure the cruise lines will still try to make their profits elsewhere (in ships' casinos, bars, and spas, for instance), the upfront price you pay for your cruise—covering your cabin, entertainment, and meals—is darn low. Generally speaking, prices these days tend to drop the closer you get to the scheduled departure date, so if price is your main concern (rather than having to schedule aboard a certain ship for a certain week), there's little benefit in booking 3, 4, or 9 months early, as there once was. Even during the holidays, like the week between Christmas and New Year's, during Presidents' Day week, and around Thanksgiving, you're likely to find cabins available on most ships a month or more before sailing. Though cruise line brochures still list the inflated rates they've traditionally printed, it's a farce. In fact, we've heard from a reliable industry insider that many lines are planning to phase out brochure rates altogether. In the meantime, just like those airbrushed brochure models dancing on deck and lounging in the sun, **brochure rates are not real. Just ignore them. You'll always pay less.** Exceptions? Small-ship lines like American Canadian Caribbean and Windjammer Barefoot Cruises, which tend to print realistic rates.

As for booking, cruise lines tend to do what they've been doing for years, relying on traditional travel agents, and now travel websites too, to sell their product, rather than retaining huge in-house reservations departments. In addition to the huge, well-known online sellers, most traditional travel agencies also have their own websites, sometimes relying on them for a chunk of their sales, sometimes using them more as advertising, yet do most of their business in person or over the telephone, the old-fashioned way. Both kinds offer low rates, but the difference lies in customer service—the Web-focused sites don't offer it. For tips on using both options to their best advantage, see "Agents & the Web: Finding the Best Deals," later in this chapter.

2 The Prices in This Guide

Unlike other cruise guides, which print cruise line brochure rates despite knowing how useless they are in the real world, we've come up with a new approach, working with Just Cruisin' Plus (✆ 800/888-0922 or 615/833-0922; www.just cruisinplus.com), a full-service travel agency specializing in cruises and vacations, to present to you a sample of the **actual prices** people are paying for cruises aboard all the ships in this book. You can see the difference for yourself. The brochure rate for a 7-night western Caribbean cruise aboard Royal Caribbean's beautiful *Radiance of the Seas* is $2,009 for a low-end outside cabin. In reality, however, the actual prices available during our sampling period (Nov 2003 cruises, priced in mid-Apr) were able to get that same cabin for $649. Can we say huge difference?

In the ship-review chapters, we've listed these realistic prices for every ship, and in the "Price Comparisons: Brochure Rates vs. Discounted Rates" table in this chapter, we've shown how the brochure prices for every ship stack up against what consumers actually pay. The table gives prices for the lowest-priced **inside cabins** (that is, ones without windows) and lowest-priced **outside cabins** (that is, with windows) aboard each ship; the ship reviews in chapters 6 through 8 also provide sample discount prices for the cheapest **suites.** Remember that cruise ships generally have many different categories of cabins within the basic divisions of inside, outside, and suite, all priced differently. The rates we've listed represent the *lowest-priced* (which usually equates to smallest) in each division. If you're interested in booking a roomier, fancier cabin or suite, the price will be higher, with rates for high-end inside cabins being close to those for low-end outsides, and rates for high-end outsides being close to those for low-end suites.

Remember that rates are always subject to the basic principles of supply-and-demand, so those listed here are meant as a guide only and are in no way etched in stone—the price you pay may be higher or lower, depending on when you book, when you choose to travel, whether any special discounts are being offered by the lines, and a slew of other factors. All rates are cruise only, per person, based on double occupancy, and, unless otherwise noted, include port charges (the per-passenger fee each island charges the cruise line for entry). Government fees and taxes are additional.

Price Comparisons: Discounted Rates vs. Brochure Rates

Cruise Line	Ship	Itinerary (number of nights/region)	Lowest-Priced Inside Cabin (discounted/brochure)	Lowest Priced Outside Cabin (discounted/brochure)
ACCL	Grande Mariner	11/Carib	$2,655 / $2,655	$2,455 / $2,455
Carnival	Carnival Conquest	7/W. Carib	$579 / $1,749	$729 / $1,899
	Carnival Destiny	7/S. Carib	$449 / $1,749	$599 / $1,899
	Carnival Glory	7/W. Carib	$599 / $1,749	$699 / $1,899
	Carnival Legend	8/W. Carib	$729 / $1,899	$899 / $2,099
	Carnival Spirit	8/E. Carib	$459 / $1,899	$699 / $2,099
	Carnival Triumph	7/W. Carib	$529 / $1,749	$679 / $1,899
	Carnival Victory	7/W. Carib	$479 / $1,749	$629 / $1,899
	Celebration	4/W. Carib	$369 / $899	$419 / $979
	Fantasy	4/Bahamas	$259 / $899	$309 / $979
	Fascination	4/W. Carib	$259 / $899	$299 / $979
	Holiday	4/W. Carib	$369 / $899	$419 / $979
	Imagination	4/W. Carib	$299 / $899	$359 / $999
	Inspiration	7/W. Carib	$449 / $1,449	$549 / $1,599
	Jubilee	7/W. Carib	$399 / $1,449	$499 / $1,599
	Paradise	7/W. Carib	$429 / $1,449	$579 / $1,599
	Sensation	4/W. Carib	$299 / $899	$349 / $979
Celebrity	Century	7/E. Carib	$520 / $1,650	$660 / $1,810
	Constellation	7/S. Carib	$575 / $1,810	$675 / $2,110
	Galaxy	11/E. Carib	$1,150 / $2,079	$1,350 / $2,479
	Horizon	11/E. Carib	$1,000 / $1,779	$1,200 / $2,179
	Infinity	14/Panama Canal	$1,600 / $3,000	$2,150 / $3,900
	Millennium	7/E. Carib	$625 / $1,810	$775 / $2,110
	Summit	10/S. Carib	$1,100 / $2,439	$1,250 / $2,899
	Zenith	14/W. Carib	$1,250 / $1,859	$1,450 / $2,259
Clipper	Nantucket Clipper	7/S. Carib	N/A	$2,020 / $2,020
	Yorktown Clipper	9/Panama Canal	N/A	$2,850 / $2,850
Costa	CostaAtlantica	7/W. Carib	$799 / $1,599	$999 / $1,949
	CostaMediterranea	7/E. Carib	$649 / $1,049	$749 / $1,349
Crystal	Crystal Harmony	11/Panama Canal	$2,195 / $4,315	$3,225 / $5,715
	Crystal Serenity	11/E. Carib	N/A	$4,560 / $6,020
	Crystal Symphony	12/Panama Canal	N/A	$3,098 / $6,200
Cunard	QE2	12/Panama Canal	$3,055 / $4,019	$3,815 / $5,019
	Queen Mary 2	11 S. Carib	$1,999 / $1,999	$2,749 / $2,749
Disney	Disney Magic	7/E. Carib	$799 / $1,499	$1,059 / $1,899
	Disney Wonder	4/Bahamas	$459 / $899	$689 / $1,149

Price Comparisons: Discounted Rates vs. Brochure Rates

Cruise Line	Ship	Itinerary (number of nights/region)	Lowest-Priced Inside Cabin (discounted/ brochure)	Lowest Priced Outside Cabin (discounted/ brochure)
Holland America	Maasdam	7/W. Carib	$499 / $1,607	$569 / $1,995
	Noordam	14/S. Carib	$1,418 / $2,565	$1,713 / $3,133
	Oosterdam	7/W. Carib	$699 / $1,607	$739 / $1,995
	Rotterdam	10/Panama Canal	$1,099 / $2,326	$1,299 / $2,889
	Veendam	7/W. Carib	$547 / $1,649	$599 / $1,995
	Volendam	10/W. Carib	$799 / $2,306	$989 / $2,869
	Westerdam	N/A	N/A	N/A
	Zaandam	7/W. Carib	$499 / $1,607	$569 / $1,995
	Zuiderdam	7/W. Carib	$599 / $1,607	$739 / $1,995
Norwegian	Norway	7/E. Carib	$303 / $853	$473 / $1,183
	Norwegian Dawn	7/W. Carib	$678 / $1,678	$778 / $1,908
	Norwegian Dream	7/W. Carib	$460 / $1,260	$575 / $1,490
	Norwegian Majesty	7/W. Carib	$529 / $1,279	$579 / $1,479
	Norwegian Sea	7/W. Carib	$527 / $1,277	$677 / $1,527
	Norwegian Sky	7/S. Carib	$559 / $1,359	$709 / $1,639
	Norwegian Sun	7/W. Carib	$727 / $1,477	$877 / $1,707
	Norwegian Wind	7/W. Carib	$513 / $1,363	$613 / $1,593
Oceania	Regatta	14/Panama Canal	$1,589 / $3,261	$1,769 / $3,661
Princess	Coral Princess	10/Panama Canal	$1,299 / $1,999	$1,599 / $2,324
	Dawn Princess	7/S. Carib	$599 / $1,229	$699 / $1,569
	Golden Princess	7/E. Carib	$599 / $1,339	$699 / $1,639
	Grand Princess	7/W. Carib	$599 / $1,339	$699 / $1,639
	Island Princess	10/Panama Canal	$1,349 / $1,999	$1,649 / $2,324
	Sun Princess	10/S. Carib	$999 / $1,674	$1,198 / $1,964
Radisson Seven Seas	Radisson Diamond	7/S. Carib	N/A	$1,858 / $3,505
	Seven Seas Mariner	9/S. Carib	N/A	$3,866 / $5,065
	Seven Seas Navigator	7/W. Carib	N/A	$2,258 / $4,305
	Seven Seas Voyager	7/W. Carib	N/A	$2,008 / $3,805
Royal Caribbean	Adventure of the Seas	7/S. Carib	$709 / $1,709	$848 / $2,099
	Brilliance of the Seas	10/W. Carib	$1,249 / $1,919	$1,449 / $2,299
	Enchantment of the Seas	4/W. Carib	$349 / $919	$435 / $1,099
	Explorer of the Seas	7/E. Carib	$699 / $1,649	$849 / $2,099
	Grandeur of the Seas	7/W. Carib	$586 / $1,499	$686 / $1,799
	Majesty of the Seas	4/Bahamas	$249 / $999	$289 / $1,219
	Mariner of the Seas	7/E. Carib	$679 / $2,029	$949 / $2,479
	Navigator of the Seas	7/W. Carib	$649 / $1,649	$799 / $2,099
	Nordic Empress	7/W. Carib	$374 / $1,638	$474 / $1,868
	Radiance of the Seas	7/W. Carib	$549 / $1,679	$649 / $2,099

Price Comparisons: Discounted Rates vs. Brochure Rates

Cruise Line	Ship	Itinerary (number of nights/region)	Lowest-Priced Inside Cabin (discounted/brochure)	Lowest Priced Outside Cabin (discounted/brochure)
	Rhapsody of the Seas	7/W. Carib	$549 / $1,499	$649 / $1,799
	Serenade of the Seas	7/S. Carib	$599 / $2,029	$699 / $2,404
	Sovereign of the Seas	4/Bahamas	$236 / $999	$266 / $1,079
	Splendour of the Seas	12/Panama Canal	$1,249 / $2,249	$1,499 / $2,879
	Voyager of the Seas	7/W. Carib	$649 / $1,649	$799 / $2,099
Royal Olympia	Olympia Explorer	13/Panama Canal	$1,981 / $3,145	$2,560 / $4,110
	Olympia Voyager	16/Panama Canal	$3,090 / $2,560	$4,290 / $3,395
Seabourn	Seabourn Legend	14/Panama Canal	N/A	$4,797 / $7,995
	Seabourn Pride	7/S. Carib	N/A	$2,922 / $4,495
SeaDream	SeaDream I	7/S. Carib	N/A	$2,450 / $4,900
	SeaDream II	5/S. Carib	N/A	$1,999 / $4,900
Silversea	Silver Cloud	7/S. Carib	N/A	$2,571 / $3,395
	Silver Whisper	13/Panama Canal	N/A	$6,710 / $7,895
	Silver Wind	7/E. Carib	N/A	$3,696 / $4,595
Star Clippers	Royal Clipper	7/S. Carib	$1,375 / $1,675	$1,595 / $1,895
	Star Clipper	7/S. Carib	$1,375 / $1,675	$1,595 / $1,895
Windjammer	Amazing Grace	13/S. Carib	N/A	$1,400 / $1,400
	Legacy	6/S. Carib	N/A	$1,100 / $1,100
	Mandalay	13/S. Carib	$1,900 / $1,900	$2,098 / $2,098
	Polynesia	6/S. Carib	$900 / $900	$1,200 / $1,200
	Yankee Clipper	6/S. Carib	N/A	$900 / $900
Windstar	Wind Spirit	7/S. Carib	N/A	$2,358 / $3,895
	Wind Surf	7/E. Carib	N/A	$2,358 / $3,895

The discounted prices listed here represent the actual rates consumers booking approximately 7 months ahead were paying through Just Cruisin' Plus for the lowest-priced inside and outside cabins aboard each ship. These prices are shown only as an example of the kinds of discounts available. Discounts shown may not apply when you book — or, you may even get a larger discount. It's all a matter of supply-and-demand (and timing). All rates are per person, based on double occupancy, and include port charges but not taxes.

3 The Cost: What's Included & What's Not

Overall, a cruise adds up to great value and convenience when you consider that your main vacation ingredients—accommodations; meals and most snacks; stops at ports of call; a packed schedule of activities; use of gyms, pools, and other facilities; and shows, cabaret, jazz performances, and more—are covered in the cruise price. Just don't think it's all free. Especially these days, with base cruise prices so low, cruise lines are pushing a slew of added-cost onboard extras as a way of increasing their revenue. So, when figuring out your budget, you have to be sure to figure in the additional costs you'll incur for shore excursions, gratuities, bar drinks and specialty coffee, spa treatments, souvenirs, and even fresh flowers and custom-tailored suits if your self-restraint is low. If you're the gambling type, you're a prime candidate for increasing your ship's revenue

Put Aside Some Money for Crew Gratuities

Almost all cruise lines have the same kind of deal with their staff that restaurants do in the United States: They pay them minimal salaries on the assumption that they'll make most of their pay in tips. Generally, each passenger can expect to tip about $70 during a weeklong cruise, either by handing out gratuities directly or, as is becoming more prevalent, by agreeing to have them added automatically to his onboard account at the end of the cruise. For more on tipping, see chapter 3, "Things to Know Before You Go."

stream, whether your game is craps or bingo, scratch-off cards or Caribbean stud poker. Sources tell us that many onboard slot machines have even been rigged to work faster, so passengers spend more money.

Some of the most luxurious and expensive lines—Silversea, Seabourn, and SeaDream Yacht Club—come closest to being truly all-inclusive by including all alcoholic beverages and gratuities in their cruise rates. Radisson Seven Seas includes gratuities as well, but offers free wine only at dinner. Aside from these aberrations, though, you can expect to shell out at least another $250 to $500 per person for an average 7-night cruise, and easily double that if, for instance, you have a bottle of wine with dinner every night, a couple of cocktails after, go on three $75 shore excursions, hit the ships' $25 per person alternative restaurants a few times, try your luck at bingo, and buy some trinkets in the onboard shops or at the ports of call. Of course, just as at a hotel, you'll also pay extra for items such as ship-to-shore phone calls and e-mails, massages, manicures, facials, haircuts, fancy coffees, dinner in the alternative restaurants, and medical treatments in the ship's infirmary. Port charges may be included in your cruise price, but if they're not, you'll have to figure this into the total cost.

If you're not cruising from a port you can drive to—such as New Orleans, New York, Charleston, or Miami—then you'll have to figure in **airfare to the ship,** which is rarely included in cruise prices. Depending on where you're flying from and when you purchase your tickets, this can run from as little as $100 to over $500.

4 Money-Saving Strategies

From last-minute deals to early-booking discounts, from sharing cabins to senior and frequent-cruiser discounts, there are a lot of ways to save money on your cruise. Read on to find out how.

LAST-MINUTE BOOKING MAKES SENSE

Used to be that booking 3 to 9 months in advance would often get you the best price, and many cruise lines would still like you to believe that's true since the earlier ships fill up, the easier they can breathe. However, this hasn't been the case for several years. While pricing policies differ from line to line, and even from week to week, **there's now little incentive to book early.** As Mike Driscoll, editor of influential industry newsletter *Cruise Week,* told us, "In today's volatile political environment, what do you have to lose when it comes to booking late?"

Read our lips: supply-and-demand. Cruise lines need to fill their ships to make money, so as sailing dates get close and berths remain empty, prices are

Average Cost of Onboard Extras

Just so you're not shocked when your shipboard account is settled at the end of your trip, here are some average prices for onboard extras.

Laundry	75¢–$6 per item
Self-service laundry	$1–$1.50 per load
Pressing	$1–$4 per item
Massage (50-min. session)	$84–$116 plus tip
Facial	$84–$130 plus tip
Men's shampoo and haircut	$26–$32 plus tip
Women's shampoo and set	$26–$50 plus tip
Manicure	$21–$54 plus tip
Pedicure	$34–$76 plus tip
Spa treatments	$13–$243 plus tip
5-inch-x-7-inch photo purchased from ship's photographer	$7–$10
Scotch and soda at an onboard bar	$3.50–$6
Bottle of domestic beer	$3
Bottle of imported beer	$3.50–$5
Bottle of wine to accompany dinner	$10–$300
Bottle of Evian water, 1.5 liters	$2.95
Bottle of Evian water, 0.5 liters	$1.95
Can of Coca-Cola	$1.50
Ship-to-shore phone call or fax	$4–$15 per minute
Sending e-mails	50¢–$1 per minute
Shore excursions	$20–$200
Ship souvenirs (logo T-shirts, key chains, etc.)	$3–$50
Sunscreen, 6-ounce bottle	$10
Disposable camera	$15–$20

slashed, slashed, and slashed again to fill cabins and get revenue flowing, even if it's less revenue than the cruise lines had originally hoped for. Since the Caribbean is overflowing with ships these days, the only thing you may sacrifice when booking late is a measure of choice: You'll probably get the cruise line you want, and the ship and itinerary too (especially if you can be a little flexible with your sailing date), but you may have to accept a different cabin category than the one you had in mind. If you've got to have something as specific as a balcony cabin in the forward section of a Grand-class Princess ship sailing in the southern Caribbean the first week of June, you may not find exactly what you want 3 weeks prior to the sailing date.

If you do need to fly to the ship, getting airfare at the last minute may be tough. You may find nothing available, depending on where you're sailing from (sure, there are tons of flights to Miami and Fort Lauderdale, but fewer to San Juan and other ports), or you may have to pay so much for the flight that it cancels out your

Price Protection: Making Sure Your Deal Is the Best Deal

It's a little-known fact that if the price of your cabin category goes down after you've booked it, a few cruise lines—namely Royal Caribbean, Celebrity, Princess and ultraluxury lines, Radisson, Cunard, and Crystal—will in some cases agree to make up the difference, in effect guaranteeing you the lowest rates up until the day of sailing. This is especially true if you haven't yet paid in full and if your cruise is still 60 days or more away. Naturally, you have to qualify for the newer lower rate, which may only be offered to residents of a certain state, to senior citizens, or to some other special group. And, to get around having to rebook passengers at lower rates, some lines like Princess and Holland America are offering deeply discounted promotions 6 weeks or so before a sailing that are restricted to new bookings only.

Some lines are trying to accommodate passengers by offering insurance policies that allow rebooking at lower rates without the penalties (or at lower penalties) that would normally apply for canceling and rebooking within 60 or 70 days of sailing. If you purchase their insurance, Holland America, for instance, will rebook passengers at lower available rates if the new lower fare is at least 10% less than the original fare. Windstar offers a similar policy.

Keep in mind, insurance or not, no law requires lines to rebook you at a lower rate; the same rules apply here as in any other retainer arrangement—you know you can't walk into a grocery store and demand a refund on the peas you bought last month because they went on sale today.

If a line does reduce rates just before the cruise you booked, don't expect them to call and let you know you're entitled to money back. To find out about lowered rates, you and/or your agent would need to monitor the prices on a weekly basis and then call the cruise line to inquire about their rebooking policies and/or fees. Since agencies make a percentage commission on your total cruise price, don't expect most of them—especially Web-based sellers and impersonal discounters who work only over the phone—to go too far out of their way to refund your money. This is where a trusted travel agent comes into play, someone who will look out for your best interests because he or she wants you to come back again.

savings on the cruise. Also, if you were planning to use frequent-flier miles, you'll likely discover that frequent-flier seats are all taken on the flights you need. And you may have to fly a multileg route instead of a direct one.

A few more caveats to consider: **Most last-minute deals are completely nonrefundable;** if you book a week before the cruise, for example, the full fare is due up front and you get zip back if you change your mind a few days later. Also, booking late generally isn't a good strategy if you're looking for a specific cabin category (say a family suite or a specific balcony cabin) during ultrapopular times like **holidays** (New Year's, Thanksgiving, Easter, and Presidents' Day week in Feb), when many cabins get booked up months in advance.

You'll find last-minute deals advertised online and in the travel section of many Sunday newspapers, especially the *Miami Herald, LA Times,* and *New York Times.* You should also check with a travel agent or discounter that specializes in cruises. See "Agents & the Web: Finding the Best Deals," later in this chapter.

For those who prefer to plan ahead, the cruise lines continue to offer substantial **early-booking discounts** as well, though they're generally not as low as you'd get by waiting till the last minute. Price aside, when booking early you naturally have much more assurance of getting exactly what you want in terms of cruise line, ship, and everything else.

SENIOR-CITIZEN DISCOUNTS

The cruise industry offers some discounts to seniors (usually defined as anyone 55 years or older), so don't keep your age a secret, and always ask your travel agent about these discounts when you're booking. For discounts in general, the best organization to belong to is **AARP,** 601 E St. NW, Washington, DC 20049 (**℃ 800/424-3410;** www.aarp.org), the biggest outfit in the United States for people 50 and over. Carnival, for instance, offers savings to AARP members of up to $100 per cabin on 7-night and longer cruises.

REPEAT-PASSENGER DISCOUNTS

If you've cruised with a particular cruise line before, you're considered a valued "repeater," and most lines will reward you with 5% to 10% discounts on future cruises, as well as (depending on how many times you've sailed) cabin upgrades, invitations to private cocktail parties, priority check-in at the terminal, free Internet access, logo souvenirs, special mailings and newsletters, and maybe even a free cruise if you've racked up enough sailings. On some upscale ships, repeaters are admitted into a secret society of sorts, given special lapel pins (or sometimes hats and windbreakers), provided with the services of a special concierge, and often invited to dine one night with the captain or another officer. Just about every line offers something for repeat guests, with lines such as Holland America, Crystal, Celebrity, Silversea and Seabourn among the most generous. The catch to all of this is that repeat-passenger discounts often cannot be combined with other pricing deals, particularly in the case of the mainstream lines. So, considering how low cruise prices are these days, chances are the rate you see advertised in the Sunday travel section will be lower than what your repeater discount would be.

If you're really a serious repeater, though, the generous booty you get on the small upscale ships can add up. After you sail a total of 140 days with Seabourn, for instance, you're entitled to a free 14-day cruise, while Silversea passengers get a free 7-night cruise after sailing 350 days. After the 15th Crystal cruise, you get a business-class air upgrade and a $250 shipboard credit, among other perks. Some of the small adventure-oriented lines offer similar deals. ACCL, for instance, gives passengers an 11th cruise free after their 10th paid cruise of at least 12 nights.

GROUP DISCOUNTS

Based on supply-and-demand, some cruise lines offer reduced rates to groups occupying a certain number of cabins (typically at least 8–15), double occupancy. If a ship isn't selling well, a group has a lot more incentive to wheel and deal with a cruise line, but if a ship is selling well, group deals may not be available. Also, last-minute discounts may end up being better than group deals worked out earlier, though Carnival now guarantees that if individual fares fall below what a group has already paid, group members get the difference back in the form of a shipboard credit.

Traditionally, the groups get one cabin free and can then deduct a percentage of that cabin's cost from all the others—for example, eight $1,000 cabins add up to $8,000 total, but the free cabin allows the travelers to divide that cost by nine instead of eight, lowering the per-cabin rate to $888. This makes cruise ships a good bet for family reunions and the like, especially if travelers have a good agent who is willing to coordinate travel for widely scattered family members or friends.

Some high-volume cruise agencies may create groups of their own, booking blocks of cabins on particular ships and then selling them individually to their customers. Aside from the savings, you'll never know you're part of a group.

SAVING MONEY BY SHARING A CABIN

All but the small adventure lines offer cabins that can house three or four passengers, two in regular beds and two in sofa beds and/or bunk-style berths that pull down from the ceiling or wall. Disney, Carnival, Royal Caribbean, and NCL go one better by offering family cabins that can accommodate five people— Disney's cabins even have 1½ bathrooms. The rates for third, fourth, and fifth passengers in a cabin, whether adults or children, are typically 50% or more off the normal adult fare, so families or friends who are willing to be a bit (or a lot) crowded can save big. You can also look into sharing a suite on most ships; many can accommodate five to seven people, and some are almost outlandishly roomy.

SAVING MONEY ON ODDBALL CABINS

Read the fine print in the cruise line brochures, since you never know what obscure special deals may apply to you. Carnival, for instance, offers really low rates on *Carnival Destiny* if you book one of the dozen category-6 cabins that are directly above the disco, which are on the receiving end of a lot of noise. The brochure calls them Night Owl Staterooms ("If you love to party late into the night"), and if you're planning on being in the disco yourself, dancing into the wee hours, you may want to consider these cabins, which are discounted at about 50% less than other, quieter cabins in the same category. Also, look for cabins with obstructed views (usually because of lifeboats hanging just outside the windows), which are often discounted too.

AVOIDING THE SINGLE PENALTY

Cruise lines base their rates on two paying passengers sharing a cabin, so passengers wanting to travel alone, in their own cabin, are often socked with something called the **single supplement,** which entails a charge of between 50% and 100% *more than* the standard cruise fare. In today's ultracompetitive environment, however, some lines are quietly foregoing or reducing this kind of supplemental charge if a ship isn't filling up on a particular sailing and its departure date is approaching. Unfortunately, there's no way to predict this trend.

If you do encounter a single penalty on the cruise you want to book, consider taking advantage of the **cabin-share service** offered by some cruise lines, whereby they'll match you with a same-gender roommate and thus pull in their regular revenue for the cabin. Fewer lines are offering such programs these days, though you can still arrange shares through Windjammer Barefoot Cruises and Holland America. Keep in mind, you won't be able to get any info about your roommate until you walk through the cabin door. The silver lining: If the cruise

Weigh Value Against Price

While you want the best price, of course, it's important not to make price your only concern. Value—what you get for your money—is just as important as the dollar amount you pay. The advertised prices you see in newspapers and on website home pages are usually for the lowest-grade cabin on a ship; a better cabin—one with a window or maybe a private veranda—will cost more.

line can't find a roommate for you, you'll probably get the cabin at the regular double occupancy rate anyway.

FINDING SPECIAL DEALS ON SPECIAL CRUISES

Repositioning cruises, when ships leave one cruise region and sail to another (for instance, heading from Alaska to the Caribbean, in stages), are often discounted, and two-for-one deals are not uncommon. Keep in mind that since most repositioning cruises require crossing great stretches of ocean, they are usually longer and tend to have fewer stops at ports of call, spending considerable time at sea.

Depending on when you go, cruise lines also offer discounts to passengers who book **back-to-back cruises** on the same ship, a decent option if you want a longer (say, 2-week) vacation, since many ships vary their itineraries from week to week, visiting different ports and sometimes different regions, such as the eastern Caribbean one week and the western Caribbean the next. Policies vary from line to line. Seabourn offers 10% to 50% savings if you combine two or more cruises. Windstar offers the same deal if you book two weeklong cruises back-to-back. Most common are discounts like the one Carnival offers: a $100-per-cabin discount on the total cruise price when two 7-night cruises are combined.

5 Agents & the Web: Finding the Best Deals

Today, practically everybody has a website, and the difference between so-called **Web-based cruise sellers** and more **traditional travel agencies** is that the former rely on their sites for actual bookings, while the latter use theirs as glorified advertising space to promote their offerings, doing all actual business in person or over the phone. With a few exceptions the cruise lines also have **direct-booking engines** on their own sites, but we don't recommend using them since agents and Web-based sellers may have negotiated group rates with the lines, be part of a consortium with whom a line is doing an upgrade promotion, or have other deals going that enable them to offer you lower rates. Though it may sound peculiar, the cruise lines actually prefer that you book through third parties, since having agents and sites do the grunt work allows the lines to maintain small reservations staffs and, simultaneously, maintain goodwill in a system that works—something they have to consider, because the vast majority of cruises are booked through agencies of one type or another. Typically, cruise lines report that only about 5% to 10% of their bookings are direct—more than in years past, but still a smallish chunk of the biz.

WHICH OFFERS BETTER PRICES?

As far as cruise prices go, there's no absolutely quantifiable difference between the real live travel agents and Internet-based cruise sellers. Sometimes you'll get the best price on the Web and sometimes you'll get it through an agent—especially in the current market, where prices offered to agents and sites tend to be very similar across the board. Some agencies, online or off, get better prices from certain cruise lines because they sell a high volume of that line's product, and are also sometimes able to offer special 1-day sales on a line's ships for the same reason. However, today's low prices mean the lines have little incentive to cut a million different deals with a million different agencies—when you're selling a weeklong cruise for $399, what's the point of pitting one agent against another, with one selling the cruise for $379 and another for $419?

WHICH PROVIDES BETTER SERVICE?

It all depends on your level of experience as a cruiser and as an Internet user. Most websites give you only a menu of ships and itineraries to select from, plus a basic search capability that takes into account only destination, price, length of trip, and date, without consideration of the type of cruise experience each line offers. If you've cruised before and know exactly what you want, no problem. If, on the other hand, you have limited experience with cruising and with booking on the Web, it may be better to see a traditional agent, who can help you wade through the choices and answer your questions.

Of course, you *are* reading this book, so you'll be approaching the booking process with a good idea of what the various cruise lines will give you. If you've decided exactly which ship and itinerary you want, you could go online and arrange your cruise in about 10 minutes through one of the cruise-only sites or through one of the larger travel generalists such as Travelocity, Expedia, or MyTravel. However, unless you've sailed on the ship already and want to book it again, some details you simply won't know, such as which cabins have their views obstructed by lifeboats; which are near loud areas such as discos and the engine room; and, in general, what the major differences are between cabin categories. Detailed information on these matters is spotty at best on the Web, and if there at all, either is not highlighted (you'd have to know to look for it) or is buried under layers of commands and dead ends that could have you sitting at your computer for what feels like eons figuring it all out.

It's in situations like these where an experienced cruise agent is invaluable—someone who's sailed on or inspected a variety of ships and booked many customers aboard in the past, passengers who have reported back about what they did and didn't like. These agents will also be able to tell you about options you may not otherwise have known existed (alternative deals, special promotions, pre- and post-cruise stays in port or add-on trips, and so on), help out and act as an intermediary should any problems arise with your booking, arrange tuxedo rental for formal nights if needed, order special extras such as a bottle of champagne in your cabin when you arrive, and in general make your planning easy.

Keep in mind, though, that you need to find an agent who really knows the business—and this applies to every type of agent: those who work out of their home or an agency office, those who work for large conglomerates and deal mostly over the phone, and those who man 800 numbers associated with Web-based sellers. Many times (though not always), representatives of large phone and Web sellers are little more than order-takers: They may not know much more than pricing, and may never even have been on a cruise themselves. This system works okay for selling air travel, where the big question is coach or first-class, case closed; but a lot more variables are associated with booking a cruise,

C Be Savvy & Beware of Scams

With the number of offers a potential cruise buyer sees, it can be difficult to know if an agency is or isn't reliable, legit, or, for that matter, stable: A lot of travel agencies have gone out of business in the past few years, and the last thing you need is your vacation plans screwed up as a result. It pays to be on your guard against fly-by-night operators and agents who may lead you astray, but there's no great secrets involved here—the same basic principles apply to buying a cruise as they do to buying a car or any other big-ticket item.

- **Get a referral.** A recommendation from a trusted friend or colleague (or from this guidebook) is one of the best ways to hook up with a reputable agent.
- **Use the cruise lines' agent lists.** Many cruise line websites include agency locator lists, naming agencies around the country with whom they do business. These are by no means comprehensive lists of all good or bad agencies, but an agent's presence on these lists is usually another good sign of experience.
- **Beware of snap recommendations.** If an agent, whether brick-and-mortar or online, suggests a particular cruise line without asking you a single question first about your tastes, beware. Since agents work on commissions from the lines, some may try to shanghai you into cruising with a company that pays them the highest rates, even though that line may not be right for you. Be prepared: Read through the cruise line reviews in chapters 6 through 8 so you'll be able to say to sneaky agents, "But Frommer's says . . . "
- *Always* **use a credit card to pay for your cruise.** It gives you more protection in the event the agency or cruise line fails. When your credit-card statement arrives, make sure the payment was made to the cruise line, not the travel agency. If you find that payment was actually made to the agency, it's a big red flag that something's wrong. If you insist on paying by check, you'll be making it out to the agency, so it may be wise to ask if the agency has default protection. Many do.
- **Always follow the cruise line's payment schedule,** and never agree to a different schedule the travel agency comes up with. The lines' terms are always clearly printed in their brochures and usually require an initial deposit, with the balance due no later than 75 to 45 days before departure. If you're booking 2 months or less before departure, the full payment is usually required at the time of booking.
- **Keep on top of your booking.** If you ever fail to receive a document or ticket on the date it's been promised, inquire about it immediately. If you're told that your cruise reservation was canceled because of overbooking and that you must pay extra for a confirmed and rescheduled sailing, demand a full refund and/or contact your credit-card company to stop payment.

and the decisions you make at booking are the major determinants in whether you have the vacation of a lifetime or one that you'll be grinding your teeth over from boarding to debarkation.

So, how do you know an agent is any good? The best way, of course, is to use one who has been referred to you by a reliable friend or acquaintance. This is particularly valuable these days, when agents are being pressed to squeeze more profit from every sale, making them less likely to take the time to discuss options. Unless you have a personal relationship with the agent, it's often chop-chop: Pick it, book it, done. When searching for a good agent, it can't hurt if they're **Master Cruise Counselors (MCC)** or **Accredited Cruise Counselors (ACC),** designations doled out by the Cruise Lines International Association (CLIA), an industry trade organization. To get these designations, agents have to complete coursework on the cruise industry and the process of booking cruises, and inspect a certain number of ships. Being a member of CLIA, or not being a member, doesn't say much about an agency; some crummy agencies are members, some big successful ones aren't. It can't hurt if an agent has a CTC designation after their names, which means they are **Certified Travel Counselors,** and have taken many hours' worth of travel-related courses through the Institute of Certified Travel Agents (ICTA). Many of the cruise lines' websites list **preferred agencies** (generally broken down or searchable by city or state), as does the CLIA site, at **www.cruising.org**. Many of the most reliable large cruise-only travel agencies also advertise in the bimonthly *Cruise Travel* magazine. Look for it on your newsstand, or call for a subscription (✆ **800/877-5893;** www. travel.org/CruiseTravel). In the sections below, we list some of the best agencies and also evaluate the major cruise-selling websites.

6 Recommended Agencies & Websites

Out of some 25,000 U.S. travel agencies, 15% (or about 3,000 agencies) sell 90% of all cruise travel in North America; about 30% of those are considered cruise-only. Agencies come in all shapes and sizes, from small neighborhood stores to huge chain operations. Like banking, telecommunications, and media, the travel industry has been rife with consolidation these past few years, so even that mom-and-pop travel agency on Main Street may turn out to be an affiliate of a larger agency.

Even though you'll get similarly low rates from everyone these days—traditional agency or Web-based—we can't stress enough that service counts for something too. There's value in knowing and trusting a travel agent you've worked with in the past or one who comes highly recommended by someone you trust. A good agent will be there for you if problems arise.

TRADITIONAL AGENCIES SPECIALIZING IN MAINSTREAM CRUISES

To give you an idea of where to begin, here's a sampling (by no means comprehensive) of both cruise-only and full-service agencies that have solid reputations selling cruises with mainstream lines such as Princess, Carnival, Royal Caribbean, Celebrity, Holland America, and Norwegian. A few are affiliated with the big chains; most are not. While all have websites to promote current deals, the agencies listed primarily operate from a combination of walk-in business and toll-free telephone-based business.

• **Admiral of the Fleet Cruise Center,** 3430 Pacific Ave. SE, Suite A-5, Olympia, WA 98501 (✆ **800/877-7447** or 360/438-1191; www.olympia cruisecenter.com)

• **Cruise Brothers,** 950 Wellington Ave., Cranston, RI 02910 (✆ **800/827-7779** or 401/941-3999; www.cruisebrothers.com)

• **The Cruise Company,** 10760 Q St., Omaha, NE 68127 (✆ **800/289-5505** or 402/339-6800; www.thecruisecompany.com)

• **Cruise Connections Canada,** 208-1090 W. Pender, Vancouver, BC V6E 2N7, Canada (✆ **800/661-WAVE;** www.cruise-connections.com)

• **Cruise Escapes,** 14474 Midway Rd., Dallas, TX 75244-3509 (✆ **800/288-1190** or 972/404-0505; www.cruiseescapes.com)

• **Cruise Holidays,** 7000 NW Prairie View Rd., Kansas City, MO 64151 (✆ **800/869-6806** or 816/741-7417; www.cruiseholidayskc.com)

• **Cruises By Brennco,** 508 E. 112th St., Kansas City, MO 64131 (✆ **800/955-1909** or 816/942-1000; www.brennco.com)

• **Cruises Only,** 220 Congress Park Dr., Delray Beach, FL 33445 (✆ **800/278-4737;** www.cruisesonly.com), is part of the MyTravel family of cruise companies, which also include CruiseOne and Cruises Inc.

• **Cruise Value Center,** 6 Edgeboro Rd., Ste. 400, East Brunswick, NJ 08816 (✆ **800/231-7447;** www.cruisevalue.com)

• **Dynamic Travel & Cruises,** 2325 E. Southlake Blvd., Southlake, TX 76092 (✆ **800/766-2911** or 817/481-8631; www.dynamictravel.com)

• **Golden Bear Travel/Mariner Club,** 16 Digital Dr., Novado, CA 94949 (✆ **800/551-1000** or 415/382-8900; www.goldenbeartravel.com)

• **Hartford Holidays,** 129 Hillside Ave., Williston Park, NY 11596 (✆ **800/828-4813** or 516/746-6670; www.hartfordholidays.com)

• **Just Cruisin' Plus,** 5640 Nolensville Rd., Nashville, TN 37211 (✆ **800/888-0922** or 615/833-0922; www.justcruisinplus.com)

• **Kelly Cruises,** 1315 W. 22nd St., Suite 105, Oak Brook, IL 60523 (✆ **800/837-7447** or 630/990-1111; www.kellycruises.com)

• **Mann Travel & Cruises,** 4400 Park Rd., Charlotte, NC 28209 (✆ **866/591-8129;** www.manntravels.com)

• **Vacation Store,** 100 Sylvan Rd., Suite 600, Woburn, MA 01801 (✆ **800/887-8111;** www.thevacationstore.com)

TRADITIONAL AGENCIES SPECIALIZING IN LUXURY CRUISES

This sampling of reputable agencies, both cruise-only and full-service, specializes in selling ultraluxury cruises such as Cunard, Seabourn, Silversea, Crystal, Radisson Seven Seas, and Windstar.

• **Altair Travel,** 2025 S. Brentwood Blvd., St. Louis, MO 63144 (✆ **800/844-5598** or 314/968-9600; www.altairtravelinc.com)

• **Concierge Cruises & Tours,** 13470 N. Sunset Mesa Dr., Marana, AZ 85653 (✆ **800/940-8385** or 520/572-6377)

• **Cruises of Distinction,** 2750 S. Woodword Ave., Bloomfield Hills, MI 48304 (✆ **800/434-6644** or 248/332-2020; www.cruisesofdistinction.com)

• **Cruise Professionals,** 130 Dundas St. East, Ste. 103, Mississauga, Ontario L5A 3V8, Canada (✆ **800/265-3838** or 905/275-3030; www.cruise professionals.com)

- **Golden Bear Travel/Mariner Club,** 16 Digital Dr., Novado, CA 94949 (℅ **800/551-1000** or 415/382-8900; www.goldenbeartravel.com)
- **Jean Rose Travel,** 140 Intracoastal Pointe Dr., Jupiter FL 33477 (℅ **800/ 441-4846** or 561/575-2901)
- **Largay Travel,** 5 F Village St., Southbury, CT 06488 (℅ **800/955-6872** or 203/264-6581; www.largaytravel.com)
- **Pisa Brothers,** 630 Fifth Ave., New York, NY 10111 (℅ **800/729-7472** or 212/265-8420; www.pisabrothers.com)
- **Strictly Vacations,** 108 W. Mission St., Santa Barbara, CA 93101 (℅ **800/ 447-2364;** www.strictlyvacations.com)

Formerly known as Allied Percival International, or API, **Virtuoso,** 500 Main St., Ste. 400, Fort Worth, TX 76102 (℅ **800/401-4274;** www.virtuoso.com), is a consortium of more than 250 member agencies, including some on the list above. To find an agency in your area, call their toll-free number or e-mail **information@ virtuoso.com.**

WEB-BASED AGENCIES SPECIALIZING IN MAINSTREAM CRUISES

The following sites are reputable Web-based cruise specialists. All allow searches by destination, date of travel, length of cruise, and price range, as well as cruise line or ship if you know exactly what you want, and all allow you to book online for at least some if not most lines. In many cases, though, this does not involve a live connection with the cruise line's reservations database, so you'll have to wait up to 24 hours for a confirmation via e-mail, fax, or phone call. Sometimes you can research your cruise online but have to call an 800 number when you're ready to get down to business. Keep in mind, these websites are constant works in progress, adding new features all the time.

- **Cruise.com** (www.cruise.com; ℅ **800/800-9552,** 800/303-3337, or 888/ 333-3116)
- **Cruise411.com** (www.cruise411.com; ℅ **800/553-7090**)
- **11th Hour Vacations** (www.11thhourvacations.com; ℅ **864/331-1140**)
- **Expedia** (www.expedia.com; ℅ **800/397-3342**)
- **Icruise.com** (www.icruise.com; ℅ **888/909-6242** or 212/929-6046)
- **Moment's Notice** (www.moments-notice.com; ℅ **888/241-3366** or 718/ 234-6295; deals hot line 718/621-4548); charges an annual $25 membership fee
- **Spur of the Moment Cruises** (www.spurof.com; ℅ **800/343-1991**)
- **Travelocity** (www.travelocity.com; ℅ **877/815-5446**) is the largest Web-based cruise seller in the world.

7 Choosing Your Cabin

Once you've decided which ship you're interested in, and have tracked down a good rate through an agent or an online cruise seller, the next thing you have to decide is what kind of cabin you need. In this section, we'll give you some tips for doing just that.

THE MONEY QUESTION

When it comes right down to it, choosing a cabin is really a question of money. From a windowless lower-deck cabin with upper and lower bunks to a 1,400-square-foot suite with a butler and mile-long private veranda, cruise ships can offer a dozen or more different cabin categories that represent different cabin

Getting a Sneak Preview

If you want to get a look at the types of cabins that are available, go online to use the **360-degree tours of cabins and public rooms** that are available on some sites. MyTravel's site, **www.mytravel.com**, has an amazing selection of 360s that includes almost all the ships reviewed in this book, with the exception of the adventure, European, and smaller lines. Many of the cruise lines' sites also offer these tours, or at least still photos of their different cabin categories.

---

sizes, different locations on the ship, different amenities, and, of course, vastly different prices.

It's traditionally been a rule of thumb that the higher up you are and the more light that gets into your cabin, the more you pay; the lower you go into the bowels of the ship, the cheaper the fare. However, on some of the more modern ships, that old rule doesn't always ring true. On ships launched recently by Carnival, for instance, designers have scattered their most desirable suites on midlevel decks as well as top decks, thereby diminishing the prestige of an upper-deck cabin. For the most part, though, and especially on small ships, where most cabins are virtually identical, cabins on higher decks are still generally more expensive, and outside cabins (with windows or balconies) are more expensive than inside cabins (those without).

EVALUATING CABIN SIZE

Inch for inch, cruise ship cabins are smaller than hotel rooms. Of course, having a private balcony attached to your cabin, as many do these days, will make your living space that much bigger.

A roomy **standard cabin** is about 170 to 180 square feet, although some of the smallest are about 85 to 100 square feet. Disney has some of the more spacious standard cabins at sea, at 226 square feet (they call them "family suites," but they're still the most common accommodation aboard their ships). Celebrity's standards are spacious enough at around 170 to 175 square feet, with those on its Millennium-class ships sometimes as big as 191 square feet. Carnival and Holland America's are about 185 square feet, with some going up to a roomy 197 and 220 square feet, respectively. By way of comparison, equivalent standard cabins on a good number of ships on the Norwegian and Royal Caribbean lines are quite a bit smaller—try 120 to 160 square feet—and can be cramped. Cabins on the small-ship lines such as Windjammer, Clipper, and ACCL can be very snug—on the order of 70 to 100 square feet.

All the standard cabins on the high-end lines are roomy—in fact, many of the high-end ships are "suite only." Windstar's cabins, for instance, are 188 square feet; those on Seabourn's *Legend* and *Pride* are 277 square feet. On Radisson's *Seven Seas Navigator,* cabins are about 246 square feet, plus a 55-square-foot balcony; and on Silversea's *Silver Shadow* and *Silver Whisper,* cabins are 287 square feet, plus a 58-square-foot balcony. Across the board, from mainstream to luxe, **suites and penthouses** are obviously the most spacious, measuring about 250 square feet up to over 1,400 square feet, plus private verandas.

Most cruise lines publish schematic drawings in their brochures, with square footage and, in some cases, measurements of length and width, which should give you some idea of what to expect. (We also include square footage ranges for inside cabins, outside cabins, and suites in the cruise ship descriptions in chapters 6–8.) Consider measuring off the dimensions on your bedroom floor and imagining your temporary oceangoing home, being sure to block out part of that space for the bathroom and closet. As a rough guideline, within a cabin of around 100 square feet, about a third of the floor space is gobbled up by those functional necessities.

Now, while you're sitting there within the chalk marks (or whatever) thinking, "Gee, that's really not a lot of space," remember that, like a bedroom in a large house, your cabin will in all likelihood be a place you use only for sleeping, showering, and changing clothes. Out beyond the door, vast acres of public spaces await, full of diversions. So unless you plan on holing up for most of your cruise, watching movies on your cabin TV and ordering room service, you probably don't need a palatial space.

THE SCOOP ON INSIDE CABINS VS. OUTSIDE CABINS

Whether you really plan to spend time in your cabin is a question that should be taken into account when deciding whether to book an inside cabin or an outside cabin (that is, one without windows or one with windows or a balcony). If you plan to get up bright and early, hit the buffet breakfast, and not stop till the cows come home, you can probably get away with booking an inside cabin and save yourself a bundle. Inside cabins are generally not as bad or as claustrophobic as they sound. Most cruise lines today design and decorate them to provide an illusion of light and space. These are not the steerage dormitories you saw in *Titanic*. Many, in fact—such as those aboard most of the Carnival and Celebrity fleets—are the same size as the outside cabins.

If, on the other hand, you want to lounge around and take it easy in your cabin, maybe ordering breakfast from room service and eating while the sun streams in—or, better yet, eating out *in* the sun, on your private veranda—then an outside cabin is definitely a worthwhile investment. Remember, though, that if it's a view of the sea you want, be sure when booking that your window or balcony doesn't just give you a good view of a lifeboat or some other obstruction (and remember, there are likely to be balconies on the deck right above your balcony, so they're more like porches than actual verandas). Some cruise line brochures tell you which cabins are obstructed (as we do in our reviews in this book), and a good travel agent or a cruise line's reservation agent can tell you which cabins on a particular ship might have this problem.

OTHER CABIN MATTERS TO CONSIDER

You may choose to work with your agent to find the right cabin for you—that's what they're for, after all—but if possible, try to go into your talks with some idea of what kind of cabin category you'd like, or at least with a list of must-haves and/or must-avoids. Unless you're booking at the last minute (like a few weeks or less before sailing), as part of a group, or in a cabin-share or cabin-guarantee program (which means you agree to a price, and find out your exact cabin at the last

---

Book Low-End Cabins on Luxury Ships

Rather than booking upper-end cabins on budget ships, some savvy cruisers book lower-end cabins aboard luxury cruise ships. That way they can enjoy the benefits of sailing on an upscale ship while paying the lowest amount possible for the privilege.

MODEL CABIN LAYOUTS

Typical Outside Cabins

- Twin beds (can usually be pushed together)
- Some have sofa-bed or bunk for third passenger
- Shower (tubs are rare)
- TV and music
- Window or porthole, or veranda

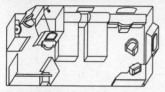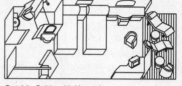

Outside Cabin

Outside Cabin with Veranda

Typical Suites

- King, queen, or double beds
- Sitting areas (often with sofa-beds)
- Large bathrooms, usually with tub, sometimes with Jacuzzi
- Refrigerators, sometimes stocked
- TVs w/VCR and stereo
- Large closets
- Large veranda

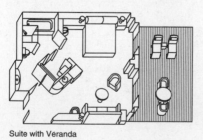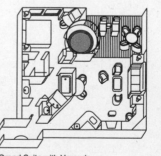

Suite with Veranda

Grand Suite with Veranda

Thanks to Princess Cruises for all photos and diagrams.

minute), your agent can tell you what your exact cabin number is when you book the cruise. Before agreeing to a certain cabin, be sure it suits your particular needs. For instance, are elevators close by? That gives convenience, but it can also be

READING A SHIP'S DECK PLAN

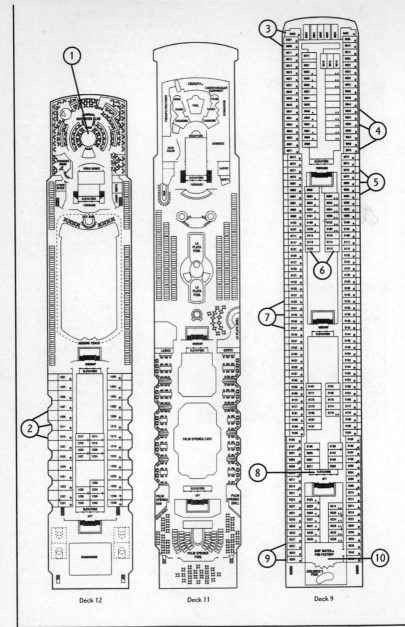

Deck 12   Deck 11   Deck 9

noisy. Is your cabin on the Promenade Deck? Such cabins are often costly and sound just grand, but passengers walking or talking outside may distract you (though they can't see in on most ships, due to the use of double-sided glass). Is your cabin above, below, or adjacent to any noisy public rooms or sports facilities,

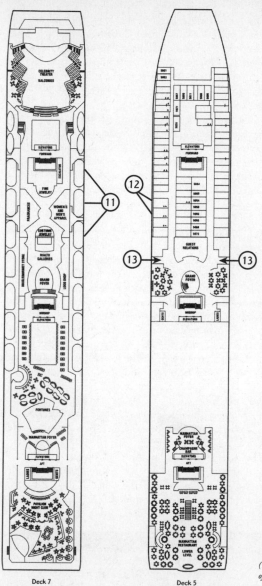

Deck 7

Deck 5

Some cabin choice considerations:

1. **Note the position of the ship's disco** and other loud public areas, and try not to book a cabin that's too close or underneath. This disco is far from any cabins — a big plus.

2. **Cabins on upper decks** can be affected by the motion of the sea. If you're abnormally susceptible to seasickness, keep this in mind.

3. **Ditto for the cabins in the bow.**

4. **Outside cabins without verandas** appear as solid blocks of space.

5. **Outside cabins with verandas** are shown with a line dividing the two spaces.

6. **Inside cabins** (without windows) can be real money-savers.

7. **Cabins amidships** are the least affected by the motion of the sea, especially if they're on a lower deck.

8. **Cabins that adjoin elevator shaftways** might be noisy (though proximity makes it easier to get around the ship).

9. **Cabins in the stern** can be affected by the motion of the sea, and tend to be subject to engine vibration.

10. **Cabins near children's facilities** may not be the quietest places, at least during the day.

11. **Check that lifeboats** don't block the view from your cabin. The ones in this example adjoin public rooms, and so are out of sight.

12. **Cabins for travelers with disabilities** are ideally located near elevators and close to the ship's entrances (#13).

(Thanks to Celebrity Cruises for use of Mercury's deck plan.)

such as the disco, children's playrooms, a basketball court, or the ship's engines? Is the view out the cabins' windows obstructed by lifeboats or other ship equipment? You can see from the deck plans included in the cruise line brochures what's where, and if some cabins in your chosen category are in a questionable spot, be sure to inquire. See the "Reading a Ship's Deck Plan" figure on p. 64 for visual reference. Here are a few more tips:

- **Don't be distracted by fancy language.** Increasingly, cruise lines use the terms "deluxe" and "standard" for their cabins. These terms can vary from line to line and are pretty much meaningless, except to suggest that deluxe is larger, is better located, and has more amenities. Compare square footage, amenities, and location on the ship, and look at the still and 360-degree photos on the cruise line's website or on a site such as **www.mytravel.com**. Is the price difference worth it?

- **Keep cabin position in mind if you suffer from seasickness.** If stability is important to you, a midships location on a middle deck is best because it's a kind of fulcrum point, the area least affected by the vessel's rocking and rolling in rough seas. In general, the best and most expensive cabins on any vessel are amidships and generally high up; however, the higher cabins are subject to more motion and swaying. The cheaper cabins are down below in the bow and stern; those toward the stern may suffer from engine vibrations as well as ocean movement.

- **Picky about bed sizes? Inquire ahead.** Beds vary little in size from cabin to cabin and ship to ship. While a few cabins have a proper queen-size bed, the vast majority has narrow, not especially long twins that can be pushed together to make one larger bed. Some, however, cannot: Their frames are built right into the wall. This is often the case with most of the smaller ships.

- **Book early if you want cabins that will be in demand.** Cabins with third and fourth berths (usually pull-down bunks or a sofa bed) are in particular demand by families, so they tend to disappear fast. Families who can afford it often book suites or two connecting cabins. This is especially desirable for those who are traveling with teenagers. Also, the lowest-priced cabins and the best in the house—the top suites and penthouses—tend to get booked up early.

- **Need a bathtub? Study up.** Most cabins have showers only. Conversely, a few (such as those on Radisson's *Seven Seas Navigator* and Silversea's *Shadow* and *Whisper*) feature a shower *and* a tub. Some deluxe cabins and suites offer whirlpool tubs.

- **Addicted to TV? Make sure your cabin has one.** Though most ships now have TVs in all cabins (often with satellite programming), some of the smaller lines do not. We've listed which do and don't in the "Cabins & Rates" tables in chapters 6 through 8. VCRs in cabins are much rarer than TVs, though they do pop up sometimes in suites.

8 Booking Your Air Travel

Except during special promotions, airfare is rarely included in the cruise rates for Caribbean cruises, as it often is on Europe and Asia itineraries. So if you can't drive to your port of embarkation and need to fly to get to Miami, Fort Lauderdale, San Juan, New Orleans, or one of the other home ports, you'll have to either purchase airfare on your own through an agent or online, or buy it as a package with your cruise. The latter is often referred to as an **air add-on** or **air/sea package.** You can usually find information on these programs in the back of cruise line brochures and on their websites, along with prices on flights from more than 100 U.S. and Canadian cities to the port of embarkation. Here are the pros and cons to booking your airfare through the cruise line.

- **Pros:** When you book through the cruise line, you usually get round-trip transfers between the airport and the ship. A uniformed cruise line employee will be in the airport to direct you to the right bus, and your luggage will be taken from the airport to the ship. The cruise line will know your airline schedule and, in the event of delayed flights and other unavoidable snafus, will do what they can to make sure you get to the ship. In such situations, people who book their air transportation and transfers separately are on their own.
- **Cons:** Odds are it will be more expensive to book through the line than on your own. In the past, cruise lines offered more competitive fares, but the airlines aren't giving them the bulk discounts they used to, meaning prices have gone up. Consequently, fewer passengers are now booking the lines' air packages. Also, if you book through the lines, you probably won't be able to use any frequent-flier miles you've accumulated, and the air add-on could require a circuitous routing—with indirect legs and layovers—before you finally arrive at your port of embarkation.

If you choose to arrange your own air transportation, make absolutely sure that airfare is not included as part of your cruise contract. It rarely is with Caribbean itineraries, but if it is, you're often granted a deduction (usually around $250 per person) off the cruise fare. Passengers who book their own air can still buy **transfers from the airport to the ship** through their cruise line, but it's often cheaper to take a taxi, as is the case in Miami and Fort Lauderdale.

9 Prebooking Your Dinner Table & Arranging Special Diets

In addition to choosing your cabin when booking your cruise, on most ships you can also choose an **early or late seating** for breakfast, lunch, and dinner, and sometimes even put in a request for the size table you're interested in (tables for 2, 4, 8, 10, and so on). Assignments for breakfast and lunch aren't necessarily important, since almost every ship also serves a casual breakfast in its buffet restaurant throughout the morning. At night, though, early seatings allow you to get first dibs on shipboard nightlife (or, conversely, promptly hit the sack), while late seatings allow you to linger a little longer over your meal. Lately, though, more lines—especially Norwegian and, to a slightly lesser extent, Princess—are junking this traditional early-late paradigm (in at least some of their restaurants) in favor of **open-seating dining** in which you simply show up when hunger pangs strike. For a more detailed discussion, see "Introducing Shipboard Dining," in chapter 4, "The Cruise Experience."

If you follow a **special diet**—whether vegetarian, low-salt, low-fat, heart-healthy, kosher, halal, or any other, or if you have certain food allergies—make this known to your travel agent when you book or at least 30 or more days before the cruise, and make sure your diet can be accommodated at all three meals (sometimes special meal plans will cover only breakfast and dinner). The vast majority of ships offer vegetarian meals and health-conscious choices as part of their daily menus these days (Crystal even offers kosher as part of daily offerings), but it can't hurt to arrange things ahead of time. A cruise is not the place to go on an involuntary starvation diet.

10 Booking Pre- & Post-Cruise Hotel Stays

Cruise lines often offer hotel stays in the cities of embarkation and debarkation, and since most of these cities are tourist attractions in their own right, you may want to explore Miami before you sail, drive to Disney World from Port

Canaveral, or spend some time in San Juan or New Orleans. The cruise lines' package deals usually include hotel stays and transportation from the hotel to the ship (before the cruise) or from the docks to the hotel (after the cruise). Inquire with your travel agent, and compare what the line is offering with what you may be able to arrange independently. Nowadays especially, you may be able to get a hotel stay much cheaper.

11 Cancellations & Insurance

Given today's soft-economy and volatile world situation, cancellation and insurance are hot topics, and ever-changing cruise line policies and procedures mean that it pays to stay informed.

What should you do if the cruise you've booked is canceled before it departs? A cruise could be canceled because of shipyard delays (if you've booked an inaugural cruise), or because of an impending hurricane, act of war, the outbreak of an infectious disease, mechanical breakdowns (such as nonfunctioning air-conditioning or an engine fire), or the cruise line going out of business.

In today's competitive market, cruise lines have been making extraordinary efforts to appease passengers who are disappointed by cancellations by the line, rescheduling the canceled cruise and offering big discounts on future cruises—after all, they don't want the bad press they'd get if they cheated hundreds or thousands of passengers. There are, however, no set rules on how a line will compensate you in the event of a cancellation.

Now, if the shoe's on the other foot and you need to cancel your own cruise, you'll generally get a refund—most lines give you every cent back if you cancel at least 2 to 3 months before your departure date, although details vary from line to line. If you cancel closer to departure, you'll usually get a partial refund up until anywhere from 15 to 7 days before the cruise. After that, you won't get any refund at all, even if you cancel for medical reasons. Exceptions? In early 2003, in response to the impending war with Iraq and the general uneasiness in the Middle East, many lines liberalized their cancellation and insurance policies for their European cruises, and, in some cases, all their itineraries, including the Caribbean, in order to encourage bookings. They covered cancellations for any reason whatsoever up to a day before sailing, issuing full (or 90%) credits for a future cruise. At press time, most of the beefed-up policies were in effect until year-end 2003 (we'll have to see if they're extended beyond that). For example, SeaDream Yacht Club will allow you to cancel your cruise for any reason up to the day of departure and get a credit for a future cruise, redeemable within the next 2 years.

For all of these reasons—worries about travel, worries about cruise lines canceling or going belly up, sudden illness or other emergencies, missed flights that cause you to miss the ship, or even if you just change your mind—you may want to think about purchasing **travel insurance.** This can also help you out if you're worried about medical problems occurring during your trip. Except for the small ships of lines such as American Canadian Caribbean, Windjammer, and Clipper Cruise Line, most cruise ships have an infirmary staffed by a doctor and a nurse or two, but in the event of a dire illness, the ship's medical staff can only do so much. Therefore, you may want a policy that covers **emergency medical evacuation** and, if your regular insurance doesn't cover it, the potential cost of major medical treatment while away from home.

There are policies sold through the cruise lines (with details varying from line to line) and others sold independently. Both have pros and cons.

C Onboard Medical Care

Medical services are available for a fee aboard almost all cruise ships, and though they mostly deal with seasickness and the common cold, you can visit the infirmary for more serious ailments. You may have read about the flurry of Norwalk virus outbreaks on a handful of cruise ships in fall 2002. A flu-like gastrointestinal illness that causes vomiting, stomach cramps, diarrhea, and general nausea for a few days, it's not pleasant, but it's certainly not fatal either. However, it is highly contagious, especially when infected people inhabit enclosed spaces such as airplanes and ships. Should you be concerned? No more than you should when boarding an airplane or checking into a hotel. The Norwalk virus (more accurately called the Norovirus) is more common than the common cold, and since the spate of highly publicized cases in 2002, ships have stepped up their already vigilant sanitation routines, disinfecting railings and gym equipment, reminding crew and passengers to wash their hands more frequently, and offering antibacterial soaps and wipes throughout the ship. Some lines have also hired outside consultants to help them detect potential breeding grounds for contagions and make sure that their ships stay ultraclean. Ships' medical staffs and crew are now more aware of the illness, and anyone showing symptoms is immediately quarantined.

As on land, a fee is charged for most visits to a ship's medical clinic. Note that the quality of ships' staffs and facilities can vary. Shipboard doctors are not necessarily certified in the United States, and aren't always experts in important areas such as cardiology. Further, many doctors at sea earn far less working on a cruise ship than they would if they practiced on land, which makes you wonder if the cruise lines are getting the best people. The author of an extensive *New York Times* article concluded that Holland America and Princess had the best onboard medical facilities (and they pay the doctors a decent wage, too).

Princess Cruises' Grand-class ships and *Coral Princess,* for instance, have a staff of one or two doctors and two to five nurses and are outfitted with high-tech medical equipment that links the ships' medical staff via special cameras and a live-video system with the emergency department at the Cleveland Clinic in Florida or the University of Texas Medical Branch at Galveston (or any medical center requested). Holland America's *Amsterdam* also has a video hookup to the University of Texas hospital. Princess's *Sea Princess,* Carnival's *Spirit,* and Holland America's new *Zuiderdam* and *Oosterdam* have a teleradiology system, which allows X-rays to be transmitted to a shoreside medical facility. Of course, ships big and small can also call ahead to arrange medical assistance at the closest shore point in the event of an emergency, and, in dire circumstances, may have helicopters pick up and evacuate a seriously ill passenger. Although the captain does his utmost to get help or head for the nearest port, depending on where the ship is during such an emergency, you can't be sure how long it may take to get reliable care.

CRUISE LINE POLICIES VS. THIRD-PARTY INSURERS

A good travel agent can tell you about policies sold through the cruise lines and ones sold independently of the lines. No matter which you choose, it's absolutely crucial to read the fine print because terms vary from policy to policy.

Both kinds typically reimburse you in some way when your trip is affected by unexpected events (such as canceled flights, plane crashes, dockworkers' strikes, or the illness or death of a loved one, as late as the day before or day of departure) but not by "acts of God," such as hurricanes and earthquakes (the exception being if your home is made uninhabitable, putting you in no mood to continue with your cruise plans). Both also typically cover **cancellation of the cruise** for medical reasons (yours or a family member's); **medical emergencies** during the cruise, including evacuation from the ship; lost or damaged luggage; and a cruise missed due to airline delays (though some cover only delays over 3 hr.). Neither kind of policy will reimburse you if your travel agent goes bankrupt, so using a travel agent you're very familiar with or who has been recommended to you is the safest precaution you can take (and, of course, *always use a credit card,* never a check; if a corrupt travel agent cashes it, or a decent one just goes out of business, then you could be screwed). Most cancellation policies also do not cover cancellations due to work requirements.

THIRD-PARTY COVERAGE   Even though agents get a commission for selling both cruise line policies and independent policies, most agents and industry insiders believe that non–cruise line policies are the best bet because some, such as Access America (see below), will issue insurance to those with **preexisting medical conditions** if the condition is stable when purchasing the insurance (a doctor would have to verify this if you ever made a claim) and if you purchase the policy within 14 days of your initial deposit on the cruise. They also offer **supplier-default coverage** that kicks in if a cruise line goes bankrupt. This is an especially relevant issue these days, considering that in fall 2001 both Renaissance Cruises and American Classic Voyages went belly up (due to financial strains compounded by the post–Sept 11 travel downturn); and in 2000, budget lines Premier and Commodore both went out of business in the face of price competition from mainstream lines with newer, flashier ships.

Still, you shouldn't be afraid to book a cruise. A well-connected travel agent should see the writing on the wall months before a cruise line fails—commissions will slow or stop being paid, phone calls won't be returned, and industry trade publications will report on any problems. The less customer-service-driven cruise sellers may not stop pushing a troubled cruise line, however, and may continue selling these lines up to the very last minute.

According to the Fair Credit Billing Act, if you paid by credit card (and again, you should), you'll generally get your money back if you dispute the charge within 60 days of the date the charge first appears. If you paid in full 4 months before the cruise, you'll likely be out of luck going the credit-reimbursement

---

Read the Fine Print

Many aggressively commission-driven travel agents and Web-based cruise sellers automatically add insurance coverage to the bill, but you're not in any way required to buy it—the decision is totally yours. Be sure to check your cruise contract before paying.

Insuring Your Jewels

If you're worried about keeping your jewelry and valuables safe on board, that usually falls under the riders attached to your homeowner's policy—though be sure to check your fine print. Of course, you should guard your jewels carefully, confining them to your in-cabin safe or the purser's safe when not wearing them, or just save the aggravation and leave them at home. If precedent means anything, though, we've taken about 100 cruises over the past 10 years and have never had one thing disappear from our cabins.

route and may have to resort to litigation. Also, while many lines post a multimillion-dollar bond with the Federal Maritime Commission, creating a fund from which they can reimburse creditors should they fail financially, it's no guarantee you'll get all or any of your money back. Technically, the bond covers cruise payments for all passengers embarking from U.S. ports, but since the line would have banks or other vendors to pay off first, you'd likely get only pennies on the dollar, if that. Still, it's better that a cruise line have a bond than not—and if you learn that a line is having trouble making bond payments, it may be a sign of serious financial woes.

Policies are available from reputable insurers such as **Access America,** Box 90315, Richmond, VA 23286 (© **800/284-8300;** www.accessamerica.com), and **Travel Guard International,** 1145 Clark St., Stevens Point, WI 54481 (© **800/826-1300** or 715/345-0505; www.travelguard.com), whose websites maintain lists of the lines they cover; those not included may be considered financially shaky.

CRUISE LINE COVERAGE   Cruise lines offer their own policies, many of them administered by New York–based BerkelyCare (including those of Carnival, Royal Caribbean, Princess, Norwegian, Celebrity, Costa, Silversea, Seabourn, Cunard, Radisson, and Crystal). If you opt for this type of policy out of sheer convenience (the cost is added right onto your cruise fare), keep in mind they do not cover you in the event of a cruise line bankruptcy (though using a credit card can save you here; see above) or for cancellation of your cruise due to preexisting medical conditions, which is usually defined as an unstable condition existing within 60 days of your buying the insurance. Some lines' policies, including Carnival, Costa, Silversea, and Crystal, will issue a cruise credit for the penalty amount if a medical claim is deemed preexisting, and issue you cash if you cancel for a covered reason. Generally, the cancellation penalty imposed by the cruise line would be 100% of the cruise fare, for example, if you cancel a few days before the cruise (assuming you've paid in full), or it could be just $300 if you cancel right after making the initial cruise deposit.

Sounds like the third-party policies win hands down, right? Well, to make it just a little more complicated, a handful of cruise line policies are actually better in some areas than outside policies. For example, since 1995, **Princess Cruises** has had an insurance policy that allows you to cancel for all the reasons that an outside policy would (illness, injury) and get cash reimbursement or they will let you cancel for any reason whatsoever (from fear of flying to a bad hair day) up until day of departure and have 75% to 90% of the normal penalty for canceling your cruise applied toward a future trip. (So, for example, Princess's penalty amount for canceling a cruise 3 days before departure, if paid in full, is 100% of the cruise fare; if you cancel between 30–15 days before departure, the penalty on a $1,000 cruise is $500, so even if you cancel for any reason at all you get 75%–90% of that back in cruise credits, and the other $500 back as a cash refund.) **Norwegian** introduced a similar policy in 2001, the same year **Celebrity** and **Royal Caribbean** started offering their "any reason" policy, which provides a cruise credit for 75%. For an extra $250 above their standard insurance fee, high-end **Silversea** allows you to cancel cruises for any reason up to 1 day before sailing and get a credit for 100% of the penalty amount (including airfare if booked through Silversea), applicable toward any cruise within the following 12 months. **Crystal** offers a similar plan: An optional $200 insurance upgrade allows travelers to cancel their cruise for any reason up until 3 days before departure and receive a 90% cruise credit good for any cruise within 12 months. Many other lines offer similar cancellation plans. The cruise lines using the BerkelyCare policies (see above) also reimburse passengers for days missed on a cruise—say, if you missed your flight and had to join up with the cruise 2 days later—covering hotel costs during the missed days and transportation to the ship (though typically only to a max of $500).

12 Putting Down a Deposit & Reviewing Tickets

In this age of last-minute booking, you typically need to pay in full when making your reservation. If you're booking several months or more ahead of time, then you have to leave a deposit to secure the booking. Depending on the policy of the line you selected, the amount will either be fixed at a predetermined amount or represent a percentage of the ticket's total cost. More often than not, within 7 days of making the booking, a fixed $100 deposit is required on a 3- or 4-night cruise, a $250 deposit is required on 7- and 8-night cruises, and a $300 to $400 deposit is needed for a 10- to 14-night cruise. Upscale lines, because they cost more, may require a larger deposit or a percentage of the cruise price. For instance, Windstar requires a $750 deposit within 7 days, and Seabourn requires a 25% deposit within 7 days, or sooner, of making your reservation.

The balance of the cruise price is due anywhere from about 60 to 90 days before you depart; holiday cruises may require final payments earlier, perhaps 90 days before departure. The payment schedule for groups is different. Booking at the last minute usually requires payment in full at the time of booking.

Credit-card payments are made direct to the cruise line, but payments by check are made out to the agency, which then passes payment on to the cruise line. As we've said repeatedly, it's preferable by far to pay by credit card, for the added protection it offers.

Carefully review your ticket, invoice, itinerary, and/or vouchers to confirm that they accurately reflect the departure date, ship, and cabin category you booked. The printout usually lists a specific cabin number; if it doesn't, it designates a cabin category. Your exact cabin location will then be assigned to you when you board ship.

3

Things to Know Before You Go

You've bought your ticket and you're getting ready to cruise. Here's the lowdown on some details you need to consider before you go.

1 Passports & Visas

Good news in the convenience category: **Visas** are not generally required for American, Canadian, and European citizens visiting the Caribbean islands or ports in Mexico, though depending on the itinerary, you may be asked to fill out a tourist card or other form on the plane, at the airport, or in the cruise terminal, especially if you're flying to a non-U.S. port to start your cruise. **Passports** aren't necessarily required by most Caribbean islands either, though you must carry proof of your U.S. citizenship (such as an expired U.S. passport, a certified copy of your birth certificate, a Certificate of Naturalization, a Certificate of Citizenship, or a Report of Birth Abroad of a U.S. Citizen) plus a photo ID, such as a driver's license. (Note that a driver's license is not acceptable as a sole form of identification.) Your travel agent will help you determine if you need a passport for the islands you'll be visiting on your itinerary, and the documents your cruise line sends with your tickets will also provide information, but our advice is, carry your passport anyway. In these days of heightened security, it just makes sense, and besides, at press time, the U.S. Bureau of Citizenship and Immigration Services (BCIS)—formerly the Immigration and Naturalization Service (INS)—was trying to establish a regulation that would require all passengers to show a passport when boarding a ship on embarkation day. Also, cruise lines are now generally requiring **two forms of ID** at boarding. (See "Checking In & Boarding," in chapter 4, for more on the process.)

If you don't currently have a passport, the **U.S. State Department website** (www.travel.state.gov/passport_services.html) provides information on obtaining one. If you're leaving within a few weeks and need **expedited passport service,** here are the basics:

- **If this is your first passport,** your fastest option is to apply in person at one of 14 passport centers in major cities around the country, most of which operate by appointment only and are specifically for people traveling imminently (generally within 2 weeks). These centers are listed at **www.travel.state.gov/agencies_list.html**. You'll need to bring a completed passport application, an ID, proof of citizenship (see list above), and two passport-size photos. To download an application, go to **www.travel.state.gov/download_applications.html**.
- **If you don't live near a passport center,** you can apply for expedited service at a local passport acceptance facility, located in post offices, courthouses, and so on, and then follow up through overnight mail. To search for the facility nearest you, go to **http://visa.his.com**.

No Vaccinations Required

Travel to the Caribbean islands does not generally warrant inoculations against tropical diseases, though you may want to check the **Centers for Disease Control (CDC)** Caribbean travelers' page (www.cdc.gov/travel/caribean.htm) to see what it suggests. In early 2003, for instance, the CDC advised yellow fever inoculations for travelers visiting rural Trinidad and Tobago, and chloroquine to prevent malaria when visiting Haiti and the Dominican Republic.

- **If you need to renew an expired passport,** you can go to one of the 14 passport centers or send a renewal form by overnight mail. Go to **www.travel.state.gov/passport_renewal.html** for information and download-able renewal forms.
- **If you're really panicking,** contact a service such as **Travisa** (© **800/222-2589** on the East Coast, **800/766-0608** in the Midwest, **800/421-5468** on the West Coast; www.travisa.com), which is in the business of expediting passport and visa applications. It'll cost in the neighborhood of $195 to $285 total (depending on how fast you need your documents), and if it's your first passport, you'll still have to go to a passport acceptance facility to show proof of citizenship and ID, but at least you'll have experienced help in your corner. To be sure the agency you contact is reputable, check with the **Better Business Bureau** (www.bbb.org) or the **American Society of Travel Agents** (www.astanet.com).

Further information is available on the State Department passport services website listed above. You can also inquire at your local passport acceptance facility or call the **National Passport Information Center** (© **888/362-8668** or 900/225-5674), but be aware that the center charges for calls: a flat fee of $5.50 for the 888 number and 55¢ per minute for the 900 number. Fees for new passports are $85 adult, $70 children. Renewals cost $55, and expedited service costs an additional $60.

As you would before any trip abroad, make two photocopies of your documents and ID before leaving home. Take one set with you as a backup (keeping it in a different piece of luggage from your originals) and keep one at home.

After using your proof of citizenship as ID to board ship at the beginning of your cruise, you may be asked to turn your papers over to ship officials for the duration of the voyage, allowing them to facilitate clearance procedures quickly at each port. Your documents are returned to you after departing the last foreign port of call, en route back to the U.S.

All non-U.S. and non-Canadian citizens must have valid passports, alien-registration cards, and the requisite visas when boarding any cruise ship or aircraft departing from and/or returning to American soil. Noncitizens also need to present an ongoing or return ticket for an airline or cruise ship as proof that they intend to remain on local shores only for a brief stay.

2 Money Matters

Know how they say cruises are all-inclusive vacations? They're lying. True, the bulk of your vacation expenses are covered in your fare, but there are plenty of extras. We've detailed what's included and what's not in "The Cost: What's

Included & What's Not," in chapter 2. In this section, we'll examine the way monetary transactions are handled on board and in port.

ONBOARD CHARGE CARDS

Cruise ships operate on a cashless basis. Basically, this means you have a running tab and simply sign for what you buy on board during your cruise—bar drinks, meals at specialty restaurants, spa treatments, shore excursions, gift-shop purchases, and so on—and pay up at the end with a credit card or cash. Very convenient, yes—and also very, very easy to forget your limits and spend more than you intended to.

Shortly before or after embarkation, a purser or check-in clerk in the terminal or on board will take an imprint of your credit card and issue you an **onboard charge card,** which on most ships also serves as your room key and as your ship ID, which you swipe through a scanner when leaving and returning to the ship from port. Some ships issue separate cards for these functions, or a card and an old-fashioned room key. Some adventure lines that carry 100 or fewer passengers (such as American Canadian Caribbean Line) rely on the honor system and don't even use room keys; guests wear ACCL nametags to identify themselves and simply check "in" or "out" on a board at the gangway when they leave and reboard the ship in port.

On the last night of your cruise, an itemized account of all you've charged will be slipped beneath your cabin door. If you agree with the charges, they'll automatically be billed to your credit card. If you'd rather pay in cash or if you dispute any charge, you'll need to stop by the office of the ship's cashier or purser, where there's usually a long line. Have fun!

BRINGING CASH ASHORE

The cashless system works just fine on board, but remember: **You'll need cash in port.** Many people get so used to not carrying their wallets aboard ship that they get off in port and find themselves without any money in their pockets— an annoyance if your ship is docked and it just means trudging back aboard for cash, but a *major* annoyance if your ship is anchored offshore and ferrying passengers back and forth by tender.

You can put any shore excursions you sign up for on your room tab, and credit cards are accepted at most port shops (as are traveler's checks), but we recommend having some real cash, ideally in small denominations, to cover the cost of taxi rides, tips to tour leaders, or purchases you make from craft markets and street vendors. Information on **local currency** is included in chapters 11 and 12, but for the most part, you don't have to worry about exchanging money as the U.S. dollar is widely accepted and is the legal currency of the U.S. Virgin Islands, Puerto Rico, and (oddly enough) the British Virgin Islands. Even on more offbeat islands such as Guadeloupe and Les Saintes, where they may prefer Euros, we've never had our U.S. dough turned away.

If you're running low on cash, **ATM machines** are in nearly every cruise port covered in this guide, in some cruise terminals, and on board many of the megaships. Expect a hefty fee for using ATMs on board ship (up to $5 in addition to what your bank charges you), and remember that you'll get local currency from machines in the Caribbean, so don't withdraw more than you'll need.

Many lines, such as Carnival and Royal Caribbean, will cash traveler's checks at the purser's desk, and sometimes personal checks of up to about $200 if issued in the U.S. With an American Express card, you can typically cash a check for up to $250.

Gratuities for the crew are not normally included in the cruise rates, though many lines these days are either automatically adding a suggested gratuity to your end-of-cruise bill or offering passengers the option of charging gratuities. Where this is not the case, you should reserve some cash so that you can be generous at the end of your cruise. See "Tipping, Customs & Other End-of-Cruise Concerns," later in this chapter, for guidelines. Information on how each line deals with gratuities is included in the "Service" section of each line review in chapters 6 through 8.

3 Keeping in Touch While at Sea

Some people take a cruise to get away from it all, but others are communication addicts. For them, today's megaships offer a spectrum of ways to keep in touch, though they're anything but cheap.

PHONING HOME

Aside from the adventure lines, almost all ships today have **direct-dial telephones** in their cabins. From most, you can call anywhere in the world via satellite, but it'll cost you between $4 and $15 a minute, with $8 or $9 being about average. It's cheaper by far to call home from a public telephone in port; we've listed where to find them close to the docks in the "Coming Ashore" sections of chapters 11 and 12.

In addition to your cabin phone, each ship has a central phone number, fax number, and e-mail address, which you'll sometimes find in the cruise line's brochure and usually in the documents you'll get with your tickets. Distribute these to family members or friends in case they have to contact you in an emergency. It also can't hurt to leave behind the numbers of the cruise line's headquarters and/or reservations department, both of whom will be able to put people in touch with you.

INTERNET & E-MAIL AT SEA

Over the past 5 years, cruise lines have hustled to add computer rooms and Internet cafes to their ships to satiate passengers' desire to stay connected to work and home 24-7. Decked out with state-of-the-art flat-screen monitors, these centers offer e-mail capabilities and Internet access, have Net-cams so that users can send their vacation pictures to friends, and are often open 24 hours. Many offer classes for computer novices, to get them up and running.

E-mail services are usually available in one of two ways: either through temporary accounts you set up once aboard ship (with rates averaging roughly $1–$4 per message) or through your AOL, Earthlink, Hotmail, Yahoo, or other personal account, which you can access through the Web at a per-minute charge that averages about 50¢ to $1—expensive, yes, but it's still loads cheaper than the per-minute charge of a phone call from ship to shore. Some lines (such as Disney and Norwegian) offer a kind of all-you-can-eat package, charging a flat fee for unlimited use during the course of your cruise—aboard Disney's ships, $40 for 3- or 4-night cruises, $90 for 7-night cruises. Currently, every ship reviewed in the mainstream chapter (chapter 6) is wired, as are most of the luxury ships (though *Radisson Diamond* and Windstar's *Wind Spirit* only offer e-mail, not Internet access). None of the ships in the alternative/sailing ship category offer access, though the Star Clippers' ships are connected for e-mail.

The trend today is to offer more personal Internet connections. SeaDream's two luxury yachts offer Internet connectivity through cabin TVs, and Royal

Caribbean's Radiance-class, Celebrity's Millennium-class, and Holland ica's new *Zuiderdam* and *Oosterdam* offer a **dataport** in every cabin so that can plug in their laptops and e-mail or surf the Net in privacy (though at a higher cost than in the ship's Internet centers). **Wireless Internet** is another new trend, offered aboard NCL's *Norwegian Dawn,* and Princess's *Dawn, Grand, Golden,* and *Sun Princess.* Expect these trends to continue. All ships reviewed in this book run on 110 AC current (both 110 and 220 on many), so you won't need an adapter.

KEEPING ON TOP OF THE NEWS

CNN junkies take note: Most ships have the station as part of their regular TV lineup, as well as, occasionally, other news stations. Many ships also maintain the tradition of reprinting headline news stories pulled off the wire and slipping them under passengers' doors each morning.

4 Packing

One of the great things about cruising is that even though you'll be visiting several countries on a typical weeklong itinerary, you need to unpack only once: You check into your cabin on day one, unpack, and settle in. The destinations come to you.

Just what do you need to pack? To some extent, that depends on the kind of cruise you're taking. Overall, though, cruise ship life mirrors that on land—and these days, for Americans especially, that mostly means casual. Here are some pointers.

DAYTIME CLOTHES

Across the board, casual daytime wear means shorts, T-shirts, bathing suits, and sundresses. Remember to bring a coverup and sandals if you want to go right from your deck chair to one of the restaurants or to some activity in a public room. When in port, the same dress code works, but err toward modesty if you're straying from the beach area (that is, something more than a skimpy bikini top). Bring good walking shoes or sandals so that you can explore the islands as comfortably as possible, as well as aqua-socks if you plan to snorkel or participate in watersports or shore excursions that require them, such as Jamaica's Dunn's River Falls trip. (Aqua-socks are cheap to buy, but many cruise lines rent them for about $5 a pair.)

If you plan on hitting the gym, don't forget sneakers and your workout clothes. And it can't hurt to bring along one pair of long casual pants and a long-sleeved sweatshirt (mostly to deal with air-conditioning), as well as an umbrella or lightweight raincoat in case the weather turns dicey.

EVENING CLOTHES

As America as a whole gets more casual—witness "business casual" law offices and the baseball-cap-and-furs-wearing Park Avenue set—cruise lines are responding by toning down or turning off their dress codes.

Norwegian Cruise Line has pretty much ditched the concept of **formal nights** completely (though an "optional formal" captain's cocktail night allows many people to choose to dress up, so you have sequins and suits next to chinos and polo shirts). Other lines (Disney, for instance) have toned formality down to the point where a sports jacket is considered formal, but most mainstream and luxury ships still have two traditional formal nights during any 7-night itinerary— usually the second and second-to-last nights of the cruise, the former for the captain's cocktail party. Imagine what you'd wear to a nice wedding: Men are encouraged to wear tuxedos or dark suits; women, cocktail dresses, sequined jackets, gowns, or other fancy attire. If you just hate dressing up, women can get away with a blouse and skirt or pants. And of course, jewelry, scarves, and other accessories can dress up an otherwise nondescript outfit.

The other nights are much more casual, and are designated either **semiformal** (or informal) or **casual,** though lately many lines have done away with semiformal nights and have just gone with a combination of formal and casual. Semiformal calls for suits or sports jackets for men and stylish dresses or pantsuits for women; casual nights call for chinos or dress pants and collared shirts for men, and dresses, skirts, or pantsuits for women.

The suggested dress codes are usually described in the back of a cruise line's brochure, but you'll still witness a wide variety of outfits. Invariably, one person's "formal" is quite different from another's. Almost anything goes, but passengers are asked not to wear baseball caps, shorts, and T-shirts for dinner in the formal dining rooms—though some inevitably do and are rarely turned away. And pretty much every major line—Carnival, Celebrity, Costa, Holland America, NCL, Princess, and Royal Caribbean—offers a nightly **casual dining option** where full dress-down is the norm.

Despite the casual trend, there's usually a contingent of folks on board who like to get all decked out for dinner—including us. It's part of the fun; after all, how many chances do you get these days to dress like you're in a Fred Astaire/ Ginger Rogers movie? Put on the tux and opera shoes, plunk yourself down in some heavily trafficked lounge an hour or two before dinner, and do some old-fashioned people-watching. It's a veritable fashion show! If you bring your good jewelry, it's wise to keep it under lock and key when you're not wearing it. Most cabins have personal safes operated by a digital code, a credit card, or, once in a while, a key lock. If your cabin doesn't have one (usually it's the older ships that don't), the ship's purser can hold onto your valuables.

Fashion rules don't apply with ultracasual **small-ship lines** such as Windjammer and American Canadian Caribbean, where shorts, T-shirts, and sandals can take you through the day and into the evening (although most people tend to dress up a tad more for dinner). Windstar and Star Clippers encourage a "smart casual" look, and have a no-jackets-required rule the entire week, though some men don sport jackets and women put on dresses for dinner. Similarly, passengers aboard Clipper Cruise Line go casual during the day and usually dress up a little at dinnertime.

SUNDRIES

Like hotel rooms, most cabins (especially those aboard the newest and the most high-end ships) come with toiletries such as soap, shampoo, conditioner, and lotion, although you still may want to bring your own products—the ones

Tuxedo Rentals

If you don't own a tux or don't want to bother lugging one along, you can often arrange a rental through the cruise line or your travel agent for about $75 ($110 with shirts, plus maybe another $10 for shoes). In some cases, a rental offer arrives with your cruise tickets; if not, a call to your travel agent or the cruise line can facilitate a rental. If you choose this option, your suit will be waiting for you in your cabin when you arrive.

provided often seem watered down. If you forget something, note that all ships in this book except those operated by ACCL have at least one small shop on board, selling razor blades, toothbrushes, sunscreen, film, and other sundries, usually at inflated prices.

Most cabins also have **hair dryers** (the "Cabins & Rates" charts in chapters 6–8 tell you which have them and which don't), but they tend to be weak, so don't expect miracles—if you have a lot of hair, bring your own. All ships reviewed in this book run on 110 AC current (both 110 and 220 on many), so you won't need an adapter.

You don't need to pack a **beach towel,** as they're almost always supplied on board (exceptions: Windjammer and ACCL), but sometimes they're kinda small and thin, so bring your own if you like large and fluffy. Bird-watchers will want their binoculars and manuals, golfers their clubs unless they intend to rent, and snorkelers their gear (which can also be rented, usually through the cruise lines).

Aside from the small ships, most vessels have a **laundry service** on board and some **dry cleaning,** too, with generally about a 24-hour turnaround time; a price list will be in your cabin. Cleaning services tend not to be cheap—$1 or 1.50 per pair of socks, $2.50 to $3 for a T-shirt, and $9 to dry-clean a suit—so if you plan to pack light and wear the same outfit several times, **self-service laundry rooms** are on board some ships (Carnival, Crystal, Princess, and Holland America, among others).

If you like to read but don't want to lug hefty novels on board, most ships of all sizes have **libraries** stocked with books and magazines. Some are more extensive than others, of course—the *QE2*'s is huge and well stocked, for instance. Most ships also stock paperback bestsellers in their shops.

5 Tipping, Customs & Other End-of-Cruise Concerns

We know you don't want to hear about the end of your cruise before you've even gone, but it's best to be prepared. Here's a discussion of a few matters you'll have to take care of before heading back to home sweet home.

TIPPING

Most cruise lines pay their service staff low base wages with the understanding that the bulk of their income will come from tips. Each line has clear guidelines for gratuities, which are usually printed in your cruise documents and the daily schedule, and/or announced toward the end of the cruise. Traditionally, cabin stewards will leave little white envelopes (marked for cabin attendants, dining stewards, and waiters, along with suggested tipping percentages and amounts) in a spot where you'll be sure not to miss them. Today, however, more and more lines are automatically adding tips to each passenger's onboard account. Norwegian, Princess, and Carnival do it this way, with the amount adjustable if you request it at the purser's desk before the end of the cruise. Some lines, such as Crystal, Star Clippers, Disney, and Windjammer, give you the option of paying cash directly to staff or adding gratuities onto your account. Some small lines pool the tips and divide them equitably among all crew. Ultraluxury lines Silverseas, Seabourn, and Radisson include tips in the cruise rates. Holland America and Windstar promote their "tipping not required" policies, but "required" is the operative word, and tipping really is expected.

Suggested tipping amounts vary slightly with the line and its degree of luxury. As a rule of thumb, however, each passenger (not each couple) should expect to tip about $3.50 per day for their cabin steward, $3.50 for their dining room waiter, and about $2 for their assistant waiter, or about $9 per person (child or adult) per day—pretty close to what the lines that automatically add gratuities tack on ($10 per person per day on Norwegian and Princess; $9.75 a day on Carnival). Wine stewards and bartenders are usually rewarded with a 15% surcharge that's automatically added onto each bill. Some lines suggest you tip the maitre d' about $5 per person for the week and slip another couple of bucks to the chief housekeeper, but it's your choice; if you've never even met these people, don't bother. Tipping the captain and officers is a no-no: They're on full salary.

On lines that follow traditional person-to-person gratuity policies, tip your waiter and assistant waiter during the cruise's final dinner, and leave your cabin steward his or her tip on the final night or morning, just before you disembark. Tip spa personnel immediately after they work on you, but note that on some lines (Celebrity, Costa, Cunard, Holland America, NCL, and Windstar), Steiner's spa personnel automatically add a tip to your account unless you indicate otherwise, so inquire first before forking over your 15% (or whatever amount you prefer).

DISEMBARKING

It's a good idea to begin packing before dinner on your final night aboard. Be sure to fill out the luggage tags given to you and attach them securely to each piece. You'll be asked to leave your luggage outside your cabin door before you retire that night (by midnight or so), after which deck hands will pick it up and spirit it away (*read:* toss it into elevators and bins, then down the gangway to the terminal—so carry bottles of rum and other breakables off the ship yourself). At debarkation, your bags will be waiting for you at the terminal, organized by the colored or numbered tags you attached. If you don't use this system, you'll have to lug your bags off yourself.

Ships normally arrive in port on the final day between 6 and 8am, and need at least 90 minutes to unload baggage and complete docking formalities. So no one disembarks much before 9am, and sometimes it may be 10am before you're allowed to leave the ship, usually via debarkation numbers assigned based on flight times. (Not surprisingly, suite passengers get expedited debarkation.) Have breakfast. Have coffee. Have patience.

In the cruise ship terminal, claim your luggage and then pass through Customs before exiting. This normally entails handing the officer your filled-out declaration form as you breeze past, without even coming to a full stop. There are generally porters available in the terminals (to whom it's traditional to pay at least $1 per bag carried), but you may have to haul your luggage through Customs before you can get to them.

U.S. CUSTOMS

The U.S. government allows U.S. citizens $1,200 worth of duty-free imports from the U.S. Virgin Islands, including five liters of alcohol (of which 1 liter should be a product of those islands); those who exceed their exemption are taxed at a 5% rate, rather than the normal 10%. The limit is $800 for the French islands of Guadeloupe and Martinique and $600 if you return directly from the following islands/countries: Antigua and Barbuda, Aruba, The Bahamas, Barbados, Belize, Bonaire, the British Virgin Islands, Costa Rica, Curaçao, Dominica, the Dominican Republic, Grenada, the Grenadines, Haiti, Jamaica, Nevis, Panama, Saba, St. Eustatius, St. Kitts, St. Lucia, St. Martin, and Trinidad and

Tobago. Since you may be visiting both foreign and U.S.-territory ports, things get more complicated: If, for instance, your cruise stops in the U.S. Virgin Islands and The Bahamas, your total limit is $1,200, of which no more than $600 can be from The Bahamas. If you visit only Puerto Rico, you don't have to go through Customs at all, since it's an American commonwealth. Note that you must declare on your Customs form all gifts received during your cruise.

U.S. citizens or returning residents at least 21 years of age who are traveling directly or indirectly from the U.S. Virgin Islands are allowed to bring in free of duty 1,000 cigarettes. Duty-free limitations on articles from other countries are generally 1 liter of alcohol, 200 cigarettes (one carton), and 100 cigars (not Cuban). You can mail **unsolicited gifts** to friends and relatives on the U.S. mainland at the rate of $200 per day from the U.S. Virgin Islands, $100 per day from other islands, or of any value from Puerto Rico. Most meat or meat products, fruit, plants, vegetables, or plant-derived products will be seized by U.S. Customs agents unless they're accompanied by an import license from a U.S. government agency.

Joint Customs declarations are possible for family members traveling together. For instance, for a husband and wife with two children, total duty-free exemption on goods from the U.S. Virgin Islands is $4,800.

Keep receipts for all purchases you make abroad. Sometimes merchants suggest making up a false receipt to undervalue your purchase, but be aware that you could be involved in a sting operation—the merchant may be an informer to U.S. Customs. It's unlikely, but possible.

We've found clearing Customs in Florida to be a painless and speedy process, with Customs officials rarely asking for anything more than your filled-out Customs declaration form as they nod you through the door. Of course, better safe than sorry. If you're carrying a particularly new-looking camera or expensive jewelry and are the worrying sort, you may want to consider carrying proof that you purchased them before your trip; again, it's unlikely you'll need it, but it is possible.

Also, to be on the safe side, if you use any medication containing controlled substances or requiring injection, carry an original prescription or note from your doctor.

For more specifics, visit the **U.S. Customs Service** website at **www.customs. ustreas.gov**; citizens of the U.K. should visit the **U.K. Customs and Excise** website at **www.hmce.gov.uk**.

4

The Cruise Experience

Cruise ships are like miniature societies, cities at sea, floating summer camps for adults. Evolved from the days when ocean liners were designed to make the best of getting from point A to point B, cruise ships today are attraction-filled destinations in themselves, with nonstop entertainment and activities, plentiful food and drink, and opportunities to be as sociable or private as you want to be. While the cruise experience varies from ship to ship, the common denominator is choice. You can run from an aerobics class to line-dancing, then to an art auction, and then to bingo or an informal seminar all before lunch, or choose to do nothing more than sunbathe all day on a quiet corner of a deck, all while traveling from one port to another. Unpack once, settle in, and enjoy the ride.

In the pages that follow, we'll give you a taste of cruise life, starting from the beginning.

1 Checking In & Boarding

It's cruise day. If you've flown into your city of embarkation, uniformed ushers will be standing at the ready at baggage claim, holding signs with your cruise line's or ship's name on it, waiting to direct you to buses bound for the terminal. (Though you also have the option of getting there on your own, via taxi or some other method.) In all likelihood, another group of travelers is vacating your ship as your plane is touching down, so don't feel rushed unless you're really late. Even if your ship has been berthed at port since early in the morning, new passengers are often not allowed on board until about 1pm since all previous passengers need to be checked out with their luggage, cabins need to be cleaned, supplies loaded, and paperwork and customs documents completed properly.

If you've driven to the cruise port, it's just a matter of parking and then trundling your luggage to the terminal. We've included information on parking in chapter 10, "The Ports of Embarkation," but always double-check with your travel agent or cruise line before you set out for the port.

When you arrive at the port and step into the cruise terminal, you'll feel like a celebrity—sometimes complete with red carpet—and an army of smiling cruise line employees is always there to direct you to the check-in desks. Whether you arrive by car, bus, or taxi, your luggage will be taken from you before check-in, scanned, and delivered to your cabin, sometimes arriving by the time you do but often lagging by a few hours, depending on how big the ship is and how much luggage needs to be delivered. For this reason, it's a good idea to keep a small bag with you containing a change of clothes, and maybe a swimsuit and a pair of sunglasses, so you don't end up waiting around to get out on deck, use the pool, or otherwise get comfortable. Porters usually wait at the terminal to help you handle your luggage. If you use their services, it's customary to tip a dollar or two per bag.

Once in the terminal, you'll hand over your cruise tickets, show ID (two forms generally; see "Passports & Visas," in chapter 3, for information on acceptable ID), and give an imprint of your credit card to establish your onboard account. Depending upon when you arrive and the crowd situation, you may find yourself waiting in line for as much as an hour, but usually it's less.

For security reasons, cruise lines do not allow unofficial visitors on board ship, so if friends or relatives brought you to the pier, you'll have to say your good-byes on land.

2 Welcome to Your Cabin

Once on board, you may be guided to your cabin (you don't need to tip the person who leads you, though we usually give him a buck or two, especially if he's carried your day-bag), but in most cases you'll have to find it on your own. Soon after you do, your cabin steward will probably stop by to introduce him- or herself, inquire if the configuration of beds is appropriate (that is, whether you want separate twin beds or a pushed-together double), and give you his or her extension so that you can call if you need anything. The brochures and **daily programs** in your cabin will answer many questions you may have about the day's activities, what you'll need to wear to dinner that night, and what the ship's safety procedures are. There may also be a **deck plan** that will help you find your way around the ship. If not, you can pick one up at the guest services desk—signs near the staircases and elevators should be able to guide you there.

With a few notable exceptions, cruise ships have **direct-dial telephones** in cabins, along with instructions on how to use them, and a directory of phone numbers for the departments or services on board. You can call anywhere in the world from most cabins' phones, via satellite, but it's nowhere near cheap. Charges range from around $4 to about $15 a minute, with $8 or $9 being about average. It's cheaper to call home from a public telephone in port, or to send an e-mail from the Internet center, which most ships have these days. (See "Keeping in Touch While at Sea" in chapter 3 for more info.)

Most ships sailing the Caribbean have North American–style **electrical outlets** (twin flat prongs, 110 AC current), although some ships have outlets for both European current (220 AC) and North American. Keep in mind, there's often only one outlet for your curling iron or hair dryer, and it's usually not in the bathroom, but above the desk or dresser.

Most ships also have **in-cabin safes** for storing your valuables, usually operated via a self-set combination. On ships that don't offer them, you can generally check items at the purser's desk.

It's guaranteed you'll attend a **lifeboat safety drill** either just before or after sailing. It's required by the Coast Guard, and attendance is mandatory. Check to make sure your cabin has enough life preservers for everyone in your party, since you'll have to wear them to the drill. (Hope you look good in orange.) If you need extra—or for that matter if you need additional blankets or pillows—let your steward know ASAP.

3 Introducing Onboard Activities

Most ships that carry more than 800 passengers offer an extensive schedule of activities from morning till night every day, especially during days at sea, when the ship isn't visiting a port. To keep track of the games, contests, lessons, and classes, most ships print a **daily program,** which is placed in your cabin the

A History of Cruising

It wasn't until the late 19th century that British shipping companies realized they could make money not just by transporting travelers, cargo, mail, and immigrants from point A to point B, but by selling a luxurious experience at sea. It's generally accepted that the first cruise ship was Peninsular & Oriental Steam Navigation Company's *Ceylon,* which in 1881 was converted to a lavish cruising yacht for carrying wealthy, adventurous guests on world cruises. A few years later, in 1887, North of Scotland, Orkney & Shetland Steam Navigation's *St. Sunniva* was launched as the first steamer built expressly for cruising.

The Germans joined the cruise trade in 1891 when the Hamburg-America Line sent its *Augusta Victoria* on a Mediterranean cruise, and during the early 1900s, more and more players entered the picture, spending warmer seasons crossing the Atlantic and Pacific and offering pleasure cruises the rest of the year. During these boom years, competition became fierce between famous shipping lines such as **Cunard,** White Star, Hamburg-America, French Line, North German Lloyd, **Holland America,** Red Star Line, and others, which all sought to attract customers by building the largest, fastest, or most luxurious new ships, with extravagant appointments you'd never find on a modern cruise ship—stained-glass ceilings, frescoes, ornate wooden stairways, and even plaster walls. (Oddly, onboard activities and entertainment were relatively sparse amid all the grandeur. Besides lavish social dinners, about the only pastimes were reading, walking around the deck, and sitting for musical recitals.) These same ships, with their first-class ballrooms, smoking lounges, and suites decorated with the finest chandeliers, oriental rugs, and artwork, also carried immigrants in inexpensive, bare-bones steerage accommodations, with second-class cabins available between these two polar extremes. This multiclass system survived until the late 1960s, and even today you can see vestiges of it in the *QE2*'s dining rooms, which are assigned to passengers depending on the level of cabin they book.

Soon after Cunard launched its popular 2,165-passenger *Mauretania* and *Lusitania* in 1906, the White Star Line's J. Bruce Ismay envisioned a trio of the largest and most luxurious passenger vessels ever built, designed to appeal to rich American industrialists. The first of these sisters, the 2,584-passenger, 46,000-ton *Olympic,* was in service by 1911, introduced with such fanfare that the 1912 launch of the second sister, *Titanic,* was not nearly as anticipated, though the ship quickly became the most famous of all time, through the most tragic of circumstances.

The Brits and Germans continued building bigger and bigger ships up until **World War I,** when almost all vessels were requisitioned to carry soldiers, supplies, and weaponry, including the *Olympic,* which did time as a hospital ship. Many other grand ships were lost in the conflict, including Cunard's *Lusitania* and the third of Ismay's trio, launched in 1914 as the *Britannic* and sunk by a mine in 1916. (Interestingly, Celebrity Cruises' *Millennium* features a dining room designed around some of the *Olympic*'s original ornate wooden wall panels, salvaged before the ship was scrapped in 1935.)

After World War I, the popularity of cruising increased tremendously, and more ships were routed to the Caribbean and Mediterranean for long, expensive cruises. For instance, Cunard's *Mauretania* and its new running mate *Aquitania* were yanked off the Atlantic for a millionaire's romp through the Med, carrying as few as 200 pampered passengers in the lap of luxury. As they headed to warmer climes, many ships' traditional black hulls were painted white to help them stay cool in those pre-air-conditioning days. This became a tradition itself, to the point where in the 1960s and 1970s nearly all the Caribbean's ships were painted a dazzling white.

By the 1930s, shipboard activities and amenities were becoming much more sophisticated, with morning concerts, quoits, shuffleboard, bridge, Ping-Pong, motion pictures, and the first "swimming baths" (*read:* pools) appearing on board, though these were often no more than burlap or canvas slung over wooden supports and filled with water. The first permanent outdoor pools appeared in the 1920s, and in the 1930s, the large outdoor pool on the *Rex* actually included a patch of sand to evoke the Lido beach in Venice. When the great French liner *Normandie* made its maiden voyage in 1935, its first-class dining room boasted the cruising world's first air-conditioning system.

World War II saw the great liners again called into service, and many never made it back to civilian life (including *Normandie,* which burned and capsized in New York while being converted into a troopship). Cunard's *Queen Elizabeth* and *Queen Mary* and Holland America's *Nieuw Amsterdam,* on the other hand, completed distinguished wartime service and sailed on into the postwar years.

Shipboard travel boomed in the 1950s, and for the first time, pleasure cruising became accessible to the growing middle class, with onboard life enhanced by pool games, bingo, art classes, dance lessons, singles' parties, and midnight buffets—all of which you'll still find on ships today. By the 1960s, however, jet airplanes had replaced ships as the public's transportation of choice, and the boom was over. Increasingly expensive to maintain, many of the great 1950s liners were sent to the scrap yards.

The industry seemed doomed; but in the early 1960s, two Norwegian cargo and tanker ship operators, Christian and Knut Kloster, offered Caribbean cruises aboard the 11,000-ton *Sunward* from a home port in Miami, and soon the Caribbean cruise trade exploded. **Royal Caribbean Cruise Line** was formed in January 1969, and in the late '60s and early '70s, **Royal Viking, Carnival, Princess, Costa,** and **Holland America** joined the lucrative circuit. It was in 1968, on board Costa's *Carla C.* (at the time chartered to Princess Cruises and sailing Mexican Riviera and Panama Canal cruises from Los Angeles) that American writer Jeraldine Saunders was inspired to write the novel *The Love Boat,* later made into a popular television series that introduced millions to cruising.

previous evening, usually while you're at dinner. A cruise director and his or her staff are in charge of the festivities and do their best to ensure that a good time is had by all. Smaller ships offer activities, too—often with less hoopla—that may include wine tastings, trivia contests, port talks by the cruise director or captain, and occasional presentations by guest speakers or onboard historians or naturalists.

ONBOARD GAMES

The ships in the Carnival, Royal Caribbean, Norwegian, Princess, Celebrity, and Costa fleets have **wacky poolside contests,** scheduled for an hour or two most afternoons. You might even say they sometimes go overboard (har har), but you'll certainly be in stitches watching blindfolded pillow fights, belly-flop contests, stuff-the-most-Ping-Pong-balls-(or fruit)-into-your-bathing-suit contests, and pool relay races that require team members to pass bagels to one another with their teeth.

And it's not just the classic party ships that let their hair down. Many other lines indulge their guests in the tomfoolery, too. At its weekly deck parties, Holland America, for example, sometimes features a nearly obscene and absolutely hilarious rendition of the pass-the-balloon-from-between-my-knees-to-yours relay race. All ages participate, and you'll want to check your pride at the door before you volunteer for this one.

Game-show simulations, such as the **Newlywed/Not-So-Newlywed Game,** are ever popular. Volunteer yourself or just listen to fellow passengers blurt out the truth about their personal lives—just like on *Oprah!* Carnival's newest ships—*Paradise, Triumph,* and *Spirit*—stage very realistic *Who Wants to Be a Millionaire?* and *Jeopardy*-style **game shows,** complete with buzzers, contestant podiums, and digital point-keeping. Some ships stage a game in which passengers break into teams and compete to be the first to produce the increasingly risqué items the emcee calls for: a five-dollar bill, a compact, a beer belly, a bra, and then, inevitably, a man dressed as a woman.

If you're a performer at heart, volunteer for the weekly **passenger talent show** held aboard many ships. Among the more bizarre displays we've seen recently: an elderly lady aboard *Norwegian Sun,* wearing red hot pants and heels and lip-syncing Shirley Temple's "On the Good Ship Lollipop." Or, head to the nightclub one evening and wiggle your way into the **hula-hoop or twist competitions.** Cerebral types can sign up for **trivia quizzes,** do puzzles, or join **chess, checkers, bridge, and backgammon tournaments.**

Winners get more than a good time, too. Prizes such as champagne, T-shirts, mugs, or key chains—maybe even an onboard credit or a massage at the spa—all make getting involved a worthwhile proposition. In its *Who Wants to Be a Mouseketeer?* show, Disney even gives a free 7-night cruise to big winners who answer all 10 Disney trivia questions correctly.

SHIPBOARD CASINOS

All but the smallest, most adventure-oriented ships have casinos, with the biggest, flashiest, most Vegas-style ones on the Carnival, Royal Caribbean, Celebrity, and Princess megaships, which have literally hundreds of slot machines, and dozens of roulette, blackjack, poker, and craps tables. Smaller luxury lines such as Windstar and Seabourn have casinos as well, albeit scaled-down ones, with maybe a dozen slots and a couple of blackjack and poker tables, while adventure-oriented lines such as ACCL, Clipper, Star Clippers, and Windjammer have no casinos at

What Is This Horse Racing?

Sure, today's cruise ships have ice-skating rinks and rock-climbing walls, but when you look at your daily program and see horse racing advertised at 3pm, don't expect the real thing. A popular (and very goofy) cruise game from way back, these races are run by toy horses mounted on poles, moved around a track based on rolls of the dice. Passengers bet on the outcome, and the end of the cruise features an "owners cup" race and best-dressed horse show.

all. Stakes aboard most ships are relatively low, with maximum bets rarely exceeding $200. Average minimum bets at blackjack and poker tables are generally $5 or $10; the minimum at roulette is typically 50¢ or $1.

Gambling is legal once a ship has sailed a certain distance out to sea (the distance varies from place to place), but local laws almost always require onboard casinos to close down whenever a ship is in port. Big gamblers should keep this in mind when cruising to Bermuda, where ships stay in port for 3 whole days, with no gambling whatsoever during that period.

Children are not permitted to enter onboard casinos; the minimum age is generally 21.

Most ships also have a **card room,** which is usually filled with serious bridge or poker players and is sometimes supervised by a full-time instructor. Most ships furnish cards for free, although some charge $1 or so per deck.

CLASSES, LESSONS & DEMONSTRATIONS

For years, lists of shipboard classes read as if they'd been lifted straight out of the Eisenhower-era home-entertainment playbook: napkin-folding, vegetable-carving, scarf-tying, mixology, and the like. You'll still find these aboard most ships (old habits die hard), but these days, ships also offer informative, if basic, **seminars** on subjects such as personal investing, health and nutrition, arts and crafts, handwriting analysis, and introduction to basic computer word processing and photo software. Restaurant staff on some ships may also conduct a **cooking demonstration** or **wine tasting.** There's usually a $5 to $15 charge for wine tastings and sometimes for arts-and-crafts materials.

Line, country, and ballroom dancing lessons are usually held a few times a week, taught by one of the onboard entertainers. Demonstrations by the salon and spa staff on hair and skin care are common, too, though they have an ulterior motive: getting passengers to sign up for not-so-cheap spa treatments.

ART AUCTIONS

You'll find shipboard art auctions either a fun way to buy pictures for your living room or an incredibly annoying and blatantly tacky way for the cruise lines to make more money by selling a lot of marginally interesting or just plain awful originals and some good but fantastically overpriced lithographs and animation cels—not that we're taking sides, of course. Whatever your position, they're big business on mainstream and ultraluxury lines, held three or four times a week for an hour or two at a time, with enticements such as free champagne to attract passengers. From a stage or in one of the ship's lounges, the auctioneer (a salesman for an outside company that arranges the shows) briefly discusses a selection of the hundreds of works displayed around the auction space, sometimes paintings by well-known artists like Peter Max and Erté; lithographs by greats

C The Birth of a Megaship

Ever wonder where cruise ships come from? Not from the cruise ship stork, that's for sure. No, they come from shipyards, and these days it takes about 18 months to build a 90,000-gross-ton, 2,000-passenger cruise ship, from the day the first building block is laid—the skeleton of a megaship is created from some 60 to 70 steel building blocks—to the day sea trials are completed and the ship is officially delivered to the cruise line. During those 18 months, the ship is the center of its own universe, with designers, architects, welders, plumbers, painters, carpenters, and countless others all working like bees on their own piece of the puzzle. A passenger ship is not just an architectural structure, such as a house or an office building; it has to be seaworthy too, balanced and hearty in the face of harsh winds and salty seas—not to mention an aesthetically pleasing and fun place to spend a vacation.

The whole process comes to a head on the day a new ship leaves the yard, and it's never as simple as casting off a line and putting the key in the ignition—there are still thousands of details to check before a ship takes on passengers. In some cases, too, the journey from the yard to the open sea is a great challenge in itself. For instance, ships built at Germany's Meyer Werft, one of Europe's major shipyards, must sail 40 miles from the yard to the North Sea, down the relatively narrow Ems River.

As project director for Royal Caribbean's *Radiance of the Seas,* marine engineer and naval architect Atle Ellefsen knows all about the building of a new ship. Here's how he saw it from the deck of *Radiance* as she cast off from Meyer Werft in January 2001:

"The crazy dash down the river yesterday was one of the most exciting experiences of my life. After many days of delays due to bad weather, finally the moment had come to seize the tide and go. We left the yard at midnight. The lock opened to the river, and we eased out slowly, stern first. Thousands of cars and people lined the banks of the Ems to watch. There were hot-dog stands strung with lights and beer carts set up across from the yard. The minute the bow cleared the lock, we blew three long and one short blasts on the ship's whistles. Everybody cheered and camera flashes raced among the crowd. Music,

such as Dalí, Picasso, and Miró; animation cels, often by Disney; and many pieces by artists you've never heard of. The art, framed or unframed, is duty-free to U.S. citizens and is packed and mailed home for the lucky winner.

4 Introducing Onboard Entertainment

Entertainment is a big part of the cruise experience on almost all ships, but especially on the megaships of Carnival, Royal Caribbean, Celebrity, Costa, Princess, NCL, and Holland America, which all offer an extensive variety throughout the day. Afternoons, you can dance on deck with the **live dance band,** which we'll lay 10-to-1 will be jamming calypso music or tunes by Bob Marley and Jimmy including Rod Stewart's 'Sailing,' blared from huge speakers mounted on the promenade deck. It was surreal.

"Then the lock closed. We had to follow the race of the tide, so Captain Thomas Teitge immediately got up to speed and soon encountered the first bend in the river. Because of a back current created when the lock closed behind us, the bow veered to starboard. I was on the starboard bridge wing, looking down at a riverbank approaching at a highly worrying speed. The bow thrusters went on full, churning up literally hundreds of tons of mud, a brown chocolate gravy boiling up and bellowing onto the shore side, flooding acres of flat fields. Just feet from the ship's side, small trunks of dead trees and bushes stuck out of the water, telling the shallowness of the small river. I thought that was it. But we had to follow the tide running and the captain hauled the hull back on course again and executed the remaining transit with surgical precision. What was most impressive was the speed and how we sailed: 3 knots backwards, stern first. We decided it was more efficient to pull the ship with its Azipod propellers and have the bow thrusters correct our course like a rudder.

"Passing Weener and going further toward the sea, it was 1:30am and still there were thousands lining the route, watching the spectacle of a huge ship inching past them, like a skyscraper in a bathtub. Despite the freezing cold, people were clapping and cheering, music was blaring, camera flashes snapped like firecrackers, and flashlights waved back and forth. We felt like pop stars!

"In the morning, we arrived in the town of Leer, just a few miles from the North Sea, and moored along a field to wait for the new high tide. When I drew apart my curtains after a half-night's sleep, again I looked out onto hundreds of spectators, schoolchildren and couples, standing and gazing at us from the dyke surrounding the ship. Finally, we moved on again, now in broad daylight. Three helicopters hovered above, at least four planes circled us, and the music, whistles, cheering, and waving continued. At last, we arrived at Eemshaven. Soon sea trials would start, and then in a few weeks, the journey across the Atlantic to Miami would begin."

And *Radiance of the Seas* was born.

Buffett. Or put on your waltzing shoes and head inside to one of the lounges for some **big-band dancing;** lines such as Holland America, Crystal, and NCL often feature a Glenn Miller–style group playing 1940s dance tunes.

Pre-dinner entertainment starts to heat up around 5pm, and continues all night to accommodate passengers dining early and late. Head to the piano bar for a cocktail or do some pre-dinner dancing to a **live jazz quartet** or big band.

Usually twice in any weeklong cruise, there's apt to be **Vegas-style musical revues** performed early and late in the main show lounge, with a flamboyant troupe of anywhere from 4 to 16 male and female dancers decked out in feather boas, sequins, and top hats sliding, kicking, and lip-syncing their way across the stage as a soloist or two belts out show tunes. You'll hear favorites from *Phantom of the Opera, Cats, Hair, Grease, Footloose, A Chorus Line,* and the classic Rodgers and Hammerstein musicals, spiced with ubiquitous pop songs such as the Village People's "YMCA." If you're the type that hits all the Broadway shows when you're in New York, these revues certainly won't compare, propelled as they are by elaborate sets, lights, and frequent costume changes rather than by any trace of a storyline (except aboard the Disney ships, which offer musicals with characters and stories based on Disney classics).

Nights when the shows aren't scheduled may feature a **magic show,** complete with sawing in half a scantily clad assistant and pulling rabbits from a hat; **acrobatic acts** (always a big hit); **headlining soloists,** some of them quite good (such as singer Jane L. Powell, a perennial NCL favorite whose amazing range takes her from Louis Armstrong to Bette Midler); or **guest comedians or specialty acts,** such as the aerialist duo Majestic or the amazing a cappella singing group the Knudsen Brothers, both of whom we saw recently on Royal Caribbean's *Explorer of the Seas.*

The **disco** gets going around 9 or 10pm and works it until 2 or 3am or sometimes later, letting you shake your booty to the best of '70s, '80s, '90s, and current pop. Sometimes a live band plays until about midnight, when a DJ takes over until the wee hours; sometimes there's only a DJ. A **karaoke session** may also be thrown in for an hour or two, usually in the evening but occasionally in the afternoon.

An alternative to the disco or the main show may be a pianist or jazz trio in one of the ship's romantic nightspots, or a **themed party** such as NCL's Miami salsa ¡Fuácata! bash or the '50s sock hops put on by many lines. Disney's ships offer a comedic **dueling-pianos act** several times per evening in one of their adults-only lounges, with the pianists taking requests and sometimes dragging audience members up to sing. Night owls who love a good laugh can catch the **R- and/or X-rated comedians** who do late-night shows around midnight. Or, for a quiet evening, lines such as Holland America, Celebrity, Crystal, and Disney have cinemas showing **recent-release movies.**

To prove that not all innovative entertainment has to be big, Celebrity's ships have been featuring strolling **vocal quartets** that roam around the ships in the evening, performing wherever people are gathered. On Royal Caribbean's *Adventure, Explorer,* and *Voyager of the Seas,* jugglers, magicians, and other **street performers** meander through the four-deck-high Royal Promenade, the main hub of activity on these ships.

Ships carrying 100 to 400 passengers have fewer entertainment options, but are no less appealing if you like things mellow. The high-end lines may feature a quartet or pianist performing before dinner and maybe a small-scale Broadway revue afterward, plus dancing in a quiet lounge. The small adventure-oriented ships may have a solo performer before and after dinner, or local musicians and/or dancers aboard for an afternoon or evening of entertainment.

5 Shipboard Gyms, Spas & Sports

If your idea of a perfect vacation starts with a run on the treadmill, a set of bicep curls, or a game of pickup basketball—or if a relaxing hot rock massage is more your thing—the newest ships in the Celebrity, Royal Caribbean, Princess, Carnival, Norwegian, and Holland America lines have the biggest and best-equipped spa, fitness, and sports facilities. Since the early 1990s, cruise lines have prioritized their spa and fitness areas, moving them out of windowless corners of bottom decks and into prime, spacious top-deck positions with lots of windows opening onto soothing ocean views. They offer state-of-the-art workout machines and spa treatments that run from the basic to the bizarre. Sports areas are also getting supersized on some ships, and options you'd never have imagined possible on a ship just a few years ago are becoming almost commonplace.

GYMS: AN ANTIDOTE TO THE MIDNIGHT BUFFET

The well-equipped fitness centers on the megaships may feature a dozen or more treadmills and just as many stationary bikes, step machines, upper- and lower-body machines, and free weights—Celebrity's newest ships even have virtual-reality stationary bikes. When it comes to big, the huge two-story Nautica gyms on the 2,642-passenger *Carnival Destiny, Triumph,* and *Victory* take the cake, with dozens of exercise machines facing floor-to-ceiling windows and tons of space to work out in—there's even a pair of hot tubs and an aerobics room on the upper level.

The roomy aerobics studios on Princess's *Golden, Grand, Coral,* and *Island Princess;* NCL's *Norwegian Dawn, Sun,* and *Sky;* Royal Caribbean's Radiance- and Voyager-class ships; and Holland America's and Carnival's post-1990 ships are like the kind you have at your gym back home, with mirrors and special flooring, and offer at least a couple of **aerobics and stretch classes** per day, including the latest trendy classes such as boxing, spinning, pilates, yoga, and tai chi. Sound great? Well sure, except that many lines are charging about $10 per session for anything but the basic aerobics and stretch classes. In the spirit of revenue, revenue, revenue, we've also been noticing that aerobics rooms are being used too often for spa demonstrations (to entice passengers to book expensive treatments) and personal training sessions that cost around $75 a pop.

Older ships, usually those built before 1990, often do not devote nearly as much space and resources to fitness areas. Gyms on such ships are generally smaller and more spartan, but you'll find at least a couple of treadmills, a stationary bike or step machine, and some free weights on all but the smallest, most adventure-oriented cruise lines—Windjammer, Star Clippers, Clipper, and ACCL. On ships with limited or no gym facilities, aerobics and stretching classes will often be held out on deck or in a lounge.

ONBOARD SPORTS OPTIONS

If you're into sports, the megaships pack the most punch, with jogging tracks; outdoor volleyball, basketball, and paddle-tennis courts; and several pools for water polo, volleyball, aqua aerobics, and swimming. The most mega of the megas—Royal Caribbean's enormous Voyager-class ships—go entirely off the deep end, packing a bona fide ice-skating rink, an outdoor rock-climbing wall, an in-line skating track, a full-size basketball court, miniature golf, and lots more. The line's Radiance-class ships also offer rock climbing.

WATERSPORTS

Small ships are the best equipped for watersports enthusiasts. The Windstar, Seabourn, and SeaDream ships and Star Clippers' *Royal Clipper* have **retractable watersports platforms** that, weather permitting, can be lowered from the stern into calm waters when the ship is anchored, allowing passengers to step practically right from their cabins to snorkel, windsurf, kayak, sail, water-ski, go on banana-boat rides, and swim, all free of charge. The SeaDream yachts and Radisson's *Radisson Diamond* even have jet skis for passenger use.

GOLF

Many cruises are offering the opportunity to tee off both on board and on shore. For the casual golfer, a few ships—Royal Caribbean's Radiance- and Voyager-class ships, *Splendour of the Seas* and *Legend of the Seas;* and Princess's *Island, Coral, Golden* and *Grand Princess*—have **miniature-golf courses** on board. For the more serious swingers, the newest, most technologically advanced ships such as Royal Caribbean's Radiance- and Voyager-class ships; Celebrity's entire fleet; Holland America's *Zuiderdam* and *Oosterdam;* and Princess's *Island, Coral Golden, Grand, Sea, Sun,* and *Dawn Princess* have **golf simulators** that allow you to play the great courses of the world without ever leaving the ship, watching the electronic path of a ball they've actually hit (for about $25 per half-hour).

Many more lines, including Norwegian, Crystal, Princess, Radisson, and Cunard, have **outdoor golf cages,** a putting green, and/or a net-enclosed driving range on most or all of their ships where you can whack at real golf balls any time of the day. Golf cages aboard Celebrity, Costa, and Carnival vessels are mostly reserved for the onboard golf pro, who uses them for private golf lessons—you wanna play, you gotta pay. Pros are available aboard these and several other lines to offer **golf instruction** and pointers; half-hour lessons are about $30 to $40, hour-long lessons are about $80, and videotaping is available.

In port, even more ships have **golf excursions** to well-known courses such as Mahogany Run in St. Thomas (U.S. Virgin Islands) and Mid Ocean in Bermuda; packages typically include greens fees, cart, and transportation between the ship and course, and range from $100 to $200 per person.

SPORTS FOR COUCH POTATOES

No need for all you sports-loving couch potatoes to be deprived. NCL's *Norwegian Sky* and *Sun;* Royal Caribbean's Radiance- and Voyager-class ships; Carnival's Conquest-, Spirit-, and Destiny-class vessels; Disney's *Magic* and *Wonder;* Holland America's *Zuiderdam* and *Oosterdam,* and Princess's *Star, Golden,* and *Grand Princess* all have **dedicated sports bars** with large-screen televisions broadcasting ESPN and live NFL games. During popular sporting events such as the Super Bowl, many lines outfit a public area or bar with televisions for game viewing. If you want to watch the game from the comfort of your cabin, no problem: ESPN is available on cabin TVs on Royal Caribbean, Celebrity, Disney, Norwegian, Crystal, Radisson, and Princess ships.

ONBOARD SPAS: TAKING RELAXATION ONE STEP FURTHER

If your idea of a heavenly vacation is spending half of it under a towel being massaged and kneaded with some soothing mystery oil, choose a cruise ship with a well-stocked spa. Generally, you'll find these aboard ships built after 1990.

Shipboard spas are big business these days; the largest, newest, and best of them are perched on top decks and boast great views from 8 or 10 treatment rooms, where you can choose from dozens of massages, mud packs, and facials, as well as some much more esoteric treatments, many of Asian origin and offered as part of high-priced packages.

Celebrity Cruises offers some of the most attractive spas and fitness facilities at sea aboard the Millennium- and Century-class ships (though the quality of service isn't always as impressive as the aesthetics are). Called the AquaSpa, these spacious health meccas incorporate Japanese, Turkish, and Moorish motifs. The focal point in each is a huge **thalassotherapy pool,** a bubbling cauldron of warm, soothing seawater that's a great place to relax before a massage (use of it is complimentary for adults on the Millennium-class ships, but on the Century-class

Making Your Appointment at the Spa

Hurry up! On the megaships, people sometimes line up 20 and 30 deep to sign up for spa excursions on the first afternoon; so if you don't get there by the second day at the latest, there's a good chance the only appointment you'll be able to get will be totally undesirable, such as during dinner or at some ungodly hour of the morning. Or you may not get one at all. Celebrity and Windstar allow you to prebook spa packages with your travel agent, though exact appointment times can't be reserved until you board the ship.

ships, it's available only to those who sign up for spa treatments). Other great features include the huge, gorgeously appointed Persian Garden steam room aboard the Millennium class, a larger version of the beautifully tiled rooms aboard the earlier ships.

The soothing ShipShape spas on **Royal Caribbean**'s Radiance-, Voyager-, and Vision-class ships are also among the most attractive around. Adjacent to each is a spacious solarium with a pool, deck chairs, floor-to-ceiling windows, and a retractable glass ceiling—a peaceful place to repose before or after a spa treatment, or any time at all. The *Radiance* sports an African theme, while on the *Brilliance* it's Indian. NCL's new *Norwegian Dawn* also has a wonderful indoor pool complex, with a large lap pool, hot tub, and water-jet relaxation pool.

Most of the smaller upscale ships also have at least some semblance of a spa and a beauty salon. For instance, Windstar Cruises' *Wind Surf* carries only 300 passengers but boasts an impressive spa, and Radisson's 490-passenger *Navigator* and 708-passenger *Mariner* have respectable spas with six and eight treatment rooms, respectively. Only the very smallest ships in the Caribbean (the Windjammer, ACCL, and Clipper vessels) lack spas.

The spas and hair salons on just about every ship in this book (more than 100 of them) are staffed and operated by the London-based firm **Steiner;** exceptions include the **Judith Jackson** spas on Radisson Seven Seas. Some ships also have **Mandara** spas (namely those of the NCL and Silverseas lines), but, alas, so much for healthy competition: Mandara was fully acquired by Steiner in December 2002, though it continues to operate as its own brand, with a focus on Asian-influenced treatments. A sampling of treatments and their standard Steiner rates are shown here:

- 50-minute full-body massage: $84 to $116
- 25-minute back-and-legs massage: $55 to $72
- Manicure: $21 to $54
- Pedicure: $34 to $76 (ridiculous!)
- 50-minute facial: $84 to $130
- Bikini wax: $21 to $28
- 50- to 70-minute Ionithermie slimming treatment: $102 to $130

Note that these prices do not include a tip (typically 15%), and that rates can vary by as much as $20 from ship to ship, though the length of the treatment is the same. Treatments are charged to your onboard account, and Steiner adds a tip directly onto your tab if you're cruising with Celebrity, Costa, Cunard, and NCL, as opposed to your writing in the amount of the tip, so make sure you're okay with the service before signing on the dotted line.

The young, mostly British women (and occasionally men) Steiner employs are professional and charming, but we've found the quality of the treatments to be inconsistent, ranging from disappointing (we felt we'd had big dollops of oil and cream smeared on us with no rhyme or reason) to excellent, when all we wanted was more, more, more. Like any spa on land or sea, the enjoyment factor depends largely on the expertise and finesse of the individual masseuse/ masseur. Massages are a pretty safe bet, quality-wise, but we've found other treatments to be disappointing and not worth the money. Fifty bucks for a mediocre pedicure—are you joking? You can get a much better one in New York for half that. Ditto for the manicures. Likewise, when we've asked questions about some of the more exotic (and expensive) treatments—such as the Ionithermie facials or slimming/detox treatments, which use electrodes to allegedly stimulate cells and release toxins—it's clear most spa staffers don't have much of a clue beyond their memorized descriptions (probably because, at least in our opinion, they're a load of hooey). Unfortunately, the larger and snazzier cruise ship spas become, the more quality control seems to suffer—50-minute massages become 45, and tired masseuses, who often work 12-hour shifts, often seem less than motivated.

There are exceptions, of course. A masseuse Heidi had on a recent *Norwegian Sun* cruise gave her a fabulous shiatsu (so good she signed up for a second), and an excellent masseur she had on a *Sovereign of the Seas* cruise was a trained sports therapist and a student of chiropractic. Matt had a deep-tissue sports massage on Princess's *Coral Princess* that was a real killer, verging on painful (as it was supposed to be), but totally fulfilling.

Steiner isn't shy about pushing its extensive and expensive collection of creams, exfoliants, moisturizers, toners, and masks, either; ditto for Mandara. Get a facial and you'll wind up with an itemized list of four or five products that they recommend you buy to get the same effect at home—products that can easily add up to over $200. Needless to say, the therapists work on commission, and with cruise lines struggling to increase profits, spa managers are under more pressure than ever to have staff push products and additional services. In the name of research (and a little vanity), on a cruise a few years ago, Heidi grudgingly bought a tube of La Therapie cleanser, a bottle of toner, and a pot of moisturizer. The grand total? Sure enough, over $200. They lasted about 6 months, and while she liked the products, the price has prevented her from ever doing this again. The sales pitch is just a little too shameless, coming just as you're drifting around in your semiconscious massage trance. Just make with the back rub already!

6 Introducing Shipboard Dining

In no other area is cruising experiencing as much change as in its dining rituals. In just the past few years, traditional five-course, assigned-seating meals in formal dining rooms have been supplanted on many vessels by **casual dining options** that allow passengers not only to dress down but also to dine with complete flexibility, choosing when, with whom, and where they want to eat, with several different restaurant options. In mid-2000, Norwegian Cruise Line got the ball rolling with its Freestyle Cruising scheme, which boils down to passengers being able to dine anytime between 5:30pm and midnight in any of several venues, with the last seating at 10pm. Princess followed suit with its own versions of ultraflexible dining, although it's not as extreme as NCL's (see line reviews for more details).

Formal or casual aside, some things never change: There are still copious amounts of food everywhere you turn. Cruise ships big and small are offering ever more choices, but the megaships are nothing short of floating smorgasbords. You can get elegant **multicourse meals** served in grand two-story dining rooms; Japanese, Italian, and Tex-Mex cuisine served in intimate **specialty restaurants;** ultracasual meals served in the ship's cafe; **midnight buffets** served under the stars; and 24-hour pizza, ice cream, pastry, specialty coffee, and even sushi to top it all off. Carnival offers pizza and Caesar salad 24 hours a day, and Celebrity and Norwegian even deliver pizza to your cabin! Disney has a hot dog counter by the pool, and Royal Caribbean's Voyager-class ships have entire 1950s-style diners out on deck. The smaller ships have fewer choices, but lately all the upscale lines are offering alternatives, too.

All but the most cost-conscious cruise lines will attempt to satisfy reasonable culinary requests, so if you follow a **special diet,** inform your line as early as possible, preferably when booking your cruise, and make sure they'll be able to satisfy your request at all three meals. **Vegetarian dishes** and a selection of **healthier, lighter meals** (labeled as such on the menu) are available as a matter of course on just about every ship at breakfast, lunch, and dinner.

TRADITIONAL DINING

Though casual dining is all the rage, most ships still continue to offer formal, traditional dinners in at least one restaurant, generally from about 6:30 to 10pm. Ships carrying fewer than 400 passengers generally have one **open-seating dinner,** where guests can stroll in when they want and sit with whomever they choose; those carrying more than 400 passengers typically have two **assigned seatings** in one, two, or even three main dining rooms. Under Princess's flexible dining plan, its ships offer a combination of both, with one restaurant on each ship offering open restaurant-style seating and another offering traditional early and late seating. (On ships with three restaurants, two are open-seating.) Putting a unique twist on things, the *Disney Magic* and *Disney Wonder* have two seatings in three main themed dining rooms that passengers (and their servers) rotate through over the course of the cruise.

Most ships still require you to reserve either the early or late seating when booking your cruise. Your choice may be confirmed at the pier during check-in or soon after you get to your cabin. **First seatings** (served at around 6:30pm) are for those who prefer dining early and are ready to leave the dining room once the dishes are cleared; elderly passengers and families with children tend to choose this seating. If you choose **second seating** (served at around 8:30pm), you won't have to rush through pre-dinner showering and dressing after an active day in port, and the meal tends to be more leisurely, allowing you to linger over coffee and after-dinner drinks.

If you get assigned to the first seating and you want the second, or vice versa, tell your maitre d', who will probably be at or near his or her station in the dining room during your initial embarkation. Most can accommodate your wishes, if not on the first night of sailing, then on the second.

Seven-night cruises offering traditional dining generally have two **formal nights** per week, when the dress code in the main dining room calls for dark suits or tuxedos for men and cocktail dresses or fancy pantsuits for women. Other nights in the main dining rooms are designated informal and/or casual. Ten- to 14-night cruises have three formal nights. (See "Packing" in chapter 3 for more information.)

Though some ships still offer early- and late-seatings for breakfast and lunch (served around 7 and 8:30am and noon and 1:30pm, respectively), most ships are now offering open-seating setups within certain hours.

Smoking is prohibited in virtually all ships' dining rooms.

DINNER COMPANIONS: THE GOOD, THE BAD & THE UGLY

The prevalence of flexible dining aboard many of today's ships means you may only dine with the same people once or twice (if at all), but on ships that stick to traditional fixed-seating schemes, your dinner companions can either make or ruin your cruise. For meeting and mingling with other passengers, we suggest trying for a table that seats at least six—the more people, the greater your chances of finding stimulating conversation. Rotate seats during the week so that you can chat with new people and keep things lively. If you get stuck with a couple of yahoos who seem to offend every bone in your body or if your table doesn't have any chemistry at all, don't just suffer in silence. Explain to the maitre d' as soon as possible that your table assignment isn't working, and request a change. You will usually be accommodated. If you want privacy, you can request a table for two, but unless you're sailing aboard one of the smaller, more upscale ships, don't get your hopes up: Tables aboard megaships generally seat between 4 and 10, with tables for couples few and far between.

SPECIALTY DINING

If you want fine dining and more formality, but with fewer fellow diners in tow, you can take advantage of the intimate, **reservations-only restaurants** most lines have added in recent years, seating around 100 guests. Following the trend of socking passengers with extra charges to make up for lower fares, the cost for dining at these restaurants ranges from Disney's reasonable $5 up to the more typical $20 to $25 per person. Frankly, sometimes the food isn't any better than in the main dining rooms (especially in Holland America's, Carnival's, and Costa's specialty restaurants), but the venues are at least quieter and more intimate. The best, without a doubt, are on the Celebrity, Crystal, Silversea, and Radisson ships. NCL's specialty restaurants are pretty damn good, too. Here's what's available on each of the lines.

Specialty Dining: Who's Got What

Cruise Line & Ships	Type of Specialty Restaurants	Extra Charge
Carnival		
Spirit and Conquest classes	Steakhouse/Seafood	$25 per person
Celebrity		
Millennium class	Continental	$25 per person
Costa		
CostaAtlantica, CostaMediterranea	Italian	$23 per person
Crystal		
Crystal Harmony	Asian, Italian	"suggested" $6 tip
Crystal Serenity	Asian, Sushi, Italian	"suggested" $6 tip
Disney		
Disney Magic, Disney Wonder	Italian	$5 per person

Cruise Line & Ships	Type of Specialty Restaurants	Extra Charge
Holland America		
Rotterdam, Volendam, Zaandam, Oosterdam,	Italian	no extra charge
Zuiderdam	Pacific Northwest	$20 per person
Norwegian		
Dawn	Steakhouse	$17.50 per person
	French/Continental	$12.50
	Pan-Asian	$10
	Sushi	a la carte pricing, $10–$12
	Teppanyaki	a la carte pricing, $10–$12
	Tapas, Italian	no extra charge
Majesty, Sea	French/Continental	$10 per person
Sky	French/Continental, Pan-Asian, Italian	$10 per person
Sun	French/Continental, Pan-Asian, Italian	$10 per person
	Sushi, Teppanyaki	a la carte pricing $10–$12
	Tapas	no extra charge
Oceania		
Regatta, Insignia	Italian, Grill	no extra charge
Princess		
Golden, Grand Princess	Italian	$15 per person
	Tex-Mex	$8 per person
Coral, Island Princess	Italian	$15 per person
	New Orleans	$10 per person
Sun class	Steakhouse	$8 per person
	Sit-down pizzeria	no extra charge
Radisson		
Seven Seas Mariner	French, International	no extra charge
Seven Seas Voyager	French, American	no extra charge
Diamond, Seven Seas Navigator	Italian	no extra charge
Royal Caribbean		
Radiance class	Italian, Steakhouse	$20 per person
Voyager class	Italian	$20 per person
Seabourn		
Legend, Pride	French, Italian, Asian, and others*	no extra charge
Silversea		
Wind, Cloud, Shadow, Whisper	French, Italian, Asian, and others*	no extra charge

* *Seabourn and Silversea host varying theme nights in one restaurant aboard each ship.*

CASUAL DINING

If you'd rather skip the formality and hubbub of the main dining room, all but the tiniest ships serve breakfast, lunch, and dinner in a casual **buffet-style cafe restaurant,** so you never have to put on a tie if you don't want to. Usually located on the Lido Deck, with indoor and outdoor poolside seating, these restaurants serve a spread of both hot and cold items. On the megas, a grill may be nearby where at lunchtime you can get burgers, hot dogs, and often chicken; sometimes you can find specialty stations offering taco fixings or Chinese food. On most ships, breakfast and lunch buffets are generally served for a 3- to 4-hour period, so guests can stroll in and out whenever they desire, but many of the mainstream lines also keep portions of their Lido cafes open almost round the clock. Some ships, like NCL's new *Dawn* and HAL's new *Zuiderdam,* also offer diners or cafes open 20 to 24 hours. Most lines serve dinner buffet-style as well in the Lido restaurants, but some offer a combination of sit-down service and buffet.

BETWEEN-MEAL SNACKING

Throughout the day, if hunger pangs get the best of you between lunch and dinner, the megaships have **pizza** (pizzerias on Carnival's ships operate 24 hr. daily and serve Caesar salad, too) and **self-serve frozen yogurt and ice-cream machines** (cheapo Princess doesn't; they sell only Häagen-Dazs). The upscale lines and some of the megas (such as Celebrity and Holland America) offer **afternoon tea service,** serving finger sandwiches, pastries, and cookies along with tea and coffee. Carnival and several others do their own, less fancy versions (kinda like "low tea"). Small-ship lines such as Star Clippers, Windstar, Clipper, and Windjammer serve pre-dinner snacks and hors d'oeuvres on deck or in the main lounge or bar area.

Some lines, such as Princess, Royal Caribbean, Norwegian, and Carnival, also have a **patisserie and/or cappuccino bar** on board their ships, but they're not free. Specialty coffees and ultrarich desserts go for about $1 to $4 each.

Some lines (such as Royal Olympia) maintain the tradition of offering classic **midnight buffets** nightly; but in recent years, because of all the other onboard dining choices and people's healthier eating habits, more and more lines are featuring such extravaganzas only once or twice a week, offering heaps of elaborately decorated fruits, vegetables, and pastries, as well as shrimp and other treats (if you're lucky), with an ice sculpture to top off the festive mood. Sometimes the nighttime feast will be focused on a culinary theme, such as Tex-Mex, Caribbean, or chocolate. On nights when there's no buffet, smaller snack stations will be set up instead. Some lines (such as Celebrity and Disney) have done away with midnight buffets completely, opting instead to have waiters cruise their ships with trays of hors d'oeuvres—which keeps drinkers where the cruise lines want them: at the bar, running up their tabs.

If you'd rather not leave your cabin, most ships offer **24-hour room service** from a limited menu. Suite guests can often order the same meals being served in the dining room.

7 Shopping Opportunities on Ship & Shore

Even the smallest ships have at least a small shop on board selling T-shirts, sweatshirts, and baseball caps bearing the cruise line logo. The big new megaships, though, are like minimalls, offering as many as 10 different stores selling items such as toiletries and sundries (film, toothpaste, candy, paperback books, and even condoms), as well as totes, T-shirts, mugs, toys, key chains, and other cruise line logo souvenirs. You'll find formal wear such as sequin dresses and jackets, silk dresses and scarves, purses, satin shoes, cummerbunds, ties, and tuxedo shirts, as well as perfume, cosmetics, jewelry (costume and the real stuff), and porcelain figurines.

A few ships have name-brand stores. All four of Celebrity's Millennium-class ships have a trendy DKNY boutique and a Michel Roux culinary-theme shop, for instance, while you'll find a Tommy Hilfiger boutique aboard Royal Caribbean's *Explorer of the Seas.* Carnival's *Paradise, Elation, Inspiration, Imagination, Sensation, Fascination, Ecstasy,* and *Fantasy* have Fossil boutiques on board, selling mostly watches. The Disney ships, of course, have shops selling Disney souvenirs, clothing, and toys. And appropriately, Cunard's *QE2* and new *QM2* each have a Harrods shop offering lots of those cute stuffed bears, green totes, and biscuits.

All merchandise sold on board while a ship is at sea is tax free; to maintain that tax-free status, the shops are closed whenever a ship is in port. Prices can vary, though: Some items—booze, for instance—sell for as much as a third less than the same items on shore, while others—disposable cameras, sunscreen, candy, and snack foods—cost substantially more. By midcruise, there are often good sales on a selection of T-shirts, tote bags, jewelry, and booze.

See "Best Ports for Serious Shoppers" in "The Best of Cruising" chapter for the best shopping islands.

Before each port of call, the cruise director or shore-excursion manager gives a **port talk** about that place's attractions. Now, it's no secret that many cruise lines have mutually beneficial deals with certain shops in every port (generally of the touristy chain variety), so on the big, mass-market ships especially, a good 75% of the port info disseminated will be about shopping. Better bring along your own guidebook (this one!) if you want information on history or culture. The lines often recommend a list of shops in town where they say the merchandise is guaranteed, and if the stone falls out of the new ring you bought at one of them once you get home, the cruise lines say they'll try to help you get a replacement. Don't hold your breath, though; the whole thing is a bit ambiguous. If you're not an expert on jewelry or whatever else it is you want to buy, it may be safer to shop at these stores; however, you won't get much of a taste for the local culture in one of them. Browsing at outdoor markets and in smaller craft shops is a better way to get an idea of the port's local flavor.

Part 2

The Cruise Lines & Their Ships

Detailed, in-depth reviews of all the cruise lines offering Caribbean, Bermuda, and Panama Canal itineraries, with discussions of the type of experience they offer and the lowdown on all their ships.

5

The Ratings
(and How to Read Them)

Okay, this is it: the point where you get to decide which ship is going to be your home, favorite restaurant, entertainment center, and means of transportation for the duration of your Caribbean getaway.

People feel very strongly about ships. For centuries, mariners have imbued their vessels with human personalities, and even though cruise passengers are typically aboard for only a week at a time, they really do bond with their vessels. They find themselves in the gift shop, buying T-shirts with the ship's name emblazoned on the front. They get to port and the first question they ask other cruisers they meet is, "Which ship are you sailing on?"—and after engaging in a friendly comparison, they walk away believing their ship is the best. We know people who have sailed the same ship a dozen times or more, and feel as warmly about it as though it were their own summer cottage. That's why, when looking at the reviews, you want to look for a ship that says "you." In this part of the book, we'll fill you in on what each one has to offer.

1 Cruise Line Categories

To make your selection easier (and to make sure you're not comparing apples and oranges), we've divided the cruise lines into four distinct categories, given each category a chapter of its own, and rated each line only in comparison with the other lines in its category (see more about this in "How to Read the Ratings," below). The categories are as follows:

THE MAINSTREAM LINES (chapter 6)   This category includes the most prominent players in the industry, the jack-of-all-trades lines with the biggest ships, carrying the most passengers and providing the most diverse cruise experiences to suit many different tastes, from party-hearty to elegant and refined. With all the competition in the industry today, these lines tend to offer good prices too. **Lines reviewed:** Carnival Cruise Lines, Celebrity Cruises, Costa Cruises, Disney Cruise Line, Holland America Line, Norwegian Cruise Line, Oceania Cruises, Princess Cruises, Royal Caribbean International, and Royal Olympia Cruises.

THE ULTRALUXURY LINES (chapter 7)   These are the Dom Perignon of cruises, offering elegant, refined, and doting service, extraordinary dining, spacious cabins, and high-toned entertainment aboard intimately sized, finely appointed vessels—and at a high price. **Lines reviewed:** Crystal Cruises, Cunard, Radisson Seven Seas Cruises, Seabourn Cruise Line, SeaDream Yacht Club, Silversea Cruises, and Windstar Cruises.

SOFT-ADVENTURE LINES & SAILING SHIPS (chapter 8)   If you don't like crowds, want to visit out-of-the-way ports that the bigger ships ignore, or prefer a good book and conversation to a large ship's roster of activities, these small, casual ships—some of them sailing ships, some of them engine-powered—may be your cup of tea. **Lines reviewed:** American Canadian Caribbean Line, Clipper Cruise Line, Star Clippers, and Windjammer Barefoot Cruises.

THE EUROPEAN LINES . . . PLUS (chapter 9)   Several good European lines also operate in the Caribbean, catering to both European and Americans guests. The other lines in this chapter are relatively minor if notable players in the region. **Lines reviewed:** First European Cruises, Mediterranean Shipping Cruises, ResidenSea, and Sea Cloud Cruises.

2 Reading the Reviews & Ratings

Each cruise line's review begins with **The Line in a Nutshell** (a quick word about the line in general) and **The Experience,** which is just what it says: a short summation of the kind of cruise experience you can expect to have aboard that line. Following this, the **Ratings Table** judges the individual elements of that line's cruise experience compared with the other lines in the same category (see below for ratings details). The text that follows fleshes out these summations, providing all the details you need to get a feel for what kind of vacation the cruise line will give you.

The individual **ship reviews** give you details on each vessel's accommodations, facilities, amenities, comfort level, upkeep, and vital statistics—size, year launched and most recently refurbished, number of cabins, number of officers and crew, and so on—to help you compare. Size is described both by the length of the ship, which is pretty self-explanatory, and by its tonnage, which is not actual weight but rather the ship's **gross register tonnage (GRT),** which is a measure of the interior space (or volume) used to produce revenue on a ship: 1 GRT equals 100 cubic feet of enclosed, revenue-generating space. Among the crew/officers statistics, an important one is the **passenger/crew ratio,** which tells you approximately how many passengers each crewmember is expected to serve—though this doesn't literally mean a waiter for every two or three passengers; "crew" in this instance includes everyone from officers to deckhands to shop clerks. The ratio is merely another way to compare lines—one crewmember to every two passengers is of course more desirable than one crewmember to every three or four passengers, in terms of getting personalized service.

Note that when several vessels are members of a class—built on the same design, with usually only minor variations in decor and, sometimes, attractions—we've grouped the ships together into one class review.

Each cruise line review also includes a chart showing **itineraries** for each ship the line has assigned to Caribbean, Bermuda, or Panama Canal routes for 2004. Often, a single ship sails on alternating itineraries—for instance, doing an eastern Caribbean route on one cruise and a western Caribbean route the next, ad infinitum until season's end. When this is the case, we've listed both itineraries and noted that they alternate. Consult your travel agent for exact sailing dates.

For those of you who are thinking about taking a non-Caribbean cruise at some point, we've also noted other itineraries sailed by the ships in different seasons. You can find more details on many of these itineraries in *Frommer's Alaska Cruises & Ports of Call* and *Frommer's European Cruises & Ports of Call.*

HOW TO READ THE RATINGS

To make things easier on everyone, we've developed a simple ratings system based on the classic customer-satisfaction survey, rating both the cruise line as a whole and the individual ships as poor, fair, good, excellent, or outstanding on a number of important qualities. The **cruise line ratings** cover all the elements that are usually consistent from ship to ship within the line (overall enjoyability of the experience, dining, activities, children's program, entertainment, service, and value), while the individual **ship ratings** cover those things that vary from vessel to vessel—quality and size of the cabins and public spaces, comfort, cleanliness and maintenance, decor, number and quality of dining options, gyms/spas, and children's facilities—plus a rating for the overall enjoyment of the onboard experience. To provide an overall score, we've given each ship an overall **star rating** (for example, ✮✮½) based on the combined total of our poor-to-outstanding ratings, translated into a 1-to-5 scale:

1	=	Poor	4	=	Excellent
2	=	Fair	5	=	Outstanding
3	=	Good			

In instances where the category doesn't apply to a particular ship (the Windjammer and ACCL ships, for instance, don't have gyms or spas, and none of the adventure ships has children's facilities), we've simply noted "not applicable" (N/A) and absented the category from the total combined score, as these unavailable amenities will be considered a deficiency only if you're a gym fan or you plan to travel with kids.

Now for a bit of philosophy: The cruise industry today offers a profusion of experiences so different that it makes comparing all lines and ships by the same set of criteria completely ludicrous. Think about it: Would you compare a Mercedes to an SUV? A jumbo jet to a hang glider? A Park Avenue apartment to an A-frame in Aspen? No, you wouldn't. That's why, to rate the cruise lines and their ships, **we've used a sliding scale,** rating lines and ships on a curve that compares them only with others in their category—mainstream with mainstream, luxe with luxe, adventure with adventure. Once you've determined what kind of experience is right for you, you can look for the best ships in that category based on your particular needs. For example, if you see in the "Soft-Adventure Lines & Sailing Ships" chapter that Star Clippers achieves an "outstanding" rating for its dining experience, that means that among the lines in that category/chapter, Star Clippers has the best cuisine. It may not be up to the level of, say, the ultraluxurious Seabourn (it's not), but if you're looking for an adventurous cruise that also has great food, this line would be your best bet.

3 Evaluating & Comparing the Listed Cruise Prices

As we explain in detail in chapter 2, the cruise lines' brochure prices are almost always wildly inflated—they're the "sticker prices" cruise line execs would love to get in an ideal world but, in reality, passengers typically pay anywhere from 10% to 50% less. Instead of publishing these inflated brochure rates, then, we've worked with **Just Cruisin' Plus** (✆ **800/888-0922** or 615/833-0922; www.just cruisinplus.com), a full-service travel agency specializing in cruises and vacations, to provide you with samples of the **actual prices** customers were paying through Just Cruisin' Plus for cruises on all ships reviewed in this book (Nov 2003 cruises, priced in mid-Apr). Each ship review includes per diem prices (the total cruise price divided by the number of days to represent the per-person, per-day

Ships at a Glance

Cruise Line	Ship	Frommer's Star Rating
ACCL (soft adventure): A family-owned New England line operating tiny, no-frills ships that travel to offbeat places, carrying casual, down-to-earth older passengers.	Grande Mariner	★★½
Carnival (mainstream): The Wal-Mart of cruising, Carnival specializes in colorful, jumbo-size resort ships that deliver plenty of bang for the buck. If you like the flash of Vegas and the party-hearty of New Orleans, you'll love Carnival's brand of flamboyant fun.	Carnival Conquest	★★★½
	Carnival Destiny	★★★★½
	Carnival Glory	not yet in service
	Carnival Legend	★★★★
	Carnival Spirit	★★★★
	Carnival Triumph	★★★★½
	Carnival Victory	★★★★½
	Celebration	★★★½
	Elation	★★★½
	Fantasy	★★★½
	Fascination	★★★½
	Holiday	★★★½
	Imagination	★★★½
	Inspiration	★★★½
	Jubilee	★★★½
	Paradise	★★★½
	Sensation	★★★½
Celebrity (mainstream): Celebrity offers the best of two worlds: If you like elegance without stuffiness, fun without bad taste, and pampering without a high price, Celebrity is king.	Century	★★★★½
	Constellation	★★★★★
	Galaxy	★★★★½
	Horizon	★★★★
	Infinity	★★★★★
	Millennium	★★★★★
	Summit	★★★★★
	Zenith	★★★★
Clipper (soft adventure): These casual, comfortable small ships focus on offbeat ports and learning.	Nantucket Clipper	★★★½
	Yorktown Clipper	★★★½
Costa (mainstream): Costa's Italian-flavored mid- and megaships offer a moderately priced, festive, international experience, albeit a humble one in the food and service department.	CostaAtlantica	★★★½
	CostaMediterranea	★★★½

Year Built	Gross Tonnage	Passenger Capacity (Double Occupancy)	Passenger/Crew Ratio	Wheelchair Access	2004 Caribbean/Bahamas/Bermuda Itineraries	Full Review on Page
1998	99	100	5.5 to 1	no	11-night E. Carib, Virgin Islands, Caicos/Bahamas, Central America	340
2002	110,000	2,974	2.5 to 1	yes	7-night W. Carib	124
1996	101,353	2,642	2.6 to 1	yes	7-night S. Carib	131
2003	110,000	3,700	2.6 to 1	yes	7-night E. & W. Carib	124
2002	88,500	2,124	2.3 to 1	yes	8-night E., S. & W. Carib, 6-night Bermuda	127
2001	88,500	2,124	2.3 to 1	yes	8-night S. & W. Carib	127
1999	102,000	2,758	2.6 to 1	yes	7-night E. & W. Carib	131
2000	102,000	2,758	2.6 to 1	yes	7-night E. & W. Carib, 6-night Bahamas	131
1987	47,262	1,486	2.2 to 1	yes	4- & 5-night W. Carib	136
1998	47,262	1,486	2.2 to 1	yes	7-night W. Carib	134
1990	70,367	2,040	2.2 to 1	yes	3- & 4-night Bahamas	134
1994	70,367	2,040	2.2 to 1	yes	3-night Bahamas, 4-night W. Carib	134
1985	46,052	1,452	2.2 to 1	yes	4- & 5-night W. Carib	136
1995	70,367	2,040	2.2 to 1	yes	4- & 5-night W. Carib	134
1996	70,367	2,040	2.2 to 1	yes	7-night W. Carib	134
1986	47,262	1,486	2.2 to 1	yes	7-night S. Carib	136
1998	70,367	2,040	2.2 to 1	yes	7-night E. & W. Carib	134
1993	70,367	2,040	2.2 to 1	yes	4- & 5-night W. Carib	134
1995	70,606	1,750	2 to 1	yes	7-night E. & W. Carib	151
2002	91,000	1,950	2 to 1	yes	7-night S. Carib	147
1996	77,713	1,896	2 to 1	yes	10- & 11-night E. & W. Carib, 7-night S. Carib	151
1990	46,811	1,354	2.1 to 1	yes	7-night Bermuda, 7-night W. Carib, 11-night E. Carib	154
2001	91,000	1,950	2 to 1	yes	14-night Panama Canal	147
2000	91,000	1,950	2 to 1	yes	7-night E. Carib	147
2001	91,000	1,950	2 to 1	yes	10-night E. Carib, 11-night W. Carib	147
1992	47,225	1,374	2.1 to 1	yes	7-night Bermuda	154
1984	1,471	100	3.2 to 1	no	7-night E. Carib, 7-night Belize/Honduras	347
1988	2,354	138	3.5 to 1	no	8-night Central America, 7- & 9-night E. Carib	347
2000	85,000	2,112	2.3 to 1	yes	7-night E. & W. Carib	162
2003	85,000	2,112	2.3 to 1	yes	7-night E. & W. Carib	162

Ships at a Glance (continued)

Cruise Line	Ship	Frommer's Star Rating
Crystal (luxury): Fine-tuned and fashionable, Crystal gives passengers pampering service and scrumptious cuisine aboard ships large enough to offer generous fitness, dining, and entertainment facilities.	Crystal Harmony	★★★★ ½
	Crystal Serenity	N/A
	Crystal Symphony	★★★★ ½
Cunard (Euro): A legendary line, offering highbrow British-style cruising on real ocean liners.	QE2	N/A
	Queen Mary 2	N/A
Disney (mainstream): Family ships where both kids and adults are catered to equally, and with style.	Disney Magic	★★★★ ½
	Disney Wonder	★★★★ ½
First European (Euro): Midsize Euro ships.	European Vision	N/A
Holland America (mainstream): Holland America has been in business since 1873, and has managed to hang on to more of its seafaring history and tradition than any line today except Cunard. It offers a moderately priced, classic, and casual yet refined cruise experience.	Maasdam	★★★★
	Noordam	★★★ ½
	Oosterdam	not yet in service
	Rotterdam	★★★★ ½
	Veendam	★★★★
	Volendam	★★★★ ½
	Westerdam	not yet in service
	Zaandam	★★★★ ½
	Zuiderdam	★★★ ½
Mediterranean Shipping (Euro): Low-priced Euro line.	Lirica	N/A
Norwegian (mainstream): NCL makes its mark with its always-casual, open-seating dining, and while its older ships aren't perfect, its newer ones are much better—*Sky, Sun,* and *Dawn* give the newest Royal Caribbean and Princess ships a run for their money.	Norway	★★★
	Norwegian Dawn	★★★★ ½
	Norwegian Dream	★★★
	Norwegian Majesty	★★★
	Norwegian Sea	★★ ½
	Norwegian Sky	★★★★
	Norwegian Sun	★★★★
	Norwegian Wind	★★★
Oceania (mainstream): New casual premium line operating two smallish, intimate ships.	Insignia	not yet in service
	Regatta	not yet in service

Year Built	Gross Tonnage	Passenger Capacity (Double Occupancy)	Passenger/Crew Ratio	Wheelchair Access	2004 Caribbean/Bahamas/Bermuda Itineraries	Full Review on Page
1990	49,400	940	1.7 to 1	yes	10-, 11- & 12-night Carib/Panama Canal; 7-, 12- & 14-night W. Carib; 10- & 12-night E. Carib	282
2003	68,000	1,080	1.7 to 1	yes	7-night W. Carib, 10- & 11-night E. Carib	285
1995	51,044	940	1.7 to 1	yes	7-, 11- & 12-night W. Carib; 11-night W. Carib/Panama Canal; 14-night Carib	282
1969	70,327	1,740	1.8 to 1	yes	15-night E. Carib	286
2003	150,000	2,620	2.1 to 1	yes	8-, 10- & 11-night Carib	287
1998	83,000	1,754	1.8 to 1	yes	7-night E. & W. Carib	172
1999	83,000	1,754	1.8 to 1	yes	3- & 4-night Bahamas	172
2001	58,600	1,500	2.1 to 1	yes	7-night Carib	375
1993	55,451	1,266	2.1 to 1	yes	7-night E. Carib, 7- & 11-night W. Carib, 10-night S. Carib	191
1984	33,930	1,214	2.4 to 1	yes	14-night S. Carib	194
2003	85,000	1,848	2.3 to 1	yes	7-night E. & W. Carib	182
1997	56,652	1,316	2.2 to 1	yes	10-night E. & S. Carib	186
1996	55,451	1,266	2.1 to 1	yes	7-night W. Carib	191
1999	63,000	1,440	2.2 to 1	yes	7-night W. Carib, 10-night S., E. & W. Carib	188
2004	85,000	1,848	2.3 to 1	yes	10-night S. Carib	182
2000	63,000	1,440	2.2 to 1	yes	7-night E. & W. Carib	188
2002	85,000	1,848	2.3 to 1	yes	7-night E. & W. Carib	182
2003	58,600	1,590	2.1 to 1	yes	7-night E. & W. Carib	379
1962	76,049	2,032	2.3 to 1	yes	7-night E. Carib	217
2002	92,250	2,224	2 to 1	yes	7-night Florida/Bahamas	202
1992	50,760	1,748	2.8 to 1	yes	7-night W. Carib	213
1992	40,876	1,460	2.7 to 1	yes	7-night W. Carib, 7-night Bermuda	210
1988	42,276	1,504	2.4 to 1	yes	7-night W. Carib, 7-night Bermuda	215
1999	77,104	2,002	2.7 to 1	yes	7-night S. Carib	207
2001	78,309	1,960	2.7 to 1	yes	7-night W. Carib	207
1993	50,760	1,748	2.8 to 1	yes	7-night W. Carib	213
1998	30,200	684	2 to 1	yes	not yet announced	222
1998	30,200	684	2 to 1	yes	12- & 14-night E. & W. Carib/Panama Canal	222

Ships at a Glance *(continued)*

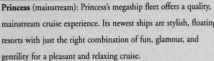

Cruise Line	Ship	Frommer's Star Rating
Princess (mainstream): Princess's megaship fleet offers a quality, mainstream cruise experience. Its newest ships are stylish, floating resorts with just the right combination of fun, glamour, and gentility for a pleasant and relaxing cruise.	Caribbean Princess	★★★★ ½
	Coral Princess	★★★★ ½
	Dawn Princess	★★★★
	Golden Princess	★★★★ ½
	Grand Princess	★★★★ ½
	Island Princess	N/A
	Sun Princess	★★★★
Radisson Seven Seas (luxury): Radisson carries passengers in style and extreme comfort. Its brand of cruising is casually elegant and subtle, and its cuisine is near the top.	Radisson Diamond	★★★ ½
	Seven Seas Mariner	★★★★ ½
	Seven Seas Navigator	★★★★
	Seven Seas Voyager	★★★★ ½
ResidenSea (luxury): A condo at sea.	The World	N/A
Royal Caribbean (mainstream): Fun, well-rounded, activity-packed cruises on attractive, glamorous, but (for the most part) not too over-the-top-glitzy megaships. There's so much going on you might not notice how small the cabins are.	Adventure of the Seas	★★★★ ½
	Brilliance of the Seas	★★★★ ½
	Enchantment of the Seas	★★★ ½
	Explorer of the Seas	★★★★ ½
	Grandeur of the Seas	★★★ ½
	Jewel of the Seas	not yet in service
	Majesty of the Seas	★★★ ½
	Navigator of the Seas	★★★★ ½
	Nordic Empress	★★★ ½
	Radiance of the Seas	★★★★ ½
	Rhapsody of the Seas	★★★ ½
	Serenade of the Seas	N/A
	Sovereign of the Seas	★★★
	Splendour of the Seas	★★★ ½
	Voyager of the Seas	★★★★ ½
Royal Olympia (mainstream): Greek line, offering fast new ships and a destination- and learning-oriented experience	Olympia Explorer	★★★★
	Olympia Voyager	★★★★
Seabourn (luxury): Seabourn's ships are floating pleasure palaces, giving passengers doting service and nearly the finest (if not *the* finest) cuisine at sea.	Seabourn Legend	★★★★
	Seabourn Pride	★★★★

Year Built	Gross Tonnage	Passenger Capacity (Double Occupancy)	Passenger/Crew Ratio	Wheelchair Access	2003 Caribbean/ Bahamas/Bermuda Itineraries	Full Review on Page
2004	116,000	2,600	2.4 to 1	yes	7-night E. & W. Carib	235
2003	91,627	1,970	2 to 1	yes	10-night Panama Canal	231
1995	77,000	1,950	2.2 to 1	yes	10-night E. & S. Carib	239
2001	109,000	2,600	2.4 to 1	yes	7-night E. & S. Carib	235
1998	109,000	2,600	2.4 to 1	yes	7-night W. Carib	235
2003	91,627	1,970	2 to 1	yes	10-night Panama Canal	231
1997	77,000	1,950	2.2 to 1	yes	10-night E. & S. Carib	239
1992	20,295	350	1.7 to 1	yes	4-, 5-, 6- & 7-night S. Carib	299
2001	50,000	700	1.6 to 1	yes	3-night Bahamas/Key West, 4-, 5- & 7-night E. Carib, 7-night W. Carib	294
1999	30,000	490	1.5 to 1	yes	5-, 6-, 7-, 9-, 10- & 11-night E., W. & S. Carib; 7- & 9-night Bermuda, 4-night Bahamas/Key West	297
2003	50,000	700	1.6 to 1	yes	5-, 6- & 7-night W. Carib; 10- & 11-night S. Carib	294
2002	43,000	390	1.2 to 1	yes	Varies weekly	380
2001	142,000	3,114	2.7 to 1	yes	7-night S. Carib	253
2002	90,090	2,100	2.5 to 1	yes	4-, 10- & 11-night W. Carib	249
1997	74,137	1,950	2.5 to 1	yes	4- & 5-night W. Carib	257
2000	142,000	3,114	2.7 to 1	yes	7-night E. & W. Carib	253
1996	74,137	1,950	2.5 to 1	yes	7-night W. Carib, 8-night Bermuda/Carib	257
2004	90,090	2,100	2.5 to 1	yes	Not yet announced at press time	249
1992	73,941	2,354	2.9 to 1	yes	3- & 4-night Bahamas	260
2003	142,000	3,114	2.7 to 1	yes	7-night E. & W. Carib	253
1990	48,563	1,600	2.4 to 1	yes	7-night Bermuda, 7-night W. Carib	262
2001	90,090	2,100	2.5 to 1	yes	7-night E. & W. Carib	249
1997	78,491	2,000	2.5 to 1	yes	7-night W. Carib	257
2003	90,090	2,100	2.5 to 1	yes	7-night E. Carib	249
1988	73,192	2,276	2.7 to 1	yes	3- & 4-night Bahamas	264
1996	69,130	1,804	2.5 to 1	yes	4- & 5-night W. Carib, 11- & 12-night Panama Canal	257
1999	142,000	3,114	2.7 to 1	yes	7-night W. Carib	253
2002	25,000	836	2.3 to 1	yes	12-night Panama Canal	271
2000	25,000	836	2.3 to 1	yes	7-night W. Carib, 15-night Panama Canal, 16-night Amazon	271
1992	10,000	208	1.5 to 1	yes	7-night E. Carib, 14-night E. & W. Carib	308
1988	10,000	208	1.5 to 1	yes	7-night E. & S. Carib	308

Ships at a Glance *(continued)*

Cruise Line	Ship	Frommer's Star Rating
Sea Cloud Cruises (Euro): A deliciously exotic sailing experience that will spoil small-ship lovers forever.	Sea Cloud I	N/A
	Sea Cloud II	N/A
SeaDream (luxury): An upscale yet casual line without the traditional regimentation.	SeaDream I	★★★★
	SeaDream II	★★★★
Silversea (luxury): Silversea caters to guests who won't settle for anything but the best, and offers free-flowing Moët & Chandon champagne, Bulgari bath products, and exceptional service.	Silver Cloud	★★★★
	Silver Whisper	★★★★★
	Silver Wind	★★★★
Star Clippers (soft adventure): With the sails and rigging of classic clipper ships and some of the cushy amenities of modern megas, a cruise on this line's 170- to 228-passenger ships offers adventure with comfort.	Royal Clipper	★★★★
	Star Clipper	★★★ ½
Windjammer (soft adventure): Ultracasual and delightfully carefree, this eclectic fleet of cozy, rebuilt sailing ships (powered by both sails and engines) lures passengers into a fantasy world of pirates-and-rum-punch adventure.	Amazing Grace	★★ ½
	Legacy	★★★ ½
	Mandalay	★★★
	Polynesia	★★★
	Yankee Clipper	★★★
Windstar (luxury): The no-jackets-required policy aboard Windstar sums up the line's casually elegant attitude. The ships feel like private yachts—they're down-to-earth, yet service and cuisine are first-class.	Wind Spirit	★★★ ½
	Wind Surf	★★★★

cost, including port charges but not including taxes) for the following three basic types of accommodations:

- Lowest-priced inside cabin (one without windows)
- Lowest-priced outside cabin (one with windows)
- Lowest-priced suite

Remember that cruise ships generally have several categories of cabins within each of these three basic divisions, all priced differently, and that the prices we've listed represent the *lowest* categories for inside and outside cabins and suites. Remember, too, that these prices are meant as a guide only and are in no way etched in stone—the price you pay may be higher or even lower, depending on

Year Built	Gross Tonnage	Passenger Capacity (Double Occupancy)	Passenger/Crew Ratio	Wheelchair Access	2003 Caribbean/ Bahamas/Bermuda Itineraries	Full Review on Page
1931	2,532	69	1.1 to 1	no	6- & 13-night E. and S. Carib	378
2001	3,000	96	1.7 to 1	no	6- & 13-night E. and S. Carib	378
1984	4,260	110	1.2 to 1	no	4-, 5- & 7-night E. Carib	315
1985	4,260	110	1.2 to 1	no	4-night E. Carib, 7-night E. & S. Carib, 10-night S. Carib	315
1994	16,927	296	1.4 to 1	yes	7-night Bermuda; 7-, 9- & 11-night W. Carib; 9-night E. Carib	323
2001	28,258	388	1.3 to 1	yes	7-night Bermuda; 6- & 8-night W. Carib; 6-, 7-, 9- & 14-night S. Carib; 14-night W. Carib	322
1994	16,927	296	1.4 to 1	yes	7-, 11- & 12-night E., W. & S. Carib	323
2000	5,000	227	2.2 to 1	no	7-night S. Carib	354
1992	2,298	170	2.5 to 1	no	7-night E. & S. Carib	356
1955	1,525	94	2.4 to 1	no	12-night E./S. Carib	369
1959	1,165	120	2.8 to 1	no	5-night S. Carib, 5-night Virgin Islands	367
1923	420	72	2.6 to 1	no	5-night E. Carib, 12-night E. Carib	371
1938	430	126	2.8 to 1	no	5-night E. Carib	371
1927	327	64	2.2 to 1	no	5-night E. Carib	371
1988	5,350	148	1.6 to 1	no	7-night E. Carib	332
1990	14,745	308	1.9 to 1	no	7-night E. & S. Carib	330

when you choose to travel, when you book, what specials the lines are offering, and a slew of other factors. Other travel agencies and online sites may also be able to obtain similar rates.

See chapter 2, "Booking Your Cruise & Getting the Best Price," for more details on pricing and to compare our discount prices with the cruise lines' published brochure rates (in the "Price Comparisons: Brochure Rates vs. Discounted Rates" table). Take a look at that chapter; seeing how much you'll probably save can be a real eye-opener, and should do away entirely with that nasty sense of sticker shock most people get when they start looking at cruise line brochure prices.

6

The Mainstream Lines

These are the shopping malls of cruise ships—they're big, bustling, exciting affairs and attract a cross section of mostly American guests. There's lots to eat, lots to buy on board, and lots of other people sharing the experience with you. You can always hide out on your cabin balcony, though—these ships have hundreds of them—or stake out the corner of a darkened lounge or secluded patch of deck far away from the pool to commune quietly with the sea and your vacation. The theme on these ships is choice, and lots of it.

Granted, the term "mainstream" covers a lot of ground, and that's the point. These ships are generalists, attempting to offer a little something for almost everyone—all ages, backgrounds, and interests. You'll find people with no couth and lots of tattoos downing cans of beer, as well as genteel types with graduate degrees and subscriptions to *Smithsonian* who like to sip sherry. It's a mixed-bag kind of crowd, if there ever was one.

Since the mainstream category is the most popular, it's the one that's seen the most growth, innovation, and investment in recent years, meaning the ships are, as a general rule, remarkably new—and also remarkably **big.** This is the category where the **megaships** reside, those hulking 1,200- to 3,200-passenger floating resorts that offer the widest variety of activities and entertainment. Most of the lines in this chapter (but particularly the "Big Four"—Carnival, Royal Caribbean, Princess, and Norwegian) have been pumping billions into building newer, bigger, and fancier ships, offering a wide variety of different cabins—inside (no windows), outside (with windows), suites, and cabins with private balconies and without. They'll have both formal and several informal dining options, a wide array of entertainment (heavy on the Vegas-style stuff), Internet centers with e-mail access, and more activities than you can possibly squeeze into a day. The lines are on a constant quest to outdo each other with cool stuff you'd never expect to find on a cruise ship, from rock-climbing walls to pottery studios, water slides, and multi-million-dollar art collections (we're talking Warhols and van Goghs). Choose from a dizzying number of things to do, from line-dancing lessons to bingo games, game-show-style contests, singles mixers, port talks, galley tours, spa demos (a ploy, of course, to get you to sign up for one of the expensive spa treatments), art auctions, and nutty contests by the pool that pit passengers against each other to try and stuff the most Ping-Pong balls down their bathing suits, or swim across the pool with a bagel in their mouths (no kidding). Overall, the atmosphere is very social.

Within this category, the more elegant and refined of the lines are commonly referred to as **premium,** a notch up in the sophistication department from others that are described as **mass-market.** Quality-wise, for the most part they're all on equal footing and, overall, are more alike than they are different, especially in areas such as dining and entertainment.

The same can be said for Royal Olympia Cruises and the new Oceania Cruises, whose fleets of midsize ships don't have tons in common with the Carnivals and Royal Caribbeans of the world. Still, these lines fit better in this chapter than any other because they offer well-rounded cruises for a fairly diverse mix of passengers.

Frommer's Ratings at a Glance: The Mainstream Lines

1 = poor   2 = fair   3 = good   4 = excellent   5 = outstanding

Cruise Line	Enjoyment Factor	Dining	Activities	Children's Program	Entertainment	Service	Worth the Money
Carnival	4	3	3	4	4	3	5
Celebrity	5	4	5	3	3	5	5
Costa	3	2	4	2	3	2	3
Disney	4	3	3	5	5	3	4
Holland America	4	3	3	2	4	5	5
Norwegian	4	4	4	3	4	3	5
Oceania	*	*	*	*	*	*	*
Princess	4	3	4	3	4	4	4
Royal Caribbean	5	4	5	4	4	4	5
Royal Olympia	4	3	4	N/A	3	4	4

Note: Cruise lines have been graded on a curve that compares them only with the other mainstream lines. See "How to Read the Ratings," in chapter 5, for a detailed explanation of the ratings methodology.
* Oceania had not yet offered its inaugural cruises at press time.

DRESS CODES   Dress-down Fridays have come to sea! The age of black tie and pearls is quickly transforming into cargo shorts and sandals. Maybe there will be a backlash, but for now the mainstream lines are looking the other way when passengers stroll into the main dining rooms wearing jeans. In fact, Norwegian Cruise Line has become the first line to completely do away with "mandatory" formal nights, though it's officially optional on the night of the captain's cocktail party (and, surprisingly, many do dress up). Aside from Oceania, the rest of the lines in this chapter still officially have 2 formal nights a week that call for dark suits or tuxedos for men and cocktail dresses, sequined numbers, or fancy pantsuits for women—and there still are *some* people who like to get all gussied up. The other 5 nights are some combination of semiformal and casual (mostly casual). On these nights, slacks and polo shirts will work for men, and dresses, pantsuits, or skirts and tops for women. Guests are asked not to wear shorts and T-shirts in the formal dining rooms, but you'll see that some people do anyway. Daytime is casual.

1 Carnival Cruise Lines

3655 NW 87th Ave., Miami, FL 33178-2428. (C) **800/327-9501** or 305/599-2200. Fax 305/406-4740. www. carnival.com.

THE LINE IN A NUTSHELL The Wal-Mart of cruising, Carnival specializes in colorful, jumbo-size resort ships that deliver plenty of bang for the buck. If you like the flash of Vegas and the party-hearty of New Orleans, you'll love Carnival's brand of flamboyant fun.

THE EXPERIENCE Nobody does it better in the party department. The line with the most recognized name in the biz serves up a very casual, down-to-earth, middle-American Caribbean vacation. While food and service are pretty average, there sure are a lot of choices to keep most people satisfied, from round-the-clock entertainment to sushi bars, upscale supper clubs on the Spirit-class ships, and the smoke-free atmosphere of *Paradise.*

The line's decor, like its clientele, has mellowed a bit since its riotous, partying beginnings, but each ship is still an exciting collage of textures, shapes, and images. Where else but on these floating playlands would you find life-size mannequins of Hollywood stars such as Marilyn Monroe and Humphrey Bogart, a San Francisco trolley car, or real oyster-shell wallpaper? The outrageousness of the decor is part of the fun: Carnival ships provide a fantasyland you can't get at home. Call it whatever you want, but don't call it dull.

Pros
- **Fun, theme-park ambience** and fanciful decor are unmatched.
- **Large standard cabins:** At 185 square feet or larger, Carnival's standard inside and outside cabins are among the roomiest in the mainstream category.
- **Melting pot at sea:** Passengers range from 20-something singles and honeymooners to families with young kids to even grandparents.
- **An insomniac's delight:** When passengers on most ships are calling it a night, Carnival's guests are just getting busy with diversions such as midnight adult comedy shows, raging discos, and 24-hour pizza parlors.

Cons
- **You're never alone:** Not in the hot tubs, on shore excursions, in the pool, while sunbathing, at the gym, at the frozen-yogurt machine . . .
- **Limited port info:** Port lectures and information handouts revolve around shopping; there's next to nothing on history and culture.
- **No enrichment lectures:** Activities are pretty much confined to fun and games on the pool deck; no guest speakers or wine tasting classes like most other mainstream lines offer.

Compared with the other mainstream lines, here's how Carnival rates:

	Poor	Fair	Good	Excellent	Outstanding
Enjoyment Factor				✓	
Dining			✓		
Activities			✓		
Children's Program				✓	
Entertainment			✓		
Service			✓		
Worth the Money				✓	

Booked aisle seat.

Reserved room with a view.

With a queen – no, make that a king-size bed.

With Travelocity, you can book your flights and hotels together, so you can get even better deals than if you booked them separately. You'll save time and money without compromising the quality of your trip. Choose your airline seat, search for alternate airports, pick your hotel room type, even choose the neighborhood you'd like to stay in.

Travelocity

Visit www.travelocity.com
or call 1-888-TRAVELOCITY

CARNIVAL: BIG LINE, BIG FUN

Carnival has enjoyed an extended run as Big Kahuna of the cruise world. The assets of its parent company, Carnival Corporation, are enormous and growing: In addition to its own fleet of 19 ships, Carnival Corp. holds full ownership of Cunard, Seabourn, Costa, Windstar, and Holland America Line—all told, more than 50% of the North American cruise industry. And, most recently, Carnival beat out Royal Caribbean to acquire P&O Princess, adding yet another major cruise brand to its cruise dynasty. When all is said and done, Carnival Corp. will operate a combined fleet of 66 ships, with another 17 scheduled for delivery over the next few years, equating to 100,000 and 42,300 berths, respectively.

The origins of the Miami-based company were as precarious as they were accidental. Company patriarch Ted Arison, a somewhat reclusive billionaire who passed away in 1999, had sold an air-freight business in New York in 1966 and intended to retire to his native Israel to enjoy the fruits of his labor—after a few more little ventures. After he negotiated terms for chartering a ship, he assembled a group of paying passengers, then discovered that the ship's owner could no longer guarantee the vessel's availability. According to latter-day legend, a deal was hastily struck whereby Arison's passengers would be carried aboard a laid-up ship owned by Knut Kloster, a prominent Norwegian shipping magnate. The ship was brought to Miami from Europe, and the combination of Arison's marketing skill and Kloster's hardware created an all-new entity that, in 1966, became the corporate forerunner of Norwegian Cruise Line.

After a bitter parting of ways with Kloster, Carnival got its start in 1972 when Arison bought *Empress of Canada,* known for its formal and somewhat stuffy administration, and reconfigured it into Carnival's first ship, the anything-but-stuffy *Mardi Gras.* After a shaky start—the brightly painted ship, carrying hundreds of travel agents, ran aground just off the coast of Miami on its first cruise—Arison managed to pick up the pieces and create a company that, under the guidance of astute and tough-as-nails company president Bob Dickinson and chairman Micky Arison (Ted's son), eventually evolved into the most influential trendsetter in the cruise ship industry. The rest is history, as they say.

Today, Carnival's fleet includes 19 ships, most of which cruise the Caribbean and Bahamas year-round. The 110,000-ton 2,974-passenger *Carnival Glory,* sister to *Conquest,* is slated to debut in July 2003 (just before this book hits the stores); a third sister, *Carnival Valor,* will follow in fall 2004; and a fourth, *Carnival Liberty,* a year after that. A fourth Spirit-class ship, the 88,500-ton *Carnival Miracle,* is set to debut in spring 2004.

PASSENGER PROFILE

In the old days, Carnival was as party-oriented as a college frat house, with about the same vibe: Heidi sailed in 1996 when more than 500 graduating high-school seniors practically took over (and ruined) a cruise on *Celebration.* She still gets nightmares. Guidelines implemented in early 1997 put a stop to all of that, mandating that no one under 21 can sail unless sharing a cabin with an adult over 25, with exceptions made for married couples and young people traveling with their parents in separate cabins. So, while you'll still find teen groups on board (especially Mar–June), things are not what they were.

Today, Carnival's passengers are a melting pot—couples, singles, and families; young, old, and lots in between—and span the whole range from Ralph Lauren shirts and Gucci glasses to Mötley Crüe T-shirts and tattoos. Carnival estimates about 30% of passengers are under age 35, another 40% are between 35 and 55,

---

Carnival's Vacation Guarantee
Unhappy with your Carnival cruise? Dissatisfied guests may disembark at their first non-U.S. port of call and, subject to some restrictions, get a refund for the unused portion of their cruise and reimbursement for coach-class airfare back to their ship's home port. To qualify, passengers must inform the ship's purser before their first port of call.

---

and 30% are over age 55. At least half of all passengers are first-time cruisers. While it's one of the best lines to choose if you're single, Carnival's ships certainly aren't overrun by singles—families and couples are definitely in the majority. The line's 2-, 3-, 4-, and 5-night cruises tend to attract the most families with kids and the highest number of 20- and 30-something single friends traveling together in groups.

Regardless of their age, passengers tend to be young at heart, ready to party, and keyed up for nonstop, round-the-clock activities. Many have visited the casinos of Las Vegas and Atlantic City and the resorts of Cancún and Jamaica, and are no strangers to soaking in sardine-can hot tubs, sunbathing, hitting the piña coladas and beer before lunch, and dancing late into the night.

The typical Carnival passenger likes to dress casual, even at dinner, with jogging suits, jeans, and T-shirts just as prevalent as Dockers, sundresses, and Hush Puppies on all but formal nights—and even on formal nights, it's not uncommon for some passengers to run back to their cabins to change out of their dressier duds and put on shorts or jeans before heading out to the discos and bars. Tuxedos are in the minority here.

DINING

Carnival has often been at the forefront of cruise innovation, but in the dining department, the line doesn't offer the degree of flexibility that NCL, and to a lesser extent Princess, does. Yes, there's **casual buffet dining** as an alternative to the main restaurants fleetwide (as most lines offer these days), but the line still offers only formal dinner seatings rather than allowing passengers to eat when and where they want. Granted, there are four different seatings on most ships rather than the traditional two, but you can choose only to dine early (5:45 and 6:15pm) or late (8 or 8:30pm), with the line selecting your exact time. The Spirit-class ships retain the traditional two seatings.

Carnival's food quality and presentation, while much improved from its early days, is still pretty average, and for the most part on par with Royal Caribbean, Princess, and NCL. Carnival's fare is fine if you've got humble-enough tastes. You'll find interesting dishes, such as honey-basted filet of salmon, roasted quail, and West Indian pumpkin soup, on the dinner menus, in addition to such all-American favorites as surf and turf and prime rib, plus pasta dishes, grilled salmon, broiled halibut, and Thanksgiving-style turkey served with all the trimmings. Unfortunately, the preparation is uneven (like it often is on lines such as Royal Caribbean), and it sometimes takes two or three tries to get your meat cooked the way you like it. At lunch, you'll now find appetizers such as sushi and fried calamari, and entrees such as focaccia filled with arugula, roasted peppers, and fresh mozzarella, and a linguini dish in a light tomato sauce with julienne of tomatoes and hickory smoked ham. **Healthier "Nautica Spa" options** and **vegetarian choices** are also on each menu.

Despite the hectic pace and ambience, dining service is usually friendly and somewhat classier than in earlier years, if not always the most efficient. The staff still presents dessert-time song-and-dance routines, although the parades of flaming Cherries Jubilee and Baked Alaska have, for safety reasons, been curtailed. Sophistication goes only so far, however: The line still has its waiters handle all wine service, rather than employing sommeliers.

Carnival Spirit, which debuted in spring 2001, was the line's first to have a **reservations-only restaurant,** a two-level venue serving steaks and other dishes for a $25-per-person cover charge (plus tip and not including wine). Subsequent Spirit-class ships—and all future Carnival ships—will feature the same. At the opposite end of the alternative-dining spectrum, guests aboard all Carnival ships can opt to have any meal in the **buffet-style Lido restaurants** at no extra charge. For an unstructured and casual dinner, walk in any time between about 6 and 9:30pm for serve-yourself entrees such as chicken, pasta, and stir-fry. It's barely a cut above Cracker Barrel, but it's casual and available anytime. At lunch, buffets in the Lido feature the usual suspects—salads, meats, cheeses, pastas, grilled burgers, and chicken filets, and several hot choices such as fish and chips, roast turkey, or stir-fry. The buffets also feature specialty stations at lunch, serving up things such as pasta or Chinese food or a Cajun fish dish. At times, the buffet line gets backed up as passengers wait for bins to be restocked and servers scramble to fill them.

But wait, there's more: Carnival ships give you **24-hour pizza** (anywhere from 500–800 pies are flipped a day!); calzones that are surprisingly tasty; Caesar salad with or without chicken; and self-serve soft ice cream and frozen yogurt, as well as a complimentary **sushi bar** (on *Fascination, Inspiration, Ecstasy, Elation, Paradise, Fantasy, Imagination, Jubilee, Celebration, Carnival Conquest,* and *Carnival Glory*) and a deli on some vessels. There are nightly **midnight buffets,** with a gala, pull-out-all-the-stops buffet once per cruise. The newest ships also have specialty (*read:* not free) **coffee and pastry bars.**

All ships offer **24-hour room service** from a limited "beef and brie on a baguette" kind of menu, and kids can select from **children's menus.** For kids under age 21, there are convenient Fountain Fun Cards that can be purchased for unlimited soft-drink purchases ($10 for a 3-night cruise, up to $26 for 8-day voyages). There's an adult version too, charging between $17 for 3-night cruises and $39 for 8-nighters.

ACTIVITIES

Carnival doesn't skimp in the keeping-busy department, so there's never a dull moment—you can run from one activity to the next all day long if you want to, though there's not as much variety as aboard lines such as Norwegian and Celebrity (*read:* no enrichment lectures or wine-tasting seminars). By day, the main pool decks are the heart of the action, and between the blaring bands and microphone-wielding social hosts whipping up interest in pillow-fighting competitions, belly-flop contests, or Austin Powers dancing lessons, you'll barely be able to hear yourself think. Lest things get too out of hand, uniformed security guards watch over the pool deck and bars. On all but the line's oldest ships, it's a little quieter up on the second tier of the Sun Deck, and each ship has a quieter pool and sunbathing area at the stern, sans loudspeakers. Spirit-class vessels have a second midships pool separated by plastic glass dividers and a bar that tend to keep most of the noise out and provide a more serene lounging space; one of the four pools on the Conquest-class ships is quieter and covered by a retractable glass roof.

Handy Hot Line

Carnival offers a **24-hour hot line** for help with unexpected snafus or emergencies. Call ✆ **877/885-4856** toll free, or 305/406-4779.

Slot machines begin clanging at 8am in the **casinos** when the ships are at sea, and waiters and waitresses in bright pink and blue uniforms start tempting passengers with trays of fruity theme cocktails long before the lunch hour. There are **line-dancing and ballroom classes,** trivia contests, facial and hairdo demonstrations, singles and newlywed parties, game shows, shuffleboard, bingo, art auctions, and movies. You can spend some time in the roomy **gyms** on the Fantasy-, Destiny-, Spirit-, and Conquest-class ships (gyms are tiny afterthoughts on the three oldest ships) or playing volleyball on the top deck, or treat yourself to one of dozens of relaxing treatments in the Steiner-managed **spas.** All ships have covered and lighted **golf driving nets,** with golf pros sailing on board to give lessons with video analysis starting at $25 for a 15-minute session and $80 for an hour.

Not surprisingly, with this pace, you won't find any focus on quiet times except in the subdued, handsome-looking library/game rooms and **24-hour Internet centers** on each ship. There are no educational lectures on art, history, or other cerebral topics, such as you'll find aboard Celebrity, Norwegian, HAL, and other lines.

CHILDREN'S PROGRAM

Carnival is right up there with the best ships for families—the line estimates that about 350,000 kids sailed aboard its ships in 2002. A few hundred children per cruise is pretty normal, and there can be as many as 700 to 800 on Christmas and New Year's cruises. There are a lot of children around in summer too, when it'll be difficult to find a kid-free hot tub or even a kid-free disco for that matter (not an issue for the ships with teen clubs). On Carnival's post-1990 ships, the **child facilities** are fairly extensive, with the Conquest-class, Spirit-class, and Destiny-class ships and *Elation, Paradise,* and *Fantasy* offering the biggest and brightest playrooms in the fleet, featuring a climbing maze, arts and crafts, oodles of toys and games, a 16-monitor video wall showing movies and cartoons, and computer stations loaded with the latest educational and entertainment software.

The **Camp Carnival program** offers supervised kids' activities on sea days from 9am to 10pm (and 2–10pm on port days) for ages 2 through 15 in four age groups: toddlers 2 to 5, juniors 6 to 8, intermediates 9 to 11, and teens 12 to 15. Eight to 12 counselors organize the fun and games, which include face painting, computer games, puzzles, fun with Play-Doh, picture bingo, pirate hat–making, and pizza parties for toddlers. For juniors, there's PlayStation 2, computer games, ice-cream parties, story time and library visits, T-shirt coloring, and swimming. For intermediates, there are scavenger hunts, trivia and bingo, Ping-Pong, video-game competitions, arts and crafts, computer games, dance classes, and talent shows. There are even **"homework help" sessions** available for kids who need to keep up while on vacation. **Teen clubs,** which had been phased out a few years back due to a supposed lack of interest, are being phased back in for big kids between 12 and 18. Besides karaoke parties, computer games, scavenger hunts, talent shows, card and trivia games, and Ping-Pong, there are movies and dance parties in the teen clubs, and most ships are also equipped with iMacs. Of course, teens can also hang out in the video arcades—the newest ships have virtual-reality games. On *Triumph* and *Destiny*, you'll also find big-screen TVs.

As if that's not enough, the entire fleet has children's wading pools, and for bigger kids there's that great signature snaking slide at the main pool of each ship.

Supervised children's activities are offered from 7 to 10pm nightly, after which time group, **slumber-party-style babysitting** for ages 4 months through age 11 is available till 3am in the playroom. No private babysitting is available. In addition to these hours, Carnival also now offers group babysitting between 8am and noon (sometimes as late as 6pm, depending on when the ship arrives in port) on port days for the under 2 set, for $6 per hour for the first child, $4 per hour for each additional child. And yes, counselors will change diapers! Parents with kids age 8 and under checked into the children's program get free use of beepers, in case their kids need to contact them. Strollers are available for rent fleetwide (except on *Celebration*).

Mom and Dad can get an earlier start on their kid-free evening on formal nights, when the counselors supervise **kids' mealtime** in the Lido restaurant between about 6 and 7pm in a special section reserved for kids. The children's dining room menu, printed on the back of a fun coloring/activity book (crayons are provided), features the usual favorites—hot dogs, hamburgers, french fries, chicken nuggets, pepperoni pizza, peanut-butter-and-jelly sandwiches, banana splits, Jell-O, and a daily special.

A **turndown service** for kids includes complimentary chocolate-chip cookies on their pillows at bedtime on the first and last nights of their cruise. Cribs are available with prior notice. Children must be at least 4 months old to sail on board.

ENTERTAINMENT

Aboard its newer megaships, Carnival has spent millions on stage sets, choreography, and sound equipment. The theaters on the Destiny-class, Spirit-class, and Conquest-class ships are spectacular three-deck extravaganzas, and the casinos are so large you'll think you landed in Vegas; but even aboard its smaller, older ships, Carnival consistently offers some of the most lavish entertainment extravaganzas afloat.

Carnival megaships each carry about 8 to 16 flamboyantly costumed dancers (fewer on *Celebration, Jubilee,* and *Holiday*) for twice-weekly **Vegas-style musicals.** One or two live soloists carry the musical part of the show, while dancers lip-sync the chorus. A 6- to 10-piece orchestra of traditional and digital instruments deftly accompanies the acts each night, sometimes enhanced by synchronized recorded music. You'll also find comedians, jugglers, acrobats, rock 'n' roll bands, country-and-western bands, classical string trios, pianists, and Dorsey- or Glenn Miller–style big bands, all performing, if not simultaneously, at least during the same cruise, and sometimes on the same night. Special entertainment may include a local mariachi band when a ship's in port late in Cozumel.

Deals for Seniors

AARP members receive a $100-per-cabin discount on Carnival's 7-night-plus cruises, and $50 on 3-, 4-, and 5-night Bahamas and Caribbean cruises. Seniors should mention their membership when booking their cruise.

Carnival Fleet Itineraries

Ship	Itineraries
Carnival Conquest	**7-night W. Carib:** Round-trip from New Orleans, year-round, visiting Montego Bay (Jamaica), Grand Cayman, and Cozumel, with 3 days at sea. **Non-Caribbean Itineraries:** None.
Carnival Destiny	**7-night S. Carib:** Round-trip from San Juan, year-round, visiting St. Thomas, Martinique, Barbados, and Aruba, with 2 days at sea. **Non-Caribbean Itineraries:** None.
Carnival Glory	**7-night E. Carib:** Round-trip from Port Canaveral, year-round, visiting Nassau, St. Thomas, and Sint Maarten, with 3 days at sea. Alternates with **7-night W. Carib:** Round-trip from Port Canaveral, year-round, visiting Key West, Belize, and Cozumel and Progreso/Merida (Mexico), with 2 days at sea. **Non-Caribbean Itineraries:** None.
Carnival Legend	**8-night E. Carib:** Round-trip from New York, Sept–Oct 2003 and Apr–Sept 2004, visiting San Juan, St. Thomas, and Tortola (BVIs), with 4 days at sea. **8-night S. Carib:** Round-trip from Fort Lauderdale, Nov 2003–Apr 2004 and Oct 2004–Mar 2005, visiting Sint Maarten, Barbados, and Martinique, with 4 days at sea. Alternates with **8-night W. Carib:** Round-trip from Fort Lauderdale, Nov 2003–Apr 2004 and Oct 2004–Mar 2005, visiting Belize, Limon (Costa Rica), and Colón (Panama), with 4 days at sea. **6-night Bermuda:** Round-trip from Philadelphia (Oct 21, 2003) and Baltimore (Oct 28, 2003), visiting King's Wharf/West End, with 2 days at sea. **Non-Caribbean Itineraries:** None.
Carnival Spirit	**8-night S. Carib:** Round-trip from Miami, Nov 2003–Mar 2004, visiting Sint Maarten, Barbados, and Martinique, with 4 days at sea. Alternates with **8-night W. Carib:** Round-trip from Miami, Nov 2003–Mar 2004, visiting Belize, Limon (Costa Rica), and Colón (Panama), with 4 days at sea. **Non-Caribbean Itineraries:** Panama Canal repositioning cruises, Hawaii, Alaska.
Carnival Triumph	**7-night E. Carib:** Round-trip from Miami, year-round, visiting San Juan, St. Thomas, and Sint Maarten, with 3 days at sea. Alternates with **7-night W. Carib:** Round-trip from Miami, year-round, visiting Cozumel, Grand Cayman, and Ocho Rios (Jamaica), with 3 days at sea. **Non-Caribbean Itineraries:** None.
Carnival Victory	**7-night E. Carib:** Round-trip from Miami, Nov 2003–May 2004, visiting San Juan, St. Thomas, and Sint Maarten, with 3 days at sea. Alternates with **7-night W. Carib:** Round-trip from Miami, Nov 2003–May 2004, visiting Cozumel, Grand Cayman, and Ocho Rios (Jamaica), with 3 days at sea. **6-night Bahamas:** Round-trip from Norfolk, VA (Oct 5 and 11, 2003, and June 10, 2004), and Charleston, SC (Oct 20, 2003, and May 31, 2004), visiting Freeport and Nassau, with 2 days at sea. **Non-Caribbean Itineraries:** New England/Canada.
Celebration	**4-night W. Carib:** Round-trip from Galveston, TX, year-round, visiting Cozumel, with 2 days at sea. Alternates with **5-night W. Carib:** Round-trip from Galveston, TX, year-round, visiting Cozumel and Playa del Carmen, with 2 days at sea. **Non-Caribbean Itineraries:** None.
Elation	**7-night W. Carib:** Round-trip from Galveston, TX, year-round beginning Sept 2003, visiting Progreso/Merida and Cozumel (Mexico) and Belize, with 3 days at sea. **Non-Caribbean Itineraries:** None.
Fantasy	**3-night Bahamas:** Round-trip from Port Canaveral, year-round, visiting Nassau, with 1 day at sea. Alternates with **4-night Bahamas:** Round-trip from Port Canaveral, year-round, visiting Freeport and Nassau, with 1 day at sea. **Non-Caribbean Itineraries:** None.

Ship	Itineraries
Fascination	**3-night Bahamas:** Round-trip from Miami, year-round, visiting Nassau, with 1 day at sea. Alternates with **4-night W. Carib:** Round-trip from Miami, year-round, visiting Key West and Cozumel, with 1 day at sea. **Non-Caribbean Itineraries:** None.
Holiday	**4-night W. Carib:** Round-trip from New Orleans, year-round, visiting Cozumel, with 2 days at sea. Alternates with **5-night W. Carib:** Round-trip from New Orleans, year-round, visiting Playa del Carmen and Cozumel, with 2 days at sea. **Non-Caribbean Itineraries:** None.
Imagination	**4-night W. Carib:** Round-trip from Miami, year-round, visiting Key West and Cozumel, with 1 day at sea. Alternates with **5-night W. Carib:** Round-trip from Miami, year-round, visiting Belize and Key West, with 2 days at sea. **Non-Caribbean Itineraries:** None.
Inspiration	**7-night W. Carib:** Round-trip from Tampa, year-round, visiting Grand Cayman, Belize, and Costa Maya and Cozumel (Mexico), with 2 days at sea. **Non-Caribbean Itineraries:** None.
Jubilee	**7-night S. Carib:** Round-trip from San Juan, year-round beginning Sept 2003, visiting St. Thomas, Antigua, St. Lucia, Dominica, St. Kitts, and Tortola (BVIs). **Non-Caribbean Itineraries:** None.
Paradise	**7-night E. Carib:** Round-trip from Miami, year-round, visiting Nassau, Santa Domingo (Dominican Republic), and St. Thomas, with 3 days at sea. Alternates with **7-night W. Carib:** Round-trip from Miami, year-round, visiting Belize, Isla Roatan (Honduras), Grand Cayman, and Cozumel, with 2 days at sea. **Non-Caribbean Itineraries:** None.
Sensation	**4-night W. Carib:** Round-trip from Tampa, year-round, visiting Cozumel, with 2 days at sea. Alternates with **5-night W. Carib:** Round-trip from Tampa, year-round, visiting Grand Cayman and Cozumel, with 2 days at sea. **Non-Caribbean Itineraries:** None.

Besides the main theater, most entertainment happens somewhere along the indoor Main Street–like promenade (except on the Spirit-class ships, which are more spread out). Called the "Something-or-other Boulevard" or "Something-or-other Way," it stretches along one entire side of each ship and is lined with just about the entire repertoire of the ships' nightclubs, bars, lounges, patisseries, and disco and casino. One bar on all the Fantasy-, Destiny-, and Spirit-class ships welcomes cigar smoking, and fleetwide (except aboard the nonsmoking *Paradise*), cigars are sold at the pool bar and during midnight buffets.

By day, entertainment includes a Caribbean-style calypso or steel-drum band performing Bob Marley tunes and other pop songs on a deck poolside, and a pianist, guitarist, or string trio playing in the atria of the line's newest ships.

SERVICE

All in all, a Carnival ship is a well-oiled machine, and you'll certainly get what you need—but not much more. When you board, for instance, you're welcomed by a polite and well-meaning staff at the gangway, given a diagram of the ship's layout, and then pointed in the right direction to find your cabin on your own, carry-on luggage in tow. Chalk it all up to the size of the line's ships. It's a fact of life that service aboard all megaliners is simply not as attentive as that aboard smaller vessels—with thousands of guests to help, your dining-room waiter and cabin steward have a lot of work ahead of them and have little time for chitchat. Lines can get long at the breakfast and lunch buffets and, at certain times, at the pizza counter, though there always seem to be plenty of drink waiters and waitresses roaming the pool decks, looking to score drink orders.

Service certainly doesn't benefit from Carnival's **automatic tipping policy.** Gratuities for the crew are automatically added to your account at the end of your cruise to the tune of $9.75 per person per day fleetwide, and they're divvied up among the staff automatically. You can adjust the amount—or eliminate it completely and hand out cash in envelopes—by visiting the purser's desk. As aboard Norwegian and Princess ships, which use the same system, waiters and cabin stewards don't seem as eager to please as they did when the tip carrot was hanging directly over them.

There is a **laundry service** aboard each ship for washing and pressing only (with per-piece charges), as well as a handful of **self-service laundry rooms** with irons and coin-operated washers and dryers. Be sure to bring your own shampoo: a small basket of trial-size toiletries is stocked in each cabin bathroom, but its contents are not automatically refilled.

The Conquest Class: Carnival Conquest • Glory (preview)

The Verdict

Like a stretch model of the slightly shorter Destiny-class vessels and souped up with a supper-club concept from the Spirit series, *Carnival Conquest* also brings the fleet's largest children's and teen's facilities—all packaged in an eye-pleasing decor of warm colors and Impressionist images.

Carnival Conquest *(photo: Carnival Cruise Lines)*

Specifications

Size (in tons)	110,000	Officers	Italian/Internat'l
Number of Cabins	1,487	Crew	1,160 (Internat'l)
Number of Outside Cabins	917	Passenger/Crew Ratio	2.5 to 1
Cabins with Verandas	556	Year Launched	2002
Number of Passengers	2,974	Last Major Refurbishment	N/A

Frommer's Ratings (Scale of 1–5)   ★★★★ ½

Cabin Comfort & Amenities	4.5	Dining Options	4
Ship Cleanliness & Maintenance	5	Gym & Spa Facilities	5
Public Comfort/Space	4.5	Children's Facilities	4.5
Decor	4	Enjoyment Factor	4

The 110,000-ton 2,974-passenger *Carnival Conquest* is the largest Carnival vessel to date, with sisters *Carnival Glory* following in mid-2003, *Carnival Valor* in fall 2004, and *Carnival Liberty* a year later. The $500-million Conquest-class ships closely resemble the Destiny series, though they stretch about 60 feet longer and add Spirit-class features such as supper clubs. If all berths are occupied, each Conquest liner can carry a bowl-you-over 3,700 passengers (plus more than 1,000 crew). These mondo megas boast more than 20 bars and lounges, Carnival's largest children's facilities, and an entire, separate zone dedicated to teens.

Cabins & Rates

Cabins	Per Diems from	Sq. Ft.	Fridge	Hair Dryer	Sitting Area	TV
Inside	$83	185	yes	yes	no	yes
Outside	$104	185–220	yes	yes	yes	yes
Suite	$300	275–345	yes	yes	yes	yes

CABINS   *Carnival Conquest's* standard outside cabins measure a roomy 220 square feet. These categories (6A and 6B) take up most of the Riviera and Main decks. Of the ship's outside cabins, 60% (556 of 917) offer balconies. The standard balcony cabins (categories 8A–8E) measure a still ample 185 square feet plus a 35-square-foot balcony. For those who simply must have a bigger balcony, a little extra dough buys an "extended balcony" (60 sq. ft.) or "wrap-around large balcony." There's only a handful of these category-9A accommodations, and they're tucked all the way aft on Upper, Empress, and Verandah decks. The 42 suites are a full 275 square feet plus a 65-square-foot balcony, and bigger still are the 10 Penthouse Suites at 345 square feet plus an 85-square-foot balcony. Most of the suites are sandwiched in the middle of the ship on Deck 7 and between two other accommodations decks, eliminating the danger of noisy public rooms above or below. Specially designed family staterooms, at a comfortable but not roomy 230 square feet, are located one deck below the children's facilities, and a couple of them can be connected to the room next door. In lieu of a private veranda, these family staterooms feature floor-to-ceiling windows for ocean views.

All categories of cabins come with a TV, safe, hand-held hair dryer (not the wall-mounted, hand-scorching variety), mini-fridge, desk/dresser, chair and stool, and bathroom with shower. A handy new amenity in standard bathrooms is the makeup/shaving mirror. Curiously, telephones do not have voice mail.

Connecting cabins are available. There are 28 cabins for passengers with disabilities.

PUBLIC AREAS   Unlike earlier Carnival ships, *Conquest* is brighter and more playful—a sort of Mardi Gras feel instead of the dark and glittery Las Vegas look. Architect Joe Farcus was inspired by the great Impressionist and post-Impressionist artists—not only their paintings but also their color palette—so *Conquest* bursts with sunny yellows and oranges and vivid blues and greens. The general arrangement closely resembles that of the Destiny class with a pair of two-story main dining rooms (one midships, one aft), a three-deck-high showroom in the bow, and a secondary lounge in the stern.

As on the Destiny ships, here, too, passengers step across the gangway and into the base of a soaring, nine-deck-high atrium. This Artists' Lobby—as it's known on *Conquest*—is decked out in a large mural collage of the most recognizable works by masters such as Claude Monet, Paul Gauguin, and Edgar Degas, and backlit flowers of Murano glass pop from the granite-topped atrium bar. The perky flowers and Impressionist montage are picked up along the interior promenade and other public areas of a vessel that sports 22 bars and lounges. Many of these rooms, dedicated to artists, are clustered on the Atlantic and Promenade decks.

The 1,500-seat Toulouse-Lautrec Show Lounge stages Carnival's big production shows in an ambience of lipstick red, gold, and posters depicting Parisian cabaret dancers. Degas Lounge, the secondary entertainment venue, hosts a dance band and late-night comedians. Bronze sculptures of ballerinas with real tulle tutus pose in niches around this room, where classical music is perhaps the only genre that isn't played. Combos belt out oldies, country, and requests in Vincent's (as in van Gogh), the sunniest room on the ship with pale wood floors and sunflower murals. A Matisse painting inspired the Blue Piano Bar, nestled beside a wine bar.

Nobody does disco better than Carnival, and Henri's Dance Club is the best of the best. Here you can groove on an enormous floor in a jungle ambience straight from the exotic paintings of Henri Rousseau, or just perch with a drink on the lotus-shaped barstools. One deck down is Alfred's Bar, named for the pioneering Impressionist Alfred Sisley, and the room is the ship's most elegant with its wood paneling and dark, rich colors. Web surfers have to troop through Alfred's to access the Internet Cafe, oddly tucked away off a back corner of the room.

Tahiti Casino sprawls across 8,500 square feet. The area is decorated with reproductions of Gauguin's Polynesian beauties and packs in almost 300 slot machines and about two dozen gaming tables. Tucked off to one side is the sports bar, a dark, fun, little Tiki-hut type hideaway with carved-wood tables and chairs that practically shouts "Mai tai!"

The ship boasts by far the biggest children's facilities in the fleet: at 4,200 square feet, Children's World is more than triple the space of the kiddie areas on Destiny-class ships. It sits atop the spa (instead of sharing the same deck as on the Destiny vessels) and holds an arts-and-crafts center, video room, library, computer lab, and PlayStation 2 game units. The enclosed adjacent deck offers a dipping pool. The ship's nod to teenagers is a big nod. Teen facilities on earlier ships were, at most, a room, but here's a space so large it forms its own secondary promenade branching off Impressionist Boulevard. The Montmartre zone has a soda bar and separate dance floor flowing into a large video games area.

DINING OPTIONS *Conquest's* pair of two-story main restaurants are named Monet and Renoir. The monumental sunflower marking the entrance to Monet is by the Murano glass artist Luciano Vistosi, while artwork in the Renoir Restaurant is inspired by the cafe scene in the painting *Lunch at the Restaurant Fournaise.* (How many art-savvy Carnival passengers will give a hoot?) Broiled lobster tail pops up on the menu once a cruise, and there are six desserts nightly. Low-fat, low-salt Spa Carnival Fare, vegetarian dishes, and children's selections are available.

Casual dining, from breakfast through dinner (plus a 24-hr. pizzeria) is at the two-story Restaurant Cezanne on the Lido Deck. Separate buffet lines (more than on the Destiny ships, to alleviate crowding) are devoted to Asian and American dishes, deli sandwiches, salads, and desserts. A new concept (on Cezanne's upper level) is Sur Mer: Carnival modestly describes this as a fish-and-chips shop, but the choices include goodies such as calamari, lobster salad, and bouillabaisse. There's no charge here or for the stand-up sushi bar down on Impressionist Boulevard, but the pastries, cakes, and specialty coffees at the patisserie cost a couple bucks each.

Carnival Conquest borrows the by-reservation supper club from the Spirit-class ships. The Point serves USDA prime-aged steaks, crab claws from Joe's Stone Crab Restaurant on Miami Beach, and other deluxe items for a

$25-per-person cover charge. On the Spirit ships, the club sits under a glass portion of the ship's funnel, but *Conquest*'s room has low ceilings and a more intimate feel. The best food and most refined service on board are here, where dinner is meant to stretch over several hours and several bottles of wine (for which there's an extra charge).

There's also 24-hour room service with new menus including items such as a focaccia sandwich with grilled zucchini, fresh mozzarella, and portobello mushrooms, plus the standard tuna salad, cookies, fruit, and so on.

POOL, FITNESS & SPA FACILITIES   *Conquest*'s four swimming pools include the main Sun Pool with its two whirlpools and a stage for live music. If you don't love reggae and calypso, don't go here. This space is where all the action (and noise) of pool games plus the occasional outbreak of line dancing occurs. (Anyone for the Electric Slide?) Carnival's trademark twisty slide shoots into the Star Pool one deck up. The aft Sky Pool, covered by a retractable glass dome, usually provides a more restful setting, although the pizzeria and burger grill are here (along with two more whirlpools). The fourth pool is the one for kiddies outside Children's World.

The ship's 12,000-square-foot health club and salon with separate steam and sauna rooms for men and women perches high on Deck 11. Called the Carnival Spa, it's run by Steiner, the company that controls most cruise-ship spas. Today's latest treatments are offered, from hot (well, warmed) rock massages to hair and scalp massages. On the fitness side, you'll find the usual aerobics offerings, plus fancier stuff like pilates and spinning (for $10 a class). These spas, like the Spirit-class, are Carnival's only spas to have an appealing decor; they're totally spartan on other vessels. The entrance is sleekly contemporary, with a glossy blue-tile floor and red-tile appointment desk. The hot tub, in a glass-enclosed space jutting into the fitness room, faces a wall of fake boulders and greenery, straight out of *The Flintstones*.

The jogging track loops above an open deck so that no cabins underneath get pounded.

The Spirit Class: Carnival Spirit • Legend

The Verdict

Bright and fun like the larger Destiny-class vessels, with the same multistory dining and entertainment venues, the Spirit class also boasts some impressive firsts, such as a reservations-only restaurant and wedding chapel.

Carnival Spirit *(photo: Gero Mylius, Indav Ltd.)*

Specifications

Size (in tons)	88,500	Crew	930 (Internat'l)
Number of Cabins	1,062	Passenger/Crew Ratio	2.3 to 1
Number of Outside Cabins	849	Year Launched	
Cabins with Verandas	682	*Spirit*	2001
Number of Passengers	2,124	*Legend*	2002
Officers	Italian/Internat'l	Last Major Refurbishment	N/A

Frommer's Ratings (Scale of 1–5)   ★★★★

Cabin Comfort & Amenities	5	Dining Options	4
Ship Cleanliness & Maintenance	4	Gym & Spa Facilities	4
Public Comfort/Space	4	Children's Facilities	4
Decor	4	Enjoyment Factor	4

When the $375-million *Carnival Spirit* debuted in April 2001, she ushered in a new class for the fun-ship line. Bigger than Carnival's eight Fantasy-class ships and smaller than its three Destiny-class vessels, the 2,124-passenger, 88,500-ton, 960-foot *Spirit*, *Pride* (which doesn't sail in the Caribbean this year), and *Legend* update Carnival's rubber-stamp style with a handful of innovations and more elegance, placing them closer to the newest Royal Caribbean and Princess vessels than to Carnival's earlier fun ships. The Spirit ships eliminate the cluster of nightclubs in favor of stretching the music venues from bow to stern on Decks 2 and 3, and there's an appealing new supper club. A state-of-the-art "teleradiology" system enables the ship's doctors to digitally transmit X-rays and other patient information to medical facilities on shore for consultation on a broad range of medical situations.

Interestingly, the Spirit-class ships bear more than a little resemblance to Costa's 4-year-old *CostaAtlantica* and newer sister *Mediterranea:* Their hull and superstructure were built from identical plans, and Carnival design guru Joe Farcus did the decor for them all.

A fourth Spirit-class ship, *Carnival Miracle,* is set to debut in spring 2004.

Cabins & Rates

Cabins	Per Diems from	Sq. Ft.	Fridge	Hair Dryer	Sitting Area	TV
Inside	$91	185	no	yes	some	yes
Outside	$112	185	no	yes	yes	yes
Suite	$291	275–300	yes	yes	yes	yes

CABINS The Spirit-class ships have verandas on more than 60% of their cabins, though most are pretty small, with a white plastic chair, a small table, and a deck chair. (Cabins with larger balconies are amidships and aft on Decks 6, 7, and 8.) Their 213 inside cabins and outsides without balconies are a roomy 185 square feet (standard outsides with balconies are the same size plus a 40-sq.-ft. balcony). Of the 44 category-11 suites, most measure 275 square feet, plus an 85-square-foot balcony, while 10 located at the stern of Decks 4 through 8 measure 245 square feet, plus a jumbo wraparound 220-square-foot balcony. The six category-12 suites measure 300 square feet, plus a 115-square-foot balcony. On Deck 4, all category-5A cabins have lifeboats obstructing the view, though they do have sliding-glass doors that allow you to lean out into the fresh air.

In a subtle departure from the minimalist, somewhat cold cabin decor of the rest of Carnival's older ships, the Spirit's cabins are warmer and more sophisticated, with toasted-caramel wood-tone furniture and mango- and coral-hued upholstery, drapes, and bedspreads. Lighting fixtures are more stylish but don't throw a lot of light on the desk mirror, which usually doubles as a makeup mirror. Also, there are none of those great little reading lights over the beds like the rest of the fleet offers, just lamps on the night tables.

All cabins, even the least expensive inside ones, have a decent amount of storage space in both closets and drawers (with small leather handles that some people find difficult to grab hold of), plus a safe, TV, desk and stool, chair, bathroom with a shower stall that is a tad larger than that on other ships, and glass shelves on either side of the large mirror to stash your toiletries. Just about all cabins have a small sitting area with a sofa and coffee table (some insides have only a chair and table), and all have a real hair dryer (stored in the desk/vanity drawer).

Connecting cabins are available. There are 16 cabins for passengers with disabilities.

PUBLIC AREAS Carnival designer Joe Farcus works his whimsy once again aboard the Spirit-class ships, blending marble, wood-veneer walls, tile mosaic work, buttery leathers, rich fabrics, copper and bronze, Art Nouveau and Art Deco themes, and all manner of glass lighting fixtures. These ships are glitzy and blinding in the same fun Vegas way as the rest of the Carnival fleet.

A guitar player with synthesized backup performs throughout the day at the lower-level lobby bar that anchors each ship's spectacular, jaw-dropping, nine-deck atrium, even more of a central hub than aboard earlier Carnival ships owing to its placement amidships. Just about all the indoor action is on Decks 2 and 3, where you'll find the piano bar (on *Spirit*, it's a neat Oriental-style spot with carved rosewood detailing, paper-lantern lighting fixtures, a red lacquer piano, and rich Chinese silk walls), large sports bar, disco, jazz nightclub (where karaoke and other contests are held), cafe (where you can purchase specialty coffees and pastries), combination library and Internet center, elegant string of shops, modern-style wedding chapel, and photography studio where passengers can make appointments for formal portraits—honeymooners take note. (Photographs can be digitally enhanced with borders, and a variety of photo-related souvenirs are sold.) The lounge tucked into the bow on Deck 1, at the end of a corridor of cabins (called the Versailles Lounge on *Spirit* and Firebird Lounge on *Legend*), is so well hidden it's often empty.

The three-level showrooms are something to see; on *Spirit*, Farcus had Verdi's Egypt-themed opera *Aida* in mind when he covered it head to toe in brightly painted gold-and-blue King Tut–style sarcophagi and hieroglyphics. Sightlines are severely limited from parts of the Deck 2 and Deck 3 level, so arrive early if you want a decent view. The disco is a two-story barrel-shaped place with a giant video wall; on *Spirit*, the funky spot has a Jackson Pollock–inspired splatter-painted design.

The ships' broad outdoor promenade is wonderfully nostalgic, but unfortunately does not wrap around the entire ship; near the bow you are channeled through a door and it suddenly (and oddly) becomes enclosed and narrower, turning into a cute but kind of odd jungle-themed area lined with comfy chairs and small tables with views through jumbo-size portholes. The kids' playroom and a video arcade are tucked away in the far forward reaches of the bow on Decks 4 and 5. The playroom is decent-size, but nowhere near the size and scope of what you'll find on the newer Conquest-class fleetmates or Royal Caribbean's Radiance- and Voyager-class ships or Disney's *Magic* and *Wonder*, with a handful of iMacs and Sony PlayStations. The video arcade is huge, with 30-plus machines, including air hockey and foosball.

DINING OPTIONS The Spirit ships have one sprawling, two-story, 1,300-seat formal dining room (offering traditional early and late seatings) and a huge, well-laid-out indoor/outdoor casual buffet restaurant. Menu items range from standard American to French, Italian, and Asian, but don't expect to be bowled over by the preparation and service unless Denny's is your idea of gourmet. On a recent cruise, desserts were disappointing.

The Spirit ships are the first in the Carnival fleet to also offer an alternative reservations-only restaurant for more intimate dining. Charging $25 per person, the two-story Nouveau Supper Club sits high up at the uppermost section of the atrium, directly forward of the ships' smokestack, and has a ceiling of glazed glass. Service is more gracious, and dedicated sommeliers are on hand to take your wine order. Menus are leather-bound, and elegant table settings feature beautiful Versace plates. Tables for two and four are available, and two musicians serenade diners with soft ballads. There's even a dance floor. The menu includes steaks, from New York Strip to porterhouse and prime rib, as well as dishes such as grilled lamb chops, Chilean sea bass, and stone crabs from Miami's famous Joe's Stone Crab (though those served here are frozen—not fresh like at Joe's). The experience is intentionally designed to be slow and lingering, so don't go if you're looking for a fast meal. The food and service are the best you'll find on Carnival. Only drawback: Rowdy crowd noise sometimes filters up from the atrium bar below.

As aboard the rest of the fleet, there's delicious 24-hour pizza and Caesar salad offered from a counter in the buffet restaurant. You can get a tasty deli sandwich from the New York Deli all day long, and self-serve frozen yogurt and soft ice cream are also on hand. Caviar and champagne combos are available in certain bars on each ship.

POOL, FITNESS & SPA FACILITIES Till now, Carnival's spas have had a bland, institutional look, so the ones aboard the Spirit-class ships are a welcome change—*Spirit*, for instance, sports a Greek-inspired motif of white fluted columns and images of Greek gods on the walls. The multilevel gyms are based loosely on a Greek amphitheater, and though they're more than adequate, with dozens of machines, they're a bit more cramped than the huge spaces on the Destiny-class ships.

In general, there are lots of places for sunbathing across the three topmost decks, including the area around the two main pools amidships on the Lido Deck, as well as around a third pool on the aft end of this deck. All told, there are four hot tubs (including one in the gym), plus a jogging track, combination volleyball/basketball court, and shuffleboard. A fun, snaking water slide for kids and adults is sequestered high up and aft on a top deck, and adjacent is a small, sort of forlorn, fenced-in kids' wading pool. With no shade up on this part of the ship, don't forget to put sunscreen on your kiddie's delicate skin—or your own, for that matter.

The Destiny Class:
Carnival Destiny •
Triumph • Victory

Carnival Destiny *(photo: Carnival Cruise Lines)*

The Verdict

These three behemoths capture the classic Carnival whimsy with mind-boggling design features, yet have a somewhat mellower color scheme than the line's older ships—but let's not split hairs, they're still bright.

Specifications

Size (in tons)				
		Triumph	508	
Destiny	101,353	*Victory*	508	
Triumph	102,000	Number of Passengers		
Victory	102,000	*Destiny*	2,642	
Number of Cabins		*Triumph*	2,758	
Destiny	1,321	*Victory*	2,758	
Triumph	1,379	Officers	Italian/Internat'l	
Victory	1,379	Crew	1,000 (Internat'l)	
Number of Outside Cabins		Passenger/Crew Ratio	2.6 to 1	
Destiny	806	Year Launched		
Triumph	853	*Destiny*	1996	
Victory	853	*Triumph*	1999	
Cabins with Verandas		*Victory*	2000	
Destiny	480	Last Major Refurbishment	N/A	

Frommer's Ratings (Scale of 1–5)　　　　　★★★★ ½

Cabin Comfort & Amenities	5	Dining Options	3.5
Ship Cleanliness & Maintenance	4	Gym & Spa Facilities	5
Public Comfort/Space	4.5	Children's Facilities	4
Decor	4	Enjoyment Factor	4.5

Taller than the Statue of Liberty, these 13-deck ships cost $400 to $440 million apiece and carry 2,642 passengers based on double occupancy and 3,400-and-change with every additional berth filled (and some cruises do indeed carry a full load). All three are nearly identical, though *Triumph* and *Victory* are a tad larger than *Destiny* (having an additional deck at top) and are reconfigured in a few minor ways. *Destiny* was the first cruise ship ever built to exceed 100,000 tons, and her sheer size and spaciousness inspired the cruise industry to build more in this league: After her debut, Princess launched the 109,000-ton Grand class, Royal Caribbean introduced the massive 142,000-ton Voyager class, Cunard began construction of the 150,000-ton *Queen Mary 2,* and Carnival's newest class, the 110,000-ton Conquest ships, debuted.

Cabins & Rates

Cabins	Per Diems from	Sq. Ft.	Fridge	Hair Dryer	Sitting Area	TV
Inside	$76	185	no	yes	no	yes
Outside	$97	220	no	yes	yes	yes
Suite	$282	275–345	yes	yes	yes	yes

CABINS   The Destiny-class sisters, along with the new Conquest-class ships, have the line's biggest standard outside cabins, with the category-6A and -6B cabins (which take up most of the Riviera and Main decks) measuring 220 square feet; the rest of the fleet's standard outsides measure 185 square feet—still very roomy. If that's not enough, more than 60% of the Destiny sisters' outside cabins (480–508 of them) have sitting areas and private balconies. That's compared to a paltry 54 private verandas out of 618 outside cabins on Carnival's Fantasy-class ships.

There are two categories of suites: Veranda Suites measuring 275 square feet, plus a 65-square-foot balcony, and Penthouse Suites where you can live like a king with 345 square feet, plus an 85-square-foot balcony. Both are located on Deck 7, smack dab in the middle of the ship. Specially designed family staterooms, at a comfortable but not roomy 230 square feet, are located convenient to children's facilities, and many of them can be connected to the stateroom next door. In lieu of a private veranda, these family-friendly staterooms feature floor-to-ceiling windows for ocean views. All standard cabins have a TV, safe, hair dryer, desk, dresser, chair and stool, and bathroom with shower.

A total of 25 cabins on *Destiny* and 27 on *Triumph* and *Victory* are wheelchair accessible. Connecting cabins are available.

PUBLIC AREAS   At the time these ships were designed, Carnival interior designer Joe Farcus never had so much public space to play with, and he took full advantage. The ships are dominated by staggering nine-deck atria with casual bars on the ground level, and the three-deck-high showrooms are a sight—*Destiny's* was the first of this magnitude on any cruise ship, and subsequent models tread a fine line between outrageous and relatively tasteful: for example, *Triumph's* wacko chandelier, which looks like DNA strands made from crystal golf balls, topped with little Alice-in-Wonderland candleholders. The ships' mondo casinos span some 9,000 square feet and feature more than 300 slot machines and about two dozen gaming tables. A photography studio enables passengers to make appointments for formal portraits, which is especially nice for honeymooners. Photographs can be digitally enhanced with borders, and photo-related souvenirs are sold.

Many of the ships' 12-plus bars and entertainment venues are located along the bustling main drag of the Promenade Deck. The Sports Bar on each ship boasts multiple TV monitors projecting different sporting events simultaneously. Each ship has a wine bar, a cappuccino cafe, and a piano bar, which aboard *Triumph* is a bizarre New Orleans–themed place called the Big Easy, sporting thousands of real oyster shells covering its walls (collected from New Orleans' famous Acme Oyster House—only on Carnival!). Each also has a sprawling disco with a wild decor: On *Victory,* an arctic motif features black faux-fur bar stools, while *Triumph's* decor is much more reserved, with wacky little Barney-purple chairs and glass panels and tubes filled with bubbling water throughout. One deck below is an elegant lounge for a drink or a cigar: On

Triumph, it's a clubby place called the Oxford Bar, with dark wood paneling, leather furniture, and gilded picture frames (too bad you can hear the disco music pounding above late at night). High tea is often served here, though it's really too big for that kind of old-world, intimate ritual. The ships' Internet centers are adjacent to this lounge.

Each ship has several shopping boutiques, a spacious beauty salon, a library, and a card room, plus a large children's playroom and video arcade.

Note: As part of *Victory's* oceans-of-the-world theme, sculpted seahorses support the staircase railings throughout the ship. All fine and dandy, but their protruding snouts are hazardous if you don't watch where you're going. Heidi got a wicked black-and-blue mark on her leg to prove it.

DINING OPTIONS   Each ship has a pair of two-level dining rooms with ocean views from both the main floor and the mezzanine level, as well as a two-story indoor/outdoor casual buffet restaurant that includes two specialty food stations that make Asian stir-fry and deli-style sandwiches to order. There's also a grill section for burgers, fries, and kielbasa-size hot dogs, a salad bar, and a dessert island. Specialty coffee bars and patisseries sell gourmet goodies for about $2 to $5 a pop, and caviar and champagne combos are available in certain bars on each ship. Oddly, on our last *Triumph* cruise, we could find absolutely no cookies aboard except for sale at the patisserie. This is a development we don't like one bit.

POOL, FITNESS & SPA FACILITIES   Along with the Conquest-class ships, facilities are the most generous among the Carnival vessels, with four pools (including a kids' wading pool); seven whirlpools; and a 214-foot, two-deck-high, corkscrew-shaped water slide.

The tiered, arena-style decks of the sprawling midships Lido pool area provide optimal viewing of the band and stage, pool games, and all the hubbub that happens in this busy part of the ship. Along with two whirlpools, *Destiny* has swim-up bars at two of its main pools; *Triumph* and *Victory* eliminated the swim-up bars in exchange for more deck space, larger pools, and the addition of a wading area a few inches deep surrounding the pools. Unfortunately, this area can be very difficult to get across, due to a lack of obvious "corridors" through all the deck chairs. The aft pool area on all three ships features two whirlpools and a retractable roof that covers it all, enabling deck activities and entertainment to continue even in rainy weather. On *Triumph* and *Victory,* the big stage adjacent to the main Continent pool is even bigger than the one on *Destiny,* and it has been reconfigured to allow more space for guests at deck parties, and to make the pool deck more open and visually appealing. Another modification is the placement of a small performance stage aft on the Lido Deck near the New World pool.

Even though the ships' huge gyms aren't as large as those on Royal Caribbean's Voyager class, Carnival's are much roomier and actually feel bigger. The two-deck-high, 15,000-square-foot spa and fitness centers feature more than 30 state-of-the-art exercise machines, including virtual-reality stationary bikes. There's a juice-bar-cum-aerobics room, men's and women's saunas and steam rooms, and a pair of hot tubs. Spas offer all the latest treatments (at the latest high prices), but as on all Carnival ships (except for the newer Spirit and Conquest classes), they're surprisingly drab, and the only place to wait for your masseuse is on a cold, high-school-locker-room bench, wrapped in a towel—no robes are provided. So much for ambience.

The well-stocked 1,300-square-foot indoor/outdoor children's play center has its own pool and is nicely sequestered on a top deck, out of the fray of the main pool deck areas. The ships also have virtual-reality video arcades that promise hours of fun.

The Fantasy Class: Fantasy • Sensation • Fascination • Imagination • Inspiration • Elation • Paradise

Fantasy *(photo: Carnival Cruise Lines)*

The Verdict

These time-tested favorites are the line's original megas, and their whimsical decor and endless entertainment and activities spell excitement from the get-go.

Specifications

Size (in tons)	70,367	*Sensation*	1993
Number of Cabins	1,020	*Fascination*	1994
Number of Outside Cabins	618	*Imagination*	1995
Cabins with Verandas	54	*Inspiration*	1996
Number of Passengers	2,040	*Elation*	1998
Officers	Italian/Internat'l	*Paradise*	1998
Crew	920 (Internat'l)	Last Major Refurbishment	
Passenger/Crew Ratio	2.2 to 1	*Fantasy*	2000
Year Launched		All Others	N/A
Fantasy	1990		

Frommer's Ratings (Scale of 1–5)   ★★★½

Cabin Comfort & Amenities	4	Dining Options	3
Ship Cleanliness & Maintenance	4	Gym & Spa Facilities	3.5
Public Comfort/Space	4	Children's Facilities	4
Decor	3.5	Enjoyment Factor	4

These Fun Ships and their risqué names offer a successful combination of hands-on fun and a glamorous, fantasyland decor, with acres of teak decking plus all the diversions, distractions, and entertainment options for which Carnival is famous. They really are fun! (Or are they cheesy? It's such a fine line.) Each was built on the same cookie-cutter design at Finland's Kvaerner Masa shipyard (at a cost of $225 million–$300 million each), and they are nearly identical in size, profile, and onboard amenities, with different decorative themes. These ships have been run hard and they're starting to look a bit worn out compared to their newer fleetmates.

From the first ship of the series *(Fantasy)* to the last *(Paradise)*, the ships' decor evolved toward a relatively mellow state. *Fantasy,* which was refurbished in late 2000, features a new Roman-themed entertainment promenade inspired (loosely of course) by the ancient city of Pompeii, with a faux-stone floor, terra-cotta urns, Doric columns, and electric torches—but where's the flowing lava?

Fascination is big on flashy fantasy, with a retina-shattering chrome atrium and a heavy Broadway and Hollywood movie-star theme, with life-size (though worn-looking) mannequins of legends such as John Wayne and Marilyn Monroe, while *Sensation* avoids obvious razzle-dazzle in favor of artwork enhanced with ultraviolet lighting, sound, and color. Aboard *Imagination,* miles of fiber-optic cable make the mythical and classical artwork glow in ways the Greek, Roman, and Assyrian designers of the originals never would have imagined. *Inspiration* was reportedly inspired by artists such as Toulouse-Lautrec and Fabergé and architects such as Frank Lloyd Wright—though in a . . . brighter style.

Paradise is just that if you're a nonsmoker. Launched in 1998, the ship, with design motifs in some rooms based vaguely on the great Atlantic ocean liners, is the industry's only completely smoke-free ship. Neither passengers nor crew may light up anywhere aboard, not even on the open decks. Those caught trying are fined $250, booted off at the next port of call, and left to fly home at their own expense. To date, several dozen passengers and a handful of crewmembers have been discharged. You'll notice that apparently smoking and drinking really do go hand in hand because the bars and discos on *Paradise* are noticeably less bustling than those on other Carnival ships.

Cabins & Rates

Cabins	Per Diems from	Sq. Ft.	Fridge	Hair Dryer	Sitting Area	TV
Inside	$64	185	no	no	no	yes
Outside	$78	185	no	no	no	yes
Suite	$228	330	yes	no	yes	yes

CABINS   Accommodations range from lower-deck inside cabins with upper and lower berths to large suites with verandas, king-size beds, sitting areas, and balconies. As with the entire fleet, standard cabins here are roomy at 185 square feet and minimalist in design, with stained-oak trim accents and conventional, monochromatic colors such as salmon red—subdued compared to the flamboy-ance of the public areas. The cabins are not big on personality but are functional and well laid out.

There are 26 demi-suites and 28 suites, all with private verandas. The 28 330-square-foot suites each have a whirlpool tub and shower, an L-shaped sofa that converts into a foldaway bed, a whirlpool bath, a safe, a minibar, a walk-in closet, and sliding-glass doors leading to a 70-square-foot private balcony, and are positioned midway between stern and bow, on a middle deck subject to the least tossing and rocking during rough weather.

All cabins, even the least expensive inside ones, have enough storage space to accommodate a reasonably diverse wardrobe, and feature safes, TVs, desk and stool, chair, reading lights for each bed, and bathrooms with roomy showers and generous-size mirrored cabinets to store your toiletries.

About 20 cabins on each ship are suitable for passengers with disabilities. Connecting cabins are available.

DINING OPTIONS In addition to a pair of big one-story dining rooms with windows, there's a large indoor/outdoor casual buffet restaurant. You'll also find specialty coffee bars and patisseries on *Fantasy* and *Paradise* selling gourmet goodies for about $2 to $5 a pop. There's a complimentary sushi bar serving fresh, tasty sushi in late afternoons on *Paradise, Fascination, Imagination,* and *Inspiration,* with sake available for an extra charge. Caviar and champagne combos are available in certain bars on each ship.

PUBLIC AREAS Each ship boasts the same configuration of decks, public lounges, and entertainment venues, including a six-story atrium flanked by glass-sided elevators, casinos, new Internet centers, and at least eight bars, plus several (usually packed) whirlpool tubs. The cluster of disappointing shops on each ship is surprisingly cramped and won't be winning any design awards.

POOL, FITNESS & SPA FACILITIES Although totally blah in the decor department, the 12,000-square-foot spas and fitness areas are well equipped. Each has a roomy, mirrored aerobics room and a large, windowed, Pepto Bismol–colored gym with (last time we counted) seven treadmills, five stationary bikes, two rowing machines, two step machines, and dozens of free weights. Each has men's and women's locker rooms and massage rooms (both areas surprisingly drab and institutional feeling), as well as a sauna and steam room, whirlpools, and three swimming pools, one of which has a spiraling water slide. The Sun Deck of each ship offers an unobstructed ⅛-mile jogging track covered with a rubberized surface.

Holiday • Jubilee • Celebration

The Verdict

Fun ships, yes, but these older Carnival vessels are outdated and frumpy compared to their slick, glamorous newer sisters.

Jubilee *(photo: Carnival Cruise Lines)*

Specifications

Size (in tons)		Officers	Italian/Internat'l
Celebration/Jubilee	47,262	Crew	
Holiday	46,052	*Celebration/Jubilee*	670 (Internat'l)
Number of Cabins		*Holiday*	660 (Internat'l)
Celebration/Jubilee	743	Passenger/Crew Ratio	2.2 to 1
Holiday	726	Year Launched	
Number of Outside Cabins		*Holiday*	1985
Celebration/Jubilee	453	*Jubilee*	1986
Holiday	447	*Celebration*	1987
Cabins with Verandas	10	Last Major Refurbishment	
Number of Passengers		*Holiday*	1998
Celebration/Jubilee	1,486	*Celebration/Jubilee*	1999
Holiday	1,452		

Frommer's Ratings (Scale of 1–5)　　　🐠🐠🐠

Cabin Comfort & Amenities	3	Dining Options	3
Ship Cleanliness & Maintenance	3	Gym & Spa Facilities	2
Public Comfort/Space	3	Children's Facilities	3
Decor	3	Enjoyment Factor	4

While these mid-1980s ships, built for about $100 million to $170 million apiece, can't compare with their new post-1990 sisters in the style and amenities departments, they still successfully offer that wild-and-crazy brand of Carnival fun. *Celebration* and *Jubilee* are identical sisters, while *Holiday* is virtually the same with a few differences (such as the configuration of cabins in the aft of the Main and Empress decks). Though about half the size of the newer Destiny-class ships, they're still not small in any normal sense. But if you want a slightly cozier ship—and can do without the latest high-tech bells and whistles—you'll find these ships more intimate and easier to explore than a megaship (and a good thing, too, because they sail short itineraries, giving you less time to settle in and start having fun). Their per diem rates are also often a little lower than the rest of the fleet's.

The decor encompasses all the colors of the rainbow, with healthy doses of chrome, brass, and mirrors a la the late 1970s, early-1980s disco scene. There's no atrium, and the Pool Deck of each ship can get crowded and cramped at high noon. Refurbishments over the past few years on *Celebration* and *Jubilee* included replacing hot tubs with new models; installing new carpeting, tile, counters, and equipment for the buffet restaurants; and adding a new video-game arcade and a photo gallery. The cramped Lido buffet restaurants on both have been remodeled, creating a more open area; teak flooring was replaced with tile and carpeting, and a new pizzeria was also installed. *Holiday's* 1998 enhancements were similar, and also included refurbishment of the spa, gym, and several entertainment areas.

Cabins & Rates

Cabins	Per Diems from	Sq. Ft.	Fridge	Hair Dryer	Sitting Area	TV
Inside	$92	186	no	no	no	yes
Outside	$105	186	no	no	no	yes
Suite	$217	374	yes	no	yes	yes

CABINS　Like the standard cabins in the entire Carnival fleet, they're big. Done in blond wood tones with pinky-red accenting, they're clean and uncluttered, though nothing to write home about, and are all virtually identical. Beds can be configured as twins or doubles, and each cabin has piped-in stereo music as well as a wall-mounted TV. The medium-size bathrooms have showers.

At 374 square feet, the 10 suites on the Verandah Deck of each ship are as large and comfortable as those offered aboard vessels charging a lot more. Each has a whirlpool tub and shower, an L-shaped sofa that converts into a foldaway bed, a safe, a minibar, a walk-in closet, and sliding-glass doors leading to an 87-square-foot private balcony.

Just over a dozen cabins are wheelchair accessible. There are no connecting cabins.

PUBLIC AREAS   You may need to keep your sunglasses on even when you're inside: Public areas explode with color in that original outrageous Carnival way. We're talking healthy doses of fuchsia, black, red, chrome, brass, glass, and neon. On *Celebration,* there's a bar designed like the inside of a trolley car, and the Red Hot Piano Bar is just that—all red. One of *Jubilee's* lounges has a wooden gazebo painted in pastels and covered with lights, and on *Holiday* one bar features an authentic British bus from 1934. In all, the ships have seven bars, six entertainment lounges, a casino, a disco, a library, and a video arcade. There's also a children's playroom, a beauty salon, and boutiques. Elevators interconnect all eight decks.

DINING OPTIONS   Two main one-story dining rooms and one casual indoor/outdoor buffet restaurant serve breakfast, lunch, and dinner. On *Celebration* and *Jubilee,* you'll find a complimentary sushi bar open in late afternoons, with sake available for an extra charge.

POOL, FITNESS & SPA FACILITIES   Even though the gyms and spas were remodeled and expanded in 1998 and 1999, you can tell fitness just wasn't a big priority when these ships were built—they're tiny and drab, with a sauna for men and women and a small hair salon. Each ship has two hot tubs and three pools, including a small wading pool for children and a pool with a snaking water slide.

2 Celebrity Cruises

1050 Caribbean Way, Miami, FL 33132. ℂ **800/437-3111** or 305/539-6000. Fax 800/722-5329. www.celebrity-cruises.com.

THE LINE IN A NUTSHELL   Celebrity offers the best of two worlds: If you like elegance without stuffiness, fun without bad taste, and pampering without a high price, Celebrity is king.

THE EXPERIENCE   With the most elegant big ships in the industry, Celebrity offers a refined cruise experience, yet one that is fun and active. Each ship is spacious, glamorous, and comfortable, mixing sleekly modern and Art Deco styles and throwing in cutting-edge art collections to boot.

An exceedingly polite and professional staff contributes greatly to the elegant mood. Dining-wise, Celebrity shines with its dashing alternative restaurants on the Millennium-class ships. Featuring the signature cuisine of celebrity chef Michel Roux, they're the best at sea for both quality of food and their gorgeous decor.

Like all the big-ship lines, Celebrity offers lots for its passengers to do, but its focus on mellower pursuits and innovative programming sets it apart. Niceties such as roving a cappella groups lend a warmly personal touch, while expert-led seminars on personal investing, divorce-coping strategies, and handwriting analysis offer a little more cerebral meat than the usual.

Celebrity gets the "best of" nod in a lot of categories: The AquaSpas on the line's megaships are the most attractive at sea, the art collections the most compelling fleetwide, the lounges the most plush, and the onboard activities among the most varied. Celebrity pampers suite guests with butler service, and treats all guests to in-cabin pizza delivery.

Pros

- **Spectacular spas:** Beautiful and well equipped, the spas on the Millennium- and Century-class ships are the best at sea today.
- **Best alternative restaurants at sea:** Service, food, and wine are simply excellent; and the Millennium-class restaurants' elegant decor incorporates artifacts from cherished old liners, such as *Olympic, Normandie,* and SS *United States.*
- **Innovative everything:** Entertainment, spas, and cuisine are some of the most innovative in the industry. The latest: a few adults-only cruises.

Cons

- **Lots of potential extra costs:** Between the heavily promoted (if optional) art auctions, the many boutiques, pricey spa treatments, wine tastings, Cova Cafés, logo beach towels, and $25 cover charge in the alternative restaurants, there are a lot of things vying for your dollars (as on all mainstream lines today).

Compared with the other mainstream lines, here's how Celebrity rates:

	Poor	Fair	Good	Excellent	Outstanding
Enjoyment Factor					✓
Dining				✓	
Activities					✓
Children's Program			✓		
Entertainment			✓		
Service					✓
Worth the Money					✓

CELEBRITY: THE BEST OF TWO WORLDS

What's not to love? Celebrity offers moderately priced cruises that feel like they should cost a lot more.

Celebrity's roots go back to the powerful Greek shipping family Chandris, whose patriarch John D. Chandris founded a cargo shipping company in 1915. The family expanded into the cruise business in the late 1960s and by 1976 had the largest passenger-cruise fleet in the world. In the late 1970s, they introduced the down-market Chandris-Fantasy Cruises, which served a mostly European market. Fantasy dissolved in 1989 just as the Chandris family pushed into the Caribbean marketplace in a big, big way by creating Celebrity Cruises, building great ships that got better each time. The company's rise to prominence was so rapid and so successful that in 1997 it was courted and acquired by the larger and wealthier Royal Caribbean Cruises, Ltd., which now operates Celebrity as a sister line to Royal Caribbean International. So far it's been a fortuitous marriage: Reservations, bookkeeping, maintenance, and provisioning were merged, but Celebrity has maintained its own very fine identity. With their crisp navy-blue-and-white hulls and rakishly angled funnel decorated with a giant X (actually the Greek letter *chi*, as in Chandris, the line's founding family), the profiles of Celebrity's 10 ships rank among the industry's most distinctive.

PASSENGER PROFILE

Celebrity tries to focus on middle- to upper-middle-income cruisers, and even wealthy patrons who want the best megaship experience out there (while happily nestled in one of the line's amazing Penthouse Suites); but these days, with Celebrity's rates comparable to those of Carnival and Royal Caribbean, you'll find a very wide range of folks aboard, those who appreciate the elegance of its ships, and those who could care less. Clients who choose their cruise based on more than just price like Celebrity because it's not Carnival and because it offers a well-balanced cruise, with lots of activities and a glamorous, exciting atmosphere that's both refined (think champagne and cozy lounges) and fun (think "dress your husband up in women's clothes" contests).

Most passengers are couples in their mid-30s and up (the average age in 2002 was 49), with decent numbers of honeymooners and couples celebrating anniversaries, as well as families with children in summer and during the holidays.

DINING

While Celebrity loves touting **executive chef Michel Roux** and his food, and while the dining service is tops in the mainstream category, the cuisine in the main dining rooms isn't really *that* much better than what's being served these days on the newest Royal Caribbean, Princess, and Disney ships. When you're serving dinner to 800 people at once, it can only be so good. What *is* a million times better is the cuisine, service, and ambience offered in the intimate **alternative restaurants** on the Millennium-class ships. Here, Michel Roux and his impressively high service and food standards are able to really shine, making the experience well worth the $25 cover charge. There seem to be more waitstaff than diners in the restaurants, which seat just over 100 passengers; Caesar salads and zabaglione are prepared tableside, and an excellent cheese trolley is presented at the end of the meal (the fine selection, from blues to sharps and mild goat cheeses, is flown in from Paris). At a recent dinner at *Infinity's* elegant SS *United States* restaurant, charming maitre d' Jean Pierre Hervio carved our crispy roasted Long Island duckling with the finesse of a concert pianist. The ultragracious

Frenchman spent 6 years as a maitre d' for Michel Roux at his exquisite Waterside Inn outside London, serving the likes of Princess Diana, Sean Connery, and King Hussein of Jordan, and now rotates among the four Millennium-class ships training sommeliers, teaching waiters to flambé and carve, and generally keeping standards high. He's a pro at making diners feel comfortable in such an elegant setting.

Menus are similar throughout the four specialty restaurants, with the Ocean Liners restaurant on the *Constellation,* for example, featuring appetizers such as a creamy lobster broth, tartare of salmon garnished with quail eggs, and goat cheese soufflé with tomato coulis, followed by entrees such as sea bream cooked in a salt crust, shrimp scampi flambéed in Armagnac, Steak Diane, and rack of lamb coated with a mushroom duxelle and wrapped in a puff pastry. For dessert, you can't go wrong with Grand Marnier soufflé, pumpkin and almond tart, or a plate of Michel Roux's favorite bite-size desserts. Wines by the glass and bottle are suggested with each dish, and while many are pricey (the most expensive glass is $33!), some are affordable, and Mr. Roux knows how to pick an exquisite wine.

In the main dining rooms, a dinner menu is likely to feature something along the lines of escargots a la bourguignon, filet of halibut on a bed of zucchini spaghetti enhanced with an apple cider beurre blanc, duckling a l'orange, or a center cut tenderloin of beef enhanced with a juniper berry sauce. To balance such heartiness, at every meal Celebrity offers lighter **"spa" fare,** such as a broiled King Salmon or roast pork loin stuffed with sun-dried tomatoes and presented with its natural juice flavored with three mustards (calories, fat, cholesterol, and sodium are listed on the back of the menu); and a **vegetarian menu** is available upon request, featuring such dishes as pumpkin vichyssoise and smoked Mexican lasagna, which on a recent cruise were not particularly well prepared (vegetarians may be better off ordering the veggies sans meat off the regular menu).

As with most lines today, **alternative casual dining** is available in the Lido restaurant on most nights. Soups and salads are offered buffet-style, while waiters serve entrees such as salmon, steak, pasta, and chicken between 6:30 and 8:30pm by reservation only (although if there's space, walk-ins are accepted too), unlike Carnival and Royal Caribbean, which offer completely buffet-style alternative restaurants. Celebrity's breakfast and lunch buffets are superior to those of most mainstream megaships: They offer pretty much what you'd expect of mainstream megaships, though the impressive and delicious spread of homemade breads and pastries are better.

Light breakfast eaters or those looking for a pre- or post-breakfast snack, will want to grab an incredibly good croissant from **Café Cova** (the croissants are free but you can also pony up a few bucks for a latte or cappuccino). The ships also have outdoor grills for burgers and such. Each Millennium-class ship has an AquaSpa Cafe in a corner of the thalassotherapy pool area where you can get already-plated, low-cal treats at lunch such as vegetarian sushi and pretty salads with tuna or chicken, or enjoy a quick spa breakfast of things like bagels and lox, fresh fruit, cereal, and boiled eggs.

A nice touch that appears on all formal nights, plus one other night, is a late-night culinary soiree known as **Gourmet Bites,** in which a series of upscale canapés and hors d'oeuvres, such as fish tempura and roasted garlic lemon chicken, are served by roving waiters in the ship's public lounges between midnight and 1am. On other nights, themed midnight buffets may offer up Oriental, Italian, Tex-Mex, or tropical smorgasbords, with a spread of fancifully carved fruits.

At least once per cruise fleetwide, the line offers what it calls **Elegant Tea,** in which white-gloved waiters serve tea, finger sandwiches, scones, and desserts from rolling trolleys. The line's 24-hour room service allows passengers to order off the lunch and dinner menus during those hours. And not only is Celebrity's pizza tasty and available throughout the afternoon fleetwide, but you also can get it delivered to your cabin (in a box and pouch like your local pizzeria uses) between 3 and 7pm and 10pm and 1am daily.

Wine-wise, Chef Roux's choices are offered in a wide price range to suit every budget, with many French choices.

ACTIVITIES

On Celebrity, there's a lot to do and a lot not to do, and the ships offer opportunities for both. A wide variety of activities is offered, but the cruise staff isn't in your face promoting them as they are on lines such as Carnival. Celebrity takes a higher road. As the cruise director on *Millennium* recently described it to us, "Celebrity is steering away from the standard cruise ship schlock." The occasional silly games and contests are the exception now, not the rule.

If you like to stay busy, activities during days at sea are fairly standardized across the fleet, and may include one of the fascinating, complimentary **enrichment lectures** often offered by experts on topics such as personal investing and women's health issues. There are generally two to three expert speakers on board per cruise. Celebrity also has the tried-and-true **wine tastings** (at $8 per person), horse racing, bingo, bridge (the Millennium-class ships have nice ocean-view card rooms), art auctions, trivia games, arts and crafts, spa and salon demos, and ballroom and line-dancing lessons. Activities are not without a dose of token cruise tomfoolery. Afternoons in the main pool area, silly pool games such as the **Mr. Celebrity contest** are held, where cheeky guys strut their stuff around the pool as a panel of bathing-suit-clad female volunteers rate them. During the day, a live pop band plays on the Pool Deck. The line has also introduced its own version of the *Who Wants to Be a Millionaire?* game show, complete with podiums, buzzers, an emcee, and prizes.

If you prefer curling up with a good book in some quiet nook, you'll have no problem finding one. On *Horizon* and *Zenith,* the aft-tiered decks and the forward Marina Deck are perfect places for quiet repose, as are the Fleet and America's Cup observation lounges. On *Galaxy* and *Mercury,* you can find some peace in the far corners of the Sky Deck and on the aft Penthouse Deck. On the *Millennium* sisters, the uppermost deck aft, near the jogging track, harbors a cluster of deck chairs away from the main-pool fray. Inside there are many hideaways, including **Michael's Club,** the edges of Rendez-Vous Square, and lounge chairs at the spa's thalassotherapy pool (on all but *Horizon* and *Zenith*). All the ships have 18 workstations for e-mail and Internet access, but only on the Millennium-class ships are they in one, great, ocean-view computer center location. On the *Century, Galaxy, Mercury, Zenith,* and *Horizon,* clusters of computers are in several different locations (these ships after all were not built with Internet cafes in mind). The Millennium-class ships also offer Internet connectivity in every cabin and suite for guests who bring their laptops. You'll also enjoy the interactive system wired to all cabin TVs fleetwide (which is a great way for Celebrity to get you to spend more money!). Besides ordering room service from on-screen menus, you select the evening's wine in advance of dinner, play casino-style games, or browse in "virtual" shops for a wide selection of merchandise for delivery directly to your home at the end of your cruise. You can also order pay-per-view movies including some adult titles (free movies are shown on the TV, too).

CHILDREN'S PROGRAM

Although it did not originate that way, Celebrity has evolved into a cruise line that pampers kids as well as adults, especially during the summer months and holidays, when 400 children on a Caribbean cruise is typical. If there are more than 12 kids aboard, a limited program is offered during off-season periods as well. Each ship has a playroom (called the Ship Mates Fun Factory on the Millennium-class and the Century-class ships, and the Children's Playroom on *Horizon* and *Zenith*), supervised activities practically all day long, and private and group babysitting for kids 3 and older. *Galaxy, Mercury,* and Millennium-class ships also have wading pools, and the Millennium-class's indoor/outdoor facilities are by far the best in the fleet.

During kid-intensive seasons, namely summers, activities are geared toward four age groups between the ages of 3 and 17. Kids ages 3 to 6, dubbed "Ship Mates," can enjoy treasure hunts, clown parties, T-shirt painting, dancing, movies, ship tours, and ice-cream-sundae-making parties. "Cadets," ages 7 to 9, have T-shirt painting, scavenger hunts, board games, arts and crafts, ship tours, and computer games. Your 10- to 12-year-old may want to join the "Ensign" activities, such as karaoke, computer games, board games, trivia contests, arts and crafts, movies, and pizza parties. For teens ages 13 to 17 who don't think themselves too cool to participate, the "Admiral T's" group offers talent shows, karaoke, pool games, and trivia contests. The Century-class and Millennium-class ships have attractive teen discos/hangout rooms. Special activities offered in the summer include summer-stock theater presentations, which involve three age groups: the Ship Mates and Cadets sing, dance, and act, and the Ensigns direct and produce the plays. The Young Mariners Club offers kids the chance to get a behind-the-scenes look at the cruise ship, with activities and tours related to the entertainment, food and beverage, and hotel departments. Junior Olympics are held poolside and the whole family is encouraged to cheer on the kids who compete in relay races, diving, and basketball free throws. There are also masquerade parties, where Ship Mates and Cadets make their own masks and then parade around the ship.

The minimum age for sailing is six months.

On formal nights during summers and holidays (and other times of the year if there are enough kids on board), a complimentary **parents' night out** program allows mom and dad to enjoy dinner alone while the kids are invited to a pizza party with the counselors. **Group babysitting** in the playroom is available for ages 3 to 12 between noon and 2pm on port days, and every evening from 10pm to 1am for children ages 3 to 12, for $6 per child per hour. **Private in-cabin babysitting** by a crewmember is available on a limited basis for $8 per hour for up to two children (kids must be at least 6 months old); make your request 24 hours in advance.

ENTERTAINMENT

Although entertainment is not a prime reason to sail with Celebrity, the line does offer a nice selection of varied, innovative performances. For instance, on many cruises a **strolling a cappella group** performs in lounges and public areas fleetwide in the afternoons and before and after dinner, delighting passengers with well-known songs old and new, performed in a fun, entertaining style. On a recent cruise, a strolling magician entertained small groups of guests enjoying drinks in one of the public lounges. You'll typically find a harpist playing at dinner and often in the atrium and at the Cova Café, and sometimes a classical trio serenading guests in the atrium.

Celebrity also offers the popular favorites, such as Broadway-style musicals led by a sock-it-to-'em soloist or two and a team of lip-syncing dancers in full Vegas-esque regalia. On the Millennium-class and the Century-class ships, these shows are performed on some of the best-equipped, highest-tech stages at sea, with hydraulic orchestra pits, trap doors, turntables, sets that move along tracks in the stage floor, lasers, and a video wall showing images that coincide with the performance. Showrooms aboard all Celebrity ships have excellent acoustics and sightlines that are among the most panoramic and unobstructed at sea.

Other nights in the showroom you'll find magicians, comedians, cabaret acts, and passenger talent shows.

When you tire of Broadway-style entertainment, you'll find that all the ships have cozy lounges and **piano bars** where you can retreat for a romantic nightcap. In these more intimate lounges, the music is often laid-back jazz or music from the big-band era, spiced with interpretations of contemporary Celine Dion– or Whitney Houston–type hits. There's also the elegant and plush Michael's Club for a cordial and some quiet conversation. (Originally created as cigar lounges, the clubs are billed as piano bars now that the cigar craze has fizzled.) Each ship has late-night disco dancing, usually until about 3am. You'll also find karaoke and recent-release movies in the theater on the Millennium-class and Century-class ships.

Each ship has a rather spacious casino, and while they may not be as Vegasy as the ones on Carnival, they're bustling enough to put gamblers in the mood.

SERVICE

Overall, service is polite, attentive, cheerful, and especially professional. Waiters have a poised, upscale-hotel air about them, and their manner contributes to the elegant mood. There are very professional sommeliers in the dining room, and waiters are on hand in the Lido breakfast and lunch buffet restaurants to carry passengers' trays from the buffet line to a table of their choice. Poolside, attendants are on hand to periodically pass out refreshing chilled towels along with sorbet. Celebrity, along with Royal Caribbean, is one of the few big-ship lines to still handle tipping by having passengers give crew cash at the end of the cruise (as opposed to automatically adding a set gratuity to passengers' onboard charge accounts), which definitely seems to keep the waiters and cabin stewards more motivated to please.

If you occupy a suite on any of the ships, you'll get a tuxedo-clad **personal butler** who serves afternoon tea, complimentary cappuccino and espresso, and complimentary pre-dinner hors d'oeuvres, bringing them right to your cabin. If you ask, he'll handle your laundry, shine your shoes, make sewing repairs, and

---

Know Where the Children Are

If you plan on spending quiet time in your cabin during the day, you may want to avoid booking one of the cabins near the children's playroom, which on all but the Millennium-class ships are located next to cabins. Their locations are marked on brochure deck plans.

Ⓒ Celebrity Art: Take a Walk on the Wild Side

Celebrity's ships have the most impressive and striking (and sometimes downright weird) art collections at sea, featuring works by Robert Rauschenberg, Damien Hirst, Jasper Johns, David Hockney, Pablo Picasso, Andy Warhol, Sol LeWitt, Helen Frankenthaler, and many others. Public areas on *Mercury* alone contain more than 400 works of art, including paintings, tapestries, cartoonish murals, and stark metal sculptures, with standouts including Christian Marclay's record-cover collages, Anish Kapoor's hallucinatory *Mirror,* and Lawrence Weiner's puzzling poetic lines painted on walls throughout the ship. *Millennium* features Jonathan Borofsky and Kenny Hunter sculptures, Anne Chu and Stephen Balkenhol ceramics, and Michalis Katzourakis and Horst P. Horst photos, among many, many others, while on *Infinity* you'll find a Dale Chihuly chandelier and works by Wolfgang Tillmans. *Summit* boasts an extensive collection of sculpture including *Woman With Fruit,* a large bronze of a rotund woman by noted Colombian artist Fernando Botero (the sculpture overlooks the ship's thalassotherapy pool area), as well as an ART sculpture by LOVE artist Robert Indiana, a mirrored flower by Jeff Koons, and a series of truly ugly but fascinating beaded busts by Liza Lou. There's also photography that includes a fun series of Barbie photos by David Levinthal, which can be found in the ship's shopping arcade. *Constellation* also has a Botero woman, *Venere Addormentata,* at the entrance to its AquaSpa, as well as a five-panel glass/mirror installation in its atrium by Iceland-born artist Olafur Eliasson, among its noteworthy works. The line's older ships are no slouches either: *Horizon* is hung with an amazing number of Warhol silk screens, while *Zenith* has etchings by David Hockney, woodcuts by Roy Lichtenstein, and silk screens and collotypes by Christo. Aboard all the ships, these compelling works sometimes greet you at unexpected moments, and may even make you pause and reflect—a rare cruise ship phenomenon.

deliver messages. For instance, on one sailing with Heidi's mother, the butler brought her a glass of juice each night after learning that she needed it to take her medication. Your butler will serve you a full five-course dinner if you'd rather dine in your cabin one night, and will even help you organize a cocktail party for your cruising friends, in either your suite or a suitable public area. (You foot the bill for food and drinks, of course.)

Other hedonistic treats bestowed upon suite guests include a bottle of champagne on arrival, personalized stationery, terry robes, a Celebrity tote bag, oversize bath towels, priority check-in and debarkation, express luggage delivery at embarkation, and complimentary use of the soothing indoor thalassotherapy pools on the Century-class ships, whose use otherwise carries a charge. Suite guests can even book an in-cabin massage daily between the hours of 7am and 8pm.

Celebrity Fleet Itineraries

Ship	Itineraries
Century	**7-night W. Carib:** Round-trip from Fort Lauderdale through Apr, visiting Ocho Rios (Jamaica), Grand Cayman, Cozumel, and Key West, with 2 days at sea. Alternates with **7-night E. Carib:** Round-trip from Fort Lauderdale through Apr, visiting San Juan, St. Thomas, Sint Maarten, and Nassau, with 2 days at sea. **Non-Caribbean Itineraries:** Europe.
Constellation	**7-night S. Carib:** Round-trip from San Juan, Nov–Apr, visiting Sint Maarten, St. Lucia, Barbados, Antigua, and St. Thomas, with 1 day at sea. **Non-Caribbean Itineraries:** Europe.
Galaxy	**11-night E. Carib:** Round-trip from Baltimore, Oct–Nov 2003 and Apr 2004, visiting Charleston, SC, St. Thomas, Sint Maarten, San Juan, and Nassau, with 5 days at sea. Alternates with **10-night W. Carib:** Round-trip from Baltimore, Sept–Nov 2003, visiting Key West, Cozumel, Belize City (Belize), Coco Cay (private Bahamian island), and Nassau, with 4 days at sea. **7-night S. Carib:** Round-trip from San Juan, Dec 2003–Mar 2004, visiting St. Thomas, St. Kitts, Barbados, Aruba, and Margarita Island (Venezuela), with 1 day at sea. **Non-Caribbean Itineraries:** New England/Canada.
Horizon	**7-night Bermuda 1:** Round-trip from New York, through Aug 2003, visiting St. George's and Hamilton, with 2 days at sea. **7-night Bermuda 2:** Round-trip from Philadelphia, Sept–Oct 2003, visiting St. George's and Hamilton, with 2 days at sea. **7-night W. Carib:** Round-trip from Tampa, Nov–Dec 2003, visiting Key West, Costa Maya and Cozumel (Mexico), and Grand Cayman, with 2 days at sea. **11-night E. Carib:** Round-trip from Tampa, Jan–Mar 2004, visiting Grand Turk (Turks and Caicos), San Juan, St. Thomas, Sint Maarten, Tortola (BVIs), and Key West, with 4 days at sea. **Non-Caribbean/Bermuda Itineraries:** None.
Infinity	**14-night Panama Canal:** East- and westbound between San Diego and Fort Lauderdale, Oct–Apr, visiting Cabo San Lucas and Acapulco (Mexico), Puntarenas (Costa Rica), Cartagena (Colombia), and Aruba, with 8 days at sea, including a full Canal transit. **Non-Caribbean Itineraries:** Hawaii, Alaska.
Millennium	**7-night E. Carib:** Round-trip from Fort Lauderdale, Nov 2003–Apr 2004, visiting San Juan, Catalina (Dominican Republic), St. Thomas, and Nassau, with 2 days at sea. **Non-Caribbean Itineraries:** Europe.
Summit	**10-night S. Carib:** Round-trip from Fort Lauderdale, Oct–April, visiting Sint Maarten, St. Lucia, Barbados, St. Kitts, and St. Thomas, with 4 days at sea. Alternates with **11-night S. Carib:** Round-trip from Fort Lauderdale, Oct–Apr, visiting Key West, Cozumel, Puerto Limon (Costa Rica), Colón (Panama), Cartagena (Colombia), Aruba, and Grand Cayman, with 4 days at sea. **Non-Caribbean Itineraries:** Alaska, Panama Canal repositionings.
Zenith	**7-night Bermuda:** Round-trip from New York, Sept–Oct 2003 (and almost certainly Apr–Oct 2004, though that hadn't been announced at press time), visiting Hamilton and St. George, with 2 days at sea. **Non-Caribbean Itineraries:** South America and Panama Canal.

At press time, itineraries were only available through April 2004.

Celebrity is the only mainstream line providing the use of cotton robes in all cabins fleetwide, as well as minifridges stocked with drinks and snacks (if consumed, each item is billed on passengers' onboard accounts).

Laundry and dry-cleaning services are available fleetwide for a nominal fee, but there are no self-service laundry facilities.

The Millennium Class: Millennium • Infinity • Summit • Constellation

The Verdict

Total knockouts, Celebrity's newest and biggest offer all the leisure, sports, and entertainment options of a megaship and an atmosphere that combines old-world elegance and modern casual style. Without a doubt, they're the classiest megas at sea.

Millennium *(photo: Celebrity Cruises)*

Specifications

Size (in tons)	91,000	Passenger/Crew Ratio	2 to 1
Number of Cabins	975	Year Launched	
Number of Outside Cabins	780	*Millennium*	2000
Cabins with Verandas	590	*Infinity*	2001
Number of Passengers	1,950	*Summit*	2001
Officers	Greek	*Constellation*	2002
Crew	999 (Internat'l)	Last Major Refurbishment	N/A

Frommer's Ratings (Scale of 1–5)   ✶✶✶✶✶

Cabin Comfort & Amenities	5	Dining Options	5
Ship Cleanliness & Maintenance	5	Gym & Spa Facilities	5
Public Comfort/Space	5	Children's Facilities	4
Decor	5	Enjoyment Factor	5

The Golden Age of sea travel may have ended about the same time top hats went out of style, but who's saying we can't have a new, more casual golden age of our own? Celebrity's Millennium-class ships may just be the vessels to ring it in.

In creating its newest ships, Celebrity took the best ideas from the wonderful *Century, Galaxy,* and *Mercury* and ratcheted them up, in terms of both scale and number: bigger ships, bigger spas and theaters, more veranda cabins, more dining options, more shopping, more lounges, and more sports and exercise facilities, plus more of the same great service, cuisine, and high-style onboard art for which the company was already known. Plus, they have state-of-the-art gas-turbine propulsion systems that produce less pollution and offer a smoother, quieter ride for passengers. With all this, who cares if the yellow and red accents on the ships' exteriors give the otherwise elegant vessels a sort of Ronald McDonald look?

Cabins & Rates

Cabins	Per Diems from	Sq. Ft.	Fridge	Hair Dryer	Sitting Area	TV
Inside	$89	170	yes	yes	yes	yes
Outside	$110	170–191	yes	yes	yes	yes
Suite	$260	251–1,432	yes	yes	yes	yes

CABINS Improving upon Celebrity's already-respectable cabins, the Millennium-class ships push the bar up yet another notch, with their elegant striped, floral, or patterned fabrics in shades such as butterscotch and pinkish terra cotta, along with Deco-style lighting fixtures and marble desktops. As with the rest of the fleet, standard inside and outside cabins are a roomy 170 square feet, and come with a small sitting area, stocked minifridge, TV, safe, ample storage space, cotton robes, and shampoo and soap dispensers built right into the shower. Only thing missing? Individual reading lights above the beds (though there are table lamps on nightstands).

Premium and Deluxe staterooms have slightly larger sitting areas and approximately 40-square-foot verandas. The 12 simply titled "Large" ocean-view staterooms in the stern measure in at a very large 271 square feet and have two entertainment centers with TVs/VCRs, a partitioned sitting area with two convertible sofa beds, and very, very, *very* large 242-square-foot verandas facing the ships' wake. Note, the category-1A and -2A balcony cabins on the Sky Deck are somewhat in the shadows of the overhanging deck above (where the buffet restaurant, pool deck, and spa are located), which juts out farther than the three decks below it. Also, the balconies at the aft and forward end of the Sky Deck are not completely private, since they jut out farther than the balconies above (keep your clothes on!).

In the suite category, Celebrity has gone all out, offering not only 24-hour butler service, but four levels of accommodation, from the 251-square-foot Sky Suites with balconies to the eight 467-square-foot Celebrity Suites (with dining area, separate bedroom, two TV/VCR combos, and whirlpool bathtub, but no verandas) and the 538-square-foot Royal Suites (also with a separate living/dining room, two TV/VCR combos, a standing shower and whirlpool bathtub, and a huge 195-sq.-ft. veranda with whirlpool tub). At the top of the food chain are the massive Penthouse Suites, which measure 1,432 square feet. They're as good at it gets, with herringbone wood floors, a marble foyer, a computer station, a Yamaha piano, and a simply amazing bathroom with ocean views and a full-size hot tub. Did we mention a 1,098-square-foot veranda that wraps around the stern of the ship and features whirlpool tub and full bar? (The only downside is you sometimes feel the vibrations of the engines a few decks below.) If these suites have a Park Avenue feel, it's no wonder. The designer, Birch Coffey, also does apartments for New York's elite.

Connecting cabins are available, and passengers requiring use of a wheelchair have a choice of 26 cabins, from Sky Suites to balcony cabins and inside staterooms.

PUBLIC AREAS There's simply nothing else at sea like the Grand Foyer atrium. The stunning hub of all four ships, each rectangular, three-deck area features a translucent, inner-illuminated onyx staircase that glows beneath your feet. All around are giant silk flower arrangements and topiaries. Off on the port side, guests can ride between decks on ocean-view elevators (on a recent Panama Canal cruise one passenger decided the elevators provided the best views on the ship and spent the day riding up and down). Overlooking the Foyer and the ocean, an attractive Internet center has 18 computer stations. These ships are masterpieces of rich velveteen and suedes, golden brocades, burled woods, and ornate topiaries.

In each ship's bow is the elegant three-deck theater, partially illuminated by what looks like torches all around the room, an amazingly realistic trick produced by projecting blue and orange lights on a strip of thin cloth that's blown by a fan from below. The effect gives the rooms a warm, flickering, elegant glow. Seating on all three levels is unobstructed, except in the far reaches of the balconies.

For specialty coffees and freshly baked pastries, the appealing Cova Café is a bustling, Italian-style cafe you could almost imagine being in Venice, with rich fabrics, cozy banquettes, and wood-frame chairs. You'll also find elegant martini, champagne, and caviar bars, as well as brighter, busier lounges for live music. For the *real* dancing, though, head up to the 100% stunning observation lounge/ disco. Three circular levels break up the windowed room, which, without the use of any barriers, make the huge space seem more intimate.

Other rooms include the cool music library, a cozy hideaway open 24 hours a day with private listening stations and a stock of some 1,500 CDs (one annoying thing, though: Apparently the headsets were getting lifted, and you now need to go all the way down to the purser's office to get one); the two-deck library, staffed by a full-time librarian; an ocean-view florist/conservatory (created with the help of Paris-based floral designer Emilio Robba and mostly filled with silk flowers and trees, some of which are for sale); and the huge, high-tech conference center and cinema. Celebrity's signature Michael's Club is a quiet, dignified piano bar, replete with fake fireplace and comfy leather club chairs (not much used during the day, it's a great place to snuggle up with a good book), and excellent for an after-dinner drink. The casinos are extensive, *Millennium*'s decorated in an opulent beaux art design, with faux-marble columns and mythological Greco-Roman sculptures, rich damask curtains, mosaic floor tiling, and wall frescoes.

The ships' Emporium Shops are among the most extensive at sea (bordering on overkill, though they're always packed with shoppers), with names such as Escada Sport, Tommy Hilfiger, Swarovski (crystal), Fendi (purses), and a Michel Roux gourmet shop. There's also plenty of less expensive souvenir stuff.

For kids, the Shipmates Fun Factory has both indoor and outdoor soft-surface jungle gyms, a wading pool, a ball-bin, a computer room, a movie room, an arts-and-crafts area, a video arcade, a teen center, and more.

DINING OPTIONS   The main dining rooms are beautiful two-level spaces that are very much in the style of Celebrity's earlier Century-class ships. A huge window in the stern and oversize round windows along both sides admit natural light, and a central double staircase provides a dramatic entrance (though the only downside to these lovely rooms is the vibrations felt from the engines a few decks below). The *Summit*'s dining room boasts a 7-foot bronze *La Normandie*, an Art Deco sculpture that originally overlooked the grand staircase on the SS *Normandie* ocean liner, in the center of its lower level. The piece, which is supposed to depict the goddess Athena, but looks an awful lot like George Washington in drag, was residing near the pool at the Fountainebleau Hotel in Miami before it was purchased by the line.

However, the pièce de résistance on these ships is their alternative, reservations-only restaurants, which offer dining experiences unmatched on any other ship today. *Millennium*'s is the Edwardian-style Olympic restaurant, whose main attraction is several dozen hand-carved and gilded French walnut wall panels that were made by Palestinian craftsmen for the A La Carte restaurant aboard White Star Line's *Olympic,* sister ship to the *Titanic,* which sailed from 1911 to 1935. *Infinity*'s SS *United States* restaurant features etched-glass panels from the

1950s liner of the same name, which claimed fame for its speed crossing the Atlantic from New York—a record that has never been broken. (The ship is still around, though it sits disused and moldering at a pier in Philadelphia.) The *Summit's* Normandie restaurant features original gold-lacquered panels from the smoking room of the legendary *Normandie,* while the *Constellation's* Ocean Liners restaurant has artifacts from a variety of luxury liners, including sets of original red and black lacquered panels from the 1920s *Ile de France,* which add a whimsical Parisian air. The dining experience Celebrity has created to match these gorgeous rooms is nothing short of amazing: 134 guests (but never seated all at once, and 75 a night is typical) are served by a staff of about 23, including 8 dedicated chefs, 6 waiters, 5 maitre d's, and 4 sommeliers, all trained personally by executive chef Michel Roux and his senior staff. Dining here is a 2- to 3-hour commitment. Gracious service includes domed silver covers dramatically lifted off entrees by several waiters in unison when meals are delivered. Cuisine is a combination of Roux specialties with original recipes from the ships the restaurants are named after (such as the Long Island duckling featured on the original SS *United States*), and includes the first use of tableside flambé cooking at sea. A great cheese selection is offered from a marble-topped trolley, and in the menu, Roux suggests wines for each course (and they're not cheap). For atmosphere, a pianist or a piano/violin duo in period garb performs early-20th-century salon music. It's $25 a person to dine there, but in this case, it's well worth it—you'd pay a fortune for this experience if you had it on land. No children under age 12 are allowed and reservations are required.

The huge but well-laid-out indoor-outdoor buffet restaurant on all four ships is open for breakfast, lunch, and dinner, offering regular buffet selections plus pizza, pasta, and ice-cream specialty stations. Waiters often carry passengers' trays to their tables and fetch coffee, a service level few other megaships match.

POOL, FITNESS & SPA FACILITIES The spas on the Millennium-class ships are gorgeous and simply sprawling, with 25,000 square feet taken up with hydrotherapy treatment rooms, New Agey steam rooms and saunas (some chamomile-scented, some mint-scented, some with a shower that simulates a tropical rainforest, some with heated tiled couches and eucalyptus scents). A large bubbling thalassotherapy pool, with soothing pressure jets, in a solarium-like setting, is under a glass roof that also shelters a seating area where guests can grab a casual breakfast or lunch from the AquaSpa Cafe. The pool is free to all adult guests (unlike the one on the Century-class ships, which is $10 a day), and on *Infinity,* it's surrounded by cabanas in which you can enjoy a snooze or a massage. Lots of pricey spa packages, from $200 to $400, combine a complement of Eastern- or Western-influenced treatments using things such as coconut and frangipani scented oil and heated massage rocks to pamper guests, though they sound a lot more appealing than they are. On a recent cruise, Heidi splurged for the $344 Tropical Milk Treat, billed as a 4-hour 4-part wrap, massage, pedicure, and manicure treatment; it turned out to be 3 hours, and with a rushed wrap and a lousy pedicure. Some of the therapists seem inexperienced, tired (you would be too after a 10- to 12-hr. day), and less than enthusiastic. (This is often true with Steiner spas on other lines, too, but it's more disappointing on Celebrity, which promotes its spas so heavily.) Stick with the basic massages ($109); you can't go wrong with a classic shiatsu.

Next door to the spa there's a very large gym with dozens of the latest machines and free weights, and a large aerobics floor.

Up top, the Sports Deck has facilities for basketball, volleyball, quoits, and paddle tennis. Just below, on the Sunrise Deck, are a jogging track and a golf simulator. Below that is the well-laid-out Pool Deck, where you'll find two pools, four hot tubs, a couple of bars, and a multistoried sunning area. Head up to the balcony level above the pool, at the stern or bow of the ship, for quieter sunbathing spots.

The Century Class: Century • Galaxy • Mercury

The Verdict

Mercury *(photo: Matt Hannafin)*

Three of the most attractive and all-around appealing megaships at sea. Down-to-earth and casual, this trio also manages to be elegant and exciting.

Specifications

Size (in tons)			
Century	70,606	*Mercury*	220
Galaxy	77,713	Number of Passengers	
Mercury	77,713	*Century*	1,750
Number of Cabins		*Galaxy*	1,896
Century	875	*Mercury*	1,896
Galaxy	948	Officers	Greek
Mercury	948	Crew	International
Number of Outside Cabins		*Century*	843
Century	571	*Galaxy*	900
Galaxy	639	*Mercury*	900
Mercury	639	Passenger/Crew Ratio	2 to 1
Cabins with Verandas		Year Launched	
Century	61	*Century*	1995
Galaxy	220	*Galaxy*	1996
		Mercury	1997

Frommer's Ratings (Scale of 1–5)   ★★★★ ½

Cabin Comfort & Amenities	5	Dining Options	4
Ship Cleanliness & Maintenance	4	Gym & Spa Facilities	5
Public Comfort/Space	5	Children's Facilities	4
Decor	5	Enjoyment Factor	5

With these three sisters, beginning with the *Century* in 1995, Celebrity ushered in some of the most beautiful ships to be built in modern times. Known collectively as the Century class, they're more or less equivalent in size and amenities. Of the three ships, the one that's the most dissimilar to its mates is the first, *Century.* It's lighter by 7,000 tons and has a capacity for 120 fewer guests, a smaller children's playroom (and no wading pool), and a brighter, glitzier feel, flaunting its high-techness with things such as video monitors blended into the decor. *Galaxy* and *Mercury* are warmer and more reminiscent of classic ocean liners, but with a modern feel. The decor casts a chic and sophisticated mood, with lots of warm wood tones as well as rich, tactile textures and deep-toned fabrics, from faux zebra skin and chrome to buttery soft leathers, velvets, and futuristic-looking applications of glass and marble.

It's difficult to say what's most striking on these three ships. The elegant spas and their 15,000-gallon thalassotherapy pools? The distinguished Michael's Club lounges with their leather wingbacks and velvet couches? The two-story old-world dining rooms set back in the stern, with grand floor-to-ceiling windows allowing diners to spy the ship's wake glowing under moonlight? An absolutely intriguing modern-art collection unmatched in the industry?

Take your pick—you won't go wrong. (***Note:*** At press time, *Mercury's* 2004 itineraries had not yet been announced, and it was unclear whether the ship would be in the Caribbean.)

Cabins & Rates

Cabins	Per Diems from	Sq. Ft.	Fridge	Hair Dryer	Sitting Area	TV
Inside	$74	170–175	yes	yes	no	yes
Outside	$94	170–175	yes	yes	some	yes
Suite	$350	246–1,433	yes	yes	yes	yes

CABINS   Simple yet pleasing decor is cheerful and based on light-colored furniture and monochromatic themes of muted purple-blue, green, or pinky red. Standard inside and outside cabins are larger than the norm (although not as large as Carnival's 185-footers), and suites, which come in four categories, are particularly spacious, with marble vanity/desk tops, Art Deco–style sconces, and rich inlaid wood floors. Some, such as the Penthouse Suite, offer more living space (1,219 sq. ft., expandable to 1,433 sq. ft. on special request) than you find in many private homes, plus such wonderful touches as a private whirlpool bath on the veranda. Royal Suites run about half that size (plus 100-ft. balconies) but offer touches such as French doors between the bedroom and seating area, both bathtub and shower in the bathroom, and TVs in each room. *Galaxy* and *Mercury's* 246-square-foot Sky Suites offer verandas that, at 179 square feet, are among the biggest aboard any ship—bigger, in fact, than those in the more expensive Penthouse and Royal suites on these ships (you may want to keep your robe on, though, as people on the deck above can see down onto part of the Sky Suite verandas). All suite bathrooms have bathtubs with whirlpools and magnified makeup mirrors.

All cabins are outfitted with built-in vanities/desks, stocked minifridges (accounts are billed for any snacks or drinks consumed), hair dryers, cotton robes, radios, and safes. Closets and drawer space are roomy and well designed, as are the bathrooms, and all standard cabins have twin beds convertible to doubles.

Cabin TVs are wired with an interactive system that allows guests to order room service from on-screen menus, select wine for dinner, play casino-style games, or go shopping.

Connecting cabins are available. Eight of the cabins aboard each ship (one inside and seven outside) were specifically designed for passengers with disabilities.

PUBLIC AREAS   All three ships are designed so well that it's never hard to find a quiet retreat when you want to be secluded but don't want to be confined in your cabin.

Each vessel boasts a cozy Michael's Club piano bar, decorated like the parlor of a London men's club. These ex-cigar bars (Celebrity phased out the focus on stogies when that faze dried up in recent years) are great spots for a fine cognac or a good single-malt Scotch while enjoying soft background music. On *Century* and *Galaxy,* Michael's Club piano bar maintains its wood-paneled clubbiness somewhat better than aboard the *Mercury,* where it wraps around the main atrium and lets onto a very uncozy view of the shopping below. Still, you can't beat the high-backed, buttery-leather chairs.

For those who don't find that clubby ambience appealing, Tastings Coffee Bar offers an alternative, with specialized upscale java. There's also the popular Rendez-Vous Square, arranged so that even large groups can achieve a level of privacy and couples can find a nook of their own. Champagne bars appear aboard *Galaxy* and *Mercury,* and the latter also sports a nice, modern Deco-looking martini bar set in the ship's aft atrium, about which our only complaint is the audible clanging of the casino's slot machines, which seems to get trapped and amplified by the atrium's drum shape. Various other bars, both indoor and outdoor, are tucked into nooks and crannies throughout all three ships.

The multistoried, glass-walled nightclubs/discos are spacious, sprawling, and elegant in a clean, modern way, yet designed with lots of cozy nooks for romantic conversation over champagne. Each of the three ships has double-decker theaters with unobstructed views from almost every seat (though avoid those at the cocktail tables at the back of the rear balcony boxes, unless you have a really long neck) and state-of-the-art equipment such as cantilevered orchestra pits and walls of video screens to augment the action on the stage.

Libraries aboard the ships are comfortable, but not as big or well stocked as they could be. The onboard casinos are larger and more comprehensive than those aboard the line's older *Horizon* and *Zenith.*

DINING OPTIONS   The two-story formal dining rooms on all three ships are truly stunning rooms reminiscent of the grand liners of yesteryear, with wide, dramatic staircases joining the two levels and floor-to-ceiling walls of glass facing astern to a view of the ship's wake. If you lean toward the dramatic, don a gown or tux and slink down the stairs nice and slow like a 1940s Hollywood star—there aren't many places you can do that these days.

Each ship also has an indoor/outdoor buffet restaurant open for breakfast, lunch, and dinner, as well as pizza and ice-cream stations.

POOL, FITNESS & SPA FACILITIES   Resort decks aboard these vessels feature a pair of good-size swimming areas rimmed with teak benches for sunning and relaxation. Even when the ships are full, these areas don't seem particularly crowded. Aboard *Galaxy* and *Mercury,* retractable domes cover one of the swimming pools during inclement weather.

The ships' spacious, windowed, 10,000-square-foot AquaSpa and fitness facilities are some of the best at sea today. The gym wraps around the starboard side of an upper forward deck like a hook, the large spa straddles the middle, and a very modern and elegant beauty salon faces the ocean on the port side. You'll feel as though you've booked yourself into an exclusive European spa resort. The focal point of these spas is a 115,000-gallon thalassotherapy pool, a bubbling cauldron of warm, soothing seawater. After a relaxing 15- or 20-minute dip, choose a massage or facial, or if you're a gambler (because the fancy stuff is hit or miss in the quality department), something more exotic, such as a Rasul treatment (a mud pack and steam bath for couples), herbal steam bath, or a variety of water-based treatments involving baths, jet massages, and soft whirling showers. There are also saunas and steam rooms (including *Mercury*'s impressive Turkish Hammam, with its uniformly heated surfaces and beautiful tile work). As aesthetically pleasing to the eye as they are functional, each of the AquaSpas employs a design theme—a Japanese bathhouse on *Century* and *Galaxy*, and a Moroccan motif on the *Mercury*.

In the generously sized gyms, you can get lost in the landscapes unfolding on the color monitors of the ships' high-tech, virtual-reality stationary bikes. (You can even ride through the virtual water traps and make squishy sounds as you come up the other side—fun!) There are also aerobics classes in a separate room and an outdoor jogging track on an upper deck, a golf simulator, and one deck that's specifically designed for sports.

Horizon • Zenith

The Verdict

Combining the gentility of classic cruising with the fun and glamour of today's exciting megaships, these midsize, casually elegant ships are a very pleasing package.

Horizon *(photo: Celebrity Cruises)*

Specifications

Size (in tons)		*Zenith*	1,374
Horizon	46,811	Officers	Greek
Zenith	47,225	Crew	International
Number of Cabins		*Horizon*	645
Horizon	677	*Zenith*	628
Zenith	687	Passenger/Crew Ratio	2.1 to 1
Number of Outside Cabins		Year Launched	
Horizon	529	*Horizon*	1990
Zenith	541	*Zenith*	1992
Cabins with Verandas	0	Last Major Refurbishment	
Number of Passengers		*Horizon*	1998
Horizon	1,354	*Zenith*	1999

Frommer's Ratings (Scale of 1–5)   ✪✪✪✪

Cabin Comfort & Amenities	4	Dining Options	3
Ship Cleanliness & Maintenance	4	Gym & Spa Facilities	3
Public Comfort/Space	4	Children's Facilities	3
Decor	4	Enjoyment Factor	4

In this day of mondo ships carrying 2,000 to 3,000 passengers, these midsize sisters carrying just about 1,350 guests are wonderfully more intimate. An exceptionally wide indoor promenade gives passengers the feeling of strolling along a boulevard within the ship's hull. Like their megaship sisters, these two smaller ships boast distinctive art collections with pieces by the likes of Warhol and Hockney, and after $4.5-million refurbishments a few years back, they also offer such signature Celebrity elements as Michael's Club lounges, patisseries, martini bars, art galleries, a new boutique selling upscale accessories and clothing, and enlarged spa facilities. Still, next to the stylish new decor you'll find chrome and other shiny remnants of the original early-1990s scheme rearing their ugly heads in places such as the main dining rooms, giving the ships two distinct personalities. Though these ships are very appealing in many ways, they are starting to show some wear and tear, and can't exactly compete with the line's new Millennium-class ships. (To spruce up some areas, *Zenith* is scheduled for a 2-week dry-dock in late 2004.)

Cabins & Rates

Cabins	Per Diems from	Sq. Ft.	Fridge	Hair Dryer	Sitting Area	TV
Inside	$91	172	no	yes	no	yes
Outside	$109	172	no	yes	some	yes
Suite	$173	270–500	yes	yes	yes	yes

CABINS   As on the Century-class ships, accommodations offer a generous amount of space, with all inside and standard outside cabins measuring 172 square feet, with the exception of some oddly shaped smaller insides amidships on the Caribbean Deck. The muted blue, green, or burnt orange fabrics and accouterments are tasteful, subdued, and relatively well maintained. All cabins on both ships have roomy bathrooms, spacious closets, stocked minifridges (accounts are billed for any snacks or drinks consumed), hair dryers, and cotton robes, and many have additional upper and lower berths for families or friendly foursomes.

Eight cabins on *Horizon* and six on *Zenith* are positioned all the way aft, with windows facing a classically romantic view of the ship's wake. Bear in mind, on *Zenith,* the children's playroom is right in the midst of these cabins (on *Horizon,* it's adjacent to cabins amidships on the Florida Deck), so if you're planning on quiet daytimes in your cabin and will sail during school holidays, you may not want to book one of them.

The 20 roomy suites on each ship are about 25 square feet bigger than most of the suites on the Century-class ships (the only difference being that *Horizon* and *Zenith* do not have any private verandas). Each suite has a marble bathroom with whirlpool tub, a sitting area, a minibar, and butler service. *Horizon* has a pair of Presidential Suites (no great shakes in the looks department) measuring 340 square feet and *Zenith* has two Royal Suites at 500 square feet, each with large sitting rooms (and on *Zenith,* a dining table and chairs), marble bathrooms, walk-in closets, VCR, CD player, minibar, and butler service.

Regardless of category, each accommodation has a safe, TV, glass-topped coffee table, desk, and marble-topped vanity. The solitary lamp on the nightstand by the bed(s) is pretty inadequate for nighttime reading. Be careful when booking if views are important to you: Most of the category-7 outside cabins on the Bermuda Deck *(Horizon)* and Bahamas Deck *(Zenith)* have views blocked by lifeboats. Cabins on the Florida Deck have portholes.

There are a handful of connecting cabins. Four cabins are wheelchair accessible.

PUBLIC AREAS   Late-1990s refurbishments improved on the original late-1980s interior design; but there are still remnants of the latter remaining, so the ships you'll see today are a schizophrenic mix of a nautical, clubby, plush, and warm ambience and an '80s modern, metallic feel. Layout differences between the two ships are minimal—*Zenith* has a larger Forward Observation Deck, for instance. Neither has a multideck atrium, nor excessive flashiness.

Without a doubt, the most attractive spaces on the ships are the elegant Michael's Club lounges added a few years ago, with wingback chairs, leather couches, brocade fabrics, and even faux fireplaces. The *Horizon* has tasseled pillows, dried flower topiaries, and Oriental carpets. Opening off the same short hallway aboard both ships is a library and a card room. Another appealing place is the spacious, nautical-themed bar/observation lounge on the Marina Deck, called Fleet Bar on *Zenith* and the America's Cup Club on *Horizon*. Both have floor-to-ceiling windows, navy-blue furniture, and honey-brown wood accents.

Amidships is the Rendezvous Lounge and Rendezvous Bar, where, especially on formal nights, guests can show off their finery and relax with cocktails before heading to the adjacent dining room. There's a really elegant martini bar in the same area, plus an art gallery offering the same kind of works you'll see at onboard art auctions. The Zodiac Club is a lounge by day and disco by night. The attractive Cova Café offers specialty coffees and chocolates as well as champagne, wine, and liquors in a lovely setting. The modern, minimalist, two-level Celebrity Show Lounge aboard each ship has good sightlines from all but seats on the edges of the balcony level.

On *Horizon*, the kids' playroom is a small, windowless space down on Deck 4, while on *Zenith* it's a deck higher, with windows. Both also have video arcades.

DINING OPTIONS   The dining rooms are the most chrome-intensive places on board (ceiling, railing, chair frames, and pillars), smacking of that sort of 1980s-era wedding-hall look, yet they're still comfortable and pleasing enough, with banquette seating for tables along the sides of the rooms. The indoor/outdoor buffet restaurants, serving breakfast, lunch, and dinner, were refurbished a few years back and now feature separate islands for drinks and food, keeping lines to a minimum; they also now feature darker wood detailing and fabrics for a more elegant look.

POOL, FITNESS & SPA FACILITIES   *Horizon* and *Zenith* have ample space dedicated to recreation, including two good-size swimming pools that never seem to be overcrowded, even when the ships are full. The newly renovated top-deck spa and fitness areas have floor-to-ceiling windows and resemble the spas aboard Celebrity's larger ships, and while they don't offer as many of the more exotic treatments or have the thalassotherapy pool featured on the larger ships, they have several spa-treatment rooms and a Seraglio steam/mud room (like the Rasul on the larger ships). The gyms are on the small side—too small, for instance, to hold fitness classes (they're held instead in one of the nightclubs).

The ships' beautiful tiered decks at the stern offer many quiet places for lounging in view of the ships' hypnotic wake when underway. Each has a cluster of three hot tubs aft on Deck 8; the *Zenith* also features a bank of wooden deck chairs with canvas umbrella-like shades over them (though a bit worn these days), like minicabanas in the south of France.

Other recreation facilities and options include a putting green, a golf driving net used for lessons with the pro, and a jogging track.

3 Costa Cruises

200 South Park Rd., Ste. 200, Hollywood, FL 33021-8541. ℂ 800/462-6782 or 954/266-5600. Fax 954/266-2100. www.costacruises.com.

THE LINE IN A NUTSHELL   Costa's Italian-flavored mid- and megasize European-styled ships offer a festive, international experience—albeit a humble one in the food department.

THE EXPERIENCE   For years, Costa has played up its Italian heritage and history as the factor that primarily distinguishes it from its all-American competition, though today the line employs far fewer Italian crewmembers than in years past (mostly it's just the officers and maitre d's that hail from Italy today), and the new *CostaMediterranea* and *CostaAtlantica,* sister ships designed by Carnival's Joe Farcus, are definitely a step into more mainstream American megaship territory, as are the soon-to-be launched *CostaFortuna* and *CostaMagica,* an even newer class for the line.

Still, you'll find more pasta dishes on the menu than other lines offer, more opera singers among the entertainment offerings, and Italian-oriented activities such as boccie ball. Plus, the line's strength in the Italian-American market definitely helps distinguish it from the Royal Caribbeans, Carnivals, and Norwegians of the world, and the number of Europeans sailing aboard (fewer in the Caribbean than on the line's Mediterranean sailings, but still significant at about 15%) means you get a passenger mix that's much more international than on most other lines, too. Unfortunately, Costa's disappointing food and sometimes-amateurish dining service also separate it from its peers.

Pros

- **Italian flavor:** Entertainment, activities, and cuisine are presented with a festive Italian flair.
- **Very active:** There are a lot of activities, and Costa passengers love to participate, creating a very fun and social environment from morning till night.

Cons

- **Disappointing dining:** While some of the authentic Italian pasta dishes work, overall the cuisine is not great and ranks below that of Celebrity, Carnival, Royal Caribbean, Norwegian, Princess, and Holland America.
- **So-so service:** Compared to that of its peers, the service, especially in the dining room, is rushed and often sloppy. Sometimes you get the feeling they think they're doing you a favor.

Compared with the other mainstream lines, here's how Costa rates:

	Poor	Fair	Good	Excellent	Outstanding
Enjoyment Factor			✓		
Dining		✓			
Activities				✓	
Children's Program		✓			
Entertainment			✓		
Service		✓			
Worth the Money			✓		

COSTA: CONTINENTAL FLAVOR IN THE CARIBBEAN

Costa's origins are as Italian as could be. In 1860, Giacomo Costa established an olive-oil refinery and packaging plant in Genoa. After his death, his sons bought a ship called *Ravenna* to transport raw materials and finished products from Sardinia through Genoa to the rest of Europe, thereby marking the founding of the Costa Line in 1924. Between 1997 and 2000, Carnival Corporation bought up shares in Costa until it became whole owner. Today, despite its glossy corporate veneer, the Costa organization is still very much in the family, though its Italianness comes off more as a marketing idea than a way of life—your cabin steward and waiter, for instance, probably won't hail from Italy, though they may still greet you with a "bon giorno."

The Costa fleet includes a number of older, rebuilt ships from the '60s through the '80s, plus a spate of newly built megaships. Of the current fleet of 10, 2 of the 4 megaships, the new 2,112-passenger *CostaMediterranea* and sister *CostaAtlantica,* are marketed to Americans for Caribbean sailings (several of Costa's ships are marketed only to European passengers). The rest of the year, May to November, the pair sails with the rest of the fleet in Europe, where about 80% of the cruisers are European. At press time, a new class of ships was to debut in November 2003 with the 105,000-ton *CostaFortuna,* with sister *CostaMagica* slated for a late 2004 launch. These ships share the same hull design as *Carnival Triumph* and *Victory,* with a few differences in layout of some public rooms.

PASSENGER PROFILE

Costa attracts passengers of all ages who want lots of action and who deliberately avoid all-American megaships like those of Carnival. Costa passengers are impressed with Italian style and appreciate a sense of fun and cultural adventure (relatively speaking, of course). Italian-Americans are heavily represented aboard every Caribbean cruise, and in general passengers like to participate and have a good time. We've never seen as many guests crowding around a dance floor, eagerly watching contests, or joining in for a go at boccie ball or mask painting as we've seen on *CostaAtlantica.*

In the Caribbean, Costa appeals to retirees and young couples alike, although there are more passengers over 50 than under. Typically you won't see more than 40 or 50 kids on any one cruise except during holidays such as Christmas and spring break, when there may be as many as 300 children on board (remember, these ships aren't in the Caribbean in summer, when more families with kids travel). While about 80% to 90% of passengers are from North America, there's usually a healthy percentage from Europe and South America as well. Because of the international mix, morning announcements and some entertainment are translated into five languages: English, Italian, German, French, and Spanish. While it can be tedious to listen to, the line goes out of its way to keep announcements to a minimum.

DINING

While the pasta is the authentic stuff and worthy of some praise, the rest of the cuisine on the Caribbean-bound ships leaves a lot to be desired. On a recent cruise, a salad billed as offering hearts of palm included just one little piece, French onion soup topped with a thin piece of what appeared to be Wonder

Bread and a triangle of Velveeta, and the lobster chunks in the linguine all' aragosta were peanut-size—when you could find them at all. Vegetables were often dried out, sauces and meat were bland, and little effort put was into presentation and service, which is friendly enough, but often amateurish.

Daily menus feature a main entree choice from a region of Italy, such as Pappardelle alla Cacciatora (wide flat pasta tossed with porcini mushrooms and carrots in a cream sauce) or a risotto dish. One or two **pasta dishes** are also on each dinner menu, such as *crespelle al prosciutto e formaggio* (pasta crepe filled with ham and cheese and topped with cream sauce) or *fagottini ai quattro formaggi* (ribbon pasta stuffed with meat, ricotta, and spinach in a four-cheese sauce). Much of the pasta is made from scratch on the ship (lasagna and cannelloni, for instance), while the fettuccini, spaghetti, and raviolis are shipped in from Italy. Keep in mind that because it's made the Italian way, the pasta is heavier and richer than some Americans are used to, but it's definitely the highlight of the food aboard. **Pizza,** offered from the buffet restaurant around lunchtime, is also homemade and authentic (very thin without a lot of gooey cheese), and tastes much better than it looks. Otherwise, expect cruise staples such as poached salmon, lobster tail, grilled lamb chops, and beef tenderloin, plus **vegetarian dishes** such as roasted vegetable frittata or spaghetti with a zucchini cheese sauce. There is a light **"healthy" recommendation,** such as *Petto di Tacchino al Forno* (roasted breast of turkey), and several staples offered each night, such as a Caesar salad, baked or grilled fish, sirloin steak, and a linguine with seafood sauce.

On the second formal night, flaming baked Alaska is paraded through the dining room and complimentary champagne is poured—though don't expect the good stuff. Other desserts include tiramisu, gelatos, *zabaione* (meringue pie), and chocolate soufflé, which was the best dessert we had while aboard.

Costa is big on themes, and in keeping with the line's Italian origins, three of the seven **theme nights** on a typical Caribbean cruise focus on Italian food and some aspect of Italian lore, legend, and ambience. **Festa Italiana** turns the ship into an Italian street festival where guests are encouraged to wear the colors of the Italian flag and participate in boccie ball, pizza-dough-tossing contests, tarantella dance lessons, Venetian-mask making, and Italian karaoke. **Notte Tropical** is a deck party with a Mediterranean twist, where guests can enjoy ethnic dancing and ice-carving demonstrations amid the typical Caribbean deck party trimmings. On **Benuento A Bordo,** the first formal night, women passengers are presented with a silver necklace by the waiters. The highlight of many cruises is **Roman Bacchanal Toga Night,** when at least some of the guests don togas (usually a bedsheet fastened with a belt around the waist) along with a good sense of humor. Even the cruise director, who is usually American or British during Caribbean sailings, is likely to threaten, "No sheet, no eat." So, whether you look good in a toga or not, you'll probably be wearing one at dinner. So traditional are these toga nights that some repeat passengers bring their own.

Informal, **buffet-style dinners** and **reservations-only alternative restaurants** (with a $23 cover charge) are offered on both ships. Dishes in the alternative venue include the likes of *aragosta con rigatoni al pomodoro fresco* (rigatoni served with lobster and tomatoes) and a *costolette d'agnello arrosto con tortino di patate* (grilled lamb chops). The ambience is very nice and romantic in these restaurants, but the cuisine isn't much better than you'll get in the regular dining room. Daily **midnight buffets** focus on a theme, such as pastry, and are filling, though nothing special.

Life on Costa's Private Island

On all eastern Caribbean itineraries, passengers spend 1 day at Costa's private beach, **Catalina Island** (formerly called Serena Cay), a deserted island off the coast of the Dominican Republic. This relaxing patch of paradise offers a long beach, with a rocky shoreline in places (less so in the crowded area adjacent to the tender dock). For more privacy, keep walking down the beach and it becomes wonderfully peaceful. The palm-tree-fringed beach offers not only sunbathing, but also activities such as volleyball, beach Olympics, and snorkeling. Music and a beach barbecue round out the day.

A local island vendor rents jet skis and offers banana-boat rides. There's a strip of shops selling jewelry, beachwear, and other souvenirs, and the local vendors running them aren't shy about trying to entice you to buy something. The ship sets up a cabana to do massages on the beach, but locals often roam around offering them too. For $25 (a fraction of what the ship charges), a local woman gave Heidi a great foot and shoulder massage. A couple of locals also sell coconuts for $2 apiece; they hack the end off and plunk in a straw or two, and you can drink the wonderful coconut milk inside. After you're finished, take it back and they'll whack the thing into pieces with a machete and scrape out the tender coconut meat for you.

All of Costa's main dining rooms (and show lounges) are designated as completely nonsmoking.

ACTIVITIES

More than anything else, Costa is known for its lineup of festive activities—some reflecting its Italian heritage—and passengers on these ships love to participate. Nights are given over to Italian and Mediterranean theme nights (see "Dining," above); daytime activities include **Italian language and cooking classes,** as well as traditional cruise staples such as jackpot bingo, bridge, arts and crafts, dance classes, shuffleboard, art auctions, horse racing, Ping-Pong, and fun poolside competitions in which teams have to put on Roman-style costumes or don silly hats. Each ship also has a combo library and Internet center, as well as a large card room. Aerobics and stretch classes are held by the pool or in the indoor aerobics studio, and the music is often blaring at full blast. Live steel-drum music is featured throughout the day, too. Luckily, there is lots of deck space across three or four levels for sunbathing, so you can escape the noise if you want to. On *Mediterranea* and *Atlantica,* there's a fun all-ages water slide operating a couple of hours a day.

For avid duffers, **private golf lessons** and **videotaped golf-swing analysis** are available on board with a PGA member golf instructor (30-min. lessons are $35; hour-long lessons are $60). There are also a driving net and daily putting tournaments, and the pro will accompany guests who sign up for golfing shore excursions to some of the best courses in the Caribbean, such as Mahogany Run in St. Thomas.

Costa Fleet Itineraries

Ship	Itineraries
CostaAtlantica	**7-night E. Carib:** Round-trip from Fort Lauderdale, Dec 2003–Apr 2004, visiting San Juan, St. Thomas, Catalina Island*, and Nassau, with 2 days at sea. Alternates with **7-night W. Carib:** Round-trip from Fort Lauderdale, Dec 2003–Apr 2004, visiting Key West, Cozumel, Ocho Rios (Jamaica), and Grand Cayman, with 2 days at sea. **Non-Caribbean Itineraries:** Europe.
Costa-Mediterranea	**7-night E. Carib:** Round-trip from Fort Lauderdale, Nov 2003–Mar 2004, visiting San Juan, St. Thomas, Catalina Island*, and Nassau, with 2 days at sea. Alternates with **7-night W. Carib:** Round-trip from Fort Lauderdale, Nov 2003–Mar 2004, visiting Key West, Cozumel and Pregresso/Merida (Mexico), and Grand Cayman, with 2 days at sea. Apr 4 sailing replaces Grand Cayman with Freeport, Bahamas. **Non-Caribbean Itineraries:** Europe.

*Costa's private island, off the coast of the Dominican Republic

A **Catholic mass** is held almost every day in each ship's chapel. For married couples, vow-renewal ceremonies are conducted on board in Port Everglades and St. Thomas.

CHILDREN'S PROGRAM

Costa's kids' programs and facilities are not nearly as extensive as those available on other lines such as Disney or Royal Caribbean, and there are usually far fewer children on board in the first place. At least two full-time youth counselors sail aboard each Costa ship, with additional staff whenever more than a dozen kids are on the passenger list. Both ships offer **supervised activities** for kids 3 to 17, divided into two age groups unless enough children are aboard to divide them into three (3–5, 6–12, and 13–17 years). The **Costa Kids Club,** for ages 3 to 12, includes such activities as Nintendo, galley and bridge tours, arts and crafts, scavenger hunts, Italian-language lessons, bingo, board games, face painting, movies, kids' karaoke, and pizza and ice-cream-sundae parties. The ships each have a pleasant children's playroom and a teen disco. If enough teens are on board, the **Costa Teens Club** for ages 13 to 17 offers tennis, foosball, darts competitions, and karaoke.

When ships are at sea in the Caribbean, supervised Kids Club hours are from 9am to noon, 3 to 6pm, and 9 to 11:30pm. The program also operates during port days, but on a more limited basis.

Two nights a week, a great complimentary **Parents' Night Out program** runs from 6 to 11:30pm during which kids 3 and older (they must be out of diapers) are entertained and given a special buffet or pizza party while mom and dad get a night out alone. All other times, **group babysitting** for ages 3 and up is available every night from 9 to 11:30pm at no cost, and from 11:30pm to 1:30am for $10 per child per hour. No private, in-cabin babysitting is available.

Children must be at least 3 months old to sail with Costa.

ENTERTAINMENT

Although the passengers are American and international, and the location is the Caribbean, the main entertainment focus aboard Costa ships is Italian, with concerts, operatic solos, puppet or marionette shows, mime, acrobatics, and cabaret that, although produced with an Italian bent, do not require audiences to actually know the language. On a recent cruise, soloist Richard Ianni wowed the audience with a wonderful operatic voice and favorites ranging from "Volare" to classic arias. Sometimes, popular Italian-American entertainers such as Al Martino and Don Cornell are featured.

The Caribbean-bound ships have two-tiered, half-moon-shaped theaters. The ones on *CostaMediterranea* and *Atlantica* have fog machines, three video screens, some 250 lights, and all sorts of moving and sliding stage sections, which allow them to present more elaborate Broadway-style song-and-dance revues than the line's older ships. The ships have glitzy casinos as well as hopping discos, which often get going only after 1am.

SERVICE

While service is efficient in most areas, the crew doesn't seem to be as eager to please or as friendly as staff on cruise lines such as Carnival, Royal Caribbean, and Celebrity. Cabin service works best, while the dining staff, though undeniably hardworking, seems to lack experience and finesse when compared to that of other lines in the mainstream category. Waiters rush around in a frenzy and service is often slipshod. On a recent cruise, half the passengers at a table would often receive their entrees 10 minutes before the other half. Wine and water were dribbled across the table, and dirty dishes sometimes remained after new courses were brought. Other service areas that were disappointing on a recent cruise included the distribution of luggage on embarkation day; suitcases were heaped in chaotic piles outside of passenger elevators making it next-to-impossible to maneuver around them (most other lines seem to have a better system).

Unlike in the past, when most Costa crew was Italian, today the waiters and cabin stewards are an international group such as you'd find on Carnival or Royal Caribbean, while officers and the maitre d's are mostly Italians.

There are **no self-service laundry facilities** on any of the Costa ships.

CostaAtlantica • CostaMediterranea

The Verdict

These 2,112-passenger ships are megas with a European ambience and a head-turning decor. They have more of a whimsical Carnival-style spin and more cutting-edge features than those aboard the line's older ships, including cabin balconies, a water slide, and a two-level gym.

CostaAtlantica *(photo: Costa Cruises)*

Specifications

Size (in tons)	85,000	Crew	920 (Internat'l)
Number of Cabins	1,056	Passenger/Crew Ratio	2.3 to 1
Number of Outside Cabins	843	Year Launched	
Cabins with Verandas	742	*Atlantica*	2000
Number of Passengers	2,112	*Mediterranea*	2003
Officers	Italian/Internat'l	Last Major Refurbishment	N/A

Frommer's Ratings (Scale of 1–5)

★★★½

Cabin Comfort & Amenities	4	Dining Options	3
Ship Cleanliness & Maintenance	4	Gym & Spa Facilities	4
Public Comfort/Space	4	Children's Facilities	3
Decor	4	Enjoyment Factor	3

The *CostaMediterranea* and *CostaAtlantica* represent a new chapter for Costa, being a kind of European version of the "Fun Ships" operated by sister company Carnival (in fact, Carnival's designer, Joe Farcus, was the man behind the design of these ships, as well as for coming fleetmates *CostaMagica* and *CostaFortuna*). At nearly 1,000 feet long, the pair cut a sleek profile, and their bright yellow smokestack creates a distinctive look, sitting up top like a giant barrel, emblazoned with a big blue Costa **C**. The *Atlantica,* the first of the pair to debut, was a first for Costa in several ways and set the tone for all of the line's future ships, with lots of cabin balconies, a two-story spa and fitness center, and a stunning cafe based on Venice's Caffè Florian.

As much as the ships represent new things for Costa, though, *Atlantica* and *Mediterranea* also have their share of design flaws including the wide outdoor promenade on Deck 3 that, at the bow, mysteriously becomes part of an interior promenade featuring an odd garden motif with little marble tables and wicker chairs along its edges (same as on the *Carnival Spirit* and *Legend*). It never gets much use. Also, the high, glazed-glass windbreaks at the forward end of Decks 9 and 10 prohibit any good view of the bow.

At press time, *CostaMediterranea* was slated to debut in June of 2003, with the same layout and public rooms as sister *Atlantica.*

Cabins & Rates

Cabins	Per Diems from	Sq. Ft.	Fridge	Hair Dryer	Sitting Area	TV
Inside	$93	158	yes	yes	no	yes
Outside	$107	175	yes	yes	yes	yes
Suite	$286	272–367	yes	yes	yes	yes

CABINS The *CostaAtlantica* and *Mediterranea* have balconies on over 75% of their cabins (700+). All cabins feature caramel-color wood tones and warm autumn-hued fabrics that create a pleasant environment. Bathrooms have good storage space. All cabins have minifridges, hair dryers, safes, and more than adequate storage space. All outside cabins have sitting areas with couches. The views from all category-4 cabins on Deck 4 are completely obstructed by lifeboats, and on Deck 5 the category-7 balcony cabins directly above are partially obstructed by the tops of the lifeboats. Avoid these cabins.

The 32 Panorama Suites on Deck 6 measure 272 square feet, plus a 90-square-foot balcony, and have attractive wooden coffee tables, chairs, and desks, plus large couches that can double as a bed, two separate floor-to-ceiling closets, lots of drawer space, and large bathrooms with bathtubs, marble counters, and double sinks. Adjacent is a dressing room with a vanity table, drawers, and a closet. The Grand Suites are the largest accommodations aboard. Six are located amidships on Deck 7 and measure 372 square feet plus 118-square-foot balconies; the other eight are aft on Decks 4, 6, 7, and 8 and measure 367 square feet, plus 282-square-foot balconies.

About 30 pairs of cabins have connecting doors. There are eight cabins accessible to wheelchairs.

PUBLIC AREAS   When you first lay eyes on the *Atlantica*'s atrium, an Alice in Wonderland–like fantasyland, it's a jarring scene of fire-engine red, gold, and green furniture and colorful, Roman-style ceiling murals punctuated by three long icicle-like chandeliers reaching down toward the La Dolce Vita bar. Soon, though, you'll grow attached to the buttery-soft red leather chairs (including several pairs of pleasantly absurd ones with towering tall backs) and huge framed black-and-white photographs of 1940s and 1950s movie stars, which fill the space and spread into the adjacent Via Veneto lounge, which leads to the two-story dining room. In general, the ship has a busy feel, with stairway carpeting and rails presenting a zigzaggy pastiche of bright colors and shapes.

Interiors on the *Mediterranea* are inspired by noble 17th- and 18th-century Italian palazzo, and heavy on dance and theatre imagery. The eye-catching atrium and main lobby area on this ship feature the major characters from the commedia dell'arte, who have done so much to promote Naples and the city's legends.

The *Atlantica*'s 12 passenger decks are all named after movies by the Italian film director Federico Fellini, such as *8½, Roma, La Strada, Amarcord, La Dolce Vita,* and *Ginger and Fred.* A cute idea, but a better one would have been adding some signage in stairwells and at elevators so passengers know where they are and where the various public rooms are located—you'll have to guess your way around until about day 5, when you'll finally have had enough practice to remember.

Among the ships' numerous bars and lounges is the red-and-gold Madame Butterfly lounge on the *Atlantica,* where the waitstaff wear Mandarin-style jackets and passengers gather for pre-dinner cocktails, bingo, and after-dinner entertainment such as the Mr. *CostaAtlantica/Mediterannea* contest and group dances (a la "YMCA") led by the cruise staff. The *Atlantica*'s Dante's Disco is a darkish, two-story, cavelike place with a video-screen wall, fog machines, and a translucent dance floor—exactly what you want in a bona fide nightclub. The Corallo Lounge, used for late-night comedy acts, karaoke, and cocktail parties, has bizarre walls covered with coral. The three-level Caruso theater has red velvet high-backed seating and a very high-tech and elaborate stage with risers, an orchestra pit, set tracks, and a center-stage turntable. A big glitzy casino features a festive Vegas-style mood, and a roomy, elegant card room is designed in a red-and-gold motif.

A kids' playroom, teen center, and large video arcade are squirreled away far forward on Decks 4 and 5. A five-station Internet center is in the elegant library, and everywhere, the great door handles are in the shape of Costa's classic barrel-like funnels. You'll also find a chapel where Mass is held, as well as conference rooms.

DINING OPTIONS   Aside from an elegant two-story dining room, there's a two-story alternative, reservations-only restaurant high up on Deck 10 called Club Atlantica, charging guests $23 per person for the privilege of dining (suite guests can go free of charge once per cruise). Its atmosphere is its best feature, with dim lights, candlelight, fresh flowers, soft live music, and lots of space between tables. We found the food to be spotty on a recent cruise, though. The *Corzetti al pesto* (pasta with basil sauce) was very good, while the sea bass and flounder entrees were not great. Service was amateurish all the way around. All in all, it wasn't worth the price.

C **Preview: *CostaFortuna* & *CostaMagica***

At press time, a new class of ship for Costa was in the works. The 2,718-passenger, 105,000-ton *CostaFortuna* was scheduled to debut in November of 2003, to be followed by sister *CostaMagica* a year later. Of the 1,358 cabins, 853 will offer ocean views, 522 of them with private balconies; the ships share the same hull design as the *Carnival Triumph* and *Victory*. Carnival design guru Joe Farcus is behind their decor, so expect lots of color and whimsy. The ships are being built by Fincantieri at Genoa's Sestri Ponente shipyards, and will be the largest cruise ships to ever fly the Italian flag, as well as the largest passenger ships ever built by the historic yard, whose largest previous vessel was the famed 45,911-ton trans-Atlantic liner *Michelangelo*, inaugurated in 1965. With this in mind, the interior design and names of public areas on the *CostaFortuna* will reflect the legendary Italian liners that used to offer regular passenger services between Italy and the Americas.

Now, Caffè Florian, that's an impressive place. Modeled on the famous 18th-century cafe of the same name in Venice's St. Mark's Square, it's the *Atlantica*'s most stunning room, with gilt moldings, intricate walls and ceiling murals, delicate red velvet wood-frame chairs, and white marble tables. (*Mediterranea* also has a cafe, but it's not a Florian's.) You can get specialty coffees, teas, and cocktails served on elegant silver trays with delicate china and a fresh flower. An English-style afternoon tea is also offered for $7.50 a person. A live trio, which performs the same repertoire as the musicians in the real Caffè Florian in Venice, serenades guests with classical music.

The ship has a sprawling indoor/outdoor casual breakfast and lunch buffet restaurant where, 6 nights a week, you can have an informal buffet-style dinner. Soft ice cream and pizza made with herbs and fresh mozzarella are served from stations in the buffet restaurant.

POOL, FITNESS & SPA FACILITIES   *Atlantica* and *Mediterranea* are the first Costa vessels to have a two-story ocean-view spa and fitness center, and a retractable glass roof over its main pool. The gym is a pleasant tiered affair with machines on many different levels and a hot tub in the center. The spa offers your typical menu of treatments, including 50-minute massages, facials, and reflexology treatments. Three pools are on Deck 9, a bright yellow-and-blue area for fun in the sun; the main pool amidships by the band stage is the loudest and most action-packed. There's a neat water slide near the aft pool (and adjacent to a kids' wading pool) for all ages, a total of three hot tubs, a golf driving net, and a combo volleyball, basketball, and tennis court. If you explore, you'll find lots of deck space for sunbathing and hiding away with a deck chair and a good book.

4 Disney Cruise Line

P.O. Box 10210, Lake Buena Vista, FL 32830. © **800/951-3532** or 888/325-2500. Fax 407/566-3541. www. disneycruise.com.

THE LINE IN A NUTSHELL Though Carnival, Royal Caribbean, Celebrity, and Princess all devote significant attention to kids, it took Disney to create vessels where both kids and adults are really catered to equally, and with style. If you love Disney, you'll love these two floating theme parks.

THE EXPERIENCE Both classic and ultramodern, the line's two ships are like no others in the industry, designed to evoke the grand transatlantic liners but also boasting a handful of truly innovative features, including extra-large cabins for families, several restaurants through which passengers rotate on every cruise, fantastic Disney-inspired entertainment, separate adult pools and lounges, and the biggest kids' facilities at sea. In many ways, the experience is more Disney than it is cruise (for instance, there's no casino); but on the other hand, the ships are surprisingly elegant and well laid out, with the Disneyisms sprinkled around subtly, like fairy dust, amid the Art Deco and Art Nouveau design motifs. Head to toe, inside and out, they're a class act.

Disney's is nothing if not organized, so its 3- and 4-day cruises aboard *Disney Wonder* are designed to be combined with a Disney theme park and hotel package to create a weeklong land/sea vacation. You can also book these shorter cruises (as well as *Disney Magic*'s weeklong cruises) separately.

Pros
- **Kids' program:** In both the size of the facilities and the range of activities, it's the most extensive at sea.
- **Entertainment:** The line's family-oriented musicals are some of the best onboard entertainment today.
- **Family-style cabins:** All have sofa beds to sleep families of at least three, and the majority have 1½ bathrooms.
- **Spacious feel:** Though the ships can carry up to 3,325 passengers with all berths full, they rarely feel crowded; and with most kids' facilities located on Deck 5, the other decks don't have a summer-camp feel.
- **Innovative dining:** No other ships have diners rotating among three different but equally appealing sit-down restaurants.

Cons
- **Limited adult entertainment:** There's no casino or library, and adult nightclubs tend to be quiet after busy family days.
- **Small gyms:** Considering the ships' large size, their gyms are tiny.

Compared with the other mainstream lines, here's how Disney rates:

	Poor	Fair	Good	Excellent	Outstanding
Enjoyment Factor				✓	
Dining			✓		
Activities			✓		
Children's Program					✓
Entertainment					✓
Service			✓		
Worth the Money				✓	

DISNEY: THE OLD MOUSE & THE SEA

For at least half a century now, Disney has been in the business of merging modern-day expectations and cutting-edge technology with a nostalgic sense of American culture: for childhood innocence, for the frontier, for an idealized turn-of-the-century past, for our mythic heroes. And whether you're a fan or a critic, it's indisputable that at this point the company itself has become a part of our culture. There are probably few people alive—and certainly few Americans—who could fail to recognize Disney's more high-profile creations: Mickey, Donald Duck, Sleeping Beauty, "When You Wish Upon a Star." They've become part of our national identity. And that's why *Disney Magic* and *Disney Wonder* work so well. In nearly every aspect of the onboard experience, they have what most other ships lack: a cultural frame of reference that's recognized by almost everyone.

Many Disney passengers purchase their cruises as part of 7-day **seamless land/sea packages** that combine 3- or 4-night cruises with 4- or 3-night precruise park stays. Disney buses shuttle passengers between Orlando and the ship—about an hour's drive, during which an orientation video imparts some info about the cruise experience. At Disney's swank cruise terminal at Port Canaveral, check-in is made easier and faster because guests who have come from the resorts already have their all-purpose, computerized Key to the World cards, which identify them at boarding, get them into their cabins, and serve as their onboard charge cards. (If you're just doing the cruise, you get your Key to the World card when you arrive at the terminal.) You don't have to worry about your luggage, either: It's picked up at the resort and delivered to your cabin soon after you board.

PASSENGER PROFILE

Disney's ships attract a wide mix of passengers, from honeymooners to seniors, but naturally a large percentage is made up of young American families with children (with a smallish number of foreign passengers as well). Because of this, the overall age demographic tends to be younger than that aboard many of the other mainstream ships, with many passengers in their 30s and early-to-mid 40s. According to Disney Cruise Line president Matt Ouimet, the bulk of the line's passengers are first-time cruisers, and since the line attracts so many families (sometimes large ones), about 50% of bookings are for multiple cabins.

DINING

Disney's dining concept sets it apart from the big-ship crowd. While the food is average cruise fare, the neat catch is that there are **three restaurants** that passengers (and their servers) rotate among for dinner over the course of the cruise. On one night, passengers dine on roasted duck breast, garlic-roasted beef tenderloin in a green peppercorn sauce, or herb-crusted sea bass in *Magic's* elegant 1930s-era Lumiere's restaurant or *Wonder's* equally elegant nautical-themed Triton's. On another night, they enjoy the likes of potato-crusted grouper, baby back ribs, or mixed grill in the tropical Parrot Cay restaurant. And on the third, they nosh on maple-glazed salmon, pan-fried veal chop, or roasted chicken breast with potato dumplings at Animator's Palate, a bustling eatery with a gimmick: It's a sort of living animation cel, its walls decorated with black-and-white sketches of Disney characters that over the course of the meal gradually become filled in with color. Video screens add to the illusion, and the waiters even disappear at some point to change from black-and-white to full-color vests. It's kinda corny, but fun.

Each restaurant has an early and a late seating, and similar groups are scheduled to rotate together as much as possible (for example, families with young children, adults alone, and families with teens). A **vegetarian option** is offered at all meals, and kosher, halal, low-salt, low-fat, and other **special diets** can be accommodated if you request them when you book your cruise, or soon thereafter; once you're aboard, a chef and head server will meet with you to determine your exact needs. Kids' menus start with appetizers such as fruit cocktail and chicken soup before heading on to such familiar entree items as meatloaf, ravioli, pizza, hot dogs, hamburger, and mac-and-cheese. The wine list is fair, and includes bottles by Silverado Vineyards, owned by members of the Disney family.

Both ships also have a romantic **adults-only restaurant** called Palo, serving Italian specialties such as ravioli, tortellini, risotto, and pumpkin-filled raviollini, as well as excellent gourmet pizzas—the one with roasted peppers, arugula, and goat cheese is mighty fine. A decent selection of Italian wines is available, and the dessert menu includes a fine chocolate soufflé and a weird-but-tasty dessert pizza. The restaurant itself is horseshoe-shaped and perched way up on Deck 10 to offer a 270-degree view. Service is attentive but not overly formal, and you don't have to dress up, though a jacket for men may be nice. Reservations are essential, and should be made immediately after you board, as the docket fills up fast. Here's the good news: It's cheap—just $5 per person, including tip.

Breakfast and lunch are served in several restaurants, both sit-down and buffet. In addition, *Magic*'s 7-night cruises also offer a champagne brunch, an afternoon tea, themed dinners, buffets, and casual dinners on nights 2 though 6 in Topsiders, the indoor/outdoor buffet.

Magic's 7-night itineraries have one formal night and one semiformal night. The rest of the evenings are casual (no jackets or ties necessary). *Wonder* is casual throughout the cruise, though (on both ships) sports jackets are recommended for men dining in Palo and Lumiere's/Triton's.

ACTIVITIES

Unlike on pretty much every other cruise ship, there's no casino of any kind on board, nor even a card room. These are family ships. Activities on both vessels include basketball, Ping-Pong, and shuffleboard tournaments; sports trivia contests; weight-loss, health, and beauty seminars; bingo, Pictionary, and other games; wine tastings; singles mixers; and a chance to navigate the Segway Human Transporter (that two-wheeled, self-balancing scooter that's been in the news these past couple years) through a designated area on Deck 10 ($15 for 20 min.). Each ship also has a spa and a surprisingly small gym for ships this size. During sea days aboard *Magic,* there are also tours, informal lectures on nautical themes and Disney history, and home entertaining and cooking demos. Film buffs and Disney aficionados will appreciate backstage theater tours, drawing and animation workshops, and talks from people involved with Disney's Broadway, film, and television productions. All these activities are complimentary except wine tasting, which costs a hefty $12 per person. There are also dance classes, movies, and that cruise stalwart the Not-So-Newlywed Game, which Disney calls "Match Your Mate." All 7-night itineraries offer a captain's cocktail party with complimentary drinks once per cruise, and all 3- and 4-night cruises host non-alcoholic welcome receptions starring Disney characters. You

Ⓒ Castaway Cay: A Well-Oiled Machine

A port of call on all Disney cruises, Castaway Cay is the line's 1,000-acre, 3-mile-by-2-mile private island in the Bahamas, rimmed with idyllically clear Bahamian water and fine sandy beaches. Disney has developed less than 10% of the island, but in that 10% guests can swim and snorkel, rent bikes and boats, get their hair braided (for two bucks!), shop, send postcards, have a massage, try out a Segway Human Transporter on the pier, or just lounge in a hammock or on the beach. Barbecue burgers, ribs, fish, and chicken are available at Cookie's Bar-B-Q, and several bars are scattered around near the beaches.

The island's best quality is its accessibility. Unlike the private islands of Holland America, Royal Caribbean, Princess, Costa, and NCL, which require ships to anchor offshore and shuttle passengers back and forth on tenders, Castaway Cay's dock allows *Magic* and *Wonder* to pull right up so that guests can step right off the ship and head for the island attractions, either on foot or via the shuttle tram. Families can head to their own beach, lined with lounge chairs and pastel-colored umbrellas, where they can swim, explore the island's 12-acre snorkeling course, climb around on the offshore water-play structure, or rent a kayak, paddle boat, banana boat, sailboat, and other beach equipment. Teens have a beach of their own, where they can play volleyball, soccer, or tetherball; go on a "Wild Side" bike, snorkel, and kayak adventure; or design, build, and race their own boats. Parents who want some quiet time can drop preteens at Scuttle's Cove, a supervised children's activity center for ages 3 to 12. Activities include arts and crafts, music and theater, scavenger hunts, and an excavation site where little ones can check out a 35-foot reproduction whale skeleton and go on their own dig, on which they can make plaster molds of what they find. Meanwhile, Mom and Dad can walk or hop the shuttle to quiet, secluded Serenity Bay, a mile-long stretch of beach in the northwest part of the island, at the end of an old airstrip decorated with vintage prop planes for a 1940s feel. Thirty- and 50-minute massages are available here in private cabanas open to a sea view on one side (sign up for your appointment at the onboard spa on the first day of your cruise to ensure that you get a spot), and the Castaway Air Bar serves up drinks.

Adult- and child-size bicycles can be rented for $6. A 2½-mile out-and-back bike/walking path begins at Serenity Bay, but don't go looking for scenery or wildlife—at best, all you'll see will be the occasional bird or leaping lizard. Parasailing is available for $70 (45 min.; over age 8 only). All-terrain strollers with canopies are available free of charge.

can catch the big game (and lots of small ones) at the **ESPN Skybox bar,** a two-story sports bar with both regulation-size and wide-screen TVs, including a huge one in a side room that's arranged like a small theater. Nacho chips and fixings are free during all open hours. Beer is not, though if you buy a 22-ounce ESPN souvenir glass, you get refills at any bar aboard at the 16-ounce price.

Disney Fleet Itineraries

Ship	Itineraries
Disney Magic	**7-night E. Carib:** Round-trip from Port Canaveral year-round, visiting Sint Maarten, St. Thomas, and Castaway Cay*, with 3 days at sea. Alternates with **7-night W. Carib:** Round-trip from Port Canaveral year-round, visiting Key West, Grand Cayman, Cozumel, and Castaway Cay*, with 2 days at sea. **Non-Caribbean Itineraries:** None.
Disney Wonder	**3-night Bahamas:** Round-trip from Port Canaveral year-round, visiting Nassau and Castaway Cay*. Alternates each sailing with **4-night Bahamas:** Round-trip from Port Canaveral year-round, visiting Nassau and Castaway Cay and spending a 3rd day either at sea or at Freeport. **Non-Caribbean Itineraries:** None.

*Disney's private Bahamian island

CHILDREN'S PROGRAM

Not surprisingly, with potentially hundreds of kids on any given sailing (900, reportedly, on our last sailing), Disney's kids' facilities are the most extensive at sea, with at least 50 counselors supervising the fun for five age groups. Nearly half a deck (comprising two huge play spaces and a nursery) is dedicated to kids. The **Oceaneer Club,** for ages 3 to 7 (with separate activities for ages 3–4 and 5–7), is a kid-proportioned playroom themed on Captain Hook. Kids can climb and crawl on the bridge, ropes, and rails of a giant pirate ship, as well as on jumbo-size animals, barrels, and a sliding board; get dressed up from a trunk full of costumes; dance with Snow White and listen to stories by other Disney characters; or play in the kiddie computer room. The interactive **Oceaneer Lab** offers kids ages 8 to 12 a chance to work on computers, learn fun science with microscopes, build from an enormous vat of Legos, do arts and crafts, hear how animation works, and construct their own radio show. Activities are arranged for two groups, ages 8 to 9 and 10 to 12, and both rooms are open till at least midnight, and till 1am on certain days. Kids can eat lunch and dinner with counselors in the Topsiders and Beach Blanket restaurants all but the first evening of the cruise. A soft-drink package is available for children 12 and under, allowing unlimited fountain soda refills for $15 and $20 for the 3- and 4-night sailings, and $35 for the 7-night cruise. (By comparison, a single soda goes for $1.50.)

For teens (13–17), the teen coffee bar called **Common Grounds** is the place to buy a cappuccino or virgin margarita, plop down into the big comfy chairs, flip through a magazine, slip on headphones and listen to one of the cafe's music CDs, work in the teen Internet center, or play in the adjacent video arcade. Dance parties and workshops on digital photography and video techniques are offered on all cruises.

Neither ship offers private babysitting services. Instead, the **Flounder's Reef Nursery** for kids ages 3 months to 3 years operates from 6pm to midnight daily, and also for a few hours during the morning and afternoon (hours vary according to the day's port schedule). No other line offers such extensive care for babies. Stocked with toys and decorated with *Little Mermaid*–themed bubble murals and lighting that gives an "under the sea" look, the area also has one-way portholes that allow parents to check on their kids without the little ones seeing them. The price is $6 per child per hour, and $5 for each additional child in a family (with a 2-hr. minimum).

And lastly, how's this for peace of mind: Parents get a tuned beeper when they first check in to the kids' program or nursery so that counselors can contact them anywhere on the ship if their child needs them.

ENTERTAINMENT

Disney's fresh, family-oriented entertainment is some of the very best at sea today. After-dinner performances by Broadway-caliber entertainers in the nostalgic Walt Disney Theatre include *Disney Dreams,* a sweet musical medley of Disney classics, taking the audience from *Peter Pan* to *The Lion King;* and *Hercules, A Muse-ical Comedy,* a salute to the popular Disney film that's part story, part song, and part stand-up comedy (with lots of pop-culture references and enough slyness to keep adults entertained as well). *Magic's* 7-night itineraries also feature *Morty the Magnificent,* a musical adventure/love story featuring Morty the Magician and his assistant/girlfriend, Daphne. On both ships, the stage design allows for lots of magic, with actors flying above the boards and disappearing in and out of trap doors, but the most refreshing thing about these shows is that they have *story lines*—rare almost to the point of extinction in the cruise world, which mostly presents musical revues.

Who Wants to Be a Mouseketeer? is a fun **audience-participation show** based on the millionaire quiz show. On Disney's version, the questions are all Disney trivia and the prizes are shipboard credits and a 7-night cruise for the big winner. Family game shows and karaoke take place nightly in the **Studio Sea family nightclub,** and adults (18 and older) can take advantage of the **adults-only entertainment area** in the forward part of Deck 3, with its three themed nightclubs: one quiet, with piano music or soft jazz; one a dance club; and one a comedy room featuring a dueling pianos act with lots of audience participation. Two other nightspots include the **Promenade Lounge,** where live jazz is featured daily; the **ESPN Skybox** sports bar, open till midnight; and the **Buena Vista Theater,** where movies are shown day and evening.

SERVICE

Just as at the parks, Disney staff hails from some 60 countries, including the United States. Service in the dining rooms is efficient and precise, but leans toward friendly rather than formal. Maintenance workers and stewards keep public areas and cabins exceptionally clean and well maintained, and inconspicuous security guards are on duty 24 hours a day to make sure nothing gets out of hand (you know how Mickey can get after one too many martinis . . .). Overall, things run very smoothly.

Services include **laundry** and **dry cleaning** (the ships also have self-service laundry rooms) and 1-hour photo processing. Tips can be charged to your onboard account, or you can give them out in the traditional method: cash.

Disney Magic •
Disney Wonder

Disney Magic *(photo: Disney Cruise Line)*

The Verdict

The only ships on the planet that successfully re-create the grandeur of the classic transatlantic liners, albeit in a modern, Disneyfied way.

Specifications

Size (in tons)	83,000	Crew	950 (Internat'l)
Number of Cabins	877	Passenger/Crew Ratio	1.8 to 1
Number of Outside Cabins	625	Year Launched	
Cabins with Verandas	378	*Magic*	1998
Number of Passengers	1,754*	*Wonder*	1999
Officers	International	Last Major Refurbishment	N/A

* Note: Double-occupancy figure. With children's berths filled, capacity can go as high as 3,325.

Frommer's Ratings (Scale of 1–5)

ⓇⓇⓇⓇ ½

Cabin Comfort & Amenities	5	Dining Options	4.5
Ship Cleanliness & Maintenance	5	Gym & Spa Facilities	3
Public Comfort/Space	4	Children's Facilities	5
Decor	5	Enjoyment Factor	5

These long, proud-looking ships carry 1,754 passengers at the rate of two per cabin, but since Disney is a family company and its ships were built expressly to carry three, four, and five people in virtually every cabin, the ship could theoretically carry a whopping 3,325 passengers. Typically, though, every single bed will not be filled, and getting up past about 2,600 passengers is not common.

Cabins & Rates

Cabins	Per Diems from	Sq. Ft.	Fridge	Hair Dryer	Sitting Area	TV
Inside	$114	184–214	yes	yes	yes	yes
Outside	$151	226–268	yes	yes	yes	yes
Suite	$197	259–1,029	yes	yes	yes	yes

CABINS   The Disney ships offer the family-friendliest cabins at sea, with standard accommodations equivalent to the suites or demi-suites on most ships—they're about 25% larger than the industry standard. All of the 877 cabins have at least a sitting area with a sofa bed to sleep families of three or four, many also have a bunk to sleep five, and nearly half have private verandas. One-bedroom suites have private verandas and sleep four or five comfortably; two-bedroom suites sleep seven. Outside cabins that don't have verandas have jumbo-size porthole windows.

The decor is virtually identical from cabin to cabin, combining modern design with nostalgic ocean-liner elements such as a steamer-trunk closet for kids, globe- and telescope-shaped lamps, map designs on the bedspreads, and a framed black-and-white 1930s shot of Mr. and Mrs. Walt Disney aboard the fabled ocean liner *Rex*. Warm wood tones predominate, with Deco touches in the metal and glass fittings and light fixtures. The majority of cabins have two bathrooms—a sink and toilet in one and a shower/tub combo and a sink in the other. Both, while compact, have ample shelf space. This is something you won't find in any other standard cabin industry-wide, and it's a great boon for families. All cabins have a minifridge, hair dryer, safe, TV, shower-tub combo, sitting area, and lots of storage space.

One-bedroom suites are done up with wood veneer in a definite Deco mood. Sliding frosted-glass French doors divide the living room from the bedroom, which has a large-screen TV, queen-size bed (which can be split to make two twins), chair and ottoman, dressing room, makeup table, and whirlpool tub in the bathroom. A second, guest bathroom is located off the living room, which also has a bar and a queen-size sofa bed. The veranda extends the length of both rooms. Two-bedroom and Royal suites are also available.

There are 214 connecting cabins on each ship, and 16 cabins are fitted for wheelchair users.

PUBLIC AREAS   Both ships have several theaters and lounges, including an adults-only area with a comedy club, piano/jazz lounge, and disco. There's also a family-oriented entertainment lounge called Studio Sea for karaoke, game shows, and dancing; the Promenade Lounge for jazz in the evenings; a 24-hour Internet cafe with eight flat-screen stations; and a sports bar, the ESPN Skybox, located in the ship's forward funnel, which is a fake, there simply to make the ship prettier. A 270-seat cinema shows recent-release and classic Disney movies. The children's facilities, as you'd expect, are the largest of any ship at sea (see "Children's Program," above, for details).

Throughout, both ships have some of the best artwork at sea, owing to Disney's vast archive of animation cels, production sketches, costume studies, and inspirational artwork, featuring characters we've all grown up with. Other art—notably the "Disney Cruise Line Seaworthy Facts" near the photo shop and A-to-Z of seagoing terms near the theater—was created specifically for the ships and gets a big, big thumbs up. Canned music pumped into the public areas and corridors tends toward big-band music and crooner tunes or surf-type pop.

DINING OPTIONS   Disney's unique rotation dining setup has guests sampling three different restaurants at dinner over the course of their cruise, with an adults-only specialty restaurant also available, by reservation only (see "Dining," above). At breakfast and lunch, the buffet-style spread in *Magic's* Topsiders and *Wonder's* Beach Blanket restaurants offers deli meats, cheeses, and rice and vegetable dishes, as well as a carving station, salad bar, and a dessert table with yummy chocolate-chip cookies. Overall, though, compared to other ships this size, these food stations offer slim pickings and are cramped and poorly designed, although seating is plentiful and spills onto attractive wooden tables and chairs out on deck.

Options for afternoon noshing poolside include Pinocchio's Pizzeria; Pluto's Dog House for hot dogs, hamburgers, and fries; and Scoops ice-cream bar. There's 24-hour room service from a limited menu, but no midnight buffet unless you count the spread offered at the late-night deck party held once per cruise. Instead, hors d'oeuvres are served to passengers in the bars around midnight.

POOL, FITNESS & SPA FACILITIES   The Pool Deck of each ship has three pools: Mickey's Kids' Pool, shaped like the mouse's big-eared head, with a great big white-gloved Mickey hand holding up a snaking yellow slide; Goofy's Family Pool, where adults and children can mingle; and the Quiet Cove Adult Pool, with whirlpools and poolside Signals Bar.

Just beyond the adult pool area is a spa and the tiny, surprisingly drab fitness center (tiny compared to those aboard Carnival, Holland America, and most of the other mainstream lines), with a small aerobics room, six treadmills, dumbbells, and a handful of cycle, elliptical, and Cybex machines. The gyms are so much of an afterthought that it's even difficult to find them, via a circuitous route through the spa. Nice view once you get there, though: The gyms' forward windows look down into the bridge, where you can watch the officers at work. The 8,500-square-foot, Steiner-managed Vista Spa & Salon is much more impressive, with attractive tiled treatment rooms, changing rooms with comfy chaise longues, a sauna, and a steam room. Both ships have an outdoor Sports Deck with basketball and paddle tennis. There's also shuffleboard and Ping-Pong, and joggers and walkers can circuit the Promenade Deck, which is generally unobstructed (though the forward, enclosed section may be closed off when the ship is arriving and departing port because it's adjacent to the anchor mechanisms).

5 Holland America Line

300 Elliott Ave. W., Seattle, WA 98119. © 877/724-5425 or 206/281-3535. Fax 800/628-4855. www.holland america.com.

THE LINE IN A NUTSHELL   Holland America has been in business since 1873, and has managed to hang on to more of its seafaring history and tradition than any line today except Cunard. It offers a moderately priced, classic, and casual yet refined cruise experience.

THE EXPERIENCE   Holland America consistently delivers a solid product with old-world elegance. Though the line has been retooling itself to attract younger passengers and families, it still caters mostly to older folks, and so generally offers a more sedate and stately experience than other mainstream lines, plus excellent service and cuisine.

Aside from the new *Zuiderdam* and *Oosterdam,* the line's first megaships, HAL's well-maintained vessels are midsize and cozy, and all have excellent (and remarkably similar) layouts that ease passenger movement. Decor tends toward the stylish and classic, though the newer ships have been getting much bolder with their color palate. Throughout the public areas you'll see flowers that testify to Holland's place in the floral trade, Indonesian fabrics and woodcarvings that evoke the country's relationship with its former colony, and seafaring memorabilia that often harks back to Holland America's own history.

Pros

- **Great service:** HAL's primarily Indonesian and Filipino staff is exceptionally gracious and friendly.
- **Traditional classic ambience:** With the exception of too-bright *Zuiderdam,* the ships' classy decor and impressive art collections lend them a more traditional ocean-liner ambience than you'll find with nearly any other line.
- **Chocolate!** The once-per-cruise dessert extravaganzas and the occasional spreads of sweets guarantee you'll gain a few pounds.
- **Great gyms:** Except on the old *Noordam,* HAL's gyms are some of the largest, most attractive, roomiest, and best stocked at sea today.

Cons

- **Sleepy nightlife:** While there are always a few stalwarts and a couple of busy-ish nights, these aren't party ships. If you're big on late-night dancing and bar-hopping, you may find yourself partying mostly with the entertainment staff.
- **Fairly homogenous passenger profile:** Although younger faces are starting to pepper the mix (especially on *Zuiderdam*'s 7-night cruises), most HAL passengers still tend to be low-key, fairly sedentary, 55-plus North American couples.

Compared with the other mainstream lines, here's how HAL rates:

	Poor	Fair	Good	Excellent	Outstanding
Enjoyment Factor				✓	
Dining				✓	
Activities			✓		
Children's Program		✓			
Entertainment				✓	
Service					✓
Worth the Money					✓

HOLLAND AMERICA: GOING DUTCH

One of the most famous shipping companies in the world, Holland America Line was founded in 1873 as the Nederlandsch-Amerikaansche StoomvAart Maatschappij (NASM, or Netherlands-American Steamship Company). Its first ocean liner, the original *Rotterdam,* took her maiden, 15-day voyage from the Netherlands to New York City in 1872.

By the early 1900s, the company had been renamed Holland America Line and was one of the major lines transporting immigrants from Europe to the United States, as well as providing passenger/cargo service between Holland and the Dutch East Indies via the Suez Canal. During World War II, the company's headquarters moved from Nazi-occupied Holland to Dutch-owned Curaçao, then the site of a strategic oil refinery, and after the war the company forged strong links with North American interests. The line continued regular transatlantic crossings up until 1971, and then turned to offering cruises full-time. In 1983, it began building the fleet of midsize ships that exists today; and in 1989, it was acquired by Carnival Corporation, which improved the line's entertainment and cuisine while maintaining its overall character and sense of history. Today, all the line's vessels are named for other classic vessels in the line's history—*Rotterdam,* for example, is the sixth HAL ship to bear that name—and paintings of older HAL ships by maritime artist Stephen Card appear in the stairways on all the ships except *Noordam.*

PASSENGER PROFILE

For years, HAL was known for catering to an almost exclusively older crowd, with most passengers in their 70s on up. Today, following intensive efforts to attract younger passengers, about 40% of the line's Caribbean guests are under age 55, with a few young families peppering the mix, especially in summers and during holiday weeks. Still, it's no Carnival or Disney, and HAL's older ships especially were designed with older folks in mind—some even have fold-down seats in the elevators.

Passengers tend to be amiable, low-key, better educated than their equivalents aboard sister line Carnival, and much more amenable to dressing up—you'll see lots of tuxedos and evening gowns on formal nights. Though you'll see some people walking laps on the Promenade Deck, others taking advantage of the ships' large gyms, and some taking athletic shore excursions, these aren't terribly active cruises, and passengers overall tend to be sedentary. HAL has a very high repeat-passenger rate, so many of the people you'll see aboard will have sailed with the line before.

The line attracts many groups traveling together, from incentive groups to social clubs and religious groups on a lark. In general, most passengers are married couples, but about 20% on any given cruise may be single, divorced, or widowed people traveling with friends. Only about 30 or 40 per cruise will be traveling entirely on their own. Solo travelers' parties encourage mixing, and you can ask to be seated with other solo passengers at dinner. On cruises of 10 nights or longer, gentlemen hosts sail aboard to provide company for single women, joining them at dinner as well as serving as dance partners.

DINING

Much improved over the years, Holland America's cuisine skirts close to the top of the mainstream heap, though it's not up to the gold standard of Celebrity's specialty restaurants. Appetizers include sevruga caviar, prawns in spicy wasabi cocktail sauce, deep-fried hazelnut brie, and duck and black-bean quesadillas; the soup-and-salad course always includes several options, from a plain house salad and minestrone to Bahamian conch chowder and chilled watermelon soup; and main courses are heavy on **traditional favorites** such as broiled lobster tail, grilled salmon, beef tenderloin, roast turkey, seared tuna steak, grilled pork chop, and filet mignon. Those wanting something less substantial can try **light and healthy dishes** such as seared duck breast, pan-seared grouper, and fresh fruit medley. Some vegetarian entrees are available on the main menu, but you can also ask for a **full vegetarian menu,** with half a dozen entrees and an equal number of appetizers, soups, and salads. (Don't miss the tofu stroganoff and celery-and-stilton soup if they're offered—yum.) Children can enjoy tried-and-true staples such as pizza, hot dogs, burgers with fries, chicken fingers, and tacos, plus chef's specials such as pasta and fish and chips. The **wine list** comprises about 70% U.S. vintages, with the rest from Europe, Chile, and Australia. **Dessert menus** feature some wonderful chocolate creations, plus delicate items such as a tropical trifle with salmonberries, raspberries, pineapple, kiwi, and coconut cream.

Once a week, a **barbeque buffet dinner** is offered as an option on the Lido Deck. As has become industry standard, **casual dining** is available each night in the ships' buffet-style Lido restaurants, which also serve breakfast and lunch and are, with the exception of the older *Noordam,* some of the best-laid-out buffets at sea, with separate stations for salads, desserts, drinks, and so on, keeping lines and crowding to a minimum. Dinners here are offered open-seating from about 6 to 8pm. Tables are set with linens and a pianist provides background music, but service is buffet-style, with waiters on hand to serve beverages. The set menu features the basics: Caesar salad, shrimp cocktail, or fresh-fruit-cup appetizer, French onion soup, freshly baked dinner rolls, and four entree choices, which may include salmon, sirloin steak, roast chicken, and lasagna, served with a vegetable of the day and a baked potato or rice pilaf. At lunch, the buffet restaurants offer deli sandwiches, pasta, salads, stir-fry, burgers, and sometimes Mexican dishes. Pizza and ice-cream stations are open till late afternoon. Out on the Lido Deck, by the pool, a **grill** serves hamburgers, hot dogs, veggie and turkey burgers, and a special of the day, such as knockwurst or spicy Italian sausage, between 11:30am and 5pm. A **taco bar** nearby offers all the fixings for tacos or nachos, but it's open only till 2:30pm (so much for nachos and beer after your shore excursion).

Rotterdam was the first HAL ship to have an **alternative, reservations-only restaurant,** and subsequent vessels have followed suit. Restaurants aboard *Rotterdam, Volendam,* and *Zaandam* seat fewer than 100 passengers and specialize in Italian cuisine, and (at least at press time) carry no extra cover charge. At dinner, a choice of half a dozen antipasti dishes may include a classic Italian bruschetta or antipasto, calamari, and Caesar salad. Pasta selections include the likes of tortellini with mushroom and sun-dried-tomato pesto sauce and penne with prosciutto and basil. For your main course, you can choose from at least six entrees such as a grilled chicken breast with mushroom and gorgonzola; tenderloin scaloppini; filet mignon with a mushroom and red-wine sauce; prawns, scallops, and fresh fish in a Tuscan bean stew; and, if you want something less fancy, pizza with goat cheese, mushrooms, and spinach. On *Zuiderdam* and *Oosterdam,* the menu is Pacific Northwest, with main dishes such as roasted salmon, sesame-crusted halibut, and rack of lamb. The cover charge here is $20 per person (spelling the beginning of the end for free specialty dining on HAL). Alternative restaurants are also open for lunch on sea days. You must reserve ahead on all ships, and we advise you to do so as soon as you get aboard.

Half Moon Cay

Half Moon Cay, Holland America's private 2,500-acre resort on the Bahamian island of San Salvador, is a beach destination all the way, and is a port of call on most of the line's Caribbean and Panama Canal cruises. Passengers can take it easy on one of the many beach chairs or blue canvas cabanas (a boon to shade-worshipers) or do a little windsurfing, snorkeling, kayaking, scuba diving, deep-sea fishing, parasailing, sailboarding, or aqua-cycling. The ships' activities staffs also organize volleyball, tug-of-war, and other games for adults, and sandcastle building and treasure hunts for kids and teens. Facilities around the island include a food pavilion, a few bars, an ice-cream stand, a kids' play area, a post office selling exclusive Half Moon Cay stamps, a cute chapel for vow-renewal ceremonies, and several "tropical mist stations" to help you keep cool. For a special treat, you can get a **massage on the beach** from the Steiner spa therapists, who set up a pair of tents on the sand. Choose from options including full body, half body, and scalp massages. Chair massages are also available on the beach at $1 per minute (10-min. minimum).

With no docking facilities on the island, ships must anchor offshore and ferry passengers in by tender, which means there's a slim chance that rough seas could force cancellation of the whole visit—as happened to us on a 2002 *Veendam* cruise.

Around midnight, daily, a spread of snacks is available in the Lido restaurant, and at least once during each cruise the dessert chefs get to go wild in a midnight **Dessert Extravaganza.** Cakes are decorated with humorous themes, marzipan animals guard towering chocolate castles, and trays are heavy with chocolate-covered strawberries, truffles, cream puffs, and other sinful things.

Room service is available 24 hours a day and ranks among the fastest and most efficient at sea. **Afternoon teas** are well-attended events, with waiters passing around teeny sandwiches and cookies in one of the main lounges; once per cruise, a special Royal Dutch High Tea features teatime snacks and music provided by the ships' string trio, making it one of the most truly "high" among the generally disappointing high teas offered on mainstream lines.

Free hot canapés are served in some of the bars/lounges during the cocktail hour, and free iced tea and lemonade are served on deck, one of many thoughtful touches provided at frequent intervals by the well-trained staff. All ships but *Noordam* have **Java Cafes,** a comfy cluster of seating around a small coffee bar serving complimentary espresso, cappuccino, caffe creme, and latte in the morning and afternoon. *Zuiderdam* and *Oosterdam* serve specialty coffees for a charge in the new Windstar Cafe, a tall-ship-themed venue that also serves snacks and light meals 20 hours a day, from 5am to 1am.

Smoking is not permitted in any HAL dining areas, including the main dining rooms and the enclosed portion of Lido restaurants.

Holland America Fleet Itineraries

Ship	Itineraries
Maasdam	**7-night E. Carib 1:** Round-trip from Fort Lauderdale, Nov–Dec 2003, visiting Grand Turk (Turks and Caicos), San Juan, St. Thomas, Nassau, and Half Moon Cay*, with 1 day at sea. **7-night E. Carib 2:** Round-trip from Fort Lauderdale, Jan 2004, visiting Grand Turk (Turks and Caicos), San Juan, Tortola (BVIs), and Half Moon Cay*, with 2 days at sea. **7-night W. Carib:** Round-trip from Fort Lauderdale, Nov 2003–Jan 2004, visiting Grand Cayman, Cozumel, Key West, and Half Moon Cay*, with 2 days at sea. **10-night S. Carib 1:** Round-trip from Fort Lauderdale, Jan–Apr and Nov 2004, visiting Sint Maarten, St. Lucia, Trinidad, Martinique, Tortola (BVIs), and Half Moon Cay*, with 2 days at sea. **10-night S. Carib 2:** Round-trip from Fort Lauderdale, Feb, Apr, and Nov 2004, visiting Aruba, Curaçao, Dominica, Tortola (BVIs), and Half Moon Cay*, with 4 days at sea. **11-night W. Carib/Canal:** Round-trip from Fort Lauderdale, Jan–Apr and Oct–Dec 2004, visiting Puerto Limon (Costa Rica), San Blas Islands (Panama), Grand Cayman, Key West, and Half Moon Cay*, with 5 days at sea, including a partial crossing of the Panama Canal. **Non-Caribbean Itineraries:** New England/Canada, Greenland/W. Europe.
Noordam	**14-night S. Carib:** Round-trip from Tampa, Jan–Mar 2004, visiting San Juan, Tortola (BVIs), Guadeloupe, Barbados, St. Lucia, Isla Margarita (Venezuela), Bonaire, Aruba, and Grand Cayman, with 4 days at sea. **Non-Caribbean Itineraries:** Europe.
Oosterdam	**7-night E. Carib 1:** Round-trip from Fort Lauderdale, Dec 2003, visiting Nassau, St. Thomas, St. Kitts, and Half Moon Cay*, with 2 days at sea. **7-night E. Carib 2:** Round-trip from Fort Lauderdale, Jan–Apr 2004, visiting Tortola (BVIs), Sint Maarten, and Half Moon Cay*, with 3 days at sea. **7-night E. Carib 3:** Round-trip from Fort Lauderdale, Oct–Dec 2004, visiting Tortola (BVIs), San Juan, Grand Turk (Turks and Caicos), and Half Moon Cay*, with 2 days at sea. **7-night W. Carib 1:** Round-trip from Fort Lauderdale, Dec 2003, visiting Key West, Cozumel, Grand Cayman, and Half Moon Cay*, with 2 days at sea. **7-night W. Carib 2:** Round-trip from Fort Lauderdale, Jan–Apr and Oct–Dec 2004, visiting Ocho Rios (Jamaica), Grand Cayman, Cozumel, and Half Moon Cay*, with 2 days at sea. **Non-Caribbean Itineraries:** Panama Canal repositioning cruises, Alaska.
Rotterdam	**10-night S. Carib/Canal:** Round-trip from Fort Lauderdale, Oct–Dec 2003, Jan–Apr and Nov–Dec 2004, visiting Curaçao, Aruba, Puerto Limon (Costa Rica), and Half Moon Cay*, with 4 days at sea including a partial crossing of the Panama Canal. **10-night E. Carib:** Round-trip from Baltimore (Apr), Philadelphia (May), and New York (May), visiting San Juan, Sint Maarten, Tortola (BVIs), and Half Moon Cay*, with 5 days at sea. **Non-Caribbean Itineraries:** Europe, New England/Canada.
Veendam	**7-night W. Carib 1:** Round-trip from Tampa, Oct–Dec 2003, Jan–Apr and Oct–Dec 2004, visiting Key West, Belize City (Belize), Santo Tomas de Castilla (Guatemala), and Cozumel, with 2 days at sea. Alternates with **7-night W. Carib 2:** Round-trip from Tampa, Oct–Dec 2003, Jan–Apr and Oct–Dec 2004, visiting Grand Cayman, Montego Bay or Ocho Rios (Jamaica), and Cozumel, with 3 days at sea. **Non-Caribbean Itineraries:** Panama Canal repositioning cruises, Alaska.

Ship	Itineraries
Volendam	**7-night W. Carib:** Round-trip from Fort Lauderdale, Oct 2003, visiting Grand Cayman, Cozumel, Key West, and Half Moon Cay*, with 2 days at sea. **10-night S. Carib 1:** Round-trip from Fort Lauderdale, Oct–Dec 2003, visiting Sint Maarten, St. Lucia, Trinidad, Martinique, Tortola (BVIs), and Half Moon Cay*, with 2 days at sea. **10-night S. Carib 2:** Round-trip from Fort Lauderdale, Nov–Dec 2004, visiting Bonaire, Isla Margarita (Venezuela), St. Lucia, Dominica, St. Thomas, and Half Moon Cay*, with 3 days at sea. **10-night W. Carib:** Round-trip from Fort Lauderdale, Jan–Mar and Oct–Nov 2004, visiting Grand Turk (Turks and Caicos), Grand Cayman, Cozumel and Veracruz (Mexico), Key West, and Half Moon Cay*, with 3 days at sea. **10-night E. Carib:** Round-trip from Fort Lauderdale, Jan–Mar and Oct–Dec 2004, visiting Grand Turk (Turks and Caicos), St. Thomas, Tortola (BVIs), Dominica, Barbados, and Half Moon Cay*, with 3 days at sea. **Non-Caribbean Itineraries:** Panama Canal repositioning cruises, Alaska.
Westerdam	**10-night S. Carib:** Round-trip from Fort Lauderdale, Dec 2004, visiting Sint Maarten, St. Lucia, Trinidad, Martinique, Tortola (BVIs), and Half Moon Cay*, with 2 days at sea. **Non-Caribbean Itineraries:** Europe.
Zaandam	**7-night E. Carib:** Round-trip from Port Canaveral, Oct–Dec 2003, Jan–Apr and Oct–Dec 2004, visiting Tortola, St. Thomas, and Half Moon Cay*, with 3 days at sea. **7-night W. Carib:** Round-trip from Port Canaveral, Oct–Dec 2003, Jan–Apr and Nov–Dec 2004, visiting Cozumel, Grand Cayman, Half Moon Cay*, and either Ocho Rios or Montego Bay (Jamaica), with 2 days at sea. **Non-Caribbean Itineraries:** Panama Canal and Pacific coastal repositioning cruises, Alaska.
Zuiderdam	**7-night E. Carib 1:** Round-trip from Fort Lauderdale, Sept–Dec 2003, visiting Nassau, St. Thomas, St. Kitts, and Half Moon Cay*, with 2 days at sea. **7-night E. Carib 2:** Round-trip from Fort Lauderdale, Jan–June 2004, visiting Tortola (BVIs), St. Thomas, and Half Moon Cay*, with 3 days at sea. **7-night E. Carib 3:** Round-trip from Fort Lauderdale, July–Dec 2004, visiting Tortola (BVIs), St. Thomas, Grand Turk (Turks and Caicos), and Half Moon Cay*, with 2 days at sea. **7-night W. Carib:** Round-trip from Fort Lauderdale, Apr–Oct 2004, visiting Key West, Cozumel, Grand Cayman, and Half Moon Cay*, with 2 days at sea. **Non-Caribbean Itineraries:** None.

HAL's private Bahamian island.

ACTIVITIES

Though varied and fun, onboard activities tend to be low-key. You can take line-dance or ballroom dance lessons; take an informal class in photography, vegetable carving, or creative napkin folding; play bingo or bridge; sit in on a trivia game or Pictionary tournament; participate in Ping-Pong, golf-putting, basketball free-throw, or volleyball tournaments; take a gaming lesson in the casino; attend a kitchen and backstage theater tour or a bad-hair workshop, skin-care clinic, or weight-loss/fitness seminar; go high-toned at a wine tasting; or go low-toned at the goofy pool games, which may be as innocuous as a relay race or as totally goofy as a contest to see how many Ping-Pong balls women can stuff in their one-pieces before time's up. Some cruises feature model shipbuilding contests in which you can use only junk you can find around the ship, with seaworthiness tested in one of the ship's hot tubs. Each ship's **Internet center** is open 24 hours a day for surfing the net and sending e-mail, with payment either by the minute or by paying a flat fee for open access.

Activities pick up a bit at night, with pre-dinner cocktails and dancing. After dinner, you may attend a Fabulous Fifties party or a country-and-western night, take part in a slot-machine tournament or Night-Owl Pajama Bingo, or take in a show or movie (see "Entertainment," below).

CHILDREN'S PROGRAM

While Holland America's **Club HAL** program offers a typical range of onboard activities for kids, these are still ships designed primarily for adults, with few kids typically aboard except during summers and holiday weeks, when there may be as many as 150 kids aboard. Activities are programmed for three age brackets (5–8, 9–12, and 13–17, though these barriers sometimes blur if a limited number of kids are aboard) and include arts and crafts, youth sports tournaments, movies and videos, scavenger hunts, disco for teens, storytelling for younger kids, miniature golf, charades, "candy bar bingo," Ping-Pong, and pizza, ice-cream, and pajama parties. Each evening, kids receive a program detailing the next day's activities. Activities are not scheduled while a ship is in port, though the line does offer kids' activities on its private beach, Half Moon Cay (see box above). The ratio of supervisors to kids is 1 to 30.

Volendam, Zaandam, Rotterdam, and *Veendam* all have a small multipurpose room that's sometimes used for kids' activities, while *Maasdam, Zuiderdam,* and *Oosterdam* have dedicated "KidZone" playrooms and separate teen centers that are an improvement (with computers, a large-screen TV for movies, an audio system, video games, and a dance floor) but still can't compete with the ball-jumps, padded climbing and crawling areas, and fanciful decor of kids' facilities aboard Disney, Royal Caribbean, Carnival, Celebrity, Princess, and NCL. All the HAL ships except *Noordam* have small video-game rooms.

In-cabin **babysitting** is sometimes (but not always) available on days at sea from volunteers among a ship's staff. If a staff member is available, the cost is $8 an hour for the first child, and $5 per hour for additional kids. Inquire at the guest services desk.

There is no age minimum for children to sail aboard.

ENTERTAINMENT

Don't expect HAL's shows to knock your socks off, but hey, at least they're trying. Each ship features small-scale **Vegas-style shows,** with live music, laser lights, and lots of glimmer and shimmer, and some sailings of *Volendam* feature a show based on the Barry Manilow song "Copacabana." Overall, though, you'll find better quality entertainment in the soloists, trios, and quartets playing jazz, pop, and light-classical standards.

Recent-release movies are shown an average of twice a day in an onboard cinema, with free popcorn available for the full movie effect. There's also a **crew talent show** once a week, in which crewmembers (Indonesians 1 week, Filipinos the next) present songs and dances from their home countries. On one 2002 cruise, a performance of "My Way" by 14 crewmembers wielding tuned bamboo angklung rattles was a real highlight of the cruise—it was, in fact, one of the most thoroughly bizarre things we'd seen in recent memory, and lots of fun. At the other end of the entertainment spectrum, **passenger-participation shows** include the Rockin' Rolldies show, with passengers lip-syncing to tunes from the '50s and '60s. A **1950s-style sock hop** follows immediately after, with twist and hula-hoop contests.

Aboard each ship, one of the public rooms becomes a disco in the evening, with a small live band generally playing before dinner and a DJ taking over for after-dinner dancing. The new *Zuiderdam* has the line's first dedicated disco, but it's one of the most stunningly ugly in the industry today. What were they thinking?

SERVICE

Holland America is one of the few cruise lines that maintains a training school (a land-based facility in Indonesia known within HAL circles as "ms Nieuw Jakarta") for the selection and training of staffers, resulting in service that's efficient, attentive, and genteel. The soft-spoken, primarily Indonesian and Filipino staffers smile more often than not and will frequently remember your name after only one introduction, though they struggle occasionally with their English. (Be cool about it: Remember, you probably can't speak even a word of Bahasa Indonesia or Tagalog.) During lunch, a uniformed employee may hold open the door of a buffet, and at dinnertime, stewards who look like vintage hotel pageboys walk through the public rooms ringing a chime to formally announce the two seatings.

Although Holland America proudly touts its **no-tipping-required policy,** it's more diplomacy than anything else. In fact, as aboard most other ships, tips are expected (staff doesn't get paid a very large base salary); it's just that on Holland America ships you won't be bombarded by guidelines and reminders. Note that unlike most other lines, HAL doesn't automatically include a 15% gratuity in bar bills. Bartenders are paid on a different scale than other servers, but if you want to give a little extra, you can tip in cash or handwrite a gratuity onto your tab.

Onboard services on every ship in the fleet include **laundry** and **dry cleaning.** Each ship—except the new *Zuiderdam,* oddly enough—also maintains several **self-service laundry rooms** with irons.

The Vista Class: Zuiderdam • Oosterdam (preview) • Westerdam (preview)

The Verdict

Zuiderdam, Holland America's first foray into megasize ships, is a bit of a hodge-podge, marrying traditional HAL style with a partying Caribbean feel—or at least trying to.

Zuiderdam *(photo: Holland America Line)*

Specifications

Size (in tons)	85,000	Crew	800 (Indonesian/ Filipino)
Number of Cabins	924	Passenger/Crew Ratio	2.3 to 1
Number of Outside Cabins	788	Year Launched	
Cabins with Verandas	623	*Zuiderdam*	2002
Number of Passengers	1,848	*Oosterdam*	2003
Officers	Dutch/British	Last Major Refurbishment	N/A

Frommer's Ratings (Scale of 1–5)   ★★★½

Cabin Comfort & Amenities	4.5	Dining Options	4
Ship Cleanliness & Maintenance	4	Gym & Spa Facilities	4.5
Public Comfort & Space	4	Children's Facilities	3
Decor	3	Enjoyment Factor	3

Built on the same hull as Carnival's Spirit-class ships and Costa's *CostaAtlantica*, *Zuiderdam* (named for the southern point of the compass, and with a first syllable that rhymes with "eye") is the first of a new series of 85,000-ton, 1,848-passenger ships that will offer 7-night itineraries year-round in the Caribbean—a first for Holland America. The line hopes she'll help it finally shed its image as your grandmother's cruise line, and compete better for the all-important baby-boomer and family cruise dollars. Can't fault them for that, and you can't fault them for experimenting with *Zuiderdam*'s design to try and make her more widely appealing. However, you can fault them for not doing it very well.

Yes, *Zuiderdam* has touches of the classic understated HAL style, and passengers coming to the line for the first time may well consider her exciting and elegant. And yes, the ship is as spacious as the line claims, and longtime HAL fans may look forward to experiencing the range of new public rooms and diversions with which they've filled all that extra tonnage. Contrary to the line's marketing campaign, though, space isn't everything. The trick is using it well, and in that regard *Zuiderdam* seems caught in a major identity crisis, undecided about whether she wants to be an elegant traditional cruise ship or a theme park version of one, with a color palette that would give Carnival a run for its money. On the one hand, spaces like her two-level Vista Dining Room are restrained and stylish, with simple gilt chandeliers and high-backed floral-pattern leather chairs. On the other, there are rooms like the Northern Lights Disco, a modernist nightmare with a low ceiling, a tacky mock-iceberg centerpiece, and black-and-white upholstery that was intended to mimic the aurora borealis but in fact looks like the spots on a Holstein cow. It's the first dedicated disco ever for Holland America, and so exemplifies a more general problem: Concepts HAL has used before come off fairly well here, but those it's trying for the first time are hit-and-miss. This is true for the ship's children's facilities as well, larger and better than those on any other HAL ship but lacking the kind of real "kid" feel that makes the playrooms on some competing lines (such as Disney, Carnival, Royal Caribbean, Princess, and NCL) so much fun.

Okay, sure, design isn't everything, and if you can keep in mind how little money you're paying for your cruise, you'll likely have a fine or even great time. For us, though, the chintziness of some of the spaces aboard really detracts from the overall experience, and the bright colors come off as unnatural, like a 60-something banker trading in his Mercedes and suits for a red Corvette and tight jeans. Sister ship *Oosterdam*—named for the eastern point of the compass and scheduled for a June 2003 debut, after this book goes to press—will have a slightly different style, though probably no less bright.

Three additional sisters, the first dubbed *Westerdam* (the 3rd HAL ship to bear that name) and the other two as yet unnamed, are scheduled to debut in April 2004, October 2005, and May 2006. All descriptions in this review refer to *Zuiderdam*.

Cabins & Rates

Cabins	Per Diems from	Sq. Ft.	Fridge	Hair Dryer	Sitting Area	TV
Inside	$86	185	yes	yes	no	yes
Outside	$106	194–200	yes	yes	yes	yes
Suite	$238	298–1,000	yes	yes	yes	yes

CABINS   Cabins in all categories are comfortable and (as aboard every HAL ship but *Noordam*) are among the industry's largest, with a simple decor that's heavy on light woods and clean lines, with subtly floral bedding. Overall, more than two-thirds of them have verandas, with the deluxe veranda suites and state-rooms in the stern notable for their deep balconies, nearly twice the size of those to port and starboard. You get a romantic view of the ship's wake from back here, too, but since the decks are tiered back here, residents of the cabins above you can see right down—so don't get *too* romantic.

Standard outside and veranda cabins all have a small sitting area (which in the latter category can be curtained off from the sleeping area) and a tub in the bath-room—a relatively rare thing in standard cabins these days. Closet space in all categories is more than adequate for 7-night cruises, with nicely designed fold-down shelves and tie rack. Dataports allow passengers to access e-mail and the Internet from every cabin, using their own laptops.

Suites run from the comfortably spacious Superior Veranda Suites (with wide verandas, large sofa bed, walk-in closet, separate shower and bath, and extra windows) to the Penthouse Veranda Suites, extremely large multi-room affairs with a flowing layout and decor reminiscent of 1930s moderne style, pantries, palatial bathrooms with oversize whirlpool bath, and ridiculously large private verandas with a second, outdoor whirlpool. Guests in every suite category have use of a concierge lounge whose staff will take care of shore excursion reserva-tions and any matters about which you'd normally have to wait in line at the front desk. The lounge is stocked with reading material, coffee, and juice, and a continental breakfast is served daily.

Each ship has 99 connecting cabins. Twenty-eight cabins are wheelchair-accessible.

PUBLIC AREAS   Public rooms on *Zuiderdam* run the gamut from the tradi-tional to the modern, from the lovely to the not-so-lovely, with several rooms looking like they were thrown together at the last minute. Among the more tra-ditional spaces is the signature Explorer's Lounge, a venue for quiet musical per-formances and high tea, here dressed up with slightly brighter colors and more modern furniture than aboard other HAL ships. The top-of-the-ship Crow's Nest lounge, an observation lounge during the day and nightclub/disco at night, offers wide-open views, comfortable leather recliners toward the bow (a perfect reading perch during days at sea), and even a few rococo thrones on the star-board side, good for "wish you were here" cruise photos.

Lower Promenade Deck is the hub of indoor activity on these ships. In the bow, the three-deck, bordello-red Vista Lounge is the venue for large-scale pro-duction shows, while the new Queen's Lounge at midships hosts comedians and other cabaret-style acts. Between the two, you'll find a casino, a comfortably modern piano bar, and our favorite room, the Sports Bar, which looks as little like the standard rah-rah sports-hero-and-pennants sports bar as you can imag-ine, with comfortable free-form leather seating, brushed-metal vase-shaped table lamps, and "Humorous Sports Figures" artwork by Jan Snoeck. Tres chic. Only the multiple TVs give away the place's true identity. There's also the Northern Lights disco, which is, to put it bluntly, butt-ugly (see description above). The hallway leading to the room is more interesting, decorated with posters from classic Hollywood studios signed by the stars. Lighting along the hall is motion-activated, coming on sequentially as you walk through.

One deck up, the traditional Ocean Bar wraps around the understated three-deck atrium, with bay windows to port and starboard looking out onto the promenade and the room's namesake. Moving forward, you pass through the shopping arcade, whose displays spill right into the central corridor courtesy of retractable walls, forcing you to browse as you walk from stem to stern. How crass a sales pitch is that? It gets a big, big thumbs-down from us. Once you get through, you come to the traditional-looking library with its ocean-liner-style writing tables and very non-traditional (but cool) funky blonde-wood swivel chairs with spring-adjusting back support. The nearby Internet Center is conversely modern—too much so, with perforated metal walls, chrome and glass furniture, and a circuit board–patterned ceiling that make it resemble a set from a grade-B 1970s sci-fi movie.

Other public rooms include the Main Deck's Atrium Bar, a very comfortable small-scale nook vaguely reminiscent of a 1930s nightclub; the wicker-furnitured outdoor Lido Bar on the Lido Deck (which unfortunately lacks the charm of similar spaces on the line's older ships); and the KidZone and WaveRunner children/teen centers. Art in the public areas includes some nice humorous paintings by Hans Leijerzapf, maritime artwork by Stephen Card, replica 18th-century Dutch engravings and commedia dell'arte statues, and, notably, glasswork by Peter Bremers and enlarged, rippling photographs of Venice set into the floor forward of the Explorer's Lounge.

Ocean-view elevators at midships, which were intended to provide inspiring views of the sea, somehow manage to be dark, boxy, and downright claustrophobic. Much better views are to be had from outdoor areas forward on Decks 5, 6, and 7, and from an area just forward of the gym, above the bridge. You can even check a ship's compass here.

DINING OPTIONS   The main Vista Dining Room is a two-deck affair, decorated traditionally but with nice touches of modernism in the high-backed black wooden chairs, whose leather backs sport an enlarged 17th-century floral design. Very sharp. The ship's alternative restaurant, the 130-seat Odyssey, serving Pacific Northwest cuisine at lunch and dinner, wraps partially around the three-deck atrium in a design that's a bit too open for our taste. Aside from this quibble, the design is appealing enough, with marble floors, bright white linens, gorgeous Bvlgari place settings, and ornate, organically sculpted chairs by Gilbert Lebigre, who also created the ship's beautiful, batik-patterned elevator doors. Ask for a table by the windows or in the aft corner for a cozier experience.

Diners wanting something more casual can opt for the well-laid-out Lido buffet restaurant; the outdoor Grill for burgers, dogs, and the like; or the Windstar Cafe, open 20 hours a day and serving specialty coffees (for a cost), snacks, and light meals in a tall-ship-themed atmosphere.

POOL, FITNESS & SPA FACILITIES   As aboard all the HAL ships reviewed in this book except *Noordam*, the Vista-class ships boast some of the largest gyms around, with all the requisite cardio equipment and weight machines arranged in an arc around the cardio floor. Also, a basketball/volleyball court is on the Sports Deck, and a computerized golf simulator is one deck down, on the Observation Deck. The Greenhouse Spa is fully 50% larger than any other in the HAL fleet, and besides offering the usual massage, mud, and exotic treatments, it has a couple of HAL firsts: a thermal suite (a series of saunas and other heat-therapy rooms) and a hydrotherapy pool, which uses heated seawater and high-pressure jets to alleviate muscle tension. Unfortunately, the pool area's bright faux-Moorish columns, contrastingly dull all-weather decking, and unconvincing cloud-like ceiling just doesn't create the soothing mood of some competitors' facilities, notably the elegant thalassotherapy pools aboard Celebrity's Century- and Millennium-class ships and the wonderful indoor spa-pool on NCL's new *Norwegian Dawn*.

Outdoors, the wraparound Promenade Deck is lined with classy wooden deck chairs—a nice touch of classic steamship style—and is popular with walkers and joggers. The main pool deck is the hub of outdoor activity on sea days, with hot tubs, music, and pool games, and can be covered with a sliding roof in inclement weather. The centerpiece of the area is a giant polar-bear-and-cub statue, an odd choice considering the ship will be in the Caribbean year-round. Another pool, in the stern on the Lido Deck, is a quieter alternative.

Rotterdam

The Verdict

A modern throwback to the glory days of trans-Atlantic travel without the stuffiness or class separation, this attractive flagship offers great features, from classic art to rich mahogany woodwork and elegant yet understated public rooms.

Rotterdam *(photo: Holland America Line)*

Specifications

Size (in tons)	56,652	Officers	Dutch/British
Number of Cabins	658	Crew	593 (Indonesian/Filipino)
Number of Outside Cabins	381	Passenger/Crew Ratio	2.2 to 1
Cabins with Verandas	161	Year Launched	1997
Number of Passengers	1,316	Last Major Refurbishment	N/A

Frommer's Ratings (Scale of 1–5)   ⟨★★★★ ½

Cabin Comfort & Amenities	4.5	Dining Options	4
Ship Cleanliness & Maintenance	4	Gym & Spa Facilities	4.5
Public Comfort & Space	5	Children's Facilities	3
Decor	5	Enjoyment Factor	4.5

Rotterdam and near-twin *Amsterdam* (which doesn't sail in the Caribbean this year) combine classic elegance with contemporary amenities and provide a very comfortable cruise, especially on itineraries of 10 nights or longer. *Rotterdam* is the sixth HAL ship to bear that name, and is popular with passengers who previously sailed aboard the legendary *Rotterdam V*, which was sold off in 1997.

Cabins & Rates

Cabins	Per Diems from	Sq. Ft.	Fridge	Hair Dryer	Sitting Area	TV
Inside	$109	182	no	yes	yes	yes
Outside	$129	197	no	yes	yes	yes
Suite	$259	225–937	yes	yes	yes	yes

CABINS   Unlike the beige color schemes of *Noordam, Maasdam,* and *Veendam,* the decor on *Rotterdam* is livelier, with corals, mangos, blues, and whites brightening things up. The standard cabins are among the most spacious at sea and offer enough hanging and drawer space for 10-night-plus cruises. Bathrooms are generous as well, with bathtubs in all but the standard inside cabins. Each cabin has a sitting area, a desk, a safe, two lower beds convertible to a queen, and great reading lights above each bed.

Veranda Suites are 225 square feet and have a 59-square-foot private veranda; Deluxe Veranda Suites measure 374 square feet and have a 189-square-foot veranda and a dressing room. Both have sitting areas, whirlpool tubs, and minibars, and are kept stocked with fresh fruit. The four Penthouse Suites measure 937 square feet and have a 189-square-foot veranda, living room, dining room, guest bathroom, and an oversize whirlpool tub. All suite guests have use of a concierge lounge whose staff will take care of shore excursion reservations and any matters about which you'd normally have to wait in line at the front desk. The lounge is stocked with reading material, and a continental breakfast is served daily.

There are 108 connecting cabins aboard. Twenty-one cabins are wheelchair-accessible.

PUBLIC AREAS   The ship has a great, easy-to-navigate layout that allows passengers to move easily among public rooms. Most of the inside public areas are concentrated on two decks; ditto for the pools, sunning areas, spa, sports facilities, and buffet restaurant, which are all on the Lido and Sports decks.

Overall, the ship gives you the feeling of an elegant old hotel, with dark red and blue upholstery and leathers, damask fabrics, mahogany tones, and gold accents. Artwork is everywhere, from the stairwells to the walkways on the Promenade and Upper Promenade decks. The overall theme is continental and Asian, with a large reproduction Flemish clock greeting passengers as they enter the atrium.

The Ocean Bar serves complimentary hot hors d'oeuvres before dinner nightly, and passengers pack into the bar to listen and dance to a lively trio. More elegant is the Explorer's Lounge, which has a string ensemble performing a classic repertoire. Nearby is the open-sided piano bar, featuring a red lacquered baby grand piano. Unfortunately, the string group can be easily heard from this lounge, as can the sound of jingling coins from the nearby casino's slot machines.

As aboard all the Holland America ships, the Crow's Nest doubles as an observation lounge and disco, and includes among its decorations a group of life-size terra-cotta human and horse figures, copies of ancient statues discovered in Xian, China. The lounge has entrances on both sides and curves around a dance floor and bar. There are plenty of cocktail tables and seating, especially given the light-to-moderate use the room gets when not hosting special events such as line-dance classes.

The casino is more subtle than those on the older *Maasdam* and *Veendam,* though it's big enough to pass through without a problem and lively enough to entice gambling fans to drop a few bills. The main showroom, perhaps the brightest of the rooms, is done in red and gold and is more a nightclub than a theater. Sit on the banquettes for the best sightlines, as alternating rows of individual chairs sit lower and don't permit most passengers to see over the heads of those in front of them. The balcony offers decent sightlines.

Other public rooms include a spacious library and large card room, a movie theater, and a computer room with eight flat-screen computer terminals for e-mailing or surfing the Net.

DINING OPTIONS The attractive two-level formal dining room has floor-to-ceiling windows and an elegant, nostalgic feel, and never feels crowded.

The Odyssey, seating fewer than 100 diners, is a romantic, intimate Italian restaurant with an elegant air. Just be careful of those funky chairs; they tip forward if you lean too far toward your soup. Food tends to be better and taste fresher here than in the main restaurant, and dishes are cooked to order.

As in the rest of the fleet, casual buffet-style breakfast, lunch, and dinner are offered in the Lido restaurant, a bright, cheerful place done in corals and blues, where lines can get long during prime times. Generally, though, the Lido is well laid out, with separate salad, drink, deli, dessert, and stir-fry stations. There's a taco bar poolside at lunchtime, and pizza is available in the afternoon.

POOL, FITNESS & SPA FACILITIES *Rotterdam* has a spacious, well-equipped gym with a very large separate aerobics area, floor-to-ceiling ocean views, plenty of elbowroom, and a decent spa. There's a pair of swimming pools: one amidships on the Lido Deck, with a retractable glass roof and a pair of hot tubs, and another smaller, less trafficked and thus more relaxing one in the stern, letting on to open views of the ship's wake. The great wraparound Promenade Deck is lined with wooden deck chairs—a quiet and nostalgic spot for a snooze or some reading. There's a combo volleyball and tennis court on the Sports Deck, and Ping-Pong tables on the Lower Promenade in the sheltered bow. Golf putting contests are held in the atrium.

Volendam • Zaandam

The Verdict

These handsome ships represent a successful marriage of HAL's usual elegance and gentility with a well-done dose of classy modern pizzazz.

Volendam *(photo: Holland America Line)*

Specifications

Size (in tons)	63,000	Crew	647 (Indonesian/ Filipino)
Number of Cabins	720	Passenger/Crew Ratio	2.2 to 1
Number of Outside Cabins	581	Year Launched	
Cabins with Verandas	197	*Volendam*	1999
Number of Passengers	1,440	*Zaandam*	2000
Officers	Dutch/British	Last Major Refurbishment	N/A

Frommer's Ratings (Scale of 1–5)   ❀❀❀❀ ½

Cabin Comfort & Amenities	4.5	Dining Options	4
Ship Cleanliness & Maintenance	4	Gym & Spa Facilities	4.5
Public Comfort/Space	5	Children's Facilities	3
Decor	5	Enjoyment Factor	4.5

Introduced at the turn of the century, *Volendam* and *Zaandam* marked Holland America's first steps into a more diverse, mainstream future, offering an experience designed to attract the vital 40-something boomers while still keeping the line's core older passengers happy. The ships have alternative restaurants, Internet centers, and huge gyms that many lines attracting younger crowds can't match, but their overall vibe is more traditional than Carnival, Princess, and Royal Caribbean—and, for that matter, than the line's newer and much more glitzy *Zuiderdam*. These are classy, classic ships, but with just a touch of funk to keep things from seeming too old-fashioned—note the autographed Bill Clinton saxophone and Iggy Pop guitar in *Zaandam's* elegant Sea View Lounge.

Cabins & Rates

Cabins	Per Diems from	Sq. Ft.	Fridge	Hair Dryer	Sitting Area	TV
Inside	$71	186	no	yes	yes	yes
Outside	$81	196	no	yes	yes	yes
Suite	$216	284–1,126	yes	yes	yes	yes

CABINS   In a word, roomy: These standard cabins are among the largest in the industry, and with a much more modern, daring look than on the line's older ships. Fabrics are done in salmon-red, burgundy, gold, and bronze, and walls in a striped pale-gold fabric, hung with gilt-framed prints. Bathrooms are roomy and well designed, with adequate storage shelves and counter space. All outside cabins have shower/tub combos (short tubs, but tubs nonetheless), while inside cabins have only showers. Cabin drawer space is plentiful, and closets are roomy, with great shelves that fold down if you want to adjust the configuration of space. There's a storage drawer under each bed.

All cabins have sitting areas; TVs with CNN, CNNfn, TNT, and a couple of movie channels; and hair dryers. Minifridges don't come standard except in suites, but can be rented for $2 a day (inquire before your cruise if you're interested). Highly functional bed headboards have reading lights and the controls for music channels and for every light in the cabin.

On the Verandah and Navigation decks, 197 suites and minisuites have balconies, including the single gorgeous Penthouse Suite, which measures in at 1,126 square feet, including veranda, and is adorned with one-of-a-kind pieces such as 19th-century Portuguese porcelain vases and early-20th-century Louis XVI marble table lamps. All suites and minisuites provide terry bathrobes for passengers to use during the cruise, and are kept stocked with fresh fruit.

There are 108 connecting cabins available, as well as 21 wheelchair-accessible cabins.

PUBLIC AREAS   *Volendam's* public areas are floral-themed; *Zaandam's* sport musical motifs. Aboard *Volendam,* each aft staircase landing has a still-life painting of flowers, and a spot outside the library has a collection of elaborate delft tulip vases (ironically, with fake silk tulips). You could even call the gorgeous graduated colors in the show lounge seating florally themed, with colors from magenta to marigold creating a virtual garden in bloom. *Zaandam's* theme is exemplified by one of the more bizarre and inspired atrium decorations we know of—a huge, mostly ornamental baroque pipe organ decorated with figures of musicians and dancers—as well as by numerous musical instruments scattered around the ship in display cases, from a classic Ornette Coleman–style plastic Grafton sax in the Sea View Lounge to the elaborate Mozart harpsichord display (with busts and a candelabra) outside the card room. The display of electric guitars in the atrium stair tower (signed by Queen, Eric Clapton, the Rolling

Stones, and others) might represent a little too much wishful thinking on HAL's part about a lower average passenger age.

In general, as aboard almost the entire HAL fleet, public areas are very easy to navigate. Corridors are broad, and there's little chance of getting lost or disoriented. Surfaces and fabrics overall are an attractive medley of subtle textures and materials, from tapestry walls and ceilings to velveteen chairs, marble tabletops, and smoky glass. *Volendam* even has a red-lacquer piano and suede walls woven to resemble rattan. *Zaandam's* pianos are all funky: The one in the piano bar is painted to look as though it's made of scrap lumber and rusty nails; the one in the Lido restaurant is painted in wildly bright colors.

The warm and almost glowingly cozy Explorer's Lounge is a favorite area, along with the nearby Sea View Lounge and the adjacent piano bar, with its round, pill-like leather bar stools and plush sofas. On busy nights, the Ocean Bar can get crowded by the bar, but if you're seated across the room or near the dance floor, where a live jazz band plays danceable music before and after dinner, there's plenty of space.

The ships' signature space, the top-deck Crow's Nest observation lounge and disco, is all warm colors and soft lines—no "disco-ball and mirrors" decor here—and wrapped in floor-to-ceiling windows. It's a popular spot for pre-dinner cocktails and after-dinner dancing.

As on the other HAL vessels, the ships' main showrooms are two-story affairs with movable clusters of single seats and banquettes on the ground level in front of the stage so passengers can get comfortable.

Both vessels have impressive art and antiques sprinkled throughout their public areas. The booty on *Volendam* includes an authentic Renaissance fountain outside the casino (the ship's most pricey piece), an inlaid marble table in the library, and a small earthenware mask dating back to 1200 B.C. that's kept in a display case near the Explorer's Lounge. On *Zaandam,* an area outside the library features reproductions of Egyptian jewelry and a huge repro Egyptian statue fragment.

Both ships have a cinema and coffee cafe, and a 24-hour Internet center located between the card room and the spacious and much-used (but not terribly well-stocked) library. There's also a video arcade, and the small Sky Room up on the Sports Deck is sometimes used as a children's center.

DINING OPTIONS   The two-story main dining rooms are glamorous affairs framed with floor-to-ceiling windows and punctuated by dramatic staircases. A classical trio serenades guests from a perch on the top level. On the bottom level, two tables in the stern corners, by the windows, are prime, with a semisecluded feel. Just outside the second level of the dining room is a place you ladies won't want to miss: a wonderful powder room with ocean views and lots of elbow room for primping, with vanity tables and stools in one room and the toilets and sinks adjacent.

Both ships also feature Italian-themed, reservations-only Marco Polo alternative restaurants with seating for fewer than 100 guests, so intimate and elegant that you may forget you're on a big cruise ship (and there's no cover charge either). *Volendam's* is covered with small eclectic Rembrandt, Henry Moore, Matisse, and Picasso prints, as well as works by some lesser-known artists (the ship's principal architect, Frans Dingemans, says he designed the room to resemble a European artist's bistro), while *Zaandam's* is more traditional, decorated with still lifes and gold-trimmed furniture. The food is as tasty as the rooms are appealing, but watch those wobbly chairs; lean forward too much and you'll feel like you're going to topple right over.

The Lido buffet restaurants are efficiently constructed, with separate stations for salads, desserts, and beverages, cutting down on the chance of monstrously long lines. A sandwich station serves its creations on delicious fresh-baked breads.

POOL, FITNESS & SPA FACILITIES   The gyms on these ships are downright palatial and among the best at sea, with floor-to-ceiling windows surrounding dozens of state-of-the-art machines, and so much elbow room that you might wonder if some equipment is out getting serviced. Hey, no complaints here. The adjacent aerobics areas are huge too—nearly as big as the ones at our gyms back home. The spas and hair salons are adequate, but not as mind-blowing.

Three pools are on the Lido Deck: a small and quiet aft pool (behind the Lido buffet restaurant) and the main pool and wading pool, located under a retractable glass roof in a sprawling area that includes the pleasant, cafelike Dolphin Bar, with rattan chairs and shade umbrellas. There are more isolated areas for sunbathing above the aft pool on a patch of the Sports Deck and in little slivers of open space aft on most of the cabin decks. The Sports Deck also has a pair of practice tennis courts, as well as shuffleboard. Joggers can use the uninterrupted Lower Promenade Deck to get their workout.

The Statendam Class: Maasdam • Veendam

The Verdict

Some of the most attractive mid-size ships out there. Functional, appealing public areas are enlivened with just a dash of glitz, collections of mostly European and Indonesian art and artifacts, and shipping memorabilia.

Veendam *(photo: Holland America Line)*

Specifications

Size (in tons)	55,451	Passenger/Crew Ratio	2.1 to 1
Number of Cabins	633	Year Launched	
Number of Outside Cabins	485	*Maasdam*	1993
Cabins with Verandas	149	*Veendam*	1996
Number of Passengers	1,266	Last Major Refurbishment	
Officers	Dutch/British	*Maasdam*	2002
Crew	602 (Indonesian/ Filipino)	*Veendam*	N/A

Frommer's Ratings (Scale of 1–5)   ✸✸✸✸

Cabin Comfort & Amenities	4	Dining Options	4
Ship Cleanliness & Maintenance	4	Gym & Spa Facilities	4
Public Comfort/Space	5	Children's Facilities	3*
Decor	4	Enjoyment Factor	4.5

* Children's facilities are in the process of being upgraded.

These two nearly identical vessels (plus sister ships *Statendam* and *Ryndam,* which don't currently sail in the Caribbean) are, like all the HAL ships but the older *Noordam,* extremely well laid out and easy to navigate. Touches of marble, teak, polished brass, and multimillion-dollar collections of art and maritime artifacts lend a classic ambience, and many decorative themes emphasize the Netherlands' seafaring traditions. The onboard mood is low-key (though things get dressy at night), the cabins are large and comfortable, and there are dozens of comfortable nooks all over the ships in which you can curl up and relax.

Cabins & Rates

Cabins	Per Diems from	Sq. Ft.	Fridge	Hair Dryer	Sitting Area	TV
Inside	$71	186	no	yes	yes	yes
Outside	$86	197	no	yes	yes	yes
Suite	$238	284–1,126	yes	yes	yes	yes

CABINS   Cabins are roomy, unfussy, and comfortable, with light-grained furniture and floral or Indonesian batik-patterned curtains separating the sleeping area from the sitting area. The same prints are used for bedspreads and curtains too, reflecting Holland's colonial history and floral preoccupation. White-gloved stewards add a hospitable touch, and music channels and TVs showing CNN, CNNfn, TNT, and a rotating series of movies keep passengers entertained. All cabins have twin beds that can be converted to a queen and, in some cases, a king. About 200 cabins can accommodate a third and fourth passenger on a foldaway sofa bed and/or an upper berth. Closets and storage space are larger than the norm, and bathrooms are well designed and well lit, with bathtubs in all but the lowest category. Personal safes come standard, but minifridges don't except in suites, though you can request one through your travel agent for a few dollars extra.

Outside cabins have picture windows and views of the sea, though those on the Lower Promenade Deck have pedestrian walkways and, consequently, pedestrians between you and the ocean. Special reflective glass prevents outsiders from spying in during daylight hours. To guarantee privacy at nighttime, you have to close the curtains. No cabin views are blocked by dangling lifeboats or other equipment.

Minisuites are larger than those aboard some of the most expensive lines (such as SeaDream). Full suites are 563 square feet, and the Penthouse Suite sprawls across a full 1,126 square feet. All come with terry bathrobes for passengers to use during the cruise, and are kept stocked with fresh fruit.

There are 52 connecting cabins aboard each ship. Six cabins are outfitted for passengers with disabilities, and public areas are also wheelchair friendly, with spacious corridors, wide elevators, and wheelchair-accessible public toilets.

PUBLIC AREAS   For the most part, public areas are subdued, consciously tasteful, and soothing. The Sky Deck offers an almost 360-degree panorama where the only drawback is the roaring wind. One deck below, almost equivalent views are available from the gorgeous Crow's Nest nightclub. With floor-to-ceiling windows and cozy clusters of seating, this romantic venue is perfect for pre-dinner cocktails; after dinner, it becomes the ships' disco and nightclub. The ships' small, three-story atria are pleasant enough and refreshingly unglitzy, housing the passenger-services and shore-excursions desks as well as officers' offices.

Showrooms are modern, stylish, two-story affairs. Unlike on most ships, which have rows of banquettes or theater-like seats, the lower levels are configured with cozy groupings of cushy chairs that can be moved, as well as banquettes. The balcony, however, has very uncomfortable bench seating, with low backs that make it impossible to lean back without slouching.

Each vessel has a large, tranquil library with floor-to-ceiling windows, a small selection of books and board games that can be signed out, and writing tables with HAL-logo stationery. *Maasdam*'s has paintings of the five previous HAL ships to carry that name. Next door, there's a spacious card room and an Internet center with eight flat-screen stations.

A cozy piano bar is nestled in a quiet nook next to the elegant Explorer's Lounge, a popular venue for high tea in the afternoon and for elegant light classical and parlor music after dinner. A live band plays for dancers before dinner in the very popular Ocean Bar, and the nice-size casinos are spacious though not as pleasingly designed as aboard the line's newer ships. A small movie theater shows films three times a day.

Maasdam has a small children's and teen's area on the top deck; *Veendam* offers children's activities in a bland multipurpose room when enough kids are aboard to warrant it.

DINING OPTIONS   These ships have elegant, two-story, ocean-view main dining rooms at the stern, with dual staircases swooping down to the lower level for grand entrances, and a music balcony at the top, where a duo or trio serenades diners. Ceilings are glamorous with their lotus-flower glass fixtures, and two smaller attached dining rooms are available for groups.

The casual indoor/outdoor buffet restaurant is well laid out, with separate stations for salads, desserts, and drinks, which helps keep lines to a minimum. The restaurant serves breakfast, lunch, and dinner daily, and its pizza and ice-cream stations are open until just before dinner. An outdoor grill on the Lido Deck serves burgers and other sandwich items throughout the afternoon, and a nearby station allows you to make your own tacos or nachos at lunchtime.

POOL, FITNESS & SPA FACILITIES   Both ships have a sprawling expanse of teak-covered aft deck surrounding a swimming pool. One deck above and centrally located is a second swimming pool plus a wading pool, hot tubs, and a spacious deck area with a sliding-glass roof for protection from inclement weather. Imaginative, colorful tile designs and a dolphin sculpture in this area add spice, and the attractive Dolphin Bar, with umbrellas and wicker chairs, is one of our favorite spaces on board, the perfect spot for a drink and snack in the late afternoon after a shore excursion.

The Sports Deck of each ship has combo basketball/tennis/volleyball courts, and the Lower Promenade Deck offers an unobstructed circuit of the ship for walking, jogging, or just lounging in the snazzy, traditional-looking wooden deck chairs. The ships' roomy, windowed Ocean Spa gyms are some of the most attractive and functional at sea, with a couple of dozen exercise machines, a large aerobics area, steam rooms, and saunas. The Steiner-managed spas lack pizzazz, but offer the typical menu of treatments (see chapter 4, "The Cruise Experience," for a discussion of spa options). There's an attached beauty salon.

The Forward Observation Deck is accessible only via two stairways hidden away in the forward (covered) portion of the Promenade Deck, and so gets little use. There's no deck furniture, but standing in the very bow as the ship plows through the ocean is a wonderful experience.

Noordam

The Verdict

This midsize 1980s ship is the oldest and coziest in the fleet, offering a comfortable, calm, glitz-free cruise experience and a slice of the (recent) past.

Noordam *(photo: Holland America Line)*

Specifications

Size (in tons)	33,930	Officers	Dutch/British
Number of Cabins	607	Crew	510 (Indonesian/ Filipino)
Number of Outside Cabins	409	Passenger/Crew Ratio	2.4 to 1
Cabins with Verandas	0	Year Launched	1984
Number of Passengers	1,214	Last Major Refurbishment	2001

Frommer's Ratings (Scale of 1–5)   ★★★½

Cabin Comfort & Amenities	4	Dining Options	4
Ship Cleanliness & Maintenance	4	Gym & Spa Facilities	3
Public Comfort/Space	3	Children's Facilities	2
Decor	4	Enjoyment Factor	4

Noordam is the line's oldest ship, built in the pre-Carnival days, and is either nostalgically evocative of the pre-megaship era or deficient in modern frills, depending on your point of view. Tiered aft decks offer lots of nooks for sunbathing and recall traditional ship style. In general, outside deck space and interior public rooms are not the kind of wide-open, flowing spaces you see on most newer ships (and all the more recent HAL ships), but are more like clusters attached to one another, creating cozy, intimate areas. Compared to the newer ships, *Noordam* is pared down in scope and scale.

Overall, *Noordam* passengers tend to be even more sedate and low-key than those aboard the line's larger ships, and more conscious than usual of getting value for their dollars. If you're planning on traveling with children, you'd be wiser to opt for *Maasdam* or the new *Zuiderdam,* which have dedicated children's facilities.

Cabins & Rates

Cabins	Per Diems from	Sq. Ft.	Fridge	Hair Dryer	Sitting Area	TV
Inside	$101	152	no	no	no	yes
Outside	$122	177–219	no	no	some	yes
Suite	$182	294	yes	no	yes	yes

CABINS   Though smaller than those on any other HAL ship, standard cabins are a decent size and are representative of the line's typically comfortable, low-key style. Bedding, upholstery, and carpeting are done in earth tones that border on drab, and the furniture is vaguely Art Deco. Storage space is more than adequate, and bathrooms are compact and well designed.

Most cabins on the Boat and Navigation decks have views obstructed by lifeboats, and those on the Upper Promenade Deck look out onto the promenade's stream of walkers, joggers, and passersby. Cabins near the stern are subject to more than their share of engine noise and vibration. Many cabins have bathtub/shower combos and all have TVs and music channels. There are no in-cabin safes, but valuables can be kept at the purser's desk. Minifridges can be requested through your travel agent and placed in cabins for a nominal fee.

There are 24 connecting cabins. Four category C deluxe cabins on the Boat Deck are suitable for people with disabilities. Elevators are wheelchair accessible.

PUBLIC AREAS   Public areas are done up in teak, polished rosewood, and discreet colors, with bouquets of fresh flowers liberally scattered throughout. The ship has a movie theater, library, Internet center, and card room, and her 15-foot-wide teak promenade allows deck-chair sitters, strollers, and joggers to mingle in the open air. Some passengers consider it the ship's most endearing feature, a lovely reminiscence of the classic ocean liners.

The ship has some unfortunate design flaws. For example, the showroom isn't large enough to seat all the passengers from each dinner seating, so is sometimes standing-room-only, with some sightlines blocked. And, in general, the ship's choppy clusters of public areas and decks can be confusing.

DINING OPTIONS   The single, one-story dining room is pleasant, though dull compared to the more glamorous two-story deals on the line's newer ships. There's also an indoor/outdoor buffet restaurant that serves breakfast, lunch, and dinner, along with a poolside grill for sandwiches.

POOL, FITNESS & SPA FACILITIES   The ship has two outside pools, a wading pool, and one hot tub. You can walk or jog on the broad, unobstructed Upper Promenade Deck. The gym and spa are small, as they are on most ships built in the 1980s and earlier: The windowed gym is located on one of the topmost decks and has rowing machines, weight machines, and stationary bicycles; the attached spa is really just a couple of treatment rooms for massages and facials, plus a steam room and sauna. Aerobics classes are held on the decks or in a public room. A Sports Deck up top features a pair of practice tennis courts and shuffleboard. A beauty salon/barber shop is located on the Main Deck.

6 Norwegian Cruise Line

7665 Corporate Center Dr., Miami, FL 33126. ✆ **800/327-7030** or 305/436-4000. Fax 305/436-4126. www. ncl.com.

THE LINE IN A NUTSHELL   NCL makes its mark with its always-casual, open-seating dining, and overall its new ships are standouts—*Sky, Sun,* and *Dawn* give the newest Royal Caribbean and Princess ships a run for their money.

THE EXPERIENCE   NCL has just come out of a major expansion mode, launching four new ships in the span of about 3 years, and it continues to roll out exciting innovations, especially in the dining department. The 2,000-passenger *Norwegian Sky,* 1,960-passenger *Norwegian Sun,* and 2,224-passenger *Norwegian Dawn* and *Star* represent the new, higher-quality NCL, while the line's four other midsize vintage-1980s vessels, carrying about 1,500 passengers each, stand for its more budget-conscious, catch-as-catch-can past.

There's no doubt NCL has remade itself, and quite impressively too. The line has quietly phased out its sports and music theme cruises, and in May 2000, it launched its "Freestyle Cruising" concept, a revolutionary ultraflexible dining program that appeals to people who don't like the regimentation and formality of traditional cruise dining. Now offered fleetwide, "freestyle" means all restaurants on the ships operate with a casual dress code and have open seating between about 5:30 and 10pm every evening.

Pros

- **Flexible dining:** NCL's dining policy lets you dine when you want and dress how you want.
- **Restaurants galore:** Not only is dining flexible, but with so many places to have dinner, you won't know where to turn. *Sky* has 6 restaurants, *Sun* 9, and *Dawn* has 10, and each of the other ships has 5.
- **Above-average entertainment:** While NCL offers the same mixed bag of options (from Vegas medleys to soloists, pianists, and so on), their talent is generally very good, from a hip cast of dancers to the powerful voice of singer Jane L. Powell, who is frequently featured across fleet.

Cons

- **Small cabins:** On all but *Norwegian Sun* and *Dawn,* standard cabins are a tight squeeze at about 150 square feet or less, compared to Carnival's 185-square-foot standard cabins.
- **No balconies** on *Majesty* and *Sea.*
- **Tinny:** We hate to pick on these guys, but overall, the interiors of *Majesty* and *Sea* feel pretty flimsy and cheap.

Compared with the other mainstream lines, here's how NCL rates:

	Poor	Fair	Good	Excellent	Outstanding
Enjoyment Factor				✓	
Dining				✓	
Activities				✓	
Children's Program			✓		
Entertainment			✓		
Service			✓		
Worth the Money					✓

NCL: INNOVATION KING

Talk about pulling yourself up by your bootstraps. Norwegian was one of the pioneers of the North American cruise market, beginning in the days of the now-defunct Kloster Cruises. But after these auspicious beginnings, the line spent many years relegated to the industry's back seat behind biggies Carnival and Royal Caribbean. Today, though, with its casual dining scheme and new ships, the line is serious about remaking itself into the great cruise line it once was.

In 1966, Knut Knutson, the Norwegian owner of Kloster, had a cruise ship but no marketing system, and Ted Arison, an Israeli, had a great North American marketing system but no ships. Together, they formed what was then known as Norwegian Caribbean Line, launching 3- and 4-day cruises from Miami to the Bahamas. In 1972, Arison and his entourage split from the company to form Carnival Cruise Lines, now the giant of the industry.

Over the years that followed, NCL had its difficulties, financial and otherwise, but by 1997, the hardest times seemed to be past, and a major program of expansion and marketing was put in place. Several of its ships were "stretched" (literally cut in half and reassembled with the addition of a new midsection); all its ships were renamed to include the word *Norwegian;* the line purchased Orient Lines, whose 800-passenger m/v *Marco Polo* does not sail in the Caribbean; and then, in August 1999, it debuted the first new NCL ship in 6 years, the megaship *Norwegian Sky.* Since then, three more brand-new ships have debuted, and the new ships of NCL are quite impressive (wish we could say the same thing about its older ships, *Norway* excluded). Except for the *Norwegian Star,* which spends the year cruising the Hawaiian Islands, the entire fleet spends all or some time in the Caribbean.

In late 2002, NCL announced it was taking over the unfinished hull (and parts) of two former "Project America" ships that were being built by American Classic Voyages and building them as their own; the first as-of-yet-unnamed ship is set to debut in spring 2004. As they're American-built and -flagged, the vessels will be legally able to offer cruises made up entirely of American ports. This emphasis on all-American vessels was perhaps responsible for another new NCL acquisition that sent a spasm of joy through classic-ship lovers everywhere: In April 2003, NCL announced that it had purchased the **SS *United States,*** built in 1952 to be the fastest, safest ship at sea, and (in those Cold War years) one able to be converted into a military transport at a moment's notice. On her maiden voyage, she averaged 35.5 knots and broke the transatlantic record with a time of 3 days, 10 hours, and 40 minutes, a record that has never been broken. Her top speed, rumored to have approached 50 knots, was kept secret as a matter of national security. Jet travel killed her bread-and-butter transatlantic business in the 1960s, and in 1969, the vessel was laid up; she has spent the past 7 years at a Philadelphia pier, gutted of her interior furnishings and slowly rusting. Preservationists have been working all along to save her from the scrap heap, and apparently they've succeeded. According to NCL, the line has now begun evaluating the extent of renovations needed to convert the *United States* into a modern cruise ship, with initial plans calling for her to be rebuilt entirely from the inside out, complying with current international safety regulations and creating an interior that's in tune with modern tastes. No target relaunch date has as yet been announced, though indications are that it will be a while. The ship is expected to offer itineraries visiting mainland U.S. ports where cruises are not currently available.

Concurrent with its announcement of the SS *United States* purchase, NCL also announced that it had purchased the classic, American-built **SS *Independence,*** formerly of the bankrupt American Hawaii Cruises, at federal auction from the U.S. Maritime Administration. No further details have been announced on possible renovation and redeployment.

Today, NCL is 100% owned by Singapore-based Star Cruises, a successful company with the moola to make serious investments in NCL's future. The new management team Star installed in 2000 has made NCL once again an important presence in the cruise industry.

PASSENGER PROFILE

NCL as a rule attracts a diverse lot, and passengers in general are younger, more price-conscious, and more active than those aboard lines such as HAL, Celebrity, and Princess. Typical NCL passengers are couples ages 25 to 60, and include a fair number of honeymooners and families with kids during summers and holidays. (Kids under 2 sail free.) The atmosphere aboard all NCL vessels is informal and well suited to the party-maker taking a first or second cruise.

Active vacationers particularly like the line because of its enhanced sports programs. For instance, snorkeling lessons are often held in the ships' pools. Scuba programs, run by independent concessionaires, are offered on some cruises, including resort certification. For the more sedentary sports fan, all major weekend games, including NFL playoffs, are broadcast via ESPN and CNN into passengers' cabins and in each vessel's sports bar, where multiple screens sometimes broadcast different games simultaneously.

DINING

The food in the specialty restaurants of NCL's newest ships is among the best of the mainstream ships, but more exciting than how the food tastes is how NCL handles the whole business of dining. In early 2000, after NCL's association with Star Cruises was cemented, management introduced a new flexibility concept called **Freestyle Cruising,** wherein all the restaurants on all NCL ships (except the old *Norway*) follow an **open-seating policy** each and every evening, allowing you to dine when and with whom you like (strolling in any time between 5:30–10pm), and dressed however you like, too. While management says anything goes *except* jeans, shorts, and tank tops, we have seen some of that too in the main restaurants. The point is, here more than on any other mainstream line, you're free to pretty much dress as you please. Of course, since anything goes, this means you'll now see a guy in jeans and a baseball cap seated next to a lady in a dress and pearls. Welcome to the new face of cruising! The night of the captain's cocktail party is officially an **optional formal night,** meaning you don't have to wear a suit, tie, or fancy dress, but for those who would like to, this is the night to do so. On a recent cruise, lots of people chose to dress up; we were surprised (and delighted!). Soon after NCL launched theirs, Princess introduced a more flexible dining setup too, although not to this extreme.

In the main dining rooms, you can usually count on such choices as grilled swordfish with lemon-caper sauce, salmon or poached sea bass, beef Wellington, broiled lobster tail, chicken Parmesan, fettuccine Alfredo, or perhaps a Jamaican jerk pork roast, Wiener schnitzel, or roast prime rib. The wine lists appeal to standard mid-American tastes, and prices aren't offensively high. Once a week, the main dining rooms serve an amusing **President's Menu.** Created by former White House chef Henry Haller, it features some former presidents' and first ladies' favorite dishes, such as President Nixon's North Atlantic Crab Soup and

ⓒ A Private Norwegian Island (So to Speak)

Great Stirrup Cay, NCL's private island, is a stretch of palm-studded beachfront in the southern Bahamas, and was the very first private resort developed by a cruise line in the Caribbean. Loaded with bar, lunch, and watersports facilities, the sleepy beach turns into an instant party whenever one of the NCL vessels is in port. Music is either broadcast or performed live, barbecues are fired up, hammocks are strung between palms, and rum punches are spiced and served. Passengers can ride paddleboats, sail Sunfish, go snorkeling or parasailing, hop on a banana boat, get a massage at one of the beachside stations, or do nothing more than sunbathe all day long. Pleasingly, the island is not overdeveloped and manages to retain more of a natural feel than some of the other lines' islands.

Betty Ford's Garden Salad with Olive Oil Dressing. Try to keep a straight face while ordering something called Nancy Reagan's Poached Sea Bass in Champagne and Saffron Sauce. We dare you.

In addition to one or two main dining rooms, each ship has at least two smaller reservations-only alternative **specialty restaurants,** one Italian and one French/Continental (called Le Bistro), with the line's newest ships offering even more, from pan-Asian restaurants to Japanese, Pacific Rim, and Spanish (tapas).

The food in **Le Bistro** (where you'll pay a $10–$12.50 per-person cover charge) is better than that in the main dining rooms, and includes items such as a yummy Caesar salad (made for you right at your table, or at least nearby), a delicious salmon filet in sorrel cream sauce, a juicy beef tenderloin, and a marvelously decadent chocolate fondue served with fresh fruit. Often, tables are available for walk-ins, but make your reservations—available only a day in advance—as soon as possible to be on the safe side.

A light spa cuisine choice and a vegetarian entree are available at lunch and dinner. Children's menus feature the popular standards: burgers, hot dogs, grilled cheese sandwiches and french fries, spaghetti and meatballs, ice-cream sundaes, and even something you may not expect: vegetable crudités and cheese dip. Kids Soda packages, which feature unlimited fountain sodas, personalized soda cup, and special straw, can be purchased once you board ship for $16 on a 7-day cruise, $10 on a 4-day cruise, and $8 on a 3-day cruise. (If purchased separately, a can of soda goes for $1.50, and fountain sodas are $1.) There are souped-up versions of these packages with more goodies, like a baseball cap and T-shirt.

All NCL vessels offer daily midnight buffets and each also has an ice-cream bar open a few hours a day. Fleetwide, you can also drool over the popular **Chocoholic Extravaganza midnight buffet,** offering everything from tortes to brownies and lots of stuff with chocolate sauce smeared all over it. All the ships serve pizza (from one of the restaurant areas in the afternoon and through room service 24 hr. a day), and a coffee bar serves specialty coffees and other beverages on all vessels but *Norwegian Sea.* Room service is available 24 hours a day.

ACTIVITIES
Adult activities are one of NCL's strongest points. You'll find the most action aboard *Sky, Sun,* and *Dawn,* but all the ships offer impressive rosters. You can take

NCL Fleet Itineraries

Ship	Itineraries
Norway	**7-night E. Carib:** Round-trip from Miami, year-round, visiting Sint Maarten, St. Thomas, and Great Stirrup Cay**, with 3 days at sea. **Non-Caribbean Itineraries:** None.
Norwegian Dawn	**7-night Bahamas & Florida:** Round-trip from New York, year-round, visiting Port Canaveral, Miami, Nassau, and Great Stirrup Cay**, with 2 days at sea. Passengers also have the option of sailing round-trip from Port Canaveral, thus including New York as a port of call. **Non-Caribbean Itineraries:** None.
Norwegian Dream	**7-night W. Carib:** Round-trip from New Orleans, Nov 2003–Mar 2004, visiting Cozumel and Cancun (Mexico), Roatan (Honduras), and Belize City (Belize), with 2 days at sea. **Non-Caribbean Itineraries:** Europe.
Norwegian Majesty	**7-night W. Carib:** Round-trip from Charleston, SC, Nov 2003–Apr 2004, visiting Grand Cayman, Cozumel, and Key West, with 3 days at sea. **7-night Bermuda:** Round-trip from Boston, Sept–Oct 2003 and May–Oct 2003, visiting St. George, with 2 days at sea. **Non-Caribbean/Bermuda Itineraries:** None.
Norwegian Sea	**7-night W. Carib:** Round-trip from Houston, TX, Nov 2003–Apr 2004, visiting Cozumel and Cancun (Mexico), Roatan (Honduras), and Belize City (Belize), with 2 days at sea. **7-night Bermuda:** Round-trip from New York (Sept 2003) and Philadelphia (Oct 2003), and visiting Hamilton, King's Wharf, and St. George, Bermuda, with 2 days at sea. **Non-Caribbean/Bermuda Itineraries:** New England.
Norwegian Sky	**7-night S. Carib 1:** Round-trip from San Juan, Oct 2003–Apr 2004, visiting St. Thomas, Dominica, Barbados, St. Lucia, and St. Kitts, with 1 day at sea. Alternates with **7-night S. Carib 2:** Round-trip from San Juan, Oct 2003–Apr 2004, visiting St. Thomas, Antigua, Martinique, Sint Maarten, and Tortola (BVIs), with 1 day at sea. **Non-Caribbean Itineraries:** Panama Canal and Pacific coastal repositioning cruises, Alaska.
Norwegian Sun	**7-night W. Carib 1:** Round-trip from Miami, Oct 2003–Mar 2004, visiting Ocho Rios or Montego Bay (Jamaica), Grand Cayman, and Costa Maya and Cozumel (Mexico), with 2 days at sea. **Non-Caribbean Itineraries:** Panama Canal and Pacific coastal repositioning cruises, Alaska.
Norwegian Wind	**7-night W. Carib:** Round-trip from Miami, Oct 2003–Apr 2004, visiting Grand Cayman, Roatan (Honduras), Belize City (Belize), and Cozumel, with 2 days at sea. **Non-Caribbean Itineraries:** Panama Canal repositioning cruises, Alaska.

*At press times, itineraries were only available through April 2004. **NCL's private Bahamian island.*

cha-cha lessons or Filipino or German classes; play bingo, shuffleboard, or basketball; attend an art auction or spa or beauty demonstration; sit in on **enrichment lectures** about classic ocean liners, nutrition, or personal investing; or listen to the live poolside calypso band. There are galley and bridge tours, snorkeling demonstrations in the pool, makeovers, talent shows, wine tastings (for $10 a person), and trivia contests, plus silly poolside competitions to keep you laughing all afternoon long. Internet cafes offer e-mail and Internet access fleetwide.

Those of you who like to work out at odd hours will appreciate NCL's **24-hour gyms;** the newest ships have all the newest classes, from cardio kickboxing to spinning (though there's a $5 charge for the latter). All of NCL's ships (except *Norwegian Majesty*) have golf driving cages where guests can practice their putting and swinging at their leisure. In port, NCL's Dive-In program offers at least one snorkeling and one scuba excursion at almost every Caribbean port, escorted by the ship's certified instructors.

CHILDREN'S PROGRAM

NCL's Kids Crew program offers year-round supervised activities for children ages 2 to 17, dividing children into four age groups: Junior Sailors, ages 2 to 5; First Mates, ages 6 to 8; Navigators, ages 9 to 12; and teens, ages 13 to 17. Activities vary across the fleet, but may include sports competitions, dances, face painting, treasure hunts, magic shows, arts and crafts, cooking classes, T-shirt painting, and even a Circus at Sea. Children get their own *Cruise News* detailing the day's events. Unlimited soda packages are $16 for kids under age 17 on 7-night cruises, and a "Teen Passport" coupon book is available for teens—for $30 they get up to 20 nonalcoholic drinks such as Virgin Daiquiris.

Each ship has a playroom called "Kids Korner" (*Norwegian Sea*'s is called "Porthole"), and with each new ship the line introduces, the kids' facilities get better. The facilities on the new *Sky, Sun,* and *Dawn* are the best by far, huge spaces that include a separate teen center and a wading pool, as well as a large, well-stocked playroom. On sea days, the playrooms are open between 9am and noon, 2 to 4:30pm, and then 7:30 to 10pm; port days the hours are 3 to 5pm and 7:30 to 10pm.

Once per 7-night cruise is **"Mom and Dad's Night Out,"** when kids dine with counselors. **Group babysitting** for kids as young as age 2 is offered nightly for $5 per child per hour, plus $3 an hour for each additional child, between 9am and 5pm on port days and every night 10pm and 1am (however, counselors do not do diapers; parents are given beepers so that they can be alerted when it's time for the dirty work!). Private, in-cabin babysitting is no longer offered.

ENTERTAINMENT

NCL offers some of the best entertainment in the mass market. A recent cruise on *Norwegian Sun* had an impressive roster of talent, from the always-awesome singer **Jane L. Powell** and her excellent accompanying band, who have appeared on NCL ships for years; to an excellent **piano-playing singer** whose renditions of Billy Joel and Cat Stevens songs transported you to another time and place; and to a Bill Cosby–style comedian who kept everyone in stitches. The **Vegas-style productions** were also very good, with 4 or 5 dancers out of a total of about 18 sharing the lead singing roles; set designs, costumes, and choreography were impressive. The cast even included a ballroom-dancing pair and an acrobat couple. Overall, *Sun* offered the best entertainment we've seen at sea in years, along with *Dawn* and her very entertaining India-inspired Bollywood song and dance medley. While the newer *Sun, Dawn,* and *Sky* have the best-equipped show lounges, all the vessels contain a fully equipped theater where abridged productions of such shows as *Crazy for You, Grease, 42nd Street, The Will Rogers Follies,* and *Dreamgirls* are presented.

Serious gamblers should consider only *Sky, Sun,* and *Dawn* because these three ships boast the fleet's biggest and splashiest casinos.

All the ships have bars where you can slip away for a quiet rendezvous, and small tucked-away corners for more intimate entertainment, including pianists and cabaret acts. Music for dancing is popular aboard all the ships and takes place before or after shows, and each ship has a late-night disco.

SERVICE

Overall, and especially on the new ships, NCL's service has been improving and is more consistently good than in the past. Generally, room service and bar service fleetwide are speedy and efficient. Waiters are accommodating, but NCL's

automatic tipping policy ($10 per adult and $5 per child under age 12 per day is automatically added to your account, though the amount can be adjusted if you go to the purser's desk) has definitely created a less personal level of service in the two main dining rooms. On a recent cruise, there definitely seemed to be less incentive to get the pepper mill to the table right away or bring a requested wine list before we finished our appetizers. Waiters seemed to be either frantically dealing with a lot of tables at once, or during a lull almost forgetting to come back to the table to fill water or check on things. On the other hand, in the alternative restaurants, Le Bistro and *Sun's* Il Adagio (Horizons on *Sky*), service was very sharp and very attentive.

Service in the well laid-out buffet restaurants on *Sky, Sun,* and *Dawn* is efficient; lines move quickly and bins are continually filled; on NCL's older ships, conditions are more cramped and lines often get backed up. Cabin service is efficient, though, again, because of the automatic tipping, your steward may not be as eager to bother introducing himself at the start of the cruise, and generally there is less schmoozing and small talk.

NCL ships offer **laundry and dry-cleaning service** but do not have self-service launderettes.

Norwegian Dawn

The Verdict

Really original megaships don't come along too often these days, but *Dawn* is one of them, with a mix of classy and fun spaces, a lively Miami-esque atmosphere, awesome kids' facilities, and more restaurant options than you can shake a stick at.

Norwegian Dawn *(photo: NCL)*

Specifications

Size (in tons)	92,250	Officers	Norwegian
Number of Cabins	1,112	Crew	1,126 (Internat'l)
Number of Outside Cabins	759	Passenger/Crew Ratio	2 to 1
Cabins with Verandas	509	Year Launched	2002
Number of Passengers	2,224	Last Major Refurbishment	N/A

Frommer's Ratings (Scale of 1–5)

★★★★ ½

Cabin Comfort & Amenities	4	Dining Options	5
Ship Cleanliness & Maintenance	5	Gym & Spa Facilities	4
Public Comfort/Space	5	Children's Facilities	5
Decor	4.5	Enjoyment Factor	4.5

After a few years of real innovation in shipbuilding and onboard amenities that began around 1995 and culminated with Royal Caribbean's enormous Voyager-class ships in 1999, new vessels in general fell into a certain sameness. Most of them offered mountains of balcony cabins, an alternative restaurant or two, a cigar bar, and either wildly outrageous decor or a more traditional, woody feel. Nice, sure. Entertaining, yes. But nothing really new. With the introduction of *Norwegian Dawn,* though, NCL has bucked that trend and moved into the vanguard of cruise innovation.

Like to eat? *Dawn* has—get this—*10 different restaurants* onboard, from fancy steakhouses and teppanyaki restaurants to casual Tex-Mex and burger joints. Want something other than the generic Caribbean theme so prevalent on many ships? *Dawn* comes with a healthy dose of Latin Miami in her music and decor, which complements innovative itineraries that depart from New York and visit Miami, Nassau, Great Stirrup Cay (NCL's private Bahamian island), and Port Canaveral, Florida, for trips to the Kennedy Space Center and Orlando's theme parks. Want the biggest suites aboard any ship, anywhere? *Dawn's* Garden Villas spread out over a mind-blowing 5,350 square feet and feature private gardens, multiple bedrooms with extravagant baths, separate living rooms, full kitchens, and private butler service. Zowie! Zowie, too, on the price: $26,000 a week! (For 6 guests.) Normal cabins, on the other hand, come at normal prices.

Onboard programs are innovative too, featuring fewer of the ho-hum napkin-folding classes that once defined ship life and more computer- and health/nutrition-oriented workshops. The production shows in the striking Stardust Theater have a fresh feel too (incorporating hip-hop, India-inspired Bollywood themes, lots of Latin music, and even the occasional hint of storyline into honest-to-God exciting musical revues), and 1 night per cruise features a Miami dance party with musicians from the South Beach scene. For kids, the T-Rex Kids' Center is a knockout, huge and so completely kid-centric that we wished we were 5 again, and the buffet restaurant's Kids' Cafe—a miniaturized version of the adult cafe, accurate down to tiny chairs and a miniature buffet counter—is just the cutest thing going.

Don't get us wrong, this isn't paradise: Though many spaces aboard the ship approach high style (the elegant Gatsby's Champagne Bar, for instance), hints of NCL's recent near-budget past still hide in the wings, including the individually wrapped butter pats used even in the fancy restaurants, fast-food-style napkin dispensers in the buffet, and spindly metal-frame chairs and end tables in most cabins. But those are minor quibbles. Overall, this ship is a winner.

Cabins & Rates

Cabins	Per Diems from	Sq. Ft.	Fridge	Hair Dryer	Sitting Area	TV
Inside	$97	142	yes	yes	yes	yes
Outside	$111	158–166	yes	yes	yes	yes
Suite	$318	229–5,350	yes	yes	yes	yes

CABINS Though not overly large compared to some in the industry (particularly those of Carnival and Holland America's ships), standard cabins on *Dawn* are larger than elsewhere in the NCL fleet. Decor is a mix, with stylish elements like cherry-wood wall paneling and snazzy rounded lights, kitschy elements like bright island-colored carpeting, and cheap touches like spindly chairs and end tables, and wall-mounted soap dispensers in the bathrooms. Each comes with a small TV and minifridge, a tea/coffeemaker (an amenity rarely offered), private safe, and cool, retro-looking Aliseo hair dryers hanging in a coiled silver wall mount. Closet and drawer space provide more than enough space for weeklong sailings, and bathrooms in all categories are well-designed, with large sinks whose faucets swing out of the way, a magnifying mirror inset in the regular mirror, adequate though not exceptional counter/shelf space, and (in all but inside cabins) shower, toilet, and washstand compartments (shower and toilet are behind their own little doors). Balconies in standard cabins accommodate two metal pool chairs and a small table, but aren't terribly roomy.

Minisuites provide about 60 more feet of floor space, with a large fold-out couch, a curtain between the bed and the sitting area, and a bathtub, while the four so-called "Romance Suites" (in the stern on Deck 10) really are, with 288 square feet of space, stereo with CD/DVD library, bathroom with separate shower and tub, nice wooden deck chairs on the balcony, and a romantic view over the ship's wake. Penthouse Suites offer the same, plus gorgeous bathrooms with whirlpool tub and tiled, sea-view shower stall; a larger balcony; and a walk-in closet. Those on Deck 11 offer a separate kids' room and bathroom. Those facing the bow on Decks 9 and 10 have large windows and deep balconies, but safety requirements mandate that instead of a nice glass door, they're accessed via an honest-to-God steel bulkhead that's marked, "For your own safety, open only when the vessel is in port." The ship's four Owner's Suites are huge, with two balconies (one facing forward, as just described, and another, more accessible one on the side), living and dining areas, powder room, guest bath, and 750 square feet of space; compared to the two Garden Villas up on Deck 14, however, these suites are peasant's quarters. The Garden Villas are, in a word, HUGE, the biggest at sea today, with three bedrooms, enormous living rooms, private Italian gardens with hot tub, panoramic views all around, private butler service, grand pianos, and totally extravagant sea-view bathrooms with whirlpool tubs. They're priced beyond the range of . . . well, pretty much everybody.

There are 140 connecting cabins, including many options for linking suites with standard ocean-view cabins. Twenty cabins are wheelchair-accessible.

PUBLIC AREAS   From the moment you step aboard into *Dawn's* large, broad, skylit atrium lobby, with its java cafe at ground level and a top-notch salsa band performing on its large stage, you'll be in a party mood. Public areas throughout are fanciful and extremely spacious, done in a mix of bright, Caribbean- and Miami-themed decor and high style Art Deco, with lots of nooks and some downright wonderful lounges and bars mixed in among all the restaurant choices. Art throughout mixes primitivist folk paintings, modern art depicting famous world buildings like the Petronas Towers and the Great Pyramids, and Andy Warhol silk-screens. There's even art outdoors, with landscapes, Matisse Dancers, and other themes painted along the length of the Promenade Deck.

Deck 7, the main entertainment deck, starts with the three-deck Stardust Theater in the bow, its thousand seats sloping down to a large stage flanked with opera boxes, where percussionists perform during the ship's Bollywood production shows. Moving toward the stern, Dazzles Lounge and Nightclub is a venue for smaller-scale cabaret entertainment and dancing. Toward the stern, behind the atrium, the Pearly King's Pub is a British-themed bar with old repro pub signs, a portrait of the queen, fish and chips in the evening, piano entertainment, and a big-screen TV for sports. Pleasant enough (if often smoky), but its big flaw is that it serves as a de facto corridor, so it gets more traffic than a cozy space should. Behind this bar, all by itself in the stern and taking up the full width of the ship, are the Galleria Shops, a veritable department store at sea.

Deck 6 is almost entirely taken up by restaurants, but in among them is the spacious Dawn Club Casino (which doesn't seek to trap you with a convoluted layout, as aboard many other ships); Gatsby's Champagne Bar, a very high-style, cathedral-ceiling space with a sweeping staircase, piano entertainment, and Art Deco representations of the Empire State Building and other famous New York skyscrapers; and the Havana Club, an almost private room for cigars. port, cognacs, and whiskey, with seating for only 12.

The ship's Internet center is wrapped around the atrium on Deck 9 and is tricky to reach, accessible during normal circumstances only via the atrium stairs, next to the Salsa restaurant. For those wanting flexibility in their Web-surfing, *Dawn* features a Wi-Fi wireless system that lets you log on from various places on board using your own or a rented laptop and an NCL network card.

Deck 12 features a complex of "sit-down" rooms, including a comfortable cin-ema with traditional theater seats, a library, a card room, a reading room, a "lifestyles" room (used for classes, private functions, and so on), several meeting rooms, and a small wedding chapel. Forward of these is Spinnaker's Lounge, a nau-tically themed observation lounge/disco with bright, amoeba-shaped chairs and couches in the starboard rear corner—totally Alice in Wonderland, totally fun.

Up top, on Deck 13, the Star Bar is a 1930/'40s-themed nightclub with a marble-topped bar, brown leather seating around small cocktail tables, artwork depicting the Rat Pack, Bogart, James Cagney, Groucho Marx, and other Hol-lywood legends. A piano player entertains in the evening.

For kids, *Dawn* has some of the better facilities at sea, with a huge, brightly colored crafts/play area, a big-screen TV room stuffed full of beanbag chairs, a huge ball-jump/crawling maze play-gym, a computer room, and a nursery with tiny little beds. Outside, the T-Rex pool area is right out of *The Flintstones*, with giant polka-dotted dinosaurs hovering around faux rock walls, slides, a paddling pool, and even a kids' Jacuzzi. The nearby teen center is large and very con-sciously private (accessed down hallways screened off from adult eyes), with computers, a dance floor and sound/video system, a soda bar, leopard-print loveseats, and Lichtenstein-style pop art on the walls. Next door, a video arcade has 24 pinging machines, mostly of the shoot-'em-up variety.

DINING OPTIONS   *Dawn* is all about its restaurants. Main dining rooms include the elegant, chandelier-lit Venetian, offering a traditional European-style dining experience; the Aqua, a lighter, more modern space ringed with Matisse Dancers reproductions and serving contemporary dishes, some designed by for-mer White House executive chef Henry Haller; and Impressions, decorated in the style of a 19th-century French dining room, with rich burled wall paneling and reproductions of Impressionist paintings throughout. The menu here varies.

The three alternative restaurants aboard carry a cover charge. Cagney's, perched way up on Deck 13, is a 1930s-themed steakhouse with an open kitchen, floor-to-ceiling windows, and a woody decor that includes faux-brick walls, frosted glass wall lamps, period photos, and newspaper headlines. Its menu is totally carnivorous, featuring USDA-certified Angus beef (cover charge is $18 per person). Bamboo is a pan-Asian restaurant with a very open feel (maybe too open, looking a bit like a slightly high-end food court), separate conveyor-belt sushi bar and sake bar, and 18-seat Japanese teppanyaki room, where meals are prepared from the center of the table as guests look on. (Cover charge for Bamboo is $10; a la carte pricing in teppanyaki room is $10–$15.) Though not nearly as cozy and snuggly as the same on the *Sun* and *Sky, Dawn*'s Le Bistro serves classic and nouvelle French cuisine in a classic atmosphere, with lily pad–pattern carpeting, floral tapestry upholstery, fine place settings, and original Impressionist paintings by van Gogh, Matisse, Renoir, and Monet adorning the walls (cover charge is $12.50 per person). Just next door, the Wine Cellar is not a cellar at all but is, in fact, right out in the open, separated from the corridor only by a railing. Wine tastings are conducted here, and tables for 2 and 10 operate as an extension of Le Bistro, with the same cover charge.

More casual dining venues include Salsa, a Tex-Mex/tapas restaurant that encircles the atrium on Deck 8. It's a great spot for a meal or just to sip sangria and eat chips while watching the house band perform in the atrium each evening. Blue Lagoon, on Deck 7, is an even more casual spot, open 24 hours a day to serve burgers, fish and chips, stir-fry, and other snacks. Typical buffet fare (and occasional pleasant surprises such as an all-vegetarian Indian buffet) is served in Deck 12's Garden Cafe, part of which becomes La Trattoria in the evenings, a casual restaurant serving pizza, pastas, and other Italian items. Beer-drinkers take note: Its bar serves McEwans, Double Diamond, Fosters, and several other uncommon options. Out on deck, the Bimini Bar & Grill serves the typical burgers, dogs, and fries during the day.

POOL, FITNESS & SPA FACILITIES   The main pool area has the feel of a resort, ringed by flower-shaped "streetlamps" and terraces of deck chairs leading down to the central pool and hot tubs. A huge bar running almost the width of the ship serves ice cream on one side, drinks on the other. Nice space, but the real plaudits go to the El Dorado Spa's indoor pool complex, an elegant, Mayan-themed space with a large lap pool, hot tub, jet-massage pool, and sunny windowed seating areas furnished with wooden deck chairs. It's one of our favorite spaces aboard any new ship this year, harking back to the classic indoor pools on the transatlantic liners. The rest of the spa is similarly stylish, with a sunlit entranceway that rises three decks high and is decorated with plants and Mayan reliefs, a juice bar, and 21 rooms offering the standard massages and beauty/relaxation treatments. The gym, by way of contrast, is blah: large, with a room for cycling classes, an aerobics studio, a very large free-weights area, and dozens of aerobics and weight machines, but it won't win any awards in the design department.

Outside on Deck 13, the jogging track is larger than the usual ones on land, with 3½ laps equaling 1 mile. Just above, Deck 14 has a sports court for basketball and volleyball, two golf-driving nets, and facilities for shuffleboard and deck chess. There's acres of open deck space for sunning aft on Deck 14 and forward on the tiered Sun Deck, where a lone hot tub looks out over the bow.

Norwegian Sky •
Norwegian Sun

The Verdict

The snazzy *Sky* was pretty impressive when she debuted with six restaurants, an Internet cafe, a cigar bar, and lots of cabin balconies; but the newer *Sun* is even better, with nine really good restaurants including a delectable sushi bar.

Norwegian Sky *(photo: NCL)*

Specifications

Size (in tons)		Officers	Norwegian
Sky	77,104	Crew	(Internat'l)
Sun	78,309	*Sky*	1,000
Number of Cabins	1,001	*Sun*	968
Number of Outside Cabins	574	Passenger/Crew Ratio	2.7 to 1
Cabins with Verandas		Year Launched	
Sky	257	*Sky*	1999
Sun	432	*Sun*	2001
Number of Passengers	2,002/1,960	Last Major Refurbishment	N/A

Frommer's Ratings (Scale of 1–5)   ⋆⋆⋆⋆

Cabin Comfort & Amenities	3/4*	Dining Options	4/4.5*
Ship Cleanliness & Maintenance	4	Gym & Spa Facilities	4
Public Comfort/Space	4	Children's Facilities	3.5
Decor	4	Enjoyment Factor	4

* Cabins and dining options differ on the two ships.

With the debut of *Norwegian Sun* in fall of 2001, several of the features of older sister *Norwegian Sky* were improved upon, namely the size and storage capacity of the cabins. *Sun's* outside balcony cabins are 172 square feet as opposed to the *Sky's* 150, and *Sun* has 32 267-foot minisuites not offered on *Sky*. Still, *Sky* marked NCL's entry into the modern megaship world, and made a splash, followed by the even more impressive *Sun*. Both ships are loaded with today's must-have features, from cabin balconies to an Internet cafe and a cigar bar— and, most importantly, *Sky* has six restaurants and *Sun* nine, all of which operate under the line's new casual dining policy.

Cabins & Rates

Cabins	Per Diems from	Sq. Ft.	Fridge	Hair Dryer	Sitting Area	TV
Inside	$80	121–147*	yes	yes	yes	yes
Outside	$101	149–154*	yes	yes	yes	yes
Suite	$211	321–512*	yes	yes	yes	yes

* Measures for Sky only. Measures for Sun are 118–191, 154–173, and 264–570 square feet.

CABINS   *Sun's* roomy cabins are an improvement over *Sky's* smaller, storage-challenged numbers. Plus, *Sun* also has a greater variety of suites (56 to *Sky's* 14), *Sun's* 32 minisuites measure a roomy 264 to 301 square feet, plus 68- to 86-square-foot balconies) and have walk-in closets, sitting areas, and bathtubs, while her 20 355- to 570-square-foot Penthouse and Owner's suites (with 119- to 258-sq.-ft. balconies) include the services of a butler and concierge who will get you on the first tender in ports, make dinner reservations, and generally try to please your every whim. The pair of penthouses also has a separate living room and dining area.

Though an improvement over *Sky's* cabins in storage and space, the layout of the *Sun's* category BA, BB, and BC balcony cabins, which take up most of Decks 8 through 10, is awkward because one of the twin beds and the closet-dresser unit are positioned too close together; a person dragging a suitcase or pushing a stroller certainly couldn't get by easily. The cabins just need to be about a foot wider. Other than that, the decor is pleasant with caramel wood veneers, attractive gilt-framed artwork, and navy, gold, and Kelly green fabrics and carpeting. Storage space is plentiful, so much so that on a recent cruise we couldn't even manage to fill up all the shelves. The bathrooms have a pair of shelves above the counter and a real useful one in the shower, though otherwise the skinny shower stalls are a tight squeeze for all but Kate Moss–types. Cabins at the forward end of *Sun's* Deck 6 have large portholes that look out on the ship's wraparound Promenade Deck, popular with walkers and runners, so you'll probably want to have your curtains closed most of the time unless you like being peeped on.

Sky's cabins are pretty too, done up in wood tones and pastels; but all cabins, even suites, have only a two-panel closet and a small bureau with four slim drawers. Be prepared to use your suitcase to store whatever. Oh, and watch out for those reading lamps above the beds: Their protruding shades make sitting up impossible. On *Sky,* the 200-plus balcony cabins measure 154 square feet, plus a 48-square-foot veranda, and the vast majority of standard outside and inside cabins are almost 40 square feet smaller than Carnival's standard cabins. Bathrooms are compact, with tubular shower stalls and slivers of shelving.

It's worth noting that *Sky's* hull was originally built a few years back by Costa, who'd planned for the cabins to have portholes and no balconies. Costa sold the hull to NCL after the shipyard went bust, and, unwilling to bring out a megaship without balconies, NCL compromised, working around the existing portholes and adding balconies, resulting in an odd door-and-porthole combo (most ships have sliding-glass doors) between cabin and balcony.

Every cabin on both *Sky* and *Sun* has a small sitting area, a minifridge (not stocked), a hair dryer, TVs, and a desk and chair. The *Sun* also has coffee- and tea-making accouterments in each cabin. Bathrooms are equipped with shampoo and liquid-soap dispensers attached right to the wall (and the shampoo is halfway decent too), so no need to fumble with the small bottles most ships provide. Suites are stocked with robes.

There are many connecting cabins, and 6 cabins on *Sky* and 20 on *Sun* are equipped for wheelchairs.

PUBLIC AREAS   The ships are bright and sun-filled due to an abundance of floor-to-ceiling windows. Surrounding the understated three-level atrium on several levels is a bar, clusters of chairs creating relaxing pockets, and an area where a pianist performs. The color scheme overall is a pleasing, but not too jarring, pastiche of mostly cool blues, sages, deep reds, and soft golds blended with marble, burled-wood veneers, and brass and chrome detailing.

The ships have nearly a dozen bars, including a sports bar, a wine bar, a nightclub/disco centrally located amidships, two large poolside bars, a coffee bar, an Internet cafe, and a dark and cozy cigar club with the most comfortable thick buttery leather chairs and couches around. With soft ballads coming from the adjacent piano bar setting the background music, the cigar bar is the most appealing place on the ship for quiet conversation (unless, of course, you can't stand smoke). Many of the balcony seats in the two-story show lounge have obstructed views of the stage, and decor-wise, this isn't one of the ships' most impressive spaces. Still, the lights are low most of the time, and the focus is on the stage, where it should be. There's a large attractive observation lounge wrapped in windows on one of the top two decks; at night it's a venue for live music. The casinos are large and flashy enough, though not as over the top as those you'll find on Carnival's and Royal Caribbean's ships. The layout of the shops is attractive, with a wide streetlike corridor (with a mural-painted ceiling) cutting between the main boutiques and a long jewelry counter, in a way, forcing passengers to browse whether they want to or not as the passage is the only way to get between the casino and show lounge.

Sun has a wedding chapel—a small, but pleasant, room also used for religious services.

For kids, the ships' huge children's area includes a sprawling playroom with ridiculously high ceilings, a teen center with a large movie screen and a pair of foosball games, and a video arcade. Each also has a wading pool.

DINING OPTIONS   Above all else, *Sun* and *Sky* excel in the restaurant department. For breakfast, lunch, and dinner, there are two elegant dining rooms, whose elegance belies their often casually dressed customers and often somewhat blasé waitstaff (remember, the tipping carrot is gone from the NCL ships, and service does feel a lot less personalized in the main restaurants because of it). The rooms have lots of tables for two and four. A large, well-organized indoor/outdoor casual buffet restaurant serves all three meals, plus snacks in between, such as pizza and jumbo really yummy homemade cookies. For dinner, you can also choose from six alternative restaurants on *Sun* and three on *Sky:* Both have a Le Bistro, an elegant space with lots of windows and several comfy round booths with cushy pillows as well as regular tables ($10 cover charge). Both ships also have an Italian venue (Horizons on *Sky* and Il Adagio on *Sun*), a long skinny space between the two main restaurants, where the lighting is low and the views are good from every seat—the row of raised round booths along the wall and the tables for two at the windows ($10 cover charge). The shrimp scampi and veal chop with wild mushroom ragout are tasty, and so is the homemade mushroom ravioli and Mediterranean seafood cocktail. Caesar salads are prepared from scratch tableside, and the warm chocolate hazelnut cake is to die for.

On *Sky,* Ciao Chow serves Asian; highlights include such dishes as Asian spiced shrimp and squid Caesar salad, and, at lunch, a create-your-own Oriental soup and a handmade sushi and sashimi bar. *Sun's* sushi bar serves expertly prepared, fresh-tasting maki and California rolls (at about $2 per roll) along with nigiri sushi and sashimi (most are $2 or $3 for two pieces) with authentic Japanese place settings; you can get a delicious and filling combo platter for $8. The adjacent teppanyaki venue does lunch and dinner just like Benihana, with the theatrical cutting and flinging of shrimp, chicken, beef, and whatever else you order from the the a la carte menu. Nearby is *Sun's* tapas restaurant, an attractive room decorated with tile mosaic and terra-cotta pottery, and serving a somewhat odd combination of very mediocre-tasting appetizer-like snacks, from fried seafood balls to ribs, olives, seafood salad, and falafel, along with sangria and a selection of Mexican (not Spanish) beer. At dinnertime, live Spanish music is featured; lunch is more casual (and on a recent cruise, the service was very slow and somewhat confused; there's no cover charge here). Pacific Heights is a health-oriented dinner venue, where calorie, fat, protein, and other similar stats are listed on the menu, and, okay, if not bland, entrees are offered, including spaghetti and turkey meatballs, and grilled pork chops with applesauce and roasted cabbage rolls. The high point of this restaurant is the view: Its booths are along a floor-to-ceiling glass wall on one of the upper decks (no cover charge here).

Both ships offer pizza throughout most of the day (on *Sky*, it's available in Ciao Chow, and on *Sun* it's in the buffet restaurant), and it's also available from room service 24 hours a day. Reservations are required for dinner in all of the specialty restaurants, though you can sometimes get a table as a walk-in.

POOL, FITNESS & SPA FACILITIES   The well-stocked ocean-view gyms on these ships are open 24 hours a day, and the adjacent aerobics room has floor-to-ceiling windows, too, and a great selection of classes, from spinning to kickboxing. Nearby, the spa and beauty salon offer ocean views as well, with lovely gilded Buddha statuary dotting the area on *Sky* and no design motif at all in *Sun's* spa. Unless you count the ocean, that is; on *Sun*, while you wait to be led to your treatment room, you can wait in a serene sitting area that has a wall of glass facing the hypnotic sea. As spas go, getting a great masseuse is hit or miss; we had a hit on *Sun* recently. Heidi got the best shiatsu massage of her life, so good she signed up for a second.

Out on deck is a pair of pools with a cluster of four hot tubs between them. One deck up are the combo basketball/volleyball court, a pair of golf driving nets, and shuffleboard. On *Sun*, the kids' wading pool and some cute mini-chaise longues are conveniently tucked along the starboard side of the Sports Deck (near a door to the interior of the ship); on *Sky*, it's in a more desolate spot far forward on the Sports Deck, where there's also a fifth hot tub.

Norwegian Majesty

The Verdict

Though *Majesty* really doesn't excel in any one area, it's still an understated, informal midsize ship, with good food and enough entertainment and activity options to keep everyone occupied.

Norwegian Majesty *(photo: NCL)*

Specifications

Size (in tons)	40,876	Officers	Norwegian
Number of Cabins	730	Crew	620 (Internat'l)
Number of Outside Cabins	481	Passenger/Crew Ratio	2.7 to 1
Cabins with Verandas	0	Year Launched	1992
Number of Passengers	1,460	Last Major Refurbishment	1999

Frommer's Ratings (Scale of 1–5)   𝄢𝄢𝄢

Cabin Comfort & Amenities	3	Dining Options	2
Ship Cleanliness & Maintenance	4	Gym & Spa Facilities	3
Public Comfort/Space	4	Children's Facilities	3
Decor	4	Enjoyment Factor	3

By normal standards, the 1992 vintage *Norwegian Majesty* would be thought of as a fairly new ship, but the explosive growth in the cruise business over the past decade has made her seem dated before her time. An extensive 1999 refurbishment and reconstruction spruced up the outside decking, carpets, and cabin decor, and added many new rooms by literally sawing the ship in half like a magician's assistant and putting it back together with a new preconstructed midsection grafted into its middle. While hardly dazzling, the humble *Majesty* is an appealing midsize in today's sea of monster megaships, two and three times as large.

Cabins & Rates

Cabins	Per Diems from	Sq. Ft.	Fridge	Hair Dryer	Sitting Area	TV
Inside	$76*	108	no	yes	no	yes
Outside	$83*	108–145	some	yes	no	yes
Suite	$168*	235	yes	yes	yes	yes

* Rates for Bermuda itineraries are higher on average.

CABINS   *Norwegian Majesty* was originally built to be a Baltic ferry, but was transformed into a cruise ship before she ever left the shipyard. She was intended for short 3- and 4-day jaunts from Miami to the Bahamas, Key West, and Cozumel—short itineraries that didn't really require large cabins. Today, though, *Majesty* does 7-night Bermuda cruises from Boston in summers, and in winters it sails 7-night Caribbean cruises out of Charleston, South Carolina; on these longer voyages some folks may find the accommodations to be a bit, shall we say, intimate. The ship has 22 price categories, although there are just two cabins in the Penthouse Suite category. The suites (18 of them) are more than adequate, with bathtubs and tile bathrooms, sitting areas, and enough room to move. Most Superior Oceanview Staterooms are barely adequate at 145 square feet, but in lower inside and outside categories (which make up a good portion of the total cabins) it gets even tighter at a ridiculous 108 square feet. All cabins have hair dryers, safes, and televisions (with ESPN, CNN, two movie channels, and an in-house station), and cabins far forward and far aft have minifridges (those in the ship's newer midsection do not). Many cabins can accommodate a third and fourth passenger.

Some cabins on the Norway and Viking decks have views that are obstructed by lifeboats. On the Promenade Deck, you are likely to open your curtain in the morning and see a jogger's head bob by. The best cabins (other than suites) are the category C rooms on the Majesty Deck, especially the ones in the bow that have windows offering sweeping vistas of the sea ahead.

There are no connecting cabins. There are seven cabins equipped for passengers with disabilities.

PUBLIC AREAS *Norwegian Majesty* is among the easiest ships to find your way around, and you are never far from something to do. Public areas aren't glitzy, decorated instead with a pleasant mixture of blues, lavenders, ivories, and lots of teak and brass.

The Royal Observatory Lounge, a bow-facing room with great views, is the scene of live entertainment nightly, including karaoke. This room is easy to miss, tucked away in the bow on a deck with no other public rooms except the Kids Corner all the way back in the stern.

The rest of the ship's nightlife is on Decks 5 and 6, except for the Frame 52 Disco on Deck 7 aft. The disco is small and not as technically advanced as some, but it serves its purpose and hops until about 3am nightly.

The Palace Theater could be described as intimate; it could also be described as claustrophobic. Either way, the sightlines are not good, with support columns all around the room. The low ceiling prevents dancers from getting too energetic.

The Polo Club, just outside the theater, is a good place to have a drink before the show or before (or after) dinner. It usually features a pianist/vocalist. On the opposite end of the long, narrow room is the Monte Carlo Casino, which was totally redone when the ship was stretched, and is now darker and moodier, a decent place for you and your money to have a parting of the ways, though nowhere near as impressive as the casinos aboard the line's newest ships, *Sky, Sun,* and *Dawn.*

A coffee bar sits next door to the Le Bistro alternative restaurant. Shops are forward from the lobby, and there's also a card room, a small video arcade, a library, and a meeting room.

The Rendezvous Lounge piano bar and Royal Fireworks dance lounge, for adult contemporary sounds, abut each other in the bow. Both rooms tend to be underused by passengers, who have no other reason to find themselves in that end of the ship.

DINING OPTIONS Both the Seven Seas and the Four Seasons dining rooms get quite crowded. Le Bistro, the line's signature alternative restaurant, is a small, intimate room off the corridor that links the two main dining rooms. It charges a $10 cover per person.

Although many ships put their buffet restaurant in the stern, this ship's indoor/outdoor Cafe Royale is in the bow, with panoramic windows that allow passengers to see what's ahead. The room is smallish and can be crowded at mealtimes, with long lines. There are outdoor tables on the Sun Deck by the pool, but if you want to stay inside and the Cafe Royale tables are taken, slip down the stairs into the Royal Observatory, another bow-facing room with great views; at dinnertime, it's also now used as another reservations-only alternative restaurant, this one serving Italian cuisine. In the stern, Piazza San Marco serves pizza, hot dogs, and burgers.

POOL, FITNESS & SPA FACILITIES Joggers and walkers can circle the ship on the wraparound Promenade Deck 7, which is also home to the Bodywave spa and fitness center. These facilities are not extensive by any means: The workout room is basic and has several weight stations and cardiovascular stations, and there's a separate aerobics room across the hall. On deck, there are two pools and a splash pool for kids, nicely sequestered on the aft end of the Norway Deck.

Norwegian Dream •
Norwegian Wind

The Verdict

These two ships are pleasant enough ways to sail if the price is low enough, but their lack of wide-open spaces and the way public rooms lead into one another makes them feel either cozy or cramped—take your pick.

Norwegian Wind *(photo: NCL)*

Specifications

Size (in tons)	50,760	Crew	614 (Internat'l)
Number of Cabins	874	Passenger/Crew Ratio	2.8 to 1
Number of Outside Cabins	716	Year Launched	
Cabins with Verandas	74	*Norwegian Dream*	1992
Number of Passengers	1,748	*Norwegian Wind*	1993
Officers	Norwegian	Last Major Refurbishment	2001

Frommer's Ratings (Scale of 1–5)   ★★★

Cabin Comfort & Amenities	3	Dining Options	3
Ship Cleanliness & Maintenance	4	Gym & Spa Facilities	3
Public Comfort/Space	3	Children's Facilities	3
Decor	4	Enjoyment Factor	3

Cruise ship years are a lot like dog years, which means these 12- and 13-year-old ships are *ooooold.* Originally built as much smaller vessels, they were "stretched" in 1998 at Germany's Lloyd Werft shipyard, with a new 130-foot midsection inserted into each, raising their tonnage from 41,000 to 50,760 and increasing their capacity from around 1,200 passengers to over 1,700. At the time, that was a nifty technological feat, but cutting-edge these ships are not. On the plus side, they provide more of an "at sea" feeling than aboard many of today's supersize megaships, with many open decks and a lot of glass letting on to ocean views. Renovations in 2001 added restaurants that allow them to offer the choices promised by NCL's Freestyle dining program.

Cabins & Rates

Cabins	Per Diems from	Sq. Ft.	Fridge	Hair Dryer	Sitting Area	TV
Inside	$66	130–150	no	no	no	yes
Outside	$82	160–176	no	no	some	yes
Suite	$251	270–385	yes	yes	yes	yes

CABINS   Over 80% of cabins aboard these ships are outside, most with sitting areas and picture windows. At 160 to 176 square feet, the outside deluxe staterooms are smaller than the outside cabins of competitors such as Holland America and Carnival. Inside cabins are even smaller, ranging in size from 130 to 150 square feet. The top-of-the-line Owner's Suites are 271 square feet, plus a 65-square-foot balcony, but even that is smaller than you'll find on many more modern ships (and that measurement includes the square footage of their balconies, to boot). Clustered on the Sun Deck, each of these suites has a balcony and a living room, convertible double-bed sofa, separate bedroom, minifridge, stereo with CD library, DVD player, and bathroom with tub and shower. The six 384-square-foot Superior Deluxe Penthouse Suites amidships on the Norway Deck have partially obstructed views because of the overhang from the restaurant above. Avoid them.

In general, cabin decor is pleasant and breezy, with wood accents and pastels evocative of the West Indies, and similar to what you'll find on Royal Caribbean's ships. Unfortunately, storage space is minimal: Two people can just barely manage, and when a third or fourth person shares a cabin, it can get truly cramped. Bathrooms are also small. The small sitting area in each cabin is a nice touch, though, and even inside cabins have a small couchette, through their presence means less maneuvering space around the bed. All cabins have TVs showing ESPN and CNN. Lifeboats block the views of the category F and G cabins at midships on the Norway Deck.

Thirteen cabins are wheelchair accessible, and 35 are equipped for passengers with hearing impairments, with a light panel on the wall that signals the doorbell, phone, and any emergency on the ship; there's also a vibrating alarm clock and a fire alarm light.

PUBLIC AREAS   Both forward and aft, the ships' upper decks cascade down in tiers, and walls of glass line the length of both vessels, letting in a lot of light. Unfortunately, chintzy materials were used in the passageways and stairways, lending the ships a somewhat tinny feel. Both ships also have layout idiosyncrasies owing to their late-'90s stretching, forcing you to walk through some public rooms and up and down stairs in order to get from one end of the ship to another.

Most lounges and other public areas are concentrated on the Star Deck, with a few one flight down on the International Deck. The dark, Vegas-style casinos are glitzy, but are on the small side. Lucky's Bar and the Dazzles disco on the Star Deck see the most late-night action, with many folks also spending lots of time at the Sports Bar and Grill, whose giant-screen TVs broadcast various games. On the International Deck, the library is small and feels like an afterthought. The Observatory Lounge on the Sports Deck, a sequestered ocean-view spot behind the gym and spa, functions as the disco (but if you're there during the day, keep in mind the basketball/volleyball court is just overhead).

DINING OPTIONS   There are three main dining rooms plus two alternative restaurants: Le Bistro and the Sports Bar & Grill. The most appealing venue is the Terraces restaurant, a cozy, three-level restaurant with a 1930s supper-club feel and floor-to-ceiling windows facing aft over the stern. The Four Seasons restaurant is also an attractive spot, with tiered seating and curved walls of windows. Couples who want a romantic dinner should try and reserve one of the ocean-view tables for two. The Sun Terrace restaurant is a trattoria serving traditional Italian fare, while Le Bistro is an intimate reservations-only Italian/continental restaurant serving just 78 guests. The entrances to three of these four restaurants are located on the International Deck, and congestion here is common at dinnertime.

Unlike most ships, neither *Wind* nor *Dream* has a traditional casual buffet restaurant. Instead, the Four Seasons restaurant offers a buffet at breakfast, while sit-down breakfasts and lunches are served in the Sun Terrace and Terraces dining rooms. You can also grab a continental-style breakfast at the somewhat cramped and inconveniently located indoor/outdoor Sports Bar and Grill, as well as hamburgers, hot dogs, and salad for lunch; dishes like chili con carne and stir-fry spicy chicken for dinner; and snacks throughout the day. The outdoor Pizzeria adjacent to the main swimming pool offers a limited breakfast buffet, plus pizza, pasta, and a salad bar at lunch.

POOL, FITNESS & SPA FACILITIES   With their attractive dark wooden decking and crisp blue-and-white striped canvas umbrellas, the pool decks have a sort of European beach-resort feel. Each ship has two pools, the larger of which, on the Sun Deck, has a swim-up bar and two hot tubs. The main problem here is that high walls added when the ships were stretched cut off sea views for those lounging poolside, and create a closed-in, somewhat claustrophobic feeling. For panoramic views of sea and sky, you have to walk up to the Sports Deck or to the small pool aft on the International Deck, where rows of deck chairs surround an almost purely decorative keyhole-shaped pool.

Gyms on both ships are cramped and inadequately equipped considering the vessels carry some 1,700 passengers. On a recent cruise, people sometimes had to wait to use the four treadmills, four stairsteppers, and four stationery bikes. The small spa offers the typical range of treatments as well as his and hers saunas. Both the gym and spa are located right underneath the Sky Deck's basketball/volleyball court, so expect some intense banging when a game is in progress.

The Sports Deck has Ping-Pong tables and a golf driving range. Joggers can work out on the wraparound Promenade deck.

Norwegian Sea

The Verdict

If you're looking for something intimate and down-to-earth, the midsize, middle-aged *Norwegian Sea* offers an ultracasual cruise and a great itinerary.

Norwegian Sea *(photo: NCL)*

Specifications

Size (in tons)	42,276	Officers	Norwegian
Number of Cabins	755	Crew	630 (Internat'l)
Number of Outside Cabins	512	Passenger/Crew Ratio	2.4 to 1
Cabins with Verandas	0	Year Launched	1988
Number of Passengers	1,504	Last Major Refurbishment	2003

Frommer's Ratings (Scale of 1–5)   ⭐⭐½

Cabin Comfort & Amenities	3	Dining Options	2
Ship Cleanliness & Maintenance	3	Gym & Spa Facilities	2
Public Comfort/Space	3	Children's Facilities	2
Decor	3	Enjoyment Factor	2

Norwegian Sea isn't a bad ship exactly, but it's definitely not one of our favorites. It's too young to be a classic, too old to be contemporary—it's a relic at 16 years old and just doesn't have a lot of character, though it's better since a face-lift in early 2003, which included adding new carpeting, upholstery, and some granite and wood flooring throughout, as well as the addition of a fifth restaurant.

But if you don't need the Ritz, the *Sea* offers laid-back 7-night cruises out of Houston to four interesting western Caribbean ports, including Cozumel and Cancún, Mexico; Roatan, Honduras; and Belize City, Belize.

Cabins & Rates

Cabins	Per Diems from	Sq. Ft.	Fridge	Hair Dryer	Sitting Area	TV
Inside	$75	113	no	yes	no	yes
Outside	$97	115	some	yes	some	yes
Suite	$361	222	yes	yes	yes	yes

CABINS   When NCL built the ship in 1988, it didn't waste space on the cabins. The rooms are small by any measure, with most insides measuring at about a skinny 113 square feet, and outsides (such as categories GG and F) just 115 square feet, although in most cases they do provide adequate drawer and hanging space for two people. Their decor is pleasant enough, and their sound-proofing is great—we heard the couple next door only once. Things get cozy (that's real-estate language for "cramped") in the standard cabins, especially the inside ones, the cheapest of the bunch. With two fold-down upper bunks and two regular berths, they allow you to cram four people into a space that's adequate for one. But if the choice is going as an anchovy or not going at all, then break out the capers. In general, bathrooms are tiny: We found a new way to turn off the shower without using our hands. It was strictly inadvertent, but it illustrates just how little room there is to maneuver.

There are four Owner's Suites, which recently got new carpets, curtains, and chairs, and three Deluxe Suites—these are the best and most spacious accommodations, if you can afford them. They have sitting areas, bathtubs, and minifridges. Note that many cabins on both the Star and Norway decks have their views either entirely or partially obstructed by lifeboats.

All cabins have hair dryers and TVs with ESPN and CNN. Some cabins have personal safes; if yours doesn't, the purser can put your valuables in a safe-deposit box.

There are no connecting cabins. Four cabins are wheelchair accessible.

PUBLIC AREAS   This is not a glitzy ship, and some parts of her look the most spartan of anything in the NCL fleet. *Sea* is a good choice for first-time cruisers looking to test the waters and not spend a lot of money; if you're an experienced and somewhat sophisticated cruiser, on the other hand, run, run, run as fast as you can from the frumpy, tinny *Sea!*

The two-deck-high lobby has a water-and-crystal sculpture, along with a cascading fountain splashing into a marble-lined pool. We found lots of quiet little nooks in the wide, bright elevator lobbies (not to be confused with the tiny, dark elevators). On some decks there are chairs and tables near the windows in these spaces. You can also sit outside Oscar's, the smoky little piano bar off the atrium; retreat to the not-very-well-stocked library; or play a game in the card room just off the roomy casino, with its card tables and nearly 200 slot machines (including one that exhorts anyone within 50 yards to "Round 'em up—it's a stampede!"). In addition to an Internet cafe, this ship, like the rest of the NCL fleet, offers wireless Wi-Fi Internet access via a network card, so you can go online with your laptop in various designated locations throughout the ship.

Gatsby's is another little bar, tucked away on Deck 10 aft. Recently redone in more romantic shades of reds and greens (used to be black and white), the intimate little wine-and-cigar bar now has wood paneling and new tables and chairs. The Cabaret Lounge is the main showroom, and you'd better get there early for a seat without an obstructed view. The newly refurbished Stardust Lounge is a cabaret-style room that offers some alternative entertainment. There's also a disco that heats up late at night; it may be small, but it works.

There's a playroom for children.

DINING OPTIONS The two main restaurants, the 280-passenger Four Seasons and the larger, 476-passenger Seven Seas, are unremarkable; and the casual dining restaurant, the depressing Big Apple Cafe, has the most convoluted, exasperating buffet line we've ever seen, and brings back memories of an elementary-school cafeteria. Still, the food is better than it looks, and the specialty station outside the main buffet is delightful, serving pick-your-own-ingredients omelets for breakfast and soup for lunch. Le Bistro, high up on the Sun Deck, is the more cozy and intimate reservations-only alternative restaurant, and you shouldn't miss dining there at least once, even with the $10 cover charge. A new alternative venue was added to the ship in early 2003. Called The Pasta Café, it offers traditional Italian fare and seats 40 guests—with no cover charge. All four of the ship's original restaurants were recently spruced up with carpeting, upholstery, and new color schemes.

There's also an ice-cream bar.

POOL, FITNESS & SPA FACILITIES There are many ships to choose from when it comes to fitness and spa programs; this is not one of them. The 24-hour fitness room is on the small side and has your basic equipment, and the "full-service" spa has two treatment rooms, one each for men and women. There are also his-and-hers saunas.

Outside, it's not always easy to find a deck chair near the pool. Go up one flight to the Sun Deck and it gets easier—the farther from the pool and band, the less crowded it is. And you are never too far from one of the outdoor bars. There are two nice pools on deck (one is quite large) and a couple of whirlpools. The Promenade Deck features a ¼-mile jogging and walking track, and adjacent to the spa and gym is a golf driving net. There's also Ping-Pong and shuffleboard.

Norway

The Verdict

She sure ain't what she used to be, but there's enough left to make the experience refreshingly nostalgic and rewarding (and who can complain about the low rates!).

Norway (photo: Heidi Sarna)

Specifications

Size (in tons)	76,049	Officers	Norwegian
Number of Cabins	1,016	Crew	900 (Internat'l)
Number of Outside Cabins	656	Passenger/Crew Ratio	2.3 to 1
Cabins with Verandas	62	Year Launched	1962
Number of Passengers	2,032	Last Major Refurbishment	2001

Frommer's Ratings (Scale of 1–5)   ☆☆☆

Cabin Comfort & Amenities	2	Dining Options	2.5
Ship Cleanliness & Maintenance	3	Gym & Spa Facilities	3
Public Comfort/Space	3	Children's Facilities	2
Decor	3	Enjoyment Factor	4

Built in 1962 as SS *France,* one of the most stylish vessels ever to cross the Atlantic, *Norway's* long sleek hull and razor-thin bow show her pedigree and draw admiring glances from anyone in sight, just like the much more formal *QE2* does, the other great old liner still plying the high seas. When rebuilt as *Norway* in 1981, she successfully introduced megaship cruising and became the unofficial flagship of the Caribbean. Today, however, both her French Line elegance and her bold innovations from 1981 have clearly faded, leaving a ship that's had many face-lifts as a misfit of sorts and a pale glimpse of what she used to be. Still, having enticed thousands to cruising, she retains a very loyal following of passengers and is a good choice for first-time cruisers or anyone craving a taste of what cruising used to be for bargain-basement rates.

Unlike the rest of the NCL fleet, *Norway* doesn't do Freestyle Cruising, but instead clings to the traditional dining setup with assigned tables and mealtimes. You also won't find soaring atria, rock-climbing walls, hundreds of balconies, or 10 different restaurants to choose from, but *Norway* does offer something that today's floating resorts could never offer—a tangible, if faint, sense of history. Her stunning profile crowned with twin-sculpted funnels and a couple of preserved public rooms help keep her history alive. The windowless, circular Windward dining room, the former first-class dining room of *France,* remains mostly intact from her early days, with its wooden paneling and the celestial dome overhead casting a warm, amber glow over diners (try whispering across the room to someone under the dome when it is empty). The other vestige of the past is the Club Internationale, once an elegant first-class lounge, with its ultrahigh ceiling, pillars, multilevel floor, and modest pale golden yellow and teal furniture—it's one of the prettiest rooms at sea. Despite some unfortunate large sculptures in the corners and a Caribbean-bright ceiling, ambience and elegance ooze from this room. Formal afternoon tea served here creates a real sense of class, and evening jazz music makes this a delightful space for pre- and post-dinner dancing.

Historical value aside, *Norway's* immense size allows for a variety of activities, from sports to shopping to swimming to listening to cruising's only ship's historian. Like her fleetmates, she offers many entertainment options, including pull-out-the-stops, Vegas-style, song-and-dance revues in the main show lounge. Her size will limit access to certain smaller ports, and monstrous lines upon disembarkation can severely limit time ashore; so if your interest is in visiting more remote islands, this isn't the vessel for you.

Oddly enough, *Norway* was retired for a few months in fall of 2001 (and transferred to Star Cruises' Asia arm); many admirers sadly watched her sail away from New York City (forever, we all thought), only to have NCL bring her back to the fleet a short time later to resume Caribbean cruises. Go figure.

Cabins & Rates

Cabins	Per Diems From	Sq. Ft.*	Fridge	Hair Dryer	Sitting Area	TV
Inside	$43	88	No	No	No	Yes
Outside	$68	143	Some	No	Some	Yes
Suite	$89	209	Yes	Some	Yes	Yes

Sizes vary dramatically within each category on this ship.

CABINS   As aboard all old ships, there's a vast array of jigsaw-puzzle-like cabin sizes and configurations, some of them quirkily charming because of floor plans that were designed before cruise lines came up with the idea of standardization. The good news is that since the *Norway* is an older ship built for transatlantic journeys, many cabins are bigger than average and offer better drawer and closet space. You can choose from 20 cabin categories, ranging from spacious Owner's Suites with balconies overlooking the bow to miniscule inside cells with upper and lower berths smaller than any cabins built within the past 15 years. Note the sheer, or curving, of the lower Cabin Deck corridors; it's a rare and special treat to see this classic design today.

Cabins are furnished traditionally and plainly, some with a few whispers of the ship's former glamour (a handful still have the original etched-glass mirrors). Bathroom size and amenities tend to be surprisingly large, especially in some of the middle- and high-grade original cabins. Plumbing fixtures tend to be a bit more solid than the cheaper plastic models installed aboard many newer ships, and many of the bathtubs are big enough for you and a floating model of *Norway.* All cabins have CNN, and a November 2001 refit replaced tired carpets and all cabin fabrics. However, when a fire sprinkler system was added to corridors in late 1998, many of the pipes and hardware were left exposed (it was too costly to rip out ceilings to hide them).

Usually the first cabins to sell out are the new 100 or so luxury cabins and suites on the two uppermost glass-enclosed decks placed on top of the ship in 1990. Half have verandas, but the partitions are flimsy and don't extend all the way up or down, actually making the cheaper suites with just an inviting wall of windows much more private. Views from the cabins on the Olympic and Fjord decks are obstructed completely or partially by lifeboats, and cabins on the International Deck can hear joggers overhead starting at 9:30am sharp.

There are about 100 cabins for singles, a rarity today, and 7 cabins that are wheelchair accessible.

PUBLIC ROOMS   The *Norway* has 12 passenger decks, with many of the lounges located on the International Deck. Two bustling interior promenades, which can get crowded during busy times, make it easy to move from end to end of the ship; and at sunset, it's nice to walk along the floor-to-ceiling windows looking out onto the Caribbean.

While stripping away its former appealing ocean-liner qualities, a series of refits over the years has also left the ship lacking cohesion. The modern and slick sports bar, adorned with large photos of sports stars, sticks out like a sore thumb; dancing at night is offered here in an atmosphere that seems more akin to a cafeteria than a lounge. The vast Monte Carlo Room is a gambler's heaven, with a couple hundred slot machines and seven blackjack tables, while the tacky, modern disco Dazzles is built over what was a pool. The balconied, two-story Saga Theatre has some bad seats; but its sound, lighting, and audiovisual facilities are state-of-the-art, and much of the room is original. If you want company, the ship's secondary cabaret lounge, the North Cape Lounge, accommodates 750 passengers. Sadly, there is simply no place to sit inside and look out at the ocean—especially unfortunate given the ship's several days at sea each week.

The nicest room left is undoubtedly the Club Internationale, an elegant lounge with very high ceilings and a lovely ambience that brings the ship's past into focus. In contrast to the Club I, the Windjammer Bar is an intimate, dark, and nautically themed bar where a pianist holds forth with nightly melodies and memories, and the occasional guest singer from the audience. A library cum Internet cafe, as well as a variety of shops, is located on the International Deck.

Though *Norway* is not the best ship for kids because of its complex layout and lack of cutting-edge facilities, there are a playroom and organized activities, so families should definitely not write this diverse ship off.

DINING OPTIONS   Two large, very busy dining rooms, the Windward and Leeward, keep passengers fed and happy during two separate sittings, though they do get loud and crowded during dinner (try the Windward at lunch, when you can enjoy the room with fewer other passengers). Food preparation and presentation are generally better on *Norway* than on the *Majesty* and *Sea,* that's for sure, and are on par with NCL's newest ships, *Sky, Sun,* and *Dawn,* though there are fewer venues. *Norway's* one alternative restaurant, Le Bistro, provides a nice change of pace from the main dining rooms. Squeezed onto the aft section of the International Deck, the Great Outdoor buffet restaurant is pretty unappealing, with its confusing, feed-the-herd setup, crowded plastic tables, and average food.

POOL, FITINESS & SPA FACILITES   *Norway* has two large outdoor pools and its lovely tiered decks offer ample room for sunning. There's also a cushioned, ¼-mile circuit for jogging, and games include table tennis, skeet shooting, shuffleboard, golf tees and nets, and basketball.

The fitness center, with floor-to-ceiling windows, and separate Roman Spa are excellent and located on two different decks with roomy facilities, an indoor pool, exercise equipment, two steam rooms, and two saunas, plus body-jet showers and a whirlpool.

It may be a bit of a hassle to reach the Roman Spa, seemingly located next to the boilers deep within the ship, because only two elevators go there from the top decks. (Consider getting some exercise on the way and taking the stairs rather than waiting what seems like a lifetime for the elevators.) Once there, however, you'll find one of the best spas at sea, with 16 treatment rooms and the first hydrotherapy baths on any cruise ship.

Sadly, as with many ships today, much of the outside decking is covered in either a beige, rubberized surface or a jarring blue AstroTurf.

7 Oceania Cruises (preview)

8120 NW 53 St., Miami, FL 33166. (C) **800/531-5658** or 305/514-2300; fax 305/514-2222. www.oceania cruises.com.

Renaissance Cruises launched in 1988; made news in the '90s by bucking the travel agent system and going directly to consumers; built a fleet of new, medium-size ships; and then abruptly went belly-up in late 2001, its ships put up for auction to the highest bidder. Princess scooped up a couple of them (which now operate as *Pacific Princess* and *Tahitian Princess*), and now a new cruise line, founded by former Renaissance CEO Frank Del Rio and former Crystal president Joseph Watters, is starting up with two others, the former *R1* and *R2* (which will become *Regatta* and *Insignia,* respectively). Named Oceania Cruises, the new line will sail its inaugural cruises with one ship *(Regatta)* in July 2003, just after this book goes to press, and will offer a series of Caribbean sailings in 2004. Its second ship, *Insignia,* was originally scheduled to enter the fleet in October 2003, but is now set to debut in April 2004.

While we're certainly not going to prognosticate on the quality of experience the line will offer once it's up and running, here's the skinny on what we've heard so far:

- Oceania will position itself to offer "premium" cruises, which translates into English as something like Holland America or Celebrity, though on a much smaller and more intimate scale since the ships carry only 684 passengers.
- The onboard vibe will be casual luxe (no tuxedos need apply).
- There will be a prominent onboard enrichment program, probably very similar to the one offered by Crystal since it's being developed by two former Crystal execs (expect informal lectures by writers, historians, and the like).
- The ships will feature port-intensive itineraries, visiting an island almost every day.
- The ships will remain in port till midnight on some nights to allow passengers a taste of the local restaurant scene and nightlife.

Time will tell how all of this plays out. Check this space next year for a full review.

Oceania Fleet Itineraries

Ship	Itineraries
Regatta	**12-night E. Carib:** Round-trip from Miami, Dec 2003–Mar 2004, visiting Tortola and Virgin Gorda (BVIs), Nevis, Dominica, Antigua, St. Barts, and the Dominican Republic, with 4 nights at sea. **14-night E. & W. Carib/Canal:** Between Miami and Puerto Caldera, Costa Rica, Jan 2 and Feb 6, 2004, visiting Tortola (BVIs), Nevis, St. Barts, Antigua, St. Lucia, Aruba, and the San Blas Archipelago (Panama), with 6 days at sea including a full Canal crossing. **14-night W. Carib/Canal:** Round-trip from Miami, Nov 25 only, visiting Port Antonio (Jamaica), the San Blas Archipelago (Panama), Puerto Limon (Costa Rica), Roatan (Honduras), Santo Tomas (Guatemala), Belize City (Belize), and Cozumel/Playa Del Carmen, with 6 days at sea including a partial Canal crossing. **Non-Caribbean Itineraries:** Europe, Mexican Riviera.

Regatta • Insignia (preview)

The Verdict

With their smallish size, understated decor, and serene atmosphere, these ships are more like quiet boutique hotels than cruise ships, and provide an ultra-comfortable, laid-back way to see the Caribbean in style.

Regatta *(photo: Oceania)*

Specifications

Size (in tons)	30,200	Officers	European
Number of Cabins	349	Crew	373 (E. European/ Internat'l.)
Number of Outside Cabins	314	Passenger/Crew Ratio	2 to 1
Cabins with Verandas	233	Year Launched	1998
Number of Passengers	684	Last Major Refurbishment	2002/2003

As these ships had not yet begun service with Oceania at press time, **Frommer's Ratings** *have not yet been established. The review that follows is based on onboard experiences during the vessels' service with Renaissance Cruises, updated to reflect changes Oceania made after taking possession. These changes included installation of new teak decking, a new pool, and new deck furniture and interior furnishings.*

Like all of the former Renaissance vessels (including the former *R3* and *R4*, which now sail as Princess's *Pacific Princess* and *Tahitian Princess,* respectively), the former *R1* and *R2* are comfortable and spacious vessels decorated mostly in warm, dark woods and rich fabrics. They're traditional and sedate, with an emphasis on intimate spaces rather than the kind of grand, splashy ones you'll find on most megaships. Think country club and you'll have it about right. The atmosphere also promises to be relaxed and clubby, with no formal nights that demand tuxedos and gowns.

Cabins & Rates

Cabins	Per Diems From	Sq. Ft.	Fridge	Hair Dryer	Sitting Area	TV
Inside	$114	158	no	yes	yes	yes
Outside	$126	165–216*	no	yes	yes	yes
Suite	$229	322–962*	yes	yes	yes	yes

* *Including veranda.*

CABINS Judging by their layout with Renaissance and by photos we've seen of the new Oceania decor, staterooms aboard *Regatta* and *Insignia* are straightforward, no-nonsense spaces with a hint of modern European city hotel: plain off-white walls, dark wood trim and furniture, and rich carpeting. As part of the Oceania refit, bedding is being replaced with 300-thread-count Egyptian cotton sheets and thick duvets, and balconies are getting new teak decking for a more classic nautical look. All cabins have televisions, safes, vanity with mirror, hair dryers, phones, TVs, full-length mirror, and French-milled toiletries.

Suites include minibars, bathtubs, and a small area with cocktail table for intimate in-room dining. Ten Owner's Suites measure 786 to 982 square feet and are located at the ship's bow and stern, featuring wraparound balconies, queen-size beds, whirlpool bathtubs, minibars, living rooms, and guest bathrooms. Owner's, Vista, and Penthouse suites feature butler service.

Thirty-two connecting cabins are available. There are three wheelchair-accessible cabins.

PUBLIC AREAS   Overall, these are elegant yet homey ships, with dark wood paneling, fluted columns, ornate iron railings, gilt-framed classical paintings, Oriental carpets, frilly moldings, marble and brass accents, and deep-hued upholstery contributing to a kind of "English inn at sea" look. In the bow, the spacious Horizons lounge has floor-to-ceiling windows on three sides and is used for dancing in the evenings and for various activities during the day. The 345-seat show lounge offers cabaret and variety acts, musical recitals, magic shows, and comedy; and the casino offers blackjack, poker tables, roulette, and slots. Other notable spaces include a martini bar, a 24-hour Internet center, and a library decorated in a traditional English style with warm red upholstery, Oriental carpets, mahogany paneling, and a faux marble fireplace.

DINING OPTIONS   Oceania's cuisine will be overseen by master chef Jacques Pépin, once personal chef to Charles de Gaulle and more recently one of America's best-known chefs and food writers. The Grand Dining Room, the main restaurant aboard each ship, will feature his French-inspired continental cuisine, with a string quartet providing music at dinner. The restaurant operates on an open-seating basis, rather than requiring you to sit with the same dinner companions every night. As an alternative, passengers can make a reservation at the Toscana Italian restaurant or the Polo Grill, serving chops, seafood, and cuts of slow-aged beef. The Tides Cafe serves casual buffet breakfast and lunch, and in the evening is transformed into Tapas at Tides, serving a selection of tapas and other Spanish and international dishes, along with cocktails and live entertainment. If none of those tickles your fancy, room service delivers 24 hours a day.

POOL, FITNESS & SPA FACILITIES   The attractive pool deck, dotted with navy-blue canvas umbrellas, offers a pair of hot tubs and plenty of deck chairs for sunbathing, and will be fitted with new teak decking before the ships' first cruises. A small jogging track is on Deck 10, and the Sun Deck has shuffleboard and a golf driving cage, and more sunbathing space. The fully equipped spa offers a variety of treatments, including aromatherapy massages, hot-stone treatments, and a fog shower that's half steam room, half gentle waterfall. Just forward of the spa on Deck 9 is an outdoor thalassotherapy whirlpool overlooking the bow. A decent ocean-view gym and beauty salon are nearby.

8 Princess Cruises

24305 Town Center Dr., Santa Clarita, CA 91355. ✆ 800/PRINCESS or 661/753-0000. Fax 661/259-3108. www.princess.com.

THE LINE IN A NUTSHELL   With a Caribbean fleet composed entirely of stylish new megaships (including some of the biggest in the world), Princess offers a quality mainstream cruise experience with a nice balance of tradition and innovation, relaxation and excitement, casualness and glamour.

THE EXPERIENCE   If you were to put Carnival, Royal Caribbean, Celebrity, and Holland America in a big bowl and mix them together, then add a pinch each of British and California style, you'd come up with Princess. Its Caribbean ships are a lot less glitzy and frenzied than Carnival's, more stylish than NCL's (though not as cutting-edge and witty as Celebrity's), and more youthful and entertaining than Holland America's. Dining, entertainment, and activities are geared for a wide cross section of cruisers: The more tradition-minded can spend some time in the library, join a bridge tournament, enjoy a traditional dinner in a grand dining room, and then take in a show; those seeking something different can learn the basics of Photoshop, work toward their PADI scuba certification, then dine in an intimate Italian or New Orleans–style restaurant and take in a set of small-group jazz after. The vessels' large (and sometimes huge) size means they can offer a plethora of bars, lounges, and theaters, many of which are built on a surprisingly intimate scale, with the kind of quiet nooks and calm spaces you more typically find on much smaller vessels.

Pros

- **Lots of dining choices and flexibility:** Each ship offers two or three main dining rooms plus an intimate alternative restaurant or two and a 24-hour buffet. The line's "Personal Choice" program allows you to dine at a fixed time and place or wing it as you go along.
- **Excellent lounge entertainment:** Princess books top-quality entertainers for its piano lounges and smaller showrooms.

Cons

- **Pottery Barn decor:** More of a qualifier than a con: The line's ships are very pleasant, yes, but the sea of beiges and blues is so safe that it can be a bit of a yawn. Artwork in public areas and cabins tends toward bland.
- **Small gyms:** For such large vessels, the gyms are surprisingly small and can even feel cramped.
- **Pricey ice cream:** No free soft-serve here. Unlike other lines, Princess's parlors sell only Häagen-Dazs.

Compared with the other Mainstream lines, here's how Princess rates:

	Poor	Fair	Good	Excellent	Outstanding
Enjoyment Factor				✓	
Dining			✓		
Activities				✓	
Children's Program			✓		
Entertainment				✓	
Service				✓	
Worth the Money				✓	

PRINCESS: SMART CASUAL

With the exception of Carnival, few other cruise lines have managed to start so small and grow so startlingly. In 1962, company founder Stanley McDonald chartered the *Yarmouth* as a floating hotel for the Seattle World's Fair, and then in 1965, chartered the long-gone *Princess Patricia* for cruises between Los Angeles, Alaska, and Mexico's Pacific coast, naming his company after the ship. In 1974, Princess Cruises was snapped up by British shipping giant P&O, and in the 1970s, it gained enormously by associating itself with the TV series *The Love Boat,* which created a bull market in new cruisers anxious to experience high-seas romance, whether they got to meet Charo or not. The twin 640-passenger ships used in the series finally left the Princess fleet in 1999 and 2002 after more than 25 years of service, and largely took any remaining traces of the *Love Boat* (as gimmick, as theme, as marketing tool . . .) with them. Today, Princess is a line of huge modern megaships, the largest of which are exceeded in passenger ship history only by Royal Caribbean's Voyager-class ships and—upon her expected launch in January 2004—by Cunard's *Queen Mary 2.*

Princess is also, apparently, a hot commodity. In November 2001, P&O Princess and Royal Caribbean announced a merger agreement that would have created the world's largest cruise fleet, but the ink was hardly dry on the rhetoric when Carnival Corporation, the 500-pound gorilla of the cruise world, stepped in with its own bid to take over the line—a bid that was finally approved at a meeting of P&O shareholders in April 2003. Already the dominant force in the industry (with ownership of the Carnival brand as well as Holland America, Cunard, Seabourn, Costa, and Windstar), Carnival Corp. will, after the merger, operate a combined fleet of 66 ships, with another 17 scheduled for delivery over the next few years. Can you say monopoly? The good news is, Carnival has historically avoided monkeying with the identities of its component brands, so we don't expect to see any significant changes to Princess's proven formula.

PASSENGER PROFILE

As is the case with almost all cruise lines, passengers in their 50s, 60s, and older make up the majority of passengers on Princess cruises, though the number of cabins filled by younger 30- and 40-somethings and their families is growing steadily, particularly on weeklong cruises and most particularly during summer school holidays. Overall, Princess passengers are less rowdy and boisterous than those aboard Carnival and not as staid as those aboard Holland America. All the ships on Caribbean itineraries have extensive kids' facilities and activities, making them suitable for families; while their balance of formal and informal makes them a good bet for a romantic vacation too, with opportunities for doing your own thing mixed in among more traditional cruise experiences. For serious romance—the movie kind, with the uniformed captain performing the ceremony—look to the *Golden, Grand,* and *Coral Princess,* all of which have wedding chapels on board. *Grand* was the first cruise ship to have one, and now Royal Caribbean's *Adventurer, Explorer,* and *Voyager,* Carnival's *Spirit,* and NCL's *Sun* and *Dawn* have them as well, though Princess's ships (including the West Coast–based *Star Princess*) remain the only ones where the captain conducts ceremonies.

DINING

All of Princess's Caribbean-based ships offer a wide variety of dining options, but, in general, their cuisine doesn't quite live up to the number and attractiveness of their restaurants. Some dishes exceed expectations and others fall flat, but most sit squarely in the "average to good" range, approximately on par with what's served aboard Royal Caribbean and Norwegian.

One place where the line shines is in the flexibility of its **Personal Choice Dining** program, which allows passengers to choose between dining at a set time, with set dining companions, in one of the ship's two or three main restaurants, or just wandering into an identical or similar restaurant anytime during a 4½-hour window to be seated by the maitre d'. (*Note:* If you're not sure which option you'll prefer once you're on board, it's easier to switch from traditional to anytime dining rather than the other way around.)

Whether you choose traditional or flexible dining, your menu will be the same, with several appetizers, soup and salad, and a choice of four or five dinner entrees that may include prime rib, lobster, king crab legs, turkey with all the trimmings, mahimahi filet with dill butter sauce, rack of lamb with Dijon sauce, Cornish hen, sautéed frogs' legs, or duck a l'orange. There are always **healthy choices** and **vegetarian options,** too, plus staples such as broiled Atlantic salmon, grilled chicken, and grilled sirloin steak.

Whether you choose the traditional or flexible plan, you also have the option of dining at one of your ship's **alternative restaurants** at an additional charge: Italian and Southwestern restaurants on Grand-class ships ($15 and $8, respectively), a steakhouse ($8) and sit-down pizzeria on Sun-class ships, and Italian and New Orleans–style restaurants on *Coral* and *Island Princess* ($15 and $10, respectively). See the individual ship reviews later in this section for more details. Reservations are recommended for all the alternative restaurants because seating is limited.

Because passengers are unlikely to have the same waitstaff every night throughout their cruise, all waiter and assistant-server **gratuities are automatically added** to passengers' onboard accounts as part of a $10 per-person, per-day total (which also covers your cabin steward). Though this may seem to remove the incentive for staff to go the extra mile, we didn't experience any drop in service quality on our most recent cruise. All tip amounts can be adjusted up or down by visiting the purser's desk at any time during your cruise. Passengers choosing the flexible option but wishing to be served by the same waiter nightly in the main restaurant can generally be seated in his or her section by making a reservation.

Unlike the no-dress-code dress code that's part of NCL's "Freestyle" dining plan, Princess maintains the tradition of holding two **formal nights** per week, with the other nights designated smart casual, which is defined as "an open-neck shirt and slacks for gentlemen and a dress, skirt and blouse, or trouser suit outfit for ladies." However, men should take our advice and pack at least a jacket. Otherwise, you may be down in the gift shop buying one, after you realize *everyone on the ship except you* decided to dress for dinner. Trust us on this: We speak from experience.

Fleetwide, passengers can choose **casual dining** at breakfast, lunch, and dinner in the 24-hour, buffet-style Horizon Court restaurant. At breakfast, you'll find the usual: fresh fruit, cold cuts, cereal, steam-table scrambled eggs, cooked-to-order fried eggs, meats, and fish. At lunch, you'll find several salads, fruits, hot and cold dishes, roasts, vegetarian choices, and sushi. Evenings (7:30pm–4am), the space becomes a very casual (no reservations required) sit-down restaurant serving the same menu of pastas, seafood, poultry, and red meats every night, along with a chef's special of the day. The food here is as good as you'll find in the main dining rooms, and the atmosphere is strictly casual. The Horizon Court's **kids' menu** offers goodies such as burgers, hot dogs, fish sticks, chicken fingers, and, of course, pb&j sandwiches. Kids can also enjoy a buffet salad and desserts such as chocolate brownies, jumbo cookies, and fruit salad.

To round out the weight-gain options, each ship also has a **poolside grill** or two serving burgers, hot dogs, and pizza; a **patisserie** serving coffee and pastries; an **ice-cream bar** serving Häagen-Dazs for a charge; and **24-hour room service.**

ACTIVITIES

Princess offers onboard activities designed to appeal to a wide range of ages and tastes, with traditional sedate shipboard activities like bingo, cards, and trivia games; more active pursuits such as Ping-Pong and shuffleboard tournaments, aerobics classes, and water volleyball; activities designed to part you from your cash, such as art auctions and beauty and spa demonstrations; plus recent-release big-screen movies, dance lessons, and more. In January 2003, the line introduced its **ScholarShip@Sea program** aboard the new *Coral Princess,* offering classes in cooking, computer skills (such as basic Photoshop and Excel), finance, photography, and, in an industry first, paint-your-own ceramics and pottery-making, with an onboard kiln to produce finished pieces by the end of your cruise. Other classes being contemplated include underwater archaeology, nutrition, geography, natural history, the performing arts, and marine biology, each taught by a guest expert. Large-group seminars are free, while small-group and individual classes carry a charge of around $20 per person. Charges for paint-your-own ceramics are calculated based on the piece you create ($20 for a coffee mug, up to $70 for a ceramic box with lid); pottery-throwing classes cost $40. If all goes according to plan, the line should have the program in operation on its other ships by year-end 2003.

For active types, the Grand-class ships and the new *Coral* and *Island Princess* offer **basketball/volleyball courts,** 9-hole **miniature-golf courses,** and virtual-reality **golf simulators** (the latter also available on the Sun-class ships). The Grand-class ships also appeal to video junkies with the biggest and best **virtual-reality game rooms** at sea, while those who prefer a good read in a comfortable library will be happy on any of the line's ships, which preserve the old steamship tradition of large, well-stocked facilities for long days at sea. Each ship also has a **24-hour Internet center** allowing passengers to send and receive e-mail and surf the Web for 50¢/minute. If you'd prefer to work in your cabin, *Grand, Golden, Sun,* and *Dawn Princess* offer wireless laptops for rent at the purser's desk.

While the general pitch of activities isn't as frenzied on Princess as it is aboard Carnival or Royal Caribbean, the ships aren't anywhere near sedate either. There are always a couple of **silly pool games** in the afternoon (such as a belly-flop contest or a stuff-the-most-Ping-Pong-balls-into-your-bathing-suit contest), the perennial Newlywed/Not-so-Newlywed game, an Island Night Deck Party with the requisite conga line, and late-night discos in case you didn't get in your workout during the day.

Princess's **"New Waves"** program is one of its most ambitious offerings, allowing equally ambitious passengers the chance to earn **PADI scuba-diving certification** while on board. You can complete all academics, pool diving, and open-water diving during your cruise (about a 21-hr. commitment, with classes scheduled so that you still have time to explore the ports; $359); complete all academic requirements before you sail, via video or CD-ROM tutorials ($359); or complete the academics and the pool dives through your local dive center, and concentrate only on the open-water dives during your vacation ($189 if you're being referred by a PADI instructor, $199 if by a non-PADI instructor). Advanced lessons are available for divers who are already certified. The program is offered aboard all 7-night Caribbean sailings, and the cost includes all equipment rentals. You can sign up after you board, but it's best to sign up in advance by calling the PADI New Waves Dive Line (© **888/919-9819**) or by going to **www.newwaves.com**. If you opt to pursue this, approach it with the seriousness it deserves, and plan to spend some time studying.

CHILDREN'S PROGRAM

Princess's **"Princess Kids"** program offers activities year-round for three age groups: Princess Pelicans (ages 3–7), Princess Pirateers (ages 8–12) and teens (ages 13–17), supervised by a staff of up to 23 counselors, depending upon the number of children aboard. Each ship in the Caribbean has a spacious indoor/outdoor **children's playroom** with a splash pool, a ball jump, an arts-and-crafts corner, game tables, and computers or games consoles, plus a **teen center** with computers, video games, a dance floor, and a sound system. The two-story affairs on *Golden* and *Grand* have a larger fenced-in outside deck dedicated to kids only, including a teen section with a hot tub and private sunbathing area; the new *Coral* and *Island Princess* have a small swimming pool for adults adjacent to the outdoor kids deck, allowing parents to relax while their kids play.

Traditional activities include arts and crafts, scavenger hunts, game tournaments, movies and videos, coloring contests, pizza and ice-cream parties, karaoke, dancing, swimming and snorkeling lessons, tours of the galley or behind the scenes at the theater, hula parties complete with grass skirts, and teenage versions of *The Dating Game*. **Learning activities** on your cruise may include environmental education programs developed by the National Wildlife Federation, the California Coastal Commission, the Center for Marine Conservation, and the Miami Seaquarium, which teach about oceans and marine life through printed materials, specially created films, and (for the Seaquarium program) activities led by youth counselors who have completed special training at the Miami park. The kids' equivalent of an **onboard guest lecturers** program is also offered occasionally, allowing children to go stargazing with an astronomer, work on their drawing with an animator, and so on.

In the Caribbean, children must be at least 6 months of age to sail. When kids are registered in the youth program, their parents are given pagers so that they can be contacted if their children need them. Parents may also rent **walkie-talkies** through the purser's desk if they want two-way communication with their kids. Two **special dinner evenings** allow parents a date night while younger kids dine together in a separate restaurant, and teens have their own group night in one of the main dining rooms, complete with photographs and an after-dinner show. Younger kids can then be taken straight to **group babysitting** in the children's center (available nightly 10pm–1am for kids 3–12; $5 per hour, per child). Princess does not offer private in-cabin babysitting.

On days in port, Princess offers children's center activities from 8am to 5pm, allowing parents to explore the islands while their kids do their own thing. On Princess's private Bahamas beach, Princess Cays, kids can be checked in at a play area supervised by the shipboard youth staff.

ENTERTAINMENT

Stem to stern, Princess has some of the best entertainment at sea, with variety acts on the ships' main stages ranging from Vegas-style musical revues and cabaret singers to ventriloquists, acrobats and aerialists, stand-up comics, and New Agey violinists. The Grand-class ships and *Coral Princess* offer three shows

Princess Cays: Private Island Paradise

Most of Princess's eastern and western Caribbean itineraries offer a stop at Princess Cays, the line's "private island" (a misnomer; since it's really a 40-acre strip off the southwestern coast of Eleuthera in the Bahamas, pretty much cut off from the rest of the island). A ½-mile of shoreline allows passengers to swim, snorkel, and make use of Princess's fleet of Hobie Cats, Sunfish, banana boats, kayaks, and paddle-wheelers; there's live music, a dance floor, and a beach barbecue; and anyone who wants to get away from it all (or sleep off too many rum punches) can head for the several dozen great tree-shaded hammocks at the far end of the beach. You can charge items to your onboard account at the Princess shop, which sells T-shirts and other clothing plus souvenirs of the mug-and-key-chain variety, but bring cash with you too, since local vendors set up stands around the island to sell conch shells and crafts (such as shell anklets and straw bags) and to offer hair braiding.

If you want to rent watersports equipment, be sure to book it aboard ship before arriving at the island (or even online, before your cruise), to ensure that you get what you want.

nightly in their main theater and two smaller venues, plus quieter music in a few lounges. The Sun-class ships offer entertainment in two showrooms. Fleetwide, the discos are always hopping, a deck band plays at various times during the day, and at several venues (including the Wheelhouse Lounge and the atrium), you'll find a pianist, guitarist, or string quartet providing live background music.

One of Princess's entertainment strengths is the quality of performers in its **piano lounges,** with longtime favorites such as Barty Brown packing the rooms night after night.

For those who would rather participate, there are regular **karaoke** nights and a **passenger talent show.** The ships' **casinos** are among the most comfortable at sea, very large and well laid out.

SERVICE

Overall, service is efficient and lines (especially on the Grand-class ships) are short, even in the busy Horizon Court buffet restaurants. As is true generally of staff aboard all the mainstream lines, you can expect them to be friendly and amenable, but not world-class—for the most part, these are simply hard-working staff doing their jobs, not career waiters and hotel staffers. Cabin steward service is the most consistent, with dining service only slightly behind. Bar service can occasionally be on the dodgy side, with language barriers sometimes frustrating attempts to get your drink just right. On the plus side, if you become a regular at a certain spot, staff are apt to remember what you want after a couple of days. Through the line's Captain's Circle loyalty program, cruisers who have sailed with Princess before are issued specially colored onboard keycards and cabin-door nameplates (gold after taking one to five cruises, platinum after five) so that staffers will know to be extra helpful. Platinum Captain's Circle members also get expedited embarkation and free Internet access throughout their cruise.

Princess Fleet Itineraries

Ship	Itineraries
Caribbean Princess	**7-night W. Carib:** Round-trip from Fort Lauderdale, year-round beginning Apr 2004, visiting Grand Cayman, Ocho Rios or Montego Bay (Jamaica), Cozumel, and Princess Cays*, with 2 days at sea. Alternates weekly with **7-night E. Carib:** Round-trip from Fort Lauderdale, year-round beginning Apr 2004, visiting St. Thomas, Sint Maarten, and Princess Cays*, with 3 days at sea. **Non-Caribbean Itineraries:** None.
Coral Princess	**10-night Panama Canal:** Round-trip from Fort Lauderdale, Sept 2003–Apr 2004, visiting Cartagena (Colombia), Limon (Costa Rica), Grand Cayman, and Cozumel, with 4 days at sea including a partial crossing of the canal. **Non-Caribbean Itineraries:** Alaska.
Dawn Princess	**7-night E. Carib:** Round-trip from San Juan, Oct 2003–Apr 2004, visiting Barbados, St. Lucia, Sint Maarten, St. Thomas, and Tortola (BVIs), with 1 day at sea. **7-night S. Carib:** Round-trip from San Juan, Oct–Apr, visiting St. Thomas, St. Kitts, Grenada, Caracas (Venezuela), and Aruba, with 1 day at sea. **Non-Caribbean Itineraries:** Panama Canal repositioning cruises, Alaska, Hawaii, Mexican Riviera.
Golden Princess	**7-night E. Carib:** Round-trip from Fort Lauderdale, Oct 2003–May 2004, visiting Sint Maarten, St. Thomas, and Princess Cays*, with 3 days at sea. **7-night S. Carib 1:** Round-trip from San Juan, beginning May 2004, visiting Barbados, St. Lucia, Antigua, Sint Maarten, and St. Thomas, with 1 day at sea. Alternates weekly with **7-night S. Carib 2:** Round-trip from San Juan, beginning May 2004, visiting St. Thomas, St. Kitts, Grenada, Caracas (Venezuela), and Aruba, with 1 day at sea. **Non-Caribbean Itineraries:** Europe, New England/Canada.
Grand Princess	**7-night W. Carib:** Round-trip from Fort Lauderdale, Oct 2003–May 2004, visiting Cozumel and Costa Maya (Mexico), Grand Cayman, and Princess Cays*, with 2 days at sea. **Non-Caribbean Itineraries:** Europe.
Island Princess	**10-night Panama Canal:** Round-trip from Fort Lauderdale, Oct 2003–Apr 2004, visiting Cartagena (Colombia), Limon (Costa Rica), Grand Cayman, and Cozumel, with 4 days at sea including a partial crossing of the canal. **Non-Caribbean Itineraries:** Alaska.
Sun Princess	**10-night E. Carib:** Round-trip from Fort Lauderdale, Oct 2003–Apr 2004, visiting Princess Cays*, St. Thomas, Sint Maarten, St. Vincent, Barbados, and Antigua, with 3 days at sea. Alternates with **10-night S. Carib:** Round-trip from Fort Lauderdale, Oct 2003–Apr 2004, visiting Curaçao, Isla Margarita (Venezuela), Barbados, Dominica, St. Thomas, and Princess Cays*, with 3 days at sea. **Non-Caribbean Itineraries:** Panama Canal repositioning cruises, Alaska, Hawaii, Mexican Riviera.

Princess's private beach, on the Bahamian island of Eleuthera.

Gratuities for all service personnel are automatically added to passengers' shipboard accounts at the rate of $10 per person per day. Adjustments (up or down) can be made by visiting or calling the purser's desk at any time; typically, parents adjust their children's tips down to around $5. Passengers who wish to tip more traditionally—dispensing cash in person—can also make arrangements for this through the desk.

All of the Princess vessels in the Caribbean offer **laundry** and **dry-cleaning** services, and also have **self-service laundromats.**

Coral Princess • Island Princess (preview)

The Verdict

Beautiful, spacious, and at the same time surprisingly intimate, *Coral* and *Island* offer great onboard learning experiences, a nice range of entertainment options and venues, and interesting itineraries.

Coral Princess *(photo: Matt Hannafin)*

Specifications

Size (in tons)	91,627	Crew	981 (Internat'l)
Number of Cabins	987	Passenger/Crew Ratio	2 to 1
Number of Outside Cabins	879	Year Launched	
Cabins with Verandas	727	*Coral Princess*	2003
Number of Passengers	1,970	*Island Princess*	2003
Officers	British/Italian	Last Major Refurbishment	N/A

Frommer's Ratings (Scale of 1–5)   ★★★★ ½

Cabin Comfort & Amenities	5	Dining Options	4
Ship Cleanliness & Maintenance	5	Gym & Spa Facilities	4
Public Comfort/Space	5	Children's Facilities	4
Decor	4	Enjoyment Factor	4.5

For the past half-dozen years, we cruise writers have had to live with the fact that balcony-heavy 2,000-passenger megaships pretty much all look alike from the outside: giant slabs of steel rising straight up out of the water, pocked with row after row of cabin verandas and lacking the graceful lines of yesteryear's ocean liners. There have been exceptions, of course—Royal Caribbean's Radiance-class ships come to mind, as do Disney's *Magic* and *Wonder*. And now we can add to that short list the new *Coral Princess* and *Island Princess*, with their clean, flowing lines, tiered and less-obtrusive balconies, and futuristic-looking jet-engine-style gas-turbine funnels, which give you the impression the ships are going to fly right out of the water and into orbit.

Further refining Princess's vision of megasize ships with an intimate feel, *Coral* and *Island* are a fifth larger than the line's Sun-class ships, yet carry only 20 more passengers apiece based on double occupancy—which translates to more room for you. They're both classic and modern in atmosphere, with Internet centers and Times Square–style news tickers right around the corner from woody, almost Edwardian lounges. The vessels' onboard life also mixes typical cruise activities with innovation. Old fashioned? Then sequester yourself in one of the library's cushy chairs with a book or some headphone music, or join the crowds in the card room for a game of bridge. Looking for something different? Then attend one of the lectures, demonstrations, or hands-on classes offered as part of the ships' ScholarShip@Sea program, which aims to slip a little learning into the average cruise experience via seminars on photography, finance, computers, cooking, and numerous other topics (see program description under "Activities," above). A pottery studio on Deck 12 offers passengers the chance to hand-paint a range of ceramic items or hand-throw your own free-form designs, and while this can be a little pricey, we think it's an absolutely fabulous idea—so much so that the pottery staff on *Coral* might even remember us, we were there so often.

Built to *juuuuussst* be able to squeeze through the Panama Canal (with approximately 2 ft. of space on each side), these ships are extremely spacious and well laid out, and never feel crowded even when full. Our favorite spaces: the clubby Wheelhouse Bar for a before-dinner drink; the bar at the New Orleans–themed Bayou Restaurant, for jazz till around midnight; the Lotus Pool, a peaceful solarium done up in Balinese style, where your book will have to be damn good to keep you from dozing off; the Princess Theater in mid- or late afternoon on sea days, for recent-release big-screen movies; the remarkable Universe Lounge, a truly innovative performance space; and, of course, the private verandas that are part of 83% of the outside cabins on each ship. Be forewarned, though, that most of the verandas are set up in descending tiers—a positive in terms of soaking up the sun, a negative if your idea of fun is sitting out there in your birthday suit. Keep that robe closed!

Island Princess is scheduled to debut just after this book goes to press, so all descriptions in this review refer to *Coral Princess.*

Cabins & Rates

Cabins	Per Diems from	Sq. Ft.	Fridge	Hair Dryer	Sitting Area	TV
Inside	$129	160	yes	yes	no	yes
Outside	$159	168–257*	yes	yes	no	yes
Suite	$354	323–591*	yes	yes	yes	yes

* *Includes veranda.*

CABINS As is true with the entire Princess fleet, an initial look at the list of 33 cabin categories available on these ships gives the impression that you have a wide range of choices, when, in fact, you actually have fewer than 10 configurations to choose from. The other 20-plus categories reflect differences in location—such as midships versus aft, upper deck versus lower—and thus price, though sometimes there can be as little as a $30 difference between them. Seems like there should be easier ways of arranging things, doesn't it? In fact, there must be, as most ships have half or a third as many categories. Decor also sticks to Princess's fleetwide standard, with upholstery and walls done in easy-on-the-eyes earth tones and off-whites, all trimmed in butterscotch wood. All have safes, hair dryers, minifridges, and TVs broadcasting CNN, CNBC, ESPN, TNT, movies, and shows from the Discovery Channel, Nickelodeon, the BBC, National Geographic, A&E, and E! Entertainment television—among the widest selections at sea today. Inside and standard outside cabins are serviceable, but don't expect much room to stretch out—at 160 and 168 square feet respectively, they're on the low end of average in the mainstream category, much larger than on Princess's Sun-class ships and some ships in the Costa and NCL fleets, but nowhere near the 185 to 195 square feet you get with the newer Carnival and Holland America ships. Outside cabins E311 to E623 on Emerald Deck have views obstructed by dangling lifeboats, a fact that's clearly stated in the line's brochures. Standard cabin bathrooms have smallish shower stalls and adequate counter space.

Minisuites provide substantially more space without jumping into the cost stratosphere, and have larger balconies and sizable sitting areas with sofa beds and two televisions, one facing the sitting area and the other the bed—an odd touch since there's no partition, creating total cacophony if you have both on simultaneously. Bathrooms have bathtubs and more counter space than in standard cabins. Storage space in both standard outsides and minisuites is more than adequate, with a large shelved closet and open-sided clothes rack facing a small dressing alcove by the bathroom door. Sixteen full suites have curtained-off sitting and sleeping areas, very large balconies, a wet bar, whirlpool tubs and separate showers in the bathroom, and a walk-in closet.

Twenty cabins on each ship are wheelchair-accessible. There are 18 connecting cabins.

PUBLIC AREAS   Layout is one of the areas in which these vessels really shine, with decks and public areas arranged so that it's always easy to find your way around. Most indoor public spaces are on Decks 6 and 7, starting with the large Princess Theater in the bow. Unlike the ornately decorated two- and three-deck theaters on many new ships, this is a classic sloping one-level space, decorated with no theme whatsoever and with a good view from every one of the comfortable theater seats, which have little flip-up tables in their arms to hold drinks or, when the room is used for lectures or other enrichment activities, your notebook. (*Tip:* During lectures, the ceiling lights may be left on, and it can get very hot in the back rows where the ceiling is lower. In such cases, try to get a seat toward the front of the theater.) Farther aft, the Explorer's Lounge is a smaller-scale show lounge for comedians, karaoke, game shows, and dancing, decorated to evoke the romantic European explorers of the 19th century, with vaguely Islamic tile motifs, African and Asian art pieces, primitivist exotic paintings on the walls, and a dark, woody atmosphere. Important sports events are broadcast here on multiple large screens. In the very stern, the new Universe Lounge is a truly innovative multipurpose space, hosting TV-style cooking demonstrations (with a full kitchen onstage), computer classes (with hookups for 50 computers around the room), lectures, and full-blown production performances on three low interconnected stages, which revolve and rise and segment and contort and do more things than you think a stage could—it's a regular three-ring circus. Shows are tailored to utilize all these options, with much of the action taking place at floor level for a true floor-show feel.

Some standout bars and lounges include the maritime-themed Wheelhouse Bar, decorated in classic dark woods, with heavy leather and corduroy armchairs and love seats, faux marble pillars, domed ceiling lights, and small end-table lamps. Though large, the mood of the room is intimate, and the arrangement of the seating allows a feeling of privacy for small groups or couples. In the evening, a small band performs smooth jazz and pop numbers for dancing, and some afternoons the ship's string quartet performs classical repertoire. At one entrance to the lounge, a small museum displays memorabilia from P&O history, including an original brass bell from the SS *Oronsay,* children's dolls from the SS *Orsova* and SS *Strathnaver,* postcards sent from the legendary SS *Canberra,* and so on. Nearby, the low-key four-deck atrium is surrounded by the ships shops; the Internet center with its news ticker; Churchill's cigar lounge, a cozy room with big windows, armchairs and sofas seating just 10 people, and a humidor under a portrait of the room's namesake; and Crooner's, a Rat Pack–themed piano bar with a Vegas/martini vibe. A real live crooner performs at the piano each evening.

One level down, the ship's library and card room are both exceptionally large and comfortable, though the layout—with entrances both from the atrium and from the midships elevators/stair tower—means that people often use the rooms as a passageway, adding an unwelcome touch of bustle. A London-themed casino and a wedding chapel round out the adult public room offerings, while at the stern on Deck 12, there's the bright and very kid-scaled Fun Zone and Pelican's Playhouse children's center and smallish Off Limits teen center, with computers and a dance floor. Outside are a children's play area and the small Pelican Pool, which is officially for kids and their parents, but after hours is fair game for anyone, and usually deserted. The ship's bright pottery studio is hidden away back here as well, giving it the feel of a playroom for grown-ups.

DINING OPTIONS   To accommodate Princess's Personal Choice concept, two similar dining rooms—the Provence and the Bordeaux—are dedicated to traditional fixed-seating dining and to anytime Personal Choice dining, respectively. Both rooms are spacious, understated, one-level affairs with lots of elbow room, but be careful about your choice of chairs: Of the three varieties, the ones with solid arms are unusually narrow. If you're not, go for the open-armed or armless variety.

There are two specialty restaurants aboard. Sabatini's Trattoria is a traditional Italian restaurant with a light, airy decor; open kitchen; cushioned wicker balloon-back chairs; and Italian scenes in faux tilework on some walls. Dinners here are 16-course extravaganzas, with all dishes brought automatically—you just select your main course. Brunches aren't much less over-the-top, with a seafood buffet and a large selection of egg dishes. Next door, the Bayou Cafe is a New Orleans–themed restaurant with a subdued, woody ambience, faux brick walls, lantern lighting, primitivist New Orleans murals on the walls, and tables spaced wide apart for a spacious feel. Dinners here include appetizers such as barbecued alligator ribs; soups such as "mud-bug" bisque; and main courses such as seafood gumbo, fried catfish, grilled jumbo prawns, and chicken-and-chorizo jambalaya. A jazz trio plays during dinner, then continues on till midnight for patrons of the attached bar. Tables are sprinkled with Mardi Gras beads for extra atmosphere. Dining here costs $10, which also covers a free Hurricane drink.

The ships' 24-hour Horizon Court buffet restaurants are comfortable enough, though the circular layout of food stations—and no clear path through them— often leads to light chaos. Overlooking the main pool, the Grill serves burgers, dogs, and the like in the afternoon, with very good pizza available one deck down (just forward of the pool) and Häagen-Dazs and fresh juices available aftward at the Lotus Pool's ice-cream bar and juice bar. Inside, at the bottom of the atrium, La Patisserie is a pleasant lounge/cafe serving regular coffee free and specialty coffees at extra cost, with cookies and sweets free for the taking. As the room is almost at sea level, it's a great spot from which to watch the waves go by.

POOL, FITNESS & SPA FACILITIES   The ships' main pool areas are spacious but surprisingly plain, with a main pool and three large hot tubs surrounded by sunning areas and with a tiny, low-key stage at one end where a steel-drum duo performs during the day. Moving toward the stern, the Lotus Pool is a much more interesting area, decorated with a Balinese motif that gives a sense of tranquillity (though if there are lots of kids aboard, that tranquillity probably won't last). Stylish wooden deck chairs here (and more traditional "Royal Teak" ones on the wraparound Promenade Deck) are much more classy than the white plastic ones around the main pool. A sliding-glass roof protects the Lotus Pool during inclement weather. Up on the Sports Deck, the splash pool is a wading pool for adults.

Fitness facilities include a surprisingly small gym with bikes, treadmills, Stair-masters, a selection of free weights, and Cybex weight machines, plus a relatively large separate aerobics room. Up on the top decks, there's a basketball/volleyball court, a computerized golf simulator, and a 9-hole miniature-golf course located in open air but behind a windowless wooden door that makes it look permanently closed. It's not; just go on in.

In the stern on Deck 14, the Balinese-themed Lotus Spa offers the usual massage, mud, and beauty treatments, and features a thermal suite (a unisex room offering various heat treatments) and a lovely sea-view salon. For what it's worth—since the spa is run by Steiner (the company that runs almost all cruise ship spas) and since personnel change regularly—we had one of our best cruise ship massages on *Coral Princess,* an almost painful deep-tissue sports massage that left us feeling completely loose and refreshed. On the downside, spa staff repeatedly suggested we sign up for a hot-stone massage or "Asian Lotus Ritual" instead, even though we showed up at the reservation desk having already decided what we wanted. Ostensibly, this was because the sports massage can be very painful (which it can), but could it be just a coincidence that the two therapies they suggested were $50 and $100 more expensive? Hmmm . . .

The Grand Class: Grand Princess • Golden Princess • Caribbean Princess (preview)

Grand Princess *(photo: Princess Cruises)*

The Verdict

These huge, well-accoutered vessels are very easy to navigate, never feel as crowded as you'd expect, and are amazingly intimate for their size.

Specifications

Size (in tons)		Grand/Golden	2,600
Grand/Golden	109,000	Caribbean	3,100
Caribbean	116,000	Officers	British/Italian
Number of Cabins		Crew	Internat'l
Grand/Golden	1,300	Grand/Golden	1,100
Caribbean	1,557	Caribbean	1,200
Number of Outside Cabins		Passenger/Crew Ratio	
Grand/Golden	928	Grand/Golden	2.4 to 1
Caribbean	1,105	Caribbean	2.6 to 1
Cabins with Verandas		Year Launched	
Grand/Golden	710	Grand Princess	1998
Caribbean	881	Golden Princess	2001
Number of Passengers		Caribbean Princess	2004

Frommer's Ratings (Scale of 1–5)   ★★★★ ½

Cabin Comfort & Amenities	5	Dining Options	4
Ship Cleanliness & Maintenance	4	Gym & Spa Facilities	5
Public Comfort/Space	5	Children's Facilities	4
Decor	4	Enjoyment Factor	4.5

When she was launched, the 109,000-ton, 2,600-passenger *Grand Princess* was the world's biggest and most expensive cruise ship, costing $450 million, but things change fast in the cruise industry: Within a year, she was eclipsed by Royal Caribbean's 142,000-ton *Voyager of the Seas*. Still, *Grand* and her sister *Golden Princess* (as well as *Star Princess*, which doesn't currently sail in the Caribbean, and *Caribbean Princess*, due for delivery in Apr 2004) are massive ships, with 18 decks soaring higher than the Statue of Liberty from pedestal to torch, hulls too wide to fit through the Panama Canal, and sterns with their elevated, space-age discos stretching from port to starboard and resembling the handle on a giant shopping cart. They look like nothing else at sea, intimidating from afar by dint of their sheer size but inside extremely well laid out, very easy to navigate, and surprisingly cozy. In fact, their public areas never feel as crowded as you'd think they would with almost 4,000 people aboard, including passengers and crew. The ultramodern ships even manage to offer a few areas with traditional accents that recall a grander era of sea travel, including the clubby and dimly lit Explorer's and Wheelhouse lounges and the elegant three-story atrium, where classical string quartets perform on formal nights and during embarkation.

Cabins & Rates

Cabins	Per Diems from	Sq. Ft.	Fridge	Hair Dryer	Sitting Area	TV
Inside	$86	160	yes	yes	no	yes
Outside	$100	165–257*	yes	yes	no	yes
Suite	$338	323–1,314*	yes	yes	yes	yes

* Includes veranda.

CABINS   Though cabins on these vessels are divided into some 35 categories, there are actually fewer than 10 configurations. For the most part, the category differences reflect location—such as amidships versus aft—and thus price, with some price differences being only $30 or so.

There are 710 cabins with verandas (only Royal Caribbean's Voyager-class ships and the new *Coral* and *Island Princess* have more, with 757 and 727, respectively), but as on the newer *Coral* and *Island Princess*, most verandas are tiered, affording less privacy. Cabins are richly decorated in light hues and earth tones, and all have safes, hair dryers, and minifridges, as well as TVs broadcasting CNN, CNBC, ESPN, TNT, movies, and shows from the Discovery Channel, Nickelodeon, the BBC, National Geographic, A&E, and E! Entertainment television. Storage is adequate and features more closet shelves than drawer space. Robes for use during the cruise are available on request.

A standard outside cabin without a balcony, such as categories F and FF, ranges from 165 to 210 square feet, while insides, such as category JJ, measure 160 square feet. Balcony cabins range from 165 to 257 square feet. At 323 square feet, the 180 minisuites on each vessel are smaller than the 32 minisuites on the Sun-class ships, but are comfortable and also offer two TVs, a sitting area, a chair and desk, a balcony, a walk-in closet, and a minifridge, but only one bathroom. Two Grand Suites measure 782 square feet and feature all the above amenities plus two bathrooms, one with the toilet, the other with a shower and separate whirlpool tub. The two Grand Suites even have fireplaces (though not real wood-burning ones, of course) plus hot tubs. There are two Family Suites that can sleep up to eight, with two bathrooms. Minibars in the suites are stocked once on a complimentary basis with soda, bottled water, beer, and liquor.

Lifeboats partially or completely obstruct the views from most cabins on the Emerald Deck. There are no connecting cabins except among the Family Suites, but a large number of cabins can accommodate a third passenger in an upper berth. Each ship has 28 wheelchair-accessible cabins, more than any other. (Public areas are also very accessible; Skywalkers disco even has a wheelchair lift up to the elevated dance floor.)

PUBLIC AREAS   Even sailing with a full load of passengers (as many as 3,100 if all additional berths in every cabin are filled), you'll wonder where everyone is. These are huge ships with a not-so-huge feeling. Because of their smart layout, six dining venues, expansive outdoor deck space divided into four main sections, multiple sports facilities, gigantic virtual-reality game room, four pools, and nine hot tubs, passengers are dispersed rather than concentrated into one or two main areas.

Coupled with this smart layout is the ship's sophisticated yet low-key decor. Like the Sun-class ships, the Grand-class offers contemporary and upscale (if mostly a bit plain) public areas, done up with caramel-colored wood tones and pleasing color schemes of warm blue, teal, and rust, with some brassy details and touches of marble.

While the decor is soothing, the entertainment is pretty hot. Gamblers will love each ship's sprawling and dazzling casino, among the largest at sea at 13,500 square feet. The three main entertainment venues include a well-equipped two-story theater for Vegas-style musical revues that feature more than a dozen dancers, a quartet of singers, and a small live orchestra; a second one-level show lounge for smaller-scale entertainment such as hypnotists and singers (this room has major sightline problems caused by structural columns and a shallow pitch in the seating); and the travel-themed Explorer's Club, with murals of Egyptian and African scenes and a band, variety performer, or karaoke nightly. There's also the clubby, old-world Wheelhouse Lounge, offering laid-back pre- and post-dinner dancing in an elegant setting, as well as a woody sports bar and a wine bar selling caviar by the ounce and vintage wine, champagne, and iced vodka by the glass.

Skywalkers multilevel disco/observation lounge, sequestered 150 feet above the ship's stern like a high-tech tree house, is a unique spot offering floor-to-ceiling windows with two impressive views: forward for a look over the ship itself, or back toward the sea and the giant vessel's very impressive wake. It's well positioned away from any cabins (so the noise won't keep anyone up), and there's a funky moving sidewalk that gets you there—it's our favorite disco at sea. Check out the view at sunset.

For kids, the two-story, indoor/outdoor Fun Zone kids' play area has tons of games and toys, as well as computers and a ball jump—after Disney, it's one of the best kids' areas you'll find at sea. A separate teen center has three more computers, plus video games, a dance floor, and a sound system. On the second (outdoor) level, there's a splash pool and a minibasketball setup, as well as a teens-only sunbathing area with deck chairs and a hot tub. Both ships have cavernous and truly amazing arcades, with hang gliding, downhill skiing, fly-fishing, motor-cycle-riding machines, virtual-reality rides, and dozens more. Rides are all priced differently—from 50¢ up to $3.50—and are paid for with a sort of game debit card, available for $20.

Each ship also has a library, a small writing room, a card room, and a 25-terminal Internet center. There's also an attractive wedding chapel where the captain himself performs about six or seven bona fide, legal marriages every cruise. It's equipped with a Web cam so that friends, family, or anyone else can see live images (updated every 60 sec. or so) on the Princess website; click on "Ships," then on the misleading "Live Bridge Cams," and then choose one of the wedding chapels from among the bridge views.

DINING OPTIONS The ships each have three pleasant, one-story main dining rooms, laid out on slightly tiered levels. By way of some strategically placed waist-high dividers, they feel cozy, although the ceilings are a tad on the low side. The 24-hour Horizon Court casual restaurant offers buffet-style breakfasts and lunches, and is designed to feel much smaller than it actually is. With clusters of buffet stations serving stir-fry, beef, turkey, pork, and lots of fruit, salads, cheeses, and more, lines are kept to a minimum and you're hardly aware of the space's enormity. This restaurant turns into a sit-down bistro from 7:30pm to 4am, with the same dinner menu each night. If you like the idea of New York strip sirloin at midnight, this is the place to go.

For a more intimate yet still casual meal, there are two alternative, reservations-required restaurants. Sabatini's specializes in Italian cuisine, featuring specialty pizzas, antipasto, homemade pasta, and salads served tableside. The food is excellent and copious, and the service is first-rate—which justifies the $15-per-person cover charge. On *Golden* and *Grand*, a very casual Southwestern restaurant serves Tex-Mex favorites such as tequila prawns, chicken fajitas, and white-bean enchiladas, and has live entertainment. Its $8 cover includes a 16-ounce margarita. *Caribbean Princess* will offer a Caribbean-themed alternative restaurant instead.

POOL, FITNESS & SPA FACILITIES The Grand-class ships have around 1.7 acres of open deck space, so it's not hard to find a quiet place to soak in the sun. Our favorite spot on a hot, humid day is portside aft on the deck overlooking the swimming pool, where the tail fin vent blows cool air. It's like having an outdoor air-conditioner.

The ships have four great swimming pools, including one with a retractable glass roof for inclement weather; another aft, under the disco, that feels miles from the rest of the ship; and another touted as a swim-against-the-current pool although, truth be told, there really isn't enough room to swim steadily if others are in the pool, and the jets are kept at a level barely powerful enough to keep a 150-pound person in place. The fourth pool is for kids. Other recreational offerings include a Sports Deck with a jogging track and paddle tennis, a fun nine-hole putting green, and computerized simulated golf. *Caribbean Princess* will offer "dive-in movies" (as well as sporting events) on a large screen built into the vessel at the midships pool.

Spa, gym, and beauty-parlor facilities are located in a large, almost separate part of each ship, on the forward Sun Deck, surrounding the lap pool and its tiered, amphitheater-style wooden benches. As is the case fleetwide with Princess, the ocean-view gym is surprisingly small for a ship of this size, although there's an unusually large aerobics floor.

The Sun Class: Dawn Princess • Sun Princess

The Verdict

These relaxed, pretty ships are pleasant and comfortable, great for families and for grown-ups who like to enjoy the good life without too much flash.

Sun Princess *(photo: Princess Cruises)*

Specifications

Size (in tons)	77,000	Crew	900 (Internat'l)
Number of Cabins	975	Passenger/Crew Ratio	2.2 to 1
Number of Outside Cabins	603	Year Launched	
Cabins with Verandas	410	*Dawn Princess*	1997
Number of Passengers	1,950	*Sun Princess*	1995
Officers	British/Italian	Last Major Refurbishment	N/A

Frommer's Ratings (Scale of 1–5)   ⓖⓖⓖⓖ

Cabin Comfort & Amenities	4	Dining Options	4
Ship Cleanliness & Maintenance	4	Gym & Spa Facilities	4
Public Comfort/Space	5	Children's Facilities	4
Decor	5	Enjoyment Factor	4

The Sun-class sisters are a great choice when you want a calmer, more genteel cruise than you'd get from Carnival, Royal Caribbean, or NCL, but aren't attracted to the more chic, modernist ambience of Celebrity. They're pretty ships but not totally stunning, spacious but not overwhelming. We were surprised at how easy it was to find our way around—by the end of the first day, we had the important landmarks memorized.

The decor of these ships is done in a style that's a combo of classic and modern, using materials such as varnished hardwoods, marble, etched glass, granite, and textured fabrics. The look doesn't sock you between the eyes with its daring; in fact, it's a bit plain-Jane: comforting and quiet, and (so far) aging gracefully. Light color schemes predominate, with lots of beiges, as opposed to the darker and bolder hues of Carnival and Celebrity, for example.

Cabins & Rates

Cabins	Per Diems from	Sq. Ft.	Fridge	Hair Dryer	Sitting Area	TV
Inside	$86	135–148	yes	yes	no	yes
Outside	$100	147–183*	yes	yes	no	yes
Suite	$296	365–678*	yes	yes	yes	yes

* Includes veranda.

CABINS   Though cabins on these vessels are divided into some 28 categories, there are actually fewer than 10 configurations—for the most part, the category differences reflect location (amidships versus aft, and so on), and thus price. More than 400 cabins on each vessel boast private balconies, though at about 3-feet-x-8½-feet, they're small. And that leads to the main point here: The staterooms on these ships are cramped. Standard outside cabins, such as categories BC and BD, are 178 square feet including their balconies, while Carnival's standards, by comparison, are nearly 186 square feet *without* balconies—on these ships, what little balcony space you gain is deducted from your room space.

Guests in each ship's six suites enjoy as much as a sprawling 678 square feet of space, as well as robes to use while aboard (regular cabin passengers can request them too) and minibars stocked once on a complimentary basis with soda, bottled water, beer, and liquor. The 32 minisuites on each ship are gorgeous, with a separate bedroom area divided from the sitting area with a curtain. Each has a pullout sofa, a chair and desk, a minifridge, two TVs, a walk-in closet, and a whirlpool tub and shower in a separate room from the toilet and sink.

All cabins have minifridges, safes, and hair dryers, plus TVs broadcasting CNN, CNBC, ESPN, TNT, movies, and shows from the Discovery Channel, Nickelodeon, the BBC, National Geographic, A&E, and E! Entertainment television.

Nineteen cabins on each vessel are wheelchair accessible. There are no connecting cabins on these ships, but quite a few will accommodate third or fourth passengers in upper berths.

PUBLIC AREAS   These ships have a decidedly unglitzy decor that relies on lavish amounts of wood, glass, marble, and collections of original paintings, statues, and lithographs. The one-story showrooms offer unobstructed viewing from every seat, and several spaces in the back are reserved for wheelchair-users. The sound systems are good, and lighting is state-of-the-art. The smaller Vista Lounge also presents entertainment, with good sightlines and comfortable cabaret-style seating. The elegant, nautical-motif Wheelhouse Bar is done in warm, dark wood tones and features small bands, sometimes with a vocalist; it's the perfect spot for pre- or post-dinner drinks.

There's a dark and sensuous disco; a bright, spacious casino; a wine bar selling caviar by the ounce and vintage wine, champagne, and iced vodka by the glass; and lots of little lounges for an intimate rendezvous, such as the Atrium Lounge and a second lounge located on the same deck, immediately aft.

DINING OPTIONS   In these ships' two dining rooms there are no dramatic, sweeping staircases for making an entrance; instead, the rooms feel intimate, broken up by dividers topped with frosted glass. Each ship also has two alternative dining venues: a sit-down pizzeria on Dolphin Deck, open approximately 11am to 2:30pm and 7pm to 1am for casual and quiet dining, with tables seating two, four, and six (sorry, no takeout or delivery, but pizza is also available by the slice in the Horizon Court 4–7pm daily); and an outdoor steakhouse set out of the wind just outside the Horizon Court, overlooking the main pool. Passengers can choose from four cuts of beef—rib-eye, New York strip, porterhouse, and filet mignon—with starters such as chili, blooming onion, jalapeño poppers, and fresh Caesar salad, plus the usual sides of baked potato or fries, sautéed mushrooms, creamed spinach, and corn on the cob. It's open from 6 to 10pm, reservations are recommended, and the cover charge is $8 per person. The 24-hour Horizon Court buffet restaurant offers an ultra-casual option for all meals, including sit-down bistro-style dinners from 7:30pm to 4am.

POOL, FITNESS & SPA FACILITIES   The center of the action for any Caribbean cruise is the pool, and these ships have plenty of space to party on the Riviera Deck. In total, there are four adult pools and one kids' wading pool, and hot tubs scattered around the Riviera Deck. Three spacious decks are open for sunbathing.

The ships' gyms are appealing, and though they're on the small side for vessels of this size, they're actually roomier than the ones on the much larger *Golden* and *Grand Princess*. Aerobics, stretching, and meditation classes are available in the conversely very roomy aerobics room, and the nearby spas offer the usual massages, mud treatments, and facials. The teak Promenade Deck provides space for joggers, walkers, and shuffleboard players, and a computerized golf center called Princess Links simulates the trickiest holes at some of the world's best golf courses.

9 Royal Caribbean International

1050 Caribbean Way, Miami, FL 33132. © **800/327-6700** or 305/539-6000. Fax 800/722-5329. www.royal caribbean.com.

THE LINE IN A NUTSHELL   Cruises on these fun, activity-packed, and glamorous but not too over-the-top-glitzy megaships offer great diversions, from Solariums to huge kids' playrooms, and even miniature golf and rock climbing.

THE EXPERIENCE   Royal Caribbean offers some of the best-looking and best-designed (not to mention incredibly activity-packed) megaships in the biz, appealing to a wide range of people—except for the older *Nordic Empress,* the company's vessels are all megaships with similar features such as multistory atria and mall-like shopping complexes, two-story (or more) dining rooms and show-rooms, and wide-open public areas (and conversely small cabins on the fleet's older ships). The line offers lots of activities, a varied and well-executed enter-tainment repertoire, and enough glamour and glitz to keep things exciting, but not so much that they overwhelm the senses. Decor-wise, these ships are a shade or two toned down from the Carnival brood, and while at the end of the day the onboard experience is similar, the Royal Caribbean ships are less in-your-face than their Carnival counterparts. The Voyager-class ships are the world's largest, with an almost city-like feel, while the Radiance class is Royal Caribbean's classi-est to date, bringing it much closer to a Celebrity-like sophistication than a Carnival-style, party-on Vegas feel.

Pros

- **Activities:** With rock-climbing walls, miniature golf, and basketball courts among the many diversions, these ships are tops in the keeping-busy department.
- **Attractive public rooms:** Lounges, restaurants, and outdoor pool decks are well designed, spacious, glamorous, and just plain inviting: not too flam-boyant, but compelling.
- **Great solariums:** The indoor-outdoor solariums on the Vision-, Voyager- and especially the Radiance-class ships are oh-so-relaxing oases, each cen-tered around a theme (for example, Venice, Africa, and so on), a pool, and a pair of enormous whirlpool tubs.

Cons

- **Small cabins:** No two ways to slice it: At just about 120 to 160 square feet, most cabins (except aboard the Voyager- and Radiance-class ships) are downright teeny: With NCL's, overall they're the smallest in the mainstream category.

Compared with the other mainstream lines, here's how RCI rates:

	Poor	Fair	Good	Excellent	Outstanding
Enjoyment Factor					✓
Dining			✓		
Activities					✓
Children's Program				✓	
Entertainment					✓
Service				✓	
Worth the Money					✓

ROYAL CARIBBEAN: ROCK CLIMBING, ANYONE? HIP SHIPS
Royal Caribbean was the first company to launch a fleet specializing exclusively in Caribbean ports of call—hence the company name. In the late 1980s, the company expanded its horizons beyond the Caribbean, offering cruises to Europe, Alaska, and the Pacific, in the process tagging the "International" onto its name.

What began in 1969 as a consortium of Norwegian ship owners with big eyes for the North American cruise market has blossomed into an immensely profitable multinational corporation with a fleet of state-of-the-art megaships that carry a staggering number of vacationers. In 1988, the Pritzker family (creative force behind the Hyatt empire) bought a major stake in the company, and funds from the sale, coupled with all the credit-worthiness of Hyatt, helped finance the line's massive 1990s building spree, which began in 1988 with the 73,192-ton *Sovereign of the Seas*. The ship ushered in a new generation of megaships, and was the largest passenger ship built in the previous 50 years. Along with her newer, near clones, *Monarch* and *Majesty of the Seas, Sovereign* tripled Royal Caribbean's cabin capacity in a mere 4 years. Beyond sheer size, though, the ships were innovative, featuring such now-standard features as soaring multi-story atria with glass-sided elevators; fountains splashing into marble pools; and observation lounges perched 10 or more stories above sea level, wrapped around the rear smokestack in a style reminiscent of big-windowed airport control towers. With the introduction of the groundbreaking 142,000-ton, 3,114-passenger Voyager-class ships in late 1999, Royal Caribbean ushered in yet another age—the age of the super-size megaships—and they still hold the title of the biggest passenger ships ever built. In 1997, Royal Caribbean acquired the smaller and more high-end Celebrity Cruises, which it continues to operate as a separate brand. In early 2002, Royal Caribbean lost out to Carnival for a bid to merge with P&O Princess.

Currently, Royal Caribbean has 17 ships in its fleet, with another due in late 2003 and another in spring 2004.

PASSENGER PROFILE
You'll find all walks of life on a Royal Caribbean cruise: passengers in their 20s through 60s, mostly couples (a good number of them honeymooning), and some singles traveling with friends, but also lots of families—more than 300,000 kids sailed with Royal Caribbean in 2001. While the majority of passengers come from somewhere in North America, because of the novelty factor the world-record-huge Voyager-class ships attract more foreigners than the other ships, including many Asians and Latin Americans. There are books in the library in French, Spanish, and Dutch; and in-cabin documents (such as room-service menus) are in five languages, including Italian and Portuguese.

Recently, the line has been making a big push for younger, hipper, more active passengers with its Iggy Pop "Lust for Life" TV ads, which portray the ships as a combination of hyperactive urban health club, chic restaurant district, and adventure-travel enabler, able to turn passengers into real, live explorers and adventurers—which of course is a bit of a stretch. Overall, passengers are active, social, and looking for a good time (no matter what their age), and want something a little less glitzy, theme-parkish, and party-animal-oriented than is offered by RCI's main competitor, Carnival. The line's shorter 3- and 4-night cruises tend to attract more of the partying crowd, as is the case with most short cruises.

Ⓒ Getting the Royal Treatment on a Private Island

Many of Royal Caribbean's cruises stop for a day at the line's two private beach resorts—Coco Cay (Little Stirrup Cay) in the Bahamas and Labadee, an isolated and sun-flooded peninsula along Haiti's north coast. At Coco Cay, an otherwise uninhabited 140-acre landfall in the Bahamas' Berry Islands, you'll find lots of beach, hammocks, food, drink, and watersports, with the line organizing such activities as limbo contests, water-balloon tosses, relay races, and volleyball tournaments. For snorkelers, Royal Caribbean even built and sank a replica of one of Bluebeard's schooners.

Labadee is isolated on a scenic 270-acre peninsula kept completely walled off from the rest of poverty-stricken Haiti, but nevertheless is a rarity among cruise lines' private islands in that it gives you a real glimpse of island culture. At the straightforwardly named "Folkloric Show," a large, colorfully costumed, and very talented troupe performs Haiti's distinctly African brand of dancing, drumming, and song, while acoustic mento-style bands perform at the various bars and restaurants, providing a wonderfully relaxed, happy soundtrack to the whole island. (Mento is a musical style of the Caribbean that predates the more widely known ska and reggae styles.) Five beaches are spread around the peninsula, and are progressively less crowded the farther you walk from the dock, where enormous tenders make the short ride to and from the ship. At Columbus Cove, the Arawak Cay children's aqua park is full of floating trampolines, inflatable iceberg-shaped slides, and water see-saws. Kayaking and parasailing are offered from a dock nearby. At the center of the peninsula, the Haitian Market and Artisan's Market are the port's low points, full of cheesy Africanesque statues and carvings, with touts trying to lure you in with "Sir, let me just show you something over here." Steer clear unless you're desperate for a souvenir. When we were here last, a painter near the dock had much more interesting work for sale.

On both Labadee and Coco Cay, organized children's activities include beach parties, volleyball, seashell collecting, and sand-castle building.

DINING

The cuisine on Royal Caribbean has been improving over the past few years, especially on the newer ships. A recent dinner on *Radiance of the Seas* was impressive, while one on *Explorer of the Seas* fell on the good side of average, and one on *Grandeur of the Seas* was pretty mediocre. Overall, meals are pretty inconsistent (good one day, so-so the next), as is true on most mainstream lines. Dinners are offered in two seatings in the main dining rooms, with typical entrees including poached Alaskan salmon, oven-roasted crispy duck served with a rhubarb sauce, sirloin steak marinated with Italian herbs and served over a chunky tomato stew, and shrimp scampi. At lunch and dinner, there's always a **light and healthy option** such as an herb-crusted baked cod with steamed red-skinned potatoes and vegetables, or a pasta tossed with smoked turkey, Portobello mushrooms, and red-pepper pesto, as well as a **vegetarian option** such as vegetable strudel served in a puff pastry with black-bean salsa.

The Voyager-class ships each have one intimate, reservations-only **alternative restaurant,** while the Radiance-class ships have two of them. They're attractive and intimate getaways, and food and service are the best on board; but at $20 a pop, you may not want to do it more than once.

Fleetwide, an open-seating **casual dinner option** is offered every night 6:30 to 9:30pm in the buffet-style Windjammer Cafe on the Pool Deck, with meals following the general theme of dinners in the main restaurants (Italian, Caribbean, and so on) and the room made a bit more inviting through dimmed lighting and the addition of tablecloths. Long open hours mean this option rarely gets crowded. You can also eat breakfast and lunch in the Windjammer if you don't want the formality of the main dining room, though lines can grow long for these meals (much less so on the Voyager- and Radiance-class ships, which have lots of separate food stations to diffuse crowding).

Ice cream and a couple of toppings are available throughout the day from a station in the Windjammer and on the Voyager ships' central promenade. There are also three pull-out-all-the-stops midnight buffets per week (and **"Midnight Treats"** hors d'oeuvres served the other days) that sometimes look better than they taste, as well as pretty decent pizza served afternoons and late night for those suffering from post-partying munchies. The Voyager-class ships also feature an honest-to-God **Johnny Rockets diner** on board for burgers and milkshakes.

A fairly extensive kids' menu (which is fun in and of itself, with word and picture games and pictures to color in, crayons included) features the usual options: burgers, hot dogs, fries, fish sticks, burritos, oven-fried lemon chicken, spaghetti and meatballs, and pizza, plus lots of desserts.

Room service is available 24 hours a day from a fairly routine, limited menu. However, during normal lunch and dinner hours, a cabin steward can bring many items served in the restaurant to your cabin.

ACTIVITIES

You'll have no problem keeping yourself occupied on a Royal Caribbean cruise, as activities are the line's forte. Of course, if you want to remain glued to a deck chair and do nothing, that's no problem either.

Royal Caribbean ships are known for their sports facilities. The Radiance- and Voyager-class ships and *Splendour of the Seas* feature **miniature-golf courses** right on board; there are **ice-skating rinks** and **in-line skating tracks** on the Voyager-class ships; and the Radiance-, Voyager-, and Vision-class ships all have combo basketball/volleyball courts on deck. Fleetwide, you'll also find rock-climbing walls (which started on the Voyager- and Radiance-class ships and should be installed on the others by year-end 2003), plus lots of the typical cruise fare: bingo, shuffleboard, horse racing, line- and ballroom dancing lessons, napkin folding, spa and beauty demonstrations, art auctions, and outrageous poolside contests, such as a men's sexy legs contest that's designed to draw big laughs. If shopping can be considered an activity, Royal Caribbean beats out Carnival with its impressive selection of boutiques clustered around the atrium.

For those whose goal is to *not* gain 5 pounds at the buffet, the line's ShipShape fitness program rewards passengers who participate in aerobics, dance classes, basketball free-throw contests, Ping-Pong tournaments, early morning walkathons, and other activities with such prizes as T-shirts and baseball caps. Gyms are well equipped across the fleet, but unfortunately some of the best classes—such as yoga and cardio-kickboxing—carry a let's-gouge-the-passengers $10 fee.

Royal Caribbean Fleet Itineraries

Ship	Itineraries
Adventure of the Seas	**7-night S. Carib 1:** Round-trip from San Juan, year-round, visiting Aruba, Curaçao, Sint Maarten, and St. Thomas, with 2 days at sea. Alternates Apr–Oct with **7-night S. Carib 2:** Round-trip from San Juan, visiting St. Thomas, Antigua, St. Lucia, Sint Maarten, and Barbados, with 1 day at sea. **Non-Caribbean Itineraries:** None.
Brilliance of the Seas	**11-night W. Carib:** Round-trip from Miami, Nov 2003–Apr 2004, visiting Key West, Cozumel, Grand Cayman, Ocho Rios (Jamaica), Aruba, and Curaçao, with 4 days at sea. Alternates Nov–Dec 2003 with **10-night W. Carib** (same ports as above, minus Key West) and Jan–Apr 2004 with **10-night W. Carib/Panama Canal:** Round-trip from Miami, visiting Grand Cayman, Aruba, and Puerto Limon (Costa Rica), with 6 days at sea including a partial Canal crossing. **4-night W. Carib:** Round-trip from Miami, Nov 10, 2003, only, visiting Key West and Cozumel, with 1 day at sea. **Non-Caribbean Itineraries:** Europe.
Enchantment of the Seas	3 alternating itineraries: **4-night W. Carib:** Round-trip from Fort Lauderdale, Sept 2003–Apr 2004, visiting Key West and Cozumel, with 1 day at sea. **5-night W. Carib 1:** Round-trip from Fort Lauderdale, Sept 2003–Apr 2004, visiting Key West, Cozumel, and Belize City (Belize), with 1 day at sea. **5-night W. Carib 2:** Round-trip from Fort Lauderdale, Sept 2003–Apr 2004, visiting Ocho Rios (Jamaica) and Grand Cayman, with 2 days at sea. **Non-Caribbean Itineraries:** None.
Explorer of the Seas	**7-night E. Carib:** Round-trip from Miami, year-round, visiting San Juan, Sint Maarten, St. Thomas, and Nassau, with 2 days at sea. Alternates with **7-night W. Carib:** Round-trip from Miami, year-round, visiting Labadee (Haiti)*, Ocho Rios (Jamaica), Grand Cayman, and Cozumel, with 2 days at sea. **Non-Caribbean Itineraries:** None.
Grandeur of the Seas	**7-night W. Carib:** Round-trip from New Orleans, Nov 2003–Apr 2004, visiting Cozumel and Progreso (Mexico), and either Grand Cayman or Key West, with 3 days at sea. **8-night Bermuda/Carib:** Boston to San Juan, Oct 31, 2003, only, visiting King's Wharf (Bermuda), St. Thomas, and Sint Maarten, with 3 days at sea. **Non-Caribbean Itineraries:** Europe, New England/Canada.
Majesty of the Seas	**3-night Bahamas:** Round-trip from Miami, year-round, visiting Nassau and Coco Cay**. **4-night Bahamas:** Round-trip from Miami, year-round, visiting Nassau, Coco Cay**, and Key West. **Non-Caribbean Itineraries:** None.
Mariner of the Seas	**7-night E. Carib:** Round-trip from Port Canaveral, year-round, visiting Nassau, St. Thomas, and Sint Maarten, with 3 days at sea. Alternates with **7-night W. Carib:** Round-trip from Port Canaveral, year-round, visiting Labadee*, Ocho Rios (Jamaica), Grand Cayman, and Cozumel, with 2 days at sea. **Non-Caribbean Itineraries:** None.
Navigator of the Seas	**7-night E. Carib:** Round-trip from Miami, year-round, visiting Nassau, St. Thomas, San Juan, and Labadee (Haiti)*, with 2 days at sea. Alternates with **7-night W. Carib:** Round-trip from Miami, year-round, visiting Labadee (Haiti)*, Ocho Rios (Jamaica), Grand Cayman, and Cozumel, with 2 days at sea. **Non-Caribbean Itineraries:** None.
Nordic Empress	**7-night Bermuda:** Round-trip from New York, Sept–Oct 2003 and May–Oct 2004, visiting King's Wharf and Hamilton. **7-night W. Carib:** Round-trip from Tampa, Nov 2003–Apr 2004, visiting Grand Cayman, Belize City (Belize), and Cozumel, with 3 days at sea. **Non-Caribbean Itineraries:** None.
Radiance of the Seas	**7-night E. Carib:** Round-trip from Fort Lauderdale, Nov 2003–Apr 2004, visiting San Juan, Sint Maarten, St. Thomas, and Nassau, with 2 days at sea. Alternates with **7-night W. Carib:** Round-trip from Fort Lauderdale, Nov 2003–Apr 2004, visiting Key West, Cozumel and Costa Maya (Mexico), and Grand Cayman, with 2 days at sea. **Non-Caribbean Itineraries:** Panama Canal and Pacific coastal repositioning cruises, Alaska, Hawaii.
Rhapsody of the Seas	**7-night W. Carib:** Round-trip from Galveston, year-round, visiting Key West, Cozumel, and Grand Cayman, with 3 days at sea. **Non-Caribbean Itineraries:** Mardi Gras cruise visiting New Orleans, Feb 22.

Royal Caribbean Fleet Itineraries

Ship	Itineraries
Serenade of the Seas	**7-night E. Carib:** Round-trip from San Juan, Nov 2003–Apr 2004, visiting St. Thomas, Sint Maarten, Antigua, St. Lucia, and Barbados, with 1 day at sea. **Non-Caribbean Itineraries:** Coastal Canada.
Sovereign of the Seas	**3- & 4-night Bahamas:** Round-trip from Port Canaveral, year-round, visiting Coco Cay** and Nassau, with 1 day at sea on 4-nighters. **Non-Caribbean Itineraries:** None.
Splendour of the Seas	**11- & 12-night Panama Canal:** Round-trip from Galveston, TX, Nov 2003–Feb 2004, visiting Cozumel, Puerto Limon (Costa Rica), Belize City (Belize), Cristobal Pier (Panama), and Grand Cayman, with 5 days at sea, including time spent on the Canal. 12-night itinerary includes visit to Montego Bay (Jamaica). **4- & 5-night W. Carib:** Round-trip from Galveston, TX, Mar–Apr 2004, visiting Cozumel, with 2 days at sea. 5-night itineraries also visit Costa Maya (Mexico). **Non-Caribbean Itineraries:** Europe.
Voyager of the Seas	**7-night W. Carib 1:** Round-trip from Miami, year-round, visiting Labadee (Haiti)*, Ocho Rios (Jamaica), Grand Cayman, and Cozumel, with 2 days at sea. Alternates with **7-night W. Carib 2:** Round-trip from Miami, year-round, visiting Belize City (Belize), Cozumel and Costa Maya (Mexico), and Grand Cayman, with 2 days at sea. **Non-Caribbean Itineraries:** None.

*Royal Caribbean's private beach on Haiti. **Royal Caribbean's private Bahamian island.*

CHILDREN'S PROGRAM

Year-round and fleetwide, Royal Caribbean offers its **"Adventure Ocean"** supervised kids' programs for children **ages 3 to 17** (divided into Aquanauts, ages 3–5; Explorers, ages 6–8; Voyagers, ages 9–11; Navigators, ages 12–14; and older teens ages 15–17). Male and female youth staff all have college degrees in education, recreation, or a related field. Each ship has a children's playroom, a teen center and disco, and a video arcade; and activities include movies, talent shows, karaoke, pizza and ice-cream parties, bingo, scavenger hunts, game shows, volleyball, face painting, beach parties, and the **"Adventure Science"** program, which teaches and entertains kids with fun yet educational scientific experiments. A new partnership with Crayola (the crayon people) focuses more activities on art projects made with the company's materials, including modeling clay, glitter, glue, markers, paint, and, of course, crayons. The scope of the kids' facilities on the Voyager- and Radiance-class ships far exceeds that of the rest of the fleet (and at 22,000 sq. ft., they're the largest on the *Navigator* and *Mariner of the Seas*), though the kids' areas on the other vessels are still quite impressive size-wise—on par with or better than Carnival's *Elation, Paradise,* and Destiny-class ships. For instance, the kids' areas on the older *Sovereign of the Seas* are gigantic.

Slumber-party-style **group babysitting** for children 3 and up is available in the kids' playroom nightly between 10pm and 1am, and from noon until sailing on days the ship is in port. The hourly charge is $5 per child (kids must be at least 3 years old and potty-trained). Private, in-cabin babysitting by a crewmember is available from about 8am to 2am and must be booked at least 24 hours in advance through the purser's desk. The charge is $8 per hour for up to two children in the same family, and $10 per hour for a maximum of three kids in the same family (children must be at least 6 months old).

So that Mom and Dad can get a break and the kids can have more fun, the new Adventure Ocean dinner program invites kids to dine with counselors in the Windjammer Cafe, the Solarium, or Johnny Rockets diner (depending on the ship) from 6 to 7pm on 3 nights of a 7-night cruise and once or twice on shorter cruises. A complete child's menu is offered.

Children must be at least 6 months old to sail with Royal Caribbean.

ENTERTAINMENT

The line doesn't scrimp in the entertainment department, with **music and comedy acts,** sock hops, toga parties, **talent shows,** karaoke, elaborate **Vegas-style shows,** and occasional name soloists such as Maureen McGovern, Clint Holmes, and Frankie Avalon. On a recent *Radiance* cruise, the Platters performed to rave reviews, and a recent *Explorer* cruise featured the amazing aerialist act Majestic as well as the Knudsen Brothers, a five-member a cappella group that mixes great harmonies and human-beat-box rhythms. Royal Caribbean uses **12- to 16-piece bands** for its main showroom, and the large-cast revues are among the best you'll find at sea. The newer the ship, the larger and more sophisticated the stage, sound, and lighting equipment, with some boasting a wall of video monitors to augment live performances.

Aside from its showrooms and huge glitzy casinos, Royal Caribbean is big on signature spaces, with each ship offering the nautical, woodsy Schooner Bar as well as the **Viking Crown Lounge,** an observation-cum-nightclub set high on a top deck and boasting panoramic views of the sea and ship in all directions. The first Viking Crown Lounge appeared on *Song of Norway,* literally built onto the side of the funnel. Naysayers predicted it would shake right off the stack; of course it didn't, but it has migrated over the years to a more stable but still lofty position.

Besides these spots, there are bars and lounges with live music in the atrium, by the pool, and in other places throughout the ships.

SERVICE

Overall, service in the restaurants and cabins is friendly, accommodating, and efficient, despite some language-barrier problems. (Sign language often comes in handy.) You are often greeted with a smile by someone polishing the brass in a stairwell or may encounter a busboy going out of his way to bring coffee and water to your table in the buffet breakfast, even though it's officially self-service. Still, some crewmembers look like they need a vacation—bad—and don't always hide their lack of enthusiasm (like on a recent *Grandeur* cruise). And, of course, big, bustling ships such as Royal Caribbean's are no strangers to crowds, lines (more so on Vision-class ships and older than on the Voyager- and Radiance-class ships), and harried servers are not able to get to you exactly when you'd like them to. Them's the breaks on a megaship.

Laundry and **dry-cleaning services** are available on all the ships, but none have self-service laundromats.

The Radiance Class: Radiance • Brilliance • Serenade of the Seas (preview) • Jewel of the Seas (preview)

Radiance of the Seas *(photo: RCCL)*

The Verdict

Megaship masterpieces! Royal Caribbean's most elegant vessels to date combine shippy lines and nautical decor with a lot of the fun and games—rock climbing and miniature golf, to name a few—associated with their famous Voyager-class sisters.

Specifications

Size (in tons)	90,090	Passenger/Crew Ratio	2.5 to 1
Number of Cabins	1,050	Year Launched	
Number of Outside Cabins	813	*Radiance*	2001
Cabins with Verandas	577	*Brilliance*	2002
Number of Passengers	2,100	*Serenade*	2003
Officers	International	Last Major Refurbishment	N/A
Crew	857 (Internat'l)		

Frommer's Ratings (Scale of 1–5) ✮✮✮✮ ½

Cabin Comfort & Amenities	4	Dining Options	4.5
Ship Cleanliness & Maintenance	5	Gym & Spa Facilities	5
Public Comfort/Space	5	Children's Facilities	4
Decor	5	Enjoyment Factor	5

There's a revolution brewing at Royal Caribbean. Okay, maybe that's a bit of a stretch, but the stunning Radiance-class ships are different from the line's older ships in some subtle and not-so-subtle ways. When you first board, you'll see Royal Caribbean's signature wiry modern art sculpture filling the bright, nine-deck-high atrium space with its spindly stainless steel tentacles. Don't be deceived: *Radiance, Brilliance,* and *Serenade* aren't just another of Royal Caribbean's peaches-and-cream tropical-themed ships, nor are they just a smaller version of the theme-park-esque Voyager-class ships. Venture a little further and you'll see that they have a much more nautical interior, with dark wood paneling, caramel-brown leathers, and fabrics and carpeting done in deep blues. Outside, her sleek exterior lines are filled with glass—some 110,000 square feet of it, covering about half of the ship's exterior. The Centrum atrium, from Decks 5 through 10 portside, is an uninterrupted wall of glass facing the sea, with four banks of glass elevators. The Viking Crown Lounge, Singapore Sling's piano bar, Crown & Anchor Lounge, Sky Bar, Windjammer Cafe, and Champagne Bar are wrapped in glass, too. All this glass was no accident because the ships were built to sail worldwide itineraries where viewing from the ship is a prime attraction—in Alaska, for instance, where the windows will let passengers view the glaciers and passing waterways while still enjoying the ships' indoor offerings.

A large entertainment complex, the Colony Club, is a classy wood-and-leather hideaway that recalls a classic yacht, university club, or cigar bar (stogie smoking is allowed in the area's Calcutta Card Club). Several of the seating nooks off the atrium are nautically styled too, while cabins done in navy blues and warm wood tones mark a Royal Caribbean first. Another first for the line are the modem jacks in every cabin, allowing passengers to bring laptops from home and plug them right in for e-mail and Internet access (on all Radiance- and Voyager-class ships). There are Internet connections in every crew cabin as well.

Just as the decor and design of *Radiance, Brilliance,* and *Serenade* are new, her mechanics are also cutting-edge. Like the Voyager-class ships, they have an Azipod propulsion system that increases maneuverability with two propeller pods that can move like a rudder, twirling almost 360 degrees. The ships' environmentally friendly GE gas turbine engines are cleaner than the standard diesels and virtually vibration-free; you can't miss the giant green GTV (for gas turbine vessel) painted on either side of *Radiance's* stern—so much for SS (steamship) or even MV (motor vessel). Seems we're in a new era.

At press time, *Serenade* was scheduled to debut in July 2003, and the fourth Radiance-class sister, *Jewel of the Seas,* was slated for a spring 2004 debut. The line is considering building a fifth and sixth Radiance-class ship, but at press time was undecided.

Cabins & Rates

Cabins	Per Diems from	Sq. Ft.	Fridge	Hair Dryer	Sitting Area	TV
Inside	$78	170	yes	yes	yes	yes
Outside	$93	170	yes	yes	yes	yes
Suite	$314	293–1,035	yes	yes	yes	yes

CABINS   Royal Caribbean cabins are finally a decent size! At 170 square feet, inside and outside cabins are roomy and inviting, compared to the small 138- to 153-square-footers on the Vision-class ships. Some 75% of outside staterooms measure at least 180 square feet and boast 40-square-foot verandas, while the rest have jumbo-size portholes. Nearly as impressive as the cabins' size is their appealing decor. A welcome change from the line's Miami Vice pinks, mints, and baby blues, these cabins sport attractive navy blues and copper tones. Another first is the Internet computer jacks in each cabin, so guests can go online with their laptops.

All but a handful of suites are located on Deck 10, including the best, the Royal Suite, measuring 1,035 square feet and offering a separate bedroom, living room (complete with a baby grand piano), dining table, bar, entertainment center, and 172-square-foot balcony. Six Owner's Suites measure 512 square feet and have 57-square-foot balconies, a separate living room, and walk-in closet and bar, while 35 Deluxe Suites are 293 square feet, with sitting areas and 66-square-foot balconies. Three 586-square-foot Royal Family Suites have 140-square-foot balconies and two bathrooms and can accommodate six people in two separate bedrooms (one with 3rd and 4th berths) and another two on a pullout couch in the living room. Suite guests are treated to complimentary in-cabin butler service in addition to cabin stewards, and there's also a Concierge Club on Deck 10 that guests can visit to request services or grab a newspaper.

All cabins have minifridges, hair dryers, interactive televisions (for buying shore excursions, checking your onboard account, and looking up stock quotes), small sitting areas with minicouches, lots of drawer space, roomy closets, bedside reading lights, vanity/desks with pullout trays to accommodate laptops, and TVs offering CNN, ESPN, Discovery, the Cartoon Network, plus lots of pre-taped movies and sitcoms. Bathrooms are small, with Royal Caribbean's traditional hold-your-breath-and-slip-in shower stalls, but do have lots of storage space.

One snag: On each ship, Cabin Decks 7 through 10 are narrower than the rest of the ship, resulting in cabin balconies on Deck 10 (many of them suites) being shaded by the overhang of the deck above. Meanwhile, cabin balconies on the aft and forward ends of Deck 7, being indented, look out onto the top of Deck 6 instead of directly out onto the sea. Balconies on cabins 7652 to 7670 and 7152 to 7170, also aft on Deck 7, are not completely private since the dividers between them don't go all the way to the edge of the space (so keep your clothes on; your neighbors can look right over at you).

Connecting cabins are available. There are 14 wheelchair-accessible cabins.

PUBLIC AREAS Overall, these ships are stunners. Our favorite place on the ship is the Colony Club, a cluster of five intimate lounges on Deck 6, featuring low lighting, inlaid wood flooring, cozy couches and seating clusters, and Oriental-style area rugs. The best is the romantic Singapore Sling's piano bar and lounge, which is stretched across the ship's stern, with a bank of floor-to-ceiling windows protruding out toward the sea. For amazing views, don't miss having a cocktail here on a moonlit night. Adjacent is the lovely Colonial-style Bombay Billiard Club, boasting Jatoba-wood herringbone floors, redwood veneer paneling, and a pair of ultra-high-tech, $90,000 pool tables gimbaled on motion-sensitive, motorized gyroscopes that counteract the ship's movements to keep the tables as level as possible—so no excuses for missing those shots!

On *Radiance,* the trendy Books, Books & Coffee cafe, with comfy high-back, spiral-top, red suede sofas, is the place to order a specialty coffee and a decadent pastry, go online at one of the three Internet stations, or browse the books and souvenirs that are for sale (the other sisters have cafes for specialty coffees too, but not combined with a mini-Internet center and book shop). The exotic African motif of *Radiance's* Solarium, with its stone elephants, waterfalls, and faux thatched-roof umbrellas, is as compelling as that of the Aurora Theater, with its cool, austere ambience. It's refreshingly different from most, with warm wood tones, seating in deep sea-blues and greens, and a handmade blue-black curtain inspired by the northern lights, along with indirect lighting and fiber optics that all come together to create a quiet, ethereal look. On *Brilliance,* the theater follows a Pacific island volcanic theme, exploding with vibrant purples, reds, and golds, while the East Indian theme Solarium is stunning with ceremonial stone elephants and hot tubs topped with grand pink terra-cotta and sandstone canopies.

Standing sentry at the Mast Bar on *Radiance,* on the balcony level above the main pool, is a 12-foot-high cedar totem pole carved for the ship by the famous Native Alaskan artist Nathan Jackson of Ketchikan. How many ships have you seen sporting a totem pole? Other public areas include the attractive Casino Royale, holding more than 200 slot machines and dozens of gaming tables; a baseball-themed sports bar with interactive games on the bar top in front of each stool; the nautically themed Schooner Bar, stretching between the atrium and Colony Club; a 12-station, 24-hour Internet center; a small library; a conference-center complex with a small movie theater; and, high up on Deck 13, Royal Caribbean's signature Viking Crown Lounge, which is divided into two main areas, a quiet lounge and a large disco with a rotating bar. Even the ships' high-style public bathrooms, with their marble counters and floors and funky portholelike mirrors, are impressive.

The huge kids' area on Deck 12 includes a sprawling playroom divided into several areas, a video arcade, and an outdoor pool with a water slide. Teens have their own nightclub, with a DJ booth, music videos, and a soda bar.

DINING OPTIONS The two-story main dining rooms are glamorous and elegant; on *Radiance* and *Brilliance* they're almost like a 1940s movie set. Four willowy silk-covered columns dominate the main floor, and a wide double staircase dramatically connects the two decks—all that's missing are Cary Grant and Katherine Hepburn.

The nautical Windjammer Cafe, with mahogany and teak finishes, ship models and nautical paraphernalia, and navy-blue carpeting and upholstery adding a yachtlike ambience, takes self-serve buffet dining to new levels, with 11 food stations (9 inside and 2 outside) set up as islands to keep the lines down and the crowds diffused. It really works. If you prefer taking your meals while reclining, there's a small strip of cozy tables with oversize rattan chairs and big squishy cushions between the indoor and outdoor seating areas.

The cozy 90-seat Chops Grille is an ocean-view venue done in dark woods with chocolate-brown, burgundy and red leather-, chenille- and mohair-upholstered chairs and high-backed booths. You can order steaks here and watch them being cooked in the open kitchen. Adjacent is the 130-seat Portofino, an Italian restaurant that also has ocean views. Service is more refined and gracious in these two venues than in the main dining room, but be prepared to wait a longer time between courses, as you would in any fine restaurant. (Oh, and be prepared to fork over $20 per person to dine in either of these places, too.) Up on the Sport Deck, the Seaview Cafe is a casual lunch and dinner venue with checkered floors, rattan chairs, and lots of light, serving quick meals such as fish and chips, popcorn shrimp, and burgers.

A counter in the Solarium serves freshly made pizza by the slice, and the Books, Books & Coffee cafe (on Radiance; it's called Latte-tudes Café on *Brilliance*) offers cappuccino and pastry.

POOL, FITNESS & SPA FACILITIES Like the Voyager-class and Vision-class ships, the Radiance ships offer tons of recreation outlets as well as lots of space to flop on a deck chair and sunbathe. There are three pools (including the Solarium pool and a kids' wading pool with water slide) and four hot tubs. As aboard most megaships, the Pool Deck resembles a sardine can on sunny days at sea, and deck chairs can be scarce during the prime hours before and after lunch.

The Sports Deck has a combo basketball, volleyball, and paddle-tennis court; a nine-hole miniature-golf course; a jogging track; golf simulators; and a rock-climbing wall attached to the funnel, with five climbing tracks and training available. The sprawling ocean-view gym has a huge aerobics floor and 18 sea-facing treadmills and eight elliptical steppers among its dozens of machines.

Radiance's Africa-themed Solarium is decorated with 15-foot sculpted rock elephant waterfalls, bronze statues of wild animals, and original watercolor paintings and stone reliefs of African scenes. Faux-thatched roofs cover the hot tubs, and a profusion of live foliage surrounds the pool, which has a counter-current pump for lap swimming and a retractable glass roof for inclement weather. *Brilliance's* theme is East Indian, and it also features grand stone elephants, these in ornate Indian headdresses, as well as stone reliefs, bronze statues, and a peacock created from ceramic tiles. The *Serenade* will have a Balinese theme, and the *Jewel*, a Thai. The adjacent (and popular) pizza counter adds a little pandemonium to the otherwise serene scene, but this is still a great spot to settle into a padded wooden chaise longue and doze away the afternoon.

In the adjacent spa are 13 treatment rooms and a special steam-room complex that features heated tiled chaise longues and special showers simulating tropical rain and fog.

The Voyager Class: Voyager • Explorer • Adventure • Navigator • Mariner of the Seas

The Verdict

Vegas meets theme park meets sports club meets cruise ship—these biggest-in-the-world vessels are real winners if you like your vacations larger than life. As we overheard one little boy say to his father, "This doesn't look like a ship, Daddy. It looks like a city!"

Explorer of the Seas *(photo: Matt Hannafin)*

Specifications

Size (in tons)	142,000	Year Launched	
Number of Cabins	1,557	*Voyager*	1999
Number of Outside Cabins	939	*Explorer*	2000
Cabins with Verandas	757	*Adventure*	2001
Number of Passengers	3,114	*Navigator*	2002
Officers	Scandinavian	*Mariner*	2003
Crew	1,176 (Internat'l)	Last Major Refurbishment	N/A
Passenger/Crew Ratio	2.7 to 1		

Frommer's Ratings (Scale of 1–5)   ★★★★ ½

Cabin Comfort & Amenities	4	Dining Options	4.5
Ship Cleanliness & Maintenance	4	Gym & Spa Facilities	5
Public Comfort/Space	5	Children's Facilities	5
Decor	4	Enjoyment Factor	5

The 3,114-passenger, 142,000-ton Voyager-class ships are an architectural marvel and mark many cruise ship firsts. They're currently the largest cruise ships in the world, rising over 200 feet above the sea and spreading 50 feet wider than any other passenger ship; they contain over 538,000 square feet of carpet and 15,000 chairs on their 17 decks, 14 of which are accessible to passengers; and they've got features you won't find anywhere else: believe it or not, a rock-climbing wall stuck to the side of the funnel, a full-size ice-skating rink featuring ice-ballet performances twice a night and skating for passengers at all other times, an outdoor in-line skating track (skates can be rented or you can bring your own), a wedding chapel, and a 1950s-style diner sitting right out on deck. As if that's not enough for you, there's also nine-hole miniature-golf courses, driving ranges, and golf simulators; regulation-size basketball, paddle-ball, and volleyball courts; and sprawling two-level gyms and spas. And did we mention they also have whopping three-story dining rooms, bars whose walls are aquariums filled with tropical fish (cool!), florist shops (you never know when you'll need a dozen roses), about 3 miles of public corridors (bring your walking shoes—it can feel like a real hike if you're walking from one end of the ship to the other), and a "peek-a-boo" bridge on Deck 11 that allows guests to watch the crew steering the ship?

What really sets these ships apart from any other passenger ship, though, are the four-story, boulevard-like promenades that run the length of four football fields from fore to aft, lined with shops, bars, cafes, and entertainment venues and anchored at each end by soaring 10-story atria. They provide a great place to people-watch, and weirdly enough, you can watch from your cabin if you want to: Three decks of inside cabins above the promenade have views from bay windows of the "street scene" below. The stroll-able feel they lend to the ships leads to our major conclusion: These vessels are a perfect compromise for couples who can't decide between a tropical cruise and a city experience. They may, in fact, be the first ships to really live up to the old "city at sea" cliché. Of course, they're more city than sea: Often, you can easily forget you're on the ocean.

And certainly enough people are aboard to warrant the comparison too: Each ship carries 3,114 guests at double occupancy, but since many staterooms have third and fourth berths, total capacity for each vessel can (and sometimes does) reach as high as 3,838. Remarkably, though, the ships never feel crowded. On our last sailing (on *Explorer*), we found many public rooms nearly empty during the day and didn't have to wait in line for anything all week, even though over 3,200 passengers were aboard. As we heard one woman comment to her companion, "I know there are 3,000 people on this ship, but where are they all?" Kudos go to the crew for efficiency, and also to Royal Caribbean for a design that not only features enough appealing public areas to diffuse crowds comfortably, but also encourages passenger foot traffic to flow in several different directions, rather than be funneled through one or two central hallways. This keeps crowding down and also means you don't tend to find yourself in the same spots day after day—it's entirely possible to be aboard for 6 days, turn a corner, and find yourself in a room you've never seen before.

A new Voyager-class sister, *Mariner of the Seas,* is scheduled to be launched in November 2003, long after this book goes to press.

Cabins & Rates

Cabins	Per Diems from	Sq. Ft.	Fridge	Hair Dryer	Sitting Area	TV
Inside	$93	160	yes	yes	no	yes
Outside	$114	173–180	yes	yes	some	yes
Suite	$393	277–1,188	yes	yes	yes	yes

CABINS   Voyager-class cabins are a vast improvement over the small cabins on the line's earlier ships, running 172 square feet for a standard ocean-view cabin (including balcony), and 160 square feet for an inside cabin. Still, bathrooms are on the cramped side, with little storage space, few amenities (soap and shampoo only), and only a thin sliver of counter, though there's more space out in the cabin on shelves above the desk. The cylindrical shower stalls, though tight for large-size people, have neat sliding doors that keep the water and warmth in. All cabins also have minifridges, safes, hair dryers (hidden in a drawer of the vanity and actually powerful enough to do their job), and TVs offering CNN, ESPN, Discovery, the Cartoon Network, and lots of pre-taped movies and sitcoms.

Of the 1,557 cabins, 939 have ocean views and 757 have verandas. There's one huge Penthouse Suite, 10 Owner's Suites, and 4 Royal Family Suites accommodating a total of eight people, with two bedrooms plus a living room with sofa bed and a pair of bathrooms. There are also smaller and cheaper family cabins with sitting areas and sofa beds, which sleep six. The superior and deluxe ocean-view cabins have balconies and sitting areas, many with sofa beds. As is the norm with Royal Caribbean, cabin color schemes are pastel-based and pleasant, but they're nothing innovative. (Thoughtfully rounded corners on the beds are appreciated, though.) For voyeurs, the 138 atrium cabins on the second, third, and fourth levels of the four-story Royal Promenade have windows facing the action below (and curtains and soundproofing to keep most of the light and noise out, when you want some downtime).

Connecting cabins are available. Twenty-six cabins are wheelchair accessible, as are all elevators.

PUBLIC AREAS   The bustling, four-story Royal Promenade provides a focus to each ship, running like Main Street down the length of the ship and designed to resemble Memphis's Beale Street or New Orleans's Bourbon Street. Like them, it's lined with shops, bars, and cafes, including an elegant champagne bar; a comfy Irish bar with "sidewalk" seating; a large sports bar that gets big, raucous crowds when games are broadcast (and puts out free hot dogs and nachos to keep them there); an arcade stocked with classic 1980s video games; a bright cafe that serves pizza, cookies, pastries, and coffee 24 hours a day; and a self-serve soft ice-cream station with lots of toppings. The ships' various musical groups perform along the promenade in the evenings, and on our last cruise the Tuesday-night concert was a major highlight, with the ship's big band presenting a set heavy on Glenn Miller tunes. As at Disney World, clowns, jugglers, and actors dressed as turn-of-the-century cops or 1930s cocktail waitresses and street cleaners also stroll about in the evening, entertaining and interacting with passengers.

Elsewhere in the bars-and-entertainment category, there are some 30 places aboard each ship to grab a drink, including the large Viking Crown nightclub, the golf-themed 19th Hole bar, and the elegant jazz club on the top decks; the dark, romantic, nautically themed Schooner Bar; and the clubby cigar bar, tucked away behind a dark door and hosting blackjack games on formal evenings. Aboard each ship, the gothic castle/dungeon-themed disco is entered though a theme-parky "secret passage," while the huge three-story showrooms occupy the opposite end of the kitsch spectrum: beautifully designed, with simple, elegant color schemes and truly lovely stage curtains, the one on *Adventure* decorated with peacock designs, the one on *Explorer* depicting a chorus of women standing under golden boughs, amid a rain of leaves.

Each ship has a two-story library-cum-computer-room with about 18 computer stations and Web cams that allow you to send your picture as an electronic postcard. There are also sprawling kids' areas with huge ocean-view playrooms, teen discos, and jumbo arcades with a pair of air-hockey tables mixed in among dozens of primarily shoot-'em-up video games. Families with science-minded kids will appreciate *Explorer*'s pair of working $1.5 million laboratories, where scientists from the University of Miami's Rosenstiel School of Marine & Atmospheric Science conduct research on wind patterns, water chemistry, UV and solar radiation, and air pollution via sensors attached to the ship's mast and hull. Over the course of each cruise, these scientists present talks on their research and show off their labs to passengers on organized free tours. Amusingly, cabin TVs have a channel that shows images from various cameras mounted around the ship. In the oceanography lab, the camera is mounted at a spot to which passengers eyes are drawn during their tour. It took us a minute to realize what we were seeing when we turned on the TV one day and were confronted with a group of people seemingly staring right at us, completely immobile for minutes on end.

The best spots for chilling out with a book during days at sea include the sea-view Seven of Hearts card room and Cloud Nine Lounge on Deck 14. Those *really* wanting to get away from people can retreat up the curving stairway to Deck 15's Skylight Chapel, which gets almost no traffic and is even free of piped-in music. (Though it also lacks windows.)

DINING OPTIONS   The three-level main dining rooms on these ships are among the most stunning and classy aboard any of today's megaships, with designs that follow a general European theme. Each level—linked by a large open area and grand staircase at its center—is considered a separate restaurant, though service and menus are consistent throughout. A pianist or piano trio entertains from a platform in the aft end of the room and a huge crystal chandelier hangs overhead, both setting an elegant mood.

For a dining alternative, the ocean-view Portofino restaurant serves Italian meals in a cozy setting (and at an additional $20 per person charge), but be sure to reserve a table as soon as you get aboard, as they book up fast.

The pleasant, spacious Island Grill and Windjammer casual buffet restaurants are joined into one large space but have separate lines and stations to keep things moving. There's no outdoor seating per se, but the ship's main pool area is on the same deck, just outside the restaurants' entrances.

Another casual option for lunch, dinner, and late-night snacks is the wildly popular Johnny Rockets, a 1950s-style diner set out on deck and offering burgers, shakes, fries, and the like, with an excellent veggie burger to satisfy non-meateaters. The international waitstaff is cute enough in their '50s-style soda-jerk clothes, but we could do without the cutesy lip-sync-and-dance routines to songs like "YMCA" and "Respect." Food is free, but shakes will cost you $3.60 a pop.

POOL, FITNESS & SPA FACILITIES   Each ship has a well-equipped ocean-view gym, though the arrangement of machines and the many pillars throughout give them a cramped feel when full. Each has a large indoor whirlpool and a huge aerobics studio (among the biggest on any ship), and their two-level spa complexes are among the largest and best accoutered at sea, with peaceful waiting areas where New Agey tropical-bird-song music induces total relaxation—until you get your bill. (Steiner, the company that manages spas aboard most cruise ships, keeps rates steep in 'em all.)

While crowds tend to disperse among the ships' myriad venues, on sunny days things can get tight out on the main pool decks, creating a kind of tenement-style sunbathing scene. As aboard Carnival's Destiny-class ships, deck chairs are squeezed into every level of the multistoried, amphitheater-like decks, and the vibe can be electric (or at least loud) when the pool band starts playing. Guests seeking something more peaceful can usually find it in the adjacent Solarium, with a second swimming pool and two enormous whirlpool tubs under a sliding roof that offers protection from inclement weather. Behind the Johnny Rockets diner, a kids' pool area has a water slide, wading pool, hot tub for adults, and dozens of adorable half-size deck chairs for the kids.

Deck 13 is the hub of sports action, with the much-touted rock-climbing wall, skating track, miniature-golf course, and basketball court. Appointments must be made to use the more popular options (especially the wall), but this is a good thing as it eliminates lines.

The Vision Class: Enchantment • Grandeur • Rhapsody • Splendour of the Seas

The Verdict

These ships are glitzy and exciting without going overboard, though they're on the frumpy side compared to the newer, snazzier Radiance- and Voyager-class ships.

Rhapsody of the Seas *(photo: RCCL)*

Specifications

Size (in tons)		Rhapsody	229
Splendour	69,130	Number of Passengers	
Grandeur	74,137	*Splendour*	1,804
Enchantment	74,137	*Grandeur*	1,950
Rhapsody	78,491	*Enchantment*	1,950
Number of Cabins		*Rhapsody*	2,000
Splendour	902	Officers	Norwegian/Int'l
Grandeur	975	Crew	International
Enchantment	975	*Splendour*	720
Rhapsody	1,000	*Grandeur*	760
Number of Outside Cabins		*Enchantment*	760
Splendour	575	*Rhapsody*	765
Grandeur	576	Passenger/Crew Ratio	2.5 to 1
Enchantment	576	Year Launched	
Rhapsody	593	*Splendour*	1996
Cabins with Verandas		*Grandeur*	1996
Splendour	231	*Enchantment*	1997
Grandeur	212	*Rhapsody*	1997
Enchantment	212	Last Major Refurbishment	N/A

Frommer's Ratings (Scale of 1–5)   ★★★½

Cabin Comfort & Amenities	3	Dining Options	3
Ship Cleanliness & Maintenance	4	Gym & Spa Facilities	4
Public Comfort/Space	4	Children's Facilities	4
Decor	3.5	Enjoyment Factor	4

From the incredible amounts of glass that give the ships their light (each contains about 2 acres of glass canopies, glass windbreaks, skylights, and floor-to-ceiling windows with sweeping views) to the colorful and whimsical artwork (though in some cases, dated and dusty) that livens every turn; from the high-tech, high-energy theaters and casinos to the dizzying number of entertainment options, these ships are pretty fine. The glitz and glass of the sun-filled atria, with white marble staircases that wind down to a landing and bandstand, are the first thing passengers see when coming aboard, and they set the tone for the rest of the cruise.

The ships are well designed with roomy public areas and a focus on important places such as the Solarium with its indoor pool and hot tubs and hushed ambience, the hoppin' multilevel disco, the well-equipped Internet center, and the sprawling outdoor decks where it's not difficult to find a quiet corner.

The six Vision-class vessels (including *Legend of the Seas,* which globe-trots in Alaska, Mexico and the South Pacific, and *Vision* which sails out of Los Angeles) evolved slightly over the 3 years between the first and latest, but for the most part they have similar features, though *Grandeur* and *Enchantment of the Seas,* for example, have more brassy-looking artwork and flashier, more metallic decorative themes than their sisters.

Cabins & Rates

Cabins	Per Diems from	Sq. Ft.	Fridge	Hair Dryer	Sitting Area	TV
Inside	$78	138–146	no	no	yes	yes
Outside	$93	153	some	no	yes	yes
Suite	$236	241–1,140	yes	no	yes	yes

CABINS   To be polite, cabins are "compact." Granted, they're noticeably larger than the cramped cubicles that were standard issue aboard the company's older ships (*Nordic Empress's* standard outside cabins, for instance, are a tiny butter-your-hips-to-get-in 122 sq. ft.), but they're still cramped when compared to the competition—37 to 52 feet smaller than Carnival's standard cabins, for example. For big, check out the Royal Suites on each of these ships—they measure a mammoth 1,150 square feet. They even have a grand piano and huge marble bathroom with double sinks, a big whirlpool bathtub, and a glass-enclosed shower for two. For something in between, the 190-square-foot category D cabins that take up most of an entire deck are roomy, with small sitting areas (with pullout couches), minifridges, and tons of storage space.

In keeping up with the Joneses of today's balcony-loving industry, nearly one-fourth of the cabins aboard each ship have private verandas. About a third can accommodate third and fourth passengers, too. Regardless of the ship you opt for, your cabin's color scheme will be awash in a sea of numbing beige and washed-out pastels that alternate with varnished hardwood trim.

All cabins have an impressive amount of storage space, safes, music channels, and TVs offering CNN, ESPN, Discovery, the Cartoon Network, and lots of pre-recorded movies and sitcoms. Bathrooms are not the largest you'll ever see, with shower stalls that are a tight squeeze for anyone thicker than a super model (though they do have a nice multilevel built-in shelf).

Connecting cabins are available. Each vessel has between 14 and 17 staterooms equipped for wheelchair users.

PUBLIC AREAS Warm woods and brass, gurgling fountains and green foliage, glass and crystal, buttery leathers, and eye-catching, if not flamboyant (and in some cases, plain old ugly), artwork and textures highlight the public areas. Some evoke a private Roman villa, others are deliberately glitzier and flashier, and different areas of the ships were designed to evoke different places in America—for example, a wine bar in New York or a gambling hall in Las Vegas.

The layout of the Promenade and Mariner decks—the main indoor public decks on each ship—allows for easy passage. Corridors are wide and bright. Focal points on the six ships are the soaring seven-story atria known as "Centrum." A sloped two-deck-high skylight crowns each. Glass elevators, a la Hyatt, take passengers up through Centrum into the stunning Viking Crown Lounge, a glass-sided aerie high above the waves. Accessorized with a superb sound-and-light system, it's high on everybody's list of favorite wave-watching and sightseeing spaces, especially during transits of the Panama Canal. The shopping arcade, Boutiques of the Centrum, is like a shipboard Fifth Avenue or Rodeo Drive, and is much more extensively stocked (and appealing to look at) than Carnival's Fantasy-class shopping complexes, which are cramped and off the beaten track.

The Schooner Bar, another Royal Caribbean signature, is a casual piano bar with lots of wood and rope, befitting its nautical name, and is a great place for a pre-dinner drink or late-night unwinding. Ditto the Champagne Terrace at the foot of the atrium. Listen and dance to a trio while sipping fine wine or a glass of bubbly.

In deliberate contrast to such massive showcase spaces, each ship contains many hideaway refuges, including an array of cocktail bars, a library, and card rooms. Hundreds of potted plants and more than 3,000 original artworks (though some tired and dusty) aboard each ship add humanity and warmth.

Full musical revues are staged in glittery, two-story showrooms, where columns obstruct views from some balcony seats. Each has an orchestra pit that can be raised and lowered hydraulically to provide dramatic effects during cabaret shows. The ship's casinos are Vegas-style flashy and consciously over-accessorized with hundreds of gambling stations so densely packed that it's sometimes difficult to move and always difficult to hear.

DINING OPTIONS The large dining rooms aboard the vessels span two decks and are interconnected with a very grand staircase and flanked with walls of glass nearly 20 feet high. Each has a decor that's contemporary and tasteful (somewhat reminiscent of a banquet hall), replete with lots of stainless steel, mirrors, and dramatic chandeliers. A pianist plays at a grand piano throughout dinner service. Like the rest of the fleet, the Vision-class ships have a large indoor/outdoor buffet restaurant called Windjammer, serving breakfast, lunch, and dinner.

POOL, FITNESS & SPA FACILITIES The Steiner-managed ShipShape Spas on these ships are some of the most attractive around, giving soothing respite from the hubbub of ship life. They offer a wide selection of treatments as well as the standard steam rooms and saunas. Adjacent to the spas are spacious Solariums, each with a pool, lounge chairs, floor-to-ceiling windows, and a retractable glass ceiling. These bright, comfortable spots, each with an inventive design motif (for example, Roman, Egyptian, or Moorish), are a peaceful place to lounge before or after a spa treatment, or any time at all. The gyms are surprisingly small and cramped considering the ships' size, and don't compare to those on Carnival's, Holland America's, and Celebrity's megaliners.

Each ship has a higher-than-expected amount of open deck space. One of the most dramatic is the Sun Deck, which manages to incorporate two swimming pools (one covered by a retractable glass roof), whirlpools, and the Windjammer buffet-style restaurant. There's usually blaring rah-rah music by the pool, along with silly contests of the belly-flop genre, which most passengers seem to love dearly. A jogging track, shuffleboard, and Ping-Pong round out the on-deck options, and Royal Caribbean's new signature rock-climbing walls are scheduled to be installed by year-end 2003.

Majesty of the Seas

The Verdict

This ship is huge, and while she definitely feels dated compared to her spiffy new Voyager- and Radiance-class sisters, she manages to maintain an easygoing style, with her light color scheme and spread-out public areas.

Majesty of the Seas *(photo: RCCL)*

Specifications

Size (in tons)	73,941	Officers	Norwegian/Int'l
Number of Cabins	1,177	Crew	825 (Internat'l)
Number of Outside Cabins	732	Passenger/Crew Ratio	2.9 to 1
Cabins with Verandas	62	Year Launched	1992
Number of Passengers	2,354	Last Major Refurbishment	N/A

Frommer's Ratings (Scale of 1–5)   ★★★½

Cabin Comfort & Amenities	3	Dining Options	2
Ship Cleanliness & Maintenance	4	Gym & Spa Facilities	3
Public Comfort/Space	4	Children's Facilities	4
Decor	4	Enjoyment Factor	3

This ship, and her mirror-image twin *Monarch of the Seas,* which sails to Mexico from Los Angeles and is not reviewed in this edition, was built in western France in 1992. She has a clean and distinguished profile and interior, and a dazzling lineup of public spaces spread out over her 14 passenger decks. Decor-wise, she's dated in a parachute-pants-wearing, big-haired, 1980s kind of way, with more brass, chrome, and neon than the newer RCI ships. All in all, though, the *Majesty* works just fine for the short itineraries she operates.

Cabins & Rates

Cabins	Per Diems from	Sq. Ft.	Fridge	Hair Dryer	Sitting Area	TV
Inside	$62	120	no	no	no	yes
Outside	$72	120	some	no	some	yes
Suite	$324	382–670	yes	no	yes	yes

CABINS   The worst feature of much of the RCI fleet—tiny cabins—is no less in evidence on this ship. Standard cabins, scattered over nine decks, average a way-too-snug 120 square feet. Bathrooms aren't much better in the size department. In 62 of the outside cabins, the cramped feeling is somewhat relieved by verandas. More than 100 cabins have upper and lower berths in order to house four, albeit quite tightly. Suites are larger, of course, and moderately more comfortable than the standard cabins. The Royal Suites and the Owner's Suites are significantly larger. All cabins sport Royal Caribbean's signature pastel fabrics and blond woods, and have safes, music channels, and TVs offering CNN, ESPN, Discovery, the Cartoon Network, and lots of pre-recorded movies and sitcoms.

Connecting cabins are available. Four cabins on each ship can accommodate wheelchair users.

PUBLIC AREAS   Public areas—including one of the largest casinos afloat—are wisely clustered aft of the atrium to minimize noise in the forward section of the ships, where most cabins are located. Broadway musicals and Hollywood films inspired the names and decor of most rooms: the Brigadoon dining room, the Ain't Misbehavin' Nightclub, the A Chorus Line Lounge, the April in Paris Lounge, and so on. Although this is a monstrous ship, she's so well designed that passengers don't seem to get lost very often; and only when you find yourself standing in long lines (or taking the stairs instead of the elevators to the Viking Crown Lounge, or strolling the wraparound Promenade Deck) do you realize just how big she is.

A dramatic five-story atrium, with a color scheme that glows in a metallic shade of either bronze or champagne, is the ship's interior focal point. A sweeping staircase curves down onto the ground floor and makes for a grand scene. Up on the topmost deck, some 150 feet above sea level, sits the glass-enclosed Viking Crown Lounge, clearly the ship's signature piece with its amazing panoramic views. It's a great place for a pre-dinner drink and the place to go to dance into the wee hours. The ship also has a host of other bars and cubbyholes scattered throughout.

There's an impressive Internet center off the atrium, open 24 hours a day, as well as a paneled library, a massive two-story showroom with lots of tiered seating, and a large shopping court with a variety of souvenir and clothing shops.

The kids' facilities are sizable, with a separate ocean-view teen disco, video arcade, and children's playroom all aft on the Sun Deck.

DINING OPTIONS   The ship has two one-story main dining rooms, as well as a large indoor/outdoor buffet restaurant, all serving breakfast, lunch, and dinner. They're pleasant enough, but not nearly as grand or elegant as the dining rooms on the Vision-, Voyager-, and Radiance-class ships.

POOL, FITNESS & SPA FACILITIES   Two good-size swimming pools, each ringed with lounge chairs, are located on the Sports Deck. Looking at this space when it's empty, you'd think there's all the room in the world, but when the ship is full, the rows of sunbathers resemble sardines in a tin.

The gym is fairly spacious, with a wall of windows facing aft. The spa has a handful of massage and treatment rooms offering a wide range of treatments, as well as separate saunas for men and women. In size and style, though, it can't hold a candle to the spas on the Vision-, Voyager-, and Radiance-class ships. Other sports and fitness facilities include an unobstructed jogging track, a basketball court, shuffleboard, Ping-Pong, and Royal Caribbean's new signature rock-climbing walls, scheduled to be installed by year-end 2003.

Nordic Empress

The Verdict

This midsize ship is an appealing, easy-to-navigate package. Public rooms are well laid out and the decor is just glittery enough to keep the mood festive.

Nordic Empress *(photo: RCCL)*

Specifications

Size (in tons)	48,563	Officers	Scandinavian
Number of Cabins	800	Crew	671 (Internat'l)
Number of Outside Cabins	471	Passenger/Crew Ratio	2.4 to 1
Cabins with Verandas	69	Year Launched	1990
Number of Passengers	1,600	Last Major Refurbishment	N/A

Frommer's Ratings (Scale of 1–5)   ✮✮✮½

Cabin Comfort & Amenities	3	Dining Options	3.5
Ship Cleanliness & Maintenance	4	Gym & Spa Facilities	3
Public Comfort/Space	4	Children's Facilities	4
Decor	4	Enjoyment Factor	4

This once-hefty 48,000-ton vessel looks small when compared to the megaships forming the rest of Royal Caribbean's modern fleet. Originally intended to sail for Admiral Cruises, a now-defunct subsidiary of Royal Caribbean during its early days, *Nordic Empress* was retained by Royal Caribbean to serve the 3- and 4-day cruise market, for which the ship was specifically created (which may explain her very small cabins); today though, she spends winters doing 7-night Caribbean cruises and summer doing weeklong voyages to Bermuda. She's an attractive ship and is consistently flooded with sunlight from big windows, which dominate most of the ship's stern, and a thoughtful layout makes it easy to navigate throughout. On the downside, she has all the brass, chrome, and neon to prove her 1980s pedigree; and after more than a decade of nonstop service, there's no hiding some rough edges, such as the tired-looking atrium fountain sculpture, which has become a little yellowed.

Cabins & Rates

Cabins	Per Diems from	Sq. Ft.	Fridge	Hair Dryer	Sitting Area	TV
Inside	$53	130	no	no	no	yes
Outside	$68	130	no	no	some	yes
Suite	$203	194–596	yes	no	yes	yes

CABINS   Cabins are small at not more than an embarrassing 130 square feet, equivalent in size and amenities to those aboard *Sovereign, Majesty,* and *Monarch.* Drawer and closet space is limited, and you may find yourself just keeping some things in your suitcase. As aboard most of the fleet, inside cabins are arranged in mazelike clusters that can make finding your cabin a challenge, at least at the beginning of a cruise.

Although small, the cabins are carefully designed, which makes them seem more livable. A large number of them are inside, however, and are downright claustrophobic, practically guaranteeing that passengers will spend more time on deck or in public areas. Bathrooms are cramped and showers coffinlike, though there's a surprisingly good amount of storage space in them. Upper-end cabins and suites have verandas; outside cabins without them offer rectangular picture windows. Even if you upgrade to one of the smaller suites, you won't gain that much additional elbow room, although amenities are better and locations within the vessel are more convenient.

All cabins have safes, music channels, and TVs offering CNN, ESPN, Discovery, the Cartoon Network, and lots of pre-taped movies and sitcoms. Though clean, on a recent visit the cabins showed some wear and tear, including stained carpeting and scuffed and peeling furniture.

Connecting cabins are available. Four cabins are wheelchair accessible.

PUBLIC AREAS   Considering the relatively small size of this vessel, the inclusion of a six-deck atrium was an astonishing design choice. Light floods in from above and from big windows flanking five decks on either side, and a splashing fountain is ringed with tropical plants and artwork based on Nordic themes.

Nordic Empress boasts her own version of Royal Caribbean's signature Viking Crown Lounge and disco. Positioned at the ship's stern like all the others and sitting 11 stories above the waterline, this version is unique because of its two-story, barrel-like shape. It's wrapped in windows and the tiny pencil-point star-like lights in the ceiling create a neat scene in the evenings, when the place is dark and the music is rocking. With a relatively mellow and unjarring decor in spite of its 1980s-style chrome and mauve motif, the ship's spacious three-level casino is a roomy place to while away the evening, and offers cozier places to play than on most ships.

The two-story Strike Up the Band Showroom is very Atlantic City and very, very pink, while the Carousel Pub is covered in dark mauve and centered around, you guessed it, a carousel theme. In all, there are five bars, three entertainment lounges, a disco, a video-game room, a playroom, and a conference area.

DINING OPTIONS   The ship's attractive two-level dining room is surrounded by windows, and its center is a dramatic sweeping staircase. There's also Royal Caribbean's signature indoor/outdoor buffet-style restaurant, the nautically inspired Windjammer, serving breakfast, lunch, and dinner for those who want to avoid the more formal main restaurant.

POOL, FITNESS & SPA FACILITIES   On the Sun Deck, where virtually everything seems to happen, there are three hot tubs, a generous swimming pool fed by a fountain, a wading pool for children, and enough shady spots to get a break from the sun. When the sun goes down, the Sun Deck transforms from sunbathing space into a starlit dance floor. The fountain, a gazebo, and sail-like canopies create a cozy, almost clubby ambience.

Although the ship's exercise area isn't the largest at sea, it's got floor-to-ceiling windows and enough equipment to satisfy most users. There's a sauna, plus massage, and the ship has an unobstructed jogging track. Royal Caribbean's new signature—the rock-climbing wall—is scheduled to be installed by year-end 2003.

Sovereign of the Seas

Sovereign of the Seas *(photo: RCCL)*

The Verdict

A trendsetter in its heyday, this ship is now dated, but she still promises and delivers action-packed, ultracasual (shorts and jeans in the dining room at night are common) 3- and 4-night cruises for the whole family.

Specifications

Size (in tons)	73,192	Officers	Norwegian
Number of Cabins	1,138	Crew	840 (Internat'l)
Number of Outside Cabins	722	Passenger/Crew Ratio	2.7 to 1
Cabins with Verandas	0	Year Launched	1988
Number of Passengers	2,276	Last Major Refurbishment	1997

Frommer's Ratings (Scale of 1–5)   ☆☆☆

Cabin Comfort & Amenities	3	Dining Options	2
Ship Cleanliness & Maintenance	4	Gym & Spa Facilities	3
Public Comfort/Space	3	Children's Facilities	4
Decor	4	Enjoyment Factor	3

When she was launched in 1988, *Sovereign of the Seas* was the largest passenger vessel built during the previous 50 years and the largest cruise ship in history. Today, in terms of gross tonnage, she's only slightly more than half the size of her giant fleetmates, *Voyager, Explorer, Adventure,* and *Navigator of the Seas.* Talk about the march of progress (or at least size).

Like her 1980s contemporaries, *Sovereign* is pretty dated in comparison to the swank newcomers in the industry, and has her share of bumps and bruises accumulated from her hectic year-round 3- and 4-night cruise schedule. Plus, we've noticed that on ships doing these pack-in-the-partying short runs, the crew tends to slack off a bit in areas like cleanliness (discarded straw wrappers and soda cans, for instance, seem to linger longer on tables and by chaise longues).

Cabins & Rates

Cabins	Per Diems from	Sq. Ft.	Fridge	Hair Dryer	Sitting Area	TV
Inside	$59	120	no	no	no	yes
Outside	$66	120–157	no	no	some	yes
Suite	$304	382–670	yes	no	yes	yes

CABINS   Light, pastel colors try to make the cabins appear larger than they are, but there's no disguising their paltry 120-square-foot size—put four family members or friends in there (as is pretty common) and it's like camping in a pup tent. The 84 larger staterooms on the Commodore Deck are roomier at 157 square feet, and the dozen top suites range up to 670 square feet; none have balconies.

Overall, cabin decor is spartan and uninspired, relatively clean, but worn. Cabins have limited storage space (remember, though, this ship's itineraries are only 3 and 4 nights long, so you won't be carrying much) but do have TVs offering CNN, ESPN, Discovery, the Cartoon Network, and lots of pre-taped movies and sitcoms. Cabin categories R, A, B, C, and D have personal safes; for everyone else, there are lockboxes at the purser's desk. Nice adjustable reading lamps are above each bed. All cabins on the Mariner Deck have views obstructed by lifeboats, and you can see the tops of these same boats from the windows of all cabins on the Commodore Deck.

Soundproofing isn't the greatest; in some cabins, you can hear every word your neighbors say above a whisper. Cabin bathrooms have seen better days, unless you don't mind rickety soap dishes, leaky showers, and peeling caulking around the tub. But, hey, ships relegated to the rough-and-tumble 3- and 4-night cruise route are subjected to more wear and tear, and you can tell (even the crew often seems more worn down on short cruises).

Connecting cabins are available. Six cabins are wheelchair accessible.

PUBLIC AREAS   Public areas are clustered toward the stern, with cabins mainly in the forward half of the ship, an arrangement that creates the illusion that this large vessel is more intimate than she is. A wide-open, crowd-friendly, five-story atrium connects most of the public areas; and there are four huge spaces (including the casino) for after-dinner entertainment, a layout that keeps any one area from getting too crowded. A collection of well-laid-out shops is grouped around the atrium.

The two-story, main show-lounge, Follies, is roomy and well planned, with lots of cocktail-table-and-chair clusters for two and a huge stage. Sightlines are good except from parts of the balcony. There are two other large nightclubs for dancing and live music, plus Royal Caribbean's nightlife trademark, the panoramic Viking Crown Lounge and disco encircling the smokestack 14 stories above sea level. The popular Schooner piano bar is located next to the sprawling, glitzy, chrome-covered, pink-themed casino (whose noise you can hear from the edge of the Schooner). You'll find these lounges, like the entire ship, populated by people wearing everything from cutoff shorts and flip-flops to nice dresses and suits. It's a real mixed bag.

The children's play area is downright huge, although a bit on the spartan side. There's a separate, and also extremely large, teen center and disco, as well as a third space for younger kids and a video arcade with about a dozen machines.

A very impressive computer nook on the Main Deck, adjacent to the purser's desk, has 12 computers equipped with Web cams that allow you to send e-mail postcards of yourself.

DINING OPTIONS   The ship offers a pair of one-story dining rooms that are pleasant enough, but a bit banquet-hall looking compared to the warm and elegant two- and three-story rooms on the line's newer ships. Also, the two-level Windjammer Cafe, with limited seating outside on a wedge of jarring green AstroTurf deck, is far forward on the Sun Deck, away from the pool.

POOL, FITNESS & SPA FACILITIES   The deck layout and two good-size swimming pools are stylish and impressive when they're empty, but the large number of passengers aboard this ship almost guarantees that they'll fill up, becoming a wall-to-wall carpet of people. Anyone have a shoehorn so we can wedge ourselves into one of those two hot tubs?

That said, there are many patches of more isolated deck space all over the ship, from the quiet slices of tiered aft deck to two levels of far-forward deck space, many spots sporting a profusion of live plants (there's a full-time plant caretaker on board). Lounge-flopping sunbathers beware: The beach towels on this ship are hand-towel size.

The Sports Deck, up high in the stern, has six Ping-Pong tables, a pair of golf putting greens, and, one deck above, basketball. The half-moon-shaped gym is bright and has floor-to-ceiling windows. Treadmills, stationary bikes, step machines, and free weights line the perimeter of the room, facing the sea, and the inner part of the room serves as the aerobics space. The adjacent spa and the gym are wedged between the Sports Deck above and the engine room below, which was not the smartest design move: A masseuse told us that when the ship pulls out of port, the massage tables vibrate and the tranquillity of the spa is disrupted. (Heidi had one of her best massages at sea on *Sovereign,* but it was while the ship was docked.)

A rock-climbing wall—Royal Caribbean's signature sports facility these days—is scheduled to be installed by year-end 2003.

10 Royal Olympia Cruises

805 Third Ave., New York, NY 10022-7513. © **800/872-6400** or 212/397-6400. Fax 888/662-6237. www.royalolympiacruises.com.

THE LINE IN A NUTSHELL This Greek line's ships generally stick to the Mediterranean, but its two newest vessels offer Caribbean, Panama Canal, and Mexico/Central America cruises, plus sailings in and around South America. It's a little touch of Greece among the Caribbean's palms and white-sand beaches, and a more destination- and learning-oriented experience than is available from any of the other mainstream lines.

THE EXPERIENCE Like mini-versions of today's megaships, the high-speed, 840-passenger sister ships *Olympia Voyager* and *Olympia Explorer* offer an almost megaship-style variety of entertainment options, activities, and cabin choices, yet stand apart with itineraries that visit more remote ports and onboard enrichment programs that are the best of any mainstream line in the Caribbean. The ships have a top speed of 28 knots (versus 22–24 for most megaships) and offer a more casual, low-key experience. Theme itineraries are offered throughout the year, including several that visit Mayan sites on the equinox, and others that are built around solar eclipses. Maya-themed cruises visit Mayan sites in Honduras, Guatemala, Belize, and Mexico's Yucatán Peninsula, and have archaeologists and historians aboard to lead discussions.

Pros

- **Cultural and scientific enrichment programs:** These comprehensive learning programs are the major factor distinguishing the *Olympia Voyager* and *Explorer* from the competition.
- **Well-organized and diverse shore excursions:** Between two and nine excursions are available at every port (four is about average), with some devoted to sites of historic or cultural interest and others to snorkeling and/or beach excursions.
- **Among the fastest ships afloat:** With a max speed of 28 knots, these ships are able to reach more distant ports than your average megaships.

Cons

- **Paltry fitness facilities:** Don't expect much in the working-out department: You can count the machines on one hand.

Compared with the other mainstream lines, here's how ROC rates:

	Poor	Fair	Good	Excellent	Outstanding
Enjoyment Factor				✓	
Dining			✓		
Activities				✓	
Children's Program	N/A*				
Entertainment			✓		
Service				✓	
Worth the Money				✓	

* Royal Olympia offers no children's program in the Caribbean.

ROYAL OLYMPIA: SPANAKOPITA, ANYONE?

Royal Olympia—named Royal Olympic until the International Olympic Committee went bonkers and accused the line of copyright infringement (can we say "petty"?)—was formed in 1995 through a merger of two Greek cruise lines, Sun Line and Epirotiki Cruises. Today, it's controlled primarily by Cyprus-based Louis Tourist Agency Ltd., which also operates another cruise line, hotels, and retail stores.

Known through the '90s for operating older, secondhand ships such as the much-beloved *Stella Solaris* (which was the line's only vessel in the Caribbean for many years), Royal Olympia headed in a new direction in 2000 by launching the sleek, high-speed *Olympia Voyager,* with sister ship *Olympia Explorer* debuting in late 2002 after long delays arising from disputes between the cruise line and the German shipyard.

PASSENGER PROFILE

Royal Olympia's passengers have, over the years, been primarily well-traveled senior couples, many of whom have sailed with the line before. The *Voyager* and *Explorer* are designed to attract a wider and generally younger group in the 35 to 55 range, though their longer itineraries almost guarantee that they're filled with time-rich retirees. Summers and holidays, you'll see families with kids on board.

DINING

Due to their relatively small size, *Voyager* and *Explorer* lack the multiple specialty restaurants that are all the rage on larger ships, sticking instead with a more traditional arrangement, with passengers taking all their meals in the main dining room or having a more casual breakfast and lunch (and sometimes dinner, on long tour days) in the buffet-style Lido Café. Lunches in the dining room are full five-course affairs, and dinner menus offer three continental entrees plus spa cuisine (low cholesterol, reduced salt), Pacific Rim cuisine, and a special **Mediterranean vegetarian menu** that offers a full range of Greek-influenced appetizers and main courses, such as *bourekakia* (pastries filled with aubergine and Greek cheese) and meatless *moussaka* (sliced, layered aubergine, potato, and zucchini with tomato, onion, and herbs, topped with cream sauce and baked). Lunch and dinner menus both usually offer **Greek specialties** such as *arnaki psito* (roasted lamb marinated with island spices), *sfyrida all spetsiota* (baked sea bass in tomatoes with potatoes), and *spanakopita* (spinach pie). **Dessert** includes Mediterranean favorites such as *galaktoboureko* (custard wrapped in phyllo pastry) and baklava (layered phyllo with honey-nut syrup), plus a sugar-free dessert and an assortment of domestic and international cheeses and fresh fruit.

The Lido Café offers an early-riser's coffee and danish, a buffet breakfast and lunch (with the usual fare for breakfast and salads, cold cuts, sandwiches, several meat and fish dishes, and various desserts at lunch), coffee and tea 24 hours a day, and a late-night buffet from 11pm to midnight.

Both ships also offer a **poolside pasta bar** and a **casual grill and pizza bar.** Daily **afternoon tea** and pastries are available, buffet-style, in both ships' casual dining areas, and a more formal afternoon tea, with piano accompaniment, is served in the observation lounge.

ACTIVITIES

At the top of the activity list is the line's top-notch **enrichment program,** with experts sailing aboard Mayaribbean and South American sailings, offering commentary and leading a series of **lectures** (many with accompanying slide presentations), **round-table discussions** (with audience participation), and **documentary film** presentations. Lecturers on archaeology, astronomy, geology, zoology, history, and diplomacy are chosen to complement each sailing, with some well-known names filling the list, including Captain Loren McIntyre, discoverer of the source of the Amazon River; engineer, political scientist, and historian Dr. Sergei Khrushchev, son of former Soviet premier Nikita Khrushchev; and astronaut M. Scott Carpenter, who flew the second American manned orbital flight in 1962. Passengers are encouraged to interact with the lecturers, both at the formal presentations and informally during the course of the cruise. Aboard select sailings, a **Seafaring Gourmet program** features culinary demonstrations by guest chefs (such as André Soltner of New York's Lutèce restaurant and the French Culinary Institute) and wine tastings and food-pairing seminars led by members of *Wine Enthusiast* magazine's editorial staff and tasting panel.

Extensive reading material in the form of pamphlets, maps, diagrams, and reprints of articles is provided at the beginning of the cruise to supplement the lectures and discussions. Throughout the cruise, additional printed material is distributed, and books written by the lecturers are sometimes available for sale. **Excursions** are offered that complement the cruise theme; for example, trips to key Mayan sites depart from most ports on the Maya regions itineraries.

Other cultural and science-related activities offered during the cruise may include classical piano or guitar concerts, stargazing sessions at night, and gatherings at sunset to search for "the green flash," an atmospheric phenomenon that occurs just after sunset.

In addition to the enrichment programs, the ships offer such leisure activities as arts-and-crafts classes, wine tastings, Ping-Pong and shuffleboard tournaments, dance instruction, perfume seminars, bingo, and hair, beauty, and massage demonstrations. Those who want to limber up in the mornings can participate in various exercise sessions, including group walk-a-mile workouts around the deck, stretching classes, and low-impact aerobics.

Both ships have modern discos on their top decks.

CHILDREN'S PROGRAM

A low-key children's program is operated whenever 10 or more children are aboard, as well as on all summertime and holiday sailings, when you'll naturally find the highest number of kids. Programming is dependent on the amount of free time spent aboard ship—most Royal Olympia itineraries are destination-intensive, so there's not a lot of downtime that needs filling up—and may include children's movies, pizza parties, and games.

Babysitting is not officially offered, but it can be arranged privately with onboard staff.

ENTERTAINMENT

Twice nightly, a troupe of singers and dancers performs in one of the lounges, joined occasionally by a comedian, a magician, and/or a guest musician such as

Royal Olympia Fleet Itineraries

Ship	Itineraries
Olympia Explorer	**12-night Panama Canal:** Port Canaveral to Los Angeles, Nov 25, 2003, visiting San Andres (Columbia), Colón and Balboa (Panama), Puntarenas (Costa Rica), Acapulco, Puerto Vallarta, Mazatlan, and Cabo San Lucas (Mexico), with 5 days at sea, including a full crossing of the Canal. **Non-Caribbean Itineraries:** Europe, Hawaii, South and Central America.
Olympia Voyager	**16-night Amazon:** Round-trip from Fort Lauderdale, Dec 2003–Jan 2004, visiting Tortola (BVIs), Barbados, Trinidad, St. Thomas, Puerto Ordaz (Venezuela), Devil's Island (French Guyana), and Macapa Pilot Station, Boca da Valeria, Manaus, and Santaram (Brazil), with 5 days at sea, including cruising days on the Amazon and Orinoco Rivers. **15-night Panama Canal:** Round-trip from Fort Lauderdale, Dec 2003–Jan 2004, visiting San Andres (Columbia), Colón, Balboa, and the San Blas Islands (Panama), Puntarenas (Costa Rica), Acapulco and Cozumel (Mexico), and Belize, with 7 days at sea, including 2 Canal crossings. **7-night W. Carib:** Round-trip from Fort Lauderdale, Jan only, visiting Cozumel, Playa del Carmen, and Progreso (Mexico), Roatan (Honduras), Belize, and Santo Tomas de Castilla (Guatemala). **Non-Caribbean Itineraries:** Panama Canal repositioning cruises, Hawaii, Europe.

pianists Michael Fennelly or Roger Rundle, lyric soprano Stephani Bissinger, or guitarist Jonathan Sargent. At some ports, **local entertainers** are invited on board to perform—in Honduras, there may be a children's folk dance troupe; in Cozumel, a mariachi band.

Greek-flavored musical entertainment is provided at poolside during lunchtime and some evenings. A Greek violin and piano duo also performs during daily afternoon tea and in the dining room at night, where they often move from table to table playing Greek tunes. On **Greek Night,** held once per 7-night cruise, the crew and many of the passengers dress in the blue and white colors of the Greek flag. Festivities begin at sunset with an ouzo party in the Lido Café accompanied by bouzouki music, followed by a dinner featuring a five-course, all-Greek meal. The evening culminates with a gala celebration featuring the ship's various entertainers along with members of the crew. At the conclusion of the show, passengers are invited to come onstage and dance.

SERVICE

Royal Olympia's Greek dining-room staff tends to stay with the line longer than is normal with other ships, and it shows in their fast and efficient service and in a level of pampering greater than one would expect on a moderately priced cruise. For instance, in the buffet restaurant and during the dining room's buffet breakfast, waiters will carry passengers' trays to their tables.

Butler service is part of the deal when you book *Explorer's* and *Voyager's* top-of-the-line Sky Suites. They'll make spa and shore excursion appointments, serve breakfast and lunch en suite, arrange private cocktail parties, and generally satisfy guests' every whim.

Voyager and *Explorer* both offer **laundry and pressing services,** but no dry cleaning or self-service laundries.

Olympia Voyager • Olympia Explorer

The Verdict

Stylish, souped-up, modern (if small-ish) cruise ships for people who want to pair great, port-intensive itineraries and learning opportunities with a casual cruise experience.

Olympia Voyager *(photo: Matt Hannafin)*

Specifications

Size (in tons)	25,000	Officers	Greek
Number of Cabins	418	Crew	360 (Internat'l)
Number of Outside Cabins	292	Passenger/Crew Ratio	2.3 to 1
Cabins with Verandas		Year Launched	
Voyager	12	*Voyager*	2000
Explorer	24	*Explorer*	2002
Number of Passengers	836	Last Major Refurbishment	N/A

Frommer's Ratings (Scale of 1–5)   ★★★★

Cabin Comfort & Amenities	4	Dining Options	3.5
Ship Cleanliness & Maintenance	5	Gym & Spa Facilities	2
Public Comfort/Space	4	Children's Facilities	N/A
Decor	4	Enjoyment Factor	4

The debut of *Voyager* in June 2000 signaled a new phase for Royal Olympia, which has been known for adventurous itineraries, excellent service, and wonderful enrichment programs, but also for its fleet of older, creakier, secondhand ships. By contrast, *Voyager* and sister *Explorer*, which debuted in 2002 after many delays, are new, new, new, from their sleek, high-tech hull design and propulsion system to their bright, modern interiors, designed by the people behind many of the beautiful rooms aboard Celebrity's ships. Additionally, it's obvious that the ships were designed with the North American market in mind—all ship signs are in English, which is also the language of choice on board. Even the ships' names on their bows are in English.

    Voyager and *Explorer* are two of the fastest passenger ships currently sailing, able to reach up near 30 knots, which makes them ideal for the kind of far-flung itineraries in which the line specializes. On one of its first sailings, a short hop out of Athens into the Greek islands, *Voyager* hit 29.5 knots and passed three ships that had left the port of Piraeus hours ahead of it. We sat in the stern, watching the three huge plumes of water churned up behind us, then had to be careful not to lose our hats to the wind when we walked up to the bow. These are speedy ships. The downside? When leaving port, expect some vibration in the stern.

Cabins & Rates

Cabins	Per Diems from	Sq. Ft.	Fridge	Hair Dryer	Sitting Area	TV
Inside	$152	140	yes	yes	no	yes
Outside	$197	140	yes	yes	no	yes
Suite	$427	215–258	yes	yes	yes	yes

CABINS   Call them "cruise ship modern," and very much in the same smooth style as that found aboard many modern megaships. All are decorated in light wood tones countered by stark, appealingly minimalist white walls hung with abstract paintings. Standard cabins, at about 140 square feet, are not huge but are well laid out and provide better style and more amenities than those aboard many comparably sized ships. They have huge floor-to-ceiling mirrors that make them seem airier than they really are, plus safes, TVs, minifridges, and a good amount of well-designed storage space—essential on the long itineraries the ships sometimes follow—with nifty sliding shoe racks and sock bins. Bathrooms are smallish but smartly designed. Inside staterooms are comparable with standard outsides, sans natural light.

Voyager offers only 12 veranda cabins, which are designated as Deluxe Sky Suites and measure 258 square feet, plus a huge 117-square-foot balcony. Sixteen 215-square-foot Bay Window Suites offer a nice seating area in a bay window that allows views down the length of the ship and, owing to the ship's speed and the cabins' windy position toward the bow, are probably a better idea than balconies. Still, on *Explorer* they were replaced by 215-square-foot balcony cabins with 50-square-foot verandas. All suites have a sitting area, a teensy bathtub (knees up!), and great modern art that echoes the pieces elsewhere on the ships. Deluxe Sky Suites have a nice Japanese-looking lattice screen between the beds' "pillow area" and the windows.

Cabins in the stern on the Venus and Dionysius decks (Decks 3 and 4) get some vibration and noise when the ships get up to speed, but not more so than that on the average slower ship. On *Voyager*, the two aft-most cabins on Deck 3 are two-room affairs that are perfect for families; the second room, though without windows, has a convertible couch that sleeps two. *Explorer* has a similar pair of family cabins on Deck 2 forward.

There are no connecting cabins and no cabins specifically designated for single passengers. Four cabins are wheelchair accessible.

PUBLIC AREAS   In its whole history up till now, Royal Olympia's fleet has consisted exclusively of old, classic-style ships, which generally were built to offer roomy public areas—a must when passengers were cooped up inside during cold Atlantic crossings. Perhaps it was this history that informed the design of *Voyager* and *Explorer*, which offer some startlingly spacious interiors considering the ships' overall smallish size. The central area of the main entertainment deck offers a nice, airy piano bar, two small shops, a card room, and a library (with three e-mail/Internet-enabled computer stations on *Explorer* only), all opening off a winding, open corridor that in some places has pillars rather than walls as the only boundary between it and the public rooms, adding to the open feeling. Stairs leading between decks have two inspiring Greece-themed poems adorning their walls.

A disco is perched on each ship's topmost deck, and is a fairly standard circular observation-lounge-by-day, tea-in-the-afternoon, disco-by-night kind of room, filled with small swiveling chairs that look like they should shoot up on little pistons when you sit in them, but don't. One level below is a single-level main lounge where small-scale revues and music and magic acts are staged. Each ship's casino is split into two small sections on each side of the small, two-level reception atrium, one side with about 40 slot machines and the other with four poker tables, roulette, and a bar. A comfortable Cigar Room rounds out the public room offerings, with great recliner-like couches and a scattering of chairs mixed with a faux fireplace and incongruous modern art that nevertheless works well with the design.

Although there's a small children's playroom on the brochure deck plan, don't expect much: It's actually a multipurpose room that's converted to a bare-bones playroom only if more than 10 kids are on board.

DINING OPTIONS   In the main dining room, romantic couples should try to wrangle one of the tables for two in the stern, flanking the captain's table. They're great, romantic spots, giving a real panorama of the ship's wake. At the opposite end of the dining spectrum, a pizza station near the pool up on deck serves good personal pies, breads, and light salads, while the adjacent bar has Amstel on tap. One deck below is the buffet restaurant, open for breakfast, lunch, and late-night snacks, with a small but wonderful outdoor seating area that offers a view of the ship's wake.

POOL, FITNESS & SPA FACILITIES   Honesty is the best policy: These ships were not designed for hardcore sports and fitness folks. Their gyms are very small and not terribly pretty, with only three windows. Exercise equipment consists of two treadmills, one step machine, four weight machines (two in a separate, grim, windowless area), a small selection of free weights, and a sauna and Turkish bath.

Small spas, just next to the gyms, are run by the Greek spa company Flair Limited rather than by the ubiquitous Steiner (which runs the spas on most cruise ships), and offer a range of massage, beauty, steam, mud, and aquatherapy treatments at lower prices than Steiner's. A beauty salon sits on the port side of the gym/spa areas.

Outside, the main area of activity on each ship is the open three-deck stern, with a single small pool flanked by wading areas and showers. These aft-facing levels are by far the most popular outdoor spaces aboard, as they offer protection from the winds the ships produce when they get up to speed. A bar, pizza station, and outdoor dining area lie just forward of the pool under a huge awning that creates a nice tent effect. Other than this, there are two side decks with lounge chairs that can get very breezy when the ship's moving, and an area circling the nightclub on the top deck, forward, that's sometimes closed to passengers while underway. There's neither a jogging track nor any other location where you can get in a good walk.

7

The Ultraluxury Lines

On these top-shelf cruises, guests don't line up for a look at an ice sculpture or a slice of pepperoni pizza en route to St. Thomas or Nassau; they sip a '98 Bordeaux with their filet de boeuf in truffle sauce while sailing to Les Saintes or St. Barts. They order jumbo shrimp from the room-service menu, and take indulgent baths in ritzy marble-covered bathrooms. There are no midnight buffets, dancing waiters, belly-flop contests by the pool, assigned dinner seating (except on the Crystal ships), or many of the other typical cruise ship trappings, but instead, doting service, the best food and wine you'll find at sea, and a calm, elegant retreat to call home for a week or two.

These cruise lines' ships are the closest thing you'll find to five-star. Mostly small and intimate, these are the sports cars of cruise ships, and they cater to discerning travelers who don't blink at paying top dollar to be pampered with fine gourmet cuisine and spacious suites with walk-in closets. Formal nights see the vast majority of guests dressed in tuxedos and sparkling dresses and gowns dining in elegant rooms with the finest linens, stemware, and china. The only exceptions here are the yachts of Windstar Cruises and SeaDream, which take a much more casual approach that suits their more laid-back decor. Aboard all the lines, delicious French, Italian, and Asian cuisine often rivals that of respected shoreside restaurants and is served in high style by large staffs of doting, gracious waiters who know how to please. A full dinner can even be served to you in your cabin, if you like. Still, you shouldn't expect the kind of five-star experience you'd get on land; none of these ultraluxe ships offer the level of service and cuisine you'd find at a Four Seasons or Ritz Carlton hotel. Plus, the luxe lines have been affected by the tough economy like everyone else, so you may find that your seviche is heavier on the snapper than on lobster chunks, or bed linens are no longer ritzy Italian Frette linens. But while it won't quite be a three-star Michelin experience, the ultraluxe lines are as good as it gets at sea. And they're pretty darn good.

Entertainment and organized activities are more dignified than on other ships—you won't see any raunchy comedy routines or bordering-on-obscene pool games here—and are more limited as guests tend to amuse themselves, enjoying cocktails and conversation in a piano bar, or small-scale Broadway-inspired song-and-dance medleys.

With the exception of the large Crystal ships and Cunard's *QE2* and *QM2*, these high-end vessels tend to be small and intimate, carrying just a few hundred passengers. You're not likely to feel lost in the crowd, and staff will get to know your likes and dislikes early on. The onboard atmosphere is much like a private club, with guests trading traveling tales and meeting for drinks or dinner.

While the high-end lines are discounting more than ever these days, they can still cost twice as much (or more) than your typical mainstream cruise. Expect to pay at least $1,500 per person for a week in the Caribbean, and easily more if you opt for a large suite or choose to cruise during the busiest times of the

Frommer's Ratings at a Glance: The Ultraluxury Lines

1 = poor   2 = fair   3 = good   4 = excellent   5 = outstanding

Cruise Line	Enjoyment Factor	Dining	Activities	Children's Program	Entertainment	Service	Worth the Money
Crystal	5	5	5	3	4	4	5
Cunard**	4	4	4	2	3	4	4
Radisson Seven Seas	4	4	4	N/A*	3	5	4
Seabourn	5	4	2	N/A*	2	4	4
SeaDream	5	4	3	N/A*	3	5	5
Silversea	5	5	4	N/A*	3	5	5
Windstar	5	3	2	N/A*	2	3	4

Note: Cruise lines have been graded on a curve that compares them only with the other lines in the Ultraluxury category. See "How To Read the Ratings," in chapter 5, for a detailed explanation of the ratings methodology. * Lines with N/A rating for children's programs have no program whatsoever. ** Cunard rating based on *QE2*. At press time, the new *QM2* was not yet in service, so could not be rated.

year. Many extras are often included in the cruise rates. For instance, Silversea's, Seabourn's, and SeaDream's rates include unlimited wine, liquor, and beverages, along with tips, a stocked minibar, and one complimentary shore excursion per cruise. Radisson's rates include tips, wine with dinner, one-time stocked minibar, and unlimited soda and bottled water, and Crystal now includes all soft drinks in its rates.

Most people attracted to these types of cruises are sophisticated, wealthy, relatively social, and used to the finer things in life. Most are well traveled, though not necessarily adventurous, and tend to stick to five-star experiences. These ships are not geared to children, although every so often a few (or a few dozen during holiday weeks) may show up. In this event, babysitting can often be arranged privately with an off-duty crewmember. The larger Crystal ships do have playrooms, and as many as 100 children are not uncommon during holiday cruises.

DRESS CODES With the exception of Windstar and SeaDream, these are the most formal cruises out there. You need to bring the tux and the sequined gown—guests dress for dinner on the 2 or 3 formal nights on these cruises. Informal nights call for suits and usually ties for men (though Seabourn, for instance, now officially doesn't require ties except on formal nights) and smart dresses, skirts, or pantsuits for ladies; sports jackets or nice shirts for men and casual dresses or pantsuits for women are the norm on casual nights. That said, like the rest of the industry, even the high-end lines are relaxing their dress codes, heading closer to lines such as Windstar and SeaDream, which espouse a casual "no jackets required" policy during the entire cruise. All the ultraluxe lines now have casual dining venues, so if you just want to throw on a sundress, or polo shirt and chinos, and be done with it, you'll be fine. Even in the formal dining room (albeit on a casual night) on a recent *Seven Seas Navigator* cruise, several 60-plus passengers wore jeans, sneakers, and T-shirts (even if they were the $50 kind).

1 Crystal Cruises

2049 Century Park E., Suite 1400, Los Angeles, CA 90067. ℂ 800/446-6620 or 310/785-9300. Fax 310/785-0011. www.crystalcruises.com.

THE LINE IN A NUTSHELL   Fine-tuned and fashionable, Crystal's three dream ships (two newly refurbished and one brand new) offer top-shelf service and cuisine on ships large enough to offer lots of outdoor deck space, generous fitness facilities, tons of activities, multiple restaurants, and more than half a dozen bars and entertainment venues.

THE EXPERIENCE   Crystal has the three largest truly upscale ships in the industry. Carrying 940 to 1,080 passengers, they aren't huge, but they're big enough to offer much more than their high-end peers. You won't feel hemmed in and you likely won't be twiddling your thumbs from lack of stimulation. Service is excellent and the line's Asian cuisine is tops. Unlike Seabourn's small ships, which tend to be more calm and staid, Crystal's sociable California ethic and large passenger capacity tend to keep things mingly, chatty, and more active.

Pros

- **Four or five restaurants:** In addition to the formal dining room, there are two or three alternative restaurants (including, on *Serenity,* two with cuisine by famed chef Nobu Matsuhisa), plus a poolside grille, an indoor cafe, and a casual restaurant that puts on great theme luncheon buffets.
- **Best Asian food at sea:** The ships' reservations-only Asian restaurants serve up utterly delicious, authentic, fresh Japanese food, including sushi. At least once per cruise, an Asian-theme buffet lunch offers an awesome spread.
- **Fitness choices:** There's a nice-size gym, paddle-tennis courts, shuffleboard, Ping-Pong, a jogging circuit, golf-driving nets, and a putting green.
- **Computer learning:** No other ship has as much, with 30-plus computer stations, complimentary training classes, and Web and e-mail access.

Cons

- **Least all-inclusive of the luxe lines:** Only non-alcoholic drinks are included in the rates, not tips, booze, and so on.
- **Formality:** If you're not nuts about dressing up nearly every night, think twice about Crystal. Some passengers even get gussied up during the day.
- **Cabin size:** Accommodations (especially on *Harmony* and *Symphony*) are smaller than those aboard Silversea, Seabourn, and Radisson.
- **Cabin bathroom size:** Compared to other luxe ships, bathrooms are tiny (especially on *Harmony*), and counter and storage space limited.

Compared with the other ultraluxury lines, here's how Crystal rates:

	Poor	Fair	Good	Excellent	Outstanding
Enjoyment Factor					✓
Dining					✓
Activities					✓
Children's Program			✓		
Entertainment				✓	
Service				✓	
Worth the Money					✓

CRYSTAL: SPARKLING & SPACIOUS

Established in 1990, Crystal Cruises has held its own and even established its own unique place in the high-stakes, super-upscale cruise market. Its ships are the largest true luxury vessels aside from Cunard's venerable *QE2* and new *QM2,* and while not quite as generous in the stateroom department (cabins are smaller than those on Radisson, Silversea, and Seabourn; and Crystal doesn't include complimentary champagne and wine in the rates), they provide a truly refined cruise for discerning guests who appreciate really good service and top-notch cuisine. No doubt about it, Crystal is one of our favorite lines.

Crystal is the North American spinoff of Japan's largest container shipping enterprise, Nippon Yusen Kaisha (NYK). Despite these origins, a passenger aboard Crystal could conceivably spend an entire week at sea and not even be aware that the ship is Japanese-owned, -built, and -funded. More than anything else, Crystal is international, with a strong emphasis on European service. The Japanese exposure is more subtle, and you'll feel it in the excellent Asian cuisine and tasty sake served in the alternative restaurants and at the Asian-theme buffets. A Japanese concierge is on board to attend to the handful of Japanese passengers you'll see on many cruises, so the majority of English-speaking passengers don't have to sit through announcements and activities being translated into Japanese.

Both *Crystal Harmony* and *Symphony* (the slightly larger of the pair built 5 years after Harmony) are decorated in a light, predominately pastel color scheme. The line's newest and long-awaited third ship, the 68,000-ton, 1,080-passenger *Crystal Serenity,* which at press time was to debut in July 2003, offers a similar style, though with a fifth restaurant and more cabin balconies.

PASSENGER PROFILE

Few other cruise lines attract as loyal a crop of repeat passengers: On many cruises more than 50% hail from affluent regions of California and most step aboard for their second, third, or fourth Crystal cruise with a definite sense of how they want to spend their time on board. There's commonly a small contingent of passengers (about 15% of the mix) from the United Kingdom, Australia, Japan, Mexico, Europe, and South America. Most passengers are well-heeled couples, stylish but not particularly flamboyant, and over 55. A good number of passengers step up to Crystal from lines such as Princess and Holland America. Passengers tend to be well traveled, although not particularly adventurous.

Many Crystal passengers place great emphasis on the social scene before, during, and after mealtimes, and many enjoy dressing up (sometimes way up) for dinner and adorning themselves with the biggest and best diamonds they own. You'll see no shortage of big rocks and gold Rolexes. The onboard jewelry and clothing boutiques do a brisk business, and it's obvious that women on board have devoted much care and attention to their wardrobes and accessories. On formal nights—at least three of which occur during every 10- or 11-day cruise—the majority of men wear tuxes and many women wear floor-length gowns, although your classic black cocktail dress is just fine. As on most ships, dress codes are much more relaxed during the day.

There are rarely many kids on board except during the holidays (and summers in Alaska and Europe), when you may see as many as 100, a lot more than what you'll get on the other lines in this chapter.

DINING

One of Crystal's best features is its diverse and high-quality cuisine, with Italian- and Asian-themed reservations-only restaurants aboard each ship in addition to the main formal dining rooms. The line's Asian venues are among the best at sea. In *Harmony's* Kyoto, the superb Japanese food includes everything from sushi platters to teriyakis, while *Symphony's* Jade Garden showcases the Asian cuisine of Wolfgang Puck's acclaimed Santa Monica restaurant, Chinois on Main. Just when we thought it couldn't get any better, master chef **Nobuyuki "Nobu" Matsuhisa,** known for his restaurants in New York, Miami, L.A., London, Paris, and other cities, has partnered with Crystal to create menus for *Serenity's* Sushi Bar and its Pan-Asian restaurant Silk Road. Dishes will feature Nobu's eclectic blends of Japanese cuisine with Peruvian and European influences. In the Sushi Bar, sample the salmon tartar with sevruga caviar or the yellowtail sashimi with jalapeño; in Silk Road, choices include lobster with truffle yuzu sauce and chicken with teriyaki balsamic. While Nobu himself will make occasional appearances on *Serenity,* chef Toshiaki Tamba, personally trained by Nobu, will oversea the restaurants.

Aboard all three ships, famed restaurateur Piero Selvaggio showcases the cuisine of his award-winning Santa Monica and Las Vegas Valentino restaurants at the Italian "Valentino at Prego." There's a suggested $6 cover charge in each of the specialty restaurants.

Besides these intimate, alternative reservations-only restaurants, Crystal offers an ultracasual dining option at the poolside Trident Grill several evenings per cruise between 6 and 9pm, offering an open-air ambience and serving dishes such as grilled shrimp, Cobb salad, and gourmet pizza. Spa hours are extended on the evenings the Grill is open, so guests can go from a relaxing massage right to a light meal on deck. The Grill also serves casual lunches (beef, chicken, and salmon burgers; wraps and tuna melts; pizza, hot dogs, and fries; fruit; and a special of the day) daily between 11:30am and 6pm for those who'd like something simple and easy poolside. You can place your order at the counter and either have a seat at the adjacent tables or head back to your deck chair and let a waiter bring you your lunch. You don't even have to change out of your bathing suit.

Dinner is served in two seatings in the main dining rooms. Cuisine selections include dishes such as coq au vin (braised chicken in burgundy red-wine sauce with glazed onions and mushrooms over a bed of linguine), Black Angus beef tenderloin with burgundy wine gravy, oven-baked quail with porcini mushroom and bread stuffing, or seared sea scallops served with a light lobster beurre blanc over a bed of risotto. At lunch and dinner, there's a light selection—lower in cholesterol, fat, and sodium—such as grilled fresh halibut served with steamed vegetables and herbed potatoes, as well as an entree salad—for example, a mixed salad with grilled herb-marinated chicken breast, lamb, or filet mignon. **Vegetarian selections** are also featured, such as spinach and ricotta cannelloni or a brochette of Mediterranean vegetables. **Kosher dishes** are also available, and sugar-free, gluten-free, and low-fat options are now part of all menus, even at buffets. Virtually any special diet can be accommodated.

In a kind of homage to the California wine industry, Crystal offers one of the most sophisticated inventories of California **wines** on the high sea, as well as a reserve list of two dozen or so rare wines and a extensive selection of French wines. Many bottles are in the $20-to-$60 range, and some go as high as $800.

Lunches and breakfasts are open seating in the dining room and the Lido buffet restaurant. Service by the team of ultraprofessional, gracious, European male waiters is excellent, and the staff sometimes seem to be more nattily attired than the passengers. In the main dining room—and to a somewhat lesser degree in the alternative restaurants—table settings are lavish and include fine, heavy crystal and porcelain. Even in the Lido restaurant, waiters are at hand to serve you your salad from the buffet line, prepare your coffee, and then carry your tray to wherever it is you want to sit. Buffets always include made-to-order salads and pastas.

Excellent themed luncheon buffets—Asian, Mediterranean, Western barbecue, or South American/Cuban, for instance—are generously spread out at lunchtime by the pool, and an extra-special gala buffet is put on once per cruise in the lobby/atrium. No expense or effort is spared to produce elaborate food fests, with heaps of jumbo shrimp, homemade sushi, Greek salads, shish kebabs, beef satay, stir-fry dishes, and more.

The Bistro serves a late continental breakfast from 9:30 to 11:30am and is open between 11:30am and 6pm for complimentary grazing at the buffet-style spread of cheeses, cold cuts, fruit, cookies, and pastries. You can also sip an almond mocha, a hazelnut latte, an espresso, and a fruit shake at no extra charge, or purchase a glass of pinot grigio or a nice merlot.

For afternoon tea, it's the ultrachic Palm Court on one of the uppermost decks. A sprawling space with floor-to-ceiling windows and pale-blue and white furniture in leather and rattan, the area gives off an overall light, soft, and ethereal ambience. Pre-dinner and midnight canapés in the lounges include the delicious likes of foie gras, caviar, and marinated salmon.

There is, of course, 24-hour room service, as well as complimentary unlimited non-alcoholic drinks everywhere aboard, from cappuccino to soda and bottled water.

ACTIVITIES

Crystal offers an interesting selection of activities that can fill your day if you care to be so busy. You can count on several enrichment lectures throughout a cruise, such as a historian presenting a slide show and speaking about the Panama Canal and how it was built, a former Ambassador speaking about regional politics, or a movie critic talking to guests about Hollywood film. Most speakers are not celebrities, but well-known personalities do occasionally show up. Recent guests have included TV journalist Garrick Utley, who appears regularly on CNN; award-winning CBS news correspondent Ike Pappas; Broadway star Joel Grey; singer Maureen McGovern; entertainer Lucie Arnaz (daughter of Lucille Ball and Desi Arnaz); comedian Jonathan Winters; and Olympic gold medalists such as speed skater Dan Jansen.

During almost one-third of its cruises each year, Crystal offers its Wine & Food Festival, in which a respected wine expert conducts at least two complimentary tastings, and guest chefs such as Andre Soltin or John Ash conduct cooking demonstrations for guests and then present the results of those lessons at dinner. There are also music-theme cruises from time to time, featuring the likes of soloists and chamber orchestras from New York's famed Julliard School performing classical music; jazz and blues musicians; and even '70s-era groups to get guests groovin' to that decade's popular hits.

Guest teachers teach swing, rumba, and merengue dance lessons on some cruises. Group lessons are complimentary, and private lessons can sometimes be arranged with the instructors for about $50 per hour per couple. Crystal is also big on organizing bridge and paddle-tennis competitions, game-show-style contests, and trivia games, as well as providing mid-afternoon dance music with the resident dance trio or quartet; serving tea to the accompaniment of a harpist; offering interesting arts and crafts such as glass-etching; and even presenting guest fashion shows. Commonly, a golf expert sails on board, too, conducting complimentary group golf lessons by the driving nets several times per cruise (again, private lessons can be arranged; prices start at $50 per hour). A variety of free aerobics classes is also offered in the fitness center, including pilates and yoga.

Kudos to the line's Computer University; no other line offers anything as extensive. Each ship has a well-stocked 24-hour computer lab with some 30 computer workstations, plus other computers recently installed in several public areas. Passengers can send and receive e-mail via their personal accounts (AOL, Hotmail, and so on) or through a special personal shipboard address they're given with their cruise documents. Computer use is free of charge, but there's an initial $5 fee to set up an onboard e-mail account and a charge of $2.75 every time you send or receive an e-mail from that account, of up to about seven to eight pages in length. You can even rent a laptop computer for use in the comfort of your stateroom ($5 a day), which are all wired for Internet access.

A complimentary **30-course computer curriculum** is offered on all cruises, with topics such as a basic introduction to using the computer, understanding the Internet, creating spreadsheets using Excel, and creating and posting websites (which go live immediately so that you can post text and photos for your friends back home; posting a website costs $40).

CHILDREN'S PROGRAM

Crystal is a sophisticated cruise line that focuses its attention on adults, but more than any other line in the luxury end of the market, it also does its part to cater to the little people. Each ship has a bright children's playroom, primarily used during holiday and summer cruises (mostly in Alaska and Europe), when some 100 kids may be aboard. All three ships have Sony PlayStation video games and personal computers. *Symphony* and *Serenity* also have video arcade/teen centers. During busy times, counselors are on hand to supervise activities such as scavenger hunts, arts and crafts, karaoke, and other games to take place during several hours in the morning and in the afternoon, for ages 3 to 17. For children as young as 8 months, in-cabin babysitting can be arranged privately through the concierge at an hourly rate of $7.50 for one child, $10 for two kids, and $12.50 for three kids. Note that children 11 and under pay 50% of the minimum fare when accompanied by two full-fare guests.

The minimum age for sailing is 6 months.

ENTERTAINMENT

Onboard entertainment is good (and plentiful), but it's certainly not the high point of the cruise. Shows in the horseshoe-shaped, rather plain Galaxy Lounge encompass everything from classical concertos by accomplished pianists to comedy. A troupe of spangle-covered, lip-syncing dancers and a pair of lead singers perform Vegas-style shows. From time to time, celebrity entertainers such as Marvin Hamlisch and Tommy Tune perform on board.

After dinner each night, a second large, attractive lounge is the venue for ballroom-style dancing to a live band, with a coterie of gentleman hosts aboard each sailing to provide dance (and dinner) partners for single ladies. *Harmony* also has a small, separate (and usually pretty empty) disco featuring karaoke a couple of nights per cruise. (On *Symphony*, the disco is part of the Starlight Club.) A pianist in the dark, paneled, and romantic Avenue Saloon—our favorite room on board—plays popular show tunes and pop hits before and after dinner, from "New York, New York" to "My Funny Valentine." On all three ships, you can also enjoy cigars in the Connoisseurs Club, a movie theater showing recent-release movies several times a day (as well as serving as a venue

Crystal Fleet Itineraries

Ship	Itineraries
Crystal Harmony	**11-night Carib/Canal:** Fort Lauderdale to Puerto Caldera (Costa Rica), Oct 2003, visiting Tortola (BVIs), St. Barts, St. Lucia, and Aruba *or* St. Thomas/ St. John, Sint Maarten, St. Lucia, and Curaçao, with 6 days at sea including a full Canal transit. **10-night Carib/Canal:** Puerto Caldera (Costa Rica) to Fort Lauderdale, Oct 2003, visiting Aruba, Sint Maarten, and St. Thomas/St. John, with 6 days at sea including a full Canal transit. **12-night Carib/Canal:** Puerto Caldera (Costa Rica) to New Orleans, Nov 2003, visiting Curaçao, St. Lucia, and Tortola (BVIs), with 7 days at sea including a full Canal transit. **11-night Carib/Canal:** Between New Orleans and Puerto Caldera (Costa Rica), Nov– Dec 2003, visiting Key West, Cozumel/Playa del Carmen, and Aruba *or* Aruba, Antigua, and St. Thomas/St. John, with 7 days at sea including a full Canal transit. **12-night W. Carib:** Round-trip from New Orleans, Dec 2003, visiting Key West, St. Thomas/St. John, Aruba, and Cozumel/Playa del Carmen, with 7 days at sea. **14-night W. Carib:** Round-trip from New Orleans, Dec 2003, visiting Cozumel/Playa del Carmen, Curaçao, St. Lucia, St. Barts, Tortola (BVIs), and Key West, with 7 days at sea. **7-night W. Carib:** Round-trip from Fort Lauderdale, Oct–Nov 2004, visiting Key West, Cozumel, Nassau, and Freeport, with 2 days at sea. **10-night E. Carib:** Round-trip from Fort Lauderdale, Nov–Dec 2004, visiting Tortola (BVIs), Martinique, Sint Maarten, and St. Thomas, with 5 days at sea. **11-night W. Carib/Canal:** Fort Lauderdale to Puerto Caldera (Costa Rica), Nov 2004, visiting St. Barts, Martinique, Barbados, and Aruba, with 6 days at sea including a full Canal transit. **10-night W. Carib/ Canal:** Puerto Caldera (Costa Rica) to Fort Lauderdale, Nov 2004, visiting Aruba, Grand Cayman, Cozumel, and Key West, with 6 days at sea including a full Canal transit. **12-night E. Carib:** Fort Lauderdale to New Orleans, Dec 2004, visiting Nassau, Antigua, Martinique, Curaçao, and Cozumel, with 6 days at sea. **14-night Carib:** Round-trip from New Orleans, Dec 2004, visiting Key West, St. Thomas/St. John, Antigua, Barbados, Curaçao, and Cozumel, with 7 days at sea. **Non-Caribbean Itineraries:** Hawaii, South Pacific, Australia and New Zealand, Asia, Alaska, Mexican Riviera.
Crystal Serenity	**11-night E. Carib:** Round-trip from Fort Lauderdale, visiting Tortola (BVIs), Antigua, St. Lucia, Sint Maarten, and St. Thomas/St. John, with 5 days at sea. **10-night E. Carib:** Round-trip from Fort Lauderdale, visiting St. Thomas/ St. John, Barbados, St. Lucia, Guadeloupe, and Dominica, with 4 days at sea. **7-night W. Carib:** Round-trip from Fort Lauderdale, Nov 2004, visiting Key West, Freeport, Nassau, and Cozumel, with 2 days at sea. **10-night Carib:** Round-trip from Fort Lauderdale, Nov–Dec 2004, visiting Nassau, St. Thomas, St. Barts, Martinique, Barbados, and Antigua, with 3 days at sea. **Non-Caribbean Itineraries:** Panama Canal repositioning cruises, Mexican Riviera, Europe.
Crystal Symphony	**14-night Carib:** Round-trip from Fort Lauderdale, Dec 2003, visiting Nassau, Tortola (BVIs), Sint Maarten, St. Lucia, Curaçao, Aruba, and Cozumel/Playa del Carmen, with 6 days at sea. **12-night W. Carib/Canal:** Fort Lauderdale to Puerto Caldera (Costa Rica), Jan 2004, visiting Tortola (BVIs), St. Barts, Martinique, Barbados, and Aruba, with 6 days at sea including a full Canal transit. **11-night W. Carib/Canal:** Puerto Caldera (Costa Rica) to Fort Lauderdale, Jan 2004, visiting Curaçao, Martinique, Antigua, and St. Barts, with 6 days at sea including a full Canal transit. **11-night W. Carib/Canal:** Between Fort Lauderdale and Puerto Caldera (Costa Rica), Jan–Feb 2004, visiting St. Thomas/ St. John, St. Kitts, St. Lucia, and Curaçao, with 5 days at sea including a full Canal transit. **11-night Carib/Canal:** Fort Lauderdale to Puerto Caldera (Costa Rica), Mar 2004, visiting La Romana (Dominican Republic), Aruba, and Cozumel, with 7 days at sea including a full Canal transit. **11-night Carib/Canal:** Puerto Caldera (Costa Rica) to Fort Lauderdale, Mar 2004, visiting Aruba, Sint Maarten, and St. Thomas, with 7 days at sea including a full Canal transit. **7-night W. Carib:** Round-trip from Fort Lauderdale, Feb, Apr, and Dec 2004, visiting Key West, Freeport, Nassau, and Cozumel, with 2 days at sea. **Non-Caribbean Itineraries:** Europe, New England/Canada, South America.

for lectures and religious services), and cabin TVs that feature a wonderfully varied and full menu of movies.

Gamblers will have no problem feeling at home in the roomy casinos, which are supervised directly by Caesars Palace Casinos at Sea. Note that the one on *Symphony* is nearly twice as large as the one on *Harmony.*

SERVICE

The hallmark of a high-end cruise like Crystal is its service, so the line's staff is better-trained and more attentive than that aboard most other cruise lines, and is typically an international cast: The dining room and restaurant staffs hail from Italy, Portugal, and other European countries, and have trained in the grand restaurants of Europe and North America; and the cabin stewardess who tidies your stateroom is likely to be from Scandinavia, Hungary, or some other European country. Overall, the dining/bar staff is best, outshining the cabin stewardesses, though everyone, even the staff manning the information and concierge desks in the lobby, is endlessly good-natured and very helpful—a rare find, indeed. Guests in Penthouse Suites are treated to the services of male butlers. (We might note that the Crystal ships are among the few that have not only a small pool for their crewmembers, but a hot tub too, located at the bow of the ship on Deck 5. It pays to keep the crew happy!) As far as **tipping** goes, passengers can pay in cash or charge gratuities to their onboard accounts.

In addition to laundry and dry-cleaning services, self-serve laundry rooms are available.

Crystal Harmony • Crystal Symphony

The Verdict

These gracious, floating pleasure palaces are small enough to feel intimate and personal, yet large enough for a whole range of entertainment, dining, and fitness diversions.

Crystal Harmony *(photo: Crystal Cruises)*

Specifications

Size (in tons)		Number of Passengers	940
Harmony	49,400	Officers	Norwegian/Japanese/Int'l
Symphony	51,044	Crew	545 (Internat'l)
Number of Cabins	480	Passenger/Crew Ratio	1.7 to 1
Number of Outside Cabins		Year Launched	
Harmony	461	*Harmony*	1990
Symphony	480	*Symphony*	1995
Cabins with Verandas		Last Major Refurbishment	
Harmony	260	*Harmony*	2002
Symphony	276	*Symphony*	2001

Frommer's Ratings (Scale of 1–5)   ★★★★ ½

Cabin Comfort & Amenities	4	Dining Options	5
Ship Cleanliness & Maintenance	4	Gym & Spa Facilities	5
Public Comfort/Space	4.5	Children's Facilities	3
Decor	4	Enjoyment Factor	5

Plush, streamlined, extravagantly comfortable, and not as overwhelmingly large as the megaships being launched by less glamorous lines, these ships compete with the high-end Silversea, Radisson, and Seabourn vessels, although Crystal's ships are almost five times as large as Seabourn's, with a broader choice of onboard diversions and distractions. *Harmony* has a few flawed features (including a small casino) that were "corrected" in 1995 with the design of the ship's newer twin, *Crystal Symphony,* a slightly bigger ship with all outside cabins and a larger atrium. In late 2001, *Symphony* underwent a thorough sprucing up during a 10-day dry dock, with her penthouses and Jade restaurant getting complete overhauls. In late 2002, *Harmony* underwent an even more extensive multi-million dollar overhaul, emerging with a larger spa and fitness center, a new Connoisseur Club cigar bar, several remodeled lounges, and an overall freshening up of carpeting, furniture, and wall finishes.

Cabins & Rates

Cabins	Per Diems from	Sq. Ft.	Fridge	Hair Dryer	Sitting Area	TV
Inside*	$200	183	yes	yes	yes	yes
Outside	$293	198–215	yes	yes	yes	yes
Suite	$788	287–782	yes	yes	yes	yes

* Harmony only.

CABINS   Despite their high price tag, the majority of Crystal's cabins are smaller than the smallest aboard any of the Silversea, Radisson, or Seabourn vessels. They're still quite comfortable though, and cabins with balconies on both ships start at 198 square feet, plus 48-square-foot verandas.

Deck 10 holds the ships' spectacular, attractively styled penthouses; the best measure more than 750 square feet, plus nearly 200-square-foot balconies, and have full-fledged Jacuzzis in their living rooms (with ocean views to boot!), dark wood furniture, sofas upholstered in silk and satin, plus Oriental rugs and entertainment centers with 35-inch flat-screen TVs, and DVD and CD players. They also enjoy the services of a doting butler in addition to a stewardess. The other two categories are about 287 and 396 square feet, plus 72- to 98-square-foot balconies.

Overall, color schemes in most staterooms mix pastel pinks, mints, blues, and beiges with pale wood tones, and are cheerful, breezy, and light. Each cabin has a sitting area, TV with some of the best programming you'll find at sea (including CNN, ESPN, and tons of movies and documentaries), VCR, stocked mini-bar (snacks and beverages consumed are charged to your onboard account except in the Penthouse Suites on Deck 10, where they're complimentary), hair dryer, and safe. While drawer space is adequate in all cabins, the hanging closets are smaller and tighter than you'd expect on ships of this caliber. Bathrooms have both shower and bathtub (a short little one in the lower category cabins), and are mostly tiled. Those on *Harmony* are compact (we're being generous) and don't offer a lot of storage space or convenient towel racks; those on *Symphony* are larger and better designed. We found the cabins to be not entirely sound-proof; we could hear our neighbors talking and hear their television quite easily.

Of the cabins without verandas, most have large rectangular windows; on *Harmony*, 14 have rounded portholes instead. All of these inside porthole cabins are positioned near the bow on Deck 5, below the show lounges, and forward of the ship's main dining room. The E Category cabins located amidships on both vessels on Decks 7 and 8 have views obstructed by lifeboats. *Harmony* has 19 inside cabins; *Symphony* has none.

Four cabins on *Harmony* and seven on *Symphony* are wheelchair accessible; only a handful of cabins on either are connecting.

PUBLIC AREAS   Throughout each ship, you'll find marble, brass, glass, and hardwood paneling mingling with flowers and potted plants (especially palms). In that classic California style, the color schemes are light and airy; furniture and walls are done in mostly grays, lavenders, champagnes, and blues. Passenger throughways are wide and easy to navigate. The atrium/lobby areas are the most dazzling areas of the ships, though they're smaller and more subdued than those aboard your average glittery megaship.

Each ship has six-plus bar/entertainment lounges, as well as a roaming staff that wanders the public areas throughout the day and much of the night, offering to bring drinks to wherever you happen to be sitting. The dark Avenue Saloon, where polished mahogany, well-maintained leather upholstery, and a live pianist draw passengers in, is one of the prime before- and after-dinner cocktail spots (and our personal favorite, by far). There are also two large entertainment lounges, one for Vegas-style material and another for ballroom dancing to a live band.

Each ship has a large theater for movies and slide lectures, and a hushed library that's outfitted with comfortably upholstered chairs and a worthy collection of books, periodicals, and videos. *Harmony* has a bright kids' playroom, while *Symphony* has both a playroom for younger kids and a video arcade/teen center for older kids.

DINING OPTIONS   Designed with curved walls and low, vaulted ceilings, the ships' main dining rooms are elegant and spacious, with white Doric columns, high-backed chairs, and mirrored ceilings with lotus-flower lighting fixtures. Tables are not too close together, and there are well over 20 tables for two, mostly along the side or near the ocean-view windows.

The ships' two themed, reservations-only alternative restaurants—Prego, an Italian restaurant, on both; Kyoto, a Japanese restaurant, on *Harmony;* and Jade, a pan-Asian restaurant, on *Symphony*—are right up there with the best at sea. Personally, our favorite is the Japanese Kyoto, with completely authentic sushi platters, miso soup, beef teriyaki, and pork dishes. The accouterments help set the tone, too—chopsticks (and little chopstick rests), sake served in tiny sake cups and decanters, and sushi served on thick blocky glass platters. Our only complaint: Sometimes service is a bit harried in the alternative restaurants—nothing another waiter or two wouldn't remedy. There's a $6 cover charge. *Symphony's* two alternative restaurants are on the main entertainment deck with the rest of the action, and are much more interesting and colorful than *Harmony's*, which are on the Lido Deck. *Symphony's* Jade Garden Asian venue was completely remodeled in late 2001, adding new paneling, carpet, furniture, and bamboo-framed Asian artwork; even the staff got new uniforms.

✆ Preview: *Crystal Serenity*

At press time, the 1,080-passenger, 68,000-ton *Crystal Serenity* was slated to debut in July of 2003, just after this book is at the printer, so we'll have to make do with a preview. Similar in style and layout to sisters *Harmony* and *Symphony*, the slightly larger *Serenity* will surely be as big a hit as her sisters, featuring an even greater space-per-guest ratio, as well as an expanded spa, gym, and computer classroom, and a second tennis court. In addition to the elegant main dining room and casual indoor/outdoor buffet restaurant, *Serenity* will have three alternative restaurants, including an Italian and a Pan-Asian venue and a sushi bar operated under the guidance of renowned master chef Nobuyuki (see "Dining" section, above). There are more penthouses, staterooms are larger, and about 85% of all outside staterooms and suites have private balconies (368 out of a total 540 staterooms). *Serenity* will also have a wine cellar, a learning center, and, like *Symphony*, both a separate teen club and a children's playroom.

The ships also have casual indoor/outdoor buffet restaurants open for breakfast and lunch, and the poolside Trident Grill serves ultracasual dinners several evenings per cruise. The Bistro is open from 9:30am to 6pm for continental breakfast, snacks, specialty coffees, and more.

POOL, FITNESS & SPA FACILITIES   These ships offer a lot of outdoor activities and spacious areas in which to do them. There are two outdoor swimming pools separated by a bar, ice-cream counter, and sandwich grill, as well as two hot tubs. One of the pools is refreshingly oversize, stretching almost 40 feet across one of the sun decks; the other can be covered with a retractable glass roof (and *Harmony*'s has a swim-up bar). The gym and separate aerobics area aboard each ship are positioned for a view over the sea. The Steiner-managed spa and beauty salons on both ships are accessorized with Feng Shui features including gurgling fountains, incense, wind chimes, crystals, and mirrors to create an atmosphere of peace and relaxation. *Symphony*'s 2002 refurbishment included an enlargement of the spa and fitness center, adding a dedicated aerobics room, more treatment rooms, and an outdoor relaxation area for quiet repose before or after a massage.

On deck, there's a pair of golf driving nets, a putting green, a large paddle-tennis court, Ping-Pong tables, and a broad, uninterrupted teak Promenade Deck for walkers and joggers.

The ships' gorgeous and generous tiered afterdecks provide quiet places for an afternoon spent dozing in a deck chair or for quiet repose while leaning against the railing and allowing yourself to become entranced by the ship's wake.

2 Cunard

6100 Blue Lagoon Dr., Miami, FL 33126. Ⓒ 800/5-CUNARD or 305/463-3000. Fax 305/463-3010. www.
cunard.com.

Can you say "history"? Can you say "God Save the Queen"? Cunard, more than
160 years old at this writing, is a bona fide cultural icon, a tangible reminder of
the days when Britannia really did rule the waves, and that's what sets it apart
from the pack. During the 1980s and '90s, the company had its ups and downs,
operating a wildly divergent fleet of large and small ships, maintaining bad relations with travel agents, and generally going to pot; but this all changed in the
late 1990s, when Cunard finally got its act together and then, predictably, was
scooped up by Carnival Corporation. Say what you will about "Carnivore's"
near-monopoly of the cruise industry, but they did manage to refocus Cunard
on what it does best: operating classic ocean liners for a clientele that wants fine
service, fine dining, and fine manners in a traditional environment.

Cunard currently has two ships in its fleet, the venerable *QE2* and the smaller
Caronia, which will be leaving the fleet in November 2004, sold to U.K.-based
Saga Group. The big news in the cruise world, though, is the soon-to-be-launched
QM2—a new *Queen Mary* for a new millennium. Scheduled to debut in January
2004, she'll be the first true ocean liner constructed in decades, similar in profile
and ambience to *QE2* but much more modern and much, much larger. At
150,000 gross register tons, she'll outsize Royal Caribbean's behemoth Voyager-
class ships (currently the largest passenger ships in the world) by about 8,000 tons,
and at 1,132 feet long, she'll stretch the length of nearly four football fields.

At this writing, *QE2* is scheduled for only one Caribbean cruise this season
(during the 2003 Christmas/New Year's week), so we couldn't justify providing
a full review. Let's leave it at this: She's a classic. Don't expect perfection (it's hard
to keep up appearances on a ship this old), but do expect old-world service and
a classic, nostalgic seagoing experience. During the 1980s and '90s, she was the
only ship still offering regular transatlantic crossings between the U.K. and New
York, but in 2004 she's being replaced on that route by *QM2*, which will also
sail a number of Caribbean cruises in her inaugural season. *QE2* will instead
head off on a 110-day world cruise that will take her to 38 ports in 25 different
countries, with as-yet-unannounced shorter sailings to follow. All in all, her days
are probably numbered, and we wouldn't gamble on her serving more than 5 or
6 more years with Cunard. Sail her while you can. Another new vessel, the

Cunard Fleet Itineraries

Ship	Itineraries
Queen Elizabeth 2	**15-night E. Carib:** Round-trip from New York, Dec 2003, visiting Fort Lauderdale, St. Lucia, Martinique, Barbados, Sint Maarten, and St. Thomas, with 7 days at sea.
Queen Mary 2	**11-night E. & S. Carib:** Round-trip from Fort Lauderdale, Jan–Feb 2004, visiting San Juan, St. Kitts, Martinique, Barbados, St. Lucia, Dominica, and St. Thomas, with 3 days at sea. **10-night E. & W. Carib:** Round-trip from Fort Lauderdale, March 2004, visiting Cristobal (Panama), Cartagena (Colombia), Aruba, Sint Maarten, and St. Thomas, with 4 days at sea. **8-night E. Carib:** Round-trip from New York, May 2004, visiting Sint Maarten, Martinique, and St. Thomas, with 4 days at sea. **10-night E. Carib:** Round-trip from New York, Nov–Dec 2004, visiting Sint Maarten, Martinique, Barbados, St. Lucia, and St. Thomas, with 4 days at sea.

85,000-ton, 1,968-passenger *Queen Victoria,* is scheduled to enter service in 2005 and will operate round-trip from Southampton in the United Kingdom.

Since *QM2* has not yet launched, and since her onboard experience will be so much different than what's been available till now on Cunard's older ships, the review that follows is shorter than our normal format and a bit speculative, based on our experiences of Cunard in the past and our knowledge of what the line is planning for the future.

Queen Mary 2 (preview)

QM2 *(photo: Cunard)*

Once she launches in January 2004, *QM2* will automatically become the most famous ship in the world, scheduled to sail a series of high-profile cruises from U.S. ports, assume *QE2*'s traditional routes across the Atlantic, and serve as a floating hotel during the 2004 Athens Olympics. All told, the ship will have 14 decks of sports facilities, bars, lounges, shops, pools, and restaurants, and be designed to handle the rough north Atlantic seas in style. In a wonderful touch of continuity, one of the three 7-foot, 1,400-pound ship's whistles from the original *Queen Mary* will be installed on the new Queen, along with an exact replica mounted alongside. The whistle (original or repro) will be audible up to 10 miles away.

True to her position as the newest and most modern ship built for the oldest and most venerable cruise line, *QM2* will be a mix of tradition and innovation. Like *QE2* before her, she'll maintain a vestige of the old steamship class system at dinner, with passengers assigned to one of the three **reserved-seating restaurants** according to the level of cabin accommodation they've booked: Passengers in the very best suites dine in the Queen's Grill; those in the Deck 10 Junior Suites dine in the Princess Grill; and guests in standard staterooms dine in the three-deck Britannia Restaurant, with its sweeping grand staircase, Wedgwood china, and Waterford crystal glassware. All guests also have the option of dining in one of four **alternative restaurants:** an Asian restaurant, an Italian trattoria, a Carvery, and the Chef's Galley, where an open kitchen allows passengers to watch the chefs at work.

Opening off the promenade, the **Winter Garden** was designed to resemble London's Kew Gardens, with lush greenery and blooming flowers, a large waterfall, and piano music—the total Victorian experience. The room will be used for various activities and entertainment, as well as for daily afternoon high tea (with fresh-brewed tea, scones, clotted cream, fresh pastries and finger sandwiches, and white glove service) and pre-dinner canapés. For a more casual vibe, the British-style **Golden Lion Pub** serves a selection of fine lagers, ales, and pub snacks, and is used as a venue for televised sports events.

Moving from the 19th century into the 21st, the ship will also offer the first **planetarium** at sea, a 500-seat hall presenting virtual reality trips to the stars (and, more prosaically, aboard a virtual roller coaster) and courses on celestial navigation. It will also function as a regular cinema and lecture hall for the ship's

enrichment program, which offers workshops, seminars, and lectures on fashion, foreign languages, watercolor techniques, antiques, film making, art history, and other subjects. Seven much smaller classrooms are also used for more intimate presentations. Technology classes are offered in the Computer Centre, where guests can also do the usual Internet surfing and e-mail checking. However, they don't have to leave their cabin to do this unless they want to, as every stateroom aboard is wired for direct Internet access. Interactive TVs in cabins also offer dozens of movies, rerun onboard seminars, and allow booking of shore excursions.

Another seagoing first will be the ship's 20,000-square-foot **Canyon Ranch SpaClub,** the first onboard spa operated by the acclaimed health resort of the same name. Beyond the usual spa treatments, the SpaClub will also offer stress-relief classes and workshops on diet, healthy aging, and disease prevention. Facilities include a thalassotherapy pool with a waterfall, a whirlpool, and a thermal suite with herbal and Finnish saunas and an aromatic steam room. While adults relax here, kids can enjoy the **Play Zone children's area,** with separate areas for kids ages 2 to 7 and 8 to 12, a nursery staffed with English nannies, a splash pool, various toys and activities, and computer terminals.

Cabins are overwhelmingly outside, with only 20% lacking windows. Of the outside cabins, 94% have private balconies. Standard staterooms measure a roomy 200 square feet, while suites range from 388 square feet up to the grand duplexes' 1,650 square feet, with a large balcony downstairs, master bedroom upstairs, two marble baths with separate whirlpool tub and shower, a guest bathroom with shower, private exercise equipment, and glass walls at the stern, facing the ship's wake. Guests in all suites and junior suites have the service of a concierge, while those in full suites also get butler service.

3 Radisson Seven Seas Cruises

600 Corporate Dr., Suite 410, Fort Lauderdale, FL 33334. (C) **866/213-1272.** Fax 954/772-3763. www. rssc.com.

THE LINE IN A NUTSHELL Radisson carries passengers in style and extreme comfort. Its brand of luxury is casually elegant and subtle, service is as good as it gets, and its cuisine is near the top.

THE EXPERIENCE Radisson's ships are spacious, and its cuisine is some of the best at sea, whether in the formal dining rooms or their alternative restaurants. Even if what tickles your fancy isn't on the menu, the chef will prepare it for you. These ships tend to be less stuffy than Seabourn and Silversea, with low-key entertainment, few distracting activities, friendly but absolutely spot-on service, an extremely relaxing onboard vibe, and a generally casual dress code—you can chuck your tux for the most part, although on formal nights they certainly aren't uncommon. Passengers tend to be unpretentiously wealthy. When last we sailed, our social circle included an Atlantic City nightclub owner, a retired recycling executive, a graphic artist, a theatrical casting director, and a woman who owned a string of Taco Bell franchises—all of them aboard to enjoy a quiet, relaxed vacation.

Pros

- **Great dining:** Cuisine is superb, and the main dining room and alternative restaurants operate on an open-seating basis, the latter by reservation.
- **Lots of private verandas:** *Radisson Diamond* has private balconies in almost 70% of her cabins, the all-suite *Seven Seas Navigator* has them in 90% of hers, and the all-suite *Mariner* and *Voyager* have them in every single stateroom. There are no windowless cabins on any of the line's ships.
- **Amazing bathrooms on *Navigator* and *Voyager*:** Bigger and better than those on Seabourn and Crystal, cabin bathrooms all have separate shower stalls and full-size bathtubs long enough for normal-size humans.

Cons

- **Less all-inclusive than other luxe lines:** While the line does include gratuities, wine with dinner, and unlimited soda and bottled water, it doesn't throw in any complimentary shore excursions, and the only free liquor is a one-time loading up of your cabin minibar. Silversea, Seabourn, and SeaDream offer more freebies.
- **Few activities:** The lack of distracting activities is why many people sail with Radisson, but if you need constant entertainment, look elsewhere.

Compared with the other ultraluxury lines, here's how Radisson rates:

	Poor	Fair	Good	Excellent	Outstanding
Enjoyment Factor			✓		
Dining			✓		
Activities			✓		
Children's Program	N/A*				
Entertainment		✓			
Service					✓
Worth the Money					✓

* Radisson offers no children's program in the Caribbean, though Navigator does offer one on her April–June Bermuda cruises.

RADISSON: LOW-KEY ELEGANCE

Radisson Hotels began Radisson Seven Seas Cruises with the much-publicized launch of the catamaran-style *Radisson Diamond* in 1992, and today owns six luxurious, globe-trotting ships, including four that comprise its fleet in the Caribbean: *Diamond, Seven Seas Navigator* (1999), *Seven Seas Mariner* (2001), and *Seven Seas Voyager* (2003). The small, 180-passenger *Song of Flower* sails exotic itineraries worldwide, including Asia, the Mediterranean, and Northern Europe, and the 320-passenger *Paul Gauguin* spends the year doing 7-night cruises in French Polynesia. Additionally, Radisson operates a series of Antarctic cruises each January and February aboard the chartered expedition ship *Explorer II*. In 2003, the line announced that, at some point in the near future, it would be dropping the "Radisson" from its name, and would operate henceforth simply as Seven Seas Cruises. No timetable for this change has yet been set.

PASSENGER PROFILE

This line appeals primarily to well-traveled and well-heeled passengers in their 50s and 60s, but younger passengers and honeymooners pepper the mix. Many passengers are frequent cruisers who have also sailed on Silversea, Seabourn, and Crystal, or are taking a step up from Holland America, Celebrity, or one of the other mainstream lines. Though they have sophisticated tastes (and can do without inane activities such as napkin-folding classes), they also appreciate a somewhat less formal ambience. On recent *Navigator* and *Diamond* cruises, casual nights in the formal dining room saw some passengers dressed in polo shirts and jackets and others in nice T-shirts with khakis and sneakers. Still, you're also likely to find some women in full makeup, coiffed 'do, and coordinated jewelry, shoes, and handbags strolling the pool deck, and many men sporting gold Rolexes the size of Texas.

Radisson Diamond is heavily marketed to meeting and convention groups, which either charter the ship outright or book a block of cabins on a regular cruise. (A company spokeswoman estimated that about 25% of her passengers in a given year are part of such groups.) Despite her small size, the vessel is spacious enough that business groups don't generally impinge on other passengers' experience, holding their meetings in the otherwise lightly used meeting rooms on Deck 7 and mixing well in the evenings with the rest of the usually business-friendly passengers. There's always a chance, however, that having really big groups aboard can lead to a balkanized onboard feel, since the ship carries only 350 passengers total.

DINING

Superb menus are designed for a sophisticated palate, and cuisine overall is some of the best in the cruise industry. Nice red and white house wines are complimentary at dinner, and each ship has an extensive menu of vintages from Germany, Italy, and Chile.

In the main restaurants, elaborate and elegant meals are served in a single, open seating by a staff of mostly Europeans. Appetizers may include oven-roasted pheasant salad or avocado fritters in a spicy sauce, with main entrees including enticing dishes such as zucchini-wrapped chicken breast stuffed with olives and tomatoes, herb-crusted roast leg of lamb, and fresh fish. Each dinner menu offers a **vegetarian option** such as a vegetable curry (plus vegetarian appetizers), and a **light and healthy choice** such as grilled tuna steak in a leek-and-tomato vinaigrette. When you've had enough of fancy, several standards called **simplicity dishes** are also available daily: spaghetti with tomato sauce, filet

Radisson Fleet Itineraries

Ship	Itineraries
Radisson Diamond	**7-night S. Carib:** Round-trip from San Juan, Jan–Mar and Nov 2004, visiting St. Barts, Dominica, Barbados, Martinique, St. Kitts, and St. Thomas. **6-night S. Carib:** Round-trip from San Juan, Jan 2004, visiting St. Barts, Dominica, Barbados, Martinique, and St. Kitts. **5-night S. Carib:** Round-trip from San Juan, Feb–Apr and Nov 2004, visiting St. Barts, St. Kitts, Sint Maarten, and St. Thomas. **4-night S. Carib:** Round-trip from San Juan, Mar–Apr and Nov 2004, visiting St. Barts, St. Kitts, and St. Thomas. **Non-Caribbean Itineraries:** Repositioning cruises, Europe.
Seven Seas Mariner	**3-night Bahamas/Key West:** Round-trip from Fort Lauderdale, Dec 2003 and Dec 2004, visiting Nassau and Key West. **7-night E. Carib 1:** Round-trip from Fort Lauderdale, Dec 2003, visiting Grand Turk (Turks and Caicos), St. Thomas, St. Kitts, St. Barts, Sint Maarten, and Nassau, with 2 days at sea. **7-night E. Carib 2:** Between Fort Lauderdale and San Juan, Apr and May 2004, visiting Great Exuma (Bahamas), Tortola (BVIs), St. Kitts, St. Barts, and St. Thomas, with 1 day at sea. **4- & 5-night E. Carib:** Round-trip from San Juan, Apr 2004, visiting St. Barts, St. Kitts, and St. Thomas, with Sint Maarten added on 5-night itineraries. **7-night W. Carib:** Round-trip from Fort Lauderdale, Dec 2004, visiting Cozumel and Progreso (Mexico), Grand Cayman, and Key West, with 2 days at sea. **Non-Caribbean Itineraries:** Panama Canal and Pacific coastal repositioning cruises, Alaska, Asia.
Seven Seas Navigator	**11-night S. & W. Carib:** San Juan to Fort Lauderdale, Dec 2003 and Mar 2004, visiting Curaçao, Aruba, Colón (Panama), Puerto Limon (Costa Rica), Grand Cayman, and Key West, with 3 days at sea. **9-night E. & S. Carib:** Round-trip from Fort Lauderdale, Jan 2004, visiting Grand Turk (Turks and Caicos), Tortola (BVIs), St. Kitts, St. Barts, St. Thomas, and Great Exuma (Bahamas), with 2 days at sea. **10-night E. & W. Carib:** Fort Lauderdale to San Juan, Jan 2004, visiting Key West, Cozumel and Costa Maya (Mexico), Port Antonio (Jamaica), La Romana (Dominican Republic), St. Thomas, and Sint Maarten, with 1 day at sea. **5-night E. Carib:** Round-trip from San Juan, Jan 2004, visiting St. Kitts, St. Barts, Sint Maarten, and St. Thomas. **6-night E. & S. Carib:** Round-trip from San Juan, Feb 2004, visiting St. Kitts, St. Barts, Dominica, Sint Maarten, and St. Thomas. **7-night E. & S. Carib:** San Juan to Fort Lauderdale, Feb 2004, visiting St. Kitts, Dominica, Sint Maarten, St. Thomas, and Great Exuma (Bahamas), with 1 day at sea. **7-night W. Carib 1:** Round-trip from Fort Lauderdale, Feb–Apr 2004, visiting Cozumel and Progreso (Mexico), Grand Cayman, and Key West, with 1 day at sea. **10-night E./S. Carib:** Fort Lauderdale to San Juan, Feb 2004, visiting Grand Turk (Turks and Caicos), Tortola (BVIs), St. Barts, Dominica, Barbados, St. Kitts, and St. Thomas, with 1 day at sea. **9-night Bahamas/Bermuda:** Round-trip from Fort Lauderdale, Apr 2004, visiting Charleston (SC), Nassau, and Hamilton, with 2 days at sea. **7-night Bermuda:** Round-trip from New York, May–Sept 2004, visiting Hamilton, St. George's, and Norfolk (VA), with 2 days at sea. **10-night S. & W. Carib:** San Juan to Tampa, Nov 2004, visiting Aruba, Colón (Panama), Puerto Limon (Costa Rica), Grand Cayman, and Key West, with 2 days at sea. **7-night W. Carib 2:** Round-trip from Tampa, Nov 2004, visiting Cozumel and Progreso (Mexico), Grand Cayman, and Key West, with 1 day at sea. **10-night W. Carib 1:** Round-trip from Tampa, Nov–Dec 2004, visiting Cozumel and Progreso (Mexico), Grand Cayman, La Romana (Dominican Republic), and Key West, with 3 days at sea. **10-night W. Carib 2:** Tampa to West Palm Beach, Dec 2004, visiting Cozumel, Roatan (Honduras), Puerto Limon (Costa Rica), Colón (Panama), San Andres (Colombia), and Grand Cayman, with 2 days at sea. **4-night Bahamas/Key West:** Round-trip from West Palm Beach, Dec 2004, visiting Nassau and Key West. **Non-Caribbean Itineraries:** New England/Canada, Scandinavia.

Radisson Fleet Itineraries *(continued)*

Ship	Itineraries
Seven Seas Voyager	**5-night W. Carib:** Round-trip from Fort Lauderdale, Nov 2003, visiting Key West and Cozumel and Progreso (Mexico), with 1 day at sea. **7-night W. Carib:** Round-trip from Fort Lauderdale, Nov–Dec 2003, visiting Cozumel and Progreso (Mexico), Grand Cayman, and Key West, with 1 day at sea. **5- & 6-night W. Carib:** Round-trip from Fort Lauderdale, Dec 2004, visiting Cozumel and Progreso (Mexico), Grand Cayman, and Key West, with 1 day at sea. **10-night E. & S. Carib:** Fort Lauderdale to San Juan, Dec 2004, visiting Grand Turk (Turks and Caicos), Tortola (BVIs), St. Barts, Dominica, Barbados, St. Kitts, and St. Thomas, with 2 days at sea. **11-night S. & W. Carib:** San Juan to Fort Lauderdale, Dec 2004, visiting Curaçao, Aruba, Colón (Panama), Puerto Limon (Costa Rica), Grand Cayman, and Key West, with 3 days at sea. **Non-Caribbean Itineraries:** Panama Canal repositioning cruises, Europe.

mignon, and grilled chicken breast or salmon. **Special diets** (kosher, halal, low-fat, low-salt, and so on) can be accommodated at all meals, but you must make arrangements before your cruise, either when booking or as soon as possible after. **Alternative restaurants** include the Italian/Mediterranean Don Vito's on *Diamond,* Portofino on *Navigator,* and Latitudes on *Mariner* and *Voyager,* serving antipasti choices such as marinated salmon rings or Bresaola carpaccio with Parmesan cheese and mushrooms, pasta courses that may feature a jumbo-prawn risotto, and main courses such as a grilled lobster or osso buco. *Mariner's* and *Voyager's* 110-seat Signatures alternative restaurants are directed by chefs from Paris's famed **Le Cordon Bleu** cooking school. All alternative venues are intimate spaces with tables for two or four. Make reservations early in the cruise, to guarantee yourself a table.

Breakfasts include made-to-order omelets, as well as a typical selection of hot and cold breakfast foods. **Lunch** entrees include a spicy paella, as well as rich homemade soups and a spread of cheeses, cold cuts, salads, and plenty of tropical fruits, including mango and papaya. Caesar salads are tossed to order, and there's usually an extensive indoor/outdoor buffet at lunchtime. If you don't want to get out of your bathing suit at lunch, there's a poolside sandwich grill on all ships, with waiters serving guests hamburgers and fries at tables clustered on deck.

Hot hors d'oeuvres are served in the lounges before dinner, and if you take advantage of the 24-hour room service, a steward will come in and lay out a white tablecloth along with silverware and china, whether you've ordered a full-course dinner, a personal pizza, or just a plate of fruit. Plus, you can always get virtually anything by request. **Specialty coffees,** soft drinks, and mineral water are complimentary at all times.

ACTIVITIES

Days not spent exploring the ports are basically unstructured, with most passengers lazing around the pool or on one of the side decks. During the day, there may be dance classes poolside (which don't generally attract hordes of passengers), and passengers are free to whack some balls into the ships' golf nets. Inside, you'll find **wine tastings,** art auctions, bridge (instructors sail with most cruises), bingo, and seminars led by **guest experts** on subjects such as hand-writing analysis and relationships (each cruise carries one or more lecturers, drawn from the ranks of former diplomats, writers, anthropologists, and naturalists chosen to complement the sailing region). *Navigator, Mariner,* and *Voyager* all have **Internet centers,** with an instructor offering classes on the latter two. Those with a penchant for high-end **shopping** don't have to leave the ship to splurge, with items like $500 Alfred Dunhill humidors, $18,500 sapphire-studded gold Cartier watches, and $700 gold Mont Blanc pens sold in the onboard boutiques, along with sundries and souvenirs.

As the smallest ship in the line's Caribbean fleet, *Diamond* offers fewer activities, and less in the way of shopping too. It's more of an amuse-yourself ship, where you're provided with a plush setting and a staff that brings you luxurious food and drink whenever they're needed, but after that you're on your own. Arm yourself with a good book and/or an interesting companion. Videotapes and books are available from the library on all four ships, 24 hours daily.

CHILDREN'S PROGRAM

These ships are geared to adults, and mature ones at that. There's no child care, though short, ad hoc children's activity sessions may be planned on holiday cruises, when a small number of children may be aboard.

Minimum age for children to sail aboard is 1 year, and the line reserves the right to limit the number of children under age 3 on each sailing.

ENTERTAINMENT

As on other relatively small ships, entertainment is low-key and modest, consisting mainly of a few headline crooners, musicians, and enrichment lecturers. In the evenings, most passengers are content exploring the cocktail circuit, crooning along in the piano bar, or dancing to the ships' elegant musical groups. All three ships offer **musical revues** of varying size and complexity in their show lounges, with more elaborate presentations on *Mariner, Navigator,* and *Voyager* than on *Diamond.* Though they're certainly not a high point of the cruises, they add a nice touch to the evenings. A show on a recent *Navigator* cruise featured hits from the 1930s and 1940s up through the 1980s, including a Village People segment that most people seemed to enjoy—even a 70-plus woman in a wheelchair and oxygen tank, bobbing her head happily to the song "Feel My Body." A recent *Diamond* cruise featured a Broadway-themed show and a '50s/'60s/'70s-themed show, with four talented singers/dancers doing their thing on the ship's small stage, sans props or sets. (Kudos to their tight harmonies!) Another night featured Welsh **comedian** Kenny Smiles, a Radisson regular. Don't sit in the front row unless you want to be pulled into his act. Occasional sailings offer themed entertainment, which last year included a Doo-Wop cruise featuring The Platters, and a "Spotlight on Classical Music" cruise featuring Anna Maria Alberghetti. Check with the line or through your travel agent if you're interested in sailing on one of these cruises.

Each ship has a **casino.** *Navigator's, Mariner's,* and *Voyager's* have nearly 50 slots plus three blackjack tables, one poker table, one craps table, and a roulette wheel. As on the Seabourn ships, *Diamond's* is considerably smaller and plainer.

SERVICE

Service is a major plus with Radisson, with staff striving to fulfill every passenger request with a smile. You rarely, if ever, hear the word "no," and since the passenger-to-crew ratio is high (about 1.5 to 1 on *Navigator, Mariner,* and *Voyager,* and 1.7 to 1 on *Diamond*), you rarely have to wait for someone else to get served first. The mostly European stewardesses ably and unobtrusively care for your cabin, and room service is speedy and efficient. The mostly European restaurant waitstaff is supremely gracious and professional, with an intimate knowledge of the menu. Bar staff will often remember your drink order after the first day.

Voyager, Navigator, and *Mariner* all have self-serve laundries in addition to standard laundry and dry-cleaning services. *Diamond* offers only the latter.

Gratuities are included in the cruise rates, but many passengers end up leaving more anyway at the end of their trip.

Seven Seas Mariner • Seven Seas Voyager

The Verdict

The 700-passenger, all-suite *Mariner* and *Voyager* are Radisson's largest ships, boasting balconies on every single stateroom, plus more of Radisson's great pampering treatment.

Seven Seas Mariner *(photo: Radisson)*

Specifications

Size (in tons)		Officers	International
Mariner	50,000	Crew	445 (Internat'l)
Voyager	42,000	Passenger/Crew Ratio	1.6 to 1
Number of Cabins	350	Year Launched	
Number of Outside Cabins	350	*Mariner*	2001
Cabins with Verandas	350	*Voyager*	2003
Number of Passengers	700	Last Major Refurbishment	N/A

Frommer's Ratings (Scale of 1–5)   ✮✮✮✮ ½

Cabin Comfort & Amenities	5	Dining Options	4
Ship Cleanliness & Maintenance	5	Gym & Spa Facilities	3
Public Comfort/Space	5	Children's Facilities	N/A
Decor	4.5	Enjoyment Factor	4

The all-suite *Seven Seas Mariner,* which entered service in March 2001, was the first vessel built by any line to offer a private balcony on every single stateroom, and was designed to be exceedingly spacious. Sister ship *Seven Seas Voyager,* which entered service in April 2003, continues this theme and offers improvements in some areas where we found *Mariner* lacking, particularly public room warmth and bathroom layout. In addition, *Voyager* was designed with an efficient one-corridor approach, making for extremely smooth traffic flow in the public areas.

Cabins & Rates

Cabins	Per Diems from	Sq. Ft.	Fridge	Hair Dryer	Sitting Area	TV
Suite	$287	252–1,204*	yes	yes	yes	yes

* *These measurements for* Seven Seas Mariner *only. Suites on* Voyager *measure 306–1,216 square feet.*

CABINS   *Mariner* and *Voyager* are the only all-suite, all-balcony ships at sea, with Deluxe Suites representing the vast majority of the available accommodations. On *Mariner,* they measure 252 square feet, plus a 49-square-foot balcony;

on *Voyager,* they've been enlarged to 306 square feet, with a 50-square-foot balcony.

Mariner's suites, designed with blond woods and rich fabrics, are certainly above average, but they lack some of the inspiration and imagination that distinguish those on the earlier *Seven Seas Navigator.* For instance, while the Penthouse Suites are quite spacious (376-sq.-ft., plus a 73-sq.-ft. balcony), with a wonderful L-shaped sofa in the living area, they feel strangely spartan. Overall, the marble bathrooms aren't as spacious as the awesome ones on *Navigator,* either, and lack that ship's separate shower/bathtub facilities in the standard suites. What suites lack in inspiration, though, they make up for in diversity, ranging from the Deluxe Suites all the way up to the two forward-facing Master Suites, which measure 1,204 square feet plus two balconies that measure 798 square feet all told. Those wanting a really large outdoor space without spending a large fortune should look into the ship's Horizon Suites, located in the stern and opening onto expansive views of the ship's wake. Their 163-square-foot balconies are disproportionately huge compared to the 359-square-foot cabin size. Balconies overall are a little less than private—walls separating them do not extend to the edge of the ship's rail, making it possible to lean out and see what your neighbor is up to.

Voyager's suites are similarly excellent and with a warmer feel to boot, as well as bathrooms similar to *Navigator's,* featuring a separate bathtub and shower. Penthouse Suites, however, are not all that much bigger than Deluxe Suites, and the balconies are about two-thirds the size of what you get on *Mariner.* The terrific aft Horizon Suites (here known as Horizon View Suites) are essentially the same size as standard Deluxe Suites, but with an oversize balcony letting onto a great aft view, making these a great value. On *Voyager,* the largest suites are still the Master Suites, but the balance between interior and exterior space has been changed, with a total area loss in the bargain (1,216 sq. ft. inside + 187 outside = only 1,403 sq. ft., about 30% less space than on *Mariner*). Guests who have sailed on *Mariner* would be well served to compare floor plans before selecting their suites on *Voyager.*

All cabins on both ships feature cotton bathrobes, hair dryer, TV/VCR, stocked refrigerator, safe, and large walk-in closet. Additionally, those on *Voyager* offer CD/DVD players and e-mail connections. Butler service comes standard in *Mariner's* Master, Mariner, and Grand suites and *Voyager's* Master, Grand, Voyager, Seven Seas, and Penthouse suites.

Several dozen suites can accommodate three guests; there are no connecting suites on *Mariner,* but 24 are connecting on *Voyager.* Six suites on *Mariner* and four on *Voyager* are wheelchair friendly.

PUBLIC AREAS   While virtually every room aboard *Mariner* has a clean, fresh appearance, combining smooth blond woods with rich leathers and fabrics and an abundance of glass, marble, and stainless steel, the ship's extremely high space-per-guest ratio can, at times, create a feeling of perhaps too much room. The one-corridor design on *Voyager* helps alleviate this problem. Some guests say the smaller *Navigator* feels much cozier overall.

Mariner does have some particularly attractive spaces, such as the two-story Constellation Theater, the specialty restaurants Signatures and Latitudes (whose eclectic decor really works, with whitewashed walls and Mission-style sconces mixing nicely with Oriental and African motifs), and the Observation Lounge, which, surprisingly, is one of the least-utilized spaces on board. Sitting high up in the bow on Deck 12, it features a semicircular bar, plush chairs and sofas, and a 180-degree view of the sea, and is particularly attractive at night.

On Deck 7, the casino is adjacent to a row of boutiques and the photo shop, forward of the seven-deck atrium, which has three glass-enclosed elevators surrounding a curved stairway. One deck below at the stern is the sleek indoor/outdoor Horizon Lounge, which connects to Signatures alternative restaurant on the port side and the Connoisseur Club cigar lounge on the starboard side. Amidships on Deck 6 are the well-stocked library, a card and conference room (popular with bridge players), and the computer center, Club.Com, with 17 terminals offering Internet and e-mail access. One very nice feature is that guests are charged only for transmission time, meaning you can compose a document in Word or another program free of charge, then open your e-mail and paste it in, and only incur a cost while you're in active e-mail mode.

Continuing forward on Deck 6, you encounter the Stars Nightclub/Disco, connected to the ship's casino directly above via a spiral staircase that sort of cuts the room in half. Compared to the discos on most megaships, this one is determinedly unglitzy—no flashing lights, no video monitors, and no glass dance floor, though its marble-topped bar is nice.

On *Voyager,* the two main interior public decks are Decks 4 and 5. The Compass Rose restaurant is centrally located on Deck 4. Just forward is the Voyager lounge, which gets lots of activity both before dinner and late at night, when it serves as the disco. The casino has been repositioned just opposite this lounge, meaning it gets much greater walk-by traffic. The two-deck Constellation Theater, forward on Decks 4 and 5, is beautifully laid out, with terrific sight lines from virtually every seat. Moving aft, you find the Internet Cafe/Club.com, the shops, and the very handsome Latitudes Restaurant. At the aft end of Deck 5 are the larger Horizon Lounge and the entrance to the stunningly lovely Signatures Restaurant. On Deck 6, there's a smallish library (open to walk-by traffic, so it's not real quiet), the photo shop, and the spa/beauty salon.

DINING OPTIONS *Mariner* and *Voyager* have four restaurants, with the main dining room, the Compass Rose, serving all three meals in single open seatings. Casual breakfast and lunches are available in the indoor/outdoor La Veranda Restaurant, up near the top of the ship on Deck 11.

There are two reservations-only (but no-charge!) restaurants that are open for dinner only. Signatures features world-ranging cuisine prepared in classic French style by chefs trained at Paris's famous Le Cordon Bleu School. On *Mariner,* Latitudes offers multiple tasting dishes served in succession; aboard *Voyager,* it has American regional specialties from the Northwest to California, Texas, Illinois, Florida, New York, and Hawaii. Menus change nightly, with wine and music to match. On *Voyager,* Latitudes has an open galley, allowing guests to watch as items are prepared.

In the evening, half of La Veranda is turned into an excellent candlelit, white-tablecloth Mediterranean Bistro with a combination of waiter and self-service dining. Grilled food is available poolside, and room service runs 24 hours—guests can even have the Compass Rose dinner menu served course by course in their suites during dinner hours.

POOL, FITNESS & SPA FACILITIES Each ship's one pool and three hot tubs are located on Deck 11. Deck chairs are set up around the roomy pool area, as well as on the forward half of the deck above, where you'll also find a paddle-tennis court, golf driving nets, shuffleboard courts, and an uninterrupted jogging track. As aboard *Navigator* and *Diamond*, sunbathing doesn't seem to be the biggest priority for Radisson guests, so deck chairs should be readily available, even on sea days in warm cruising areas.

Each ship's Judith Jackson spa is located in an attractive but rather small area, with a modest number of amenities. On the plus side (and unlike the therapists on many ships), the Judith Jackson therapists don't neutralize your relaxing massage by pitching various pricey oils and aromatherapy products the moment it's over. A small ocean-view gym and separate aerobics area are located in the same area, as well as a beauty salon.

Seven Seas Navigator

The Verdict

Awash in autumn hues and deep blues, the warm and appealing 490-passenger *Navigator* is an ideal size for an ultraluxe cruise: small enough to be intimate and large enough to offer plenty of elbow room, more than a few entertainment outlets, and some of the best cabin bathrooms at sea.

Seven Seas Navigator *(photo: Radisson)*

Specifications

Size (in tons)	30,000	Officers	International
Number of Cabins	245	Crew	324 (Internat'l)
Number of Outside Cabins	245	Passenger/Crew Ratio	1.5 to 1
Cabins with Verandas	215	Year Launched	1999
Number of Passengers	490	Last Major Refurbishment	N/A

Frommer's Ratings (Scale of 1–5)   ✧✧✧✧

Cabin Comfort & Amenities	5	Dining Options	4
Ship Cleanliness & Maintenance	4	Gym & Spa Facilities	4
Public Comfort/Space	4	Children's Facilities	N/A
Decor	4	Enjoyment Factor	4.5

Navigator has well-laid-out cabins and public rooms, and if you've been on the Silversea ships, you'll notice a similar layout (especially in the Star Lounge and Galileo Lounge), since the ships were all designed by the same architects and built in the same yard, Italy's Mariotti. While *Navigator*'s interior is very attractive, her exterior is a little ungainly: Her hull was originally built to be a Russian spy ship with a four-deck-high superstructure, but three additional decks were added when Radisson came into the picture, creating a top-heavy profile.

Cabins & Rates

Cabins	Per Diems from	Sq. Ft.	Fridge	Hair Dryer	Sitting Area	TV
Suite	$323	301–1,067	yes	yes	yes	yes

CABINS   *Navigator* is an all-suite, all-outside ship, so there's not a bad room in the house. Each elegant suite is done up in shades of deep gold, beige, and burnt orange, with caramel-toned wood furniture and a swath of butterscotch suede just above the beds. Nearly 90% of them have private balconies, with only suites on the two lowest passenger decks having bay windows instead. Of these, the only ones with obstructed views are those on the port side of Deck 6 looking out onto the promenade. The standard suites are a roomy 301 square feet; the 18 top suites range from 448 to 1,067 square feet, plus 47- to 200-square-foot balconies. Passengers in the Master, Grand, and Penthouse A & B suites are treated to butler service in addition to regular service by the staff of all-female room stewardesses. Each suite has a huge marble bathroom with a separate shower stall, a long tub, lots of counter space, and wonderful bath products from spa guru Judith Jackson. Along with those on Silversea's *Silver Whisper,* and those on the new *Seven Seas Voyager,* they're the best bathrooms at sea today.

Every suite also has a sitting area with couch, terry robes, a pair of chairs, desk, vanity table and stool (with an outlet above for a hair dryer or curling iron), TV/VCR showing CNN and ESPN among other channels, minibar stocked with two complimentary bottles of wine or spirits, private safe, and a wide walk-in closet with a tall built-in dresser. The safe is on top of the dresser, so don't do what Heidi did: leave the safe door open, bend over to rummage through a drawer, and then Bam!, smack your head on the way back up. She gave herself quite a lump.

PUBLIC AREAS   The ship's attractive decor is a marriage of classic and modern design, with contemporary wooden furniture, chairs upholstered in buttery leather, walls covered in suede, and touches of stainless steel, along with silk brocade draperies, dark wood paneling, burled veneer, and marble. The ship has lots of intimate spaces, so you'll never feel overwhelmed the way you sometimes do on larger ships.

Most of the public rooms are on Decks 6 and 7, just aft of the three-story atrium and main elevator bank (whose exposed wiring and mechanics could have been better disguised). The well-stocked library has 10 computers with e-mail and Internet access. A card room is adjacent. Across the way, the cozy Navigator Lounge, paneled in mahogany and cherry wood, is a popular place for pre-dinner cocktails—which means it can get tight in there during rush hours. Next door is the Connoisseur Club cigar lounge, a somewhat cold and often underutilized wood-paneled room with umber leather chairs. Down the hall is the roomier Stars Lounge, with a long, curved, black-granite bar and clusters of oversize ocean-blue armchairs around a small dance floor. A live music duo croons pop numbers here nightly. The attractive dark-paneled casino with its striking mural is bound to attract your eye, even if you don't gamble.

Galileo's Lounge, surrounded by windows on three sides, is our favorite spot on board in the evening, when a pianist is on hand and the golden room glows magically under soft light. When the doors to the deck just outside are open on a balmy, star-soaked night, dancers spill out from the small dance floor, creating a truly romantic, dreamy scene. By day, Galileo's is a quiet venue for continental breakfast, high tea, seminars, and meetings, and is also a perfect perch from which to view the seascape.

The stage of the twinkling two-story Seven Seas Lounge is large enough for the kind of sizable, Vegas-style, song-and-dance revues typical of much larger ships (you won't find them on Seabourn's ships, or on Radisson's *Diamond,* for that matter). While sightlines are good from the tiered rows of banquettes on the first level, views from the sides of the balcony are severely obstructed.

The cheerful windowed Vista observation lounge is used for meetings and is another great scenery-viewing spot. It opens directly out to a huge patch of forward deck space just over the bridge.

DINING OPTIONS   There are two restaurants, the formal Compass Rose dining room and the more casual Portofino Grill, which serves buffet-style breakfast and lunch and is transformed every evening into a very cozy, dimly lit, reservations-only restaurant, specializing in northern Italian cuisine and with many tables for two. The Compass Rose, a pleasant, wide-open room done in warm caramel-colored woods, offers a single open seating at all meals. There's also a casual grill on the pool deck for burgers, grilled-chicken sandwiches, fries, and salads at lunchtime.

POOL, FITNESS & SPA FACILITIES   The ocean-view gym is bright and roomy for a ship of this size, and a separate aerobics room offers impressively grueling classes, such as circuit training and step. A pair of golf nets and two Ping-Pong tables are available for guest use, but they're situated high on Deck 12 in an ash-plagued nook just behind the smokestacks, and are accessible only by a hard-to-find set of interior crew stairs. The whole area looks like an afterthought. At the pool area, a wide set of stairs joins a balcony of deck chairs to a large pool and pair of hot tubs on the deck below.

Adjacent to the gym, *Navigator's* 6-room Judith Jackson spa is surprisingly uninspired decor-wise, but provides some 16 quality treatments, including a relaxing 20-minute hair-and-scalp oil massage and a 1-hour, four-hand massage, with two therapists.

Radisson Diamond

The Verdict

The little houseboat that could! Despite a weird look and some design flaws, *Diamond* is as comfortable as an old shoe, and attracts a loyal clientele that appreciates her mix of casual and luxury.

Radisson Diamond *(photo: Matt Hannafin)*

Specifications

Size (in tons)	20,295	Officers	European
Number of Cabins	175	Crew	206 (Internat'l)
Number of Outside Cabins	175	Passenger/Crew Ratio	1.7 to 1
Cabins with Verandas	121	Year Launched	1992
Number of Passengers	350	Last Major Refurbishment	2001

Frommer's Ratings (Scale of 1–5)   ★★★½

Cabin Comfort & Amenities	4	Dining Options	4
Ship Cleanliness & Maintenance	3.5	Gym & Spa Facilities	3
Public Comfort/Space	4	Children's Facilities	N/A
Decor	3	Enjoyment Factor	4

First, let's get some things out of the way: (a) *Radisson Diamond* is weird looking; (b) she has some flaws in her interior layout, including several windowless public rooms and some odd, underused spaces; and (c) she's a terrible slowpoke, with a cruising speed that rarely exceeds 12.5 knots—about 40% slower than most other cruise ships. Nonetheless, she's a great little ship that succeeds in spite of herself, and like many of the other luxe vessels, she has an extremely loyal repeat clientele. On our last cruise, the most loyal was one 10-time *Diamond* cruiser, from whom we borrowed the "comfortable as an old shoe" quote above.

Basically a gigantic catamaran, the ship has a wide, six-deck superstructure that rides 28 feet above the water, balanced on a pair of slim, pontoonlike hulls. At 103 feet wide, she's only 2 feet narrower than Cunard's *QE2,* even though the latter measures much more than twice her 420-foot length. In port, this width makes *Diamond* look deceptively large compared to massive megaships moored nearby. The design is touted as providing the utmost in stability, but, in fact, feels no more stable than a well-balanced monohull ship. She rides well in calm seas, but in choppy waters will roll enough to cause discomfort for those susceptible to motion sickness. If weather gets really rough, high waves slamming against the underside of the passenger decks can create a loud and unpleasant shuddering sensation.

Though she offers service and cuisine on a level with Seabourn and Silversea, *Diamond* is quite informal, with an elegant though low-key interior design, extraordinarily low passenger density, and wide, comfortable outside decks that make you feel as if you're visiting a friend's home or a small, high-end, family-run hotel rather than sailing on a cruise ship. Even though there are only a handful of public rooms, you'll sometimes wonder where all the people are.

Cabins & Rates

Cabins	Per Diems from	Sq. Ft.	Fridge	Hair Dryer	Sitting Area	TV
Suite	$265	193–472	yes	yes	yes	yes

CABINS   All cabins (which the line insists on calling "suites," even though they really aren't) are outsides measuring a largish 243 square feet, though in the case of the 121 balcony cabins, this measure includes the balcony. (Fleetmates *Navigator* and *Voyager*'s standard cabins are much larger at about 300 sq. ft., plus balcony.) Teak-decked balconies aren't huge, at about 50 square feet, but are extremely private, with a full steel wall separating you from your neighbors. The 54 cabins without balconies have big, rectangular windows, and views are wide open and unobstructed from every cabin. Aside from the balcony/window difference, standard cabins are all nearly identical, with small sitting areas, a queen or two twin beds covered with wonderful thick duvets, a makeup table and mirror, TVs broadcasting CNN and other channels, a VCR, a minibar/fridge stocked free of charge one time, terry bathrobes, and a safe. Though the cabins are sizable, the sitting area is a bit cramped in balcony cabins, and closet space is minimal though adequate since the ship sticks mostly to itineraries of a week or less. Drawer space is plentiful. The subdued decor is done in a mix of modern and Art Deco styling, with blond wood trim, pastel colors and spot artwork, and quilted wall hangings behind the beds.

Bathrooms have marble countertops, granite floors, bathtub/showers, and hair dryers. Though large enough, they're not as opulent as you might expect, with tiny bathtubs and little counter space, though they have shelves to accommodate toiletries. All bathrooms come stocked with Judith Jackson soap, shampoo, conditioner, lotion, and bath gel.

Four Master Suites range from 436 and 472 square feet, plus balconies, have extra-large sitting areas, and come with butler service. Master Suites 903 and 904 have two bathrooms.

About half of the cabins on Deck 8 can accommodate a third person on a foldaway couch. Two cabins are wheelchair-friendly.

PUBLIC AREAS *Diamond* is an extremely simple ship to navigate, with all public rooms opening off the understated six-story atrium with its wide, curving stairway. As on the Seabourn ships (built at around the same time), the ship's overall decor is not as drop-dead gorgeous as aboard the more high-style Crystal and Silversea ships, tending to be more comfortable than sleek, with many heavy wood chairs and simple, easy-on-the-eye color schemes.

During the day, many passengers relax on the extremely wide teak decks. In the evenings, all activity is divided between the Windows Lounge, The Club, and the Splash Bar, a partially covered (and remarkably well-stocked) bar just aft of the pool.

The Windows Lounge, as the name implies, is a split-level (effectively three-tier), wood-paneled showroom with comfortable brown-leather chairs and sofas and a dramatic forward view of the sea through floor-to-ceiling windows. It's an oddly configured room, arranged in a kind of T formation: You enter through the upstairs bar level, and the stage, orchestra pit, dance floor, and main seating stretch port to starboard on the lower level, with two small balconies on either side. Because space is tight, shows here tend to be small-scale: comedians or musical revues featuring four talented singers/dancers, whose frequent costume changes take the place of any sets or props. There's piano music here at teatime and before dinner, dancing to the jazzily elegant Diamond Five Orchestra after, and a usually sparsely attended disco session late at night.

The ship's other main public room is The Club, an entirely windowless but nonetheless elegant Art Deco piano lounge with diffused lighting and paneled walls, furnished with black marble tables and clusters of beautiful, comfortable, cream-colored leather chairs and couches spaced widely apart—good if you're looking for quiet, romantic privacy, but definitely not conducive to keeping the room lively. For lively, sidle up to the piano to hear Kemble, *Diamond*'s long-time one-name pianist, of whom *Rolling Stone* once said (to paraphrase), "If Liberace had a son, he'd be Kemble." He's a hoot and a half, extremely talented, and adds immeasurably to the overall *Diamond* experience.

Other public areas include the small and unimpressive Chips Casino and the rarely used, skylit top level of the atrium, furnished with card tables and a ridiculously overstuffed white-leather couch into which you sink about 8 inches, then immediately fall asleep. (The vessel's Master Suites have these same couches—talk about luxurious.)

Public areas of Deck 7 are devoted to a convention/meetings center that doubles as utilitarian (*read:* blandly decorated—very) public space: The Constellation Center, the largest meeting room, is also used for art auctions and movies; and two boardrooms double as the ship's library and video library, from which guests can take books and films on the honor system 24 hours a day. A small five-station computer center offers e-mail, but no Internet connection. You have to use the ship's address, you cannot access your own account, and—shades of 1930s pageboys!—any e-mail you get in reply is printed out and hand-delivered to your stateroom.

DINING OPTIONS Bar none, the ship's most notable space is its romantic main dining room, one of the loveliest at sea today, with an entire wall of windows at the stern, an Art Deco mural wrapping around the ceiling, and soaring, stylized Deco columns. Though large enough to comfortably accommodate all guests at its single open seatings, the room achieves an intimate feel through subtle dividers that break it into several smaller areas, all with widely spaced tables and champagne-toned, scroll-back chairs, with candles adding a soft glow at dinner.

The Grill, on Deck 10, is a very casual setting for breakfast and lunch, with seating either inside at the chunky wooden tables and chairs or outside at any of the 34 tables on the wide port and starboard decks. At lunch, an extensive buffet with both staple items and specialties is set up inside and out. Come dinnertime, the Grill is decked out with red-checkered tablecloths and transformed into Don Vito's, a boisterous, casual, reservations-only venue serving northern Italian cuisine, along with singing waiters and waitresses, dancing, audience participation, lots of free-flowing red wine, and lots of laughs. Plan to be up late: The experience stretches out to almost 3 hours.

POOL, FITNESS & SPA FACILITIES One of *Diamond*'s best features is her extraordinarily wide teak decks, with sunbathing space beside the pool and hot tub, on the huge aft deck (with shuffleboard courts, Ping-Pong, and a golf driving net and putting area), in a forward observation area above the bridge, and in various nooks. Shade-seekers can snuggle into port and starboard areas in the shadow of the dangling lifeboats.

The ship lacks a traditional wraparound promenade deck, but there's a small jogging track on Deck 11 that wraps around the ship's small Steiner-managed spa/beauty salon and its decent-size ocean-view gym (13 laps = 1 mile). Stretch classes are held daily, and aerobics and yoga are added occasionally.

The ship's large, hydraulically lowered watersports platform is, at present, nonfunctional and off-limits to passengers—unfortunate since its space in the stern could be a prime sunbathing spot. As a makeshift measure, a floating marina is moored beside one of the ship's pontoons when waters are calm, allowing guests to swim, go kayaking, or take out a WaveRunner—you can even make a run right under the ship, between its pontoons, which is an incredibly weird thing to do.

4 Seabourn Cruise Line

55 Francisco St., Suite 710, San Francisco, CA 94133. ℂ 800/929-9595 or 415/391-7444. Fax 415/391-8518. www.seabourn.com.

THE LINE IN A NUTSHELL Small and intimate, these quiet, comfortable megayachts lavish all guests with personal attention and very fine cuisine.

THE EXPERIENCE Strictly upper-crust Seabourn caters to guests who are well mannered and prefer their fellow vacationers to be the same. Generally, they aren't into pool games and deck parties, preferring a good book and cocktail chatter, but maybe they'll go for recent enhancements such as free mini-massages on deck and soothing Eucalyptus oil baths drawn in suites upon request.

Due to the ships' small size, guests mingle easily and enjoy mellow pursuits such as trivia games and presentations by guest lecturers. With 157 crewmembers to just 208 guests (a higher ratio than on almost any other line), service is very personal; staff members greet you by name from the moment you check in, and your wish is their command.

Pros

- **Top-shelf service:** Staff seems to know what you need before you ask.
- **Totally all-inclusive:** Unlimited wines and spirits are included, as are gratuities.
- **Excellent dining:** Even the breakfast buffets are exceptional, and having dinner on the outside decks of the Veranda Café, with the churning wake shushing just below you, is divine.
- **Remote ports of call:** These small ships are able to visit less-touristed Caribbean ports that larger ships can't.

Cons

- **Limited activities and nightlife:** There's not a whole lot going on, but then many guests like it that way.
- **Shallow drafts mean rocky seas:** Rough seas in the Caribbean are relatively rare, but not unheard of. Because the ships are small, they can get tossed around a lot more (and in less-rough waters) than larger vessels.
- **Aging vessels:** When compared to the new ships being built by its competitors, Seabourn's 12- to 16-year-old *Legend* and *Pride* lack luster and suffer from some unfortunate design decisions, namely the configuration of the pool and sunbathing deck.
- **No balconies:** The sliding-glass doors that have been added to many of the suites are an improvement, but no substitute for the real thing.

Compared with the other ultraluxury lines, here's how Seabourn rates:

	Poor	Fair	Good	Excellent	Outstanding
Enjoyment Factor					✓
Dining					✓
Activities		✓			
Children's Program	N/A*				
Entertainment		✓			
Service				✓	
Worth the Money				✓	

* Seabourn has no children's program.

SEABOURN: THE CAVIAR OF CRUISE SHIPS

Seabourn was established in 1987, when luxury-cruise patriarch Warren Titus and Norwegian shipping mogul Atle Brynestad commissioned a trio of ultra-upscale 10,000-ton vessels from a north German shipyard. They sold out to industry giant Carnival Corporation in 1991, though the line maintains strong links with its Norwegian roots, registering each of its ships in the country and even stocking suite minibars with bottles of Norwegian Ringnes pilsner. In the spirit of streamlining, in 2001, Carnival Corporation sold the line's *Sea Goddess* vessels to Seabourn's original owner, Brynestad, and in 2002, transferred the line's 758-passenger *Seabourn Sun* to sister line Holland America. The *Goddess* ships now sail for SeaDream Yacht Club—see the review on p. 315—and *Seabourn Sun* now sails as HAL's *Prinsendam.*

Today, Seabourn finds itself struggling to remain atop the ultraluxury market that it dominated for years, with lines such as Radisson, Silversea, and Crystal building newer, bigger ships with more contemporary design and more in the way of entertainment and onboard activities. But Seabourn hasn't resigned itself to fourth fiddle just yet, and is, in fact, focusing more than ever on its strengths: doting, personalized service; fine food and wine; and a laid-back atmosphere on ships small enough to venture into exotic harbors where megaships can't go. In fact, the line now officially calls itself "The Yachts of Seabourn." New French balconies (sliding-glass doors) were added to 36 of the ships' suites in 2000 to better compete with the competition's balcony cabins, and in early 2002, even more enhancements were introduced, from complimentary mini-massages on deck to Molton Brown toiletries in suite bathrooms and fancy Eucalyptus oil or Dead Sea salt baths drawn on request. At least one shore excursion is complimentary on each cruise.

PASSENGER PROFILE

Seabourn's guests are well-traveled seniors mostly in their 60s and 70s, and are used to the five-star treatment. The average household income here is in excess of $250,000, and many have net worths in the millions. You are likely to encounter former CEOs, lawyers, investment bankers, real-estate tycoons, and entrepreneurs. The majority of passengers are couples, and there are always a handful of singles as well, usually widows or widowers. A number of European and Australian guests usually spice up the mix, but no matter what their nationality, these are experienced globe-trotting travelers. While some adult children and their parents travel together, don't expect to find children or even young adults on these ships. There is nothing to appeal to them, and the passengers prefer it that way.

DINING

While Seabourn's cuisine is very, very good and remains one of the line's strong points, Crystal, Silversea, and Radisson offer equal or superior dining, as do the elegant alternative restaurants aboard mainstream Celebrity Cruises' Millennium-class ships.

Fleetwide, dining is offered in a single open seating in the main dining rooms, allowing guests to dine whenever they choose and with whomever they want, between about 7 and 10pm. Dinner service is high-style, with waiters dramatically lifting silver lids off dishes in unison and almost running at a trot through the elaborate, six-course European service. But while the service is usually attentive and unobtrusive, on a recent cruise it was uneven. Sometimes the waiters moved *too* fast—we would have liked to linger longer between courses. Other times, service seemed slow. Food, which is prepared to order, didn't always arrive at the table simultaneously for all diners—polite tablemates had to wait. And condiments, dressings, and sauces sometimes came several minutes after the food. Overall, though, the waitstaff was quite accommodating, going out of its way to please.

Celebrity restaurateur Charlie Palmer, of New York's Aureole fame, is behind the ships' menus, with the ships' chefs training in Palmer's shoreside restaurants. Four entrees change nightly. One night may feature dishes such as pan-roasted halibut with asparagus risotto, sautéed pheasant, grilled venison chops, and grilled lamb loin. There's also a **vegetarian selection** such as soy-glazed shiitakes, a **spa choice** (called "Simplicity") with entrees like crab lasagna with tomato basil coulis, and a standing a la carte menu with such staples as Caesar salad, angel-hair pasta, baked salmon, chicken breast, New York strip steak, grilled beef filet, and broiled lamb chops. If nothing on the menu appeals to you, just ask for something you'd prefer: If the chef has the ingredients aboard, he'll prepare whatever you'd like. Want to dine alone as a couple? Not a problem. The maitre d' will be aware of preferences, and will also be aware of solo travelers who may like company.

Formal nights (two per weeklong cruise) are very formal, with virtually every male present in a tuxedo and ladies in sequins and gowns. On other nights, things have relaxed somewhat as Seabourn seeks to attract a younger crowd (younger, as in 50-somethings), and ties are not required. Regardless, passengers always look very pulled together. One night on each itinerary includes a **festive buffet dinner** served out on deck by the pool (jumbo shrimp and caviar can also be ordered poolside, or anywhere else, at no charge—aren't you salivating just reading this?), and silver-service **Beach barbecues**—complete with china and linen, and, of course, champagne and **caviar**—are also a big hit in remote ports such as Virgin Gorda, Jost Van Dyke, or tiny Mayreau in the Grenadines.

As a **casual alternative** for breakfast and lunch, the newly redecorated Veranda Café, with indoor and outdoor seating, offers a combination buffet and table-service menu. At breakfast, omelets are made to your specifications and an impressive fresh-fruit selection includes papaya, mango, raspberries, and blackberries; at lunch, you'll find salads, sandwich makings, fresh pasta, and maybe jumbo shrimp, smoked salmon, and smoked oysters, plus hot sliced roast beef, duck, and ham on the carving board. Many evenings per cruise, the Veranda Café also serves a more intimate and casual dinner, its outdoor seating offering a rare opportunity to dine with the sea breezes and night sky surrounding you; Caribbean, Italian, Thai, and Surf & Turf menus are featured. Dine here for the atmosphere, not the food—it's better in the main dining room.

Complimentary wines (about 18 on any given cruise) and **champagne** from the House of Heidsieck are served at lunch and dinner, as well as at any time and place on the ships (ditto for spirits and soft drinks); an extensive—and expensive—list of other vintages is also available. Desserts are varied and scrumptious, including ice-cream balls dipped in the most delectable milk, dark, and white chocolate.

Room service is available 24 hours a day on all ships. During normal lunch or dinner hours, your private multi-course meal can mirror the dining room service, right down to the silver, crystal, and porcelain, though don't expect all five courses to actually arrive separately. On a recent cruise, my shrimp cocktail and salad were served together, followed 5 minutes later by my main course;

Seabourn Fleet Itineraries

Ship	Itineraries
Seabourn Legend	**14-night W. Carib/Canal:** Between Fort Lauderdale and Puerto Caldera, Costa Rica, Nov 2003–Feb 2004 and Nov–Dec 2004, visiting Belize City and Hunting Cay (Belize); Roatan (Honduras); Puerto Quepos, Playa Flamingo, and either Puerto Limon or Puerto Moin (Costa Rica); and Gamboa and Fuerte Amador (Panama), with 6 days at sea including a transit of the Panama Canal. **14-night E. Carib:** Round-trip from Fort Lauderdale, Dec 2003–Jan 2004, visiting St. Thomas, St. John, Martinique, Les Saintes, St. Martin, St. Barts, San Juan, and Virgin Gorda (BVIs), with 5 days at sea. **7-night E. Carib 1:** Fort Lauderdale to St. Thomas, Feb 2004, visiting St. John, St. Kitts, Nevis, and St. Croix, with 2 days at sea. **7-night E. Carib 2:** Round-trip from St. Thomas, Mar 2004, visiting Martinique, Nevis, St. Kitts, St. Croix, and St. John, with 1 day at sea. **Non-Caribbean Itineraries:** Europe.
Seabourn Pride	**7-night E. & S. Carib 1:** Fort Lauderdale to Barbados, Nov–Dec 2003 and Oct and Dec 2004, visiting Virgin Gorda (BVIs), St. Barts, and St. John or St. Thomas, with 3 days at sea. **7-night S. Carib/Orinoco River:** Round-trip from Barbados, Nov–Dec 2003 and Nov–Dec 2004, visiting Tobago, Puerto Ordaz (Venezuela), Grenada, and Mayreau (Grenadines), with 2 days at sea. **7-night E. & S. Carib 2:** Round-trip from Barbados, Nov–Dec 2003 and Nov–Dec 2004, visiting Nevis, St. Barts, St. Martin, Les Saintes, and Bequia, with 1 day at sea. **14-night E. Carib:** Round-trip from Fort Lauderdale, Dec 2003–Jan 2004, visiting St. John, St. Thomas, St. Lucia, Martinique, Les Saintes, Nevis, St. Barts, and San Juan, with 5 days at sea. **Non-Caribbean Itineraries:** Europe, New England/Canada, South America.

dessert and coffee were never offered (of course, we could have called again if we'd really wanted it). Outside of mealtimes, the room-service menu is more limited, with burgers, salads, sandwiches, and pastas. In-cabin breakfasts are popular, and you can have your eggs prepared any way you like them.

ACTIVITIES

The Seabourn ships don't offer too much in the way of organized activities, but typically offer trivia contests, galley tours, **wine tastings,** and the occasional card games and tournaments. The lack of in-your-face, rah-rah activities is what most passengers like about Seabourn, though each ship does have a cruise director to organize things. Public announcements are few, and, for the most part, passengers are left alone to pursue their own personal peace.

Each of the ships has a retractable **watersports marina** that unfolds from its stern, weather and sea conditions permitting, allowing passengers direct access to the sea for water-skiing, windsurfing, sailing, snorkeling, banana-boat riding, and swimming. Each cruise features at least one and often two **guest lecturers** discussing upcoming ports as well as other random topics. Noted chefs, scientists, historians, authors, or statesmen may be aboard, or maybe a wine connoisseur, composer, anthropologist, TV director, or professor, presenting lectures and mingling with guests. From time to time, the line manages to bring aboard celebrities; past guests have included Alan Arkin, Tom Smothers, Gregory Hines, Alex Trebek, Paul Theroux, and Jill Eikenberry.

The ships each have four computers in a small business center for guests to e-mail and surf the Internet. Movies are available for viewing in cabins, and movies are sometimes shown out on deck as well, under the stars (and with popcorn too!).

CHILDREN'S PROGRAM

These ships are not geared to children, but there are no restrictions against them (as long as they're at least 1 year old), so you may occasionally see a young child. He or she will probably be a very bored child, however, since the line provides no special programs, no special menus, and no special kids' concessions. In a pinch, you may be able to arrange to have an available crewmember provide babysitting service.

ENTERTAINMENT

There are two roomy entertainment lounges, and both have small stages where a cabaret singer or two, solo instrumentalist (harpist, pianist, violinist), quartet, or maybe a comedian or puppeteer performs. As Seabourn continues to try to loosen up a bit, though, lighter, more fun and participatory entertainment is replacing the more traditional fare, especially in the Caribbean. On a recent cruise, we were delighted to watch three performers doing a lively 1950s/1960s rock 'n' roll show, one playing the goofy, gum-chewing, bobby-sock-wearing coed who exhorted the audience to come up on the dance floor (several couples did). Another night, a hilarious Steve Allen–style comedian/pianist delighted the audience with his wisecracking wit and musical talents.

Before dinner, a pianist plays and sings for cocktailers in The Club; adjacent is the small, rather drab casino with a handful of card tables and slots. You'll also find a pianist playing in the observation lounge on Deck 8, strictly as background music for passengers more interested in drinks and quiet conversation.

Due to the ships' small size, there are obviously no big production shows with sets and elaborate costume changes like those you'd find on the larger ships of Silversea, Radisson, and Crystal. This seems to please most guests, who choose a Seabourn cruise exactly because it isn't large enough to offer splashier shows.

SERVICE

With the minor exception of some uneven dining service and the occasional forgetful cabin stewardess, the service staff is outstanding: friendly, courteous, eager to please, discreet, and highly competent. Most are European (many Norwegian) and most have gained experience at the grand hotels of Europe; the cabin staff is all female. They're among Seabourn's most valuable assets. All **gratuities** are included in the rates.

If you don't want to deal with lugging your luggage to the airport (or your car), Seabourn offers a service where you can ship your bags directly to the ship.

Laundry and **dry cleaning** are available. There are also complimentary **self-service laundry rooms,** though on a recent *Legend* cruise, the dryers were malfunctioning; one didn't heat at all, while the other took 2 hours to (almost) dry a normal load.

Seabourn Pride •
Seabourn Legend

The Verdict

These smallish megayachts remain among the top in the market, though they're in a class by themselves—they just don't offer the same experience as the larger and newer ships of ultraluxury lines such as Radisson, Silversea, and Crystal, which have more entertainment options and brighter decor.

Seabourn Legend *(photo: Seabourn Cruise Line)*

Specifications

Size (in tons)	10,000	Crew	157 (Internat'l)
Number of Cabins	100	Passenger/Crew Ratio	1.5 to 1
Number of Outside Cabins	100	Year Launched	
Cabins with Verandas	6	*Pride*	1988
Number of Passengers	208	*Legend*	1992
Officers	Norwegian	Last Major Refurbishment	2000

Frommer's Ratings (Scale of 1–5)   ★★★★

Cabin Comfort & Amenities	4	Dining Options	3.5
Ship Cleanliness & Maintenance	4	Gym & Spa Facilities	3
Public Comfort/Space	5	Children's Facilities	N/A
Decor	3	Enjoyment Factor	4

Got the time? Got the money? Come aboard these sleek, attractive ships for a cruise to just about any Caribbean port you'd want to visit. Even with just 208 passengers, you may not see half of your cruisemates between the lifeboat drill and debarkation, and that's one of the great things about these ships: You can be as social or as private as you wish, with no rowdiness or loud music and no one exhorting you to get involved. While you're aboard, your ship is your floating boutique hotel or your private yacht. You make the call.

Cabins & Rates

Cabins	Per Diems from	Sq. Ft.	Fridge	Hair Dryer	Sitting Area	TV
Suite	$417	277–575	yes	yes	yes	yes

CABINS Everything about a Seabourn cabin has the impeccably maintained feel of an upscale Scandinavian hotel. All cabins are outside, with ocean views, and measure 277 square feet. Almost all are identical. Color schemes, a bit on the dull side, are either ice-blue or champagne-colored, with lots of bleached oak or birch wood trim, as well as mirrors and spotlight lighting. While only the top six Owner's Suites have proper balconies, 36 regular suites on Decks 5 and 6 have wonderful French balconies with sliding doors and a few inches of balcony for your feet. While you can't fit a chair on one, they do allow sunlight to pour into the cabin, as well as offer a great view up and down the length of the ship. You can sit on the sofa or in a chair and read while sunning yourself out of the wind and out of view. You can also sleep with the doors wide open, going to sleep with the sounds and smells of the ocean—unless, of course, the officers on the bridge decide to lock the doors. If seas get even a little choppy or the wind picks up a hair, a flick of a switch locks your door automatically and there's not a darn thing you can do about it. (Remember, these ships are small, so you're not that far above the water line. They like to avoid waves and sea spray getting into those lovely suites.)

The two Classic Suites measure 400 square feet, and two pairs of Owner's Suites are 530 and 575 square feet and have verandas, dining areas, and guest powder rooms. Their dark wood furnishings make the overall feeling more like a hotel room than a ship's suite, but, as is true of any cabins positioned near the bow of relatively small ships, they can be somewhat uncomfortable during rough seas. Owner's Suites 05 and 06 have obstructed views.

The best features of the suites are their bathrooms and walk-in closets, with plenty of hanging space for Seabourn's extended cruises. Drawer space, on the other hand, is minimal. White marble bathrooms include a tub and shower (depending on the ship, 10–14 suites have only showers), and lots of shelf, counter, and cabinet space. Those on *Seabourn Pride* have twin sinks; those on *Legend* have single sinks. Terry bathrobes, slippers, and umbrellas are provided for guest use, though on a recent cruise, the stewardess forgot to provide our robes for the first 2 days. Fresh fruit and a flower complete the scene.

The coffee table in the sitting area can be pulled up to become a dining table, and the complimentary minibar is stocked upon arrival with two bottles of liquor or wine of your choice (a request form comes with your cruise documents) and a chilled bottle of Piper Heidsieck champagne. Unlimited bottled water, beer, and soft drinks are restocked throughout the cruise. Ice is replenished twice daily (more often on request), and bar setups are in each room. There's a desk, hair dryer, safe, radio/CD player (music and book CDs are available for borrowing), and TV/VCR with CNN plus several in-house movie channels. Videos are available in each ship's small library.

Connecting cabins are available. Some are marketed as 554-square-foot Double Suites, and that's exactly what they are: two 277-square-foot suites, with one converted to a lounge. There are four wheelchair-accessible suites.

PUBLIC AREAS   A double, open-spiral, brass-railed staircase links the public areas, which are, overall, duller than you'd expect on ships of this caliber. Step onto most ships today and you'll "oooh" and "ahhh" at the decor. Not so here, where the minimalist Scandinavian design ethic is in play. For the most part, public rooms are spare and almost ordinary looking. Art and ornamentation are conspicuous by their absence, with the exception of the small lobby area in front of the purser's desk on Deck 5, where attractive murals of ship scenes liven up the curved walls.

The forward-facing observation lounge on Sky Deck is the most attractive public room, a quiet venue all day long for reading or cards, the spot for afternoon tea (during which a pianist provides background music), and a good place for a drink before meals. A chart and compass on the wall outside will help you pinpoint the ship's current position, and a computerized wall map lets you track future cruises.

The Club piano bar in the stern offers great views during daylight hours, is packed before dinner, and sometimes offers after-dinner entertainment such as a "Name That Tune" game or a cabaret show for the hearty few who stay up past 10pm. Hors d'oeuvres are served here both before and after dinner. A tiny, cramped casino is adjacent, with a couple of blackjack tables, a roulette wheel, and about 10 slots. The downstairs show lounge is a dark, tiered, all-purpose space for lectures, the captain's cocktail party, and featured entertainers such as singers, comedians, and pianists.

One of the best places for a romantic, moonlit moment is the isolated patch of deck far forward in the bow on Deck 5, where a lone hot tub also resides.

DINING OPTIONS   The formal restaurant, located on the lowest deck, is a large low-ceilinged room with elegant candlelit tables. (With the lights low, you can hardly notice the old bright peach and gray paint job on the columns and moldings.) It's open for breakfast, lunch, and dinner; officers, cruise staff, and sometimes guest lecturers host tables at dinnertime. If you're not in the mood for the formal dining room, the recently spruced-up Veranda Café serves a combination buffet and full-service breakfast and lunch; the fresh-fruit selection at breakfast is very impressive. On non-formal nights, it's open for dinner, too, on a reservations-only basis, with restaurateur Charlie Palmer creating the menus, as he does in the main restaurant. Dishes are prepared around themes such as "Steak House Traditions," including steaks, fish, and chicken grilled with creamed spinach and potatoes; and "Citrus & Ginger Asian," a combination of Japanese, Thai, and Chinese flavors. In good weather, it's a real treat and very romantic to dine at one of the arc of awning-covered tables located aft, overlooking the wake, with the wind and surf serenading you.

A special of the day—pizza with pineapple topping or fresh ingredients for tacos—is also available at the pleasant Sky Bar overlooking the Lido, for those who don't want to change out of their swimsuits.

POOL, FITNESS & SPA FACILITIES   The outdoor pool, which gets little use, is awkwardly situated in a shadowy location aft of the open Deck 7, between the twin engine uptakes and flanked by lifeboats that hang from both sides of the ship. A pair of whirlpools is located just forward of the pool. A third hot tub is perched far forward on Deck 5; it's wonderfully isolated and a perfect spot (as is the whole patch of deck here) from which to watch a port come into sight or fade away.

A retractable, wood-planked watersports marina opens out from the stern of each ship so that passengers can hop into sea kayaks or go windsurfing, waterskiing, or snorkeling right from the vessel. An attached steel mesh net creates a protected saltwater pool when the marina is in use.

The gym and Steiner-managed spa are roomy for ships this small, and are located forward of the Lido. There's a separate aerobics area that offers classes such as yoga and pilates as well as more traditional stuff, plus two saunas, massage rooms, and a beauty salon.

5 SeaDream Yacht Club

2601 S. Bayshore Dr., Penthouse 1B, Coconut Grove, FL 33133. ℂ 800/707-4911 or 305/856-5622. Fax 305/856-7599. www.seadreamyachtclub.com.

THE LINE IN A NUTSHELL Intimate cruise-ships-turned-yachting-vessels, SeaDream's two small ships deliver an upscale yet casual experience without the regimentation of traditional cruise itineraries and activities.

THE EXPERIENCE SeaDream—a new line created by Seabourn founder Atle Brynestad with that line's two *Sea Goddess* ships—will entice those who value impeccable service, a mellow atmosphere, and a good batch of sevruga Malossol caviar. But the line is seeking another kind of traveler as well: one who straddles a WaveRunner, barhops in Monte Carlo, and enjoys a spontaneous mountain-bike trek. But this isn't just the wealthy man's *Survivor* episode. Pampering is still a major focus, and the line's flexible itineraries and fluid daily schedules should appeal to landlubbers used to doing vacations.

Pros

- **Flexible itineraries:** Captains have the authority to duck inclement weather by visiting a different port or to extend a stay off an island because of perfect snorkeling conditions.
- **Truly all-inclusive:** Unlimited wines and spirits as well as tips are included in the rates.
- **Late-night departures from key ports:** Instead of leaving port around cocktail hour—just when things begin to get interesting—the ships will stay late or even overnight in places like St. Barts to allow passengers a night of carousing on terra firma.
- **Cool tech stuff:** These ships were built in the mid-1980s, but they've been outfitted for the 21st century. Every cabin is equipped with a flat-screen TV, Internet access, and CD and DVD players; and jet skis, MP3 players, and Segway Human Transporters are available for passenger use.

Cons

- **Rough seas:** While the intimacy of these ships can be a selling point, their size can be a detriment: They bob like buoys in even mildly rough waters, and the diesel engines sometimes produce a shimmying sensation.
- **Limited entertainment:** When you're not sipping a late-evening drink in Virgin Gorda or St. Barts, you're probably watching the lounge act, but don't expect Broadway-style pyrotechnics and scantily clad chorus girls. A piano player and a sidekick are the sum total of the ship's entertainment.

Compared with the other ultraluxury lines, here's how SeaDream rates:

	Poor	Fair	Good	Excellent	Outstanding
Enjoyment Factor					✓
Dining				✓	
Activities			✓		
Children's Program	N/A*				
Entertainment			✓		
Service					✓
Worth the Money					✓

* SeaDream offers no children's program.

SEADREAM: YOUR YACHT AWAITS

In mid-2001, Norwegian entrepreneur Atle Brynestad, who founded Seabourn in 1987 and chaired the company for a decade, bought out Carnival Corporation's stake in Seabourn's *Sea Goddess I* and *Sea Goddess II,* then worked with former Seabourn and Cunard president and CEO Larry Pimentel to form the SeaDream Yacht Club, reintroducing the ships as twin yachts. *SeaDream II* was redesigned and refitted at a Bremerhaven, Germany, shipyard and was unveiled in Miami in February 2002. Her sister ship debuted in April 2002, following her own refurbishment.

The mantra from management is that these vessels are *not* cruise ships. They are yachts and have been painstakingly renovated to invoke the ambience of your best friend's private vessel, on the theory (as president and CEO Pimentel told us recently) that "cruising is about what happens inside the vessel; yachting is about what happens outside." Toward this end, deck space has been expanded and refurbished with such touches as queen-size Sun Beds and captain's chairs with high-powered binoculars. The Main Salon feels cozier, too, with fabrics and art handpicked by Linn Brynestad, the owner's spouse. The dress code steers clear of the traditional tux and sequins dress-up night by favoring "yacht casual" wear. Some men wear jackets, but never ties. Itineraries are designed so that ships stay overnight in three-quarters of the ports they visit because, as Pimentel explained, "There's no sense in leaving a port at 5 if it doesn't start really happening till 11."

Although the company is new and the ships offer many new features, there is plenty that past Seabourn cruisers will recognize, including the crew, 80% of whom worked on the *Goddess* ships. Meticulous attention to detail and personalized service are still the ships' greatest assets.

PASSENGER PROFILE

Most passengers are in their 40s to 60s, are 70% American (with Brits and other Europeans making up most of the remainder), and are not veteran cruisers. In theory, they have refined tastes but balk at the rigid structure of cruise itineraries. They're happy to strike up a game of backgammon beside the pool, or venture into town with the chef in search of the evening's special fish. They want top-notch service and gourmet food, but are secure enough to dispense with a stuffy atmosphere. At least that's the plan.

So far, more than 50% of business comes from full charters of the ships, often by large (rich) families. Smaller groups can take advantage of a deal that gives one free cabin for every four booked, up to a maximum of 25 cabins. Still, groups of 50 are a significant presence on ships this size, so when booking, inquire whether there will be any large groups aboard, to avoid the "in crowd/out crowd" vibe.

DINING

Dining is a high point of a SeaDream cruise. Dishes such as the sautéed foie gras with cassis glaze and candied apples won raves on a recent cruise, and a coconut soufflé with vanilla sauce was still being discussed in the Top of the Yacht Bar hours after dinner.

Daily five-course dinners include five entrees that change nightly, with a **healthy selection** among them. In addition, there's a **vegetarian option** and a la carte items such as linguini with pesto and rosemary marinated lamb chops. The kitchen will prepare **special requests** provided that the ingredients are on board. **Local specialties,** such as fresh fish from markets in various ports, are likely to be incorporated into the menu.

Dining is offered from 7:30 to 10pm in the main dining room on Deck 2, where open seating offers a nice variety of tables, from the nine-seat captain's table to cozier places for two (though during the evening rush, it's not easy to snag one). Guests can venture "out" for dinner by requesting a spot in advance at one of several private alcoves on Deck 6, or even on the bridge. These special dining ops may not be advertised heavily on board—you'll have to ask for them. The partially covered, open-sided Topside Restaurant on Deck 5 serves breakfast and lunch daily, with guests choosing from a buffet or menu. Unlike the practice on the former *Sea Goddesses,* there are no formal evenings. At dinner in the Dining Salon, jackets are not required; some men wear them, but many just stick to collared shirts.

Room service is available 24 hours a day for those who don't want to pause their DVD player. Another new feature is a **raid the pantry** concept that allows guests to sneak to the Topside Restaurant's buffet area at any hour for sandwiches, cookies, and other snacks one shouldn't be eating in the middle of the night.

Dining highlights from the old *Sea Goddess* cruises are carried over here, including lavish **beach barbecues,** called the Caviar and Champagne Splash, on Jost Van Dyke and Virgin Gorda. As you lounge on a quiet beach gazing out toward the anchored ship, you'll see the captain standing at the bow of a Zodiac boat zooming toward the beach, looking like George Washington crossing the Delaware, but in decidedly better weather and absolutely bluer water. The captain's soldiers, 20-something European stewards in Hawaiian shirts, hop into the surf carrying a life preserver that doubles as a floating serving tray for an open tin of sevruga Malossol caviar, encircled by little dishes of sour cream, chopped egg, and minced onion. Two stewards perform ceremonial running front flips into the surf with champagne bottles in hand, then pop off the corks in unison. Meanwhile, other crewmembers are tending the barbecues, preparing grilled lobster tails, barbecued spare ribs, carved roast beef, baked potatoes, salads, and fresh fruit. Passengers feast under umbrellas at tables set with proper china and hotel silver brought ashore by the staff. It doesn't get much better than this.

The line's **open-bar policy** means that unlimited alcoholic beverages are served throughout the vessels, though cabin minifridges are stocked only with complimentary beer and soft drinks. If you want wine and spirits for your minifridge, you'll have to pay. Advance requests for favorite libations are encouraged. Each ship's wine cellar includes some 3,500 bottles, of which an excellent selection is complimentary. For the connoisseur, a separate wine list lists extra-cost vintages, including (when we were aboard) a $395 Château Mouton-Rothschild 1993.

ACTIVITIES

Considering the small size of these ships, they have a surprising array of indoor and outdoor activities. The best part is that few of them are organized and none of them require an announcement over the ship's intercom (*read:* peace and quiet). Cabins offer DVD and CD players, flat-screen TVs, and Internet accessibility. Internet access is also available in the library. Guests have access to portable MP3 players that (talk about a homey touch) were programmed by CEO Pimentel's 18-year-old sons, who loaded them with 170 hours of music from all genres, from pop to jazz to classical. There are about 25 on each ship; pick them up at the reception desk.

Outdoor enthusiasts are encouraged to take advantage of the toys at each ship's **Watersports Marina,** which is outfitted with sea kayaks, Sunfish, and

SeaDream Fleet Itineraries

Ship	Itineraries
SeaDream I	**7-night E. Carib 1:** Between St. Thomas and Antigua, Nov–Dec 2003, visiting St. Barts; St. Martin; and Tortola, Virgin Gorda, and Jost Van Dyke (BVIs). **7-night E. Carib 2:** Round-trip from St. Thomas, Dec 2003, visiting St. Kitts; St. Barts; Anguilla; and Tortola, Virgin Gorda, and Jost Van Dyke (BVIs). **7-night E. Carib 3:** Round-trip from St. Thomas, Dec 2003, Dec 2004, visiting Nevis, Guadeloupe, Antigua, St. Martin, and either St. Croix (Dec 2003) or Virgin Gorda (Dec 2004). **7-night E. Carib 4:** Round-trip from St. Thomas, Jan–Feb and Nov–Dec 2004, visiting St. John, St. Kitts, St. Barts, Anguilla, and Virgin Gorda and Jost Van Dyke (BVIs). **7-night E. Carib 5:** Between St. Thomas and San Juan, Feb–Apr and Nov 2004, visiting St. Martin, Antigua, Nevis, St. Barts, and Virgin Gorda and Jost Van Dyke (BVIs). **4-night E. Carib:** Round-trip from San Juan, Mar and Nov 2004, visiting St. Martin and Virgin Gorda and Jost Van Dyke (BVIs). **5-night E. Carib:** Round-trip from San Juan, Mar and Nov 2004, visiting St. Barts, St. Martin, and Virgin Gorda and Jost Van Dyke (BVIs). **Non-Caribbean Itineraries:** Europe.
SeaDream II	**4-night E. Carib:** Round-trip from San Juan, Nov 2003 and Feb 2004, visiting St. Martin and Virgin Gorda and Jost Van Dyke (BVIs). **5-night E. Carib:** Round-trip from San Juan, Nov 2003 and Feb 2004, visiting either (a) St. Barts, St. Kitts, Antigua, and Virgin Gorda (BVIs); (b) Nevis, Guadeloupe, St. Martin, and Jost Van Dyke (BVIs); or (c) St. Barts, St. Martin, and Virgin Gorda and Jost Van Dyke (BVIs). **7-night S. Carib 1:** Round-trip from Barbados, Dec 2003 and Dec 2004, visiting Tobago, Grenada, Carriacou, Bequia, Mayreau, and St. Lucia. **7-night S. Carib 2:** Barbados to St. Thomas, Jan 2004, visiting Grenada, Bequia, St. Lucia, Guadeloupe, St. Barts, and Virgin Gorda (BVIs). **10-night S. Carib:** Round-trip from Barbados, Dec 2003, visiting Tobago, Grenada, Carriacou, St. Vincent, Dominica, St. Lucia, Martinique, Bequia, and Mayreau. **7-night E. Carib 1:** Round-trip from St. Thomas, Nov–Dec 2003, visiting St. Croix, St. Kitts, St. Barts, Anguilla, and Virgin Gorda and Jost Van Dyke (BVIs). **7-night E. Carib 2:** Round-trip from St. Thomas, Dec 2003, visiting Nevis, Guadeloupe, Antigua, St. Martin, and Virgin Gorda and Jost Van Dyke (BVIs). **7-night E. Carib 3:** Round-trip from St. Thomas, Jan–April 2004, visiting St. Martin, Nevis, Antigua, St. Barts, and Virgin Gorda and Jost Van Dyke (BVIs). **7-night E. Carib 4:** Round-trip from Antigua, Feb 2004, visiting St. Kitts, Nevis, Guadeloupe, Dominica, Martinique, and Les Saintes. **7-night E. Carib 5:** Round-trip from Antigua, Feb–Mar 2004, visiting St. Barts; St. Martin; Tortola, Virgin Gorda, Jost Van Dyke (BVIs); and Anguilla. **7-night E. Carib 6:** Round-trip from Antigua, Mar 2004, visiting St. Kitts, Nevis, Guadeloupe, Dominica, Martinique, and Les Saintes.

WaveRunners (keep in mind, if seas are at all choppy, the marina isn't lowered). **Mountain bikes** are carried aboard ship for guest use onshore. Golf lovers can head toward the bow on Deck 6 to practice their swing on a **golf simulator.** The newest toy: a **Segway Human Transporter,** an upright two-wheel Jetsons-like scooter. Five are available on each yacht, and you can take a spin at $49 an hour, either on your own or on special Segway shore excursions, which instantly make you the center of attention at every port where they're offered.

One to two shore excursions are offered per port (at additional cost), with possibilities including a regatta on St. Martin and visits to The Baths on Virgin Gorda. Guests can also join the captain on a kayaking or snorkeling jaunt he may be leading to a quiet Virgin Gorda cove, meet up with the chef to scout for local produce, or follow the bartender for a night out to a local watering hole such as Foxy's on Jost Van Dyke.

CHILDREN'S ACTIVITIES

Though the only actual restriction is that children under age 1 are prohibited, these ships are by no means kid-friendly. There are no babysitting services or child-related activities, nor any third berths in the cabins (though a number of cabins can be connected to form a double-size suite with accommodation for four). Teens, on the other hand, may enjoy these cruises' emphasis on watersports and unstructured activities.

ENTERTAINMENT

Tunes are served up nightly on a white glass-topped Yamaha in the Piano Bar. Three nights a week in the Main Salon, guests can catch a spirited **cabaret vocalist** with digitized accompaniment followed by dancing, and management plans to hire **local bands** in the Caribbean. A **casino** on Deck 4 has two poker tables, four slot machines, and two electronic poker machines.

On one evening during each cruise, a screen is set up on deck for a **movie under the stars,** which passengers can view from poolside (or even from the pool).

SERVICE

Given the small number of guests and large number of crew, everyone is quick to satisfy whims and commit your name to memory, though make sure that your first drink is your favorite; you may find fresh ones reappearing automatically throughout the evening. The dining room waitstaff is courteous and knowledgeable, though a bit harried as most passengers, even though seating is open, tend to dine about the same time each evening. As aboard the Silversea ships, cabin bathrooms are stocked with Bvlgari amenities. **Laundry, dry cleaning, and pressing** are available, but there is no self-service laundry.

SeaDream I • SeaDream II

The Verdict

The service, cuisine, and intimacy of the old *Sea Goddess* ships in an even better package, with flexible itineraries and laid-back atmosphere designed to pry landlubbers from their resorts and out to sea.

SeaDream II *(photo: SeaDream Yacht Club)*

Specifications

Size (in tons)	4,260	Crew	89 (Internat'l)
Number of Cabins	55	Passenger/Crew Ratio	1.2 to 1
Number of Outside Cabins	55	Year Launched	
Cabins with Verandas	0	*SeaDream I*	1984
Number of Passengers	110	*SeaDream II*	1985
Officers	Scandinavian	Last Major Refurbishment	2002

Frommer's Ratings (Scale of 1–5)   ★★★★

Cabin Comfort & Amenities	5	Dining Options	3.5
Ship Cleanliness & Maintenance	4	Gym & Spa Facilities	4
Public Comfort/Space	4	Children's Facilities	N/A
Decor	4	Enjoyment Factor	4.5

Care for a chronology? The year is 1984, and Sea Goddess Cruises begins offering luxury small-ship cruises for very affluent travelers. Unfortunately, not enough affluent travelers are interested, and within 2 years the line sells out to Cunard, which takes over operation of its two vessels and retains a similar approach, featuring impeccable service and cuisine. In 1998, Carnival Corporation purchases Cunard and transfers the Sea Goddess ships to its Seabourn division, which operates similar-size luxury vessels. Then, in August 2001, Carnival sells the ships to Atle Brynestad, founder of Seabourn Cruises. Brynestad then brings aboard former Seabourn and Cunard president and CEO Larry Pimentel as co-owner, chairman, and CEO of the new line, and hires a raft of other ex-Cunard executives to fill the company's top spots.

Man, the business world is complicated. But since this line is geared to affluent travelers, we thought you might be interested. Now let's get to the details.

Cabins & Rates

Cabins	Per Diems from	Sq. Ft.	Fridge	Hair Dryer	Sitting Area	TV
Suite	$350	195–450	yes	yes	yes	yes

CABINS   All of the 54 one-room, 195-square-foot, ocean-view suites are virtually identical, with the bedroom area positioned alongside the cabin's large window (or portholes in the case of Deck 2 suites) and the sitting area inside, the exact opposite of most ship cabin layouts. Soundproofing between cabins is good and engine noise minimal, since all cabins are located forward and amidships.

Each cabin has twin beds that are convertible to queens, plenty of mirrors, a complementary stocked minibar and minifridge, a telephone, fresh flowers, terry robes, plush towels branded with the SeaDream logo, multiple jet massage showers, and a hair dryer. The light-colored wood cabinetry, furniture, and softgoods are all brand-new. Beds are outfitted with luxurious Belgian linen, made of Egyptian cotton. Tech items include CD and DVD players, portable MP3 players (25 are available from the reception desk), and a flat-screen TV with Internet capability. Passengers can also use the TVs to browse and buy from the SeaDream Collection, which includes the usual logo items but also lets you bring part of your SeaDream experience home—for instance, the Hadeland crystal glasses and Porsgrund china used aboard ship (produced in workshops owned by SeaDream's founder) or the brand of mountain bikes, WaveRunners, jet skis, and so on that are carried aboard the vessels. TVs channels include news-centric offerings such as CNN, CNBC, and Bloomberg.

There are 16 staterooms that are connectable to form eight 390-square-foot Commodore Club Staterooms. The gorgeous 450-square-foot Owner's Suite has a bedroom, living room, dining area, main bathroom with bathtub and separate ocean-view shower, and guest bathroom.

These ships are not recommended for passengers requiring the use of a wheelchair: Doorways leading to staterooms are not wide enough, many thresholds in public areas are several inches tall, and tenders that shuttle passengers from ship to shore in many ports cannot accommodate wheelchairs. Though there are elevators, they don't reach all decks.

PUBLIC AREAS   The SeaDream yachts retain much of *Sea Goddess's* former sophisticated decor. Stained wood floors, Oriental carpets, and striking exotic floral arrangements delight the eye. The Main Salon and its small but popular alcove bar remain the focus of the cocktail hour. One deck above in the Piano Bar, a singing pianist taps out his favorites along with any that you may request. Next door are the ship's small casino, a gift shop, and a library furnished with comfy chairs and area carpets and stocked with everything from military history to Oprah Book Club favorites.

The new favorite place to socialize has to be the Top of the Yacht Bar, which has been stunningly redone in teak flooring, rattan furniture, and contrasting blue-striped cushions. The bar area is partially covered and offers alcove seating. As you walk aft on Deck 6, you reach the pride of the remodeling, an area once covered in artificial turf. Today, slightly elevated queen-size Sun Beds allow for uninterrupted ocean viewing while guests read, sunbathe, or nap. Management encourages guests to sleep on deck and will outfit beds with blankets. Also new is the large collection of original artwork by exclusively Scandinavian artists, located throughout the ship and commissioned or otherwise chosen by Linn Brynestad.

DINING OPTIONS   Dinners are served in the main dining room. On 1 or 2 nights during the trip, a festive dinner is served in the open-sided, teak-floored Topside Restaurant, and some special meals are served on the beach during port calls. (See "Dining," above, for details.)

POOL, FITNESS & SPA FACILITIES   Much of the redesign of these ships was informed by the experience one would have on a yacht. Since yachting is about being outdoors, the open spaces on the SeaDream ships have been vastly improved. Stake an early claim to a Sun Bed, because they're prime real estate. Eight of them are aftward on Deck 6, and more are forward, near the golf simulator. Aft on Deck 3 is the pool area, with comfortable lounge chairs and umbrellas, tables, a bar, and, not too far away, a hot tub. A covered deck above has more chairs.

Toward the bow on Deck 4 are the newly refurbished beauty salon, spa, and gym, the latter of which has four treadmills with flat-screen TVs, an elliptical machine, two stationary bikes, and free weights (and lowish ceilings if you're on the tall side). Classes include aerobics, yoga, and tai chi. The uninterrupted ocean views add a calming diversion while you're burning calories. The teak-lined spa, the Asian Spa and Wellness Center, has three treatment rooms and features the usual decadent (and pricey) suspects, including wraps, facials, and massages, plus more exotic options such as hot lava rock massages, a spice and yogurt scrub, and a cucumber and aloe wrap. A full-day treatment package is offered, which you can enjoy in the spa or in the privacy of your own stateroom for $500 a person.

6 Silversea Cruises

110 E. Broward Blvd., Fort Lauderdale, FL 33301. ✆ 800/722-9955. Fax 954/522-4499. www.silversea.com.

THE LINE IN A NUTSHELL   It doesn't get better than free-flowing Moët & Chandon champagne and marble bathrooms stocked with wonderful Bvlgari bath products. These gorgeous ships offer the best of everything.

THE EXPERIENCE   Fine-tuned and genteel, a Silversea cruise caters to guests who won't settle for anything but the best. The food and service are the best at sea, and the ships' Italian-style decor is warm and inviting. Nothing seems to have been forgotten in the creation of the plush Silversea fleet. Tables are set with Christofle silver and Schott-Zwiesel crystal. These are dignified vessels for a dignified crowd that likes to dress for dinner. If you want the VIP treatment 24-7, this is your cruise line.

Pros

- **Doting service:** Gracious and ultraprofessional, the Silversea crew knows how to please well-traveled guests with high expectations.
- **Truly all-inclusive:** Unlimited wines and spirits, including the house champagne (Moët & Chandon), as well as tips, are included in the rates.
- **Excellent cuisine:** Rivaling the best restaurants ashore, cuisine is as exquisite as it gets at sea. Excellent theme dinners in the casual Terrace Cafe focus on Asian, French, Italian, or anything else the chef dreams up. Buffets are bountiful and the room-service menu includes such extravagant snacks as jumbo shrimp.
- **Large staterooms and great bathrooms:** At 287 square feet, plus 58-square-foot balconies, *Silver Whisper*'s staterooms are bigger than Seabourn's and Crystal's, and the huge marble bathrooms are the best at sea (along with those on *Seven Seas Navigator* and *Voyager*).

Cons

- **Stuffy crowd:** Of course, not every guest fits that bill, but expect a good portion of the crowd on any cruise to be, shall we say, reserved.

Compared with the other ultraluxury lines, here's how Silversea rates:

	Poor	Fair	Good	Excellent	Outstanding
Enjoyment Factor					✓
Dining					✓
Activities			✓		
Children's Program	N/A*				
Entertainment		✓			
Service					✓
Worth the Money				✓	

* Silversea has no children's program.

SILVERSEA: THE CROWN JEWELS

When Silversea Cruises introduced the 296-passenger *Silver Cloud* and *Silver Wind* in 1994, the new line joined Seabourn right at the top of the heap, with features such as stateroom balconies and a two-level show lounge giving them the edge and raising the bar for ultraluxury cruising. With the introduction of the larger, even more impressive *Silver Shadow* and *Silver Whisper* in 2000 and 2001, that bar was raised even higher, with larger staterooms and huge marble bathrooms, dimly lit and romantic cigar lounges, and more entertainment lounges—all in all, the absolute height of style, paired with itineraries that spanned the globe.

After the September 11, 2001, terrorist attacks, though, things seemed to hit a rough patch. Like many lines, Silversea began pulling its ships in closer to home (offering more itineraries in the Caribbean, for instance), but it also took the extraordinary step of laying up *Silver Cloud* from fall 2003 through April 2004 due to decreased demand (for the same reason, sister *Silver Wind* was laid up for all of 2002 and half of 2003). Other cutbacks fleetwide—from lesser-quality bed linens replacing the original Italian Frette linens when they wear out, to a discontinuing of pre-dinner cocktail parties with the chef in the Terrace Cafe—are making us wonder what lies ahead for this line and its posh ships.

PASSENGER PROFILE

While Silversea's typical passenger mix is 60-plus, shorter cruises and Caribbean sailings often skew the mix a tad younger, adding at least a handful of 30- and 40-something couples to the pot. Typically, about 85% of passengers are American and they're well traveled, well heeled, well dressed, and not afraid to flaunt five-carat diamonds and gold Rolexes the size of Texas. Most guests are couples, though singles and small groups of friends traveling together are usually part of the scene too. Many have cruised with Silversea before, and they expect the best of everything.

DINING

Gourmet foodies should consider a Silversea cruise for the food alone. The cuisine is well prepared and presented, and creative chefs continually come up with a wide variety of dishes in the ships' two restaurants. Each has a formal open-seating venue and a more casual one.

The Restaurant is the elegant main dining room. While the cuisine is not as impressive as that of the more intimate and casual Terrace Cafe, The Restaurant offers more choice, and entrees such as a pan-fried filet of lemon sole and roast lamb saddle with artichoke-garlic stuffing are very good. The wine list in both restaurants is excellent, and several complimentary wines are suggested at each meal from more than 40 choices. You can also choose one of the wines not included in the complimentary list—a $745 1990 Château Margaux, anyone? The sky's the limit on a Silversea cruise.

Hit it on a sunset departure from port, and the candlelit and windowed Terrace Cafe alternative restaurant becomes a window to the passing scenery and haven for some of the best food at sea. Reservations are required for the fixed theme menu that's offered most nights. The Asian night starts with sushi and sashimi, while a French feast begins with foie gras and two excellent French wines, and is followed by a scallop and ratatouille salad, beef tenderloin, and a warm chocolate tart with raspberries. Other theme meals may focus on Italian cuisine or even all things asparagus, as a creative chef came up with on a recent cruise. These are not mass-market meals, but well-thought-out creations from

Silversea Fleet Itineraries

Ship	Itineraries
Silver Cloud	**7-night Bermuda:** Round-trip from New York, Sept 2004, visiting Bermuda and Newport (RI), with 2 days at sea. **11-night W. Carib:** Round-trip from Fort Lauderdale, Nov 2004, visiting Key West, Santo Tomas (Guatemala), Roatan (Honduras), Puerto Limon (Costa Rica), San Andres (Colombia), and Cozumel/Playa del Carmen, with 4 days at sea. **9-night W. Carib:** Fort Lauderdale to Colón, Panama, visiting Key West, Port Antonio (Jamaica), Aruba, Santa Marta and Cartagena (Colombia), and the San Blas Islands (Panama), with 2 days at sea. **7-night W. Carib:** Colón, Panama, to Curaçao, Nov 2004, visiting Puerto Limon (Costa Rica), the San Blas Islands (Panama), Cartagena (Colombia), and Aruba, with 1 day at sea. **9-night E. Carib:** Curaçao to Fort Lauderdale, Dec 2004, visiting Grenada, St. Lucia, Antigua, St. Barts, and Virgin Gorda (BVIs), with 3 days at sea. **Non-Caribbean Itineraries:** Europe, New England/Canada.
Silver Whisper	**7-night Bermuda:** Round-trip from New York, Oct 2003, visiting Hamilton, with 2 days at sea. **8-night W. Carib:** Round-trip from Fort Lauderdale, visiting Key West, Grand Cayman, and Cozumel, with 3 days at sea. **6-night W. Carib:** Fort Lauderdale to Montego Bay, Jamaica, Nov 2003, visiting Cozumel/Playa del Carmen, and Belize City (Belize), with 2 days at sea. **7-night S. Carib 1:** Montego Bay, Jamaica, to Curaçao, Nov 2003, visiting Puerto Limon (Costa Rica), Colón (Panama), Aruba, and Cartagena and Santa Marta (Colombia), with 1 day at sea. **9-night S. Carib:** Curaçao to Barbados, Dec 2003, visiting Tortola (BVIs), St. Barts, Antigua, Dominica, St. Lucia, and Grenada, with 2 days at sea. **7-night S. Carib 2:** Round-trip from Barbados, Dec 2003, visiting Martinique, Guadeloupe, Dominica, St. Lucia, and Bequia, with 1 day at sea. **6-night S. Carib:** Round-trip from Barbados, Dec 2003, visiting Curaçao, Los Roques and Isla Margarita (Venezuela), and Grenada, with 1 day at sea. **14-night S. & E. Carib:** Barbados to Fort Lauderdale, Dec 2003, visiting Tobago, Dominica, St. Kitts, San Juan, Tortola (BVIs), St. Barts, Dominican Republic, and Nassau, with 4 days at sea. **14-night W. Carib:** Fort Lauderdale to New Orleans, Jan 2004, visiting Key West, Cozumel/Playa del Carmen, Belize City (Belize), San Andres Island (Colombia), Puerto Limon (Costa Rica), Colón (Panama), and Port Antonio (Jamaica), with 5 days at sea. **9-night W. Carib:** New Orleans to Colón, Panama, Jan 2004, visiting Key West, Port Antonio (Jamaica), Cartagena (Colombia), and the San Blas Islands (Panama), with 3 days at sea. **10-night S. Carib/Canal:** Puntarenas, Costa Rica, to Antigua, Mar 2004, visiting the San Blas Islands (Panama), Cartagena (Colombia), Aruba, Bonaire, and St. Kitts, with 4 days at sea, including a partial Canal passage. **7-night S. Carib 3:** Antigua to Barbados, Apr 2004, visiting Martinique, Bequia, Grenada, Isla Margarita (Venezuela), and Trinidad, with 1 day at sea. **Non-Caribbean Itineraries:** Europe, New England/Canada, Asia, South America.
Silver Wind	**7-night S. & E. Carib:** Between Barbados and Fort Lauderdale, Feb and Apr 2004, visiting St. Lucia, St. Kitts, Virgin Gorda (BVIs), and either St. Barts or Dominica, with 2 days at sea. **11-night W. & S. Carib:** Fort Lauderdale to Puerto Caldera, Costa Rica, Feb 2004, visiting Port Antonio (Jamaica), Santa Margarita and Cartagena (Colombia), and the San Blas Islands and Flamingo Island (Panama), with 5 days at sea including a transit of the Panama Canal. **12-night W. Carib/Canal:** Puerto Caldera, Costa Rica, to New Orleans, Mar 2004, visiting the San Blas Islands (Panama), Cartagena (Colombia), Port Antonio (Jamaica), Roatan (Honduras), and Cozumel/Playa del Carmen, with 5 days at sea including a transit of the Panama Canal. **12-night W. Carib:** New Orleans to Fort Lauderdale, Mar 2004, visiting Cozumel, Montego Bay (Jamaica), La Romana (Dominican Republic), San Juan, and Key West, with 5 days at sea. **Non-Caribbean Itineraries:** Europe, New England/Canada.

highly trained chefs. Tables for two are never a problem in the Terrace Cafe and usually not in the larger main restaurant either, though you may have to wait for one.

Burgers and sandwiches are served poolside at lunchtime in addition to service in the other two restaurants, and once per cruise, passengers are invited into the galley for the traditional galley brunch, which features more than 100 delectable dishes, from stone crab claws to pickled herring, Hungarian goulash, Rabbit a la Provencale, and German Bratwurst. A red carpet is rolled out, literally, through the galley, and it's a most festive affair, with the chef on hand to chat with guests about the feast.

ACTIVITIES

Aside from trivia games, card tournaments, stretch and aerobics classes, and bridge tours, Silversea excels in its more cerebral pursuits. Wine-tasting seminars are excellent, and the line's enrichment lectures are varied and interesting. They include guest lecturers such as Fred McLaren, a retired Navy captain and professor, who does a slide show and talk on his adventures diving 12,500 feet down in a Russian MIR submersible to explore the remains of the *Titanic*. There are also language classes, and golf and computer-learning lessons.

Lighter activities include a dip in the pool or two hot tubs, or a visit to the golf driving net, the Internet center, or the Bvlgari boutique, which on a recent *Shadow* cruise (not sailing in the Caribbean this year) offered $1,600 pink leather purses and a snooty clerk to match.

And the ships' Balinese-inspired Mandara spa beckons with its flower-strewn copper foot bowls, warm massage rocks, and other Asian-inspired treatments. Unfortunately, on a recent *Shadow* cruise, waiting in line for an hour to sign up for the overpriced $185 hot lava rock massage or one of the other pricey treatments sure wasn't very relaxing. Stick with the basic massages and facials and you won't be disappointed.

CHILDREN'S PROGRAM

These ships are not geared to children, though every so often one or two are aboard. Babysitting may be arranged with an available crewmember (no guarantee); otherwise, no activities or services are offered specifically for children. The minimum age for sailing is 12 months.

ENTERTAINMENT

For evening entertainment, the ships each have a small casino, a duo entertaining each evening in the nightclub adjacent to the show lounge, a pianist in another lounge, and dozens of in-cabin movies, including oldies and current films. The small-scale song-and-dance revues in the two-level show lounges are a pleasant after-dinner diversion, but don't expect the talent to knock anyone's Gucci socks off; low-brow Carnival or Royal Caribbean do much better at Vegas-style entertainment. It's the nonstandard stuff that Silversea excels in. Popular theme cruises from time to time feature classical musicians, golf experts, and guest chefs from Relais & Châteaux hotels and restaurants conducting demonstrations. The pace is calm, and that's the way most Silversea guests like it; most are perfectly content to spend their after-dinner hours with cocktails and conversation.

SERVICE

The gracious staff knows how to please discerning guests. Staff members are friendly and remember your name, but are never obtrusive or pushy. Waiters and stewardesses are as discreet as the guests are, and chances are you'll never hear the word "no." The room-service menu includes such decadent choices as jumbo shrimp cocktail, and you can order it as many times as you like. Unlimited wines, spirits, and soft drinks are included in the rates, as are gratuities.

Laundry and **dry cleaning** are available. There are also **self-service laundry rooms.**

Silver Whisper

The Verdict

The most beautiful, well-run ship you can find in the ultraluxe market, the *Whisper* is as good as it gets if you're on a quest for mighty fine cuisine, service, and suites.

Silver Whisper *(photo: Silversea Cruises)*

Specifications

Size (in tons)	28,258	Crew	295 (Internat'l)
Number of Cabins	194	Passenger/Crew Ratio	1.3 to 1
Number of Outside Cabins	194	Year Launched	
Cabins with Verandas	157	*Whisper*	2001
Number of Passengers	388	Last Major Refurbishment	N/A
Officers	Italian		

Frommer's Ratings (Scale of 1–5)   ⭐⭐⭐⭐⭐

Cabin Comfort & Amenities	5	Dining Options	5
Ship Cleanliness & Maintenance	5	Gym & Spa Facilities	4
Public Comfort/Space	5	Children's Facilities	N/A
Decor	5	Enjoyment Factor	5

With this ship, Silversea sets the bar very high for the rest of the ultraluxe ships. Not only is Silversea ultra-all-inclusive, with unlimited wines and spirits covered in the rates along with gratuities, but in *Whisper,* all the right chords are struck. The ship is small enough to be intimate, but large enough to offer a classy two-story show lounge, dark and romantic cigar lounge, spacious indoor/outdoor buffet restaurant, impressive spa and gym, and some really great suites.

Cabins & Rates

Cabins	Per Diems from	Sq. Ft.	Fridge	Hair Dryer	Sitting Area	TV
Suite	$516	287–1,435*	yes	yes	yes	yes

* Includes balconies.

CABINS   The suites on this all-suites ship don't leave anything to be desired. Private balconies are attached to three-quarters of the plush staterooms, which have a walk-in closet, minibar, sitting area, and huge marble-covered bathroom with double sinks, Bvlgari toiletries, and a separate shower stall and extra-long bathtub (only Radisson's *Seven Seas Navigator* and *Voyager* have equally wonderful bathrooms). The vast majority of the suites measure 287 square feet, while the largest of the four two-bedroom Grand Suites measures 1,435 square feet and comes with three bathrooms, a pair of walk-in closets, an entertainment center, two verandas, and a living room and dining area. The color scheme in the suites is focused on rich blues and soft golds, along with coppery-brown wood tones—a welcome contrast to the bland champagne-colored Seabourn suites.

PUBLIC AREAS   This classy ship is bathed in lots of deep Wedgwood blue and golden peach fabrics and carpeting, along with warm caramel wood tones. The low-key main lobby area, where the purser's desk resides, branches out into a pair of attractive four-deck-high staircases with shiplike railings. All told, there are three roomy lounges, including two with floor-to-ceiling windows. The ship has a two-story show lounge. Overall, fabrics throughout the public rooms are a rich medley of blood-red velveteens and golden brocades, as well as strong blues and teals. The cigar lounge is dark, cozy, and plush—even nonsmokers can't help but be drawn to the ambience. There's also a small casino and attached bar, plus an Internet center, a card room, a library, a boutique, and a pool bar.

DINING OPTIONS   In The Restaurant, the main dining room, a live trio plays romantic oldies, and guests are invited to take a spin around the small dance floor. Breakfast, lunch, and dinner are served here in high style, while a more casual buffet-style breakfast and lunch are offered in the indoor/outdoor Terrace Cafe. Still, service is doting, and waiters rush to carry plates to tables and are on hand to do drinks and clear plates moments after you finish eating. A special pasta or other dish is prepared made-to-order by a chef for guests who do lunch in the Terrace Cafe. Come evenings, the theme meals on most nights are wonderful. On *Whisper,* these theme meals begin in the adjacent Le Champagne lounge at about 7:30pm, where canapés such as fresh Parmesan cut from the wheel and prosciutto are served along with cocktails, while the sous-chef introduces the evening's meal and a sommelier discusses the featured wines.

POOL, FITNESS & SPA FACILITIES   Old-style wooden chaise longues padded with royal blue cushions line the open decks (though like many new ships, some decks are covered with a jolting grass-green AstroTurf in lieu of beautiful teak). There's a pool, two hot tubs, and a golf driving net.

Silver Cloud • Silver Wind

The Verdict

Small and intimate, these luxe ships are a dream. Big enough to offer a two-story show lounge and several other entertainment outlets, and cozy enough that you'll feel like you practically have the vessel to yourself.

Silver Cloud *(photo: Silversea Cruises)*

Specifications

Size (in tons)	16,927	Officers	Italian
Number of Cabins	148	Crew	210 (Internat'l)
Number of Outside Cabins	148	Passenger/Crew Ratio	1.4 to 1
Cabins with Verandas	110	Year Launched	1994
Number of Passengers	296	Last Major Refurbishment	N/A

Frommer's Ratings (Scale of 1–5)   ★★★★

Cabin Comfort & Amenities	4	Dining Options	4
Ship Cleanliness & Maintenance	4	Gym & Spa Facilities	4
Public Comfort/Space	4	Children's Facilities	N/A
Decor	4	Enjoyment Factor	5

These small ships are pure pleasure, being both super-intimate and large enough to have multiple entertainment venues, two restaurants, and lots of outdoor deck space. They were built in the mid-1990s, just in time to get in on must-have fashions such as balconies.

After taking the *Wind* out of service for all of 2002 and half of 2003 due to decreased demand following the September 11, 2001, terrorist attacks, at press time, Silversea announced that the *Cloud* would be laid up from fall 2003 through April 2004 for the same reasons. While laid up, the *Wind* received a face-lift of sorts, including an expanded spa, a new gym, Internet cafe, and wine bar. Plus, staterooms were freshened up with new linens, furniture, and wall art. Similar refurbishments are expected during the *Cloud*'s hiatus.

Cabins & Rates

Cabins	Per Diems from	Sq. Ft.	Fridge	Hair Dryer	Sitting Area	TV
Suite	$367	240–1,314*	yes	yes	yes	yes

* *Includes balconies.*

CABINS   Like their sisters, *Cloud* and *Wind* are all-suite ships, with balconies on more than three-quarters of the staterooms. All 148 suites have sitting areas, roomy walk-in closets, bathtubs, vanities, TVs and VCRs, and stocked minibars; while the top of the lot, the Grand Suites, have two bedrooms, two living rooms, three televisions, two bathrooms, and a full-size Jacuzzi tub. Color schemes revolve around creamy beige fabrics and golden brown wood. Swirled peachy-gray marble covers bathrooms from head to toe, and though indulgent enough, that can't hold a flame to the larger, simply decadent loos on newer fleetmate *Whisper*. Goose-down pillows ensure a good night's rest.

PUBLIC AREAS   Public areas, inside and out, are spacious and open. High tea is served in the windowed Panorama Lounge by day, and in the evening, a pianist plays there. Broadway-style production numbers are performed in the attractive two-story Venetian show lounge, and, on most nights, a dance band plays oldies or a DJ spins rock 'n' roll in the intimate and dimly lit adjacent bar. There's a small casino, too. On the *Cloud*, a small library also hosts a few computers with Internet access. The ships' two boutiques include a Bvlgari shop with the requisite $250 silk scarves and $30,000 gold and diamond-studded watches. An observation lounge is positioned on the far-forward part of a top deck and is oddly not attached to the ship's interior, so you must go out on deck to enter. Not a problem, of course, unless it's pouring rain or incredibly windy.

DINING OPTIONS   The formal, open-seating dining venue, called The Restaurant, is delicately decorated in pale pink and gold; and elegant candlelit tables are set with heavy crystal glasses, chunky Christofle silverware, and doily-covered silver show plates. Rivaling the best restaurants in New York or Paris, dishes such as grilled tournedos of beef with foie gras and truffles, and marinated crab with leek salad and star anise are simply delicious. Several nights a week, the indoor/outdoor Terrace Cafe, where buffet-style breakfast and lunch are served, is transformed into a venue for more casual evening dining, featuring a rotating repertoire or themes (from Asian to French and Italian). Still elegant, the dimly lit spot is very romantic.

POOL, FITNESS & SPA FACILITIES   There is a pool and two hot tubs. The ocean-view gym is compact, but adequate for a ship of this size (though tall folks should beware of the low ceiling when considering a go on the treadmill). The small spa offers a variety of massages and facials. At press time, the *Wind* was set to get an enhanced spa and gym.

7 Windstar Cruises

300 Elliott Ave. W., Seattle, WA 98119. ℂ 800/258-7245 or 206/281-3535. Fax 206/281-0627. www.windstarcruises.com.

THE LINE IN A NUTSHELL The no-jackets-required policy defines this line's casually elegant attitude. These sleek, small ships really do feel like private yachts—they're down-to-earth, yet service and cuisine are first-class.

THE EXPERIENCE Windstar offers a truly unique cruise experience, giving passengers the delicious illusion of adventure aboard its fleet of four- and five-masted sailing ships, along with the ever-pleasant reality of first-class cuisine, service, and itineraries. This is no barefoot, rigging-pulling, paper-plates-in-lap, sleep-on-the-deck kind of cruise, but a refined yet down-to-earth, yachtlike experience for a sophisticated, well-traveled crowd who wouldn't be comfortable on a big ship with throngs of tourists.

On board, fine stained teak, brass details, and lots of navy-blue fabrics and carpeting lend a traditional nautical ambience. While the ships' proud masts and white sails cut a traditional profile, they're also ultra-state-of-the-art, controlled by a computer so that they can be furled or unfurled at the touch of a button. In the Caribbean, at least once per week if at all possible, the captain shuts off the engines and moves by sail only, to give passengers a real taste of the sea. Under full sail, the calm tranquillity is utterly blissful.

Pros

- **Cuisine:** The ambience, service, and imaginative cuisine created by renowned Los Angeles chef Joachim Splichal is very good. Seating in the restaurants is open, and guests can usually get a table for two.
- **Informal and unregimented days:** This line offers the most casual high-end cruise out there—an approach much loved by passengers who enjoy fine service and cuisine but want to leave their jackets and pantyhose at home.
- **Itineraries:** The ships typically visit a port every day, and they're wonderfully less touristed than many of those called on by the megaships.

Cons

- **Limited activities and entertainment:** This is intentional, but if you need lots of organized hoopla to keep you happy, you won't find much here.
- **No verandas:** If they're important to you, you're out of luck.
- **A little worn around the edges:** But that's not surprising, since each ship is 14 to 18 years old.

Compared with the other ultraluxury lines, here's how Windstar rates:

	Poor	Fair	Good	Excellent	Outstanding
Enjoyment Factor					✓
Dining			✓		
Activities		✓			
Children's Program	N/A*				
Entertainment		✓			
Service			✓		
Worth the Money				✓	

Windstar has no children's program.

WINDSTAR: CASUAL ELEGANCE UNDER SAIL

Launched in 1986, Windstar Cruises combines the best of 19th-century clipper design with the best of modern yacht engineering. As you see a Windstar ship approaching port, with its four or five masts the height of 20-story buildings, you'll think the seafaring days of Joseph Conrad or Herman Melville have returned. But Captain Ahab wouldn't know what to do with a Windstar ship. Million-dollar computers control the triangular sails with their at least 21,489 square feet of Dacron, flying from masts that tower up to 204 feet above deck. The ships are beautiful, and so is the experience on board—the line's ad slogan, "180° From Ordinary," is right on target.

The catalyst behind the formation of the company was flamboyant French entrepreneur Jean Claude Potier, a native Parisian who, in a 25-year-span, was instrumental in leading the French Line, the Sun Line, and Paquet during their transition into the modern cruise age. Warsila Marine Industries in Helsinki developed the original designs for the ships, and they were built at Le Havre, France. Today, the line is owned by Carnival Corporation. It's the most high-end among the competing sailing cruise ships in the Caribbean.

Sadly, in December of 2002, the 1987-built *Wind Song* caught fire in the waters of French Polynesia, where it was based year-round. Though no one was injured, the ship was declared a complete loss. Windstar has no immediate plans to replace the ship, instead transferring *Wind Star* from the Caribbean to cover *Song's* itineraries. This leaves only the *Spirit* and *Surf* spending any time in the Caribbean.

PASSENGER PROFILE

People who expect high-caliber service and very high-quality cuisine but dislike the formality of the other high-end ships (as well as the mass-mentality of the megaships) are thrilled with Windstar. Most passengers are couples in their 30s to early 60s (with the average around 50), with a smattering of parents with adult children and some single friends traveling together.

The line is not the best choice for first-timers, since it appeals to a specific sensibility, and it's definitely not a good choice for singles or families with children under 15 or 16.

Overall, passengers are sophisticated, well traveled, and more down-to-earth than passengers on the other high-end lines. Most want something different from the regular cruise experience, eschew the "bigger is better" philosophy of conventional cruising, and want a somewhat more adventurous, port-intensive Caribbean cruise. These cruises are for those seeking a romantic escape and who like to visit islands and ports not often touched by regular cruise ships, including the Grenadines, the Tobago Cays, the British Virgin Islands, Belize, Honduras, and relatively isolated dependencies of Guadeloupe, such as Les Saintes.

About a third of all passengers on most cruises have sailed with the line before (a figure that represents one of the best recommendations for Windstar), and about 20% are first-time cruisers. There are usually a handful of honeymoon couples on board any given sailing. Windstar caters to corporate groups, too. In 2002, for example, about 25% of cruises on all four of the line's ships had corporate groups aboard, and half of those were full-ship charters, the majority in Tahiti.

DINING

Windstar's cuisine is among the better prepared in the Caribbean market and is a high point of the cruise, although it doesn't quite match the caliber of Silversea, Seabourn, or Radisson. It was created by renowned chef/restaurateur

Windstar Fleet Itineraries

Ship	Itineraries
Wind Spirit	7-night E. Carib: Round-trip from St. Thomas, Dec 2003–Apr 2004, visiting St. John; Sint Maarten; St. Barts; and Tortola, Jost Van Dyke, and Virgin Gorda (BVIs). **Non-Caribbean Itineraries:** Europe.
Wind Surf	7-night E. Carib: Fort Lauderdale to St. Thomas, Nov 2003, visiting Freeport, Half Moon Cay*, Grand Turk (Turks and Caicos), and Virgin Gorda and Jost Van Dyke (BVIs), with 2 days at sea. **7-night E. & S. Carib 1:** St. Thomas to Barbados, Dec 2003–Apr 2004, visiting Culebra (Puerto Rico), St. Martin, Les Saintes, St. Lucia, and Grenada, with 1 day at sea. **7-night E. & S. Carib 2:** Barbados to St. Thomas, Dec 2003–Apr 2004, visiting Bequia and Mayreau (Grenadines), Dominica, St. Barts, and Virgin Gorda (BVIs), with 1 day at sea. **Non-Caribbean Itineraries:** Europe.

*Holland America/Windstar's private Bahamian island.

Joachim Splichal, winner of many culinary awards (including some from the James Beard Society) and owner of Los Angeles's Patina Restaurant and Pinot Bistro. At its best, Splichal's food is inventive and imaginative. Appetizers may include golden fried Brie served with cranberry sauce and crispy parsley or a sweet shrimp and crab salad. Among the main courses, you may see a grilled local fish served with a roast corn salsa and sweet plantains, sautéed jumbo prawns served with garlic spinach and spaghetti, or an herb and peppercorn–coated prime rib of beef. Desserts such as an apple tart with raspberry coulis and chocolate crème brûlée are beyond tempting. An impressive **wine list** includes California, Australian, New Zealand, Spanish, French, and South African vintages.

Vegetarian dishes and **healthy choices** designed by light-cooking expert Jeanne Jones (called the "Sail Light" entrees) are available for breakfast, lunch, and dinner; fat and calorie content is listed on the menu. The light choices may feature Atlantic salmon with couscous and fresh vegetables, or a Thai country-style chicken with veggies and oriental rice. The vegetarian options may feature a fresh garden stew or a savory polenta with Italian salsa.

The once-a-week **evening barbecues** on the pool deck are wonderful parties under the stars, and an ample and beautifully designed buffet spread offers more than you could possibly sample in an evening. The setting is sublime, with tables set with linens and, often, a live Caribbean-style band performing on board.

At breakfast and lunch, meals can be ordered from a menu or selected from a buffet. Made-to-order omelets and a varied and generous spread of fruits are available at breakfast, and luncheons may feature a tasty seafood paella and a hot pasta dish of the day.

Wind Spirit has two (and *Wind Surf,* three) open-seating dining rooms: one or two are casual and breezy and used during breakfast and lunch, while the other is a more formal room that's the stage for dinner, served between 7:30 and 9:30pm. Tables seat two to eight. You can often get a table for two, but you may have to wait at rush hour.

Windstar's official dress code is **no jackets required,** which is a big draw for guests. In the main restaurant, guests dress casually elegant: trousers and nice collared shirts for men, pants or casual dresses for women.

The **24-hour room service** offers hot and cold breakfast items (cereals and breads, eggs and omelets) in the morning, and a limited menu of sandwiches, fruit, pizza, salads, and other snacks during the rest of the day. You can also order from the restaurant's dinner menu during dining hours.

ACTIVITIES

Since these ships generally visit a port of call every single day of the cruise and guests spend the day exploring ashore, few organized activities are offered, and the daily schedules are intentionally unregimented—the way guests prefer it. Weather and conditions permitting, the ships anchor and passengers can enjoy kayaking, sailing, water-skiing, snorkeling, windsurfing, banana-boat rides, and swimming from the **watersports platform** that's lowered from the stern when the ship is at anchor.

The company's organized island tours tend to be more creative than usual, and the one or two cruise directors (who double as shore excursions managers and jacks-of-all-trades) are usually knowledgeable and able to point passengers toward good spots for bird-watching, snorkeling, or a nice meal. Brief orientation talks are held before port visits.

Still, a handful of scheduled diversions are available aboard ship, such as gaming lessons in the casino and walk-a-mile sessions and stretch classes on deck. Chances are a vegetable-carving or food-decorating demonstration may take place poolside, as well as clothing or jewelry sale items on display. *Wind Surf* has a proper Internet/business center with eight computers; the *Spirit* has one computer in the library with e-mail access only.

The pool deck, with its hot tub, deck chairs, and open-air bar, is conducive to sunbathing, conversations, or quiet repose. The ships each maintain an open-bridge policy, so you're free to walk right in to chat with the captain and officers on duty. There's an extensive video and CD collection from which passengers can borrow for use in their cabins.

CHILDREN'S PROGRAM

Because children are not encouraged to sail with Windstar, no activities are planned for them. There are often a handful of teenagers on board who spend time sunbathing or holed up in their cabins, watching movies. The minimum age for children to sail is 6 months.

ENTERTAINMENT

For the most part, passengers entertain themselves. Often, a piano/vocalist duo performs before and after dinner in each ship's main lounge. **Local entertainers,** such as steel bands, calypso bands, or a group of limbo dancers, are sometimes brought aboard at a port of call. A very modest casino offers slots, blackjack, and Caribbean stud poker. After dinner, passengers often go up to the pool bar for a nightcap under the stars, and sometimes after 10 or 11pm, disco/pop music is played in the lounge if guests are in a dancing mood.

SERVICE

Windstar is a class operation, as reflected in its thoughtful service personnel. The staff smiles hello and makes every effort to learn passengers' names. Dining staff is efficient and first-rate as well, but not in that ultraprofessional, militaryesque, five-star-hotel, Seabourn kind of way. That's not what Windstar is all about. Officers and crew are helpful, but not gushing. The line operates under a **tipping-not-required policy,** although generally guests do tip staff as much as on other ships; on Windstar, as on Holland America, there's just less pressure to do so.

Wind Surf

The Verdict

An enlarged version of Windstar's 148-passenger ships, the 308-passenger *Wind Surf* is a sleek, sexy, supersmooth sailing ship offering an extensive spa and lots of suites along with an intimate yachtlike ambience.

Wind Surf (photo: Windstar Cruises)

Specifications

Size (in tons)	14,745	Officers	English/Dutch
Number of Cabins	154	Crew	163 (Internat'l)
Number of Outside Cabins	154	Passenger/Crew Ratio	1.9 to 1
Cabins with Verandas	0	Year Launched	1990
Number of Passengers	308	Last Major Refurbishment	2000

Frommer's Ratings (Scale of 1–5)　　　★★★★

Cabin Comfort & Amenities	4	Dining Options	3.5
Ship Cleanliness & Maintenance	3.5	Gym & Spa Facilities	5
Public Comfort/Space	4	Children's Facilities	N/A
Decor	4	Enjoyment Factor	4.5

Previously sailing under the Club Med banner (as *Club Med I* until 1997), *Wind Surf* was designed by the same French architect who worked on the other Windstar vessels, and, for the most part, is an enlarged copy of them. Despite a passenger capacity more than double that of her sister ships (308 vs. 148), *Wind Surf* maintains the feel of a private yacht.

Cabins & Rates

Cabins	Per Diems from	Sq. Ft.	Fridge	Hair Dryer	Sitting Area	TV
Outside	$337	188	yes	yes	no	yes
Suite	$513	376	yes	yes	yes	yes

CABINS　All cabins are very similar and display a subtle nautical ambience. They're roomy, but nowhere near as large as your typical high-end ship suite. Beds can be adapted into either a one-queen-size or two-twin-size format. Each cabin has a VCR and TV showing CNN and lots of movies (and sometimes ESPN), a CD player, a minibar, ocean-view portholes, and bathrobes, and is stocked with fresh fruit. Like the ships' main public rooms, the cabins' decor is based on navy-blue fabrics and carpeting, along with wood tones—attractive but simple, well constructed and utilitarian. Large desk/bureaus are white with dark brown trim and the rest of the cabinetry is a medium wood tone. Storage space is compact but adequate. Largish, teak-trimmed bathrooms are artfully designed and more appealing than those aboard many other luxury ships, and contain a hair dryer, plenty of towels, and more than adequate storage space. As part of *Wind Surf*'s 1998 metamorphosis, cabins were completely reconfigured for a reduced passenger capacity of 312 instead of *Club Med*'s 386. This included repartitioning total cabin space to allow for 30 suites on Deck 3 (its original layout had only one), making the vessel the most suite-heavy of the Windstar fleet. (A combination of two standard staterooms, each suite has a large space containing a sitting area and sleeping quarters, plus his-and-hers bathrooms, each with a shower and a toilet.) In late 2000, the installation of a new gangway replaced two staterooms on Deck 2, bringing the passenger capacity down further, to 308.

There are no connecting cabins. The ship has two elevators (unlike the other Windstar ships, which have none), but still is not recommended for people with serious mobility problems.

PUBLIC AREAS Because *Wind Surf*'s passenger-space ratio is 30% greater than those of her sister ships, her two main public spaces—the bright and airy Wind Surf Lounge, where passengers gather in the evening for cocktails and to listen to a three- to five-person band play their favorite requests, and the Compass Rose piano bar, popular for after-dinner drinks—are also roomier than comparable public spaces on the other ships. The Wind Surf Lounge was refurbished in late 2000 to create a more intimate space with better sightlines to the stage. The dance floor was relocated, cozier seating clusters were added, new carpeting and fabrics were installed, and the adjoining casino was enhanced.

A brand-new business center, created in late 2000 on the sunny Bridge Deck amidships, serves as both a computer center and a meeting room for about 60 people (replacing the dark conference room that used to be down on Deck 1), and has eight computer terminals offering Internet and e-mail access.

Other public areas include a pool bar, a library, and a gift shop.

DINING OPTIONS The ship offers three dining venues: the restaurant on Main Deck and two more casual alternative restaurants, the Bistro and Veranda, on Star Deck. The restaurant has many tables for two; it offers open-seating dinners between 7:30 and 9:30pm. The cozy Bistro serves sit-down dinners and combination buffet and a la carte lunches.

As on the other Windstar ships, a combo buffet and a la carte breakfast and lunch are served in the glass-enclosed Veranda, which also has outdoor seating. An outdoor barbecue station with a retractable sailcloth awning is just aft of the Veranda. Here, guests can get grilled lobster, shrimp, ribs, hamburgers, hot dogs, sausages, and vegetables.

POOL, FITNESS & SPA FACILITIES *Wind Surf* has the most elaborate fitness and spa facilities in the Windstar fleet (the line's three 148-passenger ships have no spa and only a tiny gym) and, in fact, they outclass facilities on other similar-size ships. There's a well-stocked windowed gym on the top deck, a "sports" pool for aqua aerobics and scuba lessons (passengers can get resort certification), and an aerobics room one deck below that's also used for yoga and golf swing practice. A staff of 10 doles out aromatherapy plus a variety of massages and other treatments in the attractive WindSpa. There's also a sauna and a steam room. Spa packages, geared to both men and women, can be purchased in advance through your travel agent, with appointment times made once you're on board.

There's another pool on the Main Deck, as well as two hot tubs. For joggers, a full-circuit teak promenade wraps around the Bridge Deck.

Wind Spirit

The Verdict

One of the most romantic, cozy-yet-roomy small ships out there, this vessel looks chic and offers just the right combination of creature comforts and first-class cuisine, along with a casual, laid-back, unstructured ethic.

Wind Spirit (photo: Windstar Cruises)

Specifications

Size (in tons)	5,350	Officers	British/Dutch
Number of Cabins	74	Crew	89 (Internat'l)
Number of Outside Cabins	74	Passenger/Crew Ratio	1.6 to 1
Cabins with Verandas	0	Year Launched	1988
Number of Passengers	148	Last Major Refurbishment	N/A

Frommer's Ratings (Scale of 1–5)   ✮✮✮½

Cabin Comfort & Amenities	4	Dining Options	3.5
Ship Cleanliness & Maintenance	3.5	Gym & Spa Facilities	2
Public Comfort/Space	4	Children's Facilities	N/A
Decor	4	Enjoyment Factor	4.5

Despite this ship's high-tech design and a size significantly larger than that of virtually any private yacht afloat, it nonetheless has some of the grace and lines of classic clipper ships—from the soaring masts to the needle-shaped bowsprit—with practically none of the associated discomforts. Getting around is usually easy, except that there's no inside access to the breakfast and luncheon restaurant; during high winds or rain, access via an external set of stairs can be moderately inconvenient.

Though the ship got a light face-lift in 2003 (receiving new towels, sheets, and carpeting along with some fresh coats of paint), the fact is she's 16 years old and can't help but show some wear and tear, so don't expect a flawless, spit-shined vessel, but rather a hard-worked, lived-in ship with a lot of charm.

Cabins & Rates

Cabins	Per Diems from	Sq. Ft.	Fridge	Hair Dryer	Sitting Area	TV
Cabins	$337	188	yes	yes	no	yes
Suite	$513	220	yes	yes	yes	yes

CABINS   All cabins are very similar: subtly nautical and roomy, but not as large as your typical high-end ship suite. Beds can be adapted into either a one-queen-size or a two-twin-size format. Each cabin has a VCR and TV showing CNN and movies (and sometimes ESPN), a CD player, a minibar, a pair of large round portholes with brass fittings, bathrobes, a compact closet, and fresh fruit. Teak-decked bathrooms, largish for a ship of this size, are better laid out than those aboard many luxury cruise liners, and contain a hair dryer, plenty of towels, and compact but adequate storage space. Like the ship's main public rooms, cabins are based on navy-blue fabrics and carpeting, along with wood tones—attractive but simple, well constructed, and utilitarian. Large desk/ bureaus are white with dark brown trim and the rest of the cabinetry is a medium wood tone. The ship has one Owner's Cabin measuring 220 square feet.

Although all the cabins are comfortable, cabins amidships are more stable in rough seas. Note that the ship's engines, when running at full speed, can be a bit noisy.

Connecting cabins are available. This line is not recommended for passengers with serious disabilities or those who are wheelchair bound. There are no elevators on board, access to piers is often by tender, and there are raised doorsills.

PUBLIC AREAS   There aren't a lot of public areas on this small ship, but they're more than adequate as passengers spend most of their time in port. The four main rooms include two restaurants, a library, and a vaguely nautical-looking lounge, with several cozy, somewhat private partitioned-off nooks and clusters of comfy caramel-colored leather chairs surrounding a slightly sunken wooden dance floor. In one corner is a bar, and, in another, a piano and equipment for the onboard entertainment duo. This is where passengers congregate for port talks, pre- and post-dinner drinks, dancing, and local dance performances. The second bar is out on the pool deck, and also attracts passengers before and after dinner for drinks under the stars. There's a piano in the corner of the deck (which doesn't get much play), but mostly this is your typical casual pool bar, and the place where cigars can be purchased and smoked.

The small wood-paneled library manages to be both nautical and collegiate at the same time. Guests can read, play cards, or check out one of the hundreds of videotapes (CDs are also available from the purser's office nearby). You can send and receive e-mail via a computer in the library.

DINING OPTIONS   The yachtishly elegant, dimly lit main restaurant is styled with nautical touches such as teak trim and paneling and pillars wrapped decoratively in hemp rope, while carpeting and fabrics are navy blue. It's the sole dinner venue, and it serves lunch occasionally too. The Veranda breakfast and lunch restaurant is a sunny, window-lined room whose tables extend from inside onto a covered deck (unfortunately, you do have to go outside on deck to get to the indoor part of the restaurant, so if it's raining, you get wet).

POOL, FITNESS & SPA FACILITIES   The swimming pool is tiny (as you might expect aboard such relatively small-scale ships) and there's an adjacent hot tub. The deck chairs around the pool can get filled during sunny days, but there's always the crescent-shaped slice of deck above and more space outside of the Veranda restaurant and a nice patch of deck forward of the bridge. On Deck 4, there's an unobstructed wraparound deck for walkers.

There's a cramped gym in a cabin-size room, and an adjacent coed sauna. But count your blessings; considering how small this ship is, it's a bonus that there's any workout room at all. Massages and a few other types of treatments are available out of a single massage room next to the hair salon on Deck 1. We should add that one of the best massages we've had at sea was on a Windstar ship.

8

Soft-Adventure Lines & Sailing Ships

Often more adventure tour than Love Boat, the vessels in this chapter are about as far as you can get from the typical cruise and still be on a ship. All of them are small and intimate, carrying only 60 to 200 passengers, and are designed to take you close to nature, island culture, and the sea. Of the lines reviewed here, **American Canadian Caribbean Line (ACCL)** and **Clipper** operate motorized coastal cruisers that are like hostels and B&Bs at sea, respectively, while **Star Clippers** and **Windjammer** both operate sailing ships, the former with a yacht-like vibe, the latter more like summer camp for adults. There may not be TVs in the cabins and you won't find a casino or glitzy dance revue; instead, you'll find people who have booked this type of ship because they want to meet their fellow passengers, develop friendships, and—aboard ACCL, Clipper, and Star Clippers—actually learn something about the places they're visiting. (Passengers on Windjammer Barefoot Cruises are . . . well, they're looking for a good time.) Food will be relatively basic, and you won't find room service, midnight buffets, or overly doting stewards, but you will get very personal attention, as crew and passengers get friendly fast. (None of the lines includes gratuities in fares; all tipping is at passenger discretion.) These ships generally visit a port every day, concentrating on small, out-of-the-way islands that the big cruise ships would run aground trying to approach; and shore excursions often include hiking, snorkeling, bird-watching, and history-oriented tours . . . plus beach parties for the Windjammer folks, naturally.

DRESS CODES Leave the jackets, ties, pumps, and pearls at home. Aboard these ultracasual ships you can get away with a polo shirt and khakis (or shorts) at pretty much any time, and on Windjammer you could show up to dinner in your bathing suit and not feel out of place.

Frommer's Ratings at a Glance: The Soft-Adventure Lines

1 = poor   2 = fair   3 = good   4 = excellent   5 = outstanding

Cruise Line	Enjoyment Factor	Dining	Activities	Children's Program	Entertainment	Service	Worth the Money
American Canadian Caribbean	4	3	4	N/A*	3	3	3
Clipper	4	4	4	N/A*	3	4	4
Star Clippers	5	4	4	N/A*	4	4	4
Windjammer	4	3	3	3**	3	3	5

Note: Cruise lines have been graded on a curve that compares them only with the other lines in the Soft-Adventure and Sailing Ships category. See chapter 5 for the ratings methodology. * Lines have no children's program whatsoever. **Applies only to the Windjammer *Legacy* and *Polynesia*; other vessels have no children's program. See ship reviews for details.

1 American Canadian Caribbean Line

461 Water St., Warren, RI 02885. ℂ 800/556-7450 or 401/247-0955. Fax 401/247-2350. www.accl-smallships.com.

THE LINE IN A NUTSHELL   A family-owned New England line, ACCL operates tiny, no-frills ships that travel to offbeat places and attract a well-traveled, extremely casual, and down-to-earth older crowd.

THE EXPERIENCE   ACCL's innovative and extremely informal small ships offer a cruise experience that gets passengers closer to the real life of the islands than is typical with the big-ship lines. Navigating hinterlands such as the cays off the coast of Belize and Guatemala, the Virgin Islands, and remote out-islands in the Bahamas, the line focuses on encounters with indigenous cultures and exploring the natural wonders of the region. Many of ACCL's generally friendly older passengers have sailed with the line before, and appreciate its ships' lack of glitz—which is putting it mildly. The ships are, in fact, about the most bare-bones vessels you'll find in terms of amenities, service, and meals, and are the only ships featuring a BYOB policy.

Pros

- **Casual and unpretentious:** If you're looking for a relatively cost-effective, do-it-yourself adventure at sea, these tiny yet innovative vessels are tops.
- **Innovative itineraries and ships:** Itineraries are one of a kind and imaginative, and the ships' technical innovations allow an up-close experience of out-of-the-way islands.
- **BYOB policy:** ACCL's BYOB policy provides substantial savings on bar bills. The bus or van that transports passengers from the airport or hotel to the ship stops at a reasonably priced liquor store en route so those interested can stock up on their alcoholic beverage of choice.

Cons

- **No frills:** Cabins are tiny, decor is bland, bathrooms are minuscule, there are no beach towels (bring your own), and meals are served family-style.
- **No place to hide:** When the ships are at or near full capacity, they're very, very full. Your cabin is your only sanctuary, and thin cabin walls will make you feel closer to your fellow passengers than you may prefer.
- **Minimal port information:** For a line that's so destination-oriented, ACCL's ships have a surprising lack of books and naturalists/historians to provide background on the islands' history, culture, and nature.

Compared with the other soft-adventure lines, here's how ACCL rates:

	Poor	Fair	Good	Excellent	Outstanding
Enjoyment Factor				✓	
Dining			✓		
Activities				✓	
Children's Program	N/A*				
Entertainment			✓		
Service			✓		
Worth the Money			✓		

* *ACCL offers no children's program.*

ACCL: TINY SHIPS, BIG ADVENTURE

Master shipbuilder and ACCL founder/builder/captain Luther Blount began his career in 1949, and has designed and built more than 300 vessels in his Warren, Rhode Island, shipyard. Blount built his first cruise ship, the 20-passenger *Canyon Flyer,* in 1966, and over the years has gradually increased both size and capacity while remaining faithful to his original concept that small is the only way to cruise. His company now operates a fleet of three vessels, the newest two of which, *Grande Caribe* and *Grande Mariner,* are, he told us, "about as perfect as I can build for what I'm doing." Each vessel's unusually shallow 6½-foot draft combines with more than 20 patented Blount innovations to allow it to sail into narrow, shallow waterways and nudge directly up onto pristine, dockless beaches, disembarking passengers onto shore via a ramp that extends from the bow. Who needs a pier?! For 2004, *Grande Mariner* will be the line's only ship in the Caribbean.

All said, American Canadian Caribbean is a delightfully rare find. It's one of the few family-owned cruise lines (now past age 85, Blount keeps a hand in the business—he even lives on his shipyard's grounds—but has turned over most day-to-day responsibility to his daughter Nancy) and one of the few cruise entities that designs, builds, maintains, and markets its own ships. If you sail this line, you'll bypass the typical tourist-trap ports in favor of waters normally traveled only by private yachts and other adventure lines. Just be sure you know what you're getting into, because this ship, with its spartan, communal, rough-and-ready lifestyle, just isn't for everyone.

PASSENGER PROFILE

This casual ship appeals to an unpretentious, sensible, early-to-bed crowd of mostly senior couples in their 60s through 80s, with the average age being 72. While some are physically fit, there are usually a few walking with canes and using hearing aids. Besides senior couples, there may be a few mother-daughter traveling companions. All are attracted by the ship's casual atmosphere (wash-and-wear fabrics, durable windbreakers, and easy-to-care-for sportswear is about as fancy as these folks get on vacation) and want to avoid overrun Caribbean ports such as St. Thomas, heading instead to more isolated havens where they can comb the beach or become quietly acquainted with regional culture. That said, passengers tend to be less adventurous than those on other small-ship lines, so ACCL doesn't offer hard-core activities such as water-skiing and excursions in inflatable Zodiac boats.

ACCL has one of the most loyal followings of any line, so it's not unusual to have 65% to 70% repeaters on the average cruise. Many passengers have been on other small-ship lines, such as Lindblad Expeditions, Clipper, Cruise West, and Glacier Bay/Voyager (the latter two, incidentally, operating several ships that were originally built and sailed as ACCL vessels), as well as some of the bigger, more luxurious lines. Travel programs for seniors, such as Elderhostel, are also popular with the typical ACCL passenger.

The ship will not appeal to the vast majority of young couples, singles, honeymooners, and families. Children under age 14 are prohibited, and the line offers no children's facilities or activities. Passengers sailing solo can take advantage of the line's **"Willing to Share"** program. See the "A Few Good Deals & One Extra Charge" box below for more info.

Warning: Ceilings on all ACCL ships are set at about 6 feet, 4 inches—something to take into consideration if you're very tall.

DINING

Wholesome, all-American food is well prepared, but overall is nothing special. The daily menu, with selections for all three meals, is posted every morning on the blackboard in the dining room. Meals are served promptly at 8am, noon, and 6pm every day and are announced by one of the waitresses clanging a bell as she passes through the corridors and lounge. Rather than wandering in gradually, everyone typically arrives within a few minutes. Mixing with your fellow passengers at meals is mandatory since dining is open seating, communal-style for all meals, at tables primarily seating eight (no tables for two and just one or two set for four).

Early risers will find "eye-opener" coffee and fruit juices available beginning at 6:30am in the lounge. At **breakfast,** waiters deliver melon slices and a different hot dish every morning (such as scrambled eggs with bacon, Belgian waffles, pancakes, French toast, and cheese omelets). Passengers can also choose from a buffet of hot or cold cereal, yogurt, and fruit. **Lunch** is the lightest meal of the day and consists of homemade soup (such as tomato basil, vegetable, or beef orzo) along with turkey, ham and cheese, and tuna sandwiches on freshly baked bread, plus a salad, chips, fruit, and dessert. **Dinners** begin with a salad and fresh bread followed by a main entree such as roast beef or chicken, along with vegetables and rice or potatoes, plus dessert. Fresh fish is common, especially on itineraries that include Belize, but also in the Caribbean—one cook recalls a fisherman in St. Lucia coming up to the ship and asking if they'd like to buy some fresh tuna. When asked how they knew it was fresh, the man said, "Give me 10 minutes," then went off and caught one. The same fisherman now supplies the ship whenever it's in port. Occasional theme nights spotlight dishes from Italy, the Caribbean, the American West, and so forth, and there's usually a barbecue on the top deck at least once per cruise, weather permitting.

With only one entree per meal, anyone wanting an **alternative meal** (such as fish instead of beef) can be accommodated only if he or she notifies the kitchen before 10am. In general, owing to the average passenger age, ACCL cooks try to keep things low in salt and fat. Other special dietary needs (such as vegetarian) can also be met if you give advance notice.

A variety of teas, as well as coffee and hot chocolate, is available round the clock, as are fresh fruit, pretzels and other snacks at the bar, and biscotti at the coffee station. **Fresh-baked cookies and muffins** are served between meals, and any baked goods left over from breakfast, lunch, and dinner are also left out for passenger noshing.

Because the line has a BYOB policy, all alcoholic beverages—which guests can buy at a liquor store en route from the airport or hotel to the ship—are kept in the lounge; beer and wine are stored in a cooler near the bar and there are separate shelves for liquor bottles. This is a real money-saving system for passengers—a bottle of rum we bought in Panama City, for example, cost less

---

Saving Your Soles on ACCL Excursions

ACCL doesn't always select beach stopovers because of their soft and glistening sands. Many expeditions to remote places include stops at gravel-and/or coral-covered beaches, so it's a good idea to pack a pair of nylon or rubber sandals or aqua-socks to wear on the beach and in the water.

A Few Good Deals & One Extra Charge

Unlike most other cruise lines, ACCL's brochure rates are very rarely discounted. That said, they do offer a few good deals.

Cabin shares: When three passengers share a cabin, each is granted a 15% discount. (Only some cabins can accommodate three; in those that do, expect it to be *very* tight.)

"Willing to Share" program: If you're traveling solo and are willing to share a cabin with another solo passenger, you'll pay the normal double-occupancy fare rather than the 175% single-occupancy fare. If there turns out not to be another solo aboard, you get the cabin for the cheaper rate.

Back-to-back and repeater deals: If you book two back-to-back cruises, you get 10% off the cost of the second trip. The line also gives passengers an 11th cruise free after their 10th paid cruise of at least 12 nights.

Port charges: Expect to pay between $150 and $200 per person on top of your fare, because port charges are not bundled into the cruise rates.

---

than $4 (about the cost of one drink on most ships). To avoid drinking someone else's booze, all bottles and cans are labeled with the passengers' cabin number. Soft drinks, along with tonic and soda water, are provided free of charge at the bar. On the first and last night of each cruise, hour-long welcome and goodbye parties offer an open stocked bar (for all drinks but beer), as well as jumbo-shrimp cocktails, smoked salmon, or something similar.

The line has no room service.

ACTIVITIES

With the exception of a few printed quizzes, occasional arts and crafts, and bridge and galley tours, daytime activities are oriented toward recreational pursuits off the ship during calls at remote islands and beaches. Because some of the areas frequented by ACCL are among the richest repositories of underwater life in the Western Hemisphere (especially those off the coast of Belize), there are frequent opportunities for **snorkeling** (with masks and fins provided free of charge), as well as swimming directly from a platform at the stern of the ship. During winters in the Caribbean, *Mariner* hauls along a **Sunfish** (minisailboat) and **kayaks** for passengers to use, as well as a Blount-designed 24-passenger **glass-bottom boat,** which is used at some islands to view coral formations and tropical fish. These are boarded directly from the platform in the stern—you just step aboard.

The amount of time spent at each island varies from a few hours to an entire morning or afternoon, and the ship usually remains anchored or docked at night, allowing passengers to explore restaurants and/or nightspots ashore. The typically short distance between islands is covered during daylight, often in the early morning. The cruise director (who also doubles as the purser and supervises housekeeping) is in charge of all passenger activities. Select cruises, including those to Belize, typically carry full-time naturalists aboard, but the line does not consistently have the variety or quality of onboard experts you'll find on rival Clipper. If this is important to you, inquire with the line's reservations agents which cruises will have experts aboard; they always know well in advance. Because no list of recommended background reading is supplied before the

ACCL Fleet Itineraries

Ship	Itineraries
Grande Mariner	**11-night E. Carib:** Between Antigua and Sint Maarten, Dec 2003, visiting Bird Island, St. Kitts, Nevis, Saba, St. Barts, Anguilla, Sint Maarten, Sandy Island, Isle Pinel, and Tintamarre Island. **11-night Virgin Islands:** Round-trip from St. Thomas, Jan 2004, visiting St. John, Tortola, Salt Island, Virgin Gorda, Anegada, Little Jost Van Dyke, and Norman Island. **11-night Caicos/Bahamas:** Between Caicos and Nassau, Feb 2004, visiting Providenciales, the Mayaguana Islands, Plana Cays, Acklins Island, Long Island, Exumas, Galliot Cay, White Point, Staniel Cay, Hawksbill Cay, Norman's Cay, and Allan's Cay. **11-night Bahamas:** Round-trip from Nassau, Feb–Mar 2004, visiting Spanish Wells, Harbour Island, Governor's Harbour, Norman Island, Exuma Cays, Staniel Cay, White Point, Galliot Cay, and Allan's Cay. **11-night Belize/Barrier Reef/Guatemala:** Round-trip from Belize City, Mar–Apr 2004, visiting Goff Cay, Tobaco Range, Maho Cay, Laughing Bird Cay, Placencia, Punta Gorda, El Gofete, and Water Cay (all in Belize), Livingston and Punta Icacos (Guatemala), with a bus tour to the Quirigua Ruins. **11-night Belize:** Round-trip from Belize City, Mar–Apr 2004, visiting Goff Cay, Tobaco Range, Laughing Bird Cay, Placencia, Lime Cay, Utila, Punta Gorda, West Snake Cay, Tom Owens Cay, and Northwest Pelican Caye (all in Belize), Punta Icacos (Guatemala), and Roatan (Honduras). **Non-Caribbean Itineraries:** Intracoastal Waterway, Great Lakes, Erie Canal.

cruise (and because there's only a small library aboard, in the lounge), passengers should do their own research ahead of time and bring appropriate guidebooks.

Instead of a daily printed schedule, the agenda of activities and ports of call is posted every morning on a bulletin board, and the cruise director runs through the day's schedule after breakfast.

Aside from the destination-oriented activities, the main evening events are card playing and a **movie** from the ship's video collection, shown after dinner on the large-screen TV in the lounge.

CHILDREN'S PROGRAM

The minimum age for children on board is 14 years old, and there are no special facilities even for those who clear that mark. Unless your teenage child or grandchild is particularly self-reliant and enjoys the company of older folks, he or she probably wouldn't enjoy a cruise with this line.

ENTERTAINMENT

Amusement is mostly of the do-it-yourself nature, such as board games, puzzles, and reading. The **BYOB cocktail hour** is a time for songs (accompanied on the lounge piano, assuming there's a passenger aboard who plays), announcements, and an occasional informal talk about an upcoming sight or experience. Sometimes, **local entertainers,** such as Garifuna dancers in Belize or soca or reggae musicians in the Virgin Islands, will be invited aboard for an evening or will perform for passengers in port.

SERVICE

Generally, the ship's staff is made up of Americans, many of whom hail from the Northeast, including Rhode Island, ACCL's home state. Deckhands and day workers may be hired on from the area in which the ship is sailing, adding a touch of internationalism. For many members of the service staff, serving aboard the vessel is like a summer job—the equivalent of working as a camp counselor in Maine—and they probably won't be doing this type of thing as a career. What they lack in experience, though, they make up for in enthusiasm and friendliness. As on most small ships, all of them double on many jobs that bigger ships have segregated into separate departments. You may see your cabin attendant waiting tables at dinner, for instance.

Service is adequate in the dining room—about what you'd find at a friendly local restaurant. Cabins are made up once a day after breakfast, and towels are changed every other day. There's no laundry service or room service, nor is there an onboard doctor or medical facilities—ships this size are not required to provide them because they always sail close to land, which allows them to get sick passengers ashore quickly.

Grande Mariner

The Verdict

Functional and no-frills, *Grande Mariner* is a well-thought-out vehicle for transporting passengers to remote ports—no more, no less.

Grand Mariner *(photo: ACCL)*

Specifications

Size (in tons)	99*	Officers	American
Number of Cabins	50	Crew	18 (American/Int'l)
Number of Outside Cabins	41	Passenger/Crew Ratio	5.5 to 1
Cabins with Verandas	0	Year Launched	1998
Number of Passengers	100	Last Major Refurbishment	N/A

* A different system of measuring GRTs (gross registered tons) has been employed with ACCL's vessels, which makes comparison with other similarly sized ships in this chapter difficult. Comparing passenger capacity will give a more accurate estimate of size.

Frommer's Ratings (Scale of 1–5)   ✮✮✮½

Cabin Comfort & Amenities	2	Dining Options	2
Ship Cleanliness & Maintenance	4	Gym & Spa Facilities	N/A
Public Comfort/Space	3	Children's Facilities	N/A
Decor	2	Enjoyment Factor	3

Grande Mariner (and sister ship *Grande Caribe*, which currently doesn't sail in the Caribbean) is the culmination of 30 years of ACCL's "small ship equals good ship" corporate philosophy, and though she's definitely the most comfortable and appealing vessel the line has ever built, she's still as basic as cruise ships come, with tiny, spartan cabins and no-fuss decor. Seaworthy and practical, she has all the innovative exploratory features for which ACCL is known—a shallow draft and bow ramp that allow her to pull right up to pristine beaches, a retractable pilothouse that lets her sail under low bridges on inland waterways, and a platform in the stern for swimming and launching the ship's glass-bottom boat and sailboat. Her ventilation system pumps air directly into each cabin from outside rather than circulating it throughout the ship, and the ship is a lot quieter than previous company vessels due to the use of twin-screwed, 1,400-horsepower engines mounted on cushioned bearings.

Cabins & Rates

Cabins	Per Diems from	Sq. Ft.	Fridge	Hair Dryer	Sitting Area	TV
Inside	$223	80–120	no	no	no	no
Outside	$241	80–120	no	no	no	no

CABINS   Spartan in design and amenities—four bare walls, soap and towels only, no TV or radio, minimal space for storing clothes—the ship's 50 compact cabins are somewhere between cozy and claustrophobic. However you describe them, couples have minimal room to maneuver (watch out for flying elbows!) and no space to stretch out in the minuscule head-style bathrooms—which, in layman's terms, means the toilet and sink are in the shower stall. Passengers around 6 feet or taller, beware of the low bridge over the toilet—one of our taller researchers banged his head twice. Some cabins aboard *Mariner* have a solid door between the bathroom and cabin; others have only a curtain. ACCL plans to add doors to bathrooms in cabins over the next few years, along with artwork to liven up the cabins, but this almost certainly won't be done for 2004. If a solid door is important to you, be sure you make this known when you book. Cabins are generally arranged with two single beds, but most cabins on the Main Deck can be arranged with a double. Cabins on the Lower Deck and several in the forward section of the Main Deck have upper and lower berths (i.e., bunk beds).

The cabins on the Sun Deck are the only ones with sliding picture windows; eight of these (60–62A, 60B, 70A and B, and 80 and 81B) also have doors onto the outside deck, rather than to the inside corridor. All other cabins have sealed picture windows except the six on the Lower Deck and cabins 10A, 10B, 30A, 30B, 31A, and 31B on the Main Deck, which have tiny "deadlight" portholes. All doors lock from the inside only—there are no keys, which is normal for these kinds of small, friendly ships. Most cabins have a small half-length cabinet for hanging clothes, plus five coat hooks, a narrow three-drawer unit, a storage space under the beds, and a wooden storage cabinet between beds.

Cabins on the Main Deck behind the dining room are susceptible to vibrations from the engines, located right below them. Cabins on the Sun Deck closest to the lounge may be susceptible to some noise from that room. There are no connecting cabins. None of the cabins are wheelchair accessible and the ship has no elevators, but there is a stair lift for those who have difficulty walking between decks.

PUBLIC AREAS   *Mariner* has three decks total, and larger public spaces than aboard past ACCL vessels. The main public area is the lounge on the Sun Deck, with wraparound windows that allow it to serve as a viewing area during the day. It's furnished with couches and chairs, a large-screen TV, a bar, board games and puzzles, and a random selection of books and magazines (bring your own books if you like to read), and serves as an auditorium for occasional lectures, arts-and-crafts classes, the lively BYOB pre-dinner cocktail hour every evening, and video movie and documentary screenings.

As on the other ships in this category, there's no onboard shop, but logo items—caps, T-shirts, and so on—are available for purchase from the cruise director.

During the day, many passengers view the passing ocean scene from the open top deck, which is furnished with deck chairs and partially covered by a large awning for protection from the intense tropical sun. On the Sun Deck, open decks along the port and starboard sides, a small area in the bow, and a quiet open area in the stern are also open for passenger use.

DINING OPTIONS All meals are served in a single small dining room, located next to the galley on the Main Deck. Polished wood accents give the room a semi-warm feel, but you can't call it fancy.

POOL, FITNESS & SPA FACILITIES *Mariner* has no exercise facilities, swimming pools, or spas. Passengers can walk around the Sun Deck's narrow but passable perimeter (12½ laps = 1 mile), but otherwise any exercise you get will be in port, or on the occasional swim from the ship's stern platform.

2 Clipper Cruise Line

11969 Westline Industrial Dr., St. Louis, Missouri 63146-3220. ☎ **800/325-0010** or 314/655-6700. Fax 314/655-6670. www.clippercruise.com.

THE LINE IN A NUTSHELL   Clipper's down-to-earth, comfortable small ships focus on offbeat ports of call, learning, and mingling with your fellow passengers. It's the ideal small-ship cruise for people who've tried Holland America or one of the other mainstream lines but want a more intimate cruise experience.

THE EXPERIENCE   Clipper caters to mature, seasoned, easygoing, relatively affluent, and well-traveled older passengers seeking a casual and educational vacation experience. You won't find any glitter, glitz, or Vegas-style gambling here; instead, you'll get an experience of the nature, history, and culture of the ports visited, courtesy of the naturalists who sail with every Caribbean sailing. A cruise director helps organize the days, answers questions, and assists passengers. Because these are small ships, the ambience is intimate and conducive to making new friends easily. On the downside, as with many other American-crewed small ships, cruise rates are not cheap.

The line's two primary Caribbean ships, *Nantucket Clipper* and *Yorktown Clipper,* are small and nicely appointed, with comfortable cabins, sizable lounges and dining rooms, and an overall relaxed feel. Like other small ships, they're able to access remote hideaways in the southern Caribbean, the British Virgin Islands, and Central America; but they also suffer the typical problems of small ships, such as stability: When a ship this size hits rough water, you know it. (Bring the Dramamine!)

Pros

- **Interesting ports of call:** Their small size enables the ships to visit remote ports that most ships can't get close to, such as the British Virgin Islands and Grenadines.
- **Great learning opportunities:** Historians, naturalists, and guest lecturers sail aboard, offering lectures and accompanying guests on shore excursions.
- **Informal atmosphere:** No need to dress up here—everything's casual.
- **Young, enthusiastic American crew:** While they may not be the most experienced, they're sweet and hardworking, and add a homey feel to the trip.

Cons

- **No stabilizers:** If you hit choppy waters and you're prone to seasickness, good luck.
- **Noisy engines:** If you can help it, don't book a cabin on the lowest deck (Main Deck), where noise from the engines can get quite loud.

Compared with the other soft-adventure lines, here's how Clipper rates:

	Poor	Fair	Good	Excellent	Outstanding
Enjoyment Factor				✓	
Dining				✓	
Activities				✓	
Children's Program	N/A*				
Entertainment			✓		
Service				✓	
Worth the Money				✓	

* Clipper offers no children's program.

CLIPPER: CASUAL SHIPS, ENLIGHTENING TRIPS

Based in St. Louis, of all places, Clipper was founded in 1982 and is a subsidiary of deluxe-tour operator INTRAV. The line operates differently than most others in that its ships rarely ply the same itineraries for more than a few weeks at a time, instead moving from region to region, with no one place serving as a real home port—it's as if the ships were on a constant trip around the world, boarding passengers to sail different segments of one very long itinerary. Longer seasons in the Caribbean and Alaska are the exceptions to this rule.

Although Clipper's ships carry a similar number of passengers and visit many of the same out-of-the-way ports as those of competitor American Canadian Caribbean Line, they're different breeds: While Clipper's ships lack some of ACCL's wonderful exploratory features (such as the ability to nudge right up onto a beach to disembark passengers), they're much more comfortable and homey than ACCL's spartan, bare-bones vessels.

Clipper's primary Caribbean ships are the 100-passenger, 1,471-ton *Nantucket Clipper* and the 138-passenger, 2,354-ton *Yorktown Clipper,* both reviewed in the following pages. In addition, a single 13-night Belize/Central America itinerary is being offered in September 2003 aboard the 122-passenger, 4,364-ton **Clipper Adventurer,** a former Russian expedition/research vessel that Clipper bought in 1998 and converted into a truly beautiful, almost country-club comfortable yet tough and exploratory cruiser. She's one of our favorite small ships, but since she sails only one Caribbean trip, we haven't included a full review in this book. For more details on the ship, check out *Frommer's European Cruises & Ports of Call.*

PASSENGER PROFILE

The majority of Clipper passengers are well-traveled 45- to 75-year-old couples (and occasionally singles) who are attracted by the casual intimacy of small ships and by the opportunity to actually learn something about the places they visit. Most are well educated, though not academic; casual; and adventurous in the sense that they're up for a day of snorkeling and hiking, but are happy to get back to their comfortable ship afterward. As a company spokesman noted a few years back, "Our aim is to offer an experience that adds something special to one's understanding of the world while providing a sense of enjoyment."

Clipper attracts a remarkably high number of repeat passengers: On any given cruise, 40% or more of the passengers will have sailed with the line before. Many have also sailed with other small-ship lines, such as Lindblad Expeditions, Cruise West, and ACCL.

DINING

The fare is all-American, prepared by attendees of the Culinary Institute of America, and incorporates local ingredients whenever practical. While relatively simple in ingredients and presentation, it's the equal of all but the best cuisine served aboard the mainstream megaships.

Breakfast is served in both the lounge and the dining room, with cereals, fruit, toast, and pastries in the former and a full breakfast menu in the latter. Similarly, at **lunch** you can get a full meal in the dining room or create your own sandwich from an assortment of cold cuts in the lounge. Set lunches offer a hot luncheon platter (perhaps crab cakes, baby back ribs, or pasta primavera); a lighter, cold entree (such as cobb salad, chicken Caesar salad, or seafood salad); and one or another kind of omelet—and there's always the option of a platter of fresh fruit and cottage cheese.

Dinner is served in a single open seating in the dining room, at tables set up for four to six, and offers four courses with five main entree options: seafood (perhaps herb-marinated halibut, stuffed lobster tail, or Chilean sea bass), a meat entree (such as roast duck, veal Marsala, or prime rib), a pasta entree, a "starch and vegetables" entree (such as steamed vegetables over saffron rice), and a **vegetarian option** (such as marinated grilled portobello mushroom, vegetarian lasagna, or 10-vegetable couscous). Clipper can accommodate **special diets** or restrictions if you give them warning before your cruise.

Weather permitting, there's a **barbecue** on deck at least once during each weeklong cruise, and **snacks** are available throughout each day in the lounge, including mighty fine "Clipper Chipper" chocolate-chip cookies (whose recipe is actually posted on the line's website, in case you're interested). As aboard almost all small ships, the ships don't have room service unless you're too ill to attend meals.

Though the onboard dress code is casual at all times, many passengers will put on sports jackets and dresses for dinner, and some men wear ties for the captain's welcome-aboard and farewell parties.

ACTIVITIES

By design, these ships don't offer much in the way of typical cruise ship activities; instead, their activities are designed to focus your attention on the islands and marine environments you're visiting, giving you the opportunity to return home from your vacation not only relaxed but also enriched.

Each day of the Caribbean itineraries is spent in port, with several organized excursions offered in each (at extra cost, as is the case with almost all lines). At least one naturalist always sails with the ship, and occasionally a historian as well. Typically, these experts will accompany passengers on their excursions: The historian will trek along while visiting St. Kitts's Brimstone Hill Fortress, for instance, or one of the naturalists will snorkel with passengers in St. Lucia's Anse Chastanet marine park. Throughout the cruise, these same staff members also offer a series of **informal lectures,** which on our last trip included talks on reef fish identification, the nature and geology of the Caribbean islands, American Revolution history in the Caribbean, and plant life. Experts may also offer free informal **shore walks** on certain islands. Naturally, passengers have the option of skipping all of this and just lying on the beach (towels are provided by the line) or, in many ports, snorkeling, for which gear is provided free.

When arriving at some of the more undeveloped islands, passengers go ashore via inflatable, steel-floored landing boats and often have to step from these boats into the surf when disembarking. You may want to bring along a pair of aquasocks to protect your feet.

CHILDREN'S PROGRAM

These ships have no facilities or programs of any kind for children. If you want to bring a young niece, nephew, or grandchild, they'll be expected to behave like young adults. Most teenagers would be bored to death aboard a Clipper Cruise. Babysitting is not available. There is no minimum age for children to sail.

ENTERTAINMENT

By way of entertainment, Clipper's Caribbean itineraries offer blue skies, blue waters, sandy beaches, schools of brightly colored tropical fish, island culture, a smattering of fascinating historical sites, and the occasional diving pelican or

Clipper Fleet Itineraries

Ship	Itineraries
Nantucket Clipper	**7-night E. Carib:** Round-trip from St. Thomas, Dec 2003–Jan 2004, visiting Jost Van Dyke, Tortola, Virgin Gorda, Norman Island, and Christmas Cove (all BVIs); Salt Island (Turks and Caicos); and St. John. **7-night Belize/Honduras:** Belize City, Belize, to Puerto Cortes, Honduras, Jan–Feb 2004, visiting Cocoa Plum Cay (Belize), Livingston and Puerto Barrios (Guatemala), and Roatan and Cayos Cochinos (Honduras). **Non-Caribbean Itineraries:** Intracoastal Waterway, Mid-Atlantic Coast, New England/Canada, Chesapeake Bay, Great Lakes.
Yorktown Clipper	**8-night Central America:** Between San Jose, Costa Rica, and Panama City, Nov–Dec 2003, visiting Curu Wildlife Refuge/Carara National Park, Manuel Antonio National Park/Quepos, Marenco Biological Station, and the Darien Jungle (Costa Rica), with 2 days at sea including a guaranteed daylight transit of the Panama Canal. **9-night E. Carib:** Round-trip from St. Thomas, Dec 2003, visiting Culebra, Ponce, and Vieques (Puerto Rico); Tortola, Virgin Gorda, Norman Island (BVIs); and St. John. **7-night E. Carib:** Round-trip from St. Thomas, Jan 2004, visiting St. John; Jost Van Dyke, Tortola, and Virgin Gorda, Norman Island, and Christmas Cove (all British Virgin Islands); and Salt Cay (Turks and Caicos). **Non-Caribbean Itineraries:** Baja, Alaska, Pacific Northwest.

leaping dolphin. If your response to this is "That's all?", then this isn't the line for you. As is true of the vast majority of small-ship companies, Clipper offers no casino, no dancing girls, no comedy and/or magic acts—nothing, in fact, that's standard issue on the megaships except the occasional recent-release movie (shown in the lounge) and performances by local musicians who are brought aboard for the evening. A weeklong cruise not long ago saw passengers entertained by a steel-drum band, an acoustic island-music trio, and a full modern island band, as well as a tropical fashion show in which one of the models was none other than a recent Miss St. Kitts. Royalty!

Aboard both *Nantucket Clipper* and *Yorktown Clipper,* the Observation Lounge is the central (in fact, only) public social area aside from the open decks. You'll find a bar, ample cushy seating, and a piano there, as well as a small library well stocked with books on island history, culture, nature, and geography, plus a smattering of bestsellers.

SERVICE

Service staff aboard Clipper's ships is basically collegiate or post-collegiate Americans having an adventure before getting on with whatever it is they're getting on with. In other words, these aren't the same folks you'll find serving at the Four Seasons. They're amateurs—willing to work and happy to help, but don't expect them to click their heels when you cross the threshold. Not that you'd want them to—which, we think, is the point. As Clipper's demographic base is generally couples over 50, we suspect a subtle plot on the line's part is to staff its ships with young men and women of approximately the same age as passengers' children and grandchildren; but unlike those real offspring, these substitutes *actually do what you tell them to.* A refreshing change!

There is neither room service nor any laundry facilities or services.

Nantucket Clipper • Yorktown Clipper

The Verdict

Like a pair of your favorite walking shoes, these low-frills yet comfortable small ships carry well-traveled passengers to off-the-beaten-track ports in search of nature, history, and a nice rum punch or two.

Yorktown Clipper *(photo: Clipper Cruise Line)*

Specifications

Size (in tons)		Officers	American
Nantucket	1,471	Crew	American
Yorktown	2,354	*Nantucket*	32
Number of Cabins		*Yorktown*	40
Nantucket	51	Passenger/Crew Ratio	
Yorktown	69	*Nantucket*	3.2 to 1
Number of Outside Cabins		*Yorktown*	3.5 to 1
Nantucket	51	Year Launched	
Yorktown	69	*Nantucket*	1984
Cabins with Verandas	0	*Yorktown*	1988
Number of Passengers		Last Major Refurbishment	N/A
Nantucket	100		
Yorktown	138		

Frommer's Ratings (Scale of 1–5)   ★★★½

Cabin Comfort & Amenities	3	Dining Options	4
Ship Cleanliness & Maintenance	4	Gym & Spa Facilities	N/A
Public Comfort/Space	3	Children's Facilities	N/A
Decor	3	Enjoyment Factor	4

The impression we kept coming back to when discussing the spacious lounges and cozy cabins of these ships was that someone had taken one of the Holland America or Princess ships and shrunk it to one-fiftieth its normal size. Though not boasting the many bright public rooms of those large vessels, the four-deck *Yorktown* and *Nantucket Clipper* offer similar clean styling redone in more casual and easy-to-live-with colors, while also offering a small ship's ability to take passengers into shallow-water ports and other out-of-the-way locations far from the megaship crowd.

Cabins & Rates

Cabins	Per Diems from	Sq. Ft.	Fridge	Hair Dryer	Sitting Area	TV
Outside	$316	93–140	no	yes	no	no

CABINS   Although small (an average cabin size on *Nantucket Clipper* is 93–123 sq. ft.; the average on the *Yorktown* is 110–140 sq. ft.), cabins are very pleasantly styled, with blond-wood writing desk, chair, and bed frames; "better than a bare wall"—style paintings; and a goodly amount of closet space, plus additional storage under the beds. There are no phones or TVs, but each cabin does have music channels. Cabins have no safes as such, but two drawers in the closet can be locked, and passengers can lock valuables in each ship's safe, located on the bridge.

Cabins come in six categories, differentiated mostly by their location rather than their size. (See chapter 2, "Booking Your Cruise & Getting the Best Price," for more information about cabin categories.) Each has two beds, permanently fixed in either an L-shaped corner configuration or set parallel to one another, with floor space between (the L-shaped arrangement is more comfortable for passengers over 6 ft., 2 in.; the parallel beds are abutted by both the wall and a headboard and are not much longer than 6 ft., 4 in.). Some cabins have twin beds that can be pushed together to make a double, and some contain upper berths that fold down from the wall to accommodate a third person. Each ship has three or four large suitelike cabins measuring 163 to 204 square feet.

All cabins have picture windows except for a few category-1 cabins on the Main Deck, which have portholes. All cabins on each ship's Promenade Deck and a handful at the stern on the Lounge Deck open onto the outdoors (rather than onto an interior corridor), and whereas we normally prefer this simply because it makes us feel closer to nature, here it doesn't matter because the doors open out—meaning you can't leave the door open to breezes without blocking the deck walkway. It's worth noting that passengers in the Promenade Deck cabins should also be careful when opening their doors from the inside, lest they inadvertently brain fellow passengers who are taking a walk around the deck.

Cabin bathrooms are compact, though not nearly as tiny as aboard rival American Canadian Caribbean Line. Toilets are wedged between the shower and sink area and may prove tight for heavier people. Bathrooms have showers but no tubs.

Nantucket Clipper has four connecting cabins. Neither ship has cabins designated for single occupancy. There are no cabins suitable for travelers with disabilities, and no elevators between decks.

PUBLIC AREAS   Each ship has four decks and only two indoor public areas: the dining room and the Observation Lounge. The pleasant lounge has big windows, a bar, a small but informative library, a piano that gets little use, and enough space to comfortably seat everyone on board for lectures and meetings. It's the main hub of onboard activity. Other than that, there are no cozy hideaways other than your cabin. There is, though, plenty of outdoor deck space for those liking to linger over a sunset or under the stars.

DINING OPTIONS   All meals are served in the one dining room, which is spacious and comfortable. Snacks are also offered in the lounge throughout the day, along with coffee, tea, and other drinks.

POOL, FITNESS & SPA FACILITIES   Neither ship has a swimming pool nor any workout machines. For exercise, you can jog or walk around the deck (18 laps = 1 mile), and when anchored in calm waters, you can sometimes go swimming and snorkeling right from the ship, courtesy of a small platform that's lowered into the water.

3 Star Clippers

4101 Salzedo Ave., Coral Gables, FL 33146. © **800/442-0553** or 305/442-0550. Fax 305/442-1611. www. star- clippers.com.

THE LINE IN A NUTSHELL   With the sails and rigging of classic clipper ships and some of the cushy amenities of modern megas, a cruise on this line's 170- to 228-passenger ships offers adventure with comfort.

THE EXPERIENCE   On Star Clippers, you'll have the best of two worlds. On the one hand, the ships offer comfortable, almost cushy public rooms and cabins. On the other, they espouse an unstructured, let-your-hair-down, hands-on ethic—you can climb the masts (with a harness, of course), help raise the sails, crawl into the bow netting, or chat with the captain on the open-air bridge.

On board, ducking under booms, stepping over coils of rope, leaning against railings just feet above the sea, and watching sailors work the winches are constant reminders that you're on a real working ship. Furthermore, listening to the captain's daily talk about the next port of call, the history of sailing, or some other nautical subject, you'll feel like you're exploring some of the Caribbean's more remote stretches in a ship that really belongs there—an exotic ship for an exotic locale. In a sea of look-alike megaships, *Star Clipper* and newer *Royal Clipper* stand out, recalling a romantic, swashbuckling era of ship travel.

Pros
- **Hands-on experience:** You never have to lift a finger if you don't want to, but if you do, you're free to help out.
- **Comfortable amenities:** Pools, a piano bar and deck bar, a bright and pleasant dining room serving tasty food, and a clubby, wood-paneled library balance out the swashbuckling spirit. *Royal Clipper* also boasts a gym, a small spa, and marble bathrooms.
- **Rich in atmosphere:** On these ships, the ambience is a real treat.
- **Offbeat itineraries:** While not as far-flung as those offered by ACCL or Clipper, Star Clippers' itineraries do take passengers to some of the Caribbean's more remote islands, such as the Grenadines and French West Indies.

Cons
- **Rocking and rolling:** Even though the ships have ballast tanks to reduce rolling, you'll feel the motion if you run into rough seas, as is the case with any small ship.
- **No fitness equipment on *Star Clipper*:** The newer *Royal Clipper* has a fitness center, but on *Star Clipper* you're out of luck for anything but a massage.

Compared with the other adventure lines, here's how Star Clippers rates:

	Poor	Fair	Good	Excellent	Outstanding
Enjoyment Factor					✓
Dining			✓		
Activities			✓		
Children's Program	N/A*				
Entertainment				✓	
Service				✓	
Worth the Money				✓	

* *Star Clippers offers no children's program.*

STAR CLIPPERS: COMFY ADVENTURE

Clipper ships—full-sailed, built for speed, and undeniably romantic—reigned for only a brief time on the high seas before being driven out by steam engines and iron (and then steel) hulls. During their heyday, however, these vessels, including famous names such as *Cutty Sark, Ariel,* and *Flying Cloud,* engendered more romantic myths than any before or since, and helped open the Pacific Coast of California during the gold rush of 1849, carrying much-needed supplies around the tip of South America from Boston and New York.

By the early 1990s, despite the nostalgia and sense of reverence that had surrounded every aspect of the clippers' maritime history, nothing that could be technically classified as a clipper ship had been built since *Cutty Sark* in 1869. Enter Mikael Krafft, a Swedish-born industrialist and real-estate developer with a passion for ship design and deep, deep pockets, who invested vast amounts of personal energy and more than $80 million to build *Star Flyer* and *Star Clipper* at a Belgian shipyard in 1991 and 1992.

To construct these 170-passenger twins, Krafft procured the original drawings and specifications of Scottish-born Donald McKay, a leading naval architect of 19th-century clipper-ship technology, and employed his own team of naval architects to solve such engineering problems as adapting the square-rigged, four-masted clipper design to modern materials and construction. In mid-2000, Krafft went a step further, launching the 228-passenger *Royal Clipper,* a five-masted, fully rigged sailing ship inspired by the famed *Preussen,* a German clipper built in 1902. The *Royal Clipper* now claims the title of the largest clipper ship in the world, and she's a stunning sight.

When compared with Windjammer Barefoot Cruises, which operates original (if modernized) sailing ships, and Windstar Cruises, which operates less authentic electronically controlled sailing ships, Star Clippers is smack dab in the middle—more luxurious and a bit more expensive than the bare-boned, no-frills Windjammer and less formal and expensive than Windstar (though the posh *Royal Clipper* gets pretty close to Windstar level). Overall, the experience is quite casual, and salty enough to make you feel like a fisherman keeling off the coast of Maine, without the physical hardship of actually being one. As Krafft put it on a recent sailing, "If you want a typical cruise, you're in the wrong place."

All the Star Clippers vessels are at once traditional and radical. They're the tallest and among the fastest clipper ships ever built, and are so beautiful that even at full stop they seem to soar. As opposed to ships such as Windstar's *Wind Surf,* a bulkier cruise vessel that just happens to have sails, Star Clippers' ships do generally rely on sails alone for about 25% to 35% of the time; the rest of the time, the sails are used with the engines. Each ship performs superlatively—during *Star Clipper*'s maiden sail in 1992 off the coast of Corsica, she sustained speeds of 19.4 knots, thrilling her owner and designers, who had predicted maximum speeds of 17 knots. The new *Royal Clipper* was designed to make up to 20 knots under sail (14 max under engine alone), and on a recent cruise, she easily hit 15 knots one afternoon. During most cruises, however, the crew tries to keep passengers comfortable and decks relatively horizontal, so the vessels are kept to speeds of 9 to 14 knots with a combination of sail and engine power.

PASSENGER PROFILE

With no more than about 230 passengers aboard the largest ship in the fleet, each Star Clippers cruise seems like a triumph of individuality and intimacy. The line's unusual niche appeals to passengers who might recoil at the lethargy and/or sometimes forced enthusiasm of cruises aboard larger, more typical vessels. Overall, the company reports that a whopping 60% of passengers on average are repeaters back for another Star Clippers cruise.

While you're likely to find a handful of late-20-something honeymoon-type couples, the majority of passengers are well-traveled couples in their 40s to 60s, all active and intellectually curious professionals (such as executives, lawyers, and doctors) who appreciate a casual yet sophisticated ambience and enjoy mixing with fellow passengers. During the day, polo shirts, shorts, and topsiders are standard issue, and for dinner, many passengers simply change into cleaner and better-pressed versions of the same, with perhaps a switch from shorts to slacks for most men. However, men in jackets and women in snazzy dresses aren't uncommon on the night of the captain's cocktail party.

With a nearly even mix of Europeans and North Americans on a typical Caribbean cruise, the international onboard flavor is as intriguing as the ship itself, with the sounds of English, German, and French mingling like the notes of a song. There also are usually passengers from Germany, Austria, Switzerland, France, and the U.K. Announcements are made in English and often German, too.

DINING

Although the quality can still be inconsistent, Star Clippers' cuisine has evolved and improved through the years as the line has poured more time and effort into it, with an enhanced menu that includes four well-presented entree choices at each evening meal. All meals are open seating, with tables for four, six, and eight in the restaurant; the dress code is always casual. **Breakfast and lunch** are served buffet style and are the best meals of the day. The continental cuisine reflects the line's large European clientele and is dominated at breakfast and lunch by cheeses (such as brie, French goat cheese, and smoked Gouda), as well as marinated fish and meats. Breakfasts also include a hot-and-cold buffet spread and an omelet station, where a staff member will make your eggs the way you like them. Late-afternoon snacks served at the Tropical Bar include such munchies as crudités, cheeses, and chicken wings.

Dinners consist of appetizers, soup, salad, dessert, and a choice of five main entree choices: seafood (such as lobster and shrimp with rice pilaf), meat (beef curry, for example), vegetarian, a chef's special, and a light dish. Dinner choices such as fusilli in a tomato sauce, grilled Norwegian salmon, and herb-crusted rack of lamb are tasty, but tend toward the bland side. Most dinners are sit-down, and service can feel a bit rushed and frenetic during the dinner rush. Breakfast and lunch don't get as crowded since passengers tend to eat at staggered times. Waiters and bartenders are efficient and friendly, and depending on the cruise director, may dress in costume for several theme nights each week.

Built for Speed

Every other week, when *Royal Clipper* and *Star Clipper* itineraries overlap off the coast of Dominica, the ships engage in a race under sail alone. It's great fun (and a great photo op) to watch the captain running energetically around the bridge, barking orders to staff. A small but really loud minicannon is fired to start the race, and then each ship blasts her horn three times, whipping passengers into a competitive frenzy. Not to handicap the race too much, but the larger and more powerful *Royal Clipper* usually ends up the winner—on a recent cruise, she hit 14.5 knots doing so.

A worthwhile selection of **wines** is available on board, with a heavy emphasis on medium-priced French, German, and California selections. Coffee and tea are available from a 24-hour coffee station in the piano bar.

On *Star Clipper,* **room service** is available only for guests who are sick and can't make it to the dining room; on *Royal Clipper,* passengers staying in the 14 suites and Owner's Suites get 24-hour room service.

ACTIVITIES

If you want action, shopping, and dozens of organized tours, you won't find much of what you're looking for on these ships and itineraries—in fact, their absence is a big part of the line's allure. For the most part, enjoying the experience of being on a sailing ship and socializing with fellow passengers and crewmembers is the main activity, as it is on most any ship this size. Plus, the ships are in port every single day, so boredom is not an issue.

The friendliness starts at the get-go, with smiling waitstaff offering guests complimentary fruit drinks as they board. Throughout the cruise, the captain gives **informal talks on maritime themes,** and at least once a day, the cruise director speaks about the upcoming ports and shipboard events (though port info may not be as in-depth as you'd expect; on a recent *Royal Clipper* cruise, the cruise director provided only very scant information). Within reason, passengers can lend a hand with deck duties, observe the mechanics of navigation, **climb the masts** (at designated times and with a safety harness), and have a token try at handling the wheel when circumstances and calm weather permit. Each ship maintains an open-bridge policy, allowing passengers to wander up to the humble-looking navigation center at any hour of the day or night (you may have to ask to actually go into the chart room, though).

Other activities may include a brief engine-room tour, **morning exercise classes** on deck, excursions via tender to photograph the ship under sail, in-cabin movies, and hanging out by the pools (three on *Royal Clipper,* two on *Star Clipper*). Of course, sunbathing is a sport in and of itself. Best spot for it? In the bowsprit netting, hanging out over the water. It's sunny, it's a thrill in itself, and it's the perfect place from which to spot dolphins in the sea just feet below you, dancing in the bow's wake. Massages are available on both ships, too, at a reasonable $62 an hour: On *Star Clipper,* they're doled out in a spare cabin or a small cabana on deck; *Royal* has a dedicated massage room, divided into two areas by a curtain.

Port activities are a big part of these cruises. Sailing from one island to another and often arriving at the day's port of call sometime after 9am (but usually before 11am, and usually after a brisk early-morning sail), the ships anchor offshore and shuttle passengers back and forth by tender. On many landings, you'll have to walk a few feet in shallow water between the tender and the beach.

Activities in port revolve around beaches and watersports, and are all complimentary. Partly because owner Mikael Krafft is an avid scuba diver and partly because itineraries focus on waters that teem with marine life, each ship offers (for an extra charge) the option of **PADI-approved scuba diving.** Certified divers will find all the equipment they'll need on board. Even uncertified/ inexperienced divers can pay a fee for **scuba lessons** that will grant them resort certification and allow them to make a number of relatively simple dives. There's also **snorkeling** (complimentary equipment is distributed at the start of the cruise), water-skiing, windsurfing, and banana-boat rides offered by the ship's watersports team in all ports. The ships carry along Zodiac motorboats for this

Star Clippers Fleet Itineraries

Ship	Itineraries
Royal Clipper	**7-night S. Carib 1:** Round-trip from Barbados, Nov 2003–Apr 2004, visiting Grenada, Tobago Cays, St. Vincent, Bequia, St. Lucia, and Martinique. **7-night S. Carib 2:** Round-trip from Barbados, Oct 2003–Apr 2004, visiting St. Lucia, Les Saintes, Antigua, St. Kitts, Dominica, and Martinique. **Non-Caribbean Itineraries:** Europe.
Star Clipper	**7-night S. Carib:** Round-trip from Sint Maarten, Nov 2003–Apr 2004, visiting St. Barts, Nevis, Guadeloupe, Dominica, Les Saintes, and Antigua. **7-night E. Carib:** Round-trip from Sint Maarten, Nov 2003–Apr 2004, visiting Virgin Gorda, Norman Island, Sopers Hole, and Jost Van Dyke (BVIs); Anguilla; St. Kitts; and St. Barts. **Non-Caribbean Itineraries:** Europe.

purpose, and *Royal Clipper* has a retractable marina at its stern for easy access to the water. Because there are few passengers on board and everything is so laid back, no sign-up sheets are needed for these activities; guests merely hang out by the gangway or on the beach until it's their turn.

Ships tend to depart from their ports early so that they can be under full sail during sunset. Trust us on this one: Position yourself at the ship's rail or dawdle over a drink at the deck bar to watch the sun melt into the horizon behind the silhouetted ships' masts and ropes. It's something you won't forget.

CHILDREN'S PROGRAM

An experience aboard a sailing ship can be a wonderfully educational and adventurous experience, especially for self-reliant children at least 10 years old. That said, this is not generally a line for young kids (though the line has no age restrictions), with no supervised activities and no babysitting unless a well-intentioned crewmember agrees to volunteer his or her off-duty hours. The exception is during holiday seasons such as Christmas, when families are accommodated and some children's activities are organized by the watersports staff.

ENTERTAINMENT

Some sort of featured entertainment takes place each night after dinner by the Tropical Bar, which is the main hub of activity on both ships. There's a **crew talent show** one night that's always a big hit with passengers; other nights may offer a trivia contest, dance games, or a performance by **local entertainers** (such as a steel-drum band) who come on board for the evening. A keyboard player is on hand to sing pop songs before and after dinner, but the twangy renditions of tunes such as "Chattanooga Choo Choo" and "Day-O" don't really fit in with the ships' otherwise rustic ambience. Most nights, disco music is put on the sound system and a section of the deck serves as an impromptu dance floor, with the action usually quieting down by about 1am.

A couple of movies are shown each day on cabin TVs if you feel like vegging, and one night they may show a film about clipper ships out on deck. Besides that, it's just you, the sea, and the conversation of your fellow passengers.

SERVICE

Service is congenial, low-key, unpretentious, cheerful, and reasonably attentive. During busy times, expect efficient but sometimes distracted service in the dining rooms, and during your time on deck, realize that you'll have to fetch your own bar drinks and whatever else you may need. *Royal Clipper* has a second bar on the top deck adjacent to the pools, but even on *Star Clipper,* you're never more than a 30-second walk from a cool drink.

The crew is international, hailing from Poland, Switzerland, Russia, Germany, Romania, Indonesia, the Philippines, and elsewhere, and their presence creates a wonderful international flavor on board. Crewmembers are friendly and usually good-natured about passengers who want to help with the sails, tie knots, and keep the deck shipshape. Because English is not the mother language of some crewmembers, though, certain details may get lost in the translation.

Officers, the cruise director, and the watersports team may dine with passengers during the week, and if you'd like to have dinner with the captain, just go up to the bridge one day and ask; he may oblige you (it depends on the captain). Unlike other small-ships lines such as ACCL, Clipper, and Windjammer, Star Clippers has a nurse aboard all sailings. **Laundry service** is available on both ships; *Royal Clipper* also offers **dry cleaning.**

Royal Clipper

Royal Clipper *(photo: Star Cruises)*

The Verdict

This stunning, fully rigged, five-masted, square-sail clipper is a sight to behold, and the interior amenities, from marble bathrooms to an Edwardian-style three-level dining room, are the company's most plush.

Specifications

Size (in tons)	5,000	Officers	International
Number of Cabins	114	Crew	105 (Internat'l)
Number of Outside Cabins	108	Passenger/Crew Ratio	2.2 to 1
Cabins with Verandas	14	Year Launched	2000
Number of Passengers	228	Last Major Refurbishment	N/A

Frommer's Ratings (Scale of 1–5)　　　　　★★★★

Cabin Comfort & Amenities	4	Dining Options	4.5
Ship Cleanliness & Maintenance	5	Gym & Spa Facilities	4
Public Comfort/Space	4	Children's Facilities	N/A
Decor	3	Enjoyment Factor	5

Clipper's biggest and poshest ship to date—and at 439 feet in length, one of the largest sailing ships ever built—the 5,000-ton, 228-passenger *Royal Clipper* boasts more luxurious amenities than the line's older ships, including marble bathrooms, roomier cabins, a small gym and spa, and three pools. In fact, the ship even gives the somewhat tired-looking 14- to 18-year-old Windstar ships a run for their money in the amenities department, while still offering a more rustic ambience. With five masts flying 42 sails that together stretch to 56,000 square feet, *Royal Clipper* is powerful too, able to achieve 20 knots under sail power only, and 14 knots under engine power. (Still, as on *Star Clipper,* the sails are more for show, and typically the engines are also in use 60%–80% of the time, especially at night.) Engines or not, for true sailors and wannabes, the web of ropes and cables stretched between *Royal Clipper's* sails, masts, and deck—along with the winches, *Titanic*-style ventilators, brass bells, wooden barrels, and chunky anchor chains cluttering the deck—are constant and beautiful reminders that you're on a real ship. So are the creaking, rolling, and pitching. (Though that can sometimes get a little too much: In mid-Feb 2000, the ship spent a week in dry dock while 150 tons of ballast were removed to ease its rolling tendency.)

The bottom line: This ship is a big winner for those who like the good life, but in a gloriously different way than any mainstream megaship could ever offer.

Cabins & Rates

Cabins	Per Diems from	Sq. Ft.	Fridge	Hair Dryer	Sitting Area	TV
Inside	$196	113	no	yes	no	yes
Outside	$228	148	no	yes	no	yes
Suite	$470	255–320	yes	yes	no	yes

CABINS   The ship's 114 cabins are gorgeous and roomy, done up in a nautical motif with navy-blue and gold fabrics and dark wood paneling. All but six are outsides with portholes and measure some 20 to 30 feet larger than cabins aboard *Star Clipper;* they're equivalent in size to the standard cabins on many Royal Caribbean and Norwegian Cruise Line ships, though they're about 40 square feet smaller than Windstar cabins. (On the other hand, they're about 50 sq. ft. larger than the typical cabins on Windjammer's ships.) Bathrooms are marble in all but the six inside cabins, and all have brass and chrome fittings and plenty of elbow room, as well as brass lighting fixtures, a vanity/desk, hair dryer, safes, telephones, and TVs. One problem: There are no full-length closets in the cabins—but then again, who's bringing an evening gown?

Some 22 cabins on the Main and Clipper decks have a pull-down third berth, but unfortunately it's only about 2 feet above the beds, so even when folded up, it juts out enough so that you can't sit up in bed without bumping your head.

Six tight 113-square-foot inside cabins on the Clipper Deck (category 6) and four outside cabins in the narrow forward section of the bow on the Commodore Deck (category 5) tend to be the best cabin bargains, if you're looking to save a buck. (See chapter 2, "Booking Your Cruise & Getting the Best Price," for more information about cabin categories.)

The 14 Deluxe Suites located forward on the Main Deck are exquisite, with private balconies, sitting areas, minibars, and whirlpool tubs. The Main Deck also has two Owner's Suites measuring 320 square feet; they're connectable, so you could conceivably book them together to create a 640-square-foot suite. Each boasts a pair of double beds, a sitting area, a minibar, and—count 'em—*two* marble bathrooms. Neither suite has a balcony. Suite guests get 24-hour butler service.

There are no connecting cabins, nor any wheelchair-accessible cabins.

PUBLIC AREAS   *Royal Clipper* is like no other small sailing ship we've ever set foot on, with a comfy, almost frilly interior that belies her shippy exterior, and a three-level atrium and elegant multilevel dining room that are more like what you'd find on a much larger ship. Like the cabins, the decor of the ship's main lounge, library, and corridors follows a strong nautical thread, with navy-blue and gold upholstery and carpeting complementing dark wood paneling.

The open-air Tropical Bar, with its long marble and wood bar, is the hub of evening entertainment and pre-dinner hors d'oeuvres and drinks, while the more elegant piano lounge just inside hosts the weekly captain's cocktail party. (As on *Star Clipper*, the ceiling of the piano bar is the glass bottom of the main swimming pool, so shave those legs, girls!) A clubby library is adjacent to the Tropical Bar aft on the Main Deck, and far forward on this deck is an observation lounge, where you'll find one computer with e-mail capability, but not Internet access. On a recent cruise, we didn't see one person set foot in this room.

On the lowest deck, under the waterline and adjacent to the gym, is a little lounge called Captain Nemos, where an underwater spotlight allows you to see fishy creatures swim past the portholes.

DINING OPTIONS   Compared to the dining room on *Star Clipper*, the one on *Royal Clipper* is much plusher in its deep-red velveteen upholstery and dark paneling, and is spread out over three levels. With its brilliant blue sea-scene murals, white moldings and fluted columns, frilly ironwork railings and staircase, and dark-red upholstery, it's vaguely reminiscent of a room on an early-20th-century ocean liner—and somewhat out of place on an otherwise rustic ship. The buffet table is in the center on the lowest level, with seating fanning out and up. Breakfast and lunch are buffet style and dinner is sit-down. You may notice that the low overhang from the staircase makes maneuvering around the buffet table in the dining room a bit tricky.

POOL, FITNESS & SPA FACILITIES   Considering her size, *Royal Clipper* offers amazing recreation facilities, with three pools, a gym, and a small spa. (By contrast, *Star Clipper* has two pools and no gym or spa.) The spa boils down to one massage room divided by only a curtain into two treatment areas. Leave your American inhibitions behind because not only do you get no modesty towel with these European-style rubs, but the room is so small that you can hear the muffled whispers and massage strokes of the other person on the other side of the curtain. Still, the treatments are expertly doled out at a reasonable $62 an hour.

The ship also has a retractable watersports marina at its stern for easy access to kayaking and sailing.

Star Clipper

The Verdict

With the sails and rigging of a classic clipper ship and the creature comforts of a modern mega, the 170-passenger *Star Clipper* offers a wonderfully rustic and cozy way to do the Caribbean.

Star Clipper (photo: Star Clippers)

Specifications

Size (in tons)	2,298	Officers	International
Number of Cabins	85	Crew	72 (Internat'l)
Number of Outside Cabins	79	Passenger/Crew Ratio	2.5 to 1
Cabins with Verandas	0	Year Launched	1992
Number of Passengers	170	Last Major Refurbishment	N/A

Frommer's Ratings (Scale of 1–5)   ⭐⭐⭐½

Cabin Comfort & Amenities	3	Dining Options	3.5
Ship Cleanliness & Maintenance	4	Gym & Spa Facilities	3
Public Comfort/Space	3	Children's Facilities	N/A
Decor	3	Enjoyment Factor	5

Life aboard *Star Clipper* means life on the teak deck—because the ship has few other hideaways, that's where most passengers spend their days. For that reason, these decks were planned with lots of passenger space; and although they're cluttered in places with the winches, ropes, and other equipment necessary to operate these working ships, there are lots of nooks where you can have some personal space: Even with a full load, the ship rarely feels too crowded, except at dinner. Much of the sail-trimming activity occurs amidships and near the bow, so if you're looking to avoid all bustle, take yourself off to the stern.

Cabins & Rates

Cabins	Per Diems from	Sq. Ft.	Fridge	Hair Dryer	Sitting Area	TV
Inside	$196	97	no	yes	no	no
Outside	$228	118–129	no	yes	no	yes

CABINS   Cabins are compact, but feel roomy for ships of this size and were designed with a pleasant nautical motif—blue fabrics and carpeting, portholes, brass-toned lighting fixtures, and a dark wood trim framing the off-white furniture and walls. The majority of cabins have portholes, two twin beds that can be converted into a double, a small desk/vanity with stool, and an upholstered seat fit into the corner. Storage space is more than adequate for a 7-night casual cruise in a warm climate, with both a slim floor-to-ceiling closet and a double-width closet of shelves; there's also storage space below the beds, desk, night-stand, and chair. Each cabin has a telephone, hair dryer, and safe, and all but the six smallest windowless inside cabins have a color television showing news and a selection of popular movies.

Standard bathrooms are very small but functional, with marble walls, a nice mirrored storage cabinet that actually stays closed, and a narrow shower divided from the rest of the bathroom by only a curtain; surprisingly, the rest of the bathroom stays dry when the shower's being used. The sink is fitted with water-saving (but annoying) push valves that release water only when they're pressed.

The eight Deluxe Cabins measure about 150 square feet, open right out onto the main deck, and have minibars and whirlpool bathtubs. Because of their location near the Tropical Bar, though, noise can be a problem, especially if there are late-night revelers at the bar. *Take note:* The ship's generator tends to drone on through the night; cabins near the stern on lower decks get the most of this noise, though it sometimes filters throughout the lowest deck. Note that four cabins shares walls with the dining room, and cabins 311 and 310 actually open right into the dining room itself (so be sure and be dressed before peeking out-side to see what's on the menu).

Note that the only difference between the cabins in categories 2 and 3 is a quieter location and a few square feet of space.

None of the units is a suite except for one carefully guarded (and oddly con-figured) Owner's Suite in the aft of the Clipper Deck that's available to the public only when it's not being set aside for special purposes. There are also no connecting cabins, and no cabins designed for wheelchair accessibility. Lacking an elevator, these ships are not recommended for passengers with mobility problems.

PUBLIC AREAS The handful of public rooms include the dining room; a comfy piano bar; the outside Tropical Bar (sheltered from the sun and rain by a canopy); and a cozy, paneled library with a decorative, nonfunctioning fireplace and a good stock of coffee-table books, tracts on naval history and naval architecture, a cross section of general titles, and a computer with e-mail access. Receiving messages is free, and debit cards for sending messages can be purchased from the purser.

The roomy yet cozy piano bar has comfy banquette seating and is a romantic place for a drink. That area and the outdoor Tropical Bar are the ship's hubs of activity.

Throughout, the interior decor is pleasant but unmemorable, mostly white with touches of brass and mahogany or teak trim—not as upscale-looking as *Royal Clipper* (or vessels operated by Windstar), but cozy, appealing, well designed, and shipshape.

DINING OPTIONS All meals are served in the single dining room, which has mahogany trim and a series of thin steel columns that pierce the center of many of the dining tables—mildly annoying, but necessary from an engineering standpoint. The booths along the sides, seating six, are awkward when couples who don't know each other are forever getting up and down to let their tablemates in and out. With tables only for six and eight, and no assigned seating, each evening you can dine with a different set of friends, or maybe make some new ones. The new *Royal Clipper*'s roomier dining-room layout avoids this problem.

POOL, FITNESS & SPA FACILITIES The ship's two small pools are meant more for dipping than swimming. Both have glass portholes, the one amidships peering from its depths into the piano bar. The pool near the stern tends to be more languid and is thus the favorite of sunbathers, whereas the one amidships is more active, with more noise and splashing and central to the action. At both, the ship's billowing and moving sails occasionally block the sun's rays, although this happens amidships much more frequently than it does at the stern.

While there's no gym of any sort, aerobics and stretch classes are frequently held on deck between the library and the Tropical Bar.

4 Windjammer Barefoot Cruises

1759 Bay Rd., Miami Beach, FL 33139 (P.O. Box 190-120, Miami Beach, FL 33119). © **800/327-2601** or 305/672-6453. Fax 305/674-1219. www.windjammer.com.

THE LINE IN A NUTSHELL Ultracasual and delightfully carefree, this eclectic fleet of cozy, rebuilt sailing ships (powered by both sails and engines) lures passengers into a fantasy world of pirates-and-rum-punch adventure.

THE EXPERIENCE When you see that the captain is wearing shorts and shades and is barefoot like the rest of the laid-back crew, you'll realize Windjammer's vessels aren't your typical cruise ships. Their yards of sails, pointy bowsprits, chunky portholes, and generous use of wood create a swashbuckling, storybook look; and while passengers don't have to fish for dinner or swab the decks, they are invited to help haul the sails, take a turn at the wheel, sleep out on deck whenever they please, and (with the captain's permission) crawl into the bow net. With few rules and lots of freedom, this is the closest thing you'll get to a real old-fashioned Caribbean adventure, visiting off-the-beaten-track Caribbean ports of call. The ships are ultra-informal, and hokey yet endearing rituals make the trip feel like summer camp for adults. Add in the line's tremendous number of repeat passengers (and a few of its signature rum swizzle drinks) and you have an experience that's ultra-casual, ultra-fun, and downright chummy.

Pros

- **Informal and carefree:** You can wear shorts and T-shirts (and go barefoot) all day—even to dinner and to the bar.
- **Friendly and down-to-earth:** Crew and passengers mix and mingle, and in no time the ships feel like one big happy family at sea.
- **Adventurous:** With the sails flapping and wooden decks surrounding you, it's no great leap of faith to feel like a pirate on the bounding main.
- **Cheap:** Windjammer's rates are lower than those of Star Clippers and significantly lower than those of Windstar Cruises, and bar drinks are a steal.

Cons

- **Tiny cabins:** No polite way to say it: Cabins are cramped.
- **Mal de mer:** If you're prone to seasickness, these ships may set you off and running; luckily, most of each day is spent in port.
- **Loose port schedule:** Sailings usually follow the routes described in the brochures, but one destination may be substituted for another if a particularly adverse wind is blowing, or if there's a storm.

Compared with the other soft-adventure lines, here's how Windjammer rates:

	Poor	Fair	Good	Excellent	Outstanding
Enjoyment Factor				✓	
Dining			✓		
Activities			✓		
Children's Program			✓*		
Entertainment			✓		
Service			✓		
Worth the Money					✓

* *Children's program is available on* Legacy *and* Polynesia *only.*

WINDJAMMER: LETTING IT ALL HANG OUT

When British poet Thomas Beddos wrote, "The anchor heaves, the ship runs free, the sails swell full, to sea, to sea," he might as well have been describing the Windjammer operation. There's no pretense here: On these authentic vessels, which have withstood the test of time and tide, you can taste the salt air as it blows among the riggings and feel the sails stretch to the wind, propelling you toward adventure.

With five sailing ships and one diesel-driven, passenger-carrying supply vessel, Windjammer has the largest fleet of its kind at sea today (the runner-up is reportedly the Norwegian government). In this age of homogenous, cookie-cutter megaships that barrel their way through the Caribbean headed to crowded ports, the line's tiny, eclectic, and appealingly imperfect vessels are a breath of fresh, rustic air. From an inspired if unintentional beginning, Windjammer has grown into one of the major lines for people who want a down-to-earth cruise alternative.

The famous and now semiretired **Captain Mike Burke**—Cap'n Mike, as he's been known for the past half century—founded the company in 1947 with one ship, and for years ran down-and-dirty party cruises popular with singles, purchasing sailing ships rich in history but otherwise destined for the scrap yard and transforming them into one-of-a-kind cruise vessels.

Legend has it that Burke, released from navy submarine duty in 1947, headed for Miami with $600 in back pay, intending to paint the town red. He succeeded. The next morning, he awoke with a blinding headache and no money, on the deck of a 19-foot sloop moored somewhere in the Bahamas. Mike Burke had apparently bought himself a boat. Using a mostly empty bottle of Scotch, he christened the boat *Hangover,* and the rest is history. He lived aboard to save money, and then started ferrying friends out for weekends of sailing and fishing. Demand escalated, and Burke quit his full-time job to become a one-man cruise line. Some people collect antique cars; Mike Burke collects tall ships.

Burke worked on a principle that anyone who's ever bought an old house will understand: Buy them cheap and decrepit, fix 'em up, and then stand back and admire your handiwork. His six children (including company president Susan) have assisted him in his ventures, renovating the vessels at the line's old shipyard near Miami and at a new yard in Trinidad. Burke says that the saddest thing he's ever seen is a tall ship permanently tethered to a pier, serving as a museum.

Are these cruises fun? No cruise can be all bad when it includes complimentary Bloody Marys in the morning, rum swizzles at sunset, and wine (albeit really cheap wine) with dinner. The bar operates on a doubloon system—a kind of debit card for drinks—and beverages are cheap, cheap, cheap.

Swimming pools? There's no need, because the crystal-clear Caribbean is the swimming hole. Shuffleboard? Are you kidding? That's for those other cruise ships. Work the sails? Steering the wheel? Well, no. The crew handles that, although passengers are sometimes invited to lend a hand. This is a barefoot adventure, not a Shanghai special: Your duty is to sit back and live it up, not winch up a topsail whenever the captain barks an order.

This is a T-shirt-and-shorts adventure that's ultra-laid-back: There are no keys for the cabins, rum punch is served in paper cups, daily announcements are written in magic marker on a bulletin board, chances are the purser doubles as the nurse and gift-shop manager, and itineraries are only partially finalized before a ship's departure and may vary based on wind and tides. Vessels tend to sail during the late afternoon or night, arriving each morning in port to allow passengers to enjoy the local terrain and diversions. Favored waters include the Grenadines and the Virgin Islands—mini-archipelagos that offer some of the most challenging and beautiful sailing in the hemisphere—as well as esoteric landfalls such as cone-shaped Saba, historic Statia, or mysterious Carriacou, sites almost never visited by larger ships.

Just as aboard Star Clippers and Windstar, Windjammer's ships use their engines as much or more than their sails, since it's just not practical to rely on the wind if you hope to maintain any kind of schedule. You can still take joy in the sheer beauty of the sails, though, and get a thrill when they do catch the wind, stretching taut from the masts. If at all possible, the captain will navigate under sail alone for at least a short while, but, in general, you'll always hear a certain amount of engine noise. If you're hoping for the silence of true sailing, you may be disappointed.

Windjammer still remains, for the most part, a let-your-hair-down, party-on scene and a great way to see some of the Caribbean's more offbeat islands; but since Mike Burke's children have taken over control of the company, they've made an effort to offer a more wholesome, mainstream experience—it's just not the same wild-and-crazy Windjammer that used to advertise in *Hustler* and promised its passengers they'd get a "bang" out of their vacation. A few years back, the company added an activities mate (aka cruise director) to organize more activities for passengers, and food quality has improved as well. The line also began offering a kids' program on *Legacy* and *Polynesia* during the summer months for ages 6 to 12, when you'll see up to 40 kids on a sailing. This on ships that only carry about 120 passengers total—ouch! Other innovations to keep things fresh include new theme cruises and new itineraries, including a Bahamas itinerary on *Legacy* out of Miami, the first time the line has sailed out of Florida since the 1970s. A few behavioral restrictions have been imposed, too. For instance, you can't climb the masts anymore—the line dislikes being sued by passengers who've had one too many rum swizzles and fallen off—but you're still welcome to have that one rum swizzle too many. Just be sure to keep your feet on deck while you're doing it—or, if you're adventurous and if your captain allows it, sit out in the bow rigging, as a bunch of us did one memorable night a few years back, after much, much champagne.

So has Windjammer gone soft? No more so than the rest of us. As one long-time captain told us, the line has just had to change its approach to keep up with what people want. After all, it's not the '70s anymore. This principle applies to the ships as well. *Legacy,* introduced in 1997, was the first "modern" Windjammer, somewhat larger and less woody than the rest, and probably the shape of things to come as the line's older ships are slowly retired—as *Flying Cloud* was in late 2002. Despite any changes, though, the rum still flows freely and the wind still blows through the rigging, and what more could a wannabe pirate really want? Yo-ho-ho, y'all.

PASSENGER PROFILE

Can we say nutty, quirky, nonconformist? That's why Windjammer is so appealing: It's different—a rare concept in today's mostly homogenous megaship cruise world. Unlike some "all things to all people" lines, Windjammer is for a particular kind of informal, fun-loving, down-to-earth passenger, and though some compare the experience to a continuous frat party, we wouldn't go that far. In fact, the passenger and age mix gives lie to that description. From honeymooning couples in their 20s to grandparents in their 70s, the line attracts a

Randy Singles at Sea: Jammers' Singles Cruises

Windjammer is not what you'd call a strait-laced cruise line during normal sailings, so it really means something that when the ships offer theme cruises, the level of permissive wackiness actually goes up. Writer Jonathan Siskin sent us the following three messages from various cyber cafes in the Caribbean, while in port during one of *Polynesia*'s 5-night Caribbean singles cruises. While he's had some pretty interesting assignments in his day, he said his singles cruise on the *Poly* was the most bizarre by far. It's a tough job, but someone's got to do it . . .

10/9/2000

Hello Heidi and Matt: Last evening as I boarded the ship I was greeted by this message on the bulletin board: "Welcome on board. Now it's time to relax, kick off your smelly shoes and grab a rum swizzle." For our first singles icebreaker game, each male and female was asked to pick a word out of a hat (there were two hats, one for males and the other for females). While I have played some wacky games in my life, this was my first X-rated word game. I eagerly unfolded my piece of paper to reveal the word "blow." It didn't take long to locate my match, a comely flight attendant with American Airlines in possession of the word "job." Free drinks for all matches! Whoopee! Others had words like rock, multiple, and monkey. You figure it out. Tonight's instructions are: "Wear your pajamas (or whatever else you wear to sleep in) to dinner—no birthday suits allowed!" Don't you wish you were on board? Bye for now. —JS

10/11/2000

Heidi and Matt: As to your question, yes my "blow" partner was very cute, but unfortunately every guy on the ship is chasing after her. I call her Wild Wendy. More fun and games last night before dinner. First there were crab races followed by a dirty joke recital and then a very

broad range of adventurers who like to have fun and don't want anything resembling a highly regimented vacation. Passengers are pretty evenly divided between men and women, and 15% to 20% overall are single. Due to her long itineraries and less romantic appearance, passengers aboard the *Amazing Grace* commissary ship tend to be older than those aboard the sailing ships, mostly 60-plus.

Many passengers love the Windjammer experience so much that they return again and again. The record is still held by the late "Pappy" Gomez of Cleveland, Ohio, who sailed with Windjammer more than 160 times, but many, many others have sailed with the line 30 to 50 times. The line's supply officer told us he never steps aboard one of the ships without seeing passengers he's sailed with before. There's even a reunion of sorts called the **Jammer Fest** that has Windjammer die-hards flocking to Miami for a weekend blitz: The party is on Windjammer; passengers pick up their hotel and airfare. Shows you just how far a Windjammer fan will go to keep the party alive.

Young children should probably not go (in fact, the line doesn't accept passengers under 6), nor should anyone prone to seasickness (there's quite a bit of bizarre "erotic tarts eating" contest called Queen of Tarts. Competing couples had to devour tarts strategically placed on the various (clothed) body parts of their partner. Talk about indigestion. The night culminated with a wild masquerade party built around the letter "p" as passengers were instructed to dress up as either pimps, prostitutes, pirates, or priests. More later! —JS

10/14/2000

Well, it's all over and here I am about to head for the airport. So what's the "score," you're wondering? Well, most singles (including yours truly) remained unattached for the duration of the cruise and had to be content musing over what might have been. I learned that many passengers were on their second and in some cases third or fourth singles cruise, and they still had not made a love connection, yet gave every indication they enjoyed the experience and would be back again for another try. But, hey, can you just send me on a regular cruise next time? You know, old married people, lap blankets, midmorning bullion, bingo. I'm exhausted. Ciao for now. —JS

Note: Windjammer does its best to make sure there are equal numbers of guys and gals on each singles cruise, so everybody gets a fair shot. After that, it's up to you. Besides singles cruises, Windjammer also schedules gay-only theme cruises, culinary cruises, painting and photography cruises, murder mystery cruises, spa/yoga cruises, golf cruises, cruises themed around island rum and beer, bird-watching and botanical cruises, and jazz cruises visiting the St. Lucia Jazz Festival and the Dominican World Creole Festival. Chartered cruises on Windjammer's ships include occasional nudist cruises, swingers' cruises, Jimmy Buffett–themed parrothead cruises, and (yawn) corporate charters.

that the 1st days out) or anyone wanting to be pampered (there's none of that during any day out). These ships are not for people with disabilities, either.

DINING

When it comes to dining, "slide over and pass me the breadbasket" about sums it up. Family-style and informal, there's nothing gourmet about the food, which ranges from mediocre to quite tasty. All breads and pastries are homemade, and at dinner, after soup and salad are served, passengers can choose from two main entrees, such as curried shrimp and roast pork with garlic sauce. Don't be surprised if the waiters ask for a show of hands to see who wants what. Unlimited carafes of cheap red and white wine are complimentary. Tasty **breakfasts** include all the usual, plus items such as eggs Benedict, and **lunches** include items such as lobster pizza and apple salad. Both of these meals are served buffet style. At certain islands, the crew lugs ashore a picnic lunch for an **afternoon beach party,** and each sailing usually includes an **on-deck barbecue** one evening. There are two open seatings for **dinner,** marked by the clang of a loud barnyard-style bell, usually around 6:30 and 8pm.

Many dishes overall are rooted in Caribbean tradition. The chef will accommodate **special diets,** including vegetarian and low-salt. And don't be shy if it's your birthday: The chef will make you a free cake and serve it at dinner.

ACTIVITIES

Windjammer deliberately de-emphasizes the activities that dominate life aboard larger vessels, although it may occasionally host an on-deck crab race, knot-tying demonstration, or talk on astronomy or some aspect of sailing. Otherwise, your entertainment is up to you. If the weather's fine and you want to help trim the sails, you may be allowed to lend a hand.

Just about every day is spent in port somewhere. Generally at least once per cruise, on one of the ships' **beach visits**—to Jost Van Dyke, perhaps—the activities mate organizes a hike around the island or **team games** reminiscent of mid-1960s cocktail-party movies (think Cary Grant and Audrey Hepburn in the nightclub scene in *Charade*). It's the usual embarrassing stuff: Passengers twirl hula-hoops while dressed in snorkel gear; pass cucumbers to each other, clasping them only with their thighs; or flop onto slippery foam mats and try to swim to and around a landmark. Silliness, in other words—but it does make for instant camaraderie. After all, after someone's seen you act this dumb, they've seen it all. In other ports, there may also be organized hikes.

Snorkeling gear (mask, fins, snorkel, and carrying bag) rents for $25 per week, and one-tank **scuba dives** cost around $50 at the ports of call. (Novice divers pay $85 for a "resort course.") All scuba expeditions are conducted by outside agencies, not by Windjammer, and passengers are required to sign a liability release before participating.

CHILDREN'S PROGRAM

No children under 6 are allowed aboard any ship in the Windjammer fleet, and we wouldn't recommend these ships for kids much younger than 10. Aboard most of the ships, teenagers divert themselves the same way adults do, with conversation, shore excursions, reading, and watching the wide blue sea. Otherwise, few concessions are made for their amusement. Babysitting is not available.

The Stowaway Gimmick, Some Deals & Some Charges

Stowaways: Rather than fork over a bundle for a hotel the night before your cruise, you can stay aboard your docked ship for a relatively modest $55 per person, double occupancy. That's fine, and a good deal, but it's actually a gimmick: The cruises are 5 nights long, and most passengers opt for the sixth night as a stowaway, so what it comes down to is Windjammer getting dozens of people to pay extra for a night that other cruise lines just bundle into their cruise prices.

Past Passengers Club: A $25 membership fee entitles clients to the Windjammer newsletter, $25 discounts when you book two cruises back-to-back, and notice of other discounts and special sailings.

Children's rates: Children 6 to 12 sharing a cabin with two adults pay 50% of the adult fare. In June, July, and August on *Legacy* and *Polynesia*, children 6 to 12 are free and teens pay 50% of the adult fare.

Port charges: Five-night cruises generally run $65 per person. Port charges for 13-day outings cost $150 per person.

This situation is markedly different aboard *Legacy* and *Polynesia,* which have a **"Junior Jammers" kids program,** and now draw as many as 40 kids a cruise in the summer—a full third of the passenger total, so pretty much guaranteed to cramp an old salt's party. Here, younger children are divided into roughly compatible age brackets and kept involved for 12 hours a day with a roster of summer-camp-style activities, while activities for teens focus on sailing, navigating, and kayaking. There are also introductory scuba classes for 8- to 10-year-olds and 11- to 16-year-olds.

Unlike most megaship lines, which require passengers to be at least 21 years old unless accompanied by parents, Windjammer's minimum unaccompanied age is 17. The spring-break crowd loves these ships.

ENTERTAINMENT

Part entertainment, part education, the **Captain's Story Time** held each morning out on deck is the first event of the average day on a Windjammer ship. It's a short talk that's 20% ship business; 40% information about the day's port call, activities, or sailing route; and 40% pure humor (on one trip we took, a joke about a cat and a certain part of a woman's anatomy was par for the course). At these morning meetings, the captain will come out and shout "Good morning, everybody!" and the passengers—many of whom have taken these trips before and know the drill—bark back in chorus, "Good morning, Captain SIR!" The Windjammer crowd loves every minute of it. In fact, the line's accessible and down-to-earth captains are often a part of the entertainment themselves— passengers love them and are like groupies at a rock concert, whether fawning over quiet, charming, and Marlboro-Man-handsome Captain Matt, who is often at the helm of *Mandalay,* or chatting with the more fatherly Captain Casey, who, as a senior captain, rotates among all the ships of the fleet.

In general, social interaction is centered on the bars and top sun deck. There's typically a **passenger talent show** one night; a local pop band is brought on board for a few hours of dancing once or twice a week; and there's a weekly barbecue buffet dinner and **costume party**—a Windjammer tradition that has passengers decked out as cross-dressers, pirates, and other characters. Bring your own get-up or rummage through the pile of shabby costumes the crew hauls out before the party. Either way, it's a ball! Otherwise, there's almost no organized nightlife.

At about 5pm every day, gallons of complimentary rum swizzles are dispensed along with hors d'oeuvres that may include homemade plantain chips and salsa, spicy meatballs, chicken fingers, and cheese and crackers. Guests gather on deck, often still in their sarongs and shorts, mingling in the fresh sea air as island music plays in the background. On one of our trips, a woman sang a silly song she wrote about the cruise and the people she had met, as the line's supply officer accompanied her on his flute.

After dinner, head up to the on-deck bar (drinks are cheap: $2 for a Red Stripe or Heineken and $3.50 for the most expensive cocktail) or grab a chair or mat and hit the deck. Generally, the ships stay late in one or two ports so that passengers can head ashore to an island watering hole.

Windjammer Fleet Itineraries

Ship	Itineraries
Amazing Grace	**12-night E./S. Carib:** Flexible itinerary between Grand Bahama and Trinidad, year-round; may visit Antigua, Barbados, Bequia, Conception, Cooper Island, Dominica, Dominican Republic, Grand Turk, Great Inagua, Grenada, Guadeloupe, Les Saintes, Jost Van Dyke, Marie Galante, Martinique, Nevis, Norman Island, St. Barts, St. Kitts, St. Lucia, Sint Maarten, Tobago, Tortola, and Virgin Gorda. **Non-Caribbean Itineraries:** None.
Legacy	**5-night S. Carib:** Round-trip from Aruba, Oct–Nov 2003, visiting Bonaire, Curaçao, Klein Curaçao, and Morrocoy National Park. **5-night Virgin Islands:** Round-trip from St. Thomas, Dec 2003–May 2004, visiting Buck Island, Jost Van Dyke, Norman Island, St. John, Tortola, and Virgin Gorda. **7-night Panama/San Blas Islands:** Round-trip from Panama City, summer, visiting Playa Francis, Isla Grande, Isla Verde, Cayos Hollandes, Porvenir, and Portobello. **Non-Caribbean Itineraries:** None
Mandalay	**5-night E. Carib:** Between Grenada and St. Lucia, Sept–Nov 2003, visiting Carriacou, Union Island, Mayreau, Tobago Cays, Bequia, and St. Vincent. **12-night E. Carib:** Between Grenada and Antigua, Dec 2003–May 2004, visiting Bequia, Carriacou, Dominica, Les Saintes, Martinique, Mayreau, Nevis, St. Lucia, St. Vincent, and Tobago Cays. **5-night Panama:** Round-trip from Colon, probably June–Sept 2004, visiting Portobello, Playa Francis, Isla Grande, Isla Verde, Cayos Hollandes, and Porvenir. **Non-Caribbean Itineraries:** None.
Polynesia	**5-night E. Carib:** Round-trip from Sint Maarten, Dec 2003–May 2004, visiting Anguilla, Nevis, Saba, St. Barts, St. Kitts, Tintamarre, and St. Eustatius. **Non-Caribbean Itineraries:** None
Yankee Clipper	**5-night E. Carib:** Round-trip from Grenada, year-round, visiting Bequia, Carriacou, Mayreau, St. Vincent, Tobago Cays, and Union Island. **Non-Caribbean Itineraries:** None.

The fact is, nobody—not even Windjammer's staff—knows where the line's ships go, at least not far ahead of time. But really, it doesn't matter: The islands are always small and beautiful, and the ambience is always wacky. We were aboard for a week once and couldn't remember where we'd been when we got home. We still aren't sure, but we do know we had a great time. A company spokeswoman says this is fairly common.

SERVICE

Windjammer tends to attract a staff that shares founder Mike Burke's appreciation for the wide-open sea and barely concealed scorn for corporate agendas and workaday priorities. Many are from the same Caribbean islands the line's ships visit. Service is friendly and efficient but not doting, matter-of-fact and straightforward rather than obsequious. Unlike more upscale cruise lines, with Windjammer there's no master/servant relationship between passengers and staff—the crewmembers just happen to steer the ship or serve dinner or drinks, and will chat like regular folks when they're not. They're a good bunch.

Legacy

The Verdict

The brightest, newest, and most spacious of Windjammer's ships, *Legacy* is a real winner in our book, with comfortable cabins, good-size private bathrooms, a cheerful dining saloon with large round booths, and a sprawling expanse of outdoor deck space. Even when full, the ship doesn't feel crowded.

Legacy *(photo: Windjammer)*

Specifications

Size (in tons)	1,165	Officers	Am./Brit./Aust.
Number of Cabins	61	Crew	43 (Internat'l)
Number of Outside Cabins	61	Passenger/Crew Ratio	2.8 to 1
Cabins with Verandas	0	Year Launched	1959
Number of Passengers	122	Last Major Refurbishment	1998

Frommer's Ratings (Scale of 1–5)   ★★★½

Cabin Comfort & Amenities	2	Dining Options	3
Ship Cleanliness & Maintenance	4	Gym & Spa Facilities	N/A
Public Comfort/Space	4	Children's Facilities	N/A*
Decor	3	Enjoyment Factor	5

*Legacy *has a children's program but no dedicated facilities.*

Rebuilt and relaunched in 1997 as the line's largest and most modern ship, *Legacy* was originally built in 1959 as a motored research vessel for the French government, designed with a deep keel that gave her additional balance during North Atlantic and North Sea storms. At the time, she was one of several government-owned ships sending weather reports to a central agency in Paris, which used them to predict storm patterns on the French mainland. The advent of global satellites made the vessel obsolete, and she was bought in 1988 by Windjammer, which over the course of a decade poured over $10 million into a massive reconfiguration at the family-managed Windjammer shipyard in Trinidad. Four steel masts and 11 sails were added, plus accouterments the vessel needed for 7-day barefoot jaunts through the Caribbean. Although still tiny compared to a megaship, at 1,165 tons she's larger than any other vessel in the Windjammer fleet, and is the only one that offers some itineraries from the mainland USA.

Some hard-core Windjammer veterans consider *Legacy* a wimpy addition to the venerated rough-and-tumble fleet, feeling that it's just not a real yo-ho-ho pirate adventure without their cramped, bare-bones lifestyle. When the vessel was launched, stalwart Windjammer fans wondered whether her comfort level and (gasp!) children's program meant the old days were gone forever. It was like seeing a group of 30- or 40-somethings returning to their favorite college-era dive bar and finding it newly sheathed in wood paneling, with brass lamps in place of the neon lights and light jazz on the jukebox instead of "Born to Run."

Well, here's the scoop: Though she is indeed the most comfortable of the Windjammer lot, she still embraces that irreverent Windjammer spirit. It takes only a glance at the carved wooden figurehead on the ship's prow—an image of line founder Cap'n Mike Burke in a tropical-print shirt, beer in one hand and a ship's wheel in the other—to see that this is still very much a laid-back, partying vessel. She's just a cushier one.

Cabins & Rates

Cabins	Per Diems from	Sq. Ft.	Fridge	Hair Dryer	Sitting Area	TV
Outside	$183	85	no	no	no	no
Suite	$241	160	no	no	yes	yes

CABINS Cabins aboard *Legacy* are a little larger and more comfortable than those aboard the line's older ships, but if you're used to sailing aboard typical large cruise ships, they'll probably seem cramped. Berths are either doubles or bunk beds, and if you're in the upper portion of the latter, watch your head: More than one passenger has woken up and knocked himself silly on the metal porthole cover, which projects from the wall when open. You'd do well to sleep with your feet toward it.

Suites—both the Admiral Suites and Burke's Berth, which is the best in the house—offer windows instead of portholes, plus space for a third occupant. There are a handful of single cabins, plus triple- and quad-berth options in the Commodore-class cabins, though this affords a minimum of personal space. Burke's Berth is the only cabin aboard that has an entertainment center, a bar, and a vanity.

Storage in all cabins is perfectly adequate for this type of T-shirt-and-shorts cruise, with each containing a small closet/drawer unit and having additional space under the bed. Bathrooms offer enough maneuvering space, but it's a crapshoot on the small, curtained showers—some have a raised lip that contains the runoff and some don't, making for a perpetually wet bathroom floor. Lip or no, small and spartan or not (compared to those offered on larger and glitzier ships), these facilities are still far better than the head-style facilities aboard the other Windjammer sailing ships.

There are no connecting cabins, and as with all the Windjammer ships, *Legacy* has no wheelchair-accessible cabins, and is not a good option for people with disabilities.

PUBLIC AREAS The top deck, with a large canopied area at its center, is the social focus of the cruise, the space where the rum swizzles are dispensed at sunset, where visiting bands perform at night, and where the captain conducts his daily morning "Story Time" session. The ship's bar is also located on this deck, as is the requisite barrel of rum—a real barrel, from which the bartender siphons off what he needs every day.

The Poop Deck offers the best sunbathing space, although shade from the raised sails could force you to move often. Passengers lounge on patio-style white plastic recliners or on the blue cushions strewn about, which many passengers also use to sleep out on deck under the stars, something the line fully encourages.

Navigation of the ship is often from a ship's wheel mounted out in open air near the bow. When seas are calm and sailing is easy, the crew offers passengers a chance to steer. Unlike the practice on most larger cruise ships, *Legacy's* bow is generally open to passengers, allowing you (if the captain approves) to do your Leonardo DiCaprio "King of the World" bit, or, even better, to climb out on the netting that projects to the tip of the bowsprit and lounge there while the blue Caribbean Sea splashes and sprays below you. Don't miss this opportunity if it's offered—trust us.

The only other interior public room is a small and not terribly appealing lounge that offers a TV/video arrangement and a smattering of books and board games. In an entire week aboard, the only person we saw using this room was a 10-year-old boy watching movies. Everyone else was outside, playing.

DINING OPTIONS   All meals are served in the comfortable aft dining room, fitted with large circular tables (a bummer if you're stuck in the middle, three or four people from freedom) and decorated with faux tropical plants. Evening hors d'oeuvres are served out on deck.

POOL, FITNESS & SPA FACILITIES   As aboard the rest of the line's ships, there are none. No pool, spa, no gym, no jogging track. Aboard ship, the most exercise you're likely to get is if you volunteer to help hoist the sails. In port, however, you'll have such options as snorkeling, scuba diving, sea kayaking (the ship carries its own kayaks aboard), and hiking to help you work off dessert.

Amazing Grace

The Verdict

If you're looking for a slow, easy, and cheap tour of the Caribbean and like the novelty of being on a supply ship as it does its rounds, a trip on this semi-charming tub is bound to create lasting memories.

Amazing Grace *(photo: Windjammer)*

Specifications

Size (in tons)	1,525	Officers	British/American
Number of Cabins	46	Crew	40 (Internat'l)
Number of Outside Cabins	46	Passenger/Crew Ratio	2.4 to 1
Cabins with Verandas	0	Year Launched	1955
Number of Passengers	92	Last Major Refurbishment	1995

Frommer's Ratings (Scale of 1–5)   ★★½

Cabin Comfort & Amenities	2	Dining Options	2.5
Ship Cleanliness & Maintenance	2.5	Gym & Spa Facilities	N/A
Public Comfort/Space	3	Children's Facilities	N/A
Decor	3	Enjoyment Factor	3

Amazing Grace, the only engine-only Windjammer vessel, is the closest thing to a banana boat in the cruise industry, moving doggedly and regularly through most of the Caribbean, meeting up with the line's sailing ships in various ports to drop off provisions.

Built as the *Pharos* in Dundee, Scotland, in 1955, the *Grace* mostly carried supplies to isolated lighthouses and North Sea oil rigs, but once or twice it was pressed into service as a weekend cruiser for the queen of England. The vessel was acquired by Windjammer in 1988 and still retains some vestiges of her British past despite many modernizations. If you come aboard expecting to be treated like royalty, however, you'll be sorely disappointed. This is not a fancy vessel, and the lack of organized activities on her long 13-night trips forces you to create your own mischief. Because of her large hold and deep draft, she's the most stable vessel in the fleet.

Guests are noticeably more sedentary, definitely older, and less party-oriented than those aboard the line's more raffish sail-powered vessels. Most tend to turn in by 10pm. As one bartender on the ship told us a while back, "If we have a young person aboard, they probably made a mistake."

Cabins & Rates

Cabins	Per Diems from	Sq. Ft.	Fridge	Hair Dryer	Sitting Area	TV
Outside	$107	45	yes	no	yes	no
Suite	$221	375	yes	no	yes	yes

CABINS   Cabins are utterly without frills and very small, but they're still a tad roomier than others in Windjammer's fleet. About half contain the varnished paneling from the ship's original construction; the others are more modern, with almost no nostalgic value. Although there's a sink in each cabin, some do not contain toilets and showers, requiring you to use the shared facilities. Don't reject these bathroomless cabins out of hand, though, since they're also the ones with the original varnished paneling. Non-honeymooners often rent the Honeymoon Suite near the stern because of its slightly larger size. There's also the funky, wood-paneled Burke's Berth, *Grace's* version of a Penthouse Suite. Its two rooms feel a lot like a rustic hunting lodge (minus the taxidermy), with neat features like a marble-and-teak bathroom with a sunken tub, skylights above the double bed, entertainment center, big aquarium that's normally filled with tropical fish, and even a private porch area at the stern.

There are no connecting cabins and no wheelchair-accessible cabins.

PUBLIC AREAS   You can have a lot of fun aboard this ship, although there's no avoiding the fact that it is indeed a glorified freighter. A bar/lounge faces forward across the bow, another sits in open air on the stern, and there's a TV room for between drinks. Some of the greatest authenticity preserved from the ship's early days is a piano room and a smoking room/library, which sports etched-glass doors and mahogany walls. Because large sections of this vessel (the storage areas) are off-limits to passengers, many people tend to gravitate to the deck areas (including the lovely Promenade Deck) for reading, napping, or whatever.

DINING OPTIONS   The ship's single dining room has booth-type tables that seat up to eight passengers.

POOL, FITNESS & SPA FACILITIES   There's no swimming pool, gym, or fitness facility. Instead, you'll get your exercise during snorkeling and scuba sessions at the ports of call.

Mandalay • Yankee Clipper • Polynesia

The Verdict

Bound by wood and sails, these odd-ball little ships have led fascinating and long lives, and today promise adventure, good times, and offbeat ports for a bargain price.

Yankee Clipper *(photo: Windjammer)*

Specifications

Size (in tons)		Polynesia	112
Mandalay	420	Officers	Brit./Am./Aust.
Yankee Clipper	327	Crew	International
Polynesia	430	Mandalay	28
Number of Cabins		Yankee Clipper	29
Mandalay	36	Polynesia	45
Yankee Clipper	32	Passenger/Crew Ratio	2.2–2.8 to 1
Polynesia	50	Year Launched	
Number of Outside Cabins		Mandalay	1923
Mandalay	36	Yankee Clipper	1927
Yankee Clipper	32	Polynesia	1938
Polynesia	10	Last Major Refurbishment	
Cabins with Verandas	0	Mandalay	1982
Number of Passengers		Yankee Clipper	1984
Mandalay	72	Polynesia	2002
Yankee Clipper	64		

Frommer's Ratings (Scale of 1–5)   ✹✹✹

Cabin Comfort & Amenities	2	Dining Options	3
Ship Cleanliness & Maintenance	3	Gym & Spa Facilities	N/A
Public Comfort/Space	3	Children's Facilities	N/A*
Decor	3	Enjoyment Factor	5

*Polynesia *has a children's program but no dedicated facilities.*

Despite different origins and subtle differences in the way they react to the wind and weather, all of these sailing ships share many traits, so we've opted to cluster them into one all-encompassing review. All are roughly equivalent in amenities, activities, and onboard atmosphere; and because each has been extensively refurbished, they have more or less equivalent interior decors. As for their capabilities as sailing ships, Captain Stuart Larcombe, who has served aboard them all, told us that the award goes to *Mandalay* (now that *Flying Cloud,* once a spy ship for the Allied navy in World War II, has been retired). For adventure and interesting ports of call, though, they're all absolutely top-notch, and we advise selecting your ship based on itinerary rather than the ships' minor physical differences.

What make the ships most unique are their histories. *Mandalay* was once the *Hussar IV,* the fourth in a line of same-name yachts built for financier E. F. Hutton, and was, by some accounts, the most sumptuous private yacht in the world. Later, she was commissioned as a research vessel by Columbia University, which sailed her for 1.25 million miles trying to develop theories about continental drift, which have since been proven correct. It's estimated that by the early 1980s, half the knowledge of the world's ocean floor was gathered by instruments aboard this ship.

Yankee Clipper, once the only armor-plated sailing yacht in the world, was built in 1927 by German industrial and munitions giant Krupp-Werft. Allegedly, Hitler once stepped aboard to award the Iron Cross to one of his U-boat commanders. Seized by the United States as booty after World War II, the ship eventually became George Vanderbilt's private yacht and the fastest two-masted vessel sailing off the California coast, once managing 22 knots under full sail. Burke bought the ship just before it was due to be broken down for scrap, then gutted, redesigned, and rebuilt it, stripping off the armor in the process. Renovations in 1984 added a third mast, additional deck space, and cabin modifications. Although not as streamlined as she was originally, she's still a fast and very exciting ship.

Polynesia, built in Holland in 1938, was originally known as *Argus,* and served as a fishing schooner in the Portuguese Grand Banks fleet. Windjammer bought her in 1975, gave her a good scrubbing to wash out the fish smell, and performed a complete reconfiguration of the cabins and interior spaces, adding lots of varnished wood. Less stylish-looking than many of her thoroughbred siblings, she nonetheless remains one of Windjammer's most consistently popular ships, on the one hand due to her handful of annual singles cruises, on the other because she's one of only two Windjammer ships (along with *Legacy*) that offers a children's program.

Cabins & Rates

Cabins	Per Diems from	Sq. Ft.	Fridge	Hair Dryer	Sitting Area	TV
Inside	$150	40–70	no	no	no	no
Outside	$150	40–70	no	no	no	no
Suite	$217	95	some	no	yes	some

CABINS   There's no getting around it: Cabins are cramped, just as they would have been on a true 19th-century clipper ship. Few retain any glamorous vestiges of their original owners, and most are about as functional as they come, though wood paneling in *Mandalay* and *Yankee Clipper*'s cabins gives a pleasantly rustic feel. They're all adequate enough, however, and it's the adventurous thrill of sailing on one of these ships that you come for, not luxurious accommodations.

Each cabin has a minuscule bathroom with a shower, many of which function with a push-button—for every push you get about 10 seconds' worth of water—that you'll wind up keeping your finger on the whole time while trying to wash with one hand. On many vessels, hot water is available only during certain hours of the day, whenever the ships' galleys and laundries aren't using it. Be prepared for toilets that don't always function properly, and retain your sense of humor as they're repaired.

Storage space is limited, but this isn't a serious problem because few passengers bring much with them. Many cabins have upper and lower berths, some have lower-level twins, and a few have doubles (so much for romance). Standard cabins on *Mandalay* and *Polynesia* are insides; on *Yankee Clipper,* they're outsides with portholes. Deck and Captain's cabins on *Mandalay* are outsides with portholes; aft deck cabins share a bathroom but are kind of nifty because they have a skylight and a little balcony. They're good for families, couples sailing together, and people who are willing to balance lack of private bathroom against double beds and some extra amenities, such as a minibar. *Polynesia* offers three windowless cabins that sleep four people.

Some vessels have a limited number of suites with minibars that, although not spacious by the standards of larger ships, seem to be of generous proportions when contrasted with the standard cabins. *Polynesia's* recent refit included the creation of 10 windowed suites on Deck A (the highest cabin deck), with twin beds that can be converted to doubles; before her renovation, the ship had only 2 suites.

Connecting cabins are available on *Mandalay* only. There are no wheelchair-accessible cabins on any of these ships.

PUBLIC AREAS   What glamour may have been associated with these ships in the past is long gone, lost to the years or in the gutting and refitting they required before entering Windjammer service. There's still a lot of rosewood, mahogany, and other woods left; but today it mixes with more practical steel rather than gilt, and makes an appropriate backdrop for passengers so laid-back that few bother to ever change out of their bathing suits and T-shirts. The ships' teak decks are the most popular areas on these ships, and many passengers adopt some preferred corner as a place to hang out.

DINING OPTIONS   Dining rooms are cozy, and paneled to a greater or lesser extent in wood, though overall they've been designed for efficiency. All are air-conditioned except aboard *Mandalay,* whose dining room is open-air, kept cool by evening breezes. *Polynesia's* extensive recent refit redecorated her dining saloon and bar with an appropriately Polynesian look, incorporating bamboo and tiki masks.

POOL, FITNESS & SPA FACILITIES   These ships are too small to offer health clubs, saunas, or the fitness regimens so heavily promoted aboard larger ships, and none has a swimming pool. You'll get an adequate amount of exercise, however, during hikes, snorkeling, diving and swimming off the side of the ships, and scuba sessions conducted at the ports of call.

9

European Lines . . . Plus

Welcome to the melting pot chapter. The cruise lines here don't cater primarily to Americans, as do all the other lines in this book—in fact, Europeans make up the majority of passengers on these ships, with Yanks in the minority for a change. If you're looking for something a little different in your Caribbean cruise, these may be right up your alley, providing an opportunity to immerse yourself in one culture while visiting several others. Say goodbye to Budweiser and baseball caps and helllllloooooo to baguettes, pickled herring, and sandals with socks.

The vessels in this chapter are **midsize** (or small, in the case of the Sea Cloud ships), and are, thus, more intimate than the sprawling mainstream megaships. Otherwise, they offer a similar level of formality and a varied daily repertoire of activities and entertainment, from bridge tournaments to dancing lessons and song-and-dance revues—though sometimes you may not recognize a lot of the songs. Casinos on board tend to be a bit quieter than on the American ships.

English is the first language of all the ships in this chapter, and most European passengers speak some English as well, but **shipboard announcements** may be translated into in several languages (French, German, Spanish, Dutch, Swedish, Japanese, and so on), which means they can sometimes go on for a *looooong* time. It can be annoying, but at least the English version is always first. Imagine if you had to wait till the fifth version till you understood anything! Shore excursions usually have separate buses for each language.

In general, Europeans and South Americans tend to eat later and party further into the wee hours, so **dining hours** may be adjusted accordingly. European kids tend to be less segregated than Americans, following Mom and Dad into the casino, the disco, or even the steam room rather than herding into a children's center. While a lot of smokers will usually be on board, lounges and dining rooms do offer **separate smoking sections.** Expect much of the entertainment to be less verbal and more physical (magicians, acrobats, puppeteers, singers, and dancers rather than, say, comedians) so that speakers of many languages can appreciate it.

DRESS CODES As on the mainstream American lines, weeklong cruises on these ships generally feature 2 formal nights, but you won't find too many passengers in tuxedos or fancy sequined gowns. Rather, expect your fellow passengers to be casually well dressed, with jackets and trousers for the men and a variety of skirts, dresses, and pants outfits for the ladies. As on most other ships, guests are asked not to wear shorts and T-shirts in the formal dining room. Daytime is casual.

1 First European Cruises

95 Madison Ave., Ste. 609, New York, NY 10016. © **888/983-8767** or 212/779-7168. Fax 212/779-0948. www.first-european.com.

THE LINE IN A NUTSHELL   Relatively new to cruising, First European is the U.S. arm of Europe-based Festival Cruises, founded in 1986 by George F. Poulides of the Greek Poulides shipping dynasty. Its fleet includes three attractive new ships all launched since 1999, with the 1,566-passenger *European Vision* the only one offering Caribbean cruises to the American market.

THE EXPERIENCE   *European Vision* is a midsize melting pot, with no more than 10% to 20% of the passenger mix being North American (often less), and the rest mostly from Europe, but also South America and Asia. The international ambience is charming and exotic, and the sea of different languages flowing through the ship is almost musical.

First European Cruises came into being in 1997, and 2 years later, the French-flagged *Mistral* debuted as the line's first stab at a new ship. While *Mistral* was an overall success, the larger *Vision* was able to improve upon her older sister's shortcomings, offering more cabin balconies, an **Internet center,** and a casual buffet restaurant open 24 hours a day. There's also a main dining room and an intimate **reservations-only alternative venue.** Her spa was one of the first to offer the multi-chamber steam rooms that have become more common in the past few years, with one chamber misting eucalyptus, one chamomile, and another a mixture of jasmine and lavender. Between them are contoured, tiled longues facing a wall of windows—a great spot for watching the ship depart a port. Adjacent is a roomy oceanview gym, a separate aerobics area, a beauty salon, and treatment rooms. Other public rooms include a large show lounge, several smaller entertainment lounges, a low-key casino, a sprawling top-deck disco, a specialty coffee cafe, and, out on deck, two pools, a golf simulator and **miniature-golf** course (plus lessons offered by an onboard **golf pro**), a combo volleyball/basketball court, and even a **climbing wall.** For kids, the ship has a playroom and a teen center.

Of the ship's 783 cabins, 132 are 235-square-foot suites with 50-square-foot **balconies,** sitting areas, walk-in closets, bathtubs, robes, and a fruit basket. Standard cabins measure 150 square feet. All staterooms have **stocked minibars** (with charges for any snacks or drinks you consume automatically billed to your onboard account), safe, hair dryer, compact but well-laid-out bathrooms, desk/vanity combo, and TV. Designed with blond wood tones and blue, burgundy, and goldish fabrics, the smart, minimalist layout offsets the cabins' relatively small size—Carnival's standard cabins, by comparison, measure 185 square feet. A new **"Hilton Floating Resort"** program, created and marketed in cooperation with the famous hotel company, provides guests booking special suites with such services as priority check-in and checkout, plus additional dining, entertainment, and excursion benefits.

THE FLEET   Along with *European Vision,* First European operates the 1,500-passenger *European Stars* (2002) in the Mediterranean and Adriatic, the 1,200-passenger *Mistral* (1999) in the Baltic and Scandinavia, and the older 720- passenger *Azur* (1971) in the eastern Mediterranean.

First European Fleet Itineraries

Ship	Itineraries
European Vision	**7-night Carib:** Round-trip from Santo Domingo (Dominican Republic). **Non-Caribbean Itineraries:** Europe.

2 Mediterranean Shipping Cruises

420 Fifth Ave., New York, NY 10018. © 800/666-9333 or 212/764-4800. Fax 212/764-1486. www.msc cruisesusa.com.

THE LINE IN A NUTSHELL   The cruise wing of Mediterranean Shipping Company, one of the world's largest container ship operations, Mediterranean Shipping Cruises (MSC) is an Italian line that operates one brand-new midsize cruise ship in the Caribbean and several older ones in Europe. In the Caribbean, it offers a pair of low-priced, port-packed, 11-night itineraries catering to Europeans and North Americans.

THE EXPERIENCE   For the past several years, MSC has operated one of the old "Big Red Boats" of defunct Premier Cruises, running long, low-priced Caribbean jaunts for a crowd that tends to be half European (many of them younger, sometimes with children) and half American (many of them older and a bit more conservative than the Europeans). In 2003, though, the line launched its first purpose-built ship, m/s *Lirica,* a modern, midsize, 58,600-gross-ton, 1,590-passenger vessel. Very similar in design to First European's *European Vision,* with 130 balcony suites among its 795 cabins, the ship could win a larger American passenger base for this very Italian line. *Lirica* will be deployed in the Mediterranean during the summer months and in the Caribbean during the winter season in 2003. A sister ship, m/s *Opera,* is due to be launched in 2004.

Med Shipping's **cuisine** is a fairly standard mixture of international and Italian specialties, served in *Lirica's* two restaurants or in the buffet restaurant. **Activities** on a typical cruise include bingo, bridge, dance lessons, arts and crafts, language classes, and gambling in the casino. As might be expected on a ship with a variety of nationalities, much of the **entertainment** is visual—dancers, magicians, and jugglers, for example, rather than stand-up comedians—plus the usual musical revues. Movies are shown daily, but if you decide to drop in, check the daily program beforehand, as the movie could be in English, Italian, Spanish, or German. A **children's center** offers a modest selection of activities and a small wading pool, but, in general, few efforts are made to segregate children into their own areas. Children's programs are offered depending on the number of children aboard, mostly during the holidays and summer.

Service is above average for a ship that operates these kinds of inexpensive cruises. Many of the career staffers are from Italy and are attentive without being servile, pleasant without being effusive.

THE FLEET   *Lirica* is the line's only ship in the Caribbean for 2003. Three other vessels sail in the Mediterranean.

Mediterranean Shipping Cruises Itineraries

Ship	Itineraries
Lirica	**11-night W. Carib:** Round-trip from Fort Lauderdale, Jan–Apr. **11-night E. Carib:** Round-trip from Fort Lauderdale, Jan–Apr. **Non-Caribbean Itineraries:** Europe.

3 ResidenSea

5200 Blue Lagoon Dr., Suite 790, Miami, FL 33126. ℂ **800/970-6601** or 305/779-3399 (vacation stays); ℂ 305/264-9090 (residential purchase). www.residensea.com.

THE LINE IN A NUTSHELL   This relatively new line is running with a novel idea: the oceangoing equivalent of condos and timeshares. All it takes is an ultraluxury cruise ship, accommodations as big and plush as Fifth Avenue apartments, an ongoing itinerary that circles the globe, and some seriously well-heeled guests.

THE EXPERIENCE   We always knew cruise ships were floating hotels, but ResidenSea takes the idea literally with its floating condo, *The World*, which debuted in April 2002. At press time, studio and one- to three-bedroom apart-ments that range from 259 to 3,242 square feet are still available for purchase, with studios starting at a tidy $900,000 and multi-room apartments starting at $1,700,000, plus maintenance fees. For those less commitment-minded, studio and two- to six-bedroom apartments, most with balconies, can be rented for any length of time (3 days minimum), with embarkation and debarkation at the port of your choice. Nightly fares begin at $450 for studios, $1,800 for multi-room apartments, double occupancy, and include food, beverages, gratu-ities, and port charges for two guests. Apartments come with full kitchens, a washer/dryer, an entertainment system, Internet access, a terrace with hot tub, Wedgwood china, Christofle flatware, and Frette linens. Meals and beverages for owner-residents can be purchased a la carte or in package plans.

Owner or renter, everyone aboard *The World* can sample any of the ship's four open-seating restaurants (French fusion, grill, Mediterranean, and Asian); sample deli items from Fredy's, which doubles as a gourmet market; get a treatment or 10 at the 7,015-square-foot Clinique La Prairie health spa; or use the many sports and fitness options, which include a full-size tennis court, swimming pools, jogging track, and a retractable marina offering activities such as water-skiing, sailing, and kayaking. The World Golf Club by Simon Holmes Golf Academy includes two full-shot driving ranges, a golf simulator, putting greens, and full-time pros who accompany residents and guests on excursions to the best courses in the regions visited. A crew of about 320 caters to residents and guests, and, of course, a 24-hour concierge and 24-hour room service are available. Meals can even be prepared in the apartments by an onboard chef, for an addi-tional charge.

The World was designed by some of the same naval architects who worked on the SeaDream yachts, Silversea's *Silver Cloud* and *Silver Wind,* and Seabourn's *Pride, Spirit,* and *Legend.* The idea for the floating condo was the brainchild of Norwegian shipping magnate Knut U. Kloster, Jr., the former chairman of Royal Viking Line and Norwegian Cruise Lines. The crowd targeted is a mix of Americans (about 40%) and Europeans, Asians, Latin Americans, and any big

ResidenSea Fleet Itineraries

Ship	Itineraries
The World	**Cruises of Any Length:** Northern Europe, United Kingdom, Canary Islands, Mediterranean, Canada, New England, Caribbean, Central America, Mexico, Hawaii.

spender of any nationality. Crisscrossing the globe, itineraries are timed to coincide with major international events such as the Cannes Film Festival, the Grand Prix in Monaco, and the British Open. The ship stays in port as long as 5 days at a stretch to make sure guests have the time to leisurely sightsee and meet up with friends or family. You can sail on *The World* for any length of time, from 5 days to 50 or 150. While at sea, guests can fill their day by attending seminars on history, science, and art topics, or classes on everything from music to bridge and dancing.

THE FLEET   *The World* is the line's first and only ship.

4 Sea Cloud Cruises

32–40 N. Dean St., Englewood, NJ 07631. ℂ **888/732-2568** or 201/227-9404. Fax 201/227-9424. www. seacloud.com.

THE LINE IN A NUTSHELL   These sailing ships offer a deliciously exotic experience that will spoil small-ship lovers forever. *Sea Cloud I,* built in 1931, and *Sea Cloud II,* a modern replica of her older sister, attract a mixed European and American crowd that keeps things interesting.

THE EXPERIENCE   German-based Sea Cloud Cruises caters to a well-traveled clientele looking for a five-star sailing adventure. A typical Caribbean cruise draws about 30% to 40% American passengers, 20% German, 20% British, and the rest from elsewhere in Europe.

If grand living like the super rich is your idea of a jaunt through the Caribbean, then *Sea Cloud I* and *II* are definitely worth considering. The 69-passenger *Sea Cloud I* was built as *Hussar* in 1931 by Wall Street tycoon E. F. Hutton for his heiress wife Majorie Merriweather Post (who, when later divorced, took over the ship and renamed it *Sea Cloud,* enjoying it with future husbands). No expense was spared in designing the four-masted sailing ship and its owner's cabins, which have now been restored to their original grandeur, dripping with **marble, gold detailing,** and **mahogany.** Post herself took up residence in cabin number 1, an indulgent museum-like room with a French antique white and gold-leaf bed, marble fireplace and bathroom, chandeliers, and intricate moldings everywhere. Even if you don't splurge for one of the owner's staterooms, you can still enjoy the dark wood paneling, brass trimmings, and nautical paintings in the restaurant. On the larger *Sea Cloud II,* an elegant lounge is designed with rich mahogany woodwork, ornate ceiling moldings, leather club couches, and overstuffed bucket chairs. *Cloud II* has several opulent suites, one with burled wood paneling and a canopy bed. Otherwise, on both ships, the standard cabins are very comfortable, but ordinary in comparison. Those on *II* have small sitting areas, and all cabins have marble bathrooms with showers, TV/VCRs, telephones, safes, hair dryers, and bathrobes.

Sea Cloud Fleet Itineraries

Ship	Itineraries
Sea Cloud I & II	**6- to 13-night E. & S. Carib:** Several different itineraries from Antigua and Barbados, Nov–Apr. **Non-Caribbean Itineraries:** Europe.

The dining room on each ship accommodates all guests in one open seating, and fine **wines and beer are complimentary at lunch and dinner.** Breakfast and some lunches are offered buffet style, while the more **formal dinners** are served on elegant candlelit tables set with white linens, china, and silver. Most men wear jackets nightly, though the 2 formal nights on each cruise are not black-tie affairs; jackets and ties work just fine. Most cruises also feature a **barbecue night** out on deck.

These being small sailing ships, **organized activities are few;** it's the ships themselves that entertain, and watching the crew work the riggings, plus visits to less-touristed ports such as Les Saintes, Dominica, Bequia, Mayreau, Tobago, and St. Barts. Only 1 day of each cruise is spent at sea. As on the Star Clippers' vessels, the outside decks of both ships are covered with lines, winches, cleats, brass compasses, wooden deck chairs, and other shippy accouterments, providing a wonderfully nostalgic and nautical setting, and a **sailing class** is offered on every cruise. *Cloud II* also has a **library** and a **small gym.** Evenings may include piano music and mingling over cocktails. Other occasional activities may include a guest lecturer who sails on board; **local musicians** who come aboard for a few hours; and **"open houses,"** where guests enjoy champagne and caviar on the Main Deck before touring each other's cabins (with the residents' permission, of course!).

THE FLEET   The two *Clouds* are closest in look and style to Star Clippers' tall ships, though smaller and more upscale. The 69-passenger, 2,532-ton, four-masted *Sea Cloud I* (1931) is in a class by itself, while its newer incarnation, 96-passenger, 3,849-ton, three-masted schooner *Sea Cloud II* (2001), is a wonderful copy.

The company's other vessels, 90-passenger *River Cloud I* (1996) and 88-passenger *River Cloud II* (2001), traverse the rivers of Europe.

Part 3

The Ports

With advice on things you can see and do on your own and via organized shore excursions in 36 ports of call, plus information on the five major ports of embarkation and the other alternative home ports now being used by the cruise lines.

The Ports of Embarkation

Hands down, the busiest of the ports of embarkation is **Miami**, followed by Port Everglades in **Fort Lauderdale;** Port Canaveral at **Cape Canaveral,** directly east of Orlando; **Tampa,** on Florida's west coast; and **New Orleans,** which is popular for ships sailing to Mexico and the western Caribbean. We profile all of these in detail in this chapter. **San Juan, Puerto Rico,** is both a major port of embarkation in the eastern Caribbean and a major port of call, so we include its review in chapter 11. These ports are tourist destinations themselves, so most cruise lines now offer special deals to extend their passengers' vacations with a stay either before or after their cruise. These packages, for 2, 3, or 4 days, often offer hotel and car-rental discounts, as well as sightseeing packages. Have your travel agent or cruise specialist check for the best deals. In this chapter, we describe the major ports of embarkation, tell you how to get to them, and suggest things to see and do there, including shopping and hitting the beach. We also recommend a sampling of restaurants and places to stay.

The big news this year is **alternative ports of embarkation,** U.S. population centers where the lines are positioning ships to more easily allow passengers to drive rather than fly to their cruise (or, at the least, to allow a wider range of flight options). For the Caribbean, the most significant of these alternative ports are **Galveston,** Texas; **New York City;** and **Charleston,** South Carolina. We've included brief descriptions of each at the end of this chapter.

Note that **hotel prices** listed here are winter rates for standard double rooms unless stated otherwise. Prices in the off-season will be lower. In addition to the hotels listed in this chapter, the following **motel chains** also have branches in all the mainland port cities unless noted otherwise:

- **Best Western,** © 800/780-7234; www.bestwestern.com
- **Clarion,** © 877/424-6423; www.clarioninn.com (no Galveston branch; Houston only)
- **Comfort Inn,** © 800/424-6423; www.comfortinn.com (no New Orleans branch)
- **Comfort Suites,** © 800/424-6423; www.comfortsuites.com (no Galveston branch; Houston only)
- **Courtyard by Marriott,** © 800/321-2211; www.courtyard.com (no Galveston branch; Houston only)
- **Days Inn,** © 800/329-7466; www.daysinn.com
- **Doubletree,** © 800/222-8733; www.doubletree.com
- **Econo Lodge,** © 800/424-6423; www.econolodge.com
- **Holiday Inn,** © 800/465-4329; www.holiday-inn.com
- **Howard Johnson,** © 800/466-4656; www.hojo.com (no Galveston branch; Houston only)
- **Motel 6,** © 800/466-8356; www.motel6.com (no Miami branch)
- **Quality,** © 800/424-6423; www.qualityinn.com (no Galveston branch; Houston only)
- **Red Roof Inns,** © 800/733-7663; www.redroof.com (no Galveston branch; Houston only)

All the ports in this chapter can be reached by train as well as by air and car. **Amtrak** (© **800/872-7245;** www.xamtrak.com) has a New York–Miami route that stops at Miami, Fort Lauderdale, and Orlando (for Cape Canaveral); a New York–Tampa route that stops at Orlando and Tampa; a Los Angeles–Orlando route that stops at Orlando, New Orleans, and Houston (for Galveston); and a route from Chicago to New Orleans.

For more information about each destination, check *Frommer's Florida, Frommer's South Florida, Frommer's New Orleans, Frommer's Puerto Rico, Frommer's New York City, Frommer's Philadelphia & the Amish Country,* and *Frommer's The Carolinas & Georgia.*

1 Miami

It's the most Latin city in the U.S., with a hot-hot-hot club scene, sparkling beaches, crystal clear waters, and more palm fronds, glittering hotels, and red sports cars than you can shake a stick at; and on top of all that, Miami is also the undisputed cruise capital of the world. More cruise ships, especially supersize ones, berth here than anywhere else on earth, and more than three million cruise passengers pass through yearly. Not surprisingly, the city's facilities are extensive and state-of-the-art, and Miami International Airport is only 8 miles away, about a 15-minute drive.

Industry giants Carnival and Royal Caribbean both have long-term agreements with the port, and to accommodate the influx of new ships over the past few years, Miami has spent $76 million on major improvements to Terminals 3, 4, and 5, and added a 750-space parking facility.

GETTING TO MIAMI & THE PORT

The **Port of Miami** is at 1015 N. America Way, in south Florida. It's on Dodge Island, reached via a four-lane bridge from the downtown district. For information, call © **305/371-7678** or head online to **www.miamidade.gov/portof miami.**

BY PLANE   **Miami International Airport** is about 8 miles west of downtown Miami and the port. If you've arranged air transportation and/or transfers through the cruise line (see chapter 2, "Booking Your Cruise & Getting the Best Price"), a cruise line rep will direct you to shuttle buses to the port. Taxis are also available; the fare is about $18. Some leading taxi companies include **Central Taxicab Service** (© **305/532-5555**), **Diamond Cab Company** (© **305/545-5555**), and **Metro Taxicab Company** (© **305/888-8888**).

SuperShuttle (© **305/871-2000**) charges about $9 per person, with two pieces of luggage ($2–$5 each additional piece), for a ride within Dade County, which includes the Port of Miami. Their vans operate 24 hours a day.

BY CAR   The Florida Turnpike (a toll road) and Interstate 95 are the main arteries for those arriving from the north. Continue south on I-95 to I-395 and head east on I-395, exiting at Biscayne Boulevard. Make a right and go south to Port Boulevard. Make a left and go over the Port Bridge. Coming in from the northwest, take Interstate 75 to State Road 826 (Palmetto Expressway) south to State Road 836 east. Exit at Biscayne Boulevard. Make a right and go south to Port Boulevard. Make a left and go over the Port Bridge. Parking lots right at street level face the cruise terminals. Parking runs $10 per day. Porters can carry your luggage to the terminals.

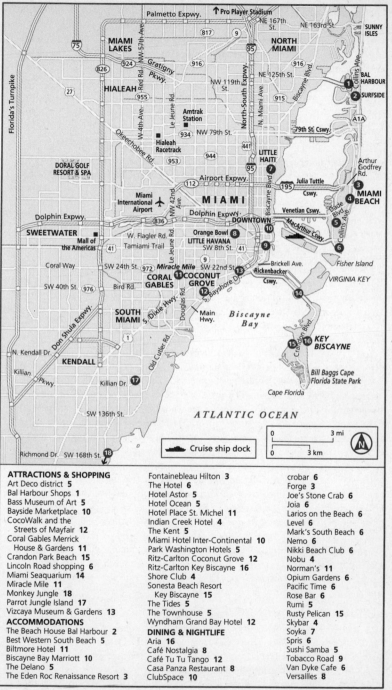

ATTRACTIONS & SHOPPING

Art Deco district **5**
Bal Harbour Shops **1**
Bass Museum of Art **5**
Bayside Marketplace **10**
CocoWalk and the
Streets of Mayfair **12**
Coral Gables Merrick
House & Gardens **11**
Crandon Park Beach **15**
Lincoln Road shopping **6**
Miami Seaquarium **14**
Miracle Mile **11**
Monkey Jungle **18**
Parrot Jungle Island **17**
Vizcaya Museum & Gardens **13**

ACCOMMODATIONS

The Beach House Bal Harbour **2**
Best Western South Beach **5**
Biltmore Hotel **11**
Biscayne Bay Marriott **10**
The Delano **5**
The Eden Roc Renaissance Resort **3**

Fontainebleau Hilton **3**
The Hotel **6**
Hotel Astor **5**
Hotel Ocean **5**
Hotel Place St. Michel **11**
Indian Creek Hotel **4**
The Kent **5**
Miami Hotel Inter-Continental **10**
Park Washington Hotels **5**
Ritz-Carlton Coconut Grove **12**
Ritz-Carlton Key Biscayne **16**
Shore Club **4**
Sonesta Beach Resort
Key Biscayne **15**
The Tides **5**
The Townhouse **5**
Wyndham Grand Bay Hotel **12**

DINING & NIGHTLIFE

Aria **16**
Café Nostalgia **8**
Café Tu Tu Tango **12**
Casa Panza Restaurant **8**
ClubSpace **10**

crobar **6**
Forge **3**
Joe's Stone Crab **6**
Joia **6**
Larios on the Beach **6**
Level **6**
Mark's South Beach **6**
Nemo **6**
Nikki Beach Club **6**
Nobu **4**
Norman's **11**
Opium Gardens **6**
Pacific Time **6**
Rose Bar **6**
Rumi **5**
Rusty Pelican **15**
Skybar **4**
Soyka **7**
Spris **6**
Sushi Samba **5**
Tobacco Road **9**
Van Dyke Cafe **6**
Versailles **8**

EXPLORING MIAMI

A sizzling, multicultural mecca, Miami offers the best in cutting-edge restaurants, unusual attractions, entertainment, shopping, beaches, and the whole range of hotels, from luxury to boutique, kitschy to charming. South Beach is a people-watching paradise.

VISITOR INFORMATION   Contact the **Greater Miami Convention and Visitors Bureau,** 701 Brickell Ave., Suite 2700, Miami, FL 33131 (*© **888/76-MIAMI** for a free vacation planner and 305/539-3000 for questions), or visit their website at **www.miamiandbeaches.com.**

GETTING AROUND   See "Getting to Miami & the Port," above, for taxi contact information. The meter starts at $1.50, and ticks up another $2 each mile and 30¢ for each additional minute, with standard flat-rate charges for frequently traveled routes. **Metromover** (*© **305/770-3131**), a 4⅓-mile elevated line, circles downtown, stopping near important downtown attractions and shopping and business districts. It runs daily from about 5am to midnight, and is fun if you've got time to kill. The fare is 25¢.

HITTING THE BEACH

A 300-foot-wide sand beach runs for about 10 miles from the south of Miami Beach to Haulover Beach Park in the north. (For those of you who like to get an all-around tan, Haulover is a known nude beach.) Although most of this stretch is lined with a solid wall of hotels, beach access is plentiful, and you are free to frolic along the entire strip. A wooden boardwalk runs along the hotel side from 21st to 46th streets—about 1½ miles.

You'll find lots of **public beaches** here, wide and well maintained, with lifeguards, toilet facilities, concession stands, and metered parking (bring lots of quarters). There are also public parking garages on 7th and 13th streets. Prices range from $7 to $24. Lifeguard-protected public beaches include 21st Street, at the beginning of the boardwalk; 35th Street, popular with an older crowd; 46th Street, next to the Fontainebleau Hilton; 53rd Street, a narrower, more sedate beach; 64th Street, one of the quietest strips around; and 72nd Street, a local old-timers' spot. On the southern tip of the beach is family-favorite South Pointe Park, where you can watch the cruise ships. Lummus Park, in the center of the Art Deco district, is the best place for people-watching and model-spotting. The beach between 11th and 13th streets is popular with the gay crowd. The beach from 1st to 15th streets is popular with seniors.

In Key Biscayne, **Crandon Park,** 4000 Crandon Blvd. (*© **305/361-5421**), is one of metropolitan Miami's finest white-sand beaches, stretching for some 3½ miles. There are lifeguards, and you can rent a cabana with a shower and chairs for $20 per day. Saturday and Sunday the beach can be especially crowded. Parking nearby is $4 per car and $10 for campers, minivans, SUVs, and buses.

ATTRACTIONS

Miami's best attraction is a part of the city itself. Located at the southern end of Miami Beach below 20th Street, South Beach's **Art Deco district** is filled with outrageous and fanciful 1920s and 1930s architecture that shouldn't be missed (oh, and the characters strolling about in teeny-tiny beachwear are pretty interesting, too). This treasure-trove, called "the Beach" or "SoBe," features more than 900 pastel, Pez-colored buildings in the Art Deco, Streamline Moderne, and Spanish Mediterranean Revival styles. The district stretches from 6th to 23rd streets, and from the Atlantic Ocean to Lennox Court. Ocean Drive boasts many of the premier Art Deco hotels.

Also in South Beach is the **Bass Museum of Art,** 2121 Park Ave. (© **305/ 673-7530;** www.bassmuseum.org), with a permanent collection of Old Masters, along with textiles, period furnishings, objets d'art, ecclesiastical artifacts, and sculpture. Rotating exhibits include pop art, fashion, and photography. The museum is open from 10am to 5pm Tuesday, Wednesday, Friday, and Saturday; 10am to 9pm on Thursday; and 11am to 5pm on Sunday. Admission is $6 for adults, $4 seniors and students.

The adjoining **Coral Gables** and **Coconut Grove** neighborhoods are fun to visit for their architecture and ambience. In Coral Gables, the Old World meets the new as curving boulevards, sidewalks, plazas, fountains, and arched entrances evoke Seville. Today, the area is an Epicurean's Eden, boasting some of Miami's most renowned eateries as well as the University of Miami and the ½-mile-long **Miracle Mile,** a 5-block retail mecca (see "Shopping," below). You can even visit the boyhood home of George Merrick, the man who originally developed Coral Gables. The **Coral Gables Merrick House & Gardens,** 907 Coral Way (© **305/460-5361**), has been restored to its 1920s look and is filled with Merrick memorabilia. At press time, the property was closed for renovation but was expected to reopen in fall 2003. For updates, call the Coral Gables Historical Resources Department at © **305/460-5093.**

Coconut Grove, South Florida's oldest settlement, remains a village surrounded by the urban sprawl of Miami. It dates back to the early 1800s, when Bahamian seamen first sought to salvage treasure from the wrecked vessels stranded along the Great Florida Reef. Mostly people come here to shop, drink, dine, or simply walk around and explore. But don't miss the **Vizcaya Museum & Gardens,** 3251 S. Miami Ave. (© **305/250-9133;** www.vizcayamuseum. com), a spectacular 70-room Italian Renaissance–style villa. It is open every day except Christmas. The $10 admission fee includes a free guided tour.

THE ANIMAL PARKS   Just minutes from the Port of Miami in Key Biscayne, the **Miami Seaquarium,** 4400 Rickenbacker Causeway (© **305/361- 5705;** http://miamiseaquarium.com), is a delight. Performing dolphins such as Flipper, TV's greatest sea mammal, perform along with "Lolita the Killer Whale." You can also see endangered manatees, sea lions, tropical-theme aquariums, and the gruesome shark feeding. It's open daily from 9:30am to 6pm. Admission is $24 for adults and $19 for children 3 to 9 (free for children under 3).

At **Monkey Jungle,** 14805 SW 216th St., Miami (© **305/235-1611;** www. monkeyjungle.com), the trick is that the visitors are caged and nearly 500 monkeys frolic in freedom and make fun of them. The most talented of these freeroaming primates perform shows daily for the amusement of their guests. The site also contains one of the richest fossil deposits in South Florida, with some 5,000 specimens. It's open daily from 9:30am to 5pm. Admission is $15 for adults, $10 for children 4 to 12, and free for children under 4.

Parrot Jungle Island, 1111 Parrot Jungle Trail (© **305/2-JUNGLE;** www. parrotjungle.com), is actually a botanical garden, wildlife habitat, and bird sanctuary all rolled into one. Children can enjoy a petting zoo and a playground. It's open daily from 9:30am to 6pm. Admission is $24 for adults, $19 for children 3 to 10, and free for children under 3. *Note:* Parrot Jungle Island has recently moved, reopening at this new location in July 2003.

ORGANIZED TOURS

BY BOAT From September through May, **Heritage Schooner Cruises** (© **305/442-9697;** www.heritageschooner.com) offers daily 2-hour jaunts at 1:30, 4, and 6:30pm aboard the 85-foot schooner *Heritage of Miami II*, departing from the Bayside Marketplace. Tickets cost $20 for adults and $10 for children under 12. On Friday, Saturday, and Sunday evenings, 1-hour tours at 8, 9, 10, and 11pm show off the lights of the city.

ON FOOT An **Art Deco District Walking Tour,** sponsored by the Miami Design Preservation League (© **305/672-2014;** www.mdpl.org), leaves every Thursday at 6:30pm and Saturday at 10:30am from the Art Deco Welcome Center at 1001 Ocean Dr., Miami Beach. The 90-minute tour costs $15.

SHOPPING

Most cruise ship passengers shop right near the Port of Miami at **Bayside Marketplace,** 401 Biscayne Blvd. (© **305/577-3344;** www.baysidemarketplace. com), a mall with 150 specialty shops, street performers, live music, and some 20 eateries, including a Hard Rock Cafe and others serving everything from Nicaraguan to Italian food. Many restaurants have outdoor seating right along the bay for picturesque views of the yachts harbored there. It can be reached via regular shuttle service from the port or by walking over the Port Bridge.

You can find a Miami version of Rodeo Drive at **Bal Harbour Shops,** 9700 Collins Ave. (© **305/866-0311;** www.balharbourshops.com). Shoppers will find big-name stores from Chanel and Prada to Lacoste and Neiman Marcus (and Florida's largest Saks Fifth Avenue).

In South Beach, **Lincoln Road,** an 8-block pedestrian mall, runs between Washington Avenue and Alton Road, near the northern tier of the Art Deco district. It's filled with popular shops such as Gap and Banana Republic, interior-design stores, art galleries, and even vintage-clothing outlets, as well as coffeehouses, restaurants, and cafes. Despite the recent influx of commercial anchor stores, Lincoln Road still manages to maintain its funky, arty flair, attracting an eclectic, colorful crowd.

Coconut Grove, centered on Main Highway and Grand Avenue, is the heart of the city's boutique district and features two open-air shopping and entertainment complexes, **CocoWalk** (www.cocowalk.com) and the **Streets of Mayfair.**

In Coral Gables, **Miracle Mile,** actually a ½-mile stretch of SW 22nd Street between Douglas and Le Jeune roads (aka 37th and 42nd aves.), features more than 150 shops.

For a change of pace from the fast-paced glitz of South Beach or the serene luxury of Coral Gables, head for **Little Havana,** where pre-Castro Cubans commingle with young artists who have begun to set up performance spaces in the area. It's located just west of downtown Miami on SW 8th Street. In addition to authentic Cuban cuisine, the cafe Cubano culture is alive and well.

WHERE TO STAY

Thanks to its network of highways, you can stay virtually anywhere in Greater Miami and still be within 10 to 20 minutes of your ship.

DOWNTOWN Two hotels—the 34-story **Hotel Inter-Continental Miami,** 100 Chopin Plaza (© **800/327-3005** or 305/577-1000; http://miami.inter-conti.com; rates: $199–$229), and the **Biscayne Bay Marriott,** 1633 North Bayshore (© **800/228-9290** or 305/374-3900; www.marriott.com; rates:

$149–$400)—are right across the bay from the cruise ship piers, near Bayside Marketplace, a mecca of shops and restaurants.

SOUTH BEACH   The Art Deco, comfy-chic **Hotel Astor,** 956 Washington Ave. (*©* **800/270-4981** or 305/531-8081; www.hotelastor.com), originally built in 1936, reopened in 1995 after a massive renovation. In December 2002, the hotel opened a new restaurant, Metro Kitchen and Bar (which replaced Astor Place), and also made significant renovations to its guest rooms and public areas. Rates: $145 to $900. The Astor is only 2 blocks from the beach, but if that's still too far for you, try the upscale **Hotel Ocean,** 1230–1238 Ocean Dr. (*©* **800/783-1725** or 305/672-2579; www.hotelocean.com). Rates: $200 to $280. If you're on a budget but want a cozy Deco feel, try the **Best Western South Beach,** which comprises four buildings—the Kenmore, Taft, Belaire, and Davis—right next door to the Astor at 1020–1050 Washington Ave. (*©* **305/ 532-1930;** www.bestwestern.com/southbeach). Rates: $85 to $145. The **Delano,** 1685 Collins Ave. (*©* **800/555-5001** or 305/672-2000; www.ian schragerhotels.com), is a sleek, postmodern, and self-consciously hip celebrity hot spot, but it's worth at least a peek. Rates: $475 to $675. **The Hotel,** 801 Collins Ave., at the corner of Collins and 8th Street (*©* **305/531-5796;** www. thehotelofsouthbeach.com), formerly known as The Tiffany Hotel until the folks behind the little blue box threatened to sue, is a Deco gem, as well as being the most fashionable hotel on South Beach, thanks to the whimsical interiors designed by haute couturier Todd Oldham. Rates: $275 to $425. The **Town-house,** 150 20th St. (*©* **877/534-3800** or 305/534-3800; www.townhouse hotel.com), is a funky newcomer with exercise bikes in the hallways and CD players and dataports in all rooms. Rates: $115 to $195. **The Kent,** 1131 Collins Ave. (*©* **800/688-7678** or 305/604-5068; www.islandoutpost.com), is part of Chris Blackwell's Island Outpost chain, and attracts a less upwardly mobile yet no less chic crowd of young, hip travelers. Rates: $130 to $350 suite. The trendy **Shore Club,** 1901 Collins Ave. (*©* **877/640-9500** or 305/695-3100; www.shoreclub.com), is where you'll find Miami's very first Nobu, the Japanese restaurant that took Manhattan by storm some years ago. Rates: $295 to $775.

MIAMI BEACH   At the **Indian Creek Hotel,** 2727 Indian Creek Dr., at 28th Street (*©* **800/491-2772** or 305/531-2727; www.indiancreekhotelmb.com), each room is an homage to the 1930s Art Deco age. Rates: $70 to $160. The **Eden Roc Renaissance Resort,** 4525 Collins Ave. (*©* **800/327-8337** or 305/ 531-0000; www.edenrocresort.com; rates: $259–$400), and the **Fontainebleau Hilton,** next door at 4441 Collins Ave. (*©* **800/548-8886** or 305/538-2000; www.fontainebleau.hilton.com; rates: $209–$309), are both popular, updated 1950s resorts evoking the bygone Rat Pack era, with spas, health clubs, outdoor swimming pools, and beach access. **The Beach House Bal Harbour,** 9449 Collins Ave., in Surfside (*©* **877/782-3557** or 305/535-8600; www.rubell hotels.com/beach.html), brings a taste of Nantucket to Miami with soothing hues, comfortable furniture, oceanfront views, and a Ralph Lauren–decorated interior. Rates: $229 to $379.

COCONUT GROVE   Near Miami's City Hall and the Coconut Grove Marina, the **Wyndham Grand Bay Hotel,** 2669 S. Bayshore Dr. (*©* **800/327-2788** or 305/858-9600; www.wyndham.com), overlooks Biscayne Bay. Rates: $239 to $319 suite. The **Ritz-Carlton Coconut Grove,** 3300 SW 27th Ave. (*©* **800/241-3333** or 305/644-4680; www.ritzcarlton.com), the third and smallest of Miami's Ritz-Carlton hotels, opened with a quiet splash in fall 2002. It's surrounded by 2 acres of tropical gardens and overlooks Biscayne Bay and the Miami skyline. Decorated in an Italian Renaissance design, the hotel's understated luxury is a welcome addition to an area known for its gaudiness. Biscaya Grill is its extremely elegant restaurant—we're talking footstools for women to put their purses on!

CORAL GABLES   The famous **Biltmore Hotel,** 1200 Anastasia Ave. (© **800/ 448-8355** or 305/445-1926; www.biltmorehotel.com), was restored a few years ago, but despite renovations, it exudes an old-world, stately glamour and is rumored to be haunted by ghosts of travel days past. Rates: $339 to $509. The **Hotel Place St. Michel,** 162 Alcazar Ave. (© **800/848-HOTEL** or 305/444- 1666; www.hotelplacestmichel.com), is a three-story establishment reminiscent of an inn in provincial France. Rates: $165.

KEY BISCAYNE   The **Sonesta Beach Resort Key Biscayne,** 350 Ocean Dr. (© **800/SONESTA** or 305/361-2021; www.sonesta.com/keybiscayne), offers relative isolation from the rest of congested Miami. Rates: $260 to $310. The **Ritz-Carlton, Key Biscayne,** 455 Grand Bay Dr. (© **800/241-3333** or 305/ 365-4500; www.ritzcarlton.com), offers a to-die-for spa, not to mention equally stunning ocean views. Rates: $325 to $850 suite.

WHERE TO DINE

DOWNTOWN   Up Biscayne Boulevard near the burgeoning Miami Design District is **Soyka,** 5556 NE 4th Court (© **305/759-3117**), the hip downtown sibling of South Beach's News and Van Dyke cafes. Dinner main courses: $11 to $24.

SOUTH BEACH   Join the celebs and models for pan-Asian cuisine at **Nemo,** 100 Collins Ave. (© **305/532-4550**). Dinner main courses: $24 to $36. Take time to stroll down the pedestrian mall on Lincoln Road, which offers art galleries, specialty shops, and several excellent outdoor cafes such as **Spris,** a pizzeria at 731 Lincoln Rd. (© **305/673-2020**), and the **Van Dyke Cafe,** 846 Lincoln Rd. (© **305/534-3600**). Prices at Spris range from $5 to $14; main courses at the Van Dyke from $9 to $17. The standout culinary trendsetter on Lincoln Road, however, is **Pacific Time,** 915 Lincoln Rd. (© **305/534-5979**), where you can enjoy a taste of the Pacific Rim with a deliciously modern South Beach twist. Dinner main courses: $20 to $32. The newest haute eateries-cum-lounges imported from New York (or at least inspired by its hot spots) include **Rumi,** 330 Lincoln Rd. (© **305/672-4353**), inspired by Lotus, Manhattan's restaurant of the moment, and oozing with lots of mirrors, mushy coaches, and even a queen-size Murphy bed (dinner main courses $18–$30); **Sushi Samba,** 600 Lincoln Rd. (© **305/673-5337**), which features a delectable fusion of South American and Japanese cuisine (dinner main courses $14–$39; sushi priced by the piece); and **Nobu,** 1901 Collins Ave. (© **305/695-3232**), the now nearly legendary name in Nouvelle Japanese cuisine. Dinner main courses: $8 to $36.

At the legendary **Joe's Stone Crab,** 11 Washington Ave., between South Point Drive and 1st Street (© **305/673-0365**), about a ton of stone-crab claws are served daily during stone-crab season from October to May (the place is usually closed May 15–Oct 15), and people are kept waiting for up to 2 hours for a table. Crab prices vary depending on the market rate, but start around $23 per order. If the sky's the limit in the budget department, try **Mark's South Beach** in the Hotel Nash, 1120 Collins Ave. (© **305/604-9050**), for fine dishes such as slow-roasted salmon with horseradish. Dinner main courses: $22 to $43. Even if Gloria Estefan weren't co-owner of **Larios on the Beach,** 820 Ocean Dr. (© **305/532-9577**), the crowds would still flock to this bistro, which serves old-fashioned Cuban dishes such as *masitas de puerco* (fried pork chunks). Dinner main courses: $11 to $25.

COCONUT GROVE   If you'd like to people-watch while you eat, head for **Café Tu Tu Tango,** 3015 Grand Ave., Suite 250 (© **305/529-2222**), on the second floor of CocoWalk. Designed to look like a disheveled artist's loft, it has original paintings (some half-finished) on easels or hanging from the walls. Tapas courses range from $3 to $9.

CORAL GABLES   **Norman's,** 21 Almeria Ave. (© **305/446-6767**), possibly the best restaurant in the entire city of Miami, is run by its namesake, Norman Van Aken, a James Beard–award winning chef and pioneer of New World and Floribbean cuisine. Dinner main courses: $29 to $40.

KEY BISCAYNE   The surf and turf is routine at the **Rusty Pelican,** 3201 Rickenbacker Causeway (© **305/361-3818**), but it's worth coming for a drink and to catch the spectacular sunset view. Dinner main courses: $16 to $41. **Aria,** 455 Grand Bay Dr., at the Ritz-Carlton (© **800/241-3333** or 305/365-4500), serves gorgeous (not to mention delicious) Mediterranean fare. Dinner main courses: $22 to $34.

LITTLE HAVANA   One reason to visit Little Havana is to enjoy its excellent Hispanic cuisine. **Casa Panza Restaurant,** 1620 SW 8th St. (© **305/643-5343**), a taste of old Seville in Little Havana, is a feast for the senses with flamenco dancers, tempting tapas, and a lively atmosphere that reels in crowds nightly. At 11pm, everyone, no matter what their religion, is given a candle to pray to La Virgen del Rocio, one of Seville's most revered saints—it's a party with piety! Dinner main courses: $6 to $14. Another place to check out is **Versailles,** 3555 SW 8th St. (© **305/444-0240**), a late-night (open till 2am Sun–Fri, 4am Sat) palatial, mirrored diner serving all the Cuban mainstays in large and reasonably priced portions. Dinner main courses: $8 to $20.

MIAMI AFTER DARK

Miami nightlife is as varied as its population, and its sizzling nightlife is no stranger to A-list celebrities from Leonardo DiCaprio and Gwyneth Paltrow to Al Pacino, Sylvester Stallone, and Madonna. Look for the klieg lights to direct you to the hot spots of South Beach. While the blocks of Washington Avenue, Collins Avenue, and Ocean Drive are the main nightlife thoroughfares, you're more likely to spot a celebrity in a more off-the-beaten-path eatery such as **Joia,** 150 Ocean Dr. (© **305/674-8871**), a popular, chic Italian eatery with a new upstairs lounge called Pure Lounge (that's anything but); or **The Forge,** 432 41st St. (© **305/538-8533**), an ornately decorated rococo-style steakhouse boasting one of the finest wine selections around.

Restaurants and bars are open late—usually until 5am. Also popular are the hotel bars, such as the Delano's **Rose Bar** and the Shore Club's hot, hauter-than-thou celeb magnet **Skybar,** 1901 Collins Ave. (© **877/640-9500** or 305/695-3222; www.shoreclub.com). Command central all hours of the night for the chic elite include the restaurants-cum-lounges **Rumi, Sushi Samba,** and **Nobu,** listed above in the "Where to Dine" section.

As trends come and go, so do clubs, so before you head out for a decadent night of disco, make sure the place is still in business! At press time, some of the clubs at which to see, be seen, and, of course, dance, included **crobar,** 1445 Washington Ave. (© **305/531-5027**); **Level,** 1235 Washington Ave. (© **305/ 532-1525**); and **Opium Gardens,** 136 Collins Ave. (© **305/531-5535**), an open-air nightclub that's a magnet for the trendoid brass (be sure to check out its new hot V-VIP lounge, called Prive). For a Playboy Mansion–type scene by day, check out the **Nikki Beach Club,** 1 Ocean Dr. © **305/538-1111**), complete with tiki huts and teepees.

But South Beach isn't the only place for nightlife in Miami. Not too far from the Miami River is the city's oldest bar, **Tobacco Road,** 626 S. Miami Ave. (© **305/374-1198**), a gritty place that still attracts some of the city's storied, pre–Miami Vice natives. **ClubSpace,** 142 NE 11th St. (© **305/372-9378**), occupies a very large warehouse in Downtown Miami and is vaguely reminiscent of a funky, SoHo-style dance palace. Down in Little Havana is **Café Nostalgia,** 2212 SW 8th St. (© **305/541-2631**), where salsa is not a condiment but a way of life.

Other nocturnal options abound in **Coconut Grove** and **Coral Gables** and, slowly but surely, the downtown/Design District areas. Check the *Miami Herald, Miami New Times,* and **www.miami.citysearch.com** for specific events.

2 Fort Lauderdale

Broward County's **Port Everglades** is the second-busiest cruise port in the world, drawing over 3.5 million cruise passengers in 2002. It boasts the deepest harbor on the eastern seaboard south of Norfolk, 12 ultramodern cruise ship terminals, and an easy access route to the Fort Lauderdale-Hollywood International Airport, less than a 5-minute drive away.

The port itself is fairly free of congestion, offering covered loading zones, drop-off and pickup staging, and curbside baggage handlers. Terminals are comfortable and safe, with seating areas, snack bars, lots of taxis, clean restrooms, and plenty of pay phones. Parking lots have recently been expanded to offer a total of 4,500 spaces.

GETTING TO FORT LAUDERDALE & THE PORT

Port Everglades is located about 23 miles north of Miami within the city boundaries of Fort Lauderdale, Hollywood, and Dania Beach. I-595 will take you right onto the grounds. For information, contact **Port Everglades** (© **954/523-3404;** www.broward.org/port).

BY AIR   Small and extremely user-friendly, the **Fort Lauderdale-Hollywood International Airport** (© **954/359-6100**) is less than 2 miles from Port Everglades (5 min. by bus or taxi), making this the easiest airport-to-cruiseport trip in Florida. (Port Canaveral, by contrast, is about a 45-min. drive from the Orlando airport.) If you've booked air or transfers through the cruise line, a representative will show you to your shuttle after you land. If you haven't, taking a taxi to the port costs less than $10.

BY CAR   The port has three passenger entrances: Spangler Boulevard, an extension of State Road 84 East; Eisenhower Boulevard, running south from the 17th Street Causeway/A1A; and Eller Drive, connecting directly with Interstate 595. Interstate 595 runs east-west, with connections to the Fort Lauderdale-Hollywood Airport, Interstate 95, State Road 7 (441), Florida's Turnpike, Sawgrass Expressway, and Interstate 75. Parking is available at the port in two large garages. The 2,500-space Northport Parking Garage, next to the Greater Fort

Fort Lauderdale

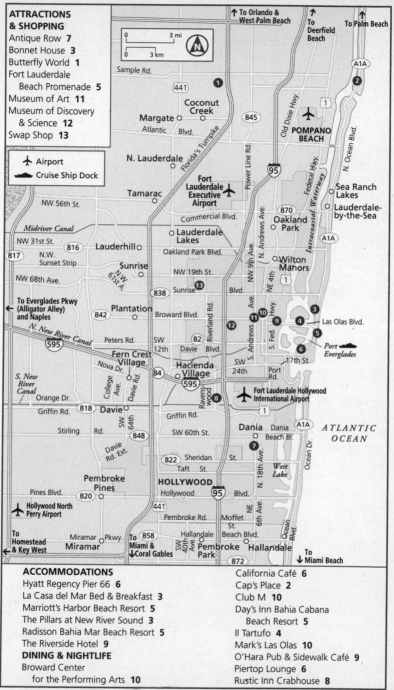

ATTRACTIONS & SHOPPING
Antique Row **7**
Bonnet House **3**
Butterfly World **1**
Fort Lauderdale
  Beach Promenade **5**
Museum of Art **11**
Museum of Discovery
  & Science **12**
Swap Shop **13**

✈ Airport
🚢 Cruise Ship Dock

↑ To Orlando &
West Palm Beach

↑ To
Deerfield
Beach

↑ To Palm Beach

A1A

Sample Rd.

441

Coconut
Creek

Margate

845

Atlantic   Blvd.

N. Lauderdale

POMPANO
BEACH

Tamarac

Fort
Lauderdale
Executive
Airport

Power Line Rd.

Old Dixie Hwy.

1

Federal Hwy.

Sea Ranch
Lakes

870

Lauderdale-
by-the-Sea

NW 56th St.

Commercial Blvd.

Oakland
Park

A1A

Midriver Canal

NW 31st St.   816

Lauderdale
Lakes

Lauderhill

Oakland Park Blvd.

NW 9th Ave.

N. Andrews Ave.

Wilton
Manors

817

N.W.
Sunset Strip

Sunrise

NW 19th St.

NE 4th

NW 68th Ave.

N.W.
61st A.

838

Sunrise   13   Blvd.

1

To Everglades Pkwy
(Alligator Alley)
and Naples

842

Plantation

Broward Blvd.

Riverland Rd.

12   11   10   9

3

4   Las Olas Blvd.

595

Peters Rd.

SW
12th

82

Davie   Blvd.

S. Andrews Ave.

S. Fed. Hwy.

5

6

Port
Everglades

N. New River Canal

Fern Crest
Village

Nova Dr.

84

Hacienda
Village

595

SW
24th

Port
Rd.

17th St.

S. New
River
Canal

College Ave.

Davie Rd.

Orange Dr.

Ravenswood Rd.

8

Fort Lauderdale Hollywood
International Airport

Griffin Rd.   818

Davie

SW
64th

Griffin Rd.

1

ATLANTIC
OCEAN

Stirling   Rd.

848

SW 60th St.

Dania   Dania
Beach Bl.

7

A1A

Davie
Rd. Ext.

822

Sheridan   St.

Taft   St.

N. 18th Ave.

West
Lake

Ocean Dr.

Pembroke
Pines

HOLLYWOOD

Pines Blvd.

820

Hollywood   95   Blvd.

441

Pembroke Rd.

Moffet
St.

NE
6th Ave.

Hollywood North
Perry Airport

Miramar   Pkwy.

858

Hallandale

Beach Blvd.

Ocean
Blvd.

To
Homestead
& Key West

Miramar

To
Miami &
↓Coral Gables

SW
40th Ave.

Pembroke
Park

Hallandale

872

To
↓ Miami Beach

ACCOMMODATIONS
Hyatt Regency Pier 66 **6**
La Casa del Mar Bed & Breakfast **3**
Marriott's Harbor Beach Resort **5**
The Pillars at New River Sound **3**
Radisson Bahia Mar Beach Resort **5**
The Riverside Hotel **9**
DINING & NIGHTLIFE
Broward Center
  for the Performing Arts **10**

California Café **6**
Cap's Place **2**
Club M **10**
Day's Inn Bahia Cabana
  Beach Resort **5**
Il Tartufo **4**
Mark's Las Olas **10**
O'Hara Pub & Sidewalk Café **9**
Piertop Lounge **6**
Rustic Inn Crabhouse **8**

Lauderdale/Broward County Convention Center, serves Terminals 1, 2, and 4. The 2,000-space Midport Parking Garage serves Terminals 18, 19, 21, 22, 24, 25, and 26. Garages are well lit, security patrolled, and designed to accommodate RVs and buses. The 24-hour parking fee is $12 daily.

EXPLORING FORT LAUDERDALE

Fort Lauderdale Beach, a 5-mile strip along Florida A1A, gained fame in the 1950s as a spring-break playground, popularized by the movie *Where the Boys Are.* But in the 1980s, partying college kids (who brought the city more mayhem than money) began to be less welcome as Fort Lauderdale sought to attract a more mainstream, affluent crowd, a task at which it has largely been successful.

In addition to miles of beautiful wide beaches, Fort Lauderdale has more than 300 miles of navigable natural waterways, in addition to innumerable artificial canals that permit thousands of residents to anchor boats in their backyards (and which has led to the city to be referred to as the "Venice of the Americas"). You can easily get on the water by renting a boat or hiring a private, moderately priced water taxi.

VISITOR INFORMATION   The **Greater Fort Lauderdale Convention & Visitors Bureau,** 1850 Eller Dr., Suite 303, Fort Lauderdale, FL 33316 (© **954/765-4466;** www.sunny.org), is an excellent resource, distributing a comprehensive guide on accommodations, events, and sightseeing in Broward County.

GETTING AROUND   For a taxi, call **Yellow Cab** (© **954/565-5400**). Rates start at $2.75 for the first mile and $2 for each additional mile. **Broward County Mass Transit** (© **954/357-8400**) runs bus service throughout the county. One-day passes are $2.50. **Water Taxi** (© **954/467-6677**) offers all-day passes for $5.

HITTING THE BEACH

Backed by an endless row of hotels and popular with visitors and locals alike, the **Fort Lauderdale Beach Promenade** underwent a $30 million renovation not long ago, and it looks marvelous. It's located along A1A, also known as the Fort Lauderdale Beach Boulevard, between SE 17th Street and Sunrise Boulevard. The fabled strip from *Where the Boys Are* is **Ocean Boulevard,** between Las Olas and Sunrise boulevards. On weekends, parking at the oceanside meters is difficult to find.

Fort Lauderdale Beach at the Howard Johnson is a perennial local favorite. A jetty bounds the beach on the south side, making it rather private, although the water gets a little choppy. High-school and college students share this area with an older crowd. One of the main beach entrances is at 4660 N. Ocean Dr. in Lauderdale-by-the-Sea.

ATTRACTIONS

The Museum of Discovery & Science, 401 SW Second St. (© **954/467-6637;** www.mods.org), is an excellent interactive science museum with an IMAX theater. Check out the 52-foot-tall "Great Gravity Clock" in the museum's atrium. Admission is $14 for adults, $12 for children, and $13 for seniors and students. It's open from 10am to 5pm Monday through Saturday; Sundays noon to 6pm.

The **Museum of Art,** 1 E. Las Olas Blvd. (© **954/763-6464;** www.museum ofart.org), is a truly terrific small museum whose permanent collection of 20th-century European and American art includes works by Picasso, Calder, Warhol,

Mapplethorpe, Dalí, Stella, and William Glackens. African, South Pacific, Pre-Columbian, Native American, and Cuban art are also on display. Admission is $7 for adults, $6 for seniors, and $5 for students. Kids under 6 are free. The museum is open 10am to 5pm Tuesday through Saturday and noon to 5pm on Sunday.

Bonnet House, 900 N. Birch Rd. (© **954/563-5393;** www.bonnethouse. org), a plantation-style home and 35-acre estate, survives in the middle of an otherwise highly developed beachfront condominium area, offering a glimpse into the lives of Fort Lauderdale's pioneers. Guided tours are offered Wednesday through Sunday. From December through April, hours are 10am to 4pm. From May to November, hours are 10am to 3pm. Bonnet House is closed for tours on Monday and Tuesday. Cost is $10 adults, $9 seniors, $8 students, and free for children under 6.

Butterfly World, Tradewinds Park South, 3600 W. Sample Rd., Coconut Creek, west of the Florida Turnpike (© **954/977-4400;** www.butterflyworld. com), cultivates more than 150 species. In the park's walk-through, screened-in aviary, visitors can watch newborn butterflies emerge from their cocoons and flutter around as they learn to fly. It's open from 9am to 5pm Monday through Saturday and 1 to 5pm Sunday. Admission is $15 adults, $10 kids 4 to 12, and free for kids under 4.

ORGANIZED TOURS

BY BOAT   The Mississippi-style riverboat *Jungle Queen,* Bahia Mar Yacht Center, Florida A1A (© **954/462-5596;** www.junglequeen.com), is one of Fort Lauderdale's best-known attractions. Dinner cruises and 3-hour sightseeing tours take visitors up the New River past Millionaires' Row, Old Fort Lauderdale, the new downtown, and the Port Everglades cruise ship port. Call for prices and departure times.

Water Taxis of Fort Lauderdale, 651 Seabreeze Blvd. (© **954/467-6677;** www.watertaxi.com), operates a fleet of old port boats that offer taxi service on demand around this city of canals, carrying up to 72 passengers each. You can be picked up at your hotel and shuttled to the dozens of restaurants and bars on the route for the rest of the night. The service operates daily from 6:30am to midnight. The cost is $4 per person per trip, $5 for a full day. Opt for the all-day pass—it's worth it.

SHOPPING

Not counting the discount "fashion" stores on Hallandale Beach Boulevard, visitors should know about a few other shopping places, including **Antique Row,** a strip of U.S. 1 around North Dania Beach Boulevard (in Dania, about 1 mile south of Fort Lauderdale-Hollywood International Airport) that holds about 200 antiques shops. Most shops are closed Sunday.

The **Swap Shop,** 3291 W. Sunrise Blvd. (© **954/791-SWAP;** www.florida swapshop.com), is one of the world's largest flea markets. In addition to endless acres of vendors, there's a mini-amusement park, a 13-screen drive-in movie theater, and even a free circus, complete with elephants, horse shows, high-wire acts, and clowns. It's open daily.

WHERE TO STAY

Fort Lauderdale Beach has a hotel or motel on nearly every block, and the selection ranges from run-down to luxurious.

Located very close to the port, the **Hyatt Regency Pier 66,** 2301 SE 17th St. (© **800/233-1234** or 954/525-6666; http://pier66.hyatt.com), is a circular landmark with larger rooms than some equivalently priced hotels in town. Its famous Piertop Lounge, a revolving bar on its roof, is often filled with cruise ship patrons. Rates: $219 to $259.

Located just south of Fort Lauderdale's strip, **Marriott's Harbor Beach Resort,** 3030 Holiday Dr. (© **800/222-6543** or 954/525-4000; www.marriott harborbeach.com), is set on 16 acres of beachfront property. All rooms have private balconies overlooking either the ocean or the Intracoastal Waterway. Rates: $349 to $429.

Radisson Bahia Mar Beach Resort, 801 Seabreeze Blvd. (© **800/327-8154** or 954/764-2233; www.radisson.com/ftlauderdalefl), is scattered over 42 acres of seacoast. A four-story row of units is adjacent to Florida's largest marina. Rates: $144 to $169. The **Riverside Hotel,** 620 E. Las Olas Blvd. (© **800/325-3280** or 954/467-0671; www.riversidehotel.com), which opened in 1936, is a local favorite. Try for one of the ground-floor rooms, which have higher ceilings and more space. Rates: $129.

The Spanish Mediterranean–style **La Casa del Mar Bed & Breakfast,** 3003 Granada St. (© **954/467-2037;** www.lacasadelmar.com), has 10 individually furnished rooms and is only a block away from Fort Lauderdale Beach. Rates: $110 to $145. **The Pillars at New River Sound,** 111 N. Birch Rd. (© **800/800-7666** or 954/467-9639; www.pillarshotel.com), is a small 23-room hotel, the best of its size in the region. Rates: $169 to $199. Several **Best Western hotels** (www.bestwestern.com) in the area are reasonably priced and within 5 miles of the airport and port: Best Western Inn, 1221 W S.R. 84 (© 800/528-1234 or 954/462-7005; rates: $62–$199); Best Western Marina Inn & Yacht Harbor, 2150 SE 17th St. (© 800/327-1390 or 954/525-3484; rates: $89–$249); Best Western Oceanside Inn, 1180 Seabreeze Blvd. (© 800/367-1007 or 954/525-8115; rates: $79–$199). Call the **Greater Fort Lauderdale Convention & Visitors Bureau** (© **954/765-4466;** www.sunny.org) for a copy of *Superior Small Lodgings,* a guide to other small accommodations in the area.

WHERE TO DINE

California Café, at the Hyatt Pier 66 Hotel, 2301 SE 17th St. (© **954/728-3500**), serves brick-oven pizza and pasta dishes at affordable prices. Dinner main courses: $16 to $32.

Cap's Place, 2765 NE 28th Court (© **954/941-0418;** www.capsplace.com), is a famous old-time seafood joint, offering good food at reasonable prices. The restaurant is on a peninsula; you get a ferry ride over (see their website for directions). Dolphin (not the mammal but a local saltwater fish also known as mahimahi) and grouper are popular and, like the other meat and pasta dishes here, can be prepared any way you want. Dinner main courses: $14 to $25.

Il Tartufo, 2400 E. Las Olas Blvd. (© **954/767-9190**), serves oven-roasted specialties and other Italian standards, plus a selection of fish baked in rock salt. Dinner main courses: $15 to $22.

Mark's Las Olas, 1032 E. Las Olas Blvd. (© **954/463-1000**), is the showcase of Miami restaurant mogul Mark Militello. The continental gourmet menu changes daily and may include Jamaican jerk chicken with fresh coconut salad or a superb sushi-quality tuna. Dinner main courses: $14 to $42.

Garlic crabs are the specialty at the **Rustic Inn Crabhouse,** 4331 Anglers Ave. (© **954/584-1637;** www.crabhouse.com), located west of the airport. This riverside dining choice has an open deck over the water. Dinner main courses: $10 to $19.

The restaurant and patio bar at the **Day's Inn Bahia Cabana Beach Resort,** 3001 Harbor Dr./A1A (© **954/524-1555;** www.bahiacabanaresort.com), is charming and laid-back, serving inexpensive American-style dishes on a covered open-air deck overlooking Fort Lauderdale's largest marina; the Fort Lauderdale water taxi makes a stop here. Dinner main courses: $8 to $17.

FORT LAUDERDALE AFTER DARK

From the area's most famous bar, the revolving **Piertop Lounge,** in the Hyatt Regency at Pier 66 (© **954/525-6666**), you'll get a 360-degree panoramic view of Fort Lauderdale. The bar completes a revolution every 66 minutes, and has a dance floor and live music, including blues and jazz.

On weekends, it's hard to get into **Club M,** 2037 Hollywood Blvd. (© **954/ 925-8396**), one of the area's busiest music bars, featuring a DJ and live bands on weekends playing blues, rock, and jazz.

O'Hara Pub & Sidewalk Café, 722 E. Las Olas Blvd. (© **954/524-1764**), is often packed with a trendy crowd who come to listen to live R & B, pop, blues, and jazz. Call their jazz hot line (© **954/524-2801**) to hear the lineup.

The **Broward Center for the Performing Arts,** 201 SW Fifth Ave. (© **954/ 462-0222;** www.browardcenter.org), hosts top opera, symphony, dance, and Broadway productions. Call the 24-hour Arts Entertainment Hot Line (© **954/ 357-5700**) for schedules and performers, or look for listings in the *Sun-Sentinel* or the *Miami Herald.*

3 Cape Canaveral & Cocoa Beach

Known as the "Space Coast" because of nearby Kennedy Space Center, the Cape Canaveral/Cocoa Beach area boasts 72 miles of beaches, plus fishing, golfing, surfing, and close proximity to Orlando's theme parks, only about an hour west—which is exactly why long-underutilized **Port Canaveral** is now busier than ever before, offering many 3- and 4-night cruise options (often sold as packages with pre- or post-cruise visits to the Orlando resorts) as well as week-long itineraries. This year, Port Canaveral has even become a port of call, with NCL's *Norwegian Dawn* visiting on her round-trip Florida/Caribbean itineraries from New York.

Outside the port area, Cape Canaveral is . . . well, it's no Miami. Highways, strip malls, chain stores, and tracts of suburban homes predominate from the port area south into Cocoa Beach, where most of the hotels, restaurants, and beaches discussed here are located. The central areas of Cocoa Beach are mildly more interesting, with some great '50s/'60s condo and hotel architecture, but stylish they're not.

GETTING TO CAPE CANAVERAL & THE PORT

Port Canaveral is located at the eastern end of the Bennett Causeway, just off State Road 528 (the Bee Line Expressway), the direct route from Orlando. From the port, the 528 turns sharply south and becomes State Road A1A, portions of which are known as Astronaut Boulevard and North Atlantic Avenue. For information about the port, contact the **Canaveral Port Authority** (© **888/767-8226** or 321/783-7831; www.portcanaveral.org).

BY AIR   The nearest airport is the **Orlando International Airport** (© **407/ 825-2001;** www.orlandoairports.net), a 45-mile drive from Port Canaveral via the State Road 528 Bee Line Expressway. Cruise line representatives will meet you if you've booked air and/or transfers through the line. **Cocoa Beach Shuttle** (© **800/633-0427** or 321/784-3831) offers shuttle service between Orlando's airport and Port Canaveral; the trip costs $22 per person each way.

BY CAR   Port Canaveral and Cocoa Beach are about 45 miles east of Orlando and 186 miles north of Miami. They're accessible from virtually every interstate highway along the East Coast. Most visitors arrive via Route 1, Interstate 95, or State Road 528. At the port, park in the North Lots for north terminals nos. 5 and 10 and the South Lots for nos. 2, 3, or 4. Parking costs $10 a day for vehicles up to 20 feet, $20 a day for vehicles 20 feet and over.

EXPLORING CAPE CANAVERAL & COCOA BEACH

Port Canaveral probably wouldn't be on the cruise industry's radar if it weren't so close to Orlando, and most passengers shuttle directly from theme park to pier rather than spending any significant time here. Nevertheless, anyone interested in the space program and its history should plan to arrive a day early (or stay a day after) to check out Kennedy Space Center and the Astronaut Hall of Fame.

VISITOR INFORMATION   Contact the **Florida Space Coast Office of Tourism,** 8810 Astronaut Blvd./A1A, Suite 102, Cape Canaveral, FL 32920 (© **800/872-1969** or 321/868-1126; fax 321/868-1139; www.space-coast.com). Their office is in the Sheldon Cove building, right on the corner of Central Boulevard and the A1A, and is open Monday to Friday from 8am to 5pm.

GETTING AROUND   For taxis, call **Comfort Travel** (© **800/567-6139** or 321/784-8294) or **Brevard Yellow Cab** (© **321/723-1234**).

THE ORLANDO THEME PARKS

All it took was a sprinkle of pixie dust in the 1970s to begin the almost-magical transformation of Orlando from a large swath of swampland into the most visited tourist destination in the world. Today it's home to three giants—Walt Disney World, Universal Orlando, and SeaWorld—whose local offerings include seven of the eight most popular theme parks in the United States.

Many cruises from Port Canaveral are sold as land-sea packages that include park stays, but if you decide to visit Orlando before or after your cruise, it's essential to plan ahead. Otherwise, the number of attractions begging for your time and the hyper-commercial atmosphere can put a serious dent in your psyche as well as your wallet and stamina. Even if you had 2 weeks, it wouldn't be long enough to hit everything, so don't even try. Stay selective, stay sane. That's our motto.

It would take a significant portion of this book to detail everything to do in Orlando, but we list some basic information on the major theme parks below. If you plan to spend a considerable amount of time here, we suggest picking up a copy of *Frommer's Walt Disney World & Orlando 2004.*

WALT DISNEY WORLD

Walt Disney World is the umbrella above four theme parks: the **Magic Kingdom, Epcot, Disney–MGM Studios,** and **Animal Kingdom,** which combined drew over 37 million guests in 2002 despite a decline in international visitors, according to *Amusement Business* magazine. Besides its theme parks, Disney has an assortment of other venues, including three water parks, several entertainment venues, and a number of shopping spots.

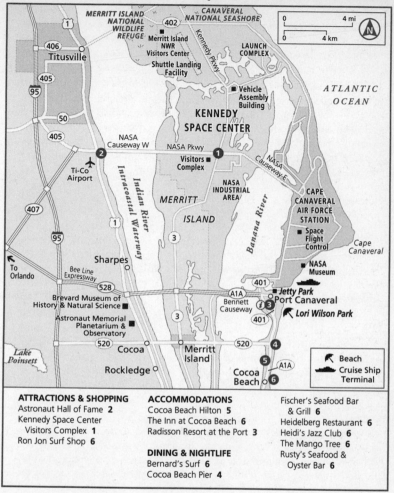

ATTRACTIONS & SHOPPING
Astronaut Hall of Fame **2**
Kennedy Space Center
 Visitors Complex **1**
Ron Jon Surf Shop **6**

ACCOMMODATIONS
Cocoa Beach Hilton **5**
The Inn at Cocoa Beach **6**
Radisson Resort at the Port **3**

DINING & NIGHTLIFE
Bernard's Surf **6**
Cocoa Beach Pier **4**

Fischer's Seafood Bar
 & Grill **6**
Heidelberg Restaurant **6**
Heidi's Jazz Club **6**
The Mango Tree **6**
Rusty's Seafood &
 Oyster Bar **6**

VISITOR INFORMATION Located southwest of Orlando off Interstate 4, west of the Florida Turnpike. For information, vacation brochures, and videos, call ✆ **407/934-7639;** for general information, call ✆ 407/824-2222; www. disneyworld.com.

TICKET PRICES At press time, **1-day/1-park tickets,** for admission to the Magic Kingdom, Epcot, Animal Kingdom, or Disney–MGM, were $52 for adults, $42 for children 3 to 9. And those prices don't include Orlando's 6% sales tax. (Ouch!) Discounted multiday, multipark passes are available; many land-sea cruise packages include these passes.

OPERATING HOURS Park hours vary and are influenced by special events and the economy, so call ahead or go to **www.disneyworld.com** to check. Generally, expect Animal Kingdom to be open from 8 or 9am to 5 or 6pm; Epcot to be open 10am to 9pm; and Magic Kingdom and Disney–MGM to be open 9am to 5 or 7pm. All may open or close earlier or later.

The Parks

MAGIC KINGDOM   The most popular theme park on the planet offers some 40 attractions, plus restaurants and shops, in a 107-acre package. Its symbol, Cinderella Castle, forms the hub of a wheel whose spokes reach to seven "lands" simulating everything from an Amazonian jungle to Colonial America. If you're traveling with little kids, this is the place to go.

EPCOT   This 260-acre park (the acronym stands for Experimental Prototype Community of Tomorrow) has two sections. **Future World** is centered on Epcot's icon, a giant geosphere that looks like a big golf ball. Major corporations sponsor the park's 10 themed areas, and the focus is on discovery, scientific achievements, and tomorrow's technologies in areas running from energy to undersea exploration. The **World Showcase** is a community of 11 miniaturized nations surrounding a 40-acre lagoon. All of these "countries" have indigenous architecture, landscaping, restaurants, and shops; and cultural facets are explored in art exhibits, dance or other live performances, and innovative films. This park definitely appeals more to adults than children, but it has few thrill rides. If that's a requirement, go elsewhere. *Note:* Hiking through this park will often exhaust even the fittest person—some folks say Epcot really stands for "Every Person Comes Out Tired"—so we recommend splitting your visit over 2 days if possible.

DISNEY–MGM STUDIOS   You'll probably spy the Earful Tower—a water tower outfitted with gigantic mouse ears—before you enter this 110-acre park, which Disney bills as "the Hollywood that never was and always will be." You'll find pulse-quickening rides such as the Aerosmith-themed **Rock 'n' Roller Coaster** and the **Twilight Zone of Terror,** and movie- and TV-themed shows such as **Jim Henson's Muppet*Vision 3D,** as well as some wonderful street performers. Adults and kids both love it, and, best of all, it can be done comfortably in 1 day.

ANIMAL KINGDOM   This 500-acre park opened in 1998, combining animals, elaborate landscapes, and a handful of rides. It's a conservation venue as much as an attraction, though, so it's easy for most of the animals to escape your eyes here (unlike at Tampa's Busch Gardens, the state's other major animal park). The thrill rides are better at Busch, but Animal Kingdom has much better shows, such as **Tarzan Rocks!** and **Festival of the Lion King.** The park is good for both adults and children and can be done in a single outing, but if you come on a hot summer day, come early or it's unlikely you'll see many of the primo animals, who are smart enough to seek shade.

UNIVERSAL ORLANDO

Universal Orlando is Disney World's number-one competitor in the ongoing Orlando area "anything you can do we can do better" theme brawl. Although it's a distant second in terms of attendance, it's unquestionably the champion at entertaining teenagers and the older members of the thrill-ride crowd, with two major parks—the original **Universal Studios Florida** and the newer **Islands of Adventure**—plus an entertainment district and several resorts.

VISITOR INFORMATION   Located at Universal Boulevard, Orlando, off Interstate 4. For information, call © **800/837-2273** or 407/363-8000; www. universalorlando.com.

TICKET PRICES   A **1-day/1-park ticket** costs $52 (plus 6% sales tax!) for adults, $43 for children 3 to 9; a Universal Orlando Bonus Pass gets you 5 consecutive days at Universal Studios and Islands of Adventure for $90 for adults, $77 for children 3 to 9 (available online only).

OPERATING HOURS   The parks are open 365 days a year, generally from 9am to 6pm, though often later, especially in summer and around holidays, when they're sometimes open until 9pm. Call before you go for hours on the days you're visiting.

The Parks

UNIVERSAL STUDIOS FLORIDA   Even with fast-paced, grown-up rides such as **Back to the Future, Terminator,** and **Men in Black Alien Attack,** Universal Studios Florida is fun for kids. And as a plus, it's a working motion-picture and TV studio, so occasionally filming is being done at Nickelodeon's sound stages or elsewhere in the park. A talented group of actors portraying a range of characters from Universal films usually roam the park. You can do the park in a day, although you'll be a bit breathless when you get to the finish line.

ISLANDS OF ADVENTURE   This 110-acre theme park opened in 1999 and it is, bar none, *the* Orlando theme park for thrill-ride junkies. With areas themed on Dr. Seuss, Jurassic Park, and Marvel comics, the park successfully combines nostalgia with state-of-the-art technology. Roller coasters roar above pedestrian walkways and water rides slice through the park. **The Amazing Adventures of Spider-Man** is a 3-D track ride that is arguably the best all-around attraction in Orlando; the **Jurassic Park River Adventure**'s 70-foot drop scared creator Steven Spielberg into jumping ship before going over; and **Dueling Dragons** draws more raves from coaster crazies than any other in Orlando. Unless it's the height of high season, the park can be done in a day. It is not, however, a park for families with young kids: 9 of the park's 14 major rides have height restrictions. If, however, you have teens, or are an adrenaline junkie, this is definitely the place for you.

SEAWORLD

VISITOR INFORMATION   The park entrance is at the intersection of Interstate 4 and State Road 528 (the Bee Line Expressway), 10 minutes south of downtown Orlando and 15 minutes from Orlando International Airport. For information, call © **800/423-8368** or 407/351-3600; www.seaworld.com).

TICKET PRICES   A **1-day ticket** costs $52 for ages 10 and over, $43 for children 3 to 9, plus 6% sales tax; age 2 and under, free.

OPERATING HOURS   The park is usually open 9am to at least 6pm, and later during summer and holidays when there are additional shows at night.

A 200-acre marine-life park, SeaWorld explores the deep in a format that combines conservation awareness with entertainment—pretty much what Disney is attempting at Animal Kingdom, but SeaWorld got here first, and its message is subtler and a more integrated part of the experience. The park is fun for everyone from small children to adults (who doesn't like dolphins and whales?) and is easily toured in a single day. The pace is much more laid-back than at Universal or Disney, so it makes for a nice break if you're in the area for several days. SeaWorld has a handful of high-tech roller coasters such as **Journey to Atlantis** and **Kraken,** but all in all, the park can't compete in this category with Disney and Universal. On the other hand, those parks don't let you discover the crushed-velvet texture of a stingray or the song of a sea lion, not to mention the killer whale **Shamu,** the park's star attraction, and the six other resident Orcas.

KENNEDY SPACE CENTER & THE ASTRONAUT HALL OF FAME

Set amid 150,000 acres of marshy wetlands favored by birds, reptiles, and amphibians, the **Kennedy Space Center** (© 321/449-4444; www.kennedy spacecenter.com) is where astronauts left for the moon in 1969, where the shuttles have lifted off since 1981 (including the ill-fated *Columbia* in 2003), and where America's components of the International Space Station are sent into orbit. Even if you've never really considered yourself a science or space buff, you can't help but be impressed by the achievements the place represents.

Security restrictions mean that most of the center is off-limits, but the **Visitors Complex** is designed to offer a glimpse of the works, with real NASA spacecraft; exhibits; hands-on activities for kids; a daily Q & A with a real astronaut; IMAX movies; a Space Shuttle mock-up; a Launch Status Center where presentations are given on current shuttle missions; an outdoor rocket garden displaying now-obsolete Redstone, Atlas, Saturn, and Titan rockets; and more. There's also the obligatory gift shop and several ridiculously pricey stops where you can grab a bite. Plan to eat before or after your visit.

Some visitors stick to the visitor center, but for a more complete insight into the space age, take the **bus tour** of the larger complex. Buses depart at 15-minute intervals, but the wait to get aboard can easily take an hour or more, so figure this into your planning. In the past, buses have stopped at three sites around the complex, with visitors allowed to spend as much time at each as they liked before catching the next bus back; but at press time, new security restrictions had put Launch Complex 39 and the International Space Station Center off-limits, leaving only one stop still open to the public—the **Apollo/Saturn V Center.** Here, visitors experience a narrated simulation of the Apollo 8 launch while looking into an actual Mission Control room that was used for the mission. Following the show, visitors enter an enormous hall where an entire Saturn V rocket is on display, held up horizontally by huge metal supports. Numerous exhibits cover various aspects of the Apollo program, and a lunar module hangs from the ceiling above the snack bar.

A privately owned operation until 2002, the **Astronaut Hall of Fame,** located 6 miles west of the Space Center visitors complex on State Road 405, near the intersection with U.S. 1, focuses on the heroic human element of the space program, and holds the world's largest collection of astronaut memorabilia. Film presentations introduce visitors to the origins of rocketry and to the sheer power of the rockets themselves; displays of personal memorabilia offer insight into the astronauts' lives; and displays of NASA memorabilia are just plain awesome: actual Mission Control terminals at which you can sit to access interactive information; Jim Lovell's logbook from Gemini VII; and, most mind-blowing of all, the actual Apollo 14 command module *Kitty Hawk,* whose plaque bears the inscription "This spacecraft flew to the moon and back January 31 February 9, 1971." Nuff said.

But let's get down to brass tacks. The Astronaut Hall of Fame offers one main thing the rest of the KSC Visitors Complex doesn't: the chance to pretend you're an astronaut through various simulations. In the **G-force simulator,** two wannabe spacemen at a time are strapped tightly into pods at opposite ends of what looks like a giant barbell, which then whirls around on its axis so fast that your cheeks start to flap, just like in the movies. A film projected in the pod simulates a high-speed test flight. Just across the room, the **3D 360 simulator** takes a group of passengers on a simulated shuttle flight from Earth to the new International Space Station, along the way pitching you backward, forward, sideways, and upside down. At the **Walk on the Moon simulator,** visitors are strapped into a harness, which is then counterbalanced to their weight so that they can bounce around as if weightless, doing their "one small step for man" imitation. Next door, the **Mission to Mars simulator** bumps you over the surface of the red planet in a rover. Not bad, but of the group, it's the simulator to skip if you've got limited time. Now, the warnings: Simulators are off-limits to folks under 48 inches, which is okay because smaller kids would probably freak out anyway. Also, if you tend to suffer from motion sickness, you'll probably want to avoid everything except the weightlessness simulation. Lastly, on the off-chance you're there on a slow day, be sure to allow at least a few minutes between simulations, even if you've got a cast-iron constitution. Trust us on this one.

Kennedy Space Center is accessible via State Road 405, just off U.S. 1. The Visitors Complex, including the Astronaut Hall of Fame, is open daily, except Christmas and certain launch days, from 9am to 5:30pm. The last bus tour departs at 2:15pm at the Visitors Complex. Admission to the Visitors Complex is $28 adults, $18 children 3 to 11, and to the Hall of Fame, $14 adults, $10 children. Combined tickets are available for $33 adults, $23 children. Parking at the Visitors Complex and Hall of Fame is free, and there is no shuttle between the two. Be sure to pick up maps as you enter each branch, and expect to spend most of the day to get a full experience.

HITTING THE BEACH

Though the Cape Canaveral/Cocoa Beach area doesn't have the spectacular beach culture of Miami, it doesn't lack for pleasant coastline. The following beaches (or "parks" in the local lingo) are located within an easy drive of the port area.

Closest to the cruise ship port and actually part of the larger port complex, the clean, nicely landscaped **Jetty Park,** 400 E. Jetty Rd. (© **321/783-7111; www.jettypark.com**), is the most elaborate and possibly the nicest of the local beaches, perched at a point from which the whole expanse of the Cape Canaveral/Cocoa Beach coastline stretches away to the south. It's some view. A massive stone jetty juts seaward as protection for the mouth of Port Canaveral, and alongside is an elevated platform from which fishermen dangle their lines right into the surf. A snack bar, bathrooms, showers, picnic facilities, a children's playground, and fishing and beach equipment rental are available. Parking costs $3 per car. Follow the signs after entering the port area, near where State Road 528 and the A1A intersect.

A series of beaches are accessible (and generally signposted) off the A1A heading south from the port. The **Cocoa Beach Pier** area, off the A1A at Meade Avenue, is a great surfing spot with volleyball, an open-air bar, and a party atmosphere. **Lori Wilson Park,** farther south at 1500 N. Atlantic Ave., is another nicely landscaped area on the order of Jetty Park, with bathrooms and showers; a rustic boardwalk with some shaded picnic areas and benches; a nature center; and The Hammock, a ¼-mile boardwalk nature trail that winds through ferns, twisted trees, and other *Jurassic Park*-looking foliage, while butterflies flutter by and spiders eye them from their webs. Parking is free.

SHOPPING

Let's be unkind: You could shop here, but why bother? The offerings in Cape Canaveral and Cocoa Beach are mostly the kind of national mall shops that you've probably got at home, so save your energy and dollars for the Caribbean.

An exception—as much for the experience as for the goods—is the **Ron Jon Surf Shop,** 4151 N. Atlantic Ave./A1A (© **321/799-8888;** www.ronjons.com). Inside the pink and green, South Beach–looking Art Deco building is enough au courant beachwear to transform you and a good-size army into surfer dudes. The store also rents beach bikes, body boards, surfboards, kayaks, beach chairs, and other equipment by the hour, day, or week. It's open 24 hours a day, 365 days a year.

WHERE TO STAY

Only a 5-minute drive from the port, **Radisson Resort at the Port,** 8701 Astronaut Blvd./A1A (© **800/333-3333** or 321/784-0000; www.radisson.com/cape canaveralfl), offers comfortable rooms and very comfortable two-room suites that are a great option for families, featuring a kitchenette with microwave, fridge, and place settings; living room with sofa bed and giant TV; and bedroom with a Jacuzzi and second giant TV. The great jungle-motif front courtyard has a large amoeba-shaped pool and a second courtyard has tennis courts. Cruise passengers who are arriving by car can leave their vehicles free in the hotel's lot during their cruise and take the free Radisson shuttle to and from the port. Rates: $109 rooms; $129 suites.

At the other end of the spectrum, **The Inn at Cocoa Beach,** 4300 Ocean Beach Blvd., just off the A1A behind the Ron Jon Surf Shop (© **800/343-5307** or 321/799-3460; www.theinnatcocoabeach.com), is almost entirely couples-oriented, presenting itself as more of a personalized inn than a traditional hotel. Almost all of its 50 comfortable, B&B-style rooms face the ocean, with rocking chairs on their balconies and king- or queen-size beds, TVs, and large bathrooms. A bar off the lobby operates on the honor system (just sign for what you take), and two lobby dogs and six tropical birds in cages around the property add to the homey, low-key atmosphere. Rates: $90 to $250.

Located near Lori Wilson Park on the A1A (and, for you '60s TV fans, near a street called I Dream of Jeannie Lane), the **Cocoa Beach Hilton,** 1550 N. Atlantic Ave./A1A (© **800/526-2609** or 321/799-0003; www.cocoabeach hilton.com), is the most upscale of the beachfront mainstream hotels, though it looks more like a downtown business hotel that's been transplanted to the seashore. Rooms are spacious but have smallish picture windows only; none offers a balcony. Rates: $89 to $205.

WHERE TO DINE

In the heart of Cocoa Beach, the Fischer Family restaurants, **Bernard's Surf, Fischer's Seafood Bar & Grill,** and **Rusty's Seafood & Oyster Bar** (all at © **321/783-2033;** www.bernardssurf.com), are all bunched up together at 2 S. Atlantic Ave., at Minuteman Causeway Road. At Bernard's, opened in 1948, photos testify to the many astronauts—and Russian cosmonauts too—who have celebrated their safe return to Earth with the restaurant's steak and seafood, the latter provided by the Fischer family's own boats. Fischer's Seafood Bar & Grill is a *Cheers*-like lounge popular with the locals, serving fried combo platters, shrimp and crab claw meat, and the like. Rusty's is another casual option, with spicy seafood gumbo, raw or steamed oysters, burgers and sandwiches, pasta, and so on. Another Rusty's branch is on the south side of Port Canaveral harbor at 628 Glen Cheek Dr. (© **321/783-2033**), serving the same menu but with views of the fishing boats and cruise ships heading in and out of the port. Bernard's main courses $15 to $25; Fischer's main courses $9 to $16, sandwiches and salads $4 to $8; Rusty's main courses $10 to $20, sandwiches and salads $4 to $9.

The Mango Tree, 118 N. Atlantic Ave./A1A, between N. 1st and N. 2nd streets (© **321/799-0513**), is the most beautiful and sophisticated restaurant in Cocoa Beach, serving gourmet seafood, pasta, chicken, and continental dishes in a plantation-home atmosphere. Dinner main courses: $14 to $30.

In downtown Cocoa Beach, the **Heidelberg Restaurant,** 7 N. Orlando Ave./ A1A at the Minuteman Causeway (© **321/783-6806**), serves German and Continental dinner cuisine such as beef filet stroganoff, goulash, roast duck, sauerbraten, and grilled loin pork chops in a middling-elegant atmosphere. The adjoining Heidi's Jazz Club (see "Port Canaveral After Dark," below) has music nightly except Mondays. Dinner main courses: $16 to $23.

PORT CANAVERAL AFTER DARK

The Cocoa Beach Pier, 401 Meade Ave., off the A1A, a ½-mile north of State Road 520 (© **321/783-7549**; www.cocoabeachpier.com), juts out 800 feet over the Atlantic, offering a casual beer-and-fruity-drinks atmosphere, an open-air bar with live music most nights, an ice-cream shop, sit-down seafood restaurants, and an arcade, plus beach equipment rentals and volleyball right next door on the sand.

At the Heidelberg restaurant (see "Where to Dine," above), **Heidi's Jazz Club,** 7 N. Orlando Ave./A1A at the Minuteman Causeway (© **321/783-4559**; www.heidisjazzclub.com), offers live jazz and blues Tuesday through Sunday, with featured performers on selected Friday and Saturday evenings and an open jam session Sundays at 7pm. See their website for a schedule of performances.

4 Tampa

Tampa was a sleepy port until Cuban immigrants founded Ybor City's cigar industry in the 1880s. A few years later, Henry B. Plant built a railroad to carry tourists into town and constructed his garish Tampa Bay Hotel (now the Henry B. Plant Museum). During the Spanish-American War, Teddy Roosevelt trained his Rough Riders here and walked the Ybor City streets with Cuban revolutionary José Marti. A land boom in the 1920s gave the city its charming, Victorian-style Hyde Park suburb (now a gentrified area, just across the Hillsborough River from downtown), and the go-go 1980s and 1990s brought skyscrapers, a convention center, a performing-arts center, and lots of shopping and dining options to the downtown area.

On the western shore of Tampa Bay, **St. Petersburg** is the picturesque and pleasant flip side of Tampa's busy business, industrial, and shipping life. Originally conceived and built primarily for tourists and wintering snowbirds, it's got a nice downtown area, some quality museums, and a few good restaurants.

The **Port of Tampa** is set amid a complicated network of channels and harbors near historic Ybor City and its deepwater Ybor Channel. Ships sailing from here head primarily to the western Caribbean, the Yucatán, and Central America.

GETTING TO TAMPA & THE PORT

The **Tampa Port Authority** is located at 1101 Channelside Dr. (© **813/905-7678**; www.tampaport.com). Cruise Terminal 2 is located at 651 Channelside Dr.; Terminal 3, 815 Channelside Dr.; Terminal 6, 1333 McKay St.; and Terminal 7, 2303 Guy N. Verger Blvd.

BY AIR   Tampa International Airport (© **813/870-8700**) lies 5 miles west of downtown Tampa, near the junction of Florida 60 and Memorial Highway.

If you haven't arranged transfers with the cruise line, the port is an easy 15-minute taxi ride away; the fare is $17 per person via **Central Florida Limo** (© 813/396-3730). **Travel Ways** (© 800/888-1428) also runs a bus service, which costs $16 per person from the airport to Garrison Seaport Center.

BY CAR Tampa lies 188 miles southwest of Jacksonville, 50 miles north of Sarasota, and 245 miles northwest of Miami. From I-75 and I-4: To Terminals 2 and 6 take I-4 West to Exit 1 (Ybor City), go South on 21st Street, then turn right on Adamo Drive (Hwy. 60) and then left on Channelside Drive; for Terminal 7 go south on 21st Street (21st St. merges with 22nd St. after crossing Adamo Dr.), turn right on Maritime Boulevard, and then go left on Guy N. Verger to Hooker's Point. From Tampa International Airport: To Terminals 2 and 6, follow signs to I-275 North, go to I-4 East and then to Exit 1 (Ybor City), go South on 21st Street, turn right on Adamo Drive (Hwy. 60), and then turn left on Channelside Drive; for Terminal 7, use directions from I-75 above. The port has ample parking (at $8 per day), with good security.

EXPLORING TAMPA

Tampa is best explored by car, as only the commercial district can be covered on foot. If you want to go to the beach, you'll have to head to neighboring St. Petersburg.

VISITOR INFORMATION Contact the **Tampa/Hillsborough Convention and Visitors Association, Inc. (THCVA),** 400 N. Tampa St., Suite 1010, Tampa, FL 33602 (© 800/44-TAMPA or 813/223-2752; www.visittampabay. com). You can also stop by the **Tampa Bay Visitor Information Center,** 3601 E. Busch Blvd. (© 813/985-3601), north of downtown in the Busch Gardens area.

GETTING AROUND Taxis in Tampa do not normally cruise the streets for fares; instead, they line up at public loading places, such as the airport, cruise terminal, and major hotels. **Yellow Cab** (© 813/253-0121) or **United Cab** (© 813/253-2424 or 813/251-5555) charge about $1.75 per mile.

The **Hillsborough Area Regional Transit/HARTline** (© 813/254-HART) provides regularly scheduled bus service between downtown Tampa and the suburbs. Fares are $1.15 for local services and $1.50 for express routes; exact change is required.

ATTRACTIONS

BUSCH GARDENS Yes, admission prices are high, but Busch Gardens remains Tampa Bay's most popular attraction. The 335-acre family entertainment park, at 3000 E. Busch Blvd. (© 888/800-5447 or 813/987-5171; www. buschgardens.com), features thrill rides, animal habitats, live entertainment, shops, restaurants, and games. The park's zoo ranks among the best in the country, with nearly 3,400 animals.

Montu, the world's tallest and longest inverted roller coaster, is part of **Egypt,** the park's ninth themed area, which also includes a replica of King Tutankhamen's tomb and a sand-dig area for kids. **Timbuktu** is a replica of an ancient desert trading center, complete with African craftspeople at work. It also features a sandstorm ride, Dolphin theater with daily shows, a boat-swing ride, a roller coaster, and a video-game arcade. **Morocco,** a walled city with exotic architecture, has Moroccan craft demonstrations and a sultan's tent with snake charmers. **The Congo** features white-water raft rides; Kumba, the largest steel

Tampa

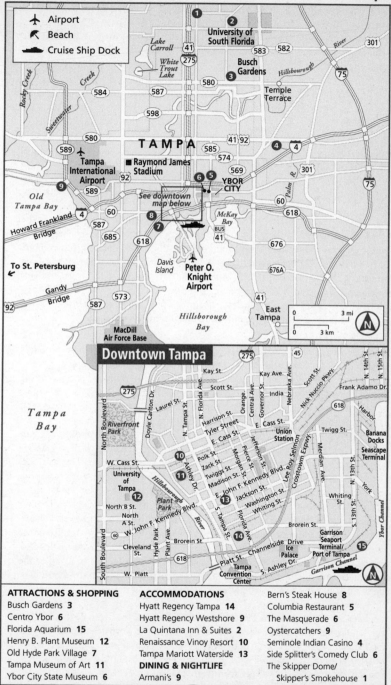

Airport

Beach

Cruise Ship Dock

Lake Carroll

White Trout Lake

Rocky Creek

Sweetwater Creek

584

587

598

580

Tampa International Airport

Old Tampa Bay

Howard Frankland Bridge

To St. Petersburg

Gandy Bridge

589

589

60

587

685

573

587

92

4

T A M P A

Raymond James Stadium

See downtown map below

Davis Island

MacDill Air Force Base

Peter O. Knight Airport

Hillsborough Bay

1

2

University of South Florida

Busch Gardens

3

Temple Terrace

583

582

301

75

580

587

574

585

569

301

92

41

41

92

4

4

618

60

676

676A

41

East Tampa

YBOR CITY

McKay Bay

BUS 41

75

618

0   3 mi
0   3 km
N

Downtown Tampa

Tampa Bay

275

45

Kay St.

Scott St.

Kay Ave.

India

Frank Adamo Dr.

275

North Boulevard

Riverfront Park

Doyle Carlton Dr.

Laurel St.

N. Tampa Ave.

N. Florida Ave.

Harrison St.

Tyler Street

E. Cass St.

Polk St.

Zack St.

Twiggs St.

Madison St.

Ashley Dr.

Hillsborough River

Plant Park

University of Tampa

North B St.

North A St.

W. Cass St.

W. John F. Kennedy Blvd.

Cleveland St.

Hyde Park Ave.

Plant Ave.

Brorein St.

60

South Boulevard

618

W. Platt

Platt St.

Tampa Convention Center

Orange

Central Ave.

Governor St.

Pierce St.

Jefferson St.

Morgan St.

E. John F. Kennedy Blvd.

Jackson St.

Washington St.

Whiting St.

S. Tampa St.

Florida Ave.

S. Ashley Dr.

Channelside Drive

Ice Palace

Union Station

Nebraska Ave.

Scott St.

Nick Nuccio Pkwy.

Lee Roy Selmon Crosstown Expwy.

Twigg St.

Meridian Ave.

Brorein St.

Garrison Seaport Terminal/ Port of Tampa

618

Harbor

Banana Docks

Seascape Terminal

N. 14th St.

N. 15th St.

N. 13th St.

S. 13th St.

Whiting St.

York

Ybor Channel

Garrison Channel

10

11

12

13

14

15

N

ATTRACTIONS & SHOPPING
Busch Gardens 3
Centro Ybor 6
Florida Aquarium 15
Henry B. Plant Museum 12
Old Hyde Park Village 7
Tampa Museum of Art 11
Ybor City State Museum 6

ACCOMMODATIONS
Hyatt Regency Tampa 14
Hyatt Regency Westshore 9
La Quintana Inn & Suites 2
Renaissance Vinoy Resort 10
Tampa Mariott Waterside 13
DINING & NIGHTLIFE
Armani's 9

Bern's Steak House 8
Columbia Restaurant 5
The Masquerade 6
Oystercatchers 9
Seminole Indian Casino 4
Side Splitter's Comedy Club 6
The Skipper Dome/
  Skipper's Smokehouse 1

roller coaster in the southeastern United States; and Claw Island, a display of rare white Bengal tigers in a natural setting.

Rhino Rally is the newest addition. It's an off-road adventure in 16-passenger "Ralliers," or Land Rovers, that travel a bumpy course that allows views of Asian elephants, buffalo, antelope, and more. Hang onto your hat when a flash flood whisks away the bridge—and your vehicle.

The Serengeti Plain is an open area with more than 500 African animals roaming in herds. This 80-acre natural grassy veldt can be viewed from the tram ride, the Trans-Veldt Railway, or the Skyride. **Nairobi** is home to a natural habitat for various species of gorillas and chimpanzees, a baby-animal nursery, a petting zoo, reptile displays, and Curiosity Caverns, where visitors can observe animals active at night. **Bird Gardens,** the original core of Busch Gardens, offers rich foliage, lagoons, and a free-flight aviary holding hundreds of exotic birds, including golden and American bald eagles, hawks, owls, and falcons. This area also features Land of the Dragons, a children's adventure.

Crown Colony, a multilevel restaurant overlooking the Serengeti Plain, is the home of a team of Clydesdale horses, as well as the Anheuser-Busch hospitality center. **Akbar's Adventure Tours,** which offers a flight simulator, is located here.

To get to the Gardens, take Interstate 275 northeast of downtown to Busch Boulevard (Exit 33), and go east 2 miles to the entrance on 40th Street (McKinley Ave.). Admission is $52 for adults and $43 for kids 3 to 9 (plus 7% tax). Parking is $7. Park hours are at least 10am to 6pm; hours are extended during summer. See the website for opening and closing times.

OTHER ATTRACTIONS   Only steps from the Garrison Seaport Center, the **Florida Aquarium** (✆ 813/273-4000; www.flaquarium.net) celebrates the role of water in the development and maintenance of Florida's topography and ecosystems, with more than 10,000 aquatic plants and animals. An overriding theme follows a drop of water as it bubbles through Florida limestone and winds its way to the sea. Admission is $15 for ages 13 and older, $12 for seniors, and $10 for children 3 to 12. Children under 2 are admitted free.

Thirteen silver minarets and distinctive Moorish architecture make the stunning **Henry B. Plant Museum,** 401 W. Kennedy Blvd. (✆ 813/254-1891; www.plantmuseum.com), the focal point of the Tampa skyline. This national historic landmark, built in 1891 as the Tampa Bay Hotel, is filled with European and Oriental furnishings and decorative arts from the original hotel collection.

Ybor City is only about a mile or so from the cruise ship docks. It's Tampa's historic Latin enclave and one of only three national historic districts in Florida. Once known as the cigar capital of the world, Ybor offers a charming slice of the past with its Spanish architecture, antique street lamps, wrought-iron balconies, ornate grillwork, and renovated cigar factories. Stroll along 7th Avenue, the main artery (closed to traffic at night), where you'll find cigar shops, boutiques, nightclubs, and the famous 100-year-old **Columbia Restaurant** (see "Where to Dine," below).

The **Ybor City Museum State Park,** 1818 9th Ave., between 18th and 19th streets (✆ 813/247-6323; www.ybormuseum.org), is primarily devoted to the area's cigar history, with a collection of cigar labels, cigar memorabilia, and works by local artisans. Admission is $2 per person. Children under 6 are admitted free. The museum is open daily from 9am to 5pm.

At **Centro Ybor,** a shopping/entertainment complex between 7th and 8th avenues and 16th and 17th streets (✆ 813/242-4660; www.thecentroybor.com), you'll find a multiscreen cinema, several restaurants, a comedy club, a large open-air bar, a bunch of typical mall-type stores, and GameWorks, a high-tech entertainment center designed by Steven Spielberg's Dreamworks and Universal Studios. The Ybor City Chamber of Commerce has its **Cigar Museum & Visitor Center** here (on 8th Ave. next to Centro Espanol).

The permanent collection of the **Tampa Museum of Art,** 600 N. Ashley Dr. (© **813/274-8130;** www.tampamuseum.com), is especially strong in ancient Greek, Etruscan, and Roman artifacts, as well as 20th-century art. The museum grounds, fronting the Hillsborough River, contain a sculpture garden and a decorative fountain. It's open 10am to 5pm Tuesday to Saturday (till 8pm every 3rd Thurs), and 1 to 5pm on Sunday. Admission is $7 adults, $6 seniors, $3 for students with ID cards and children over 6, and free for kids under 6.

ORGANIZED TOURS

BY BUS   Swiss Chalet Tours, 3601 E. Busch Blvd. (© **813/985-3601**), operates guided tours of Tampa, Ybor City, and the surrounding region. Four-hour (10am–2pm) tours run most every day, and cost $40 for adults, $35 for children 3 to 12. Seven-hour tours, which also run virtually every day (10am–5pm), visit Tampa, Clearwater, and St. Petersburg. Cost is $70 for adults and $65 for children. Reservations for both tours must be made 1 day in advance.

ON FOOT   Ybor City walking tours are available through the **Ybor City Museum** (see "Other Attractions," above). Tours are $5 for ages 6 and older.

HITTING THE BEACH

You have to start at **St. Petersburg,** across the bay, for a north-to-south string of interconnected white sandy shores. Most beaches have restrooms, refreshment stands, and picnic areas. You can either park on the street at meters (usually 25¢ for each half-hour) or at one of the four major parking lots located from north to south at **Sand Key Park** in Clearwater, beside Gulf Boulevard (also known as Rte. 699), just south of the Clearwater Pass Bridge; **Redington Shores Beach Park,** beside Gulf Boulevard at 182nd Street; **Treasure Island Park,** on Gulf Boulevard just north of 108th Avenue; and **St. Pete Beach Park,** beside Gulf Boulevard at 46th Street.

SHOPPING

On and around 7th Avenue in Ybor City, you'll find lots of **cigar stores** selling handmade stogies, as well as a variety of interesting boutiques and shops.

Some 60 upscale shops, plus restaurants and movie theaters, are located at **Old Hyde Park Village,** an outdoor, European-style market at Swann and Dakota avenues near Bayshore Boulevard (© **813/251-3500;** http://oldhyde parkvillage.com). There's nothing particularly "Tampa" about it, but if you need a new Brooks Brothers suit or Ann Taylor dress for your cruise, it'll do.

WHERE TO STAY

TAMPA   Tampa has two Hyatts. The **Hyatt Regency Westshore,** 6200 Courtney Campbell Causeway (© **800/233-1234** or 813/874-1234; http://grand tampabay.hyatt.com), sits in a 35-acre wildlife preserve at the Tampa end of the long causeway traversing Tampa Bay, about 2 miles from the airport and 8 miles from downtown. In addition to regular rooms and suites, 45 Spanish-style town houses/villas are set about a ½-mile from the main hotel building. Rates: $175 to $255. The **Hyatt Regency Tampa,** Two Tampa City Center at 211 N. Tampa St. (© **800/233-1234** or 813/225-1234; http://tamparegency.hyatt.com), sits in Tampa's commercial center and caters mostly to the corporate crowd. Rates:

$125 to $219. The other big downtown hotel, the **Tampa Marriott Waterside,** 700 S. Florida Ave. (℗ **800/228-9290** or 813/221-4900; www.marriotthotels. com), opened in 2000. About half of the rooms have balconies overlooking the bay or city (the best views are high up on the south side). Rates: $129 to $189.

La Quinta Inn & Suites, 3701 E. Fowler Ave. (℗ **800/687-6667** or 813/ 910-7500; www.laquinta.com), is a motel with a pinch of upscale. Rooms have coffeemakers and dataports, and the place is located only 1½ miles from Busch Gardens. Rates: $90 to $110.

ST. PETERSBURG Overlooking Tampa Bay, the **Renaissance Vinoy Resort,** 501 Fifth Ave. NE, at Beach Drive (℗ **800/HOTELS1** or 727/894-1000; www. renaissancehotels.com), is the grande dame of the region's hotels. Built as the grand Vinoy Park in 1925, this elegant Spanish-style establishment reopened in 1992 after a meticulous $93-million restoration. Many of the guest rooms offer lovely views of the bay. Accommodations in the new wing ("The Tower") are slightly larger than those in the hotel's original core. Rates: $199 to $349.

WHERE TO DINE

On the 14th floor of the Hyatt Regency Westshore Hotel, **Armani's,** 6200 Courtney Campbell Causeway (℗ **813/207-6800**), is a stylish northern Italian restaurant with a panoramic view of the city skyline and the bay. Jackets are recommended but not required. Dinner main courses: $18 to $35. At **Bern's Steak House,** 1208 S. Howard Ave. (℗ **813/251-2421**), the steaks are close to perfect. You order according to thickness and weight. Dinner main courses: $17 to $60.

In Ybor City, the nearly 100-year-old **Columbia Restaurant,** 2117 7th Ave. E., between 21st and 22nd streets (℗ **813/248-4961**), occupies an attractive tile-sheathed building that fills an entire city block, about a mile from the cruise docks. The aura is pre-Castro Cuba. The simpler your dish is, the better it's likely to be. Filet mignons; roasted pork; and the black beans, yellow rice, and plantains are flavorful and well prepared. Catch a flamenco show on the dance floor Monday through Saturday. Dinner main courses: $15 to $25.

The best fish in Tampa is served at **Oystercatchers,** in the Hyatt Regency Westshore Hotel complex, 6200 Courtney Campbell Causeway (℗ **813/207-6815**). Pick the fish you want from a glass-fronted buffet or enjoy mesquite-grilled steaks, chicken rollatini, and shellfish. Dinner main courses: $20 to $30.

TAMPA AFTER DARK

Nightfall transforms **Ybor City,** Tampa's century-old Latin Quarter, into a hotbed of music, ethnic food, poetry readings, and after-midnight coffee and dessert. Seventh Avenue, one of its main arteries, is closed to all but pedestrian traffic Wednesday through Saturday evenings. **The Masquerade,** 1503 E. 7th Ave. (℗ **813/247-3319**), set in a 1940s movie palace, is just one of the many nightclubs that pepper the streets here. Other options include **Side Splitters Comedy Club,** 12938 N. Dale Mabry Hwy. (℗ **813/960-1197**), which features stand-up pros most nights of the week. Ticket prices are $12 for general admission and $14 for preferred admission.

In North Tampa, **Skipper's Smokehouse,** 910 Skipper Rd., at the corner of Nebraska Avenue (℗ **813/971-0666;** www.skipperssmokehouse.com), is a favorite evening spot, with an all-purpose restaurant and bar (with oysters and fresh shellfish sold by the dozen and half-dozen) and live music back in the Skipper Dome, a sprawling deck sheltered by a canopy of oak trees.

Northeast of town, at Exit 5 off the I-4, the **Seminole Casino,** 5223 N. Orient Rd., at Hillsborough Road (© 813/621-1302; www.casino-tampa.com), is open 24 hours every day of the year, with poker, bingo, and slots.

For more on Tampa nightlife, the Tampa/Hillsborough Arts Council maintains **Artsline** (© 813/229-ARTS), a 24-hour information service about current and upcoming cultural events.

5 New Orleans

New Orleans may be best known as a world-class party town, but by some yardsticks, it's also the busiest seaport in the nation, visited by thousands of cargo vessels transporting grains, ores, machinery, and building supplies, as well as by a number of cruise ships bound for ports in the western Caribbean, including Cancún, Playa del Carmen, and Cozumel. You can watch the parade of cargo ships pass by you as you steam downriver to the ocean, against the backdrop of Louisiana's Mississippi River delta.

GETTING TO NEW ORLEANS & THE PORT

The **Julia Street Cruise Ship Terminal** sits at the foot of Julia Street on the Mississippi River, in the convention center district, a 10-minute walk or a short streetcar or taxi ride away from the edge of the French Quarter. For information, call the **Port of New Orleans** at © 504/522-2551 or check out **www.portno.com**.

BY AIR   **New Orleans International Airport** (© 504/464-0831) is about 15 miles northwest of the port. Cruise line representatives meet all passengers who have booked transfers through the line. For those who haven't, a taxi to the port costs about $28 for two passengers and takes about 45 minutes. **Airport Shuttle** (© 866/596-2699 or 504/592-0555) runs vans at 10- to 12-minute intervals from outside the airport's baggage claim to the port and other points in town. It costs $10 per passenger each way; it's free for children under 6.

BY CAR   Take the I-10 downtown. Take the Tchoupitoulas/St. Peters Street exit, the last one before you cross the Mississippi. Stay to the right, and head toward the New Orleans Convention Center. Turn right onto Convention Center Boulevard, then left onto Henderson Street, which will take you to Port of New Orleans Place. Turn left and continue on to the Cruise Ship Terminal. You can park your car in long-term parking at the port; inquire through your cruise line. You must present a boarding pass or ticket before parking.

EXPLORING NEW ORLEANS

The **French Quarter** is the oldest part of the city and still the most popular for sightseeing. Many visitors never leave its confines, but by venturing outside the Quarter, you'll be able to feel the pulse of the city's commerce, see river activities that keep the city alive, stroll through spacious parks, drive or walk by the impressive homes of the **Garden District,** and get a firsthand view of the bayou/lake connection that explains why New Orleans grew up here in the first place.

VISITOR INFORMATION   Contact the **New Orleans Metropolitan Convention and Visitors Bureau,** 1520 Sugar Bowl Dr., New Orleans, LA 70112 (© 800/672-6124 or 504/566-5011; www.neworleanscvb.com), for brochures, pamphlets, and information. In New Orleans, the **New Orleans Welcome Center** is located at 529 St. Ann St. in the French Quarter (© 800/672-6124). *Note:* The bureau will move into a new building at 2020 St. Charles Ave. in mid-2003. Its phone numbers will remain the same.

GETTING AROUND   Taxis are plentiful. If you're not near a taxi stand, call **United Cabs** (© **504/522-9771**) and a car will come in 5 to 10 minutes. The meter begins at $2.50 plus $1 for each additional person, and rises to $1.60 per mile thereafter.

Streetcar lines run the length of St. Charles Avenue. The nostalgic cars with wooden bench seats operate 24 hours a day and cost $1.25 per ride (you must have exact change). A transfer from streetcar to bus costs 25¢. You board at the corner of Canal and Carondelet streets in the French Quarter, or at intervals along St. Charles. A **VisiTour Pass,** which gives you unlimited rides on all streetcar and bus lines, sells for $5 for 1 day, $12 for 3 days. You can buy passes through selected hotel information counters and retail stores; you'll find a list at **www.regionaltransit.org/passes/buyvisitourpass.php**.

Where the trolleys don't run, a **city bus** will. For route information, call © **504/248-3900** or pick up a map at the Regional Transit Authority office (2817 Canal St.). Most buses charge $1.25 per ride (plus 25¢ for a transfer), although some express buses charge $1.50.

The **Vieux Carré Minibus** takes you to French Quarter sights. The route is posted along Canal and Bourbon streets. The minibus operates weekdays between 5am and 6:30pm, weekends 8am to 6:30pm, and costs $1.25.

From Jackson Square (at Decatur St.), you can take a 2¼-mile, 30-minute **horse-drawn carriage** ride through the French Quarter. **Royal Carriage Tour Co.** (© **504/943-8820**) offers group tours for $10 per person in open-topped surreys suitable for up to eight passengers at a time, daily from 9am to midnight. Private rides for up to four passengers in a Cinderella carriage go for $50 a pop.

ATTRACTIONS

At the well-designed **Aquarium of the Americas,** 1 Canal St., at the Mississippi River (© **800/774-7394** or 504/581-4629), a 400,000-gallon tank holds a kaleidoscope of species from the deep waters of the nearby Gulf of Mexico. Admission is $14 for adults, $10 for seniors, $6.50 for children under 12; open 9:30am to 6pm Sunday through Thursday, 9:30am to 7pm Friday and Saturday.

Incorporating seven historic buildings connected by a brick courtyard, the **Historic New Orleans Collection,** 533 Royal St., between St. Louis and Toulouse (© **504/523-4662**), evokes New Orleans of 200 years ago. The oldest building in the complex escaped the tragic fire of 1794. The others hold exhibitions about Louisiana's culture and history. All are open from 10am to 4:30pm daily. Admission is free.

Founded in 1950, the **New Orleans Pharmacy Museum,** 514 Chartres St., at St. Louis (© **504/565-8027;** www.pharmacymuseum.org), is just what the name implies. In 1823, the first licensed pharmacist in the United States, Louis J. Dufilho, Jr., opened an apothecary shop here. Today you'll find old apothecary bottles, voodoo potions, pill tile, and suppository molds, as well as the old glass cosmetics counter and a jar of leeches, in case you feel the need to be bled. It's open Tuesday through Sunday 10am to 5pm; admission $2 adults, $1 seniors and students, free for children under 12.

Constructed in 1795 through 1799 as the Spanish government seat in New Orleans, **The Cabildo,** 701 Chartres St., at Jackson Square (© **800/568-6968** or 504/568-6968), was the site of the signing of the Louisiana Purchase transfer. It's now the center of the Louisiana State Museum's facilities in the French Quarter, with a multiroom exhibition that traces the history of Louisiana from

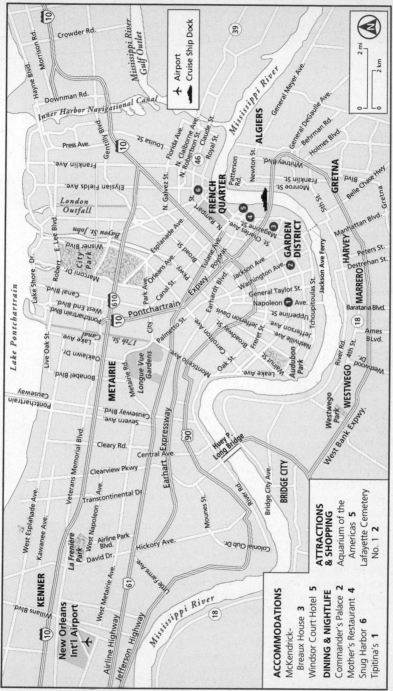

Greater New Orleans

Airport
Cruise Ship Dock

2 mi
2 km

Mississippi River Gulf Outlet

Crowder Rd.

Morrison Rd.

Hayne Blvd.

Downman Rd.

Inner Harbor Navigational Canal

Press Ave.

Franklin Ave.

Gentilly Blvd.

Louisa St.

Florida Ave.

N. Claiborne Ave.

N. Robertson St.

Claude St.

Royal St.

Elysian Fields Ave.

N. Galvez St.

Esplanade Ave.

Broad St.

N. Rampart

Tulane Ave.

Poydras

FRENCH QUARTER

Patterson Rd.

Newton St.

Mississippi River

ALGIERS

General Meyer Ave.

General DeGaulle Ave.

Behrman Rd.

Holmes Blvd.

Whitney Blvd.

Monroe St.

Franklin St.

5th St.

GRETNA

Belle Chase Hwy.

Gretna Blvd.

Manhattan Blvd.

HARVEY

Peters St.

Destrehan St.

MARRERO

Barataria Blvd.

Ames Blvd.

Westwood Dr.

WESTWEGO

River Rd.

West Bank Expwy.

4th St.

London Outfall

City Park

Bayou St. John

Wisner Blvd.

E. Lee Blvd.

Robert E. Lee Blvd.

Marconi Dr.

Lake Shore Dr.

Canal Blvd.

West End Blvd.

Pontchartrain Blvd.

Pontchartrain

City Park Ave.

Orleans Ave.

Canal St.

Esplanade Expwy.

Earhart Blvd.

Jackson Ave.

Washington Ave.

St. Charles Ave.

Magazine St.

GARDEN DISTRICT

General Taylor St.

Napoleon Ave.

Tchoupitoulas St.

Jackson Ave Ferry

Upperline St.

Lake Pontchartrain

610

Palmetto St.

City Pkwy.

Carrollton Ave.

Broadway St.

Jefferson Davis

Nashville Ave.

Jefferson Ave.

Freret St.

Leake Ave.

Walnut St.

Audubon Park

Napoleon Ave.

METAIRIE

Metairie Rd.

Longue Vue Gardens

17th St.

Lake Ave.

Live Oak Dr.

Oaklawn Dr.

Bonabel Blvd.

Pontchartrain Causeway

Severn Ave.

Causeway Blvd.

Cleary Rd.

Central Ave.

Clearview Pkwy

Transcontinental Dr.

Veterans Memorial Blvd.

West Napoleon Ave.

Mounes St.

Earhart Expressway

Westwego Park

Huey P. Long Bridge

Bridge City Ave.

BRIDGE CITY

River Rd.

Colonial Club Dr.

West Esplanade Ave.

Kawanee Ave.

La Freniere Park

Airline Park Blvd.

David Dr.

Hickory Ave.

Little Farms Ave.

KENNER

Willians Blvd.

New Orleans Int'l Airport

West Metairie Ave.

Airline Highway

Jefferson Highway

Mississippi River

61

90

18

18

39

46

10

ACCOMMODATIONS
McKendrick-Breaux House **3**
Windsor Court Hotel **5**

DINING & NIGHTLIFE
Commander's Palace **2**
Mother's Restaurant **4**
Snug Harbor **6**
Tipitina's **1**

ATTRACTIONS & SHOPPING
Aquarium of the Americas **5**
Lafayette Cemetery No. 1 **2**

exploration through Reconstruction, covering all aspects of life, including ante-
bellum music, mourning and burial customs, immigrants, and the changing
roles of women in the South. It's open Tuesday through Sunday 9am to 5pm;
admission $5 adults, $4 students and seniors, free for children under 13.

Also on Jackson Square, **The Presbytère,** 751 Chartres St. (© **800/568-6968**
or 504/568-6968), was planned as housing for the clergy but is now a Mardi
Gras museum that traces the history of the annual event, with everything from
elaborate Mardi Gras Indian costumes to Rex Queen jewelry from the turn of
the century on display. A re-creation of a float allows you to pretend you are
throwing beads to a crowd on a screen in front of you. It's open Tuesday through
Sunday 9am to 5pm; admission $5 adults, $4 seniors and students, free for children under 13.

The collections of the **New Orleans Historic Voodoo Museum,** 724
Dumaine St., at Bourbon (© **504/523-7685** or 504/522-5223), celebrate the
occult and the mixture of African and Catholic rituals first brought to New
Orleans by slaves from Hispaniola. A gift shop and voodoo parlor are stocked
with apothecary ingredients, and the staff can provide you with psychic services.
Admission is $7 for adults; $5.50 for college students, military personnel, and
seniors; $4.50 for high-school kids; and $3.50 for grade-school children. It's
open daily from 10am to 8pm. A new location at 217 North Peter's St. contains
a collection of more contemporary voodoo artifacts.

While we're on the subject of the undead, there's the issue of New Orleans'
cemeteries: Since the city is prone to flooding, bodies have been interred above-
ground since its earliest days, in sometimes very elaborate tombs that are definitely worth a visit. **St. Louis Cemetery No. 1,** Basin Street between Conti and
St. Louis streets, at the top of the French Quarter, is the oldest extant cemetery
(1789) and the most iconic. The acid-dropping scene from *Easy Rider* was shot
here, prompting the city to declare that no film would ever, ever, *ever* be shot
again in one of its cemeteries. In the Garden District, **Lafayette Cemetery
No. 1,** 1427 Sixth St., right across the street from Commander's Palace Restaurant, is another old cemetery that's been beautifully restored. Though both of
these cemeteries are usually full of visitors during the day, you should exercise
caution when touring, as they've seen some crime over the years.

ORGANIZED TOURS

ON FOOT   There are a lot of tours offered in New Orleans, but **Historic New
Orleans Walking Tours** (© **504/947-2120**) is the place to go for authenticity,
offering tours of the French Quarter, the Garden District (including Lafayette
Cemetery), and a cemetery and voodoo tour. Prices are about $10 to $15 per
person.

A daily guided **voodoo-and-cemetery walking tour** of the French Quarter
departs from the original **New Orleans Historic Voodoo Museum,** 724
Dumaine St., led by a folk historian and acclaimed storyteller who calls herself
Bloody Mary (© **504/486-2080**). The walking tours are all $22 and include
museum admission.

BY BUS   Gray Line, 1 Toulouse St. (© **800/535-7786** or 504/587-0861),
offers a 2-hour bus tour that gives a fast overview of the city. Tours cost $24 for
adults and $12 for children, and require advance booking.

SHOPPING

Despite what you may think while making your first walk down Bourbon Street,
there's more to New Orleans shopping than tourist traps selling cheap T-shirts,

The French Quarter

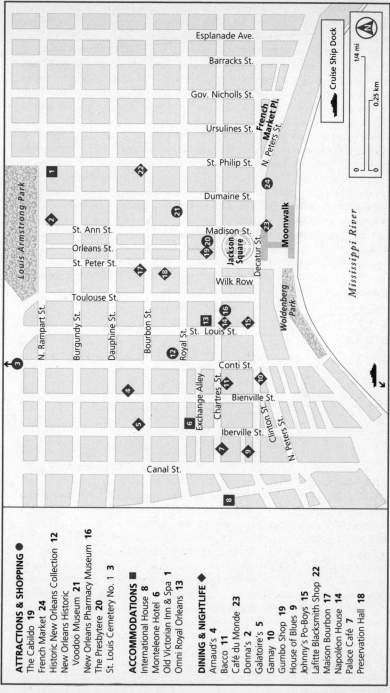

Esplanade Ave.

Barracks St.

Gov. Nicholls St.

Ursulines St.

French Market Pl.

N. Peter's St.

St. Philip St.

Dumaine St.

St. Ann St.

Madison St.

Orleans St.

Jackson Square

St. Peter St.

Wilk Row

Decatur St.

Moonwalk

Toulouse St.

Woldenberg Park

Mississippi River

N. Rampart St.

Burgundy St.

Dauphine St.

Bourbon St.

Royal St.

St. Louis St.

Conti St.

Exchange Alley

Chartres St.

Bienville St.

Clinton St.

N. Peter's St.

Iberville St.

Canal St.

Cruise Ship Dock

1/4 mi

0.25 km

alligator snow globes, and other souvenir items—although there are plenty of those too (most of them with an absolutely mind-boggling selection of hot sauces). The city's antiques stores are especially good.

On Decatur Street across from Jackson Square, **The French Market** has shops selling candy, cookware, fashion, crafts, toys, New Orleans memorabilia, and candles. There is a lot of kitsch, but some good buys are mixed in, and it's always fun to stroll through and grab a few beignets at Café du Monde (see "Snacks & Sweets," below). The French Market is open from 10am to 6pm; Café du Monde is open 24 hours.

From Camp Street down to the river on **Julia Street,** you'll find many of the city's best contemporary art galleries. Of course, some of the works are a bit pricey, but there are good deals to be had if you're collecting, and fine art to be seen if you're not.

Magazine Street is the Garden District's premier shopping street, with more than 140 shops among the 19th-century brick storefronts and cottages. You'll find antiques, art galleries, boutiques, crafts, and more. The greatest concentration of stores is between Felicity and Washington streets, but if you're so inclined, you could shop your way from here all the way to Audubon Park, hopping over the dry patches on the city bus. Be sure to pick up a copy of *Shopper's Dream,* a free guide and map to most of the stores. It's available all along the street.

WHERE TO STAY

In the Garden District, the **McKendrick-Breaux House,** 1474 Magazine St. (© **888/570-1700** or 504/586-1700; fax 504/522-7138), was built at the end of the Civil War by a wealthy plumber and Scottish immigrant, and today is one of the best guesthouses for value. It's been completely restored to its original charm, with each room furnished with antiques, family collectibles, and fresh flowers. Rates: $125 to $195.

In the Central Business District, just outside the French Quarter and close to the cruise ship terminal, the **International House,** 221 Camp St., just west of Canal (© **800/633-5770** or 504/553-9550; www.ihhotel.com), is a very modern, minimalist hotel that was constructed in an old beaux arts bank building. Rooms are simple with high ceilings, ceiling fans, very contemporary bathrooms, dataports, CD players with CDs, and photos and knickknacks that remind you you're in New Orleans. It's all corridors and dark and chic. Rates: $199 to $225.

About 7 blocks from the cruise ship terminal is the atmospheric **Hotel Monteleone,** 214 Royal St., between Iberville and Bienville (© **800/535-9595** or 504/523-3341; www.hotelmonteleone.com), the oldest hotel in the city and also the largest hotel in the French Quarter—because of its size you can almost always get a reservation here, even when other places are booked. Everyone who stays here loves it, probably because its staff is among the most helpful in town. Decor and floor layouts are slightly different in each of the rooms, so ask to see a few different ones. Rates: $199 to $510.

Three streets from Bourbon in the French Quarter, the **Olde Victorian Inn and Spa,** 914 N. Rampart St. (© **800/725-2446** or 504/522-2446; www.oldevictorianinn.com), was formerly known as P. J. Holbrook's, and is now owned by Keith and Andre West-Harrison (and their four dogs and one cat), who have retained the former decor and menu. The inn is a beautifully restored 1840s home, with antiques and reproductions. Some rooms have balconies, and most have fireplaces. The inn can arrange wedding packages that include a service in its courtyard; you can head off for your honeymoon cruise from there! The "spa" in the name refers to the inn's recently opened day spa. Rates: $120 to $185.

The **Omni Royal Orleans,** 621 St. Louis St., between Royal and Chartres (© **800/843-6664** or 504/529-5333; www.omnihotels.com), is a most elegant hotel located smack in the center of the Quarter. The lobby is a small sea of marble, and the rooms are sizable and elegant, full of muted tones and plush furniture, with windows that let you look dreamily out over the Quarter. Service varies, but can be exceptional. Rates: $206 to $269.

In the Central Business District, the **Windsor Court Hotel,** 300 Gravier St. (© **800/262-2662** or 504/523-6000; www.windsorcourthotel.com), was named Best Hotel in North America by *Condé Nast Traveler,* so feel free to hold it to a high standard. Accommodations are exceptionally spacious and classy, with large bay windows or a private balcony overlooking the river or the city. Downstairs, two corridors display original 17th-, 18th-, and 19th-century art, and a plush reading area with an international newspaper rack is on the second floor. Rates: $300 to $400.

WHERE TO DINE

Essentially, New Orleans is one giant restaurant. In 1997, a U.S. survey named it "the fattest city in the country," which makes sense once you've tasted what's being whipped up at 3 or 4 or 8 or 40 of the city's best restaurants. We've profiled many of the best below. Most of them are in the French Quarter.

In business since 1918 and still mighty fine, the legendary **Arnaud's,** 813 Bienville St. (© **504/523-2847**), is set up in three interconnected, once-private houses from the 1700s, and its three Belle Epoque dining rooms are lush with Edwardian embellishments. Menu items include snapper or trout topped with crabmeat, filet mignon, shrimp Arnaud, oysters stewed in cream, roasted duck a l'orange, and classic Bananas Foster. Dinner main courses: $17 to $35.

Bacco, 310 Chartres St., between Bienville and Conti (© **504/522-2426**), a great New Orleans bistro, has an elegant setting with pink faux-marble floors and Venetian chandeliers. You can feast on wood-fired pizzas, regional seafood, and such specialties as black truffle fettuccine and lobster ravioli. Dinner main courses: $19 to $25.

Galatoire's, 209 Bourbon St., at Iberville (© **504/525-2021**), feels like a bistro in turn-of-the-20th-century Paris, and is one of the city's most legendary places—one of the ones where the locals go for a good meal. Menu items include trout (meunière or amandine), rémoulade of shrimp, oysters en brochette, a savory Creole-style bouillabaisse, and a good eggplant stuffed with a purée of seafood. Dinner main courses: $18 to $28.

Gamay, in the Bienville House hotel, 320 Decatur St., at Conti (© **504/299-8800**), serves contemporary Creole cuisine in a formal setting. Entrees include the gigantic almond-crusted soft-shell crab with garlic shrimp and saffron pasta, and a Gulf fish of the day. Dinner main courses: $18 to $28.

The Gumbo Shop, 630 St. Peter St., at Chartres (© **504/525-1486**), is a cheap and convenient place to get solid, classic Creole food. The menu reads like a textbook list of traditional local food: red beans and rice, shrimp Creole, crawfish étouffée. The seafood gumbo with okra is a meal in itself, and do try the jambalaya. Dinner main courses: $6 to $17.

Johnny's Po-Boys, 511 St. Louis St., between Chartres and Decatur (© **504/524-8129**), serves pretty much anything you can think of on huge hunks of

French bread, including fried seafood (the classic), deli meats, cheese omelets, ham and eggs, and the recommended vegetarian selection: the French Fry po' boy. All items are under $11.

Not far outside the Quarter, **Mother's Restaurant,** 401 Poydras St., at Tchoupitoulas (© **504/523-9656**), has long lines and zero atmosphere, but damn, those po' boys. Customers have been flocking here since 1938 for home-made biscuits and red-bean omelets at breakfast, po' boys at lunch, and soft-shell crabs and jambalaya at dinner. Everything's between $2 and $17.

Napoléon House, 500 Chartres St., at the corner of St. Louis Street (© **504/ 524-9752**), would have been the home of the lieutenant himself if some locals' wild plan to bring him here to live out his exile had panned out. A landmark 1797 building with an incredible atmosphere, the place is a hangout for drinking and good times, but also serves food. The specialty is Italian muffuletta, with ham, Genoa salami, pastrami, Swiss cheese, and provolone. Dinner main courses: $19 to $26.

Right on the border of the French Quarter, the open kitchen at **Palace Café,** 605 Canal St., between Royal and Chartres (© **504/523-1661**), serves con-temporary Creole food with a big emphasis on seafood: catfish pecan meunière, andouille-crusted fish of the day, and lots more. Don't miss the white chocolate bread pudding. Dinner main courses: $19 to $25.

Outside the Quarter, at the corner of Washington Avenue and Coliseum Street in the Garden District, **Commander's Palace,** 1403 Washington Ave. (© **504/899-8221**), still reigns as one of the finest dining choices not only in New Orleans, but in the whole United States—the James Beard Foundation voted it the country's best restaurant in 1996. The cuisine is haute Creole. Try anything with shrimp or crawfish, or the Mississippi quail, or . . . oh hell, just try anything. Dinner main courses: $45.

SNACKS & SWEETS

Café du Monde, 800 Decatur St., right on the river (© **504/581-2914**), is basi-cally a 24-hour coffee shop that specializes in beignets, a square, really yummy French doughnut–type thing, hot and covered in powdered sugar. It's a great spot for people-watching, but if you don't want to wait for a table, you can always get a bag of beignets to go. Grab *lots* of napkins. Premoistened towelettes would be a good idea too.

NEW ORLEANS AFTER DARK

Life in "The Big Easy" is conducive to all manner of nighttime entertainment, usually raucous. There's a reason why jazz was born in this town.

Do what most people do: Start at one end of **Bourbon Street** (say, around Iberville), walk down to the other end, and then turn around and do it again. Along the way, you'll hear R & B, blues, and jazz pouring out of dozens of bars, be beckoned by touts from the numerous strip clubs, and see one tiny little storefront stall after another sporting hand-lettered signs that say OUR BEER IS CHEAPER THAN NEXT DOOR. It's a scene. Bacchanalian? Yes. Will you spend time in Purgatory for it? Maybe, but it's loads of fun. Grab yourself a big $2 beer or one of the famous rum-based Hurricanes—preferably in a yard-long green plas-tic cup shaped like a Roswell alien—and join the party.

Most of the places in this section have a cover charge that varies depending on who's performing; some are free.

Preservation Hall, 726 St. Peter St., just off Bourbon (© **504/522-2841** dur-ing the day, 504/523-8939 after 8pm; www.preservationhall.com), is a deliberately shabby little hall with very few places to sit and no air-conditioning. Nonetheless, people usually pack the place to see the house band, a bunch of mostly older musicians who have been at this for eons. Don't request "When the Saints Go Marching In" 'cause the band won't play it—even classics get to be old smelly hats when you've played them 45,000 times. There's a $5 admission fee.

Close by, **Maison Bourbon,** 641 Bourbon St. (© **504/522-8818**), presents authentic and often fantastic Dixieland and traditional jazz. Stepping into the brick-walled room, or even just peering in from the street, takes you away from the mayhem outside. There's a one-drink minimum.

Lafitte's Blacksmith Shop, 941 Bourbon St. (© **504/523-0066**), is a French Quarter pub housed in an 18th-century Creole blacksmith shop that looks like only faith keeps it standing. Tennessee Williams used to hang out here.

If you're looking to get away from the Bourbon scene and hear some real brass-band jazz, head up to **Donna's,** 800 N. Rampart St., at the top of St. Ann Street (© **504/596-6914;** www.donnasbarandgrill.com). There's no better place to hear the authentic sound that made New Orleans famous. The cover varies, but is always reasonable.

Jazz, blues, and Dixieland pour out of the nostalgia-laden bar and concert hall **Tipitina's,** way out in the Uptown neighborhood at 501 Napoleon Ave. (© **504/ 891-8477;** www.tipitinas.com).

House of Blues, 225 Decatur St. (© **504/529-2583**), is one of the city's largest live-music venues. You stand and move among the several bars that pepper the club. There's also a restaurant.

One block beyond Esplanade, on the periphery of the French Quarter, **Snug Harbor,** 626 Frenchman St. (© **504/949-0696;** www.snugjazz.com), is a jazz bistro, a classic spot to hear modern jazz in a cozy setting. Sometimes R & B combos and blues are added to the program. There's a full dinner menu.

6 Alternative Home Ports

Given the mood of the world (and particularly Americans) since the September 11, 2001, terrorist attacks, cruise lines have stepped up their search for additional home ports that allow more passengers to drive to their ships rather than fly—in the process easing flight congestion to the big cruise ports of Miami and Fort Lauderdale. At press time, there were a whopping 13 Caribbean home ports in the continental U.S., including the main ports above, the primary alternative ones below, and Houston (www.portofhouston.com); Norfolk, Virginia (www.cruisenorfolk.org); Baltimore (www.mpa.state.md.us); Jacksonville, Florida (www.jaxport.com); and Philadelphia (www.cruisephilly.com).

GALVESTON, TEXAS

Galveston is an island some 50 miles south of Houston, just off the mainland, and was one of the first big alternative ports developed for Caribbean-bound megaships. Ships departing from Galveston can reach the open sea in about 30 minutes, compared to several hours of lag time from the Port of Houston—which, like New Orleans, sits inland, on the edge of the Houston Ship Channel, above Galveston Bay. (The Port of Houston does have one advantage: It's closer to the airports. It takes 45–90 min. to travel between the Port of Galveston and the airports, depending on which airport you're using. Currently, Royal Olympia Cruises' *Olympia Voyager* and NCL's *Norwegian Sea* are sailing out of Houston to the western Caribbean.)

Until late 2002, the Port of Galveston offered just one 132,000-square-foot cruise ship terminal, but in late 2002, a warehouse adjacent to Terminal One was converted into a second terminal, offering facilities and services for 4-, 5-, 7-, 10-, and 11-night sailings, including a passenger loading bridge and 1,000-foot berth. In mid-2003, the terminal is scheduled to be upgraded to accommodate larger vessels.

The port has expanded with good reason, as Carnival's *Celebration* and *Elation* and Royal Caribbean's *Rhapsody of the Seas* are currently sailing out of Galveston to the western Caribbean year-round, with Royal Caribbean's *Splendour of the Seas* offering 10- and 11-night sailings during the winter season. Within walking distance of the terminal is the historic **Strand District,** Galveston's revitalized downtown, with shops, art galleries, museums, and eateries lining its quaint brick streets.

GETTING TO GALVESTON & THE PORT

The **Texas Cruise Ship Terminal** at the Port of Galveston is at Harborside Drive and 25th Street, on Galveston Island. It's reached via I-45 south from Houston. For information, call ✆ **409/766-6113** or check out www.portofgalveston.com or www.galveston.com.

BY PLANE   You'll fly into one of two Houston airports: **William P. Hobby Airport** (south of downtown Houston, and about 31 miles, or a 45-min. drive from the terminal) or **George Bush Intercontinental Airport** (just north of downtown Houston, and about 54 miles, or an 80-min. drive from the terminal). Information on both is available at the Houston Airport System website, **www.houstonairportsystem.org.** Bush is the larger airport and it's international. If you've arranged air transportation and/or transfers through the cruise line (see chapter 2, "Booking Your Cruise & Getting the Best Price"), a cruise line representative will direct you to shuttle buses that take you to the port. Taxis are also available. **United Cab** (✆ **713/699-0000**) charges $75 per carload from Hobby Airport and $119 from George Bush Intercontinental Airport. The following taxi companies provide service from the port to the airports only (not the other way around): **Busy Bee** (✆ **409/762-6666**) for $70 to Hobby Airport and $125 to George Bush (each additional passenger is $5); and **Yellow Cab Company** (✆ **409/763-3333**) for $70 to Hobby and $110 to Bush.

Galveston Limousine Service (✆ **800/640-4826** or 409/744-5466) provides the same service, charging $30 per person to/from Hobby and $35 to/from Bush. Round-trip rates are $50 and $60, respectively. Both companies require reservations.

BY CAR   I-45 is the main artery for those arriving from the north. To get to the terminal, follow I-45 South to Exit 1C (at Harborside Dr./Hwy. 275); it's the first exit after the causeway. Turn left (east) onto Harborside Drive and continue for about 5 miles to the cruise terminal.

PARKING   Long-term parking at the port is $40 for a 4-night cruise, $45 for a 5-night cruise, $60 for a 7-night cruise, $75 for a 10-night cruise, and $80 for an 11-night cruise. The lots are a ½-mile from the cruise ship terminal, and shuttle buses transport passengers between the lots and the terminal, where porters are available to carry luggage.

NEW YORK CITY

Up until the 1950s, New York City was one of the biggest ports in the world for both cargo and passenger vessels, its famous skyline and the Statue of Liberty offering a dramatic approach that no other ports could match. So many ships parked their noses against Manhattan's West side, that it was dubbed Luxury Liner Row. All the greats were there, from the *Normandie* to *Queen Mary* and *France,* their horns echoing across midtown. All that ended when the jet plane put the liners out of business, allowing people to cross the Atlantic in half a day rather than a week. Never again would the Port of New York see as much traffic, though today it's reclaiming a bit of its former glory as a cruise home port.

Joining a handful of lines that long based ships in NYC for summer and/or fall cruises to Bermuda, New England, and Canada are several Caribbean-bound ships. In early 2003, Norwegian Cruise Line announced the *Norwegian Dawn* would be based year-round in New York, using the Big Apple as a home port for 7-night round-trip cruises to Florida and the Bahamas. That was also the first year *Carnival Legend* was based in New York for the summer, sailing 8-night Caribbean voyages.

Like the ports of New Orleans, San Francisco, and Charleston, New York's cruise ship piers are in the heart of town. Passengers are a short stroll away from 42nd Street and Times Square and a slightly longer one from Fifth Avenue, Central Park, and many other sites. Much of the Big Apple can be explored on foot (Manhattan is only about 2 miles wide by 13 miles long, with most visitors remaining in its bottom half). If you need a break, hail one of the ubiquitous **yellow taxis** (meters start at $2 and increase 30¢ every ⅕-mile or 20¢ per 90 sec. when stuck in traffic) or hop on the red double-decker **Gray Line tour buses** that crisscross the city (© **800/669-0051** or 212/445-0848; www.graylinenewyork. com); you can join the tour loop at the Circle Line terminal just a few steps south of the cruise ship piers.

GETTING TO NEW YORK CITY & THE PORT

The **New York City Passenger Ship Terminal** is at 711 12th Avenue, between 46th and 54th streets, on the Hudson River waterfront. It's reached via the Henry Hudson Parkway (aka the West Side Hwy.) via the 54th Street vehicle ramp. For information, call © **212/246-5450** or check out www.nypst.com.

BY PLANE   You'll fly into one of three New York area airports. **John F. Kennedy (JFK) International** is east of Manhattan in the southeastern section of Queens County, 15 miles from midtown Manhattan and a 30- to 60-minute drive from the piers, depending on traffic. **LaGuardia Airport** is east of Manhattan in Queens, 8 miles from midtown Manhattan and a 20- to 40-minute drive from the piers. **Newark International Airport** is west of Manhattan in Essex and Union counties, New Jersey, about 16 miles from midtown Manhattan and a 30- to 60-minute drive from NYC. Information on all three is at the Port Authority of New York & New Jersey website, **www.panynj.gov.** Kennedy and Newark are the larger airports and accommodate both domestic and international flights. If you've arranged air transportation and/or transfers through the cruise line (see chapter 2, "Booking Your Cruise & Getting the Best Price"), a cruise line representative will direct you to shuttle buses that take you to the port. Taxis are also available. From the airport to the terminal, yellow **New York City Taxis** are usually lined up in great numbers at the airports waiting for fares. From JFK to Manhattan, yellow taxis charge a flat fee of $35 per carload, plus tolls and tip; there is no flat fee from Newark or LaGuardia. If you're traveling via yellow taxi *to* any of the airports, pay the amount on the meter (to Newark, a $10 surcharge is added to metered fare).

Carmel Car Service (© **800/9-CARMEL** or 212/666-6666) charges $27 per carload from Manhattan (including the cruise ship piers) to LaGuardia, $37 to JFK, and $36 to Newark; from Manhattan, the rates vary depending on time of day: $27 to $34 from LaGuardia, $35 to $41 from JFK, and $36 to $44 from Newark. Freelance (aka "gypsy") drivers may solicit you in the airport; to avoid being gouged, it's better to stick with a car service or the official NYC yellow taxis.

Super Shuttle (© **212/258-3826;** www.supershuttle.com) vans are another good way to get between the airports and the piers. Fares range from $13 to $22 per person each way (so, it's no bargain if you're a group of three or more). Twenty-four-hour advance reservations are recommended.

BY CAR Manhattan's Henry Hudson Parkway/West Side Highway is the main artery into the port. To get to the terminals at 48th, 50th, and 52nd streets, cars should enter via the vehicle ramp at 54th Street, directly off the highway.

PARKING Long-term parking at the port is $18 a day if parking for multiple days, or $15 for up to 10 hours. If you want to park for 9 days or more, the monthly rate is $170. The lots are on top of the three terminals, with escalators leading down. Payment is accepted in cash or travelers checks only.

CHARLESTON, SOUTH CAROLINA

One of the most important seaports and cultural centers of America's Colonial period, Charleston is one of the best preserved cities in the U.S., boasting 73 pre–Revolutionary War buildings, 136 from the late 18th century, and more than 600 built before the 1840s. Horse-drawn carriages carry visitors through cobblestone, gas-lit streets, as the fragrances of jasmine and wisteria fill the air. Cruise passengers can walk right from the cruise ship docks to the heart of the city, filled with lovely 18th-century architecture. Highlights include the **Old City Market** at East Bay and Market streets, a 3-block collection of boutiques and crafts stalls; **Fort Sumter** in Charleston Harbor, where the first shots of the Civil War were fired; and innumerable antique-filled colonial homes and manicured gardens.

For 2004, Carnival's *Carnival Victory* and NCL's *Norwegian Majesty* will homeport in Charleston, with Crystal's *Crystal Symphony,* Silversea's *Silver Whisper,* Radisson's *Seven Seas Navigator,* Celebrity's *Galaxy,* and Clipper's *Nantucket Clipper* also using the city as a port of call on several coastal itineraries.

GETTING TO CHARLESTON & THE PORT

The Port of Charleston's 18,000-square-foot cruise ship terminal is located in the peninsular city at 196 Concord St., at the foot of Market Street, in the heart of the historic district.

BY PLANE The **Charleston International Airport** (© **843/767-7009;** www.chs-airport.com) is located in North Charleston, 12 miles from the cruise ship terminal. If you've made arrangements for transfers through your cruise line, a representative will meet your arriving flight and direct you to shuttle buses. **Taxis** are available at a rate of approximately $20 for one or two passengers, with each additional person charged an additional $10. **Shuttle service** is available through the Airport Limo/Taxi Association (© **800/750-1311** or 843/ 607-5456; www.charlestonairporttaxi.com), but because the per-person rate is $10, you may as well get a taxi.

BY CAR   The Port of Charleston is located 12 miles from Charleston International Airport. **From I-95 North or South,** take I-26 (SE) toward Charleston. Exit at East Bay Street, turn left onto Market Street, then right onto Concord Street. The entrance to the terminal will be on your left. **From U.S. Highway 17,** exit at East Bay Street, turn right off the exit ramp, then left onto Market, then right onto Concord. The entrance will be on your left. **From Charleston Airport,** exit onto I-526 and connect to I-26 (Charleston). Continue to East Bay Street-Morrison Drive exit (219-B) and turn left at the bottom of the ramp. Continue onto Morrison Drive, which becomes East Bay Street. Turn left onto Calhoun Street, then right onto Washington Street, which will connect to Concord Street and the terminal.

PARKING   Parking lots are located near the terminal, with port police on hand to direct you. A shuttle bus is available to take you and your luggage right to the pier. Parking is $8 per day.

SAN JUAN, PUERTO RICO

In addition to being the embarkation port for a number of ships, San Juan is also a major port of call, so see "Puerto Rico," in chapter 11, for all information.

11

Caribbean Ports of Call

Whether you choose a certain cruise because of its itinerary, with little regard for the ship that will take you there, or whether you care more about being at sea and consider the ports of call secondary diversions, you'll want to make the most of the limited time you have in whichever port you happen to land.

Here's the good news: There are hardly any lousy Caribbean islands. Sure, depending on your likes and dislikes, you'll appreciate some more than others. Some—such as Key West and especially St. Thomas and Nassau—are much more overrun with tourists than others, but then again, they'll appeal to shoppers with their large variety of bustling stores. Others—Virgin Gorda, St. John, Jost Van Dyke, and Les Saintes, for instance—are quieter and more natural and will appeal to those who'd rather walk along a deserted beach or take a drive along a lonely, winding road in the midst of pristine tropical foliage. Prices are high at some ports—such as Bermuda, the U.S. Virgin Islands, St. Barts, St. Martin, and Aruba—while others are cheaper, such as Cozumel, Jamaica, and the Grenadines.

Choosing activities to participate in aboard ship is one thing, but when the ship pulls up to a port of call, figuring out how to make the most of your limited time there is another. Should you take an organized tour or go off on your own? And just what are the best shore excursions? Where are the best beaches? Where's the shopping? Any good restaurants or bars nearby?

We'll answer all those questions and more, as we take you to 35 ports of call, mainly in the Caribbean, but also including the Bahamas, Mexico's Yucatán Peninsula, the Panama Canal, and Key West. (See chapter 12 for coverage of Bermuda.)

SHORE EXCURSIONS VS. GOING IT ON YOUR OWN

At some ports, your best bet is to just head off exploring on your own, so in the sections that follow we'll advise you which islands are good bets for solo exploring, and whether you should go it on foot or by taxi, motor scooter, ferry, or otherwise. One downside to exploring independently is that you'll be forgoing the kind of narrative you get from a guide, and may miss out on some of the historical, cultural, and other nuances of a particular island. On the other hand, you may find your own little nuances, things that an organized tour skips over as being too minor to bother with. See the following page for a chart showing which islands are particularly strong in certain areas—dining, shopping, activities close to the port, and so on.

In other ports, touring on your own could be an inefficient use of your time, entailing lots of hassles and planning, maybe costing more, and possibly incurring some risk (because of poor roads or driving conditions, for instance). In these cases, the **shore excursions offered by the cruise lines** are the way to go. Under each port review we'll run through a sampling of both the best excursions and the best sights and activities you can see and do on your own.

Frommer's Ratings at a Glance: Caribbean Ports of Call

1 = poor   2 = fair   3 = good   4 = excellent   5 = outstanding

Port	Review on Page	Overall Experience	Shore Excursions	Activities Close to Port	Beaches & Watersports	Shopping	Dining/Bars
Antigua	428	4	3	4	5	2	4
Aruba	435	5	3	4	5	4	4
Bahamas: Freeport	450	3	2	2	3	3	3
Bahamas: Nassau	441	4	3	4	4	3	3
Barbados	456	4	3	3	3	3	3
Belize	462	4	5	2	4	2	3
Bequia	469	4	2	4	4	2	4
Bonaire	475	3	4	3	5	2	3
British Virgin Islands: Tortola	484	4	3	3	3	2	3
British Virgin Islands: Virgin Gorda	489	5	3	4	4	2	3
Cozumel (Mexico)	491	4	5	4	2	4	3
Curaçao	505	4	3	4	2	3	3
Dominica	510	3	4	3	2	3	3
Grand Cayman	518	5	5	4	5	4	3
Grenada	522	5	3	4	3	3	3
Guadeloupe	528	4	4	5	4	4	5
Jamaica: Ocho Rios	536	4	5	4	3	2	3
Jamaica: Montego Bay	541	4	5	4	3	3	3
Key West	545	4	4	5	2	3	4
Les Saintes	552	4	2	5	3	2	3
Martinique	558	4	3	3	4	3	3
Nevis	567	4	1	4	4	2	2
Playa del Carmen (Mexico)	500	4	5	3	3	2	3
Puerto Rico	573	5	2	5	3	4	4
St. Barts	587	4	3	4	4	4	3
St. Croix	632	4	4	4	4	5	3
St. John	628	4	3	4	4	2	2
St. Kitts	593	3	3	1	3	2	3
St. Lucia	598	4	4	3	4	2	3
St. Martin	604	4	3	4	4	4	4
St. Thomas	620	4	4	4	4	5	3
Tobago	617	4	3	1	4	2	2
Trinidad	612	2	2	1	2	2	3

See chapter 12 for Bermuda ratings.

Shore excursions can be a wonderful and carefree way to get to know the islands, offering everything from island tours and snorkeling and sailing excursions (often with a rum-punch party theme) to more physically challenging pursuits such as bicycle tours, hiking, kayaking, and horseback riding. Keep in mind that **shore-excursion prices** vary from line to line, even for the exact same tour; the prices we've listed are typical and are adult rates. Also note that some cruise lines may not offer all these tours, while other may offer even more. Note also that in some cases the excursions fill up fast, especially on the megaships, so don't dawdle in signing up. When you receive your cruise documents, or at the latest when you board the ship, you'll get a pamphlet with a listing of the excursions offered for your itinerary. Look it over, make your selections, and sign up the first or second day of your cruise. (In some cases, if a tour offered by your ship is booked up, you can try to book it independently once you get to port. The popular Atlantis submarine tour, for example—offered at Grand Cayman, Nassau, St. Thomas, and more—usually has an office/agent in the cruise terminals or nearby.) If there's an excursion you absolutely need to take and don't want to risk getting left out of, there are a few ways to book excursions before you sail. A company called **Port Promotions** in Plantation, Florida, is now allowing travel agents and passengers to book shore excursions online at **www.port promotions.com**. A few cruise lines do, too: At press time, Royal Caribbean, Celebrity, and Princess offered prebooking of shore excursions on their websites (www.royalcaribbean.com, www.celebrity-cruises.com, and www.princess.com) or via the printed forms sent with your cruise documents. Disney also allows guests to prebook by phone or fax.

If you want to **rent a car** in port, make reservations in advance. **Avis** (© 800/ 331-1212; www.avis.com), **Budget** (© 800/472-3325; www.drivebudget. com), and **Hertz** (© 800/654-3001; www.hertz.com) all have offices on most of the Caribbean islands in this chapter; **Dollar** (© 800/800-4000; www. dollar.com) and **National** (© 800/227-7368; www.nationalcar.com) are less well represented in the region. See "Getting Around" in the individual port listings to see which have offices where, and note that in certain ports we advise against renting at all.

DOCKING, DOLLARS & OTHER PORT DETAILS

ARRIVING IN PORT Most cruise ships arrive in port sometime before 10am, though this will vary slightly from line to line and port to port. You rarely have to clear Customs or Immigration because your ship's purser has your passport or other ID and will have done all the paperwork for you. When local officials give the word, you just go ashore. Often you can walk down the gangway right onto the pier, but if you're on a large cruise ship and the port isn't big enough, your ship will anchor offshore and ferry passengers to land via a small boat called a tender. In either case, you might have to wait in line to get ashore, but the waits will be longer if you have to tender in. Once ashore, even if you've come by tender, you aren't stuck there—tenders run back and forth on a regular basis, so you can return to the ship at any time for lunch, a nap, or whatever. Tenders all look pretty much alike, so you might be confused as to which one's heading to your ship, but officers are on duty to check your ID and make sure you get to the right boat.

SCHEDULING YOUR TIME ASHORE All shore excursions are carefully organized to coincide with your time in port. If you're going it on your own, you can count on finding taxi drivers at the pier when your ship docks. It's a good idea to arrange with the driver to pick you up at a certain time to bring you back to the port. In most ports you can also rent a car, moped/scooter, or bicycle to get around.

CUSTOM EXCURSIONS If you want to do something special in port— find a special restaurant for lunch or do some scuba diving, golf, tennis, horse-back riding, or fishing—talk with your cruise director or shore-excursion manager beforehand. Keep in mind that they'll most likely just tell you to sign up for one of their organized excursions and won't have the time or ability to help you arrange personal and private tours. This is especially true on the mega-ships. The smaller lines, however, whether high-end or adventure, will usually help you in this way. Remember, too, that your waiter, masseuse, or favorite bar-tender may know the islands you're visiting quite well (since they're there week after week), so it can't hurt to ask them about their favorite beaches and water-ing holes, and so on.

You'll need to reserve spots for many of these activities before you land, because facilities might be filled by land-based vacationers or by passengers from other cruise ships. It goes without saying that if you arrive at a port of call and find the harbor filled with ships, expect the shops, restaurants, beaches, and everything else to be crowded. Call from the docks for any reservations.

CALLING HOME Since the prices for calling home from a cruise ship are so sky-high (anywhere from $4–$15 a min.), it's a better idea to call from land, when you're in port. We've included information on where to find phones in all the port reviews. Country codes are as follows: United States and Canada, 1; Australia, 61; New Zealand, 64; the United Kingdom, 44; and the Republic of Ireland, 353.

DUTY-FREE SHOPPING The savings on duty-free merchandise can range from as little as 5% to as much as 50%. Unless a special sale is being offered, many products carry comparable price tags from island to island. If you have particular goods you're thinking of buying this way, it pays to check prices at your local discount retailer before you leave home so you'll know whether you're really getting a bargain. (Note that the U.S. dollar is widely accepted through-out the islands as well as in Bermuda, so even though we've listed each island's official local currency, there's rarely a need to exchange U.S. dollars. Credit cards and traveler's checks are also widely accepted.)

AVOIDING PROHIBITED MERCHANDISE You may be eyeing that gor-geous piece of **black-coral jewelry,** but did you know it's illegal to bring many products made from coral and other marine animals back to the United States because of laws prohibiting the trade in endangered species? (Remember, corals aren't rocks: They're living animals—a single branch of coral contains thousands of tiny coral animals, called polyps.) The shopkeeper selling it won't tell you that, of course, and it may in fact be legal for him to sell it. Nonetheless, you

---

Don't Forget Cash When Going Ashore

It's happened to both of us and it's happened to our friends, so it can hap-pen to you too: After a few days of living cash-free aboard ship, it doesn't even cross your mind to grab the greenbacks when you're going ashore. You get there and realize you're penniless. It's soooo frustrating, especially if you've had to tender in from offshore. Don't let it happen to you.

will be in violation of U.S. and international law if you bring these items back to the States. If caught, you could face stiff penalties and have your treasured mementos confiscated.

Sea turtles, too, are highly endangered, and sea horses, while not yet protected by laws, are currently threatened with extinction. The best way to appreciate and protect all of these natural beauties is with an underwater camera on a snorkeling expedition.

REBOARDING   Most passengers start heading back to the ship around 4pm or not much later than 5. By 6pm you're often sailing off to your next destination. In some cases—for instance, in Nassau, New Orleans, Key West, and the British Virgin Islands (for the smaller ships)—the ship may stay in port till after midnight so passengers can stay ashore and enjoy the island's nightlife. When actually walking back aboard, you'll generally have to present your shipboard ID and another ID as well, except aboard some of the smaller ships.

THE CRUISE LINES' PRIVATE ISLANDS

Royal Caribbean, Princess, Disney, Holland America, Norwegian, and Costa all have private islands (or patches of islands) in the Bahamas that are included as a port of call on many of their Caribbean and Bahamas itineraries and are off-limits to anyone but the line's passengers. While completely lacking in any true Caribbean culture, they do offer cruisers a guaranteed beach day with all the trimmings. We've described these islands in the cruise line reviews in chapters 6 through 9.

1 Antigua

Though it's the largest of the British Leeward Islands, Antigua (pronounced An-TEE-*gah*) is still only 23km (14 miles) long and 18km (11 miles) wide, and offers little of the polish or glitz of some Caribbean islands. And that's its greatest asset: serenity. Nice, relaxing beaches are close to port; **St. John's,** the island's capital and main town, is sleepy and undemanding; and the locals, usually friendly, sometimes wary, are easygoing. Sure, there are things to do, but nothing will raise your blood pressure. Close to port, you can shop lazily in historic, restored warehouses that now feature boutiques and restaurants; spend half an hour or so at a museum to get a sense of Antigua's past; or climb a gentle hill to the massive cathedral overlooking town. Not all of St. John's is charming, but the town is full of cobblestone sidewalks, weather-beaten wooden houses, and louvered Caribbean verandas. The island's British accent is another plus. Antigua has been independent since 1981, but the U.K. legacy lives on: Driving is on the left, half of the tourists are subjects of the queen, every little village has an Anglican church, and the island's greatest passion is for the sport of cricket.

Away from St. John's, the rolling, rustic island boasts important historic sites and lots of pretty beaches. On the southern coast, **Nelson's Dockyard,** once Britain's main naval station in the Lesser Antilles, is now a well-maintained national park. Tucked away in the arid, grassy interior, **Betty's Hope,** with its picturesque windmills, conjures up Antigua's sugar plantation past. And the **Wallings Conservation Area,** in the island's southwestern region, is the best example of the moist forests that covered Antigua before Europeans cleared the land for agriculture.

Antigua cashed in on sugar and cotton production for years. Today tourism is the main industry. Most Antiguans are descendants of African slaves brought

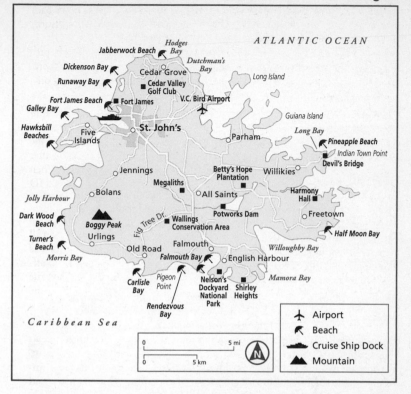

ATLANTIC OCEAN

Airport
Beach
Cruise Ship Dock
Mountain

Caribbean Sea

over centuries ago to labor in the fields. People of European, Asian, and Middle Eastern extraction are also represented in the population of 68,000.

COMING ASHORE   Most cruise ships dock at **Heritage Quay** (pronounced *key*) in St. John's, the island's only town of any size. Heritage Quay and the adjacent **Redcliffe Quay** are the main shopping areas, but duty-free stores, restaurants, taxis, and other services can be found in the surrounding blocks as well. When several ships are in port, some dock at the **Deep Water Harbour Terminal,** 1.6km (1 mile) from St. John's. From there, you can either walk or take a short taxi ride into town. A handful of smaller vessels drop anchor at English Harbour, on the south coast.

   Credit-card phone booths can be found on the dock, at both quays, and at Deep Water Harbour. If you want a more comfortable, air-conditioned place to make calls, try the Kinko's-like **Parcel Plus** (© 268/462-4854) at 14 Redcliffe St. (in Redcliffe Quay), where you can also check your e-mail ($3 for 15 min.). **Cable & Wireless** (© 268/480-4237), on the corner of Long and Thames streets, sells prepaid phone cards for as little as $4.

   You'll find **ATMs** at both quays and at the corner of Thames and St. Mary streets.

LANGUAGE   Antigua is a former British colony, so the official language is **English,** often spoken with a musical West Indian lilt.

CURRENCY   Although the **Eastern Caribbean dollar** (EC$2.70 = $1 U.S.; EC$1 = 37¢ U.S.) is Antigua's official currency, the U.S. dollar is readily accepted by most shopkeepers and cab drivers, and almost all businesses post their prices in U.S. currency. Prices quoted in this section are in U.S. dollars. Credit cards and traveler's checks are accepted by most tourist-oriented businesses as well.

INFORMATION   The **Antigua and Barbuda Department of Tourism,** at Nevis Street and Friendly Alley in St. John's (© **268/462-0480**), is open Monday through Friday from 8am to 4:30pm. Before you leave home, contact the Department of Tourism's New York office (© **888/268-4227** or 212/541-4117; www.antigua-barbuda.org) or e-mail info@antigua-barbuda.org.

CALLING FROM THE U.S.   When calling Antigua from the U.S., simply dial "1" before the numbers listed throughout this section.

GETTING AROUND

BY TAXI   Taxis meet every cruise ship. Although meters are nonexistent, rates are fixed by the government, and are posted at the taxi stand at the end of Heritage Quay's pedestrian mall. From the cruise ship dock, it's $10 to Dickenson Bay, $20 to Betty's Hope, $22 to Nelson's Dockyard, and $25 to Devil's Bridge. Settle on a fare (and the currency) before hopping in. Drivers often double as tour guides: For this added service, expect to pay about $20 per hour for up to four people, with a 2-hour minimum. Tip between 10% and 15% for all rides.

BY BUS   Buses are cheap (little more than $1 to almost anywhere on the island), but service is erratic. The privately operated vehicles, mostly 12-seat vans (all have license plates beginning with "A" or "B"), run from early morning until about 6pm. If you're adventurous and want to chew the fat with Antiguan villagers, give it a whirl.

There are two bus stations in St. John's: East Bus Station, on Independence Avenue, serves the north and east; West Bus Station, near St. John's market, is the terminus for routes to the south and west (and English Harbour).

BY RENTAL CAR   Driving is on the left side. Most roads are decent, but some are narrow and chock-full of potholes. Inadequate signage is a problem island-wide. On the bright side, you'll never have to worry about traffic jams. **Avis, Budget, Hertz,** and **National** all operate on the island. Your valid driver's license and a local temporary driving permit ($20, available from all rental agencies) are required.

SHORE EXCURSIONS OFFERED BY THE CRUISE LINES

Four-Wheel-Drive Island Tour ($66, 3 hr.): Tour the island's only remaining rainforest via a four-wheel-drive vehicle, and stop at the ruins of forts, sugar mills, and plantation houses. The excursion includes beach time.

Nelson's Dockyard at English Harbour ($37–$41, 3 hr.): After traversing the island's hilly countryside, you'll visit the site of the planet's last surviving, working Georgian dockyard. Many colonial buildings still stand, including forts, residences, and barracks; and several have been converted into restaurants, hotels, shops, and museums. The sea vistas are impressive.

Catamaran Tour ($39–$52, 3 hr.): Sail along the coast with time to swim, sunbathe, and snorkel. Lunch and equipment are included.

Jolly Roger Cruise ($39, 4 hr.): Aboard this wooden "pirate ship," you can take in some of the island's coastal sights, snorkel, dance on the poop deck, limbo, and walk the plank. Drinks and buffet lunch are included.

> ## ⓒ Frommer's Favorite Antigua Experiences
>
> **Sand, Sun, and Sloth:** It's your choice: A bustling, social strand or a tranquil, private refuge. Either is within easy reach of the dock. (See "Beaches," below.)
>
> **Salt, Sailors, and Swashbucklers:** Nelson's Dockyard, on Antigua's southern coast, is a must for history buffs. Colonial forts guard the narrow passage into the protected harbor where the British, beginning in the 1700s, maintained their most important naval station in the Lesser Antilles. Like a Caribbean version of Colonial Williamsburg, the national park, with its many restored buildings, evokes another era. (See "On Your Own: Beyond the Port Area," below.)

EXCURSIONS OFFERED BY LOCAL AGENCIES

Catamaran Cruises: Kokomo Cat Cruises (ⓒ 268/462-7245) and **Wadadli Cats** (ⓒ 268/462-4792) offer different all-day catamaran cruises every day except Monday. Prices, which include an open bar, buffet lunch, and snorkeling equipment, range from $70 to $100 (children under 12 half-price, under 2 free). Check, though, to make sure you'll be back in time to reboard your cruise ship before it leaves. Both companies offer private catamaran charters.

Miscellaneous Tours: Several reputable operators offer outback eco-adventures, Jeep safaris, kayak and snorkeling excursions, and bus tours of the island. Prices range, and discounts for children under 12 are common. Inquire at **Antigua Destination Planners** (ⓒ 268/463-1944), **Paradise Island Tours** (ⓒ 268/462-7280), and **Wadadli Island Tours** (ⓒ 268/773-0367).

ON YOUR OWN: WITHIN WALKING DISTANCE

St. John's has a number of attractions that can be easily reached on foot. To your right, just as you pass through immigration formalities, **Redcliffe Quay** is Antigua's most interesting shopping complex. Most of the sugar, coffee, and tobacco produced on the island in years past was stored in the warehouses here, and before slavery was abolished on the island in 1834, the area witnessed slave auctions. The restored buildings, with their stone foundations, wooden-slat sidings, colorful shutters, and red corrugated metal roofs, now house an array of boutiques and restaurants. For more local color, turn right (south) once you've reached Market Street and walk 5 blocks to the **Public Market.** The roof of the enclosed structure casts a strange color on the vendors' wares below, but it's still the best place to sample locally produced fruits and vegetables or to pick up some Antiguan pottery or baskets. It's at its most animated early in the morning, especially on Fridays and Saturdays. Across the street, next to the West Bus Station, fishermen hawk their catch every morning at the waterfront **Fish Market.** Chances are slim that you'll buy anything here, but stop by for the salty and sometimes saucy scene. Next retrace your steps on Market Street, walking north to the intersection of Long Street, where you'll find the **Museum of Antigua and Barbuda** (ⓒ 268/462-1469). Although not the plushest exhibition space in the Caribbean, the museum traces the history of the nation from its geological birth to the present day. Housed in a former courthouse, a neoclassical structure built in 1750, its exhibits include pre-Columbian tools and artifacts, a replica of an Arawak wattle-and-daub hut, African-Caribbean pottery, and sections dedicated to the island's naval, sugar, and slavery eras. It's open Monday to Friday from 8:30am to 4pm; Saturday from 10am to 2pm. Admission is free, but a donation of $2 is requested. A couple of blocks uphill from the museum, bordered by Church, Long, and Newgate streets, **St. John's Anglican Cathedral** (✆ 268/ 462-4686) dominates St. John's skyline with its 21m- (70-ft.-) high, aluminum-capped twin spires. The original St. John's, a simple wooden structure built in 1681, was replaced in 1720 by a brick building, which was destroyed during an 1843 earthquake. Upon its completion in 1847, the present baroque structure was not universally appreciated: Ecclesiastical architects criticized it as being like "a pagan temple with two dumpy pepperpot towers." The cavernous interior is entirely encased in pitch pine, a construction method intended to secure the building from hurricanes and earthquakes.

ON YOUR OWN: BEYOND THE PORT AREA

One of the major historical attractions of the eastern Caribbean, **Nelson's Dock-yard National Park** (✆ 268/481-5021, 268/481-5022) lies 18km (11 miles) southeast of St. John's, alongside one of the world's best-protected natural har-bors. English ships used the site as a refuge from hurricanes as early as 1671, and the dockyard played a major role during the 18th century, an era of privateers, pirates, and great sea battles. Admiral Nelson's headquarters from 1784 to 1787, the restored dockyard today remains the only Georgian naval base still in use. At its heart, the **Dockyard Museum,** housed in a former Naval Officers' House built in 1855, traces the history of the site from its beginning as a British Navy stronghold to its development as a national park and yachting center. Nautical memorabilia comprise much of the display. Uphill and east of the Dockyard, the **Dow's Hill Interpretation Center** (✆ 268/481-5045) features an entertaining 20-minute multimedia overview of Antiguan history and an observation plat-form that affords a 360-degree view of the park. Farther uphill, Palladian arches mark the **Blockhouse,** a military fortification built in 1787 that included offi-cers' quarters and a powder magazine. For an eagle's-eye view of English Har-bour, continue to the hill's summit, to the **Shirley Heights Lookout** (✆ 268/ 460-1785). Fortified to defend the precious cargo in the harbor below, Fort Shirley's barracks, arched walkways, batteries, and powder magazines are scattered around the hilltop. The Lookout, with its view of the French island of Guade-loupe, was the main signal station used to warn of approaching hostile ships.

The grounds of the national park, which represent 10% of Antigua's total land area, are well worth exploring. Bordered on one side by sandy beaches, the park is blanketed in cactus, tamarind, cinnamon, and turpentine trees, and man-groves that shelter African cattle egrets. An array of **nature trails,** which take anywhere from 30 minutes to 5 hours to walk, meander through the vegetation and offer vistas of the coast. One trail climbs to **Fort Berkeley,** built in 1704 to protect the harbor's entrance. Admission, which is $5 for adults (children under 12 are free), covers the Dockyard, the Dockyard Museum, Dow's Hill Interpre-tation Center, the Blockhouse, Shirley Heights, and the rest of the park. The complex is open daily from 9am to 5pm, and is within walking distance of cruise ships that dock at English Harbor. Free guided tours of the dockyard last 15 to 20 minutes; tipping is discretionary.

To see what's billed as the only operational 18th-century sugar mill in the Caribbean, visit **Betty's Hope,** not far from Pares village on the island's east side

(© **268/462-1469**). On-site are twin mills, the remnants of a boiling house, and a small visitor center, which opens its doors Tuesday through Saturday from 10am till 4pm. Gardeners should be able to spot golden seal bushes, neem trees, and wild tamarinds on the rolling hills. Serene cows saunter lazily on the grounds.

Not far from Betty's Hope, on the extreme eastern tip of the island, **Devil's Bridge** is one Antigua's most picturesque natural wonders. Over the centuries, powerful Atlantic breakers, gathering strength over the course of their 4,830km (3,000-mile) run from Africa, have carved out a natural arch in the limestone coastline and created blowholes through which the surf spurts skyward at high tide.

Another option for nature lovers, **Wallings Conservation Area** (© **268/462-1007**) is Antigua's largest remaining tract of tropical rainforest. Located in the southwest, this lush wilderness area features three hiking trails and numerous opportunities to spot some of Antigua's nonhuman inhabitants: birds (purple-throated caribs, Antillean crested hummingbirds, broadwinged hawks), mammals (mongooses, bats), amphibians (tree frogs), and reptiles (lizards, snakes). Vegetation includes strangler fig, hog plum, black loblolly, mango, and silk cotton trees, as well as numerous epiphytes. If you've spent your day at Nelson's Dockyard, pass through the area on the way back to your ship via the circular **Fig Tree Drive.** Although full of potholes in places, this is the island's most scenic drive. It winds through the tropical forest, passing fishing villages, frisky goats, and old sugar mills along the way.

SHOPPING

Most shops of interest in St. John's are clustered in Heritage Quay and Redcliffe Quay, and on St. Mary's Street, all within easy walking distance of the cruise ship docks. Duty-free items include English woolens and linens, as well as local pottery, straw work, and rum.

Redcliffe Quay, to your right as you pass through Customs, was a slave-trading and warehouse district before abolition. Tastefully renovated, it now contains interesting specialty shops, including **Jacaranda** on Redcliffe Street (© **268/462-1888**), which sells batik clothing, spices, and Caribbean art; **The Goldsmitty** on Redcliffe Street (© **268/462-4601**), which offers handmade gold jewelry; and **The Map Shop** on St. Mary's Street (© **268/462-3993**), which stocks old and new map prints, sea charts, and Caribbean literature.

Located at the cruise dock, **Heritage Quay** is a run-of-the-mill shopping center with 40 duty-free shops and a vendors' hall.

BEACHES

Antiguans claim that the island is home to 365 beaches, one for each day of the year. True or not, all of them are public, and quite a few are spectacular.

Closest to St. John's, **Fort James Beach,** located 5 minutes and a $7 cab fare from the cruise dock, is popular with both locals and tourists. The cordoned area is always safe, but farther from shore, undercurrents are occasionally strong. Volleyball and cricket are daily happenings. You can rent umbrellas and beach chairs, and the open-air restaurant/bar allows you to spend every minute outdoors. For a change of pace, hike up the hill to explore the authentically derelict ruins of **Fort James,** which once protected St. John's harbor. Another restaurant/bar at the summit offers splendid views of the area.

A bit farther north, a $10 cab ride from the dock, the .8km- (½-mile-) long beach at **Dickenson Bay** is the island's most bustling strand, with numerous hotels, restaurants, and watersports. It's the place to watch people, try out some watersports equipment, or just bake in a social environment. The water is calm, drinking and eating options abound, and chairs and umbrellas are available for rent.

Pleasant, picturesque spots on the less-developed southwest coast include unspoiled **Darkwood Beach** and nearby **Turner's Beach.** Showers, snorkeling equipment, and chairs are available. Restaurants serve fresh seafood, while bars keep you hydrated.

If you crave complete peace and quiet, head to Antigua's most beautiful beach, at **Half Moon Bay.** Isolated at the island's southeast extreme, this expanse is virtually undeveloped. Waves at the beach's center are great for bodysurfing, while the quieter eastern side is better for children and snorkeling. A restaurant and bar are near the parking lot.

SPORTS

GOLF   The 18-hole, par-70 **Cedar Valley Golf Club,** Friar's Hill Road (ℂ **268/462-0161**), is a 5-minute, $10 taxi ride from the cruise dock. The 5,528m (6,142-yard) golf course has panoramic views of the northern coast. Greens fees for 18 holes and use of a cart are $75. Club rental is $20.

SCUBA DIVING & SNORKELING   Antigua's dive sites include reefs, wall drops, caves, and shipwrecks. To arrange a dive contact **Dive Antigua,** at the north end of Dickenson Bay (ℂ **268/462-3483**). A two-tank dive is $72. Reef snorkeling is $25.

WATERSPORTS   Tony's Watersports (ℂ **268/462-6326**) and **Sea Sports** (ℂ **268/462-3355**), both located at Dickenson Bay Beach, offer a full range of watersports equipment. Prices are negotiable depending on season and demand, but sample fares for jet skis are $35 per half-hour and for water-skiing $25 per lap.

WINDSURFING   **Windsurfing Antigua Watersports** (ℂ **268/461-9463**), also at Dickenson Bay Beach, specializes in 2-hour introductory lessons ($60) that are limited to four people. Experienced wind sailors can rent a full rig for the day at $50, or for half a day at $40. The operation also rents Sunfish ($20 per hr.), kayaks ($10 per hr.), and snorkel gear ($10 for the day).

GREAT LOCAL RESTAURANTS & BARS

Lunch menus on the island focus on West Indian cuisine, but you can get sandwiches, salads, and burgers as well. Antigua's **local beer** is Wadadli, the island's Carib name. The **local rum** is Cavalier.

There's no better place to watch the street life of St. John's than the second-floor wraparound veranda at **Hemingway's,** on St. Mary's Street (ℂ **268/462-2763**). Across from Heritage Quay, on the main road leading from the dock, it serves tasty salads, sandwiches, burgers, seafood, and refreshing tropical drinks. The **Commissioner Grill** on Redcliffe Street (ℂ **268/462-1883**) is sunny and colorful. One of the few eateries in town that's open on Sunday, its menu features West Indian specialties at moderate prices.

If you've opted to spend all day at the beach, your best bet at Dickenson Bay is **Coconut Beach Restaurant** (ℂ **268/462-1538**), a quiet, open-air beachside refuge at the strand's southern extreme, complete with palm trees and superb seafood. Lunch $19.

If you're in English Harbour, stop for a lunch break at the rustic **Admiral's Inn,** in Nelson's Dockyard (ℂ **268/460-1027**). Built in 1788, this restored brick building originally stored barrels of pitch, turpentine, and lead used to repair ships. The menu changes daily but usually features pumpkin soup and main courses such as local red snapper, grilled steak, and lobster.

2 Aruba

More of a desert island than a rainforest, Aruba has unwaveringly sunny skies, warm temperatures, and cooling breezes, along with some of the best beaches in the Caribbean—or in the world, for that matter—miles of white sugary sand; turquoise and aqua seas; warm, gentle surf; and plenty of space.

If you tire of lolling on the beach, there's scuba diving, snorkeling, great wind-surfing, and all the other watersports you expect from a sun-and-sea vacation. On land, you can golf, ride a horse, or drive an all-terrain vehicle over the island's wild-and-woolly outback. Away from the beach, Aruba's full of cactus, iguanas, and strange boulder formations. Contrasting sharply with the southern shoreline's beaches, the north coast features craggy limestone cliffs, sand dunes, and crashing breakers.

Focused on shopping? The concentration of stores and malls in Oranjestad, the island's capital, is as impressive as any in the Caribbean. In between pur-chases, try your luck at one of the island's dozen **casinos;** two are just steps away from your ship. Or maybe grab a bite to eat: Unlike the so-so fare found in most of the Caribbean, Aruba's culinary offerings are diverse, inventive, and often outstanding.

Aruba's still part of the Netherlands, so there's a Dutch influence, which adds a nice European flavor. Though it has a few small museums, and some centuries-old indigenous rock glyphs and paintings, nobody comes to Aruba for culture or history.

Only 32km (20 miles) long and 9.7km (6 miles) across at its widest point, the island is slightly larger than Washington, D.C. It's the westernmost of the Dutch ABC islands—Aruba, Bonaire, and Curaçao—and lies less than 32km (20 miles) north of Venezuela. Aruba's capital and largest city, **Oranjestad,** is on the island's southern coast and pretty far to the west.

The Arubans are as friendly as can be. With little history of racial or cultural conflicts, locals have no cause for animosity. And everybody speaks English, as well as Dutch, Spanish, and Papiamento, the local patois.

COMING ASHORE   Cruise ships arrive at the **Aruba Port Authority,** a modern terminal with a tourist information booth, phones, ATMs, and plenty of shops. From the pier it's a 5-minute walk to the **shopping districts** of down-town Oranjestad.

LANGUAGE   The official language is **Dutch,** but nearly everybody speaks **English.** The language of the street is often **Papiamento,** a patois that combines various European, African, and indigenous American languages. **Spanish** is also widely spoken.

CURRENCY   The **Aruba florin (AFl)** is the official currency, but U.S. dollars are as widely accepted, and most items and services are priced in both curren-cies. Traveler's checks and major credit cards are almost universally accepted as well. The exchange rate is relatively stable at about 1.8 AFl to U.S.$1 (1 AFl = U.S.56¢). Prices quoted in this section are in U.S. dollars.

INFORMATION   For information, go to the **Aruba Tourism Authority,** 172 L. G. Smith Blvd., Oranjestad (© **297/5823777;** www.aruba.com). It's open Monday to Friday from 9am to 5pm.

> ### ℂ Frommer's Favorite Aruba Experiences
>
> **Pretend You're Neil Armstrong:** Alien boulders and stark terrain mark Aruba's northern coast, making you feel like a visitor to the moon. The roads are unpaved but easy to navigate in an all-terrain vehicle. You can stop at a lighthouse, an old chapel, and the ruins of a gold-smelting factory, but the major attractions are supplied by nature. (See "Shore Excursions Offered by the Cruise Lines" and "On Your Own: Touring by Rental Jeep," below)
>
> **Make like Captain Nemo:** Submerge 45m (150 ft.) beneath the sea in a modern submarine to marvel at nature's underwater splendor. (See "Shore Excursions Offered by the Cruise Lines," below.)

CALLING FROM THE U.S.   When calling Aruba from the U.S., dial the international access code (011) before the numbers listed in this section.

GETTING AROUND

BY RENTAL CAR   Excellent roads connect major tourist attractions, and all the major rental companies accept valid U.S. or Canadian driver's licenses. Rent a four-wheel-drive vehicle for the rough roads in the outback. **Avis, Budget, Dollar, Hertz,** and **National** all have offices here.

BY MOTORCYCLE OR BIKE   Scooters and motorcycles are impractical unless you plan to stick to paved roads. They're available at **George's Cycle Center,** L. G. Smith Blvd. 136 (ℂ 297/5825975). Scooters rent for $30 per day, while motorcycles go for $45 up to $100 for a Harley. You can rent mountain bikes at **Semver Cycle Rental,** Noord 22 (ℂ **297/5866851**), where rates start at $25 per day.

BY TAXI   Taxis line up at the dock to take you wherever you want to go. Cabs don't have meters, but fares are fixed, and every driver has a copy of the official rate schedule. Ask the fare before getting in the car. The dispatch office number is ℂ **297/5822116.** The fare from the cruise terminal to the beach resorts is $6 to $8. Tip between 15% and 20%.

Most drivers speak good English and are eager to give you a tour of the island. Expect to pay $35 per hour for a maximum of four passengers.

BY BUS   Aruba has good daily bus service beginning at 6am. Same-day round-trip fare between the beach hotels and Oranjestad is $2; a one-way ride is $1.15. Have exact change. The bus terminal is across the street from the cruise terminal on L. G. Smith Boulevard.

SHORE EXCURSIONS OFFERED BY THE CRUISE LINES

Four-Wheel-Drive Backcountry Aruba Tour ($95, 7½ hr.): Just like the solo tour described in "On Your Own: Touring by Rental Jeep," below, but this version does the tour in a convoy of four-passenger sports utility vehicles, with you behind the wheel and in radio contact with your guide. A stop is made for lunch and swimming.

Atlantis Submarine Journey ($79, 2 hr.): If you loved Captain Nemo and *20,000 Leagues Under the Sea,* don't miss your chance to cruise 45m (150 ft.) below the sea in a submarine. During the gentle descent, you'll pass by scuba

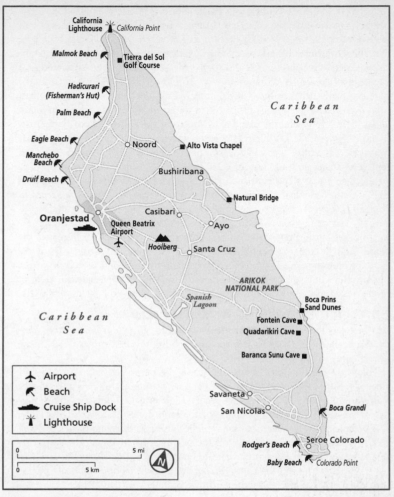

California
Lighthouse · California Point

Malmok Beach
Tierra del Sol
Golf Course

Hadicurari
(Fisherman's Hut)

Palm Beach

Eagle Beach
Noord · Alto Vista Chapel

Manchebo
Beach
Bushiribana

Druif Beach

Natural Bridge

Casibari

Oranjestad
Queen Beatrix
Airport · Ayo

Hooiberg · Santa Cruz

*Caribbean
Sea*

ARIKOK
NATIONAL PARK

*Spanish
Lagoon*

Boca Prins
Sand Dunes

Fontein Cave
Quadarikiri Cave

Baranca Sunu Cave

*Caribbean
Sea*

Savaneta

San Nicolas
Boca Grandi

Rodger's Beach · Seroe Colorado

Baby Beach · Colorado Point

✈ Airport
⤹ Beach
⚓ Cruise Ship Dock
🗼 Lighthouse

| 0 | 5 mi |
| 0 | 5 km |

divers, coral reefs, shipwrecks, and hundreds of curious sergeant majors, damselfish, parrotfish, and angelfish.

Aruba Bus Tour ($34, 3 hr.): This air-conditioned bus tour rolls along part of Aruba's wild and woolly windward coastline to the Natural Bridge (a rocky "bridge" cut by the sea and wind) and the Casibari rock formations, as well as along Aruba's hotel strip.

ON YOUR OWN: WITHIN WALKING DISTANCE

Aruba's capital has a sunny Caribbean demeanor, with Dutch colonial buildings painted in vivid colors. The main thoroughfare, **Lloyd G. Smith Boulevard,** runs along the waterfront and is crowded with marinas, shopping malls, restaurants, and bars. **Caya G. F. Betico Croes,** or Main Street, is another major shopping venue running roughly parallel to the waterfront several blocks inland. The harbor is packed with fishing boats and schooners docked next to stalls, where vendors hawk fruits, vegetables, and fish. On the other side of the Seaport Marketplace shopping mall, **Queen Wilhelmina Park,** named after one of Holland's longest-reigning monarchs, features manicured lawns, views of colorful fishing boats, and luxuriant tropical vegetation. If you're looking for a little culture, Oranjestad has a handful of museums that are worth a bit of your time. Squeezed between St. Franciscus Roman Catholic Church and the parish rectory, the small **Archaeological Museum of Aruba,** J. E. Irausquinplein 2A (© **297/5828979**), highlights the island's Amerindian heritage, with pottery vessels, shell and stone tools, burial urns, and skulls and bones on display. (Free admission. Open Mon–Fri 8am–noon and 1–4pm.) To defend the island against pirates, the Dutch erected **Fort Zoutman** in 1796. In 1867, **Willem III Tower,** named after the then-reigning Dutch monarch, was added. Since 1992, the complex has housed the modest **Museo Arubano,** Zoutmanstraat z/n (© **297/5826099**), which displays prehistoric Amerindian artifacts and remnants from the Dutch-colonial period. (Admission $1.75. Open Mon–Fri 9am–noon and 1–4pm.) *Note: The museum re-opened in May 2003 after renovations.* The small **Numismatic Museum of Aruba,** Zuidstraat 7, 1 block northeast of Fort Zoutman (© **297/5828831**), looks unpromising from the outside, but its meticulous, homemade exhibits tell the history of the world through coins. Dedicated numismatists can spend the better part of the morning perusing the 35,000 different specimens from more than 400 countries, but anyone with a passing interest in coins or history will appreciate this labor of love. (Free admission; donations appreciated. Open Mon–Fri 7:30am–3:30pm.)

ON YOUR OWN: TOURING BY RENTAL JEEP

The best way to see Aruba's desertlike terrain is to rent a four-wheel-drive vehicle. Car-rental companies have maps highlighting the best routes to reach the attractions. Here's one popular route.

Following the system of roads that traces the perimeter of the island, start clockwise from Oranjestad. Drive past the hotel strip, toward the island's northwesternmost point. Here, the **California Lighthouse** affords sweeping 360-degree views of spectacular scenery—gentle sand dunes, rocky coral shoreline, and turbulent waves. The picturesque lighthouse gets its name from the *California,* a passenger ship that sank off the nearby coast in 1916. The story that this vessel was the only ship to have heard (and ignored) the *Titanic's* distress signal is malarkey. (In fact, the *Californian* [with a final "n"] of *Titanic* infamy was torpedoed by a German submarine off the coast of Greece in 1915.)

From here on, your adventure will take you into the island's moonlike terrain, past heaps of giant boulders and barren rocky coastline. The well-maintained road that links the hotel strip with Oranjestad deteriorates abruptly into a band of rubble, and the calm, turquoise sea turns rough and rowdy.

By the time you reach the **Alto Vista Chapel,** about 8km (5 miles) from the lighthouse, chances are you'll already be coated with red dust. Don't let that stop you from peeking inside the quaint pale-yellow church that was built in 1750 and renovated 200 years later. Radiating serenity from its cactus-studded perch overlooking the sea, the chapel, Aruba's first, was built by native Indians and Spanish settlers before the island had its own priest.

Farther along the northern coast, you'll approach the hulking ruins of the **Bushiribana Gold Smelter.** Built in 1872, its massive stone walls are remnants of Aruba's gold-mining 19th century. Climb the multitiered interior for impressive sea views. Too bad the walls have been marred with artless graffiti.

Within view of the smelter, **Natural Bridge** is Aruba's most photographed attraction. Rising 7.5m (25 ft.) above the sea and spanning 30m (100 ft.) of rock-strewn waters, this limestone arch has been carved out over the centuries by the relentless pounding of the surf. Because the bridge acts as a buffer between the sandy beach and open ocean, many people come to swim and picnic.

Next, head toward the center of the island and the bizarre **Ayó and Casibari rock formations.** Looking like something out of *The Flintstones,* the gargantuan Ayó rocks served Aruba's early inhabitants as a dwelling or religious site. The reddish-brown petroglyphs on the boulders suggest mystical significance. Although the Casibari boulders weigh several tons each, they look freshly scattered by some cyclopean dice-roller. Look for the formations that resemble birds and dragons, or climb the trail to the top of the highest rock mound for a panorama of the area.

Farther east, back along the northern coast, **Arikok National Park,** Aruba's showcase ecological preserve, sprawls over roughly 20% of the island. Its premier attractions are a series of caves that punctuate the cliff sides of the area's mesas. The most popular, **Fontein Cave,** has brownish-red drawings left by Amerindians and graffiti etched by early European settlers. Stalagmites and stalactites here look like human heads and bison; park rangers stationed at the cave will point them out. The hole is an important roosting place for long-tongued bats, which nap in the damp inner sanctum. Nearby **Quadirikiri Cave** boasts two large chambers with roof openings that allow sunlight in, making flashlights unnecessary. Hundreds of small bats use the 30m- (100-ft.-) long tunnel to reach their nests deeper in the cave. You'll need a flashlight to explore the 90m- (300-ft.-) long passageway of **Baranca Sunu,** another cave in the area commonly known as the Tunnel of Love because of its heart-shaped entrance. Helmets and lights can be rented at the entrance for $6.

Heading southeast toward Aruba's behemoth oil refinery, you'll eventually come to **Baby Beach,** at the island's easternmost point. Like a great big bathtub, this shallow bowl of warm turquoise water is protected by an almost complete circle of rock, and is a great place for a dip after a sweaty day behind the wheel.

SHOPPING

Although Aruba boasts plenty of shopping, don't expect prices to be fabulously cut-rate: The days of Caribbean bargains are waning. Nevertheless, the island's low 3.3% duty can make prices on items such as jewelry and fragrances attractive. What's more, there's no sales tax.

Because the island is part of the Netherlands, **Dutch goods** such as Delft porcelain, chocolate, and cheese are especially good buys. Items from **Indonesia,** another former Dutch colony, are reasonably priced too. **Skin and hair-care products** made from locally produced aloe are also popular and practical. If you're looking for **big-ticket items,** Aruba offers the usual array of watches, cameras, gold and diamond jewelry, Cuban cigars, premium liquor, English and German china, porcelain, French and American fragrances, and crystal.

Aruba's retail activity centers on Oranjestad. About 1km (½-mile) long, **Caya G. F. Betico Croes,** better known as Main Street, is the city's major shopping venue. Downtown also teems with several contiguous shopping malls that stretch for several blocks along the harbor front. **Seaport Mall** and **Seaport Marketplace** feature more than 130 stores, 2 casinos, 20 restaurants and cafes, and a movie theater. Just down the road, **Royal Plaza Mall** is chock-full of popular restaurants and generally upscale boutiques.

BEACHES

All of Aruba's beaches are public, but chairs and shade huts are hotel property. If you use them, expect to be charged. Shade huts located at beaches where there are no hotels, such as Baby Beach, Arashi, and Malmok, are free of charge. Visitors can rent chairs at Eagle and Bay beaches.

Palm Beach, home of Aruba's glamorous high-rise hotels, is the best spot for people-watching. This stretch of white sand is also great for swimming, sunbathing, sailing, fishing, and snorkeling. It can get crowded, and with two piers and numerous watersports operators, it's also busier and noisier than Aruba's other beaches.

Separated from Palm Beach by a limestone outcrop, **Eagle Beach** stretches as far as the eye can see. The sugar-white sand and gentle surf are ideal for swimming, and although the nearby hotels offer watersports and beach activities, the ambience is relaxed and quiet. A couple of bars punctuate the expansive strand, and shaded picnic areas are provided for the public.

Baby Beach, at Aruba's easternmost tip, is a prime destination for families with young children. The protection of rock breakwaters makes this shallow bowl of warm turquoise water perfect for inexperienced swimmers. Giant sea grape bushes offer protection from the sun. The beach has a refreshment stand and washrooms, but no other facilities.

SPORTS

SCUBA DIVING & SNORKELING   Aruba is no Bonaire, but it still offers enough coral reefs, marine life, and wreck diving to keep scuba divers and snorkelers busy. The best snorkeling sites are around Malmok Beach and Boca Catalina, where the water is calm and shallow and marine life is plentiful. Dive sites stretch along the entire southern coast, but most divers head for the German freighter *Antilla,* which was scuttled during World War II off the island's northwestern tip, near Palm Beach. The island's largest watersports operators, **Pelican Adventures** (© **297/5872302**) and **Red Sail Sports** (© **297/5861603**), offer sailing, windsurfing, and water-skiing in addition to snorkeling and scuba diving. Two-tank dives are $65; one-tank dives are $45. Two-hour snorkeling trips are $37.50 and half-day snorkeling excursions sell for $49.50.

WINDSURFING   Aruba's world-class windsurfing conditions attract wind sailors from around the world. **Malmok Beach** is the island's most popular windsurfing spot. Sailed by novices and pros alike, it has slightly gusty offshore winds, minimal current, and moderate chop. **Boca Grandi,** on the extreme eastern coast, is for advanced wave sailors only. **Aruba Boardsailing Productions** (© **297/5863940**) offers 2-hour beginner lessons with equipment for $55. Equipment is $30 for 2 hours, $45 for half a day, and $55 for a full day.

GAMBLING

Aruba boasts 11 casinos, most of them casually elegant. Slot machines gear up at 10am; table games such as baccarat, blackjack, poker, roulette, and craps can start as early as noon; and bingo starts in the afternoon.

Two casinos are steps from the dock. At the Aruba Sonesta Beach Resort, the **Crystal Casino,** L. G. Smith Blvd. 82 (© **297/5836000**), is Aruba's only 24-hour casino and probably its most elegant. In addition to slots and an array of table games, it features a race and sports book room with a satellite linkup and wagering based on Las Vegas odds. The **Seaport Casino,** L. G. Smith Blvd. 9 (© **297/5836000**), also in downtown Oranjestad, fits in well with the surrounding shopping mall; you might think it's just another store.

GREAT LOCAL RESTAURANTS & BARS

Opulence and first-rate French cuisine make **Chez Mathilde,** Havenstraat 23 (© **297/5834968**), the perfect choice for special occasions. Main courses include pan-fried trout, curry mushroom chicken, wild boar, and ostrich. It's pricey, but you deserve it. Lunch $30.

Hip and happy **Cuba's Cookin',** Wilhelminastraat 27 (© **297/5880627**), serves flavorful Cuban dishes expertly prepared. Kid-friendly **Waterfront Crabhouse,** Seaport Market, L. G. Smith Boulevard (© **297/5835858**), offers grilled-cheese sandwiches and "psketti." The more sophisticated adult fare includes red snapper, Maine lobster, and crab. Lunch $10.

3 Bahamas: Nassau & Freeport

Technically, the 700 islands of the Bahamas aren't in the Caribbean—they're in the Atlantic Ocean, just north of the Caribbean and less than 161km (100 miles) from Miami. Because they're an important port of call on the cruise ship circuit and part of the West Indies, though, they're almost always lumped together with their island neighbors to the south.

If you're a seasoned cruiser, chances are you've been to the Bahamas already and might prefer an itinerary that includes more far-flung ports; but if you're new to the region, the Bahamas are a great introduction, with everything you'd expect from a fun-in-the-sun vacation—postcard-perfect beaches, a full range of water activities, and warm temperatures year-round. There's a well-developed tourist infrastructure—things work here—and economic conditions are the envy of most other West Indian islands, so you won't see the kind of poverty that plagues some Caribbean islands. In many ways, the Bahamas isn't much different from, say, some parts of Florida, but if you're looking for something on the exotic side, you'll be able to see colonial sights, British influences, and West Indian color too—you'll know right away you're not in Kansas anymore.

The Bahamas became an independent commonwealth of Great Britain in 1973. Tourism and offshore banking account for the islands' current prosperity. About 85% of Bahamians are descended from African slaves; people of European extraction make up most of the rest of the population.

LANGUAGE   **English** is the official language of the Bahamas. Most people in the tourism industry speak a standard American version of the language at work. You'll also hear an island lilt and a vocabulary that reflects British, Arawak, and African influences.

CURRENCY   The Bahamas' legal tender is the **Bahamian dollar (B$1),** whose value is always the same as that of the U.S. dollar. Both currencies are accepted everywhere on the islands, and most stores accept traveler's checks and major credit cards.

CALLING FROM THE U.S.   Calling the Bahamas from the United States is as simple as phoning between states: Just dial "1" before the numbers listed throughout this section.

NASSAU

Located 298km (185 miles) southeast of Miami, Nassau is the cultural, social, political, and economic center of the Bahamas. With its beaches, shopping, resorts, casinos, historic landmarks, and water and land activities, it's also the island chain's most visited destination—one million travelers a year make their way to the town, and Nassau is one of the world's busiest cruise ship ports. The

Nassau/Paradise Island area comprises two separate islands. Nassau is on the northeastern shore of the 34km- (21-mile-) long island of New Providence, while tiny Paradise Island, linked to New Providence by bridges, protects Nassau harbor for a 4.8km (3-mile) stretch. Although the area accounts for only 2% of the nation's land area, its 175,000 residents represent 60% of the Bahamian population.

COMING ASHORE The cruise ship docks at Prince George Wharf are in the center of town, near Rawson Square and adjacent to the main shopping areas. Your best bet for making long-distance phone calls is the Bahamas Telecommunications (BATELCO) phone center on East Street, about 4 blocks inland from Rawson Square.

INFORMATION The **Ministry of Tourism Office** is located in the British Colonial Hilton, 1 Bay St. (© 242/322-7500), and is open Monday through Friday 9am to 5pm. A smaller booth at Rawson Square is near the dock. For information before you go, call the Tourist Office in the U.S. (© **800/4-BAHAMAS;** www.bahamas.com).

GETTING AROUND

Unless you hire a horse-drawn carriage, the only way to see old Nassau is on foot. The major attractions and stores are pretty concentrated, so walking is the most convenient mode of transportation anyway. If you're really fit, you can even trek over to Cable Beach or Paradise Island.

BY TAXI Practical for longer trips, taxis are required to have working meters, but some drivers insist on flat rates. The initial meter fare is $2, and each additional quarter-mile for the first two passengers is 30¢; for third and fourth passengers, add $2 each to the meter reading. Also, a surcharge is added for luggage stowed in the trunk. Tip your driver 15%. You can hire a five-passenger cab at $23 to $25 per hour. Taxis can be hailed on the street or taken from stands. Radio cabs can be ordered at © **242/323-5111.**

BY JITNEY Jitneys, medium-size buses that travel set routes throughout the city, are the least expensive means of transport. The fare is 75¢ for adults, 50¢ for children, and exact change is required. Buses operate from early in the morning until about 8pm.

BY FERRY Ferries run from the end of Casuarina Drive on Paradise Island across the harbor to Rawson Square for $2 per person. Water taxis also operate during the day between Paradise Island and Prince George Wharf for $3 per person.

BY HORSE-DRAWN CARRIAGE Horse-drawn surreys are the regal (if touristy) way to see Nassau. Agree on a price before you start. The average charge for a 20- to 25-minute tour is $10 per person. The maximum load is two adults plus one child under the age of 12 (or three small adults—if you've been spending too much time at the ship's buffet, you don't qualify). The colorfully painted surreys are available daily from 9am to 4:30pm, except when the horses rest—usually from 1 to 3pm May through October, 1 to 2pm November through April. You'll find surreys in front of the cruise port building.

BY MOTOR SCOOTER/MOPED To rent a motor scooter, contact Ursa Investment, Prince George Wharf (© **242/326-8329**). Mopeds run about $20 an hour or $50 for a full day.

Nassau

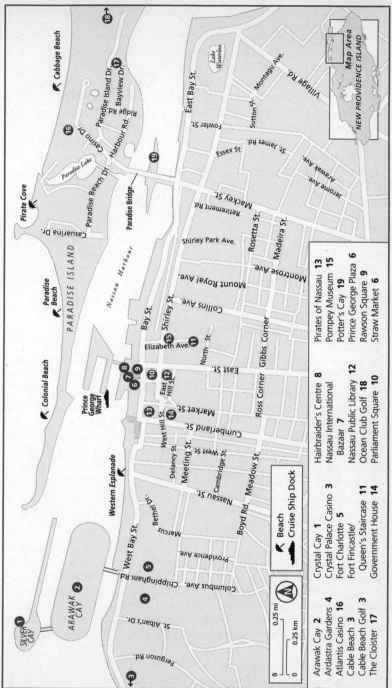

Beach ↙
Cruise Ship Dock ▲

Arawak Cay **2**
Ardastra Gardens **4**
Atlantis Casino **16**
Cable Beach **3**
Cable Beach Golf **3**
The Cloister **17**

Crystal Cay **1**
Crystal Palace Casino **3**
Fort Charlotte **5**
Fort Fincastle/
Queen's Staircase **11**
Government House **14**

Hairbraider's Centre **8**
Nassau International
Bazaar **7**
Nassau Public Library **12**
Ocean Club Golf **18**
Parliament Square **10**

Pirates of Nassau **13**
Pompey Museum **15**
Potter's Cay **19**
Prince George Plaza **6**
Rawson Square **9**
Straw Market **6**

ⓔ Frommer's Favorite Nassau Experiences

Gorging on Fresh Conch at Arawak Cay: The small man-made island across the West Bay Street shore has the freshest conch around. For a true island experience, wash it down with the local cocktail—coconut water, milk, and gin. (See "Great Local Restaurants & Bars," below.)

Taking a Walk Through Colonial History: Nassau has numerous forts, government buildings, and private establishments that keep the flavor of the islands' colonial past alive. Shops and boutiques abut the historic attractions, so you can get some culture and feed your shopping addiction at the same time. (See "On Your Own: Within Walking Distance," below.)

BY RENTAL CAR   Most vehicles have left-hand steering, and driving is British-style. If you're used to driving on the right, it may take some time to adjust. Thankfully, traffic is seldom heavy except downtown near the port. Rental-car license plates carry the letters "SD" (which stands for "suicide driver" according to joking Bahamians). **Avis, Budget, Dollar,** and **Hertz** all have offices here.

SHORE EXCURSIONS OFFERED BY THE CRUISE LINES
It's easy to get around Nassau via taxi or foot, so you can do a lot on your own. Cruise lines typically offer a variety of excursions, though, including the ones described below.

Heart of Nassau & Ardastra Gardens ($33, 2½ hr.): After touring Bay Street, the main shopping district, you'll witness Ardastra Gardens' marching flamingo review. Other stops include the Queen's Staircase and Fort Charlotte.

Harbor Cruise & Atlantis Resort ($42, 2½ hr.): A tour boat with local guide shows you the sights (such as they are) from the water, then drops you at the fanciful Atlantis Resort for a brief tour that includes a visit to Predator Lagoon, home to sharks, barracuda, and other toothy fish.

Thriller Powerboat Tour ($42, 1 hr.): A thrill-seeker's excursion, with high-speed boats roaring around the waters off Nassau, scaring the hell out of the fish. Not our personal favorite way to see . . . well, anything, but it sure is fast. Vroom.

EXCURSIONS OFFERED BY LOCAL AGENCIES
Goombay Guided Walking Tours: These 45-minute tours, arranged by the Ministry of Tourism (ⓒ **242/326-9772**), leave from the Tourist Information Booth on Rawson Square, and usually leave every hour from 10am to 2:30 pm. Make reservations in advance. The tours include descriptions of some of the city's oldest buildings, with information on Nassau's history, customs, and traditions. The cost is $10.

Scuba Diving, Sea Scootering & Shark Dives: Unpretentious and friendly **Nassau Scuba Centre,** Coral Harbour (ⓒ **242/362-1964;** www.divenassau. com), offers transportation to and from Prince Georges Wharf for cruise ship visitors, with dives at 9am and 1pm. Two-tank dives run about $75; snorkeling is $35, including equipment. For certified divers, shark dives allow you to either watch a divemaster feed sharks ($115) or don a chain-mail shark suit and feed them yourself (for a hefty $399). **Stuart Cove,** Southwest Bay Street, South Ocean (℃ **800/879-9832** in the U.S., or 242/362-4171; www.stuartcove.com), offers more options, including personal submarine excursions, which allow non-divers to move about underwater without scuba equipment ($95). The operation can be a mob scene, though, and the service is less personal than that at Nassau Scuba. The company also offers two-tank dives for certified divers ($80–$125) and snorkel excursions ($40). All programs are 3½ hours long. It's recommended to reserve ahead for both the Nassau Scuba Centre and Stuart Cove.

Walking on the Ocean Floor: If you loved Captain Nemo and *20,000 Leagues Under the Sea,* you won't want to miss **Hartley's Undersea Walk,** East Bay Street (℃ **242/393-8234**). As part of a 3½-hour yacht cruise ($150 per person), you'll don a breathing helmet and spend about 20 minutes walking along the ocean bottom through a "garden" of tropical fish, sponges, and other undersea life. You don't have to be able to swim, and you can wear your glasses, but some people find the high-pitched pinging noise annoying. Ships depart from the Nassau Yacht Haven Tuesday through Saturday at 9:30am and 1:30pm. Check-in times are 9am and 1pm, respectively.

Yacht Cruises: Located at the Paradise Island Bridge, **Nassau Cruises** (℃ **242/ 363-3000**) has three luxurious yachts that head for the secluded beaches of Blue Lagoon Island, 6.5km (4 miles) east of Paradise Island. The boats leave daily at 10 and 11:30am and return at 2pm and 4pm. A day pass ($25 for adults and $15 for children) covers the boat ride only. An all-inclusive day pass ($65 for adults and $35 for children) includes transportation to the dock, the boat ride, lunch, two daiquiris for adults, and all nonmotorized watersports.

ON YOUR OWN: WITHIN WALKING DISTANCE

Walking is the best way to see the major sites of Nassau and to get a feel for the city's character and history. Start at Prince George Wharf, where your ship is docked.

As you exit from the cruise ship wharf into the main port area, aggressive hawkers will encourage you to have your hair braided at the **Hairbraider's Centre.** This government-sponsored open-air pavilion attracts braiding experts from all over the island. If you're looking for a Bo Derek look, here's your chance. If you're not, a simple "no thanks" keeps the touts at bay.

Just across Bay Street from Rawson Square (inland from the wharf) are the flamingo-pink government buildings of **Parliament Square,** constructed in 1815. The House of Assembly, old colonial Secretary's Office, and Supreme Court flank a statue of Queen Victoria, while a bust on the north side of the square honors Sir Milo B. Butler, the Bahamas' first governor-general.

Built as a prison in 1798, the **Nassau Public Library,** located a block inland from Parliament Square, facing Shirley Street, is one of the city's oldest buildings and surely one of the more interesting libraries anywhere. Its octagonal shape was copied from a munitions storage facility, and the decidedly unpenitentiary pink paint was added after 1889, when the building reopened as a library. The books, historical prints, colonial documents, and Arawak Indian artifacts are kept in former cells.

Slaves carved the **Queen's Staircase** out of a solid limestone cliff in 1793. Originally designed as an escape route for soldiers at Fort Fincastle, each step now represents a year in Queen Victoria's 65-year reign. Lush plants and a water-fall stand guard over the staircase, which is located a few blocks up from the library on East Street and leads to **Fort Fincastle,** Elizabeth Avenue, built in 1793 by Lord Dunmore, the royal governor. An elevator climbs a 38m- (126-ft.-) high water tower, where you can look down on the arrowhead-shaped fort. Walk around on your own or hire a guide. (*Note:* You may find some of them aggressive.)

Walking downhill from Fort Fincastle and back toward the waterfront, turn left on East Hill Street past Market Street. On the left stands **Government House,** the official residence of the governor-general, built in 1801. Tropical foliage lines the grounds leading to the colonial mansion, and a statue of Columbus stands over the hillside steps.

This one's for kids, but young-at-heart parents may also enjoy the corny **Pirates of Nassau** museum at King and George streets, downhill from Government House (© 242/356-3759). Step aboard an embattled pirate ship and come face-to-face with Captain Teach and his fearsome crew as they guide you through the age of piracy in the lawless Nassau of 1716. It's open 9am to 2pm daily, and admission is a steep $12 for adults—only worth it if you're with kids, as each adult may bring two children free; each additional child is $6. Admission includes a 45-minute tour.

On Bay Street, about a block closer to the waterfront than the Pirates of Nassau, is the **Straw Market,** which burned to the ground in 2001, but reopened on the same spot. Some of the items sold at the stalls here are authentic, but much of what you see comes from Asia. There are better places to get the real thing (see "Shopping," below), but enjoy the scene anyway. Hours are roughly 7:30am to 7pm.

The modest **Pompey Museum** (© 242/326-2566), which is located adjacent to the Straw Market, at press time was scheduled to reopen in June 2003 with upgrades. Displays recount the story of Bahamian slavery, abolition, and emancipation through artifacts, historical documents, and drawings. The museum, which was formerly open Monday through Friday 10am to 4pm and Saturday 10am to noon, plans to extend its hours, possibly to as late as 8 or 9pm. Admissions of $1 for adults, 50¢ for children may be raised nominally.

If you're up for more walking, **Potter's Cay,** under the Paradise Island Bridge, provides more market color. Sloops from the less populated Out Islands bring in their fresh catch. Freshly grown herbs and vegetables are also sold, along with limes, papayas, pineapples, and bananas. Stalls sell conch in several forms: raw and marinated in lime juice, as spicy deep-fried fritters, and in salad and soup.

ON YOUR OWN: BEYOND THE PORT AREA
About 1.6km (1 mile) west of downtown Nassau, just off West Bay Street, **Fort Charlotte** covers more than 40 hilltop hectares (100 acres). The Bahamas' largest fort, it offers impressive views of Paradise Island, Nassau, and the harbor. The complex, constructed in 1788, features a moat, dungeons, underground passageways, and 42 cannons.

Parading pink flamingos are the main attraction at the lush, 2-hectare (5-acre) **Ardastra Gardens,** Chippingham Road, about 1.6km (1 mile) west of downtown Nassau (© 242/323-5806). The graceful birds obey the drillmaster's orders, and with their long-legged precision and discipline, they give the Rockettes a run for their money. The performances, accompanied by informative commentary, are presented daily at 10:30am, 2:10pm, and 4:30pm. Lory parrot feedings can be viewed at 11am, 1:30pm, and 3:30pm. Other exotic wildlife—boa constrictors, honey bears, macaws, and capuchin monkeys—are less talented but fascinating in their own right. Paths meander through tropical foliage that's sure to enchant gardeners. The gardens are open daily from 9am to 5 pm, with gates closing at 4:30pm. Admission is $20 per person.

The Cloister, on Casino Drive on Paradise Island (© **242/363-3000**), is part of a monastery built in the 13th century by French monks. In the 1920s, William Randolph Hearst bought it, had it disassembled, and moved it from France to his estate in San Simeon, California. The stones were stored for years because no one knew how to properly reassemble them. In 1962, Huntington Hartford, the A&P grocery store heir and developer of Paradise Island, bought the structure from Hearst and hired a sculptor to reconstruct it on the island. It's quite an anomaly on tropical Paradise Island, but it's a serene spot. The adjacent **Versailles Gardens** feature formal vistas, tropical flowers, and classic bronze and marble statuary. The Cloister is only open to guests staying at the Ocean Club, Comfort Suites Paradise Island, Atlantis Paradise Island, or Harborside Resort at Atlantis. There is no admission fee.

The mythical lost city of Atlantis submerged under Bahamian waters? Sure, it sounds hokey, and all the grandiloquent hype makes you want to hate the place, but **The Dig** and **Marine Habitat** at the Atlantis Paradise Island megaresort actually end up exceeding expectations. Drawing on age-old myths of the lost city, The Dig is a fantastic world of faux ancient ruins flooded by the sea. The interconnected passageways, boulevards, and chambers, now inhabited by piranhas, hammerhead sharks, stingrays, and morays, are visible through huge glass windows. Purported to be the largest man-made marine habitat in the world—"second only to Mother Nature"—the resort's sprawling 11-million-gallon lagoon system boasts more than 200 sea species and 50,000 individual creatures. Tickets for the guided "Discovery Tour," available at the resort's guest services desks, are $25 for adults, $19 for children under 12. (*Note:* This tour does not include use of the resort's beach or water slide, which are reserved for guests only.) For information, call © **242/363-3000** or check out **www.atlantis.com**.

GAMBLING

If you think your ship's casino is as good as most land-based facilities, you haven't been to the impressive, 9,290 sq. m (100,000-sq.-ft.) **Atlantis Casino** in the Atlantis Paradise Island megaresort (© **242/363-3000**), the largest gaming and entertainment complex in the Caribbean. Two astounding glass sculptures, the *Temple of the Sun* and the *Temple of the Moon,* anchor the vast facility and tie in with the resort's Lost City of Atlantis theme. Open 24 hours a day, the casino boasts almost 1,000 slot machines and 78 gaming tables for baccarat, roulette, craps, blackjack, and Caribbean stud poker. Unlike most other casinos, the Atlantis makes no attempt to hide what's going on outside: Huge windows provide panoramas of the adjacent marina and lagoons.

The 3,250 sq. m (35,000-sq.-ft.) **Crystal Palace Casino,** West Bay Street, Cable Beach (© **242/327-6200**), screams 1980s with its pink and purple rainbow decor. The only casino on New Providence Island, it's part of the Wyndham Nassau Resort. Despite tough competition from the Atlantis Casino, it stacks up well against most other casinos in the Caribbean, with 700 slot machines and more than 60 gaming tables. The oval-shaped bar extends onto the gaming floor, and the lounge offers live entertainment. It's open Sunday to Thursday from 10am to 4am, Friday and Saturday 24 hours.

Taxis will take you to either casino from the cruise pier.

SHOPPING

In 1992, the Bahamas abolished import duties on 11 luxury-good categories, including china, crystal, fine linens, jewelry, leather goods, photographic equipment, watches, and fragrances. Even so, you can end up spending more on an item in the Bahamas than you would at home. True bargains are rare, as is finding much that's really worth buying. The principal shopping area is **Bay Street** and the adjacent blocks, which are almost the first things you see when you leave your ship. Here you'll find duty-free luxury-goods stores, such as Colombian Emeralds and Solomon's Mines, plus hundreds of others selling T-shirts, tourist gimcracks, duty-free booze and cigars, and recordings of Junkanoo music.

In the crowded aisles of the **Straw Market** on Bay Street, between Market Range and Navy Lion Road, you can watch craftspeople weave and plait straw hats, handbags, dolls, place mats, and other items, but be aware that many of the items aren't of the best quality; in fact, much of it has been imported from Asia. Welcome to the global market, folks! It's tourist central, so most shopkeepers are willing to bargain, though some won't budge. If you want a really beautiful handmade straw work, walk a few blocks to **The Plait Lady,** at Victoria and Bay streets. The merchandise here is vastly superior to what's peddled in the Straw Market, and it's 100% Bahamian-made. Both **Island Tings,** Bay Street between East Street and Elizabeth Avenue, and **Seagrape,** West Bay Street at the Travelers' Rest restaurant (10 min. west of Cable Beach by car), offer Bahamian arts and crafts, Junkanoo masks, and jewelry.

The tired-looking **Nassau International Bazaar,** running from Bay Street to the waterfront near Prince George Wharf, has 30 shops that sell goods from around the globe. The stores at **Prince George Plaza,** Bay Street, sell designer merchandise and are often crowded.

Marlborough Antiques, across the street from the Hilton British Colonial on Marlborough Street, has an eclectic and interesting collection of antiques and books.

Bahamas Rum Cake Factory, at 602 E. Bay St., carries an array of Bahamian food products, including hot sauces, spices, and the eponymous dessert, which you can buy as they come out of the oven. If you can't get enough of the local rum, try a milkshake with a shot. And if you get home and want more, you can arrange worldwide cake delivery through their website, **www.bahamasrum cakefactory.com.**

BEACHES

On New Providence Island, sun worshippers make the pilgrimage to **Cable Beach,** which offers various watersports and easy access to shops, a casino, bars, and restaurants. The beach stretches for 6.4km (4 miles), and the waters can change quickly from rough to calm and clear. It's 8km (5 miles) from the port—a $10 taxi ride or 75¢ via the No. 10 bus.

More convenient for cruise ship passengers but inferior to Cable Beach, the **Western Esplanade** sweeps westward from the Hilton British Colonial hotel. Facilities include restrooms, changing facilities, and a snack bar. In the months preceding the Junkanoo carnival (celebrated on the new year), local bands practice their carnival routines here.

Paradise Beach on Paradise Island is a ferry ride away from Prince George Wharf (see "By Ferry" under "Getting Around," above). The price of admission ($3 for adults, $1 for children) includes use of a shower and locker. An extra $10 deposit is required for towels. Paradise Island has a number of smaller beaches as well, including **Pirate's Cove Beach** and **Cabbage Beach.** Bordered by casuarinas, palms, and sea grapes, Cabbage Beach's broad sands stretch for 3.2km (2 miles), but it's likely to be crowded with guests of the nearby resorts. Tranquillity seekers find something approaching solitude on the northwestern end, accessible by boat or foot only.

SPORTS

GOLF   South Ocean Golf Course, Southwest Bay Road (℃ 242/362-4391), is the best course on New Providence Island and one of the best in the Bahamas. Located 30 minutes from Nassau, this 18-hole, 6,036m (6,707-yard), par-72 beauty has some first-rate holes with a backdrop of trees, shrubs, ravines, and undulating hills. Greens fees are $100 per person with cart. Although not as challenging, the 6,336m (7,040-yard), par-72 **Cable Beach Golf Course,** Cable Beach, West Bay Road (℃ 242/327-6000), has lakes and ponds tucked picturesquely throughout, and the length encourages strong hitters to shave strokes with long, well-placed drives. Greens fees are $140 per person for 18 holes, including cart.

The 18-hole, 6,390m (7,100-yard), par-72 PGA course at the **Ocean Club** (℃ 242/363-6680) on Paradise Island was designed by Tom Weiskopf and hosts the Michael Jordan Celebrity Invitational. The visually intimidating par-4 seventh hole has water down the right side off the tee and the added difficulty of prevailing left-to-right winds. Hole 12 features wetlands and a panorama of the Atlantic, while the 17th plays entirely along the beach. The club is not open to the general public. Guests at the Ocean Club and Atlantis are charged greens fees of $245 per person, including cart. Guests at selected other hotels may be eligible to use the course if they call the day they want to play. They're charged greens fees of $255 per person, including cart.

GREAT LOCAL RESTAURANTS & BARS

Conch, Bahamian "rock lobster," and boiled fish are local specialties; pigeon peas and rice are popular side dishes. The **local beer** is Kalik, and Nassau's **local rum** is Bacardi.

ON ARAWAK CAY   You'll get all the conch you can eat on **Arawak Cay,** a small man-made island across West Bay Street from Ardastra Gardens and Fort Charlotte. Join the locals in sampling conch with hot sauce, and wash it down with a coconut water–and–gin cocktail. Gorging on the cay is a local tradition and a real Bahamian experience.

IN NASSAU   If you want fancy, **Graycliff Restaurant,** West Hill Street, next to Government House (℃ 242/322-2796), is one of the most elegant restaurants in the West Indies. It was built in the 1740s by a former privateer and became Nassau's first inn in 1844, and during the American Civil War its cellar served as a jail for war prisoners. Polly Leach, a friend of Al Capone, owned the house some time later, as did Lord and Lady Dudley, friends of the Duke and Duchess of Windsor. Royalty and celebrities have eaten in the elegant surroundings for decades, enjoying its extensive wine list and hand-rolled cigars. The continental lunches and dinners (jacket required) are expensive, but worth it if you've squirreled away for a really special meal. Call ahead for reservations. Lunch $30.

Much more modest, **Bahamian Kitchen,** Trinity Place, off Market Street, next to Trinity Church (℃ 242/325-0702), is one of the best places for good, down-home Bahamian food at modest prices. Specialties include lobster Bahamian style, fried red snapper, and curried chicken. Lunch $8.

Near Ardastra Gardens, **The Shoal,** Nassau Street (℗ **242/323-4400**), is another local favorite and a featured restaurant in the Ministry of Tourism's "Real Taste of the Bahamas" program, which highlights independent establishments that serve indigenous cuisine. Every cab driver knows the place, which really hops on Sunday mornings. Try the boiled fish breakfast.

Café Matisse, on Bank Lane at Bay Street, behind Parliament Square (℗ **242/356-7012**), is set in an old colonial home and features antique tile floors, Matisse prints, and a serene outdoor courtyard. The extensive menu includes seafood, pastas, and pizzas. It's an unbeatable respite from shopping and sightseeing in downtown Nassau. Lunch $15.

ON PARADISE ISLAND   Among the 30-plus pricey restaurants and bars in the **Atlantis Paradise Island,** on Casino Drive (℗ **242/363-3000**), two merit special mention. **Seagrapes** serves an affordable buffet of tropical foods, with a special emphasis on Cuban, Caribbean, and Cajun dishes. Lunch $16. **Five Twins,** just off the casino floor, features an elegantly minimalist sushi and satay bar. The lighting is soothingly dim, and the black-and-white marble floor complements the black lacquer dinnerware and scarlet napkins. Don't pass up the tropical-fruit soup dessert. The restaurant is not open for lunch.

FREEPORT/LUCAYA

Freeport/Lucaya on Grand Bahama Island (often referred to as GBI) is the second most popular destination in the Bahamas. Technically, Freeport is the landlocked section of town while adjacent Lucaya hugs the waterfront. Originally intended as two separate developments, the two have grown together over the years, and though they offer none of Nassau's colonial charm, they do offer plenty of sun, surf, golf, tennis, and watersports—though the frenzy of the gambling and shopping scenes here might be too much for some visitors.

It wasn't until the 19th century that the first permanent settlers arrived on the island. Most earned a living as fishermen or by harvesting timber. GBI remained sparsely populated until 1955, when American developer Wallace Groves joined British industrialist Sir Charles Hayward to build the tax-free city of Freeport for tourism and manufacturing. Today, tourism remains the lifeblood of the island's 50,000 residents.

COMING ASHORE   On Grand Bahama Island, your ship docks at a dreary port in the middle of nowhere, a $10 taxi ride from Freeport and the International Bazaar, center of most of the action.

CALLING HOME FROM THE BAHAMAS   Long-distance phones are in the port terminal.

INFORMATION   Information is available from the **Grand Bahama Tourism Board,** located in the International Bazaar in the Lucaya area (℗ **800/448-3386** or 242/352-8044). Another information booth is located at Port Lucaya (℗ **242/373-8988**). For information before you go, call the **Bahamas Tourism Board** in New York (℗ **800/4-BAHAMAS**) or visit the website at **www. bahamas.com**.

GETTING AROUND

Once you get to Freeport by taxi, you can explore the center of town on foot. If you want to make excursions to the west or east ends of the island, your best bet is to rent a car.

Freeport/Lucaya

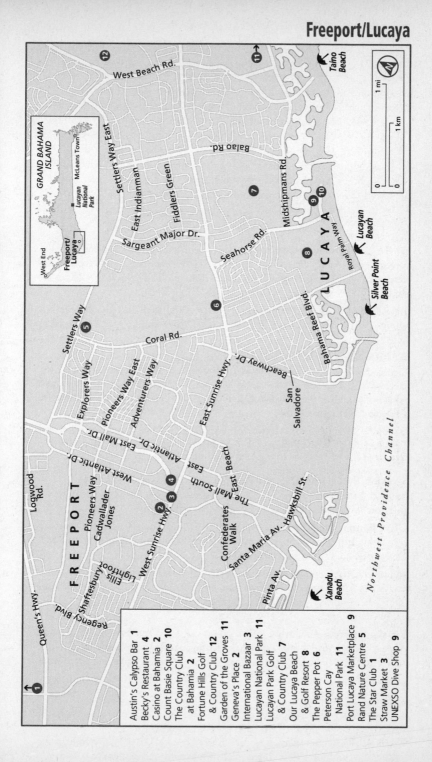

GRAND BAHAMA ISLAND

West End

Freeport/ Lucaya

Lucayan National Park

McLeans Town

West Beach Rd.

Settlers Way East

East Indianman

Fiddlers Green

Balao Rd.

Sargeant Major Dr.

Settlers Way

Explorers Way

Coral Rd.

Pioneers Way East

Adventurers Way

East Mall Dr.

West Atlantic Dr.

Pioneers Way

Cadwallader Jones

Shaftesbury

Ellis

Lightfoot

Logwood Rd.

Queen's Hwy.

Regency Blvd.

FREEPORT

West Sunrise Hwy.

East Atlantic Dr.

East Sunrise Hwy.

The Mall South

East Beach

East Mall

Confederates Walk

Santa Maria Av.

Hawksbill St.

Pinta Av.

Seahorse Rd.

Midshipmans Rd.

Bahama Reef Blvd.

Beachway Dr.

San Salvadore

LUCAYA

Royal Palm Way

Taino Beach

Lucayan Beach

Silver Point Beach

Xanadu Beach

Northwest Providence Channel

1 mi

1 km

Austin's Calypso Bar **1**
Becky's Restaurant **4**
Casino at Bahamia **2**
Count Basie Square **10**
The Country Club at Bahamia **2**
Fortune Hills Golf & Country Club **12**
Garden of the Groves **11**
Geneva's Place **2**
International Bazaar **3**
Lucayan National Park **11**
Lucayan Park Golf & Country Club **7**
Our Lucaya Beach & Golf Resort **8**
The Pepper Pot **6**
Peterson Cay National Park **11**
Port Lucaya Marketplace **9**
Rand Nature Centre **5**
The Star Club **1**
Straw Market **3**
UNEXSO Dive Shop **9**

> ### Ⓒ Frommer's Favorite Freeport/Lucaya Experiences
>
> **Touring Lucayan National Park:** About 19km (12 miles) from Lucaya, this park boasts one of the loveliest beaches on Grand Bahama, as well as caves, mangroves, and nature walks through various ecological zones. (See "Shore Excursions Offered by the Cruise Lines," below.)
>
> **Visiting the Star Club:** Built in the 1940s, this gem has hosted many famous guests over the years. A salty old joint, it's now the island's only after-hours bar and a watering hole Ernest Hemingway would have loved. (See "Great Local Restaurants & Bars," below.)

BY TAXI   The government sets taxi rates, which start at $3 and increase 30¢ for each additional ¼-mile. Cabs wait at the dock, or you can call **Freeport Taxi Company** (Ⓒ **242/352-6666**) or **Grand Bahama Taxi Union** (Ⓒ **242/352-7101**).

BY RENTAL CAR   Roads are good on GBI, and traffic is light. Remember, though, that driving is on the left side. **Avis, Dollar,** and **Hertz** all have offices here.

BY MOTOR SCOOTER OR BICYCLE   You can rent scooters or bicycles at the major hotels such as **The Royal Oasis Beach & Golf Resort,** West Sunrise Highway (Ⓒ **242/350-7000**). A two-seat scooter requires a $100 deposit and rents for about $40 a day; bicycles require a $50 deposit and cost about $12 for a half-day, $20 for a full day.

BY BUS   Public bus service runs from the International Bazaar to downtown Freeport and from the Pub on the Mall to the Lucaya area. The typical fare is 75¢ to $1.

SHORE EXCURSIONS OFFERED BY THE CRUISE LINES
Snorkel Adventure ($29–$36, 3 hr.): It's a standard snorkeling excursion, letting you swim with the fishes and explore coral formations.

Glass Bottom Boat Tour ($24, 3 hr.): Departing from Port Lucaya Marketplace, this trip allows you to view coral reefs without getting your feet wet. Divers feed the fish below as you watch.

Sanctuary Bay Dolphin Encounter ($76, 3¼ hr.): Pat a dolphin on the nose! On this excursion you can watch, touch, and photograph Flipper, or at least one of his relatives. See the UNEXSO information below for more elaborate dolphin excursions you can arrange on your own.

Kayaking Nature Adventure ($72, 6 hr.): Visit a protected island creek, kayak through a mangrove forest, explore the island's caves, and take a guided nature walk into Lucayan National Park. The excursion includes lunch and beach time.

Lucayan Beach Experience ($49, 6 hr.): The Lucayan Beach resort complex has facilities for pool volleyball, basketball, beach bowling, and body painting. The cost includes lunch. But $49 to go to the beach? C'mon.

EXCURSIONS OFFERED BY LOCAL AGENCIES
Kayak & Bike Tours: Kayak Nature Tours (Ⓒ **242/373-2485;** www.bahamas vg.com/kayak.html) offers three worthwhile and recommended excursions

suitable for cruisers. The first, to Lucayan National Park, features sea kayaking through mangroves, a nature hike, a stop at two caves, and a swim and picnic lunch at Gold Rock Beach ($69, 6 hr.). The second, to Peterson Cay National Park, includes sea kayaking to the small offshore cay, guided snorkeling, beach time, and lunch ($69, 5 hr.). The other features a leisurely bicycle ride along Taino Beach and the Settlement of Smith Point. The tour includes a visit to Sanctuary Bay, a guided walk through the tropical landscape of Garden of the Groves, and lunch ($79, 5 hr.). Guides on each of the tours are personable, informative, and professional.

Scuba, Snorkeling, Shark Dives & Dolphin Swims: In the Bahamas, reef diving takes a back seat to theme-park-style "adventure" programs, including shark-feeding dives and swim-with-dolphins adventures. One of the premier diving and snorkeling facilities in the Caribbean, the **Underwater Explorers Society (UNEXSO),** at Lucaya Beach (© **800/992-3483** or 242/373-1244; www.unexso.com), offers reef, shark, and wreck dives. Two-tank reef dives are $70, shark dives are $89, 3-hour learn-to-dive courses are $99, and snorkeling trips are $29 adults, $15 children under 12. Premier snorkeling sites include Paradise Cove and Deadman's Reef. UNEXSO also allows divers to swim alongside dolphins in the open ocean. Several different programs are available. The **Close Encounter** ($59, children under 5 free) allows guests to observe the sea mammals from an observation deck while listening to an informative presentation. Later, you can wade into the waist-high water and touch the creatures. The highlight of the **Swim with the Dolphins** experience ($149, minimum age 12, under 16 must be accompanied by an adult) is swimming alongside the animals in protected waters after a briefing on dolphin behavior. The open-ocean **Snorkel with the Dolphins** program ($169, minimum age 12, under 16 must be accompanied by an adult) allows you to dive with bottlenose dolphins in shallow waters. These programs are popular, so advance reservations are a must.

Party/Snorkel Cruises: Superior Watersports in Freeport (© **242/373-7863**) offers daily 5-hour beach party/snorkeling cruises that include equipment, lunch, and unlimited rum punch ($59 for adults, $39 for children 2–12). **Paradise Watersports,** at the Xanadu Beach Resort and Marina (© **242/352-2887**), offers a snorkeling cruise that transports passengers on a 48-foot catamaran to a coral reef ($30 adults, $15 children under 12) and a glass-bottom boat ride ($25 adults, $15 children under 12).

ON YOUR OWN: BEYOND THE PORT AREA

Nothing of note is within walking distance of the port. You must take a cab over to Freeport/Lucaya for all attractions.

One of the island's prime attractions, the 4.8-hectare (12-acre) **Garden of the Groves,** was once the private meditation garden of Freeport's founder, Wallace Groves. The tranquil park features waterfalls, flowering shrubs, about 10,000 trees, tropical birds, Bahamian raccoons, Vietnamese potbellied pigs, and West African pygmy goats. The serene hilltop chapel overlooking the pond is a popular place for exchanging vows. It's located at the intersection of Midshipman Road and Magellan Drive, Freeport (© **242/373-5668**), and is open Monday through Saturday from 9am to 4pm, Sunday 9am to 4pm; $9.95 for adults, $6.95 for ages 3 to 10.

A couple of miles east of downtown Freeport, the 40-hectare (100-acre) **Rand Nature Centre** serves as the regional headquarters of the Bahamas National Trust. Pineland nature trails meander past native flora and wild birds, including the Bahama parrot and the island's only flock of West Indian flamingos. Other highlights include native animal displays (don't miss the boa constrictors), a replica of a Lucayan Indian village, an education center, and a gift shop. It's located on East Settlers Way, Freeport (© 242/352-5438), and is open Monday through Friday, 9am to 4pm; $5 for adults, $3 for ages 5 to 12.

Peterson Cay National Park, approximately 24km (15 miles) east of Freeport and .8km (½-mile) offshore, is accessible by boat only. Coral reefs ringing the tiny island make for great snorkeling and diving, and the serene location is perfect for a picnic. For information, contact the Rand Nature Centre (© 242/352-5438).

If your ship's in port late, don't miss the free nightly concert at **Count Basie Square,** in the center of Port Lucaya's waterfront restaurant-and-shopping complex. The legendary jazz bandleader who lends his name to the square had a home on Grand Bahama, and today the square's vine-covered bandstand attracts steel-drum bands, small Junkanoo groups, and gospel singers.

SHOPPING
The **International Bazaar,** at East Mall Drive and East Sunrise Highway, next to the Casino at Bahamia, is pure 1960s Bahamian kitsch, and though relentlessly cheerful, it's a little long in the tooth. Each area of the 4-hectare (10-acre), 100-shop complex attempts to capture the ambience of a different region of the globe. Stereotypes abound. You'll find Japanese items in the "Ginza," sidewalk cafes on the "Left Bank," silk saris in "India," woodcarvings and dashikis in "Africa," serapes and piñatas in "Spain," and everything from high-end luxury goods to T-shirts throughout. Some items here run about 40% less than in the United States, though certainly not all. Buses marked INTERNATIONAL BAZAAR deliver passengers to the center's much-photographed Torii Gate, a Japanese symbol of welcome.

The **Straw Market,** beside the International Bazaar, features items with a Bahamian touch—baskets, hats, handbags, and place mats. Quality varies, so look around before buying your souvenirs.

The **Port Lucaya Marketplace,** on Seahorse Road near the UNEXSO Dive Shop, is a 2.4-hectare (6-acre) shopping-and-dining complex much like the International Bazaar. Steel-drum bands and strolling musicians add to the festive atmosphere. Many of the restaurants and shops overlook a 50-slip marina, and the boardwalk along the water is ideal for watching the dolphins at **UNEXSO** (www.unexso.com), which has a dive shop if you're in need of wet suits, underwater cameras, or more prosaic items such as swimsuits, sunglasses, and hats.

BEACHES
Grand Bahama Island has miles of white-sand beaches. **Xanadu Beach,** immediately east of Freeport at the Xanadu Beach Resort, is the premier stretch in the Lucaya area, offering most watersports equipment. It can get crowded at times. **Taíno Beach, Churchill Beach,** and **Fortune Beach** are all conveniently located on the Lucaya oceanfront. A 20-minute ride east of Lucaya, **Gold Rock Beach** may be the island's best. Secluded in Lucayan National Park, it has barbecue pits, picnic tables, and a spectacular low tide. **Barbary Beach,** slightly closer to Lucaya, is great for seashell hunters, and in May and June white spider lilies in the area bloom spectacularly.

SPORTS
GOLF With more links than any other island in the Bahamas, Grand Bahama is becoming a prime golf destination. **The Country Club at Bahamia,** The Mall South (© 242/352-6721), has two championship courses. The Emerald

Course has plenty of trees along the fairways, as well as an abundance of water hazards and bunkers. Its toughest hole is the ninth, a par-5 with 491m (545 yards) from the blue tees to the hole. The Ruby Course has a total of 6,075m (6,750 yards) if played from the championship tees. Greens fees for 18 holes are $95, including cart.

Our Lucaya Beach & Golf Resort, Royal Palm Way, F-42500, Lucaya (© 242/373-2002), also has two courses. The Lucayan course, designed by Dick Wilson, features well-protected elevated greens, fairways lined with tropical foliage, and doglegs. The par-72 links-style Reef course, designed by Robert Trent Jones, Jr., is 6,237m (6,930 yards) from the championship tees, with water traps on 13 of 18 holes. Greens fees are $105 for 18 holes, including cart. Club rentals are $48.

The course at **Lucayan Park Golf & Country Club,** at Lucaya Beach (© 242/373-1066), was recently made over and is known for its entrance and a hanging boulder sculpture. Greens are fast, and the course has a couple of par-5 holes more than 450m (500 yards) long. Total distance from the blue tees is 6,142m (6,824 yards); par is 72. Greens fees are $120 per person for 18 holes, including cart.

Fortune Hills Golf & Country Club, Richmond Park, Lucaya (© 242/373-4500), was designed as an 18-hole course, but the back 9 were never completed. You can replay the front 9 for a total of 6,224m (6,916 yards) from the blue tees; par is 72. Greens fees are $54 per person, including cart.

WATERSPORTS   Paradise Watersports, at the Xanadu Beach Resort and Marina (© 242/352-2887), offers water-skiing ($20 for 30 min.) and parasailing ($50). Water-skiing lessons are $40 for 30 minutes.

GAMBLING

The 1,860 sq. m (20,000-sq.-ft.) **Casino at Bahamia,** on the Mall at West Sunrise Highway (© 242/350-7000), offers gaming, dining, and live entertainment. The exterior looks like a Moroccan palace—a fanciful Kismet sort of conceit that's perfect next to the kitsch of the International Bazaar. Serious gamblers appreciate the variety of games: full-service sports book, double odds, craps, blackjack, minibaccarat, roulette, Caribbean stud poker, big six wheel, and hundreds of slots and video poker games. The facility's $10 million face-lift was completed in late 2001.

GREAT LOCAL RESTAURANTS & BARS

The most popular **Bahamian beer** is Kalik. Bahamian Hammerhead, another brand, is brewed on Grand Bahama. GBI's **local rums** include Don Lorenzo and Ricardo.

If you'd like a taste of the Bahamas the way they used to be, head for the **Star Club,** on Bayshore Road, on the island's west end (© 242/346-6207). Built in the 1940s, the Star was Grand Bahama's first hotel, and over the years it's hosted many famous guests. The joint's still run by the family of the late Austin Henry Grant, Jr., a former Bahamian senator and West End legend. You can order Bahamian chicken in the bag, burgers, fish and chips, or "fresh sexy" conch prepared as chowder, fritters, and salads. But come for the good times, not the food. Lunch $8. Next door, **Austin's Calypso Bar** is a colorful old dive if ever there was one.

At Freeport Harbor, near the cruise ship dock, **Pier 1** (© 242/352-6674) serves clam chowder, fresh oysters, baby shark, sand crabs, a fresh fish of the day, and more in several dining rooms. There's also a nice high-ceilinged bar. Lunch $10. **Geneva's Place,** East Mall Drive and Kipling Lane (© **242/352-5085**), offers traditional Bahamian meals. It's one of the best places to sample conch, whether it be stewed, cracked, or fried, or part of a savory conch chowder. Lunch $8. **The Pepper Pot,** East Sunrise Highway at Coral Road (© **242/373-7655**), a 5-minute drive east of the International Bazaar in a tiny shopping mall, serves takeout portions of the best carrot cake on the island, as well as a savory conch chowder, fish, pork chops, chicken souse (a traditional soup), cracked conch, sandwiches, and hamburgers. Lunch $6. **Becky's Restaurant,** at the International Bazaar, East Sunrise Highway (© **242/352-8717**), offers authentic Bahamian cuisine prepared in the time-tested style of the Out Islands. Try the souse, stewed fish, and johnnycakes. Lunch $9.

4 Barbados

No port of call in the southern Caribbean can compete with Barbados when it comes to natural beauty, attractions, and fine dining. With all it offers, you'll think the island is much bigger than it is. But what really put Barbados on world tourist maps is its seemingly endless stretches of pink and white sandy beaches, among the best in the entire Caribbean Basin.

This Atlantic outpost was one of the most staunchly loyal members of the British Commonwealth for over 300 years, and although it gained its independence in 1966, Britishisms still remain—the accent is British, driving is on the left, cricket is a popular sport, and Queen Elizabeth II is still officially the head of state.

Originally operated on a plantation economy that made its aristocracy rich, the island is the most easterly in the Caribbean, floating in the mid-Atlantic like a great coral reef. Topography varies from rolling hills and savage waves on the eastern (Atlantic) coast to densely populated flatlands, rows of hotels and apartments, and sheltered beaches in the southwest.

The people in Barbados are called Bajans, and you'll see this term used everywhere.

COMING ASHORE　The cruise ship pier, a short drive from Bridgetown, the capital, is one of the best docking facilities in the southern Caribbean. You can walk right into the modern cruise ship terminal, which has car rentals, taxi services, sightseeing tours, and a tourist information office, plus shops and scads of vendors (see "Shopping," below).

Frommer's Favorite Barbados Experiences

Renting a Car for a Barbados Road Trip: Seventeenth-century churches, tropical flowers, snorkeling, great views, and more are just a rental-car ride away. (See "On Your Own: Beyond the Port Area," below.)

Visiting Gun Hill Signal Station: If you've got less time, hire a taxi or rent a car and go to Gun Hill for panoramic views of the island. (See "On Your Own: Beyond the Port Area," below.)

Taking a Submarine Trip: Sightseeing submarines make several dives daily. (See "Shore Excursions Offered by the Cruise Lines," below.)

Barbados

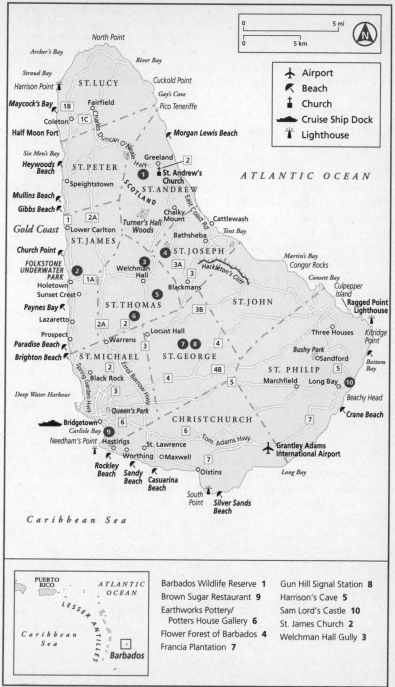

Scale:
0 — 5 mi
0 — 5 km

Legend:
- ✈ Airport
- ⚲ Beach
- ⛪ Church
- 🚢 Cruise Ship Dock
- 🗼 Lighthouse

North Point

Archer's Bay
River Bay
Stroud Bay
Cuckold Point
Harrison Point
ST. LUCY
Gay's Cove
Maycock's Bay
1B Fairfield
Pico Teneriffe
Coleton
1C
Half Moon Fort
Morgan Lewis Beach
Six Men's Bay
Greeland **2**
Heywoods Beach
ST. PETER
St. Andrew's Church
ATLANTIC OCEAN
Speightstown
ST. ANDREW
Mullins Beach
SCOTLAND
Gibbs Beach
Chalky Mount
Cattlewash
Gold Coast
1 **2A** Turner's Hall Woods
Tent Bay
Church Point
Lower Carlton
Bathsheba
ST. JAMES
3 **4** ST. JOSEPH
Martin's Bay
FOLKSTONE UNDERWATER PARK
Welchman Hall
3A
Congor Rocks
2
1A Holetown
Blackmans
Hackleton's Cliff
Consett Bay
Sunset Crest
5
Culpepper Island
Paynes Bay
ST. THOMAS
6
ST. JOHN
Ragged Point Lighthouse
Lazaretto
3B
Prospect
2A
Locust Hall
Three Houses
Kitridge Point
Paradise Beach
Warrens
7 **8** **4**
Bushy Park
Bottom Bay
Brighton Beach
3
ST. GEORGE
Sandford
ST. MICHAEL
4B
ST. PHILIP **5**
Black Rock
2
4
Marchfield
Long Bay **10**
3
5
Beachy Head
Queen's Park
Crane Beach
Bridgetown
6
CHRISTCHURCH
6
7
Carlisle Bay
9
Needham's Point Hastings
Tom Adams Hwy.
St. Lawrence
Grantley Adams International Airport
Worthing Maxwell
7
Rockley Beach
Oistins
Long Bay
Sandy Beach
Casuarina Beach
South Point
Silver Sands Beach

Caribbean Sea

Spring Garden Hwy.
Errol Barrow Hwy.
East Coast Rd.
Charles Duncan O'Neale Hwy.
Deep Water Harbour
Welchman Hall

PUERTO RICO
ATLANTIC OCEAN
LESSER ANTILLES
Caribbean Sea
Barbados

Barbados Wildlife Reserve **1**
Brown Sugar Restaurant **9**
Earthworks Pottery/ Potters House Gallery **6**
Flower Forest of Barbados **4**
Francia Plantation **7**

Gun Hill Signal Station **8**
Harrison's Cave **5**
Sam Lord's Castle **10**
St. James Church **2**
Welchman Hall Gully **3**

If you want to go into Bridgetown, about 1.6km (1 mile) from the port, instead of to the beach, you can take a hot, dusty walk of 10 to 15 minutes, or catch a taxi. The one-way fare ranges from $4 on up. Buses pass by the Harbour frequently. Bus fares are BD$1.50 (US75¢).

At a huge phone center in the terminal, you can make credit-card calls to the U.S. and other international destinations. You'll also find fax facilities and phone cards and stamps for sale.

LANGUAGE   **English** is spoken with an island lilt.

CURRENCY   The **Barbados dollar (BD$)** is the official currency, and is available in $100, $20, $10, and $5 notes and $1, 25¢, and 10¢ silver coins, plus 5¢ and 1¢ copper coins. The exchange rate is BD$1.99 to US$1 (BD$1 = US50¢). Unless otherwise specified, prices in this section are given in U.S. dollars. Most stores take traveler's checks or U.S. dollars, so don't bother to convert them if you're here for only a day.

INFORMATION   The Barbados Tourism Authority is on Harbour Road (P.O. Box 242), Bridgetown, Barbados, W.I. (✆ **888/BARBADOS** or 246/427-2623; www.barbados.org). Its cruise terminal office, which is very well run, is always open when a cruise ship is in port.

CALLING FROM THE U.S.   When calling Barbados from the United States, you need only dial a "1" before the telephone numbers listed here.

GETTING AROUND

BY TAXI   Taxis are not metered, but their rates are fixed by the government. Even so, drivers may try to get more money out of you, so make sure you settle on the rate before getting in. Taxis are identified by the letter *Z* on their license plates, and you'll find them just outside of the terminal.

BY BUS   Blue-and-yellow public buses fan out from Bridgetown every 20 minutes or so onto the major routes; their destinations are marked on the front. Buses going south and east leave from Fairchild Street, and those going north and west depart from Lower Green and the Princess Alice Highway. Fares are BD$1.50 (US75¢) and exact change is required.

Privately owned minibuses run shorter distances and travel more frequently. These bright yellow buses display destinations on the bottom-left corner of the windshield. In Bridgetown, board at River Road, Temple Yard, and Probyn Street. Fare is about BD$1.50 (US75¢).

BY RENTAL CAR   While it's a good way to see the island if you've got an adventurous streak and an easygoing attitude, before you decide to rent a car, keep in mind that driving is on the left side of the road and the signs are totally inadequate (boy, could we tell you stories!). **Hertz** has an office here. Rental cars all have an *H* on their license plates (meaning "hired"), so everyone will know you're a tourist.

SHORE EXCURSIONS OFFERED BY THE CRUISE LINES

It's not easy to get around Barbados quickly and conveniently, so a shore excursion is a good idea here.

Harrison's Cave ($58, 4 hr.): Most cruise lines offer a tour to Harrison's Cave in the center of the island (see "On Your Own: Beyond the Port Area," below, for details).

Atlantis Submarine Adventure ($89, 2½ hr.): *Atlantis* transports passengers through Barbados's undersea world, where you can watch the fishies and other colorful marine life through 28-inch windows.

Barbados Highlights Bus Tour ($36, 3 hr.): Tours take passengers by bus to Gun Hill Signal Station, St. John's Church, and Sam Lord's Castle Resort (see "On Your Own: Beyond the Port Area," below, for details).

Horseback Riding ($89, 3½ hr.): Horse treks through the heart of the island wind past old plantation houses, sugar cane fields, old sugar factories, small villages, and, if you're lucky, green monkeys scouting for food.

TOURING THROUGH LOCAL OPERATORS

Island Tours/Eco Tours: Since most cruise lines don't really offer a comprehensive island tour, many passengers deal with one of the local tour companies. **Bajan Tours,** Glenayre, Locust Hall, St. George (✆ **800/550-6288,** ext. 2225 from the U.S.; or 246/437-9389; www.funbarbados.com/Tours/bajantrs.cfm), offers an island tour that leaves between 8:30 and 9am and returns to the ship before departure. It covers all the island's highlights. On Friday they conduct a heritage tour, focusing mainly on the island's major plantations and museums. On Tuesday and Wednesday they offer an Eco Tour, which takes in the natural beauty of the island. Call ahead for information and to reserve a spot. The cost is generally around $56 per person.

Taxi Tours: If you can afford it, touring by taxi is far more relaxing than the standardized bus tour. Nearly all Bajan taxi drivers are familiar with their island and like to show off their knowledge to visitors. The standard rate is about $20 per hour per taxi (for one to four passengers). You might want to try contacting taxi owner/driver **Aaron Francis** (✆ **246/431-9059**). He's a gem—friendly, reliable, and knowledgeable.

ON YOUR OWN: WITHIN WALKING DISTANCE

About the only thing you can walk to is the cruise terminal. The modern, pleasant complex has an array of duty-free shops and retail stores, plus many vendors selling arts and crafts, jewelry, liquor, china, crystal, electronics, perfume, and leather goods.

ON YOUR OWN: BEYOND THE PORT AREA

We don't recommend wasting too much time in Bridgetown—it's hot, dry, and dusty, and the honking horns of traffic jams only add to its woes. So, unless you want to go shopping, you should spend your time exploring all the beauty the island has to offer instead. The tourist office in the cruise terminal is very helpful if you want to go somewhere on your own.

Welchman Hall Gully, St. Thomas (Hwy. 2 from Bridgetown; ✆ **246/438-6671**), is a lush tropical garden owned by the Barbados National Trust. It's 13km (8 miles) from the port (reachable by bus) and features some plants that were here when the English settlers landed in 1627.

All cruise ship excursions visit **Harrison's Cave,** Welchman Hall, St. Thomas (✆ **246/438-6640**), Barbados's top tourist attraction. Here you can see a beautiful underground world from aboard an electric tram and trailer. Admission is $13 for adults and $6 for children. If you'd like to go on your own, a taxi ride takes about 30 minutes and costs at least $25.

About 1.6km (1 mile) from Harrison's Cave is the **Flower Forest,** Richmond Plantation, St. Joseph (✆ **246/433-8152**). This old sugar plantation stands

255m (850 ft.) above sea level near the western edge of the "Scotland district," in one of the most scenic parts of Barbados. The forest is 19km (12 miles) from the cruise terminal; one-way taxi fare is about $15 and the entrance fee is $7.50.

A fine home still owned and occupied by descendants of the original owner, the **Francia Plantation,** St. George (© **246/429-0474**), stands on a wooded hillside overlooking the St. George Valley, about 16km (10 miles) from the port. You can explore several rooms. It's open 10am to 4pm Monday through Friday. Admission is $5 for adults, $2.50 for children. One-way taxi fare is about $20.

Built in 1818, the **Gun Hill Signal Station,** Highway 4 (© **246/429-1358**), one of two such stations owned and operated by the Barbados National Trust, is strategically placed on the highland of St. George and commands a wonderful panoramic view from east to west. It's 19km (12 miles) from the port; the one-way taxi ride costs about $15, and the entrance fee is $4.60. It's open Monday through Saturday, 9am to 5pm.

Sam Lord's Castle Resort, Long Bay, St. Philip (© **246/423-7350**), was built in 1820 by one of Barbados's most notorious scoundrels, Samuel Hall Lord. Legend says he made his money by luring ships onto the jagged, hard-to-detect rocks of Cobbler's Reef and then "salvaging" the wreckage. You can explore the architecturally acclaimed centerpiece of this luxury resort, which has a private sandy beach. It's a $12 taxi ride from the cruise terminal. It's open Monday through Sunday 10am to 5pm. Admission is $7.50.

If it's wildlife you want, head for the **Barbados Wildlife Reserve** (© **246/422-8826**), in St. Peter Parish on the northern end of the island. It's not exactly Animal Kingdom, but on this 1.6-hectare (4-acre) site you'll see turtles, rabbits, iguanas, peacocks, green monkeys, and a caged python.

Maybe it's the party life you crave. If so, don't miss the **Mount Gay Rum Tour** in Bridgetown (© **246/425-9066;** www.mountgay.com). You'll get a 30- to 40-minute soup-to-nuts introduction about rum in an air-conditioned rum shop (they say, of all the rum shops on the island, it's the only one with A/C). Tours are offered every half hour Monday to Friday from 9am to 3:45pm. The cost is $6 per person.

SHOPPING

The shopping-mall-size **cruise terminal** contains duty-free shops, retail stores, a convenience store, and a plethora of vendors selling arts and crafts, jewelry, liquor, china, crystal, electronics, perfume, and leather goods. Vendors sell great local hot sauce, as well as yummy Punch de Crème (you can get a free sample before buying), a creamy rum drink. For rum cake, an island specialty, the family-owned **Calypso Island Bakery** has a shop in the terminal (© **246/426-1702**). The shrink-wrapped cakes last up to 6 months and make great gifts. In general, though, you'll find a wider selection of stuff to buy and better prices in Bridgetown—last time we were there, T-shirts in the terminal were going for $15 apiece, a roll of film was $5, and a liter of J&B (yellow label) was anywhere from $10.75 to $15.15.

Good **duty-free** buys include cameras, watches, crystal, gold jewelry, bone china, cosmetics and perfumes, and liquor (including locally produced Barbados rum and liqueurs), along with tobacco products and British-made cashmere sweaters, tweeds, and sportswear. **Cave Shepherd,** Broad Street, Bridgetown (© **246/431-2121**), is the largest department store on Barbados and the best place to shop for tax-free merchandise.

Among Barbados **handcrafts,** you'll find lots of black-coral jewelry, but beware—because black coral is endangered, it's illegal to bring it back to the

United States. We suggest looking, but not buying. Local clay potters turn out different products, some based on designs centuries old. Check out the **Potters House Gallery** (© 246/425-3463) and **Earthworks Pottery** (© 246/425-0223; www.barbados.org/shops/earthworks), both on Edghill Heights, in St. Thomas parish. Crafts include wall hangings made from grasses and dried flowers, straw mats, baskets, and bags with raffia embroidery. Bajan leatherwork includes handbags, belts, and sandals.

In Bridgetown, standout stores include **Articrafts,** on Broad Street, for Bajan arts and crafts, straw work, handbags, and bamboo items; and **Colours of De Caribbean** (© 246/436-8522), at the Waterfront Marina, for tropical clothing, jewelry, and decorative objects.

BEACHES

Beaches on the island's western side—the luxury resort area called the Gold Coast—are far preferable to those on the surf-pounded Atlantic side, *which are dangerous for swimming.* The government requires that there be access to all beaches, via roads along the property line or through the hotel entrance, so all Barbados beaches are open to the public, even those in front of the big resort hotels and private homes.

ON THE WEST COAST (GOLD COAST)   Take your pick of the west coast beaches, which are about a 15-minute, $8 taxi ride from the cruise terminal. **Payne's Bay,** with access from the Coach House (© 246/432-1163) or Daphne's Restaurant (© 246/432-2731), is a good beach for watersports, especially snorkeling. There's a parking area here. This beach can get rather crowded, but the beautiful bay makes it worth it. Directly south of Payne's Bay, at Fresh Water Bay, is a trio of fine beaches: **Brighton Beach, Brandon's Beach,** and **Paradise Beach.**

Church Point lies north of St. James Church, opening onto Heron Bay, site of the Colony Club Hotel (© 246/422-2335). Although this beach can get crowded, it's one of the most scenic bays in Barbados, and the swimming is ideal. Retreat under some shade trees when you've had enough sun. You can also order drinks at the Colony Club's beach terrace.

Snorkelers in particular seek out the glassy blue waters by **Mullins Beach.** There are some shady areas, and you can park on the main road. Order food and drink at Suga Suga (© 246/422-1878). Lunch $25.

ON THE SOUTH COAST   Depending on traffic, south-coast beaches are usually easy to reach from the cruise terminal. Figure on about an $8 taxi fare. **Sandy Beach,** reached from the parking lot on the Worthing main road, has tranquil waters opening onto a lagoon. This is a family favorite, with lots of screaming and yelling, especially on weekends. Food and drink are sold here.

Windsurfers are particularly fond of the trade winds that sweep across **Casuarina Beach** even on the hottest summer days. Access is from Maxwell Coast Road, across the property of Casuarina Beach Hotel (© 246/428-3600). This is one of the wider beaches on Barbados. The hotel has food and drink.

Silver Sands Beach is to the east of the town of Oistins, near the very southernmost point of Barbados, directly east of South Point Lighthouse and near the Silver Rock Resort (© 246/428-2866). This white sandy beach is a favorite with many Bajans, who probably want to keep it a secret from as many visitors as possible. (Tough luck, Bajans!) Windsurfing is good here, but not as good as at Casuarina Beach. You can buy drinks at Silver Rock Resort's bar, called **Jibboms** (© 246/428-2866).

ON THE SOUTHEAST COAST The southeast coast is known for its big waves, especially at **Crane Beach,** a white sandy stretch backed by cliffs and palms that often appears in travel-magazine articles about Barbados. The Crane Beach Hotel (© 246/423-6220) towers above it from the cliffs, and Prince Andrew owns a house here. The beach offers excellent bodysurfing, but this is real ocean swimming, not the calm Caribbean, so be careful. At $20 from the cruise pier, the one-way taxi fare is relatively steep, so try to share the ride with other cruise passengers.

SPORTS

GOLF The 18-hole, par-72 championship course at the west coast's **Sandy Lane Golf Club,** St. James (© 246/432-1311; www.sandylane.com), is open to all. Greens fees are $195 in winter and $140 in summer for 18 holes. Carts and caddies are available. Make reservations the day before you arrive in Barbados or before you leave home. The course is a 20- to 25-minute taxi ride from the cruise terminal. The one-way fare is about $20.

WINDSURFING Experts say that Barbados windsurfing is as good as any this side of Hawaii. In fact, it's a very big business between November and April, when thousands of windsurfers from all over the world come here. **Silver Sands** is rated the best spot in the Caribbean for advanced windsurfing (skill rating 5–6). **Barbados Windsurfing Club,** at the Silver Sands Resort in Christ Church (© 246/428-6001), gives lessons and rents boards. To reach the club, take a taxi from the cruise terminal; it's an $18 one-way fare.

GREAT LOCAL RESTAURANTS & BARS

Two tips for you: Be sure to try the tasty local delicacy, flying fish (you can even get it in burger form), and, because this is a British-flavored island, the custom in restaurants is that you won't get your bill until you ask for it.

Try **Mustors** (© 246/426-5175), on McGregor Street. It's a favorite with locals and serves authentic Barbadian lunch fare. Lunch $7. For pub grub, try the hopping **Whistling Frog Pub** (© 246/420-5021), located at Time Out at the Gap Hotel (© 246/420-5021), next to the Turtle Beach Resort (© 246/428-7131). Lunch will run you about $10 at the Whistling Frog.

Brown Sugar, Aquatic Gap (off Bay St.), St. Michael, just below Bridgetown on Carlisle Bay (© 246/426-7684; www.brownsugarrestaurant.com), is an alfresco restaurant in a turn-of-the-century bungalow. The chefs prepare some of the tastiest Bajan specialties on the island. Of the main dishes, Creole-broiled pepper chicken is popular, as are the stuffed crab backs. There's a great lunch buffet for less than $20 per person.

5 Belize

Located on the northeastern tip of Central America, bordering Mexico on the north, Guatemala to the west and south, and the Caribbean to the east, Belize combines Central American and Caribbean cultures, offering both ancient Mayan ruins and a 298km (185-mile) coral reef that runs the entire length of the country—it's the largest in the Western Hemisphere and the second largest in the world, supporting a tremendous number of patch reefs, shoals, and more than 1,000 islands called cayes (pronounced "keys"), the largest and most populous being Ambergris Caye. (Both Ambergris Caye and Caye Caulker are popular with visitors, offering a barefoot informality.) The country is noted for its eco-friendly philosophy and, unlike many other Caribbean countries, is serious

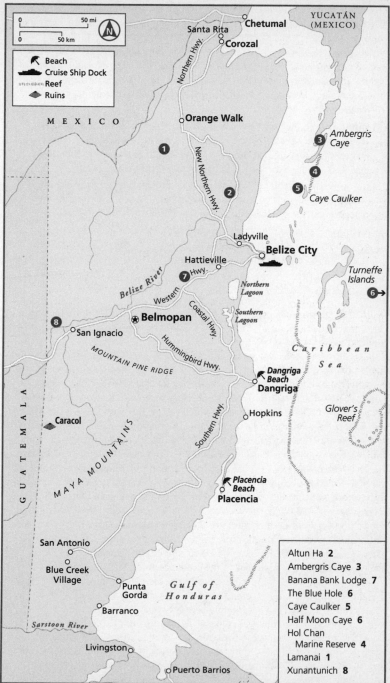

Belize

YUCATÁN
(MEXICO)

Chetumal

Santa Rita

Corozal

MEXICO

Orange Walk

1

3 Ambergris
Caye

4

5

Caye Caulker

2

Ladyville

Belize City

Hattieville

7

Northern
Lagoon

Turneffe
Islands

6

Belmopan

Southern
Lagoon

San Ignacio

8

MOUNTAIN PINE RIDGE

Western

Coastal Hwy.

Hummingbird Hwy.

C a r i b b e a n
S e a

Belize River

New Northern Hwy.

Northern Hwy.

Hwy.

Dangriga
Beach
Dangriga

Hopkins

Glover's
Reef

Caracol

G U A T E M A L A

M A Y A   M O U N T A I N S

Southern Hwy.

Placencia
Beach
Placencia

San Antonio

Blue Creek
Village

Punta
Gorda

Gulf of
Honduras

Barranco

Sarstoon River

Livingston

Puerto Barrios

0   50 mi
0   50 km

N

Beach
Cruise Ship Dock
Reef
Ruins

Altun Ha **2**
Ambergris Caye **3**
Banana Bank Lodge **7**
The Blue Hole **6**
Caye Caulker **5**
Half Moon Caye **6**
Hol Chan
   Marine Reserve **4**
Lamanai **1**
Xunantunich **8**

Frommer's Favorite Belize Experiences

Visiting Lamanai: Satisfying to both the archaeology buff and the wildlife enthusiast, a visit to this Mayan site gives you both land and water experiences. How can you pass up wonderful photo ops and howler monkeys? (See "Shore Excursions Offered by the Cruise Lines," below.)

Snorkeling or Diving at Hol Chan Marine Reserve & Shark Ray Alley: The reef is what it's all about when it comes to the waters of Belize: Friendly fish and playful stingrays make for an extremely memorable day. (See "Shore Excursions Offered by the Cruise Lines," below.)

Going Horseback Riding: Whether you're an experienced rider or have always wanted to give it a try, Banana Bank Ranch is definitely the place to go. (See "Excursions Offered by Local Agencies," below.)

Tubing in Caves: Glide down the Caves Branch River in an inner tube while wearing miner-style flashlight headbands. (See "Shore Excursions Offered by the Cruise Lines," below.)

in its dedication to conservation: One-fifth of Belize's total landmass is dedicated as nature reserves, and 7,770 sq. km (3,000 sq. miles) of its waters are protected as well.

Previously known as British Honduras, Belize gained its independence from England in 1981. It has a parliamentary democracy and is a member of the British Commonwealth. Belmopan is the capital, but **Belize City** is the economic center of the country. Trying to choose which natural or man-made wonder to explore will be the most stress you'll feel in this very laid-back, diverse, stable, and English-speaking nation, whose population of about 216,000 comprises Creoles, Garifuna (Black Carib Indians), Mestizos (a mix of Spanish and Indian), Spanish, Maya, English, Mennonites, Lebanese, Chinese, and Eastern Indians. The country has the highest concentration of **Mayan sites** among all Central American nations, including Altun Ha, Caracol, Cerros, Lamanai, Lubaantun, Xunantunich, and also nearby Tikal in Guatemala. During the classic period (A.D. 250–900), there were a million Maya in Belize, and although the civilization began to decline after A.D. 900, some Mayan centers were occupied until contact with the Spanish in the 1500s. Today, Belize has joined with El Salvador, Guatemala, Honduras, and Mexico to establish *Mundo Maya* (World of the Maya), a program dedicated to the preservation of Mayan culture.

The country gained dubious celebrity in recent years as the setting for reality TV show *Temptation Island* (even though it's not, in fact, an island), but adventurous travelers have been vacationing here for years. It's only in the past several years, as Belize has gradually developed its tourism infrastructure, that cruise lines have added the country to their ever-expanding itineraries. Although Belize is a year-round destination, the waters are especially clear from April to June; and the dry season, lasting from February to May, coincides nicely with the cruise high season.

COMING ASHORE   A new multimillion-dollar, 450-sq.-m (5,000-sq.-ft.) pier opened in Belize City in October 2001. While big ships still can't pull alongside because of shallow waters and must tender in passengers from anchorages offshore (a 20- to 30-min. trip each way), the spiffy pier area now offers a new shopping complex, with restaurants, tourist information, and even a tranquil Mayan-themed courtyard. Smaller ships, like Windstar's, skip Belize City completely and anchor offshore from the cayes and other parts of the mainland, such as Dangriga.

LANGUAGE **English** is the official language of Belize, although **Spanish,** Creole, Garifuna, and Mayan are spoken throughout the country as well.

CURRENCY The **Belize Dollar (BZ)** has a fixed exchange rate of BZ$2 to US$1 (US$1 = BZ50¢), so even after a few too many rum punches, you won't have to take out your calculator here. Most establishments, as well as taxis and vendors on the street, take U.S. dollars, and most places take credit cards too. In especially touristy areas, just be sure to ask if the price quoted is in U.S. or BZ dollars. Unless otherwise specified, prices in this section are given in U.S. dollars.

INFORMATION If you want information before you leave home, contact the **Belize Tourism Board** (© 800/624-0686 or 2-31913; www.travelbelize. org) or the **Belize Tourism Industry Association** (© 2-75717). The **Belize Audubon Society** (© 2-34987) also has a huge presence, in not only bird-watching but all areas of nature conservation, and manages many of the country's reserves.

CALLING FROM THE U.S. To make a call from the U.S. to Belize, dial the international access code (011), the country code (501), and then the number of the establishment.

GETTING AROUND

BY TAXI Taxis are available at the pier, in town, and in resort areas, and are easily recognized by their green license plates. Although the taxis have no meters, the drivers do charge somewhat standard fares, but it's always important to find out what your fare will be prior to hiring a taxi.

BY WATER TAXI From the **Marine Terminal** in Belize City (© 2-31969), water-taxi service runs to Ambergris Caye, Caye Caulker, and various other cayes. Boats leave at 9am, 10:30am, noon, and 3pm. The ride from Belize City to San Pedro, the main town on Ambergris Caye, is approximately 80 minutes and costs $45 round-trip.

BY PLANE Local airlines **Tropic Air** (© 800/422-3435 or 2-62012; www. tropicair.com) and **Maya Island Air** (© 800/225-6732 or 2-62435; www.maya islandair.com) offer hourly flights to Ambergris Caye, Caye Caulker, Placencia, and Dangriga. The flight to Ambergris Caye takes approximately 20 minutes, and, because you fly so low, you get a breathtaking view of the surrounding cayes and atolls. Keep your eyes open for stingrays and dolphins swimming below you. Flights leave from Belize City to San Pedro approximately every 90 minutes until 5pm and cost approximately $94 round-trip. The term *puddle jumper* really applies here: The planes can be as small as six-seaters and you may even get to sit next to the pilot.

BY RENTAL CAR Not recommended. Although most of the major roads and highways are paved, lots of patches are in need of repair, which makes for a very bumpy ride.

SHORE EXCURSIONS OFFERED BY THE CRUISE LINES

Lamanai ($82, 7½ hr.): Lamanai is one of the largest ceremonial centers in Belize. In the original Mayan language, its name means "submerged crocodile," and you will see various crocodile carvings throughout the site. Starting with a 45-minute drive up the Northern Highway to Tower Hill, you'll board a river-boat and head up the New River. Along the way, through the mangroves, your guide will point out crocodiles basking in the sun, a variety of birds (including jacanas and hawks), delicate water lilies, and other exotic flowers such as black orchids. You'll pass local fisherman and, surprisingly, Mennonite farms—Mennonites from Canada and Mexico began arriving in Belize in 1958 in search of land and a more isolated and simple life, and today their community numbers around 7,000. Landing at the Lamanai grounds, you'll have lunch and then tour the series of temples. There are more than 700 structures, most of them still buried beneath mounds of earth. For a view above the thick jungle, you can climb some of the temples—look in the trees for toucans and spider monkeys playing or napping. You won't mistake the roar of the howler monkey. Your guide may tell you about the red gumbo-limbo tree, whose bark becomes a shade of red and then peels off—it's jokingly referred to as the tourist tree. A small archaeological museum is on the site, as well as a few stands to buy souvenirs.

Altun Ha ($45, 4 hr.): Meaning "water of the rock," Altun Ha is a relatively small site of temples and tombs that was rediscovered in 1957 during expansion of the Northern Highway. This is one of the most extensively excavated sites and was an important trading post during the classical Mayan period. Many treasures were found here, including a carved jade head representing Kinish Ahau, the Mayan sun god. It has become one of the country's national symbols, and is depicted on the nation's currency. The tour includes lunch, and a small gift shop is on-site.

Xunantunich ($80–$92, 8 hr.): This site, near the Guatemalan border and over-looking the Mopan River, was a major ceremonial center during the classic Mayan period. After crossing the river by hand-cranked ferry, you can explore six major plazas surrounded by more than 25 temples and palaces, including "El Castillo" (the castle), the largest of the temples. Be sure to climb to the top—it's well worth it for the amazing panoramic view. There's also a new visitor's center with old excavation photos, a scale model, and a few exhibits and souvenir shops. Afterwards, you'll head to San Ignacio for lunch and enjoy a marimba band.

Hol Chan Marine Reserve & Shark Ray Alley ($92, 8 hr.): You'll head north for an hour-long speedboat ride to Hol Chan (Mayan for "little channel"), 6.4km (4 miles) southeast of San Pedro on Ambergris Caye, snorkel the reef for about an hour, and then head off to the Shark Ray Alley dive site, about 5 min-utes away, where you'll see and pet dozens of southern stingrays and nurse sharks. Guides bring goodies for them to eat, and they stick around till the food is gone. Remember to bring a disposable underwater camera—if you're going to pet a stingray, you may as well capture it on film! Lunch is on San Pedro, and you can find yourself a rum punch, go shopping, or just hang out at the beach.

Cave Tubing ($96, 6½ hr.): On arriving at Jaguar Paw, you take a 45-minute hike down a jungle trail where your guide will point out various plants and trees used by the ancient Maya for medicinal purposes. When you get to the cave, your guide will hand out flashlights and inner tubes and set you afloat, propelled by the current, through the cave system. On several occasions, you'll emerge into the sunlight before entering another cave. The float lasts about 2 hours, after which you'll have lunch. Bring a change of clothes.

Belize City Tour ($30–$38, 3 hr.): It's hardly one of the most exciting tours and definitely not a great way to see the natural side of Belize, but if you want to do something quick and easy, this is the tour. It will give you a feel for the city, its colonial architecture, and its culture through a visit to the Belize Maritime Museum and Terminal, the Government House Museum, and St. John's Cathedral, built in 1812, making it the oldest Anglican cathedral in Central America. Around lunchtime, the Mennonite farmers and craftsman are out selling their handmade furniture. Their denim overalls, checked shirts, and straw cowboy hats make them easily recognizable.

EXCURSIONS OFFERED BY LOCAL AGENCIES

Taxi Tours: Generally, the excursions offered by the cruise lines are the way to go in Belize, but if you crave a more personalized experience, you can hire a taxi driver who doubles as a guide (make sure you tell them you want a guide before getting into the taxi and negotiating a price). Tour guides must be licensed by the Belize Tourism Board and are recognizable with a photo ID. Of the many operators, one of the larger ones is **Discovery Expeditions** (© 2-30748), which offers a wide variety of tours all around the country and can arrange custom tours. For a tour of Belize City, try to snag Lasalle Tillet of **S&L Travel & Tours** (© 227-7593, 227-7594 or 227-5145). Everyone in town seems to know him, and you'll enjoy his cheerful and insightful information.

Horseback Tours: Banana Bank Lodge (© 820-2020; www.bananabank. com), located in Belmopan, about an hour's drive from the pier, offers 7-hour tours through the jungle, plains, and riverbank. Larger-than-life cowboy-owner John Carr greets each of his guests personally and makes your riding experience a memorable one. The $90 per-person cost includes a delicious traditional lunch and a tour of the grounds. Well-trained horses are matched to each rider's ability.

Fishing Excursions: Belize is a fishing mecca, with an abundance of game fish that guarantees excellent sport. The estuaries, inlets, and mouths to the many rivers are known for their tarpon, snook, and jacks; the lagoons and grass flats are known for the bonefish, permit, and barracuda; the coral reefs support grouper, snapper, jacks, and barracuda; and the deeper waters offshore are home to sailfish, marlin, bonito, and pompano. One of the largest operations is the **Belize River Lodge** (© 888/275-4843; www.belizeriverlodge.com), which offers a half-day fishing package that includes lunch and drinks ($370 for up to two guests). A favorite local fishing guide is **Richard Young, Jr.** (© 227-4385). Most guides and boatmen speak English.

ON YOUR OWN: WITHIN WALKING DISTANCE

Belize City is the hub of the country but doesn't boast the country's major attractions. The historic **harbor district** right around the pier is small and quaint. You'll find a few restaurants, and the **Baron Bliss Park and Lighthouse** is just a short stroll away. After sailing from Portugal, the eponymous baron arrived sick with food poisoning, and remained aboard his yacht for 2 months while local fisherman and administrators treated him kindly and taught him about Belize. He died soon after, but not before changing his will and leaving $2 million to Belize in a trust fund. That money made possible the building of the Bliss Institute Library and Museum and a number of health clinics and markets around the country, as well as helping with the Belize City water system. The baron is considered Belize's greatest benefactor, and Baron Bliss Day, a national holiday, is celebrated on March 9.

Outside the immediate port area, much of the rest of the city is run down and poor, with narrow, crowded streets and many old colonial structures that are in need of repair. However, since tourism is an important industry in Belize, the country is making an effort to spruce up the city and reduce crime, instituting a squad of Tourism Police to patrol popular tourist areas. Its officers are dressed in brown uniforms.

ON YOUR OWN: BEYOND THE PORT AREA

A 20-minute flight will get you to **Ambergris Caye,** the largest of Belize's 200 offshore islands and the inspiration for the Madonna song "La Isla Bonita." You know, "last night I dreamt of San Pedro . . . tropical island breeze . . . all of nature wild and free . . . blah blah blah"? The thing is, she got it about right. They have a motto here: "No shoes, No shirt . . . No problem," and that's really true. Everyone drives around in golf carts, and you can too (for about $35 for an afternoon, from rental places located along the main streets and near the little airport). Once in San Pedro (the island's main town), the beach is akin to the main street, offering plenty of shopping, restaurants, bars, and watersports.

Slightly smaller **Caye Caulker** is Belize's second most popular caye, and is even more laid back, with plenty of beachfront restaurants and bars. Despite the growth of tourism, the island retains a small village feel, with a distinct cultural flavor not found in areas with large-scale tourist development. Almost all the businesses are locally owned and you rarely see vehicles larger than golf carts on the streets. You can just hang out on the beach or dive into some watersports, including snorkeling, scuba, fishing, kayaking, windsurfing, sailing, manatee-watching, and birding.

Back in Belize City, the **Princess Hotel-Casino** is located a couple of kilometers (a mile or 2) from the cruise pier on Newtown Barricks Road (© **2-32670**); it's about 10 minutes and $5 by taxi from the pier.

SHOPPING

In general, the best buys in Belize are wooden and slate carvings, Mayan calendars, pottery, ceramics, and furniture made by the Mennonites. Near the Radisson Pier, you'll find the **National Handicrafts Sales Centre** (© **2-33833**) specializing in locally made mahogany bowls and assorted other carvings and artwork. **Marie Sharp's hot sauces and jams** seem to be served everywhere and can be purchased to take home. On Ambergris Caye, you'll find a variety of slightly more upscale gift shops, and the excursion sites all have goods available.

BEACHES

Compared to many other islands in the Caribbean, the beaches of Belize are neither the biggest nor the widest, but they are relaxing, with very clear water. Areas that offer the best beach sunbathing are in the cayes, including Ambergris Caye, Caye Caulker, Tobacco Caye, Dangriga, and Placencia. There are no beaches near Belize City.

SPORTS

WATERSPORTS   If you don't opt for one of your ship's dive excursions, local dive shops can customize an experience as well. **Hugh Parkey's Belize Dive Connection** (© **888/223-5403** or 223-4526; www.belizediving.com) is conveniently located on the Radisson Pier and offers day scuba dives and snorkel trips with a yummy lunch catered by the Fort Street Restaurant. In San Pedro, **Aqua Dives** (© **800/641-2994** or 2-63415; www.aquadives.com) is located on the beachfront and can plan a diving or snorkeling adventure.

In the center of **Lighthouse Reef Atoll,** about 80km (50 miles) due east of Belize City, the "Blue Hole" was originally a cave. The roof fell in some 10,000 years ago as the land receded into the sea, leaving an almost perfectly circular hole 300m (1,000 ft.) in diameter and 124m (412 ft.) deep. Popularized by a Jacques Cousteau television special, it's become the most famous dive site in all Belize. **Half Moon Caye,** located at the southeast corner of Lighthouse Reef Atoll, was the first reserve to be established by the Natural Parks System Act of 1981, which specifically protected the Red-footed Booby bird and its rookery. Some 98 other species of birds have been recorded on the Caye.

One of the newest national parks in Belize is **Laughing Bird Caye,** located 21km (13 miles) southeast of Placencia Village in the Stann Creek District. Although the caye was named for the original large number of laughing gulls, the birds have virtually abandoned their rookery because of excessive human encroachment. Since Laughing Bird Caye is a shelf atoll with deep channels, the scuba-diving and snorkeling opportunities are outstanding.

Many dive excursions include a barbecue lunch on **Goff's Caye.** Part of the Central Main Reef, it's a popular dive site itself.

GREAT LOCAL RESTAURANTS & BARS

The **local beer** is Belikan, and you can order it most anywhere. If you visit Altun Ha you'll recognize the site as the beer's logo (or vice versa).

IN BELIZE CITY   Around the pier you'll find several pleasant restaurants within walking distance. You can stroll to The Great House Hotel at 13 Cork St. and find **The Smokey Mermaid** (© 2-34759), situated in a lovely mango-tree-shaded patio garden. One of their specialties is the yucca-crusted snapper with a fruity salsa topping. For dessert, be sure to try their coconut pie. Lunch $10. **Chateau Caribbean,** 6 Marine Parade (© 2-30800), offers Caribbean and Asian specialties. Lunch $12.50. At the **Radisson Hotel** (© 2-33333) you have several dining choices either inside or on their deck outside overlooking the Caribbean. A buffet lunch sells for $11.50 while sandwiches and burgers can be had for about $8.

IN SAN PEDRO, AMBERGRIS CAYE   Most of the restaurants and bars here are on the beach, so you can just stroll along and stop at whatever place strikes your fancy.

ON CAYE CAULKER   Caye Caulker has about 25 restaurants, also mostly on the beach, offering Belizean and international cuisine, including fresh seafood. Lobster, conch, and red snapper are seasonal specialties.

FARTHER OUT   Heading west of Belize City, the very rustic **Cheers Bar & Restaurant** (© 1-49311) is kind of in the middle of nowhere on the Western Highway at mile 31 (about 3km/2 miles from The Belize Zoo and 26km/16 miles from Banana Bank Lodge), but the food is good, it has a nice outdoor patio, and it's frequented by tourists and locals. Leave behind a memento T-shirt to say you were here—there are dozens of them from all over the world. Still farther west, you'll find **Eva's Restaurant** at 22 Burns St., San Ignacio, about 5km (3 miles) from Xunantunich (© 9-22267). For warm hospitality, **La Palapa Restaurant,** Mayaland Villas, right off the highway in San Ignacio, about 3km (2 miles) from Xunantunich (© 9-23506), offers an outdoor, patio-style lunch setting.

6 Bequia

Bequia (meaning "Island of the Cloud" in the original Carib, and inexplicably pronounced *beck-*wee) is the largest island in the St. Vincent Grenadines, with a population of around 5,000. Sun-drenched, windswept, peaceful, and green (though

Ⓒ Frommer's Favorite Bequia Experiences

Strolling Along the Belmont Walkway: In the evenings, this walkway at water's edge makes for a terrifically romantic stroll as you make your way from one nightspot to the next. You might even pick up the company of one of the friendly port dogs, who seem more interested in companionship than panhandling. (See "On Your Own: Within Walking Distance," below.)

Visiting Brother King's Old Hegg Turtle Sanctuary: Wanna see baby turtles? This is your place. You'll see hundreds of the critters in the main swimming pool and in their own little private cubbyholes, and hear about the sanctuary's conservation efforts. Donations are gladly accepted. (See "On Your Own: Beyond the Port Area," below.)

Visiting the Lower Bay and Princess Margaret Beach: South of Port Elizabeth, this stretch of sand is frequently described by cruisers as "the best beach I've ever experienced." It's a little chunk of paradise, backed by waving palms and fronted by yachts bobbing at anchor in the distance. (See "Beaches," below.)

arid), it's a popular stop for small-ship lines such as Clipper, ACCL, Star Clippers, Windjammer, and the more upscale Seabourn, SeaDream, and Windstar, which join the many yachts in Admiralty Bay throughout the yachting season.

Very much a tourism-oriented island, Bequia is nevertheless anything but touristy. You'll find a few of the requisite cheesy gift shops in the main town, **Port Elizabeth,** but none of the typical cruise-port giants such as Little Switzerland. Instead, the town offers one of the most attractive port settings in the Caribbean, with restaurants, cozy bars, a produce market, and craft shops strung out along and around the **Belmont Walkway,** a path that skirts so close to the calm bay waters that at high tide you have to skip across rocks to avoid getting your feet wet. Many ships spend the night here or make late departures, allowing passengers to take in the nightlife.

The island's rich seafaring tradition manifests itself in fishing, sailing, boat building (though most handmade boats you'll see are scale models made for the yachting set), and even whaling, though this is whaling of more of a token, almost ritualistic sort—only about one whale is taken in any given year.

COMING ASHORE   Ships dock right in the center of the island's main town, Port Elizabeth, a stone's throw from the restaurants, bars, and shops that line the waterfront.

LANGUAGE   The official and daily-use language is **English.**

CURRENCY   The **Eastern Caribbean dollar** (EC$2.70 = US$1; EC$1 = US37¢) is used on Bequia; however, U.S. dollars are accepted by all businesses. It's always a good idea to ask if you're not sure which currency a price tag refers to. Rates quoted in this section are given in U.S. dollars.

INFORMATION   A small tourist information booth is right on the beach by the cruise dock, but frankly, you can almost see everything there is to do from the same spot. It's a pretty small island. For information before you go, contact the **Bequia Tourist Association** (Ⓒ 784/458-3286; www.bequiasweet.com) or

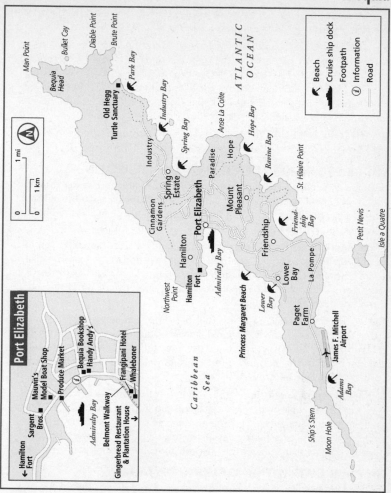

the St. Vincent & The Grenadines Department of Tourism (*©* **800/729-1726** or 212/687-4981in the U.S., 784/457-1502; www.svgtourism.com).

CALLING FROM THE U.S. To place a call to Bequia you need only dial a "1" before the numbers listed in this section.

GETTING AROUND

Ships dock right in Port Elizabeth, putting you within walking distance of all the town sights. The popular Princess Margaret Beach is within walking distance as well.

BY TAXI You'll find plenty of taxis lined up right at the cruise dock to take you around the island. The fare is approximately $20 per hour, or $5 per person per hour for groups of more than four.

BY MINIBUS The entire island of Bequia is served by a fleet of small, unofficial dollar-cab minibuses that cruise regular routes, picking up passengers when flagged down (some obvious bus stops are also scattered around). Tell the driver where you want to go and he'll tell you a price.

BY RENTAL CAR   Rentals are available at **Handy Andy's Rentals,** on the Main Road in Port Elizabeth, to the right of the dock if you're facing inland (© **784/458-3722;** fax 784/457-3402). Day rental of a small golf-cart-type vehicle is $65. A Jeep Wrangler rents for $75. **Phil's Car Rental** (© **784/458-3304**), located at the cruise ship dock, has Geo Trackers and Suzuki Sidekicks for rent for approximately $70 per day.

BY MOTORCYCLE/BICYCLE   Handy Andy's (see above) also rents Honda 250XR motorbikes for $45 and Mongoose mountain bikes for $20.

SHORE EXCURSIONS OFFERED BY THE CRUISE LINES

Bequia is very much a "relax and have a drink" kind of island, rather than one with a lot of definable, tourable attractions. Aside from a standard island tour, most excursions offered are sailing trips around the island and to neighboring Mustique and Tobago Cays.

Island Tour ($35, 3 hr.): The typical island tour is by taxi, meaning you can arrange one easily once you get ashore if your ship doesn't offer one officially. Tours generally visit beautiful Industry Bay on the island's east coast, the Old Hegg Turtle Sanctuary, and a model-boat shop, and at some point stop for a complementary drink in Spring Bay.

Sail & Snorkel Catamaran Trip ($85, 5–6 hr.): This is your typical booze cruise, though moderation is suggested if you're going to do any snorkeling. The trip sails around Bequia's coast, where you'll see the "Moonhole," a residential community set among odd rock formations, as well as the old whaling station on Petit Nevis, a small island off the coast.

Sailing Excursion to Mustique ($85, 7–8 hr.): Sail aboard a schooner to exclusive (*read:* Rich people own it) Mustique, just southeast of Bequia, for strolling, shopping, snorkeling, or simply lying on the beach. Complimentary drinks are included aboard ship. A shorter version of this tour travels between islands by powerboat rather than sailing ship—less romantic, but speedier ($65, 3–4 hr.).

ON YOUR OWN: WITHIN WALKING DISTANCE

In theory, almost the entire island of Bequia is within walking distance, but only for serious walkers. We decided to test this theory out by walking from Port Elizabeth first to Hamilton Fort, just north of town, then backtracking through the port and down to the tiny old whaling village of **Paget Farm,** near the airport on Bequia's southern tip. As the crow flies it's not much of a distance, but curving roads and hilly terrain made it a real journey that took about 4 to 5 hours round-trip, with no significant stops. If your ship is in port late and you're in good shape, it's a great way to see the island (including lovely Friendship Bay, on the east coast) and meet some of the local people along the way. Bring water.

For those wanting something less strenuous, strolling around Port Elizabeth itself is close to idyllic. The **Belmont Walkway** runs south from the docks right at the water's edge (meaning at high tide, parts of it are actually under a few inches of water), fronting many restaurants, shops, and bars. In the evenings this area is particularly romantic.

Heading north from the docks along the Main Road you'll find a homey **produce market** that also stocks some tourist items. Across the street, **Mauvin's Model Boat Shop** (© 784/458-3669) is one of the most visible reminders of the island's boat-building tradition, though now the money seems to lie in crafting

Use Your Ship's Facilities

Since Bequia is an extremely dry island and is very conscious of water conservation, it has few public washrooms. You'd be well advised to use your ship's bathroom facilities before coming ashore.

scale models of real boats for sale to the yachting crowd. Farther along the Main Road, **Sargent Bros. Model Boat Shop** (© 784/458-3344) is a larger shop offering the same type of merchandise. The workshop is a little more accessible here, so you can easily see the craftsmen creating their wares (all the work is done by hand; no power tools are employed at all), and see models in various stages of construction. At both shops, the models are amazing, lovingly constructed, and signed by the craftsman—and they're not what you'd call cheap: Prices start around $100 for a tiny model, and can go up as high as $10,000 for something really fabulous.

If you continue walking along the Main Road, you'll pass through an area with many boating supply stores and a few bars and food stands obviously geared to the local fishing and sailing trades. It's a quiet, pretty walk, even though it may well be the most "industrial" part of the island. Eventually you'll come upon a concrete walkway hanging above the water along the coast. From here the going gets rough—many sections of the walkway have been cracked and heaved drastically off-kilter by hurricanes, and it's patched here and there with planks and other makeshift materials. At the end of the walkway the road starts curving uphill and inland through a quiet residential area, and all the way up to **Hamilton Fort,** perched above Admiralty Bay and offering a lovely view of Port Elizabeth, though that's about all it offers—a few tiny fragments of battlements and five plugged canons are all that remain of the old fort. A taxi can take you here as well by another route, if you want to avoid the walk (a good idea unless you're in decent shape and very sure-footed).

ON YOUR OWN: BEYOND THE PORT AREA

At Park Beach on the island's northeast coast, 3.2km (2 miles) east of Port Elizabeth, **Brother King's Old Hegg Turtle Sanctuary** (© 784/458-3596) offers a chance to see conservation in action. Founded in 1995 by the eponymous King and dedicated to raising and releasing Hawksbill turtle hatchlings, the sanctuary is a real labor of love. A main concrete swimming pool and small plastic kiddy pools allow maturing hatchlings to socialize. Brother King and his assistants are on hand to tell you about their conservation efforts, and will gladly accept donations to help keep the place going.

Aside from this and the activities in Port Elizabeth, most of the island's other attractions are beaches, so turn to that section, below.

SHOPPING

You'll find most shopping worth doing within walking distance of the docks in Port Elizabeth. Heading south from the pier, one of the first businesses you'll come to is the **Bequia Bookshop** (© 784/458-3905), selling books on the island's and region's culture and history; books of poetry and prose by local authors; yachting guides; and a selection of other fiction and nonfiction titles; as well as truly beautiful scrimshaw pocket knives, pendants, money clips, necklaces, and pins, all made from polished camel bone rather than the traditional whale bone. Presumably, camels are not yet endangered.

ⓒ A Quiet Day on Union Island

Some small ships stop for a day at quiet, tranquil (very quiet, very tranquil) Union Island, the southernmost port of entry in the St. Vincent Grenadines. Think of your stop here as a "recovery day" rather than a whiz-bang exciting day in port: There are few facilities (none whatsoever in Chatham Bay, where ships usually tender passengers to land), few people, and few opportunities to do anything more than swim, snorkel, and do a little beachcombing. You'll likely see hundreds of conch-shell pieces along the beach, since a number of local fishermen are based here. (You can always tell if the conch was naturally thrown up on the beach or caught, since those caught have a small gash in the shell—the method the fishermen use to sever the muscle by which the conch beast holds onto its shell home.) Some enterprising fishermen set out the best shells they find on small tables, offering them to tourists for a couple bucks—you miss out on the personal thrill of finding them yourself, but they're some mighty nice shells.

Snorkeling is decent in Chatham Bay, though the waters don't yield the diversity you'll see elsewhere in the eastern Caribbean.

Sam McDowell, the artist who creates these scrimshaw items, opens his **Banana Patch Studio** for visitors by appointment. Located in the little village of Paget Farm on the southern part of the island, near the airport, the studio displays Sam's scrimshaw and whaling-themed paintings, as well as his wife Donna's shellwork. Call or fax ⓒ **784/458-3865** for an appointment.

You'll find several generic gift shops farther along, some fronting off the Belmont Walkway, including **Solana's,** for Caribelle batiks, T-shirts, and so on.

Heading in the other direction, north from the docks, you'll find the two model-boat shops described above, as well as a couple of open-air souvenir/crafts stalls, a produce market, and **Kennie's Music Shop** (ⓒ **784/458-3748**), for island sounds on CD and cassette.

BEACHES

Beaches are one of the big draws on Bequia, and all are open to the public. Tops on the list is **Princess Margaret Beach,** a golden-sand stretch lying just south of Port Elizabeth. To get there, take the Belmont Walkway to its end; from there, take the dirt path over the hill. **Lower Bay beach** is a little farther down along the same stretch of coast.

On the northeast coast, the beach at **Industry Bay** is, despite its name, windswept and gorgeous, a scene straight out of a romance novel. Trees on the hills surrounding the bay grow up to a certain height and then level out, growing sideways due to the constant wind off the Atlantic. The small, three-room **Crescent Beach Hotel** (ⓒ **784/458-3 400**) lies along this stretch, in case you want to come back after your cruise and stay a while. Along the southeast coast is **Friendship Bay,** an area that draws many European visitors.

There are no clothing-optional beaches on Bequia. Also, do not under any circumstances pick or eat the small green apples you'll see growing in some spots. These are manchineel, and are extremely poisonous.

SPORTS

Besides walking (see above) and biking (mountain bikes are available to rent from Handy Andy's Rentals right by the cruise dock), the sports here, like the rest of life on the island, center on the water. **Dive Bequia** (© 784/458-3504; www.dive-bequia.com) and **Bequia Dive Adventure** (© 784/458-3826), located along Belmont Walkway, right by the docks, specialize in diving and snorkeling.

GREAT LOCAL RESTAURANTS & BARS

The coastal stretch along the Belmont Walkway is chockablock with restaurants and bars. The local beer of St. Vincent and the Grenadines is Hairoun, which is decent but not up to the level of St. Lucia's Piton. The local rum is Sunset.

The **Frangipani Hotel Restaurant and Bar** (© 784/458-3255) is right on the water along the walkway. Lunch (served 10am–5pm) includes sandwiches, salads, and seafood platters. Dinner specialties include conch chowder, baked chicken with rice-and-coconut stuffing, and an array of fresh fish. On Thursday nights the bar hosts an excellent steel band. It's a lovely scene, with yachters, locals, cruisers from ships that have stayed late in port, and a coterie of friendly local dogs all getting to know one another over drinks or settling down for the restaurant's special barbecue. Lunch $9.

Farther along the walkway, the **Whaleboner Bar & Restaurant** (© 784/458-3233) serves a nice thin-crust pizza (with toppings such as lobster, shrimp, and generic "fish"), sandwiches, fish and chips, and cold beer, either indoors or at tables in their shaded, oceanview front yard. It's a perfect casual resting-up spot after walking around the island. Lunch $10.

The **Gingerbread Restaurant & Bar,** also right along the waterfront (© 784/458-3800), has a beautiful balcony dining room that's open throughout the day, and its downstairs cafe serves coffee, tea, and Italian ice cream at outside tables. Lunch $12. **Plantation House** (© 784/458-3425), farther along still, is the premier dining spot on the island, and serves informal lunches between noon and 2:30pm. Service and cuisine are both first-rate. Reservations are recommended.

7 Bonaire

Ever wonder what's going on under all that water you've been cruising on for days? There's no better place to find out than the island of Bonaire—"Divers Paradise," as the slogan on the island's license plates says. Avid divers have flocked to this unspoiled treasure for years for its pristine waters, stunning coral reefs (which encircle the island just feet from shore), and vibrant marine life— it's simply one of the best places in the Caribbean for diving and snorkeling.

The island also offers other adventure activities such as mountain biking, kayaking, and windsurfing; but if these options sound too strenuous, why not just marvel at the sun-basking iguanas, fluorescent lora parrots, blue-tailed lizards, wild donkeys, graceful flamingos, and feral goats? As for flora, you're likely to see more cacti in Bonaire than anywhere outside of the deserts of Mexico and the Southwest. Sprawling bushes of exotic succulents and permanently windswept divi-divi trees also abound. If you'd rather join the iguanas and just bake in the sun, Bonaire's beaches are intimate and uncrowded. In fact, the entire island is cozy and manageable. In no time at all, you'll feel it's your very own private resort.

Relying on your high-school French, you might think Bonaire ("good air") is a French island. It's not. Located 81km (50 miles) north of Venezuela and 48km (30 miles) west of Curaçao, this untrampled, boomerang-shaped refuge—39km (24 miles) long and 4.8km to 11km (3–7 miles) wide, large enough to require a motorized vehicle if you want to explore, but small enough that you won't get lost—is the "B" of the ABC Netherlands Antilles chain (Aruba and Curaçao are the "A" and the "C"). The name "Bonaire" actually comes from the Caiquetio word "bonay," which means "low country."

The Caiquetios, members of the Arawak tribe who sailed from the coast of Venezuela a thousand years ago, were Bonaire's first human inhabitants. Europeans arrived 500 years later, in 1499, when Alonso de Ojeda and Amerigo Vespucci claimed the island for Spain. The Spanish enslaved the indigenous people and moved them to other Caribbean islands. Later, the Europeans used the island to raise cows, goats, horses, and donkeys. The Dutch gained control in the 1630s, and on the back of African slave labor, Bonaire became an important salt producer.

With the discovery of oil in Venezuela early in the 20th century, Aruba and Curaçao became refining centers, and Bonaire, too, got a piece of the pie. Tourism, the island's major industry today, developed after World War II, when Bonaire won self-rule from the Netherlands (though it remains a Dutch protectorate). The people of Bonaire are a mix of African, Dutch, and South American ancestries. You'll also meet expatriates from the U.S., Britain, and Australia.

COMING ASHORE   Cruise ships dock in the port of **Kralendijk** (*Crawl*-endike), the island's capital, commercial center, and largest town (pop. about 2,500). The dock leads to Wilhelmina Park, a pleasant public space named after a former Dutch queen. **Queen Beatrix Way,** the brick-paved path along the waterfront, is lined with open-air restaurants and bars. Most of the town's shopping is a block inland on **Kaya Grandi.**

Your best bet for making **long-distance phone calls** is the 24-hour central phone company office (Telbo) at Kaya Libertador Simón Bolívar 8.

LANGUAGE   Almost everyone in Bonaire speaks **English,** which, along with **Dutch,** is a required course in the local schools. **Papiamentu** is the local patois and language of the street, a rich blend of Dutch, Spanish, Portuguese, French, English, Caribbean Indian, and several African languages. Given the island's proximity to Venezuela, you're likely to hear **Spanish** as well.

CURRENCY   Bonaire's official currency is the **Netherlands Antilles florin (NAf),** also known as the **guilder** (exchange rate: 1.78 florins = US$1; NAf1 = U.S.56¢). Each florin is divisible by 100 cents. Don't waste your time exchanging money, though, since the U.S. dollar is as widely accepted as the local currency. Prices quoted in this section are in U.S. dollars. Change may be a mixture of dollars and florins. If you need cash, several **ATMs** are located along Kaya Grandi. Traveler's checks and credit cards are widely accepted.

INFORMATION   The **Tourism Corporation Bonaire** is located at Kaya Grandi 2 in Kralendijk (© **599/717-8322** or 599/717-8649; fax 599/717-8408; www.infoBonaire.com).

CALLING FROM THE U.S.   When calling Bonaire from the United States, dial the international access code (011) before the numbers listed in this section.

GETTING AROUND

BY RENTAL CAR   Highway signs are in Dutch, and sometimes English, with easy-to-understand international symbols. Driving is on the right, the same as

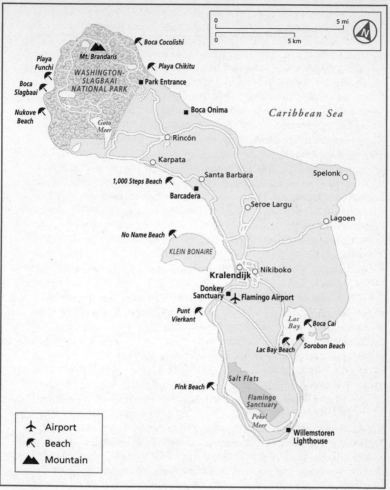

in the States and most of Europe. A valid driver's license is acceptable for renting and driving a car. **Avis, Budget, Hertz,** and **National,** as well as a number of local companies, all have offices here.

BY TAXI   Taxis greet cruise ship passengers at the pier. Although the cars are unmetered, the government establishes rates, and drivers should produce a price list upon request. Most cabs can be hired for a tour of the island, with as many as four passengers allowed to go along for the ride. Negotiate a price before leaving, but expect to pay about $25 per hour. You can get more information from the **Taxi Central Dispatch office (℃ 599/717-8100).**

BY SCOOTER OR MOPED   If you plan to stick relatively close to the port area, scooters and mopeds are practical, open-air alternatives. They can be rented from **Bonaire Motorcycle Shop,** Kaya Grandi 54 (℃ **599/717-7790), Hot Shot Scooter/Rento Fun Drive,** Kaya Bonaire 4C (℃ **599/717-2408)** or

> ## Ⓒ Frommer's Favorite Bonaire Experiences
>
> **Scuba Diving:** Diving in Bonaire is said to be easier than anywhere else on Earth. The island's leeward coast has more than 80 dive sites, and whether you're diving from a boat or right from shore, you'll see spectacular coral formations and as many types of fish as anywhere in the Caribbean. If you're not certified to dive, you can take a half-day resort course to see firsthand what divers rave about. If you'd rather just stick to snorkeling, abundant marine life is perfectly visible just beneath the crystal-clear water.
>
> **Mountain Biking Along the Western Coast:** Bike along the coast on a road carved through lava and limestone, and bordered with cactus. The road north from the island's capital and main town, Kralendijk, is relatively flat and passes several uncrowded beaches—perfect for cooling off. If you're looking for more of a challenge, pedal uphill to Bonaire's oldest town, Rincon. (See "Shore Excursions Offered by the Cruise Lines," below.)
>
> **Exploring Washington-Slagbaai National Park:** This preserve is home to a variety of exotic wildlife and vegetation and offers spectacular coastal views. At times, the towering cacti, iguanas, and thousands of jittery lizards make you think you're in Arizona; but the humidity, flamingos, and beaches make it clear you're not. (See "On Your Own: Beyond the Port Area," below.)
>
> **Making New Friends at the Donkey Sanctuary:** Miss your pooch back home? Why not lavish your love on some deserving surrogates? Donkeys were first brought to Bonaire centuries ago as beasts of burden; when more efficient modes of transport replaced them, many reverted to feral ways in the outback. More than 40 of them, most of them orphaned or injured by cars, call this oasis near the airport home, and greet you as you enter the gate, accompanying you around the tidy, brightly colored grounds. After recuperation and rehabilitation, they're returned to the wild. If you're moved by the animals' unconditional affection, you can adopt one; as a new parent, you'll receive photos and letters from your adoptee twice a year. The sanctuary is located at Punt Vierkant 5, just south of the airport in Kralendijk (Ⓒ **599/95-607-607**), and is open Tuesday through Sunday from 10am to 4pm. There's no admission charge, but donations are appreciated. The souvenir shop has donkey shirts, donkey bags, and donkey art.

Macho Scooter Rentals at the Plaza Resort Bonaire, J. A. Abraham Blvd. 80 (Ⓒ **599/717-2500**). Mopeds are about $18 a day; two-seat scooters run about $38.

BY BICYCLE For getting around town or exploring the nearby coast, try bicycling. The coastal terrain is essentially flat, but the sun can be brutal even before noon. Plan your excursion as early in the day as possible. **Cycle Bonaire,** Kaya L. D. Gerharts 11D (Ⓒ **599/717-7558**), rents 21-speed mountain bikes ($15–$20) and arranges half- ($55) and full-day ($65) tours.

SHORE EXCURSIONS OFFERED BY THE CRUISE LINES

Scuba Excursion for Certified Divers ($69, 3 hr.): Dive in the island's famous Bonaire Marine Park.

Bike Tour ($64, 3–4 hr.): This scenic ride along mostly flat and downhill terrain affords riders views of Bonaire's many species of birds, cacti, and other flora and fauna, including pink flamingos. The ride takes you along the island's northern shoreline.

Snorkeling ($39–$69, 3 hr.): The snorkeling off the coast of Bonaire is some of the best you'll find in the Caribbean. A variety of snorkeling tours include spending time at "No Name Beach," Ebo's Reef, and Karel's Hills, all located off the shore of uninhabited Klein Bonaire.

ON YOUR OWN: WITHIN WALKING DISTANCE

You can walk the length of **Kralendijk** in an hour or less. It's a sleepy town, but its residents like it that way, thank you. The **tourist office,** Kaya Grandi 2, has walking-tour maps, but because Bonaire has always been off the beaten track, Kralendijk's highlights are modest and few. You'll probably want to stroll along the seafront with its views and restaurants, and along **Kaya Grandi,** the island's major shopping district. Just south of the town dock is **Fort Oranje,** a tiny fortress that has a cannon dating from the time of Napoleon. The town has some charming Dutch Caribbean architecture—gabled roofs you might see in Amsterdam, but in cheerful Caribbean colors, especially sunny ochre and terra cotta. If your ship arrives early enough, you can visit the **waterfront produce market.**

ON YOUR OWN: BEYOND THE PORT AREA

As a day visitor, you'll probably choose to explore either the northern or southern part of the island. The coastal road north of Kralendijk is said to be one of the most beautiful in the Antilles. Turquoise, azure, and cobalt waters stretch to the horizon on your left, while pink-coral and black-volcanic cliffs loom on your right. Towering cacti, intimate coastal coves, strange rock formations, and panoramic vistas add to the beauty. The north also boasts Washington-Slagbaai National Park, an impressive, 5,400-hectare (13,500-acre) preserve that occupies the northwestern portion of the island, and Rincon, Bonaire's "other" town and oldest settlement.

NORTH OF KRALENDIJK   Soon after leaving Kralendijk, on the coast road, across from the Bonaire Caribbean Club, you'll find **Barcadera,** an old cave once used to trap goats. Take the stone steps down to the cave and examine the stalactites.

Just past the Radio Nederland towers, **1,000 Steps Beach** and dive site offers lovely views: picturesque coves, craggy coastline, and tropical waters of changing hues. Actually, there are only 67 steps; it just feels like a thousand if you're schlepping dive gear.

At the Kaya Karpata intersection, you'll see a mustard-colored building on your right. It's what's left of the aloe-processing facilities of **Landhuis Karpata,** a 100-year-old former plantation. The modest exhibits here explain the cultivation, harvesting, and processing of aloe, once a major export crop.

Thirty or 40 arduous minutes after turning right on Kaya Karpata, you'll arrive in **Rincon,** the original Spanish settlement on the island, founded in 1527. The town eventually became the home of African slaves who worked the island's plantations and salt pans. Nestled in a valley away from either coast,

Rincon was hidden from marauding pirates, who plagued the Caribbean for decades. Today, the quiet and picturesque village is home to Bonaire's oldest church, a handsome ochre-and-white structure, and to **Prisca's,** an island institution serving the best local ice cream. Try the rum raisin, peanut, pistachio, or ponche crema (a little like eggnog). The shop is located in a pistachio-colored building on Kaya Komkomber (that's Papiamentu for "cucumber").

The pride of Bonaire, located on the island's northern tip, **Washington-Slagbaai National Park** is one of the Caribbean's first national parks. Formerly two separate plantations that produced aloe and charcoal and raised goats, it now showcases the island's geology, animals, and vegetation. The park boasts more than 190 species of birds; thousands of kadushi, yatu, and prickly pear cactus; and herds of wild goats, foraging donkeys, flocks of flamingos, and what seems like billions of lizards. The scenery includes stark, desertlike hills, quiet beaches, secluded caverns, and wave-battered cliffs. You have two options: Either take the shorter 24km (15-mile) route around the park, marked with green arrows, or take the longer 35km (22-mile) track, marked with yellow arrows. You'll have plenty of opportunities to hike, swim, or snorkel either way. Admission is $10 for adults, $2 for children under 15, and the park is open from 8am to 5pm daily except for major holidays; last entry is at 3pm. Guide booklets and maps are available at the gate, where there's also a small museum. The unpaved roads are well marked and safe, but rugged; jeeps trump small cars.

On your way back to Kralendijk, take the Kaminda Onima, which traces the island's northeastern coast to **Onima,** the site of 500-year-old Caiquetio Indian inscriptions. Some of the red and brown drawings depict turtles and rain; others appear to have religious significance. You should be able to recognize snakes, human hands, and the sun among the roughly 75 inscriptions.

Before returning to Kralendijk, call on **Sherman Gibbs.** You'll find his monument to the beauty of common objects on Kaminda Tras di Montaña, the road leading back to Kralendijk. Eccentric is one way to describe Mr. Gibbs; genius is another. If you're familiar with the Watts Tower in Los Angeles, you know "junk" can be transformed into something beautiful. Sherman, who's as gentle as his pet iguanas, combines old detergent bottles, boat motors, buoys, car seats, and just about anything else that strikes his fancy to create a wondrously happy sanctuary. The wind and old fan blades power his TV.

SOUTH OF KRALENDIJK   Just minutes south of town, dazzlingly bright salt pyramids dominate the horizon. These hills, looking more like alpine snowdrifts than sodium mounds, are created when seawater is forced into lakes by the tide and then evaporates, leaving crystallized salt behind. Farther from the road, abandoned saltworks have been set aside as a **flamingo sanctuary.** Bonaire is one of the world's few nesting places for pink flamingos, a species that until recently was seriously threatened by extinction. Thanks to the reserve, the island's flamingo population during the breeding season now swells to roughly 10,000, rivaling the island's human population of 14,000. The sanctuary is completely off-limits to the public because the birds are extremely wary of humans and disturbances of any kind. But even from the road you can spot a pink haze on the horizon, and with binoculars you can see the graceful birds feeding in the briny pink-and-purple waters.

At the island's southern tip, restored slave huts stand as monuments to the inhumanity of the island's slave era. Each hut, no bigger than a large doghouse, provided crude nighttime shelter for slaves brought from Africa by the Dutch West Indies Company to cut dyewood, cultivate maize, and harvest solar salt.

On Friday afternoons, the slaves trekked 7 hours in the oppressive heat to their homes and families in Rincon for the weekend, returning to the salt pans on Sunday evenings.

Located on the eastern side of the island's southern tip, the classically picturesque **Willemstoren Lighthouse,** Bonaire's first, was built in 1837. It's fully automated today and usually closed to visitors, but its magnificent setting is the real draw. Odd little bundles of driftwood, bleached coral, and rocks in the area look like something out of *The Blair Witch Project,* but they're actually constructed by fishermen to mark where boats have been left.

A few minutes up the east coast is **Lac Bay,** a lagoon that's every bit as tranquil as the nearby windward sea is furious. The calm, shallow waters and steady breezes make the area ideal for windsurfing, and various fish come here to hatch their young. Deep inside the lagoon, mangrove trees with Edward Scissorhands roots lunge out of the water. If it weren't for the relentlessly cheerful sun, they might seem sinister. Wild donkeys, goats, and flamingos pepper the countryside along the way.

SHOPPING

Don't expect to be caught up in a duty-free frenzy in Bonaire. You'll be able to hit every store in Kralendijk before lunch, and you'll probably find greater selections and prices at other ports. The island is a great place to buy certain items, though. Consider top-of-the-line **dive watches** and **underwater cameras.** Or how about jewelry with marine themes?

You'll find most shops on **Kaya Grandi,** on the adjacent streets, or in small malls. For Tag-Heuer dive watches, Cuban cigars, Lladró porcelain, Daum crystal, and Kosta Boda glass, try **Littman Jewelers** at Kaya Grandi 33. In the centrally located Harborside Mall, **Little Holland** has silk neckties, Nautica menswear, blue Delft porcelain, and an even more impressive array of Cuban cigars. If you're an aficionado, you'll love the shop's climate-controlled cigar room with its Montecristos, H. Upmanns, Romeo & Julietas, and Cohibas. **Sparky's,** in the same mall, carries perfume and other cosmetics, including Lancôme, Esteé Lauder, Chanel, Calvin Klein, and Ralph Lauren. **Maharaj Gifthouse,** at Kaya Grandi 21, has jewelry, gifts, and more blue Delft porcelain. **Boolchand's,** at Kaya Grandi 19, has a peculiarly wide range of items, including underwater cameras, electronic goods, watches, sunglasses, and shoes.

Benetton, at Kaya Grandi 49, has smart casual wear at discounts of 20% to 30%. If batik shirts, bathing suits, or souvenir T-shirts are what you want, try **Best Buddies,** Kaya Grandi 32; **Boutique Vita,** Kaya Grandi 16; **Bye-Bye Bonaire,** Harborside Mall; or **Island Fashions,** Kaya Grandi 5.

Probably the best place for dressier women's clothing, including Hermès scarves, Oscar de la Renta resort wear, and Kenneth Cole shoes, is **The Shop at Harbour Village** at Kaya Gobernador N. Debrot 72. You can also find sunglasses, jewelry, and perfume with Cartier, Fendi, Donna Karan, and Givenchy labels.

On a hot day, nothing beats the frozen-food section at **Cultimara Supermarket,** Kaya L. D. Gerharts 13. The store offers free coffee, a wide assortment of Dutch cheeses and chocolates, straight-from-the-oven breads and pastries, and various products from the Caribbean, Europe, South America, and the United States.

BEACHES

Bonaire's beaches are narrow and full of coral, but they're clean, intimate, and uncrowded. Swimming on the tranquil, leeward coast is never a problem, but the east coast is rough and dangerous. **Pink Beach,** south of Kralendijk, is the island's best strand. Aptly named, the sand here turns a rosy hue as the sun sets. No refreshment stands or equipment rentals mar the panoramic setting, so bring your own drinks and towels. Bring sun protection too: The few palm trees offer little shade. The southern end has less exposed rock. Crowded with Bonaireans on weekends, it's yours alone during the week.

The water at **Lac Bay Beach** is only 1 to 2 feet deep, making it especially popular with families. In a protected area of Bonaire's southeast coast, it boasts windsurfing concessions and snack bars. Trees provide shade. Across the bay, white-sand **Sorobon Beach** is the island's only nude beach. It's part of the Sorobon Beach Resort, which means that as a nonguest, you'll pay for the privilege of disrobing.

North of Kralendijk, **Nukove Beach** is a small white-sand cove carved out of a limestone cliff. A narrow sand channel cuts through an otherwise impenetrable wall of elkhorn coral, giving divers and snorkelers access to the sea.

Washington-Slagbaai National Park has a number of beaches. **Boca Slagbaai,** once a plantation harbor, draws divers, snorkelers, and picnickers. Be careful venturing into the water barefoot, though: The coral bottom can be sharp. The island's northernmost beach, **Boca Cocolishi,** is a perfect spot to picnic. The calm, shallow basin is good for snorkeling, but stay very close to shore. Algae makes the water purplish, and the sand, formed by coral and mollusk shells, is black. At **Playa Chikitu,** the water is too treacherous for swimming but the cove, sand dunes, and crashing waves are secluded and beautiful. On one side of **Playa Funchi,** flamingos nest in the lagoon; on the other, there's excellent snorkeling.

Klein Bonaire, the small uninhabited island about 1km (½ mile) west of Kralendijk, boasts **No Name Beach,** which features a 270m (300-yard) white-sand strip. The finger, brain, and mustard hill corals are patrolled by parrotfish and yellowtail snappers, attracting snorkelers and divers. There are no facilities or shade on Klein Bonaire.

SPORTS

KAYAKING   For a peaceful, relaxing time, kayak through the mangroves in Lac Bay. Proceed at your own pace in the calm waters, but take time to observe the hundreds of baby fish and the bizarre tree roots. Bring protection from the sun and the ravenous mosquitoes. Divers and snorkelers can tow a lightweight sea kayak behind them as they explore the waters of the leeward coast. Guided trips and kayak rentals are available from **Discover Bonaire,** Kaya Gobernador N. Debrot 79 (© **599/717-8738**), and, in Sorobon, from **Jibe City** (© **599/717-5233**). Kayak rentals are $10 for one person and 15 for two for a half day. In December 2002, Bonaire **Boating/ABC Yachting** (© **599/790-5353;** www.abc-yachting.com) opened the **Mangrove Information & Kayak Center.** It's located on the road to Cai, Lac Bay, and provides information about the mangrove forest and offers guided mangrove tours.

MOUNTAIN BIKING   Bonaire has miles of roads, paved and unpaved, flat and hilly. The truly athletic can even follow goat paths. Take water, a map, a wide-brimmed hat, and plenty of sunscreen. Discover Bonaire (see above) conducts guided bike tours through the kunuku (outback) and Washington-Slagbaai Park.

SCUBA DIVING AND SNORKELING   Bonaire has 80 dive sites and a rich marine ecosystem that includes brain, elkhorn, staghorn, mountainous star, gorgonian, and black coral; anemones, sea cucumbers, and sea sponges; parrotfish, surgeonfish, angelfish, grouper, blennies, frogfish, and yellowtails; and morays and sea snakes. Dive shops are numerous and highly professional. Expect to pay $40 to $55 for a one-tank dive (equipment extra) and $100 for an introductory resort course (equipment included). **Great Adventures Bonaire,** Kaya Gobernador N. Debrot 72 (© **800/868-7477** in the U.S. and Canada, or 599/717-7500, ext. 295), is the island's poshest operation, upscale but unpretentious and friendly. In addition to two of the island's most beautiful boats, it boasts a first-class photo shop where you can rent underwater still and video cameras. **Bonaire Dive and Adventure,** Kaya Gobernador N. Debrot 77 (© **599/717-5433**), is popular with return visitors and offers comparable services. The resort's "Sand Penny" children's program is a godsend for parents who want to dive without worrying about the kids. **Captain Don's Habitat,** Kaya Gobernador N. Debrot 103 (© **800/327-6709** or 305/ 438-4222 in the U.S. for Maduro Dive Fanta-seas, Captain Don's North American representative, www.habitatdiveresorts.com; or 599/717-8290), attracts diving fanatics, including disciples of Captain Don Stewart, an island icon and the driving force behind the Bonaire Marine Park. The full-service shop includes a photo shop and lab and equipment repair.

Thanks to shallow-water coral reefs, snorkelers can enjoy Bonaire's awesome marine environment, too. The island's **Guided Snorkeling Program** includes a slide-show introduction to reef fish, corals, and sponges; an in-water demonstration of snorkeling skills; and a guided tour of one of several sites. The cost is $25 per person. Equipment rental is about $10 more. You can arrange a tour through any of the dive shops listed above or through **Buddy Dive Resort,** Kaya Gobernador N. Debrot 85 (© **800/GO-BUDDY** in the U.S., or 599/717-5080); **Bon Bini Divers,** at the Lions Dive Hotel Bonaire, Kaya Gobernador N. Debrot 90 (© **599/717-5425**); **Carib Inn,** J. A. Abraham Boulevard (© **599/ 717-8819**); or **Dive Inn,** Kaya C. E. B. Hellmund 27 (© **599/717-8761**).

WINDSURFING   Shallow waters, steady breezes, and protection from choppy waters make Lac Bay perfect for beginners and pros. Sorobon has two equipment-rental centers: **Jibe City** (© **599/717-5233**) and **Bonaire Windsurf Place** (© **599/717-2288**). Boards and sails are $45 for half a day, $60 for a full day. Beginner's lessons are $45, including equipment.

GREAT LOCAL RESTAURANTS & BARS

Kralendijk offers a variety of culinary options at generally reasonable prices. One of Bonaire's most popular restaurants, **Capriccio,** Kaya Isla Riba 1 (© **599/717-7230**), serves impeccably fresh Northern Italian cuisine on the harbor front. Originally from Padua and Milan, the restaurateurs offer savory salads, homemade pastas, straight-from-the-oven focaccia, thin-crust pizzas, and more substantial fare such as mahimahi braised in onion, olives, and sun-dried tomatoes, and braised duck in port wine sauce. Lunch $12. **Zeezicht Seaside Restaurant,** Kaya Jan N. E. Craane 12 (© **599/717-8434**), is a local favorite, also on the downtown waterfront. Seviche, conch sandwiches, and a gumbo of conch, fish, shrimp, and oysters are on the menu; and mermaids, fishing nets, and pirates adorn the walls. Lunch $6. To sample traditional Bonairean food in an unpretentious setting, try **Bon Awa,** Kaya Nikiboko Zuid 8 (© **599/717-5157**), with its outside tables, killer hot sauce, and outstanding homemade ice cream.

8 British Virgin Islands: Tortola & Virgin Gorda

With small bays and hidden coves that were once havens for pirates, the BVIs are among the world's loveliest cruising regions, consisting of some 40 islands located in the northeastern corner of the Caribbean, about 97km (60 miles) east of Puerto Rico. Only Tortola, Virgin Gorda, and Jost Van Dyke are of significant size. The other islets, most of them tiny rocks and cays, have names such as Fallen Jerusalem and Ginger. Norman Island is said to have been the prototype for Robert Louis Stevenson's *Treasure Island*, and Blackbeard inspired a famous ditty by marooning 15 pirates and a bottle of rum on the rocky cay known as Deadman Bay. Yo-ho-ho.

Columbus came this way in 1493, but the British Virgins apparently made little impression on him. Although the Spanish and Dutch contested it, Tortola was officially annexed by the English in 1672. Today, these islands are a British colony, with their own elected government and a population of about 17,000.

The vegetation is varied and depends on the rainfall. Palms and mangos grow in profusion in some parts, while other places are arid and studded with cacti.

Smaller cruise lines such as Seabourn, Windstar, and Windjammer Barefoot Cruises call at Tortola and the more scenic Virgin Gorda and Jost Van Dyke. Unlike port calls at St. Thomas and other major ports, visits here are less bound by rigid scheduling.

LANGUAGE **English** is spoken here.

CURRENCY The **U.S. dollar** is the legal currency, much to the surprise of arriving Brits who find no one willing to accept their pounds.

CALLING FROM THE U.S. When calling the BVIs from the United States, you need only dial a "1" before the numbers listed here.

TORTOLA

Road Town, the colony's capital, sits about midway along the southern shore of 62 sq. km (24-sq.-mile) Tortola. Once a sleepy village, it's become a bustling center since **Wickhams Cay,** a 28-hectare (70-acre) landfill development and marina, brought in a massive yacht-chartering business.

The island's entire southern coast is characterized by rugged mountain peaks. On the northern coast are beautiful bays with white sandy beaches, banana trees, mangoes, and clusters of palms.

If your ship isn't scheduled to visit Virgin Gorda but you want to, you can catch a boat, ferry, or launch here and be on the island in no time, since it's only a 19km (12-mile) trip.

COMING ASHORE Visiting cruise ships dock at **Wickhams Cay 1** in Road Town. You'll be brought ashore by tender and let off a pleasant 5-minute walk to Main Street. You should have no trouble finding your way around town.

INFORMATION The **BVI Tourist Board** office is on Wickhams Cay 1 in the Akara Building and is open Monday to Friday from 8:30am to 4:30pm (© **284/494-3134**). You can pick up a copy of the *Welcome Tourist Guide* here. For info before you go, log on to **www.britishvirginislands.com**.

GETTING AROUND

BY TAXI Open-air and sedan-style taxis meet every arriving cruise ship. To call a taxi in Road Town, call the **BVI Taxi Association** (© **284/494-2322**). Three other local taxi services, **Quality Taxi** (© **284/494-8397**), **Road Town**

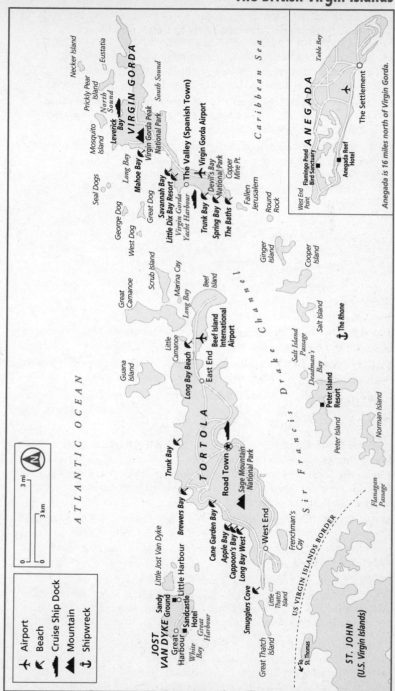

The British Virgin Islands

ATLANTIC OCEAN

Necker Island
Eustatia
Prickly Pear Island
Mosquito Island
North Sound
South Sound
Leverick Bay
VIRGIN GORDA
Long Bay
Mahoe Bay
Virgin Gorda Peak National Park
Savannah Bay
The Valley (Spanish Town)
Little Dix Bay Resort
Virgin Gorda Yacht Harbour
Virgin Gorda Airport
Devil's Bay National Park
Copper Mine Pt.
Trunk Bay
Spring Bay
The Baths
Fallen Jerusalem
Round Rock

Caribbean Sea

Seal Dogs
George Dog
West Dog
Great Dog
Scrub Island
Great Camanoe
Marina Cay
Long Bay
Beef Island
Ginger Island
Cooper Island

Little Camanoe
Long Bay Beach
East End
Beef Island International Airport

Guana Island

TORTOLA
Trunk Bay
Brewers Bay
Cane Garden Bay
Apple Bay
Cappoon's Bay
Long Bay West
Road Town
Sage Mountain National Park
West End
Frenchman's Cay
Smugglers Cove
Little Thatch Island

Drake Channel

Salt Island Passage
Deadman's Bay
Peter Island Resort
Salt Island
The Rhone

Peter Island
Norman Island

Sir Francis

Flanagan Passage

US VIRGIN ISLANDS BORDER

To St. Thomas

Great Thatch Island

ST. JOHN (U.S. Virgin Islands)

JOST VAN DYKE
Sandy Ground
Little Jost Van Dyke
Great Harbour
Little Harbour
Sandcastle Hotel
White Bay
Great Harbour

Scale:
0   3 mi
0   3 km

Legend:
✈ Airport
ᴋ Beach
▲ Cruise Ship Dock
▲ Mountain
⚓ Shipwreck

ANEGADA
Table Bay
The Settlement
Flamingo Pond Bird Sanctuary
Anegada Reef Hotel
West End Point

Anegada is 16 miles north of Virgin Gorda.

ⓒ Frommer's Favorite Tortola Experiences

Visiting Bomba's Surfside Shack: The oldest, most memorable bar on Tortola may not look like much, but it's the best party on the island. (See "Great Local Restaurants & Bars," below.)

Spending a Day at Cane Garden Bay: It's the best beach on the island, with palm trees, sand, and a great local restaurant (shack) for lunch and drinks. (See "Beaches," below.)

Hiking up Sage Mountain: It's one of the best ways to learn about Tortola's natural character. Organized shore excursions usually include hiking trips to the 534m (1,780-ft.) peak, beginning with a ride along mountain roads in an open-air safari bus. (See "On Your Own: Beyond the Port Area," below.)

Taking an Island Tour: Open-air safari buses take you on a scenic journey around the extremely hilly island. Take your ship's organized tour (see "Shore Excursions Offered by the Cruise Lines," below), or take a 2- to 3-hour taxi tour from the pier, with beach stops, for about $15 per person.

Taxi Association (ⓒ 284/494-8755), and the **Waterfront Taxi Association** (ⓒ 284/494-3456), are within walking distance of the cruise pier.

BY BUS   Scato's Bus Service (ⓒ 284/494-2365) picks up passengers (mostly locals) who hail it down. Fares for a trek across the island are about $1 to $4.

BY RENTAL CAR   We don't recommend driving here, as the roads are bad and driving is on the left. But if you're intent on it, **Avis, Dollar, Hertz,** and **ITGO** (the local Budget operator) all have offices here.

SHORE EXCURSIONS OFFERED BY THE CRUISE LINES
Island Tour ($30–$34, 3½ hr.): Hop on an open-air safari bus and embark on a scenic journey around the island. You'll enjoy some panoramic views and good photo ops, and end with a stop at Cane Garden Bay Beach for swimming, sunbathing, and just plain old relaxing.

Mount Sage & Botanical Gardens ($34, 3½ hr.): Start with a 1.6km (1-mile-) long hike up Mount Sage to the highest point in the BVIs, then make a brief visit to the J.R. O'Neill Botanical Gardens, a 1.6-hectare (4-acre) garden located in the center of Road Town.

Norman Island Snorkeling ($50, 3 hr.): Cross the Sir Frances Drake Channel by boat to Normal Island, one of the BVI's prime snorkel sites, full of coral formations, colorful fish, and a group of caves at Treasure Point, where pirate treasure is reputed to have been hidden.

EXCURSIONS OFFERED BY LOCAL AGENCIES
Bus Tours/Snorkeling/Glass-Bottom Boat Tours: Since the shore excursions here are very modest, you might consider calling **Travel Plan Tours,** Romasco Place, Wickham's Cay, Road Town (ⓒ 284/494-2872), which will take one to three people on a 3-hour guided tour of the island (about $23 a person, if there is a minimum of two people), a snorkeling excursion (about $28 a person for

groups of 10 or more), or an all-day catamaran sailing excursion ($95 per person, including lunch).

Taxi Tours: You can take a 2- to 3-hour taxi tour for about $45 for up to three people. For a taxi in Road Town, call ℂ **284/494-2322.**

ON YOUR OWN: WITHIN WALKING DISTANCE

Besides the handful of shops on Main and Upper Main streets in Road Town, there's also a **Botanic Garden** (ℂ **284/494-4557**) right in the middle of town, across from the police station. It's open daily from 8am to 6pm and features a wide variety of flowers and plants, including a section on medicinal plants.

ON YOUR OWN: BEYOND THE PORT AREA

You have mainly nature to look at on Tortola. The big attraction is **Mount Sage National Park,** which rises to 534m (1,780 ft.) (the highest point in the BVIs and USVIs) and covers 37 hectares (92 acres). It was established in 1964 to protect those remnants of Tortola's original forests not burned or cleared during its plantation era, and is both the oldest national park in the British Virgin Islands and the best present-day example of the territory's native moist forests. You'll find a lush forest of mango, papaya, breadfruit, and coconut trees; many of the plants and trees are labeled, and there are also birchberry, mountain guava, and guavaberry trees here, all of which have edible fruit. This is a great place to enjoy a picnic while overlooking neighboring islets and cays. Any taxi driver can take you to the mountain. Before going, stop at the **tourist office** (see above) and pick up a brochure with a map and an outline of the park's trails. The two main hikes are the Rain Forest Trail and the Mahogany Forest Trail. For a quiet beach day, head to **Smuggler's Cove,** a secluded, picture-perfect spot with white sand and calm turquoise water. *Note:* At press time, there is no fee for park admission, but the BVI National Trust plans to implement one soon, possibly sometime in 2003. Call ℂ **284/494-2069** or 284/494-6177 for more information.

SHOPPING

Shopping on Tortola is a minor activity compared to other Caribbean ports. Only British goods are imported without duty, and they are the best buys, especially English china. You'll also find West Indian art, terra-cotta pottery, wicker and rattan home furnishings, Mexican glassware, dhurrie rugs, baskets, and ceramics. Most stores are on Main Street in Road Town.

A good shop to visit is **Pusser's Company Store,** Main Street, Road Town (ℂ **284/494-2467**), for Pusser's rum, fine nautical artifacts, and a selection of Pusser's sports and travel clothing and upmarket gift items. The **Sunny Caribee Herb and Spice Company,** also on Main Street (ℂ **284/494-2178**), is a good spot for Caribbean spices, seasonings, teas, condiments, and handicrafts. You can buy two world-famous specialties here: West Indian Hangover Cure and Arawak Love Potion.

BEACHES

Most of the beaches are a 20-minute taxi ride from the cruise dock. Figure on about $15 per person one-way (some will charge less, about $5 per person if you've got a group), but discuss it with the driver before setting out. You can also ask him to pick you up at a designated time.

The finest beach is at **Cane Garden Bay,** which compares favorably to the famous Magens Bay Beach on the north shore of St. Thomas. It's on the northwest side of the island, across the mountains from Road Town; but it's worth the effort to get there, and is so special you might take a taxi here in the morning and not head back to your cruise ship until departure time. Plan to have lunch here at **Rhymer's** (© 284/495-4639), where the chef will cook some conch or whelk, or perhaps some barbecue spareribs. The beach bar and restaurant is open daily from 8am to 9pm, serving breakfast, lunch, and dinner, with main courses ranging from $15 to $25. Showers are available, and Rhymer's rents towels.

Surfers like **Apple Bay**, also on the northwest side, but you'll have to watch out for sharks (no joke: On a recent trip a friend saw one while surfing, and its dorsal fins were visible from the shore). A hotel here called **Sebastians** (© 284/495-4212) caters to the surfing crowd that visits in January and February, but the beach is ideal year-round. **Brewers Bay,** site of a campground, is on the northwest shore near Cane Garden Bay and is good for beach strolling and swimming. Both snorkelers and surfers come here. **Smugglers Cove** (sometimes known as Lower Belmont Bay) is a wide crescent of white sand wrapped around calm, sky-blue water, located at the extreme western end of Tortola, opposite the offshore island of Great Thatch and very close to St. John's in the U.S. Virgin Islands. Snorkelers and surfers also like this beach.

SPORTS
SCUBA DIVING   *Skin Diver* magazine has called the wreckage of the RMS *Rhône,* which sank in 1867 near the western point of Salt Island, the world's most fantastic shipwreck dive. It teems with marine life and coral formations, and was featured in the motion picture *The Deep. Chikuzen,* an 81m (270-ft.) steel-hulled refrigerator ship that sank off the island's east end in 1981, is another intriguing dive site off Tortola, although it's no *Rhône.* The hull, still intact under about 24m (80 ft.) of water, is now home to a vast array of tropical fish, including yellowtail, barracuda, black-tip sharks, octopus, and drum fish. **Underwater Safaris** (© 284/494-3235) can take you to all the best sites. It offers a complete PADI and NAUI training facility and is associated with The Moorings yacht charter company. Underwater Safaris' Road Town office is a 5-minute, $4 taxi ride from the docks. Two-tank dives sell for $84, while a one-tank dive costs $58. Equipment rental is $10.

GREAT LOCAL RESTAURANTS & BARS
On Cappoon's Bay, **Bomba's Surfside Shack** (© 284/495-4148) is the oldest, most memorable bar on Tortola, sitting on a 6m- (20-ft.-) wide strip of unpromising coastline near the West End. It's the "junk palace" of the island, covered with Day-Glo graffiti and laced with wire and rejected odds and ends of plywood, driftwood, and abandoned rubber tires. They must've spent their decorating budget on the sound system, which thumps mightily. It's open daily from 10am to midnight (or later, depending on business). Lunch $8.

Standing on the waterfront across from the ferry dock, **Pusser's Road Town Pub** (© 284/494-3897) serves Caribbean fare, English pub grub, and good pizzas. The drink to have here is the famous Pusser's Rum, the same blend of five West Indian rums that the Royal Navy served to its men for more than 300 years. Honestly, it's not the world's greatest rum, but sometimes you just have to do things for the experience. Lunch $12. **Capriccio di Mare,** Waterfront Drive (© 284/494-5369), is the most authentic-looking Italian cafe in the Virgin Islands, serving fresh pastas with succulent sauces, well-stuffed sandwiches, and great pizza. Lunch $10. For a fine roti (curries wrapped in flat bread) sans atmosphere—it's sparsely furnished and not too attractive—try **Roti Palace**

(© **284/494-4196**), in Road Town. Lunch $8. **Callaloo,** at the Prospect Reef Resort (© **284/494-3311**), is very romantic if it's a balmy day and the tropical breezes are blowing. Begin with the conch fritters or shrimp cocktail, and don't pass on the house salad, which has a zesty papaya dressing. Main dishes include fresh fish. Lunch $12. At **Pusser's Landing,** Frenchman's Cay, on the West End (© **284/495-4554**), you can enjoy grilled fish such as mahimahi, or West Indian roast chicken. Try the mango soufflé for dessert. Lunch $8. **Quito's Gazebo** (© **284/495-4837**), on Cane Garden Bay, is owned by local recording star Quito Rhymer. It's a good place for West Indian fish dishes; Quito performs Thursday to Sunday and Tuesday. Lunch $10.

VIRGIN GORDA

Instead of visiting Tortola, some small cruise ships put in at lovely Virgin Gorda, famous for its boulder-strewn beach known as **The Baths.** The third-largest island in the colony, it got its name ("Fat Virgin") from Christopher Columbus, who thought the mountain framing it looked like a protruding stomach. At 16km (10 miles) long and 3.2km (2 miles) wide, the island is about 19km (12 miles) east of Road Town, so it's easy to take a ferry or boat here if your ship only visits Tortola.

The island was a fairly desolate agricultural community until Little Dix Bay Hotel opened here in the early 1960s. Other major hotels followed, but privacy and solitude still reign supreme on Virgin Gorda.

COMING ASHORE   Virgin Gorda doesn't have a pier or landing facilities to suit any of the large ships. Most vessels anchor and send small craft ashore, disembarking passengers at **St. Thomas Bay.** Many others dock beside the pier in Road Town on Tortola and then send tenders across the channel to Virgin Gorda. Taxis are usually available at Leverick Bay.

GETTING AROUND   The best way to see the island is to call **Andy Flax** at the Fischers Cove Beach Hotel (© **284/495-5252**). He runs the Virgin Gorda Tours Association, which gives island tours for about $40 per couple. They'll pick you up at the dock if you give them 24-hour notice. Another good option is to call **Speedy's,** also known as Virgin Gorda Transport (© **284/495-5250**). The **Virgin Gorda Tourist Association** gives island tours for about $40 per couple and will pick visitors up at the dock if provided with 24-hour notice. **Taxis**

Frommer's Favorite Virgin Gorda Experiences

Visiting The Baths: House-size boulders and clear waters make for excellent swimming and snorkeling in a fabulous setting. (See "Shore Excursions Offered by the Cruise Lines" and "Beaches," both below.)

Spending a Beach Day in Spring Bay or Trunk Bay: Located near The Baths, Spring Bay has one of the best beaches on the island, with white sand, clear water, and good snorkeling. Trunk Bay, a wide sand beach that can be reached by boat or via a rough path from Spring Bay, is another good bet. (See "Beaches," below.)

Taking an Island Tour: Open-air safari buses do a good job of showing guests this beautiful island. (See "Shore Excursions Offered by the Cruise Lines," below.)

are available and will take visitors to Spanish Town (about 20 min. away) or to The Baths and area beaches for about $5 per person each way.

SHORE EXCURSIONS OFFERED BY THE CRUISE LINES

The Baths Excursion ($38, 3–4 hr.): All cruise lines stopping here offer this trip. (See "Beaches," below, for details.)

Island Tour ($42, 3–4 hr.): The open-air safari buses do a good job of showing guests this beautiful island. You'll get views of the sea, the entire erratically shaped island, and Tortola and St. Thomas, too, as you head across the island from Leverick Bay via North Sound Road, ascending at least partway up 411m (1,370-ft.) Gorda Peak. Some tours stop at the base of the mountain, from which a local guide walks visitors through the national park to the peak, where visitors can mount an observation deck and snap photos. After, visitors reboard their bus for a drive to the quaint capital, called Spanish Town. Tours usually include a stop at Copper Mine Point, where visitors can view the ruins of a 19th-century copper mine.

ON YOUR OWN: WITHIN WALKING DISTANCE

The **watersports center** in Leverick Bay rents two- and four-person dinghies starting at $50 per half day, and snorkeling equipment for $6 per day. Visitors can also hire a water taxi here to visit **Bitter End Yacht Club** (© 284/494-2746; www.beyc.com) in the North Sound area, for a lobster lunch or for a little windsurfing or sailing. The taxis pick up guests at Bitter End for the trip back; a round-trip fare costs $25 per person. There's also a local branch of the BVI's famous **Pusser's Company Store,** which includes a gift shop, restaurant, and bar.

ON YOUR OWN: BEYOND THE PORT AREA

The **Virgin Gorda Yacht Harbour** is a taxi ride away from the St. Thomas Bay pier, and has several restaurants, shops, a bank, and the local office of the BVI Tourist Board. You might also consider cabbing it to the glamorous **Little Dix Bay Resort** (© 284/495-5555), established by Laurence Rockefeller in 1965, to enjoy a lunch buffet at an outdoor pavilion that shows off Virgin Gorda's beautiful hills, bays, and sky.

SHOPPING

Souvenirs and locally produced artwork are available right in Leverick Bay, where most of the island's shopping is located. The **Palm Tree Gallery** (© 284/495-7479) carries jewelry, artwork, books, postcards, and other souvenirs.

Stores in the Yacht Harbour area include **DIVE BVI** (© 284/495-5513), which sells diving equipment and offers diving instructions for all ability levels; **Margo's Jewelry Boutique** (© 284/495-5237), which sells handcrafted gold and silver items; **Virgin Gorda Craft Shop** (© 284/495-5137), featuring locally made items; and **Wine Cellar** (© 284/495-5250), which offers oven-baked French bread and pastries, cookies, and sandwiches. The **Blue Banana Boutique** (© 284/495-6633), also in the Yacht Harbour area, sells women's swimwear and beachwear.

BEACHES

The major reason cruise ships come to Virgin Gorda is to visit **The Baths,** where geologists believe ice-age eruptions caused house-size boulders to topple onto one another to form the saltwater grottoes we see today. The pools around The Baths are excellent for swimming and snorkeling (equipment can be rented on the beach), and a crawl between and among the boulders, which in places are

☟ A Slice of Paradise: Jost Van Dyke

Covering only 10 sq. km (4 sq. miles), mountainous Jost Van Dyke is truly an offbeat, rarely visited retreat—unless you count the small yachts dotting Great Harbour. With no cruise pier, passengers are shuttled ashore via tender. Small-ship lines such as Windjammer Barefoot Cruises will sometimes throw an afternoon beach party on the beach at White Bay, with the crew lugging ashore a picnic lunch for a leisurely afternoon of eating, drinking, and swimming. If your ship stays late, don't miss a trip to **Foxy's** (☎ 284/495-9258), a well-known watering hole at the far end of Great Harbour that's popular with the yachting set as well as locals. It's your classic island beach bar, with music pounding and drinks flowing into the wee hours.

very cavelike, is more than a little bit fun. A cafe sits just above the beach for a quick snack or a cool drink before heading back to the ship. **Devil's Bay** is a great beach near The Baths, and is usually less crowded.

Also near The Baths is **Spring Bay**, one of the best of the island's beaches, with white sand, clear water, and good snorkeling. Nearby is **The Crawl**, a natural pool formed by rocks that's great for novice snorkelers; a marked path leads there from Spring Bay. **Trunk Bay** is a wide sand beach that can be reached by boat or via a rough path from Spring Bay. **Savannah Bay** is a sandy stretch north of the yacht harbor, and **Mahoe Bay**, at the Mango Bay Resort (☎ 284/495-5672), has a gently curving beach and vivid blue water.

Devil's Bay National Park can be reached by a trail from The Baths. The walk to the secluded coral-sand beach takes about 15 minutes through a natural setting of boulders and dry coastal vegetation.

SPORTS
WATERSPORTS   **Kilbrides Sunchaser Scuba,** at the Bitter End Resort at North Sound (☎ 800/932-4286 in the U.S., or 284/495-9638; www.sunchaserscuba.com), offers diving at more than 20 BVI sites, including the wreck of the RMS *Rhône.* You can purchase a video of your dive. Morning two-tank dives are $85. Afternoon dives are $60. The excursions last about 4½ hours. Wet suits rent for $5.

GREAT LOCAL RESTAURANTS & BARS
At the end of the waterfront shopping plaza in Spanish Town, **Bath and Turtle Pub,** Virgin Gorda Yacht Harbour (☎ 284/495-5239), is the island's most popular bar and pub. You can join the regulars over midmorning guava coladas or peach daiquiris and order fried fish fingers, nachos, very spicy chili, pizzas, Reubens or tuna melts, steak, lobster, and daily seafood specials such as conch fritters. Lunch $13. **Mad Dog** (☎ 284/495-5830) is a hot-dog stop near The Baths that also serves BLTs, beer, and frozen piña coladas. Lunch $5.

9 Cozumel & the Yucatán Peninsula

Check this statistic: On some days, up to 16 ships visit Cozumel simultaneously, counting those that anchor offshore and tender passengers into shore. All that activity can make the port town of **San Miguel** seem more like Times Square than the sleepy, refreshingly gritty Mexican port town it once was. San Miguel has developed at a faster rate in the past few years than just about any other Caribbean port on the map, so if you haven't been there in a while, you may not recognize the place. Still, crowds and shiny, Miami-wannabe boutiques aside, Cozumel's allure remains its proximity to the ancient Mayan ruins at **Tulum** and **Chichén-Itzá** on the mainland of the Yucatán Peninsula. Besides the ruins, the island's beaches are a big draw, along with diving and shopping for silver jewelry, local handicrafts, and T-shirts from the town's notorious beer pit, Carlos 'n Charlie's.

To see the ruins, you must take a rocky 45-minute ferry ride between Cozumel and Playa del Carmen, on the mainland, though a few cruise ships call directly on Playa del Carmen, anchoring just offshore. In recent years, a handful of other Yucatán ports have come onto the scene, including **Costa Maya** near the sleepy fishing village of Mahajual, just over 161km (100 miles) south of Playa del Carmen. Details on both Playa and Costa Maya are included later in this section. A few ships also call at **Calica**, just south of Playa, where there's little more than a pier, and at **Progreso**, on the Gulf coast of the Yucatán, where the Mayan ruins and colonial architecture of nearby Merida are the big draw. At press time, Carnival was still negotiating final terms for a new port and pier called the **Port of Cancun** at Xcaret, just down the road from Playa del Carmen.

LANGUAGE   Spanish is the tongue of the land, although **English** is spoken in most places that cater to tourists.

CURRENCY   The Mexican currency is the nuevo **peso** (new peso). Its symbol is the "$" sign, but it's hardly the equivalent of the U.S. dollar—the exchange rate is about $10 pesos to US$1 ($1 peso = about US10¢). The main tourist stores gladly accept U.S. dollars, credit cards, and traveler's checks; but if you want to change money, many banks are within a block or so of the downtown tender and ferry pier. Unless otherwise specified, prices in this section are given in U.S. dollars.

CALLING FROM THE U.S.   When calling from the U.S., you need to dial the international access code (011) and 52 before the numbers listed here.

MAYAN RUINS ON THE MAINLAND

Because all of the sites listed here are quite far from the cruise piers, most cruise passengers visit them as part of shore excursions. Admission to the sites is included in the excursion price.

The largest and most fabled of the Yucatán ruins, **Chichén-Itzá** was founded in A.D. 445 by the Mayans and later inhabited by the conquering Toltecs of central Mexico. Two centuries later, it was mysteriously abandoned. After lying dormant for 2 more centuries, the site was resettled and enjoyed prosperity again until the early 13th century, when it was once more relinquished to the surrounding jungle. The area covers 18 sq. km (7 sq. miles), so you can see only a fraction of it on a day trip.

The best known of Chichén-Itzá's ruins is the pyramid **Castillo of Kukulkán**, which is actually an astronomical clock designed to mark the vernal and autumnal equinoxes and the summer and winter solstices. A total of 365 steps, one for each day of the year, ascend to the top platform. During each equinox, light striking the pyramid gives the illusion of a giant snake slithering down the steps to join its gigantic stone head mounted at the base. The government began restoration of the site in the 1920s, and today it houses a museum, a restaurant, and a few shops. While visitors have always been free to climb up to

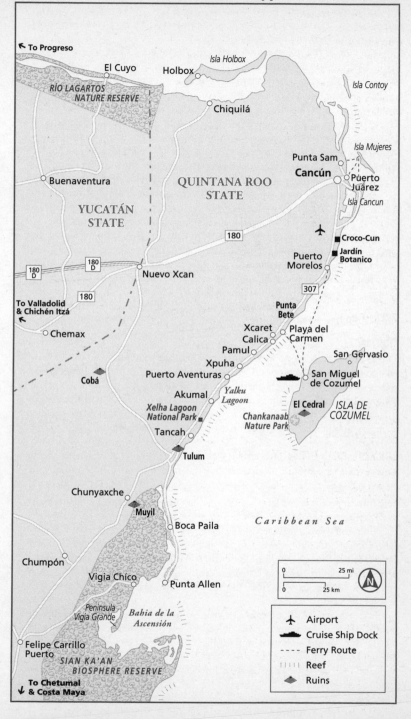

To Progreso

El Cuyo

Holbox

Isla Holbox

*RÍO LAGARTOS
NATURE RESERVE*

Chiquilá

Isla Contoy

Isla Mujeres

Punta Sam

Cancún

Puerto
Juárez

Isla Cancun

Buenaventura

**QUINTANA ROO
STATE**

**YUCATÁN
STATE**

180

Croco-Cun

Jardín
Botanico

Puerto
Morelos

180
D

180
D

Nuevo Xcan

307

To Valladolid
& Chichén Itzá

180

Chemax

Punta
Bete

Xcaret

Playa del
Carmen

Calica

San Gervasio

Pamul

Cobá

Xpuha

Puerto Aventuras

San Miguel
de Cozumel

Akumal

*Yalku
Lagoon*

*Xelha Lagoon
National Park*

El Cedral

*ISLA DE
COZUMEL*

Tancah

*Chankanaab
Nature Park*

Tulum

Chunyaxche

Caribbean Sea

Muyil

Boca Paila

Chumpón

0   25 mi

0   25 km

Vigia Chíco

Punta Allen

N

*Peninsula
Vigia Grande*

*Bahia de la
Ascensión*

Felipe Carrillo
Puerto

✈ Airport

Cruise Ship Dock

Ferry Route

Reef

Ruins

*SIAN KA'AN
BIOSPHERE RESERVE*

To Chetumal
& Costa Maya

check out the spectacular view (and suffer the vertigo on the crawl down), rumor has it that climbing to the top will soon be banned because of increasing vandalism and wear and tear on the stones.

About 129km (80 miles) south of Cancún and about a 30-minute drive from Playa del Carmen, the small walled city of **Tulum** is the single most visited Mayan ruin due to its proximity to the ports. It was the only Mayan city built on the coast and the only one inhabited when the Spanish conquistadors arrived in the 1500s. From its dramatic perch atop seaside cliffs, you can see wonderful panoramic views of the Caribbean. Tulum consists of 60 individual structures. Though nowhere near as large and impressive as Chichén-Itzá, the two cities share a similar prominent feature: a ruin topped with a temple to Kukulkán, the primary Mayan/Olmec god. Other important structures include the Temple of the Frescoes, the Temple of the Descending God, the House of Columns, and the House of the Cenote, which is a well. There's also a sliver of silky beach amidst the site, so bring your bathing suit for a quick refreshing dip. New visitor facilities include a well-stocked bookstore and a soon-to-open museum.

A 35-minute drive northwest of Tulum puts you at **Cobá,** site of one of the most important city-states in the Mayan empire. Cobá flourished from A.D. 300 to 1000, with its population numbering perhaps as many as 40,000. Excavation work began in 1972, but archaeologists estimate that only 5% of this dead city has yet been uncovered. The site lies on four lakes. Its 32 primitive hectares (81 acres) provide excellent exploration opportunities for the hiker. Cobá's pyramid, Nohoch Mul, is the tallest in the Yucatán.

COZUMEL

The ancient Mayans, who lived here for 12 centuries, would be shocked by the million cruise passengers who now visit Cozumel each year. Their presence has greatly changed San Miguel, the only town, which now has fast-food joints and a Hard Rock Cafe. Development, however, hasn't touched much of the island's natural beauty. Ashore, away from San Miguel, you'll see abundant wildlife, including armadillos, brightly colored tropical birds, and lizards. Offshore, the government has set aside 32km (20 miles) of coral reefs as an underwater national park, including the stunning Palancar Reef, the world's second-largest natural coral formation.

COMING ASHORE   Gone are the days of anchoring offshore, as there are now three piers for cruise ships to call on. The newest is **Punta Langosta,** right in the center of San Miguel, which puts you just steps from the shops, restaurants, and cafes across the street. (The ferry pier that takes tenders from Playa del Carmen is about ¼-mile away.) Other ships pull alongside the well-accoutered **International Pier** (3.2km/2 miles south of San Miguel) or at the **Puerto Maya pier** (another kilometer or so farther south), both a $4 to $5 taxi ride from town or a 30- to 45-minute walk from the heart of San Miguel. The beaches are close to the International Pier.

You can make telephone calls in Cozumel from the Punta Langosta pier or from the Global Communications phone center on the International Pier, for a few bucks a minute, or from a kiosk inside the terminal. Keep in mind, there are often lines for the phones. In town, try the **Calling Station,** Avenida Rafael Melgar 27 (© 987/2-1417), at the corner of Calle 3 in San Miguel, 3 blocks from the ferry pier.

INFORMATION   The Department of **Tourism Office,** on the second floor of Plaza del Sol (© 987/872-7563), distributes the *Vacation Guide to Cozumel*

⟳ Frommer's Favorite Cozumel Experiences

Visiting the Mayan Ruins at Chichén-Itzá or Tulum: Chichén-Itzá is the largest and most fabled of the Yucatán ruins—and the flight there, in a small plane, only adds to the experience. A few hours a day, you can climb a narrow staircase inside the main temple's inner pyramid to sneak a claustrophobic peek at a stunning jaguar throne inlaid with turquoise spots and eyes. Tulum is perched dramatically above the ocean (and in the middle of "iguana central"—they're everywhere), and tours there often include a stop at the beautiful Xel-Ha Lagoon for some swimming. (See "Mayan Ruins on the Mainland," above, and "Shore Excursions," below.)

Swimming with the Dolphins at Chankanaab: Book on your own for this once in a lifetime opportunity to be kissed, splashed, towed, and pushed through the wake like a water-skier by some of the friendliest locals you'll ever meet. For the not-so-bold, the less expensive "Dolphin Encounter" (which unlike the swimming with the dolphins, *is* offered as a shore excursion), allows you to get up close and personal with two friendly dolphins, minus the aquatic acrobatics. The encounter program does not include the overpriced but irresistible video, complete with music and slow motion close-ups. (See "On Your Own: Beyond the Port Area," below.)

Signing Up for a Jeep Trek: Explore Cozumel's jungles and sandy back roads on a fun self-drive, caravan-style adventure, and then stop at a beach for lunch and swimming. (See "Shore Excursions," below.)

and *Cozumel Island's Restaurant Guide;* both have island maps. It's open Monday to Friday from 8:30am to 5pm, and Saturday from 9am to 1pm. The Tourism booth at the ferry pier is open Monday to Saturday, from 8:30am to 4pm. For info before you go, call ℂ **800/44-MEXICO** or click on **www.islacozumel.com.mx**.

GETTING AROUND

The town of San Miguel is so small you can walk anywhere you want to go. Essentially, there's only one road in Cozumel—it starts at the northern tip of the island, hugs the western shoreline, and then loops around the southern tip and returns to the capital.

If you're driving in Cozumel, it's helpful to know that the roads parallel to the sea are called avenues, and these have the right of way. The ones running from the sea are called streets, and you have to stop at each street to give way.

BY TAXI   Taxi service is available 24 hours a day; however, like many other things in the Miami of the Yucatán, it's no bargain. The average fare from San Miguel to most major resorts and beaches is about $10 to 15; between the International terminal and downtown it's about $5. More distant island rides cost $20 and up. It's customary to overcharge cruise ship passengers, so settle on a fare before getting in—occasionally you can bargain it down. It's easy to find a cab at the pier, but you can also call ℂ **987/872-0236**.

BY RENTAL CAR If you want to drive yourself, four-wheel-drive vehicles or open-air jeeps are the best rental choice. **Avis, Budget,** and **Hertz** all have offices here. **Rent-a-Car,** Avenida 5A at Calle 2 N. (© **800/527-0700** in the U.S., or 987/872-0903), 2 blocks from the ferry pier, rents both. A four-door economy car rents for about $45 a day, with a Geo Tracker going for $80 and up, plus insurance and gas. *Note:* Most rental cars in the Caribbean have manual transmissions, so if you need an automatic, be sure to specify that when renting. A new option is the **Fun Car** or **Scoot Car,** which looks like a souped-up convertible golf cart. At $85 per day or $35 for the first hour and $10 each additional hour, these small automatic-transmission buggies can go 45 mph and are a safer option than a moped. Look for the rental booth on the ground floor of Punta Langosta shopping arcade.

BY MOPED Mopeds are a popular means of getting about despite heavy traffic, hidden stop signs, potholed roads, and a high accident rate. The best and most convenient rentals are at **Auto Rent** (© **987/872-0844**) in the Hotel El Cid La Ceiba, right next to the International Pier. The cost is about $35 per day, including helmet rental; Mexican law requires that you wear a helmet.

BY FERRY A number of passenger ferries link Cozumel with Playa del Carmen. The most comfortable are the big speedboats and water-jet catamarans run by **Aviomar** (© **987/872-0477**). They operate Monday to Saturday from 6am to 10pm, Sunday from 9am to 1pm. The trip takes 25 to 45 minutes. All the ferries have ticket booths at the main pier. One-way fares cost about $8 per person. You'll get a ferry schedule when you buy your ticket.

SHORE EXCURSIONS

It's easier to see the ruins at Chichén-Itzá, Tulum, and Cobá from Playa del Carmen because it's on the mainland and therefore closer to the ruins sites. Many ships en route to Cozumel pause in Playa del Carmen to drop off passengers who have signed up for ruins tours. After the tours, passengers either take a ferry back to the ship in Cozumel or, if the tour is by plane, get dropped off at the airport in Cozumel, near downtown. See "Mayan Ruins on the Mainland," above, for details about the ruins. If your ship is not dropping passengers off at Playa del Carmen (many don't), then keep in mind that shuttling back and forth via ferry or tender will add another hour or two to your schedule. If you're more interested in a lazy, relaxing day (and your ship doesn't go to Playa del Carmen), you may want to just hang out in Cozumel.

Chichén-Itzá Excursion ($220–$240, 6–7 hr.): Founded in A.D. 445, Chichén-Itzá is the largest and most fabled of the Yucatán ruins—and you can even climb up its tallest pyramid for wonderful views of the ancient city, much of which is still covered in foliage and earth. Due to vandalism and general deterioration, we've been told visitors will soon be forbidden to climb this pyramid, so if it is still an option when you arrive, go for it. You'll take a 45-minute flight each way on a 10- to 20-seater aircraft. The flight there is almost as interesting as the ruins. This tour may leave from Playa del Carmen. (*Note:* It can get hot. Bring plenty of water.)

The Mayan Ruins of Tulum & Xel-Ha ($99, 8 hr.): This is a very worthwhile experience. The ruins of this walled city are all the more spectacular because they're located on a cliff, dramatically perched above the ocean. This tour often includes an hour or two stop at the Xel-Ha Lagoon, a beautiful and natural setting for swimming, exploring a nature trail, or just relaxing in a hammock (in this case, the tour is 7–8 hr. long and costs another $20 or so). The tour leaves from Playa del Carmen.

Xcaret Ecological Park ($72, 8 hr.): Lying 6.4km (4 miles) south of Playa del Carmen on the coast, Xcaret (pronounced "*Ish*-car-et") is a 100-hectare (250-acre) ecological theme park where many visitors spend their entire day. It's a great place, with Mayan ruins scattered about the lushly landscaped acres. Visitors can put on life jackets for an underwater river ride, which takes them through currents running throughout a series of caves. You can also snorkel through (something we recommend highly) as well as swim with dolphins, though this costs extra. The park has a botanical garden, an aquarium, a sea turtle breeding and release facility, a dive shop, a new rotating observation tower, a Mayan village, and two theatres that put on worthwhile cultural shows on the grounds.

Jeep Trek ($86, 4½ hr.): Hop in a four-seat Jeep, draw straws to see who gets to drive, and explore the natural side of Cozumel, its jungle mangroves and sandy back roads. Much of the roller-coaster-like route is off-road, and the Jeeps travel in a convoy. Included is a visit to the La Palma ruin, where the goddess Ixchel is said to still grant wishes (you make them with your eyes closed, facing the sea), and a stop at a lovely secluded beach for swimming and a picnic lunch of tasty Mexican fare.

Horseback-Riding Tours ($85, 3–4 hr.): Worthwhile horseback-riding tours offer a chance to see Cozumel's landscape, but although they tout visits to Mayan ruins, don't get your hopes up—there's little more than a few refrigerator-size rocks here and there on Cozumel. The tour includes a guide who discusses Mayan culture and customs while exploring the inside of a cave where the Mayans gathered for ceremonial meetings. A bus transports riders to a ranch, where the ride begins; on the trip back to the ship, guests are served free and refreshingly coooolllldddd Mexican beer, as is the case on just about all bus excursions in Mexico.

ON YOUR OWN: WITHIN WALKING DISTANCE

For walkers, the classic grid layout makes getting around the town of San Miguel easy. Directly across from the downtown tender docks, the main square—**Plaza del Sol** (also called la plaza or el parque)—is excellent for people-watching. **Avenida Rafael Melgar,** the principal street along the waterfront, runs along the western shore of the island, site of the best resorts and beaches. Most of the shops and restaurants are on Rafael Melgar, although many well-stocked duty-free shops line the Malecón, the seaside promenade.

Only 3 blocks from the ferry pier on Agenda Rafael Melgar between Calles 4 and 6 N., the **Museo de la Isla de Cozumel** (© 987/872-1434) has two floors of exhibits displayed in what was Cozumel's first luxury hotel. Exhibits start in the pre-Hispanic times and continue through the colonial era to the present. Included are many swords and nautical artifacts; one of the displays showcases endangered species. The highlight is a reproduction of a Mayan house. It's open daily from 10am to 5pm, and sometimes later; admission is $3.

ON YOUR OWN: BEYOND THE PORT AREA

You can rent a motor scooter and zip around most of the island, including its wild and natural side. Stop for lunch at a beachside open-air seafood restaurant for some grilled fish and a cool drink. Scooters can be rented from several outfits, including Auto Rent (see "By Moped," above).

Outside of San Miguel is the **Chankanaab Nature Park,** where a saltwater lagoon, offshore reefs, and underwater caves have been turned into an archaeological park, botanical garden, and wildlife sanctuary. More than 10 countries have contributed seedlings and cuttings. Some 60 species of marine life occupy the lagoon, including sea turtles and captive dolphins (that you can swim with for a mere $120). Reproductions of Mayan dwellings are scattered throughout the park. There's also a wide white-sand beach with thatch umbrellas and a changing area with lockers and showers. Both scuba divers and snorkelers enjoy examining the sunken ship offshore (there are four dive shops here). The park also has a restaurant and snack stand. It's all located at Carretera Sur, Kilometer 9 (no phone). It's open daily from 9am to 5pm. Admission is $7, free for children 9 and under. The 10-minute taxi ride from the downtown tender and ferry pier (Muelle Fiscal) costs about $10.

Mayan ruins on Cozumel are very minor compared to those on the mainland. The most notable of the two, is at **San Gervasio,** reached by driving west across the island to the army air base, and then turning right and continuing north 6.4km (4 miles) to San Gervasio. This was once a ceremonial center and capital of Cozumel. The Mayans dedicated the area to Ixchel, the fertility goddess. The ruins cost $3.50 to visit, plus $1 for entrance to the access road. For $12, guides will show people what's left, including several broken columns and lintels. It's open daily from 8am to 5pm.

Another meager ruin is **El Cedral,** which lies 3.2km (2 miles) inland at the turnoff at kilometer 17.5, east of Playa San Francisco. It's the island's oldest structure, with traces of original Mayan wall paintings. The Spanish tore much of it down, and the U.S. Army nearly finished the job when it built an airfield here in World War II. Little remains now except a Mayan arch and a few small ruins covered in heavy growth. Guides at the site will show you around for a fee.

SHOPPING

You can walk from the ferry pier to the best shops in San Miguel (they start right across the street from the new Punta Langosta pier, and are 3.2km to 4.8km (2–3 miles) by taxi or foot from the International and Puerto Maya cruise ship piers). Because of the influx of cruise ship passengers, prices are relatively high here, but you can and should bargain. Silver jewelry is big business, and it's generally sold by weight. You can find some nice pieces, but again, don't expect much of a bargain. **Heritage,** Avenida Rafael Melgar 341, is one of the most important jewelers in Cozumel, and the exclusive distributor of Rolex watches on the Mexican Riviera. **Rachat & Romero,** Avenida Rafael Melgar 101, has a wide variety of loose stones, which they can mount while you wait.

Wall-to-wall shops along the waterfront in San Miguel offer all manner of souvenirs. Also, shops line the perimeter of Plaza del Sol, adjacent to the downtown ferry pier (.4km/¼-mile or so north of the Punta Langosta pier), and several shopping arcades are accessible from the plaza, including the pleasant, tree-lined **Plaza Confetti** and the peach-painted **Villa Mar complex,** with several good silver jewelry shops.

Agencia Publicaciones Gracia, Avenida 5A, a block from the downtown tender and ferry pier, is Cozumel's best source for English-language books, guidebooks, newspapers, and magazines. Viva Mexico at Avenida Rafael **Unicornio,** 5 Avenida Sur 2 (2 blocks from the ferry pier), has Mexican handicrafts. **Viva Mexico** at the intersection of Avenida Rafael Melagar and Adolfo Rosado, has beautiful local handicrafts, live music, and traditional Mexican dancers to entertain shoppers while they browse the two story boutique. **Cinco Soleils** at

Avenida Rafael Melagar and Caille 8 is also well stocked with beautiful, if pricey, handmade local goods. There is also a small tequila bar and coffee shop to re-energize the weary shopper.

If you're docking at the International Pier, a bunch of nice shops in the terminal sell everything from Mexican blankets to jewelry, T-shirts, and handicrafts of all kinds. Again, prices aren't cheap—a roll of film went for $9 at the terminal last time we were there. The pier at Puerta Maya has just undergone a major expansion and now too boasts a wide selection of well-stocked gift shops.

BEACHES

Cozumel's best powdery white-sand beach, **Playa San Francisco,** stretches for some 4.8km (3 miles) along the southwestern shoreline. It was once one of the most idyllic beaches in Mexico, but resort development is threatening to destroy its old character. You can rent equipment for watersports here, or have lunch at one of the many palapa restaurants and bars on the shoreline. There's no admission to the beach, and it's about a $10 taxi ride south of San Miguel's downtown pier. If you land at the International Pier, you're practically at the beach already.

Playa del Sol, about 1.6km (1 mile) south of Playa del San Francisco, is a fine beach but has a big reputation, so it's likely to be wall-to-wall with your fellow cruisers. **Playa Bonita** (sometimes called "Punta Chiqueros") is one of the least crowded beaches, but it lies on the east (windward) side of the island and is difficult to reach unless you rent a vehicle or throw yourself at the mercy of a taxi driver. It sits in a moon-shaped cove sheltered from the Caribbean Sea by an offshore reef. Waves are only moderate, the sand is powdery, and the water is clear.

You may want to consider **Parque Chankanaab,** a parklike beach area lined with thatched umbrellas and contoured plastic chaise longues. While the water is rough here and not ideal for swimming, the beach and scenery are very nice and the place is popular with locals. Admission is $10, and you can swim with dolphins (for a fee, of course) or rent snorkeling equipment. There's also a restaurant and bar. This beach is about a 15-minute, $12 taxi ride from the downtown pier.

If you don't want to go far, two hotel beaches are a stone's throw north of the International Pier (facing the water, they're on the right), and they welcome day visitors to use their small beach, cabanas, pools, and changing facilities. **El Cid La Ceiba** charges $10 per person for the day, and the **Park Royale** charges $25 per person for the day (9am–5pm), which includes all drinks, lunch, plus a snack bar.

SPORTS

SCUBA DIVING   Jacques Cousteau did much to extol the glory of Cozumel for scuba divers, discovering black coral in profusion, plus hundreds of species of rainbow-hued tropical fish. Underwater visibility can reach 75m (250 ft.). All this gives Cozumel some of the best diving in the Caribbean. Cruisers might want to confine their adventures to the finest spot, **Palancar Reef.** Lying about 1.6km (1 mile) offshore, this fabulous water world features gigantic elephant-ear sponges and black coral, as well as deep caves, canyons, and tunnels. It's a favorite of divers from all over the world. The best scuba outfitters are **Aqua Safari,** Avenida Rafael Melgar at Calle 5, next to the Vista del Mar Hotel (© **987/872-0101;** www.aquasafari,com), and **Diving Adventures,** Calle 51 Sur no. 2, near the corner of Avenida Rafael Melgar (© **888/338-0388** from the U.S., or 987/872-3009; www.divingadventures.net).

SNORKELING   The shallow reefs at Playa San Francisco and Chankanaab Bay are among the best snorkeling spots. You'll see a world of sea creatures parading by, everything from parrotfish to conch. The best outfitter is **Cozumel Snorkeling Center,** Calle Primera Sur (© 987/872-0539), which offers a 3-hour snorkeling tour ($40 per person), including all equipment and refreshments. They can also arrange parasailing. In addition, you can just rent snorkeling equipment at Chankanaab.

GREAT LOCAL RESTAURANTS & BARS

The **local beer** is Sol. On a hot day, a bottle of the stuff is manna from heaven.

The new **Carlos 'n Charlie's,** Avenida Rafael Melgar 11, right across from the new Punta Langosta pier (© 987/872-0191; www.carlosn-charlies.com), is Mexico's equivalent of the Hard Rock Cafe, but much wilder. Though moved into more sterile Houlihan's-style digs in a brand-new whitewashed mall, the music still blares, and dancing tourists pound back yard-long glasses of beer as if they're going out of style—just like they did at the old sawdust-covered Carlos 'n Charlie's that once roared just down the road. Many a cruise passenger has stumbled back from this place clutching a souvenir glass as though it were the Holy Grail—dubious proof of a visit to Mexico. People come here for good times and the spicy, tasty ribs. You can dine surprisingly well on Yucatán specialties and the best chicken and beef fajitas in Cozumel.

Another party spot is the **Hard Rock Cozumel** itself, at Avenida Rafael Melgar 2A (© 529/872-5273; www.hardrock.com), which serves the hard stuff as well as burgers and grilled beef or chicken fajitas. Yet another is the **Fat Tuesday,** at the end of the International Pier (© 987/872-5130), where you'll find lots of crewmembers on their day or night off (you can even hear their revelry from the ship). Join the fun and guzzle a 16-ounce margarita for $5 a pop or a 24-ounce version for $7. There's another Fat Tuesdays near the ferry pier at the entrance to the Villa Mar complex, right next to Plaza del Sol. A half block from the pier, **Las Palmeras,** Avenida Rafael Melgar (© 987/872-0532), is ideal for casual eating. If you arrive in time, it serves one of the best breakfasts in town; for lunch, it offers tempting seafood dishes or Mexican specialties.

On the main drag in town is **Lobster's Cove** (© 987/872-4022) offering tasty seafood and Mexican dishes. Just north of the ferry pier, **El Capi Navegante,** Avenida 10A Sur 312 at Calles 3 and 4, 5 blocks from the downtown tender and ferry pier (© 987/872-1730), offers the freshest fish in San Miguel, as well as a great lobster soufflé. **La Choza,** Calle Rosada Salas 198 at Avenida 10A Sur, 2 blocks from the downtown tender and ferry pier (© 987/872-0958), offers real local cooking that's a favorite of the town's savvy foodies.

PLAYA DEL CARMEN

Some cruise ships spend a day at Cozumel and then anchor offshore at Playa del Carmen for another day, but most ferry passengers to Playa from Cozumel for tours to Tulum and Chichén-Itzá, then head on to spend the day tied up at Cozumel.

The famed white-sand beach here was relatively untouched by tourists not many years ago, but today the pleasure-seeking hordes have replaced the Indian families who used to gather coconuts for copra (dried coconut meat). Shops have sprung up like weeds, but if you can tolerate the crowds, the snorkeling is still excellent over the offshore reefs. Turtle watching is another local pastime.

Avenida Juárez in Playa del Carmen is the principal business zone for the Tulum-Cancún corridor. Part of Avenida 5 running parallel to the beach has

> ### ⓒ Frommer's Favorite Playa del Carmen Experiences
>
> **Taking a Tour of Tulum or Chichén-Itzá:** Both of the tours described in the Cozumel section, under "Shore Excursions," above, are also offered here.
>
> **Spending a Day in Xel-Ha:** You'll find yourself floating around the lagoon on an inner tube without a care in the world. See "Shore Excursions" in the Cozumel section.
>
> **Spending a Day in Xcaret:** How does snorkeling through a cool underwater cave sound? See "Shore Excursions" in the Cozumel section.

been closed to traffic, forming a good promenade. Most visitors at some point head for **Rincón del Sol,** a tree-filled courtyard built in the colonial Mexican style. It has the best collection of handicraft shops in the area, some of which offer goods of excellent quality—much better than the junky souvenirs peddled elsewhere.

COMING ASHORE   Some cruise ships anchor offshore or at the pier of Cozumel, then send passengers over to Playa del Carmen by tender. Others dock at the **Puerto Calica Cruise Pier** (a former dock for freighters carrying cement), 13km (8 miles) south of Playa del Carmen. Taxis meet each arriving ship here, and drivers transport visitors into the center of Playa del Carmen—which is a good thing since there's nothing to do at Calica save for making a phone call or buying a soda.

GETTING AROUND
BY TAXI   Taxis are readily available to take you anywhere, but you can walk to the center of town, to the beach, and to most major shops.

BY RENTAL CAR   If you decide to rent a car for the day, **Avis, Budget, Hertz,** and **National** all have offices here.

SHORE EXCURSIONS
Most visitors head for the Mayan ruins or one of the local water parks the moment they reach shore (see "Shore Excursions" in the Cozumel section, above).

ON YOUR OWN: WITHIN WALKING DISTANCE
From the pier, you can walk to the center of Playa del Carmen, to the beach, and to the small but ever expanding shopping district, which has some pretty trendy boutiques and hip restaurants.

ON YOUR OWN: BEYOND THE PORT AREA
Other than the beach and shopping, the only major attractions are Xcaret and Xel-Ha (both open daily). The easiest way to get to either is to sign up for your ship's organized excursion (see above), which includes transportation; otherwise, if you're docked in Cozumel, you'll have to get ferry tickets on your own to get between the island and Playa del Carmen. If you come independently of a tour, general admission for **Xcaret** (ⓒ **998/881-2400;** www.xcaretcancun.com) is a steep $49 for adults, $25 for children 5 to 11 (free for kids 4 and under). The **Xel-Ha eco park** (ⓒ **984/875-6000;** www.xel-ha.com.mx), just a few miles farther south of Xcaret (and pronounced "Shell ha"), features a sprawling natural

lagoon filled with sparkling blue-green water and surrounded by lush foliage. The use of inner tubes and life vests are included in the admission price, and you can spend a great couple of hours wending your way from one end of the snaking body of calm water to the other, accompanied by schools of tropical fish. Snorkeling gear is available for rental. Xel-Ha has dolphins too, along with shops, restaurants, and lots of beach chairs. Admission is $25 for adults and $13 for kids. Buses from Playa del Carmen come here frequently; a taxi costs about $10 one way.

GREAT LOCAL RESTAURANTS & BARS
El Chino, Calle 4, Avenida 15 (© **984/873-0015**), is a pristine restaurant known locally for its regional Yucatán specialties, as well as standard dishes from throughout Mexico. **El Tacolote,** Avenida Juárez (© **984/873-1363**), specializes in fresh seafood and the best grilled meats in town, brought to your table fresh from the broiler on a charcoal pan to keep the food warm.

If you want to stay in the thick of things, there's a **Señor Frog's** (© **984/873-0930**), right at the ferry pier for all the beer and shots you can stomach.

COSTA MAYA
While Cozumel gets the most traffic by far, a handful of other Yucatán ports have entered the scene, including **Costa Maya** near the sleepy fishing village of **Mahajual** (just over 161km/100 miles south of Playa del Carmen). Don't confuse Costa Maya with Riviera Maya, which stretches between Cancún and Tulum. Technically, Costa Maya is the region between Punta Herrero and Xcalak near the border with Belize. Millions of dollars have been invested in a pier that opened just a couple of years ago and a lavish oceanfront shopping and restaurant complex that caters exclusively to the needs of the cruise ship passengers (no hotels are anywhere in the area). Princess, Royal Caribbean, Regal, Carnival, and Norwegian are among the lines that visit the port. The Mayan ruins of nearby Kohunlich and Chacchoben are the draw, along with silky white beaches and diving and snorkeling at the Chincorro, Mexico's largest coral atoll.

© Frommer's Favorite Costa Maya Experiences

Jungle Beach Break: A short bus ride lands you at the small but charming Uvero Beach, where you can sunbathe, kayak, rent jet skis or a mini-speedboat, or snorkel on the pristine reef. Then again, you may just want to stroll out to the end of the long pier to gaze down at the colorful sea life in the crystal blue water below. See "Shore Excursions," below.

Kohunlich Mayan Explorer: This fascinating Mayan site offers a noncommercial look at both excavated and unrestored Mayan ruins, including a ball court, foundations of residential buildings, and a stele returned to the site after being stolen by thieves. The high point (literally and figuratively) is a large temple with remarkably well-preserved stucco faces flanking the crumbling steps. Uncleared ruins just past the ball courts waiting to be unearthed make you feel like a bona fide explorer. See "Shore Excursions," below.

COMING ASHORE   Literally carved out of the jungle, this well-accoutered pier is the only major form of development for miles around, and has pretty much everything you want: sprawling restaurants (one with a balcony, the other with outdoor seating and a stage for live music), an amphitheater for cultural dance performances, two saltwater pools, a pool bar, a trampoline, and plenty of shops. And a free tram even shuttles passengers from their ship down the loooooong .5km (⅓-mile) pier to the port entrance.

GETTING AROUND

BY TAXI   A long line of shiny new taxis line up just outside the pier. Unfortunately, because any attraction of note is far, far away and there are no alternative means of transportation, the prices are steep and non-negotiable. Visiting the Mayan ruins of Kohunlich will set passengers back $65 per person round-trip, while a round-trip ride to Chacchoben comes in at $45 per person. With prices like these, unless you have a fear of crowds, we highly recommend you book the shore excursions instead (see below). About the only reasonable fare is to the nearby sleepy fishing village of Mahajual ($5 per person).

BY RENTAL CAR   No rental-car facilities are in the area, but with only one long, straight, flat road—and that still in the process of being paved—this does not seem to be too much of an inconvenience.

SHORE EXCURSIONS

The Mayan Ruins of Kohunlich ($79, 7 hr.): Located in a secluded jungle setting near the border of Belize, this ancient Mayan city was built between A.D. 200 and 900, spanning the early through the late-classical periods. The visitor center is little more than restrooms and a guard post powered by solar panels. The trail to the ruins is marked by a tree that was uprooted and replanted upside down—a means of marking sites used by the apparently brilliant, though obviously eccentric, Mexican archaeologist who first explored the site. Check out the elaborate foundations of residential dwellings of the city's elite; the Plaza of the Acropolis, where two temples are aligned with the equinox; and the Temple of the Masks from the 6th century, where 1.8m- (6-ft.-) tall stucco masks of the Mayan sun god are remarkably well preserved.

The Mayan Ruins of Chacchoben ($62, 4 hr.): Opened to the public in 1999, this collection of temples dates back to A.D. 360, or the middle of the early classical period, and played an important role as a trading center for wood, jade, and colorful birds. There are over two dozen structures, but to date less than 5% of the site has been excavated. The first temple encountered is the temple of Venus, a tribute to fertility. The pyramids are in an excellent state of preservation, and their distinctive curved edges and soft lines are particularly beautiful. Climbing to the first plateau affords an impressive view of the surrounding area.

Bike & Kayak ($48, 3 hr.): Starting off on mountain bikes, you pedal along a dirt road past a small mangrove lagoon with views of the coastline, then through the village of Mahajual (don't blink or you'll miss it), and finally arrive at the beach. After a short refreshment break, trade in your helmet for a paddle and pair up with a partner for a kayak trip out along the nearby reef. The small two-person kayaks are easily launched from the shore and easy to handle. The bike ride back includes another beach stop.

Catamaran Sail & Snorkel ($45, 2–3 hr.): Hop aboard the catamaran and pick your spot on the sun-drenched deck or in the shaded lounge. Enjoy the sail to the reef and complimentary soft drinks while your guide prepares you for the snorkeling excursion ahead. Once at the reef, don fins and a mask and enter the crystal blue water as a group exploring the pristine reef with an expert PADI-certified guide. On the way back, you can compare notes of marine life sightings over free drinks from the open bar.

Jungle Beach Break ($36): A shuttle operates between the nearby Uvero Beach and the pier, allowing you to come and go as you please every 35 minutes. But, would you ever want to leave the snow-white beaches and crystal-blue water, not to mention the chaise longues and umbrellas, open bar, free snorkel gear, paddle boats, and the sea kayaks, jet skis, and power boats you can rent? Changing rooms with showers and a snack bar are on-site (food not included). Parasailing is also available.

YOUR OWN: WITHIN WALKING DISTANCE

If you choose, you could stay right at the one-stop-shop pier complex and still get a taste of the Mayan coast. A new 650-seat amphitheatre here offers cultural shows daily, from a pre-Hispanic dance drama to a Mexican folkloric performance. There are also activities throughout the day in and around the pier, from guacamole-making classes to aqua-aerobics, games, and contests. Check the daily entertainment schedule posted near the restrooms for performance times and activities.

Immediately next to the pier is a lovely private beach club with umbrellas, chairs, hammock swings, and a small restaurant and bar. There's a small fee for day passes. Enter from the parking lot near the bus departure point.

ON YOUR OWN: BEYOND THE PORT AREA

The only town in the area is the **Mahajual** fishing village, which, until quite recently, did not even have electricity. A single main road is lined with a short row of rustic, screened-in restaurants and a miniscule grocery; across the street is a long white beach lined with fishing boats and noticeably devoid of beach umbrellas and sunbathers. Unless you're just curious, there's no real reason to go.

SHOPPING

Because the port at Costa Maya was constructed with the sole purpose of serving American and European cruise ship passengers, you can bet your last enchilada that shopping abounds. There are some 70 shops in a mall-like setting, some of them familiar to the seasoned cruiser, others unique. **Ultra Femme** specializes in fragrances and cosmetics cheaper than you'll find at the duty-free. If it's gold and jewels you're after, head over to **Tanzanite International** for a wide selection and friendly staff, or to **Diamond International** for some great bargains. Next door, you can haggle over "art in silver" at **Taxco Factory.** For something different, head over to the two nearby palapas, where local artisans craft their wares as potential buyers look on.

GREAT LOCAL RESTAURANTS & BARS

Bandito's Lobster House at the pier serves some of the freshest seviche and tastiest guacamole around. The fish, shrimp, or lobster tacos can be ordered a la carte, so you can sample one of each, while the fire-roasted Baja lobster, whole sea bass, and Mayan fajitas are full meals, and come with a slew of sides. Order a fruity tropical teaser or classic margarita to wash it all down. Next door, at **Mamacita's Taqueria,** you can enjoy casual dining and drinks while taking in the excellent views of the coast and port. Try the blackened chicken fundido to start, then the grande baja burrito or the tres taco platter.

10 Curaçao

As you sail into the harbor of Willemstad, be sure to look for the quaint "floating bridge," the Queen Emma pontoon bridge, which swings aside to open the narrow channel. Welcome to Curaçao, the largest and most populous of the Netherlands Antilles, just 56km (35 miles) north of the Venezuelan coast.

Curaçao was first discovered by the Spanish around 1499, but in 1634, the Dutch came and prospered. Because much of the island's surface is an arid desert, the settlers ruled out farming and instead developed Curaçao into one of the Dutch Empire's busiest trading posts. In 1915, when the Royal Dutch/Shell Company built one of the world's largest oil refineries to process crude from Venezuela, workers from 50 countries poured onto the island, and today it remains a melting pot, its population descended from a curious mixture of bloodlines, including African, Dutch, Venezuelan, and Pakistani. The oil refineries went into decline after World War II, and by the 1980s tourism had begun to develop, leading to the building of many new hotels. Today the island still retains a Dutch flavor, especially in Willemstad, whose harbor is bordered by rows of picture-postcard, pastel-colored gabled Dutch-colonial houses. While these structures give Willemstad a storybook appearance, the rest of the island looks like the American Southwest, its desertlike landscape dotted with three-pronged cacti, spiny-leafed aloes, and divi-divi trees bent by trade winds.

COMING ASHORE   Cruise ships dock in Willemstad at a $9 million megapier just beyond the Queen Emma pontoon bridge, which leads to the duty-free shopping sector and the famous floating market. It's a 5- to 10-minute walk from here to the center of town, or you can take a taxi from the stand. A new mega shopping/entertainment complex, Riffort Village, recently opened in the adjacent fort. The town itself is easy to navigate on foot. Most of it can be explored in 2 or 3 hours, leaving plenty of time for beaches or watersports. Although the ship terminal has a duty-free shop, save your serious shopping for Willemstad. There's a phone center at the cruise terminal.

LANGUAGE   **Dutch, Spanish,** and **English** are spoken on Curaçao, along with **Papiamento,** a patois that combines the three major tongues with Amerindian and African dialects.

CURRENCY   The official currency is the **Netherlands Antillean florin (NAf),** also called a **guilder,** which is divided into 100 cents (NAf$1.78 = US$1; NAf1 = US56¢). Canadian and U.S. dollars are accepted for purchases, so there's no need to change money. Unless otherwise noted, prices in this section are given in U.S. dollars.

INFORMATION   For visitor information, go to the **Curaçao Tourist Board,** Pietermaai (© **599/9-461-6000**). It's open Monday to Friday from 8am to 5pm. For information before you go, contact (© **800/328-7222;** www.Curacao-tourism.com).

CALLING FROM THE U.S.   When calling Curaçao from the United States, you need to dial the international access code (011) before the numbers listed here.

GETTING AROUND

BY TAXI   Taxis don't have meters, so settle on a fare before getting in. Drivers are supposed to carry an official tariff sheet. Generally, there's no need to tip. The best place to get a taxi is on the Otrabanda side of the floating bridge, or call © **599/9-869-0747.** Up to four passengers can share the price of an island tour by taxi, which costs about $30 per hour.

BY BUS A fleet of DAF yellow buses operates from Wilhelmina Plein, near the shopping center, and runs to most parts of Curaçao. You can hail a bus at any designated bus stop.

BY RENTAL CAR Driving is on the right on paved roads. **Avis, Budget,** and **Hertz** all have offices here.

SHORE EXCURSIONS OFFERED BY THE CRUISE LINES

Many excursions aren't really worth the price here—you can easily see the town on your own and hop a taxi to the few attractions on the island outside of Willemstad (see "Getting Around," above).

Hato Caves & Curaçao Museum Tour ($40, 3½ hr.): After a short bus ride to the caves and a walking tour among the grottoes, stalactites, and petroglyphs, the tour proceeds to the Curaçao Museum, founded in 1946, with displays of contemporary art and Curaçao life in the mid–19th century.

Countryside Bus Tour ($45, 2–3 hr.): This excursion takes you via bus to sights such as the Westpunt, Mount Christoffel, the towering cacti, and the rolling hills topped by landhuizen (plantation houses) built more than 3 centuries ago. You'll also stop at a beach, the Curaçao Seaquarium, and Chobolobo, an old colonial mansion where the original Curaçao liqueur is still distilled.

ON YOUR OWN: WITHIN WALKING DISTANCE

Willemstad is the major attraction here, and you can see it on foot. After years of restoration, the town's historic center and the island's natural harbor, Schottegat, have been inscribed on UNESCO's World Heritage List. Be sure to watch the **Queen Emma pontoon bridge** move. It's motorized and a man actually drives it to the side of the harbor every so often so ships and boats can pass through the channel. It's the coolest thing to see.

A statue of **Pedro Luis Brion** dominates the square known as **Brionplein,** at the Otrabanda end of the Queen Emma pontoon bridge. Born in Curaçao in 1782, Brion became the island's favorite son and best-known war hero. He was an admiral of the fleet under Simón Bolívar and fought for the independence of Venezuela and Colombia.

⌀ Frommer's Favorite Curaçao Experiences

Visiting Christoffel National Park: Hike up the 369m (1,230-ft.) St. Christoffelberg, passing cacti, iguanas, wild goats, many species of birds, and ancient Arawak paintings along the way. With 32km (20 miles) of roads, you can also see the park by car. (See "On Your Own: Beyond the Port Area," below.)

Gazing into the Mirrored Waters of the Hato Caves: Stalagmites and stalactites are mirrored in a mystical underground lake in these caves, whose limestone formations were created by water seeping through the coral. (See "On Your Own: Beyond the Port Area," below.)

Take the Hato Caves/Curaçao Liqueur Tour: This is a neat combination. A short bus ride gets you to the caves, and then to a plantation house and the liqueur factory for a tour. (See "Shore Excursions Offered by the Cruise Lines," above.)

Map labels:

Noordpunt

Westpunt

Westpunt

Playa Abao

Boca Tabla

Knip Bay

CHRISTOFFEL NATIONAL PARK

Playa Lagun

St. Christoffelberg

Santa Cruz

Santa Marta Bay

Soto

Barber

Caribbean Sea

St. Willibrordus

Daaibooi

Curaçao International Airport

Boca St. Marie

Boca Hato

Fort St. Michiel

Hato Caves

Julianadorp

Brienvengat

Blauwbaai

Caribbean Sea

Curaçao Museum

Emmastad

Santa Catarina

Piscadera Bay

St. Anna Bay

WILLEMSTAD

Seaquarium

Santa Rosa

St. Joris Bay

Punda

Montagne

Jan Thiel Bay

Spanish Water

Santa Barbara Beach

Punt Kanon Lighthouse

Curaçao Underwater Park

Ostpunt

Legend:
✈ Airport
🏖 Beach
🚢 Cruise Ship Dock
🏔 Mountain

0 5 mi
0 5 km

N

Fort Amsterdam, site of the Governor's Palace and the 1769 Dutch Reformed church, has the task of guarding the waterfront. The church still has a British cannonball embedded in it. The arches leading to the fort were tunneled under the official residence of the governor. A corner of the fort stands at the intersection of Breedestraat and Handelskade, the starting point for a plunge into the island's major shopping district.

A few minutes' walk from the pontoon bridge, at the north end of Handelskade, is the **Floating Market,** where scores of schooners tie up alongside the canal. Boats arrive here from Venezuela and Colombia, and from other West Indian islands, to sell tropical fruits and vegetables, as well as handicrafts. The modern market under its vast concrete cap has not diminished the fun of watching the activity here. Either arrive early or stay late to view these marine merchants setting up or storing their wares.

Between the I. H. (Sha) Capriles Kade and Fort Amsterdam, at the corner of Columbusstraat and Hanchi di Snoa, is the **Mikve Israel-Emanuel Synagogue.**

Dating from 1651, the Jewish congregation here is the oldest in the New World. Next door, the **Jewish Cultural Historical Museum,** Kuiperstraat 26-28 (© **599/9-461-1633**), is housed in two buildings dating from 1728. They were the rabbi's residence and the mikvah (bath) for religious purification purposes. Entry is through the synagogue and admission is $3.

You can walk from the Queen Emma pontoon bridge to the **Curaçao Museum,** Van Leeuwenhoekstraat (© **599/9-462-6051**). The building, constructed in 1853 by the Royal Dutch Army as a military hospital, has been carefully restored and furnished with paintings, objets d'art, and antique furniture, and houses a large collection from the Caiquetio tribes. On the museum grounds is an art gallery for temporary exhibitions of both local and international art.

ON YOUR OWN: BEYOND THE PORT AREA
Cacti, bromeliads, rare orchids, iguanas, donkeys, wild goats, and many species of birds thrive in the 1,800-hectare (4,500-acre) **Christoffel National Park** (© **599/9-8640363**), located about a 45-minute taxi or car ride from the capital near the northwestern tip of Curaçao. The park rises from flat, arid countryside to 369m- (1,230-ft.-) high St. Christoffelberg, the tallest point in the Dutch Leewards. Along the way are ancient Arawak paintings and the **Piedra di Monton,** a rock heap piled by African slaves who cleared this former plantation. Legend says slaves could climb to the top of the rock pile, jump off, and fly back home across the Atlantic to Africa. If they had ever tasted a grain of salt, however, they would crash to their deaths. The park has 32km (20 miles) of one-way trail-like roads. The shortest is about 8km (5 miles) long, but takes about 40 minutes to drive because of its rough terrain. One of several hiking trails goes to the top of St. Christoffelberg. It takes about 1½ hours to walk to the summit (come early in the morning before it gets hot). There's also a museum in an old storehouse left over from plantation days. The park is open Monday to Saturday from 7:30am to 4pm and on Sunday from 6am to 3pm, and guided tours are available. Admission is $10 per person.

The **Curaçao Seaquarium,** off Dr. Martin Luther King Boulevard (© **599/ 9-461-6666**), displays more than 400 species of fish, crabs, anemones, and other invertebrates, sponges, and coral. In the "shark and animal encounter," divers, snorkelers, and experienced swimmers are able to feed, film, and photograph sharks, stingrays, lobsters, tarpons, parrotfish, and other marine life in a controlled environment. Nonswimmers can see the underwater life from a 14m (46-ft.) semisubmersible observatory. Curaçao's only full-facility, white-sand, palm-shaded beach is on the Seaquarium grounds. Admission is $13 for adults and $7.25 for children 2 to 14. Hours are Monday through Sunday, 8am to 4:30pm.

Stalagmites and stalactites are mirrored in a mystical underground lake in **Hato Caves,** F. D. Rooseveltweg (© **599/9-868-0379**). Long ago, geological forces uplifted this limestone terrace, which was originally a coral reef. The limestone formations were created over thousands of years by water seeping through the coral. After crossing the lake, you enter two caverns known as "The Cathedral" and La Ventana ("The Window"), where you'll see samples of ancient Indian petroglyphs. The caves are open daily from 10am to 4pm, and professional local guides take visitors through every hour. Admission is $6.50 for adults, $5 for children 4 to 11, and free for kids 3 and under.

SHOPPING

Curaçao is a shopper's paradise, with some 200 stores lining Heerenstraat, Breedestraat, and other streets in the 5-block district called the **Punda.** Many shops occupy the town's old Dutch houses.

The island is famous for its 5-pound "wheelers" of Gouda and Edam cheese. Look for good buys on wooden shoes, French perfumes, Dutch blue Delft souvenirs, finely woven Italian silks, Japanese and German cameras, jewelry, silver, Swiss watches, linens, leather goods, liquor, and island-made rum and liqueurs, especially Curaçao liqueur, some of which has a distinctive blue color. Some stores also offer good buys on intricate lacework imported from everywhere between Portugal and China. If you're a street shopper and want something colorful, consider a carving or flamboyant painting from Haiti or the Dominican Republic; both are hawked by street vendors at any of the main plazas.

Suggested shops include **Bamali,** Breedestraat 2 (© **599/9-461-2258**), for Indonesian-influenced clothing (mostly for women); **Gandelman Jewelers,** Breedestraat 35, Punda (© **599/9-461-1854**), for a large selection of fine jewelry as well as Curaçaoan gold pieces; and **Curaçao Creations,** Schrijnwerkerstraat 14 (© **599/9-462-4516**), for Curaçao handicrafts.

BEACHES

Curaçao has some 38 beaches, ranging from hotel sand patches to secluded coves. The seawater remains an almost-constant 76°F (24°C) year-round, with good underwater visibility, but beaches here just aren't as good as others in the region. Taxi drivers waiting at the cruise dock will take you to any of the beaches, but you'll have to negotiate a fare. To be on the safe side, arrange to have your driver pick you up at a certain time and take you back to the cruise dock.

The **Curaçao Seaquarium** has the island's only full-facility, white-sand, palm-shaded beach, but you'll have to pay the full aquarium admission to get in (see "On Your Own: Beyond the Port Area," above). The rest of the beaches here are public.

A good beach on the eastern side of the island is **Santa Barbara Beach,** on land owned by a mining company between the open sea and the island's primary watersports and recreational area, known as Spanish Water. You'll also find Table Mountain and an old phosphate mine. The natural beach has pure-white sand and calm water. A buoy line protects swimmers from boats, and there are restrooms, changing rooms, a snack bar, and a terrace. You can rent water bicycles and small motorboats. It's open daily from 8am to 6pm. The beach has access to the **Curaçao Underwater Park** (© **599/9-462-4242**), which stretches from the Breezes Resort to the eastern tip of Curaçao and includes some of the island's finest reefs.

Daaibooi is a good beach about 30 minutes from town, in the Willibrordus area on the west side of Curaçao. It's free, but there are no changing facilities.

Blauwbaai (Blue Bay) is the largest and most frequented beach on Curaçao, with enough white sand for everybody. Along with showers and changing facilities, there are plenty of shady places to retreat from the noonday sun. To reach it, take the road that goes past the **Holiday Beach Hotel & Casino** (© **599/9-462-5400**), heading in the direction of Juliandorp. Follow the sign that tells you to bear left for Blauwbaai and the fishing village of San Michiel.

Westpunt is known for its gigantic cliffs and the Sunday divers who jump from them into the ocean below. This public beach is on the northwestern tip of the island. **Knip Bay,** just south of Westpunt, has beautiful turquoise waters.

On weekends, live music and dancing make the beach a lively place. Changing facilities and refreshments are available. **Playa Abao,** with crystal turquoise water, is situated at the northern tip of the island.

Warning: Beware of stepping on the hard spines of sea urchins, which are sometimes found in these waters. While not fatal, their spines can cause several days of real discomfort. For temporary first aid, try the local remedies of vinegar or lime juice.

GREAT LOCAL RESTAURANTS & BARS

Curaçao's **local beer** is the very Dutch Amstel. The **local drink** is Curaçao liqueur, some of which has a distinctive blue color.

Golden Star, Socratesstraat 2, at the corner of Dr. Hugenholtzweg and Dr. Maalweg, southeast of Willemstad (*©* **599/9-465-4795**), is the best place to go on the island for criollo, or local food. It's inland from the coast road leading southeast from St. Anna Bay, 8 minutes by taxi from the cruise dock. **La Pergola,** in the Waterfront Arches, Waterfort Straat (*©* **599/9-461-3482**), is an Italian restaurant where the menu items change virtually every day. Lunch $25. **Rijstaffel Indonesia and Holland Club Bar,** Mercuriusstraat 13, Salinja (*©* **599/9-461-2999**), is the best place on the island to sample the Indonesian rijstaffel, the traditional "rice table" with all the zesty side dishes. Lunch $22. You'll need a taxi to get to this villa in the suburbs near Salinja, near the **Super-Clubs Breezes Curacao** southeast of Willemstad.

11 Dominica

First things first. It's pronounced "Dome-ee-*nee*-ka," not "Doe-*min*-i-ka." And it has nothing to do with the Dominican Republic. The Commonwealth of Dominica is an independent country, and English, not Spanish, is the official language. The only Spanish commonly understood in Dominica is *mal encaminado a Santo Domingo* ("accidentally sent to the Dominican Republic"), the phrase stamped on the many letters that make it to their proper destination only after an erroneous but common detour.

To be sure, Dominica has some rough edges. The island is poor, so don't expect luxury or up-to-the-minute technology around every corner, and not everything man-made is as beautiful as nature's handiwork. Balancing this, though, is the fact that Dominica is the most lush and mountainous island in the eastern Caribbean. About 47km (29 miles) long and 26km (16 miles) wide, and lying between the French islands of Guadeloupe and Martinique, smack-dab in the center of the arc formed by the Antilles, it's blessed with astonishing natural wonders—crystal-pure rivers (one for every day of the year, they say), dramatic waterfalls, volcanic lakes (one gurgles and boils from the heat and tumult in the earth below), and foliage as gargantuan as any H. G. Wells ever imagined on Venus. Volcanic coral reefs, every bit as biologically complex as the rainforests onshore, ring the island, and a bit farther from land, whales mate and calve.

Much of Dominica's beauty is accessible to even the most sedentary visitor. Sitting in a rowboat, you can glide up a river through swampland crowded with mangroves and exotic birds, and impressive waterfalls are minutes from paved roads. You can also wend through astonishingly verdant rainforests along undemanding nature trails.

The island's people—primarily descendants of the West Africans brought over to work the plantations, plus some descendants of Europeans and Indians—are another great natural resource. Friendly and proud of their national independence,

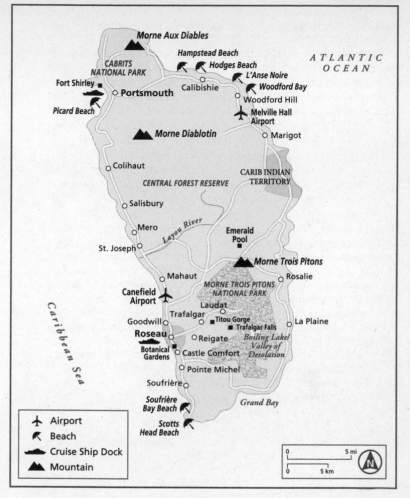

Morne Aux Diables

Hampstead Beach
CABRITS
NATIONAL PARK
Hodges Beach
Fort Shirley
Calibishie
L'Anse Noire
Portsmouth
Woodford Bay
Picard Beach
Woodford Hill

ATLANTIC
OCEAN

Melville Hall
Airport

Morne Diablotin
Marigot

Colihaut
CARIB INDIAN
TERRITORY
CENTRAL FOREST RESERVE

Salisbury

Mero
Layou River
St. Joseph
Emerald
Pool

Morne Trois Pitons
Mahaut
Rosalie
MORNE TROIS PITONS
NATIONAL PARK
Canefield
Airport
Laudat
Trafalgar
La Plaine
Goodwill
Titou Gorge
Trafalgar Falls
Roseau
Reigate
Boiling Lake
Valley of
Desolation
Botanical
Gardens
Castle Comfort
Pointe Michel

Caribbean Sea

Soufrière
Grand Bay
Soufrière
Bay Beach
Scotts
Head Beach

✈ Airport
⚓ Beach
⛴ Cruise Ship Dock
▲ Mountain

0 — 5 mi
0 — 5 km

Dominica's 72,000 citizens remain, for the most part, unchanged by tourism. Don't be surprised when you're greeted with a smile and an "okay," the island's equivalent of "hi." Unfortunately, in Roseau, the main city, drug dealers offering to sell you some of the local weed may also greet you—tourism might be a still-developing industry here, but some others are obviously a little further along.

One portion of the island's population has immeasurable ethnological significance: Concentrated in a territory in the northeast, Dominica's approximately 3,000 Carib Indians are the last remaining descendants of the people who dominated the region when Europeans arrived.

COMING ASHORE   Dominica has two cruise ship ports. The most frequented is in the heart of **Roseau,** the country's capital and largest town. The other is near the northwestern town of **Portsmouth.** Banks, restaurants, a market, a tourism office, and the recommended Dominica Museum line the road opposite Roseau's harbor. Portsmouth's port has a tourist welcome center (with

Ⓒ Frommer's Favorite Dominica Experiences

Hiking to the Emerald Pool: A 15-minute walk through a gorgeous forest brings you to this primeval pool, where you can swim or just take in the beauty of the picture-perfect waterfall, the moss-covered boulders, and the sunlight streaming through branches high overhead. (See "Shore Excursions Offered by the Cruise Lines," below.)

Paddling Up the Indian River: Minutes from Portsmouth, the gentle Indian River drains into the Caribbean from its source in the foothills of the island's tallest mountain, 1,424m- (4,747-ft.-) high Morne Diablotin. As a boatman paddles you up the twisting river, you'll pass through swampland that features giant palms and mango trees with serpentine roots. (See "Shore Excursions Offered by the Cruise Lines," below.)

Experiencing Carib Culture: Along a rugged portion of Dominica's northeastern coast, the 1,480-hectare (3,700-acre) Carib Territory is home to the world's last surviving Carib Indians. The Caribs today live like most other rural islanders—growing bananas and coconuts, fishing, and operating small shops—but their sturdy baskets of dyed and woven larouma reeds and their wooden canoes carved from the trunks of massive gommier trees are evidence of the people's links to the past. A traditional big house, called the Karbet, serves as a cultural and entertainment center. If you're lucky, you'll witness a performance of the Karifuna Cultural Group, whose youthful members are dedicated to the regeneration of Carib spirit and culture. (See "Shore Excursions Offered by the Cruise Lines," below.)

Exploring Fort Shirley/Cabrits National Park: On Dominica's northwestern coast, right by the cruise ship port of Portsmouth, the 104-hectare (260-acre) Cabrits National Park combines stunning mountain scenery, tropical deciduous forest and swampland, volcanic-sand beaches, coral reefs, and the romance of an 18th-century fort. (See "On Your Own: Within Walking Distance," below.)

---

an auditorium for speakers and films), shops, and instant access to Fort Shirley and Cabrits National Park.

LANGUAGE   **English** is Dominica's official language. Almost everyone speaks **Creole** as well, a patois that combines elements of French, English, and African language. Dominica's Creole is similar to those spoken on the neighboring French islands of Guadeloupe and Martinique.

CURRENCY   The **Eastern Caribbean dollar** (EC$2.70 = US$1; EC$1 = US37¢) is Dominica's official currency, but U.S. dollars are accepted almost everywhere. You're likely to receive change in the local currency. Several **ATMs** in Roseau, including one at the port, dispense both U.S. and EC dollars. Credit cards and traveler's checks are widely accepted. Unless otherwise specified, prices in this section are given in U.S. dollars.

INFORMATION   Dominica's **Division of Tourism** operates branches at the Roseau and Portsmouth cruise ship berths (the Roseau office is located a block from the waterfront at the old post office building on Dame M. E. Charles Blvd.). For information before you leave home, contact the **Dominica Tourist Office** (© **888/645-5637;** www.dominica.dm). Several island businesses, including restaurants, tour operators, and other service providers, have joined forces to create another site, **www.delphis.dm/home.htm**, which has scores of links and helpful information.

CALLING FROM THE U.S. When calling Dominica from the United States, simply dial "1" before the numbers listed here.

GETTING AROUND

BY RENTAL CAR Dominica's road system is extensive and relatively well maintained considering the frequent torrential rains, but driving is on the left side, and passage through the mountains can be harrowing. You need a valid driver's license and a Dominican driver's permit, which costs about $10 and is available through rental agencies. Don't get annoyed when other drivers sound their horns; honking usually indicates an oncoming vehicle (especially at sharp curves) or is meant as a friendly greeting. **Avis, Budget,** and **Hertz** all have offices here, as do the local agencies **Valley Car Rentals,** with offices in both Roseau and Portsmouth (© **767/448-3233** Roseau, 767/445-5252 Portsmouth), and **Garraway Rent-a-Car,** in downtown Roseau at 17 Old St. (© **767/448-2891**). Another option is **Auto Trade Car Rentals** (© **767/448-3425**).

BY TAXI Taxis and public minivans are designated by license plates that begin with the letters *H* or *HA*. Fleets of both await cruise ship passengers at the Roseau and Portsmouth docks. Drivers are generally knowledgeable about sites and history, and the standard sightseeing rate is $18 per hour for up to four people. The vehicles are unmetered, so negotiate a price in advance and make sure everyone's talking about the same currency. You can get more information from the **Dominica Taxi Association** (© **767/449-8533**). **Mally's Tour and Taxi Service** (© **767/448-3114**), **Julius John's** (© **767/449-1968**), and **Alwyn's Taxi and Tour Service** (© **767/235-4260**) are three reputable operators.

SHORE EXCURSIONS OFFERED BY THE CRUISE LINES

Trafalgar Falls & Emerald Pool Nature Tour ($40, 4 hr.): Drive to Morne Bruce for a panoramic view of Roseau and learn about local flora and fauna at the Botanical Gardens. Proceed to a lookout point for a majestic view of Trafalgar Falls. After refreshment at a nearby restaurant, drive to the Emerald Pool, where, after a 15-minute trail walk, you can swim in a natural pool surrounded by moss-covered boulders at the base of a picture-perfect waterfall.

Roseau & Indian River Tour ($40, 5 hr.): Drive through Roseau and fishing villages along the island's western coast to the town of Portsmouth. Embark on wooden canoes for a guided tour of the Indian River. Ferns, lianas, and reeds cluster between the trees, forming a cool green tunnel of foliage. You'll spot herons, bananaquits, and the occasional iguana. Land crabs shuffle between the roots, and fish occasionally pop out of the water. The relaxing trip features informative commentary by your boatman and a brief stop at a rainforest refreshment stand for a beer or soda, where you can also pick up a fish or bird fashioned origami-style from reed. Cruise lines often offer this excursion, but if you're in Portsmouth, locals with boats are everywhere trying to drum up business (the actual ride upstream is only about 1.6km/1 mile or so), so you can skip the middleman and hop in one for about $20 a person (or whatever you can negotiate).

Carib Indian Territory ($51, 5 hr.): Drive to the Carib Territory, where the tribe's chief will acquaint you with Carib history. Attend a performance by the Karifuna Cultural Group and view local crafts.

Champagne Scuba Dive ($51, 3 hr.): Certified divers can dive the reef named for the bubbles produced by an underwater geothermal vent. Observe corals, fish, and other marine life. Equipment is included.

D'Auchamps Gardens & Museum ($36, 3 hr.): Walk through an impressive collection of exotic plants and flowers and learn about their uses and origins. Along a marked trail through this old coffee estate you'll see cacao, avocado, breadfruit, and citrus trees, as well as heliconias, orchids, and other spectacular blooms from around the world. View Trafalgar Falls and a variety of birds. Learn about Dominica's history at the museum.

EXCURSIONS OFFERED BY LOCAL AGENCIES

Nature Tours: Dominica has several excellent tour operators who know the island's many features and intricate terrain like the backs of their hands. One truly outstanding and highly recommended operation is **Ken's Hinterland Adventure Tours,** Fort Young Hotel, Victoria St., Roseau (© **767/448-4850**), which offers tours that focus on botany, natural history, bird-watching, and whale-watching.

Carib Indian Excursions: For trips through the Carib Territory, you might want to make arrangements with **NICE** (Native Indigenous Carib Excursions; © **767/445-8669**). You can't miss with the firsthand knowledge of Carib traditions offered by NICE's operator, former Carib chief Irvince Auguiste.

See "Sports," below, for information on scuba, snorkeling, and kayaking trips.

ON YOUR OWN: WITHIN WALKING DISTANCE

IN ROSEAU   In the early 18th century, the French chose to build their largest settlement at what is now Roseau because the area has the largest expanse of flat land on the leeward coast and is well supplied with fresh water from the nearby Roseau River. The town's name comes from the river reeds (*roseaux* in French) that grow profusely around the estuary. As you come ashore, you'll see the **Dominica Museum,** which faces the bay front. Housed in an old market house dating from 1810, the museum's permanent exhibit provides a clear and interesting overview of the island's geology, history, archaeology, economy, and culture. The displays on pre-Columbian peoples, the slave trade, and the Fighting Maroons—slaves who resisted their white slave owners and established their own communities—are particularly informative. The museum is open Monday to Friday from 9am to 4pm, Saturday from 9am to noon; admission is $2.

Directly behind the museum is the **Old Market Square.** Vendors of vegetables, fruits, and other merchandise have crowded this cobbled square for centuries, and over the years the location has also witnessed slave auctions, executions, and political meetings and rallies. Today it offers primarily handicrafts and souvenirs. The **Public Market Place** at the mouth of the Roseau River, to your left as you leave the ship, is the Old Market Square's successor as the town's center of commercial activity. It's most colorful on Saturday mornings, when farmers and country vendors from the hills artfully display their fruits, vegetables, root crops, and flowers across the courtyards, sidewalks, and stalls of the marketplace.

It took more than 100 years to build the **Roseau Cathedral of Our Lady of Fair Heaven,** on Virgin Lane. Made of cut volcanic stone in the Gothic-Romanesque revival style, it was finally completed in 1916. The original funds to build the church were raised from levies on French planters, and Caribs erected the first wooden ceiling frame. Convicts on Devil's Island built the pulpit, and one of the stained-glass windows is dedicated to Christopher Columbus. The **Methodist Church** stands next door to the Cathedral on land that once belonged to Catholics who later converted to Methodism. The Protestant church's location and the "conversion" of the land caused such discomfort in the late 1800s that a street riot ensued. Things are calmer today.

On the eastern edge of Roseau, the **Botanical Gardens** lie at the base of Morne Bruce, the mountain overlooking the town. The gardens were established at the end of the 19th century to encourage crop diversification and to provide farmers with correctly propagated seedlings. London's Kew Gardens provided exotic plants collected from every corner of the tropical world, and experiments conducted to see what would grow in Dominica revealed that everything does. Unfortunately, in 1979 Hurricane David destroyed many of the garden's oldest trees. One arboreal victim, an African baobab, still pins the bus it crushed, a monument to the power of the storm. At the garden's aviary you can see sisserou and jacko parrots, part of a captive-breeding program designed to increase the ranks of these endangered species.

IN PORTSMOUTH   The cruise ship dock at Portsmouth leads directly to 104-hectare (260-acre) **Cabrits National Park,** which combines stunning mountain scenery, tropical deciduous forest and swampland, volcanic-sand beaches, coral reefs, and the romance of 18th-century **Fort Shirley** overlooking the town and Prince Rupert's Bay. Previous visitors to the area include Christopher Columbus, Sir Francis Drake, Admiral Horatio Nelson, and John Smith, who stopped here on his way to Virginia, where he founded Jamestown. Fort Shirley and more than 50 other major structures comprise one of the West Indies' most impressive and historic military complexes. Admission is $2.

ON YOUR OWN: BEYOND THE PORT AREAS

Approximately 15 to 20 minutes by car from Roseau, **Trafalgar Falls** is actually two separate falls referred to as the mother and the father falls. The cascading white torrents dazzle in the sunlight before pummeling black lava boulders below. The surrounding foliage comes in innumerable shades of green. To reach the brisk water of the natural pool at the base of the falls, you'll have to step gingerly along slippery rocks, so the nonballetic shouldn't attempt the climb. The constant mist that tingles the entire area beats any spa treatment. The rainbows are perpetual.

Titou Gorge, near the village of Laudat, offers an exhilarating swimming experience. Wending through the narrow volcanic gorge, you struggle against the cool current like a salmon swimming upstream to spawn. The sheer black walls enclosing the gorge loom 6m (20 ft.) above. At first, they seem sinister, but worn smooth by the water, they're ultimately womblike rather than menacing. Rock outcrops and a small cave provide interludes from the water flow, and eventually you reach the small but thundering waterfall that feeds the torrent.

Emerald Pool sits deep in the rainforest not far from the center of the island. After walking 15 minutes along a relatively easy trail shaded by majestic trees, you reach a 15m (50-ft.) waterfall that crashes into the pool, named for the moss-covered boulders that enclose it. You can splash in the refreshing water if you like, floating on your back to see the thick rainforest canopy and bright blue sky above you.

About 6.4km (4 miles) from Portsmouth, in the midst of orange, grapefruit, and banana groves, the **Syndicate Nature Trail** provides an excellent introduction to tropical rainforests. The easy loop trail meanders through a stunningly rich ecosystem that features exotic trees such as the lwoyé kaka and the chantannyé.

Hard-core masochists have an easy choice—the forced march through the **Valley of Desolation** to **Boiling Lake.** Experienced guides say this all-day hike is like spending hours on a maximally resistant Stairmaster; one ex-Marine drill sergeant, a master of understatement, referred to it as "arduous." No joke, the trek is part of the Dominican army's basic training (of course, you won't have to carry one of your colleagues along the way). Why would any sane person endure this hell? To breathe in the harsh, sulfuric fumes that have killed all but the hardiest vegetation? Because the idea of baking a potato in the steam rising from the earth is irresistible? Maybe to feel the thrill that comes with the risk that you might break through the thin crust that separates you from hot lava? Or could it be the final destination, the 21m- (70-ft.-) wide cauldron of bubbling, slate-blue water of unknown depth? Don't even think of taking a dip in this flooded fumarole: The water temperature ranges from 180° to 197°F (82°C–92°C). Can we sign you up?

SHOPPING

In addition to the usual duty-free items—jewelry, watches, perfumes, and other luxury goods—Dominica offers handicrafts and art not obtainable anywhere else, most notably **Carib Indian baskets** made of dyed larouma reeds and balizier (heliconia) leaves. Designs for these items originated in Venezuela's Orinoco River valley and have been handed down from generation to generation since long before the time of Columbus. Dominican designs and materials are similar to those made today in the Orinoco valley—amazing considering that there's been no interaction between the two peoples for more than 500 years. The Carib basket you buy, therefore, is more than a souvenir; it's a link to the pre-Columbian Caribbean. You can buy Carib crafts directly from the craftspeople in the Carib Territory or at various outlets in Roseau. A small, 12-inch basket will cost about $10, and you can get a bell-shaped model about 22 inches high for $30 or $35. **Floor mats** made from vertiver grass are another Dominican specialty.

At **Tropicrafts,** at the corner of Queen Mary Street and Turkey Lane in Roseau, you can watch local women weave grass mats with designs as varied and complex as those you made as a child with your Spirograph. The large store also stocks Carib baskets, locally made soaps and toiletries, rums, jellies, condiments, woodcarvings, and masks made from the trunks of giant fougère ferns. The **Rainforest Shop,** at 12 Old St. in Roseau, is dedicated to the preservation of Dominica's ecosystem and offers colorful hand-painted items made from recycled materials such as oil drums, coconut shells, and newspapers. The **Crazy Banana,** at 17 Castle St., features Dominican arts and crafts, including straw and ceramic items, as well as jewelry and Cuban cigars. For unique and sometimes whimsical objects, try **Balisier's** at 35 Great George St. Local artist Hilroy Fingal transforms throwaway items such as aluminum cans, perfume bottles, rocks, and coconut shells into things of beauty. His aesthetic is a little like Keith Haring's and every bit as fun. **Caribana,** at 31 Cork St., is one of the island's oldest craft shops. It offers items as varied as furniture, home accessories, jewelry, books, and skin-care products, and also serves as a showcase for local painters and sculptors and as a gathering place for the local arts community. **Frontline Cooperative,** at 78 Queen Mary St., specializes in books about Caribbean peoples, issues, and cooking.

BEACHES

If your sole focus is beaches, you'll likely find Dominica disappointing. Much of the seacoast is rocky, and many sandy beaches have dark, volcanic sand. But there are golden sand beaches as well, primarily on the northern coast. Head for **Woodford Bay, L'Ance Tortue, Pointe Baptiste,** or **Hampstead Beach;** all have white sand, palm trees, and azure waters protected by reefs or windswept headlands.

SPORTS

FISHING Dominica is a prime destination for anglers looking to catch marlin, wahoo, yellowfin tuna, or dorado. The island's numerous rivers flow into the Caribbean, providing an abundance of baitfish, including bonito, jacks, and small tuna that attract bigger deepwater species. **Gamefishing Dominica** (✆ **767/449-6638**) has two boats, a 10m (34-ft.) Luhrs and an 8.4m (28-ft.) Pacemaker. Coastline fishing prices start at $50 per person, with a four-passenger minimum. Deep-water half-day excursions are $450 for up to six anglers.

SCUBA DIVING Dominica's lush, beautiful scenery above water is echoed underwater in the surrounding Caribbean and Atlantic. Although the island is drained by hundreds of rivers and streams, the jagged volcanic undersea-scape prevents runoff sediment from clouding the water. Visibility ranges from 18m (60 ft.) to more than 30m (100 ft.). Most local dive operations surpass international standards set by PADI, NAUI, and SSI, and small, uncrowded excursions are the norm. **Dive Dominica** (✆ **888/262-6611** in the U.S., or 767/448-2188) is perhaps the island's best operator. Single-tank boat dives run about $45. First-time dives with instruction run about $130.

SNORKELING Dominica offers almost 30 top-notch snorkeling areas, including the popular Champagne site. Snorkelers can join a dive-boat party, participate in special snorkel excursions, or explore the coast in a sea kayak, periodically jumping overboard for a look below. The calm water on the island's leeward side is perfect for viewing the riotous colors of sponges, the corals, and the 190-plus fish species native to the area. Offshore snorkeling and equipment rental can be arranged through the dive operator listed above. Prices start at approximately $25.

GREAT LOCAL RESTAURANTS & BARS

Seafood, local root vegetables referred to as "provisions," and Creole recipes are among the highlights of Dominican cuisine. Crapaud ("mountain chicken" in English, though it's really mountain frog) is the national delicacy. For a **local beer,** try Kubuli; for a **local rum,** try Soca or Macoucherie.

IN ROSEAU Try **La Robe Créole,** 3 Victoria St. (✆ **767/448-2896**), which gets top marks for its callaloo soup (made from the spinachlike leaves of a local vegetable called dasheen, plus coconut), lobster and conch crepes, and mango chutney. The decor features heavy stone walls, solid ladder-back chairs, and colorful madras tablecloths. The restaurant is only open for dinner. **Guiyave,** 15 Cork St. (✆ **767/448-2930**), an airy restaurant on the second floor of a pistachio-colored wood-frame house, features steamed fish, conch, octopus, and spareribs. Take a table on the veranda and cool off with one of the fresh-squeezed juices. How about soursop, tamarind, sorrel, cherry, or strawberry? The down-stairs takeout counter offers chicken patties, spicy rotis, and delectable tarts and cakes. Lunch $13. The **Sutton Grille**, 25 Old St. (© **767/449-8700**), in the Sutton Place Hotel, boasts an airy dining area ensconced in 100-year-old stone walls. You can choose a table a few steps up from the bustle of downtown Roseau or one set back from the action. The menu, a veritable primer of Creole and other West Indian cookery, also offers a generous sprinkling of international and vegetarian dishes. Lunch $8.

IN PORTSMOUTH   If you disembark in Portsmouth, get a table at the **Coconut Beach Restaurant** at Picard Beach (© **767/445-5393**). It overlooks the Caribbean and the twin peaks of Cabrits National Park across Prince Rupert's Bay. The fresh seafood and Creole dishes taste even better with the tang of salt in the air. Lunch $18. The **Purple Turtle** (© **767/445-5296**) is closer to the dock and features lobster and crayfish, as well as lighter fare such as rotis, sandwiches, and salads. Lunch $10.

12 Grand Cayman

Grand Cayman is the largest of the Cayman Islands, a British colony 773km (480 miles) due south of Miami (Cayman Brac and Little Cayman are the others). It's the top of an underwater mountain, whose side—known as the **Cayman Wall**—plummets straight down for 150m (500 ft.) before becoming a steep slope that falls away for 1,800m (6,000 ft.) to the ocean floor.

Despite its "grand" name, the island is only 35km (22 miles) long and 13km (8 miles) across at its widest point. Flat, relatively unattractive, and full of scrub-land and swamp, Grand Cayman and its sister islands nevertheless boast more than their share of upscale, expensive private homes and condos, owned by millionaire expatriates from all over who come because of the tiny nation's lenient tax and banking laws. (Enron, the poster child of shady business dealings, reportedly had more than 690 different subsidiaries here to help it avoid paying U.S. taxes.)

Grand Cayman is also popular because of its laid-back civility—so civil that ships aren't allowed to visit on Sunday. **George Town** is the colony's capital and its commercial hub, and many hotels line the sands of the nation's most famous sunspot, **Seven Mile Beach.** Scuba divers and snorkelers come for the coral reefs and other formations that lie sometimes within swimming distance of the shoreline.

COMING ASHORE   Cruise ships anchor off George Town and ferry their passengers to a pier on Harbour Drive. The short tender ride can be choppy, but the landing point couldn't be more convenient: You're let off right in the heart of the shopping district. There's a **tourist information booth** at the pier, and taxis line up to meet cruise ship passengers. There's a phone center for credit-card calls on Cardinal Avenue, right in downtown.

LANGUAGE   **English** is the official language of the islands.

CURRENCY   The legal tender is the **Cayman Islands dollar** (CI82¢ = US$1; CI1 = US$1.22), but U.S. dollars are commonly accepted. Be sure to note which currency price tags refer to before making a purchase. Prices in this section are given in U.S. dollars.

INFORMATION   The **Department of Tourism** is in the Pavilion Building, Cricket Square (P.O. Box 67), George Town, Grand Cayman, BWI (© **800/346-3313** or 345/949-0623). It's open Monday to Friday from 9am to 5pm. To

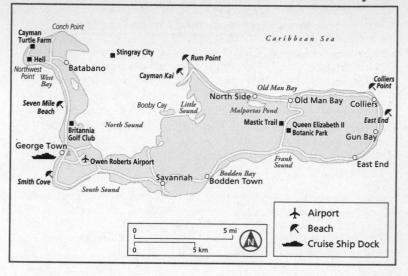

get info before you go, contact the **Cayman Islands Department of Tourism** in New York (℡ 212/682-5582; www.caymanislands.ky).

CALLING FROM THE U.S.   When calling Grand Cayman from the U.S., you need only dial a "1" before the numbers listed here.

GETTING AROUND

BY TAXI   Taxi fares are fixed; typical one-way fares range from $12 to $20. **Holiday Taxi** (℡ 345/947-1066) offers 24-hour service.

BY RENTAL CAR   The roads are good by Caribbean standards, so driving around is relatively easy, as long as you remember to drive on the left side of the road. **Avis, Budget, Dollar,** and **Hertz** all have offices here.

BY MOTOR SCOOTER OR BICYCLE   The terrain is relatively flat, so motor scooters and bicycles are another way to get around. **Soto Scooters Ltd.,** Seven Mile Beach (℡ 345/945-4465), at Coconut Place, offers Honda Elite scooters for about $30 daily, and bicycles for $15 daily.

SHORE EXCURSIONS OFFERED BY THE CRUISE LINES

Nearly all the shore excursions here are underwater adventures, which you can book through your cruise ship or on your own.

Stingray City ($45–$55, 2–3 hr.): The waters off Grand Cayman are home to Stingray City, one of the world's most unusual underwater attractions. Set in the very shallow, sun-flooded waters of North Sound, about 3.2km (2 miles) east of the island's northwestern tip, the site was discovered in the mid-1980s when local fishermen cleaned their catch and dumped the offal overboard. They noticed scores of stingrays (which usually eat marine crabs) feeding on the debris, a phenomenon that quickly attracted local divers and marine zoologists. Today, anywhere from 30 to 100 relatively tame stingrays hover in the waters around the site for their daily handouts from hordes of snorkelers (often hundreds of cruise passengers at a time, so don't be surprised if they're not hungry). Stingrays are terribly gentle creatures, and love to have their bellies rubbed, but they possess viciously barbed stingers capable of inflicting painful damage to

> **Frommer's Favorite Grand Cayman Experiences**
>
> **Swimming with Stingrays:** At Stingray City, you can hop into the water with dozens of these weird-looking but gentle sea creatures, which will swim right into your arms, like dogs. (See "Shore Excursions Offered by the Cruise Lines," above.)
>
> **Taking In the Scene on Seven Mile Beach:** Grand Cayman's famed stretch of sand is known for its watersports and its translucent aquamarine waters. (See "Beaches," below.)

anyone mistreating them. Never try to grab one by the tail. As long as you don't, you can feed and pet these velvet-skinned creatures without incident. Some tours include a quick island tour, including a stop at the Cayman Turtle Farm and a town called Hell (to look at some interesting rock formations and, of course, buy a T-shirt with that great Hell logo).

Atlantis Submarine Excursion ($86, 1½ hr.): A 45-minute ride in the submarine is usually offered. The "Atlantis Expedition" dive visits the Cayman Wall; the "Atlantis Discovery" lasts 40 minutes and introduces viewers to the marine life of the Caymans.

Island Tour via Bicycle ($69, 3 hr.): A great way to really get a feel for an island—and get some exercise—is via bicycle. You pick up your touring mountain bike at the **Beach Club Colony Hotel** (© 345/949-8100), ride along the coastline for views of Seven Mile Beach, and then journey inland en route to the north side of the island to ride along the coast again.

EXCURSIONS OFFERED BY LOCAL AGENCIES

Stingray City: If the tours on your ship get booked, about half a dozen entrepreneurs lead expeditions to Stingray City, and usually a few tour agents wait around the terminal in George Town to snare cruise passengers as they debark. One well-known outfit is **Treasure Island Divers** (© 800/872-7552 from the U.S.; www.tidivers.com), which charges $30 per person for stingray snorkeling excursions.

Taxi Tours: If you want to see the island, you can grab a taxi in port and take a tour. Taxis should cost about $40 per hour and can hold up to five people. A 3-hour tour covers all the sights in a leisurely fashion. Make sure to stop in the town called Hell and send a postcard home.

ON YOUR OWN: WITHIN WALKING DISTANCE

In George Town, **Cayman Islands National Museum,** Harbour Drive (© 345/949-8368; www.museum.ky), is housed in a veranda-fronted building that once served as the island's courthouse. Exhibits include Caymanian artifacts collected by Ira Thompson (beginning in the 1930s), and other items relating to the natural, social, and cultural history of the Caymans. There's a gift shop, theater, and cafe. Admission is $5 for adults and $2.50 for students and senior citizens.

ON YOUR OWN: BEYOND THE PORT AREA

The only green-sea-turtle farm of its kind in the world, **Cayman Turtle Farm,** Northwest Point (© 345/949-3894; www.turtle.ky), is the island's most popular land-based tourist attraction. Once a multitude of turtles lived in the waters surrounding the Cayman Islands, but today these creatures are an endangered species. The turtle farm's purpose is twofold: to replenish the waters with hatchlings and yearling turtles and, at the other end of the spectrum, to provide the local market with edible turtle meat. You can peer into 100 circular concrete tanks containing turtles ranging in size from 6 ounces to 600 pounds, or sample turtle dishes at a snack bar and restaurant. The farm is open from 8:30am to 5pm. Admission is $6 for adults, $3 for children 6 to 12.

On 26 hectares (65 acres) of rugged wooded land, **Queen Elizabeth II Botanic Park,** off Frank Sound Road, North Side (℃ 345/947-9462), offers visitors a 1-hour walk along a short (1.2km/¾-mile) trail through wetlands, swamps, dry thicket, and mahogany trees. You may spot hickatees (the freshwater turtles found only on the Caymans and in Cuba), the rare Grand Cayman parrot, or the anole lizard with its cobalt-blue throat pouch. There are six rest stations along the trail, plus a visitor center and a canteen. There's also a heritage garden, a floral garden, and a lake.

The **Mastic Trail,** west of Frank Sound Road, is a restored 200-year-old footpath through a 2-million-year-old woodland area in the heart of the island. Named for the majestic mastic tree, the trail showcases the reserve's natural attractions, including a native mangrove swamp, traditional agriculture, and an ancient woodland area. You can follow the 3.2km (2-mile) trail on your own, but we recommend taking a 3-hour guided tour. Call ℃ **345/945-6588** to make a reservation. The trail, adjacent to the Botanical Park, is about a 45-minute drive from George Town.

SHOPPING

There's duty-free shopping here for silver, china, crystal, Irish linens, and British woolen goods, but we've found most prices to be similar to those in the United States. You'll also find cigar shops and international chains such as Coach, the leather-goods store. Please don't succumb and purchase turtle or black-coral products. You'll see them everywhere, but it's illegal to bring them back into the United States and most other Western nations.

Some standout shops include **Artifacts Ltd.,** Harbour Drive, on the harbor front, across from the landing dock (℃ **345/949-2442**), for back issues of Cayman stamps; **The Jewelry Centre,** Fort Street (℃ **345/949-0070**), one of the largest jewelry stores in the Caymans; and the **Kennedy Gallery** West Shore Centre (℃ **345/949-8077**), specializing in watercolors by local artists.

BEACHES

Grand Cayman's **Seven Mile Beach,** which begins north of George Town, an easy taxi ride from the cruise dock, has sparkling white sands with a backdrop of Casuarina trees. The beach is really about 8.9km (5½ miles) long, but who are we to quibble with tradition? It's lined with condominiums and plush resorts, and is known for its array of watersports and its translucent aquamarine waters. The average water temperature is a balmy 80°F (27°C).

SPORTS

SCUBA DIVING & SNORKELING   Coral reefs and other formations encircle the island and are filled with marine life. It's easy to dive close to shore, so boats aren't necessary, but plenty of boats and scuba facilities are available, as well as many dive shops renting scuba gear to certified divers. The best dive operation is **Bob Soto's Reef Divers,** P.O. Box 1801, Grand Cayman, BWI

(© 800/262-7686 for reservations, or 345/949-2022; www.bobsotosreefdivers.
com), with full-service dive shops at Treasure Island, the Scuba Centre on North
Church Street, and Soto's Coconut in the Coconut Place Shopping Centre.
There are full-day resort courses as well as excursions for experienced divers daily
on the west, north, and south walls, plus shore diving from the Scuba Centre.
The staff is helpful and highly professional.

GREAT LOCAL RESTAURANTS & BARS

A favorite **local beer** is Stingray, and a favorite **local rum** is Tortuga.

Abanks' Club Paradise, on Harbour Drive (© 345/945-1444), is less than
a kilometer's (less than ½-mile's) walk south of the pier. It's a great open-air seaside cafe for a sandwich, chicken fingers, and a couple of cool Stingray beers or
a frozen drink. **Cracked Conch by the Sea,** West Bay Road, near Turtle Bay
Farm (© 345/945-5217), serves some of the island's freshest seafood, including
the inevitable conch, plus meat dishes such as beef, jerk pork, and spicy combi-
nations of chicken. Lunch $10. The **Crow's Nest Restaurant,** South Sound, on
the southwesternmost tip of the island, a 4-minute drive from George Town
(© 345/949-9366), is one of those places that evokes the Caribbean "the way
it used to be." There's no pretense here—you get good, honest Caribbean cookery, including grilled seafood, at great prices. Many dishes are spicy, especially
their signature appetizer—fiery coconut shrimp. Lunch $16.

The Wreck on the Rocks, North Church Street, near the beginning of West
Bay Road (© 345/949-6163), has a loyal clientele and is divided into an amus-
ingly decorated pub and a Caribbean-inspired dining room open to a view of
the harbor. In the pub, you can order such British staples as fish and chips or
cottage pie. **Ottmar's Restaurant and Lounge,** West Bay Road (© 345/945-
5879), is one of the island's top restaurants for dinner, offering such dishes as
Bavarian cucumber soup; bouillabaisse; French pepper steak; Wiener schnitzel;
and chicken Trinidad, stuffed with grapes, nuts, and apples rolled in coconut
flakes, sautéed golden brown, and served in orange-butter sauce.

13 Grenada

The southernmost nation of the British Windwards, Grenada (Gre-*nay*-dah) is
one of the lushest in the Caribbean. Called the "Spice Island," it has extravagant
fertility—a result of the gentle climate and volcanic soil—that produces more
spices than anywhere else in the world: clove, cinnamon, mace, cocoa, tonka
beans, ginger, and a third of the world's supply of nutmeg. The beaches are white
and sandy, and the populace (a mixture of English expatriates and islanders of
African descent) is friendly. Once a British Crown Colony but now independent, the island nation also incorporates two smaller islands: Carriacou and Petite
Martinique, neither of which has many tourist facilities.

St. George's, the country's capital, is one of the most colorful ports in the
West Indies. Nearly landlocked in the deep crater of a long-dead volcano, and
flanked by old forts, it reminds many visitors of Portofino, Italy. Here you'll see
some of the most charming Georgian colonial buildings in the Caribbean, many
with red tile roofs (the tiles were brought by European trade ships as ballast) and
pastel walls. Churches dot the hillside of the harbor. Frangipani and flamboyant
trees add even more color.

Crisscrossed by nature trails, Grenada's interior is a jungle of palms, oleander,
bougainvillea, purple and red hibiscus, crimson anthurium, bananas, breadfruit,
bird-song, ferns, and palms. The island's lush tropical scenery and natural

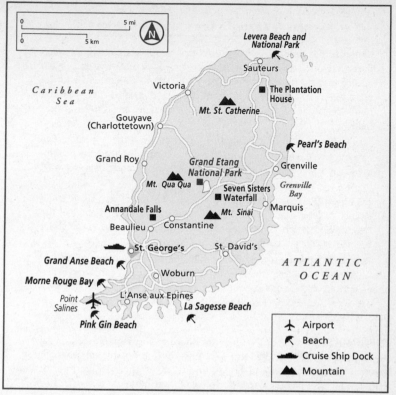

Map of Grenada

Scale	0 — 5 mi / 0 — 5 km

Caribbean Sea

Levera Beach and National Park

Sauteurs

Victoria

The Plantation House

Mt. St. Catherine

Gouyave (Charlottetown)

Pearl's Beach

Grand Roy

Grand Etang National Park

Grenville

Mt. Qua Qua

Grenville Bay

Seven Sisters Waterfall

Annandale Falls

Mt. Sinai

Marquis

Beaulieu

Constantine

St. George's

St. David's

Grand Anse Beach

ATLANTIC OCEAN

Morne Rouge Bay

Woburn

Point Salines

L'Anse aux Epines

La Sagesse Beach

Pink Gin Beach

Legend:
- ✈ Airport
- Beach
- Cruise Ship Dock
- ▲▲ Mountain

bounty attract visitors who want to snorkel, sail, fish, hike on jungle paths, or loll the day away on the 3.2km (2-mile) white-sand **Grand Anse Beach,** one of the best in the Caribbean.

COMING ASHORE Ships either dock at a pier right in St. George's or anchor in the much-photographed harbor and send their passengers to the pier by tender. A **tourist information center** at the pier dispenses island data. The Carenage (St. George's main street) is only a short walk away from the pier; a taxi into the center of town costs about $3. To get to Grand Anse, you can take a regular taxi or a water taxi (see "Getting Around," below).

You'll find a pair of credit-card phones for international calls inside the small cruise terminal and two more just outside of it. There are six more London-style red phone booths midway around the Carenage, less than a half mile from the terminal.

LANGUAGE **English** is commonly spoken on this island. **Creole English,** a mixture of African, English, and French, is spoken informally by the majority.

CURRENCY The official currency is the **Eastern Caribbean dollar** (EC$2.70 = US$1; EC$1 = US73¢). Always determine which dollars—EC or U.S.—you're talking about when discussing a price. Credit cards and traveler's checks are commonly accepted in tourist areas. Unless otherwise specified, all prices in this section are given in U.S. dollars.

ⓒ Frommer's Favorite Grenada Experiences

Hiking to the Seven Sisters Waterfalls: A hearty walk along a muddy path that winds through the thick, pristine jungle. At the end of the approximately 1.6km- (1-mile-) long trail, there's a set of beautiful waterfalls. You can even jump from the tops of two of them into the pools below. (See "Shore Excursions Offered by the Cruise Lines," below.)

Visiting Levera National Park: With beaches, coral reefs, a mangrove swamp, a lake, and a bird sanctuary, this is a paradise for hikers, swimmers, and snorkelers alike. (See "On Your Own: Beyond the Port Area," below.)

Taking the Rainforest and Grand Etang Lake Tour: Take a bus to an extinct volcanic crater some 522m (1,740 ft.) above sea level. On the way, drive through rainforests and stop at a spice estate. (See "Shore Excursions Offered by the Cruise Lines," below.)

Picnicking at Annandale Falls: A 15m (50-ft.) cascade is the perfect backdrop for a picnic among tropical flora—and you can swim in the falls afterward. (See "On Your Own: Beyond the Port Area," below.)

INFORMATION　Go to the **Grenada Board of Tourism,** on the Carenage in St. George's (ⓒ **800/927-9554** or 473/440-2279), for maps and general information. It's open Monday to Friday from 8am to 4pm. To get information before you go, contact the **Grenada Tourism Board** in New York (ⓒ **212/687-9554;** www.grenadagrenadines.com).

CALLING FROM THE U.S.　When calling Grenada from the United States, you need only dial a "1" before the numbers listed here.

GETTING AROUND

St. George's can easily be explored on foot, although parts of the town are steep as the streets rise up from the harbor.

BY TAXI　Taxi fares are set by the government. Most cruisers take a cab from the pier to somewhere near St. George's. You can also tap most taxi drivers as a guide for a day's sightseeing. The charge is about $20 per hour, but be sure to negotiate a price before setting out, and make sure you're both talking about the same currency. From the pier to Grand Anse Beach is about $15 per carload.

BY MINIVAN　Minivans, used mostly by locals, charge EC$1 to EC$6 (US73¢–U.S.$4.40). Most minivans depart from Market Square or from the Esplanade area of St. George's. The most popular run is between St. George's and Grand Anse Beach.

BY WATER TAXI　Water taxis are an ideal way to get around the harbor and to Grand Anse Beach (the round-trip fare is about $4) or from one end of the Carenage to the other (for another $2). Look for them on the Carenage by the cruise ship welcome center.

BY RENTAL CAR　We don't recommend driving here, as the roads are very narrow and winding.

SHORE EXCURSIONS OFFERED BY THE CRUISE LINES

Because of Grenada's lush landscape, we recommend spending at least a few hours touring its interior, one of the most scenic in the West Indies.

Hike to Seven Sisters Waterfalls ($35, 4 hr.): After about a 1.6km (1 mile) walk along a muddy path in the lush Grand Etang rainforest, passengers are free to take a swim in the natural pools or hop off the edge of the cascading waterfalls. It's gorgeous and lots of fun. Don't forget to wear your bathing suit and maybe a pair of Teva-type sandals.

Rainforest/Grand Etang Lake Tour ($33–$37, 3 hr.): This is a great way to experience Grenada's lush, cool, dripping-wet tropical interior. Via bus, you travel past the red-tiled roofs of St. George's en route to the bright blue Grand Etang Lake, within an extinct volcanic crater some 570m (1,900 ft.) above sea level. On the way, you drive through rainforests and stop at a spice estate. Some tours include a visit to the Annandale Falls.

Island Bus Tour ($33, 3 hr.): Typical scenic island tours take you through the highlights of the interior and along the coast, including Grand Anse Beach. Along the way you get to see the most luxuriant part of Grenada's rainforest, a nutmeg-processing station, a sugar factory, and many small hamlets. Many cruise lines also book a tour ($27, 2 hr.) that explores St. George's historical sites and forts before taking you to some of the island's natural highlights, including a private garden where some 500 species of island plants and flowers are cultivated.

Party Cruises ($33, 3 hr.): Party cruises are popular here, with no shortage of rum and reggae music. The cost includes rum punch, sodas, a beach stop, and sometimes snorkeling.

ON YOUR OWN: WITHIN WALKING DISTANCE

In St. George's, you can visit the **Grenada National Museum,** at the corner of Young and Monckton streets (© **473/440-3725**), set in the foundations of an old French army barracks and prison built in 1704. Small but interesting, it houses ancient petroglyphs and other archaeological finds, a rum still, and various Grenada memorabilia, including the island's first telegraph and two notable bathtubs: the wooden barrel used by the fort's prisoners and the carved marble tub used by Joséphine Bonaparte during her adolescence on Martinique. The most comprehensive exhibit illuminates the native culture of Grenada. The museum is open 9am to 4:30pm Monday to Friday, and 10am to 1pm Saturday; admission is $2.50 for adults and 50¢ for children.

If you're up for a good hike, walk around the historical Carenage from the cruise terminal and head up to **Fort George,** built in 1705 by the French and originally called Fort Royal. (You can pick up a rudimentary walking-tour map from the cruise terminal to help you find interesting sites along the way.) While the fort ruins and the 200- to 300-year-old canons are worth taking a peek at, it's the 360-degree panoramic views of the entire harbor area that are most spectacular, taking in your ship, the sea, and many of the red-tile-roofed buildings dotting the island. Don't forget your camera! Before or after a visit to the fort, be sure to walk along **Church Street** (which leads right to the fort) as far as St. Johns or Juille Street. Along the way, you'll see lots of quaint 18th- and 19th-century architecture framed by brilliant flowering plants; examples of Grenada's sedan porches, open-ended porches originally used as porte-cocheres to keep residents dry when going between house and carriage; **St. Andrew's Presbyterian Church,** built in 1831 with the help of the Freemasons; **St. George's Anglican**

Church, built in 1825 by the British; the **Houses of Parliament;** and the **Roman Catholic Cathedral,** rebuilt in 1884 (the tower dates back to 1818).

ON YOUR OWN: BEYOND THE PORT AREA

You can take a taxi up Richmond Hill to **Fort Frederick,** which the French began in 1779. The British retook the island in 1783 and completed the fort in 1791. From its battlements you'll have a panoramic view of the harbor and the yacht marina.

Don't miss the mountains northeast of St. George's. If you don't have much time, **Annandale Falls,** a tropical wonderland where a 15m- (50-ft.-) high cascade drops into a basin, is just a 15-minute drive away, on the outskirts of the **Grand Etang Forest Reserve.** The overall beauty is almost Tahitian. You can have a picnic surrounded by liana vines, elephant ears, and other tropical flora and spices. Annandale Falls Centre offers gift items, handicrafts, and samples of the island's indigenous spices. Nearby, a trail leads to the falls, where you can enjoy a refreshing swim. If you've got more time and want a less crowded spot, the even better **Seven Sisters Waterfalls** are farther into Grand Etang, an approximately 30-minute drive and then a 1.6km or so (1-mile) hike along a muddy trail. It's well worth the trip and you'll really get a feel for the power and beauty of the tropical forest here. The falls themselves are lovely, and you can even climb to the top and jump off into the pool below. Be careful, though: It's awfully slippery on those rocks. If you want to skip the jumping, you can still enjoy a relaxing swim in the cool water after the sweaty hike.

Opened in 1994, 180-hectare (450-acre) **Levera National Park** has several white sandy beaches for swimming and snorkeling, although the surf is rough. Offshore are coral reefs and sea-grass beds. Inland, the park contains a mangrove swamp, a lake, and a bird sanctuary—perhaps you'll see a rare tropical parrot. It's a hiker's paradise. The interpretation center (© **473/442-1018**) is open Monday to Sunday from 8am to 4pm. About 24km (15 miles) from the harbor, the park can be reached by taxi, bus, or water taxi.

SHOPPING

The local stores sell luxury imports, mainly from England, at prices that are not quite down at duty-free level. This is no grand Caribbean merchandise mart, so if you're cruising on to such islands as Aruba, St. Martin, or St. Thomas, you might want to postpone serious purchases. On the other hand, you can find some fine local handicrafts, gifts, and art here.

Spice vendors besiege you wherever you go, including just outside of the cruise terminal. If you're not interested, a polite "I just bought some from another vendor" usually works. But you really should take at least a few samples home with you. The spices here are fresher and better than any you're likely to find in your local supermarket, so nearly everybody comes home with a hand-woven basket full of them. Nutmeg products are especially popular. The Grenadians use every part of the nutmeg: They make the outer fruit into a tasty liqueur and a rich jam, and ground the orange membrane around the nut into a different spice called mace. You'll also see the outer shells used as gravel to cover trails and parking lots. **Arawak Islands,** Upper Belmont Road, has different fragrances distilled from such island plants as frangipani, wild lilies, cinnamon, nutmeg, and cloves. You'll also find body oils, soaps, an all-natural insect repellent that some clients insist is the most effective (and safest) they're ever used, and some mighty fine hot sauce. We regretted not buying more the last time we were there, but then we found their mail-order website (**www.arawak-islands.com**).

Some worthwhile shops include **Art Fabrik,** Young Street (© **473/440-0568**), for batik shirts, shifts, shorts, skirts, T-shirts, and the like; **Sea Change Bookstore** (© **473/440-3402**), the Carenage, for recent British and American newspapers; and **Tikal,** Young Street (© **473/440-2310**), for handicrafts from Grenada and around the world.

BEACHES

Grenada's **Grand Anse Beach,** with its 3.2km (2 miles) of wide sugar-white sands, is one of the best beaches in the Caribbean, with calm waters and a great view of St. George's to make the scene complete. There are several restaurants beachside, and you can also join a banana-boat ride or rent a Sunfish sailboat. From the port, it's about a 10-minute, $10 taxi ride, although you can also take a water taxi from the pier for only $4 round-trip.

SPORTS

SCUBA DIVING & SNORKELING   Grenada offers an underwater world rich in submarine gardens, exotic fish, and coral formations. Visibility is often up to 36m (120 ft.). Off the coast is the wreck of the nearly 180m (600-ft.) ocean liner *Bianca C.* Novice divers should stick to the west coast; the more experienced might search out the sites along the rougher Atlantic side. **Sanvic's Watersports,** directly on the beach in the Grenada Grand Beach Resort, Grand Anse Beach (© **473/444-4371**, ext. 638), is the premier scuba-diving outfit, also offering snorkeling trips. They will pick you up at the pier in a courtesy bus and bring you back to the cruise ship later. American-run **Eco-Dive,** at Coyaba Beach Resort on Grand Anse Beach (© **473/444-4129**), gives Sanvic's serious competition, offering scuba diving and snorkeling jaunts to reefs and shipwrecks teeming with marine life. Diving instruction is available. (*Note:* Grenada doesn't have a decompression chamber. In the event of an emergency, divers must be taken to the facilities on Barbados or Trinidad.)

GREAT LOCAL RESTAURANTS & BARS

A favorite **local beer** is Carib; a favorite **local rum** is Clarkecourt.

Your last chance to enjoy food from old-time island recipes, many now fading from cultural memory, may be at **The Plantation House** (aka **the Betty Mascoll Morne Fendue Plantation House**), at St. Patrick's (© **473/442-9330**), 40km (25 miles) north of St. George's. The house was built in 1912 of chiseled river rocks held together by a mixture of lime and molasses. Betty Mascoll was born that same year and lived here right up until her recent death. You dine as an upper-class family did in the 1920s. Lunch is likely to include a yam-and-sweet-potato casserole or curried chicken with lots of island-grown spices. The most famous dish is the legendary pepper-pot stew, which includes pork and oxtail, tenderized by the juice of grated cassava. The new proprietor, Dr. Jean Thompson, and the veteran staff need time to prepare, so it's imperative to call ahead. They serve a fixed-price ($16) lunch Monday to Saturday from 12:30 to 3pm.

The Nutmeg, the Carenage, located right on the harbor over the Sea Change Shop (© **473/440-2539**), is a casual hangout for the yachting set and a favorite with expatriates and visitors. The menu is extensive. Lunch $10.

Rudolf's, the Carenage (© **473/440-2241**), serves great steak, flying fish, and mahimahi, and prepares conch and shrimp in several different ways. After a fire in July 2002, the restaurant began operating out of the Cinnamon Hill Hotel (© 473/444-4301), but it should be back at the Carenage by the time you read this. Lunch $11.

14 Guadeloupe

Take the things you love about France—sophistication, great food, and an appreciation of the good things in life—add the best of the Caribbean—nice beaches, a relaxed pace, and warm, friendly people—and combine with efficiency and modern convenience. Voilà! Guadeloupe. And once you leave the crowded, narrow streets of Pointe-à-Pitre, the commercial center and main port, you'll see that the island is more developed and modern than many others in the region.

Guadeloupe's **Creole cuisine,** a mélange of French culinary expertise, African cooking, and Caribbean ingredients, is reason enough to get off the ship, regardless of how much you're enjoying the food on board. And if **shopping** is your favorite sport, you'll have ample opportunity to stock up on French perfumes, clothes, and other luxury products. For the more adventurous, there's a volcano, scuba diving, surfing, and hiking to spectacular mountain waterfalls. Of course, you can always work on your tan at one of the island's many beaches. Or maybe you just want to sit at a sidewalk cafe, sip your espresso while glancing through a copy of *Le Monde,* and watch the world go by.

Guadeloupe, the political entity, is an overseas region of France that includes the islands of St. Barthélemy (St. Barts), St. Martin, Les Saintes, La Désirade, Marie-Galante, and Guadeloupe itself. The name Guadeloupe, however, usually refers to two contiguous islands—Basse-Terre and Grande-Terre—separated by a narrow seawater channel, the Rivière Salée. Nestled between Antigua and Dominica, these two islands are shaped like a 1,373-sq.-km (530-sq.-mile) butterfly. The eastern wing, the limestone island of Grande-Terre, is known for its white-sand beaches, rolling hills, sugar cane fields, and resort areas. Pointe-à-Pitre, your port of debarkation, is here. The butterfly's larger, volcanic western wing, Basse-Terre, is dominated by the National Park of Guadeloupe, a mountainous rainforest replete with waterfalls and La Soufrière, a brooding, still occasionally troublesome volcano. The capital of Guadeloupe, also called Basse-Terre, is at the southern tip of this western wing.

Almost half of Guadeloupe's population of 410,000 is under the age of 20. About 80% of Guadeloupeans are descended from African slaves, with people of European and East Indian ancestry making up most of the remaining 20%.

Today, sugar and rum are the island's main exports.

COMING ASHORE   Cruise ships dock at the modern **Centre Saint-John Perse,** adjacent to downtown Pointe-à-Pitre, Grande-Terre's main city. The terminal has shops, restaurants, cafes, a small tourist office, and phones.

LANGUAGE   **French** is the official language, but you'll often hear islanders speaking a local **Creole** among themselves. Don't expect to get too far with only English unless you're at one of the busier tourist areas. Bring a phrase book. Guadeloupeans are nice people; meet them halfway.

CURRENCY   Guadeloupe is an overseas region of France, so the **euro** (€) is now the official currency (exchange rate: €1 = US$1.10; $1 = €.90). There are numerous **ATMs** (*distributeur de billets*) in downtown Pointe-à-Pitre. You'll have no trouble using your credit cards. Unless otherwise specified, prices in this section are given in U.S. dollars.

INFORMATION   The main **tourist office** (Office du Tourisme) in Pointe-à-Pitre is at 5 Square de la Banque, a 5-minute walk from the port (© **590/82-09-30**), and is open Monday to Friday from 8am to 5pm, Saturday 8am to

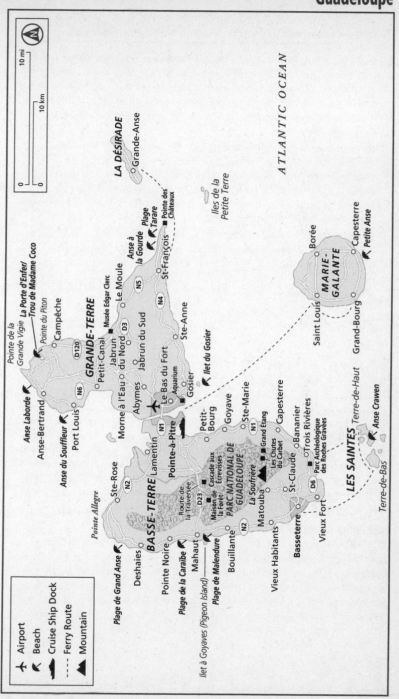

Frommer's Favorite Guadeloupe Experiences

Climbing a Volcano: Draped in thousands of banana trees and other lush foliage, La Soufrière rises 1,440m (4,800 ft.) above the surrounding sea and dominates the island of Basse-Terre. You can drive to a parking area at La Savane à Mulets, then hike the final 450m (1,500 ft; 2 arduous hr.) right to the mouth of the volcano. (See "On Your Own: Beyond the Port Area," below.)

Touring Grande-Terre's Atlantic Coast: Drive out to Grande-Terre's eastern extreme, La Pointe des Châteaux, to watch the Atlantic and Caribbean vent their fury on the rocky shore. Continue up the coast to La Porte d'Enfer and La Pointe de la Grande Vigie for splendid views of limestone cliffs and sparkling aquamarine waters. (See "On Your Own: Beyond the Port Area," below.)

Soaking Up the French-Caribbean Ambience: Walk the streets of Pointe-à-Pitre. Browse through the stores and maybe buy some perfume or "thigh-reducing cream" from one of the upscale pharmacies (look for the neon green cross). Pick up a newspaper; find a shady table at a sidewalk cafe; order a cold, fresh fruit juice; and luxuriate in your blessed life.

noon. If you want information before you leave home, contact the **Guadeloupe Tourist Office** in New Jersey (© 732/302-1223; www.frenchcaribbean.com).

CALLING FROM THE U.S. When calling Guadeloupe from the United States, dial the international access code (011) and 590 before the numbers listed in this section. The numbers listed already have a 590 prefix, but that's not the same 590: You have to dial 590 twice (bureaucracy in France is just as inscrutable as anywhere). **Telecartes** phone cards make local and international calls easier and less expensive. They're sold at post offices and other outlets marked TELECARTE EN VENTE ICI and are used in phone booths (marked TELE-COM) found all over. Many phones accept Visa, MasterCard, and other credit cards for long-distance calls.

GETTING AROUND

BY TAXI Metered taxis await cruise passengers at the Pointe-à-Pitre pier. Rates are regulated, but they can be expensive. Taxis can be hired for private tours, but you'll have a hard time finding a driver who speaks English. Negotiate a price before setting out, and make sure all terms are clear to avoid an unpleasant scene later. One recommended driver is **Alain Narcisse,** an enthusiastic, knowledgeable, English-speaking guide who offers tours of Grande-Terre, northern Basse-Terre, and southern Basse-Terre. He's often booked, so make arrangements in advance by calling © 690/35-27-29 or 590/94-55-95. General **radio cab dispatch numbers** include © 590/20-74-74, 590/82-96-69, and 590/83-09-55.

BY BUS Buses are inexpensive, comfortable, and efficient. Almost all play zouk, an upbeat local music (at reasonable decibel levels), and some have videos. Signs (ARRET-BUS) indicate bus stops, but you can wave down a driver anywhere along the road. Pay the driver or the conductor as you get off. The fare from Pointe-à-Pitre to Gosier is just over $1.

BY RENTAL CAR Guadeloupe's road system is one of the best in the Caribbean, and traffic regulations and road signs are the same as elsewhere in France. Driving is on the right. Reserve a car before leaving home, especially during the high season. **Avis, Budget, Hertz,** and **National** all have offices on the island. Your valid driver's license from home will be honored. Almost all rentals have standard transmissions. Be forewarned that Guadeloupeans are skillful but aggressive drivers; don't tarry in the passing lane.

SHORE EXCURSIONS OFFERED BY THE CRUISE LINES

Carbet Falls ($40, 4 hr.): After driving through the banana plantations and rainforests of Basse-Terre's south side, hike 30 minutes to picturesque Carbet Falls, where you're free to swim in the refreshing water. Wear sturdy walking shoes.

Pigeon Island ($50, 4½ hr.): First pass through Guadeloupe's National Park, a lush and mountainous tropical rainforest, on the Route de la Traversée. At Pigeon Island, board a glass-bottom boat for a 90-minute ride around a beautiful coral reef now designated the Cousteau Underwater Reserve. Marvel at the numerous fish, corals, and other marine life.

EXCURSIONS OFFERED BY LOCAL AGENCIES

Hiking Tours: Basse-Terre's **Parc National** has 322km (200 miles) of well-marked trails. Some meander through tropical rainforests to waterfalls and mountain pools; others focus on the La Soufrière volcano, geology, animals, and vegetation. Free maps and brochures in English can be obtained from the **National Park Office,** Habitation Beausoleil, Montéran, Boite Postal 13, St-Claude 97120 (© **590/80-24-25**). The park office will also provide visitors with a list of local agencies offering excursions.

Snorkeling Tours: To snorkel in the Cousteau Underwater Reserve, contact **Nautilus** (© **590/98-89-08**) or **Aquarus** (© **590/98-87-30**), both located at the Bouillante town dock, south of Malendure. They make guided tours in glass-bottom boats several times daily; at least 15 minutes is reserved for snorkeling and refreshments (about 90 min., $25–$30).

ON YOUR OWN: WITHIN WALKING DISTANCE

The little trolley that meets cruise ship passengers at the port is supposed to provide hassle-free transportation around Pointe-à-Pitre. Unfortunately, it's no match for the city's traffic and narrow roads. Unless you enjoy traffic jams, walk. It's a better way to browse, shop, and visit the museums.

Pointe-à-Pitre's narrow streets and congested sidewalks are bustling with activity, and its markets are among the Caribbean's most colorful. The largest, **Marché St. Antoine,** at the corner of rues Frébault and Peynier, is well known for its playful, sassy vendors, who sell tropical produce and spices in madras bags. **Marché de la Darse,** on the waterfront at the foot of place de la Banque, offers exotic fruits, vegetables, and souvenirs. The **place Gourbeyre Flower Market,** next to the cathedral, is ablaze with tropical blooms, including roses de porcelaine and alpinias. Lined with royal palms, scarlet flamboyants, and travelers palms, the renovated **place de la Victoire** commemorates Victor Hugues' defeat of the English in 1794. It's the largest public space in town and is bordered with restaurants and cafes. The nearby **Cathedral of St-Pierre and St-Paul,** built in 1871, has an iron framework designed to withstand earthquakes and hurricanes. Three churches destroyed by successive earthquakes form its foundation. The **Musée Municipal Saint-John Perse,** 9 rue de Nozières, near the corner of rue Achille-René Boisneuf (℃ **590/90-01-92**), chronicles the life of native son Alexis Léger, who won the Nobel Prize for literature under the nom de plume "Saint-John Perse" in 1960. The museum is housed in one of the city's most beautifully restored colonial mansions, an urban chalet that features ornate friezes, voluted consoles, and wrought-iron galleries. Open windows allow breezes into the main parlor, which is furnished with bourgeois furniture. In addition to many of the poet's personal effects, the museum boasts photographs documenting Guadeloupean life from the turn of the 20th century through the 1930s; you can buy postcards of some of them in the museum gift shop. The museum is open Monday to Friday from 9am to 5pm, Saturday 8:30am to 12:30pm. Admission is about $2 for adults, half price for students.

The **Musée Schoelcher,** 24 rue Peynier (℃ **590/82-08-04**), tells the story of Victor Schoelcher, the key figure in the move to abolish slavery in Guadeloupe. The powerful exhibit, housed in a renovated mansion, includes a slave-ship model, a miniature guillotine, china from Bordeaux with scenes from *Uncle Tom's Cabin,* and racist caricatures published in Parisian journals. Particularly moving is an 1845 census document that lists slaves as nothing more than plantation animals. It's open Monday to Friday from 9am to 5pm; admission is $1.50, half that for students and children.

ON YOUR OWN: BEYOND THE PORT AREA

Guadeloupe is too large to tour in 1 day. You'll have to choose among Grande-Terre, northern Basse-Terre, and southern Basse-Terre.

GRANDE-TERRE

The **Aquarium de la Guadeloupe,** near the Bas du Fort Marina just east of Pointe-à-Pitre (℃ **590/90-92-38**), is compact but has an impressive collection of exotic fish, corals, and sponges from the Caribbean and the Pacific. Come face-to-face with hugging sea horses, sleeping nurse sharks, and graceful sea turtles. Don't miss the polka-dot grouper known as *mérou de Grace Kelly.* Explanatory markers are in both French and English. The souvenir shop sells hand-painted folk art, jewelry, and fish- and sea-themed trinkets and T-shirts. It's open daily from 9am to 7pm; admission is about $5.50 for adults, $2.75 for children under 12.

La Pointe des Châteaux (Castle Point), at Grande-Terre's easternmost point, is an impressive seascape spectacle. Angry Atlantic waves bash black limestone rocks and jagged cliffs with a roughness reminiscent of Brittany's Finistère coast or England's Land's End. Follow the path leading to the point where the land falls off abruptly to the ocean for the best views of the island of La Désirade.

Farther north, **La Porte d'Enfer** is a quaint little cove and beach protected from the furious Atlantic by an outcrop of limestone cliffs. The name means "Hell's Gate," but swimming close to shore in the turquoise water is usually safe. Don't venture out too far, though; the next cove, **Le Trou de Madame Coco** (Madame Coco's hole), is where (according to legend) the sea stole Madame Coco and her parasol as she promenaded along the edge. **La Pointe de la Grande Vigie,** at the northernmost tip of the island, has paths that lead to the edge of spectacular cliffs with dramatic views of Porte de l'Enfer and, on a clear day, the island of Antigua. Cacti and other succulents grow everywhere.

Along the northern coasts of Grande-Terre and Basse-Terre, **La Réserve Naturelle du Grand Cul-de-Sac Marin** is one of the Caribbean's largest marine reserves.

BASSE-TERRE

Basse-Terre's greatest attraction is the **Parc National de la Guadeloupe,** 29,600 hectares (74,000 acres) of tropical rainforests, mountains, waterfalls, and ponds. UNESCO designated the park a World Biosphere Reserve in 1992. Its 322km (200 miles) of well-marked trails make it one of the best places for hiking in the entire Caribbean. Pick up information and maps at park entrances. Thirty minutes from Pointe-à-Pitre, **La Maison de la Forêt (Forest House;** closed Mon) lies on the Route de la Traversée, which bisects the park, and is the starting point for easy walking tours of the surrounding mountainous rainforest. English-language trail guides describe the plant and animal life. Nearby, the **Cascade aux Ecrevisses (Crayfish Falls),** a slippery 10-minute walk from the roadside, is nice for a cooling dip. To the south, the steep hike to the three falls of **Les Chutes du Carbet (Carbet Falls)** is among Guadeloupe's most beautiful excursions (one of the falls drops 20m/65 ft., the second 108m/360 ft., the third 123m/410 ft.). The middle fall, the most dramatic, is the easiest to reach. On the way up, you'll pass **Le Grand Etang (the Great Pond),** a volcanic lake surrounded by tree-size ferns, giant vining philodendrons, wild bananas, orchids, anthuriums, and pineapples.

The park's single greatest feature is the still-simmering volcano **La Soufrière,** rising to 1.440m (4,800 ft.) and flanked by banana plantations and lush vegetation. In 1975, ashes, mud, billowing smoke, and tremors proved that the volcano is still active, and today you can smell sulfurous fumes and feel the heat through the soil as steam spews from the fumaroles. The summit is like another planet: Steam rises from two active craters, large rocks form improbable shapes, and roars from the earth make it difficult to hear your companions. Go with an experienced guide (see "Hiking Tours" under "Excursions Offered by Local Agencies," above). On your way down, don't miss **La Maison du Volcan,** the volcanology museum in St-Claude.

Gardeners should save a couple of hours to visit the **Domaine de Valombreuse** (© **590/95-50-50**), a 2.4-hectare (6-acre) floral park with exotic birds, spice gardens, and 300 species of tropical flowers. Created in 1990, and close to the town of Petit Bourg, the park has a riverside restaurant and a superior gift shop. It's open daily from 9am to 6pm; admission is about $6 for adults, $3.50 for children under 12.

Parc Archéologique des Roches Gravées, on Basse-Terre's southern coast in the town of Trois-Rivières (© **590/92-91-88**), has the West Indies' largest collection of Arawak Indian petroglyphs. The animal and human images etched on boulders date from between A.D. 300 and 400. Paths and stone stairways meander through the tranquil grounds, which include avocado, banana, cocoa, coffee, guava, and papaya trees. Explanatory brochures are in French and English. It's open daily from 8:30am to 4:30pm; admission is about $1.50.

SHOPPING

Parlez-vous Chanel? Hermès? Saint Laurent? Baccarat? If you do, you'll find that Guadeloupe has good buys on almost anything French—scarves, perfumes, cosmetics, crystal, and other luxury goods—and many stores offer 20% discounts on items purchased with foreign currency, traveler's checks, or credit cards. You can also find local **handcrafted items,** madras cloth, spices, and rum at any of the local markets.

Right at Pointe-à-Pitre's port, the **Centre Saint-John Perse** has about 20 shops that frequently offer lower prices than can be found elsewhere in town.

L'Artisan Parfumeur sells French and American perfumes, as well as tropical scents. **Suzanne Moulin** features original African-inspired jewelry and crafts. **Jean-Louis Padel** specializes in gold jewelry. If you're looking for beach and resort wear, stop by **Vanilla Boutique** and **Brasil Tropique.** For something a little more provocative, look through the delicate lingerie at **Soph't.**

Rue Frébault, directly in front of the port, is one of the best shopping streets for duty-free items. **Roséblu,** 5 rue Frébault, offers china, crystal, and silver from Christoffle, Kosta Boda, and other high-end manufacturers. **Phoenicia,** 8 rue Frébault and 121 bis rue Frébault, has large selections of French perfumes and cosmetics. For men's and women's fashions, as well as for cosmetics and perfumes, browse through **Vendôme,** 8–10 rue Frébault. Across the street at the intersection of rues Frébault and Delgrès, **Geneviève Lethu** is a French version of Williams-Sonoma, with everything for preparing and serving food. If you find yourself overdosing on froufrou, duck into **Tati,** France's answer to Kmart. It's at the intersection of rues Frébault and Abbé Grégoire. This venerable old department-store chain, famous for its anti-fashion pink-plaid shopping bags, is great for inexpensive basics.

The French Antilles are where the beguine began, so if you're in the market for French Antillean music or French-language books, there are a couple of large book and music stores across from each other on rue Schoelcher: **Librairie Antillaise** at no. 41 and **Librairie Général** at no. 46. Each has a small selection of English-language books as well.

BEACHES

Beaches on Grande-Terre's southern coast have soft white sand. Those on the Atlantic coast have wilder water and are less crowded. The convenient **Bas du Fort/Gosier** hotel area has mostly man-made strips of sand with rows of beach chairs, watersports shops, and beach bars. Changing facilities and chairs are available for a nominal fee. The tiny, uninhabited **Ilet Gosier,** across Gosier Bay, is a quieter option popular with those who want to bare it all. You can take a fishing boat to the island from Gosier's waterfront. The wide strip of white sand at **Ste-Anne,** about 30 minutes from Pointe-à-Pitre, is lined with shops and food stands. **Plage Tarare,** just before the tip of Pointe des Châteaux, is the most popular nude beach.

On Basse-Terre, the **Plage de Grande Anse** is a long expanse of ochre sand. A pleasant walk north from Deshaies, it offers changing facilities, watersports, boutiques, and outdoor snack bars. Farther south, the gray expanse of **Plage de Malendure** is alive with restaurants, bars, and open-air boutiques. It's the departure point for snorkeling and scuba trips to the Cousteau Reserve off Pigeon Island.

SPORTS

SNORKELING   Beachside stands at virtually all the resorts on Grande-Terre's southern coast rent snorkeling equipment for about $8 a day. The St-François reef and the Ilet de Gosier are especially recommended.

GREAT LOCAL RESTAURANTS & BARS

Many restaurants change their hours from time to time and from season to season, so call in advance for reservations and exact hours. Most, but not all, restaurants accept major credit cards.

The **local beer** is Corsaire, while Bonka is the **local coffee. Local rums** come in a variety of flavors—bois bandé, shrubb (orange and vanilla), lemon—and are painstakingly nurtured at small rum estates such as Séverin, Longueteau, Damoiseau, Bologne, and Montebello. Local producers compare their slow, time-honored process to that used to make cognac.

ON GRANDE-TERRE

Chez Violetta-La Créole, Perinette, in Gosier (© **590/84-36-80**), was established by the late Violetta Chaville, the island's legendary high priestess of Creole cookery. Her brother continues the family tradition, serving stuffed crabs, cod fritters, and conch fricasée. It's open daily from noon to 3:30pm.

   Chez Monia at 4 rue Victor Hugues, off of rue Nozières in Pointe-à-Pitre, serves ice cream that is pure heaven in the midday heat. Flavors (*aromes*) include pear, lemon, kiwi, guava, and champagne. Three scoops in a homemade waffle cone costs about $2. Street vendors also offer superior ice cream, usually flavored with fresh vanilla and coconut, straight from their hand-cranked machines.

ON BASSE-TERRE

In Deshaies, Lucienne Salcède's family has run **Le Karacoli** (© **590/28-41-17**), one of Guadeloupe's best seaside restaurants, for almost 30 years. Sit on the beachfront terrace in the shadow of almond and palm trees and let the waves hypnotize you. In the distance, the island of Montserrat is visible. Try a rum aperitif or two, then bliss out on cod fritters, stuffed christophine, and avocado féroce before moving on to Creole lobster or conch. It's open daily from noon to 2pm; closed the entire month of September. Reservations are imperative on weekends. Lunch $30.

15 Jamaica

A favorite of North American honeymooners, Jamaica is a mountainous island 145km (90 miles) south of Cuba and about 161km (100 miles) west of Haiti. It's the third largest of the Caribbean islands, with some 11,396 sq. km (4,400 sq. miles) of predominantly green terrain, a mountain ridge peaking at 2,220m (7,400 ft.) above sea level, and, on the north coast, many beautiful white-sand beaches rimming the clear blue sea.

   One of the most densely populated nations in the Caribbean, with a vivid sense of its own identity, Jamaica has a history rooted in the plantation economy and some of the most impassioned politics in the Western Hemisphere, all of which leads to a sometimes turbulent day-to-day reality. You've probably heard, for instance, that the island's vendors and hawkers can be pushy and the locals not always the most welcoming to tourists, and while there's some truth to this, we've had nothing but positive experiences on many visits to Jamaica. So, keep an open mind.

   Most cruise ships dock at **Ocho Rios** on the lush northern coast, although more and more are opting to call at the city of **Montego Bay** ("Mo Bay"), 108km (67 miles) to the west. These ports offer comparable attractions and some of the same shopping possibilities. Don't try to do both ports in one day, however, since the 4-hour round-trip ride leaves time for only superficial visits to each.

LANGUAGE   The official language is **English,** but most Jamaicans speak a richly nuanced patois that's primarily derived from English but includes elements of African, Spanish, Arawak, French, Chinese, Portuguese, and East Indian languages.

CURRENCY   The unit of currency is the **Jamaican dollar,** designated by the same symbol as the U.S. dollar ($). For clarity, we use the symbol J$ to denote

> ### ⓒ Frommer's Favorite Ocho Rios Experiences
>
> **Tubing on the White River:** Offered by most cruise lines, this trip is just a downright fantastic experience. (See "Shore Excursions Offered by the Cruise Lines," below.)
>
> **Riding Horseback Through the Surf:** An excursion by horseback includes a ride along the beach and through the surf. (See "Shore Excursions Offered by the Cruise Lines," below.)
>
> **Riding a Mountain Bike to Dunn's River Falls:** This excursion takes you to the top of a mountain, where you hop on your mountain bike and soar downhill to the falls. (See "Shore Excursions Offered by the Cruise Lines," below.)

prices in Jamaican dollars. The exchange rate is usually US$1 = J$42; J$1 = US2¢. Visitors can pay in U.S. dollars, but always find out if a price is being quoted in Jamaican or U.S. dollars—there's a big difference! Unless otherwise specified, prices in this section are given in U.S. dollars.

INFORMATION   To get info before you go, call the **Jamaica Tourist Office** in New York (ⓒ **800/233-4582** or 212/856-9727; www.jamaica-travel.com). Information booths in the ports are discussed below.

CALLING FROM THE U.S.   When calling Jamaica from the United States, you need only dial a "1" before the numbers listed here.

OCHO RIOS

Once a small banana and fishing port, Ocho Rios is now Jamaica's cruise ship capital, welcoming a couple of ships every day during high season. Though the area has some of the Caribbean's most fabled resorts, and Dunn's River is just a 5-minute taxi ride away, the town itself is not much to see, despite there being a few outdoor local markets within walking distance. Don't expect to shop in the markets without a lot of hassle and a lot of very pushy hawking of merchandise—some of which is likely to be ganja, the locally grown marijuana. (Remember, it may be readily available, but it's still illegal.) In recent years the government has been making an effort to keep things saner around the markets, employing a veritable army of blue-uniformed "resort patrol" officers on bikes to help keep order.

COMING ASHORE   Most cruise ships dock at the port of Ocho Rios, near Dunn's River Falls. Only 1.6km (1 mile) away are important shopping areas, the Ocean Village Shopping Centre and the new Island Village and Taj Majal Shopping Centre. The route to these shopping centers from the cruise ship pier is called the "turtle walk" and is marked. There are bathrooms and a telephone center at the terminal.

INFORMATION   You'll find **tourist board offices** at the Ocean Village Shopping Centre in Ocho Rios (ⓒ **876/974-2582**), open Monday to Friday from 9am to 5pm. There's also a small information stand right at the dock.

GETTING AROUND

BY TAXI   Taxis are your best means of transport, but always agree on a fare before you get in. Your best and safest bet is to get a taxi from the pier; there will be lots of them waiting. Taxis licensed by the government display **JTB** decals,

Jamaica

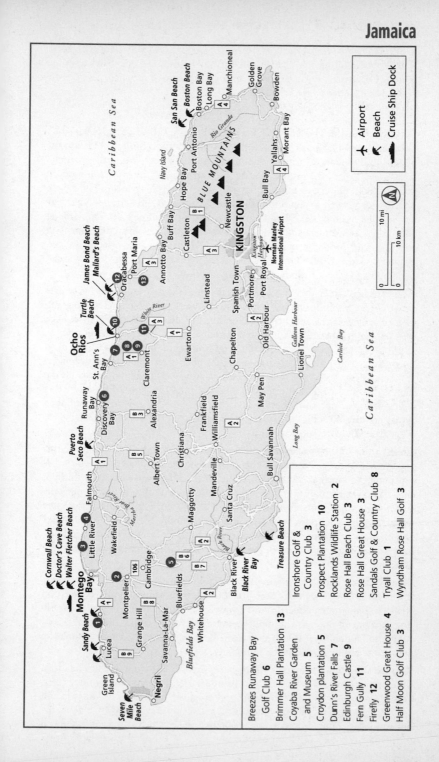

Legend:
- Airport
- Beach
- Cruise Ship Dock

Caribbean Sea

Blue Mountains

San San Beach
Boston Beach
Long Bay
Manchioneal
Golden Grove
Bowden
Port Antonio
Hope Bay
Buff Bay
Morant Bay
Yallahs
Bull Bay
Castleton
Newcastle
KINGSTON
Kingston Harbour
Norman Manley International Airport
Port Royal
Portmore
Spanish Town
Annotto Bay
Port Maria
Oracabessa
Linstead
Chapelton
Old Harbour
Galleon Harbour
Lionel Town
Carlisle Bay
Ewarton
May Pen
Spanish Town

Navy Island
Rio Grande
White River
James Bond Beach
Mallard's Beach
Turtle Beach
Ocho Rios
St. Ann's Bay
Claremont
Runaway Bay
Puerto Seco Beach
Discovery Bay
Alexandria
Albert Town
Christiana
Frankfield
Williamsfield
Bull Savannah
Long Bay

Cornwall Beach
Doctor's Cave Beach
Walter Fletcher Beach
Sandy Beach
Montego Bay
Falmouth
Little River
Wakefield
Cambridge
Montpelier
106
Grange Hill
Savanna-La-Mar
Whitehouse
Bluefields
Bluefields Bay
Green Island
Lucea
Negril
Seven Mile Beach

Martha Brae River
Maggotty
Mandeville
Santa Cruz
Black River
Black River Bay
Treasure Beach
Great River
Black River

Caribbean Sea

10 mi
10 km

Breezes Runaway Bay Golf Club **6**
Brimmer Hall Plantation **13**
Coyaba River Garden and Museum **5**
Croydon plantation **5**
Dunn's River Falls **7**
Edinburgh Castle **9**
Fern Gully **11**
Firefly **12**
Greenwood Great House **4**
Half Moon Golf Club **3**

Ironshore Golf & Country Club **3**
Prospect Plantation **10**
Rocklands Wildlife Station **2**
Rose Hall Beach Club **3**
Rose Hall Great House **3**
Sandals Golf & Country Club **8**
Tryall Club **1**
Wyndham Rose Hall Golf **3**

indicating they're official Jamaican Tourist Board taxis. All others are gypsy cabs, which you should avoid. Taxi dispatchers are at the pier and fixed rates are posted. Otherwise, if you're getting into a taxi from somewhere else on the island, always agree to the price first.

BY RENTAL CAR   We don't recommend renting a car here.

SHORE EXCURSIONS OFFERED BY THE CRUISE LINES

Dunn's River Falls Tour ($44, 4 hr.): These falls cascade 180m (600 ft.) to the beach and are the most visited attraction in Jamaica, which means they're hopelessly overcrowded when a lot of cruise ships are in port (the hordes thin out in the afternoon, though, so consider hopping a taxi there yourself later in the day). Tourists are allowed to climb the falls, and it's a ball to slip and slide your way up with the hundreds of others, forming a human chain of sorts. Don't forget your waterproof camera and your aqua-socks. (If you do, most cruise lines will rent you aqua-socks for an extra $5.) This tour usually also visits Shaw Park Botanical Gardens, Fern Gully, and other local attractions, with time allocated for shopping. Wear a bathing suit under your clothes.

River Tubing Safari ($55, 3½ hr.): This is one of the best excursions we've ever taken. After a scenic 30-minute van ride deep into the pristine jungles, the group of 20 or so passengers and a couple of guides get into the White River, sit back into big black inner tubes (they have wooden boards covering the bottom so your butt doesn't get scraped on the rocks), and begin the 4.8km (3-mile) glide downriver, passing by gorgeous, towering bamboo trees and other lush foliage. It's sometimes peaceful and sometimes exhilarating—especially when you hit the rapids! (If your ship doesn't offer this tour—at press time, only a few did—you can contact the operator directly, and they'll try to get you on a trip: **Safari Tours Jamaica,** P.O. Box 142, Ocho Rios, Jamaica; © **876/795-0482;** fax 876/974-3382; safari@cwjamaica.com.)

Chukka Cove Horseback-Riding Excursion ($86, 4 hr.): Riders will love this trip, on which after a 45-minute ride from the stables through fields, you'll gallop along the beach and take your horse bareback into the surf for a thrilling ride. *Tip:* Take the morning ride and your horse is bound to be more energetic. (Also, if you book directly with Chukka Cove [© **876/972-2506**], the same tour, including transportation there and back, is only $55. The Chukka folks also offer a 3-hr. mountain-biking tour; after being driven up picturesque Lillyfield Mountain, you glide down the 11km/7-mile route, drinking in the scenery along the way.)

Dunn's River Falls Mountain-Biking Trek ($61–$69, 4 hr.): After you're driven up to the summit of 450m- (1,500-ft.-) high Murphy Hill, above Ocho Rios, strap on your helmet, hop on your mountain bike, and enjoy a mostly downhill ride through the natural limestone and ferns, passing the eight springs that form Dunn's River Falls. Once at the bottom, you'll have time to climb the falls before heading back to the ship.

Countryside/Plantation Bus Tour ($59, 5 hr.): This tour includes a drive through the Jamaican countryside to Brimmer Hall Plantation, a working plantation property with a Great House and tropical crops, such as bananas and pimiento. On the way back, you pass the estates once occupied by Noël Coward and Ian Fleming. Often a stop at Dunn's River Falls is tacked onto the end of the tour. Another variation on this tour ($40, 4–5 hr.) stops at the Prospect Plantation instead of Brimmer Hall.

Cruise Booze

If you step inside the small cruise "terminal" in Ocho Rios, you'll find a shop called Cruise Booze, which sets up a tasting station where you can sample a ton of different rums, including a 150-proof white rum.

Snorkeling Excursion ($31, 2 hr.): A coral reef near the cruise pier is one of the best places in the area for snorkeling, with panoramic underwater visibility. You can also take a 1-hour cruise on a glass-bottom boat for a look at underwater Jamaica ($39).

Martha Brae River Rafting ($53, 5 hr.): This tour, in 9m (30-ft.), two-seat bamboo rafts, is traditionally one of the most heavily booked excursions from both Ocho Rios and Montego Bay. However, most people find it disappointing. We'd recommend the tubing and bicycling excursions instead.

ON YOUR OWN: WITHIN WALKING DISTANCE

Aside from some markets (see "Shopping," below), there's little to do close to the docks.

ON YOUR OWN: BEYOND THE PORT AREA

South of Ocho Rios, **Fern Gully** was originally a riverbed. Today, the main A3 road winds some 210m (700 ft.) through a rainforest filled with wild ferns, hardwood trees, and lianas. For the botanist, there are hundreds of varieties of ferns; for the less plant-minded, roadside stands sell fruits and vegetables, carved-wood souvenirs, and basketwork. The road runs for about 6.4km (4 miles).

Near Lydford, southwest of Ocho Rios, are the remains of **Edinburgh Castle.** This was the lair of one of Jamaica's most infamous murderers, a Scot named Lewis Hutchinson, who used to shoot passersby and toss their bodies into a deep pit. The authorities got wind of his activities, and although he tried to escape by canoe, he was captured by the navy and hanged. Rather proud of his achievements (evidence of at least 43 murders was found), he left £100 and instructions for a memorial to be built. It never was, but the 1763 castle ruins remain. To get to Lydford, take the A3 south until you reach a small intersection directly north of Walkers Wood, and then follow the signposts west.

The 1817 **Brimmer Hall Estate,** Port Maria, St. Mary's (✆ **876/994-2309**), 34km (21 miles) east of Ocho Rios, is a working plantation where you're driven around in a tractor-drawn jitney to see the tropical fruit trees and coffee plants. Knowledgeable guides tell you about the processes necessary to produce the fine fruits of the island. Afterward, you can relax beside the pool and sample a wide variety of drinks, including an interesting one called "Wow!" The **Plantation Tour Eating House** offers typical Jamaican dishes for lunch. There's also a souvenir shop with a good selection of ceramics, art, straw goods, woodcarvings, rums, liqueurs, and cigars. Tours run daily if there are enough people. Hours are 7am to 5pm daily. Admission is $15 for adults, $7.50 for children, free for kids under 5.

About 1.6km (1 mile) from the center of Ocho Rios, at an elevation of 126m (420 ft.), **Coyaba River Garden and Museum,** Shaw Park Road (✆ **876/974-6235;** www.coyabagardens.com), was built on the grounds of the former Shaw Park plantation. The Spanish-style museum displays artifacts from the Arawak, Spanish, and English settlements in the area. The gardens are filled with native flora, a cut-stone courtyard, and fountains. It's open daily from 8am to 6pm. Admission is $4 for adults, $2.25 for children.

At the 180m (600-ft.) **Dunn's River Falls,** on the A3 (© **876/974-2857**), you can relax on the beach, splash in the waters at the bottom of the falls, or climb with a guide to the top and drop into the cool pools higher up between the cascades of water. The beach restaurant provides snacks and drinks, and dressing rooms are available. If you're planning to climb the falls, wear aquasocks or sneakers to protect your feet from the sharp rocks and to prevent slipping. At the prettiest part of Dunn's River Falls, known as the Laughing Waters, scenes were shot for the James Bond classics *Dr. No* and *Live and Let Die.*

About 4.8km (3 miles) east of Ocho Rios along the A3, adjoining the 18-hole Prospect Mini Golf Course, the working **Prospect Plantation** (© **876/974-2373**) is often a shore-excursion stop. On your leisurely ride by covered jitney, you'll readily see why this section of Jamaica is called "the garden parish of the island." You'll see pimiento (allspice), banana, cassava, sugar cane, coffee, cocoa, coconut, pineapple, and the famous leucaena "Tree of Life"—plus, for what it's worth, Jamaica's first hydroelectric plant. Horseback riding is available on three scenic trails. The rides vary from 1 to 2¼ hours; you'll need to book a horse at least an hour in advance. Rates are $20 per person per hour.

Firefly, Grants Pen, 32km (20 miles) east of Ocho Rios above Oracabessa (© **876/725-0920**), was the home of Sir Noël Coward and his longtime companion, Graham Payn, who, as executor of Coward's estate, donated it to the Jamaica National Heritage Trust. The recently restored house is as it was on the day Sir Noël died in 1973.

SHOPPING

Shopping in Ocho Rios is not as good as in Montego Bay and other ports, but if your money's burning a hole in your pocket, you can wander around the **Ocho Rios Craft Park,** opposite the Ocean Village Shopping Centre off Main Street. Some 150 stalls stock hats, handbags, place mats, woodcarvings, and paintings, plus the usual T-shirts and jewelry. More luxurious items can be found at **Soni's Plaza,** on Main Street, and the **Taj Mahal** (© **876/974-6455**), located opposite the pier and looking like the Mini-Me of the original. **Coconut Grove Shopping Plaza** is a collection of low-slung shops linked by walkways and shrubs. The merchandise consists mainly of local craft items. **Island Plaza shopping complex,** right in the heart of Ocho Rios, has paintings by local artists, local handmade crafts (be prepared to do some haggling), carvings, ceramics, and even kitchenware, plus T-shirts, of course. At all of these places, prepare yourself for aggressive selling and fierce haggling. Every vendor asks too much for an item at first, which gives them the leeway to negotiate the price.

To find local handicrafts or art without the hassle of the markets, head for **Beautiful Memories,** 9 Island Plaza (© **876/974-2374**), which has a limited but representative sampling of Jamaican art, as well as local crafts, pottery, woodwork, and hand-embroidered items.

If you'd like to flee the hustle and bustle of the Ocho Rios bazaars completely, take a taxi to **Harmony Hall** (© **876/975-4222**), Tower Isle, on the A3, 6.4km (4 miles) east of Ocho Rios. One of Jamaica's Great Houses, the restored house

---

Deal or No Deal?

Some so-called duty-free prices are indeed lower than stateside prices, but then the Jamaican government hits you with a 15% "General Consumption Tax." Buyers beware.

is now a gallery selling paintings and other works by Jamaican artists. The arts and crafts here are of high quality—not the usual junky assortment you might find at the beach.

Island Village (www.islandjamaica.com), a new entertainment and shopping complex developed by Island Records' Chris Blackwell, sits on 1.6 hectares (4 acres) at the western end of Ocho Rios, between Reynolds Pier and Turtle Beach. Attractions include the ReggaeXplosion museum, a casino, an outdoor concert venue and indoor theater, shopping, and a branch of Jimmy Buffett's Margaritaville.

BEACHES

Mallards Beach, at the Renaissance Jamaica Grand Resort (© 876/974-2201) on Main Street, is shared by hotel guests and cruise ship passengers and tends to be overcrowded. Locals may steer you to the good and less-crowded **Turtle Beach,** southwest of Mallards. You might also want to check out the big **James Bond Beach** in Oracabessa, at the east end of Ocho Rios.

SPORTS

GOLF SuperClubs' 18-hole, par-72 **Breezes Runaway Bay,** at Runaway Beach near Ocho Rios on the north coast (© 876/973-2436), is one of the better courses in the area, although it's nowhere near the courses at Montego Bay. Call ahead to book tee times. Greens fees are $80 for 18 holes. Players can rent carts and clubs. The 18-hole, par-71 **Sandals Golf & Country Club** at Ocho Rios (© 876/975-0119) is also open to the public, charging $70 for 9 holes and $100 for 18. The course lies about 210m (700 ft.) above sea level. To get there from the center of Ocho Rios, travel along the main bypass for 3.2km (2 miles) until Mile End Road; turn right at the Texaco station there, and drive for 8km (5 miles).

GREAT LOCAL RESTAURANTS & BARS

The favorite **local beer** is Red Stripe; a favorite **local rum** is Appleton.

Ocho Rios Jerk Centre, on DaCosta Drive (© 876/974-2549), serves up lip-smacking jerk pork and chicken. Don't expect anything fancy; just come for platters of meat. Lunch $14. For a special lunch out, **Almond Tree Restaurant,** 83 Main St., in the Hibiscus Lodge Hotel, 3 blocks from the Ocho Rios Mall (© 876/974-2813), is a two-tiered patio restaurant overlooking the Caribbean, with a tree growing through its roof. Lobster thermidor is the most delectable item on the menu. Lunch $18.50. **Evita's Italian Restaurant,** Eden Bower Road, 5 minutes south of Ocho Rios (© 876/974-2333), is run by a flamboyant Italian and is the premier Italian restaurant in Ocho Rios. It serves pastas and excellent fish dishes, as well as unique choices such as jerk spaghetti and pasta Viagra (don't ask). Lunch $20. **Parkway Restaurant,** 60 DaCosta Dr. (© 876/974-2667), couldn't be plainer or less pretentious, but it's always packed with hungry diners chowing down on Jamaican-style chicken, curried goat, sirloin steak, lobster, filet of red snapper and other seafood, and, to top it off, banana cream pie. Lunch $10.

There are probably more great rum bars on Jamaica than churches. Among the best is **Bibi Bips,** 93 Main St. (© 876/974-8759).

MONTEGO BAY

Montego Bay is sometimes less of a hassle than the port at Ocho Rios, and has better beaches, shopping, and restaurants, as well as some of the best golf courses

> ### ⓒ Frommer's Favorite Montego Bay Experiences
>
> In addition to these, our favorite shore excursions from Ocho Rios are also offered from Montego Bay.
>
> **Visiting Rocklands Wildlife Station:** This is the place to go if you want to have a Jamaican doctor bird perch on your finger or feed small doves and finches from your hand. (See "On Your Own: Beyond the Port Area," below.)
>
> **Spend a Day at the Rose Hall Beach Club:** With a secluded beach, crystal-clear water, a full restaurant, two beach bars, live entertainment, and more, it's well worth the $8 admission. (See "Beaches," below.)

in the Caribbean, superior even to those on Puerto Rico and the Bahamas. Like Ocho Rios, Montego Bay has its crime, traffic, and annoyance, but there's much more to see and do here.

There's little of interest in the town itself except shopping, although the good stuff in the environs is easily reached by taxi or shore excursion. Getting around from place to place is one of the major difficulties here. Whatever you want to visit seems to be in yet another direction.

COMING ASHORE   Montego Bay has a modern cruise dock with lots of conveniences, including duty-free stores, telephones, tourist information, and plenty of taxis to meet all ships.

INFORMATION   You'll find the **tourist board offices** at Cornwall Beach, St. James (ⓒ 876/952-4425), open Monday to Friday from 9am to 5pm.

GETTING AROUND
BY TAXI   If you don't book a shore excursion, a taxi is the way to get around. See "Getting Around" under "Ocho Rios," above, for taxi information, as the same conditions apply to Mo Bay.

SHORE EXCURSIONS OFFERED BY THE CRUISE LINES
In addition to the tour listed below, most of those listed under Ocho Rios are also offered from Montego Bay.

Croydon Plantation Tour ($55, 4–5 hr.): Forty kilometers (25 miles) from Montego Bay, the plantation can be visited on a half-day tour on Tuesday, Wednesday, and Friday. Included in the price are round-trip transportation from the dock, a tour of the plantation, a fruit tasting in season (featuring pineapple and a variety of other tropical fruits), and a barbecued chicken lunch.

ON YOUR OWN: WITHIN WALKING DISTANCE
There's nothing really. You'll have to take a taxi to the town for shopping or sign up for an excursion.

ON YOUR OWN: BEYOND THE PORT AREA
These attractions can be reached by taxi from the cruise dock.

The most famous Great House in Jamaica is the legendary **Rose Hall Great House,** Rose Hall Highway (ⓒ 876/953-2323), located 14km (9 miles) east of Montego Bay along the coast road. The house was built about 2 centuries ago by John Palmer, and gained notoriety from the doings of "Infamous Annie" Palmer, wife of the builder's grandnephew, who supposedly dabbled in witchcraft and took slaves as lovers, killing them when they bored her. Annie also was said to have murdered several of her husbands while they slept, and eventually suffered the same fate herself. For what it's worth, many Jamaicans insist the house is haunted. The house, now privately owned, has been restored. **Annie's Pub** sits on the ground floor. The house is open daily from 9am to 5:15pm; admission is a steep $15 for adults, $10 for children under 12.

On a hillside perch 23km (14 miles) east of Montego Bay and 11km (7 miles) west of Falmouth, **Greenwood Great House,** on the A1 (© **876/953-1077**), is even more interesting to some than Rose Hall. Erected in the late 18th century, the Georgian-style building was, from 1800 to the mid-1840s, the residence of Richard Barrett, a first cousin of Elizabeth Barrett Browning. On display are the family's library, portraits of the family, and rare musical instruments. Open from 9am to 6pm daily; admission is $12 for adults and $6 for children under 12.

It's a unique experience to have a Jamaican doctor bird perch on your finger to drink syrup, or to feed small doves and finches from your hand, or simply to watch dozens of birds flying in for the evening at **Rocklands Wildlife Station,** Anchovy, St. James (© **876/952-2009**). Lisa Salmon, known as the "Bird Lady of Anchovy," established this sanctuary. It's perfect for nature lovers and birdwatchers. Rocklands is about 1.2km (¾-mile) outside Anchovy on the road from Montego Bay. It's open daily from 9am to 5:30pm, and charges $8 admission for adults and $4 for children age 5 to 12.

SHOPPING

The main shopping areas are at **Montego Freeport,** within easy walking distance of the pier; **City Centre,** where most of the duty-free shops are, aside from those at the large hotels; and **Holiday Village Shopping Centre.**

Old Fort Craft Market, a shopping complex with nearly 200 vendors licensed by the Jamaica Tourist Board, fronts Howard Cooke Boulevard up from Gloucester Avenue in the heart of Montego Bay, on the site of Fort Montego. With a varied assortment of handicrafts, this is browsing country. You'll see a selection of wall hangings, hand-woven straw items, and hand-carved wood sculptures, and you can also get your hair braided. Vendors can be extremely aggressive, so be prepared for some major hassles, as well as some serious negotiation. Persistent bargaining on your part will lead to substantial discounts.

You can find the best selection of handmade Jamaican souvenirs at the **Crafts Market,** near Harbour Street in downtown Montego Bay. Straw hats and bags, wooden platters, straw baskets, musical instruments, beads, carved objects, and toys are all available here. That "jipijapa" hat will come in handy if you're going to be out in the island sun.

For the best selection of local folk art—as well an absolutely fantastic, and reasonably priced, collection of Cuban, Jamaican, and Haitian fine art—try the **Galley of West Indian Art** on 11 Fairfield Rd. (© **876/952-4547**).

Ambiente Art Gallery, 9 Fort St. (© **876/952-7919**), stocks local artwork. At **Blue Mountain Gems Workshop,** at the Holiday Village Shopping Centre (© **876/953-2338**), you can take a tour of the workshops to see the process from raw stone to the finished product available for purchase later. **Klass Kraft Leather Sandals,** 44 Fort St. (© **876/952-5782**), offers sandals and leather accessories made on location.

BEACHES

Cornwall Beach is a long stretch of white-sand beach with dressing cabanas. Daily admission is about $2 for adults, $1 for children. A bar and cafeteria serve refreshments.

Doctor's Cave Beach (© 876/952-2566), on Gloucester Avenue across from the Doctor's Cave Beach Hotel (© 876/952-4355; www.doctorscave.com), helped launch Mo Bay as a resort in the 1940s. Admission to the beach is about $4 for adults, half price for children up to 12. Dressing rooms, chairs, umbrellas, and rafts are available.

One of the premier beaches of Jamaica, **Walter Fletcher Beach,** in the heart of Mo Bay, is noted for its tranquil waters, which make it a particular favorite for families with children. Changing rooms are available, and lifeguards are on duty. There's also a restaurant for lunch. The beach is open daily, with an admission price of about $1 for adults, half price for children.

You may want to skip the public beaches and head for the **Rose Hall Beach Club** (© 876/680-0969), lying on the main road 18km (11 miles) east of Montego Bay. It sits on .8km (½-mile) of secure, secluded, white sandy beach, with crystal-clear water. The club offers a full restaurant, two beach bars, a covered pavilion, an open-air dance area, showers, restrooms, and changing facilities, plus beach volleyball courts, various beach games, and a full watersports activities program. There's also live entertainment. The club is open daily from 9am to 5pm; admission fees are about $6 for adults, $3 for children under 12.

SPORTS

GOLF   Wyndham Rose Hall Golf & Beach Resort, Rose Hall (© 876/953-2650), has a noted 18-hole, par-71 course with an unusual and challenging seaside and mountain layout. The 90m- (300-ft.-) high 13th tee offers a rare panoramic view of the sea, and the 15th green is next to a 12m (40-ft.) waterfall, once featured in a James Bond movie. A fully stocked pro shop, a clubhouse, and a professional staff are among the amenities. Greens fees are $125.

The excellent, regal 18-hole, par-72 course at the **Tryall Club** (© 876/956-5660; www.tryallclub.com), 19km (12 miles) from Montego Bay, has often been the site of major golf tournaments, including the Jamaica Classic Annual and the Johnnie Walker Tournament. Greens fees are $115.

Half Moon, at Rose Hall (© 876/953-2560; www.halfmoon-resort.com/golf), features an 18-hole, par-72 championship course designed by Robert Trent Jones, Sr. Greens fees are $130, plus $17 for a mandatory caddy.

Ironshore Golf & Country Club, Ironshore, St. James, Montego Bay (© 876/953-3681), a well-known, 18-hole, par-72 course, is privately owned but open to the public. Greens fees are $30 plus $14 for a mandatory caddy.

HORSEBACK RIDING   The best horseback riding is offered by the helpful staff at the **Rocky Point Riding Stables,** at the Half Moon Club, Rose Hall, Montego Bay (© 876/953-2286). The stables, built in the colonial Caribbean style in 1992, are the most beautiful in Jamaica.

RAFTING   Mountain Valley Rafting, 31 Gloucester Ave. (© 876/956-4920), offers excursions on the Great River, departing from the Lethe Plantation, about 16km (10 miles) south of Montego Bay. Bamboo rafts are designed for two, with a raised dais to sit on. In some cases, a small child can accompany two adults on the same raft, although you should exercise caution when doing so. A half-day experience includes transportation to and from the pier, an hour's rafting, lunch, a garden tour of the Lethe property, and a taste of Jamaican liqueur.

GREAT LOCAL RESTAURANTS & BARS

The Pork Pit, 27 Gloucester Ave., near Walter Fletcher Beach (*©* 876/952-1046), is the best place to go for the famous Jamaican jerk pork and jerk chicken. Many beachgoers come over here for a big lunch. Picnic tables encircle the building, and everything is open-air and informal. Order half a pound of jerk meat with a baked yam or baked potato and a bottle of Red Stripe beer. Prices are very reasonable. Lunch $10.

The Native Restaurant, Gloucester Avenue (*©* 876/979-2769), continues to win converts with such appetizers as jerk reggae chicken, ackee and saltfish (an acquired taste), smoked marlin, and steamed fish. The boonoonoonoos, billed as "A Taste of Jamaica," is a big platter with a little bit of everything, including meats and several kinds of fish and vegetables. Lunch $20

16 Key West

No other port of call offers such a sweeping choice of fine dining, easy-to-reach attractions, street entertainment, and roguish bars as does this heavy-drinking, fun-loving town at the very end of the fabled Florida Keys. It's America's southernmost city, located at Mile Marker 0, where U.S. Route 1 begins, but it feels more like a colorful Caribbean outpost mixed with a dash of New Orleans.

You have only a day, so flee the busy cruise docks and touristy **Duval Street** for a walk through hidden and more secluded byways, such as **Olivia** or **William streets.** Or you might want to spend your day playing golf or going diving or snorkeling.

COMING ASHORE   Ships dock at **Mallory Square,** Old Town's most important plaza; **Truman Annex;** and the **Hilton Resort & Marina.** All three are on the Gulf of Mexico side of the island, and virtually everything is at your doorstep, including the two main arteries, Duval Street and Whitehead Street, each filled with shops, bars, restaurants, and the town's most important attractions.

LANGUAGE   Speak **English** here. Remember, you're in the U.S. of A.

CURRENCY   U.S. dollars are used here.

INFORMATION   The **Greater Key West Chamber of Commerce,** 402 Wall St. (*©* 305/294-5988; www.keywestchamber.org), lies near the cruise ship docks, and provides information for tours and fishing trips. *Pelican Path* is a free walking guide that documents the history and architecture of Old Town, and *Solares Hill's Walking and Biking Guide to Old Key West* contains a bunch of walking tours. To get info before you go, contact the **tourism board** (*©* 800/FLA-KEYS; www.fla-keys.com).

GETTING AROUND

The island is only 4 miles long and 2 miles wide, so getting around is easy. Many people who live here own bicycles instead of cars. The most popular sights, including the **Ernest Hemingway Home & Museum,** the restored bright red brick **Key West Art & History Museum at the Custom House,** and the **Harry S Truman Little White House,** are within walking distance of most ships, so you're hardly dependent on public transportation unless you want to go to the beaches on the island's Atlantic side.

BY TAXI   Island taxis operate around the clock, but are small and not suited for sightseeing tours. They will, however, take you to the beach and arrange to pick you up at a certain time. You can call one of four services: **Florida Keys**

⟨✐⟩ **Frommer's Favorite Key West Experiences**

Viewing the Sunset from Mallory Dock: More than just a sunset, It's a daily carnival. If your ship is in port late enough, don't miss it. (See "On Your Own: Within Walking Distance," below.)

Taking a Catamaran Party Cruise: The popular Fury catamarans take passengers snorkeling and then back to shore, with music, booze, and a good time. (See "Shore Excursions Offered by the Cruise Lines," below.)

Taxi (© 305/294-2227), **Maxi-Taxi Sun Cab System** (© 305/294-2222), **Pink Cabs** (© 305/296-6666), and **Island Transportation Services** (© 305/296-1800). Prices are uniform; the meter starts at about $1.75 and adds 35¢ per ¼-mile.

BY TRAM The **Conch Tour Train** (© 305/294-5161; www.conchtourtrain. com) is a narrated 90-minute tour that takes you up and down all the most interesting streets and offers commentary on 100 local sites, giving you lots of lore about the town. It's the best way to see lots of Key West in a short time. The depot is located at Mallory Square near the cruise ship docks. Trains depart every 30 minutes. Most ships sell this as an excursion, but you can also do it on your own; departures are daily from 9am to 4:30pm and cost $20 for adults, $10 for children ages 4 to 12 (free for children 3 and under). The trip has only one stop where passengers can get on and off (at the Historic Seaport). If you want more flexibility, try the **Old Town Trolley** (© 305/296-6688; www.trolleytours. com). It's less popular than the Conch Tour Train, but it lets you get off and explore a particular attraction, and then reboard another of its trains later. Professional guides spin tall tales about Key West throughout the 90-minute route. The trolleys operate 7 days a week from 9am to 4:30pm, with departures every 30 minutes from convenient spots throughout town. You can board the trolley near the cruise docks (look for signposts). Tours cost about $20 for adults, $10 for children ages 4 to 12, and are free for children under 4.

BY MOTOR SCOOTER OR BICYCLE One of the largest and best places to rent a bicycle or motorbike is **Keys Moped and Scooter Rental,** 523 Truman Ave., about a block off Duval Street (© 305/294-0399). Cruise ship passengers might opt for a 3-hour motor-scooter rental for about $12, the 9am to 5pm rental for $18, or the all day (24-hr.) rental for $23. One-speed, big-wheeled "beach-cruiser" bicycles with soft seats and big baskets for toting beachwear rent for about $4 for 8 hours.

BY BUS The cheapest way to see the island is by bus, which costs only about 75¢ for adults and 35¢ for senior citizens and children 6 years and older (kids 5 and under ride free).

BY RENTAL CAR Walking or cycling is better than renting a car here, but if you do want to rent, **Avis, Budget, Dollar,** and **Hertz** all have offices here, as do **Tropical Rent-a-Car,** 1300 Duval St. (© 305/294-8136), and **Enterprise Rent-a-Car,** 2834 N. Roosevelt Blvd. (© 800/325-8007 or 305/292-0220; www.enterprise.com). If you're visiting in winter, make reservations at least a week in advance.

Key West

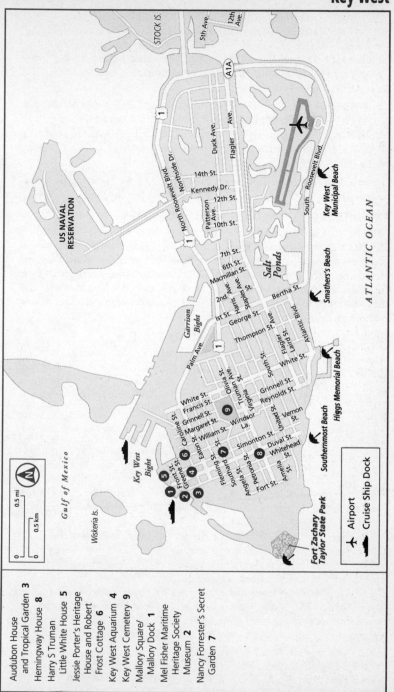

Audubon House
and Tropical Garden **3**
Hemingway House **8**
Harry S Truman
Little White House **5**
Jessie Porter's Heritage
House and Robert
Frost Cottage **6**
Key West Aquarium **4**
Key West Cemetery **9**
Mallory Square/
Mallory Dock **1**
Mel Fisher Maritime
Heritage Society
Museum **2**
Nancy Forrester's Secret
Garden **7**

SHORE EXCURSIONS OFFERED BY THE CRUISE LINES

In Key West, it's definitely not necessary to take an organized excursion since everything is so accessible by foot or tram. If you like the services of a guide, most lines offer walking tours. Also, the trams and trolleys discussed above have running narratives about Key West history and culture. Here are a couple of other popular options.

Catamaran Party Cruises ($44, 3 hr.): The popular Fury catamarans take passengers to a reef for some snorkeling and then finish the trip back to shore with music, booze, and a good time. You can also book these trips on your own (© **800/994-8898** or 305/294-8899; www.furycat.com). Their sunset sail is an option if your ship will be in port late ($30, 2 hr.).

Guided Bike Tour ($25, 2 hr.): Get the lowdown on Key West's multifaceted history and quirky culture while peddling along a 2½-mile route.

EXCURSIONS OFFERED BY LOCAL AGENCIES

Glass-Bottomed Boat Tours: The MV *Discovery* (© **800/262-0099** or 305/ 293-0099; www.discoveryunderseatours.com), a 78-foot motor craft, has 20 large viewing windows (angled at 45°) set below the water line to allow passengers to view reef life in comfort from below deck. Two-hour tours depart daily at 10:30am, 1:30pm, and sunset from Land's End Village & Marina at the western end of Margaret Street, a 6-block walk from the cruise ship docks. The cost is $30.

ON YOUR OWN: WITHIN WALKING DISTANCE

If the lines aren't too long, you'll want to see the Harry S Truman Little White House and the Ernest Hemingway Home & Museum, but don't feel obligated. If you want to see and capture the real-life mood and charm of Key West in a short time, leave the most-visited attractions to your fellow cruise ship passengers and head for the others mentioned below. All are an easy walk from the docks.

Audubon House and Tropical Garden, 205 Whitehead St., at Greene Street (© **877/281-2473** or 305/294-2116; www.audubonhouse.com), is dedicated to the 1832 Key West sojourn of the famous naturalist John James Audubon. The ornithologist didn't live in this three-story building, but it's filled with his engravings. The main reason to visit is to see how wealthy sailors lived in Key West in the 19th century, and the lush tropical gardens surrounding the house are worth the $9 price of admission.

The **Harry S Truman Little White House,** 111 Front St. (© **305/294-9911;** www.trumanlittlewhitehouse.com), the president's vacation home, is part of the 103-acre Truman Annex near the cruise ship docks. The small house, which takes less than an hour to visit, affords a glimpse of a president at play.

There may be long lines at the **Hemingway House,** 907 Whitehead St. (© **305/294-1575**), where "Papa" lived with his second wife, Pauline. Here, in the studio annex, Hemingway finished *For Whom the Bell Tolls* and *A Farewell to Arms,* among others. Hemingway had some 50 polydactyl (many-toed) cats, whose descendants still live on the grounds.

Jessie Porter Newton, known as "Miss Jessie" to her friends, was the grande dame of Key West, inviting the celebrities of her day to her house, including Tennessee Williams and her girlhood friend Gloria Swanson, as well as family friend Robert Frost, who stayed in a cottage out back. Today, you can wander the grounds, look at the antique-filled rooms, and inspect her mementos and the exotic treasures collected by six generations of the Porter family at **Jessie Porter's Heritage House and Robert Frost Cottage,** 410 Caroline St. (✆ **305/296-3573**).

On the waterfront at Mallory Square, the **Key West Aquarium,** 1 Whitehead St. (✆ **305/296-2051;** www.keywestaquarium.com), in operation since 1932, was the first tourist attraction built in the Florida Keys. The aquarium's special feature is a "touch tank" where you can feel a horseshoe crab, sea squirt, sea urchin, starfish, and, of course, conch, the town's mascot and symbol. It's worth taking a tour, as the guides are both knowledgeable and entertaining—and you'll get to pet a shark, if that's your idea of a good time.

The **Key West Cemetery** (✆ **305/292-6718**), 21 prime acres in the heart of the historic district, is the island's foremost offbeat attraction. The main entrance is at Margaret Street and Passover Lane. Stone-encased caskets rest on top of the earth because graves dug into the ground would hit the water table. There's also a touch of humor here: One gravestone proclaims "I Told You I Was Sick" and another says "At Least I Know Where He Is Sleeping Tonight." To get a better scoop on what you'll be seeing, print out the cemetery tour at **www.key west.com/cemetery.html** before you go.

The late treasure hunter Mel Fisher used to wear heavy gold necklaces, which he liked to say were worth a king's ransom. He wasn't exaggerating. After long and risky dives, Fisher and his associates plucked more than $400 million in gold and silver from the shipwrecked Spanish galleons *Santa Margarita* and *Nuestra Señora de Atocha,* which were lost on hurricane-tossed seas some 350 years ago. Now this extraordinary long-lost Spanish treasure—jewelry, doubloons, and silver and gold bullion—is displayed at the **Mel Fisher Maritime Heritage Society Museum,** near the docks at 200 Greene St. (✆ **305/294-2633;** www.melfisher.com).

Nancy Forrester's Secret Garden, 1 Free School Lane, off Simonton between Southard and Fleming streets (✆ **305/294-0015**), is the most lavish and verdant garden in town. Some 150 species of palms and thousands of species of other plants, including orchids, climbing vines, and ground covers, are planted here, creating a blanket of lush, tropical magic. It's a 20-minute walk from the docks, near Key West's highest point, Solares Hill. Pick up a sandwich at a deli and picnic at tables in the garden. Admission is $6 per person; hours are 10am to 5pm daily.

If your ship leaves late enough, you can take in a unique local celebration: **viewing the sunset from Mallory Dock.** Sunset-watching is good fun all over the world, but in Key West it's been turned into a carnival-like, almost pagan celebration. People from all over begin to crowd Mallory Square even before the sun starts to fall, bringing the place alive with entertainment—everything from string bands to a unicyclist wriggling free of a straitjacket to a juggler tossing around machetes and flaming sticks. The main entertainment, however, is that massive fireball falling out of view, a sight that's always greeted with hysterical applause.

ON YOUR OWN: BEYOND THE PORT AREA

Nothin'. That's the beauty of Key West: Everything worthwhile is accessible by foot.

SHOPPING

Within a 12-block radius of Old Town, you'll find mostly tawdry and outrageously overpriced merchandise, but if you're in the market for some Key West kitsch, this is the neighborhood for you. Shopping by cruise ship passengers has become a joke among Key West locals, but that's their problem. We say be proud of your flamingo snow globe and floppy straw hat. What else says "vacation" better?

Among the less-kitschy alternatives, a few standouts are located much farther along **Duval Street,** the main drag leading to the Atlantic, and on hidden back streets. You can reach all these stores from the cruise ship docks in a 15- to 20-minute stroll.

Haitian Art Company, 600 Frances St. (© 305/296-8932), claims to inventory the largest collection of Haitian paintings in the United States. Prices range from $15 to $5,000. **Key West Aloe, Inc.,** 524 Front St. or 540 Greene St. (© 305/294-5592), is aloe, aloe, and more aloe; the shop's inventory includes shaving cream, aftershave lotion, sunburn ointments, and fragrances for men and women based on tropical essences such as hibiscus, frangipani, and white ginger. **Key West Hand Print Fashions and Fabrics,** 201 Simonton St. (© 305/292-8951), sells bold, tropical prints—hand-printed scarves with coordinated handbags and rack after rack of busily patterned sundresses and cocktail dresses that will make you look jaunty on deck. **Key West Island Bookstore,** 513 Fleming St. (© 305/294-2904), is well stocked with books on Key West and has Florida's largest collection of works by and about Hemingway. In the rear is a rare-book section where you may want to browse, if not buy.

BEACHES

Beaches are not too compelling here. Most are man-made, often with imported Bahamian or mainland Florida sand. Those mentioned below are free and open to the public daily from 7am to 11pm. There are few facilities, just locals hawking beach umbrellas, food, and drinks.

Fort Zachary Taylor State Beach (© 305/292-6883) is the best and the closest to the cruise ship docks, a 12-minute walk away. This 51-acre man-made beach is adjacent to historic Fort Taylor, once known as Fort Forgotten because it was buried under tons of sand. The beach is fine for sunbathing and picnicking and is suitable for snorkeling. To get there, go through the gates leading into **Truman Annex** (© 305/292-6713). Watering holes near one end of the beach include the raffish **Green Parrot Bar** (© 305/294-6133) and **Meteore Smokehouse Barbecue** (© 305/294-5602).

Higgs Memorial Beach lies a 25-minute walk from the harbor near the end of White Street, one of the main east-west arteries. You'll find lots of sand, picnic tables sheltered from the sun, and fewer of your fellow cruise ship passengers. **Smathers Beach,** named in honor of one of Florida's most colorful former senators, is the longest (about 1½ miles) in town. Unfortunately, it's about a $10 one-way taxi ride from the cruise docks. The beach borders South Roosevelt Boulevard. There's no shade here.

In the 1950s, **Southernmost Beach** drew Tennessee Williams, but today it's more likely to fill up with visitors from the motels nearby. Except for a nearby restaurant, facilities are nonexistent. The beach lies at the foot of Duval Street on the Atlantic side, across the island from the cruise ship docks. It takes about 20 minutes to walk there along Duval Street from the docks. The beach boasts some white sand but is not particularly good for swimming. Nevertheless, it's one of the island's most frequented.

SPORTS

FISHING   As Hemingway, an avid fisherman, would attest, the waters off the Florida Keys are some of the world's finest fishing grounds. You can follow in his wake aboard the 40-foot *Linda D III* and *Linda D IV* (✆ **800/299-9798** or 305/296-9798; www.charterboatlindad.com), which offer the best deep-sea fishing here. Full-day charters for up to 6 people $675, half-day $450. Full-day shared charters $165 per person, half-day $110. Make arrangements as far in advance as possible.

GOLF   Redesigned in 1982 by architect Rees Jones, the 18-hole, par-70 **Key West Resort Golf Club,** 6450 E. Junior College Rd. (✆ **305/294-5232;** www. keywestgolf.com), lies 6 miles from the cruise docks, near the southern tip of neighboring Stock Island. It features a challenging terrain of coral rock, sand traps, mangrove swamp, and pines. Greens fees are $140, including cart. The course is a 10- to 15-minute, $15 taxi ride from the dock each way.

SCUBA DIVING   The largest dive outfitter is **Captain's Corner,** 125 Ann St., half a block from the dock (✆ **305/296-8865;** www.captainscorner.com). The five-star PADI operation has 11 instructors, a well-trained staff, and a 60-foot dive boat that was used by Timothy "James Bond" Dalton during the filming of *License to Kill.* To reach the departure point, walk to the end of Greene Street.

GREAT LOCAL RESTAURANTS & BARS

RESTAURANTS   All the restaurants listed below are within an easy 5- to 15-minute walk of the docks, except for Camille's and El Siboney, which are more than a mile away. Several "raw bars" near the dock area offer seafood, including oysters and clams, although the king here is conch—served grilled, ground into burgers, made into chowder, fried in batter as fritters, or served raw in a conch salad. Even if you don't have lunch, at least sample the local favorites: a slice of Key lime pie with a Cuban coffee. The pie's unique flavor comes from the juice and minced rind of the local, piquant Key lime.

Cruise ship passengers on a return visit to Key West often ask for "The Rose Tattoo," a historic old restaurant named for the Tennessee Williams film partially shot on the island. The restaurant is now the **Bagatelle,** 115 Duval St., at Front Street (✆ **305/296-6609**), one of Key West's finest. Look for daily specials or stick to the chef's better dishes, such as conch seviche (thinly sliced raw conch marinated in lime juice and herbs). Lunch $13. **Blue Heaven,** 729 Thomas St. (✆ **305/296-8666**), is a dive that serves some of the best food in town, including fresh local fish, most often grouper or red snapper. Their hot and spicy jerk chicken is as fine as that served in Jamaica. Lunch $12. **Camille's,** 1202 Simonton St., at Catherine Street (✆ **305/296-4811**), is an unpretentious, hip cafe that serves the best breakfast in town and has the best lunch value. Try a sandwich made from the catch of the day, served on fresh bread, and finish off with some of their great Key lime pie. Lunch $10. **El Siboney,** 900 Catherine St. (✆ **305/296-4184**), is the place for time-tested Cuban favorites such as ropa vieja, roast pork with garlic and tart sour oranges, and paella Valenciana. Lunch $10.

Half Shell Raw Bar, Land's End Marina, at the foot of Margaret Street (✆ **305/294-7496**), is Key West's original raw bar, offering fresh fish, oysters, and shrimp direct from its own fish market. Lunch $10. To be honest, though, we prefer the food at **Turtle Kraals Wildlife Bar & Grill,** Land's End Village, at the foot of Margaret Street (✆ **305/294-2640**). Try the tender Florida lobster, spicy conch chowder, or perfectly cooked fresh fish (often dolphinfish with pineapple salsa or baked stuffed grouper with mango crabmeat stuffing). Lunch $10.

Pepe's Café & Steak House, 806 Caroline St., between William and Margaret streets (✆ **305/294-7192**), is the oldest eating house in the Florida Keys, established in 1909. Diners eat under slow-moving paddle fans at tables or dark pine booths with high backs. At lunch (served noon–4pm), choose from zesty homemade chili, perfectly baked oysters, fish sandwiches, and Pepe's deservedly famous steak sandwiches. Lunch $8.

If something cool would go down better than a full meal, check out the **Flamingo Crossing** ice-cream shop, 1105 Duval St., at Virginia Street (© **305/296-6124**).

BARS   Key West is a bar town, and since many ships stay in town late, you'll likely have an opportunity to do some carousing. Most places recommended below offer fast food to go with their drinks. The food isn't the best on the island, but usually arrives shortly after you order it, which suits most rushed cruise ship passengers just fine. Try some of the favorite **local beer,** Hog's Breath, or some of the favorite **local rum,** Key West Gold (even though it's a cheat—it isn't actually made on the island).

Heavily patronized by cruise ship passengers, **Captain Tony's Saloon,** 428 Greene St. (© **305/294-1838**), is the oldest active bar in Florida, and is tacky as hell. The 1851 building was the original Sloppy Joe's, a rough-and-tumble fisherman's saloon. Hemingway drank here from 1933 to 1937, and Jimmy Buffett got his start here before opening his own bar and going on to musical glory. The name refers to Capt. Tony Tarracino, a former Key West mayor and rugged man of the sea who owned the place until 1988.

The current **Sloppy Joe's,** 201 Duval St. (© **305/294-5717**), is the most touristy bar in Key West, visited by almost all cruise ship passengers, even those who don't normally go to bars. It aggressively plays up its association with Hemingway, although the bar stood on Greene Street back then (see above). Marine flags decorate the ceiling, and its ambience and decor evoke a Havana bar from the 1930s.

Jimmy Buffett's Margaritaville, 500 Duval St. (© **305/296-3070**), is the third most popular Key West bar with cruise ship passengers. Buffett is the hometown boy done good, and his cafe, naturally, is decorated with pictures of himself. And, yes, it sells T-shirts and Margaritaville memorabilia in a shop off the dining room. His margaritas are without competition, but then they'd have to be, wouldn't they?

Open-air and very laid-back, the **Hog's Breath Saloon,** 400 Front St. (© **305/296-HOGG**), near the cruise docks, has been a Key West tradition since 1976. Drinking is a sport here, especially among the fishermen who come in after a day chasing the big one. Live entertainment is offered from 1pm to 2am.

For a real local hangout within an easy walk of the cruise ship docks, head to **Schooner Wharf,** 202 William St., Key West Bight (© **305/292-9520**), the most robust and hard-drinking bar in Key West, drawing primarily a young crowd, many of whom work in the tourist industry or on the local fishing boats.

17 Les Saintes

You want charming? The eight islets of Les Saintes (pronounced "lay sant") are irresistibly so: pastel-colored gingerbread houses with tropical gardens, sugarloaf hills that slope down to miniature beaches, and picturesque bays with pelicans, sailboats, and turquoise water. Only two of the islands in this French archipelago off the southern coast of Guadeloupe are inhabited: Terre-de-Bas and its more populous neighbor, Terre-de-Haut (more populous, in this case, meaning

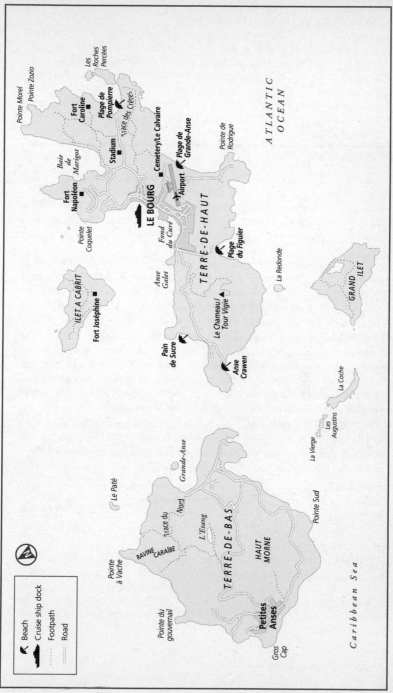

Tormented by Love? Have a Pastry

As you leave your ship, you'll spot local women selling Les Saintes' signature sweet, tartlets known as *tourments d'amour* (love's torments). Legend has it that young maidens baked these flaky-crusted, coconut-filled treats to present to their betrotheds as they returned from lengthy fishing expeditions. From time to time, the cruel and heartless sea claimed the life of a beloved, leaving a teary-eyed damsel at the dock with nothing but her pain and pastry. Is it the suffering that makes the tourments d'amour so tasty?

---

it has about 1,700 inhabitants). Terre-de-Haut (pronounced "t'air d'oh"), with only one village—the straightforwardly named Le Bourg ("town")—is the destination of most visitors. Some say it's what Saint-Tropez was like before Brigitte Bardot. For a U.S. point of reference, think Fire Island, Provincetown, Martha's Vineyard, or Sausalito with a French-Caribbean twist. Nautical and quaint are the watchwords.

But Les Saintes, also known as Iles des Saintes, isn't a fantasy park built to look enchanting. Although tourism is important to the island's economy, most people here still make their living from the sea. Les Saintois, as the locals are called, are widely regarded as the best fishermen in the Antilles, and it's this underlying saltiness that keeps the place from being cloyingly sweet.

COMING ASHORE   Cruise ships dock at **Le Bourg** in Terre-de-Haut. The village has two main streets, both parallel to the bay and lined with cafes, restaurants, and souvenir shops. **Telephones** at the dock require a télécarte, a prepaid phone card sold at the post office (a 10-min. walk from the dock; take a right) and other outlets marked TELECARTE EN VENTE ICI. Some phones now accept U.S. calling cards or major credit cards for long-distance calls.

LANGUAGE   The official language is **French,** but many islanders speak **Creole** with each other. Few locals feel comfortable with English, though, so take the opportunity to practice your high-school French. Most everyone is helpful and friendly, especially if you smile and make an effort.

CURRENCY   Les Saintes is part of the larger archipelago of Guadeloupe, an overseas region of France, so the **Euro** (€) is now the official currency (exchange rate: €1 = US$1.10; $1 = €.90). You can withdraw euros from the **ATM** next to the tourism office (see "Information" below). Unless otherwise specified, prices in this section are given in U.S. dollars.

INFORMATION   If you take a right on the main road after you leave the ship, you'll see signs for the **tourism office** (OFFICE DU TOURISME). It's less than a 5-minute walk. Most printed information available here is in French, but the maps are helpful even if you don't understand the lingo. For info before you go, contact the Tourism Board in the United States (© **410/286-8310;** www.french caribbean.com).

CALLING FROM THE U.S.   When calling Les Saintes from the U.S., dial the international access code (011) and 590 before the numbers listed here. Yes, the numbers listed here already begin with 590, but an effort by the French telephone authorities to standardize procedures requires that you dial those three digits twice. Really.

GETTING AROUND

If you're reasonably fit, there's no reason you can't walk wherever you want to go. If you're the type who runs 8km (5 miles) a day, you can hike up Le Chameau, traipse around Fort Napoléon, head over to Plage de Pompierre, and complete the Trace des Crêtes, with time for a meal or swim before returning to the ship.

BY TAXI   The island has a handful of minivans that serve as taxis. Each seats six to eight passengers, and most drivers offer 3-hour tours of the island for about $40 (be aware, though, that fluent English is not widely spoken). You'll find the cabs parked directly in front of the cruise ship dock.

BY SCOOTER   Terre-de-Haut is less than 6.4km (4 miles long) and less than 3.2km (2 miles) wide. Aside from tourist vans and the occasional private car, four-wheeled vehicles are rare (at last count, there were fewer than three dozen). Scooters rule the roads. Scores of them await you just off the dock along Le Bourg's main road. Expect to pay about $35 for a two-seater for the day. A $500 deposit (credit cards accepted) is required.

BY BICYCLE   You can rent bicycles for between $15 and $20 along Le Bourg's main road. The island is hilly, though. You'd do better to rent a scooter or walk.

SHORE EXCURSIONS OFFERED BY THE CRUISE LINES

Don't expect any. This is a wander-around-at-your-own pace kind of place. See "Sports," below, for scuba, snorkeling, and fishing excursions you can arrange through local agencies.

ON YOUR OWN: WITHIN WALKING DISTANCE

Everything is within walking distance of the dock. **Fort Napoléon** looms over Le Bourg's picturesque bay. The French started building this stone bastion after they regained Les Saintes from the British in 1815 but didn't complete it until 1867. Today it houses engaging, detailed exhibits that cover the entire history of the islands, including life before Columbus, European expansion into the New World, early French settlements, the Battle of Les Saintes, and the development of the fishing industry. You can wander through barracks, dungeons, and the grounds, which feature an impressive array of cacti and succulents. Pick up the English-language brochure that describes the vegetation when you purchase your admission ticket; adult admission is about $2.80, children under 12 pay $1.40. For 80¢, you can rent a cassette that provides excellent English commentary as you walk through the museum. The fort is open a brief 3½ hours a day, from 9am to 12:30pm, so make it your first destination.

On the hill that leads to Fort Napoléon, visit **Jerome Hoff**, a fourth-generation Santois of Alsatian ancestry who paints religious icons in a heartfelt but slightly disturbing style. He has the wild-eyed air of a John the Baptist, but he's a gentle man, retired now, who loves to talk about his 50 years of singing in the church choir. You can't miss his modest home and studio—they're surrounded by numerous quirky signs that feature colorful saints and passionate prayers.

On the route to the tourism office and the ATM, you'll pass Le Bourg's **stone church.** It's humble, but worth the couple of minutes it takes to peek inside.

If you're up for some hiking, the **Trace des Crêtes trail** traces the spine of one of Terre-de-Haut's hills just north of the airport and offers remarkable views of beaches, cliffs, and neighboring islands. Although clearly marked, the path is

Frommer's Favorite Les Saintes Experiences

Meandering Around Fort Napoléon: The French built this impressive stone fortification after they regained Les Saintes in 1815, and today it houses engaging, detailed exhibits covering the entire history of the islands. (See "On Your Own: Within Walking Distance," above.)

Trekking to the Top of Le Chameau: The highest point on Terre-de-Haut, Le Chameau is located in the southern part of the island and offers a tough (though shaded) 30- to 60-minute climb, for which you're rewarded with spectacular views. (See "On Your Own: Within Walking Distance," above.)

Sunbathing on Picture-Perfect Pompierre Beach: No beach on Terre-de-Haut is nicer than Plage de Pompierre, located only a 15-minute walk from the dock. (See "Beaches," below.)

Climbing Along the Trace des Crêtes: This trail across the center of Terre-de-Haut offers remarkable views of beaches, cliffs, the island's toylike airport, and neighboring islands. (See "On Your Own: Within Walking Distance," above.)

rocky and challenging—you have an advantage if you're part goat. Wear sunscreen and bring water.

Be sure to stop for a few minutes at the **cemetery** next to the airport. You'll notice several graves adorned with conch shells, which signify a sea-related death. On Saturday nights, refrigerator-size speakers are brought in, makeshift food stands are set up, and the cemetery becomes a huge open-air disco. In the same vicinity, **Le Calvaire** is a giant Christ statue at the summit of a hill; numerous steps ascend to great panoramas.

Chameau means camel in French, and with a bit of imagination you can see that **Le Chameau,** the highest point on Terre-de-Haut, looks sort of like the hump of a dromedary. The concrete road to the 300m (1,000-ft.) summit is off-limits to all motorized vehicles, and, mercifully, it's shaded much of the way. After 30 to 60 minutes of arduous climbing, you're rewarded with spectacular views of the entire archipelago, Guadeloupe, and Dominica. **Tour Vigie,** a military lookout dating from the time of Napoleon, crowns the mountain; unfortunately, it's usually locked.

SHOPPING

Little boutiques that sell beachwear, T-shirts, jewelry, and knickknacks line the streets. Stop by Pascal Foy's **Kaz an Nou Gallery** behind the church. You can watch him make Cases Creoles, miniature carved wooden Creole houses in candy colors. They're becoming collector's items. **Galerie Martine Cotten,** at the foot of the dock, features the work of an artist originally from Brittany who celebrates the natural beauty and fishing traditions of Les Saintes. Beyond the town hall, **Ultramarine** is a tiny cottage where you can buy unusual dolls, clothes, T-shirts, and handcrafted items from France, Haiti, and Africa. **Galerie Marchande Seaside,** a group of shops situated around a patio, is just up the street after you turn right from the pier. Art, gifts, antiques, jewelry, lace, beachwear, and ice cream are available.

BEACHES

Beaches with golden sand are tucked away in almost all of the island's coves. Calm, crescent-shaped **Plage de Pompierre** (sometimes spelled Pont Pierre) is shaded by sea grape bushes, as well as almond and palm trees. A 15-minute walk from the dock, it boasts soft white sand, shade from coconut palms, and quiet seclusion. The gentle water in the cliff-encircled cove is a stunning aquamarine. Because the bay is a nature preserve, fishing and anchoring are prohibited. It's the island's most popular sunbathing spot, so your best bet is to go early or late.

Grande Anse, near the airfield, is large, but there's no shade, and the rough surf has a strong undertow. Although swimming is discouraged, the cliffs at either end of the beach and the powerful breakers make for a dramatic seascape. The usually deserted **Figuier,** on the southern coast, has excellent snorkeling.

SPORTS

FISHING Going out to sea with a local fisherman is one way to experience Les Saintes' nautical heritage. Most of the local sailors will be delighted to take you out, if you can communicate well enough to negotiate a price. Most fishermen are stationed next to the cruise ship dock; just follow the waterfront to the fishing boats.

SCUBA, SNORKELING & OTHER WATERSPORTS For scuba diving and snorkeling, go to **La Dive Bouteille Centre Nautique des Saintes** (© 590/ 99-54-25; www.dive-bouteille.com) at the Plage de la Colline west of town past the market, or **UCPA** (© 590/99-54-94), on the other side of Fort Napoléon hill in Marigot Bay. One-tank dives run about $40. Both also rent sea kayaks and windsurfing equipment.

GREAT LOCAL RESTAURANTS & BARS

Virtually every restaurant in Terre-de-Haut offers seafood that couldn't be fresher, and many feature Creole dishes. A local favorite is smoked kingfish (*thazard fumé*). **L'Auberge Les Petits Saints aux Anarcadiers** (© 590/99-50-99) is a hillside veranda restaurant overlooking the bay. On Route de Rodrigue, it boasts a tropical garden and countless antiques. The terrace restaurant at the **Hôtel Bois Joli** (© 590/99-50-38), on the island's western tip, offers a view of Pain de Sucre, Les Saintes' petite version of Rio de Janeiro's Sugarloaf Mountain, and is fringed with palm trees. For pasta, pizza, or salad, try **La Saladerie**'s seaside terrace on the way to Fort Napoléon. **Café de la Marine** (© 590/99-53-78), on the bay and main street, serves thin-crusted pizzas and seafood. One of the island's best bakeries (*boulangeries*), **Le Fournil de Jimmy** (© 590/99-57-73), is on the same square as the town hall, across from the tourist office. If you stop in at the right time, you can get a crusty baguette hot from the oven. If you'd rather have something cold, try one of the Italian gelati at **Tropico Gelato** (© 590/99-88-12). Turn right off the dock; it's a couple of storefronts down on your right.

The Goats of Love

Don't leave anything unattended while swimming at Plage de Pompierre. Savvy goats hide out in the scrub behind the beach, patiently scoping out the action. Once you go into the water, they'll make a beeline for your unattended picnic basket and treat themselves to anything edible. They're especially fond of those tourments d'amour you just bought at the dock. Who's crying now?

18 Martinique

Fairy-tale romance and horrific disaster: Who could resist such an enticing combination? As if being the birthplace and childhood home of Empress Joséphine, sweetheart and wife of Napoleon, weren't enough, Martinique mesmerizes with the epic tragedy that befell St. Pierre one fair day in 1902: bustling cosmopolitan capital one minute, devastated volcanic graveyard of 30,000 souls the next. Love and death make quite a one-two punch, but they're just the hook. Look a bit deeper to appreciate Martinique's subtler attractions—quaint seaside villages, colonial ruins, and captivatingly beautiful rainforests and beaches.

"Madiana," or "island of flowers," was the Carib name for the island, and hibiscus, bougainvillea, and bird of paradise grow in lush profusion alongside mango, pineapple, banana, and papaya. Like Guadeloupe and St. Barts, Martinique is as French as Bordeaux, and you'll find everything from baguettes to Balenciaga here. But with African and new-world roots forever entwined, Creole cuisine and traditions continue to flourish.

About 81km (50 miles) long and 35km (22 miles) wide, the island features a diverse topography. Rainforests drape the volcanic mountains of the north; small, rounded hills and enclosed valleys mark the central plain; and white-sand beaches ring the arid, flat south.

During the 18th and 19th centuries, France and England vied for the island. In 1946, Martinique became an overseas department of France, and in 1974, it achieved regional status—the French minister of the interior appoints a prefect, but the island's citizens elect representatives to the national legislature in Paris and the regional legislature in Fort-de-France.

Most of Martinique's 380,000 residents are descendants of African slaves, but others of European, Asian, and Middle Eastern ancestry add to the melting pot. Attesting to the generally amicable relations among the various peoples, every shade of skin color is represented.

COMING ASHORE   Most cruise ships dock in the heart of Fort-de-France, at the **Pointe Simon Cruise Dock,** which has quays for two large vessels. Because Martinique is a popular port of call, ships also dock at the Passenger Terminal at the **main harbor,** a cargo port on the north side of the bay, a $10 cab ride from the center of town.

LANGUAGE   **French** is Martinique's official language, but you can get by with English at most restaurants and tourist sites. You'll also hear the island patois, **Creole,** on the street. Because many of the island's service employees work hard to improve their English, cruisers who speak no French find Martinique easier to navigate than Guadeloupe, the other big French Caribbean island. Ask for English-language brochures and commentaries when sightseeing; most sites have them.

CURRENCY   Martinique is an overseas region of France, so the **euro** (€) is now the official currency (exchange rate: €1 = US$1.10; $1 = €.90). Unless otherwise specified, prices in this section are given in U.S. dollars. There are numerous **ATMs** (*distributeur de billets*) in downtown Fort-de-France, and you'll have no trouble using your credit cards and traveler's checks. You can change money at **Change Caraïbe** (② 596/60-28-40), 4 rue Ernest Deproge, on the waterfront, or 1 block inland at **Change Point Change** (② 596/63-80-33), 14 rue Victor Hugo.

INFORMATION   The **Office du Tourisme,** on Boulevard Alfassa, on the waterfront in downtown Fort-de-France (② 596/63-79-60), is open Monday

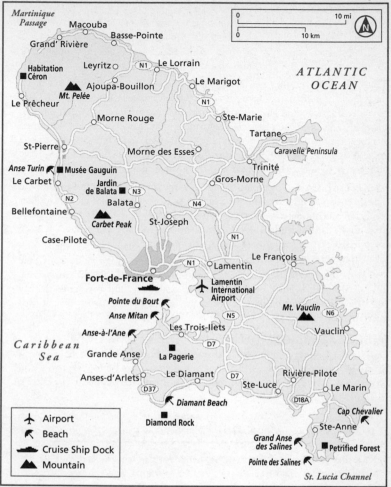

Martinique Passage

Macouba
Basse-Pointe
Grand' Rivière
Habitation Céron
Leyritz N1 Le Lorrain
Ajoupa-Bouillon
Mt. Pelée
Le Prêcheur
Le Marigot
N1
Morne Rouge
Ste-Marie
Tartane
St-Pierre
Morne des Esses
Caravelle Peninsula
Anse Turin
Musée Gauguin
Trinité
Le Carbet
Jardin de Balata N3
Gros-Morne
N2
Balata
Bellefontaine
N4
Carbet Peak
St-Joseph
Case-Pilote
N1
Le François
N1 Lamentin
Fort-de-France
Lamentin International Airport
Pointe du Bout
Mt. Vauclin N6
Anse Mitan
N5
Vauclin
Anse-à-l'Ane
Les Trois-Ilets
Caribbean Sea
Grande Anse
La Pagerie
D7
Anses-d'Arlets
Le Diamant
D7
Rivière-Pilote
D37
Ste-Luce
Le Marin
Diamant Beach
D18A
Cap Chevalier
Diamond Rock
Ste-Anne
Grand Anse des Salines
Petrified Forest
Pointe des Salines
St. Lucia Channel

✈ Airport
📍 Beach
⚓ Cruise Ship Dock
▲ Mountain

ATLANTIC OCEAN

0   10 mi
0   10 km

through Friday 8am to 5pm, and Saturday from 8am to noon. For info before you go, contact the Martinique Promotion Bureau in the U.S. (☏ **410/286-8310**; www.martinique.org).

CALLING FROM THE U.S.   When calling Martinique from the U.S., dial the international access code (011) and 596 before the numbers listed here. The numbers listed here already begin with 596, but an effort by the French telephone authorities to standardize procedures requires that you dial those three digits twice.

If you want to check your e-mail, go to **Cyber Club Caraibes** (☏ **596/71-43-21**), an Internet cafe at 16 rue François Arago 97200 Fort-de-France. The cafe is open Monday from 2pm to 8pm, Tuesday to Saturday from 10am to 10pm and Sundays 2pm to 6pm. It costs $3 for 15 minutes—cheaper than aboard ship.

GETTING AROUND

BY TAXI   Travel by taxi is convenient but expensive. Few cabs are metered, so agree on a price before getting in. Taxis wait for ships at the cruise pier, and several English-speaking drivers give tours of the island for roughly $40 an hour for up to four passengers. For a radio taxi, call © **596/63-63-62.**

BY BUS   For trips beyond Fort-de-France, collective taxi-minibuses are a cheap but iffy alternative. These privately owned minivans (look for the TC sign) generally seat eight and have flexible routes and unpredictable schedules. Often crowded and sometimes less than comfortable, they're widely used by adventurous tourists nonetheless, particularly those who speak some French. The reason? Price: A one-way ride to Grande Anse des Salines beach is about $5. Vans leave from a parking lot at Pointe Simon, in the heart of Fort-de-France.

BY RENTAL CAR   Martinique's size and myriad attractions make renting a car especially worthwhile. You drive on the right on roads that are in excellent condition and almost always scenic. You need a valid driver's license and must be at least 21. **Avis, Budget, Hertz,** and **National** all have offices here.

BY FERRY   To reach La Pagerie (Empress Joséphine's birthplace), the island's golf course, horseback-riding stables, and the resort area of Pointe du Bout, take one of the blue ferries operated by **Somatour** (© **596/73-05-53**) from Quai d'Esnambuc, east of the cruise dock, in Fort-de-France. The trip across the bay takes 15 minutes, and round-trip tickets are $6 per person. Boats leave at least once an hour.

SHORE EXCURSIONS OFFERED BY THE CRUISE LINES

Golf at the Country Club of Martinique ($115, 6 hr.): The 18-hole, par-71 course in Trois Ilets, designed by Robert Trent Jones, is both challenging and picturesque, with 5,976m (6,640 yards) of twisting fairways and fast greens.

 Frommer's Favorite Martinique Experiences

Touring "Pompeii of the Caribbean": Mount Pelée erupted in 1902, killing all but one of St. Pierre's 30,000 residents. See the havoc this not-yet-dormant volcano wreaked on the town's church, theater, and other buildings, and view smaller relics at the volcano museum. (See "On Your Own: Beyond the Port Area," below.)

Traveling back to the 17th Century: The estate ruins at Habitation Céron, near the island's northern Caribbean coast, are enormously evocative of early colonial times, when sugar was king. The old stone plantation buildings are covered with moss, and the wild gardens abound with lush vegetation and singing birds. (See "On Your Own: Beyond the Port Area," below.)

Eavesdropping on Imperial Romance: Empress Joséphine, Napoleon Bonaparte's first wife, was born and reared at La Pagerie, her family's estate near the town of Trois Îlets. Part of the sugar plantation still stands, and the museum displays personal effects of the Martinican empress, including a passionate love letter from the Little Corporal to his Petite Creole. (See "On Your Own: Beyond the Port Area," below.)

Transportation, greens fees (for 18 holes), and a golf cart are included; lunch is not. (See "Sports," later in this section, for more details on the course.)

St. Pierre and Rainforest Drive ($59, 4 hr.): Drive through Martinique's lush rainforest, visit a butterfly farm and botanical park among the ruins of the island's first sugar plantation, and then explore the ruins of St. Pierre, devastated by Mount Pelée's eruption in 1902. On the drive back to Fort-de-France, make a quick stop at the church of Balata, a replica of Paris's Sacred Heart (Sacré Coeur) Basilica.

Martinique Snorkeling ($49, 2½ hr.): Across the bay from Fort-de-France, the reef at Anse Dufour offers excellent snorkeling for experts and novices. The reef is filled with marine animals, including French grunts, blackbar soldierfish, and silversides. Snorkeling equipment is provided, as are professional instruction, supervision, and transportation.

EXCURSIONS OFFERED BY LOCAL AGENCIES

Adventure Excursions & Hiking: Martinique's lush, mountainous northern half provides myriad adventure opportunities. **Aventures Tropicales** (① **596/ 75-24-24**), based in Fort-de-France, is the island's premier adventure tour operator, offering canyoning and river-crossing in a tropical rainforest, kayaking through mangroves to uninhabited islands, hiking up Mount Pelée, and a 4WD tour through rivers, rainforests, and banana plantations. Prices vary depending on activity but generally range from $35 to $45, and some excursions require a minimum number of participants. Make arrangements before arriving on the island.

Horseback Treks: Pros and novices are both accommodated on morning horseback rides offered by **Ranch Jack,** Morne Habitué, Trois Ilets (① **596/68-37-69**). The daily promenades pass over hills, through fields, and onto beaches, as guides provide a running commentary on the history, fauna, and botany of the island. Transportation to and from the cruise dock can be arranged. The price of a half-day excursion with refreshments is about $50.

See "Sports," later in this section, for **scuba and snorkeling.**

ON YOUR OWN: WITHIN WALKING DISTANCE

Fort-de-France is a bustling, cosmopolitan town with 100,000 residents and an unmistakable French air. Part New Orleans, part French Riviera, it's full of ochre buildings, ornate wrought-iron balconies, cascading flowers, and tall palm trees. The town's narrow streets, cluttered with boutiques and cafes, climb from the bowl of the sea to the surrounding hills, forming a great urban amphitheater. There's plenty here to keep you busy.

At the eastern end of downtown, **La Savane** is a broad formal park with palms, mangoes, and manicured lawns, perfect for a promenade or rest in the shade. Its most famous feature is the **Statue of Empress Joséphine,** carved in 1858 by Vital Dubray. Like a variation on the Venus de Milo, this white marble empress is headless: Napoleon's Little Creole was unceremoniously decapitated and doused with red paint in 1995 by locals who remembered her role in reinstating slavery on the island in the early 1800s.

Across the street at 21 rue de la Liberté, the **Bibliothèque Schoelcher** (Schoelcher Library; ① **596/70-26-67**) is one of Fort-de-France's great Belle Epoque buildings. Named in honor of Victor Schoelcher, one of France's most influential abolitionists, this elaborate structure, designed by French architect Henri Pick, was first displayed at the 1889 Paris Exposition. Four years later, the red-and-blue Romanesque portal, Egyptian lotus-petal columns, iron-and-glass cupola, and multicolored tiles were dismantled and then reassembled piece by piece at the present site. The interior light, mosaics, and tile floor are glorious. The proud repository of Schoelcher's 10,000-volume book collection, as well as an impressive archive of colonization, slavery, and emancipation documents, it's open Monday through Saturday. There's no admission charge.

Another Henri Pick masterpiece, **St. Louis Cathedral,** on rue Victor Schoelcher at rue Blénac, was built in 1895. A contemporary of Gustave Eiffel (of Eiffel Tower fame), Pick used massive iron beams to support the walls, ceiling, and spire. A grand example of Industrial Revolution architecture, it's been likened to a Catholic railway station. The organ, stained-glass windows, and ornamented interior walls are well worth a look and can be viewed every morning except Saturday.

Built in 1640, **Fort St. Louis,** Boulevard Alfassa, dominates the rocky promontory east of La Savane. A noteworthy example of 17th- and 18th-century military architecture, it first defended Fort-de-France in 1674 against Dutch invaders; beginning in 1762, it was the site of numerous battles between French and English forces. Today, the bastion remains the French navy's headquarters in the Caribbean. Guided tours leave daily every 30 minutes beginning at 9:30am. Bring a picture ID. The entrance fee, payable in dollars, is $5 for adults, $2.50 for students.

The best of Fort-de-France's many museums, the **Musée Départemental Archéologie Precolombienne Préhistoire,** 9 rue de la Liberté (© 596/71-57-05), traces 2,000 years of Martinique's pre-Columbian past with more than a thousand relics from the Arawak and Carib cultures. Spread over three floors, the detailed exhibits document various pottery and tool styles, burial practices, agricultural methods, social and religious customs, and changes that occurred after the arrival of Europeans. Across the street from La Savane, it's open Monday to Friday from 8am to 5pm, and Saturday from 9am to noon. Admission is about $3 for adults, $2 for students, and 75¢ for children. The tiny gift stand sells pottery reproductions.

A less established museum, the **Musée du Carnaval** (© 596/73-49-07), next to the cruise terminal on rue des Gabares, focuses on the history, costumes, and traditions of Martinique's unique version of Carnival—pajama parades, drag marriages, junkyard jump-ups, and decorated jalopies, to name a few. English-speaking guides help you navigate the tiny museum, which is open Tuesday through Friday from 9am to 4pm, and on Saturday from 9am to noon. Admission is about $3 for adults, $2 for students, and 75¢ for kids under 12.

ON YOUR OWN: BEYOND THE PORT AREA

Martinique is much too large to tackle in a single day. You'll have to make some tough choices about which of its many museums, plantations, floral parks, and natural wonders to visit. Here are three suggested itineraries for the day.

NORTH OF FORT-DE-FRANCE   Less than 8km (5 miles) north of Fort-de-France, on the scenic Route de la Trace (Rte. N3), **L'Eglise Sacré Coeur de Balata** overlooks the capital and its bay. This quiet village church is anything but typical: Built in 1924, it's a one-fifth-scale replica of the wedding-cake-pretty Sacré Coeur Basilica that crowns Montmartre in Paris. Rather than the white stone of the Paris original, this unintentionally whimsical copy uses gray freestone.

Martinique's Carib name, Madiana, means "island of flowers." To see what the Caribs were talking about, stroll through the **Jardin de Balata** (© 596/64-48-73). Just minutes north of the Sacré Coeur church, this lush, Edenic garden showcases 200 species of plants, trees, and tropical flowers, including towering ferns, lotuses, alpinias, porcelain roses, anthuriums, and heliconias. The hillside oasis, which boasts resident hummingbirds, frogs, and lizards, is open daily from 9am to 5pm. Admission is about $6 for adults, $2.50 for kids under 12.

Yes, it's hot outside, but things could be worse. One of Martinique's must-see attractions, the village of **St. Pierre** on the northwest coast, was the cultural and economic capital of Martinique until 8am on May 8, 1902, when Mount Pelée, the hulking volcano that dominates the northern tip of the island, exploded in fire and lava. Three minutes later, all but 1 of St. Pierre's 30,000 inhabitants had been incinerated, buried in ash and lava, or asphyxiated by poisonous gas. The town once hailed as the "Paris of the Antilles" and the "Pearl of the West Indies" because of its beautiful buildings, imposing residences, and lively theaters suddenly became "the Pompeii of the Caribbean." It never regained its splendor, and today it's no more than a sleepy fishing village, home to fewer than 5,000 souls. Ruins of a church, theater, and other buildings punctuate the town, memorials to St. Pierre's former glory and the horrific fury of Pelée. In lieu of walking from one ruin to another, you can hop on the rubber-wheeled trolley known as the **Cyparis Express,** which departs from the Musée Volcanologique (see below). The 50-minute tours operate Monday to Friday from 10:30am to 1pm and from 2:30 to 7pm, departing once an hour, more or less. The fee is about $7 for adults, half that for kids. (The trolley is named in honor of Cyparis, a prisoner locked behind thick cell walls, who was the sole human to survive the eruption. Found in his dungeon 4 days after the disaster, he later toured with P. T. Barnum's circus, showing his burn scars to curious folks around North America.)

The town's touristic potential hasn't been grotesquely exploited: Aside from the ruins, the only other point of interest is the **Musée Volcanologique,** rue Victor Hugo (② **596/78-15-16**). Founded by American vulcanologist Franck A. Perret, this one-room exhibit traces the story of the cataclysm through pictures and relics excavated from the debris, including petrified spaghetti, lava-encrusted teapots, twisted musical instruments, a human skull, and distorted clocks that stopped at the hour of destruction. Open daily from 9am to 5pm, it charges adults about $1.50; children under 8 enter free.

Part sugar-plantation ruins, part tropical paradise, **Habitation Céron** (② **596/52-94-53**) is the most evocative of Martinique's historical agricultural sites. This sprawling 17th-century estate, 15 minutes north of St. Pierre, is almost as wild and tranquil as the surrounding rainforest, but its verdigris cisterns, moss-covered stone buildings, and archaic, still functioning water mill are all haunted with the ghosts of a time when sugar was king, slaves toiled in the heat, and French colonists lived in languid comfort. The site is open daily from 9:30am to 5pm. Self-guided tours of the estate cost $5.50. The on-site restaurant, housed in former slave quarters, serves crayfish, octopus, and other seafood.

A few miles south of St. Pierre, **Le Carbet** is where Columbus landed in 1502, the first French settlers arrived in 1635, and the French painter Paul Gauguin lived for 5 months in 1887. Too ill to return to France after a failed quest for "noble savages" in Panama, the artist wrote that "only in Martinique was I able to feel truly myself." An unassuming museum devoted to Gauguin and his Martinican works, the **Musée Paul Gauguin,** Anse Turin (② **596/78-22-66**), sits not far from the hut the painter once occupied. It boasts no original paintings, but it does have reproductions of the dozen pictures he composed on the island, precursors of his later, more famous Tahitian works. Other items on display include biographical texts and whiny, self-pitying letters he wrote to his wife back in France. Other exhibits include Creole costumes and contemporary island art. The museum has extensive English commentary and is open daily from 9am to 5:30pm. Admission is about $3 for adults, 75¢ for children under 10, and free for those under 8.

SOUTH OF FORT-DE-FRANCE Marie Josèphe Rose Tascher de la Pagerie was born in 1763 in the quaint little village of **Trois Ilets,** across the bay from Fort-de-France. As Joséphine, she became the wife of Napoleon Bonaparte in 1796 and Empress of France in 1804. Although reviled by some historians as ruthless and selfish, she's revered by some on Martinique as having been uncommonly gracious. Others, however, blame her for Napoleon's reintroduction of slavery. A small museum, the **Musée de la Pagerie** (✆ **596/68-33-06**), sits in the former estate kitchen building, where Joséphine gossiped with her slaves. Displays include the bed that she slept in until she departed for France at age 16, portraits of her and of Napoleon, invitations to Parisian balls, bills attesting to her extravagance as the empress, and letters, the most notable being a passionate missive from lovelorn Napoleon. The plantation house itself was destroyed in a hurricane, but the kitchen and partially restored ruins of the sugar mill and church remain (the latter is in the village itself). The museum is open Tuesday through Sunday from 9am to 5:30pm, and an English-speaking guide is usually on hand. Admission is about $3 for adults, 75¢ for children under 16. The nearby **Parc des Floralies** (✆ **596/68-34-50**) displays more than a hundred species of flowers, trees, and greenery, as well as aviaries housing exotic birds. It's open from 8:30am to 5pm Monday through Friday, and from 9:30am to 5:30pm on weekends. Admission is just over $2 for adults, about 85¢ for kids.

Diamond Rock, a craggy multifaceted protrusion in the bay south of Trois Ilets, not only resembles a diamond, but was once the jewel in the crown of the British Caribbean fleet. The British and French fought on so many fronts during the early 19th century that ships were sometimes in short supply. Only one ship was assigned to blockade the ports of Martinique, St. Pierre in the north and Fort-de-France in the south. Short of ships but not imagination, the British proclaimed Diamond Rock a man-of-war and proceeded to equip the islet with guns. No temporary gesture, it remained in service for 2 years. Birds have replaced Brits as the primary residents. On a misty day, the rock looks more like the Loch Ness Monster emerging from the depths than a diamond.

You'll have passed through a number of quaint coastal villages by this time but none sweeter than **Ste. Luce.** Absurdly picturesque with its blindingly white stucco walls, red-tile roofs, turquoise sea, and multicolored fishing boats, this town is pure sun-drenched maritime serenity. Swim or snorkel off the small, pleasant beach, meditate on horizon-dominating Diamond Rock, or check out the village boutiques and cafes. For an unhurried taste of French island life, this is as good a place as any to spend the day.

SHOPPING

Martinique offers a good selection of French luxury items—perfumes, fashionable clothing, luggage, crystal, and dinnerware—at prices that can be as much as 30% to 40% lower than those in the States. Unfortunately, because some luxury goods, including jewelry, are subject to a hefty value-added tax, the savings are ultimately less compelling. Paying in dollar-denominated traveler's checks or credit cards is sometimes good for a 20% discount. The main shopping district in Fort-de-France is bound by rue Ernest Deproge (on the waterfront), La Savane, rue Lamartine, and rue de la République, with rue Victor Hugo being the single most important stretch. Martinican goods, such as rum, Creole jewelry, madras fabric, folk paintings, and hand-woven baskets, are good buys and more representative of the island. The **open-air market** in La Savane, at rue de la Liberté and rue Ernest Deproge, has the best selection of these items. For sheer Caribbean color, stroll through the enclosed **vegetable and fruit market** on rue Isambert near rue Blénac; built in 1901, it's another work of architect Henri Pick. Stores generally open at 9am and close at 5pm; most close for lunch, usually between 1 and 3pm. On Saturdays, shops are open in the morning only; on Sundays virtually all are closed.

Duty-free divas invariably make **Roger Albert,** 7 rue Victor Hugo, their first stop. This well-known outlet frequently has the best buys on French perfume, china, and crystal. **Cadet-Daniel,** 72 rue Antoine Siger, is its chief competitor. Compare and save.

Centre des Métieres d'Art, rue Ernest Deproge, near the tourist office, is one of the best arts-and-crafts stores in Martinique. Pass over the junk and focus on the more accomplished handmade items, including ceramics, painted fabrics, and patchwork quilts.

The French consider libations an art, and aficionados consider Martinican rum among the world's finest. **La Case à Rhum,** in the Galerie Marchande, 5 rue de la Liberté, stocks all the local brands and allows sample nips to help you decide which bottle to buy.

If you find yourself across the bay in Pointe du Bout, stop by **La Belle Matadore,** Immeuble Vermeil Marina (midway between the La Pagerie Hôtel and the Méridien Hotel). This boutique takes the history and tradition of Creole jewelry seriously, and virtually every piece for sale replicates designs developed during slave days by *matadores* (prostitutes), midwives, and slaves.

BEACHES

Serious beach bunnies hop south of Fort-de-France to **Grand Anse des Salines,** widely regarded as Martinique's nicest strand. At the island's extreme southern tip, about an hour from the capital by car, it features coconut palm trees, views of Diamond Rock, and white sand that seems to go on for miles. During summer holidays and weekends, it's busy with families and children, but during the week, it's often quiet and uncrowded. Beachside stands offer refreshment. To get to the island's main **gay beach,** turn right at the entrance to Grand Anse des Salines and drive to the far end of the parking lot, near the sign for Petite Anse des Salines. Follow the path through the woods and then veer left till you find the quiet section with the good-looking guys.

Conveniently located across the bay from Fort-de-France, **Pointe du Bout** is Martinique's most lavish resort area. Aside from a marina and a variety of watersports, the area has some modest man-made, white-sand beaches. The sandy, natural beaches at nearby **Anse Mitan** and **Anses d'Arlet** are popular with both swimmers and snorkelers.

Beaches north of Fort-de-France have mostly gray (they like to call it silver) volcanic sand. The best of the bunch is **Anse Turin,** just to the side of the main Caribbean coastal road, between St. Pierre and Le Carbet. Extremely popular with locals and shaded by palms, it's where Gauguin swam when he called the island home.

Martinique has no legal nudist beaches, but toplessness is as common here as anywhere in France. As a rule, public beaches lack changing cabins or showers, but hotel lockers and changing cabanas can be used by nonguests for a charge.

SPORTS

GOLF When Robert Trent Jones, Sr., designed **Golf de la Martinique** (© 596/68-32-81) in 1976, he chose a picturesque, historic site: the seaside hills neighboring La Pagerie, the birthplace of Empress Joséphine. Thirty-two kilometers (20 miles) from Fort-de-France, this good, tough, 18-hole, 5,976m (6,640-yard), par-71 course features emerald hills, swaying palms, constant vistas of the turquoise sea, and, thankfully, year-round trade winds that help keep things cool. The par-5 12th, with a dogleg to the right, is the most difficult hole. The fairway here is narrow, the green is long, and the wind, especially between December and April, is tricky. The 15th and 16th require shots over sea inlets. Facilities include a pro shop, a golf academy, a bar, a restaurant, and tennis courts. English-speaking pros are at your service. Greens fees and cart rental run about $100 for 18 holes, $70 for 9. A set of clubs is another $17.

SCUBA DIVING & SNORKELING Favorite dives in the coastal waters off Martinique include the caves and walls of Diamond Rock and the dozen ships sunk by the 1902 volcanic eruption at St. Pierre (the most popular wreck, the metal-hulled *Roraima,* was made famous by Jacques Cousteau and rests on a slant in 45m/150 ft. of water). For cruisers, the most convenient dive operators are across the bay from Fort-de-France in Pointe du Bout. **Espace Plongée,** at the Hôtel Méridien (© 596/66-01-79), and **Planète Bleue** (© 596/66-08-79), based at the Pointe du Bout marina, are among the island's best operators. If you want to dive around St. Pierre, try **UCPA** (© 596/78-21-03). Single-tank dives with all equipment run about $40. The waters of Pointe du Bout and nearby Anse Mitan and Anse Dufour are popular with snorkelers, as are the small bays of Sainte Anne and Anses d'Arlet on the southwest coast. Snorkeling equipment from on-site vendors runs about $10.

GREAT LOCAL RESTAURANTS & BARS

Hey, it's France: Expect great food. More than any other island in the French West Indies, Martinique gives French and Creole cuisine equal billing. If you're on a mission to sample the booze of every port of call, Martinique's **local beer** is Lorraine; Clement, De Paz, and Saint James are among the island's best **rums.** Too early in the day for demon rum? Slake your thirst with Didier, the Caribbean's only naturally carbonated spring water.

IN FORT-DE-FRANCE A small, elegant restaurant located in a beautiful 19th-century mansion in the hills above Fort-de-France, **La Belle Epoque,** Route de Didier (© 596/64-41-19), serves exquisite classic French cuisine. The fixed-price lunch special, which includes an appetizer, a main course, and dessert, is a steal, costing about $25. Enhanced by the languid, colonial atmosphere, the seafood ravioli in wine and lobster sauce and rum shrimp flambé are memorable. **Le Planteur,** 1 rue de la Liberté, across the street from La Savane in the heart of town (© 596/63-17-45), offers views of the park and bay. Try the flavorful cassoulet of minced conch or the seafood stew in cream sauce.

AT POINTE DU BOUT Just minutes by car from the resorts of Pointe du Bout, **La Villa Créole,** Anse Mitan (© 596/66-05-53), serves down-home Creole staples such as *accras de morue* (codfish beignets), *boudin Créole* (Creole blood sausage), and *féroces* (avocado, codfish, and manioc hushpuppies). Don't leave your garden table without indulging in the chocolate fondant with bittersweet chocolate and pear sauce. The nearby **Au Poisson d'Or,** Anse Mitan (© 596/66-01-80), a rustic roadside eatery, offers more Creole choices such as grilled conch in coconut milk and stewed shrimp.

NEAR ST. PIERRE   Fifteen minutes north of St. Pierre, **Habitation Céron,** Anse Céron, Le Prêcheur (© **596/52-94-53**), a 17th-century sugar estate, offers Creole crayfish freshly harvested from the on-site farm. Fish, octopus, and vegetables straight from the garden are also served at the open-air, riverside tables. Lunch, $20.

19 Nevis

Off the beaten tourist track, south of St. Martin and north of Guadeloupe, Nevis is the junior partner in the combined Federation of St. Kitts and Nevis, which gained self-government from Britain in 1967 and became a totally independent nation in 1983. It's a stormy marriage, though: Nevis's 1998 referendum for separation from its larger partner failed by the slimmest of margins.

Though smaller than St. Kitts and lacking a major historical site like Brimstone Hill Fortress, Nevis is nevertheless the more appealing and upbeat of the two islands. When viewed from its sister island, about 3.2km (2 miles) away, Nevis appears to be a perfect cone, rising gradually to a height of 970m (3,232 ft.). Columbus first sighted the island in 1493, naming it Las Nieves, Spanish for "snows," because its peak reminded him of the Pyrenees. Settled by the British in 1628, the island became a prosperous sugar-growing island as well as the most popular spa island of the 18th century, when people flocked in from other West Indian islands to visit its hot mineral springs. Nevis's two most famous historical residents were **Admiral Horatio Nelson,** who married a local woman here in 1787, and **Alexander Hamilton,** who was born here and went on to find fame as a drafter of the American Federalist Papers, as George Washington's treasury secretary, and as Aaron Burr's unfortunate dueling partner. Today, the island's capital city, **Charlestown,** has a lovely mixture of port-town exuberance and small-town charm, and the popular **Pinney's Beach** is just a knockout.

COMING ASHORE   Only small ships call on Nevis, docking right in the center of Charlestown and/or dropping anchor off the coast of Pinney's Beach.

LANGUAGE   **English** is the language of both islands.

CURRENCY   The local currency is the **Eastern Caribbean dollar** (US$1 = EC$2.70; EC$1 = US37¢). Many shops and restaurants quote prices in U.S. dollars. Always determine which currency locals are talking about. We've used U.S.-dollar prices in this section.

INFORMATION   Nevis recently opened a **tourism authority office** in the historic Treasury Building on Main Street near the docks (© **869/469-7550;** www.nevisisland.com). For information before you go, call 866/55NEVIS.

CALLING FROM THE U.S.   When calling St. Kitts or Nevis from the United States, you need dial only a "1" before the numbers listed here.

GETTING AROUND

BY TAXI   The entirety of Charlestown is accessible on foot, but if you want to visit Pinney's Beach or elsewhere on the island, you can hop a taxi in Charlestown. The cost to Pinney's is about $5.50. Taxi drivers double as guides on Nevis, so if you want to take a general tour of the island, negotiate a price with your driver.

BY RENTAL CAR   Because driving is on the left side in Nevis and most of the worthwhile sites are within walking distance or easily reached by taxi, we don't recommend renting a car here.

SHORE EXCURSIONS OFFERED BY THE CRUISE LINES

Few organized excursions are offered on Nevis. Some of the small-ship lines offer a day at Pinney's Beach as part of their regular visit, and might also offer hiking and snorkeling options, but the island is so small and easy to negotiate on your own that excursions aren't really necessary. If you want some local commentary, you can hire a taxi driver to give you an island tour. (See "Getting Around," above.)

ON YOUR OWN: WITHIN WALKING DISTANCE

If your ship docks in Charlestown, you're dead center of a perfect walking-tour opportunity. Charlestown is a lovely little place, laid back in somewhat the same manner as St. John, but with some of the really rural character of sister island St. Kitts.

If you head left from the docks and walk a little ways (maybe .4km/¼-mile) along Main Street, you'll come to the **Alexander Hamilton Birthplace (② 869/ 469-5786;** www.nevis-nhcs.org/nevishistory.html), where the road curves just before the turnoff to Island Road. It's a rustic little two-level house set right on the coastline. On the first floor is the **Museum of Nevis History** and gift shop (admission $2, $1 children under 12), but in all honesty you'll do just as well to skip it and just appreciate the outside, taking a moment to read the historic plaque. Far be it from us to take a couple bucks out of the island's economy, though, so if you're feeling philanthropic, drop your two bucks and then head on for the rest of your walk.

Backtracking along Main Street, you'll pass several serviceable if unremarkable shops (see "Shopping," below). Keep walking through the center of town, saying "hi" to the occasional mama goat and kids you'll pass, and then turn left onto Government Road. One block up on the left, you'll find the **Jews' Burial Ground,** with graves from 1684 to 1768. Stones left atop the graves attest to the visitors who have been there before you to pay their respects. When we were there, the dead were being entertained with reggae music coming from the doorway of a shop across the street, while a breeze stirred the few trees on the property. All in all, not a bad resting spot.

Backtrack to Main Street, turn left, and continue on past the Grove Park Cricket Ground, bearing left when the road forks. Head up the hill (where you'll see first an abandoned hotel and then several buildings standing alone on the hill to your right), and then turn at the first right, which will bring you back behind

---

② Frommer's Favorite Nevis Experiences

Wandering Around Charlestown: The capital city is a fine place to wander around on your own, visiting the birthplace of American statesman Alexander Hamilton, the small but appealing Nelson Museum, and the 17th-century Jewish cemetery; poking your head into some of the small shops; or greeting the goats and chickens that wander past, evidently taking their own walking tours. (See "On Your Own: Within Walking Distance," above.)

Taking Some Downtime on Pinney's Beach: Lounge back, have a beer, take a swim in the reef-protected waters, do a little snorkeling, or engage in some beachcombing. Talk about relaxation. (See "Beaches," above.)

those buildings, the first of which is the inaccessible Government House and the second of which is the **Nelson Museum** (© 869/469-0408; www.nevis-nhcs. org/nelsonmuseum.html). A very small, very homemade kind of place, it's nevertheless an interesting and evocative spot, and well worth the $2 admission ($1 for children 12 and under). The museum traces the history of Admiral Horatio Nelson's career enforcing England's Navigation Acts in the Caribbean, and also houses artifacts from Nevis's Carib, Arawak, and Aceramic peoples; a small display on Nevis today; and a number of wonderful clay artworks, including a replica of the old "Coolie Man's Store," by local artist Gustage "Bush Tea" Williams. The timeline of Nelson's Caribbean career includes ship models, ceramic and bronze Nelson figures, paintings of his battles and other scenes, a scrap from the Union Jack under which the admiral was standing when he was shot, a miniature of his casket, and an actual ticket to his funeral, with wax seal. A tiny birdcage with wood enclosing box bears the inscription "In a number of letters written to Fanny Nisbet [Nelson's wife], Nelson mentioned his search for a traveling birdcage. This bird cage, though not the one Nelson finally procured, is from that period." Museum hours are 8am to 4pm Monday through Friday, Saturday 9am to noon.

Once back outside, amble slowly off in the same direction you were going (right from the gate). Keep bearing right and you'll eventually be back on Main

Street, in plenty of time to do a little shopping or stop into one of the local bars or restaurants.

ON YOUR OWN: BEYOND THE PORT AREA

The 3.2-hectare (8-acre) **Botanical Garden of Nevis** (© 869/469-3509) is located 4.8km (3 miles) south of Charlestown on the Montpelier Estate. There are several gardens, including a tropical rainforest conservatory, a rose and vine garden, a cactus garden, a tropical fruit garden, and an orchid garden. Fountains, ponds, and re-creations of Mayan sculptures dot the grounds, which are open Monday through Saturday 10am to 4pm. Admission is $9 adults, $4 children. There's a restaurant and gift shop on-site.

SHOPPING

Nevis is not a shopping hub on the order of St. Thomas or even the much more laid-back St. John. In fact, it's no kind of shopping hub at all. Still, there are a few shops worth poking your head into, all of them along Main Street, right in the port area.

Island Hopper, on Main, 1 block north of Prince Charles Street (© 869/ 469-0893), is the best shop in town for visitors, stocking a huge selection of batik clothing. **Pemberton Gift Shop,** across Main Street from Island Hopper (© 869/469-5668), is also sparse, but has a selection of T-shirts, gift items, and a shelf of CSR (Cane Spirit Rothschild), the local cane sugar liquor. **Jerveren's Fashions,** in the Cotton Ginnery complex right at the pier (© 869/469-0062), has a decent selection of T-shirts and gifts.

For stamp collectors, the **Nevis Philatelic Bureau** at the Head Post Office, on Market Street next to the public market, 1 block south and 1 block east of the docks (© 869/469-5535), has a range of Nevis stamps.

BEACHES

The name to know on Nevis is **Pinney's Beach,** located north of Charlestown. A lovely spot for swimming, snorkeling, beachcombing, or just sitting back and watching the pelicans divebomb into the surf, it's home to the Four Seasons resort, reopened in late 2000 after being obliterated by 1999's Hurricane Lenny. As a counterpoint to conspicuous luxury, the rickety **Sunshine's Bar and Grill** (© 869/469-5817), "Home of the Killer Bee," sits right on the beach, offering beer and other refreshments along with the aforementioned Bee, a "killer" drink.

GREAT LOCAL RESTAURANTS & BARS

A nice place to eat in Charleston is **Eddy's Bar & Restaurant,** on Main Street (© 869/469-5958), which sits on an upper floor and offers good sandwiches, steaks, and seafood, as well as a nice balcony's-eye view of the slowly bustling town below.

20 Panama

The Panama Canal is an awesome feat of engineering and human effort. Construction began in 1880 and wasn't completed until 1914, at the expense of thousands of lives, and the vast majority of the original structure and equipment is still in use. Transiting the canal, which links the Atlantic Ocean with the Pacific, is a thrill for anyone even vaguely interested in engineering or history.

Passing through the canal takes about 8 hours from start to finish, and is a fascinating procedure—the route is about 81km (50 miles) long and includes passage through three main locks, which, through gravity alone, raise ships over

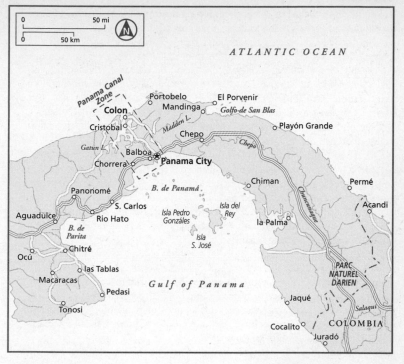

Central America and down again on the other side. Between the locks, ships pass through artificially created lakes such as the massive Gatun Lake, 26m (85 ft.) above sea level. It often costs ships about $100,000 to pass through, with fees based on each ship's weight. Your ship will line up in the morning, mostly with cargo ships, to await its turn through the canal. While transiting, there will be a running narration of history and facts about the canal by an expert who's brought on board for the day.

Cruises that include a canal crossing are generally 10 to 14 nights long, with popular routes between Florida and Acapulco, visiting a handful of Caribbean and Mexican ports and a few ports in Central America along the way, including Panama's San Blas Islands, Costa Rica's Puerto Caldera, and Guatemala's Puerto Quetzal.

COLON

In compliance with a treaty signed between the United States and Panama in 1977, canal operations passed from U.S. to Panamanian hands at the stroke of midnight on December 31, 1999. Not only did the transition go smoothly, but the canal changeover spurred government agencies and private developers in Panama to expand the canal zone's tourism infrastructure—not simply trying to attract as many ships as possible, but developing new attractions at the canal's Atlantic entrance to lure cruise passengers off their ships and into Panama's interior on shore excursions and for pre- and post-cruise stays. Even ships not transiting the canal are being wooed, with a long-term goal of making the city of Colón a home port for cruise ships sailing to the southern Caribbean.

The linchpin project in the new canal-area developments is **Colón 2000,** a $45-million private port development that opened in October 2000 in Colón, near the canal's Caribbean entrance, and that is capable of handling any size cruise vessel—even the 100,000-ton-plus ships that are too large to pass through the canal. Colón 2000's developer, Corporacion de Costas Tropicales, has created a tour company, **Adventuras 2000 (www.colon2000.com),** which offers a series of shore excursions highlighting Panama's history, culture, and diverse natural attractions (see "Shore Excursions Offered by the Cruise Lines," below). The project has opened many new jobs to locals, who are being trained as bilingual tour guides, drivers, and so on.

Colón 2000's glass-and-marble terminal building has a large lounge, an Internet cafe, a huge duty-free shopping mall (part of the Colón Free Zone, the 2nd largest tax-free zone in the world), restaurants, and craft shops. The entire complex is surrounded by landscaped parkland and is adjacent to a Radisson hotel that's scheduled to open in late 2003. Unfortunately, the town surrounding the splashy new development remains depressed. So there's no question passengers calling here should book an organized tour.

Princess, Holland America, and Royal Caribbean were some of the first lines to include Colón 2000 as a port of call on some Panama Canal itineraries. It doesn't hurt that they're getting incentives by the Panamanian government: Panama has hedged its bets by establishing a 5-year program that pays cruise ships $2.50 to $12 per passenger for calls at any Panamanian port. The incentives grow as the passenger count rises, and additional incentives are offered to lines that register their ships in Panama.

Another new development in Colón, the Cristobal Cruise Terminal (Pier 6), offers piers for two ships of any size and has a duty-free shopping area, restaurants, and telephones. A rail line here, connecting Colón and the capital of Panama City, is in the planning stages.

SHORE EXCURSIONS OFFERED BY THE CRUISE LINES

The following excursions represent a sampling of those offered from Colón:

Emberá Indian Village Tour ($87, 3½ hr.): Today, Panama's Emberá Indians live much as they did in the early 16th century, when their first tourist—Vasco Nunez de Balboa, who "discovered" the Pacific Ocean—came through. You'll travel by dugout canoe up the Chagres River, visit the Emberá village, witness a performance of traditional dance, and (surprise, surprise) have an opportunity to purchase handicrafts.

Fort San Lorenzo & Gutun Locks ($65, 4½–6 hr.): Visit the late-16th-century Fort San Lorenzo, built at the entrance to the Chagres River to protect the riches Spain was busily pillaging from the area. The tour also visits the Gutun Locks, where you'll learn about the history of the Canal.

Kayaking the Canal ($75, 3¾ hr.): From Colón, you'll travel to Sol Melina, where you'll spend about 1 hour kayaking amid the plant life, mammals, and birds, then head by bus to the Gutun Locks for a look at the Canal's workings.

Panama City Tour ($75, 4½–6 hr.): Visit the ruins of Old Panama, founded in 1519 by Pedro Arias Davila and destroyed in 1671 by the pirate Sir Henry Morgan; head to colonial Panama, built to replace the original capital; and then visit the Miraflores Locks for a look at the Canal.

The Pirates Trail ($43, 4 hr.): Founded in 1597, Portobelo was a trading town through which passed the gold from Pizarro's plunder of Peru, which made it a frequent target of British pirates, including William Parker, Sir Henry Morgan, and Edward Vernon. On this tour, you'll visit Fort San Geronimo, Fort San Felipe, the Customs House, and the Black Christ Church; learn about the area's history; and then get a view of the Canal from the Gutun Locks.

PORTS ALONG THE CANAL ROUTE

The **San Blas Islands** are a beautiful archipelago and home to the Kuna Indians, whose women are well known for their colorful, hand-embroidered stitching. If you get a chance to go ashore, the tiny women, dressed in their traditional *molas* (bright, intricately appliquéd blouses), sell all manner of this textile art in square blocks and strips, all of which are known as molas and make great pillow covers or wall hangings. They cost about $5 to $10 each, but don't try to bargain too much—these gals will only go so low before standing firm. When your ship anchors offshore at the islands, be prepared for throngs of Kunas to emerge from the far-off distance, paddling (or, in a few cases, motoring) their dugout canoes up to the ship, where they will spend the entire day calling for money or anything else ship passengers toss overboard. The Kuna seem to enjoy diving overboard to retrieve coins thrown to them, but, of course, it's a sad sight, too, watching entire families so needy. Makes you feel damn guilty for rolling in on that fancy cruise ship of yours.

In Costa Rica, many ships call at **Puerto Caldera** on the Pacific side or **Puerto Limón** on the Atlantic side. While there's nothing to see from either cargo port, both are great jumping-off points for tours that all visiting ships offer of the country's lush, beautiful rainforests, which are alive with some 850 species of birds, 200 species of mammals, 9,000 species of flowering plants, and about 35,000 species of insects. After a scenic bus ride, tours will take you on a nature walk through the forest.

In Guatemala, most Panama Canal–bound ships call at **Puerto Quetzal,** on the Pacific coast; a few may call at **Santo Tomas** on the Caribbean side. Both are used as gateways to Guatemala's spectacular Mayan ruins at Tikal. They're the country's most famous attractions and are considered the most spectacular yet discovered, with more than 3,000 temples, pyramids, and other buildings of the ancient civilization—some of them dating as far back as A.D. 300—nestled in a thick, surreal jungle setting. Excursions here are neither cheap nor easy—a 10-hour tour involves buses, walking, and a 1-hour flight, and costs about $500—but the journey is well worth the effort. Excursions to the less-spectacular Mayan sites in Honduras are also offered from Puerto Quetzal, as are several overland tours of Guatemala's interior.

21 Puerto Rico

San Juan, the capital of Puerto Rico, has the busiest ocean terminal in the West Indies and is one of the cruise trade's most important ports. While cruise groups, by their sheer size, can overwhelm many ports of call, San Juan absorbs cruise passengers with ease. The San Juan metropolitan area, home to about a third of Puerto Rico's four million people, is one of the largest and most sophisticated urban centers in the Caribbean, offering all the amenities of a modern major city: great shopping, interesting neighborhoods, beautiful people, excellent restaurants, glamorous bars and nightclubs, and fine museums. It also offers some of the drawbacks: traffic, crowded sidewalks, and, in some areas, crime (avoid the La Perla neighborhood, along the north-central edge of Old San Juan).

Frommer's Favorite San Juan Experiences

Strolling Through Historic Old San Juan: Meander through block after block of narrow cobblestone streets lined with centuries-old Spanish colonial architecture. (See "Shore Excursions Offered by the Cruise Lines" and "Walking Tour: Old San Juan," both below.)

Hiking Through El Yunque National Forest: One of Puerto Rico's most popular attractions, El Yunque covers 28,000 acres and receives up to 200 inches of rain per year. There are 240 different tropical trees, more than 50 orchid species, 150 varieties of ferns, 68 types of birds, and millions of tiny *coquí* tree frogs. You can hike, picnic, and swim in mountain streams. (See "Shore Excursions Offered by the Cruise Lines," below.)

Founded in 1521 by Spanish conquistador **Juan Ponce de León,** the city is one of the oldest in the New World. The cobblestone streets of the hilly old section of the city (**Old San Juan,** the ancient walled city on San Juan Island) are lined with brightly painted colonial town houses, ancient churches, intimate parks, and sun-drenched plazas. Like the pyramids of Egypt and the Great Wall of China, Old San Juan's Spanish colonial forts and city walls are United Nations World Heritage Sites. Another attraction is the people: Puerto Ricans are warm, quick to laugh, and proud of their multicultural heritage, a distinct blend of Amerindian, Spanish, African, and American influences that is present in the culture of the island, from salsa music to Puerto Rican cuisine.

San Juan's shopping ranks among the Caribbean's best, and the city's historic sites, beaches, gambling, and other diversions make it, overall, the number-one port of call in the region. You'll find some of the Caribbean's best restaurants here, as well as sprawling beaches with high-rise luxury hotels reminiscent of those in Miami.

Old San Juan is the prime tourist haunt, but there's much more to the metropolitan area. Other interesting neighborhoods include **Santurce,** linked with San Juan Island by a causeway; **Condado,** a strip of beachfront hotels, restaurants, casinos, and nightclubs on a peninsula stretching from San Juan Island to Santurce; **Hato Rey,** the business center; **Río Piedras,** site of the University of Puerto Rico; and **Bayamón,** an industrial and residential quarter. **Isla Verde,** another resort zone, is connected to the rest of San Juan by an isthmus.

Puerto Rico has been inhabited since about 3000 B.C., when the earliest people arrived from Florida or Central America. In 1493, Christopher Columbus landed on the island, and within 50 years, the native population had been decimated by forced labor, malnutrition, Western diseases, and warfare with the Spanish.

Puerto Rico remained part of Spain's empire for 4 centuries. Spanish rule ended in 1898, when the island was ceded to the United States in the wake of the Spanish-American War. In 1917, Puerto Ricans became U.S. citizens, and in 1952, the island became a semiautonomous commonwealth of the United States. In the last referendum on statehood, in 1998, slightly more Puerto Ricans voted for maintaining the status quo than for joining the union; a small fraction favored independence.

COMING ASHORE Cruise ships dock on the historic Old San Juan peninsula, a short walk from the Plaza de la Marina, Old San Juan's main bus station,

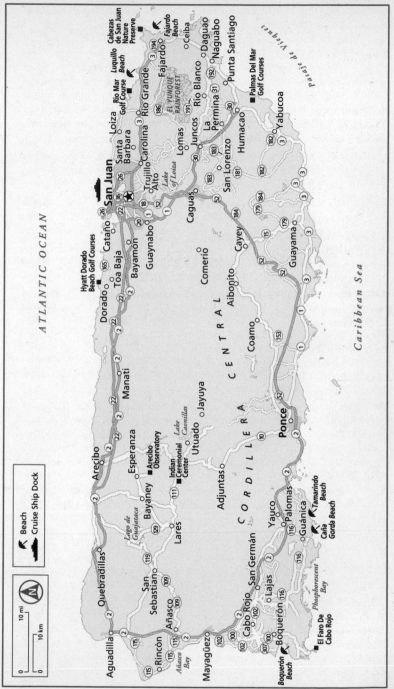

Puerto Rico

and most of the Old Town's historic treasures. A small **tourist information center** is located next to credit-card phones on Plaza de la Marina, just in front of Pier 1; the information center is open 9am to 5:30pm Thursday and Friday, 9am to 8pm Saturday through Wednesday.

During periods of heavy volume—Saturday and Sunday in midwinter, when as many as eight cruise ships dock on the same day—additional, less convenient piers are used. You'll need motorized transit (a taxi or a van supplied by the cruise line as part of the shore-excursion program) to get to the Old Town from these docks. For information about the port, contact the **Port of San Juan,** P.O. 362829, San Juan, PR 00936-2829 (© **787/723-2260**).

LANGUAGE   **Spanish** is the native tongue, but most people in the tourism industry also speak **English.** The farther you venture from San Juan, the more likely it is you'll have to practice your Spanish.

CURRENCY   Puerto Rico is part of the United States, so the **U.S. dollar** is the coin of the realm. Canadian currency is accepted, albeit reluctantly, by some of San Juan's bigger hotels. Credit cards and traveler's checks are widely accepted.

INFORMATION   For advice and maps, drop by the **Tourist Information Center** at La Casita, near Pier 1 (© **787/721-2400**). For info before you go, contact the Puerto Rico Tourism Company (© **800/223-6530;** www.prtourism.com).

CALLING FROM THE U.S.   Calling Puerto Rico from the continental United States is as simple as dialing between U.S. states: Just dial "1" before the numbers listed here.

GETTING AROUND

Driving in congested San Juan is frustrating, and parking in some areas is impossible. You're better off walking around the Old Town. Take buses or taxis to Condado, Ocean Park, and Isla Verde.

BY TAXI   Taxis operated by the **Public Service Commission (PSC)** are metered in San Juan, but the fare structure between major tourism zones is standardized. The set rates from the cruise ship piers are $6 to Old San Juan, $10 to Condado, and $16 to Isla Verde. You can also hire a taxi for an hour for $20. If a meter's used, the initial charge is $1, plus 10¢ for each additional one-thirteenth of a mile and 50¢ for each suitcase. The minimum fare is $3. After 10pm, there's a night charge (add $1 to the meter reading). For phone numbers of taxi companies, look in the Yellow Pages or call the PSC (© **787/756-1919**).

BY TROLLEY   When you tire of walking around Old San Juan, board one of the free trolleys. They depart from Plaza de la Marina and Piers 2 and 4, but you can hop on anywhere along the route.

BY BUS   The Metropolitan Bus Authority operates extensive bus service in the greater San Juan area. Bus stops are marked by signs that read PARADA, and terminals are in front of Pier No. 4. For route and schedule information, call © **787/250-6064.**

BY RENTAL CAR   Puerto Rico has expressways and thousands of miles of other paved roads, so travel by car is pretty effortless, except in metropolitan San Juan, where traffic can be heavy and nightmarish—the 500-year-old streets in the old town just weren't built with cars in mind. Driving is on the right side of the road, and all other U.S. rules apply. Signs are in Spanish, though, and the metric system is used for distance markers (kilometers rather than miles) and at

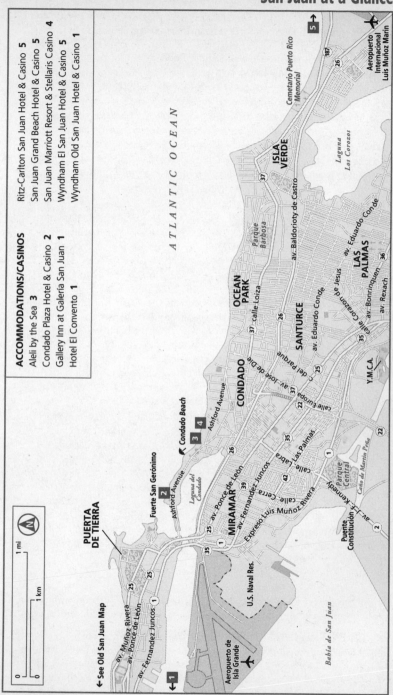

ACCOMMODATIONS/CASINOS

Aleli by the Sea **3**
Condado Plaza Hotel & Casino **2**
Gallery Inn at Galería San Juan **1**
Hotel El Convento **1**

Ritz-Carlton San Juan Hotel & Casino **5**
San Juan Grand Beach Hotel & Casino **5**
San Juan Marriott Resort & Stellaris Casino **4**
Wyndham El San Juan Hotel & Casino **5**
Wyndham Old San Juan Hotel & Casino **1**

ATLANTIC OCEAN

← See Old San Juan Map

PUERTA DE TIERRA

Fuerte San Gerónimo

av. Muñoz Rivera
av. Ponce de León
av. Fernández Juncos

U.S. Naval Res.

Aeropuerto de Isla Grande

Bahía de San Juan

MIRAMAR

av. Ponce de León
Expreso Luis Muñoz Rivera
av. Fernández Juncos

Ashford Avenue
Laguna del Condado

← Condado Beach

CONDADO

Ashford Avenue

av. José de Diego
calle Europa

calle Las Palmas
calle Cerra
calle Labra

Puente Constitución

Parque Central

av. J.F. Kennedy

Caño de Martín Peña

SANTURCE

OCEAN PARK

Parque del parque

av. Eduardo Conde
calle Loíza

av. Baldorioty de Castro
Parque Barbosa

Y.M.C.A.

LAS PALMAS

av. Eduardo Conde
Corazón de Jesús
av. Borinquen
av. Rexach

ISLA VERDE

Cementerio Puerto Rico Memorial

Laguna Los Corozos

Aeropuerto Internacional Luis Muñoz Marín

San Juan as a Port of Embarkation

Puerto Rico is the number-one port of embarkation in the Caribbean, with more than 1.2 million visitors embarking on 700 cruises every year from here. Most cruise lines have packages that include hotel rooms on the island.

GETTING TO SAN JUAN & THE PORT   **Luis Muñoz Marín International Airport** (© 787/791-1014) is on the city's east side, about 7½ miles from the port. Taxi fares from the airport are fixed at $8 to Isla Verde, $12 to Condado and Ocean Park, and $16 to Old San Juan and the cruise ships. The ride to the port takes at least 30 minutes—longer if traffic is heavy, and it often is.

ACCOMMODATIONS

IN OLD SAN JUAN   The quietly elegant **Hotel El Convento,** 100 Calle del Cristo (© 800/468-2779 or 787/723-9020; www.elconvento.com), is Puerto Rico's most famous lodging. A former Carmelite convent, it offers large rooms, many with views of the Old Town. Rates: $325 to $385 winter; $160 to $250 summer. **Wyndham Old San Juan Hotel & Casino,** 100 Brumbaugh St. (© 800/996-3426 or 787/721-5100; www.wyndham.com), is on the waterfront across the street from the cruise ship docks. Rooms are comfortable, and Old San Juan is a step away. Rates: $255 to $295. On Old San Juan's highest hill, with a sweeping view of the sea, **Gallery Inn at Galería San Juan,** 204–206 Calle Norzagaray (© 787/722-1808; www.thegalleryinn.com), was the home of a Spanish aristocrat in the 1700s. Many of the rooms open to patios, fountains, and gardens. Art is everywhere, contributing to the hotel's cultured, contemplative, bohemian ambience. Rates: $145 to $350.

IN CONDADO   The original high-rise, high-glamour section of modern San Juan, Condado boasts numerous hotels, restaurants, and nightclubs. Among its best hotels are the **Condado Plaza Hotel & Casino,** 999 Ashford Ave. (© 800/468-8588 or 787/721-1000; rates: $230–$395), and the **San Juan Marriott Resort & Stellaris Casino,** 1309 Ashford Ave. (© 800/981-8546 or 787/722-7000; www.marriott.com/marriott/SJUPR; rates: $185–$240). **Alelí by the Sea,** 1125 Sea View St., a block off Ashford Avenue (© 787/725-5313), is a small, charming option on the beach. Rooms are basic but clean; the big draws are the sound of the surf just outside your window and the rates—about $55 to $100.

gas stations (liters instead of gallons); confusingly enough, speed limits are posted in miles per hour. **Avis, Budget, Dollar,** and **Hertz** all have offices here.

SHORE EXCURSIONS OFFERED BY THE CRUISE LINES

Don't bother with organized shore excursions if it's Old San Juan you want to see—it's easy enough to get around on your own. On the other hand, if you prefer a guide or want to explore somewhere farther afield, an organized tour may be a good idea.

Old San Juan Walking Tour ($33, 2½ hr.): Visit El Morro, the most dramatic of the city's military fortifications, as well as other historic sites including Casa

Motels in Condado include the **Comfort Inn,** 1 Mariano Ramirez Bages, off Ashford Avenue at Joffre Street, Condado (📞 **787/724-4160;** www.choicecaribbean.com), and **San Juan Days Inn-Condado Lagoon Hotel,** 6 Clemenceau St., Ashford Avenue to Mariano Ramirez Street, then 2 blocks (📞 **787/721-0170;** www.the.daysinn.com/sanjuan08830).

IN ISLA VERDE   Similar to Condado in atmosphere and abundance of hotels, but more recently developed, Isla Verde has a number of dazzlingly deluxe resort complexes, including the **Wyndham El San Juan Hotel & Casino,** 6063 Isla Verde Ave. (📞 **800/468-2818,** or 787/791-1000; www.wyndham.com; rates: $195–$385), and the **Ritz-Carlton San Juan Hotel & Casino,** 6961 Rte. 187 (📞 **800/241-3333** or 787/253-1700; www.ritzcarlton.com; rates: $259–$469). At the other end of the spectrum, motels include the **Howard Johnson Carolina,** 4820 Isla Verde Ave. (📞 **787/728-1300;** www.hojo.com).

SAN JUAN AFTER DARK

The San Juan club scene is hot. In general, people get pretty dressed up, so forget about T-shirts or shorts. **Babylon,** in the Wyndham El San Juan Hotel & Casino, 6063 Isla Verde Ave. (📞 **787/791-1000**), attracts a rich and beautiful crowd, as well as hundreds of wannabes. On weekends, you may wait 2 hours to get in. For dance action in the Old Town, head for **Club Lazer,** 251 Calle del Cruz (📞 **787/725-7581**), where you can dance the night away to the sounds of salsa and merengue. In Condado, **Club Millennium,** in the Condado Plaza Hotel, 999 Ashford Ave. (📞 **787/722-1900**), draws disco devotees and features a cigar bar on the side. San Juan's exuberant gay scene is easily the Caribbean's best, and no club in town surpasses the energy of **Eros,** 1257 Avenida Ponce de León, in Santurce (📞 **787/722-1131**). Also in Santurce, you'll find the enduringly popular lesbian bar, **Cups,** 1708 Calle San Mateo (📞 **787/268-3570**).

For a mellow experience and a sophisticated atmosphere, try **Carli Café Concierto,** in old San Juan on Plazoleta Rafael Carríon (📞 **787/725-4927**), a bistro offering live piano and jazz music. **Palm Court** in the Wyndham El San Juan Hotel & Casino, 6063 Isla Verde Ave. (📞 **787/791-1000**), has a giant chandelier and an intricate, wood-paneled ceiling, and is probably the island's most glamorous meeting place.

Blanca, the Ballajá Barracks, San José Church, and San Juan Cathedral. The tour ends at Capilla del Cristo, near the Old Town's main shopping area.

El Yunque Rainforest ($30, 4–5 hr.): Get acquainted with one of Puerto Rico's premier natural wonders. After arriving at Baño Grande, a natural swimming hole, hike half an hour along the Camimitillo trail and see parrot nests, giant ferns, orchids, and palms. Listen for the song of Puerto Rico's national symbol, the tiny coquí tree frog. After a short stop at an interpretive station, proceed to Yohaku observation tower and Coca waterfall.

Tropical Horseback Riding ($82, 3½ hr.): Meet your horse, briefly learn the ropes, and then ride down a beautiful beach. Take a quick swim during the refreshment stop.

Bioluminescence Bay Kayak Tour ($77, 4½ hr.): Ride to Las Cabezas de San Juan Natural Reserve, at Puerto Rico's northeasternmost point. Under the light of the stars, paddle down mangrove-lined channels and watch the water glow as billions of single-celled organisms light up as they sense the movement of your boat.

Bacardi Rum Distillery Tour ($19, 2 hr.): Learn about the Puerto Rican sugar and rum industries. Watch giant fermenting tanks transform sugar cane into rum, and then follow the liquor from vat to barrel to bottle. Taste the finished product.

EXCURSIONS OFFERED BY LOCAL AGENCIES

If you're staying in a hotel before or after your cruise, book tours at the tour desk. Otherwise try **Rico Suntours,** 176 Calle San Jorge, San Juan (© **787/ 722-2080**), or **Castillo Tours & Travel Services,** 2413 Calle Laurel, Punta La Marias, Santurce (© **787/791-6195** or 787/726-5752). For serious adventure, rock climbing, rappelling, cave exploring, or canyoneering, your best bet is **Aventuras Tierra Adentro,** 268-A Avenida Piñero, Río Piedras (© **787/766-0470**).

WALKING TOUR   **OLD SAN JUAN**

The streets are narrow and teeming with traffic, but strolling through Old San Juan is like walking through 5 centuries of history. More than 400 Spanish colonial buildings from the 16th and 17th centuries, many featuring intricate wrought-iron balconies with lush hanging plants, have been lovingly restored here. The streets' blue paving stones were used originally as ballast by ships crossing the ocean from Spain. Although Old San Juan is a National Historic Zone, it's as vibrant today as it ever has been. Block after block, you'll find shops, cafes, museums, plazas, people, and pigeons. The crowds thin out by late afternoon, so linger around to experience Old San Juan's more sedate charms.

Begin your adventure near the post office, amid the taxis, buses, and urban hubbub of:

❶ Plaza de la Marina

The Plaza is a small park that overlooks San Juan Bay, which was one of the New World's most important harbors for trading and for military protection. Walking west from the plaza, you'll come to San Juan's showcase promenade, El Paseo de la Princesa. This renovated 19th-century walkway traces the ancient city walls past heroic statues, gurgling fountains, and landscaped gardens.

Proceed along the Paseo to:

❷ La Princesa

This gray-and-white building on the right served as one of the Caribbean's most notorious prisons for centuries.

Today it houses contemporary Puerto Rican art exhibits and the offices of the Puerto Rico Tourism Company.

Continue walking westward to the fountain near the sea's edge. Turn right and follow the promenade as it skirts the base of the:

❸ City Wall

The wall was completed in the 1700s and once formed part of the New World's most impregnable defenses against enemy invaders and pirates. Marvel at the immensity, antiquity, and engineering genius of the wall, which on average is 40 feet high and 20 feet thick.

Follow the promenade until you reach the:

❹ San Juan Gate

The Gate stands at Calle San Juan and Recinto del Oeste. Turn right through

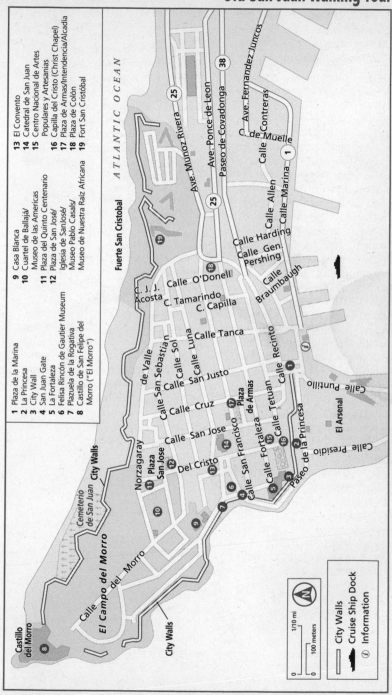

Old San Juan Walking Tour

ATLANTIC OCEAN

1 Plaza de la Marina
2 La Princesa
3 City Wall
4 San Juan Gate
5 La Fortaleza
6 Felisa Rincón de Gautier Museum
7 Plazuela de la Rogativa
8 Castillo de San Felipe del Morro ("El Morro")

9   Casa Blanca
10 Cuartel de Ballajá/
    Museo de las Americas
11 Plaza del Quinto Centenario
12 Plaza de San José/
    Iglesia de SanJosé/
    Museo Pablo Casals/
    Museo de Nuestra Raíz Africana

13 El Convento
14 Catedral de San Juan
15 Centro Nacional de Artes
    Populares y Artesanías
16 Capilla del Cristo (Christ Chapel)
17 Plaza de Armas/Intendencia/Alcadia
18 Plaza de Colón
19 Fort San Cristóbal

Castillo del Morro

El Campo del Morro

Calle del Campo del Morro

Cementerio de San Juan

City Walls

Fuerte San Cristóbal

Ave. Muñoz Rivera

Ave. Ponce de León

Paseo de Covadonga

Ave. Fernandez Juncos

C. de Muelle

C. de Contreras

Calle Allen

Calle Marina

Calle Harding

Calle Gen. Pershing

Calle Braumbaugh

Calle O'Donell

C. J. J. Acosta

C. Tamarindo

C. Capilla

Calle Tanca

Calle Recinto

de Valle

Calle San Sebastian

Calle Sol

Calle Luna

Calle San Justo

Calle Cruz

Calle Tetuan

Plaza de Armas

Calle San Jose

Calle San Francisco

Calle Fortaleza

Norzagaray

Plaza San Jose

Del Cristo

Paseo de la Princesa

Calle Puntillo

Calle Presidio

El Arsenal

N

1/10 mi

100 meters

City Walls
Cruise Ship Dock
Information

the portal. The gate was built in 1635 and served as the main entrance into San Juan. Today, it's the only remaining passage through the wall into the city.

Turn right at the first street and walk uphill along Calle Recinto del Oeste to the wrought-iron gates of:

⑤ La Fortaleza

Also known as Santa Catalina Palace, La Fortaleza is the residence of Puerto Rico's governor. Although it initially served military purposes, it's the oldest executive mansion in continuous use in the Western Hemisphere (construction began in 1533). Over the past 4 centuries, numerous additions and alterations have been made, resulting in the current amalgam of marble, mahogany, and stained glass. The architectural pastiche includes medieval, baroque, gothic, neoclassical, and Moorish elements. English-language tours are given Monday through Friday (except holidays) every hour on the hour (except noon) from 9am to 3pm.

Now retrace your steps along Calle Recinto del Oeste, downhill to Caleta de San Juan. The colonial house at number 51, on the northeast corner, is the:

⑥ Felisa Rincón de Gautier Museum

This is the former home of one of San Juan's most popular mayors. An organizer of the city's women and other dispossessed, Fela, as her many admirers called her, swept into power in 1946 and led the city for 22 years. The first woman in the Western Hemisphere to be the chief executive of a major city, she was the brains behind Head Start, the preschool program for low-income children. Watch the short English-language documentary of her life, tour the modest rooms of her home, and view some of the hundreds of pictures of Madame Mayor with the world's celebrities (© 787/723-1897; free admission; open weekdays, except holidays, 9am–4pm).

Walking back to Calle Recinto del Oeste, turn right and proceed 1 block to Caleta de las Monjas. Fork left to a panoramic view and a modern statue marking the center of:

⑦ Plazuela de la Rogativa

According to local legend, the British, while besieging San Juan in 1797, misidentified the flaming torches of a rogativa, or religious procession, as Spanish reinforcements. Frightened by the display, the would-be invaders hastily retreated. Statues in this plaza memorialize the event.

Continue westward, parallel to the city wall, passing through a pair of urn-topped gateposts. The road will fork. Bear to the right and continue climbing the steep cobblestone-covered ramp to its top. Walk westward across the field toward the neoclassical gateway leading to the:

⑧ Castillo de San Felipe del Morro ("El Morro")

This castle, whose treasury and strategic position were for centuries the envy of both Europe and the Caribbean, was where Spanish Puerto Rico defended itself against the navies of Great Britain, France, and Holland, as well as hundreds of pirate ships. First built in 1540, and substantially enhanced in 1787, the fortress was part of a comprehensive defense network. The six-level complex rises 140 feet above the sea on a rocky promontory. You can spend the better part of the morning exploring its labyrinth of dungeons, barracks, towers, ramps, and tunnels on your own. Check out the small, air-conditioned military museum and the gift shop. Both El Morro and San Cristóbal (see stop 19, below) are managed by the U.S. National Park Service, which provides continuous video presentations and scheduled guided tours in English. (It's at the western end of Calle Norzagaray; © 787/729-6960; $2 for adults, $3 for ages 13–17 and over 62, free for children; open daily 9am–5pm. Save your ticket stub, which gets you admission to Fort San Cristóbal, below.)

Retrace your steps through the treeless field to Calle del Morro, then walk uphill to the small plaza at the top of the street. On the right is:

⑨ Casa Blanca

Though it was his family home, Juan Ponce de León, the conquistador and Puerto Rico's first governor, never actually lived here: While the structure was being built, he was off looking for the Fountain of Youth, ironically dying (from battle wounds) along the way, in 1521. The city's oldest fort, Casa Blanca was San Juan's only defense against attacks until La Fortaleza was completed in 1533. Today, it features a small museum illustrating Indian life and 16th- and 17th-century colonial family life. The garden and fountains in back are a tranquil respite from the streets. (1 Calle de San Sebastián; © 787/725-1454; $2 for adults, 50¢ for children and senior citizens; open daily Tues–Sat 9am–4pm, except for an hour at noon.)

Exit through the front entrance and walk downhill, retracing your steps for a half block, then head toward the massive tangerine-colored building on your right, the:

⑩ Cuartel de Ballajá

These former military barracks once housed 1,000 Spanish soldiers and their families. Built between 1854 and 1864, the complex is the last and largest military building erected by Spain in the Western Hemisphere. The three-story quadrangular structure, constructed in a sober neoclassical style, has long arcades that enclose a large patio once used as a parade ground. Today, the building's second floor is home to the **Museo de las Americas** (Museum of the Americas), which showcases Caribbean as well as North, Central, and South American cultures. The popular art exhibits focus on housing and furniture styles, handicrafts, tools, musical instruments, toys, clothing, and religious objects. The carved wooden saints (*santos*) are especially interesting. (Cuartel de Ballajá; © 787/724-5052; free admission; open Tues–Sun 10am–4pm.)

Exit through the barracks' eastern door, where you'll immediately spot the dramatic and modern:

⑪ Plaza del Quinto Centenario (Quincentennial Plaza)

This plaza is dominated by a large, totem-pole-like column that commemorates the 500th anniversary of Columbus's arrival.

Now, walk a short block southeast to the borders of:

⑫ Plaza de San José

This plaza features a statue of Juan Ponce de León cast from an English cannon captured during a 1797 naval battle. Three sites around this square are worth visiting. Built in 1532, the **Iglesia de San José** is where Ponce de León's descendants worshipped. Despite being looted over the years, the church, on the plaza's north side, still has several treasures, including a carved crucifix presented to Ponce de León, paintings by Puerto Rican 18th-century master José Campéche, and works by Francisco Oller, who painted in the late 1800s and early 1900s. A 15th-century Flemish work in the Chapel of Belém is venerated by many who believe it works miracles. The **Museo Pablo Casals** (© 787/723-9185; $1 for adults, 50¢ for children under 12; open Tues–Sat 9:30am–4:30pm) honors the Spanish-born cellist who adopted Puerto Rico as his home (his mother and wife were Puerto Rican). Original manuscripts of Casals' music, his cello, and his piano are displayed in the main hall. The video library upstairs archives many of his performances. Casals' legacy on the island includes the annual Casals Music Festival and the Puerto Rico Symphony Orchestra. The **Museo de Nuestra Raíz Africana** (Museum of Our African Roots) compactly and ingeniously chronicles the history of Africans in

Puerto Rico. Various exhibits trace the slave experience and focus on African contributions to local music, dance, clothing, art, cuisine, religion, and language. Placards are in Spanish, but the exhibits are fascinating and often self-explanatory (© 787/724-0700, ext. 4239; free admission; open Tues–Sat 9:30am–5pm, Sun 11am–5pm).

Exiting from the plaza's southwestern corner, walk downhill along one of the capital's oldest and best-known streets, Calle del Cristo. Two blocks down, on the north side of shady Plaza de las Monjas, look for:

⑬ El Convento

The New World's first Carmelite convent, El Convento opened in 1651 with 30-foot-thick walls designed to withstand hurricanes and enemy attacks. The building remained a convent for 250 years, but fell on hard times early in the 20th century and served as a dance hall and flophouse. Today, the beautifully restored building is the Hotel El Convento, possibly Puerto Rico's most elegant hotel.

Across the street from El Convento stands the island's most famous church, the:

⑭ Catedral de San Juan

The original thatch-roofed, wooden cathedral, built in the early 1520s, was destroyed by a hurricane in 1529. Reconstruction in 1540 added a circular staircase and vaulted Gothic ceilings, but most of the current church was built in the 1800s. Look for the tomb of Ponce de León and the wax-encased mummy of St. Pio, a Roman martyr (153 Calle del Cristo; © 787/722-0861; free admission; open weekdays 8:30am–5pm).

Now walk 2 blocks south along Calle del Cristo, through one of the Caribbean's most attractive shopping districts. After passing Calle La Fortaleza, look on your left for the:

⑮ Centro Nacional de Artes Populares y Artesanias

Operated by the Institute of Puerto Rican Culture, this center displays a collection of the island's folk arts and crafts (253 Calle del Cristo; © 787/722-0621; free admission; open Mon–Sat 9am–5pm).

Continue to the southernmost tip of Calle del Cristo (just a few steps away) to the wrought-iron gates that surround a chapel no bigger than a newspaper kiosk, the:

⑯ Capilla del Cristo (Christ Chapel)

Legend has it that in 1753 a young rider lost control of his horse in a race down Calle del Cristo during the feast of St. John the Baptist and plunged over the steep precipice at the street's end. A witness to the tragedy promised to build a chapel if the young man's life was saved. Records maintain that the horseman died, but lore contends otherwise. In another version of the story, the horseman, after himself praying to God while falling over the cliff, survived to build the chapel. The delicate silver altar here can be seen through glass doors (free admission; open Mon, Wed, and Fri 10:30am–3:30pm).

Retrace your steps about a block north along the Calle del Cristo, then turn right on Calle Fortaleza. One block later, take a left onto Calle San José, then proceed another block to the capital's liveliest square, the:

⑰ Plaza de Armas

This broad, open plaza has lots of pigeons, several old men playing dominos, office workers and shoppers basking in the sun, and a 19th-century statue representing the four seasons. Originally used for military drills, the plaza now hosts folk dances and concerts on weekends. The neoclassical **Intendencia** (which houses offices of the U.S. State Department) and the Alcadía (San Juan's City Hall) flank the square.

Walk eastward along the plaza's northern border, Calle San Francisco, for 4 blocks until you reach another square:

⑱ Plaza de Colón

This park is notable for its statue of Cristóbal Colón (Christopher Columbus). Bronze plaques at the monument's base commemorate episodes in the explorer's life.

Finally, walk to the plaza's northeast corner, where Calle San Francisco meets Boulevard del Valle. Turn left and follow the signs to:

⑲ Fort San Cristóbal

Built in 1634 (and expanded in the 1770s), this fortress rises more than 150 feet above the sea. A complex maze of tunnels and moats connects the central fort with wave after wave of outlying posts. Don't miss the

Garita del Diablo (the Devil's Sentry Box), a lonely post at the edge of the sea where, legend has it, the devil himself snatched away solitary sentinels. (The Fort is uphill from Plaza de Colón on Calle Norzagaray; ℂ 787/729-6960; $3 for adults, $1 for ages 13–17 and over 62, and children under 13 are free. Note that your ticket stub from El Morro is good for admission here. Open daily 9am–5pm.)

CASINOS

Casinos are one of San Juan's biggest draws, and most large hotels have one. They're generally open daily from noon to 4am, but some never close. Dress, usually informal during the day, becomes impressive in the evenings. The **Casino at the Ritz-Carlton,** 6961 State Rd., Isla Verde (ℂ 787/253-1700), is the largest in Puerto Rico. Combining elegant 1940s decor with tropical fabrics and patterns, it's one of the plushest entertainment complexes in the Caribbean. The **Inter-Continental San Juan,** 187 Isla Verde Ave. (ℂ 800/443-2009 or 787/791-6100), is another elegant place to rendezvous. One of its Murano glass chandeliers is "longer than a bowling alley." Most convenient for cruise ship passengers, the **Wyndham Old San Juan Hotel & Casino,** 100 Brumbaugh St. (ℂ 787/721-5100), is directly across from Pier 3 and often bustling.

BEACHES

Puerto Rico is ringed by hundreds of miles of sandy beaches, and you won't have to leave San Juan to play in the surf. Perhaps the most famous beach in the Caribbean, **Condado Beach,** at the western end of Ashford Avenue, is the backyard playground of Condado's resort hotels. A favorite of families, it can get pretty crowded in winter. The beaches of **Isla Verde,** behind the hotels and condominiums along Isla Verde Avenue, are less rocky and are excellent for people-watching. If you're looking for a more picturesque, sedate scene, head to **Ocean Park,** north of McLeary Street. The waters here are sometimes choppy, but they're still swimmable. Popular with college students on weekends, the beach is also very gay-friendly. Condado Beach, Isla Verde, and Ocean Park all have white sand, palm trees, ocean breezes, beautiful bodies, and ample eating and drinking options. Snorkeling gear and other watersports equipment are available to rent.

If you're anxious to get out of the city, **Luquillo Beach,** about 30 miles east of San Juan, near the town of Luquillo, stretches along a vast coconut grove. Coral reefs protect the clear lagoon from the fierce Atlantic, and a "Sea Without Barriers" facility caters to people with physical disabilities. Be aware, however, that some sections of the beach aren't as well maintained as they once were.

All *balnearios*—government-run beaches with dressing rooms, showers, lifeguards, snack bars, and parking—are open to the public; there's a nominal charge for lockers and showers. Public beaches are closed on Mondays. However, if Monday is a holiday, the beaches will be open that day but closed the next. Hours are 9am to 5pm in winter, 9am to 6pm during the off-season. If you find a secluded spot, be vigilant about your surroundings: Solitude is nice, but there's safety in numbers.

SPORTS

DEEP-SEA FISHING   Many say that Captain Mike Benitez, who's chartered boats out of San Juan for more than 40 years, sets the standard by which other deep-sea-fishing captains are judged. Contact him at **Mike Benitez Marine Services,** P.O. Box 9066541, Puerto de Tierra, San Juan, PR 00906-6541 (© 787/723-2292; www.mikebenitezfishing.com). **Captain Bill Burleson,** P.O. Box 8270, Humacao, PR 00792 (© 787/850-7442), operates charters off the southeast coast. For both companies, expect to pay a little under $600 for a half-day excursion (up to six anglers).

GOLF   Puerto Rico is a golfer's dream, but you'll need to sign up for a ship excursion or rent a car to reach the major courses from San Juan. With 72 holes, **Hyatt Dorado Beach Resort & Country Club** (© 787/796-8916; www.hyatt. com) offers the greatest concentration of golf in the Caribbean. All four 18-hole courses at the Hyatt's Regency Cerromar and Dorado Beach properties here were designed by Robert Trent Jones, Sr. Jack Nicklaus ranks the fourth hole at the Dorado Beach East course as one of the 10 best-designed holes in the world. Greens fees are $145 for 18 holes. The **Doral Resort at Palmas del Mar** (© 787/285-2256; www.palmasdelmar.com), 45 miles east of San Juan, has two courses: the par-72 Palm course designed by Gary Player and the newer 18-hole Flamboyan course designed by Rees Jones. Greens fees at the Palm are $150 for 18 holes and $170 at the Flamboyan course. The **Westin Rio Mar Country Club** (© 787/888-6000; www.westinriomar.com), 20 miles away from San Juan in Rio Grande, also has two 18-hole courses, one designed by Tom and George Fazio, the other by Greg Norman. Greens fees are $190 and $130 for play after 2pm.

SCUBA DIVING & SNORKELING   Puerto Rico offers excellent diving and snorkeling, but the best sites aren't within easy reach of San Juan. **Caribe Aquatic Adventures,** P.O. Box 9024278, San Juan Station, San Juan 00902 (© 787/724-1882; www.caribeaquaticadventure.com), will take you to good diving and snorkeling sites around the capital or near Fajardo on the northeast coast. Caribe operates out of the Park Plaza Normandie (Av. Muñoz-Rivera, at the corner of Calle Los Rasales in Puerta de Tierra). A local reef dive is $50. Much more interesting trips to Fajardo (which include a picnic) require a minimum of three passengers (cost is $135 per person for certified divers, $115 for divers who've completed a resort course, and $85 for snorkelers). The Fajardo excursion must be booked a week in advance, the local reef dives a day in advance.

WINDSURFING, KITEBOARDING & JET-SKIING   The most popular windsurfing beach in the San Juan area is Puntas las Marias, between Isla Verde and Ocean Park. You can rent equipment and take lessons from nearby **Velauno,** 2430 Calle Loiza (© 866/778-3521 or 787/728-8716). Boards and a complete rig are $75 per day; 4-hour beginner lessons are $150. Velauno also offers kite-boarding—windsurfing powered by a large kite rather than sails. A 1-hour intro-ductory course is $49. Two-hour kite-control classes are $100. Another popular place for windsurfing is along the beachfront of the Hyatt Resorts at Dorado, about 30 miles west of San Juan. **Penfield Island Adventures** (© 787/796-1234, ext. 3768, or 787/796-2188), at the Hyatt Regency Cerromar, rents windsurfing equipment, jet skis, kayaks, and sailboats.

SHOPPING

San Juan has some great bargains—prices are often even lower than those in St. Thomas—and U.S. citizens pay no duty on items bought in Puerto Rico. Every tourist zone offers ample shopping opportunities, but the streets of the Old Town, especially **Calle San Francisco** and **Calle del Cristo,** are the major venues. Generally, shopping hours are 8am to 6pm from Monday to Thursday and Saturday, 8am to 9pm on Friday, and 11am to 5pm Sunday for some stores, though most are closed. **Local handicrafts** can be good buys, including santos (hand-carved wooden religious figures), needlework, straw work, hammocks, guayabera shirts (loose-fitting shirts), papier-mâché masks, and paintings and sculptures by local artists.

El Alcazar, 103 Calle San José, has the largest collection of antique furniture, silver, and art objects in the Caribbean. You'll need help to wade through the massive inventory, though—it fills several buildings. Smaller but still impressive, **Olé,** 105 Calle Fortaleza, has antique santos, coins, and silver. It's also the place to get a custom-fitted Panama hat. **Puerto Rican Arts & Crafts,** 204 Calle Fortaleza, has authentic handicrafts, including papier-mâché carnival masks from the town of Ponce. **José E. Alegria & Associates,** 152–154 Calle del Cristo, is half antiques shop, half gift arcade; while **Galería Botello,** 208 Calle del Cristo, once the home of late Puerto Rican artist Angel Botello, sells his paintings and sculptures, as well as antique santos.

Old San Juan's best book and music store, **Cronopios,** is at 255 Calle San José. Most books are in Spanish, but there are plenty in English too. Looking for Puerto Rican novels? Try *The House on the Lagoon,* by Rosario Ferré, or *The Renunciation,* by Edgardo Rodríguez Julia. And pick up some salsa CDs while you're browsing.

Designer outlet shops include London Fog, 156 Calle del Cristo; Polo Ralph Lauren, 201 Calle del Cristo; Coach, 158 Calle del Cristo; and Tommy Hilfiger, 206 Calle del Cristo.

GREAT LOCAL RESTAURANTS & BARS

San Juan has some of the best restaurants in the Caribbean and a variety of cuisines that only a major city can offer. A favorite **local beer** is Medalla. The most famous **local rum** is Bacardi, in all of its varieties; Don Q is also popular.

In Old San Juan, **Amadeus,** 106 Calle San Sebastián (© 787/722-8635), offers nouvelle Caribbean dishes and features an intimate courtyard in back. Lunch $15. **El Patio de Sam,** practically next door at 102 Calle San Sebastián (© 787/723-1149), is a popular gathering spot for expatriates, journalists, and shopkeepers. Lunch $9. The unpretentious **La Bombonera,** 259 Calle San Francisco (© 787/722-0658), famous for its homemade Puerto Rican meals and 1940s diner atmosphere, has attracted the island's literati and Old San Juan families for decades. San Juan's trailblazing nuevo Latino bistro, **Parrot Club,** 363 Calle Fortaleza (© 787/725-7370), blends Spanish, Taíno, and African cuisines.

In Condado, **Miró Marisquería Catalana,** 76 Condado Ave. (© 787/723-9593), serves seafood and traditional Catalonian dishes. Lunch $20. Not far away, **Ajili Mójili,** 1052 Ashford Ave. (© 787/725-9195), serves some of the island's best upmarket Puerto Rican cuisine. Lunch $14.

For stylish but relaxed beachfront dining and sublime Caribbean delicacies, no place beats **Pamela's,** 1 Calle Santa Ana (© 787/726-5010), in Ocean Park. You'll savor every bite. Lunch $16.

22 St. Barthélemy (St. Barts)

Chic, sophisticated St. Barthélemy—St. Barts to everyone in the know—is internationally renowned as one of the ritziest refuges in the Caribbean, rivaled only by Mustique as the preferred island retreat of the rich and famous. From early fans Nureyev, Baryshnikov, and Buffett to later enthusiasts Mick Jagger, Princess Di, Calvin Klein, Madonna, and Naomi Campbell, the glitterati who've played here form a veritable Who's Who of fabulousness. Despite its transformation over the past couple of decades into a celebrity hot spot, St. Barts retains its charm, serenity, natural beauty, and Gallic flavor. Just 24km (15 miles) from St. Martin and politically part of Guadeloupe, the island's 21 sq. km (8 sq. miles) of dramatic hills and pristine white-sand beaches are decidedly French, like a peaceful slice of the Côte d'Azur transplanted in the Caribbean. The roller-coaster terrain, strict zoning and construction laws, and a local consensus that stratospheric pricing is the surest way to maintain exclusivity, protects the island from massive development that would certainly change its character.

First inhabited about 3,000 years ago by Ciboney Indians, then later by Arawaks (A.D. 200) and Caribs (A.D. 1000), St. Barts was first spotted by Europeans in 1496, when Christopher Columbus named the island after his baby brother, Bartolemeo. The French took possession of the island in the mid–17th century, then in 1784 traded it to the Swedes, who built forts, houses, and roads and declared St. Barts a free port. Sweden transferred it back to France in 1878 after its colony began to falter. It wasn't until the 1980s that St. Barts began to impress jet-setting tourists. Later, tax breaks for French nationals fueled investment in tourism.

In sharp contrast to most Caribbean islands, where descendants of African slaves form the majority, St. Barts's 7,000 year-round residents are primarily of French ancestry, mostly from Brittany and Normandy. Many affluent Americans and Europeans have villas on the island, some living in the Caribbean year-round, others making seasonal visits.

COMING ASHORE   Cruise ships anchor off Gustavia, the main town, and ferry passengers to the dollhouse-size harbor and town via tenders. Phones and ATMs are in the immediate vicinity of the harbor. The post office (or PTT), which also serves as a telecommunications center, is located at the back corner of the harbor opposite the dock. You can check your e-mail at the second-floor offices of **Centre @lizes** (© 590/29-89-89), on rue de la République, a few blocks to the right of the dock. Access to the Internet is about 12¢ a minute. Be sure to ask for an American keyboard: The position of letters on French keyboards is significantly different.

LANGUAGE   **French** is the official language, but virtually everyone speaks **English** as well.

CURRENCY   St. Barts is part of the French overseas region of Guadeloupe, so the **euro** (€) is now the official currency (exchange rate: €1 = US$1.10; $1 = €.90). Prices mentioned in this section are in U.S. dollars. You'll have no trouble using credit cards and traveler's checks.

INFORMATION   The **Office Municipal du Tourisme** (© 590/27-87-27), adjacent to the dock on Quai Général de Gaulle, is open Monday through Friday from 8:30am to 12:30pm, Friday from 2pm to 5pm, and Monday through Thursday from 2pm to 5:30pm. For information before you go, get on the horn to Maison de la France in the U.S. (© 212/838-7800; www.st-barths.com).

CALLING FROM THE U.S.   When calling St. Barts from the United States, dial the international access code (011) and 590 before the numbers listed here, which *also* begin with 590. That's right: If you want to make a connection, you have to dial 590 twice. It's just one of those oddities that makes the world go round.

GETTING AROUND

BY TAXI   Taxis meet cruise ships at Gustavia's harbor. Because the island is so small, no destination is too distant. Consequently, fares seem reasonable. Dial © 590/27-66-31 for service if you don't spot a cab. The fare ranges from approximately $10 to $22, depending on your destination.

BY RENTAL CAR   If you love adventure, rent an open-sided Mini-Moke (a jeep–golf cart hybrid) or Suzuki Samurai: Zipping up and down St. Barts's jagged, picturesque hills is more thrilling than riding most amusement-park rides. Roads are in excellent condition, and local drivers are alert and competent, but tend to drive aggressively. Automatic transmissions are in short supply, so reserve in advance: If you're not already adept at using a stick shift, St. Barts is not the place to learn. **Budget** and **Avis** have offices here, as does **Europcar** (© 590/27-74-34). The island has only two gas stations: one near the airport, the other in Lorient. Both are closed on Sundays, but the airport station has a pump that accepts credit cards any time of day, any day of the week.

BY MOTOR SCOOTER   Terrified by winding roads and speeding drivers, mothers on St. Barts are loath to let their kids ride scooters. Few bikes have the power to make it up the steep hills anyway. If you have a death wish, go ahead and rent a motorbike or scooter from **Meca Moto** (© 590/52-92-49), rue du

> ### Frommer's Favorite St. Barts Experiences
>
> **Making the Scene at Le Select:** For more than 50 years this garden cafe has been the most popular gathering spot in Gustavia, and the best place to get a taste of local life. (See "Great Local Restaurants & Bars," below.)
>
> **Bronzing on the Beach:** St. Barts has several gorgeous beaches, some social, some private. (See "Beaches," below.)
>
> **Zipping Around the Island in a Mini-Moke:** Few experiences are as exhilarating as zooming along the island's roller-coaster roads in one of these open-air vehicles, half golf cart, half jeep. (See "Getting Around," above.)

Général de Gaulle, or **Tropic'all Rent** (© 590/27-64-76), rue du Roi Oscar II, both in Gustavia. Expect to pay about $30 for the day, mandatory helmet included. A $200 deposit or credit-card imprint is required.

SHORE EXCURSIONS OFFERED BY THE CRUISE LINES
Minibus Island Tour ($25, 1½ hr.): This brief excursion highlights the island's natural beauty and beaches. Stops include Gustavia, the port and main town; St. Jean, one of the more popular beaches and shopping areas; Grand Cul de Sac, the lagoon and beach favored by windsurfers; and Corossol, a tiny fishing village where the traditions of St. Barts survive.

ON YOUR OWN: WITHIN WALKING DISTANCE
Aside from shopping, eating, and hanging out in sidewalk cafes, cruisers sticking close to port can visit Gustavia's modest points of interest. **St. Bartholomew's Church,** rue Samuel Fahlberg, dates from the 1850s and features limestone and volcanic stone walls, as well as imported pitch pine pews. Its tiny Anglican, English-speaking congregation is an anomaly on this overwhelmingly French Catholic island.

Evidence of St. Barts's faint but lingering Swedish presence, the **Wall House,** rue Duquesne, is a staid, stone building near the harbor's mouth, across from the dock. Once a Swedish home, the structure was rebuilt after fire devastated it (and much of Gustavia) in 1852. Since 1989, it's housed the **Municipal Museum** (© 590/29-71-55), an unfocused but respectable introduction to the history, sociology, ethnology, economy, and ecology of the island. The most interesting items include Amerindian artifacts, rustic farm furnishings, clothing used by early French settlers, and photos documenting hurricane devastation. Admission for persons over 12 is $2; the exhibits are open Monday 2:30 to 6pm, Tuesday through Friday 8:30am to 12:30pm and 2:30 to 6pm, and Saturday 9am to 1pm.

ON YOUR OWN: BEYOND THE PORT AREA
Visiting the tiny fishing village of **Corossol** is a vibrant way to experience the St. Barts of the past. About 10 minutes by taxi from the dock, this quaint, totally un-chic hamlet is home to traditional folk who still live off the sea. It's your best bet for spotting women in traditional 17th-century bonnets and for watching

roadside vendors weave items from palm fronds. On the town's waterfront, about 30m (100 ft.) to the left of the road from Gustavia, the **Inter Oceans Museum** (© **590/27-62-97**) catalogs thousands of shells, corals, sand dollars, sea horses, sea urchins, and fish from around the world. One (now very old) man's obsession, the museum's homemade, thorough displays are completely endearing and sure to enthrall the child in everyone. Don't miss the collection of sand from beaches around the world: A cocktail umbrella is planted in each specimen. Admission is $3. Doors to this extension of the owner's home are open from 9am to 1pm and 3pm to 5pm Tuesday through Saturday.

SHOPPING

A duty-free port, St. Barts is a good place to buy liquor, perfume, and other French luxury items. Good buys on apparel, crystal, porcelain, and watches can also be found, especially during April, the biggest sale month. Moisturizer mavens can stock up on the island's own cosmetic line, Ligne St. Barth. Shops are concentrated in Gustavia and St. Jean, where the quality-to-schlock ratio is as high as anywhere in the Caribbean. Most shops and offices close for a long lunch, usually from noon to 2pm.

In Gustavia, **Carat,** rue de la République; **Fabienne Miot,** rue de la République; and **Diamond Genesis,** rue du Général de Gaulle, offer an array of fine jewelry, some handcrafted on the premises. **Dovani,** rue de la République, and **Privilège,** rue du Roi Oscar II, are your best bets for perfumes and cosmetics. **St. Barth Style,** rue Lafayette, near the corner of rue du Port, stocks fashionable beachwear, while **Mandarine,** rue de la République, carries chic but casual women's clothing. Higher-style women's fashion is available at **Roberto Cavalli,** Le Carré d'Or; **Stéphane & Bernard,** rue de la République behind Carat; and **Sorélina,** rue du Général de Gaulle. Men in search of a new shirt or trousers should try **Images Boutique** or **L'Homme et la Mer,** both on rue du Général de Gaulle. Men's and women's shoes can be found at **Human Steps,** rue de la France. **Le Comptoir du Cigare,** rue du Général de Gaulle, sells cigars from Cuba and the Dominican Republic and connoisseur-quality rums, while **Nilaya,** rue du Roi Oscar II, stocks unique, handcrafted objets d'art from Asia and elsewhere around the world.

In St. Jean, **Kiwi Saint Tropez** stocks chic beachwear, **Bleu Marine** has French and Italian women's fashions, **Elysees Caraïbes** sells high-style handbags and luggage, and **Boutique Iléna** offers erotic lingerie.

BEACHES

The 22 beaches of St. Barts are first-rate. Few are ever crowded, even during the peak season, and all are public, free, and easily accessible by taxi from the cruise pier (make arrangements with your driver to be picked up at a specific time). As St. Barts is a French island, toplessness is common at all beaches. Full nudism is officially prohibited, but bathers at several sites—Saline and Gouverneur, to name a couple (see below)—willfully flout the rules. Defying a common stereotype, most nude bathers on the island actually have attractive bodies.

If you're looking for an active beach strand, with restaurants and watersports, **Grand Cul de Sac** fits the bill. The shallow, protected waters here are warm and relatively calm. Watersports are well represented, with windsurfing especially popular. An even busier and equally social beach, **St. Jean** is actually two beaches divided by a rock promontory. Protected by a coral reef, the calm waters here attract families and watersports enthusiasts, including windsurfers. When the winds gather greater force, surfer dudes appear. Near the end of the airport's incredibly short runway, St. Jean also provides numerous eating, drinking, shopping, and people-watching opportunities. **Gouverneur,** on the south central coast, is quiet and relatively remote. Its idyllic setting and unspoiled beauty make it No. 1 with locals and discerning visitors who want privacy and serenity. Farther east, in a wild and rustic area that was once the site of salt ponds, **Saline** is reached by a 3-minute hike over a sand dune. Most famous for its adult environment and nude bathers, it also boasts great bodysurfing waves.

SPORTS

SAILING, SCUBA DIVING & SNORKELING **Marine Service,** Quai du Yacht Club (© 590/27-70-34), operates from the marina across the harbor from the busier side of Gustavia. Most dive sites served by this five-star PADI operator are a 10- to 20-minute boat ride from the harbor; depths vary from 3m to 30m (10 ft.–100 ft.). Reef dives are the rule, although one wreck dive for more experienced divers is a possibility. One-tank dives are about $55 to $60; two-tank dives are about $100, including beverages and all equipment. The operation also offers half-day snorkeling cruises (about $65, including snorkeling gear, a French snack buffet, and an open bar) and catamaran or sloop charters (starting at $540 for half a day during the low season; $650 during the winter, including cheese, fruit, beverages, and music). The cost is for a maximum of eight people and includes a crew. Prospective charterers should call Marine Service for Christmas and New Year's rates. Vendors at both St. Jean and Grand Cul de Sac rent snorkel gear and other watersports equipment—jet skis, Sunfish sailboats, and so on.

WINDSURFING Try **St. Barth Wind School** (© 590/27-71-22) near the Tom Beach Hotel at St. Jean or **Windwave Power** (© 590/27-82-57) at Grand Cul de Sac. Expect to pay about $25 an hour for a full rig.

GREAT LOCAL RESTAURANTS & BARS

Mix lots of rich, discerning diners with the French tradition of culinary expertise, and it's no wonder that so many of St. Barts's restaurants consistently receive high accolades. It's a pity that some of the best open only for dinner, well after your ship has gone out to sea. Luckily, enough serve lunch to assure you one of the best meals of your cruise.

IN GUSTAVIA More interested in seeing and being seen than in satisfying your taste buds? Make a beeline to **Le Select,** rue de la France at rue du Général de Gaulle (© 590/27-86-87), the epicenter of Gustavia's social life for more than 50 years. This cafe's tables rest in a tree-shaded garden a block from the harbor. A full bar is available to complement burgers, salads, and other simple fare. Salty locals, celebrities, and chic tourists are among the clientele. The classic, funky ambience inspired Jimmy Buffet's "Cheeseburger in Paradise." At the foot of Gustavia harbor, **La Route des Boucaniers** (© 590/27-73-00) looks like any seaside restaurant around Chesapeake Bay or on the Jersey shore, but its traditional and nouvelle Creole cuisine is anything but run-of-the-mill. Try the octopus gratin served in a potato shell or the braised scallops with passion fruit. Lunch $18. **L'Iguane,** Quai de la République (© 590/27-88-46), offers an international menu that includes sushi and light sandwiches and salads.

AT ST. JEAN **Eden Rock** (© 590/29-79-99) has three restaurants at St. Jean beach: one on the rock promontory that bisects the strand, one next to the ocean, and one in the sand, aptly dubbed the Sand Bar, which serves lunch at a cost of about $30. Traditional French cuisine, seafood, and tropical drinks are the trio's strong suits. For great pizza and friendly ambience, try **The Hideaway** (© 590/27-63-62). Lunch $20. Relax on the open-air terrace or get your order to go. If you're more in the mood for a sandwich and want to get back to the sun, head to **KiKi-e Mo** (© 590/27-90-65), an Italian gourmet shop that whips up divine light fare to go. Lunch $7.

AT GRANDE SALINE A handful of restaurants are within walking distance of Saline beach. **Grain de Sel** (© 590/52-46-05) looks no-frills, but the seafood and Creole specialties are deluxe. Lunch $20. Prettier and more upscale, but just as relaxing, **Le Tamarin** (© 590/27-72-12) specializes in beef, salmon, and tuna carpaccios; fresh grilled lobster; and inventive Creole dishes. Lunch $55.

23 St. Kitts

Somewhat off the beaten tourist track, south of St. Martin and north of Guadeloupe, St. Kitts forms the larger half of the combined Federation of St. Kitts and Nevis, which gained self-government from Britain in 1967 and became a totally independent nation in 1983. The two islands are separated by only about 3.2km (2 miles) of ocean, but the emotional distance is a little wider, with Nevis's citizens often expressing a strong urge for independence from St. Kitts.

St. Kitts—or St. Christopher, a name hardly anyone uses—is by far the more populous of the two islands, with some 35,000 people. It was the first English settlement in the Leeward Islands, and during the plantation age its 176 sq. km (68 sq. miles) enjoyed one of the richest sugar cane economies in the Caribbean. Of course, the plantation age depended on slave labor for cultivation, and today, though the bulk of the island's revenue still comes from the nationalized sugar industry, the back-breaking and low-paying work of sugar harvesting is shunned by most of St. Kitts's citizens—in their place, Guayanese workers come in for the harvesting season. Cane fields climb the slopes of a volcanic mountain range, and you'll see ruins of old mills and plantation houses as you drive around the island.

St. Kitts is lush and fertile, dotted with rainforests and waterfalls and boasting some lovely beaches along its southeast coastline, but it's also extremely poor and has suffered catastrophically in recent years, being hit with several successive hurricanes in the late 1990s. Despite efforts at wooing tourists to bring in badly needed cash, the country lags behind in amenities and infrastructure.

The island is crowned by the 1,138m (3,792-ft.) **Mount Liamuiga,** a crater that, thankfully, remains dormant. The island's most impressive landmark is the **Brimstone Hill fortress,** one of the Caribbean's most impressive forts. **Basseterre,** the capital city, is rife with old-time Caribbean architecture, and has a few worthwhile landmarks, but overall the city has little to hold the interest of visitors.

COMING ASHORE **Port Zante,** which was hit hard by successive hurricanes, has undergone a rebuilding and expansion that was completed in late 2002. The new port, which stretches from the center of town into the deep waters offshore, offers 4,050 sq. m (45,000 sq. ft.) of shopping and office space, restaurants, and a welcome center.

LANGUAGE **English** is the language of both islands.

CURRENCY The local currency is the **Eastern Caribbean dollar** (US$1 = EC$2.70; EC$1 = US73¢). Many shops and restaurants quote prices in U.S.

dollars. Always determine which currency locals are talking about. We've used U.S.-dollar prices in this section.

INFORMATION   You can get local tourist information at the **St. Kitts Tourism Authority,** Pelican Mall, Bay Road, in Basseterre (© **869/465-4040**), open Monday to Friday from 8am to 4pm. For info before you go, contact the tourism board office in the U.S. (© **800/582-6208;** www.stkitts-tourism.com).

CALLING FROM THE U.S.   When calling St. Kitts or Nevis from the United States, you just need to dial a "1" before the numbers listed here.

GETTING AROUND

BY TAXI   Taxis wait at the docks in Basseterre and in the Circus, a public square near the docks at the intersection of Bank and Fort streets. Since most taxi drivers are also guides, this is the best means of getting around the island. Taxis aren't metered, so you must agree on the price before heading out. Always ask if the rates quoted are in U.S. dollars or Eastern Caribbean dollars.

BY RENTAL CAR   We don't recommend renting a car here.

SHORE EXCURSIONS OFFERED BY THE CRUISE LINES

Brimstone Hill Tour ($39, 3 hr.): Visit this 17th-century citadel, which, at some 240m (800 ft.) above sea level, gives you an inspiring panoramic view of the coastline and the island. Tours typically include a visit to the beautiful Romney Gardens, which lie between Basseterre and the fort. You can check out the lush greenery, say hi to the cows that graze just across the hill, or shop at Carabelle Boutique.

Rainforest Adventure Hike ($58, 4 hr.): Departing from Romney Gardens, about 8km (5 miles) from Basseterre, you'll hike along a loop of trail through lush rainforest. With luck, you'll catch sight of some of the island's resident monkey population.

Beach Horseback Ride ($38, 1–2 hr.): Cruise ship passengers ride well-trained horses along the Atlantic coastline, where trade winds ensure a cool, breezy trip.

ⓒ Frommer's Favorite St. Kitts Experiences

Visiting Brimstone Hill Fortress: Begun by the British in 1690 and subsequently changing hands from British to French and back to British again, this is one of the most impressive forts in the Caribbean, with battlement after battlement leading up to a spectacular view of the sea. (See "Shore Excursions Offered by the Cruise Lines," above, and "On Your Own: Beyond the Port Area," below.)

Hiking Mount Liamuiga: The hike up this dormant volcano will take you through a rainforest and along deep ravines up to the rim of the crater at a cool 788m (2,625 ft.). (See "On Your Own: Beyond the Port Area," below.)

Rainforest Adventure Hike: Departing from Romney Gardens, about 8km (5 miles) from Basseterre, you'll hike along a loop of trail through rainforest, and get a feel for the island's lush interior. (See "Shore Excursions Offered by the Cruise Lines," above.)

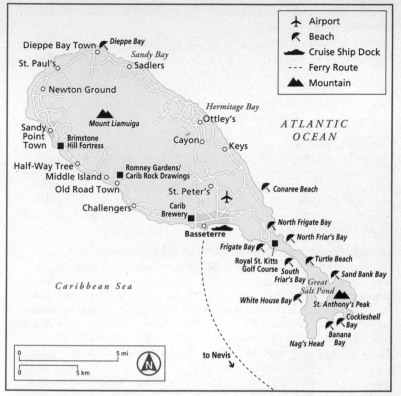

Sail & Snorkel Catamaran Trip ($68, 3–4 hr.): A sailing catamaran takes you to secluded Smitten's Bay for snorkeling among diverse reef fish and coral formations. Complimentary rum punch is served aboard the boat on your return trip.

Nevis Catamaran Trip ($94, 7 hr.): The tour stops at Smitten's Bay for snorkeling before crossing the channel to sister-island Nevis, spending time there on the beach, where a barbecue lunch is served. Food and all drinks are included in the price.

Nevis Botanical Gardens Tour ($75, 3½ hr.): Travel by water taxi to Nevis, visiting the Alexander Hamilton Museum before heading for the gardens.

EXCURSIONS OFFERED BY LOCAL AGENCIES

Rainforest Tours: For a great rainforest walk in the thickets around Romney Gardens, contact Addy of **Addy's Rainforest Safaris** (© 869/465-8069). He knows the flora and fauna of St. Kitts like the back of his hand and delivers a satisfying, personal rainforest experience, ending his tour by sharing a plate of his wife's tasty homemade banana bread and some fresh guava and passion fruit juices.

Taxi Tours: You'll find a fleet of taxis waiting in the dock as you disembark from the ship. Taxi drivers will take you on a 3-hour tour of the island for about $60. Lunch can be arranged at one of the local inns. Good inn choices are **Golden**

Lemon at Dieppe Bay (© **869/465-7260**) or **Rawlins Plantation,** Mount Pleasant (© **869/465-6221**).

ON YOUR OWN: WITHIN WALKING DISTANCE

The capital city of **Basseterre,** where the docks are located, has typical British colonial architecture and some quaint buildings, a few shops, and a market where locals display fruits and flowers—but even this description might be giving you the wrong idea about this place. The truth is, it's a very poor town, with few attractions aimed at visitors. Plans call for a revitalization, but we'll have to wait and see.

Rainforest and beaches are the real draw on St. Kitts, so you need only about a half-hour to explore in town. **St. George's Anglican Church,** on Cayon Street (walk straight up Church St. or Fort St. from the dock), is the oldest church in town and is worth a look. **Independence Square,** a stone's throw from the docks along Bank Street, is pretty, with its central fountain and old church, but there's no good reason to linger unless it's to sit in the shade and toss back a bottle of Ting, the refreshing (and very sweet) grapefruit-based local soda.

ON YOUR OWN: BEYOND THE PORT AREA

The **Brimstone Hill Fortress** (© **869/465-6211;** www.brimstonehillfortress. org), 14km (9 miles) west of Basseterre, is the major stop on any tour of St. Kitts. This historic monument, among the largest and best preserved in the Caribbean, is a complex of bastions, barracks, and other structures, ingeniously adapted to the upper slopes of a steep, 240m (800-ft.) hill. The name of the place derives from the odor of sulfur released by nearby undersea vents.

The structure dates from 1690, when the British fortified the hill to help recapture Fort Charles, located below, from the French. In 1782, an invading force of 8,000 French troops bombarded the fortress for a month before its small British garrison, supplemented by local militia, surrendered. When the British took the island back the next year, they proceeded to enlarge the fort into "The Gibraltar of the West Indies." In all, the structure took 104 years to complete.

Today the fortress is the centerpiece of a national park crisscrossed by nature trails and home to a diverse range of plant and animal life, including green vervet monkeys. It's a photographer's paradise, with views of mountains, fields, and the Caribbean Sea—on a clear day you can see six neighboring islands. From below, the fort presents a dramatic picture, poised among diabolical-looking spires and outcroppings of lava rock.

Visitors will enjoy the self-directed tours among the many partially restored structures, including the barrack rooms at Fort George. The gift shop sells prints of rare Caribbean maps and paintings of the Caribbean. Admission is $5 for adults, $2.50 for children. The park is open daily from 9:30am to 5:30pm.

The well-maintained **Romney Gardens** are located amidst the ruins of a sugar estate, just a 15-minute drive from Basseterre, in the town of Old Road. The boiling houses, a chimney, and a stone aqueduct, all enveloped in lush foliage and bright flowering plants, are all that remain of the estate. With picturesque views of the sea in the distance, the hillside gardens feature giant ferns, orchids, poinsettias, and "The Tree," a 350-year-old Saman tree. Rainforest hiking excursions depart from here, and most allow time for a short exploration of the gardens and a stop at the Caribelle Batik shop (see "Shopping," below).

The dormant **Mount Liamuiga volcano,** in the northwest area of the island, has long been known as "Mount Misery." It sputtered its last gasp around 1692, and today its summit is a major goal for hikers. A round-trip to the usually cloud-covered peak takes about 4 hours—2½ hours going up, 1½ coming down. Hikers usually make the ascent from Belmont Estate near St. Paul on the north end of St. Kitts. The trail winds through a rainforest and travels along deep ravines up to the rim of the crater at a cool 788m (2,625 ft.). Many hikers climb (or crawl) down a steep, slippery trail to a tiny lake in the caldera, some 120m (400 ft.) below the rim.

You can reach the rim without a guide, but it's absolutely necessary to have one to go into the crater. **Greg's Safaris** (© **869/465-4121;** www.skbee.com/ safaris) offers guided hikes to the crater for about $80 per person (a minimum of four hikers required), including breakfast, a picnic at the crater's rim, and a cocktail toast at the end. A half-day rainforest exploration, also with a picnic, sells for $40 per person. Another $40 half-day excursion, the Plantation Heritage tour, visits private Great Houses and sugar plantations in modified land rovers. The tour is conducted off-road and includes a picnic with Greg's homemade pastries and tropical juices.

SHOPPING

Basseterre is not a shopping town, despite the handout maps you may receive when you arrive, which show a listing of shops that would put St. Thomas's shopping hot spot, Charlotte Amalie, to shame—that is, until you look closer and see entries such as "R. Gumbs Electrical," "TDC/Finco Finance Co.," and "Horsford Furniture Store." Turns out they just listed every business on every street in town, no matter whether it's of interest to visitors or not. Strength in numbers, we suppose.

The closest thing to high-quality shopping is at **Pelican Shopping Mall,** with more than a dozen shops, as well as banking services, a restaurant, and a philatelic bureau where collectors can buy St. Kitts stamps and everyone else can mail letters. Here too, though, don't expect much—and whose idea was it to build a covered mall in the sunny Caribbean, anyway?

At Romney Gardens, you'll find **Caribelle Batik** (© **869/465-6253**), one of the island's most popular boutiques. Inside, artisans demonstrate their Indonesian-style hand-printing amid rack after rack of brightly colored clothes. Brimstone Hill and rainforest-hike shore excursions typically include a stop here. If you're coming on your own, look for signs indicating a turnoff along the coast road, about 8km (5 miles) north of Basseterre in the town of Old Road.

BEACHES

The narrow peninsula in the southeast contains the island's salt ponds and also boasts the best white-sand beaches (approach via the windy, hilly road for a dramatic and gorgeous view). You'll find the best swimming at **Conaree Beach,** 4.8km (3 miles) from Basseterre; **Frigate Bay,** with its talcum-powder-fine sand; the twin beaches of **Banana Bay** and **Cockleshell Bay,** at the southeast corner of the island; and **Friar's Bay,** a peninsula beach opening onto both the Atlantic and the Caribbean. All beaches, even those that border hotels, are free and open to the public. However, you must usually pay a fee to use a hotel's beach facilities.

SPORTS

GOLF   The **Golden Rock Golf Course,** Frigate Bay (© **869/465-7512**), is a 5-minute drive from the cruise port. Greens fees at the 9-hole, par-34 course are $30.

SCUBA DIVING & SNORKELING   One of the best diving spots is **Nagshead,** at the southern tip of St. Kitts. This is an excellent shallow-water dive for certified divers, starting at 3m (10 ft.) and extending to 21m (70 ft.). You'll see a variety of tropical fish, eagle rays, and lobster here. Another good site is **Booby Shoals,** between Cow 'n' Calf Rocks and Booby Island. Booby Shoals has abundant sea life, including nurse sharks, lobster, and stingrays. Dives here are up to 9m (30 ft.) in depth, and are good for both certified and beginning divers.

GREAT LOCAL RESTAURANTS & BARS

The favorite **local beer** is Carib, brewed right on the northern edge of Basseterre. There's a local cane sugar drink called CSR (Cane Spirit Rothschild) that tastes a bit like Brazilian cachaça, but with a slight licorice flavor.

Ballahoo Restaurant (© 869/465-4197), located in Basseterre's most picturesque intersection (The Circus, right by the cruise dock), serves some of the best baby back ribs in town. Seafood platters, such as garlic shrimp, curried conch, or fresh lobster, are served with salad and rice. Lunch $15.

24 St. Lucia

With a turbulent history shared by many of its Caribbean neighbors, St. Lucia (pronounced *Loo*-sha), second largest of the Windward Islands at about 622 sq. km (240 sq. miles), changed hands often during the colonial period, being British seven times and French seven times. Today, though, it's an independent state that's become one of the most popular destinations in the Caribbean, with some of the finest resorts. The heaviest development is concentrated in the northwest, between the capital of Castries and the northern end of the island, where there's a string of white-sand beaches. The interior boasts relatively unspoiled green-mantled mountains and gentle valleys, as well as the volcanic **Mount Soufrière.** Two dramatic peaks **(the Pitons)** rise along the southwest coast.

Castries, the capital, has grown up around an extinct volcanic crater that's now a large harbor surrounded by hills. Because of fires that devastated many of its older structures, the town today has touches of modernity, with glass-and-concrete buildings, although there's still an old-fashioned **Saturday-morning market** on Jeremie Street. The country women dress in traditional cotton headdress to sell their luscious fruits and vegetables, while weather-beaten men sit close by playing warrie (a fast game played with pebbles on a carved board) or fleet games of dominoes using tiles the color of cherries.

COMING ASHORE   Most cruise ships arrive at a fairly new pier at **Pointe Seraphine,** within walking distance of the center of Castries. Unlike piers on other islands, this one boasts St. Lucia's best shopping. You'll also find a visitor information bureau. Phone cards are sold for use at specially labeled phones.

If Pointe Seraphine is too crowded (not too likely, as six megaships can pull alongside at once), your ship might dock at **Port Castries** on the other side of the colorful harbor. There's now a shopping terminal here called La Place Careenage. At press time, the port was in the process of adding an animation center that depicts St. Lucia's history to La Place Careenage. But if you still want to shop in Pointe Seraphine, a water taxi ($1) runs between the two all day. A land taxi will cost you around $4, or you can also walk between the two. Some smaller vessels, such as Star Clippers', Seabourn's, and Clipper's, anchor off Rodney Bay to the north or Soufrière to the south and carry you ashore by tender.

There are telephones inside La Place Carnage's duty free shopping mall and at the Pointe Seraphine pier.

LANGUAGE   **English** is the official language.

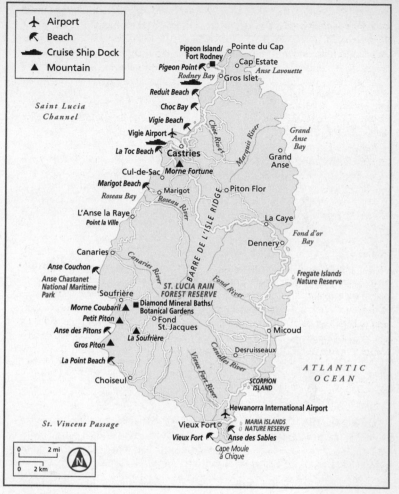

Legend:
- ✈ Airport
- 🏖 Beach
- 🚢 Cruise Ship Dock
- ▲ Mountain

Pointe du Cap
Pigeon Island/ Fort Rodney
Cap Estate
Pigeon Point
Anse Lavouette
Rodney Bay
Gros Islet
Reduit Beach
Choc Bay
Vigie Beach
Saint Lucia Channel
Vigie Airport
Grand Anse Bay
La Toc Beach
Castries
Grand Anse
Cul-de-Sac
Morne Fortune
Marigot Beach
Marigot
Piton Flor
Roseau Bay
L'Anse la Raye
La Caye
Point la Ville
Fond d'or Bay
Dennery
Canaries
Anse Couchon
Fregate Islands Nature Reserve
Anse Chastanet National Maritime Park
ST. LUCIA RAIN FOREST RESERVE
Soufrière
Morne Coubaril
Diamond Mineral Baths/ Botanical Gardens
Petit Piton
Fond
St. Jacques
Anse des Pitons
Micoud
Gros Piton
La Soufrière
Desruisseaux
La Point Beach
ATLANTIC OCEAN
Choiseul
SCORPION ISLAND
St. Vincent Passage
Hewanorra International Airport
Vieux Fort
MARIA ISLANDS NATURE RESERVE
Vieux Fort
Anse des Sables
Cape Moule à Chique

0   2 mi
0   2 km
N

CURRENCY The official monetary unit is the **Eastern Caribbean dollar** (EC$). The exchange rate is US$1 = EC$2.70; EC$1 = US73¢. Prices quoted in this section are in U.S. dollars, which are accepted by nearly all hotels, restaurants, and shops.

INFORMATION The **St. Lucia Tourist Board** is located at Vide Bouteille outside the town of Castries (© **758/452-4094**). The board runs a visitor information bureau at Pointe Seraphine, which is open Monday to Friday from 9am to 5pm. For info before you go, contact the tourism board office in the U.S. (© **800/456-3984** or 212/456-3984; www.stlucia.org).

CALLING FROM THE U.S. When calling St. Lucia from the United States, you just need to dial a "1" before the numbers listed here.

GETTING AROUND
BY TAXI Most taxi drivers have been trained to serve as guides. Their cars are unmetered, but the government fixes tariffs for all standard trips. Be sure to

---

⦿ Frommer's Favorite St. Lucia Experiences

Riding a Catamaran Along the Coast: See the lush coast of St. Lucia and the mighty Pitons via catamaran, and then ride a minibus to visit a volcano, the Diamond Baths (warm mineral baths), and sulfur springs. (See "Shore Excursions Offered by the Cruise Lines," below.)

Exploring a Banana Plantation: See how St. Lucia's leading export is grown and harvested. (See "On Your Own: Beyond the Port Area," below.)

Hiking up to Fort Rodney in Rodney Bay: The beautiful Pigeon Island on Rodney Bay offers the chance to hike up to Fort Rodney, an 18th-century English base that was used as an American signal station during World War II. From the top you can catch sight of Martinique. (See "Shore Excursions Offered by the Cruise Lines," below.)

---

determine if the driver is quoting a rate in U.S. or EC dollars. There is an official taxi association servicing both Pointe Seraphine and La Place Carenage. The taxi association will have standard fares posted. You can hire a taxi to go to Soufrière on your own, too. A taxi for four will cost about $120 for a 3- to 4-hour tour, including a beach stop, photo ops, shopping, and sightseeing. Avoid any driver who is not in uniform (which is really just a light-cotton tropical shirt).

BY RENTAL CAR　Driving is on the left, and roads are decent (but not great). The roads are not always clearly marked and are narrow. We wouldn't recommend renting a car, but if you're set on it, **Avis, Budget,** and **Hertz** all have offices here, as does **Courtesy Rent-A-Car** (© 758/452-8140).

SHORE EXCURSIONS OFFERED BY THE CRUISE LINES

Because of the difficult terrain, shore excursions are the best means of seeing this beautiful island in a day or less. In addition to the sampling below, most ships typically offer plantation tours, island bus tours, and snorkeling cruises.

Island Tour by Land & Sea ($69–$82, 8 hr.): A picturesque journey from Castries to the Piton peaks, via catamaran, takes you along St. Lucia's verdant coast. Docking at La Soufrière, you'll board a minibus and visit the volcano, the Diamond Baths (see "On Your Own: Beyond the Port Area," below), and sulfur springs. Lunch is included at a restaurant in Soufrière or on the boat.

Rainforest Bicycle Tour ($65, 4½ hr.): After being dropped off by bus in the middle of the forest, you'll ride past banana plantations and the Errard Falls waterfall, and stop to sample various fruits that grow along the roadside. Some time for swimming is usually included at the falls. A different tour takes riders to the Bike St. Lucia facility, where they can ride the 16km (10 miles) of trails at their own pace. Snorkeling time is included at the end ($86, 4½ hr.).

Pigeon Island Sea Kayaking ($64, 3 hr.): After transferring to Rodney Bay, you'll make the approximately 30-minute paddle out to the island, where you'll have time to swim, kayak some more, or make the steep climb up to Fort Rodney. From the summit, you'll have great views of the Pitons, and sometimes you'll even be able to see Martinique.

Beach Snorkel ($74, 3½ hr.): A 60-minute boat ride from Castries Harbor brings you to Anse Chastanet Marine Park, where you'll swim with an amazing variety of reef fish in a protected area.

EXCURSIONS OFFERED BY LOCAL AGENCIES

Horseback Treks: Trim's National Riding Stables, north of Castries, offers picnic trips to the Atlantic side of the island, with a barbecue lunch and drinks included. Departure is at 10am. The fee is $70 for a 2-hour ride. Nonriders can also join the excursion; they are transported to the site in a van and pay half price. To make arrangements, contact René Trim at © **758/450-8273.**

ON YOUR OWN: WITHIN WALKING DISTANCE

First, a tip: The last time we were at the duty-free marketplaces right at Castries' dock, a guy was doling out 5-minute massages for $5. If he's still there, this could save you a bundle on those expensive Steiner massages aboard the ship!

The principal streets of Castries are William Peter Boulevard and Bridge Street. Don't miss a walk through town: People are very friendly, and Jeremie Street is chockablock with variety stores of the most authentic local kind, selling everything from spices to housewares. A Roman Catholic cathedral stands on Columbus Square, which has a few restored buildings. Take a gander at the enormous 400-year-old "rain" tree, also called a "no-name" tree, which grows in the square. The nearby **Government House** is a late Victorian structure.

Beyond Government House lies **Morne Fortune,** which means "Hill of Good Luck." Actually, no one's had much luck here, certainly not the French and British soldiers who battled for Fort Charlotte. The fort switched nationalities (from French to English, and vice versa) many times. You can visit the 18th-century barracks, complete with a military cemetery, a small museum, the Old Powder Magazine, and the "Four Apostles Battery"—four grim muzzle-loading cannons. The view of the harbor of Castries is panoramic from this point. You can also see north to Pigeon Island or south to the Pitons. To reach Morne Fortune, head east on Bridge Street. Castries has a very colorful **Central Market,** right near the dock, which is also worth a visit. The airplane-hangar-size emporium sells local food, trinkets, and produce. Buy some banana ketchup or local cinnamon sticks to take home.

ON YOUR OWN: BEYOND THE PORT AREA

Bananas are St. Lucia's leading export, so if you're being taken around the island by a taxi driver, ask him to take you to one of the huge plantations. (Most island tours include a drive through one of the plantations as a matter of course.) We suggest a look at one of the three biggest: the **Cul-de-Sac,** just north of Marigot Bay; **La Caya,** on the east coast in Dennery; or the **Roseau Estate,** south of Marigot Bay.

St. Lucia's first national park, **Pigeon Island National Landmark,** was originally an island but is now joined to the northwest shore of the mainland by a very environmentally unfriendly causeway that has disrupted offshore currents, thereby upsetting the local fishing industry. The 18-hectare (44-acre) island got its name from the red-neck pigeon, or ramier, which once made this island home. It's ideal for picnics and nature walks, and is covered with lemongrass, which spread from original plantings made by British light opera singer Josset, who leased the island for 30 years and grew the grass to provide thatch for her cottage's roof. Every few years the grass, which is full of volatile oils, catches fire and immolates much of the island before it can be put out (© **758/450-0603**). Hours are 9am to 5pm daily; admission is $5 for adults, $1 for children 6 to 12.

The island's **Interpretation Centre** contains artifacts and a multimedia display of local history, covering everything from the Amerindian settlers of A.D. 1000 to 1782's Battle of Saints, when Admiral Rodney's fleet set out from Pigeon Island and defeated the French admiral De Grasse. Right below the interpretation center is the cozy **Captain's Cellar pub,** located in what was formerly a soldier's mess. From the tables outside you get wonderful views of the crashing surf on the Atlantic coast, just a few steps away.

From the center, you can walk up the winding and moderately steep path to a lookout from which you can see Martinique. In 1780, Admiral Rodney said of this spot, "This is the post the Governor of Martinique has set his eye on and if possessed by the enemy would deprive us of the best anchorage place in these islands, from which Martinique is always attackable." Remember that when planning your own assault. From the pinnacle you get a wonderful view, and the cannons that ring the space are a nice place to pose for "I was there" pictures.

On Pigeon Island's west coast are two white-sand beaches. There's also a restaurant, **Jambe de Bois** ("Leg of Wood"), named after a peg-legged pirate who once used the island as a hideout.

Pigeon Island National Landmark is open daily from 9am to 5pm. For more information, call the **St. Lucia National Trust** (© **758/452-5005**). The best way to get here is to take a taxi and arrange to be picked up in time to return to your ship (the trip is 30 min., at most, back to the docks). Some small ships anchor here and bring passengers ashore by tender.

La Soufrière, a fishing port and St. Lucia's second largest settlement, is dominated by the dramatic **Pitons,** Petit Piton and Gros Piton, two pointed peaks that rise right from the sea to 738m and 786m (2,460 ft. and 2,619 ft.), respectively. Formed by lava and once actively volcanic, these mountains are now cloaked in green vegetation, with waves crashing around their bases. Their sheer rise from the water makes them such visible landmarks that they've become the very symbol of St. Lucia.

Near the town of Soufrière lies the famous "drive-in" volcano, **La Soufrière,** a rocky lunar landscape of bubbling mud and craters seething with fuming sulfur. You can literally drive into an old crater and walk between the sulfur springs and pools of hissing steam. The fumes are said to have medicinal properties. A local guide is usually waiting nearby; if you do hire a guide, agree—then doubly agree—on what the fee will be.

Nearby are the **Diamond Mineral Baths** (© **758/452-4759**), surrounded by a tropical arboretum. They were constructed in 1784 by order of Louis XVI, whose doctors told him that these waters were similar in mineral content to the waters at Aix-les-Bains. The baths were built to help French soldiers who had been fighting in the West Indies recuperate from wounds and disease. Later destroyed, they were rebuilt after World War II. The water's average temperature is 106°F (41°C). You'll also find another fine attraction here: a waterfall that changes colors (from yellow to black to green to gray) several times a day. For about $2.60 you can bathe and benefit from the recuperative effects of the baths yourself.

SHOPPING

Many stores sell duty-free goods, and will deliver tobacco products and liquor to the cruise dock. Keep in mind, you are allowed to purchase only one bottle of liquor here (in St. Thomas, you can buy five). You'll find some good, but not remarkable, buys in bone china, jewelry, perfume, watches, liquor, and crystal. Souvenir items include designer bags and mats, local pottery, and straw hats—again, nothing remarkable. A tip: If your cruise is also calling in St. Thomas, let the local vendors know; it may make them more amenable to bargaining.

Built for cruise ship passengers, **Pointe Seraphine** has the best collection of shops on the island. You must present your cruise pass when making purchases here. Liquor and tobacco will be delivered to the ship.

Gablewoods Mall, on Gros Islet Highway, 3.2km (2 miles) north of Castries, has three restaurants and one of the densest concentrations of stores on St. Lucia. Since this mall is near some lovely beaches (and near the Sandals St. Lucia resort), it's possible to plan a day that combines shopping and sunbathing.

At **Caribelle Batik,** Howelton House, Old Victoria Road, The Morne (© 758/452-3785), just a 5-minute taxi ride from Castries, you can watch St. Lucian artists creating intricate patterns and colors through the ancient art of batik, which involves application of removable wax before dyes are applied so that the waxed area repels the dye. **Eudovic Art Studio,** Goodlands, Morne Fortune (© 758/452-2747), sells woodcarvings by St. Lucia native Vincent Joseph Eudovic and some of his pupils. Take a taxi from the cruise pier. Southwest of Soufrière, just past the small village of Choiseul, **Choiseul Craft Centre,** La Fargue (© 758/459-3226), is a government-funded retail outlet and training school that perpetuates the tradition of handmade Amerindian pottery and basketware. Some of the best basket weaving on the island is done here, using techniques practiced only in St. Lucia, St. Vincent, and Dominica. Look for place mats, handbags, woodcarvings (including bas-reliefs crafted from screw pine), and pottery. The craft center is open Monday to Friday 8:30am to 4pm and Saturday 10:30am to 2:30pm.

BEACHES

If you don't take a shore excursion, you might want to spend your time on one of St. Lucia's famous beaches, all of which are open to the public, even those at hotel properties (but you must pay to use a hotel's beach equipment). Taxis can take you to any of the island's beaches, but we recommend that you stick to the calmer shores along the western coast, since the rough surf on the windward Atlantic side makes swimming potentially dangerous.

Leading beaches include **Pigeon Island,** off the northern shore, with white sand and picnic facilities; **Vigie Beach,** north of Castries Harbour, with fine sand; **Marigot Beach,** south of Castries Harbour, framed on three sides by steep emerald hills and skirted by palm trees; and **Reduit Beach,** between Choc Bay and Pigeon Point, with fine brown sand. For sheer novelty, you might want to visit the black-volcanic-sand beach at **Soufrière.**

Just north of Soufrière is a beach connoisseur's delight, **Anse Chastanet** (© 758/459-7000), boasting an expanse of white sand at the foothills of lush, green mountains. This is a fantastic spot for snorkeling.

SPORTS

SCUBA DIVING In Soufrière, **Scuba St. Lucia,** in the Anse Chastanet Hotel (© 758/459-7000; www.scubastlucia.com), is a five-star PADI dive center offering great diving and comprehensive facilities. The hotel is at the southern end of Anse Chastanet's .4km (¼-mile) secluded beach. Some of St. Lucia's most spectacular coral reefs—many only 3m to 6m (10 ft.–20 ft.) below the surface—provide shelter for sea creatures just a short distance offshore.

)RTS **St. Lucian Watersports,** on Reduit Beach at the Rex St.
1 (© **758/452-8351**), is the best place to rent watersports equip-
range water-skiing.

GREAT LOCAL RESTAURANTS & BARS

A really, really great **local beer** is Piton—very refreshing on a hot day, like
Corona but better. A favorite **local rum** is Bounty.

IN CASTRIES At the **Green Parrot,** Red Tape Lane, Morne Fortune, about
2.4km (1½ miles) east of the town center (© **758/452-3399**), there's an emphasis on St. Lucian specialties and homegrown produce (the restaurant has trained
cruise ship chefs in the use of local products). Try the christophine au gratin (a
Caribbean squash with cheese) or the Creole soup made with callaloo (a leafy
green) and pumpkin. Lunch $10. **Jimmie's,** Vigie Cove Marina (© **758/452-
5142**), is known for its fresh-fish menu and tasty Creole cookery.

AT MARIGOT BAY **Doolittle's,** at the Marigot Beach Club (© **758/451-
4974;** www.marigotdiveresort.com/dining.htm), showcases Caribbean and
international dishes. To reach the place, you'll have to take a ferryboat across
Marigot Bay. The ferry runs from the Moorings Marigot Bay Resort about every
10 minutes throughout the day and evening. Lunch $18.

IN THE SOUFRIERE AREA **Chez Camilla Guest House & Restaurant,**
7 Bridge St., 1 block inland from the waterfront (© **758/459-5379**), is the only
really good place to eat in the village of Soufrière itself. It serves sandwiches, cold
salads, omelets, and burgers at lunch. **Dasheene Restaurant & Bar,** in the
Ladera Resort, between Gros and Petit Piton (© **758/459-7323**), serves the
most refined and certainly the most creative cuisine in St. Lucia. The chef has a
special flair with the seafood pasta and the marinated sirloin steak. Your best bet
is the catch of the day, likely to be kingfish or red snapper, grilled to perfection.
Other standouts are the dumpling-and-callaloo soup, the fresh pumpkin risotto
with red pepper coulis, and the banana-stuffed pork with ginger and coconut
sauce. The restaurant is perched atop a 300m (1,000-ft.) ridge and framed by
the rising twin peaks of the Pitons. Everything is locally produced, including the
furniture. Lunch $15.

IN RODNEY BAY **The Lime,** north of Reduit Beach (© **758/452-0761**), is
a casual local place specializing in stuffed crab backs and Creole-seasoned fish
steaks. It also serves shrimp, steaks, lamb, pork chops, and rotis (Caribbean burritos). The **Mortar & Pestle,** in the Harmony Marina Suites, Rodney Bay
Lagoon (© **758/452-8711**), offers indoor-outdoor dining with a view of the
boats moored at the nearby marina. For something truly regional, try the Barbados souse, full of marinated pieces of lean cooked pork, or the frogs' legs from
Dominica. Lunch $13.

25 St. Martin/Sint Maarten

Who can resist a two-for-one sale? On the island of St. Martin, you get two cultures, two nationalities, and two different experiences for the price of one. Occupying the bend where the Lesser and Greater Antilles meet, about 242km (150
miles) southeast of Puerto Rico, this is the smallest territory in the world that is
shared by two sovereign states: France, with 52 sq. km (20 sq. miles), and the
Netherlands, with 44 sq. km (17 sq. miles). The two nations have shared the
island in a spirit of neighborly cooperation and mutual friendship for more than

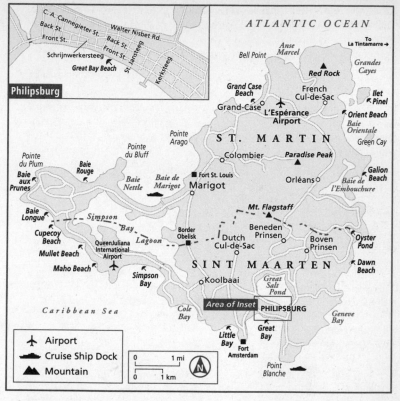

Philipsburg

ATLANTIC OCEAN

Airport
Cruise Ship Dock
Mountain

350 years. Although the border between the two sides is virtually imperceptible—a monument along the road marks the change in administration—each side retains elements of its own heritage. The French side, with some of the best beaches and restaurants in the Caribbean, emphasizes quiet elegance. French fashions and luxury items fill the shops, and the fragrance of croissants mixes with the spicy aromas of West Indian cooking. The Dutch side, officially known as Sint Maarten, reflects Holland's anything-goes philosophy: Development is much more widespread, flashy casinos pepper the landscape, and strip malls make the larger towns look as much like Anaheim as Amsterdam. The 100% duty-free shopping has turned both sides of the island into a bargain-hunter's paradise.

St. Martin's first inhabitants, the Stone Age hunter-gatherer Ciboneys, arrived as early as 1800 B.C. The first Dutch and French colonists arrived more than 100 year later, in the early 17th century, and exchanged some martial rumblings before deciding, in March 1648, to just get along, splitting the island roughly in two. Coffee, sugar, rum, and salt brought relative prosperity to the island, but not to the slaves brought over from Africa. Tourism supplanted agriculture as the major industry in the last half of the 20th century.

Today, the Dutch side holds a slight population edge: 41,000 people to the French side's 36,000. Most locals are descendants of African slaves, but residents born in France, Holland, and the U.S. occupy many of the villas and condominiums around the island.

COMING ASHORE Most cruise ships dock on the Dutch side, at A. C. Wathey Pier, about 1.6km (1 mile) southeast of **Philipsburg.** The majority of passengers are then tendered to the smaller Captain Hodge Pier at the center of town, but others choose to walk the distance or take taxis. The Wathey pier has few facilities except for some credit-card phones, whereas the Hodge Pier offers immediate access to phones, tourist information, and taxis.

Smaller vessels sometimes dock on the French side of the island, at Marina Port la Royale, adjacent to the heart of **Marigot.** The waterfront here features restaurants, shopping arcades, and a tourist office. The pier accommodates only one ship at a time, so passengers on subsequently arriving vessels are tendered ashore.

LANGUAGE Surprise, surprise: The official language on the **Dutch** side is Dutch, and the official language on the **French** side is French. Most people on both sides also speak **English.** Among locals on the street, patois is often spoken: **Papiamento** on the Dutch side, **Creole** on the French.

CURRENCY The legal tender in Dutch Sint Maarten is the **Netherlands Antilles guilder,** or NAf (NAf1.9 = US$1; NAf1 = US55¢), and the official currency on the French side is the **euro** (€1 = US$1.10; $1 = €.90). U.S. dollars are widely accepted on both sides, though, so there's no need to change money. Most prices are quoted in U.S. dollars, too, so you're spared the work of calculating exchange rates. Credit cards and travelers checks are readily accepted, as well. Prices in this chapter are given in U.S. dollars. ATMs abound in both Philipsburg and Marigot.

INFORMATION **On the Dutch side,** the Tourist Information Bureau headquarters, in the Imperial Building at 23 Walter Nisbeth Road in Philipsburg (© **599/542-2337**), is open Monday to Friday from 8am to 5pm. There's a smaller but more conveniently located satellite office at the town pier. For information before you go, call the tourist board office in the U.S. (© **800/786-2278;** www.st-maarten.com).

The Tourist Information office **on the French side** is adjacent to the pier at Marina Royale in Marigot (© **590/87-57-23**). It's open Monday to Friday from 8:30am to 1pm and 2:30 to 5:30pm. For info before you go, contact the French St. Martin Tourism Board in the U.S. (© **212/475-8970;** www.st-martin.org).

CALLING FROM THE U.S. When calling **Dutch** Sint Maarten from the United States, simply dial the international access number (011) before the numbers listed here. Calling **French** Saint Martin requires more of an effort: dial 011, then 590 before the numbers listed. Yes, 590 appears in our listed numbers, but those three digits must be dialed twice to make a connection.

GETTING AROUND

BY TAXI Taxis on both sides of the island are unmetered. Agree on a rate and currency before getting in. Dutch law requires that drivers list government-regulated fares, which assume two passengers (each additional passenger is another $4). Shorter rides, including the route between Marigot and Philipsburg, average around $12; longer trips can climb to $20-plus. Drivers, who greet cruisers in both Philipsburg and Marigot, expect at least a $1 tip for short runs, more for extended 2-hour sightseeing trips around the island. To call a taxi on the Dutch side, dial © **599/542-2359.** On the French side, dial © **590/87-56-54.**

BY MINIVAN Privately owned and operated minivans are a reasonable way to get around, if you don't mind frequent stops, potential overcrowding, and the local zouk and soca music that's usually playing (a plus or a minus, depending on your tastes). These jitneys run daily from 7am to midnight and serve much of the island. The most popular run, between Philipsburg and Marigot, has almost constant service. Fares range from about $1 to $2. The vans, which have signs to indicate their destination, can be hailed anywhere on the street.

BY RENTAL CAR   Rental cars are a great way to make the most of your day and see both sides of the island. Driving is on the right side, roads are generally in decent shape, and signage is in either international symbols or English. Parking can be a headache in both Philipsburg and Marigot, and road construction and drawbridges sometimes exacerbate congestion. Away from the two main towns, however, zipping along is a breeze. **Avis, Budget,** and **Hertz** all have offices here.

SHORE EXCURSIONS OFFERED BY THE CRUISE LINES

America's Cup Sailing Regatta ($84, 3 hr.): Get a taste of nautical exhilaration by competing in a race aboard Dennis Connor's America's Cup–winning *Stars & Stripes*. This hands-on, extremely popular excursion lets you grind winches, trim sails, and duck under booms—after you've been trained by professionals, of course. Alternatively, sit back and watch others do all the work. In either case, wear your Topsiders (or other soft-soled shoes).

Island Tour ($23, 3 hr.): See both sides of the island from the air-conditioned comfort of your minibus, stopping along the way to marvel at various panoramas. A stopover in Marigot allows some for some on-foot town sightseeing and shopping.

Ilet Pinel Snorkeling Tour ($37, 3½ hr.): After a scenic bus ride to the French town of Cul de Sac, along the northeast coast, hop on a tender to the small offshore island of Ilet Pinel for some of St. Martin's best snorkeling.

Butterfly Farm & Marigot ($38, 3½ hr.): After a scenic drive through both the French and Dutch sides of the island, walk through a surrealistic enclosed garden that features pools, waterfalls, and hundreds of exquisitely beautiful and exotic butterflies from around the world. Amusing guides identify species, describe courtship and mating rituals, and give tips on attracting butterflies to your garden at home. Afterward, absorb the Creole charm and French atmosphere of Marigot.

EXCURSIONS OFFERED BY LOCAL AGENCIES

Horseback Treks: Bayside Riding Club, Coconut Grove, next to the Butterfly Farm (© **590/87-36-64**), offers 2-hour riding expeditions ($60 per person) that conclude on an isolated beach, where horses and riders enjoy a cool post-ride romp in the water. Half-hour pony rides with a handler, for the little ones, are $25. Riders of all experience levels are welcome.

Mountain Biking Tours: Frog Legs (© **590/87-05-11**), based in Marigot, offers three tours, which vary in difficulty (5%–30% climb), time (from a little under 2 hr. to more than 4 hr.), and price ($40–$45). Some stay along the coast, others move to inland hills.

Scuba Diving: Of the island's 40 dive sites, the 1801 British man-of-war HMS *Proselyte,* which sank to a watery grave on a reef 1.6km (1 mile) off the coast, is the most popular. Other favorites include Ilet Pinel, for shallow diving; the Green Key barrier reef; and Flat Island, for its sheltered coves and geologic faults. On the Dutch side, **Pelican Watersports,** Simpson Bay (© **599/544-2640**),

C Frommer's Favorite St. Martin Experiences

Sizzling in the Sun: On the French side, colorful open-air restaurants and bars line Orient Beach, a social, very European strand humming with motorized water toys.

Dejeuner Chez Madame Claude's Mini Club: Savor the rich flavors of Creole and French cuisine on the cozy, colorfully painted upstairs terrace of Marigot's oldest restaurant. (See "Great Local Restaurants & Bars," below.)

Competing for the America's Cup: Race on and against 12m (40-ft.) yachts that once competed in the famed America's Cup race. (See "Shore Excursions Offered by the Cruise Lines," above.)

Trekking up to the Ramparts of Fort St. Louis: A 10- or 15-minute walk from the heart of Marigot will take you to the top of the fort, where you're treated to panoramic views of Marigot and beyond. (See "On Your Own: Within Walking Distance," below.)

employs some the most knowledgeable guides on the island. Dives are $45 to $90. One of the French side's premier dive operators, **Marine Time,** is in Quartier d'Orléans, not far from Coconut Grove Beach (© **590/87-20-28**). Single-tank dives with all equipment run about $45; two-tank dives are around $90.

ON YOUR OWN: WITHIN WALKING DISTANCE

Shopping, sunbathing, and gambling are the pastimes that interest most cruisers who hit this island, but folks with a taste for culture and history can make a day of it here as well.

ON THE DUTCH SIDE   Directly in front of the Philipsburg town pier, on Wathey Square, the **Courthouse** combines northern European sobriety with Caribbean brightness. Originally built in 1793 of freestone and wood, this venerable old building has suffered numerous hurricanes, but has been restored after each tempest and continues to house government offices. East of the Courthouse, at 7 Front St. (down a little shopping alley), the tiny **Sint Maarten Museum** (© **599/542-4917**) features modest, cluttered exhibits that focus on the island's history and geology. The second-floor gallery is open every day but Sunday. There's no admission fee, but donations are appreciated. The museum is open Monday through Friday, from 10am to 4pm, and Saturday 10am to 2pm. The street-level gift shop stocks handicrafts, postcards, and books.

Historically, **Fort Amsterdam** is the Dutch side's most important colonial site. Since 1631, the fort has looked out over Great Bay from the hill west of Philipsburg. The fort was the Netherlands' first military outpost in the Caribbean. The Spanish captured it 2 years later, making it their most significant bastion east of Puerto Rico. Peter Stuyvesant, who later became governor of New Amsterdam (now New York), lost his leg to a cannonball while trying to reclaim the fort for Holland. The site provides grand views of the bay, but ruins of the walls and a couple of rusty cannons are all that remain of the original fort.

ON THE FRENCH SIDE   **Fort St. Louis** is Marigot's answer to Fort Amsterdam. Built in 1767 to protect the waterfront warehouses that stored the French colony's agricultural riches, the cannons of this bastion frequently fired on hostile British raiders from Anguilla. After restorations and modification in the 19th century, the fort was eventually abandoned. In addition to the fort's cannons, crumbling walls, and French *tricouleur* flag flapping in the breeze, the short climb up the hill flanking Marigot Bay's north end affords splendid vistas. As a respite from the sun, duck into Marigot's **Museum of Saint Martin** (© 590/29-22-84), next to the Tourism Office and adjacent to the marina. Much more thorough and scholarly than its Philipsburg counterpart, this institution boasts a first-rate collection of Ciboney, Arawak, and Carib artifacts excavated from the island's Amerindian sites, plus a reproduction of a 1,500-year-old burial mound. Another display details the history of the plantation and slavery era, and early-20th-century photographs trace the island's modern development. It's open Monday through Friday 9am to 4pm, Saturday 9am to 1pm. Admission is $5 for adults, $2 for children.

GAMBLING

Slot machines and game tables can be found in the Dutch side's dozen casinos. Most of the heavy betting takes place after dark, but a handful of casinos open before noon. In the heart of Philipsburg on Front Street, **Coliseum Casino** (© 599/543-2101), **Diamond Casino** (© 599/543-2565), **Paradise Plaza Slots World** (© 599/5434-4721), and **Rouge et Noir** (© 599/542-2952) all open at 11am, early enough to snag cruisers. West of Philipsburg, **Hollywood Casino,** at the Pelican Resort on Simpson Bay (© 599/544-2503), features a panoramic view of the water and offers craps, roulette, blackjack, stud poker, and slots after 1pm. Farther west, at Maho Bay, **Casino Royale** (© 599/545-2590) has roulette, Caribbean stud poker, craps, blackjack, baccarat, minibaccarat, and slots, also after 1pm.

SHOPPING

St. Martin is a true free port—no duties are paid on any item coming in or going out—and neither side of the island has a sales tax.

ON THE DUTCH SIDE   Shops in the much busier Dutch side are concentrated in Philipsburg, along Front Street and the numerous alleys radiating from it. The district is largely nondescript, but you'll find all the usual suspects—the omnipresent jewelry and luxury-item shop **Little Switzerland** and a host of other jewelry/gift/luxury-item shops—as well as some quirky local boutiques. In general, prices in the major stores are nonnegotiable, but at small, family-run shops, you can try your luck with a little polite bargaining. The T-shirt and souvenir epicenter is in the open-air market behind the Courthouse in front of the town pier.

    Guavaberry Emporium, 8–10 Front St., sells Guavaberry "island folk liqueur," an aged rum with a distinctive fruity, woody, almost bittersweet flavor; it's available only on St. Martin. Parrot heads in search of all things Jimmy Buffett should cross the street to **Last Mango in Paradise,** 17 Front St., for CDs, T-shirts—you name it, they got it. Walking west, Old Street, off Front Street, features a couple dozen boutiques, including **Colombian Emeralds** and **The Belgian Chocolate Shop.** For cigars, **La Casa del Habano,** 24 Front St., has Cohibas, Montecristos, and the like; while **Lipstick,** 31 Front St., is your best bet for perfumes and cosmetics. Next door, **Dutch Delft Blue,** 29 Front St., stocks the distinctive blue-and-white porcelain.

ON THE FRENCH SIDE   **Marigot** features a much calmer, more charming, and sophisticated ambience, with waterfront cafes where you can rest your weary over-shopped feet. Many shops here close their doors for a 2-hour lunch break starting at noon.

The wide selection of European merchandise is skewed toward an upscale audience, but French crystal, perfume, liqueur, jewelry, and fashion can be up to 50% less expensive than in the States. At Marina Port la Royale, **Havane** offers casual and high-fashion French clothing for men; while **L'Epicerie** stocks caviar, foie gras, and a host of French wines. For chic women's clothing, especially Italian styles, start your search at **La Romana,** 12 rue de la République. **Oro de Sol Jewelers,** rue de la République, is one of many purveyors of bracelets, necklaces, and watches; while **Beauty & Scents,** rue du Général de Gaulle, has your favorite perfumes and cosmetics.

An inviting **open-air craft market** sprawls along the waterfront next to Boulevard de France every day, while on Wednesdays and Saturdays, another open-air market stretches from the base of Fort St. Louis to the wharves below, offering a colorful array of homegrown produce, tropical fruits and spices, and fresh fish. **Gingerbread & Mahogany Gallery,** Marina Port la Royale (in a narrow alleyway at the marina), deals in Haitian art by both old masters and talented amateurs.

BEACHES

Beach lovers rejoice: St. Martin has more than 30 beautiful white-sand beaches, some social, some serene. The busier ones boast bars, restaurants, watersports, and hotels, where changing facilities are usually available for a small fee. Toplessness is ubiquitous, and nudism is common on the French side, and increasingly evident on the Dutch side as well.

ON THE DUTCH SIDE **Great Bay Beach** is your best bet if you want to stay in Philipsburg. This 1.6km- (1-mile-) long stretch is convenient, but because it borders the busy capital, it lacks the tranquillity and cleanliness of the more remote beaches. The water is calm, though, and all the amenities of Philipsburg are a step away.

Just west of the airport, on the west side of the island, **Maho Beach** boasts a casino, shade palms, and a popular beachside bar and grill. The biggest attraction, however, seems to be its views of takeoffs and landings (keep your belongings outside the flight path; jumbo jets sometimes blow items into the surf). Farther west, **Mullet Beach** borders the island's golf course. Shaded by palm trees and crowded on weekends, it's popular with swimmers and snorkelers. On-site vendors rent an array of watersports equipment. Just around the corner to the west (just below the Dutch-French border), but miles away mentally, lies perfectly serene **Cupecoy Beach.** Set against a stunningly beautiful backdrop of mysterious caves and sandstone cliffs that provide morning shade, this beach has no facilities, but a vendor at the parking lot rents beach chairs and shade umbrellas. The clientele is adult, primarily in the buff, quiet, and, not infrequently, gay. The surf can be strong, and aficionados claim that the sun here is more intense than anywhere else on the island.

ON THE FRENCH SIDE Far and away the island's most visited strand, **Orient Beach,** on the northeast coast, fancies itself "the Saint Tropez of the Caribbean." Hedonism is the name of the game here: plenty of food, drink, music, and flesh (a naturist resort occupies the beach's southern tip, but nudism isn't confined to any one area). Watersports abound. South of Orient Beach, the waveless waters of Coconut Grove or **Galion Beach** are shallow 30m (100 ft.) out. Protected by a coral reef, this area is No. 1 with kids and popular with windsurfers.

On the island's west coast, just north of the Dutch border, **Long Bay** is the island's longest beach and another refuge for adults seeking peace and quiet. There are no facilities here, but this wild beach bordering some of the island's grandest mansions is popular with the rich and (sometimes) famous. The water and sand here are silky.

SPORTS

GOLF The **Mullet Bay Golf Course** (© 599/545-2850), on the Dutch side, has an 18-hole course designed by Joseph Lee that's considered one of the more challenging in the Caribbean, especially the back 9. Mullet Pond and Simpson Bay lagoon provide both beauty and hazards. Greens fees and cart rental for 18 holes is $110; for 9 holes it's $65; club rental is an additional $25. The course opens at 7am, 7 days a week.

SNORKELING Tiny coves and calm offshore waters make St. Martin a snorkeler's paradise. Dawn Beach, on the Dutch east coast, is the best snorkeling site on the island (rent equipment from **Busby's Beach Bar,** which is right on the beach), followed by **Maho** (Dutch side) and the French side's **Baie Rouge** and **Ilet Pinel,** the latter of which can be reached by ferry from Cul de Sac (about $5 per person, round-trip). Most hotels and restaurants at these sites rent equipment for about $10.

WATERSPORTS Most of the large hotels on Orient Beach offer an array of watersports adventures, often from makeshift kiosks on the beach. Two independent operators function from side-by-side positions near the Esmeralda Hotel: **Kon Tiki Watersport** (© 590/87-46-89) and **Bikini Watersports** (© 690/27-07-48). From these operators, jet skis and WaveRunners go for about $45 for 30 minutes, $80 for an hour; and parasailing $50 to $80.

GREAT LOCAL RESTAURANTS & BARS

A favorite **local beer** (on both the Dutch and French sides) is Red White and Blue, while the indigenous **rum liqueur** is the fruity and slightly bitter Guavaberry.

ON THE DUTCH SIDE As might be expected, food is usually better on the French side, but Dutch St. Maarten has a number of appealing restaurants, too. In Philipsburg, **Da Livio Ristorante,** 159 Front St. (© 599/542-2690), serves delicious seafood, veal, and pasta, including the house specialty, homemade manicotti. Dine alfresco with views of Great Bay, and check out the photos of celebrities who've sated their hunger here. Lunch $22. Next to the historic courthouse, just off Front Street at 6 Hendrikstraat, **Kangaroo Court** (© 599/542-7557) is Philipsburg's coziest coffeehouse. Stop in for a quick latte and muffin or grab a table in back for a salad, burger, or sandwich. The rich, gooey desserts can satisfy the most insatiable sweet tooth. Lunch $8. Indonesian *rijstaffel* is yours for the asking at **Wajang Doll,** 167 Front St. (© 599/542-2687). Order the 14-dish sampling of Javanese, Balinese, and Sumatran cuisine, or opt for something lighter, such as red snapper with ginger, chili, and lemongrass. Lunch $20.

ON THE FRENCH SIDE In Marigot, Madame Claude herself is running the show at **Mini Club** (© 590/87-50-69), one of the oldest restaurants in town, on the waterfront street rue des Pêcheurs. Savor the rich flavors of spicy conch stew, Creole-style fresh fish, or other West Indian and French dishes on the cozy, bright-yellow upstairs terrace. **La Brasserie de Marigot,** 11 rue du

Général-de-Gaulle (© **590/87-94-43**), is another great choice for good food at modest prices. Dishes include pot-au-feu, duck breast with peaches, and steak tartare. For light salads, sandwiches, and ice-cream concoctions, claim a harborside table at **La Vie en Rose,** at the corner of rue de la République and Boulevard de France (© **590/87-54-42**). Lunch $15.

26 Trinidad & Tobago

The southernmost islands in the Caribbean chain, Trinidad and tiny Tobago (which together form a single nation), manage to encompass nearly every facet of Caribbean life. Located less than 16km (10 miles) east of Venezuela's coast, Trinidad is large (the biggest and most heavily populated Caribbean island) and diverse, with an industrial, cosmopolitan capital city, Port of Spain, and an outgoing, vibrant culture that combines African, East Indian, European, Chinese, and Syrian influences. Little-sister Tobago is the more natural of the two, with rainforested mountains and spectacular secluded beaches.

Trinidad and Tobago won independence from Britain in 1962 and became a republic in 1976, but some British influences, including the residents' love of cricket, remain. Trinidad grew rich from oil, and the islands are still the Western hemisphere's largest oil exporters.

Trinidad's music is another local treasure. The calypso, steel-pan, and soca styles that originated here have influenced musical trends worldwide. Trinidad's rhythmic, soulful music is a main feature of **Carnaval,** the Caribbean-wide bacchanalian celebration held each year on the Monday and Tuesday before Lent. Among all the Carnaval celebrations in the Caribbean, Trinidad's is king.

Trinidad's residents are charming, are friendly, and love to talk. With a literacy rate of 97%, the populace is full of well-informed conversationalists. You'll find Trinis (as residents call themselves) happy to socialize with visitors and discuss just about anything.

LANGUAGE The official language is **English,** but like many of their Caribbean neighbors, Trinis speak English with a distinct patois. Hindi, Creole, and Spanish are also spoken among various ethnic groups.

CURRENCY The unit of currency is the **Trinidad & Tobago dollar,** sometimes designated by the same symbol as the U.S. dollar ($) and sometimes just by "TT." The exchange rate is US$1 = TT$6.22; TT$1 = US16¢. Vacationers can pay in U.S. dollars, but be sure you know what currency prices are being quoted in, and try to get change in U.S. dollars. Unless otherwise specified, prices in this section are given in U.S. dollars. Local **ATM** machines mainly dispense TT notes.

CALLING FROM THE U.S. When calling Trinidad and Tobago from the United States, you just need to dial "1" before the numbers listed here.

TRINIDAD

Trinidad is one of the most industrialized countries in the Caribbean, and it shows—if you're looking for a sleepy, quiet Caribbean retreat, go to Tobago instead. Trinidad's capital and commercial center, **Port of Spain,** is an energetic, bustling metropolis of 300,000. There are few distinct attractions—Port of Spain isn't necessarily a tourist city—but the central shopping area at the south end of Frederick Street is a colorfully crowded mix of outdoor shopping arcades and air-conditioned minimalls.

Independence Square, in the heart of Port of Spain, is the place to get a taxi, find a bank, and get good, cheap food. There are mosques, shrines, and temples here, and locals gather at Woodford Square to hear public speakers or attend outdoor meetings.

While Port of Spain is interesting and not threatening by day, it's unsafe at night, and strolling around is not recommended if your ship happens to be in port late.

COMING ASHORE   Cruise ships visiting Trinidad dock at Port of Spain's 1.6-hectare (4-acre) cruise terminal, built in the early 1990s to accommodate the island's growing cruise traffic. The complex includes a telephone and communications center, a shopping mall, tourist info, and car-rental agencies. Arriving passengers are usually greeted by steel-pan musicians and colorfully dressed dancers. Outside the terminal, there's a craft market with T-shirts, straw items, and other souvenirs.

INFORMATION   The **Tourism and Industrial Development Corporation of Trinidad and Tobago (TIDCO)** is located at 10–14 Phillips St., at the terminal in Port of Spain (© **868/623-1932** or 888/595-4TNT). It's open Monday to Friday from 8am to 4:30pm. For info before you go, contact the tourism board office in the U.S. (© **212/682-7272;** www.visittnt.com).

> ⓒ **Frommer's Favorite Trinidad Experiences**
>
> **Visiting the Asa Wright Nature Center:** This 80-hectare (200-acre) preserve, located in Trinidad's rainforest in the northern hills, features intertwined hiking trails, a bird sanctuary, and a conservation center. (See "On Your Own: Beyond the Port Area," below.)
>
> **Touring the Caroni Bird Sanctuary:** This ecological wonder features dense mangroves, remote canals, and shallow lagoons that are the breeding grounds for spectacular scarlet ibis. Visitors tour the sanctuary in guided boats. (See "Shore Excursions Offered by the Cruise Lines," below.)
>
> **Trying a Drink with Angostura Bitters:** This local specialty contains citrus-tree bark and is made from a secret recipe.

GETTING AROUND

BY TAXI Taxis are available at the cruise terminal. The registered taxi association at the Port-of-Spain is the Trinidad and Tobago Tourist Transport Association. These drivers are trained tour guides who are identified by dark pants and shirts with printed taxi association monograms. Another identifier is that these drivers' car license plates begin with the letter *H* (for "hiring car"). The Port Authority posts cab fares on a board by the main entrance (the cars don't have meters). Always establish a fare before loading into the taxi and shoving off. Private cabs can be relatively expensive.

BY VAN Maxi-taxis (minivans operating regular routes within specific zones) have a yellow stripe and are lower priced than taxis. There are also route taxis, shared cabs that travel along a prescribed route and charge about TT$2 to TT$8 (US30¢–US$1.30) to drop you at any spot along the route.

BY RENTAL CAR Driving is on the left. Trinidad has a fairly wide network of roads, and roads in town are generally well marked; but traffic is frequently heavy. None of the major rental companies have offices here.

SHORE EXCURSIONS OFFERED BY THE CRUISE LINES

Caroni Bird Sanctuary ($44, 3 hr.): This sanctuary is a pristine network of lush mangroves, quiet canals, and shallow lagoons, and is considered a world-class bird-watching preserve. Following a 30-minute drive from the cruise pier, passengers embark for the tour in flat-bottomed boats, which glide through calm canals and lagoons. Guides will point out unique flora and fauna during the ride. Heron, osprey, and scarlet ibis are among the bird species native to this area.

ON YOUR OWN: WITHIN WALKING DISTANCE

Except for the craft market right outside the terminal, and a small restaurant across the street, there isn't much to see close to the cruise pier.

ON YOUR OWN: BEYOND THE PORT AREA

Among Port of Spain's chief centers of activity, **Independence Square,** a stone's throw from the cruise complex, isn't really a square at all but parallel streets running east and west and connected at one end by a pedestrian mall. The scene here resembles a Middle Eastern bazaar, with a dense thicket of pushcarts, honking cabs, produce hawkers, and inquisitive shoppers moving to the irresistible beat of soca, reggae, and calypso music blaring from nearby stores and sidewalk stands. Some parts of the square have become run-down, and some locals consider the area less than safe. Visitors should keep an eye out for pickpockets and petty thieves.

Woodford Square, laid out by Ralph Woodford, Trinidad's early-19th-century British governor, is among the most attractive areas in town, full of large, leafy trees surrounding a rich lawn with landscaped walkways. This area has traditionally served as a center for political debates, discussions, and rallies. The **Cathedral of the Holy Trinity,** built in 1818 by Woodford, lies on the square's south side. The church's carved roof is designed as a replica of Westminster Hall in London. Inside the church is a memorial statue of Woodford himself. To reach the square, take Independence Square North and then go left on Abercromby Street, or Wrightson Road to Sackville Street.

On the square's western border is **Red House,** an imposing (and, yes, red) Renaissance-style edifice built in 1906. Today, it houses Trinidad's parliament. The building was badly damaged in 1990 when militants took the prime minister and parliament members hostage. A little farther north of the city center is **Queen's Park Savannah,** originally part of a 80-hectare (200-acre) sugar plantation but now a public park with 32 hectares (80 acres) of open land and walkways, with great shade trees. A depression at the park's northwest section, known as the Hollows, has flower beds, rock gardens, and small ponds. The area has become a popular picnic spot. Most streets heading north from the cruise complex end at the park.

There are a number of notable sights along the park's outer, western edge, including the **Magnificent Seven,** a row of seven colonial buildings constructed in the late 19th and early 20th centuries. The buildings include Queen's Royal College, White Hall (the prime minister's office), and Stollmeyer's Castle, which was designed to resemble a Scottish castle—complete with turrets.

Beyond the northern edge of Queen's Park Savannah lies the **Emperor Valley Zoo (© 868/622-3530),** featuring local animals, including tropical toucans and macaws, porcupines, monkeys, and various snakes. The zoo emphasizes colorful tropical plants, which are in evidence all over the grounds. It's open 9:30am to 5:30pm daily; admission is $1 adults, 25¢ for children.

The 28-hectare (70-acre) **botanical gardens** are east of the zoo. Laid out in 1820, the gardens are landscaped with attractive walkways and great flowering trees, among them the wild poinsettia, whose bright red blossom is the national flower. The **President's House,** built in 1875 as the governor's residence, is adjacent to the gardens.

Near Spring Hill Estate, 48km (30 miles) northeast of Port of Spain beside Blanchisseuse Road, the **Asa Wright Nature Center (© 868/667-4655; www.asawright.org)** is known to bird-watchers throughout the world. Within its 78 hectares (196 acres), set at an elevation of 360m (1,200 ft.) in Trinidad's rainforested mountains, you can see hummingbirds, toucans, bellbirds, manakins, several varieties of tanagers, and the rare oilbird. Hiking trails line the grounds, and guided tours are available. Call for a schedule.

SHOPPING

Shopping in the Port of Spain area means crafts, fabrics, and fashions made by local artists, a range of spices, and colorful artwork. Most of the shopping opportunities lie in the area around **Independence Square,** particularly near Frederick and Queen streets. Art lovers will find a handful of galleries and studios featuring the work of local and regional artists. **Art Creators,** at Seventh Street and St. Ann's Road in the Aldegonda Park section ((℃ **868/624-4369**), is a serious gallery offering year-around exhibits of both newly emerging and established artists. **Aquarela Galleries,** at 1A Dere St., exhibits the work of recognized and up-and-coming Trini artists and also publishes high-end art books. If you're in the mood for distinctive gift and apparel shopping, hire a cab to the **Hotel Normandie,** 10 Nook Ave. in the St. Ann's section (℃ **868/624-1181**), where the **Village Market shops** feature clothing and jewelry by some of the country's top designers. The market's **Greer's Textile Designs** carries colorful batiks and pricey jewelry from designer Jillian Bishop. You'll also find **Interiors** here, which sells all manner of unusual gifts.

For craft creations outside of the cruise terminal area, try the **Trinidad and Tobago Blind Welfare Association,** at 118 Duke St., with accessories and gifts of rattan and other natural materials, all made by blind craftsmen. **Art Potters Ltd.,** located at the cruise terminal, is a pottery specialist.

Music is another of Trinidad's signature products, and the latest soca and reggae can be purchased at **Rhyner's Record Shop** at 54 Prince St., Port of Spain (℃ **868/625-2476**). There's also **Crosby Records** (℃ **868/622-7622**), located in the St. James area.

BEACHES

Unlike its tiny sister Tobago, Trinidad was not blessed with many beautiful beaches. The most popular of the beaches is **Maracas Bay,** a scenic, 40-minute drive from Port of Spain. The drive takes vacationers over mountains and through a lush rainforest. As you near the beach, the coastal road descends from a cliffside. The beach itself is wide and sandy, with a small fishing village on one side and the richly dense mountains in the background. There are lifeguards, changing rooms and showers, and areas for picnics. There are also many stands selling "shark and bake" sandwiches (a local favorite made with fresh slabs of shark and fried bread).

SPORTS

GOLF The oldest and best-known golf course on the island is the 18-hole, par-72 **St. Andrews Golf Club** in the suburb of Maraval (℃ **868/629-2314**). Also known as Moka Golf Course, it was established in the late 19th century. Greens fees are $60.

GREAT LOCAL RESTAURANTS & BARS

A favorite **local beer** is Stag; a favorite **local rum** is Vat 19 Old Oak.

Trinidad is home to some of the most diverse culinary styles in the Caribbean, a result of its African, Chinese, English, French, Indian, Portuguese, Spanish, and Syrian influences. **Rafters,** at 6A Warner St. (℃ **868/628-9258**), is an old rum house with brick walls and hand-finished ceilings, which offers sandwiches, chili, and chicken in its bar. There's also an elegant dining room for more formal meals. Lunch $7. **Plantation House,** at 38 Ariapita Ave. (℃ **868/628-5551**), is an expensive, quality restaurant housed in a charming colonial house. **Solimar,** at 6 Nook Ave. near the Normandie Hotel (℃ **868/624-6267**), features a changing menu of international dishes engineered by owner Joe Brown, a peripatetic Englishman who was once a chef for the Hilton hotel chain. Lunch $28.

Cricket Wicket, 149 Tragarete Rd., is a pub with various bands performing on weekends.

TOBAGO

Tobago is the antithesis of its larger cousin, as peaceful, calm, and easygoing as Trinidad is loud, crowded, and frenetic. The island is filled with magical white-sand beaches, languid palm trees, and clear blue waters, and you'll find lots of spots for diving and snorkeling. There are also magnificent rainforests and hundreds of tiny streams and waterways carved into a steep crest of mountains that rise 600m (2,000 ft.) and snake down the island's center. The bird life and nature trails here are impressive.

COMING ASHORE   Most cruise passengers arrive at a small but orderly cruise terminal in central **Scarborough,** the island's main town. There's usually a fleet of taxis ready to go just outside of the cruise terminal, and detailed cab rates are posted inside the terminal at the main entrance. Larger ships must anchor offshore and transfer passengers to the terminal via tenders.

There are a number of phones inside the terminal, although last time we were here they weren't taking our AT&T phone card and we had to buy a local phone card.

INFORMATION   There is a small information booth at the terminal in Scarborough, open from 9am to 3pm, Monday through Friday. For info before you go, contact the **tourism board office** in the U.S. (© 212/682-7272; www.visit tnt.com).

GETTING AROUND

BY TAXI   Taxi is the preferred mode of transportation for visitors here; the island is small enough that any location worth visiting can be reached this way. Distances can be deceiving, though, because some of the roads are in very bad shape and others wind along the coast and twist through the mountains. There is no road that completely circles the island. Like Trinidad, visitors should use registered drivers who are part of the Trinidad and Tobago Tourist Transport Association network. See the Trinidad taxi section for more information.

BY RENTAL CAR   There's really no need for a cruise passenger to rent a car on Tobago.

SHORE EXCURSIONS OFFERED BY THE CRUISE LINES

Pigeon Point Beach Trip ($49, 5½ hr., including lunch): By taxi, you'll head toward Tobago's most popular beach, where you'll find a restaurant, a bar, restrooms, and small cabanas lining the beach. You have your pick of watersports, including snorkeling and banana-boat rides (for a fee, of course).

Tobago Island Explorer ($59, 7½ hr., including lunch): Passengers depart the cruise terminal via bus for a trip that starts at Fort King George and the Tobago Museum. After a tour of the museum, the excursion continues along the Windward Coast Road to the Richmond Greathouse for a guided tour. Continuing to the Speyside lookout, a photo stop is made before the tour proceeds to Jemma's Seafood Kitchen for a tasty lunch.

ON YOUR OWN: WITHIN WALKING DISTANCE

The well-restored, British-built **Fort King George,** dating from 1777, overlooks Scarborough's east side. There's no admission charge to enter the grounds. The fort offers a great view of Tobago's Atlantic coast. Other historic buildings here include St. Andrew's church (built in 1819) and the Courthouse (built in 1825). The small **Tobago Museum** (© 868/639-3970) is located in the Fort's old barracks guardhouse. Scarborough's **botanical gardens** (© 868/639-3421) are

---

ⓒ Frommer's Favorite Tobago Experiences

Visiting Pigeon Point Beach: One of the most beautiful and distinctive spots in the Caribbean, Pigeon Point is an oasis of white sand, aqua water, and tall palm trees. (See "Shore Excursions Offered by the Cruise Lines," above.)

Snorkeling at Buccoo Reef: The spot is a must-visit for its exotic fish and impressive underwater coral, which can also be observed by glass-bottom boat. (See "Beaches," below.)

Checking Out Nylon Pool: Named for its crystal-clear water, this small lagoon is located near Buccoo Reef and is filled with tropical fish. It's great for wading and swimming.

---

situated between the main highway and the town center, less than .4km (¼-mile) from the cruise dock, but they are not much more than a glorified public park with a few marked trees.

Other than this, there aren't many attractions within walking distance of the cruise terminal, and even the terminal shops are small and limited.

SHOPPING
There simply isn't much here beyond the shops inside the cruise terminal and sporadic craft merchants at the popular beaches at Fort King George. It's best to put aside the shopping excursions for another port and enjoy Tobago's relaxed atmosphere and fine beaches.

BEACHES
Pigeon Point, near the southern tip of Tobago on the Caribbean side, is the best beach on an island filled with great beaches. **Store Bay,** south of Pigeon Point, has white sands and good year-round swimming (there's a lifeguard, too). Here you'll find vendors hawking local wares and glass-bottom-boat tours departing to **Buccoo Reef.** Despite their names, **Parlatuvier** and **Bloody Bay,** on Tobago's Caribbean (west) coast, are tranquil, secluded, and beautiful.

SPORTS
GOLF About 8km (5 miles) from Pigeon Point, the championship, 18-hole, par-72 **Mount Irvine Golf Course,** at the Mount Irvine Hotel (ⓒ 868/639-8871), is among the most scenic courses in the Caribbean, overlooking the sea from gently rolling hills. The clubhouse sits on a promontory and offers great views. Greens fees are $55.

SCUBA DIVING Tobago is virtually surrounded by shallow-water reefs filled with colorful marine life, easily visible through the clear water. All kinds of diving experiences, from beginner-level dives at Buccoo Reef to drift diving for experienced divers at Grouper Ground, are offered. **Dive Tobago,** at Pigeon Point (ⓒ 868/639-0202), is the island's oldest dive operation, offering resort courses and rentals, and catering to both beginners and experienced divers.

GREAT LOCAL RESTAURANTS & BARS
There are several moderately priced restaurants in Tobago, including The **Old Donkey Cart House,** on Bacolet Street in Scarborough (ⓒ 868/639-3551),

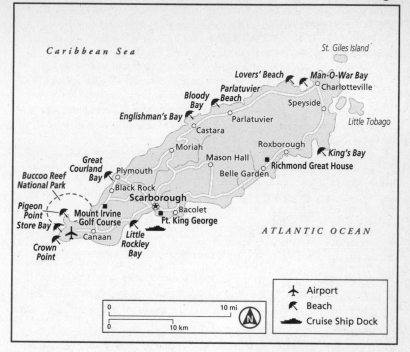

Caribbean Sea

St. Giles Island

Lovers' Beach — Man-O-War Bay
Parlatuvier — Charlotteville
Beach
Bloody — Speyside
Bay
Englishman's Bay — Parlatuvier — Little Tobago
Castara
Moriah — Roxborough
Mason Hall — King's Bay
Great — Richmond Great House
Courland — Plymouth
Buccoo Reef — Bay — Belle Garden
National Park — Black Rock
Scarborough — ATLANTIC OCEAN
Pigeon
Point — Mount Irvine — Bacolet
Store Bay — Golf Course — Ft. King George
Canaan — Little
Crown — Rockley
Point — Bay

✈ Airport
ʎ Beach
⛴ Cruise Ship Dock

0   10 mi
0   10 km

which occupies a restored colonial home that once served as Tobago's first guest-house. Today it's a bistro serving French wines, light snacks, salads, and special-ties such as armadillo and opossum (called manicou). Lunch $8.

The beach at Store Bay is lined with a row of cheap-food stands offering rotis (chicken or beef wrapped in Indian turnovers and flavored with curry), shark-and-bake, crab with dumplings, and fish lunches. **Chrystal's** (© **868/639-7648**), on the corner of Store Bay and Milford Road, is another local favorite for flying fish, shark-and-bake, and fruit juices. Lunch $5.

27 U.S. Virgin Islands: St. Thomas, St. John & St. Croix

Ever since Columbus discovered the Virgin Islands during his second voyage to the New World in 1493, they have proven irresistible to foreign powers seeking territory, at one time or another being governed by Denmark, Spain, France, England, Holland, and, since 1917, by the United States. Vacationers discovered **St. Thomas,** the largest of the islands, right after World War II and have been flocking here in increasing numbers ever since to enjoy its fine dining, elegant resorts, and, in recent years, its shopping. Tourism and U.S. government pro-grams have raised the standard of living to one of the highest in the Caribbean, and today the island is one of the busiest and most developed cruise ports in the Caribbean, often hosting more than six ships a day during the peak winter sea-son. **Charlotte Amalie** (pronounced Ah-*mahl*-yah), named in 1691 in honor of the wife of Denmark's King Christian V, is the island's capital and has become the Caribbean's major shopping center.

St. Croix, the largest of the USVIs, gets nowhere near as many visitors as St. Thomas, making for a more tranquil port experience. The island's major attraction is **Buck Island Reef National Monument,** an offshore park full of gorgeous coral reefs.

By far the most tranquil and unspoiled of the islands, however, is **St. John,** the smallest of the lot, more than half of which is preserved as the gorgeous Virgin Islands National Park. A rocky coastline, forming crescent-shaped bays and white-sand beaches, rings the whole island, whose miles of serpentine hiking trails lead past the ruins of 18th-century Danish plantations and let onto panoramic ocean views.

By far, the largest number of cruise ships dock in St. Thomas's Charlotte Amalie, but a few anchor directly off St. John or tie up at the Anne Abramson Pier in Fredericksburg, St. Croix. Those that dock in St. Thomas usually offer excursions to St. John, but if yours doesn't, it's quite easy to get there on your own via water taxi or shuttle.

LANGUAGE   English is spoken on all three islands.

CURRENCY   The **U.S. dollar** is the local currency.

INFORMATION   For information before you go, contact the **U.S. Virgin Islands Department of Tourism** (✆ **800/372-USVI;** www.usvitourism.vi).

CALLING FROM THE U.S.   When calling the Virgin Islands from the fifty states, you just need to dial a "1" before the numbers listed in this section.

ST. THOMAS

With a population of about 50,000 and a large number of American expatriates and temporary sun-seekers in residence, tiny St. Thomas isn't exactly a tranquil tropical retreat. You won't have any beaches to yourself. Shops, bars, and restaurants (including a lot of fast-food joints) abound here, and most of the locals make their living off the tourist trade. Most native Virgin Islanders are the descendants of slaves brought from Africa. In fact, Charlotte Amalie was one of the major slave-trading centers in the Caribbean.

Ⓒ Frommer's Favorite St. Thomas Experiences

Biking Around the Island: You'll get great views and a great workout too. (See "Shore Excursions Offered by the Cruise Lines," below.) Biking on Water Island is a great experience, too.

Kayaking Among the Island's Mangroves: You'll learn about the local lagoon ecosystem and get some exercise to boot. (See "Shore Excursions Offered by the Cruise Lines," below.)

Visiting the Colorful Village of Frenchtown: Have lunch in a village settled by French-speaking citizenry who were uprooted after the Swedes invaded the island of St. Barts. (See "On Your Own: Beyond the Port Area," below.)

Taking a Nature Walk: The lush St. Peter Greathouse Estate and Gardens has 200 varieties of plants and trees, plus a rainforest, an orchid jungle, and more. (See "On Your Own: Beyond the Port Area," below.)

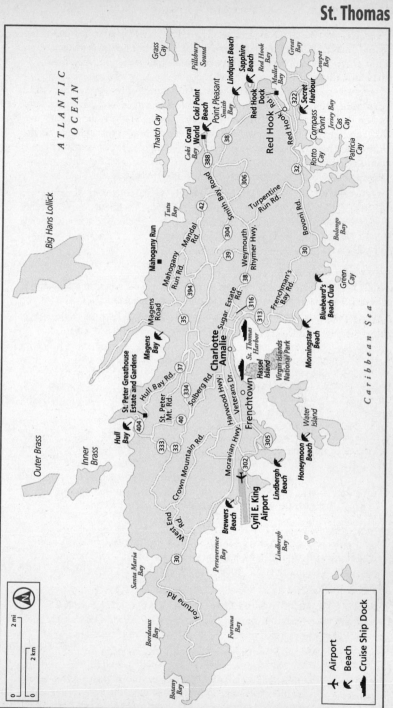

St. Thomas

ATLANTIC OCEAN

Grass Cay

Pillsbury Sound

Lindquist Beach

Sapphire Beach

Great Bay

Red Hook Bay

Coral Bay

Mullet Bay

Coupet Bay

Coki Point Beach

Coki Coral Bay World

Point Pleasant

Smith Bay

Red Hook Dock

322

Secret Harbour

Red Hook

Thatch Cay

388

38

Red Hook Rd.

Compass Point

Jersey Bay

Cas Cay

Thatch Cay

306

32

Rotto Cay

Patricia Cay

Big Hans Lollick

Tutu Bay

42

Smith Bay Road

Turpentine Run Rd.

Bovoni Rd.

Mahogany Run

304

Weymouth Rhymer Hwy.

Balongo Bay

Mandal Rd.

39

Frenchman's Bay Rd.

30

Mahogany Run Rd.

394

38

316

Bluebeard's Beach Club

Green Cay

Magens Road

35

Sugar Estate Rd.

313

St. Peter Greathouse Estate and Gardens

Magens Bay

Charlotte Amalie

St. Thomas Harbor

Morningstar Beach

Caribbean Sea

37

Hull Bay Rd.

Harwood Hwy.

Hassel Island

Virgin Islands National Park

St. Peter Mt. Rd.

334

Solberg Rd.

Veterans Dr.

Frenchtown

Hull Bay

40

404

Moravian Hwy.

Water Island

Outer Brass

333

Crown Mountain Rd.

305

Honeymoon Beach

Inner Brass

33

302

Lindbergh Beach

West End Rd.

Cyril E. King Airport

Brewers Beach

Lindbergh Bay

Santa Maria Bay

30

Perseverance Bay

Fortuna Rd.

Bordeaux Bay

Fortuna Bay

Botany Bay

N

2 mi

2 km

Airport

Beach

Cruise Ship Dock

COMING ASHORE   Most cruise ships anchor at Havensight Mall, at the eastern end of Charlotte Amalie Harbor, 1½ miles from the town center. The mall has a tourist information office, restaurants, a bookstore, a bank, a U.S. postal van, phones that accept long-distance credit cards, and a generous number of duty-free shops. Many people make the long, hot walk to the center of Charlotte Amalie, but it's not a scenic route in any way—you may want to opt for one of the open-air taxis for about $3 per person.

If Havensight Mall is clogged with cruise ships, your ship will dock at the **Crown Bay Marina,** to the west of Charlotte Amalie. A taxi is your best bet—the 30-minute walk into Charlotte Amalie feels longer on a hot day, and isn't terribly picturesque. A taxi ride into town from here costs about $4.

INFORMATION   The **U.S. Virgin Islands Department of Tourism** has offices at Tolbod Gade in Charlotte Amalie (© **340/774-8784**), open Monday to Friday from 8am to 5pm and Saturday from 8am to noon. Stop by and pick up *St. Thomas This Week,* which includes maps of St. Thomas and St. John. There's also an office at the Havensight Mall.

GETTING AROUND

BY TAXI   Taxis are the chief means of transport here. They're unmetered, but a guide of point-to-point fares around the island is included in most of the tourist magazines. The official fare for sightseeing is about $40 for two passengers for 1½ hours. For **radio-dispatch service,** call © **340/774-7457.**

BY BUS   Comfortable and often air-conditioned, government-run Vitran buses serve Charlotte Amalie and the countryside as far away as Red Hook, a jumping-off point for St. John. You rarely have to wait more than 30 minutes during the day. A one-way ride costs about 75¢ within Charlotte Amalie, $1 to outer neighborhoods, and $3 for rides as far as Red Hook. For routes, stops, and schedules, call © **340/774-5678.**

BY TAXI VAN   Less structured and more erratic are "taxi vans," privately owned vans, minibuses, or open-sided trucks operated by local entrepreneurs. They make unscheduled stops along major traffic arteries and charge the same fares as the Vitran buses. If you look like you want to go somewhere, one will likely stop for you. They may or may not have their final destinations written on a cardboard sign displayed on the windshield.

BY RENTAL CAR   No need to rent a car here.

BY FERRY   Ferries run every 2 hours from Charlotte Amalie until 5:30pm. and all day hourly from Red Hook to St. John. The ride from Charlotte Amalie takes about 45 minutes and costs $7 one-way; from Red Hook the ride is 20 minutes and costs $3. For information, call © **340/776-6282.**

SHORE EXCURSIONS OFFERED BY THE CRUISE LINES

In addition to the excursions below, plenty of organized snorkeling trips, booze cruises, and island tours are offered.

Kayaking the Marine Sanctuary ($68, 3½ hr.): Kayak from the mouth of the marine sanctuary at Holmberg's Marina and spend nearly an hour paddling among the mangroves while a naturalist explains the mangrove and lagoon ecosystem. Includes a free half-hour to snorkel or walk along the coral beach at Bovoni Point.

Water Island Bike Trip ($66, 3½ hr.): After a ferry ride to Water Island, a 5-minute bus ride brings you to the island's highest point, from which you get a nice downhill ride. Your guide will point out various historic sites and wildlife en route to Honeymoon Beach, where you can swim and enjoy a drink.

Island Tour by Minibus ($30, 3 hr.): First, drive along the impressive Skyline Drive for panoramic views of St. John and the ship harbor, then head up to the 1,400-foot Mountain Top for awesome views of Magens Bay and the British Virgin Islands. The next stop is Drake's Seat, where Sir Francis Drake is said to have perched, keeping an eye on his own ships and spying on others.

Atlantis Submarine Odyssey ($89, 2 hr.): Descend about 100 feet into the ocean in this air-conditioned submarine for views of exotic fish and sea life. (You can also book this tour independently. Call © **800/253-0493.**)

Kon-Tiki Party Cruise ($34, 3 hr.): One of the liveliest party boats in the Caribbean sails over a coral reef where you can watch coral, sponges, and other marine life through glass panels—assuming you can see through those beer goggles you may be wearing by then. Steel band music plays throughout. At Palm Fringed Bay, you'll have time to swim before heading back to the pier.

EXCURSIONS OFFERED BY LOCAL AGENCIES

St. John Yachting/Snorkeling Excursion: Many yachts and catamarans are available for snorkel and scuba excursions and champagne sails. You can join a full-day or half-day sail aboard the 49-passenger catamaran *Dancing Dolphin* (© **340/774-8899;** www.thedancingdolphin.com), visiting local beaches, coves, wrecks, and reefs. The owner, Captain Sharee Winslow, makes special accommodations for handicapped passengers and runs special sails for children as well.

For a more personal experience, the six-passenger *Fantasy* (© **340/775-5652;** www.daysailfantasy.com) departs from the American Yacht Harbor at Red Hook (on the west coast of St. Thomas) at 9:30am daily, sailing to St. John and nearby islands for swimming, snorkeling, beachcombing, or trolling. The normal full-day trip departs at 9:30am and returns at 4pm, but shorter sailings can be arranged. The cost is $110 per person, including continental breakfast, open bar, a hot lunch served on board, and snorkel gear. Only six people can be accommodated per trip.

ON YOUR OWN: WITHIN WALKING DISTANCE

Depending on your level of energy, you can either walk from the port into **Charlotte Amalie** (about 1½ miles) or take a taxi. In days of yore, seafarers from all over the globe flocked to this old-world Danish town, including pirates and, during the Civil War, Confederate sailors. The old warehouses that once held pirates' loot still stand and, for the most part, house shops. The main streets (called "Gades" here in honor of their Danish heritage) are a veritable shopping mall, usually packed with visitors. Sandwiched among the shops are a few historic buildings, most of which can be covered on foot in about 2 hours.

Before starting your tour, stop off at the so-called **Grand Hotel,** near Emancipation Park. No longer a hotel, it has a restaurant, a bar, shops, and a visitor center. There are views of the harbor below from the wood-paneled pub/restaurant at **Hotel 1829,** one street farther up Government Hill. It's a great place for a drink or some lunch.

Stray behind the seafront shopping strip (Main St.) of Charlotte Amalie and you'll find pockets of 19th-century houses and the truly charming, cozy, brick-and-stone **St. Thomas Synagogue,** built in 1833 by Sephardic Jews. There's a great view from here as well. It's located high on the steep sloping Crystal Gade.

Dating from 1672, **Fort Christian,** 32 Raadets Gade, rises from the harbor to dominate the center of town. Named after the Danish king Christian V, the structure has been everything from a governor's residence to a jail. Many pirates were hanged in its courtyard. Some of the cells have been turned into the rather minor **American-Caribbean Historical Museum,** displaying Indian artifacts of only the most passing interest. The fort is open Monday to Friday from 8am to 3pm. Admission is $8 for adults and $4 for children.

Seven Arches Museum, Government Hill (© **340/774-9295**), is a 2-century-old Danish house completely restored to its original condition and furnished with antiques. You can walk through the yellow ballast arches and visit the great room with its view of the busy harbor.

The **Paradise Point Tramway** (© **340/774-9809**) affords visitors a dramatic view of Charlotte Amalie Harbor at a peak height of 697 feet. The tramways transport customers from the Havensight area to Paradise Point, where riders disembark to visit shops and a popular restaurant and bar.

ON YOUR OWN: BEYOND THE PORT AREA

Coral World Marine Park & Underwater Observatory, 6450 Coki Point, off Route 38, 20 minutes from downtown Charlotte Amalie (© **340/775-1555;** www.coralworldvi.com), is the number-one attraction in St. Thomas. The 3½-acre complex features a three-story underwater observation tower 100 feet offshore—you'll see sponges, fish, coral, and other underwater life in their natural state through the windows. In the Marine Gardens Aquarium, saltwater tanks display everything from sea horses to sea urchins. An 80,000-gallon reef tank features exotic Caribbean marine life. Another tank is devoted to sea predators, including circling sharks. The entrance is hidden behind a waterfall.

West of Charlotte Amalie, **Frenchtown** was settled by a French-speaking citizenry who were uprooted when the Swedes invaded and took over their home of St. Barts. These settlers were known for wearing cha-chas, or straw hats. Many of the people who live here today are the direct descendants of those long-ago residents. This colorful fishing village contains several interesting restaurants and taverns. To get there, take a taxi down Veterans Drive (Rte. 30) west and turn left at the sign to the Admirals Inn.

The lush **St. Peter Greathouse Estate and Gardens,** at the corner of St. Peter Mountain Road (Rte. 40) and Barrett Hill Road (© **340/774-4999**), ornaments 11 acres on the volcanic peaks of the island's northern rim. It's the creation of Howard Lawson DeWolfe, a *Mayflower* descendant who, with his wife, Sylvie, bought the estate in 1987 and set about transforming it into a tropical paradise. It's filled with some 200 varieties of plants and trees, including an umbrella plant from Madagascar. There's also a rainforest, an orchid jungle, waterfalls, and reflecting ponds. From a panoramic deck you can see some 20 of the Virgin Islands. The house itself is worth a visit, its interior filled with local art. Admission is $10 for adults, $5 children.

SHOPPING

St. Thomas is famous for its shopping opportunities. As in St. Croix and St. John, American shoppers can bring home $1,200 worth of merchandise without paying duty—twice the amount of other Caribbean islands. You'll sometimes find well-known brand names at savings of up to 40% off stateside prices, but you'll often have to plow through a lot of junk to find the bargains. The main goodies are jewelry, watches, cameras, china, and leather.

Charlotte Amalie

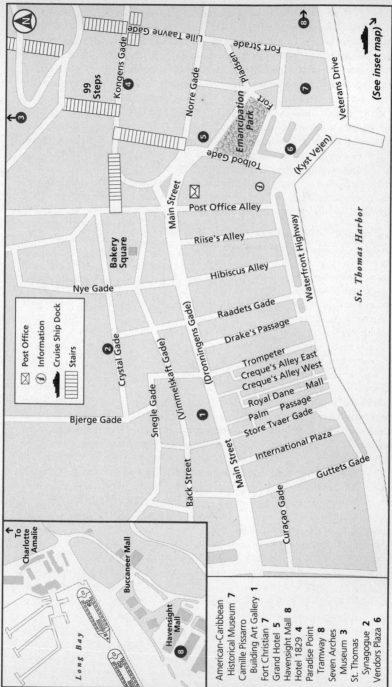

St. Thomas Harbor

Waterfront Highway

Veterans Drive

(See inset map)

Fort Strade

Emancipation Park

Fort

(Kyst Vejen)

Tolbod Gade

Lille Taavne Gade

Kongens Gade

99 Steps

Norre Gade

Post Office Alley

Main Street

Riise's Alley

Bakery Square

Hibiscus Alley

Nye Gade

Raadets Gade

Drake's Passage

Crystal Gade

(Dronningens Gade)

Trompeter
Creque's Alley East
Creque's Alley West

Royal Dane   Mall
Palm   Passage

Store Tvaer Gade

(Vimmelskaft Gade)

Snegle Gade

Bjerge Gade

International Plaza

Guttets Gade

Back Street

Main Street

Curaçao Gade

Legend
- ⊠ Post Office
- ⓘ Information
- ▮ Cruise Ship Dock
- ▥ Stairs

To Charlotte Amalie

Buccaneer Mall

Long Bay

Havensight Mall

American-Caribbean
Historical Museum **7**
Camille Pissarro
Building Art Gallery **1**
Fort Christian **7**
Grand Hotel **5**
Havensight Mall **8**
Hotel 1829 **4**
Paradise Point
Tramway **8**
Seven Arches
Museum **3**
St. Thomas
Synagogue **2**
Vendors Plaza **6**

625

Many cruise ship passengers shop at the **Havensight Mall,** where the ships dock, but the major shopping goes on along the harbor of Charlotte Amalie. **Main Street** (or Dronningens Gade, its old Danish name) is the main shopping area. Just north of Main Street is merchandise-loaded **Back Street,** or Vimmelskaft. Many shops are also spread along the Waterfront Highway (also called Kyst Vejen). Running between these major streets is a series of side streets, walkways, and alleys, all filled with shops. All the usual Caribbean mega-tourist-shops sell all the usual jewelry, watches, perfume, gift items, and so on; but there are a number of other interesting, and more unique, shops. Just do a little comparison shopping from place to place and be a little cautious of people trying to lure you into their shop and offering you a special rate if you bring in others from your group.

Upstairs at 14 Dronningens Gade, the **Camille Pissarro Building Art Gallery** is in the house where the impressionist painter Pissarro was born on July 10, 1830. In three high-ceilinged and airy rooms, you'll see all the available Pissarro paintings relating to the islands. Many prints and note cards by local artists are available, too, as well as original batiks.

Huddled under oversize parasols, hundreds of street vendors ply their trades in a designated area called **Vendors Plaza,** at the corner of Veterans Drive and Tolbod Gade. It's open Monday to Saturday from 7:30am to 5:30pm, and on Sunday if a cruise ship is expected. Food vendors set up on sidewalks outside.

MAPes MONDe (© 340/776-2886; www.mapesmonde.com) has two locations in St. Thomas—one in Riise Alley and the other at The Grand Hotel—and another at Mongoose Junction on St. John. Its elegant books, reproductions, historic maps, and archival photos of the Caribbean are a nice break from jewelry and tourist knickknacks. They also carry lovely prints, silk screens, and greeting cards featuring indigenous birds and vegetation.

BEACHES

St. Thomas has some good beaches, all of which are easily reached by taxi. Arrange for your driver to return and pick you up at a designated time. All the beaches in the U.S. Virgin Islands are public, but some still charge a fee. Mind your belongings, as St. Thomas has pickpockets and thieves who target visitors. If you're going to St. John, you may want to do your beaching there (see "Beaches," under "St. John," below).

THE NORTH SIDE   Located across the mountains, 3 miles north of the capital, **Magens Bay Beach** was once hailed as one of the world's 10 most beautiful beaches, but its reputation has faded. Though still beautiful, it isn't as well maintained as it should be and is often overcrowded, especially when many cruise ships are in port. It's less than a mile long and lies between two mountains. Admission is $3 for adults and 25¢ for children under 12. Changing facilities, bathrooms, a snack bar, snorkel gear, and float rentals are available. Magens Bay also has picnic tables and benches. There's no public transportation here, so take a taxi. The gates are open daily from 6am to 6pm (you'll need insect repellent after 4pm).

Located in the northeast near Coral World, **Coki Beach** is good, but it, too, becomes overcrowded when cruise ships are in port. Snorkelers come here often, as do pickpockets—protect your valuables. Lockers can be rented at Coral World, next door. An East End bus runs to Smith Bay and lets you off at the gate to Coral World and Coki.

Also on the north side is **Renaissance Grand Beach Resort,** one of the island's most beautiful beaches. It opens onto Smith Bay, right off Route 38, near Coral World. Many watersports are available here.

THE SOUTH SIDE   On the south side, **Morningstar** lies about 2 miles east of Charlotte Amalie at Marriott's Frenchman's Reef Beach Resort. You can wear your most daring swimwear here, and you can also rent sailboats, snorkeling equipment, and lounge chairs. The beach can be easily reached via a cliff-front elevator at the Marriott.

The **Bolongo Bay Beach Club** lures those who love a serene spread of sand. You can feed hibiscus blossoms to iguanas and rent snorkeling gear and lounge chairs. They also offer a variety of watersports, including parasailing. There's no public transportation, but it's a $9 ride by taxi from Charlotte Amalie. Unlike Magens Bay Beach (see above), where there's only a snack bar, Iggy's Restaurant is right on Bolongo's beach. **Bluebeard's Beach Club** (formerly known as Lime-tree Beach) offers a secluded setting and is a quick ride from the cruise ship pier.

Brewer's Beach, one of the island's most popular, lies in the southwest near the University of the Virgin Islands, also along the Fortuna bus route.

THE EAST END   Small and special, **Secret Harbor** sits near a collection of condos. With its white sand and coconut palms, it's a veritable cliché of Caribbean charm. No public transportation stops here, but it's an easy taxi ride east of Charlotte Amalie heading toward Red Hook.

Sapphire Beach is one of the finest on St. Thomas, set against the backdrop of the Doubletree Sapphire Beach Resort & Marina complex, where you can lunch or order drinks. Windsurfers like this beach a lot. You can rent snorkeling gear and lounge chairs here. A large reef lies close to the shore, and there are great views of offshore cays and St. John. To get here, take the East End bus from Charlotte Amalie, going via Red Hook. Ask to be let off at the entrance to Sapphire Bay; it's a short walk to the water.

SPORTS

GOLF   Designed by Tom and George Fazio, **Mahogany Run** on the north shore, Mahogany Run Road (© **800/253-7103** or 340/777-6006), is one of the most beautiful courses in the West Indies. This 18-hole, par-70 course rises and drops like a roller coaster on its journey to the sea. Cliffs and crashing sea waves are the ultimate hazards at the 13th and 14th holes. The golf course is an $8 taxi ride from the cruise dock. Greens fees are about $100.

SCUBA DIVING & SNORKELING   The waters off the U.S. Virgin Islands are rated as one of the "most beautiful areas in the world" by *Skin Diver* magazine. Thirty spectacular reefs lie just off St. Thomas alone. **Dive In!,** in the Doubletree Sapphire Beach Resort & Marina, Smith Bay Road, Route 36 (© **800/524-2090;** www.diveinusvi.com), offers professional instruction, daily beach and boat dives, custom dive packages, underwater photography and videotapes, and snorkeling trips.

GREAT LOCAL RESTAURANTS & BARS

IN CHARLOTTE AMALIE   Beni Iguana's Sushi Bar, in the Grand Hotel Court, just behind Emancipation Park in downtown (© **340/777-8744**), is the only Japanese restaurant on St. Thomas. Lunch $10. **Greenhouse,** Veterans Drive (© **340/774-7998**), attracts cruise ship passengers with daily specials, including American fare and some Jamaican-inspired dishes. Lunch $10. The

Hard Rock Cafe, 5144 International Plaza (on the 2nd floor of a pink-sided mall), on the Waterfront (© 340/777-5555), has the best burgers in town, but people mainly come for the good times and the T-shirts. Lunch $9. **Virgilio's,** 18 Dronningens Gade, entrance on a narrow alleyway running between Main and Back streets (© 340/776-4920), is the good northern Italian restaurant that serves excellent lobster ravioli. Lunch $15. **Lillian's Caribbean Grill,** 43–46 Norre Gade, in the Grand Galleria Courtyard directly across from Emancipation Park (© 340/774-7900), serves authentic Caribbean dishes. Conveniently located near the Vendor's Plaza shopping area, it makes for a nice lunch stop. Lunch $10.

IN FRENCHTOWN   At **Alexander's,** rue de St. Barthélemy, west of town (© 340/774-4349), there's a heavy emphasis on seafood—the menu even includes conch schnitzel on occasion. Other dishes include a mouthwatering Wiener schnitzel and homemade paté. Lunch $16. **Craig & Sally's,** 22 Honduras (© 340/777-9949), serves dishes that, according to the owner, are not "for the faint of heart, but for the adventurous soul"—roast pork with clams, filet mignon with macadamia-nut sauce, and grilled swordfish with a sauce of fresh herbs and tomatoes. Lunch $20.

ON THE NORTH COAST   Newly renamed (it used to be Sandra's New Terrace) but with the same Caribbean flair as always, **Glenda's Caribbean Spot,** 66–67 Smith Bay, Route 38, just east of the Coral World turnoff (© 340/775-2699), is one of the island's best-known West Indian restaurants. It oozes local color. The place made news around the world on January 5, 1997, when Bill and Hillary Clinton showed up unexpectedly for lunch. Surrounded by secret-service men, they shared a conch appetizer, then Mrs. Clinton went for the vegetable plate while the president opted for the catch of the day, which he reportedly loved.

ST. JOHN
A tiny gem of an island, lush St. John lies about 3 miles east of St. Thomas across Pillsbury Sound. It's the smallest and least populated of the U.S. Virgins, only about 7 miles long and 3 miles wide, with a total land area of some 19 square miles. The island was slated for big development under Danish control, but a slave rebellion and the decline of the sugar cane plantations ended that idea. Since 1956, more than half of St. John's land mass, as well as its shoreline waters, have been set aside as the **Virgin Islands National Park,** and today the island leads the Caribbean in eco- (or "sustainable") tourism. Miles of winding hiking trails lead to panoramic views and the ruins of 18th-century Danish plantations. Mysterious geometric petroglyphs incised into boulders and cliffs can be seen all over the island (ask a guide to point them out if you can't find them). These figures, of unknown age and origin, have never been deciphered. Since St. John is easy to reach from St. Thomas and the beaches are spectacular, many cruise ship passengers spend their entire day here.

COMING ASHORE   Cruise ships cannot dock at either of the piers in St. John. Instead, they moor off the coast at **Cruz Bay,** sending in tenders to the National Park Service Dock, the larger of the two piers. Most cruise ships docking at St. Thomas offer shore excursions to St. John's pristine interior and beaches.

If your ship docks on St. Thomas and you don't take an organized shore excursion to St. John, you can get here from Charlotte Amalie by **ferry.** Ferries leave the Charlotte Amalie waterfront for Cruz Bay at 1- to 2-hour intervals, from 9am until around 5:30pm. The last boat leaves Cruz Bay for Charlotte

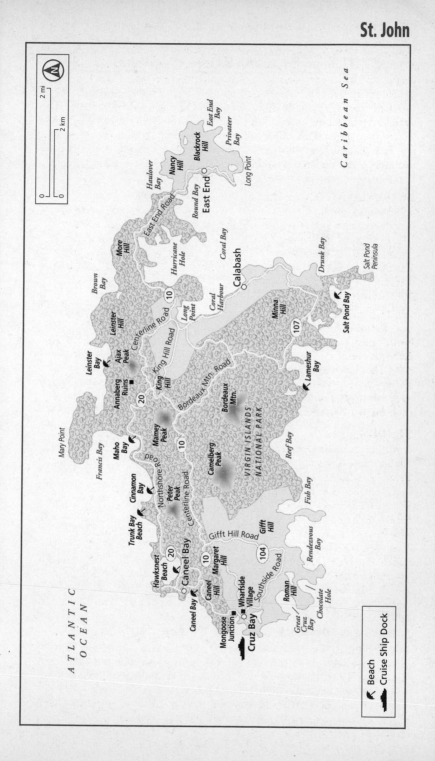

St. John

> ### ✐ Frommer's Favorite St. John Experiences
>
> **Touring the Island in an Open-air Safari Bus:** The views are spectacular from the island's coastal road, and you'll visit the ruins of a plantation and one of St. John's excellent beaches. (See "Shore Excursions Offered by the Cruise Lines," below.)
>
> **Beaching Yourself in Trunk Bay:** Although it can get somewhat crowded, it's a gorgeous beach and there's some decent snorkeling too. (See "Beaches," below.)

Amalie at 3:45pm. The ride takes about 45 minutes and costs $7 each way. Call ✆ **340/776-6282** for more information. Another ferry leaves from the Red Hook pier on St. Thomas's eastern tip more or less every half-hour, starting at 6:30am. It's a 30-minute drive from Charlotte Amalie's port to the pier at Red Hook; the ferry trip takes another 20 minutes each way. The one-way fare is $3 for adults, $1 for children under 11. Schedules can change without notice, so call in advance (✆ **340/776-6282**). You can take a Vitran bus from a point near Market Square (located near the west end of Main St. in Charlotte Amalie) directly to Red Hook for $1 per person each way, or negotiate a price with a taxi driver.

GETTING AROUND

BY TAXI   The most popular way to get around is by surrey-style taxi. Typical fares from Cruz Bay are $5.50 to Trunk Bay, $7.50 to Cinnamon Bay, and $11 to Maho Bay. Taxis wait at the pier. In the *very* unlikely event you don't see a taxi at the pier, you can call **St. John Taxi Service** at ✆ **340/693-7530.** Almost any taxi at Cruz Bay can take you on a 2-hour taxi tour of the island. Tours cost from $45 for one or two passengers, or about $16 per person for three or more riders.

BY RENTAL CAR   The extensive Virgin Islands National Park has kept the island's roads undeveloped and uncluttered, opening onto some of the most panoramic vistas anywhere. Renting a vehicle is the best way to see these views, especially if you like to linger at particularly beautiful spots. Open-sided Jeep-like vehicles are the most fun of the limited rentals here. There's sometimes a shortage of cars during the busy midwinter season, so try to reserve early. Remember to drive on the left (even though steering wheels are on the left, too—go figure). **Avis** and **Hertz** both have offices here. Your car is likely to come with just enough fuel to get you to one of the island's two gas stations, so fill 'er up: Due to the distance between stations, it's never a good idea to drive around St. John with less than half a tank of gas.

SHORE EXCURSIONS OFFERED BY THE CRUISE LINES

Island Tour ($39, 4–5 hr.): Since most ships tie up in St. Thomas, tours of St. John first require a ferry or tender ride to Cruz Bay in St. John. Then you board open-air safari buses for a tour that includes a stop at the ruins of a working plantation (the Annaberg Ruins), as well as a pause at Trunk Bay or one of the other beaches. The island and sea views from the coastal road are spectacular.

ON YOUR OWN: WITHIN WALKING DISTANCE

Most cruise ship passengers dart through Cruz Bay, a cute little West Indian village with interesting bars, restaurants, boutiques, and pastel-painted houses.

Wharfside Village, near the dock, is a complex of courtyards, alleys, and shady patios with a mishmash of boutiques, restaurants, fast-food joints, and bars. Down the road from the dock is **Mongoose Junction** (see "Shopping," below).

Located at the public library, the **Elaine Ione Sprauve Museum** (© 340/776-6359) isn't big, but it does have some local artifacts, and will teach you about some of the history of the island. It's open Monday to Friday from 9am to 5pm. Admission is free.

ON YOUR OWN: BEYOND THE PORT AREA

In November 1954, the wealthy Rockefeller family began acquiring large tracts of land on St. John. They then donated more than 5,000 acres to the Department of the Interior for the creation of the **Virgin Islands National Park,** which Congress voted into existence on August 2, 1956. Over the years, the size of the park has grown steadily; it now totals 12,624 acres, including over two-thirds of St. John's landmass plus submerged land and water adjacent to the island. Stop off first at the **visitor center** (© 340/776-6201) right on the dock at St. Cruz, where you'll find some exhibits and learn more about what you can see and do in the park. You can explore the park on the more than 20 miles of biking trails; rent your own car, Jeep, or Mini-Moke; or hike. If you decide to hike, stop at the visitor center first to watch an 18-minute video about the park and to pick up maps and instructions. You can take a taxi for about $5 to the starting point of whatever trail you select. All trails are well marked.

Within the park, try to see the **Annaberg Ruins,** Leinster Bay Road, where the Danes founded thriving plantations and a sugar mill in 1718. You'll find tidal pools, forest, hilltops, wild scenery, and the ruins of several Danish plantations. It's located off North Shore Road, east of Trunk Bay on the north shore. On certain days of the week (dates vary), guided walks of the area are given by park rangers. Check at the visitor center.

SHOPPING

Compared to St. Thomas, St. John is a minor shopping destination, but the boutiques and shops at Cruz Bay are generally more interesting than those on St. Thomas. Most of them are clustered at **Mongoose Junction** (www.usvi.net/shopping/mongoose), in a woodsy area beside the roadway, about a 5-minute walk from the ferry dock. **Bamboula** (© 340/693-8699) has an unusual and appealing collection of gifts from the Caribbean, Haiti, India, Indonesia, and Central Africa. **The Canvas Factory** (© 340/776-6196) produces its own rugged, colorful handmade canvas bags. **Donald Schnell Studio** (© 800/253-7107 or 340/776-6420) deals in handmade pottery, sculpture, and blown glass. The **Fabric Mill** (© 340/776-6194) features silk-screened and batik fabrics from around the world. **R and I Patton Goldsmithing** (© 800/626-3445 or 340/776-6548) has a large selection of locally designed jewelry, made with sterling silver, gold, and precious stones. In case you forgot your Tevas or need a new bathing suit, check out **Big Planet Adventure Outfitters** (© 340/776-6638), which stocks lots of outdoor-gear brands.

At Cruz Bay's Wharfside Village, **Pusser's Company Store** (© 340/775-6379; www.pussers.com) offers a large collection of classically designed, old-world travel and adventure clothing, along with unusual accessories and Pusser's famous (though not terribly good) rum, which was served aboard British Navy ships for over 300 years. A good, cheap gift item is packets of Pusser's coasters, on which is written the recipe for that classic Caribbean rum specialty, the Painkiller.

BEACHES

For a true beach lover, missing the great white sweep of **Trunk Bay** would be like touring Europe and skipping Paris. Trouble is, the word is a little more than out. This gorgeous beach is usually overcrowded, and there are sometimes pickpockets lurking about. The beach has lifeguards and rents snorkeling gear to those wanting to explore the underwater trail near the shore. Both taxis and "safari buses" to Trunk Bay meet the ferry as it docks at Cruz Bay.

Caneel Bay, the stamping ground of the rich and famous, has seven perfect beaches on its 170 acres, but only one—Honeymoon Beach—that's open to the public. Since it's the closest beach to Cruz Bay (and is very beautiful, if a bit narrow and windy), it's often overcrowded. Safari buses and taxis from Cruz Bay will take you along North Shore Road.

The campgrounds of **Cinnamon Bay** and **Maho Bay** have their own beaches. Snorkelers find good reefs here, and it's a great place to spot turtles and schools of parrotfish. Changing rooms and showers are available. There's also **Hawksnest Beach,** on the island's north shore. It's known as the beach locals frequent during peak tourist season.

SPORTS

HIKING   The network of trails in Virgin Islands National Park is the big thing here. The visitor center at Cruz Bay hands out free trail maps of the park. Since you don't have time to get lost—you don't want the ship to leave without you—it's best to set out with someone who knows his or her way around. Both **Maho Bay Camps** (② 340/776-6226) and **Cinnamon Bay Campground** (② 340/776-6201) conduct nature walks.

KAYAKING & WINDSURFING   The **Cinnamon Bay Watersports Center** on Cinnamon Bay Beach (② 340/776-6330) rents kayaks and 12- or 14-foot Hobie monohull sailboats, and the windsurfing here is some of the best anywhere, for both beginners and experts.

SCUBA DIVING & SNORKELING   Low Key Watersports, Wharfside Village (② 800/835-7718 or 340/693-8999; www.divelowkey.com), offers two-tank, two-location wreck dives on its own custom-built dive boats. They also arrange day-sailing charters, kayaking tours, deep-sea sportfishing, and snorkel tours, and rent watersports gear, including masks, fins, snorkels, and dive skins. **Cruz Bay Watersports,** at Palm Plaza (② 340/776-6234; www.divestjohn.com), is a PADI and NAUI five-star diving center. Snorkel tours are available daily.

GREAT LOCAL RESTAURANTS & BARS

In Wharfside Village, at Cruz Bay, the new, upscale **Cafe Wahoo** (② 340/776-6600) offers a lovely view of Cruz Bay Harbor. Lunch $11. For a more casual meal and drinks, try **The Beach Bar,** downstairs (② 340/777-4220), with the same view to go with your burgers and bar food. Lunch $8.

The Fish Trap, at Raintree Court, Cruz Bay (② 340/693-9994), is known for its wide selection of fresh fish, but also caters to vegetarians and the burger crowd. The restaurant does not serve lunch. The Italian food at **Paradiso,** Mongoose Junction (② 340/693-8899), is the best on the island—the chicken picante Willie, a spicy, creamy picante sauce over crispy chicken with linguini and ratatouille, was featured in *Bon Appétit.* The restaurant does not serve lunch.

ST. CROIX

More tranquil and less congested than St. Thomas, St. Croix is rocky and arid on its eastern end (which, incidentally, is the easternmost possession of the U.S.)

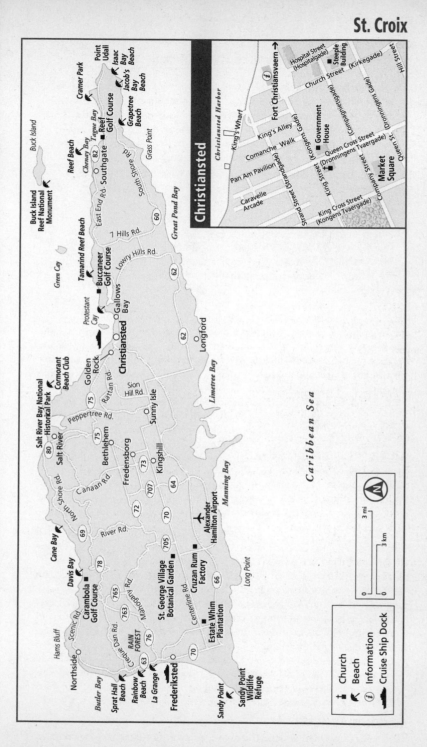

St. Croix

Christiansted

Hospital Street (Hospitalgade)
Steeple Building
Church Street (Kirkegade)
Fort Christiansvaern
Christiansted Harbor
King's Wharf
King's Alley
Comanche Walk
Pan Am Pavilion
Caravelle Arcade
Strand Street (Strangade)
King's Street (Kongens Gade)
Government House
Queen Cross Street (Dronningens Tvaergade)
King Street (Compagniesgade)
King Cross Street (Kongens Tvaergade)
Company Street (Dronningens Gade)
Queen St.
Market Square
Hill Street

Point Udall
Isaac Bay Beach
Cramer Park
Jacob's Bay Beach
Grapetree Beach
Reef
Southgate Golf Course
Tague Bay
Cheney Bay
82
Reef Beach
Grass Point
Buck Island
South Shore Rd.
East End Rd.
Great Pond Bay
60
7 Hills Rd.
Tamarind Reef Beach
Lowry Hills Rd.
Buccaneer Golf Course
Green Cay
62
Protestant Cay
Gallows Bay
Longford
62
Buck Island Reef National Monument
Christiansted
Golden Rock
Limetree Bay
Cormorant Beach Club
Salt River Bay National Historical Park
Rattan Rd.
Sion Hill Rd.
75
Peppertree Rd.
Sunny Isle
80
75
Salt River
Bethlehem
Fredensborg
73
Kingshill
North Shore Rd.
Canaan Rd.
707
64
Manning Bay
72
69
River Rd.
70
Alexander Hamilton Airport
705
Caribbean Sea
Cane Bay
78
Davis Bay
Carambola Golf Course
765
763
St. George Village Botanical Garden
Cruzan Rum Factory
66
Long Point
Hams Bluff
Scenic Rd.
Creque Dan Rd.
Mahogany Rd.
RAIN FOREST
76
Centerline Rd.
Estate Whim Plantation
70
Northside
Butler Bay
Sprat Hall Beach
Rainbow Beach
63
La Grange
Frederiksted
Sandy Point
Sandy Point Wildlife Refuge

3 mi
3 km
0
0

N

† Church
⚓ Beach
ⓘ Information
⚓ Cruise Ship Dock

633

ⓒ Frommer's Favorite St. Croix Experiences

Visiting Buck Island Reef National Monument: Within this 800-acre preserve (the only underwater national monument in the United States), you can snorkel over a series of unique marked underwater trails and experience some of the best-preserved coral reefs in the Caribbean. A snorkeling instructor guides the excursion. (See "Shore Excursions Offered by the Cruise Lines," below.)

Biking Along the Coast: On this tour, you'll pass through Frederiksted, past ruins, and through forests and rolling grasslands. (See "Shore Excursions Offered by the Cruise Lines," below.)

Strolling Through Christiansted: Because of its well-preserved 18th- and 19th-century Danish architecture (particularly evident at Fort Christiansvaern), Christiansted has been designated a National Historic Site. In the late 1700s, it was a crown colony of Denmark and one of the Caribbean's major ports. Today, many street signs are still in Danish.

---

but more lush in the west, with a rainforest of mango and mahogany, tree ferns, and dangling lianas. Rolling hills and upland pastures make up much of the area between the two extremes, and the vivid African tulips are just one of the many tropical flowers that add a splash of color to the landscape, which is dotted with the ruins of sugar cane plantations. The major St. Croix attraction are the coral reefs of **Buck Island Reef National Monument,** located offshore. There are some fine beaches here as well, including Sandy Point, Sprat Hall, and Rainbow Beach.

Although large cruise ships moor at **Frederiksted,** most of the action is really in **Christiansted,** located on a coral-bound bay about midway along the north shore and featuring more sights and better restaurants and shopping. Showing 2½ centuries of Danish influence in its architecture, the town is being handsomely restored and the entire harborfront area is a national historic site. St. Croix's population is descended from both Africa and Europe, and some families have been here for 10 generations, with roots dating back to colonial times.

COMING ASHORE Only cruise ships no longer than 350 feet can land directly at the dock at Christiansted. Others moor at newly renovated **Anne Abramson Pier** at Frederiksted, a sleepy town that springs to life only when the ships arrive. There's space for two megaships, and both piers have information centers and telephones. We suggest you spend as little time as possible in Frederiksted and head immediately for Christiansted, some 17 miles away. It's easy to explore either town on foot (it's the only way, really). You might want to consider one of the shore excursions outlined below to see more of the island, especially its underwater treasures.

Although St. Croix is relatively safe, it's wise to stay on the beaten path and watch your belongings on the beaches (as you should on any island); in late 2001, four incidences of muggings and robberies were reported involving Carnival Cruise Lines passengers and crew.

GETTING AROUND

BY TAXI Taxis are unmetered, and rates are set from point to point. The **St. Croix Taxicab Association** (ⓒ 340/778-1088) offers door-to-door service.

Taxi tours are a great way to explore the island. For one or two passengers, the cost is about $50 for 2 hours or $70 for 3 hours. It costs $20 to take a taxi from Christiansted to Frederiksted.

BY BUS   Air-conditioned buses run between Christiansted and Frederiksted about every half hour between 5:30am and 9pm. The main stop in Christiansted is on Hospital Street, near the National Park office; the main stop in Frederiksted is on Budhoe Park, near Fort Frederick and King Street. The fare is $1 for adults, 75¢ for children, and 55¢ for seniors. For more information, call © **340/778-0898.**

BY SEAPLANE   Daily seaplane shuttles between St. Croix and St. Thomas are available for $130 round-trip. It is strongly recommended to book in advance. Flights depart every 15 to 45 minutes in both directions, and flight time is a mere 18 minutes; but figure 30 minutes from dock to dock. For more information, contact **Seaborne Airlines,** 34 Strand St., Christiansted (© **340/773-6442;** www.seaborneairlines.com).

BY RENTAL CAR   We don't recommend renting a car here.

SHORE EXCURSIONS OFFERED BY THE CRUISE LINES

Buck Island Tour/Snorkeling ($60, 4–5 hr.): The most popular tour in St. Croix takes you to a tropical underwater wonderland of blue water, a dazzling rainbow of sea life, and colorful coral reefs. Transportation is provided from the Frederiksted pier to Christiansted, where a powerboat takes you over to Buck Island. An experienced guide provides snorkel lessons.

Island Tour ($36, 4 hr.): This tour is designed to give a taste of the whole island, with visits to the Whim Great House sugar plantation, Christiansted, and other major sites.

St. Croix Bike Tour ($49, 3 hr.): Bike along the coast of St. Croix, passing through the town of Frederiksted before heading out on the Northside Road, past ruins and through forests and rolling grasslands.

Hiking Tour ($30, 3 hr.): Hike through the 225-acre Butler Bay Preserve— prime bird-watching territory.

Golf at Carambola ($148, self-timed): Your cruise line will probably offer an excursion to Carambola, one of the Caribbean's most famous golf courses. If not, you can do it on your own (see "Sports," below).

EXCURSIONS OFFERED BY LOCAL OPERATORS

Horseback Tour: On this 1½-hour tour, run by **Paul and Jill's Equestrian Stables,** Sprat Hall Plantation, Route 58 (© **340/772-2880;** http://pws.prserv.net/ paul-and-jills), you'll pass ruins of abandoned 18th-century plantations and sugar mills, and climb the hills of St. Croix's western end. Tour guides give running commentaries on island fauna and history and on riding techniques. The stables, owned by Paul Wojcie and his wife, Jill Hurd (a daughter of the establishment's original founders), are set on the sprawling grounds of the island's oldest plantation, and are known throughout the Caribbean for the quality of the horses and the exceptionally scenic forest trails. The grounds also boast an exquisite tropical fruit orchard. Both beginner and experienced riders are welcome. Make reservations in advance.

ON YOUR OWN: WITHIN WALKING DISTANCE

IN FREDERIKSTED   Frederiksted is nothing great, but if you decide to hang around, you should begin your tour at russet-colored **Fort Frederik** (© 340/772-2021), next to the cruise ship pier. Some historians claim it was the first fort to sound a foreign salute to the U.S. flag, in 1776. The structure, at the northern end of Frederiksted, has been restored to its 1840 look. You can explore the court-yard and stables, visit the police museum, peruse exhibits of antique cannons and clothing, and see photographs of life on St. Croix in the days of yore. Admission is free. The fort is open Monday to Friday from 8am to 5pm.

IN CHRISTIANSTED   You can begin your visit at the **visitor bureau** (© 340/773-0495), a yellow building with a cedar roof near the harbor front. It was built as the Old Scalehouse in 1856 to replace a similar, older structure that burned down. In its heyday, all taxable goods leaving and entering the har-bor were weighed here. The scales could once accurately weigh barrels of sugar and molasses weighing up to 1,600 pounds.

The **Steeple Building** (© 340/773-1460), or Church of Lord God of Sabaoth, was completed in 1753 as St. Croix's first Lutheran church. It, too, stands near the harbor front, and contains an exhibit on island heritage in gen-eral and the church in particular, with photos and artifacts. Get there via Hospi-tal Street. The building was deconsecrated in 1831 and has served at various times as a bakery, a hospital, and a school. Admission is $3, which also includes admis-sion to **Fort Christiansvaern** (© 340/773-1460), the best-preserved colonial fortification in the Virgin Islands. The National Park Service maintains the fort as a historic monument, overlooking the harbor. Its original star-shaped design was at the vanguard of the most advanced military planning of its era. Hours are 8am to 5pm Monday to Friday and 9am to 4:45pm Saturday and Sunday.

ON YOUR OWN: BEYOND THE PORT AREA

Salt River, on the island's northern shore, is the only site that Columbus is known to have landed on in what is now U.S. territory. To mark the 500th anniversary of the arrival of Columbus, former President George Bush signed a bill creating the 912-acre **Salt River Bay National Historical Park and Eco-logical Preserve.** The landmass includes the site of the original Carib village explored by Columbus and his men, along with the only Taíno ceremonial ball court (used for ceremonial sporting events) ever discovered in the Lesser Antilles. At the Carib settlement, Columbus's men liberated several Taíno women and children held as slaves. On the way back to their vessels, the Spaniards faced a canoe filled with hostile Caribs, armed with poison arrows. One Spanish soldier was killed, and perhaps six Caribs were either slain or cap-tured. This is the first documented case of hostility between invading Europeans and Native Americans. Sailing away, Columbus named this part of St. Croix "Cape of the Arrows."

The park today is in a natural state. It has the largest mangrove forest in the Virgin Islands, sheltering many endangered animals and plants, plus an under-water canyon attracting scuba divers from around the world. The **St. Croix Envi-ronmental Association,** 3 Arawak Building, Gallows Bay (© 340/773-1989; www.seastx.org), conducts tours of the area.

The **Cruzan Rum Factory,** West Airport Road, Route 64 (© 340/692-2280), distills the famous Virgin Islands rum. Guided tours depart from the vis-itor pavilion.

Restored by the St. Croix Landmarks Society, the **Estate Whim Plantation Museum,** Centerline Road, about 2 miles east of Frederiksted (© 340/772-0598), is composed of only three rooms and is unique among the many old sugar plantations dotting the island, with 3-foot-thick walls made of stone, coral, and molasses. Also on the museum's premises are a woodworking shop, the estate's original kitchen, a museum store, servant's quarters, and tools from the 18th century. The ruins include remains of the plantation's sugar-processing plant, complete with a restored windmill.

The **St. George Village Botanical Garden of St. Croix** (© 340/692-2874) is a much-loved, popular Eden of tropical trees, shrubs, vines, and flowers, located 4 miles east of Frederiksted.

SHOPPING

Americans get a break here, since they can bring home $1,200 worth of merchandise from the U.S. Virgin Islands without paying duty, as opposed to a paltry $400 from most other Caribbean ports. And liquor here is duty-free.

The **King's Alley Complex,** a pink-sided compound created right on the Christiansted waterfront following the hurricanes of 1995, is filled with the densest concentration of shopping options on St. Croix. There are a number of worthwhile specialty shops in Christiansted as well. **Skirt Tails,** Pam Am Pavilion, is one of the most colorful and popular boutiques on the island, specializing in hand-painted batiks for both men and women. The **White House/Black Market,** King's Alley Walk, stocks women's clothing, ranging from dressy to casual and breezy—with all apparel in black and white. **Elegant Illusions Copy Jewelry,** 55 King St., sells credible copies of the baroque and antique jewelry your great-grandmother might have worn, priced from $10 to $1,000. **Larimar,** on The Boardwalk/King's Walk, specializes in its namesake, a pale-blue pectolyte stone prized for its sky-blue color, in various gold settings. **Sonya Ltd.,** 1 Company St., specializes in traditional Caribbean hook bracelets.

Folk Art Traders, 1B Queen Cross St., deals in Caribbean art and folk-art treasures, such as carnival masks, pottery, ceramics, original paintings, and hand-wrought jewelry. **Many Hands,** in the Pan Am Pavilion, Strand Street, sells Virgin Islands handicrafts, spices and teas, handmade jewelry, and more.

GAMBLING

St. Croix's first casino opened in early 2000 at the new **Divi Carina Bay Hotel,** 25 Estate Turner Hole, in Christiansted, on the east side of the island (© 340/773-9700; www.divicarina.com). By taxi, it takes approximately 45 minutes and costs about $30 per person to get to the casino from Frederiksted. The casino opens at noon.

BEACHES

Beaches are the biggest attraction on St. Croix. The drawback is that getting to them from Christiansted or Frederiksted isn't always easy. Taxis will take you, but they can be expensive. From Christiansted, you can take a ferry to the **Hotel on the Cay,** a palm-shaded island in the harbor.

NEAR FREDERIKSTED   Most convenient for passengers arriving at Frederiksted is **Sandy Point,** the largest beach in all of the U.S. Virgin Islands. Its waters are shallow and calm, perfect for swimming. You may remember this beach from the last scene of the movie *The Shawshank Redemption.* Sandy Point is also the nesting ground for endangered leatherback, hawksbill and green sea turtles, who lay their eggs every year between early April and early June. Parts of the beach are roped off during this time, but you can watch these fascinating creatures from outside of the protected areas.

On Route 63, a short ride north of Frederiksted, **Rainbow Beach** is inviting, with its white sand and ideal snorkeling conditions. **Sprat Hall** is another good beach in the vicinity, also on Route 63, about 5 minutes north of Frederiksted. You can rent lounge chairs here, and there's a bar nearby.

We highly recommend **Cane Bay** and **Davis Bay.** They're both the type of beaches you'd expect to find on a Caribbean island—palms, white sand, and good swimming and snorkeling. Cane Bay attracts snorkelers and divers with its rolling waves, coral gardens, and drop-off wall. It's near Route 80 on the north shore. Davis Beach, also off Route 80 on the north shore in the vicinity of the Carambola Beach Resort, draws bodysurfers. There are no changing facilities.

NEAR CHRISTIANSTED At the **Cormorant Beach Club,** about 5 miles west of Christiansted, palm trees shade some 1,200 feet of white sand. A living reef lies just off the shore, making snorkeling ideal.

SPORTS

GOLF St. Croix has the best golfing in the U.S. Virgin Islands, hands down. In fact, guests staying on St. John and St. Thomas often fly over to St. Croix for a day, just to play. The 18-hole, par-72 **Carambola Golf Course,** on the northeast side of St. Croix (© **340/778-5638**), was designed by Robert Trent Jones, Sr., who called it "the loveliest course I ever designed." Golfing authorities consider its collection of par-3 holes to be the best in the tropics. Greens fees are $100, including cart. The 18-hole, par-70 **Buccaneer,** 2 miles east of Christiansted (© **340/773-2100**, ext. 738), is a challenging 5,810-yard course with panoramic vistas. Players can knock the ball over rolling hills right to the edge of the ocean. Greens fees are $55 and car rentals $15. The 3,100-yard, 9-hole, par-35 course **Reef Golf Course** is located at Teague Bay on the east end of the island (© **340/773-8844**). Greens fees are $12 (yes, that's correct) plus $10 for those wishing to rent a cart

SCUBA DIVING Divers love St. Croix's sponge life, beautiful black-coral trees, and steep drop-offs near the shoreline. This island is home to the largest living reef in the Caribbean. Its fabled north-shore wall begins in 25 to 30 feet of water and drops—sometimes almost straight down—to 13,200 feet. There are 22 moored diving sites. Favorites include **Salt River Canyon,** the coral gardens of **Scotch Banks,** and **Eagle Ray,** filled with cruising eagle rays. **Pavilions** is another good dive site, boasting a pristine coral reef. The best site of all, however, is **Buck Island,** an underwater wonderland with a visibility of more than 100 feet and an underwater nature trail. All minor and major agencies offer scuba and snorkeling tours to Buck Island. **Dive St. Croix,** 59 King's Wharf (© **340/ 773-2628;** fax 340/773-7400), operates the 38-foot diver boat *Reliance.*

GREAT LOCAL RESTAURANTS & BARS

A couple of favorite **local beers** are Carib and Blackbeard's (made on St. Thomas); the favorite **local rum** is Cruzan.

IN CHRISTIANSTED **Harvey's,** 11B Company St. (© **340/773-3433**), features the thoroughly zesty cooking of island matriarch Sarah Harvey. Main dishes are the type of food Sarah was raised on: barbecue chicken, barbecue spareribs (barbecue is big here), broiled filet of snapper, and lobster when she can get it. Lunch $7. **Indies,** 55–56 Company St. (© **340/692-9440**), serves what may be the finest and freshest meals on St. Croix. The swordfish with fresh artichokes, shiitake mushrooms, and thyme is a savory treat, as is the baked wahoo with lobster curry, fresh chutney, and coconut. The restaurant is only open for dinner.

Paradise Cafe, Queen Cross St. at 53B Company St., across from Government House (© **340/773-2985**), serves burgers and New York deli-style sandwiches throughout the day—everything from a Reuben to a tuna melt. Lunch $8. **Fort Christian Brew Pub,** King's Alley Walk (© **340/713-9820**), has one of the best harbor views in Christiansted and serves beer, plus burgers, sandwiches, and Cajun cuisine. It's the only restaurant/microbrewery in the Virgin Islands. Lunch $9. **Tutto Bene,** 2 Company St. (© **340/773-5229**), serves a full range of delectable pastas, plus fish, veggie frittatas, a chicken pesto sandwich, spinach lasagna, and more. The restaurant only serves dinner.

IN FREDERIKSTED   **Le St. Tropez,** Limetree Court, 67 King St. (© **340/ 772-3000**), is the most popular bistro in Frederiksted, offering crepes, quiches, soups, and salads for lunch in its sunlit courtyard. Lunch $15. **Pier 69,** 69 King St. (© **340/772-0069**), looks like a combination of a 1950s living room and a nautical bar. It's a hangout for Christiansted's counterculture and a top spot for sandwiches and salads. Lunch $8.

Bermuda

Besides the Caribbean, the island nation of Bermuda, sitting out in the Atlantic roughly parallel to South Carolina (or Casablanca, if you're measuring from the east), is the other major cruise destination from the U.S. eastern seaboard. Most cruise ships bound for here depart from New York or Boston.

Although the Spanish discovered Bermuda in the early 16th century, it was the British who first settled here in 1609, when the ship *Sea Venture,* en route to Virginia's Jamestown colony, was wrecked on the island's reefs. No lives were lost, and the crew and passengers built two new ships and continued on to Virginia; but three crewmembers stayed behind and became the island's first permanent settlers. Bermuda became a crown colony in 1620 and remains one today, retaining a very British character—the island is divided up into parishes, driving is on the left, and horse-drawn carriages trot about, but the sun and the ubiquitous Bermuda shorts serve as proof you're in the islands. It's a genteel, sane, and orderly place; it even prohibits rental cars.

Not to say things aren't bustling when the ships are in town at Hamilton and St. George's, but a calm and controlled atmosphere reigns as visitors fan out across the island. There are many powdery soft beaches easily accessible by taxi or motor scooter; Horseshoe Bay and Elbow Beach are popular, and the many unnamed slivers of silky beach tucked into the jagged coastline are worth discovering.

Bermuda has more golf courses per square mile than any other place in the world. For shoppers, Front and Queen streets in Hamilton offer dozens of shops and department stores, most specializing in English items, including porcelain, crystal, wool clothing, and linens. For history buffs, the nearly 300-year-old St. Peter's Church and several museums are within walking distance of the pier in St. George's, and Fort St. Catherine is just about 1.5km (1 mile) away. The exhibits at the Maritime Museum, which is built into the ruins of Bermuda's oldest fort at the Royal Naval Dockyard, are impressive and varied.

Cruise ships have been sailing to Bermuda for over a century, making it one of the earliest cruise destinations. The Quebec Steamship Company, which eventually evolved into the Furness Bermuda Line, began service from New York to Bermuda in 1874 with the small steamers *Canima* and *Bermuda* and then added the *Orinoco* in 1881, the *Trinidad* in 1893, and the liner *Pretoria,* acquired from the Union Line, in 1897.

Unlike most Caribbean itineraries, on which ships visit ports for a day at most, the majority of Bermuda-bound ships spend several whole days at the island. To protect its hotel trade and to maintain a semblance of order and keep the island from getting overrun by too many tourists, the government of Bermuda allows only six cruise ships—five on weekdays and the other on weekends, sailing from New York, Boston, and Philadelphia—to visit the island on a regular basis during its season, late April through October, when the temperatures hover around 75°F (24°C) and extended rainfall is rare.

SHIPS VISITING BERMUDA   For 2004, the ships sailing regular Bermuda routes are Celebrity's *Zenith* and *Horizon,* and Royal Caribbean's *Nordic Empress,* all sailing from New York, and Norwegian's *Norwegian Majesty,* sailing from Boston. At press time, Princess had not announced which ship it would have in Bermuda. See cruise line reviews in chapter 6 for details on all these ships and itineraries.

COMING ASHORE   Cruise ships tie up at three harbors in Bermuda; most are at the docks smack dab in the middle of Hamilton or St. George's in the east end, and less often at the Royal Naval Dockyard in the west end. Exploring couldn't be easier as the ships pull right to the docks in all three places; there's no need to tender back and forth.

Several credit-card phones are in the terminal in Hamilton, and a bank of phones is just off the pier in St. George's.

CURRENCY   The legal tender in Bermuda is the Bermuda dollar (BD$) and it's pegged to the U.S. dollar on an equal basis—BD$1 equals U.S.$1. There's no need to exchange any U.S. money for Bermudian.

LANGUAGE   English is the official language.

INFORMATION   Bermuda's **Visitor Service Bureau** has several branches, including one at the ferry terminal in Hamilton (© **441/295-1480**) and one on King's Square in St. George's (© **441/297-1642**). For information before you go, check out **www.bermudatourism.com**, the official Bermuda Department of Tourism website.

CALLING FROM THE U.S.   When calling Bermuda from the U.S., you need only dial a "1" before the numbers listed here.

GETTING AROUND

BY TAXI   Taxis are regulated by meter and are clean, new, and plentiful at all three cruise piers—but boy are they expensive! Expect to pay at least $4.80 for the first mile and $1.68 for each additional mile; fares go up 25% between midnight and 6am, as well as on Sundays and holidays. If you want to go touring, the hourly rates for a taxi are $30 for up to four people, with a 3-hour minimum. When a taxi has a blue flag on its hood (locals call it the "bonnet"), drivers are qualified to serve as tour guides, and they don't charge extra for the tour. Several authorized taxi companies operate on the island, including **Radio Cab** (© **441/295-4141**), **Bermuda Industrial Union Taxi Co-op** (© **441/292-4476**), and **Sandys** (© **441/234-2344**). Taxi fares add up and you can pay $20

Frommer's Ratings: Bermuda

	Poor	Fair	Good	Excellent	Outstanding
Overall Experience					✓
Shore Excursions			✓		
Activities Close to Port				✓	
Beaches & Watersports					✓
Shopping					✓
Dining/Bars				✓	

Frommer's Favorite Bermuda Experiences

Hopping a Local Ferry in Hamilton: For a few bucks, you get a scenic ride to the Royal Naval Dockyard on the island's far west end, where you can tour the historic fortress ruins and excellent museums. (See "By Ferry," below, for where to get tickets and schedules.)

Renting a Motor Scooter and Touring the Island Independently: Bermuda's roads are well maintained (but can get crowded at rush hour), the island is scenic, and its beaches are easy to find. (See "By Moped/Motor Scooter," below, for rental information.)

Having Lunch at Waterloo House: The elegant patio restaurant at the Waterloo House, within walking distance of the cruise ship docks in Hamilton, offers idyllic views of the boats and yachts in Hamilton Harbour. (See "Great Local Bars & Restaurants," later in this chapter.)

---

or $30 before you know it; if you can, split a taxi (most are minivans) among four people.

BY BUS   Buses are a good option in Bermuda; they're cheap, they're clean, and they go everywhere. Some, however, don't run on Sundays and holidays. Bermuda is divided into 14 zones of about 3km (2 miles) each. You must have exact change or tokens to use the buses. The cash fare for trips up to three zones is $3; longer trips cost $4.50. You can purchase tokens at the Central Bus Terminal on Washington Street in Hamilton. You can also purchase day passes. The tourism offices in Hamilton and St. George's can provide bus schedules.

BY MOPED/MOTOR SCOOTER   Mopeds and motor scooters are everywhere in Bermuda, and are a popular option for visitors. Roads are well maintained, but remember that driving is on the left, traffic can be heavy in town, and scooter accidents are so common that some cruise lines forbid their employees to ride them. Rental fees are pretty standard across the island. Mopeds go for about $35 for the first day and $60 for 2 days; scooters go for about $45 for 1 day. You need a major credit card, and you must buy a one-time insurance policy costing $15. You can rent from **Wheels Cycles** (© 441/292-2245), along Front Street in Hamilton, adjacent to the cruise ship terminal; **Eve's Cycles** (© 441/236-6247), which sets up shop near the cruise terminal in Hamilton; or **Oleander Cycles** (© 441/295-0919) on Gorham Road in Hamilton.

BY FERRY   Ferries are an interesting and efficient way to get around Bermuda, and you get some sightseeing done in the process. The government-run ferries crisscross Great Sound between Hamilton and Somerset (where the Royal Naval Dockyard is located), charging only $4 one way. Service also goes between Hamilton and Paget and Warwick, across the harbor. Buy tickets and get schedules at the Ferry Terminal (adjacent to the cruise ship docks) or at the Central Bus Terminal in Hamilton. Or call for information at © 441/295-4506.

BY HORSE-DRAWN CARRIAGE   Before 1946, carriages were the only way to get around. Now they're the quaint way. Drivers congregate along Front Street in Hamilton, adjacent to the No. 1 cruise ship terminal. A single carriage accommodating one to four passengers and drawn by one horse costs $30 for 30

Bermuda

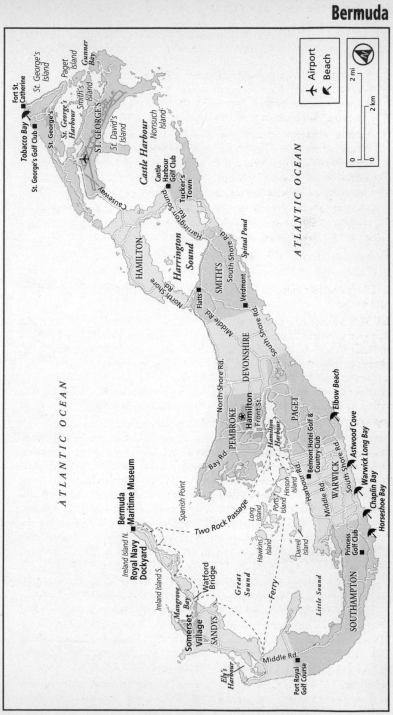

minutes. For longer rides, the fee is negotiable. Unless you make special arrangements for a night ride, you aren't likely to find any carriages after 4:30pm. For more information, contact **Terceira's Stables** at © **441/236-3014.**

BY RENTAL CAR Rental cars are not permitted on the island.

SHORE EXCURSIONS

Bermuda is truly an island made for independent exploring, offering a great combination of history, beaches, and shopping. Take your pick. Hamilton and St. George's are conducive to walking tours, and the beaches and golf courses are easily accessible by taxi, bus, or motor scooter.

Guided Walking Tour of St. George's ($21, 1 hr.): Learn about Bermuda's history, including its churches, art galleries, libraries, and private gardens.

West End Highlights ($40, 3 hr.): This minibus tour takes you from Hamilton to the Royal Naval Dockyard; en route, you'll sightsee and then explore the many exhibits at the Dockyard's museums.

Railway Biking Tour ($50, 3 hr.): Bike where the original Bermuda Railway once ran on narrow gauge tracks. The tracks are gone, but a great trail remains behind, and this excursion is a great opportunity to get views of the ocean, and the island's lush gardens and bird life. The flat route covers 8km to 13km (5–8 miles).

Snorkeling Trip ($42, 3 hr.): From Hamilton, board a boat and motor out to a snorkeling spot near the West End as the captain talks to passengers about Bermuda history and customs. Then, after an hour or so of snorkeling, the fun begins: The music is turned on, the dancing starts, and the bar opens as the boat heads back to port.

Glass-Bottomed Boat Cruise ($30, 2 hr.): See the coral reefs and colorful fish living in Bermuda's waters, then view one of Bermuda's famous shipwrecks and enjoy a rum swizzle from a fully stocked bar.

Golf Excursion ($65–$160, half-day): Excursions include tee times for 18 holes at challenging courses such as Mid Ocean Golf Club, among the best in world; Riddells Bay Golf & Country Club, a veritable golfing institution built in 1922; Port Royal Golf Course; and St. George's Golf Club, designed by Robert Trent Jones. A taxi to and from the courses may be extra and club rental is about $30 extra, but carts are included. The golf excursions are often sold directly through an onboard golf pro who organizes lessons on the ship too.

WALKING TOUR   **HAMILTON**

Hamilton was once known as the "Show Window of the British Empire," and has been the capital of Bermuda since 1815, when it replaced St. George's. Today, it's the economic hub of the island. This walking tour will introduce you to all that's noteworthy in the city.

Start at the harborfront at the:

❶ Visitors Service Bureau/Ferry Terminal

Pick up free maps and brochures of the island here.

From the bureau, you'll emerge onto **Front Street,** Hamilton's main street and shopping area. Before 1946, there were no cars here, but today, its busy traffic includes small autos, buses, mopeds, bicycles, and horse-drawn carriages.

Walk directly south of the Ferry Terminal toward the water, taking a short side street

0 | 1/8 mile

0 | 100 meters

N

✝ Church
ⓘ Information

North St.
Parsons Rd.
Ewing St.
Angle St.
Court St.
Laffan St.
Elliott St.
Elliott St.
Princess St.
Hamilton
BERMUDA
Curving Ave.
Dundonald St.
Dundonald St.
Victoria Park
Park Rd.
Cedar Ave.
Union St.
King St.
Happy Valley Rd.
Woodlands Rd.
Wesley St.
Victoria St.
Parliament St.
Richmond Rd.
8
finish here
Fort Hamilton
14
Woodbourne Ave.
Gorham Rd.
Par-la-Ville Park
Queen St.
Burnaby St.
11 ✝
Church St.
12
Bermudiana Rd.
Par-la-Ville Rd.
5 6 7
Reid St.
Court St.
4
13
Front St.
3 1 ⓘ
★ start here
2
Hamilton Harbour

1 Visitors Service Bureau/Ferry Terminal	6 Bermuda Historical Society Museum	11 Bermuda Cathedral
2 Albouy's Point	7 Perot Post Office	12 Sessions House (Parliament Building)
3 Bank of Bermuda	8 Hamilton City Hall	13 Cenotaph
4 The "Birdcage"	9 Victoria Park	14 Fort Hamilton
5 Par-la-Ville Park	10 St. Theresa's	

between the Visitors Service Bureau and the large Bank of Bermuda. You'll come to:

❷ Albouy's Point

The Point is a small grassy park with benches and trees that opens onto a panoramic vista of the boat- and ship-filled slip. Nearby is the Royal Bermuda Yacht Club, an elite rendezvous for both Bermudian and American yachting sets since the 1930s.

After taking in the view, walk directly north, crossing Point Pleasant Road, to the:

❸ Bank of Bermuda

Open Monday to Friday from 9:30am to 3pm, it has Bermuda's most extensive coin collection, with at least one sample of every coin minted in the United Kingdom since the reign of King James I in the early 17th century. You'll also see Bermuda's famous money, called "hog money." In use since the early 1600s, the hog coin is

stamped on one side with the ill-fated *Sea Venture* and on the other side with a wild hog, the main source of food for Bermuda's early settlers.

Now, head east along Front Street to the point where it intersects with Queen Street, where you'll see:

❹ The "Birdcage"

This is the perch in the middle of the intersection from which police direct traffic. It's the most photographed sight in Bermuda. If the bobby directing traffic is a man, he'll likely be wearing Bermuda shorts.

Next, continue north along Queen Street until you reach:

❺ Par-la-Ville Park

The Park was once a private garden attached to the town house of William B. Perot, the first postmaster of Bermuda, who designed the gardens in the 19th century. He collected rare and exotic plants from all over the globe, including the Indian rubber tree, which was seeded in 1847.

Also opening onto Queen Street at the entrance to the park is the:

❻ Bermuda Historical Society Museum/Bermuda Library

The museum/library is at 13 Queen St. You'll find items such as cedar furniture, collections of antique silver and china, hog money, a 1775 letter from George Washington, and more.

Next door is the:

❼ Perot Post Office

William Perot ran it from 1818 to 1862. It's said that when he went to collect mail from the clipper ships, he'd put the mail under his top hat to maintain his dignity. As he strolled through town, he'd greet friends by tipping his hat, and thereby deliver the mail, too. He started printing stamps in 1848, and today, they're extremely valuable—only 11 are known to exist.

Continue onto Queen Street, and then turn right onto Church Street to reach:

❽ Hamilton City Hall

City Hall is at 17 Church St. and dates from 1960. A white tower crowns it. The bronze weather vane on top is a replica of the *Sea Venture*.

In the back of Hamilton City Hall, opening onto Victoria Street, lies:

❾ Victoria Park

This park is a cool, refreshing 1.6-hectare (4-acre) oasis frequented by office workers on their lunch breaks. It has a sunken garden, ornamental shrubbery, and a Victorian bandstand.

Cedar Avenue is the eastern boundary of Victoria Park. If you follow it north for 2 blocks, you'll reach:

❿ St. Theresa's

This Roman Catholic cathedral is open daily from 8am to 7pm and for Sunday services. Dating from 1927, its architecture was inspired by the Spanish Mission style. It's one of a half-dozen Roman Catholic churches in Bermuda. Its gold-and-silver chalice was a gift from Pope Paul VI when he visited the island in 1968.

After seeing the cathedral, retrace your steps south along Cedar Avenue until you reach Victoria Street. Cedar now becomes Burnaby Street; continue south on this street until you come to Church Street and then turn left, until you see the:

⓫ Bermuda Cathedral

Also called the Cathedral of the Most Holy Trinity, this neo-Gothic church is the seat of the Anglican Church of Bermuda.

When you leave the cathedral, continue east along Church Street to:

⓬ Sessions House (Parliament Building)

On Parliament Street, between Reid and Church streets, it's open to the public Monday to Friday from 9am to 12:30pm and 2 to 5pm. On Fridays, you can see Bermuda's political process in action, with the speaker wearing a full wig and a black robe. Bermuda has the third-oldest parliament in the world, after Iceland's and England's.

Continue walking south along Parliament Street until you approach Front Street, where you should turn left toward the:

⓭ Cenotaph

The Cenotaph is a memorial to the Bermudians slain in World War I and World War II.

From here, continue east along Front Street until you reach King Street, and then head north to Happy Valley Road. Go right until you see the entrance (on your right) to:

⓮ Fort Hamilton

An imposing old fortress on the eastern outskirts of Hamilton, Fort Hamilton was constructed on the orders of the Duke of Wellington to protect Hamilton Harbour. It offers panoramic views of the city and harbor, although with its moat and 18-ton guns, the fort was outdated before it was even completed.

Quaint and historic, St. George's was the second English town established in the new world, after Jamestown in Virginia. King's Square, also called Market Square or the King's Parade, is the center of life here, and it's just steps from where the cruise ships dock. From here, you can begin the following walking tour, which takes you to all the major sights.

Start this walking tour at:

❶ King's Square

The Square is about 200 years old, and it's not as historic as St. George's itself. This was formerly a marshy part of the harbor, back when the shipwrecked passengers and crew of the *Sea Venture* first saw it. On the square, notice a replica of the pillory and stocks that were formerly used to punish presumed criminals.

From the square, head south across the small bridge to:

❷ Ordnance Island

Jutting into St. George's Harbour, the British once stored gunpowder and cannons here, but today the island houses the *Deliverance,* a replica of the vessel that carried the shipwrecked *Sea Venture* passengers on to Virginia. Alongside the ship is a ducking stool, a contraption used in 17th-century witch trials.

Retrace your steps across the bridge to King's Square. On the waterside stands the:

❸ White Horse Tavern

The White Horse Tavern is a restaurant jutting out into St. George's Harbour. Consider it for lunch or a drink. It was once the home of John Davenport, who came to Bermuda in 1815 to open a dry-goods store. Turns out, Davenport was a bit of a miser: Upon his death, some 75,000 English pounds' worth of gold and silver were discovered stashed away in his cellar.

Across the square stands the:

❹ Town Hall

This hall is the meeting place of the corporation governing St. George's.

Inside, a multimedia audiovisual presentation on Bermuda's history and culture is shown several times a day.

From King's Square, head east along King Street, cutting north on Bridge Street. There you'll come to the:

❺ Bridge House

Located at 1 Bridge St., the Bridge House was constructed shortly after 1700. Once the home of several governors of Bermuda, it is furnished with 18th- and 19th-century antiques, and is now home to an art gallery and souvenir shop.

Return to King Street and continue east to the:

❻ Old State House

Opening onto Princess Street, at the top of King Street, this is the oldest stone building in Bermuda, dating from 1620, and was once the home of the Bermuda Parliament.

Continue your stroll down Princess Street until you come to Duke of York Street and the entrance to:

❼ Somers Gardens

The heart of Sir George Somers, the admiral of the *Sea Venture,* is buried here.

Walk through Somers Gardens and up the steps to the North Gate onto the Blockade Alley. If you look up the hill, you'll see what's known as the "folly of St. George's," the:

❽ Unfinished Cathedral

This cathedral was intended to replace St. Peter's (see stop 12 on this walking tour). Work began in 1874, but eventually came to an end; the church was beset by financial difficulties and a schism in the Anglican congregation.

St. George's Walking Tour

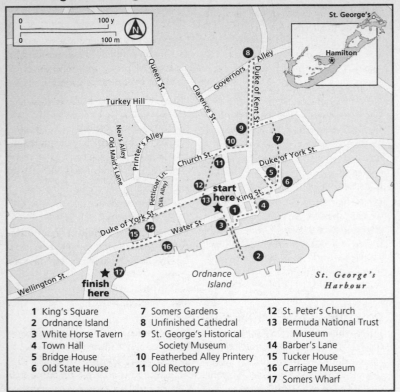

After viewing the ruins, turn left onto Duke of Kent Street, which leads down to the:

⑨ St. George's Historical Society Museum

Found at the intersection of Featherbed Alley and Duke of Kent Street, this is a wonderful example of 18th-century architecture. The house has a collection of Bermudian historical artifacts and cedar furniture.

Around the corner on Featherbed Alley is the:

⑩ Featherbed Alley Printery

This printing shop has a working replica of the type of printing press invented by Johannes Gutenberg in Germany in the 1450s.

Go up Featherbed Alley and straight onto Church Street. At the junction with Broad Lane, look to your right to see the:

⑪ Old Rectory

The rectory is at the head of Broad Alley, behind St. Peter's Church. Now a private home administered by the National Trust, a reformed pirate built it in 1705. It's open on Wednesday only, from noon to 5pm.

Next, go through the back of the churchyard entrance, opposite Broad Alley, to reach:

⑫ St. Peter's Church

The church's main entrance is on Duke of York Street. This is believed to be the oldest Anglican place of worship in the Western Hemisphere. In the churchyard, some headstones date back some 300 years. The present church was built in 1713.

Across the street is the:

⑬ Bermuda National Trust Museum

Once the Globe Hotel, headquarters of Major Norman Walker, the Confederate representative in Bermuda, today it houses relics from the island's involvement in the American Civil War (from Bermuda's perspective).

As you continue west along Duke of York Street, you'll reach:

⑭ Barber's Lane

This street honors Joseph Hayne Rainey, a former slave from South Carolina who was a barber in St. George's before eventually returning to the States, where he was elected the first black member of the U.S. House of Representatives. Nearby is Petticoat Lane, also known as Silk Alley. The name dates from the 1834 emancipation, when two former slave women who'd always wanted silk petticoats like their former mistresses finally got some—and then paraded up and down the lane to show off their new finery.

Continue until you reach:

⑮ Tucker House

Opening onto Water Street, this was the former home of a prominent Bermudian family, and now houses an excellent collection of antiques.

Diagonally across from the Tucker House is the:

⑯ Carriage Museum

Located at 22 Water St., this museum preserves some of the most interesting carriages used in Bermuda until 1946, when the automobile arrived.

End your tour across the street at:

⑰ Somers Wharf

This wharf is a multimillion-dollar waterfront restoration project that includes shops, restaurants, and taverns.

ON YOUR OWN: SANDYS PARISH

If your ship docks at the Royal Naval Dockyard, sometimes called King's Wharf, on the west end, you can walk to the sprawling complex there. Constructed by convict labor, this 19th-century fortress was used by the British Navy until 1951 as a strategic dockyard. Today, it's a major tourist attraction whose centerpiece is the **Bermuda Maritime Museum,** the most important and extensive museum on the island. Exhibits are housed in six large halls within the complex, and the displays all relate to Bermuda's long connection with the sea, from Spanish exploration to 20th-century ocean liners. You can have a look at maps, ship models, and such artifacts as gold bars, pottery, jewelry, and silver coins recovered from 16th- and 17th-century shipwrecks, such as the *Sea Venture.* A visit is a must.

ON YOUR OWN: PEMBROKE PARISH, HAMILTON AREA

From Hamilton, besides all of the great sites included in the walking tour above, a visit to the **Bermuda Underwater Exploration Institute (© 441/292-7219)** is worthwhile. Adjacent to the Hamilton docks near the roundabout on East Broadway, there are two floors of interactive exhibits about the ocean plus the highlight: a capsule that simulates a 3,600m (12,000-ft.) dive below the ocean's surface (it accommodates 21 people at a time). Open daily 9am to 5pm, admission is $10.50 for adults and $5.50 for kids ages 7 to 16.

Bermuda Welcome Wagon

If you plan to see all of Bermuda's attractions on your own, the **Heritage Passport** grants admission to eight cultural attractions (museums, historic homes, and the like) over a 7-day period. Cost is $25 for adults and $15 for children 6 to 16. You can buy the Heritage Passport at any Visitors Service Bureau or any of the participating attractions (including the National Trust Museum and the Bermuda Aquarium), or by calling © 441/236-4034.

The **Bermuda Railway Trail** offers about 29km (18 miles) of trails divided into easy-to-explore sections. It was created along the course of the old Bermuda Railway, which stretched a total of 34km (21 miles) and served the island from 1931 to 1948, until the automobile was introduced. Armed with a copy of the *Bermuda Railway Trail Guide,* available at the various visitor centers, you can set out on your own expedition via foot or bicycle (most of the moped/scooter rental agencies rent bicycles as well). Most of the trail winds along a car-free route, and there is a section of trail in St. George's and near Hamilton.

ON YOUR OWN: BEYOND WALKING DISTANCE

A mile or two from King's Square in St. George's, overlooking the beach where the shipwrecked crew of the *Sea Venture* came ashore in 1609, is **Fort St. Catherine,** which you'll want to see. Completed in 1614, and reconstructed several times after, it was named for the patron saint of wheelwrights and carpenters. The fortress houses a museum, with several worthwhile exhibits.

In Flatts Village, about halfway between Hamilton and St. George's, is the **Bermuda Aquarium, Museum & Zoo** (© 441/293-2727; www.bamz.org). There are interactive displays, huge aquariums, and seal feedings throughout the day. Open daily 9am to 4pm; admission is $10 for adults and $5 for seniors and children ages 6 to 12. Children 5 and under are free. All kids 12 and under must be accompanied by someone 13 or older.

SHOPPING

You'll get quality and lots of British items, but don't expect great deals. Nothing in Bermuda is cheap, but keep your eyes peeled for sales, especially at the department stores.

IN HAMILTON   Hamilton offers the best and widest shopping choices on the island. **Front and Queen streets** have dozens of shops and department stores, most specializing in English items such as porcelain, crystal, wool clothing, and linens. **Trimingham's** (© 441/295-1183) and **H. A. & E. Smith** (© 441/295-2288), two popular department stores on Front Street, as well as other nearby boutiques, sell Waterford, Baccarat, Kosta Boda, Orrefors, and Galway crystal vases, wine glasses, bowls, and curios; Lalique porcelain figurines; Wedgwood, Royal Doulton, Royal Copenhagen, Spode, Aynsley, and Royal Worcester fine bone china dinnerware, vases, bowls, and curios; Shetland, lamb's wool, and cashmere sweaters and skirts from Scotland and England; and Burberry's rainwear.

Archie Brown on Front Street (© 441/295-2928) specializes in sweaters, woolens, and tartans of all kinds. **A. S. Cooper & Sons** on Front Street (© 441/ 295-3961) is the island's oldest and largest china and glassware store—it has it all. **The Irish Linen Shop** on the corner of Queen and Front streets (© 441/ 295-4089) sells pure Irish linens and an eclectic array of luxury bed linens. Many other stores, along and adjacent to Front Street, sell clothing, arts and crafts, and souvenirs.

IN ST. GEORGE'S   Here you'll find many of the same kinds of shops as in Hamilton, including branches of famous Front Street stores. **King's Square,** the **Somers Wharf** complex, and **Water Street** are the main shopping areas. If you're a hard-core shopper, though, save yourself for Hamilton, which is Bermuda's shopping mecca.

SPORTS

GOLF   Bermuda has more courses per square mile than any other place in the world. They're all easily accessible via taxi, and your ship will likely have organized excursions to them if you'd rather not go it alone. The following are all 18-hole courses. Robert Trent Jones designed the par-71, 5,909m (6,565-yard) **Port Royal Golf Course,** Southampton Parish (© 441/234-0974), which lies along ocean terrain. Greens fees of $130 per person include cart and range balls. It's a public course and ranks among the very best on the island—as a matter of fact, it's rated among the best in the world. Jack Nicklaus likes to play here. **Southampton Princess Golf Club,** Southampton Parish (© 441/239-6952), is a par-54, 2,416m (2,684-yard), 18-hole course with elevated tees, strategically placed bunkers, and an array of water hazards to challenge even the most experienced golfers. Greens fees are $66 a person and include golf cart. Carts are mandatory. **St. George's Golf Club,** St. George's Parish (© 441/297-8067), is one of the island's best. This par-62, 3,639m (4,043-yard) course, designed by Robert Trent Jones, is within walking distance of historic St. George's. Greens fees are $86 per person, including cart. In 1923, Emmett Devereux, a Scotsman, designed the par-70, 5,199m (5,777-yard) course at the former **Belmont Hotel Golf & Country Club** in Warwick. At press time, the property was scheduled to reopen as the **Belmont Hills Golf Club Hotel & Villa.** The rebuilt golf course was scheduled to open in spring 2003, with the property opening its doors in late 2003 or early 2004.

SCUBA DIVING   **Blue Water Divers & Watersports Co., Ltd.,** Robinson's Marina, Southampton (© 441/234-1034), is Bermuda's oldest and largest full-service scuba-diving operation. All equipment is provided; reservations are necessary.

BEACHES

Many of Bermuda's famous powdery soft beaches (not really pink as they're touted—or maybe we're just colorblind) are easily accessible by taxi or motor scooter. **Horseshoe Bay** in Southampton Parish and **Elbow Beach** in Paget Parish are very popular and often crowded public beaches, and the many unnamed slivers of silky beach tucked into the jagged coastline are worth discovering. Hotel beaches are generally private. Elbow Beach charges $4 for visitors; the adjacent Elbow Beach Hotel offers facilities and rentals. Horseshoe Bay is a free public beach and has a place to get snacks.

Also consider these public beaches: **Astwood Cove** (Warwick Parish) is remote and rarely overcrowded—ditto for **Chaplin Bay** (Warwick and Southampton Parishes). **Warwick Long Bay** (Warwick Parish) is popular and set against a backdrop of scrubland and low grasses, and **Tobacco Bay Beach** (St. George's Parish) is popular, and is the most frequented beach on St. George's Island. You can rent snorkeling equipment by the hour here ($8 for 1 hr., or $12 for 2 hr.), but it's not as new as what you'll get on a cruise ship shore excursion.

GREAT LOCAL BARS & RESTAURANTS

You don't go to Bermuda for its cuisine, but there are some tasty local specialties, such as fish chowder laced with rum and sherry peppers (yum!!), as well as spiny Bermuda lobster, mussel pie, and wahoo steak.

IN HAMILTON   Try the **Waterloo House,** Pitts Bay Road (℃ **441/295-4480**), at the elegant Relais Châteaux hotel, within walking distance of the ship docks. Lunch is served on the outdoor patio overlooking the colorful and idyllic harbor, and many snazzy-looking businesspeople lunch here. The fish chowder is great. Lunch $25. **The Lobster Pot & Boat House Bar,** 6 Bermudian Rd. (℃ **441/292-6898**), serves great local fish and lobster dishes. Lunch $22. **The Hog Penny,** 5 Burnaby Hill (℃ **441/292-2534**), is Bermuda's most famous pub and a great choice for lunch. With its dark paneled walls and classic pub ambience, you'll think you're in merry olde England. The fresh fish and chips, tossed back with a cool pint of ale, is a good choice. Lunch $14.

IN ST. DAVID'S   Don't miss a meal at the **Black Horse Tavern,** 101 St. David's Rd. (℃ **441/297-1991**), for an authentic taste of Bermuda—or so the locals maintain. Order curried conch stew or fish chowder. Lunch $15.

IN ST. GEORGE'S   The **White Horse Pub & Restaurant,** 8 King's Square (℃ **441/297-1838**), is the oldest in St. George's and a favorite casual hangout for visitors. The terrace has great views of the square and all the hubbub below. Have an ice-cold beer and fish and chips. Lunch $13.

Index

FROMMER'S® COMPLETE TRAVEL GUIDES

Alaska
Alaska Cruises & Ports of Call
Amsterdam
Argentina & Chile
Arizona
Atlanta
Australia
Austria
Bahamas
Barcelona, Madrid & Seville
Beijing
Belgium, Holland & Luxembourg
Bermuda
Boston
Brazil
British Columbia & the Canadian
   Rockies
Brussels & Bruges
Budapest & the Best of Hungary
California
Canada
Cancún, Cozumel & the Yucatán
Cape Cod, Nantucket & Martha's
   Vineyard
Caribbean
Caribbean Cruises & Ports of Call
Caribbean Ports of Call
Carolinas & Georgia
Chicago
China
Colorado
Costa Rica
Cuba
Denmark
Denver, Boulder & Colorado Springs
England
Europe
European Cruises & Ports of Call

Florida
France
Germany
Great Britain
Greece
Greek Islands
Hawaii
Hong Kong
Honolulu, Waikiki & Oahu
Ireland
Israel
Italy
Jamaica
Japan
Las Vegas
London
Los Angeles
Maryland & Delaware
Maui
Mexico
Montana & Wyoming
Montréal & Québec City
Munich & the Bavarian Alps
Nashville & Memphis
New England
New Mexico
New Orleans
New York City
New Zealand
Northern Italy
Norway
Nova Scotia, New Brunswick &
   Prince Edward Island
Oregon
Paris
Peru
Philadelphia & the Amish Country
Portugal

Prague & the Best of the Czech
   Republic
Provence & the Riviera
Puerto Rico
Rome
San Antonio & Austin
San Diego
San Francisco
Santa Fe, Taos & Albuquerque
Scandinavia
Scotland
Seattle & Portland
Shanghai
Sicily
Singapore & Malaysia
South Africa
South America
South Florida
South Pacific
Southeast Asia
Spain
Sweden
Switzerland
Texas
Thailand
Tokyo
Toronto
Tuscany & Umbria
USA
Utah
Vancouver & Victoria
Vermont, New Hampshire & Maine
Vienna & the Danube Valley
Virgin Islands
Virginia
Walt Disney World® & Orlando
Washington, D.C.
Washington State

FROMMER'S® DOLLAR-A-DAY GUIDES

Australia from $50 a Day
California from $70 a Day
England from $75 a Day
Europe from $70 a Day
Florida from $70 a Day
Hawaii from $80 a Day

Ireland from $60 a Day
Italy from $70 a Day
London from $85 a Day
New York from $90 a Day
Paris from $80 a Day

San Francisco from $70 a Day
Washington, D.C. from $80 a Day
Portable London from $85 a Day
Portable New York City from $90
   a Day

FROMMER'S® PORTABLE GUIDES

Acapulco, Ixtapa & Zihuatanejo
Amsterdam
Aruba
Australia's Great Barrier Reef
Bahamas
Berlin
Big Island of Hawaii
Boston
California Wine Country
Cancún
Cayman Islands
Charleston
Chicago
Disneyland®
Dublin
Florence

Frankfurt
Hong Kong
Houston
Las Vegas
Las Vegas for Non-Gamblers
London
Los Angeles
Los Cabos & Baja
Maine Coast
Maui
Miami
Nantucket & Martha's Vineyard
New Orleans
New York City
Paris
Phoenix & Scottsdale

Portland
Puerto Rico
Puerto Vallarta, Manzanillo &
   Guadalajara
Rio de Janeiro
San Diego
San Francisco
Savannah
Seattle
Sydney
Tampa & St. Petersburg
Vancouver
Venice
Virgin Islands
Washington, D.C.

FROMMER'S® NATIONAL PARK GUIDES

Banff & Jasper
Family Vacations in the National
   Parks

Grand Canyon
National Parks of the American West
Rocky Mountain

Yellowstone & Grand Teton
Yosemite & Sequoia/Kings Canyon
Zion & Bryce Canyon

Frommer's® Memorable Walks

Chicago	New York	San Francisco
London	Paris	

Frommer's® With Kids Guides

Chicago	Ottawa	Vancouver
Las Vegas	San Francisco	Washington, D.C.
New York City	Toronto	

Suzy Gershman's Born to Shop Guides

Born to Shop: France	Born to Shop: Italy	Born to Shop: New York
Born to Shop: Hong Kong, Shanghai & Beijing	Born to Shop: London	Born to Shop: Paris

Frommer's® Irreverent Guides

Amsterdam	Los Angeles	San Francisco
Boston	Manhattan	Seattle & Portland
Chicago	New Orleans	Vancouver
Las Vegas	Paris	Walt Disney World®
London	Rome	Washington, D.C.

Frommer's® Best-Loved Driving Tours

Britain	Germany	Northern Italy
California	Ireland	Scotland
Florida	Italy	Spain
France	New England	Tuscany & Umbria

Hanging Out™ Guides

Hanging Out in England	Hanging Out in France	Hanging Out in Italy
Hanging Out in Europe	Hanging Out in Ireland	Hanging Out in Spain

The Unofficial Guides®

Bed & Breakfasts and Country Inns in:
- California
- Great Lakes States
- Mid-Atlantic
- New England
- Northwest
- Rockies
- Southeast
- Southwest

Best RV & Tent Campgrounds in:
- California & the West
- Florida & the Southeast
- Great Lakes States
- Mid-Atlantic
- Northeast
- Northwest & Central Plains

- Southwest & South Central Plains
- U.S.A.
- Beyond Disney
- Branson, Missouri
- California with Kids
- Central Italy
- Chicago
- Cruises
- Disneyland®
- Florida with Kids
- Golf Vacations in the Eastern U.S.
- Great Smoky & Blue Ridge Region
- Inside Disney
- Hawaii
- Las Vegas
- London
- Maui

- Mexio's Best Beach Resorts
- Mid-Atlantic with Kids
- Mini Las Vegas
- Mini-Mickey
- New England & New York with Kids
- New Orleans
- New York City
- Paris
- San Francisco
- Skiing & Snowboarding in the West
- Southeast with Kids
- Walt Disney World®
- Walt Disney World® for Grown-ups
- Walt Disney World® with Kids
- Washington, D.C.
- World's Best Diving Vacations

Special-Interest Titles

Frommer's Adventure Guide to Australia & New Zealand
Frommer's Adventure Guide to Central America
Frommer's Adventure Guide to India & Pakistan
Frommer's Adventure Guide to South America
Frommer's Adventure Guide to Southeast Asia
Frommer's Adventure Guide to Southern Africa
Frommer's Britain's Best Bed & Breakfasts and Country Inns
Frommer's Caribbean Hideaways
Frommer's Exploring America by RV
Frommer's Fly Safe, Fly Smart

Frommer's France's Best Bed & Breakfasts and Country Inns
Frommer's Gay & Lesbian Europe
Frommer's Italy's Best Bed & Breakfasts and Country Inns
Frommer's Road Atlas Britain
Frommer's Road Atlas Europe
Frommer's Road Atlas France
The New York Times' Guide to Unforgettable Weekends
Places Rated Almanac
Retirement Places Rated
Rome Past & Present

Booked aisle seat.

Reserved room with a view.

With a queen – no, make that a king-size bed.

With Travelocity, you can book your flights and hotels together, so you can get even better deals than if you booked them separately. You'll save time and money without compromising the quality of your trip. Choose your airline seat, search for alternate airports, pick your hotel room type, even choose the neighborhood you'd like to stay in

Travelocity

Visit www.travelocity.com or call 1-888-TRAVELOCIT